The Sporting Life
TRAINERS REVIEW

Flat Season 1992

Compiled by
John Bigley, Colin Havercroft and Michael Frost

Published 1992 by The Sporting Life
Orbit House, 1 New Fetter Lane, London EC4A 1AR

© 1992 The Sporting Life

ISBN 0 901091 62 6

Cover designed by ReproSharp Ltd, London EC1
Cover printed by Ark Litho Ltd, London SW19
Text printed by Mackays of Chatham, Kent

Cover picture
Collage of Leading Trainers: *Left to right: Jack Berry, John Gosden, Richard Hannon, Peter Chapple-Hyam, Geoff Lewis, Mary Reveley, Lord Huntingdon, Clive Brittain, Mark Johnston and Michael Bell* (Photographs: Phil Smith, The Sporting Life)

CONTENTS

TRAINER SECTION

J AKEHURST (Upper Lambourn, Berks)

	No. of Horses	Races Run	1st	2nd	3rd	Unpl	Per cent	£1 Level Stake
2-y-o	2	12	2	1	1	8	16.7	- 3.00
3-y-o	7	21	0	1	1	19	-	- 21.00
4-y-o+	13	51	4	3	2	42	7.8	- 26.50
Totals	22	84	6	5	4	69	7.1	- 50.50

Jan	Feb	Mar	Apr	May	Jun	Jul	Aug	Sep	Oct/Nov
0-3	0-0	1-4	1-9	1-15	0-13	0-6	2-12	1-10	0-12

Winning Jockeys	W-R	£1 Level Stake		W-R	£1 Level Stake
Mr E Reitel	1-1	+ 2.00	W Carson	1-2	+ 3.00
Kim McDonnell	1-2	+ 5.50	J Weaver	1-3	+ 6.00
M Roberts	1-2	+ 3.00	D Holland	1-13	- 9.00

Winning Courses					
Kempton	2-7	+ 5.50	Lingfield (AW)	1-7	- 4.00
Southwell (AW)	1-2	+ 7.00	Folkestone	1-12	- 8.00
Windsor	1-6	- 1.00			

Winning Horses	Age	Races Run	1st	2nd	3rd	Unpl	Win £
Hello Hobson's	2	7	2	1	1	3	6,216
Bengal Tiger	4	12	1	2	0	9	2,700
Carousel Music	5	6	1	0	0	5	2,658
Tactical Mission	4	4	1	0	2	1	2,406
Classic Account	4	3	1	0	0	2	2,324

Favourites	2-11	18.2%	- 3.00	Total winning prize-money			£16,304
1991 Form	13-95	13.7%	+ 35.63	1990 Form	4-31	12.9%	- 10.62

R AKEHURST (Epsom, Surrey)

	No. of Horses	Races Run	1st	2nd	3rd	Unpl	Per cent	£1 Level Stake
2-y-o	11	47	2	6	6	33	4.3	- 9.50
3-y-o	10	38	2	5	3	28	5.3	- 23.50
4-y-o+	34	174	24	23	14	113	13.8	- 6.89
Totals	55	259	28	34	23	174	10.8	- 39.89

BY MONTH

2-y-o	W-R	Per cent	£1 Level Stake	3-y-o	W-R	Per cent	£1 Level Stake
January	0-0	-	0.00	January	0-0	-	0.00
February	0-0	-	0.00	February	0-0	-	0.00
March	0-0	-	0.00	March	0-0	-	0.00
April	0-1	-	- 1.00	April	0-1	-	- 1.00
May	0-2	-	- 2.00	May	0-4	-	- 4.00
June	0-7	-	- 7.00	June	0-7	-	- 7.00
July	0-8	-	- 8.00	July	0-5	-	- 5.00
August	1-7	14.3	- 3.50	August	1-7	14.3	+ 0.50
September	1-11	9.1	+ 23.00	September	0-6	-	- 6.00
Oct/Nov	0-11	-	- 11.00	Oct/Nov	1-8	12.5	- 1.00

4-y-o+	W-R	Per cent	£1 Level Stake	Totals	W-R	Per cent	£1 Level Stake
January	1-3	33.3	- 1.27	January	1-3	33.3	- 1.27
February	1-4	25.0	- 2.20	February	1-4	25.0	- 2.20
March	1-9	11.1	- 3.00	March	1-9	11.1	- 3.00
April	2-26	7.7	- 9.00	April	2-28	7.1	- 11.00
May	3-19	15.8	- 3.50	May	3-25	12.0	- 9.50
June	2-26	7.7	- 11.00	June	2-40	5.0	- 25.00
July	5-26	19.2	+ 9.75	July	5-39	12.8	- 3.25
August	2-14	14.3	+ 24.50	August	4-28	14.3	+ 21.50
September	4-23	17.4	- 3.67	September	5-40	12.5	+ 13.33
Oct/Nov	3-24	12.5	- 7.50	Oct/Nov	4-43	9.3	- 19.50

DISTANCE

2-y-o	W-R	Per cent	£1 Level Stake	3-y-o	W-R	Per cent	£1 Level Stake
5f-6f	2-36	5.6	+ 1.50	5f-6f	0-4	-	- 4.00
7f-8f	0-9	-	- 9.00	7f-8f	0-15	-	- 15.00
9f-13f	0-2	-	- 2.00	9f-13f	2-16	12.5	- 1.50
14f+	0-0	-	0.00	14f+	0-3	-	- 3.00

4-y-o+	W-R	Per cent	£1 Level Stake	Totals	W-R	Per cent	£1 Level Stake
5f-6f	1-12	8.3	- 7.50	5f-6f	3-52	5.8	- 10.00
7f-8f	9-45	20.0	+ 35.08	7f-8f	9-69	13.0	+ 11.08
9f-13f	13-75	17.3	- 3.47	9f-13f	15-93	16.1	- 6.97
14f+	1-42	2.4	- 31.00	14f+	1-45	2.2	- 34.00

TYPE OF RACE

Non-Handicaps	W-R	Per cent	£1 Level Stake	Handicaps	W-R	Per cent	£1 Level Stake
2-y-o	2-33	6.1	+ 4.50	2-y-o	0-9	-	- 9.00
3-y-o	0-14	-	- 14.00	3-y-o	2-20	10.0	- 5.50
4-y-o+	5-30	16.7	- 1.47	4-y-o+	17-130	13.1	- 1.92
Selling	0-6	-	- 6.00	Selling	1-2	50.0	+ 4.00
Apprentice	0-1	-	- 1.00	Apprentice	1-11	9.1	- 6.50
Amat/Ladies	0-1	-	- 1.00	Amat/Ladies	0-2	-	- 2.00
Totals	7-85	8.2	- 18.97	Totals	21-174	12.1	- 20.92

COURSE GRADE

	W-R	Per cent	£1 Level Stake
Group 1	10-118	8.5	- 50.25
Group 2	8-52	15.4	- 4.75
Group 3	4-42	9.5	+ 6.75
Group 4	6-47	12.8	+ 8.36

FIRST TIME OUT

	W-R	Per cent	£1 Level Stake
2-y-o	0-11	-	- 11.00
3-y-o	0-9	-	- 9.00
4-y-o+	5-31	16.1	+ 28.73
Totals	5-51	9.8	+ 8.73

JOCKEYS RIDING

	W-R	Per cent	£1 Level Stake		W-R	Per cent	£1 Level Stake
T Quinn	9-47	19.1	+ 81.75	R Cochrane	2-14	14.3	- 10.47
G Carter	4-12	33.3	+ 11.33	L Carter	2-20	10.0	- 11.00
F Norton	3-20	15.0	- 7.50	R Perham	2-39	5.1	- 26.50
T Ashley	2-5	40.0	+ 2.50	J Reid	1-8	12.5	- 3.50
M Roberts	2-5	40.0	+ 3.50	A Munro	1-13	7.7	- 4.00

S Dawson	0-9	A Clark	0-2	J Lowe	0-1
N Adams	0-7	D Biggs	0-2	M Hills	0-1
W Carson	0-6	D Holland	0-2	Miss J Allison	0-1
B Rouse	0-5	J Fortune	0-2	Mr R Byrne	0-1
L Piggott	0-4	J Quinn	0-2	Mr T Jenks	0-1
J Williams	0-3	N Kennedy	0-2	N Day	0-1
L Dettori	0-3	S O'Gorman	0-2	O Pears	0-1
Pat Eddery	0-3	A Dicks	0-1	S Whitworth	0-1
R Hills	0-3	B Doyle	0-1	T Sprake	0-1
S Cauthen	0-3	C Rutter	0-1		
T Williams	0-3	G Milligan	0-1		

COURSE RECORD

	Total W-R	Non-Handicaps 2-y-o	Non-Handicaps 3-y-o+	Handicaps 2-y-o	Handicaps 3-y-o+	Per cent	£1 Level Stake
Brighton	5-17	0-1	2-4	0-1	3-11	29.4	+ 17.00
Lingfield	3-31	0-6	0-5	0-2	3-18	9.7	- 17.75
Southwell (AW)	2-4	0-0	2-3	0-0	0-1	50.0	- 0.47
Newmarket	2-12	0-0	0-0	0-1	2-11	16.7	+ 2.50
Epsom	2-15	1-2	0-1	0-0	1-12	13.3	- 8.75
Sandown	2-18	0-1	0-2	0-1	2-14	11.1	+ 1.50
Folkestone	2-21	1-6	0-2	0-2	1-11	9.5	+ 20.50
Kempton	2-21	0-4	0-5	0-1	2-11	9.5	- 6.50
Beverley	1-2	0-0	0-0	0-0	1-2	50.0	+ 3.00
Edinburgh	1-2	0-0	0-0	0-0	1-2	50.0	+ 4.00
Hamilton	1-3	0-0	0-0	0-0	1-3	33.3	- 0.25
Yarmouth	1-3	0-2	0-0	0-0	1-1	33.3	+ 4.00
Wolverhampton	1-4	0-0	0-1	0-0	1-3	25.0	+ 0.33
Doncaster	1-10	0-1	1-2	0-0	0-7	10.0	0.00
Windsor	1-13	0-3	0-5	0-0	1-5	7.7	+ 21.00
Goodwood	1-19	0-5	0-1	0-1	1-12	5.3	- 16.00

Ascot	0-12	Salisbury	0-4	Leicester	0-2
Lingfield (AW)	0-9	Warwick	0-4	Newcastle	0-1
Nottingham	0-8	Catterick	0-3	Pontefract	0-1
Bath	0-7	Chepstow	0-3	York	0-1
Newbury	0-7	Haydock	0-2		

WINNING HORSES

	Age	Races Run	1st	2nd	3rd	Unpl	Win £
Fire Top	7	9	1	2	1	5	50,770
Millsolin	4	4	3	0	0	1	13,313
Croft Valley	5	5	2	2	1	0	9,552
Mahfil	4	6	2	1	1	2	8,772
Barrish	6	7	2	0	0	5	8,720
Texan Tycoon	4	6	2	0	1	3	6,367
Sarah-Clare	4	11	2	1	2	6	5,887
Gulf Palace	7	4	1	2	0	1	5,481
Lara's Baby	4	4	2	2	0	0	4,766
Lazy Rhythm	6	5	2	0	0	3	3,998
Pharamineux	6	1	1	0	0	0	3,558
Caroles Express	4	10	1	0	0	9	3,106
Island Blade	3	7	1	1	0	5	2,954
Misty Jenni	2	3	1	0	0	2	2,954
Fay's Song	4	10	1	1	0	8	2,880
Iron Merchant	2	7	1	2	3	1	2,700
Amazon Express	3	1	1	0	0	0	2,637
Absolutely Right	4	6	1	2	1	2	2,324
Monte Bre	6	8	1	0	1	6	2,128

WINNING OWNERS

	Races Won	Value £		Races Won	Value £
Mrs A Valentine	1	50,770	Mrs Susan Crane	1	3,106
Normandy Developments London	6	22,062	The Lime St Racing Syndicate	1	2,954
G S Beccle	3	10,900	P F Roberts	1	2,954
Miss Vivian Pratt	2	9,552	S Harper	1	2,880
A D Spence	2	8,720	C F Sparrowhawk Ltd	1	2,700
Miss Clare Coyne	2	5,887	Mrs Jill Moss	1	2,637
G Burrell	1	5,481	Larabuild Contractors	1	2,383
Miss S A Hamilton	2	3,998	Automarque (Bournem'th) Ltd	1	2,324
Nicholas Roteman	1	3,558			

Favourites	10-44	22.7%	- 7.39	Total winning prize-money			£142,866
Longest winning sequence			2	Average SP of winner			6.8/1
Longest losing sequence			22	Return on stakes invested			-15.4%
1991 Form	42-301	14.0%	+ 27.04	1989 Form	33-259	12.7%	- 17.09
1990 Form	34-344	9.9%	- 129.61	1988 Form	25-250	10.0%	- 27.42

R ALLAN (Cornhill-on-Tweed, Northumberland)

	No. of Horses	Races Run	1st	2nd	3rd	Unpl	Per cent	£1 Level Stake
2-y-o	2	5	1	1	0	3	20.0	+ 10.00
3-y-o	1	4	0	0	1	3	-	- 4.00
4-y-o+	4	14	1	1	2	10	7.1	- 11.50
Totals	7	23	2	2	3	16	8.7	- 5.50

Jan	Feb	Mar	Apr	May	Jun	Jul	Aug	Sep	Oct/Nov
0-0	0-0	0-2	0-5	1-5	0-2	1-3	0-2	0-2	0-2

Winning Jockeys	W-R	£1 Level Stake			W-R	£1 Level Stake
J Weaver	1-5	- 2.50	S Webster		1-13	+ 2.00

Winning Course			
Edinburgh	2-9	+ 8.50	

Winning Horses	Age	Races Run	1st	2nd	3rd	Unpl	Win £
Sabo Song	2	2	1	1	0	0	2,358
Latvian	5	7	1	1	1	4	2,159

Favourites	0-1		Total winning prize money		£4,517

1991 Form	1-19	5.3%	- 15.50	1989 Form	1-29	3.4%	- 22.50
1990 Form	1-33	3.0%	- 30.00	1988 Form	1-33	3.0%	- 29.75

C N ALLEN (Newmarket)

	No. of Horses	Races Run	1st	2nd	3rd	Unpl	Per cent	£1 Level Stake
2-y-o	7	23	4	2	4	13	17.4	+ 7.63
3-y-o	8	41	3	3	1	34	7.3	- 12.00
4-y-o+	8	51	0	3	7	41	-	- 51.00
Totals	23	115	7	8	12	88	6.1	- 55.37

Jan	Feb	Mar	Apr	May	Jun	Jul	Aug	Sep	Oct/Nov
1-5	1-11	1-6	0-13	1-12	1-23	0-17	2-17	0-9	0-2

Winning Jockeys	W-R	£1 Level Stake			W-R	£1 Level Stake
G Forster	2-43	- 23.00	R Cochrane		1-9	- 6.37
D Harrison	1-1	+ 12.00	M Denaro		1-11	- 6.00
P McCabe	1-1	+ 7.00	G Bardwell		1-23	- 12.00

Winning Courses						
Southwell (AW)	4-23	+ 15.00	Beverley		1-2	+ 9.00
Thirsk	1-1	+ 7.00	Newmarket		1-16	- 13.37

Allen C N

Winning Horses	Age	Races Run	1st	2nd	3rd	Unpl	Win £
Toocando	2	5	2	1	2	0	6,648
Persian Traveller	2	6	2	0	1	3	4,486
Digger Doyle	3	3	1	0	0	2	2,363
Bassio	3	6	1	0	1	4	2,246
Energic	3	5	1	1	0	3	2,128

Favourites	1-9	11.1%	- 6.37	Total winning prize-money			£17,871

1991 Form	15-184	8.2%	- 76.97	1989 Form	8-151	5.3%	- 93.50
1990 Form	19-269	7.1%	-119.09	1988 Form	7-80	8.8%	- 27.25

E J ALSTON (Preston, Lancs)

	No. of Horses	Races Run	1st	2nd	3rd	Unpl	Per cent	£1 Level Stake
2-y-o	8	28	0	4	3	21	-	- 28.00
3-y-o	5	29	0	1	5	23	-	- 29.00
4-y-o+	11	119	11	16	15	77	9.2	- 23.00
Totals	24	176	11	21	23	121	6.3	- 80.00

BY MONTH

2-y-o	W-R	Per cent	£1 Level Stake	3-y-o	W-R	Per cent	£1 Level Stake
Mar/Apr	0-3	-	- 1.00	Mar/Apr	0-0	-	0.00
May	0-5	-	- 5.00	May	0-4	-	- 4.00
June	0-4	-	- 4.00	June	0-5	-	- 5.00
July	0-1	-	- 1.00	July	0-6	-	- 6.00
August	0-7	-	- 7.00	August	0-5	-	- 5.00
September	0-4	-	- 4.00	September	0-4	-	- 4.00
Oct/Nov	0-4	-	- 4.00	Oct/Nov	0-5	-	- 5.00

4-y-o+	W-R	Per cent	£1 Level Stake	Totals	W-R	Per cent	£1 Level Stake
Mar/Apr	2-21	9.5	- 4.00	Mar/Apr	2-24	8.3	- 5.00
May	3-12	25.0	+ 30.00	May	3-21	14.3	+ 21.00
June	1-19	5.3	- 13.50	June	1-28	3.6	- 22.50
July	1-18	5.6	- 12.00	July	1-25	4.0	- 19.00
August	1-19	5.3	- 15.00	August	1-31	3.2	- 27.00
September	2-18	11.1	+ 2.00	September	2-26	7.7	- 6.00
Oct/Nov	1-12	8.3	- 4.50	Oct/Nov	1-21	4.8	- 13.50

DISTANCE

2-y-o	W-R	Per cent	£1 Level Stake	3-y-o	W-R	Per cent	£1 Level Stake
5f-6f	0-25	-	- 25.00	5f-6f	0-6	-	- 6.00
7f-8f	0-3	-	- 3.00	7f-8f	0-10	-	- 10.00
9f-13f	0-0	-	0.00	9f-13f	0-12	-	- 12.00
14f+	0-0	-	0.00	14f+	0-1	-	- 1.00

4-y-o+	W-R	Per cent	£1 Level Stake	Totals	W-R	Per cent	£1 Level Stake
5f-6f	7-68	10.3	- 20.50	5f-6f	7-99	7.1	- 51.50
7f-8f	1-32	3.1	- 11.00	7f-8f	1-45	2.2	- 24.00
9f-13f	3-19	15.8	+ 8.50	9f-13f	3-31	9.7	- 3.50
14f+	0-0	-	0.00	14f+	0-1	-	- 1.00

TYPE OF RACE

Non-Handicaps	W-R	Per cent	£1 Level Stake	Handicaps	W-R	Per cent	£1 Level Stake
2-y-o	0-25	-	- 25.00	2-y-o	0-3	-	- 3.00
3-y-o	0-8	-	- 8.00	3-y-o	0-14	-	- 14.00
4-y-o+	0-14	-	- 14.00	4-y-o+	10-81	12.3	+ 5.00
Selling	0-2	-	- 2.00	Selling	0-2	-	- 2.00
Apprentice	0-0	-	0.00	Apprentice	0-11	-	- 11.00
Amat/Ladies	0-2	-	- 2.00	Amat/Ladies	1-14	7.1	- 4.00
Totals	0-51	-	- 51.00	Totals	11-125	8.8	- 29.00

COURSE GRADE

	W-R	Per cent	£1 Level Stake
Group 1	3-67	4.5	- 46.50
Group 2	2-39	5.1	- 21.50
Group 3	3-38	7.9	- 12.50
Group 4	3-32	9.4	+ 0.50

FIRST TIME OUT

	W-R	Per cent	£1 Level Stake
2-y-o	0-8	-	- 8.00
3-y-o	0-4	-	- 4.00
4-y-o+	1-11	9.1	+ 10.00
Totals	1-23	4.3	- 2.00

JOCKEYS RIDING

	W-R	Per cent	£1 Level Stake		W-R	Per cent	£1 Level Stake
K Fallon	7-67	10.4	0.00	Mr R Wilkinson	1-10	10.0	0.00
P Robinson	1-5	20.0	+ 1.00	G Baxter	1-11	9.1	- 7.00
J Weaver	1-7	14.3	+ 2.00				

L Piggott	0-10	J Quinn	0-3	C Hawksley	0-1
S Knott	0-8	P Burke	0-3	C Rutter	0-1
Mrs S Barclay	0-6	A Munro	0-2	D Moffatt	0-1
N Kennedy	0-5	B Doyle	0-2	G Duffield	0-1
D Holland	0-4	D Nicholls	0-2	J Fanning	0-1
F Norton	0-4	N Carlisle	0-2	J Williams	0-1
J Fortune	0-4	N Varley	0-2	M Roberts	0-1
M Hills	0-4	T Williams	0-2	N Adams	0-1
G Mitchell	0-3	B Crossley	0-1	S Maloney	0-1

Alston E J

COURSE RECORD

	Total W-R	Non-Handicaps 2-y-o	3-y-o+	Handicaps 2-y-o	3-y-o+	Per cent	£1 Level Stake
Carlisle	3-8	0-1	0-2	0-0	3-5	37.5	+ 24.50
Redcar	2-14	0-0	0-2	0-0	2-12	14.3	+ 3.50
Hamilton	2-17	0-2	0-3	0-0	2-12	11.8	- 0.50
Newbury	1-1	0-0	0-0	0-0	1-1	100.0	+ 4.50
Beverley	1-4	0-1	0-0	0-0	1-3	25.0	+ 5.00
Ayr	1-7	0-0	0-1	0-0	1-6	14.3	- 3.00
Haydock	1-30	0-6	0-3	0-2	1-19	3.3	- 19.00

Chester	0-16	Catterick	0-5	Southwell (AW)	0-2
Doncaster	0-14	Warwick	0-5	Thirsk	0-2
Wolverhampton	0-12	York	0-5	Chepstow	0-1
Pontefract	0-9	Newmarket	0-4	Newcastle	0-1
Leicester	0-7	Ascot	0-3		
Ripon	0-7	Kempton	0-2		

WINNING HORSES

	Age	Races Run	1st	2nd	3rd	Unpl	Win £
No Comebacks	4	17	3	0	5	9	9,268
Stack Rock	5	13	1	2	1	9	5,020
Granny Mc	5	8	2	1	1	4	4,393
Gondo	5	21	1	3	2	15	3,290
Cronk's Courage	6	14	1	5	1	7	3,019
Johnston's Express	4	11	1	0	2	8	2,669
Kummel King	4	8	1	2	0	5	2,500
Ballad Dancer	7	18	1	2	2	13	2,276

WINNING OWNERS

	Races Won	Value £		Races Won	Value £
Lionel Snowden	3	9,268	M P Russell	1	3,019
Castle Racing	1	5,020	Frank McKevitt	1	2,669
Mrs S Y Alston	2	4,393	David Hall	1	2,500
Mrs Helen O'Brien	1	3,290	Mick Graham	1	2,276

Favourites	2-12	16.7%	- 2.50	Total winning prize-money			£32,435

Longest winning sequence		1	Average SP of winner	7.7/1
Longest losing sequence		30	Return on stakes invested	-45.5%

1991 Form	12-111	10.8%	+ 6.50	1989 Form	1-58	1.7%	- 54.50
1990 Form	6-82	7.3%	- 15.50	1988 Form	10-183	5.5%	- 72.67

D W P ARBUTHNOT (Compton, Berks)

	No. of Horses	Races Run	1st	2nd	3rd	Unpl	Per cent	£1 Level Stake
2-y-o	3	20	4	3	2	11	20.0	+ 21.00
3-y-o	16	79	4	9	8	58	5.1	- 37.25
4-y-o+	11	63	4	3	4	52	6.3	- 27.50
Totals	30	162	12	15	14	121	7.4	- 43.75

BY MONTH

2-y-o	W-R	Per cent	£1 Level Stake	3-y-o	W-R	Per cent	£1 Level Stake
January	0-0	-	0.00	January	0-0	-	0.00
February	0-0	-	0.00	February	0-0	-	0.00
March	0-0	-	0.00	March	0-0	-	0.00
April	0-0	-	0.00	April	0-8	-	- 8.00
May	1-4	25.0	+ 5.00	May	1-14	7.1	- 9.50
June	1-3	33.3	+ 8.00	June	0-14	-	- 14.00
July	2-4	50.0	+ 17.00	July	2-16	12.5	- 4.75
August	0-6	-	- 6.00	August	0-10	-	- 10.00
September	0-1	-	- 1.00	September	1-12	8.3	+ 14.00
Oct/Nov	0-2	-	- 2.00	Oct/Nov	0-5	-	- 5.00

4-y-o+	W-R	Per cent	£1 Level Stake	Totals	W-R	Per cent	£1 Level Stake
January	1-1	100.0	+ 5.00	January	1-1	100.0	+ 5.00
February	0-2	-	- 2.00	February	0-2	-	- 2.00
March	1-3	33.3	+ 1.50	March	1-3	33.3	+ 1.50
April	0-7	-	- 7.00	April	0-15	-	- 15.00
May	1-9	11.1	- 1.00	May	3-27	11.1	- 5.50
June	0-5	-	- 5.00	June	1-22	4.5	- 11.00
July	0-6	-	- 6.00	July	4-26	15.4	+ 6.25
August	1-8	12.5	+ 9.00	August	1-24	4.2	- 7.00
September	0-11	-	- 11.00	September	1-24	4.2	+ 2.00
Oct/Nov	0-11	-	- 11.00	Oct/Nov	0-18	-	- 18.00

DISTANCE

2-y-o	W-R	Per cent	£1 Level Stake	3-y-o	W-R	Per cent	£1 Level Stake
5f-6f	4-16	25.0	+ 25.00	5f-6f	0-12	-	- 12.00
7f-8f	0-4	-	- 4.00	7f-8f	1-19	5.3	+ 7.00
9f-13f	0-0	-	0.00	9f-13f	3-38	7.9	- 22.25
14f+	0-0	-	0.00	14f+	0-10	-	- 10.00

4-y-o+	W-R	Per cent	£1 Level Stake	Totals	W-R	Per cent	£1 Level Stake
5f-6f	1-19	5.3	- 11.00	5f-6f	5-47	10.6	+ 2.00
7f-8f	0-21	-	- 21.00	7f-8f	1-44	2.3	- 18.00
9f-13f	3-16	18.8	+ 11.50	9f-13f	6-54	11.1	- 10.75
14f+	0-7	-	- 7.00	14f+	0-17	-	- 17.00

TYPE OF RACE

Non-Handicaps	W-R	Per cent	£1 Level Stake	Handicaps	W-R	Per cent	£1 Level Stake
2-y-o	2-6	33.3	+ 14.00	2-y-o	2-13	15.4	+ 8.00
3-y-o	0-21	-	- 21.00	3-y-o	3-51	5.9	- 13.75
4-y-o+	0-3	-	- 3.00	4-y-o+	3-57	5.3	- 38.50
Selling	1-6	16.7	- 1.50	Selling	0-0	-	0.00
Apprentice	0-1	-	- 1.00	Apprentice	0-2	-	- 2.00
Amat/Ladies	0-0	-	0.00	Amat/Ladies	1-2	50.0	+ 15.00
Totals	3-37	8.1	- 12.50	Totals	9-125	7.2	- 31.25

COURSE GRADE

	W-R	Per cent	£1 Level Stake
Group 1	1-73	1.4	- 47.00
Group 2	3-24	12.5	+ 10.00
Group 3	3-30	10.0	- 4.75
Group 4	5-35	14.3	- 2.00

FIRST TIME OUT

	W-R	Per cent	£1 Level Stake
2-y-o	1-3	33.3	+ 6.00
3-y-o	0-15	-	- 15.00
4-y-o+	1-11	9.1	- 5.00
Totals	2-29	6.9	- 14.00

JOCKEYS RIDING

	W-R	Per cent	£1 Level Stake		W-R	Per cent	£1 Level Stake
R Price	5-38	13.2	- 5.25	Paul Eddery	1-3	33.3	+ 6.00
T Quinn	3-38	7.9	- 12.50	G Bardwell	1-3	33.3	+ 23.00
Mrs D Arbuthnot	1-2	50.0	+ 15.00	A Munro	1-12	8.3	- 4.00

B Procter	0-6	D Holland	0-2	J Quinn	0-1
B Raymond	0-5	D McKeown	0-2	J Weaver	0-1
M Hills	0-5	M Roberts	0-2	K Darley	0-1
W Carson	0-5	P Robinson	0-2	L Dettori	0-1
J Lowe	0-4	S Whitworth	0-2	L Piggott	0-1
J Reid	0-4	A Garth	0-1	N Adams	0-1
R Cochrane	0-4	A McGlone	0-1	S Cauthen	0-1
D Harrison	0-3	D Biggs	0-1	S D Williams	0-1
F Norton	0-3	D Dunnachie	0-1	W R Swinburn	0-1
M Birch	0-3	G Baxter	0-1		

COURSE RECORD

	Total W-R	Non-Handicaps 2-y-o	3-y-o+	Handicaps 2-y-o	3-y-o+	Per cent	£1 Level Stake
Windsor	2-7	0-0	0-0	1-1	1-6	28.6	+ 7.25
Lingfield (AW)	2-10	0-0	0-0	0-0	2-10	20.0	+ 0.50
Chester	1-3	0-0	0-0	0-0	1-3	33.3	+ 5.00
Bath	1-4	1-1	0-2	0-0	0-1	25.0	+ 7.00
Brighton	1-4	0-2	0-1	0-0	1-1	25.0	+ 13.00
Southwell (AW)	1-4	0-0	0-0	0-0	1-4	25.0	+ 4.00
Salisbury	1-7	1-1	0-1	0-1	0-4	14.3	+ 2.00
Wolverhampton	1-7	0-0	1-3	0-0	0-4	14.3	- 2.50
Folkestone	1-9	0-0	0-4	1-2	0-3	11.1	+ 1.00
Newbury	1-11	0-0	0-1	0-2	1-8	9.1	+ 15.00

York	0-11	Kempton	0-6	Redcar	0-2
Newmarket	0-10	Lingfield	0-6	Ripon	0-2
Haydock	0-9	Doncaster	0-5	Ayr	0-1
Nottingham	0-9	Warwick	0-5	Pontefract	0-1
Ascot	0-6	Epsom	0-4	Yarmouth	0-1
Chepstow	0-6	Sandown	0-4		
Goodwood	0-6	Leicester	0-2		

WINNING HORSES

	Age	Races Run	1st	2nd	3rd	Unpl	Win £
Love Legend	7	11	1	0	2	8	6,940
La Dama Bonita	3	7	1	1	0	5	4,971
Maybe Gold	2	8	2	0	0	6	4,848
Strat's Legacy	5	6	2	0	1	3	4,814
Dark Eyed Lady	2	4	2	1	1	0	4,605
Fly For Gold	3	8	1	2	0	5	2,461
Holy Wanderer	3	8	1	0	2	5	2,363
Munday Dean	4	5	1	0	0	4	1,576
Wassl This Then	3	7	1	3	2	1	1,550

WINNING OWNERS

	Races Won	Value £		Races Won	Value £
George S Thompson	3	11,788	J S Gutkin	1	2,461
Christopher Wright	1	4,971	Michael Pescod	1	2,363
Jack Blumenow	2	4,814	N A Woodcock	1	1,576
Mrs M Gutkin	2	4,605	Mrs Josephine Carter	1	1,550

Favourites	1-8	12.5%	- 3.50	Total winning prize-money			£34,128
Longest winning sequence			2	Average SP of winner			8.9/1
Longest losing sequence			28	Return on stakes invested			-26.7%
1991 Form	12-155	7.7%	- 56.57	1989 Form	10-136	7.4%	- 50.25
1990 Form	20-147	13.6%	+ 59.75	1988 Form	3-145	2.1%	- 94.00

R W ARMSTRONG (Newmarket)

	No. of Horses	Races Run	1st	2nd	3rd	Unpl	Per cent	£1 Level Stake
2-y-o	10	24	5	2	2	15	20.8	+ 29.00
3-y-o	16	85	7	3	14	61	8.2	- 6.50
4-y-o+	7	38	2	10	1	25	5.3	- 32.25
Totals	33	147	14	15	17	101	9.5	- 9.75

Armstrong R W

BY MONTH

2-y-o	W-R	Per cent	£1 Level Stake	3-y-o	W-R	Per cent	£1 Level Stake
January	0-0	-	0.00	January	0-2	-	- 2.00
February	0-0	-	0.00	February	0-0	-	0.00
March	0-0	-	0.00	March	0-0	-	0.00
April	0-0	-	0.00	April	0-8	-	- 8.00
May	0-0	-	0.00	May	0-14	-	- 14.00
June	2-6	33.3	+ 1.75	June	3-19	15.8	+ 9.00
July	1-6	16.7	+ 3.00	July	2-20	10.0	- 13.50
August	0-2	-	- 2.00	August	0-10	-	- 10.00
September	1-5	20.0	+ 29.00	September	2-9	22.2	+ 35.00
Oct/Nov	1-5	20.0	- 2.75	Oct/Nov	0-3	-	- 3.00

4-y-o+	W-R	Per cent	£1 Level Stake	Totals	W-R	Per cent	£1 Level Stake
January	0-0	-	0.00	January	0-2	-	- 2.00
February	0-0	-	0.00	February	0-0	-	0.00
March	0-3	-	- 3.00	March	0-3	-	- 3.00
April	0-3	-	- 3.00	April	0-11	-	- 11.00
May	0-8	-	- 8.00	May	0-22	-	- 22.00
June	1-6	16.7	- 3.00	June	6-31	19.4	+ 7.75
July	1-7	14.3	- 4.25	July	4-33	12.1	- 14.75
August	0-6	-	- 6.00	August	0-18	-	- 18.00
September	0-3	-	- 3.00	September	3-17	17.6	+ 61.00
Oct/Nov	0-2	-	- 2.00	Oct/Nov	1-10	10.0	- 7.75

DISTANCE

2-y-o	W-R	Per cent	£1 Level Stake	3-y-o	W-R	Per cent	£1 Level Stake
5f-6f	1-11	9.1	- 6.00	5f-6f	1-8	12.5	- 5.00
7f-8f	4-13	30.8	+ 35.00	7f-8f	3-45	6.7	- 28.50
9f-13f	0-0	-	0.00	9f-13f	2-26	7.7	+ 18.00
14f+	0-0	-	0.00	14f+	1-6	16.7	+ 9.00

4-y-o+	W-R	Per cent	£1 Level Stake	Totals	W-R	Per cent	£1 Level Stake
5f-6f	0-2	-	- 2.00	5f-6f	2-21	9.5	- 13.00
7f-8f	0-20	-	- 20.00	7f-8f	7-78	9.0	- 13.50
9f-13f	2-12	16.7	- 6.25	9f-13f	4-38	10.5	+ 11.75
14f+	0-4	-	- 4.00	14f+	1-10	10.0	+ 5.00

TYPE OF RACE

Non-Handicaps	W-R	Per cent	£1 Level Stake	Handicaps	W-R	Per cent	£1 Level Stake
2-y-o	5-23	21.7	+ 30.00	2-y-o	0-1	-	- 1.00
3-y-o	2-35	5.7	- 21.50	3-y-o	5-48	10.4	+ 17.00
4-y-o+	0-3	-	- 3.00	4-y-o+	2-34	5.9	- 28.25
Selling	0-1	-	- 1.00	Selling	0-0	-	0.00
Apprentice	0-0	-	0.00	Apprentice	0-1	-	- 1.00
Amat/Ladies	0-0	-	0.00	Amat/Ladies	0-1	-	- 1.00
Totals	7-62	11.3	+ 4.50	Totals	7-85	8.2	- 14.25

COURSE GRADE

	W-R	Per cent	£1 Level Stake
Group 1	4-67	6.0	- 18.25
Group 2	4-18	22.2	+ 46.00
Group 3	4-32	12.5	- 14.00
Group 4	2-30	6.7	- 23.50

FIRST TIME OUT

	W-R	Per cent	£1 Level Stake
2-y-o	1-10	10.0	- 5.00
3-y-o	1-16	6.3	- 6.00
4-y-o+	0-7	-	- 7.00
Totals	2-33	6.1	- 18.00

JOCKEYS RIDING

	W-R	Per cent	£1 Level Stake		W-R	Per cent	£1 Level Stake
W Carson	6-40	15.0	- 12.25	S Cauthen	1-4	25.0	- 1.25
R Hills	2-8	25.0	+ 36.00	M Roberts	1-7	14.3	- 4.00
B Raymond	1-3	33.3	+ 5.00	L Piggott	1-13	7.7	- 10.25
N Day	1-4	25.0	+ 30.00	B Crossley	1-34	2.9	- 19.00

C K Tse	0-5	Pat Eddery	0-2	C Nutter	0-1
J Ho	0-4	R Cochrane	0-2	G Bardwell	0-1
P Robinson	0-3	R Street	0-2	J Quinn	0-1
G Duffield	0-2	W Aldwinckle	0-2	Mr L Maynard	0-1
J Williams	0-2	A Munro	0-1	N Carlisle	0-1
L Dettori	0-2	C Asmussen	0-1	S D Williams	0-1

COURSE RECORD

	Total W-R	Non-Handicaps 2-y-o	3-y-o+	Handicaps 2-y-o	3-y-o+	Per cent	£1 Level Stake
Brighton	2-3	0-0	1-1	0-0	1-2	66.7	+ 41.00
Doncaster	2-8	1-1	0-1	0-0	1-6	25.0	- 2.25
Beverley	2-9	0-1	0-3	0-0	2-5	22.2	+ 4.00
Lingfield (AW)	1-5	0-0	0-3	0-0	1-2	20.0	- 2.00
Goodwood	1-6	1-1	0-0	0-0	0-5	16.7	+ 3.00
Leicester	1-6	1-1	0-3	0-0	0-2	16.7	- 3.75
Ripon	1-6	0-1	0-0	0-0	1-5	16.7	+ 9.00
Sandown	1-7	1-1	0-0	0-1	0-5	14.3	+ 27.00
Warwick	1-7	0-0	1-6	0-0	0-1	14.3	- 3.50
Lingfield	1-8	1-1	0-6	0-0	0-1	12.5	- 3.00
Yarmouth	1-13	0-2	0-2	0-0	1-9	7.7	- 10.25

Newmarket	0-20	Newbury	0-4	Nottingham	0-1
Southwell (AW)	0-11	Ascot	0-3	Thirsk	0-1
Kempton	0-10	Windsor	0-3	Wolverhampton	0-1
York	0-7	Ayr	0-1		
Folkestone	0-6	Epsom	0-1		

WINNING HORSES

	Age	Races Run	1st	2nd	3rd	Unpl	Win £
Maroof	2	3	2	1	0	0	21,415
Arak	4	7	2	0	0	5	8,300
Kateb	3	7	2	0	0	5	5,878

Gabr	2	2	1	1	0	0	4,468
Thakawah	3	7	1	0	3	3	3,184
Gustavia	2	3	1	0	0	2	3,058
Mayaasa (USA)	3	8	1	0	1	6	2,868
Tate Dancer	3	9	1	0	3	5	2,812
Fawz	3	2	1	0	1	0	2,532
Masrur	3	7	1	1	0	5	2,212
Hadeer's Dance	2	5	1	0	0	4	2,070

WINNING OWNERS

	Races Won	Value £		Races Won	Value £
Hamdan Al-Maktoum	11	50,857	Mrs John Davall	1	2,812
Mrs Robert Armstrong	1	3,058	Khalifa Dasmal	1	2,070

Favourites	5-19	26.3%	- 3.00	Total winning prize-money	£58,796

Longest winning sequence	2	Average SP of winner	8.8/1
Longest losing sequence	41	Return on stakes invested	-6.6%

1991 Form	10-114	8.8%	- 28.89	1989 Form	21-139	15.1%	+ 31.20
1990 Form	26-155	16.8%	- 24.88	1988 Form	36-211	17.1%	- 16.63

A BAILEY (Tarporley, Cheshire)

	No. of Horses	Races Run	1st	2nd	3rd	Unpl	Per cent	£1 Level Stake
2-y-o	9	44	3	4	5	32	6.8	- 27.75
3-y-o	9	36	1	1	4	30	2.8	- 15.00
4-y-o+	11	85	11	6	11	57	12.9	- 5.33
Totals	29	165	15	11	20	119	9.1	- 48.08

BY MONTH

2-y-o	W-R	Per cent	£1 Level Stake	3-y-o	W-R	Per cent	£1 Level Stake
January	0-0	-	0.00	January	0-3	-	- 3.00
February	0-0	-	0.00	February	0-4	-	- 4.00
March	0-0	-	0.00	March	0-0	-	0.00
April	1-4	25.0	- 1.75	April	0-5	-	- 5.00
May	1-11	9.1	- 4.00	May	0-2	-	- 2.00
June	0-8	-	- 8.00	June	0-1	-	- 1.00
July	1-9	11.1	- 2.00	July	1-4	25.0	+ 17.00
August	0-2	-	- 2.00	August	0-3	-	- 3.00
September	0-5	-	- 5.00	September	0-9	-	- 9.00
Oct/Nov	0-5	-	- 5.00	Oct/Nov	0-5	-	- 5.00

4-y-o+	W-R	Per cent	£1 Level Stake	Totals	W-R	Per cent	£1 Level Stake
January	2-4	50.0	+ 16.00	January	2-7	28.6	+ 13.00
February	0-4	-	- 4.00	February	0-8	-	- 8.00
March	0-2	-	- 2.00	March	0-2	-	- 2.00
April	0-5	-	- 5.00	April	1-14	7.1	- 11.75
May	0-7	-	- 7.00	May	1-20	5.0	- 13.00
June	3-7	42.9	+ 5.67	June	3-16	18.8	- 3.33
July	3-15	20.0	+ 3.50	July	5-28	17.9	+ 18.50
August	1-18	5.6	- 5.00	August	1-23	4.3	- 10.00
September	1-11	9.1	- 4.00	September	1-25	4.0	- 18.00
Oct/Nov	1-12	8.3	- 3.50	Oct/Nov	1-22	4.5	- 13.50

DISTANCE

2-y-o	W-R	Per cent	£1 Level Stake	3-y-o	W-R	Per cent	£1 Level Stake
5f-6f	3-31	9.7	- 14.75	5f-6f	1-16	6.3	+ 5.00
7f-8f	0-12	-	- 12.00	7f-8f	0-8	-	- 8.00
9f-13f	0-1	-	- 1.00	9f-13f	0-10	-	- 10.00
14f+	0-0	-	0.00	14f+	0-2	-	- 2.00

4-y-o+	W-R	Per cent	£1 Level Stake	Totals	W-R	Per cent	£1 Level Stake
5f-6f	3-15	20.0	+ 3.50	5f-6f	7-62	11.3	- 6.25
7f-8f	2-24	8.3	- 2.50	7f-8f	2-44	4.5	- 22.50
9f-13f	6-41	14.6	- 1.33	9f-13f	6-52	11.5	- 12.33
14f+	0-5	-	- 5.00	14f+	0-7	-	- 7.00

TYPE OF RACE

Non-Handicaps	W-R	Per cent	£1 Level Stake	Handicaps	W-R	Per cent	£1 Level Stake
2-y-o	2-36	5.6	- 26.75	2-y-o	1-5	20.0	+ 2.00
3-y-o	1-14	7.1	+ 7.00	3-y-o	0-13	-	- 13.00
4-y-o+	3-11	27.3	+ 8.67	4-y-o+	8-47	17.0	+ 13.00
Selling	0-9	-	- 9.00	Selling	0-5	-	- 5.00
Apprentice	0-2	-	- 2.00	Apprentice	0-15	-	- 15.00
Amat/Ladies	0-0	-	0.00	Amat/Ladies	0-8	-	- 8.00
Totals	6-72	8.3	- 22.08	Totals	9-93	9.7	- 26.00

COURSE GRADE

	W-R	Per cent	£1 Level Stake
Group 1	2-59	3.4	- 45.00
Group 2	6-42	14.3	+ 0.42
Group 3	3-22	13.6	+ 5.50
Group 4	4-42	9.5	- 9.00

FIRST TIME OUT

	W-R	Per cent	£1 Level Stake
2-y-o	1-8	12.5	- 5.75
3-y-o	0-6	-	- 6.00
4-y-o+	1-8	12.5	- 1.00
Totals	2-22	9.1	- 12.75

JOCKEYS RIDING

	W-R	Per cent	£1 Level Stake		W-R	Per cent	£1 Level Stake
A Tucker	4-18	22.2	+ 2.67	B Doyle	1-3	33.3	+ 10.00
A Mackay	3-35	8.6	- 19.75	Miss L Eaton	1-4	25.0	+ 9.00
D Wright	2-13	15.4	+ 13.50	L Piggott	1-5	20.0	+ 2.00
P Bowe	2-16	12.5	- 3.00	G Baxter	1-8	12.5	+ 0.50

W Hollick	0-15	Donna Hayman	0-1	Miss T Bracegirdle	0-1
G Carter	0-8	F Norton	0-1	Mr A McPherson	0-1
K Fallon	0-4	G Forster	0-1	N Connorton	0-1
O Pears	0-3	J Fortune	0-1	N Day	0-1
G Bardwell	0-2	J Quinn	0-1	P Robinson	0-1
J Carroll	0-2	J Williams	0-1	Pat Eddery	0-1
L Charnock	0-2	K Darley	0-1	R Cochrane	0-1
W Carson	0-2	K L Tsui	0-1	S Davies	0-1
W Ryan	0-2	Miss C Radband	0-1	S Sanders	0-1
B Raymond	0-1	Miss Diana Jones	0-1	Wendy McLaughlin	0-1
D Nicholls	0-1	Miss I D W Jones	0-1		

COURSE RECORD

	Total W-R	Non-Handicaps 2-y-o	Non-Handicaps 3-y-o+	Handicaps 2-y-o	Handicaps 3-y-o+	Per cent	£1 Level Stake
Chester	4-28	0-7	2-5	0-1	2-15	14.3	+ 7.17
Lingfield (AW)	3-12	0-0	1-2	0-0	2-10	25.0	+ 14.00
Leicester	1-2	0-0	0-1	0-0	1-1	50.0	+ 6.50
Brighton	1-4	1-1	0-2	0-0	0-1	25.0	- 1.75
Pontefract	1-4	0-0	0-2	0-0	1-2	25.0	+ 9.00
Redcar	1-4	0-0	1-2	0-0	0-2	25.0	+ 1.00
York	1-5	0-1	0-1	0-0	1-3	20.0	+ 2.00
Hamilton	1-9	0-3	0-2	0-0	1-4	11.1	- 3.00
Wolverhampton	1-14	1-6	0-2	0-1	0-5	7.1	- 7.00
Ayr	1-20	0-6	0-2	1-3	0-9	5.0	- 13.00

Haydock	0-15	Warwick	0-3	Edinburgh	0-1
Southwell (AW)	0-9	Beverley	0-2	Epsom	0-1
Newmarket	0-6	Catterick	0-2	Kempton	0-1
Goodwood	0-5	Ripon	0-2	Lingfield	0-1
Doncaster	0-4	Ascot	0-1	Newcastle	0-1
Nottingham	0-4	Bath	0-1		
Thirsk	0-3	Carlisle	0-1		

WINNING HORSES

	Age	Races Run	1st	2nd	3rd	Unpl	Win £
Never So Sure	4	13	3	1	2	7	23,181
Rose Glen	6	11	3	1	1	6	10,177
Finmental	2	8	2	1	2	3	6,066
Falcons Dawn	5	10	2	1	1	6	5,899
Princess Roxanne	5	11	2	1	4	4	4,958
Ever So Lonely	3	11	1	0	2	8	3,493
Moodiesburn	2	6	1	1	1	3	2,385
Beechwood Cottage	9	15	1	1	2	11	2,167

WINNING OWNERS

	Races Won	Value £		Races Won	Value £
Mrs M O'Donnell	7	34,205	P Green (Huyton) & A King	1	2,553
D G Furlong	3	10,177	D W Rolt	1	2,385
A Bailey	1	3,493	Mrs A Madgwick	1	2,167
Paul Green	1	3,346			

Favourites	4-20	20.0%	- 3.08	Total winning prize-money	£58,325

Longest winning sequence		1	Average SP of winner	6.8/1
Longest losing sequence		31	Return on stakes invested	-29.1%

1991 Form	11-95	11.6%	- 32.87	1989 Form	12-210	5.7%	-100.67
1990 Form	10-180	5.6%	- 88.09	1988 Form	21-240	8.8%	- 37.88

R J BAKER (Tiverton, Devon)

	No. of Horses	Races Run	1st	2nd	3rd	Unpl	Per cent	£1 Level Stake
2-y-o	2	3	0	0	0	3	-	- 3.00
3-y-o	5	17	1	2	0	14	5.9	+ 9.00
4-y-o+	6	19	1	1	2	15	5.3	- 8.00
Totals	13	39	2	3	2	32	5.1	- 2.00

Jan	Feb	Mar	Apr	May	Jun	Jul	Aug	Sep	Oct/Nov
0-0	0-0	0-0	0-3	0-5	1-5	0-4	1-5	0-12	0-5

		£1 Level				
Winning Jockeys	W-R	Stake			W-R	£1 Level Stake
Mr R Farrant	1-1	+ 10.00	R Waterfield		1-3	+ 23.00

Winning Course		
Chepstow	2-8	+ 29.00

		Races					Win
Winning Horses	Age	Run	1st	2nd	3rd	Unpl	£
Athar	3	7	1	1	0	5	2,532
La Belle Vie	6	4	1	0	0	3	1,982

Favourites	0-1		Total winning prize-money	£4,514

17

G B BALDING (Dorchester, Dorset)

	No. of Horses	Races Run	1st	2nd	3rd	Unpl	Per cent	£1 Level Stake
2-y-o	8	39	2	1	3	33	5.1	- 19.12
3-y-o	10	70	5	6	8	51	7.1	- 22.37
4-y-o+	10	80	8	6	13	53	10.0	- 27.30
Totals	28	189	15	13	24	137	7.9	- 68.79

BY MONTH

2-y-o	W-R	Per cent	£1 Level Stake	3-y-o	W-R	Per cent	£1 Level Stake
January	0-0	-	0.00	January	0-0	-	0.00
February	0-0	-	0.00	February	0-0	-	0.00
March	0-0	-	0.00	March	0-0	-	0.00
April	0-0	-	0.00	April	1-6	16.7	+ 9.00
May	0-6	-	- 6.00	May	0-14	-	- 14.00
June	0-1	-	- 1.00	June	0-5	-	- 5.00
July	1-6	16.7	- 3.12	July	2-10	20.0	+ 5.63
August	0-5	-	- 5.00	August	0-7	-	- 7.00
September	0-13	-	- 13.00	September	2-17	11.8	0.00
Oct/Nov	1-8	12.5	+ 9.00	Oct/Nov	0-11	-	- 11.00

4-y-o+	W-R	Per cent	£1 Level Stake	Totals	W-R	Per cent	£1 Level Stake
January	1-3	33.3	+ 2.50	January	1-3	33.3	+ 2.50
February	0-1	-	- 1.00	February	0-1	-	- 1.00
March	0-0	-	0.00	March	0-0	-	0.00
April	1-10	10.0	+ 1.00	April	2-16	12.5	+ 10.00
May	0-12	-	- 12.00	May	0-32	-	- 32.00
June	0-7	-	- 7.00	June	0-13	-	- 13.00
July	2-14	14.3	+ 5.00	July	5-30	16.7	+ 7.51
August	1-15	6.7	- 7.00	August	1-27	3.7	- 19.00
September	1-10	10.0	- 8.43	September	3-40	7.5	- 21.43
Oct/Nov	2-8	25.0	- 0.37	Oct/Nov	3-27	11.1	- 2.37

DISTANCE

2-y-o	W-R	Per cent	£1 Level Stake	3-y-o	W-R	Per cent	£1 Level Stake
5f-6f	2-21	9.5	- 1.12	5f-6f	0-13	-	- 13.00
7f-8f	0-18	-	- 18.00	7f-8f	2-32	6.3	- 16.37
9f-13f	0-0	-	0.00	9f-13f	3-25	12.0	+ 7.00
14f+	0-0	-	0.00	14f+	0-0	-	0.00

4-y-o+	W-R	Per cent	£1 Level Stake	Totals	W-R	Per cent	£1 Level Stake
5f-6f	5-28	17.9	+ 5.07	5f-6f	7-62	11.3	- 9.05
7f-8f	2-17	11.8	- 0.50	7f-8f	4-67	6.0	- 34.87
9f-13f	0-26	-	- 26.00	9f-13f	3-51	5.9	- 19.00
14f+	1-9	11.1	- 5.87	14f+	1-9	11.1	- 5.87

TYPE OF RACE

Non-Handicaps	W-R	Per cent	£1 Level Stake	Handicaps	W-R	Per cent	£1 Level Stake
2-y-o	1-22	4.5	- 19.12	2-y-o	1-14	7.1	+ 3.00
3-y-o	2-21	9.5	- 3.37	3-y-o	3-46	6.5	- 16.00
4-y-o+	2-6	33.3	- 1.30	4-y-o+	6-56	10.7	- 8.00
Selling	0-4	-	- 4.00	Selling	0-1	-	- 1.00
Apprentice	0-0	-	0.00	Apprentice	0-13	-	- 13.00
Amat/Ladies	0-0	-	0.00	Amat/Ladies	0-6	-	- 6.00
Totals	5-53	9.4	- 27.79	Totals	10-136	7.4	- 41.00

COURSE GRADE

	W-R	Per cent	£1 Level Stake
Group 1	7-77	9.1	- 23.80
Group 2	3-45	6.7	- 11.00
Group 3	1-39	2.6	- 36.12
Group 4	4-28	14.3	+ 2.13

FIRST TIME OUT

	W-R	Per cent	£1 Level Stake
2-y-o	0-8	-	- 8.00
3-y-o	1-9	11.1	+ 6.00
4-y-o+	1-10	10.0	- 6.87
Totals	2-27	7.4	- 8.87

JOCKEYS RIDING

	W-R	Per cent	£1 Level Stake		W-R	Per cent	£1 Level Stake
J Williams	6-83	7.2	- 31.99	L Dettori	1-2	50.0	+ 15.00
Pat Eddery	3-5	60.0	+ 9.07	W Newnes	1-4	25.0	+ 1.50
M Roberts	1-1	100.0	+ 1.63	S Cauthen	1-7	14.3	+ 1.00
W Carson	1-1	100.0	+ 10.00	Dale Gibson	1-8	12.5	+ 3.00

Tracey Purseglove	0-16	B Raymond	0-1	Mr D Salter	0-1
N Adams	0-9	B Rouse	0-1	Mr J Rees	0-1
R Price	0-7	D Biggs	0-1	Mrs C Smallman	0-1
A Munro	0-6	D Harrison	0-1	Paul Eddery	0-1
S O'Gorman	0-5	D O'Neill	0-1	R Street	0-1
C Rutter	0-3	D Toole	0-1	S Whitworth	0-1
Iona Wands	0-3	M Hills	0-1	T Quinn	0-1
J Quinn	0-3	M Perrett	0-1	T Sprake	0-1
S Dawson	0-3	Miss C Balding	0-1	W R Swinburn	0-1
N Carlisle	0-2	Miss J Southcombe	0-1		
A McGlone	0-1	Miss K Greaney	0-1		

COURSE RECORD

	Total W-R	Non-Handicaps 2-y-o	3-y-o+	Handicaps 2-y-o	3-y-o+	Per cent	£1 Level Stake
Sandown	3-11	0-1	1-2	0-0	2-8	27.3	+ 6.57
Salisbury	3-38	0-8	1-6	0-0	2-24	7.9	- 4.00
Lingfield (AW)	2-7	0-0	1-3	0-0	1-4	28.6	+ 1.13
Newbury	2-22	0-4	0-2	1-4	1-12	9.1	- 0.50
Ascot	1-6	0-0	0-0	0-1	1-5	16.7	+ 5.00
Wolverhampton	1-6	0-1	0-1	0-1	1-3	16.7	+ 5.00
Doncaster	1-10	0-1	1-2	0-3	0-4	10.0	- 6.87
Warwick	1-10	0-0	0-2	0-1	1-7	10.0	+ 1.00
Bath	1-13	1-1	0-3	0-0	0-9	7.7	- 10.12

Balding G B

Goodwood	0-13	Brighton	0-5	Nottingham	0-2
Kempton	0-12	Folkestone	0-5	Epsom	0-1
Chepstow	0-10	Leicester	0-4	Haydock	0-1
Windsor	0-10	Lingfield	0-2	Newmarket	0-1

WINNING HORSES

	Age	Races Run	1st	2nd	3rd	Unpl	Win £
Gone Savage	4	13	4	1	2	6	13,279
Major Bugler	3	8	1	1	1	5	9,474
Chili Heights	2	8	2	0	1	5	7,266
Respectable Jones	6	9	2	0	1	6	5,618
Morley Street	8	1	1	0	0	0	3,290
Sheringa	3	6	1	1	2	2	3,199
Singers Image	3	9	1	0	0	8	2,868
Lady Lacey	5	18	1	2	6	9	2,481
Matching Green	3	7	1	0	3	3	2,246
Super Serenade	3	12	1	3	1	7	1,330

WINNING OWNERS

	Races Won	Value £		Races Won	Value £
Rex L Mead	4	13,279	Michael Jackson Bloodstock Ltd	1	3,290
Michael Kerr-Dineen	1	9,474	David Shering	1	3,199
B T Attenborough	2	7,266	Mrs K L Perrin	1	2,481
Mrs Ernest Weinstein	2	5,618	Jack Maxwell	1	1,330
Miss B Swire	2	5,114			

Favourites	3-20	15.0%	- 11.05	Total winning prize-money		£51,050
Longest winning sequence			1	Average SP of winner		7.0/1
Longest losing sequence			46	Return on stakes invested		-36.4%
1991 Form	18-247	7.3%	- 67.47	1989 Form	15-181	8.3%	- 35.36
1990 Form	18-188	9.6%	- 8.59	1988 Form	7-202	3.5%	-137.00

I A BALDING (Kingsclere, Hants)

	No. of Horses	Races Run	1st	2nd	3rd	Unpl	Per cent	£1 Level Stake
2-y-o	28	84	8	13	10	53	9.5	- 20.52
3-y-o	24	107	8	20	12	67	7.5	- 54.17
4-y-o+	18	125	20	7	18	80	16.0	+ 32.58
Totals	70	316	36	40	40	200	11.4	- 42.11

BY MONTH

2-y-o	W-R	Per cent	£1 Level Stake	3-y-o	W-R	Per cent	£1 Level Stake
Mar/Apr	0-0	-	0.00	Mar/Apr	0-11	-	- 10.00
May	0-4	-	- 4.00	May	3-23	13.0	0.00
June	0-5	-	- 5.00	June	4-26	15.4	- 4.17
July	2-15	13.3	- 6.38	July	0-22	-	- 22.00
August	3-16	18.8	+ 0.24	August	0-14	-	- 14.00
September	3-35	8.6	+ 3.62	September	1-9	11.1	- 1.00
Oct/Nov	0-9	-	- 9.00	Oct/Nov	0-2	-	- 2.00

4-y-o+	W-R	Per cent	£1 Level Stake	Totals	W-R	Per cent	£1 Level Stake
Mar/Apr	0-12	-	- 10.00	Mar/Apr	0-23	-	- 20.00
May	5-24	20.8	+ 0.25	May	8-51	15.7	- 3.75
June	2-21	9.5	+ 7.75	June	6-52	11.5	- 1.42
July	5-22	22.7	+ 40.00	July	7-59	11.9	+ 11.62
August	2-17	11.8	- 10.00	August	5-47	10.6	- 23.76
September	3-20	15.0	+ 5.00	September	7-64	10.9	+ 7.62
Oct/Nov	3-9	33.3	+ 1.58	Oct/Nov	3-20	15.0	- 9.42

DISTANCE

2-y-o	W-R	Per cent	£1 Level Stake	3-y-o	W-R	Per cent	£1 Level Stake
5f-6f	4-26	15.4	+ 12.86	5f-6f	3-11	27.3	+ 0.83
7f-8f	4-58	6.9	- 33.38	7f-8f	1-36	2.8	- 31.00
9f-13f	0-0	-	0.00	9f-13f	4-52	7.7	- 16.00
14f+	0-0	-	0.00	14f+	0-8	-	- 8.00

4-y-o+	W-R	Per cent	£1 Level Stake	Totals	W-R	Per cent	£1 Level Stake
5f-6f	4-13	30.8	+ 19.50	5f-6f	11-50	22.0	+ 33.19
7f-8f	6-34	17.6	- 10.42	7f-8f	11-128	8.6	- 74.80
9f-13f	8-47	17.0	+ 40.00	9f-13f	12-99	12.1	+ 24.00
14f+	2-31	6.5	- 16.50	14f+	2-39	5.1	- 24.50

TYPE OF RACE

Non-Handicaps	W-R	Per cent	£1 Level Stake	Handicaps	W-R	Per cent	£1 Level Stake
2-y-o	8-72	11.1	- 8.52	2-y-o	0-12	-	- 12.00
3-y-o	6-55	10.9	- 18.67	3-y-o	2-49	4.1	- 32.50
4-y-o+	6-30	20.0	- 12.17	4-y-o+	14-90	15.6	+ 49.75
Selling	0-0	-	0.00	Selling	0-0	-	0.00
Apprentice	0-1	-	- 1.00	Apprentice	0-4	-	- 4.00
Amat/Ladies	0-0	-	0.00	Amat/Ladies	0-3	-	- 3.00
Totals	20-158	12.7	- 40.36	Totals	16-158	10.1	- 1.75

Balding I A

COURSE GRADE

	W-R	Per cent	£1 Level Stake
Group 1	26-189	13.8	+ 36.70
Group 2	2-51	3.9	- 44.17
Group 3	4-56	7.1	- 35.71
Group 4	4-20	20.0	+ 1.07

FIRST TIME OUT

	W-R	Per cent	£1 Level Stake
2-y-o	2-28	7.1	- 18.00
3-y-o	3-24	12.5	+ 0.50
4-y-o+	2-18	11.1	- 10.00
Totals	7-70	10.0	- 27.50

JOCKEYS RIDING

	W-R	Per cent	£1 Level Stake		W-R	Per cent	£1 Level Stake
R Cochrane	21-112	18.8	+ 14.87	A Clark	1-1	100.0	+ 0.57
J Reid	4-49	8.2	- 28.55	C Rutter	1-3	33.3	+ 3.50
W Carson	3-7	42.9	+ 14.50	F Arrowsmith	1-4	25.0	+ 7.00
L Dettori	2-10	20.0	+ 29.00	Pat Eddery	1-4	25.0	+ 1.00
M Hills	2-15	13.3	+ 27.00				

S O'Gorman	0-47	G Baxter	0-2	L Piggott	0-1
B Raymond	0-10	G Duffield	0-2	Mrs J H Roddam	0-1
D Griffiths	0-8	Miss C Balding	0-2	N Howe	0-1
A Munro	0-5	P Robinson	0-2	P D'Arcy	0-1
W Ryan	0-5	Paul Eddery	0-2	R Fox	0-1
M Roberts	0-4	T Quinn	0-2	R Hills	0-1
G Carter	0-3	A Tucker	0-1	S Whitworth	0-1
J Williams	0-3	B Rouse	0-1	W Newnes	0-1
S Cauthen	0-3	J Lowe	0-1		

COURSE RECORD

	Total W-R	Non-Handicaps 2-y-o	3-y-o+	Handicaps 2-y-o	3-y-o+	Per cent	£1 Level Stake
Goodwood	8-29	1-7	4-12	0-1	3-9	27.6	+ 20.75
Newbury	5-38	1-11	2-8	0-1	2-18	13.2	- 10.38
Sandown	3-19	1-3	0-4	0-0	2-12	15.8	+ 1.50
Wolverhampton	2-4	2-3	0-0	0-0	0-1	50.0	+ 10.57
Warwick	2-5	0-1	1-1	0-1	1-2	40.0	+ 1.50
Doncaster	2-19	1-5	0-3	0-1	1-10	10.5	+ 20.00
Kempton	2-21	0-4	2-6	0-0	0-11	9.5	- 11.00
Ascot	2-23	0-3	0-5	0-0	2-15	8.7	+ 29.00
Bath	2-24	0-6	0-6	0-1	2-11	8.3	- 7.00
Ayr	1-3	0-0	0-1	0-0	1-2	33.3	+ 8.00
Epsom	1-5	0-0	0-2	0-0	1-3	20.0	+ 3.50
Beverley	1-6	1-3	0-1	0-0	0-2	16.7	- 4.38
Pontefract	1-6	1-1	0-1	0-2	0-2	16.7	- 4.33
Lingfield	1-9	0-3	1-4	0-0	0-2	11.1	- 7.17
Newmarket	1-9	0-3	1-3	0-0	0-3	11.1	- 7.17
York	1-14	0-2	0-1	0-0	1-11	7.1	- 8.50
Salisbury	1-27	0-8	1-5	0-0	0-14	3.7	- 22.00

Haydock	0-8	Chester	0-5	Thirsk	0-2
Leicester	0-7	Catterick	0-4	Lingfield (AW)	0-1
Folkestone	0-6	Chepstow	0-4	Newcastle	0-1
Windsor	0-6	Nottingham	0-3	Ripon	0-1
Brighton	0-5	Redcar	0-2		

WINNING HORSES

	Age	Races Run	1st	2nd	3rd	Unpl	Win £
Lochsong	4	7	4	1	1	1	134,403
Selkirk	4	5	3	1	1	0	126,601
Spinning	5	8	3	1	2	2	74,216
Knock Knock	7	11	3	2	1	5	39,879
Poker Chip	2	5	2	0	2	1	26,353
Pay Homage	4	11	1	0	2	8	14,655
Heart Of Darkness	4	11	2	0	1	8	11,481
Flashfoot	4	7	1	0	1	5	11,063
Saratoga Source	3	3	1	0	0	2	10,495
Crystal Cross	3	10	2	3	1	4	8,958
Vailmont	3	4	2	0	1	1	6,527
Fragrant Hill	4	6	1	0	0	5	5,114
Brandon Prince	4	7	1	0	1	5	4,944
Palace Pageant	2	3	1	1	0	1	3,106
Brandonhurst	2	5	1	2	0	2	2,979
Frivolous Air	2	4	1	0	0	3	2,784
Green Lane	4	11	1	2	1	7	2,658
Zenith	2	4	1	2	1	0	2,637
East Liberty	2	5	1	0	1	3	2,532
Tissisat	3	5	1	2	0	2	2,304
Abbey's Gal	2	5	1	2	1	1	2,198
Baby Wizzard	3	6	1	0	0	5	1,970
Raven Runner	3	3	1	0	0	2	1,242

WINNING OWNERS

	Races Won	Value £		Races Won	Value £
J C Smith	7	171,818	R P B Michaelson	2	7,922
George Strawbridge	6	143,623	The Queen	2	4,941
Paul Mellon	12	110,849	Jerrard Williamson	1	2,198
G M Smart	3	39,879	David Myers	1	1,970
Miss A V Hill	1	14,655	Mrs Ronald K Kirk	1	1,242

Favourites	15-39	38.5%	+ 4.39	Total winning prize-money £499,096
Longest winning sequence			2	Average SP of winner 6.6/1
Longest losing sequence			31	Return on stakes invested -13.3%
1991 Form	53-362	14.6%	- 50.22	1989 Form 41-349 11.7% - 89.91
1990 Form	48-375	12.8%	- 41.74	1988 Form 43-368 11.7% - 38.29

23

J E BANKS (Newmarket)

	No. of Horses	Races Run	1st	2nd	3rd	Unpl	Per cent	£1 Level Stake
2-y-o	2	4	0	0	0	4	-	- 4.00
3-y-o	4	13	0	1	2	10	-	- 13.00
4-y-o+	8	32	4	5	2	21	12.5	- 11.75
Totals	14	49	4	6	4	35	8.2	- 28.75

Jan	Feb	Mar	Apr	May	Jun	Jul	Aug	Sep	Oct/Nov
0-0	0-1	1-5	0-5	0-4	0-11	2-12	1-2	0-3	0-6

Winning Jockeys	W-R	£1 Level Stake				W-R	£1 Level Stake
N Day	2-6	+ 1.75					
D Biggs	1-3	+ 0.50		J Weaver		1-7	+ 2.00

Winning Courses	W-R	£1 Level Stake			W-R	£1 Level Stake
Chester	1-2	+ 7.00		Southwell (AW)	1-6	- 1.00
Lingfield (AW)	1-5	- 1.50		Newmarket	1-7	- 4.25

Winning Horses	Age	Races Run	1st	2nd	3rd	Unpl	Win £
Polonez Prima	5	10	2	2	1	5	13,630
Tanfith	5	4	1	1	1	1	4,113
Mizyan	4	4	1	1	0	2	2,448

Favourites	1-4	25.0%	- 1.25	Total winning prize-money	£20,191
1991 Form	3-61	4.9%	- 27.00		

W L BARKER (Richmond, North Yorks)

	No. of Horses	Races Run	1st	2nd	3rd	Unpl	Per cent	£1 Level Stake
2-y-o	1	3	0	1	0	2	-	- 3.00
3-y-o	1	14	0	2	3	9	-	- 14.00
4-y-o+	4	18	1	0	2	15	5.6	- 6.00
Totals	6	35	1	3	5	26	2.9	- 23.00

Jan	Feb	Mar	Apr	May	Jun	Jul	Aug	Sep	Oct/Nov
0-0	0-0	0-0	0-4	0-5	0-5	1-11	0-3	0-2	0-5

Winning Jockey	W-R	£1 Level Stake	Winning Course	W-R	£1 Level Stake
L Charnock	1-8	+ 4.00	Catterick	1-17	- 5.00

Winning Horse	Age	Races Run	1st	2nd	3rd	Unpl	Win £
Rexy Boy	5	11	1	0	2	8	2,512

Favourites	0-0	Total winning prize-money	£2,512
1991 Form	0-7		

M F BARRACLOUGH (Claverdon, Warwicks)

	No. of Horses	Races Run	1st	2nd	3rd	Unpl	Per cent	£1 Level Stake
2-y-o	0	0	0	0	0	0	-	0.00
3-y-o	5	24	2	2	1	19	8.3	- 11.00
4-y-o+	1	1	0	0	0	1	-	- 1.00
Totals	6	25	2	2	1	20	8.0	- 12.00

Jan	Feb	Mar	Apr	May	Jun	Jul	Aug	Sep	Oct/Nov
0-0	0-0	0-0	0-4	0-4	0-3	1-5	1-4	0-4	0-1

Winning Jockeys		W-R	£1 Level Stake					W-R	£1 Level Stake
E Husband		1-1	+ 6.50		N Carlisle			1-5	+ 0.50

Winning Courses									
Doncaster		1-2	+ 3.50		Windsor			1-2	+ 5.50

Winning Horse	Age	Races Run	1st	2nd	3rd	Unpl	Win £
Ganeshaya	3	12	2	2	1	7	4,938

Favourites	0-0	Total winning prize-money	£4,938

1991 Form	0-13

T D BARRON (Thirsk, North Yorks)

	No. of Horses	Races Run	1st	2nd	3rd	Unpl	Per cent	£1 Level Stake
2-y-o	17	87	11	9	7	60	12.6	+ 3.50
3-y-o	15	89	13	12	10	54	14.6	- 9.00
4-y-o+	18	147	13	16	22	96	8.8	- 48.20
Totals	50	323	37	37	39	210	11.5	- 53.70

BY MONTH

2-y-o	W-R	Per cent	£1 Level Stake	3-y-o	W-R	Per cent	£1 Level Stake
January	0-0	-	0.00	January	3-11	27.3	+ 5.10
February	0-0	-	0.00	February	2-6	33.3	+ 1.30
March	0-5	-	- 5.00	March	1-7	14.3	+ 6.00
April	0-8	-	- 8.00	April	3-10	30.0	+ 14.50
May	0-7	-	- 7.00	May	1-8	12.5	- 4.00
June	2-12	16.7	+ 2.00	June	1-10	10.0	- 6.00
July	2-13	15.4	- 4.00	July	2-12	16.7	- 0.90
August	1-10	10.0	+ 7.00	August	0-7	-	- 7.00
September	2-14	14.3	- 1.00	September	0-8	-	- 8.00
Oct/Nov	4-18	22.2	+ 19.50	Oct/Nov	0-10	-	- 10.00

Barron T D

4-y-o+	W-R	Per cent	£1 Level Stake	Totals	W-R	Per cent	£1 Level Stake
January	2-22	9.1	- 17.20	January	5-33	15.2	- 12.10
February	2-16	12.5	- 2.00	February	4-22	18.2	- 0.70
March	2-11	18.2	0.00	March	3-23	13.0	+ 1.00
April	2-16	12.5	+ 3.00	April	5-34	14.7	+ 9.50
May	2-13	15.4	+ 1.00	May	3-28	10.7	- 10.00
June	1-8	12.5	- 2.00	June	4-30	13.3	- 6.00
July	0-20	-	- 20.00	July	4-45	8.9	- 24.90
August	1-18	5.6	- 9.00	August	2-35	5.7	- 9.00
September	0-12	-	- 12.00	September	2-34	5.9	- 21.00
Oct/Nov	1-11	9.1	+ 10.00	Oct/Nov	5-39	12.8	+ 19.50

DISTANCE

2-y-o	W-R	Per cent	£1 Level Stake	3-y-o	W-R	Per cent	£1 Level Stake
5f-6f	7-59	11.9	- 6.00	5f-6f	4-24	16.7	- 3.00
7f-8f	4-28	14.3	+ 9.50	7f-8f	5-28	17.9	+ 2.90
9f-13f	0-0	-	0.00	9f-13f	3-31	9.7	- 11.90
14f+	0-0	-	0.00	14f+	1-6	16.7	+ 3.00

4-y-o+	W-R	Per cent	£1 Level Stake	Totals	W-R	Per cent	£1 Level Stake
5f-6f	3-47	6.4	- 5.00	5f-6f	14-130	10.8	- 14.00
7f-8f	8-63	12.7	- 19.20	7f-8f	17-119	14.3	- 6.80
9f-13f	1-35	2.9	- 27.00	9f-13f	4-66	6.1	- 38.90
14f+	1-2	50.0	+ 3.00	14f+	2-8	25.0	+ 6.00

TYPE OF RACE

Non-Handicaps	W-R	Per cent	£1 Level Stake	Handicaps	W-R	Per cent	£1 Level Stake
2-y-o	5-40	12.5	- 12.00	2-y-o	5-27	18.5	+ 18.50
3-y-o	7-29	24.1	+ 4.40	3-y-o	5-50	10.0	- 12.40
4-y-o+	2-20	10.0	- 15.20	4-y-o+	11-108	10.2	- 14.00
Selling	1-23	4.3	- 14.00	Selling	1-9	11.1	+ 8.00
Apprentice	0-1	-	- 1.00	Apprentice	0-11	-	- 11.00
Amat/Ladies	0-0	-	0.00	Amat/Ladies	0-5	-	- 5.00
Totals	15-113	13.3	- 37.80	Totals	22-210	10.5	- 15.90

COURSE GRADE				FIRST TIME OUT			
	W-R	Per cent	£1 Level Stake		W-R	Per cent	£1 Level Stake
Group 1	4-60	6.7	- 23.50	2-y-o	1-16	6.3	- 12.50
Group 2	5-72	6.9	- 21.00	3-y-o	4-15	26.7	+ 15.00
Group 3	7-59	11.9	- 14.90	4-y-o+	1-18	5.6	- 12.00
Group 4	21-132	15.9	+ 5.70				
				Totals	6-49	12.2	- 9.50

JOCKEYS RIDING

	W-R	Per cent	£1 Level Stake		W-R	Per cent	£1 Level Stake
Alex Greaves	19-163	11.7	- 33.20	B Doyle	1-2	50.0	+ 6.00
J Fanning	6-22	27.3	+ 12.50	B Raymond	1-2	50.0	+ 5.00
K Darley	6-41	14.6	- 3.00	J Lowe	1-8	12.5	- 3.00
V Halliday	3-36	8.3	+ 11.00				

L Charnock	0-5	D Harrison	0-1	Mrs D Kettlewell	0-1
L Dettori	0-5	D McKeown	0-1	N Connorton	0-1
S Maloney	0-4	D Moffatt	0-1	N Kennedy	0-1
Dale Gibson	0-3	G Duffield	0-1	O Pears	0-1
J Weaver	0-2	J Fortune	0-1	S Webster	0-1
Mrs A Farrell	0-2	J Williams	0-1	S Whitworth	0-1
R Cochrane	0-2	K Fallon	0-1	S Wood	0-1
S D Williams	0-2	M Hills	0-1	S Wynne	0-1
A Mackay	0-1	M Roberts	0-1	T Williams	0-1
A Shoults	0-1	Miss E Bronson	0-1	W Ryan	0-1
B Crossley	0-1	Miss I D W Jones	0-1		

COURSE RECORD

	Total W-R	Non-Handicaps 2-y-o	3-y-o+	Handicaps 2-y-o	3-y-o+	Per cent	£1 Level Stake
Southwell (AW)	10-62	0-5	6-26	0-0	4-31	16.1	- 6.80
Catterick	8-29	2-8	1-6	0-3	5-12	27.6	+ 32.50
Haydock	2-6	0-0	1-3	1-1	0-2	33.3	+ 9.50
Nottingham	2-6	1-1	0-0	1-2	0-3	33.3	+ 12.00
Carlisle	2-9	0-2	1-2	0-0	1-5	22.2	+ 8.00
Hamilton	2-12	0-3	0-0	1-2	1-7	16.7	- 3.00
Redcar	2-25	1-8	1-3	0-1	0-13	8.0	- 15.00
Thirsk	2-26	0-6	0-2	0-0	2-18	7.7	- 2.00
Beverley	2-27	0-4	0-5	0-2	2-16	7.4	- 16.90
Pontefract	1-7	0-0	0-0	1-2	0-5	14.3	0.00
Doncaster	1-12	0-2	0-0	1-4	0-6	8.3	+ 5.00
Newcastle	1-15	1-4	0-1	0-1	0-9	6.7	- 11.00
Edinburgh	1-20	0-6	0-6	0-0	1-8	5.0	- 16.00
Ripon	1-20	0-3	0-2	1-2	0-13	5.0	- 3.00

York	0-11	Leicester	0-4	Goodwood	0-1
Lingfield (AW)	0-9	Warwick	0-2	Sandown	0-1
Ayr	0-7	Windsor	0-2	Wolverhampton	0-1
Newmarket	0-7	Chester	0-1	Yarmouth	0-1

WINNING HORSES

	Age	Races Run	1st	2nd	3rd	Unpl	Win £
Early Star	3	7	2	2	1	2	12,987
Euroblake	5	24	5	5	4	10	12,308
Pop To Stans	3	11	4	2	2	3	8,982
Sea Gazer	2	5	3	0	1	1	8,934
Boldville Bash	2	11	3	0	2	6	8,461

Barron T D

Eurotwist	3	10	3	2	1	4	7,703
So So	2	7	2	2	1	2	7,083
Egg	2	12	2	1	2	7	5,221
Orient Air	4	10	2	0	1	7	5,068
Love Jazz	3	13	2	1	1	9	4,835
Touch Above	6	14	1	1	2	10	3,818
Stairway To Heaven	4	10	1	1	1	7	3,606
Glastondale	6	6	1	0	1	4	2,406
Slades Hill	5	3	1	0	0	2	2,383
East Barns	4	8	1	1	2	4	2,324
Seraphim	3	6	1	0	1	4	2,217
Shedad	4	6	1	0	2	3	2,206
Papa Westray	3	3	1	0	0	2	2,148
For The Present	2	3	1	0	0	2	1,932

WINNING OWNERS

	Races Won	Value £		Races Won	Value £
P D Savill	8	22,230	Liam Moroney	1	3,606
W G Swiers	8	20,011	J Baggott	1	2,406
E Buck	2	12,987	James E Greaves	1	2,383
W G Spink	4	8,982	Mrs M Baggott	1	2,324
Geoffrey Martin	2	7,083	Alex Gorrie	1	2,217
Mrs J Hazell	2	5,750	T D Barron	1	2,206
David Barron Racing Club	2	5,221	Miss N J Barron	1	2,148
Mrs I M Raine	2	5,068			

Favourites	9-54	16.7%	- 23.70	Total winning prize-money			£104,621
Longest winning sequence			3	Average SP of winner			6.3/1
Longest losing sequence			30	Return on stakes invested			-16.6%
1991 Form	39-331	11.8%	- 75.22	1989 Form	24-275	8.7%	- 122.25
1990 Form	58-337	17.2%	- 42.83	1988 Form	18-208	8.7%	- 31.12

R BASTIMAN (Wetherby, West Yorks)

	No. of Horses	Races Run	1st	2nd	3rd	Unpl	Per cent	£1 Level Stake
2-y-o	2	8	0	0	0	8	-	- 8.00
3-y-o	4	32	2	3	5	22	6.3	- 22.67
4-y-o+	11	81	8	4	3	66	9.9	- 1.00
Totals	17	121	10	7	8	96	8.3	- 31.67

BY MONTH

2-y-o	W-R	Per cent	£1 Level Stake	3-y-o	W-R	Per cent	£1 Level Stake
January	0-0	-	0.00	January	0-0	-	0.00
February	0-0	-	0.00	February	0-0	-	0.00
March	0-0	-	0.00	March	0-1	-	- 1.00
April	0-0	-	0.00	April	0-2	-	- 2.00
May	0-0	-	0.00	May	0-2	-	- 2.00
June	0-1	-	- 1.00	June	0-4	-	- 4.00
July	0-1	-	- 1.00	July	0-7	-	- 7.00
August	0-1	-	- 1.00	August	1-5	20.0	0.00
September	0-3	-	- 3.00	September	0-6	-	- 6.00
Oct/Nov	0-2	-	- 2.00	Oct/Nov	1-5	20.0	- 0.67

4-y-o+	W-R	Per cent	£1 Level Stake	Totals	W-R	Per cent	£1 Level Stake
January	0-3	-	- 3.00	January	0-3	-	- 3.00
February	1-1	100.0	+ 7.00	February	1-1	100.0	+ 7.00
March	0-3	-	- 3.00	March	0-4	-	- 4.00
April	1-14	7.1	- 5.00	April	1-16	6.3	- 7.00
May	1-12	8.3	- 6.00	May	1-14	7.1	- 8.00
June	1-14	7.1	+ 12.00	June	1-19	5.3	+ 7.00
July	2-11	18.2	0.00	July	2-19	10.5	- 8.00
August	0-10	-	- 10.00	August	1-16	6.3	- 11.00
September	2-9	22.2	+ 11.00	September	2-18	11.1	+ 2.00
Oct/Nov	0-4	-	- 4.00	Oct/Nov	1-11	9.1	- 6.67

DISTANCE

2-y-o	W-R	Per cent	£1 Level Stake	3-y-o	W-R	Per cent	£1 Level Stake
5f-6f	0-5	-	- 5.00	5f-6f	0-18	-	- 18.00
7f-8f	0-3	-	- 3.00	7f-8f	1-8	12.5	- 3.00
9f-13f	0-0	-	0.00	9f-13f	1-6	16.7	- 1.67
14f+	0-0	-	0.00	14f+	0-0	-	0.00

4-y-o+	W-R	Per cent	£1 Level Stake	Totals	W-R	Per cent	£1 Level Stake
5f-6f	1-23	4.3	- 14.00	5f-6f	1-46	2.2	- 37.00
7f-8f	2-29	6.9	+ 5.00	7f-8f	3-40	7.5	- 1.00
9f-13f	5-26	19.2	+ 11.00	9f-13f	6-32	18.8	+ 9.33
14f+	0-3	-	- 3.00	14f+	0-3	-	- 3.00

TYPE OF RACE

Non-Handicaps	W-R	Per cent	£1 Level Stake	Handicaps	W-R	Per cent	£1 Level Stake
2-y-o	0-3	-	- 3.00	2-y-o	0-0	-	0.00
3-y-o	0-2	-	- 2.00	3-y-o	0-18	-	- 18.00
4-y-o+	1-4	25.0	+ 4.00	4-y-o+	4-48	8.3	- 5.00
Selling	0-10	-	- 10.00	Selling	4-15	26.7	+ 14.33
Apprentice	0-0	-	0.00	Apprentice	1-19	5.3	- 10.00
Amat/Ladies	0-0	-	0.00	Amat/Ladies	0-2	-	- 2.00
Totals	1-19	5.3	- 11.00	Totals	9-102	8.8	- 20.67

COURSE GRADE					FIRST TIME OUT			
	W-R	Per cent	£1 Level Stake			W-R	Per cent	£1 Level Stake
Group 1	0-18	-	- 18.00	2-y-o		0-2	-	- 2.00
Group 2	4-29	13.8	- 2.67	3-y-o		0-3	-	- 3.00
Group 3	4-41	9.8	+ 5.00	4-y-o+		1-11	9.1	- 2.00
Group 4	2-33	6.1	- 16.00					
				Totals		1-16	6.3	- 7.00

JOCKEYS RIDING

	W-R	Per cent	£1 Level Stake			W-R	Per cent	£1 Level Stake
H Bastiman	6-62	9.7	- 19.00	A Culhane		1-1	100.0	+ 10.00
D McKeown	2-14	14.3	+ 16.33	R Hills		1-4	25.0	+ 1.00

J Quinn	0-5	L Charnock	0-3	Dale Gibson		0-1
M Hills	0-4	S Maloney	0-3	J A Williams		0-1
N Connorton	0-4	Miss L Revell	0-2	N Kennedy		0-1
P Burke	0-4	S Dawson	0-2	T Wilson		0-1
F Norton	0-3	A Garth	0-1	W Carson		0-1
K Fallon	0-3	C Hawksley	0-1			

COURSE RECORD

	Total W-R	Non-Handicaps 2-y-o	Non-Handicaps 3-y-o+	Handicaps 2-y-o	Handicaps 3-y-o+	Per cent	£1 Level Stake
Redcar	2-12	0-3	0-1	0-0	2-8	16.7	+ 3.33
Southwell (AW)	2-12	0-1	1-3	0-0	1-8	16.7	+ 5.00
Thirsk	1-5	0-0	0-0	0-0	1-5	20.0	- 3.00
Yarmouth	1-7	0-0	0-1	0-0	1-6	14.3	- 2.00
Nottingham	1-9	0-1	0-0	0-0	1-8	11.1	+ 17.00
Hamilton	1-10	0-0	0-3	0-0	1-7	10.0	- 4.00
Pontefract	1-10	0-0	0-0	0-0	1-10	10.0	- 1.00
Ripon	1-10	0-3	0-1	0-0	1-6	10.0	- 1.00

Doncaster	0-7	Wolverhampton	0-4	Chester	0-1
Edinburgh	0-7	York	0-4	Folkestone	0-1
Catterick	0-6	Carlisle	0-3	Sandown	0-1
Beverley	0-5	Haydock	0-2		
Newcastle	0-4	Brighton	0-1		

WINNING HORSES

	Age	Races Run	1st	2nd	3rd	Unpl	Win £
Golden Torque	5	9	2	2	0	5	8,070
Joseph's Wine	3	6	2	0	1	3	5,064
Sea Paddy	4	8	2	1	1	4	4,903
Ghylldale	4	7	1	0	1	5	2,826
Lady's Mantle	8	8	1	0	0	7	2,167
Company Cash	4	7	1	0	0	6	2,128
Deputy Tim	9	5	1	0	0	4	1,856

WINNING OWNERS

	Races Won	Value £		Races Won	Value £
Trevor J Smith	2	8,070	M R Handy	1	2,826
Mrs P Bastiman	3	6,920	I B Barker	1	2,167
Greg Lancaster	2	4,903	Mrs P Churm	1	2,128

Favourites	3-7	42.9%	+ 4.33	Total winning prize-money		£27,014
Longest winning sequence			1	Average SP of winner		7.9/1
Longest losing sequence			19	Return on stakes invested		-26.2%
1991 Form	14-127	11.0%	+ 4.25	1989 Form	7-56	12.5%	+ 5.50
1990 Form	12-119	10.1%	- 8.25	1988 Form	3-41	7.3%	- 26.00

B BEASLEY (Hambleton, North Yorks)

	No. of Horses	Races Run	1st	2nd	3rd	Unpl	Per cent	£1 Level Stake
2-y-o	20	64	7	4	6	47	10.9	- 9.75
3-y-o	8	45	3	1	3	38	6.7	- 25.27
4-y-o+	11	43	4	4	5	30	9.3	+ 3.00
Totals	39	152	14	9	14	115	9.2	- 32.02

BY MONTH

2-y-o	W-R	Per cent	£1 Level Stake	3-y-o	W-R	Per cent	£1 Level Stake
Mar/Apr	0-0	-	0.00	Mar/Apr	0-0	-	0.00
May	0-0	-	0.00	May	0-0	-	0.00
June	2-13	15.4	- 2.50	June	0-1	-	- 1.00
July	2-25	8.0	- 10.75	July	2-17	11.8	- 9.27
August	1-19	5.3	- 10.00	August	1-15	6.7	- 3.00
September	2-7	28.6	+ 13.50	September	0-12	-	- 12.00
Oct/Nov	0-0	-	0.00	Oct/Nov	0-0	-	0.00

4-y-o+	W-R	Per cent	£1 Level Stake	Totals	W-R	Per cent	£1 Level Stake
Mar/Apr	0-0	-	0.00	Mar/Apr	0-0	-	0.00
May	0-0	-	0.00	May	0-0	-	0.00
June	2-12	16.7	+ 22.00	June	4-26	15.4	+ 18.50
July	2-15	13.3	- 3.00	July	6-57	10.5	- 23.02
August	0-8	-	- 8.00	August	2-42	4.8	- 21.00
September	0-8	-	- 8.00	September	2-27	7.4	- 6.50
Oct/Nov	0-0	-	0.00	Oct/Nov	0-0	-	0.00

Beasley B

DISTANCE

	W-R	Per cent	£1 Level Stake		W-R	Per cent	£1 Level Stake
2-y-o				3-y-o			
5f-6f	7-49	14.3	+ 5.25	5f-6f	1-7	14.3	+ 5.00
7f-8f	0-15	-	- 15.00	7f-8f	2-26	7.7	- 18.27
9f-13f	0-0	-	0.00	9f-13f	0-11	-	- 11.00
14f+	0-0	-	0.00	14f+	0-1	-	- 1.00
4-y-o+		Per cent	£1 Level Stake	Totals		Per cent	£1 Level Stake
5f-6f	2-17	11.8	+ 13.50	5f-6f	10-73	13.7	+ 23.75
7f-8f	2-22	9.1	- 6.50	7f-8f	4-63	6.3	- 39.77
9f-13f	0-4	-	- 4.00	9f-13f	0-15	-	- 15.00
14f+	0-0	-	0.00	14f+	0-1	-	- 1.00

TYPE OF RACE

	W-R	Per cent	£1 Level Stake		W-R	Per cent	£1 Level Stake
Non-Handicaps				Handicaps			
2-y-o	3-29	10.3	- 15.25	2-y-o	1-17	5.9	0.00
3-y-o	1-16	6.3	- 14.27	3-y-o	2-25	8.0	- 7.00
4-y-o+	0-4	-	- 4.00	4-y-o+	3-30	10.0	+ 13.50
Selling	4-23	17.4	+ 3.00	Selling	0-3	-	- 3.00
Apprentice	0-0	-	0.00	Apprentice	0-4	-	- 4.00
Amat/Ladies	0-0	-	0.00	Amat/Ladies	0-1	-	- 1.00
Totals	8-72	11.1	- 30.52	Totals	6-80	7.5	- 1.50

COURSE GRADE

	W-R	Per cent	£1 Level Stake
Group 1	6-50	12.0	+ 6.00
Group 2	4-43	9.3	+ 2.50
Group 3	1-20	5.0	- 16.75
Group 4	3-39	7.7	- 23.77

FIRST TIME OUT

	W-R	Per cent	£1 Level Stake
2-y-o	3-10	30.0	+ 9.50
3-y-o	0-1	-	- 1.00
4-y-o+	0-0	-	0.00
Totals	3-11	27.3	+ 8.50

JOCKEYS RIDING

	W-R	Per cent	£1 Level Stake		W-R	Per cent	£1 Level Stake
L Charnock	5-49	10.2	- 7.50	J Carroll	1-1	100.0	+ 12.00
D Nicholls	4-35	11.4	- 20.52	G Duffield	1-2	50.0	+ 15.00
S D Williams	3-29	10.3	+ 5.00				

J Lowe	0-5	D Carson	0-1	Mr D Durrant	0-1
J Weaver	0-4	D Holland	0-1	N Connorton	0-1
P Burke	0-4	G Hind	0-1	N Day	0-1
R Cochrane	0-4	G Husband	0-1	P Turner	0-1
J Fortune	0-3	G McDonald	0-1	S Wynne	0-1
A Garth	0-2	L Piggott	0-1		
S Webster	0-2	M Tebbutt	0-1		

COURSE RECORD

	Total W-R	Non-Handicaps 2-y-o	3-y-o+	Handicaps 2-y-o	3-y-o+	Per cent	£1 Level Stake
Newcastle	5-10	2-4	0-0	0-1	3-5	50.0	+ 42.50
Thirsk	2-12	0-2	0-3	0-2	2-5	16.7	+ 13.00
Redcar	2-16	1-6	0-3	1-3	0-4	12.5	+ 4.50
Chepstow	1-1	1-1	0-0	0-0	0-0	100.0	+ 2.25
Edinburgh	1-4	0-1	1-1	0-0	0-2	25.0	− 1.50
Carlisle	1-7	0-0	1-4	0-0	0-3	14.3	− 5.27
Ayr	1-8	1-1	0-1	0-2	0-4	12.5	− 4.50
Catterick	1-9	1-3	0-2	0-1	0-3	11.1	+ 2.00

Southwell (AW)	0-12	Goodwood	0-4	Wolverhampton	0-3
Ripon	0-11	Sandown	0-4	York	0-3
Doncaster	0-9	Lingfield	0-3	Ascot	0-2
Hamilton	0-9	Lingfield (AW)	0-3	Chester	0-1
Beverley	0-7	Newmarket	0-3	Newbury	0-1
Haydock	0-6	Pontefract	0-3	Warwick	0-1

WINNING HORSES

	Age	Races Run	1st	2nd	3rd	Unpl	Win £
Viceroy	5	6	2	0	0	4	18,828
Act Of Union	3	6	1	0	0	5	7,115
Misteropogigo	2	4	2	1	0	1	5,213
Call Me I'm Blue	2	1	1	0	0	0	3,288
Arkendale Diamond	2	6	1	1	0	4	3,150
Persuasius	4	3	1	1	0	1	2,703
Norling	2	1	1	0	0	0	2,595
Jefferson Davis	3	5	1	0	1	3	2,217
Juliet Bravo	2	8	1	0	1	6	2,148
McA Below The Line	4	3	1	0	1	1	2,136
Manuleader	3	8	1	1	0	6	1,988
My Godson	2	6	1	0	0	5	1,161

WINNING OWNERS

	Races Won	Value £		Races Won	Value £
Franco Gamma	2	18,828	Peter Tierney	1	2,595
Derek Atkinson	1	7,115	Mrs Jan Hopper	1	2,148
The Confederacy Ltd	2	5,505	Mike Clynes Associates Ltd	1	2,136
Giovanni Alessi	2	5,213	Manulife Group Services Ltd	1	1,988
S A Barningham	1	3,150	Mrs M J Russell	1	1,161
J Silfverling	1	2,703			

Favourites	4-13	30.8%	− 1.77	Total winning prize-money	£52,541
Longest winning sequence			2	Average SP of winner	7.6/1
Longest losing sequence			27	Return on stakes invested	−21.1%

C R BEEVER (Grantham, Lincs)

	No. of Horses	Races Run	1st	2nd	3rd	Unpl	Per cent	£1 Level Stake
2-y-o	0	0	0	0	0	0	-	0.00
3-y-o	0	0	0	0	0	0	-	0.00
4-y-o+	4	16	1	1	2	12	6.3	- 12.00
Totals	4	16	1	1	2	12	6.3	- 12.00

Jan	Feb	Mar	Apr	May	Jun	Jul	Aug	Sep	Oct/Nov
1-9	0-1	0-1	0-2	0-3	0-0	0-0	0-0	0-0	0-0

Winning Jockey	W-R	£1 Level Stake	Winning Course	W-R	£1 Level Stake
Mrs L Pearce	1-1	+ 3.00	Southwell (AW)	1-11	- 7.00

Winning Horse	Age	Races Run	1st	2nd	3rd	Unpl	Win £
Hand Painted	8	10	1	1	1	7	2,265

Favourites	1-3	33.3%	+ 1.00	Total winning prize-money		£2,265

1991 Form	1-29	3.4%	- 18.00	1989 Form	0-29
1990 Form	1-63	1.6%	- 54.00		

M BELL (Newmarket)

	No. of Horses	Races Run	1st	2nd	3rd	Unpl	Per cent	£1 Level Stake
2-y-o	30	119	21	24	14	60	17.6	- 22.47
3-y-o	23	142	17	17	20	88	12.0	- 39.54
4-y-o+	11	66	1	4	9	52	1.5	- 58.00
Totals	64	327	39	45	43	200	11.9	-120.01

BY MONTH

2-y-o	W-R	Per cent	£1 Level Stake	3-y-o	W-R	Per cent	£1 Level Stake
January	0-0	-	0.00	January	2-3	66.7	+ 9.50
February	0-0	-	0.00	February	0-6	-	- 6.00
March	0-3	-	- 3.00	March	0-5	-	- 5.00
April	1-6	16.7	+ 1.00	April	3-13	23.1	+ 5.25
May	2-12	16.7	- 5.50	May	4-19	21.1	+ 1.75
June	2-17	11.8	- 13.17	June	2-29	6.9	- 19.50
July	7-22	31.8	+ 6.70	July	2-20	10.0	- 11.92
August	5-21	23.8	+ 11.63	August	2-21	9.5	- 5.00
September	4-19	21.1	- 1.13	September	0-13	-	- 13.00
Oct/Nov	0-19	-	- 19.00	Oct/Nov	2-13	15.4	+ 4.38

4-y-o+	W-R	Per cent	£1 Level Stake	Totals	W-R	Per cent	£1 Level Stake
January	0-0	-	0.00	January	2-3	66.7	+ 9.50
February	0-0	-	0.00	February	0-6	-	- 6.00
March	0-6	-	- 6.00	March	0-14	-	- 14.00
April	0-7	-	- 7.00	April	4-26	15.4	- 0.75
May	0-11	-	- 11.00	May	6-42	14.3	- 14.75
June	0-7	-	- 7.00	June	4-53	7.5	- 39.67
July	1-9	11.1	- 1.00	July	10-51	19.6	- 6.22
August	0-10	-	- 10.00	August	7-52	13.5	- 3.37
September	0-9	-	- 9.00	September	4-41	9.8	- 23.13
Oct/Nov	0-7	-	- 7.00	Oct/Nov	2-39	5.1	- 21.62

DISTANCE

2-y-o	W-R	Per cent	£1 Level Stake	3-y-o	W-R	Per cent	£1 Level Stake
5f-6f	11-70	15.7	- 18.42	5f-6f	1-13	7.7	- 7.00
7f-8f	10-49	20.4	- 4.05	7f-8f	8-60	13.3	- 10.42
9f-13f	0-0	-	0.00	9f-13f	7-58	12.1	- 19.12
14f+	0-0	-	0.00	14f+	1-11	9.1	- 3.00

4-y-o+	W-R	Per cent	£1 Level Stake	Totals	W-R	Per cent	£1 Level Stake
5f-6f	0-1	-	- 1.00	5f-6f	12-84	14.3	- 26.42
7f-8f	1-25	4.0	- 17.00	7f-8f	19-134	14.2	- 31.47
9f-13f	0-37	-	- 37.00	9f-13f	7-95	7.4	- 56.12
14f+	0-3	-	- 3.00	14f+	1-14	7.1	- 6.00

TYPE OF RACE

Non-Handicaps	W-R	Per cent	£1 Level Stake	Handicaps	W-R	Per cent	£1 Level Stake
2-y-o	15-84	17.9	- 27.85	2-y-o	6-28	21.4	+ 12.38
3-y-o	3-25	12.0	- 9.62	3-y-o	12-96	12.5	- 30.42
4-y-o+	0-9	-	- 9.00	4-y-o+	0-44	-	- 44.00
Selling	0-7	-	- 7.00	Selling	1-6	16.7	+ 2.00
Apprentice	0-3	-	- 3.00	Apprentice	1-16	6.3	- 9.50
Amat/Ladies	0-1	-	- 1.00	Amat/Ladies	1-8	12.5	+ 7.00
Totals	18-129	14.0	- 57.47	Totals	21-198	10.6	- 62.54

COURSE GRADE

	W-R	Per cent	£1 Level Stake
Group 1	17-153	11.1	- 55.08
Group 2	5-41	12.2	- 19.82
Group 3	9-75	12.0	- 31.09
Group 4	8-58	13.8	- 14.02

FIRST TIME OUT

	W-R	Per cent	£1 Level Stake
2-y-o	2-30	6.7	- 19.50
3-y-o	4-19	21.1	+ 13.50
4-y-o+	0-11	-	- 11.00
Totals	6-60	10.0	- 17.00

JOCKEYS RIDING

	W–R	Per cent	£1 Level Stake		W–R	Per cent	£1 Level Stake
M Hills	24-128	18.8	- 1.14	W R Swinburn	1-3	33.3	- 1.00
P Turner	4-42	9.5	- 25.87	J Weaver	1-3	33.3	- 0.25
G Duffield	3-10	30.0	+ 1.92	T Quinn	1-5	20.0	+ 1.50
E Bentley	1-2	50.0	+ 4.50	Mrs G Bell	1-5	20.0	+ 10.00
D Biggs	1-2	50.0	+ 4.00	R Hills	1-9	11.1	0.00
S Cauthen	1-2	50.0	+ 2.33				

J Quinn	0-14	C Rutter	0-2	A Culhane	0-1
F Norton	0-11	D Holland	0-2	A McGlone	0-1
A Munro	0-9	D McKeown	0-2	D Harrison	0-1
J Carroll	0-5	J Fortune	0-2	G Bardwell	0-1
A Cairns	0-4	J Reid	0-2	J Fanning	0-1
L Dettori	0-4	K Darley	0-2	M Humphries	0-1
W Newnes	0-4	K Fallon	0-2	Mr J Berry	0-1
A Mackay	0-3	K Rutter	0-2	Mr O Frei	0-1
E Johnson	0-3	L Piggott	0-2	N Day	0-1
G Baxter	0-3	M Tebbutt	0-2	N Varley	0-1
M Roberts	0-3	Pat Eddery	0-2	P D'Arcy	0-1
Mrs L Lawson	0-3	S Maloney	0-2	R Adams	0-1
N Kennedy	0-3	T O'Leary	0-2	S Wood	0-1
P Robinson	0-3	W Carson	0-2		
C Hawksley	0-2	A Clark	0-1		

COURSE RECORD

	Total W-R	Non-Handicaps 2-y-o	3-y-o+	Handicaps 2-y-o	3-y-o+	Per cent	£1 Level Stake
Newmarket	7-44	1-9	1-10	2-5	3-20	15.9	+ 3.38
Southwell (AW)	5-19	2-5	0-3	0-1	3-10	26.3	+ 12.60
Hamilton	3-8	1-2	0-0	0-1	2-5	37.5	- 0.17
Redcar	3-10	3-5	0-0	0-0	0-5	30.0	+ 0.18
Newcastle	3-12	3-4	0-1	0-2	0-5	25.0	- 6.71
Bath	2-6	0-0	0-1	0-0	2-5	33.3	+ 2.83
Haydock	2-7	2-3	0-0	0-2	0-2	28.6	- 0.75
Windsor	2-12	0-3	0-0	1-2	1-7	16.7	+ 0.25
Edinburgh	1-2	0-0	0-0	0-0	1-2	50.0	+ 1.50
Brighton	1-3	0-0	0-0	1-2	0-1	33.3	+ 3.00
Ayr	1-5	0-3	0-0	1-1	0-1	20.0	+ 3.50
Catterick	1-6	0-2	1-2	0-0	0-2	16.7	- 3.62
Lingfield	1-6	1-2	0-0	0-1	0-3	16.7	- 1.00
Sandown	1-10	1-4	0-2	0-1	0-3	10.0	- 7.00
Warwick	1-10	1-3	0-1	0-2	0-4	10.0	- 3.50
Leicester	1-11	0-3	0-0	0-0	1-8	9.1	- 4.00
Goodwood	1-13	0-5	1-1	0-1	0-6	7.7	- 9.00
York	1-13	0-3	0-1	1-2	0-7	7.7	- 4.50
Yarmouth	1-18	0-5	0-0	0-1	1-12	5.6	- 10.00
Doncaster	1-20	0-5	0-3	0-1	1-11	5.0	- 5.00

Kempton	0-11	Chester	0-6	Epsom	0-3
Nottingham	0-9	Folkestone	0-6	Thirsk	0-2
Newbury	0-8	Lingfield (AW)	0-6	Carlisle	0-1
Salisbury	0-8	Pontefract	0-6	Chepstow	0-1
Wolverhampton	0-8	Ripon	0-6		
Ascot	0-7	Beverley	0-4		

WINNING HORSES

	Age	Races Run	1st	2nd	3rd	Unpl	Win £
A-To-Z	3	2	1	0	0	1	22,869
Noyan	2	6	3	1	0	2	20,618
Blockade	3	11	4	0	3	4	16,823
Simply-H	3	14	4	3	1	6	11,905
King Paris	2	6	3	1	0	2	11,273
Captain Le Saux	2	5	2	2	1	0	10,540
Carnbrea Snip	2	8	3	0	0	5	8,344
Persian Brave	2	4	2	1	0	1	6,885
Good Reference	3	6	1	0	0	5	6,056
Buddy	3	13	2	1	1	9	4,393
Pippin Park	3	1	1	0	0	0	3,078
Ancestral Dancer	2	5	1	1	1	2	3,028
Red Kite	3	12	1	3	3	5	2,709
Go Flightline	2	4	1	1	0	2	2,700
Champenoise	4	14	1	1	0	12	2,679
Witches Coven	3	8	1	1	2	4	2,616
Regal Lover	3	10	1	2	1	6	2,611
Home From The Hill	2	5	1	0	1	3	2,532
Girl At The Gate	2	2	1	0	0	1	2,481
Soul Emperor	2	2	1	0	0	1	2,427
Princess Oberon	2	4	1	0	2	1	2,343
Roger The Butler	2	7	1	3	0	3	2,322
Moving Image	2	8	1	2	1	4	2,322
Bear With Me	3	6	1	1	1	3	2,295

WINNING OWNERS

	Races Won	Value £		Races Won	Value £
Brian Cooper	1	22,869	Robert Baker	1	2,709
Yucel Birol	3	20,618	Ian K I Stewart	1	2,700
A M Warrender	4	16,823	Mrs Daphne Kilgour	1	2,679
G L H Lederman	4	11,905	Hambleton Th'Breds Plc	1	2,616
Mrs Pauline Karpidas	3	11,273	A A Bridgewater	1	2,611
P A Philipps	2	10,540	Capt B W Bell	1	2,532
Mrs S M Crompton	3	8,344	John G Morley	1	2,481
Persian Partnership	2	6,885	R P B Michaelson	1	2,343
Alan Lillingston	1	6,056	Cheveley Park Stud	1	2,322
Fahd Salman	2	5,505	M B Hawtin	1	2,322
E & B Theatre Productions Ltd	2	4,393	Mrs T Stopford-Sackville	1	2,295
Innlaw Racing	1	3,028			

Favourites	14-49	28.6%	- 16.84	Total winning prize-money			£155,849
Longest winning sequence			2	Average SP of winner			4.3/1
Longest losing sequence			26	Return on stakes invested			-36.7%
1991 Form	43-278	15.5%	+ 9.14	1989 Form	18-142	12.7%	- 36.27
1990 Form	21-200	10.5%	- 17.64				

J A BENNETT (Wantage, Oxon)

	No. of Horses	Races Run	1st	2nd	3rd	Unpl	Per cent	£1 Level Stake
2-y-o	2	3	0	0	1	2	-	- 3.00
3-y-o	2	8	0	0	0	8	-	- 8.00
4-y-o+	7	45	1	0	6	38	2.2	- 39.00
Totals	11	56	1	0	7	48	1.8	- 50.00

Jan	Feb	Mar	Apr	May	Jun	Jul	Aug	Sep	Oct/Nov
0-2	0-3	0-0	0-6	1-6	0-10	0-8	0-7	0-7	0-7

Winning Jockey	W-R	£1 Level Stake	Winning Course	W-R	£1 Level Stake
N Carlisle	1-7	- 1.00	Hamilton	1-2	+ 4.00

Winning Horse	Age	Races Run	1st	2nd	3rd	Unpl	Win £
Verro	5	16	1	0	2	13	2,807

Favourites	0-1	Total winning prize-money	£2,807

1991 Form	2-30	6.7%	- 7.00	1989 Form	0-31
1990 Form	0-24			1988 Form	0-25

R A BENNETT (Maidenhead, Berks)

	No. of Horses	Races Run	1st	2nd	3rd	Unpl	Per cent	£1 Level Stake
2-y-o	1	2	0	0	0	2	-	- 2.00
3-y-o	0	0	0	0	0	0	-	0.00
4-y-o+	6	21	1	1	1	18	4.8	- 13.50
Totals	7	23	1	1	1	20	4.3	- 15.50

Jan	Feb	Mar	Apr	May	Jun	Jul	Aug	Sep	Oct/Nov
0-3	0-1	0-0	0-1	0-2	0-3	0-4	1-8	0-1	0-0

Winning Jockey	W-R	£1 Level Stake	Winning Course	W-R	£1 Level Stake
L Dettori	1-1	+ 6.50	Brighton	1-2	+ 5.50

Winning Horse	Age	Races Run	1st	2nd	3rd	Unpl	Win £
Anatroccolo	5	5	1	1	0	3	2,679

Favourites	0-1	Total winning prize-money	£2,679

1991 Form	1-73	1.4%	- 62.00	1989 Form	1-35	2.9%	- 14.00
1990 Form	4-116	3.4%	- 84.75	1988 Form	0-11		

C J BENSTEAD (Epsom, Surrey)

	No. of Horses	Races Run	1st	2nd	3rd	Unpl	Per cent	£1 Level Stake
2-y-o	4	10	2	0	2	6	20.0	+ 3.75
3-y-o	7	61	2	7	7	45	3.3	- 39.00
4-y-o+	6	49	4	2	4	39	8.2	- 13.00
Totals	17	120	8	9	13	90	6.7	- 48.25

Jan	Feb	Mar	Apr	May	Jun	Jul	Aug	Sep	Oct/Nov
0-0	0-3	0-2	0-11	0-18	2-14	4-18	0-19	0-14	2-21

Winning Jockeys	W-R	£1 Level Stake			W-R	£1 Level Stake
W Carson	3-24	- 1.00	G Duffield		1-4	- 1.25
T Williams	2-26	+ 3.00	T Quinn		1-9	- 1.00
J Reid	1-1	+ 8.00				

Winning Courses	W-R	£1 Level Stake			W-R	£1 Level Stake
Chepstow	2-7	+ 16.00	Newmarket		1-11	- 6.00
Windsor	2-10	+ 7.00	Goodwood		1-14	- 11.25
Lingfield	1-8	+ 9.00	Salisbury		1-15	- 8.00

Winning Horses	Age	Races Run	1st	2nd	3rd	Unpl	Win £
Mahsul	4	14	2	1	1	10	6,981
Ghurrah	3	12	1	3	1	7	3,850
Tadora	3	13	1	0	1	11	3,175
Nabjelsedr	2	3	1	0	0	2	2,950
Mahrajan	8	11	1	0	1	9	2,553
Rakis	2	4	1	0	1	2	2,553
Zinbaq	6	15	1	1	2	11	2,343

Favourites	2-9	22.2%	- 1.25	Total winning prize-money			£24,405
1991 Form	5-99	5.1%	- 62.00	1989 Form	9-111	8.1%	- 24.50
1990 Form	6-161	3.7%	-124.00	1988 Form	14-145	9.7%	- 23.75

J BERRY (Cockerham, Lancs)

	No. of Horses	Races Run	1st	2nd	3rd	Unpl	Per cent	£1 Level Stake
2-y-o	90	431	55	41	42	293	12.8	-108.20
3-y-o	29	262	38	27	31	166	14.5	- 25.57
4-y-o+	10	95	13	12	8	62	13.7	- 21.46
Totals	129	788	106	80	81	521	13.5	-155.23

BY MONTH

2-y-o	W-R	Per cent	£1 Level Stake	3-y-o	W-R	Per cent	£1 Level Stake
January	0-0	-	0.00	January	4-8	50.0	+ 18.50
February	0-0	-	0.00	February	0-1	-	- 1.00
March	3-11	27.3	+ 1.80	March	2-12	16.7	+ 0.75
April	7-38	18.4	- 11.54	April	7-34	20.6	+ 20.00
May	6-36	16.7	- 13.09	May	1-27	3.7	- 24.12
June	8-62	12.9	- 24.35	June	8-52	15.4	- 12.58
July	14-106	13.2	- 46.50	July	4-42	9.5	- 29.35
August	8-75	10.7	+ 5.33	August	4-27	14.8	- 8.27
September	6-55	10.9	+ 0.90	September	4-36	11.1	- 4.50
Oct/Nov	3-48	6.3	- 20.75	Oct/Nov	4-23	17.4	+ 15.00

4-y-o+	W-R	Per cent	£1 Level Stake	Totals	W-R	Per cent	£1 Level Stake
January	0-2	-	- 2.00	January	4-10	40.0	+ 16.50
February	0-2	-	- 2.00	February	0-3	-	- 3.00
March	2-5	40.0	+ 5.63	March	7-28	25.0	+ 8.18
April	2-9	22.2	- 2.25	April	16-81	19.8	+ 6.21
May	0-8	-	- 8.00	May	7-71	9.9	- 45.21
June	1-12	8.3	- 5.00	June	17-126	13.5	- 41.93
July	4-14	28.6	- 1.09	July	22-162	13.6	- 76.94
August	2-13	15.4	+ 2.25	August	14-115	12.2	- 0.69
September	0-15	-	- 15.00	September	10-106	9.4	- 18.60
Oct/Nov	2-15	13.3	+ 6.00	Oct/Nov	9-86	10.5	+ 0.25

DISTANCE

2-y-o	W-R	Per cent	£1 Level Stake	3-y-o	W-R	Per cent	£1 Level Stake
5f-6f	49-355	13.8	-113.20	5f-6f	32-208	15.4	- 15.07
7f-8f	6-75	8.0	+ 6.00	7f-8f	6-48	12.5	- 4.50
9f-13f	0-1	-	- 1.00	9f-13f	0-6	-	- 6.00
14f+	0-0	-	0.00	14f+	0-0	-	0.00

4-y-o+	W-R	Per cent	£1 Level Stake	Totals	W-R	Per cent	£1 Level Stake
5f-6f	4-65	6.2	- 46.62	5f-6f	85-628	13.5	-174.89
7f-8f	9-29	31.0	+ 26.16	7f-8f	21-152	13.8	+ 27.66
9f-13f	0-1	-	- 1.00	9f-13f	0-8	-	- 8.00
14f+	0-0	-	0.00	14f+	0-0	-	0.00

TYPE OF RACE

Non-Handicaps	W-R	Per cent	£1 Level Stake	Handicaps	W-R	Per cent	£1 Level Stake
2-y-o	39-297	13.1	-104.20	2-y-o	6-60	10.0	- 15.00
3-y-o	18-87	20.7	- 15.32	3-y-o	15-129	11.6	- 1.75
4-y-o+	8-26	30.8	+ 3.91	4-y-o+	4-65	6.2	- 30.37
Selling	12-87	13.8	- 5.50	Selling	3-17	17.6	+ 24.00
Apprentice	0-3	-	- 3.00	Apprentice	1-14	7.1	- 5.00
Amat/Ladies	0-1	-	- 1.00	Amat/Ladies	0-2	-	- 2.00
Totals	77-501	15.4	-125.11	Totals	29-287	10.1	- 30.12

COURSE GRADE					FIRST TIME OUT			
	W-R	Per cent	£1 Level Stake			W-R	Per cent	£1 Level Stake
Group 1	26-257	10.1	- 80.92	2-y-o		11-87	12.6	- 36.54
Group 2	13-124	10.5	- 42.32	3-y-o		6-29	20.7	+ 20.75
Group 3	26-185	14.1	- 36.39	4-y-o+		1-10	10.0	- 2.00
Group 4	41-222	18.5	+ 4.40					
				Totals		18-126	14.3	- 17.79

JOCKEYS RIDING

	W-R	Per cent	£1 Level Stake		W-R	Per cent	£1 Level Stake
J Carroll	50-360	13.9	-125.49	J Williams	1-2	50.0	+ 15.00
G Carter	26-138	18.8	+ 33.32	Miss I D W Jones	1-3	33.3	+ 1.00
Pat Eddery	8-33	24.2	+ 3.05	S Wood	1-3	33.3	+ 31.00
L Charnock	5-22	22.7	+ 26.38	J Fanning	1-4	25.0	- 1.12
D McKeown	3-15	20.0	+ 10.50	R Cochrane	1-5	20.0	+ 1.50
G Duffield	3-17	17.6	- 2.50	L Piggott	1-9	11.1	+ 1.00
N Carlisle	2-23	8.7	- 12.37	J Fortune	1-13	7.7	- 8.50
Julie Krone	1-1	100.0	+ 3.00	P Roberts	1-22	4.5	- 13.00

T Quinn	0-15	D Holland	0-2	Miss L Perratt	0-1
N Adams	0-8	M Tebbutt	0-2	N Connorton	0-1
S Haworth	0-8	Mr D Parker	0-2	N Day	0-1
Emma O'Gorman	0-7	P Robinson	0-2	P Burke	0-1
L Dettori	0-6	S Giles	0-2	Paul Eddery	0-1
M Hills	0-6	A Clark	0-1	R Fox	0-1
M Birch	0-5	C Asmussen	0-1	R P Elliott	0-1
R Hills	0-5	C Roche	0-1	S Cauthen	0-1
A Daly	0-4	G Bardwell	0-1	S D Williams	0-1
S Porritt	0-4	Gay Kelleway	0-1	S Dawson	0-1
A Munro	0-3	J Reid	0-1	S Whitworth	0-1
B Crossley	0-3	J Weaver	0-1	T Rogers	0-1
A Garth	0-2	Jaki Houston	0-1	T Sprake	0-1
A Mackay	0-2	Joanna Morgan	0-1	W Carson	0-1
Alex Greaves	0-2	K Fallon	0-1	W Ryan	0-1
Bethan Prys-Jones	0-2	M Roberts	0-1		

COURSE RECORD

	Total W-R	Non-Handicaps 2-y-o	3-y-o+	Handicaps 2-y-o	3-y-o+	Per cent	£1 Level Stake
Hamilton	13-54	6-22	4-13	1-5	2-14	24.1	+ 23.81
Southwell (AW)	9-47	4-25	2-10	0-1	3-11	19.1	+ 8.91
Edinburgh	8-43	5-24	2-8	0-0	1-11	18.6	- 9.14
Wolverhampton	6-36	1-17	1-5	3-7	1-7	16.7	+ 11.25
Ayr	6-47	1-14	5-8	0-6	0-19	12.8	- 2.61
Carlisle	5-18	2-9	2-6	0-0	1-3	27.8	+ 10.75
Warwick	5-23	2-11	1-3	1-4	1-5	21.7	+ 16.25
Redcar	5-33	3-16	0-3	0-4	2-10	15.2	+ 5.88
Beverley	5-40	3-24	1-9	0-1	1-6	12.5	- 18.75
Newmarket	4-29	0-5	1-5	1-4	2-15	13.8	+ 17.00
Haydock	4-44	1-14	2-11	1-7	0-12	9.1	- 27.00
Chepstow	3-9	1-3	2-5	0-0	0-1	33.3	- 3.20

Berry J

Lingfield (AW)	3-12	0-6	1-2	0-0	2-4	25.0	- 3.00
Newcastle	3-19	0-9	0-0	0-2	3-8	15.8	+ 1.13
Doncaster	3-22	1-10	1-3	0-2	1-7	13.6	+ 1.00
Chester	3-25	2-8	1-2	0-3	0-12	12.0	0.00
Pontefract	3-29	1-18	1-5	0-1	1-5	10.3	- 14.25
Ripon	3-30	2-16	0-5	1-4	0-5	10.0	- 18.70
Catterick	3-35	3-19	0-4	0-4	0-8	8.6	- 27.87
Folkestone	2-8	1-4	1-3	0-1	0-0	25.0	- 2.75
Newbury	2-12	2-4	0-3	0-1	0-4	16.7	- 5.84
Thirsk	2-28	1-16	1-7	0-3	0-2	7.1	- 21.50
York	2-30	2-8	0-5	0-3	0-14	6.7	- 21.10
Yarmouth	1-4	1-3	0-0	0-0	0-1	25.0	+ 17.00
Kempton	1-5	1-3	0-1	0-0	0-1	20.0	+ 4.00
Epsom	1-11	0-4	1-1	0-0	0-6	9.1	- 9.50
Nottingham	1-21	1-14	0-4	0-1	0-2	4.8	- 13.00

Goodwood	0-18	Windsor	0-10	Lingfield	0-7
Ascot	0-11	Sandown	0-9	Brighton	0-1
Bath	0-10	Leicester	0-8		

WINNING HORSES

		Races					Win
	Age	Run	1st	2nd	3rd	Unpl	£
Sabre Rattler	2	11	3	3	1	4	20,444
Fylde Flyer	3	10	2	1	2	5	19,453
Palacegate Episode	2	6	4	2	0	0	18,206
Laurel Queen	4	15	7	2	0	6	17,246
Classic Storm	2	11	7	1	2	1	16,574
Heather Bank	3	10	2	0	2	6	16,310
Lucky Parkes	2	6	4	1	0	1	15,420
Palacegate Touch	2	5	3	0	0	2	13,391
Cranfield Comet	3	17	4	1	1	11	11,649
Threepence	3	13	3	1	3	6	10,021
Paris House	3	7	1	1	0	5	8,894
Palacegate Racing	3	13	3	1	1	8	6,932
Amron	5	12	2	1	0	9	6,660
Echo-Logical	3	6	3	1	0	2	6,485
Palacegate King	3	13	3	0	2	8	6,384
Two Moves In Front	2	10	3	0	0	7	5,630
Mamma's Too	3	7	2	2	0	3	5,612
Allegrissima	2	7	3	1	0	3	5,309
Laurel Delight	2	7	2	1	1	3	5,226
Soba Guest	3	14	2	0	3	9	4,854
Trentesimo	2	9	2	1	2	4	4,737
Palacegate Prince	2	12	2	1	1	8	4,728
High Principles	3	12	2	0	4	6	4,668
Convenient Moment	2	6	2	2	0	2	4,598
Charity Express	2	10	2	1	1	6	4,551
Arctic Appeal	3	12	2	4	1	5	4,549
Another Episode	3	6	2	1	0	3	4,460
Tynron Doon	3	2	2	0	0	0	4,384
Dokkha Oyston	4	9	2	1	1	5	4,183
Cee-Jay-Ay	5	12	1	1	4	6	3,870
Windpower	3	12	1	1	1	9	3,785

Local Heroine	2	5	1	1	0	3	3,688
Memsahb	3	6	1	0	0	5	3,558
Margaret's Gift	2	8	1	2	1	4	3,002
Palacegate Sunset	2	9	1	2	0	6	2,784
Sober Lad	2	5	1	0	0	4	2,584
Tuscan Dawn	2	7	1	2	1	3	2,540
Tom Piper	2	4	1	0	0	3	2,511
Daaniera	2	6	1	0	0	5	2,500
Anusha	2	2	1	0	0	1	2,448
Kentucky Dreams	2	3	1	0	0	2	2,422
Make It Happen	2	8	1	1	2	4	2,414
Drumdonna	2	6	1	0	1	4	2,369
Pilgrim Bay	2	8	1	0	1	6	2,346
Glowing Value	2	8	1	2	2	3	2,261
Murray's Mazda	3	9	1	2	0	6	2,206
Press The Bell	2	7	1	0	2	4	2,192
Our Mica	2	9	1	0	1	7	2,167
Chateau Nord	3	12	1	1	1	9	2,128
Rhett's Choice	2	5	1	1	2	1	2,070
Super Seve	2	7	1	0	0	6	1,725
Music Dancer	3	10	1	3	2	4	1,660
Sizzling Saga	4	6	1	0	0	5	1,590
Cockerham Ranger	2	5	1	1	0	3	1,520

WINNING OWNERS

	Races Won	Value £		Races Won	Value £
Palacegate Corporation Ltd	18	56,884	Express Marie Curie Racing	2	4,551
Laurel (Leisure) Ltd	9	22,472	Mrs J M Bradford-Nutter	2	4,492
H B Hughes	3	20,444	D G Rogers	2	4,384
Blackpool Gazette & Herald Ltd	2	19,453	Mrs L J Meylan	1	3,688
D J Ayres	7	16,574	The Sussex Stud Ltd	1	3,558
Norman Harper	2	16,310	T G Holdcroft	1	3,002
Joseph Heler	4	15,420	F Viner	1	2,584
P E T Chandler	4	14,202	Miss Antonia Taverner	1	2,540
R E Sangster	4	13,806	A B Atkins	1	2,511
Cranfield Industries Ltd	4	11,649	Mrs Seamus Purcell	1	2,500
Richard Jinks	3	8,724	Mrs Norma Peebles	1	2,369
Robert Aird	4	8,044	Frank A McNulty	1	2,346
Yahya Nasib	3	6,997	F Dunne	1	2,261
Roy Peebles	2	6,660	Sydney Mason	1	2,192
Liverpool Daily Post & Echo	3	6,485	Mike Dodds	1	2,167
Murray Grubb	3	6,389	Melville Stewart Partnership	1	2,128
Heathavon Stables Ltd	3	6,328	Wentdale Const Ltd	1	1,725
J K Brown	2	5,612	J David Abell	1	1,590
B R Allen	2	4,737	Alan Berry	1	1,520
David Fish	2	4,598			

Favourites	38-105	36.2%	- 12.44	Total winning prize-money	£323,894
Longest winning sequence			3	Average SP of winner	5.0/1
Longest losing sequence			39	Return on stakes invested	-19.7%
1991 Form	143-837	17.1%	-184.88	1989 Form	92-645	14.3%	-184.22
1990 Form	127-807	15.7%	-158.61	1988 Form	70-461	15.2%	- 51.43

J D BETHELL (Middleham, North Yorks)

	No. of Horses	Races Run	1st	2nd	3rd	Unpl	Per cent	£1 Level Stake
2-y-o	6	18	1	1	1	15	5.6	- 7.00
3-y-o	5	29	0	1	3	25	-	- 29.00
4-y-o+	10	59	3	2	5	49	5.1	- 35.00
Totals	21	106	4	4	9	89	3.8	- 71.00

Jan	Feb	Mar	Apr	May	Jun	Jul	Aug	Sep	Oct/Nov
1-10	0-1	1-4	0-8	0-13	0-15	0-11	1-11	1-18	0-15

Winning Jockeys		W-R	£1 Level Stake				W-R	£1 Level Stake
A Munro		2-19	+ 2.00		D Harrison		1-6	- 3.00
J Reid		1-1	+ 10.00					

Winning Courses								
Beverley		1-3	+ 14.00		Newcastle		1-4	+ 7.00
Brighton		1-3	+ 1.00		Southwell (AW)		1-12	- 9.00

Winning Horses		Age	Races Run	1st	2nd	3rd	Unpl	Win £
Precentor		6	6	1	0	0	5	3,886
Double Echo		4	12	1	2	2	7	2,363
Spice And Sugar		2	1	1	0	0	0	2,343
Brora Rose		4	5	1	0	0	4	2,226

Favourites	1-5	20.0%	- 2.00	Total winning prize-money			£10,818
1991 Form	11-156	7.1%	- 21.62	1989 Form	11-120	9.2%	- 12.12
1990 Form	10-120	8.3%	- 48.00	1988 Form	4-63	6.3%	- 11.50

P J BEVAN (Uttoxeter, Staffs)

	No. of Horses	Races Run	1st	2nd	3rd	Unpl	Per cent	£1 Level Stake
2-y-o	0	0	0	0	0	0	-	0.00
3-y-o	1	3	0	0	0	3	-	- 3.00
4-y-o+	4	13	2	0	0	11	15.4	+ 5.00
Totals	5	16	2	0	0	14	12.5	+ 2.00

Jan	Feb	Mar	Apr	May	Jun	Jul	Aug	Sep	Oct/Nov
0-0	0-0	0-0	0-0	0-1	0-3	1-6	0-2	0-1	1-3

Winning Jockey		W-R	£1 Level Stake				W-R	£1 Level Stake
B Crossley		2-7	+ 11.00					

Winning Courses								
Chester		1-2	+ 7.00		Haydock		1-2	+ 7.00

Winning Horse	Age	Races Run	1st	2nd	3rd	Unpl	Win £
My Chiara	6	6	2	0	0	4	9,102

Favourites	0-0				Total winning prize-money		£9,102

1991 Form	1-20	5.0%	- 15.50	1989 Form	0-23
1990 Form	0-14			1988 Form	0-28

M BLANSHARD (Upper Lambourn, Berks)

	No. of Horses	Races Run	1st	2nd	3rd	Unpl	Per cent	£1 Level Stake
2-y-o	9	56	2	5	3	46	3.6	- 45.00
3-y-o	6	41	1	2	2	36	2.4	- 28.00
4-y-o+	8	76	4	10	4	58	5.3	- 35.25
Totals	23	173	7	17	9	140	4.0	-108.25

Jan	Feb	Mar	Apr	May	Jun	Jul	Aug	Sep	Oct/Nov
0-1	0-0	0-8	0-19	1-19	1-24	3-33	1-22	1-27	0-20

Winning Jockeys	W-R	£1 Level Stake			W-R	£1 Level Stake
R Cochrane	2-22	- 10.25	D Harrison		1-11	- 3.00
F Norton	1-8	- 5.00	J Quinn		1-15	- 3.00
C Avery	1-9	+ 8.00	J Reid		1-20	- 7.00

Winning Courses						
Yarmouth	2-5	+ 6.75	Folkestone		1-8	+ 9.00
Catterick	1-1	+ 2.00	Salisbury		1-9	- 1.00
Chester	1-2	+ 10.00	Newbury		1-10	+ 3.00

Winning Horses	Age	Races Run	1st	2nd	3rd	Unpl	Win £
Welshman	6	8	1	1	0	6	19,250
Spring Sunrise	2	8	2	1	1	4	5,383
Sunday's Hill	3	10	1	1	1	7	5,254
Prince Sobur	6	9	1	5	0	3	3,173
Luna Bid	9	18	1	2	1	14	2,856
Barbara's Cutie	4	18	1	0	2	15	2,532

Favourites	1-8	12.5%	- 5.25	Total winning prize-money		£38,447

1991 Form	6-136	4.4%	- 85.00	1989 Form	8-120	6.7%	- 10.50
1990 Form	5-128	3.9%	- 76.50	1988 Form	3-113	2.7%	- 87.00

G BLUM (Newmarket)

		No. of Horses	Races Run	1st	2nd	3rd	Unpl	Per cent	£1 Level Stake
2-y-o		4	15	0	0	0	15	-	- 15.00
3-y-o		8	42	4	2	1	35	9.5	- 3.92
4-y-o+		1	11	0	1	0	10	-	- 11.00
Totals		13	68	4	3	1	60	5.9	- 29.92

Jan	Feb	Mar	Apr	May	Jun	Jul	Aug	Sep	Oct/Nov
0-0	0-2	0-1	1-9	0-10	1-21	1-10	1-8	0-4	0-3

Winning Jockeys	W-R	£1 Level Stake			W-R	£1 Level Stake
D Harrison	3-14	+ 3.08	C Hawksley		1-7	+ 14.00

Winning Courses	W-R	£1 Level Stake			W-R	£1 Level Stake
Leicester	2-7	+ 3.38	Warwick		1-5	+ 16.00
Brighton	1-2	+ 4.70				

Winning Horse	Age	Races Run	1st	2nd	3rd	Unpl	Win £
Certain Lady	3	14	4	2	0	8	8,657

Favourites	1-2	50.0%	+ 0.88	Total winning prize-money	£8,657

1991 Form	6-64	9.4%	+ 17.00	1989 Form	1-75	1.3%	- 67.50
1990 Form	2-70	2.9%	- 42.00	1988 Form	3-70	4.3%	- 36.50

M J BOLTON (Shrewton, Wilts)

		No. of Horses	Races Run	1st	2nd	3rd	Unpl	Per cent	£1 Level Stake
2-y-o		0	0	0	0	0	0	-	0.00
3-y-o		2	9	0	0	0	9	-	- 9.00
4-y-o+		3	19	5	3	1	10	26.3	+ 16.00
Totals		5	28	5	3	1	19	17.9	+ 7.00

Jan	Feb	Mar	Apr	May	Jun	Jul	Aug	Sep	Oct/Nov
0-0	0-1	0-0	0-1	1-2	0-1	2-8	2-8	0-7	0-0

Winning Jockeys	W-R	£1 Level Stake			W-R	£1 Level Stake
J Lowe	3-4	+ 18.50	C Rutter		1-4	+ 1.50
W Carson	1-2	+ 5.00				

Winning Courses	W-R	£1 Level Stake			W-R	£1 Level Stake
Hamilton	2-4	+ 8.50	Sandown		1-3	+ 4.00
Windsor	1-2	+ 8.00	Salisbury		1-9	- 3.50

Winning Horses	Age	Races Run	1st	2nd	3rd	Unpl	Win £
Dawes Of Nelson	7	10	4	0	1	5	9,963
Rocquaine Bay	5	8	1	3	0	4	2,784

Favourites	1-3	33.3%	+ 2.50	Total winning prize-money			£12,747

1991 Form	1-40	2.5%	- 36.00	1989 Form	0-19
1990 Form	2-34	5.9%	- 11.00	1988 Form	0-26

C B B BOOTH (Flaxton, North Yorks)

	No. of Horses	Races Run	1st	2nd	3rd	Unpl	Per cent	£1 Level Stake
2-y-o	7	19	1	3	2	13	5.3	- 16.25
3-y-o	3	25	1	1	7	16	4.0	- 20.50
4-y-o+	5	33	1	2	1	29	3.0	- 24.00
Totals	15	77	3	6	10	58	3.9	- 60.75

Jan	Feb	Mar	Apr	May	Jun	Jul	Aug	Sep	Oct/Nov
0-5	0-3	0-0	0-6	0-5	0-7	2-10	1-10	0-12	0-19

Winning Jockeys	W-R	£1 Level Stake		W-R	£1 Level Stake
G Oldroyd	2-27	- 19.75	G Forster	1-8	+ 1.00

Winning Courses	W-R	£1 Level Stake		W-R	£1 Level Stake
Hamilton	1-6	- 3.25	Doncaster	1-10	- 1.00
Ayr	1-7	- 2.50			

Winning Horses	Age	Races Run	1st	2nd	3rd	Unpl	Win £
State Flyer	4	15	1	1	0	13	3,080
Master Copy	3	9	1	0	2	6	2,253
Montone	2	3	1	0	1	1	2,196

Favourites	1-3	33.3%	- 0.25	Total winning prize-money			£7,529

1991 Form	5-59	8.5%	- 11.70	1989 Form	4-81	4.9%	- 60.50
1990 Form	4-74	5.4%	- 48.50	1988 Form	7-95	7.4%	- 17.50

R BOSS (Newmarket)

	No. of Horses	Races Run	1st	2nd	3rd	Unpl	Per cent	£1 Level Stake
2-y-o	4	10	0	1	1	8	-	- 10.00
3-y-o	12	85	9	5	6	65	10.6	- 30.50
4-y-o+	4	14	0	0	1	13	-	- 14.00
Totals	20	109	9	6	8	86	8.3	- 54.50

Jan	Feb	Mar	Apr	May	Jun	Jul	Aug	Sep	Oct/Nov
0-0	0-1	0-2	0-13	0-14	2-14	4-26	3-24	0-8	0-7

Winning Jockeys	W-R	£1 Level Stake			W-R	£1 Level Stake
Pat Eddery	3-10	+ 7.50	J Reid		1-4	+ 2.50
M Tebbutt	2-21	- 12.00	J Quinn		1-4	+ 3.50
A Munro	1-4	+ 6.00	B Raymond		1-7	- 3.00

Winning Courses						
Wolverhampton	2-4	+ 6.50	Beverley		1-6	- 1.00
Pontefract	2-7	+ 4.50	Leicester		1-8	- 2.00
Catterick	1-1	+ 3.00	Newmarket		1-17	- 9.50
Southwell (AW)	1-3	+ 7.00				

Winning Horses	Age	Races Run	1st	2nd	3rd	Unpl	Win £
Miss Haggis	3	9	3	0	0	6	15,139
Spanish Express	3	10	2	0	2	6	5,316
Walking Possession	3	11	2	1	1	7	5,129
Forest Fairy	3	9	1	1	0	7	3,623
Liability Order	3	10	1	1	1	7	3,340

Favourites	2-5	40.0%	+ 6.50	Total winning prize-money		£32,546

1991 Form	18-194	9.3%	- 78.53	1989 Form	23-170	13.5%	+ 5.06
1990 Form	36-230	15.7%	- 40.88	1988 Form	23-141	16.3%	+ 12.77

J F BOTTOMLEY (Malton, North Yorks)

	No. of Horses	Races Run	1st	2nd	3rd	Unpl	Per cent	£1 Level Stake
2-y-o	4	23	1	4	3	15	4.3	- 15.50
3-y-o	3	16	0	2	1	13	-	- 16.00
4-y-o+	5	13	2	1	0	10	15.4	+ 13.00
Totals	12	52	3	7	4	38	5.8	- 18.50

Jan	Feb	Mar	Apr	May	Jun	Jul	Aug	Sep	Oct/Nov
2-5	0-3	0-4	0-0	0-3	1-5	0-10	0-6	0-9	0-7

Winning Jockeys		W-R	£1 Level Stake				W-R	£1 Level Stake
G Bardwell		2-13	+ 13.00		N Kennedy		1-7	+ 0.50

Winning Courses								
Southwell (AW)		2-14	+ 12.00		Wolverhampton		1-1	+ 6.50

Winning Horses		Age	Races Run	1st	2nd	3rd	Unpl	Win £
Comtec's Legend		2	8	1	0	2	5	2,344
Qualitair Flyer		10	4	1	0	0	3	2,265
Qualitair Aviator		6	1	1	0	0	0	2,226

Favourites	0-3				Total winning prize-money			£6,835

1991 Form	4-94	4.3%	- 29.00		1989 Form	5-41	12.2%	+ 0.50
1990 Form	5-108	4.6%	- 57.25					

S R BOWRING (Edwinstowe, Notts)

	No. of Horses	Races Run	1st	2nd	3rd	Unpl	Per cent	£1 Level Stake
2-y-o	3	5	0	0	0	5	-	- 5.00
3-y-o	2	14	1	3	0	10	7.1	+ 1.40
4-y-o+	6	64	8	6	6	44	12.5	+ 49.50
Totals	11	83	9	9	6	59	10.8	+ 45.90

Jan	Feb	Mar	Apr	May	Jun	Jul	Aug	Sep	Oct/Nov
1-5	0-3	0-3	1-8	1-5	3-14	1-16	1-9	1-12	0-8

Winning Jockeys		W-R	£1 Level Stake				W-R	£1 Level Stake
M Harris		4-25	+ 3.50		F Norton		1-6	+ 9.40
S Webster		3-21	+ 13.00		N Adams		1-7	+ 44.00

Winning Courses								
Southwell (AW)		5-23	+ 56.50		Beverley		1-8	- 3.00
Ripon		2-2	+ 34.40		Nottingham		1-14	- 6.00

Winning Horses		Age	Races Run	1st	2nd	3rd	Unpl	Win £
Sandmoor Denim		5	21	4	3	2	12	10,536
Strip Cartoon		4	24	3	2	2	17	6,416
Lincstone Boy		4	9	1	1	2	5	2,783
Ace Girl		3	9	1	3	0	5	1,518

Favourites	1-3	33.3%	+ 1.00		Total winning prize-money			£21,252

1991 Form	2-56	3.6%	- 19.00		1989 Form	2-75	2.7%	- 53.00
1990 Form	4-78	5.1%	- 6.00		1988 Form	7-97	7.2%	- 9.00

J M BRADLEY (Chepstow, Gwent)

	No. of Horses	Races Run	1st	2nd	3rd	Unpl	Per cent	£1 Level Stake
2-y-o	1	3	0	0	0	3	-	- 3.00
3-y-o	4	13	0	0	1	12	-	- 13.00
4-y-o+	13	62	3	5	4	50	4.8	- 23.00
Totals	18	78	3	5	5	65	3.8	- 39.00

Jan	Feb	Mar	Apr	May	Jun	Jul	Aug	Sep	Oct/Nov
0-2	2-4	0-6	0-10	0-14	1-14	0-12	0-7	0-7	0-2

Winning Jockey	W-R	£1 Level Stake				W-R	£1 Level Stake
N Adams	3-20	+ 19.00					

Winning Courses							
Nottingham	1-2	+ 9.00		Southwell (AW)		1-8	+ 3.00
Lingfield (AW)	1-6	+ 11.00					

Winning Horse		Age	Races Run	1st	2nd	3rd	Unpl	Win £
Sooty Tern		5	15	3	3	1	8	7,482

Favourites	0-4		Total winning prize-money			£7,482

1991 Form	2-58	3.4%	- 26.00	1989 Form	1-86	1.2%	- 77.00
1990 Form	4-73	5.5%	- 30.50	1988 Form	2-60	3.3%	- 18.00

G C BRAVERY (Newmarket)

	No. of Horses	Races Run	1st	2nd	3rd	Unpl	Per cent	£1 Level Stake
2-y-o	3	10	5	1	0	4	50.0	+ 33.63
3-y-o	1	6	0	1	1	4	-	- 6.00
4-y-o+	1	1	0	0	0	1	-	- 1.00
Totals	5	17	5	2	1	9	29.4	+ 26.63

Jan	Feb	Mar	Apr	May	Jun	Jul	Aug	Sep	Oct/Nov
0-0	0-0	0-0	0-1	0-0	1-4	2-4	1-5	1-1	0-2

Winning Jockeys	W-R	£1 Level Stake			W-R	£1 Level Stake
W R Swinburn	2-4	+ 9.00	N Day		1-2	+ 0.63
L Dettori	1-1	+ 16.00	M Hills		1-3	+ 8.00

Winning Courses						
Newmarket	2-7	+ 17.00	Southwell (AW)		1-2	+ 9.00
Leicester	1-1	+ 5.00	Lingfield (AW)		1-2	+ 0.63

Winning Horses		Age	Races Run	1st	2nd	3rd	Unpl	Win £
Wynona		2	5	2	1	0	2	24,205
Time's Arrow		2	4	3	0	0	1	7,070
Favourites	1-2	50.0%	+ 0.63		Total winning prize-money			£31,275

R G BRAZINGTON (Redmarley, Glos)

	No. of Horses	Races Run	1st	2nd	3rd	Unpl	Per cent	£1 Level Stake
2-y-o	0	0	0	0	0	0	-	0.00
3-y-o	0	0	0	0	0	0	-	0.00
4-y-o+	4	9	1	0	0	8	11.1	0.00
Totals	4	9	1	0	0	8	11.1	0.00

Jan	Feb	Mar	Apr	May	Jun	Jul	Aug	Sep	Oct/Nov
1-5	0-0	0-2	0-0	0-0	0-0	0-0	0-1	0-1	0-0

Winning Jockey	W-R	£1 Level Stake	Winning Course	W-R	£1 Level Stake
J Quinn	1-6	+ 3.00	Southwell (AW)	1-8	+ 1.00

Winning Horse	Age	Races Run	1st	2nd	3rd	Unpl	Win £
Give Me Hope	4	4	1	0	0	3	2,206

Favourites	0-1		Total winning prize-money	£2,206

1991 Form	0-0	1989 Form	0-4
1990 Form	0-1	1988 Form	0-6

J J BRIDGER (Liphook, Hants)

	No. of Horses	Races Run	1st	2nd	3rd	Unpl	Per cent	£1 Level Stake
2-y-o	3	22	0	0	0	22	-	- 22.00
3-y-o	6	28	0	3	1	24	-	- 28.00
4-y-o+	4	18	2	0	3	13	11.1	+ 1.63
Totals	13	68	2	3	4	59	2.9	- 48.37

Jan	Feb	Mar	Apr	May	Jun	Jul	Aug	Sep	Oct/Nov
0-1	0-2	0-3	0-6	0-8	2-12	0-9	0-10	0-10	0-7

Bridger J J

Winning Jockeys		W-R	£1 Level Stake				W-R	£1 Level Stake
T Quinn		1-1	+ 1.63	S Whitworth			1-18	- 1.00

Winning Course								
Lingfield		2-9	+ 10.63					

Winning Horse		Age	Races Run	1st	2nd	3rd	Unpl	Win £
Shades Of Jade		4	12	2	0	3	7	4,440

Favourites	1-2	50.0%	+ 0.63	Total winning prize-money				£4,440

1991 Form	0-63			1989 Form	0-43	
1990 Form	2-57	3.5%	- 18.00	1988 Form	0-63	

K S BRIDGWATER (Lapworth, Warwicks)

	No. of Horses	Races Run	1st	2nd	3rd	Unpl	Per cent	£1 Level Stake
2-y-o	1	4	1	0	0	3	25.0	+ 4.50
3-y-o	4	15	0	0	2	13	-	- 15.00
4-y-o+	9	35	1	2	3	29	2.9	- 14.00
Totals	14	54	2	2	5	45	3.7	- 24.50

Jan	Feb	Mar	Apr	May	Jun	Jul	Aug	Sep	Oct/Nov
0-1	0-2	1-5	0-4	0-7	0-5	1-11	0-11	0-6	0-2

Winning Jockeys		W-R	£1 Level Stake				W-R	£1 Level Stake
B Raymond		1-2	+ 6.50	A Tucker			1-5	+ 16.00

Winning Courses								
Beverley		1-8	+ 13.00	Warwick			1-9	- 0.50

Winning Horses		Age	Races Run	1st	2nd	3rd	Unpl	Win £
Minshaar		2	4	1	0	0	3	2,469
Peak District		6	3	1	1	0	1	2,265

Favourites	0-5			Total winning prize-money				£4,734

1991 Form	2-44	4.5%	- 13.00	1989 Form	0-24		
1990 Form	0-49			1988 Form	1-48	2.1%	- 14.00

W M BRISBOURNE (Baschurch, Salop)

	No. of Horses	Races Run	1st	2nd	3rd	Unpl	Per cent	£1 Level Stake
2-y-o	0	0	0	0	0	0	-	0.00
3-y-o	3	15	0	0	0	15	-	- 15.00
4-y-o+	1	12	2	0	2	8	16.7	+ 8.00
Totals	4	27	2	0	2	23	7.4	- 7.00

Jan	Feb	Mar	Apr	May	Jun	Jul	Aug	Sep	Oct/Nov
0-0	0-1	0-3	0-2	0-2	0-0	0-5	2-6	0-6	0-2

Winning Jockey	W-R	£1 Level Stake				W-R	£1 Level Stake
S Maloney	2-4	+ 16.00					

Winning Courses		£1 Level Stake					£1 Level Stake
Thirsk	1-2	+ 8.00	Nottingham			1-4	+ 6.00

Winning Horse	Age	Races Run	1st	2nd	3rd	Unpl	Win £
Green's Cassatt	4	12	2	0	2	8	5,407

Favourites	0-1	Total winning prize-money	£5,407

1991 Form	0-15

C E BRITTAIN (Newmarket)

	No. of Horses	Races Run	1st	2nd	3rd	Unpl	Per cent	£1 Level Stake
2-y-o	49	141	15	16	12	98	10.6	- 56.75
3-y-o	50	282	34	33	29	186	12.1	- 30.65
4-y-o+	27	173	14	14	14	131	8.1	- 67.54
Totals	126	596	63	63	55	415	10.6	-154.94

BY MONTH

2-y-o	W-R	Per cent	£1 Level Stake	3-y-o	W-R	Per cent	£1 Level Stake
January	0-0	-	0.00	January	0-0	-	0.00
February	0-0	-	0.00	February	0-4	-	- 4.00
March	0-0	-	0.00	March	0-10	-	- 10.00
April	0-2	-	- 2.00	April	7-43	16.3	+ 45.66
May	1-7	14.3	- 2.67	May	3-48	6.3	- 37.79
June	4-23	17.4	- 5.50	June	11-50	22.0	+ 20.75
July	2-31	6.5	- 26.83	July	3-44	6.8	- 33.25
August	3-19	15.8	+ 3.75	August	3-34	8.8	- 18.27
September	5-34	14.7	+ 1.50	September	3-26	11.5	- 9.25
Oct/Nov	0-25	-	- 25.00	Oct/Nov	4-23	17.4	+ 15.50

Brittain C E

4-y-o+	W-R	Per cent	£1 Level Stake	Totals	W-R	Per cent	£1 Level Stake
January	0-0	-	0.00	January	0-0	-	0.00
February	0-6	-	- 6.00	February	0-10	-	- 10.00
March	3-10	30.0	+ 7.63	March	3-20	15.0	- 2.37
April	2-19	10.5	- 9.17	April	9-64	14.1	+ 34.49
May	3-24	12.5	+ 0.50	May	7-79	8.9	- 39.96
June	3-28	10.7	- 5.50	June	18-101	17.8	+ 9.75
July	1-29	3.4	- 21.00	July	6-104	5.8	- 81.08
August	1-20	5.0	- 10.00	August	7-73	9.6	- 24.52
September	1-18	5.6	- 5.00	September	9-78	11.5	- 12.75
Oct/Nov	0-19	-	- 19.00	Oct/Nov	4-67	6.0	- 28.50

DISTANCE

2-y-o	W-R	Per cent	£1 Level Stake	3-y-o	W-R	Per cent	£1 Level Stake
5f-6f	10-75	13.3	- 33.25	5f-6f	0-12	-	- 12.00
7f-8f	5-64	7.8	- 21.50	7f-8f	12-109	11.0	- 23.96
9f-13f	0-2	-	- 2.00	9f-13f	20-143	14.0	+ 14.06
14f+	0-0	-	0.00	14f+	2-18	11.1	- 8.75

4-y-o+	W-R	Per cent	£1 Level Stake	Totals	W-R	Per cent	£1 Level Stake
5f-6f	0-12	-	- 12.00	5f-6f	10-99	10.1	- 57.25
7f-8f	6-72	8.3	- 25.17	7f-8f	23-245	9.4	- 70.63
9f-13f	7-67	10.4	- 15.37	9f-13f	27-212	12.7	- 3.31
14f+	1-22	4.5	- 15.00	14f+	3-40	7.5	- 23.75

TYPE OF RACE

Non-Handicaps	W-R	Per cent	£1 Level Stake	Handicaps	W-R	Per cent	£1 Level Stake
2-y-o	13-117	11.1	- 56.75	2-y-o	2-23	8.7	+ 1.00
3-y-o	24-150	16.0	+ 13.85	3-y-o	9-124	7.3	- 43.50
4-y-o+	4-50	8.0	- 19.37	4-y-o+	10-118	8.5	- 43.17
Selling	1-4	25.0	+ 3.00	Selling	0-3	-	- 3.00
Apprentice	0-0	-	0.00	Apprentice	0-7	-	- 7.00
Amat/Ladies	0-0	-	0.00	Amat/Ladies	0-0	-	0.00
Totals	42-321	13.1	- 59.27	Totals	21-275	7.6	- 95.67

COURSE GRADE

	W-R	Per cent	£1 Level Stake
Group 1	39-389	10.0	- 80.26
Group 2	8-58	13.8	- 19.59
Group 3	12-90	13.3	- 30.59
Group 4	4-59	6.8	- 24.50

FIRST TIME OUT

	W-R	Per cent	£1 Level Stake
2-y-o	5-48	10.4	- 27.33
3-y-o	4-49	8.2	+ 16.00
4-y-o+	3-27	11.1	- 6.37
Totals	12-124	9.7	- 17.70

JOCKEYS RIDING

	W-R	Per cent	£1 Level Stake		W-R	Per cent	£1 Level Stake
M Roberts	44-279	15.8	+ 44.03	Pat Eddery	1-2	50.0	+ 11.00
G Duffield	6-15	40.0	+ 28.48	M Hills	1-2	50.0	+ 1.00
A Munro	2-11	18.2	+ 5.00	L Piggott	1-3	33.3	- 1.33
W R Swinburn	2-11	18.2	- 4.62	P Robinson	1-8	12.5	- 4.00
G Crealock	2-52	3.8	- 41.50	L Dettori	1-15	6.7	- 8.50
B Doyle	2-80	2.5	- 66.50				

S Cauthen	0-23	R Cochrane	0-4	D Holland	0-1
M Birch	0-14	G Baxter	0-3	Dale Gibson	0-1
T Quinn	0-14	R Hills	0-3	J Lowe	0-1
Ron Hillis	0-10	G Bardwell	0-2	K Darley	0-1
W Carson	0-8	J Reid	0-2	Mrs E Mellor	0-1
B Raymond	0-6	Paul Eddery	0-2	S Dawson	0-1
D Biggs	0-6	A Mackay	0-1	T Rogers	0-1
J Quinn	0-6	A McGlone	0-1	W Ryan	0-1
G Carter	0-4	B Crossley	0-1		

COURSE RECORD

	Total W-R	Non-Handicaps 2-y-o	Non-Handicaps 3-y-o+	Handicaps 2-y-o	Handicaps 3-y-o+	Per cent	£1 Level Stake
Newmarket	7-101	3-24	3-38	0-5	1-34	6.9	- 59.25
Lingfield	5-17	1-4	1-3	0-1	3-9	29.4	+ 1.25
Yarmouth	5-32	2-9	2-7	0-1	1-15	15.6	- 9.25
Newbury	5-35	1-10	2-11	0-1	2-13	14.3	+ 12.50
Ascot	5-53	1-14	1-17	0-1	3-21	9.4	- 11.00
Beverley	4-17	0-1	2-8	0-0	2-8	23.5	+ 4.83
Epsom	4-18	1-2	1-8	0-1	2-7	22.2	+ 16.00
York	4-34	0-3	3-16	0-0	1-15	11.8	- 9.27
Doncaster	4-36	0-7	2-8	1-4	1-17	11.1	- 2.62
Warwick	3-14	0-1	1-6	0-0	2-7	21.4	+ 13.50
Kempton	3-27	0-3	2-9	0-2	1-13	11.1	- 1.12
Sandown	3-40	0-7	3-16	0-1	0-16	7.5	- 5.50
Brighton	2-13	0-1	2-4	0-1	0-7	15.4	+ 3.91
Haydock	2-13	1-2	0-3	1-1	0-7	15.4	- 2.33
Leicester	2-14	1-5	1-6	0-1	0-2	14.3	- 3.67
Goodwood	2-29	1-4	1-12	0-1	0-12	6.9	- 14.67
Ripon	1-5	0-0	1-3	0-0	0-2	20.0	- 1.75
Bath	1-7	1-3	0-2	0-0	0-2	14.3	- 2.50
Folkestone	1-17	0-4	1-5	0-0	0-8	5.9	- 10.00

Chester	0-14	Southwell (AW)	0-6	Windsor	0-2
Lingfield (AW)	0-12	Pontefract	0-5	Ayr	0-1
Wolverhampton	0-10	Chepstow	0-4	Redcar	0-1
Nottingham	0-9	Newcastle	0-2		
Salisbury	0-6	Thirsk	0-2		

WINNING HORSES

	Age	Races Run	1st	2nd	3rd	Unpl	Win £
User Friendly	3	5	5	0	0	0	402,905
Ivanka	2	5	2	1	1	1	101,909
Sayyedati	2	3	2	1	0	0	94,304
Armarama	3	5	1	3	1	0	58,833
Shambo	5	8	1	2	2	3	43,976
Gussy Marlowe	4	6	1	0	0	5	33,390
Efharisto	3	6	2	2	0	2	22,349
Spartan Shareef	3	8	2	1	0	5	16,336
Love Of Silver	2	3	2	0	0	1	16,167
Host	3	7	2	0	0	5	14,589
Robingo	3	9	3	1	0	5	13,528
Endoli	5	2	1	0	0	1	11,268
Go Executive	4	12	2	0	1	9	10,853
For Mog	3	6	1	2	0	3	10,598
Chatham Island	4	10	3	0	1	6	9,826
Sueboog	2	2	1	0	0	1	8,155
Anonymous	2	7	1	1	0	5	7,318
Luchiroverte	4	7	1	2	1	3	7,180
Beldi	3	3	1	0	1	1	6,248
Lobilio	3	11	1	3	2	5	6,108
Colossus	4	12	2	0	1	9	5,737
Wahem	2	4	1	0	1	2	5,361
Holiday Island	3	11	2	1	0	8	5,140
Andrath	4	6	1	0	0	5	4,136
Boloardo	3	5	1	1	0	3	3,818
Army Of Stars	7	9	1	1	1	6	3,785
Flute	3	5	1	0	1	3	3,753
Amazon Express	3	12	2	0	1	9	3,599
Sooty Swift	2	3	1	0	0	2	3,003
Al Ramis	3	6	1	1	0	4	3,002
Mr Martini	2	4	1	1	1	1	2,898
Fierro	2	5	1	0	0	4	2,807
Ler Cru	3	13	1	0	2	10	2,783
Garden Of Heaven	3	4	1	2	1	0	2,714
Tender Moment	4	12	1	2	1	8	2,657
Al Sadi	3	6	1	0	1	4	2,532
Nuez	3	1	1	0	0	0	2,520
American Boogie	3	8	1	0	1	6	2,442
Shamisen	2	3	1	1	0	1	2,280
Kalko	3	9	1	0	0	8	2,187
Romoosh	3	3	1	0	0	2	2,070
Lys	2	4	1	0	0	3	2,005
Secret Thing	3	4	1	0	1	2	1,932
Big Blue	3	8	1	2	1	4	1,730
Infant Protege	2	10	1	2	1	6	1,604

WINNING OWNERS

	Races Won	Value £		Races Won	Value £
W J Gredley	5	402,905	Mike Dawes	2	10,853
Ali Saeed	4	118,076	F M Kalla	2	7,431
Mohamed Obaida	5	107,993	Mrs J L Hislop	1	7,318
C T Olley	3	75,169	A J Richards	3	6,040
The Dowager Lady Beaverbrook	9	67,817	The Army Of Stars Partnership	1	3,785
Mrs C E Brittain	3	50,281	Mrs Celia Miller	2	3,334
Mrs John Van Geest	1	33,390	Circlechart Ltd	1	2,898
Luciano Gaucci	4	21,492	Ray Richards	1	2,657
Capt M Lemos	5	19,264	Saeed Manana	1	2,280
B H Voak	4	13,644	Sheikh Marwan Al Maktoum	1	2,005
Sheikh Mohammed	4	12,083	C E Brittain	1	1,618

Favourites	16-45	35.6%	+ 2.65	Total winning prize-money	£972,330
Longest winning sequence			2	Average SP of winner	6.0/1
Longest losing sequence			48	Return on stakes invested	-25.9%
1991 Form	53-545	9.7%	-121.61	1989 Form 36-508 7.1%	-205.68
1990 Form	42-507	8.3%	- 71.96	1988 Form 40-465 8.6%	-117.66

M BRITTAIN (Warthill, North Yorks)

	No. of Horses	Races Run	1st	2nd	3rd	Unpl	Per cent	£1 Level Stake
2-y-o	12	52	3	1	2	46	5.8	- 24.00
3-y-o	4	17	0	0	0	17	-	- 17.00
4-y-o+	17	154	4	11	12	127	2.6	- 99.00
Totals	33	223	7	12	14	190	3.1	-140.00

Jan	Feb	Mar	Apr	May	Jun	Jul	Aug	Sep	Oct/Nov
0-6	0-3	0-13	1-39	1-36	4-35	1-27	0-27	0-19	0-18

Winning Jockeys	W-R	£1 Level Stake		W-R	£1 Level Stake
S Maloney	2-22	- 5.00	G Bardwell	1-15	+ 2.00
K Darley	2-34	- 9.00	J Lowe	1-45	- 34.00
N Connorton	1-2	+ 11.00			

Winning Courses	W-R	£1 Level Stake		W-R	£1 Level Stake
Southwell (AW)	3-28	+ 6.00	Doncaster	1-15	- 2.00
Kempton	1-2	+ 6.00	Beverley	1-21	- 4.00
Haydock	1-11	0.00			

Brittain M

Winning Horses	Age	Races Run	1st	2nd	3rd	Unpl	Win £
Nordic Brave	6	11	2	1	1	7	7,080
Matthew David	2	9	2	0	0	7	3,631
Cost Effective	5	11	1	1	1	8	2,965
Nicky Mygirl	2	6	1	1	1	3	2,679
Grey Commander	4	16	1	2	2	11	1,256

Favourites	0-3			Total winning prize-money			£17,609

1991 Form	21-420	5.0%	-214.25	1989 Form	26-505	5.1%	-173.14
1990 Form	27-543	5.0%	-260.59	1988 Form	44-734	6.0%	-307.00

C D BROAD (Westbury-on-Severn, Glos)

	No. of Horses	Races Run	1st	2nd	3rd	Unpl	Per cent	£1 Level Stake
2-y-o	3	11	0	0	0	11	-	- 11.00
3-y-o	2	5	0	0	0	5	-	- 5.00
4-y-o+	4	18	1	1	0	16	5.6	- 3.00
Totals	9	34	1	1	0	32	2.9	- 19.00

Jan	Feb	Mar	Apr	May	Jun	Jul	Aug	Sep	Oct/Nov
0-1	0-0	0-0	0-2	0-4	1-7	0-7	0-7	0-6	0-0

Winning Jockey	W-R	£1 Level Stake	Winning Course	W-R	£1 Level Stake
R Price	1-2	+ 13.00	Wolverhampton	1-6	+ 9.00

Winning Horse	Age	Races Run	1st	2nd	3rd	Unpl	Win £
Little Big	5	3	1	0	0	2	1,298

Favourites	0-0		Total winning prize-money	£1,298

1991 Form	1-20	5.0%	+ 14.00

D BURCHELL (Ebbw Vale, Gwent)

	No. of Horses	Races Run	1st	2nd	3rd	Unpl	Per cent	£1 Level Stake
2-y-o	2	6	0	1	0	5	-	- 6.00
3-y-o	4	10	0	1	1	8	-	- 10.00
4-y-o+	14	26	1	1	5	19	3.8	- 23.75
Totals	20	42	1	3	6	32	2.4	- 39.75

Jan	Feb	Mar	Apr	May	Jun	Jul	Aug	Sep	Oct/Nov
0-3	0-0	1-4	0-5	0-9	0-8	0-5	0-6	0-1	0-1

Winning Jockey		W-R	£1 Level Stake	Winning Course		W-R	£1 Level Stake
R Cochrane		1-2	+ 0.25	Southwell (AW)		1-5	- 2.75

Winning Horse		Age	Races Run	1st	2nd	3rd	Unpl	Win £
Maamur		4	4	1	1	1	1	2,304

Favourites	1-4	25.0%	- 1.75	Total winning prize-money			£2,304

1991 Form	4-63	6.3%	+ 29.00	1989 Form	1-31	3.2%	- 28.25
1990 Form	7-75	9.3%	- 27.50				

K R BURKE (Broadway, H'ford & Worcs)

	No. of Horses	Races Run	1st	2nd	3rd	Unpl	Per cent	£1 Level Stake
2-y-o	2	12	0	0	4	8	-	- 12.00
3-y-o	3	14	0	3	1	10	-	- 14.00
4-y-o+	3	8	1	0	0	7	12.5	- 1.50
Totals	8	34	1	3	5	25	2.9	- 27.50

Jan	Feb	Mar	Apr	May	Jun	Jul	Aug	Sep	Oct/Nov
0-0	0-0	0-0	1-6	0-6	0-5	0-5	0-1	0-4	0-7

Winning Jockey		W-R	£1 Level Stake	Winning Course		W-R	£1 Level Stake
D Holland		1-3	+ 3.50	Lingfield		1-2	+ 4.50

Winning Horse		Age	Races Run	1st	2nd	3rd	Unpl	Win £
Wanda		5	2	1	0	0	1	2,634

Favourites	0-2			Total winning prize-money			£2,634

1991 Form	2-42	4.8%	- 17.00	1990 Form	0-14

P BUTLER (Lewes, East Sussex)

	No. of Horses	Races Run	1st	2nd	3rd	Unpl	Per cent	£1 Level Stake
2-y-o	4	22	0	1	0	21	-	- 22.00
3-y-o	1	7	1	2	1	3	14.3	+ 1.50
4-y-o+	3	10	2	0	0	8	20.0	+ 8.00
Totals	8	39	3	3	1	32	7.7	- 12.50

Jan	Feb	Mar	Apr	May	Jun	Jul	Aug	Sep	Oct/Nov
0-0	0-0	0-2	0-5	0-4	0-9	0-1	1-4	1-6	1-8

Winning Jockeys	W-R	£1 Level Stake		W-R	£1 Level Stake
S Drowne	2-7	+ 11.00	T Williams	1-8	+ 0.50

Winning Courses					
Chepstow	1-1	+ 8.00	Folkestone	1-8	+ 0.50
Windsor	1-4	+ 5.00			

Winning Horses	Age	Races Run	1st	2nd	3rd	Unpl	Win £
Prince Rooney	4	4	2	0	0	2	4,850
Precious Wonder	3	7	1	2	1	3	2,658

Favourites	0-2		Total winning prize-money	£7,508

1991 Form	0-28		1989 Form	0-30
1990 Form	0-11		1988 Form	0-22

N BYCROFT (Brandsby, North Yorks)

	No. of Horses	Races Run	1st	2nd	3rd	Unpl	Per cent	£1 Level Stake
2-y-o	5	31	1	3	6	21	3.2	- 23.00
3-y-o	4	41	3	4	1	33	7.3	- 9.25
4-y-o+	8	33	0	1	3	29	-	- 33.00
Totals	17	105	4	8	10	83	3.8	- 65.25

Jan	Feb	Mar	Apr	May	Jun	Jul	Aug	Sep	Oct/Nov
0-4	0-1	0-3	1-7	0-12	1-15	1-20	1-22	0-16	0-5

Winning Jockeys	W-R	£1 Level Stake		W-R	£1 Level Stake
A Munro	1-2	+ 1.75	N Kennedy	1-11	0.00
S Whitworth	1-3	+ 5.00	S Wood	1-13	+ 4.00

Winning Courses					
Lingfield (AW)	1-1	+ 2.75	Thirsk	1-6	+ 2.00
Wolverhampton	1-5	+ 6.00	Catterick	1-7	+ 10.00

Winning Horses	Age	Races Run	1st	2nd	3rd	Unpl	Win £
Miss Movie World	3	14	2	4	1	7	4,812
Kick On Majestic	3	16	1	0	0	15	2,343
Plum First	2	13	1	3	3	6	2,304

Favourites	1-4	25.0%	- 0.25	Total winning prize-money	£9,459

1991 Form	6-114	5.3%	- 48.25	1989 Form	2-149	1.3%	-118.00
1990 Form	2-169	1.2%	-141.00	1988 Form	10-151	6.6%	- 78.99

T H CALDWELL (Warrington, Cheshire)

	No. of Horses	Races Run	1st	2nd	3rd	Unpl	Per cent	£1 Level Stake
2-y-o	0	0	0	0	0	0	-	0.00
3-y-o	3	21	1	2	2	16	4.8	+ 30.00
4-y-o+	3	15	0	2	1	12	-	- 15.00
Totals	6	36	1	4	3	28	2.8	+ 15.00

Jan	Feb	Mar	Apr	May	Jun	Jul	Aug	Sep	Oct/Nov
0-4	0-4	0-2	0-4	1-3	0-6	0-6	0-1	0-3	0-3

Winning Jockey	W-R	£1 Level Stake	Winning Course	W-R	£1 Level Stake
N Kennedy	1-9	+ 42.00	Hamilton	1-2	+ 49.00

Winning Horse	Age	Races Run	1st	2nd	3rd	Unpl	Win £
Neltegrity	3	8	1	2	0	5	2,402

Favourites	0-1		Total winning prize-money	£2,402

1991 Form	0-19		1989 Form	0-4
1990 Form	0-5			

N A CALLAGHAN (Newmarket)

	No. of Horses	Races Run	1st	2nd	3rd	Unpl	Per cent	£1 Level Stake
2-y-o	11	53	5	6	3	39	9.4	- 26.00
3-y-o	15	85	9	10	8	58	10.6	- 28.25
4-y-o+	7	31	5	2	5	19	16.1	- 8.40
Totals	33	169	19	18	16	116	11.2	- 62.65

BY MONTH

2-y-o	W-R	Per cent	£1 Level Stake	3-y-o	W-R	Per cent	£1 Level Stake
January	0-0	-	0.00	January	1-2	50.0	+ 1.25
February	0-0	-	0.00	February	0-2	-	- 2.00
March	0-0	-	0.00	March	0-5	-	- 5.00
April	1-7	14.3	- 3.50	April	1-13	7.7	+ 2.00
May	0-12	-	- 12.00	May	3-19	15.8	0.00
June	0-7	-	- 7.00	June	0-22	-	- 22.00
July	0-7	-	- 7.00	July	4-13	30.8	+ 6.50
August	2-8	25.0	- 1.00	August	0-7	-	- 7.00
September	0-5	-	- 5.00	September	0-1	-	- 1.00
Oct/Nov	2-7	28.6	+ 9.50	Oct/Nov	0-1	-	- 1.00

Callaghan N A

4-y-o+	W-R	Per cent	£1 Level Stake		Totals	W-R	Per cent	£1 Level Stake	
January	0-0	-		0.00	January	1-2	50.0	+	1.25
February	0-0	-		0.00	February	0-2	-	-	2.00
March	1-3	33.3	-	0.90	March	1-8	12.5	-	5.90
April	1-7	14.3	-	1.00	April	3-27	11.1	-	2.50
May	0-8	-	-	8.00	May	3-39	7.7	-	20.00
June	1-5	20.0	+	0.50	June	1-34	2.9	-	28.50
July	2-4	50.0	+	5.00	July	6-24	25.0	+	4.50
August	0-2	-	-	2.00	August	2-17	11.8	-	10.00
September	0-2	-	-	2.00	September	0-8	-	-	8.00
Oct/Nov	0-0	-		0.00	Oct/Nov	2-8	25.0	+	8.50

DISTANCE

2-y-o	W-R	Per cent	£1 Level Stake		3-y-o	W-R	Per cent	£1 Level Stake	
5f-6f	3-39	7.7	-	21.25	5f-6f	3-14	21.4	+	14.00
7f-8f	2-14	14.3	-	4.75	7f-8f	2-25	8.0	-	16.75
9f-13f	0-0	-		0.00	9f-13f	3-38	7.9	-	22.50
14f+	0-0	-		0.00	14f+	1-8	12.5	-	3.00

4-y-o+	W-R	Per cent	£1 Level Stake		Totals	W-R	Per cent	£1 Level Stake	
5f-6f	0-0	-		0.00	5f-6f	6-53	11.3	-	7.25
7f-8f	1-8	12.5	-	2.00	7f-8f	5-47	10.6	-	23.50
9f-13f	4-21	19.0	-	4.40	9f-13f	7-59	11.9	-	26.90
14f+	0-2	-	-	2.00	14f+	1-10	10.0	-	5.00

TYPE OF RACE

Non-Handicaps	W-R	Per cent	£1 Level Stake		Handicaps	W-R	Per cent	£1 Level Stake	
2-y-o	3-29	10.3	-	9.00	2-y-o	1-7	14.3	-	3.75
3-y-o	3-24	12.5	-	8.00	3-y-o	4-42	9.5	-	9.75
4-y-o+	2-10	20.0	-	2.40	4-y-o+	3-17	17.6	-	2.00
Selling	1-17	5.9	-	13.25	Selling	2-15	13.3	-	6.50
Apprentice	0-4	-	-	4.00	Apprentice	0-3	-	-	3.00
Amat/Ladies	0-0	-		0.00	Amat/Ladies	0-1	-	-	1.00
Totals	9-84	10.7	-	36.65	Totals	10-85	11.8	-	26.00

COURSE GRADE				
	W-R	Per cent	£1 Level Stake	
Group 1	6-57	10.5	-	16.50
Group 2	2-23	8.7	-	14.75
Group 3	4-47	8.5	-	23.50
Group 4	7-42	16.7	-	7.90

FIRST TIME OUT				
	W-R	Per cent	£1 Level Stake	
2-y-o	0-11	-	-	11.00
3-y-o	1-15	6.7	-	11.75
4-y-o+	0-7	-	-	7.00
Totals	1-33	3.0	-	29.75

JOCKEYS RIDING

	W–R	Per cent	£1 Level Stake			W–R	Per cent	£1 Level Stake
Pat Eddery	5-22	22.7	− 0.40	J Carroll		1-2	50.0	+ 3.00
J Tate	3-32	9.4	− 6.50	T Williams		1-2	50.0	+ 9.00
J Reid	2-3	66.7	+ 6.25	W Newnes		1-6	16.7	− 2.75
M Roberts	2-11	18.2	− 0.50	W Ryan		1-7	14.3	− 1.50
O Pears	1-1	100.0	+ 2.75	W Carson		1-9	11.1	− 4.00
J Weaver	1-2	50.0	+ 4.00					

G Duffield	0-11	J Lowe	0-2	J Fortune	0-1
L Piggott	0-5	P Burke	0-2	J Quinn	0-1
B Raymond	0-4	Paul Eddery	0-2	J Williams	0-1
D Harrison	0-4	T Jarnet	0-2	John Francome	0-1
G Carter	0-4	A Whelan	0-1	L Charnock	0-1
A McGlone	0-3	Antoinette Armes	0-1	L Dettori	0-1
D Holland	0-3	B Crossley	0-1	Mr R Walker	0-1
K Darley	0-3	B Doyle	0-1	N Carlisle	0-1
A Mackay	0-2	D Carson	0-1	T Lucas	0-1
A Munro	0-2	Dale Gibson	0-1	T Quinn	0-1
C Hawksley	0-2	G Hind	0-1	W Thomas	0-1
F Norton	0-2	J Fanning	0-1		

COURSE RECORD

	Total W–R	Non-Handicaps 2-y-o	3-y-o+	Handicaps 2-y-o	3-y-o+	Per cent	£1 Level Stake
Brighton	2-8	0-2	0-1	1-1	1-4	25.0	+ 0.25
Lingfield (AW)	2-9	2-2	0-3	0-0	0-4	22.2	+ 7.50
Yarmouth	2-10	0-2	1-1	0-0	1-7	20.0	+ 0.50
Folkestone	2-13	0-1	1-5	0-0	1-7	15.4	− 7.40
Haydock	1-2	0-1	0-0	0-0	1-1	50.0	+ 1.50
Catterick	1-3	1-1	0-1	0-0	0-1	33.3	+ 0.75
Goodwood	1-3	0-0	1-2	0-0	0-1	33.3	+ 3.00
Newcastle	1-3	1-2	0-1	0-0	0-0	33.3	+ 0.50
York	1-3	0-1	0-1	0-0	1-1	33.3	+ 4.00
Edinburgh	1-4	0-0	1-1	0-0	0-3	25.0	+ 1.00
Sandown	1-4	0-1	0-0	0-1	1-2	25.0	+ 11.00
Leicester	1-6	0-2	0-1	0-1	1-2	16.7	+ 1.00
Southwell (AW)	1-7	0-2	0-1	0-0	1-4	14.3	− 3.75
Hamilton	1-9	0-3	0-2	0-0	1-4	11.1	− 3.00
Newmarket	1-28	0-8	1-11	0-2	0-7	3.6	− 22.50

Windsor	0-10	Lingfield	0-4	Warwick	0-3
Kempton	0-7	Beverley	0-3	Wolverhampton	0-3
Newbury	0-6	Chester	0-3	Chepstow	0-1
Nottingham	0-5	Pontefract	0-3	Doncaster	0-1
Redcar	0-5	Ripon	0-3		

WINNING HORSES

	Age	Races Run	1st	2nd	3rd	Unpl	Win £
Freddie Lloyd (USA)	3	7	3	1	1	2	32,016
Bowden Boy	4	12	3	0	3	6	8,393
Majed	4	8	2	0	1	5	4,994
Mystery Lad	3	5	2	1	0	2	4,912
Fiveofive	2	9	1	0	1	7	3,330
Naseer	3	9	1	2	1	5	2,973
Anguish	3	8	1	0	2	5	2,448
Allimac Nomis	3	7	1	0	1	5	2,422
Dublin Indemnity	3	10	1	0	0	9	2,089
Bird Hunter	2	6	1	2	0	3	2,070
Madame Cyn's Risk	2	11	1	1	2	7	1,245
Excess Baggage	2	3	1	0	0	2	1,214
Nut Bush	2	8	1	1	0	6	1,193

WINNING OWNERS

	Races Won	Value £		Races Won	Value £
Michael Hill	3	32,016	R K Carvill	1	2,089
T A Foreman	4	11,723	Yahya Nasib	1	2,070
N A Callaghan	3	7,967	Roldvale Ltd	1	1,245
Gallagher Properties Ltd	2	4,912	Frank W Golding	1	1,214
Mrs J Callaghan	2	4,870	Mrs M E Cooke	1	1,193

Favourites	6-23	26.1%	+ 1.85	Total winning prize-money			£69,297
Longest winning sequence			2	Average SP of winner			4.6/1
Longest losing sequence			33	Return on stakes invested			-37.1%
1991 Form	30-265	11.3%	- 30.99	1989 Form	32-237	13.5%	- 27.34
1990 Form	31-197	15.7%	- 17.39	1988 Form	27-256	10.5%	- 58.50

P CALVER (Ripon, North Yorks)

	No. of Horses	Races Run	1st	2nd	3rd	Unpl	Per cent	£1 Level Stake
2-y-o	6	14	0	0	0	14	-	- 14.00
3-y-o	8	43	4	1	3	35	9.3	- 8.25
4-y-o+	3	13	2	0	0	11	15.4	+ 3.50
Totals	17	70	6	1	3	60	8.6	- 18.75

Jan	Feb	Mar	Apr	May	Jun	Jul	Aug	Sep	Oct/Nov
0-1	0-0	0-1	0-2	2-15	1-12	3-14	0-9	0-8	0-8

Winning Jockeys	W-R	£1 Level Stake			W-R	£1 Level Stake
W Newnes	2-7	+ 1.75	Mrs A Farrell		1-3	+ 6.00
J Tate	2-11	+ 5.50	G Duffield		1-4	+ 13.00

Winning Courses						
Catterick	4-10	+ 26.75	Redcar		1-13	- 7.50
Beverley	1-5	+ 4.00				

Winning Horses	Age	Races Run	1st	2nd	3rd	Unpl	Win £
Leave It To Lib	5	11	2	0	0	9	5,395
Boursin	3	9	2	0	1	6	4,040
Hemsworth Lad	3	7	1	0	0	6	2,954
Pride Of Pendle	3	11	1	1	1	8	1,970

Favourites	0-1		Total winning prize-money			£14,359

1991 Form	8-109	7.3%	- 0.25	1989 Form	7-92	7.6%	- 17.00
1990 Form	18-131	13.7%	- 26.90	1988 Form	7-96	7.3%	- 54.50

M J CAMACHO (Malton, North Yorks)

	No. of Horses	Races Run	1st	2nd	3rd	Unpl	Per cent	£1 Level Stake
2-y-o	7	32	7	1	3	21	21.9	+ 23.00
3-y-o	4	14	0	3	2	9	-	- 14.00
4-y-o+	10	66	13	10	6	37	19.7	+ 23.76
Totals	21	112	20	14	11	67	17.9	+ 32.76

BY MONTH

2-y-o	W-R	Per cent	£1 Level Stake	3-y-o	W-R	Per cent	£1 Level Stake
January	0-0	-	0.00	January	0-1	-	- 1.00
February	0-0	-	0.00	February	0-1	-	- 1.00
March	0-0	-	0.00	March	0-1	-	- 1.00
April	0-1	-	- 1.00	April	0-2	-	- 2.00
May	0-1	-	- 1.00	May	0-1	-	- 1.00
June	0-0	-	0.00	June	0-3	-	- 3.00
July	3-6	50.0	+ 23.50	July	0-3	-	- 3.00
August	1-7	14.3	- 2.50	August	0-2	-	- 2.00
September	2-8	25.0	0.00	September	0-0	-	0.00
Oct/Nov	1-9	11.1	+ 4.00	Oct/Nov	0-0	-	0.00

Camacho M J

4-y-o+	W-R	Per cent	£1 Level Stake		Totals	W-R	Per cent	£1 Level Stake
January	0-0	-	0.00		January	0-1	-	- 1.00
February	0-0	-	0.00		February	0-1	-	- 1.00
March	1-3	33.3	+ 8.00		March	1-4	25.0	+ 7.00
April	6-12	50.0	+ 23.63		April	6-15	40.0	+ 20.63
May	0-5	-	- 5.00		May	0-7	-	- 7.00
June	1-6	16.7	- 2.75		June	1-9	11.1	- 5.75
July	0-4	-	- 4.00		July	3-13	23.1	+ 16.50
August	0-3	-	- 3.00		August	1-12	8.3	- 7.50
September	2-17	11.8	0.00		September	4-25	16.0	0.00
Oct/Nov	3-16	18.8	+ 6.88		Oct/Nov	4-25	16.0	+ 10.88

DISTANCE

2-y-o	W-R	Per cent	£1 Level Stake		3-y-o	W-R	Per cent	£1 Level Stake
5f-6f	1-9	11.1	+ 8.00		5f-6f	0-0	-	0.00
7f-8f	6-21	28.6	+ 17.00		7f-8f	0-7	-	- 7.00
9f-13f	0-2	-	- 2.00		9f-13f	0-6	-	- 6.00
14f+	0-0	-	0.00		14f+	0-1	-	- 1.00

4-y-o+	W-R	Per cent	£1 Level Stake		Totals	W-R	Per cent	£1 Level Stake
5f-6f	7-30	23.3	+ 17.25		5f-6f	8-39	20.5	+ 25.25
7f-8f	1-17	5.9	+ 4.00		7f-8f	7-45	15.6	+ 14.00
9f-13f	3-16	18.8	- 0.12		9f-13f	3-24	12.5	- 8.12
14f+	2-3	66.7	+ 2.63		14f+	2-4	50.0	+ 1.63

TYPE OF RACE

Non-Handicaps	W-R	Per cent	£1 Level Stake		Handicaps	W-R	Per cent	£1 Level Stake
2-y-o	2-18	11.1	+ 8.00		2-y-o	4-9	44.4	+ 16.50
3-y-o	0-8	-	- 8.00		3-y-o	0-3	-	- 3.00
4-y-o+	2-15	13.3	+ 5.00		4-y-o+	8-46	17.4	+ 7.01
Selling	1-7	14.3	- 3.50		Selling	1-3	33.3	+ 0.50
Apprentice	0-0	-	0.00		Apprentice	2-3	66.7	+ 10.25
Amat/Ladies	0-0	-	0.00		Amat/Ladies	0-0	-	0.00
Totals	5-48	10.4	+ 1.50		Totals	15-64	23.4	+ 31.26

COURSE GRADE

	W-R	Per cent	£1 Level Stake
Group 1	10-46	21.7	+ 60.75
Group 2	5-29	17.2	- 8.12
Group 3	2-20	10.0	- 13.75
Group 4	3-17	17.6	- 6.12

FIRST TIME OUT

	W-R	Per cent	£1 Level Stake
2-y-o	2-7	28.6	+ 19.00
3-y-o	0-4	-	- 4.00
4-y-o+	2-9	22.2	+ 4.75
Totals	4-20	20.0	+ 19.75

JOCKEYS RIDING

	W-R	Per cent	£1 Level Stake		W-R	Per cent	£1 Level Stake
N Connorton	11-67	16.4	− 0.24	D Holland	1-1	100.0	+ 1.75
J Fanning	2-3	66.7	+ 14.00	J Marshall	1-1	100.0	+ 2.25
S Webster	2-6	33.3	+ 14.00	S Morris	1-12	8.3	+ 9.00
L Charnock	2-10	20.0	+ 4.00				

J Lowe	0-3	K Fallon	0-1	S Maloney		0-1
A Culhane	0-1	M Roberts	0-1	S Mulvey		0-1
D Biggs	0-1	N Kennedy	0-1			
J Quinn	0-1	R Cochrane	0-1			

COURSE RECORD

	Total W-R	Non-Handicaps 2-y-o	3-y-o+	Handicaps 2-y-o	3-y-o+	Per cent	£1 Level Stake
Newcastle	4-9	1-2	0-0	0-0	3-7	44.4	+ 34.50
Thirsk	2-3	0-0	0-0	2-2	0-1	66.7	+ 4.50
Catterick	2-5	1-2	0-1	1-1	0-1	40.0	+ 3.50
York	2-8	1-2	0-2	1-1	0-3	25.0	+ 22.00
Edinburgh	1-3	0-1	0-1	0-0	1-1	33.3	− 0.62
Nottingham	1-3	0-1	0-0	0-0	1-2	33.3	− 0.25
Ayr	1-4	0-0	0-0	0-0	1-4	25.0	− 0.75
Chester	1-4	0-0	0-1	0-1	1-2	25.0	+ 3.00
Newmarket	1-4	0-0	1-2	0-0	0-2	25.0	+ 3.00
Doncaster	1-7	0-0	1-2	0-2	0-3	14.3	+ 6.00
Pontefract	1-8	0-3	0-1	0-0	1-4	12.5	− 4.50
Haydock	1-9	0-0	0-0	0-1	1-8	11.1	+ 1.00
Ripon	1-9	0-3	0-4	0-0	1-2	11.1	− 5.50
Redcar	1-13	0-4	0-2	0-2	1-5	7.7	− 10.12

Hamilton	0-5	Carlisle	0-3	Leicester	0-2
Southwell (AW)	0-4	Beverley	0-2	Lingfield (AW)	0-2
Ascot	0-3	Goodwood	0-2		

WINNING HORSES

	Age	Races Run	1st	2nd	3rd	Unpl	Win £
Blyton Lad	6	6	2	2	1	1	21,224
Nordan Raider	4	7	3	3	0	1	16,044
Hi Nod	2	9	4	1	2	2	11,438
Tusky	4	12	1	1	2	8	7,245
El Nido	4	8	3	1	0	4	6,894
Avro Anson	4	3	2	1	0	0	5,789
Dutosky	2	6	1	0	0	5	5,663
Urry Urry Urry	2	3	1	0	0	2	5,205
Sea Devil	6	10	1	2	0	7	3,720
Twilight Falls	7	7	1	0	1	5	2,559
Hot Storm	2	5	1	0	0	4	2,259

Camacho M J

WINNING OWNERS

	Races Won	Value £		Races Won	Value £
Mrs J Addleshaw	2	21,224	B P Skirton	2	5,789
Miss J A Camacho	3	16,044	Lady Matthews	1	5,205
Lord Matthews	2	12,908	E G Noble	1	3,720
Brian Nordan	4	11,438	Clifford Smith	1	2,559
H Roberts	3	6,894	G B Turnbull Ltd	1	2,259

Favourites	11-25	44.0%	+ 14.26	Total winning prize-money			£88,040
Longest winning sequence			3	Average SP of winner			6.2/1
Longest losing sequence			17	Return on stakes invested			29.3%
1991 Form	15-109	13.8%	- 11.21	1989 Form	12-97	12.4%	+ 23.75
1990 Form	20-140	14.3%	+ 63.18	1988 Form	8-105	7.6%	- 36.25

I CAMPBELL (Newmarket)

	No. of Horses	Races Run	1st	2nd	3rd	Unpl	Per cent	£1 Level Stake
2-y-o	3	6	1	0	1	4	16.7	- 1.67
3-y-o	6	20	0	0	2	18	-	- 20.00
4-y-o+	8	24	3	1	1	19	12.5	- 14.87
Totals	17	50	4	1	4	41	8.0	- 36.54

Jan	Feb	Mar	Apr	May	Jun	Jul	Aug	Sep	Oct/Nov
0-4	0-1	1-4	0-9	1-6	0-6	1-4	0-6	0-5	1-5

Winning Jockeys	W-R	£1 Level Stake			W-R	£1 Level Stake
G Mitchell	2-8	- 1.25	M Tebbutt		1-11	- 6.67
B Raymond	1-1	+ 1.38				

Winning Courses	W-R	£1 Level Stake			W-R	£1 Level Stake
Southwell (AW)	2-12	- 5.29	Leicester		1-5	- 1.00
Warwick	1-1	+ 1.75				

Winning Horses		Age	Races Run	1st	2nd	3rd	Unpl	Win £
Qualitair Rhythm		4	8	3	1	1	3	7,440
Jordywrath		2	4	1	0	1	2	1,235

Favourites	3-9	33.3%	+ 0.13	Total winning prize-money			£8,675
1991 Form	1-42	2.4%	- 37.50	1989 Form	3-68	4.4%	- 40.67
1990 Form	7-85	8.2%	- 10.62	1988 Form	4-38	10.5%	+ 3.00

H CANDY (Wantage, Oxon)

	No. of Horses	Races Run	1st	2nd	3rd	Unpl	Per cent	£1 Level Stake
2-y-o	13	25	3	2	4	16	12.0	- 11.25
3-y-o	20	102	11	9	14	68	10.8	+ 11.30
4-y-o+	14	73	7	9	4	53	9.6	+ 11.38
Totals	47	200	21	20	22	137	10.5	+ 11.43

BY MONTH

2-y-o	W-R	Per cent	£1 Level Stake	3-y-o	W-R	Per cent	£1 Level Stake
Mar/Apr	0-0	-	0.00	Mar/Apr	0-11	-	- 11.00
May	0-0	-	0.00	May	2-15	13.3	+ 21.00
June	0-1	-	- 1.00	June	1-11	9.1	- 6.00
July	1-2	50.0	+ 1.75	July	2-12	16.7	- 3.00
August	1-7	14.3	- 2.50	August	1-14	7.1	- 6.00
September	1-11	9.1	- 5.50	September	2-20	10.0	+ 8.80
Oct/Nov	0-4	-	- 4.00	Oct/Nov	3-19	15.8	+ 7.50

4-y-o+	W-R	Per cent	£1 Level Stake	Totals	W-R	Per cent	£1 Level Stake
Mar/Apr	0-9	-	- 9.00	Mar/Apr	0-20	-	- 20.00
May	1-12	8.3	+ 3.00	May	3-27	11.1	+ 24.00
June	1-12	8.3	+ 5.00	June	2-24	8.3	- 2.00
July	1-11	9.1	- 9.62	July	4-25	16.0	- 10.87
August	2-10	20.0	+ 32.00	August	4-31	12.9	+ 23.50
September	1-13	7.7	- 7.00	September	4-44	9.1	- 3.70
Oct/Nov	1-6	16.7	- 3.00	Oct/Nov	4-29	13.8	+ 0.50

DISTANCE

2-y-o	W-R	Per cent	£1 Level Stake	3-y-o	W-R	Per cent	£1 Level Stake
5f-6f	2-11	18.2	- 2.75	5f-6f	1-9	11.1	+ 8.00
7f-8f	1-14	7.1	- 8.50	7f-8f	5-47	10.6	- 8.00
9f-13f	0-0	-	0.00	9f-13f	4-41	9.8	+ 11.30
14f+	0-0	-	0.00	14f+	1-5	20.0	0.00

4-y-o+	W-R	Per cent	£1 Level Stake	Totals	W-R	Per cent	£1 Level Stake
5f-6f	0-1	-	- 1.00	5f-6f	3-21	14.3	+ 4.25
7f-8f	2-16	12.5	+ 33.00	7f-8f	8-77	10.4	+ 16.50
9f-13f	4-43	9.3	- 10.62	9f-13f	8-84	9.5	+ 0.68
14f+	1-13	7.7	- 10.00	14f+	2-18	11.1	- 10.00

Candy H

TYPE OF RACE'

Non-Handicaps	W-R	Per cent	£1 Level Stake	Handicaps	W-R	Per cent	£1 Level Stake
2-y-o	3-23	13.0	- 9.25	2-y-o	0-2	-	- 2.00
3-y-o	8-59	13.6	+ 15.30	3-y-o	2-36	5.6	- 4.00
4-y-o+	1-14	7.1	- 11.00	4-y-o+	5-51	9.8	+ 24.38
Selling	0-3	-	- 3.00	Selling	0-1	-	- 1.00
Apprentice	1-1	100.0	+ 6.00	Apprentice	1-9	11.1	- 3.00
Amat/Ladies	0-1	-	- 1.00	Amat/Ladies	0-0	-	0.00
Totals	13-101	12.9	- 2.95	Totals	8-99	8.1	+ 14.38

COURSE GRADE

	W-R	Per cent	£1 Level Stake
Group 1	4-88	4.5	- 49.00
Group 2	3-30	10.0	+ 26.00
Group 3	12-63	19.0	+ 40.93
Group 4	2-19	10.5	- 6.50

FIRST TIME OUT

	W-R	Per cent	£1 Level Stake
2-y-o	1-13	7.7	- 7.50
3-y-o	2-20	10.0	+ 6.80
4-y-o+	1-14	7.1	+ 1.00
Totals	4-47	8.5	+ 0.30

JOCKEYS RIDING

	W-R	Per cent	£1 Level Stake		W-R	Per cent	£1 Level Stake
C Rutter	10-102	9.8	- 17.37	S Dawson	2-13	15.4	+ 12.50
Antoinette Armes	5-36	13.9	+ 26.00	S Cauthen	1-1	100.0	+ 7.00
A Munro	2-12	16.7	+ 4.30	D McKeown	1-1	100.0	+ 14.00

W Newnes	0-15	G Carter	0-1	N Howe	0-1
S Drake	0-5	J Lowe	0-1	P Robinson	0-1
G Duffield	0-2	L Piggott	0-1	Pat Eddery	0-1
R Cochrane	0-2	M Roberts	0-1	T Quinn	0-1
B Raymond	0-1	Mrs C Dunwoody	0-1	W Carson	0-1

COURSE RECORD

	Total W-R	Non-Handicaps 2-y-o	Non-Handicaps 3-y-o+	Handicaps 2-y-o	Handicaps 3-y-o+	Per cent	£1 Level Stake
Chepstow	4-10	1-2	2-3	0-0	1-5	40.0	+ 36.00
Salisbury	3-17	0-3	1-6	0-0	2-8	17.6	+ 39.00
Leicester	3-21	0-3	2-7	0-0	1-11	14.3	- 1.50
Windsor	2-7	0-0	0-2	0-0	2-5	28.6	+ 11.38
Nottingham	2-11	2-2	0-1	0-0	0-8	18.2	- 2.75
Epsom	1-2	0-0	0-1	0-0	1-1	50.0	+ 4.00
Haydock	1-3	0-0	1-2	0-0	0-1	33.3	+ 12.00
Wolverhampton	1-4	0-0	1-1	0-0	0-3	25.0	+ 0.50
Warwick	1-8	0-0	1-5	0-1	0-2	12.5	0.00
Goodwood	1-9	0-2	1-3	0-0	0-4	11.1	- 6.00
Bath	1-13	0-3	1-2	0-0	0-8	7.7	- 1.20
Kempton	1-17	0-0	0-12	0-0	1-5	5.9	- 2.00

Newbury	0-20	Folkestone	0-5	Chester	0-1
Newmarket	0-20	York	0-4	Lingfield (AW)	0-1
Lingfield	0-8	Redcar	0-2	Ripon	0-1
Sandown	0-7	Beverley	0-1	Southwell (AW)	0-1
Doncaster	0-6	Brighton	0-1		

WINNING HORSES

	Age	Races Run	1st	2nd	3rd	Unpl	Win £
Venus Observed	4	6	1	0	0	5	13,940
Night Manoeuvres	3	4	1	2	1	0	10,868
Incola	6	8	4	0	0	4	10,138
Caspian Tern	3	2	2	0	0	0	5,682
Not In Doubt	3	8	2	1	1	4	5,386
Second Call	3	8	2	0	0	6	4,791
Hebridean	5	7	1	1	1	4	4,230
Hold Fast	4	6	1	0	0	5	3,322
Will Of Steel	3	7	1	3	1	2	3,273
Weaver Bird	2	2	1	0	1	0	2,952
Surprise Surprise	2	1	1	0	0	0	2,616
Pippin Park	3	7	1	0	1	5	2,553
Laundry Maid	3	6	1	0	2	3	1,660
Fancied	2	3	1	0	1	1	1,506
Gunner's Daughter	3	6	1	0	1	4	1,380

WINNING OWNERS

	Races Won	Value £		Races Won	Value £
Mrs David Blackburn	6	15,524	Kingstone Warren Partners	1	3,322
Mrs C E Gross	1	13,940	P Robinson	1	3,273
P G Goulandris	2	12,248	Mrs Henry Candy	1	2,952
C J R Trotter	3	6,451	Mrs J E L Wright	1	2,616
Fahd Salman	2	5,682	Major M G Wyatt	1	2,553
P A Deal	1	4,230	H R Mould	1	1,506

Favourites	4-13	30.8%	+ 0.13	Total winning prize-money			£74,296
Longest winning sequence			2	Average SP of winner			9.1/1
Longest losing sequence			22	Return on stakes invested			6.0%
1991 Form	16-220	7.3%	- 55.00	1989 Form	16-201	8.0%	- 37.44
1990 Form	23-189	12.2%	+ 23.20	1988 Form	20-273	7.3%	-126.62

J M CARR (Malton, North Yorks)

	No. of Horses	Races Run	1st	2nd	3rd	Unpl	Per cent	£1 Level Stake
2-y-o	5	13	0	0	0	13	-	- 13.00
3-y-o	0	0	0	0	0	0	-	0.00
4-y-o+	3	20	2	3	2	13	10.0	- 8.00
Totals	8	33	2	3	2	26	6.1	- 21.00

Jan	Feb	Mar	Apr	May	Jun	Jul	Aug	Sep	Oct/Nov
0-0	0-0	0-0	0-4	0-2	1-5	0-7	1-5	0-6	0-4

Winning Jockeys	W-R	£1 Level Stake				W-R	£1 Level Stake
W Newnes	1-2	+ 4.00	S Morris			1-27	- 21.00

Winning Courses						
Hamilton	1-2	+ 4.00	Nottingham		1-3	+ 3.00

Winning Horse	Age	Races Run	1st	2nd	3rd	Unpl	Win £
Here Comes A Star	4	15	2	3	2	8	3,595

Favourites	0-2	Total winning prize-money	£3,595

W CARTER (Epsom, Surrey)

	No. of Horses	Races Run	1st	2nd	3rd	Unpl	Per cent	£1 Level Stake
2-y-o	12	66	6	5	8	47	9.1	- 12.50
3-y-o	10	66	5	6	5	50	7.6	+ 4.50
4-y-o+	12	76	8	8	7	53	10.5	+ 4.25
Totals	34	208	19	19	20	150	9.1	- 3.75

BY MONTH

2-y-o	W-R	Per cent	£1 Level Stake	3-y-o	W-R	Per cent	£1 Level Stake
January	0-0	-	0.00	January	0-3	-	- 3.00
February	0-0	-	0.00	February	1-3	33.3	+ 3.00
March	0-3	-	- 3.00	March	0-4	-	- 4.00
April	3-11	27.3	+ 23.00	April	1-14	7.1	+ 3.00
May	0-7	-	- 7.00	May	1-8	12.5	- 3.50
June	0-12	-	- 12.00	June	2-11	18.2	+ 32.00
July	0-10	-	- 10.00	July	0-9	-	- 9.00
August	1-9	11.1	- 4.00	August	0-5	-	- 5.00
September	1-9	11.1	- 1.50	September	0-7	-	- 7.00
Oct/Nov	1-5	20.0	+ 2.00	Oct/Nov	0-2	-	- 2.00

4-y-o+	W-R	Per cent	£1 Level Stake	Totals	W-R	Per cent	£1 Level Stake
January	0-3	-	- 3.00	January	0-6	-	- 6.00
February	0-0	-	0.00	February	1-3	33.3	+ 3.00
March	0-0	-	0.00	March	0-7	-	- 7.00
April	0-7	-	- 7.00	April	4-32	12.5	+ 19.00
May	1-7	14.3	+ 6.00	May	2-22	9.1	- 4.50
June	4-14	28.6	+ 7.75	June	6-37	16.2	+ 27.75
July	2-20	10.0	- 0.50	July	2-39	5.1	- 19.50
August	0-10	-	- 10.00	August	1-24	4.2	- 19.00
September	1-13	7.7	+ 13.00	September	2-29	6.9	+ 4.50
Oct/Nov	0-2	-	- 2.00	Oct/Nov	1-9	11.1	- 2.00

DISTANCE

2-y-o	W-R	Per cent	£1 Level Stake	3-y-o	W-R	Per cent	£1 Level Stake
5f-6f	6-49	12.2	+ 4.50	5f-6f	1-15	6.7	- 10.50
7f-8f	0-17	-	- 17.00	7f-8f	2-27	7.4	- 4.00
9f-13f	0-0	-	0.00	9f-13f	1-18	5.6	- 1.00
14f+	0-0	-	0.00	14f+	1-6	16.7	+ 20.00

4-y-o+	W-R	Per cent	£1 Level Stake	Totals	W-R	Per cent	£1 Level Stake
5f-6f	0-9	-	- 9.00	5f-6f	7-73	9.6	- 15.00
7f-8f	4-36	11.1	- 16.25	7f-8f	6-80	7.5	- 37.25
9f-13f	3-21	14.3	+ 33.00	9f-13f	4-39	10.3	+ 32.00
14f+	1-10	10.0	- 3.50	14f+	2-16	12.5	+ 16.50

TYPE OF RACE

Non-Handicaps	W-R	Per cent	£1 Level Stake	Handicaps	W-R	Per cent	£1 Level Stake
2-y-o	2-38	5.3	- 17.00	2-y-o	3-12	25.0	+ 7.50
3-y-o	1-15	6.7	+ 2.00	3-y-o	4-43	9.3	+ 10.50
4-y-o+	0-2	-	- 2.00	4-y-o+	8-62	12.9	+ 18.25
Selling	1-18	5.6	- 5.00	Selling	0-5	-	- 5.00
Apprentice	0-1	-	- 1.00	Apprentice	0-9	-	- 9.00
Amat/Ladies	0-0	-	0.00	Amat/Ladies	0-3	-	- 3.00
Totals	4-74	5.4	- 23.00	Totals	15-134	11.2	+ 19.25

COURSE GRADE

	W-R	Per cent	£1 Level Stake
Group 1	8-61	13.1	+ 30.75
Group 2	6-52	11.5	- 6.00
Group 3	2-50	4.0	- 17.50
Group 4	3-45	6.7	- 11.00

FIRST TIME OUT

	W-R	Per cent	£1 Level Stake
2-y-o	0-12	-	- 12.00
3-y-o	0-10	-	- 10.00
4-y-o+	0-12	-	- 12.00
Totals	0-34	-	- 34.00

JOCKEYS RIDING

	W–R	Per cent	£1 Level Stake		W–R	Per cent	£1 Level Stake
N Gwilliams	8-77	10.4	+ 1.25	D Biggs	1-3	33.3	+ 12.00
J Reid	4-20	20.0	+ 15.50	A Munro	1-8	12.5	+ 9.00
G Carter	2-10	20.0	+ 13.00	J Quinn	1-9	11.1	- 4.50
K Darley	1-1	100.0	+ 4.00	C Hawksley	1-17	5.9	+ 9.00

B Rouse	0-6	F Norton	0-2	J Fortune	0-1
Paul Eddery	0-6	M Roberts	0-2	M Hills	0-1
R Cochrane	0-6	W Ryan	0-2	Miss Y Haynes	0-1
W Newnes	0-6	A Martinez	0-1	Mr S Swiers	0-1
L Dettori	0-5	B Raymond	0-1	Mrs S Moore	0-1
J Carroll	0-4	C Asmussen	0-1	N Adams	0-1
Dale Gibson	0-3	D Toole	0-1	S Cauthen	0-1
J Lowe	0-3	G Bardwell	0-1	T Ashley	0-1
J Williams	0-3	G Duffield	0-1	T Quinn	0-1

COURSE RECORD

	Total W–R	Non-Handicaps 2-y-o	3-y-o+	Handicaps 2-y-o	3-y-o+	Per cent	£1 Level Stake
Yarmouth	2-8	0-2	0-0	0-0	2-6	25.0	+ 24.50
Sandown	2-9	0-3	0-0	1-4	1-4	22.2	+ 2.25
Goodwood	2-10	0-2	0-1	0-0	2-7	20.0	+ 29.00
Redcar	2-11	0-5	0-0	1-2	1-4	18.2	- 0.50
Brighton	2-16	0-1	0-3	0-1	2-11	12.5	- 5.50
Haydock	1-2	0-0	0-1	0-0	1-1	50.0	+ 2.50
York	1-2	0-0	1-2	0-0	0-0	50.0	+ 15.00
Thirsk	1-5	0-1	0-0	0-0	1-4	20.0	+ 12.00
Newmarket	1-7	0-2	0-0	1-1	0-4	14.3	0.00
Ripon	1-7	1-1	0-2	0-0	0-4	14.3	+ 1.00
Wolverhampton	1-8	1-4	0-0	0-0	0-4	12.5	+ 5.00
Lingfield (AW)	1-8	0-0	0-1	0-0	1-7	12.5	- 2.00
Kempton	1-10	1-2	0-3	0-0	0-5	10.0	+ 3.00
Folkestone	1-14	0-4	0-2	0-0	1-8	7.1	+ 1.00

Leicester	0-12	Catterick	0-6	Salisbury	0-4
Windsor	0-11	Ascot	0-5	Southwell (AW)	0-4
Epsom	0-10	Warwick	0-5	Chepstow	0-3
Lingfield	0-9	Bath	0-4	Pontefract	0-3
Nottingham	0-9	Newbury	0-4	Doncaster	0-2

WINNING HORSES

	Age	Races Run	1st	2nd	3rd	Unpl	Win £
Sheila's Secret	2	12	4	1	2	5	15,182
Bobzao	3	8	1	1	0	6	11,355
Hamadryad	4	10	3	2	0	5	9,329
Akkazao	4	9	2	0	2	5	5,502
Try Leguard	3	16	2	1	2	11	5,340
Affordable	4	7	1	0	0	6	2,950
Greenwich Bambi	4	7	1	2	1	3	2,734
Cheshire Annie	3	11	1	2	0	8	2,685

Shamshom Al Arab	4	7	1	0	2	4	2,532
Petite Lass	2	5	1	0	1	3	2,520
Anar	3	9	1	0	1	7	2,448
Greenwich Chalenge	2	9	1	2	2	4	2,406

WINNING OWNERS

	Races Won	Value £		Races Won	Value £
Miss Maha Kalaji	6	17,259	J P Devaney	2	5,340
Sherwoods Transport Ltd	4	15,182	J Humphreys Turf Accountants	1	2,734
T G Mills Ltd	2	13,875	D P Delaney	1	2,685
Ernie Penfold	2	5,502	J A Bird	1	2,406

Favourites	3-15	20.0%	+ 0.75	Total winning prize-money	£64,982

Longest winning sequence		2	Average SP of winner	9.8/1
Longest losing sequence		39	Return on stakes invested	-1.8%

1991 Form	15-299	5.0%	-130.52	1989 Form	23-182	12.6%	+ 66.83
1990 Form	20-281	7.1%	-161.74	1988 Form	2-53	3.8%	+ 61.00

T CASEY (Upper Lambourn, Berks)

	No. of Horses	Races Run	1st	2nd	3rd	Unpl	Per cent	£1 Level Stake
2-y-o	2	5	0	1	0	4	-	- 5.00
3-y-o	1	3	0	0	0	3	-	- 3.00
4-y-o+	6	39	5	1	2	31	12.8	- 5.50
Totals	9	47	5	2	2	38	10.6	- 13.50

Jan	Feb	Mar	Apr	May	Jun	Jul	Aug	Sep	Oct/Nov
0-6	1-6	1-3	0-3	1-3	0-6	2-8	0-4	0-5	0-3

Winning Jockeys	W-R	£1 Level Stake		W-R	£1 Level Stake
J Reid	3-11	+ 8.50	F Norton	2-10	+ 4.00

Winning Courses					
Newmarket	1-1	+ 8.00	Newbury	1-7	- 2.00
Warwick	1-2	+ 6.00	Lingfield (AW)	1-14	- 8.00
Goodwood	1-5	+ 0.50			

Winning Horses	Age	Races Run	1st	2nd	3rd	Unpl	Win £
Aughfad	6	15	3	0	0	12	10,725
Rushanes	5	11	2	1	2	6	4,824

Favourites	0-1		Total winning prize-money	£15,549

1991 Form	5-63	7.9%	- 20.67	1989 Form	1-28	3.6%	- 17.00
1990 Form	4-74	5.4%	- 37.50	1988 Form	3-33	9.1%	- 8.00

H R A CECIL (Newmarket)

	No. of Horses	Races Run	1st	2nd	3rd	Unpl	Per cent	£1 Level Stake
2-y-o	39	80	25	13	9	33	31.3	- 4.22
3-y-o	64	262	77	52	44	89	29.4	- 22.79
4-y-o+	9	41	7	6	6	22	17.1	+ 15.08
Totals	112	383	109	71	59	144	28.5	- 11.93

BY MONTH

2-y-o	W-R	Per cent	£1 Level Stake	3-y-o	W-R	Per cent	£1 Level Stake
Mar/Apr	0-0	-	0.00	Mar/Apr	21-43	48.8	+ 8.83
May	1-3	33.3	- 1.20	May	19-56	33.9	+ 5.25
June	2-7	28.6	- 4.25	June	10-37	27.0	- 11.33
July	9-15	60.0	+ 5.69	July	13-42	31.0	- 6.83
August	2-11	18.2	- 1.06	August	3-25	12.0	- 12.95
September	5-17	29.4	- 2.43	September	6-24	25.0	- 1.46
Oct/Nov	6-27	22.2	- 0.97	Oct/Nov	5-35	14.3	- 4.30

4-y-o+	W-R	Per cent	£1 Level Stake	Totals	W-R	Per cent	£1 Level Stake
Mar/Apr	3-9	33.3	+ 9.38	Mar/Apr	24-52	46.2	+ 18.21
May	0-7	-	- 7.00	May	20-66	30.3	- 2.95
June	2-9	22.2	+ 20.00	June	14-53	26.4	+ 4.42
July	0-7	-	- 7.00	July	22-64	34.4	- 8.14
August	2-5	40.0	+ 3.70	August	7-41	17.1	- 10.31
September	0-3	-	- 3.00	September	11-44	25.0	- 6.89
Oct/Nov	0-1	-	- 1.00	Oct/Nov	11-63	17.5	- 6.27

DISTANCE

2-y-o	W-R	Per cent	£1 Level Stake	3-y-o	W-R	Per cent	£1 Level Stake
5f-6f	4-15	26.7	- 8.30	5f-6f	3-11	27.3	- 3.13
7f-8f	21-64	32.8	+ 5.08	7f-8f	13-60	21.7	- 17.08
9f-13f	0-1	-	- 1.00	9f-13f	53-162	32.7	- 0.90
14f+	0-0	-	0.00	14f+	8-29	27.6	- 1.68

4-y-o+	W-R	Per cent	£1 Level Stake	Totals	W-R	Per cent	£1 Level Stake
5f-6f	0-0	-	0.00	5f-6f	7-26	26.9	- 11.43
7f-8f	2-12	16.7	+ 4.00	7f-8f	36-136	26.5	- 8.00
9f-13f	4-23	17.4	+ 9.08	9f-13f	57-186	30.6	+ 7.18
14f+	1-6	16.7	+ 2.00	14f+	9-35	25.7	+ 0.32

TYPE OF RACE

Non-Handicaps	W-R	Per cent	£1 Level Stake	Handicaps	W-R	Per cent	£1 Level Stake
2-y-o	25-78	32.1	- 2.22	2-y-o	0-2	-	- 2.00
3-y-o	62-198	31.3	- 19.67	3-y-o	14-58	24.1	+ 1.15
4-y-o+	3-25	12.0	+ 1.38	4-y-o+	3-13	23.1	+ 15.50
Selling	0-1	-	- 1.00	Selling	0-0	-	0.00
Apprentice	2-6	33.3	- 3.07	Apprentice	0-0	-	0.00
Amat/Ladies	0-2	-	- 2.00	Amat/Ladies	0-0	-	0.00
Totals	92-310	29.7	- 26.58	Totals	17-73	23.3	+ 14.65

COURSE GRADE

	W-R	Per cent	£1 Level Stake
Group 1	57-230	24.8	- 5.31
Group 2	16-46	34.8	- 7.39
Group 3	26-78	33.3	+ 5.02
Group 4	10-29	34.5	- 4.25

FIRST TIME OUT

	W-R	Per cent	£1 Level Stake
2-y-o	8-39	20.5	- 8.71
3-y-o	23-63	36.5	- 0.05
4-y-o+	2-9	22.2	+ 6.38
Totals	33-111	29.7	- 2.38

JOCKEYS RIDING

	W-R	Per cent	£1 Level Stake		W-R	Per cent	£1 Level Stake
W Ryan	36-121	29.8	+ 25.73	S Davies	5-19	26.3	- 2.04
Pat Eddery	35-106	33.0	- 8.63	G Parkin	1-1	100.0	+ 0.20
S Cauthen	24-67	35.8	+ 3.41	K Darley	1-2	50.0	- 0.38
A McGlone	6-30	20.0	+ 1.78	R Cochrane	1-2	50.0	+ 3.00

M Roberts	0-11	B Raymond	0-3	L Dettori		0-1
W R Swinburn	0-6	Miss J Allison	0-2	Miss L S-Sackville		0-1
L Piggott	0-4	Dale Gibson	0-1	W Carson		0-1
M J Kinane	0-4	J Reid	0-1			

COURSE RECORD

	Total W-R	Non-Handicaps 2-y-o	Non-Handicaps 3-y-o+	Handicaps 2-y-o	Handicaps 3-y-o+	Per cent	£1 Level Stake
Newmarket	15-64	8-20	6-34	0-0	1-10	23.4	- 13.42
Newbury	8-22	1-2	4-14	0-0	3-6	36.4	+ 12.18
Ripon	7-12	0-1	6-10	0-0	1-1	58.3	+ 2.35
Newcastle	7-13	2-2	4-9	0-0	1-2	53.8	+ 2.22
Doncaster	7-23	2-6	5-14	0-0	0-3	30.4	+ 8.01
Wolverhampton	6-10	1-3	5-7	0-0	0-0	60.0	+ 2.00
Nottingham	6-16	1-4	5-12	0-0	0-0	37.5	+ 2.40
York	6-22	1-3	3-12	0-0	2-7	27.3	- 6.76
Windsor	5-11	0-1	3-8	0-0	2-2	45.5	+ 7.63
Yarmouth	5-16	2-7	2-6	0-0	1-3	31.3	- 3.27
Warwick	3-9	1-1	1-5	0-1	1-2	33.3	+ 1.37
Haydock	3-15	1-1	2-9	0-0	0-5	20.0	- 4.87

Cecil H R A

Leicester	3-15	0-6	3-8	0-0	0-1	20.0	-	5.72
Goodwood	3-18	2-2	1-11	0-0	0-5	16.7	-	1.08
Sandown	3-19	2-5	1-11	0-0	0-3	15.8	-	10.10
Bath	2-2	0-0	1-1	0-0	1-1	100.0	+	4.50
Thirsk	2-3	1-1	1-1	0-1	0-0	66.7	-	0.18
Pontefract	2-4	0-1	2-3	0-0	0-0	50.0	+	2.75
Chepstow	2-5	0-1	1-3	0-0	1-1	40.0	+	4.00
Redcar	2-5	0-0	2-4	0-0	0-1	40.0	+	2.67
Lingfield	2-6	0-1	1-3	0-0	1-2	33.3	-	2.36
Kempton	2-9	0-0	2-5	0-0	0-4	22.2	-	3.49
Chester	2-10	0-1	2-5	0-0	0-4	20.0	-	2.37
Ascot	2-21	0-4	1-13	0-0	1-4	9.5	+	8.00
Epsom	1-4	0-0	0-3	0-0	1-1	25.0	+	4.00
Folkestone	1-5	0-1	1-4	0-0	0-0	20.0	-	2.62
Brighton	1-8	0-1	1-6	0-0	0-1	12.5	-	5.50
Beverley	1-9	0-2	1-5	0-0	0-2	11.1	-	7.27

Catterick	0-2	Edinburgh	0-1	Southwell (AW)	0-1
Salisbury	0-2	Lingfield (AW)	0-1		

WINNING HORSES

		Races					Win
	Age	Run	1st	2nd	3rd	Unpl	£
Armiger	2	2	2	0	0	0	109,290
Perpendicular	4	3	1	0	0	2	58,536
Rudimentary	4	6	2	0	2	2	57,960
All At Sea	3	7	3	3	0	1	42,814
Twist And Turn	3	6	2	1	0	3	40,224
Pursuit Of Love	3	7	2	4	1	0	39,764
Ardkinglass	2	5	3	1	0	1	19,076
Musicale	3	2	1	0	0	1	18,353
Gondolier	4	7	1	1	1	4	18,227
Wharf	2	2	2	0	0	0	17,329
Tenby	2	2	2	0	0	0	14,607
Folia	3	4	3	0	0	1	13,003
Allegan	3	4	3	1	0	0	12,810
King's Loch	3	3	1	0	0	2	12,679
Garah	3	7	3	1	1	2	12,264
Alphard	3	4	2	0	0	2	12,014
Receptionist	3	8	3	1	3	1	11,166
Marabella Star	3	4	1	0	0	3	10,625
Peto	3	6	4	0	0	2	9,457
Tapis Rouge	3	6	3	1	1	1	9,414
Alhamad	3	6	2	2	1	1	8,215
Fetish	3	5	2	2	1	0	8,022
Rockawhile	3	4	3	0	0	1	8,004
Hatta's Mill	3	3	1	1	0	1	7,096
Citiqueen	3	5	2	1	0	2	6,562
Belgran	3	4	2	1	1	0	6,396
Balnibarbi	3	3	2	0	0	1	6,278
Magique Rond Point	2	3	1	0	1	1	6,212
Skimble	3	4	1	0	0	3	5,640
Elkhart	2	4	2	1	0	1	5,367
Mizoram	3	5	2	1	0	2	5,318

Miss Plum	3	3	2	0	0	1	5,007
Felucca	2	2	1	0	1	0	4,932
Glaisdale	3	5	2	1	1	1	4,905
Anchorage	3	6	2	2	1	1	4,612
United Kingdom	3	4	1	1	2	0	4,581
Fayfa	2	1	1	0	0	0	4,468
Wave Hill	3	4	1	1	0	2	4,013
Placerville	2	1	1	0	0	0	3,850
Dayflower	2	2	1	0	0	1	3,753
Gueca Solo	4	5	1	0	2	2	3,728
Imperial Ballet	3	3	2	0	0	1	3,557
Lead The Dance	3	5	1	1	1	2	3,460
Truben	3	5	2	1	0	2	3,450
Deserve	3	3	1	0	0	2	3,290
Lead Note	2	1	1	0	0	0	3,231
Pabouche	3	5	1	0	1	3	3,158
Pica	3	5	1	1	0	3	2,930
Mimique	3	4	1	2	0	1	2,910
Awol	3	4	1	1	2	0	2,846
Mukhamedov	2	4	1	0	0	3	2,840
Double Bass	2	3	1	2	0	0	2,819
Helvellyn	2	3	1	0	1	1	2,700
Charmed Life	3	3	1	0	1	1	2,637
Halley	3	3	1	0	0	2	2,595
Dakar Rally	2	2	1	0	0	1	2,560
Yeltsin	2	2	1	0	0	1	2,553
Sweet Quest	3	2	1	0	0	1	2,511
Flaming Arrow	4	8	1	4	0	3	2,427
Self Assured	2	5	1	2	2	0	2,406
Henpot	4	2	1	0	0	1	2,402
Wand	3	4	1	1	1	1	2,364
Betelgeuse	3	5	1	1	1	2	2,343
Informatrice	2	1	1	0	0	0	2,322
Pavonis	3	3	1	1	1	0	2,238
Intent	3	2	1	0	1	0	2,072
Kaiser Wilhelm	3	5	1	1	2	1	2,072
Kaisar	3	4	1	2	1	0	2,070
Nile Delta	3	2	1	1	0	0	2,070
Sculler	2	2	1	0	0	1	2,070
Shirley Valentine	3	6	1	2	1	2	1,618

WINNING OWNERS

	Races Won	Value £		Races Won	Value £
K Abdulla	23	234,562	Edward St George	4	8,457
Lord Howard De Walden	7	177,333	Ivan Allan	2	6,562
Sheikh Mohammed	35	136,405	S Khaled	2	6,396
Prince A A Faisal	6	24,947	Q Irshid	1	6,212
R E Sangster	3	21,911	Mrs H G Cambanis	2	6,083
Cliveden Stud	5	20,626	C A B St George	1	3,728
Sir David Wills	3	19,076	David St George	1	2,840
D K Harris	4	16,595	Terry Ellis	1	2,511
Michael Poland	1	12,679	Saeed Maktoum Al Maktoum	1	2,427
L Marinopoulos	4	10,641	H E Lhendup Dorji	1	2,402
M C Samlalsingh	1	10,625	Charles H Wacker III	1	2,072

Cecil H R A

Favourites	73-177	41.2%	- 24.54	Total winning prize-money			£735,088

Longest winning sequence		4	Average SP of winner		2.4/1
Longest losing sequence		15	Return on stakes invested		-3.0%

1991 Form	119-381	31.2%	+ 17.10	1989 Form	116-363	32.0%	+ 48.42
1990 Form	111-351	31.6%	- 8.67	1988 Form	112-370	30.3%	- 59.14

MRS J CECIL (Newmarket)

	No. of Horses	Races Run	1st	2nd	3rd	Unpl	Per cent	£1 Level Stake
2-y-o	13	35	4	8	4	19	11.4	+ 9.63
3-y-o	31	122	24	19	16	63	19.7	+ 58.69
4-y-o+	0	0	0	0	0	0	-	0.00
Totals	44	157	28	27	20	82	17.8	+ 68.32

BY MONTH

2-y-o	W-R	Per cent	£1 Level Stake	3-y-o	W-R	Per cent	£1 Level Stake
January	0-0	-	0.00	January	0-2	-	- 2.00
February	0-0	-	0.00	February	1-1	100.0	+ 1.50
March	0-0	-	0.00	March	0-1	-	- 1.00
April	0-0	-	0.00	April	2-14	14.3	- 1.00
May	0-2	-	- 2.00	May	6-26	23.1	+ 0.30
June	1-6	16.7	- 2.50	June	2-22	9.1	- 16.87
July	0-3	-	- 3.00	July	1-12	8.3	+ 3.00
August	0-1	-	- 1.00	August	2-9	22.2	- 3.49
September	1-7	14.3	+ 27.00	September	1-13	7.7	- 3.00
Oct/Nov	2-16	12.5	- 8.87	Oct/Nov	9-22	40.9	+ 81.25

4-y-o+	W-R	Per cent	£1 Level Stake	Totals	W-R	Per cent	£1 Level Stake
January	0-0	-	0.00	January	0-2	-	- 2.00
February	0-0	-	0.00	February	1-1	100.0	+ 1.50
March	0-0	-	0.00	March	0-1	-	- 1.00
April	0-0	-	0.00	April	2-14	14.3	- 1.00
May	0-0	-	0.00	May	6-28	21.4	- 1.70
June	0-0	-	0.00	June	3-28	10.7	- 19.37
July	0-0	-	0.00	July	1-15	6.7	0.00
August	0-0	-	0.00	August	2-10	20.0	- 4.49
September	0-0	-	0.00	September	2-20	10.0	+ 24.00
Oct/Nov	0-0	-	0.00	Oct/Nov	11-38	28.9	+ 72.38

DISTANCE

2-y-o	W-R	Per cent	£1 Level Stake	3-y-o	W-R	Per cent	£1 Level Stake
5f-6f	1-21	4.8	- 17.50	5f-6f	0-5	-	- 5.00
7f-8f	3-14	21.4	+ 27.13	7f-8f	7-24	29.2	+ 63.75
9f-13f	0-0	-	0.00	9f-13f	13-83	15.7	- 15.56
14f+	0-0	-	0.00	14f+	4-10	40.0	+ 15.50

4-y-o+	W-R	Per cent	£1 Level Stake	Totals	W-R	Per cent	£1 Level Stake
5f-6f	0-0	-	0.00	5f-6f	1-26	3.8	- 22.50
7f-8f	0-0	-	0.00	7f-8f	10-38	26.3	+ 90.88
9f-13f	0-0	-	0.00	9f-13f	13-83	15.7	- 15.56
14f+	0-0	-	0.00	14f+	4-10	40.0	+ 15.50

TYPE OF RACE

Non-Handicaps	W-R	Per cent	£1 Level Stake	Handicaps	W-R	Per cent	£1 Level Stake
2-y-o	4-34	11.8	+ 10.63	2-y-o	0-1	-	- 1.00
3-y-o	15-67	22.4	+ 13.69	3-y-o	9-52	17.3	+ 48.00
4-y-o+	0-0	-	0.00	4-y-o+	0-0	-	0.00
Selling	0-0	-	0.00	Selling	0-0	-	0.00
Apprentice	0-2	-	- 2.00	Apprentice	0-0	-	0.00
Amat/Ladies	0-0	-	0.00	Amat/Ladies	0-1	-	- 1.00
Totals	19-103	18.4	+ 22.32	Totals	9-54	16.7	+ 46.00

COURSE GRADE

	W-R	Per cent	£1 Level Stake
Group 1	11-76	14.5	+ 25.13
Group 2	5-25	20.0	+ 23.88
Group 3	7-40	17.5	+ 12.51
Group 4	5-16	31.3	+ 6.80

FIRST TIME OUT

	W-R	Per cent	£1 Level Stake
2-y-o	0-12	-	- 12.00
3-y-o	5-30	16.7	- 9.50
4-y-o+	0-0	-	0.00
Totals	5-42	11.9	- 21.50

JOCKEYS RIDING

	W-R	Per cent	£1 Level Stake		W-R	Per cent	£1 Level Stake
Paul Eddery	13-82	15.9	- 25.69	P Robinson	1-2	50.0	+ 0.88
M Roberts	3-7	42.9	+ 8.00	L Dettori	1-3	33.3	+ 0.50
G Duffield	3-7	42.9	+ 65.00	B Crossley	1-7	14.3	- 4.50
W Newnes	2-2	100.0	+ 15.63	J Reid	1-7	14.3	0.00
R Cochrane	2-2	100.0	+ 36.50	S Cauthen	1-7	14.3	+ 3.00

W Ryan	0-6	J Quinn	0-2	Mrs J Crossley	0-1
A Clark	0-3	P Turner	0-2	N Carlisle	0-1
D Harrison	0-3	B Raymond	0-1	Pat Eddery	0-1
L Piggott	0-3	F Norton	0-1	W R Swinburn	0-1
A McGlone	0-2	K Fallon	0-1		
J Carroll	0-2	M Hills	0-1		

COURSE RECORD

	Total W-R	Non-Handicaps 2-y-o	3-y-o+	Handicaps 2-y-o	3-y-o+	Per cent	£1 Level Stake
Leicester	3-7	1-3	2-3	0-0	0-1	42.9	+ 7.13
Ripon	2-9	0-2	1-5	0-0	1-2	22.2	- 2.12
York	2-9	0-0	2-3	0-0	0-6	22.2	- 2.00
Newbury	2-10	0-2	2-4	0-0	0-4	20.0	- 3.37
Yarmouth	2-13	0-5	2-5	0-0	0-3	15.4	+ 5.75
Newmarket	2-21	0-8	0-4	0-0	2-9	9.5	+ 34.00
Carlisle	1-1	0-0	1-1	0-0	0-0	100.0	+ 0.30
Warwick	1-2	1-1	0-0	0-0	0-1	50.0	+ 2.50
Wolverhampton	1-2	0-0	0-0	0-0	1-2	50.0	+ 8.00
Chester	1-3	0-0	0-1	0-1	1-1	33.3	+ 1.50
Folkestone	1-3	0-1	0-1	0-0	1-1	33.3	+ 1.50
Lingfield (AW)	1-3	0-0	1-3	0-0	0-0	33.3	- 0.50
Goodwood	1-4	0-1	0-1	0-0	1-2	25.0	+ 4.50
Pontefract	1-4	0-0	1-4	0-0	0-0	25.0	+ 13.00
Ascot	1-5	1-1	0-3	0-0	0-1	20.0	- 1.50
Sandown	1-5	0-0	0-3	0-0	1-2	20.0	+ 2.00
Windsor	1-5	0-0	1-4	0-0	0-1	20.0	- 2.37
Doncaster	1-6	0-1	0-3	0-0	1-2	16.7	+ 0.50
Kempton	1-6	0-0	1-3	0-0	0-3	16.7	+ 1.00
Lingfield	1-6	1-2	0-1	0-0	0-3	16.7	+ 28.00
Redcar	1-6	0-1	1-3	0-0	0-2	16.7	- 2.50

Haydock	0-7	Southwell (AW)	0-3	Newcastle	0-1
Beverley	0-3	Bath	0-2	Thirsk	0-1
Chepstow	0-3	Catterick	0-2		
Nottingham	0-3	Epsom	0-2		

WINNING HORSES

	Age	Races Run	1st	2nd	3rd	Unpl	Win £
Cambrian	3	6	3	0	0	3	37,038
Iota	3	9	3	1	3	2	10,772
High Tycoon	2	3	1	1	1	0	10,325
Kristianstad	3	4	2	1	0	1	9,543
Million In Mind	3	6	2	0	1	3	7,960
Cropton	2	2	2	0	0	0	5,700
Ambiguously Regal	3	6	1	1	1	3	5,536
Alderbrook	3	7	2	2	1	2	4,854
Pater Noster	3	2	1	0	0	1	3,590
Kinglow	3	6	1	1	0	4	3,571
Surf	3	3	1	0	1	1	3,366
Fassfern	3	5	1	0	1	3	3,097
Long Silence	3	4	1	1	0	2	2,679
Albemine	3	3	1	0	0	2	2,511
Lady Dundee	3	9	1	1	2	5	2,490
Khrisma	3	5	1	0	1	3	2,363
Mr Flood	3	5	1	3	0	1	2,128
Aremef	3	9	1	2	0	6	2,072
Rapid Repeat	2	2	1	0	0	1	2,070
Big Easy	3	5	1	2	1	1	1,907

WINNING OWNERS

	Races Won	Value £		Races Won	Value £
Sheikh Mohammed	8	57,353	V E Barclay	1	3,571
James H Stone	5	11,379	Grundy Bloodstock Ltd	1	3,366
R N Tikkoo	1	10,325	W S Farish III	1	2,679
George L Ohrstrom	2	8,633	Mrs Mark Burrell	1	2,511
The Million In Mind Partnership	2	7,960	Lord Howard De Walden	1	2,363
Lady Murless	2	5,700	Lord Petersham	1	2,072
Martin Myers	1	3,590	Lord Hartington	1	2,070

Favourites	10-35	28.6%	- 4.06	Total winning prize-money	£123,572
Longest winning sequence			2	Average SP of winner	7.0/1
Longest losing sequence			13	Return on stakes invested	43.5%
1991 Form	19-95	20.0%	- 3.45		

N CHAMBERLAIN (West Auckland, Co Durham)

	No. of Horses	Races Run	1st	2nd	3rd	Unpl	Per cent	£1 Level Stake
2-y-o	2	8	1	0	0	7	12.5	+ 18.00
3-y-o	1	2	0	0	0	2	-	- 2.00
4-y-o+	0	0	0	0	0	0	-	0.00
Totals	3	10	1	0	0	9	10.0	+ 16.00

Jan	Feb	Mar	Apr	May	Jun	Jul	Aug	Sep	Oct/Nov
0-0	0-0	0-0	0-0	0-0	0-0	0-0	0-0	0-6	1-4

	W-R	£1 Level Stake		W-R	£1 Level Stake
Winning Jockey			Winning Course		
S Wood	1-3	+ 23.00	Catterick	1-4	+ 22.00

	Age	Races Run	1st	2nd	3rd	Unpl	Win £
Winning Horse							
Public Way	2	7	1	0	0	6	3,057

Favourites	0-0		Total winning prize-money	£3,057
1991 Form	0-18		1989 Form	0-6
1990 Form	0-14		1988 Form	0-32

M R CHANNON (Upper Lambourn, Berks)

	No. of Horses	Races Run	1st	2nd	3rd	Unpl	Per cent	£1 Level Stake
2-y-o	23	122	9	13	14	86	7.4	- 44.70
3-y-o	18	106	9	12	11	74	8.5	- 64.39
4-y-o+	9	57	8	3	1	45	14.0	0.00
Totals	50	285	26	28	26	205	9.1	-109.09

BY MONTH

2-y-o	W-R	Per cent	£1 Level Stake	3-y-o	W-R	Per cent	£1 Level Stake
January	0-0	-	0.00	January	0-2	-	- 2.00
February	0-0	-	0.00	February	0-1	-	- 1.00
March	1-2	50.0	+ 3.50	March	1-6	16.7	+ 5.00
April	0-6	-	- 6.00	April	1-15	6.7	- 11.00
May	0-5	-	- 5.00	May	0-26	-	- 26.00
June	2-13	15.4	+ 14.80	June	2-19	10.5	- 6.75
July	1-19	5.3	- 12.50	July	4-12	33.3	+ 0.63
August	1-23	4.3	- 13.00	August	1-9	11.1	- 7.27
September	2-29	6.9	- 16.50	September	0-10	-	- 10.00
Oct/Nov	2-25	8.0	- 10.00	Oct/Nov	0-6	-	- 6.00

4-y-o+	W-R	Per cent	£1 Level Stake	Totals	W-R	Per cent	£1 Level Stake
January	0-3	-	- 3.00	January	0-5	-	- 5.00
February	2-5	40.0	+ 6.50	February	2-6	33.3	+ 5.50
March	2-5	40.0	+ 11.50	March	4-13	30.8	+ 20.00
April	0-5	-	- 5.00	April	1-26	3.8	- 22.00
May	1-5	20.0	+ 3.00	May	1-36	2.8	- 28.00
June	0-7	-	- 7.00	June	4-39	10.3	+ 1.05
July	2-9	22.2	+ 3.00	July	7-40	17.5	- 8.87
August	0-11	-	- 11.00	August	2-43	4.7	- 31.27
September	1-6	16.7	+ 3.00	September	3-45	6.7	- 23.50
Oct/Nov	0-1	-	- 1.00	Oct/Nov	2-32	6.3	- 17.00

DISTANCE

2-y-o	W-R	Per cent	£1 Level Stake	3-y-o	W-R	Per cent	£1 Level Stake
5f-6f	7-64	10.9	- 0.20	5f-6f	2-21	9.5	- 13.10
7f-8f	2-57	3.5	- 43.50	7f-8f	2-32	6.3	- 19.75
9f-13f	0-1	-	- 1.00	9f-13f	5-50	10.0	- 28.54
14f+	0-0	-	0.00	14f+	0-3	-	- 3.00

4-y-o+	W-R	Per cent	£1 Level Stake	Totals	W-R	Per cent	£1 Level Stake
5f-6f	4-32	12.5	+ 2.00	5f-6f	13-117	11.1	- 11.30
7f-8f	2-19	10.5	- 7.50	7f-8f	6-108	5.6	- 70.75
9f-13f	2-4	50.0	+ 7.50	9f-13f	7-55	12.7	- 22.04
14f+	0-2	-	- 2.00	14f+	0-5	-	- 5.00

TYPE OF RACE

Non-Handicaps	W-R	Per cent	£1 Level Stake	Handicaps	W-R	Per cent	£1 Level Stake
2-y-o	8-71	11.3	- 3.70	2-y-o	0-29	-	- 29.00
3-y-o	5-50	10.0	- 30.99	3-y-o	3-43	7.0	- 22.50
4-y-o+	3-7	42.9	+ 13.50	4-y-o+	5-50	10.0	- 13.50
Selling	2-25	8.0	- 12.90	Selling	0-8	-	- 8.00
Apprentice	0-0	-	0.00	Apprentice	0-1	-	- 1.00
Amat/Ladies	0-0	-	0.00	Amat/Ladies	0-1	-	- 1.00
Totals	18-153	11.8	- 34.09	Totals	8-132	6.1	- 75.00

COURSE GRADE

	W-R	Per cent	£1 Level Stake
Group 1	4-108	3.7	- 65.70
Group 2	7-61	11.5	- 30.79
Group 3	8-74	10.8	- 15.60
Group 4	7-42	16.7	+ 3.00

FIRST TIME OUT

	W-R	Per cent	£1 Level Stake
2-y-o	2-23	8.7	+ 8.50
3-y-o	0-17	-	- 17.00
4-y-o+	0-7	-	- 7.00
Totals	2-47	4.3	- 15.50

JOCKEYS RIDING

	W-R	Per cent	£1 Level Stake		W-R	Per cent	£1 Level Stake
B Doyle	5-41	12.2	- 1.00	S Whitworth	1-3	33.3	+ 3.50
Paul Eddery	3-14	21.4	+ 0.03	R Cochrane	1-4	25.0	- 1.90
P Turner	2-4	50.0	+ 7.50	M Hills	1-4	25.0	+ 22.00
Pat Eddery	2-19	10.5	- 11.77	G Carter	1-4	25.0	+ 1.00
J Quinn	2-22	9.1	- 9.75	W Carson	1-5	20.0	- 3.20
B Rouse	2-25	8.0	- 10.50	D Holland	1-6	16.7	- 2.50
D McKeown	1-1	100.0	+ 9.00	R Hills	1-11	9.1	- 3.00
M Roberts	1-2	50.0	+ 8.00	T Quinn	1-27	3.7	- 23.50

C Rutter	0-19	Dale Gibson	0-2	J Fortune	0-1
Lorna Vincent	0-11	G Bardwell	0-2	J Lowe	0-1
R Perham	0-8	G Hind	0-2	K Darley	0-1
J Williams	0-6	K Fallon	0-2	Kim McDonnell	0-1
W Newnes	0-6	R Price	0-2	L Piggott	0-1
A Munro	0-4	W Ryan	0-2	M Tebbutt	0-1
L Mahoney	0-4	Antoinette Armes	0-1	N Adams	0-1
A Tucker	0-3	B Crossley	0-1	S Cauthen	0-1
F Norton	0-3	C Hawksley	0-1	T Williams	0-1
G Duffield	0-3	G Baxter	0-1	W R Swinburn	0-1

COURSE RECORD

	Total W-R	Non-Handicaps 2-y-o	3-y-o+	Handicaps 2-y-o	3-y-o+	Per cent	£1 Level Stake
Beverley	5-15	2-3	0-2	0-1	3-9	33.3	+ 22.00
Lingfield (AW)	5-16	1-3	2-5	0-0	2-8	31.3	+ 13.50
Pontefract	2-4	2-2	0-0	0-1	0-1	50.0	+ 15.00
Ripon	2-5	0-2	2-3	0-0	0-0	40.0	+ 6.10

Channon M R

Lingfield	2-17	0-5	1-4	0-3	1-5	11.8	- 5.75
Goodwood	2-21	1-8	0-1	0-3	1-9	9.5	+ 10.50
Salisbury	2-21	0-8	2-6	0-0	0-7	9.5	- 16.64
Folkestone	1-4	1-1	0-1	0-0	0-2	25.0	+ 1.50
Southwell (AW)	1-9	1-1	0-4	0-0	0-4	11.1	+ 1.00
Brighton	1-10	0-2	0-3	0-0	1-5	10.0	- 6.50
Bath	1-12	0-3	1-4	0-1	0-4	8.3	- 9.60
Kempton	1-14	0-2	1-5	0-2	0-5	7.1	- 5.00
Sandown	1-15	1-5	0-2	0-2	0-6	6.7	- 13.20

Windsor	0-18	York	0-7	Ayr	0-2
Newmarket	0-16	Redcar	0-5	Chester	0-2
Chepstow	0-15	Newcastle	0-4	Haydock	0-2
Newbury	0-15	Catterick	0-3	Warwick	0-2
Wolverhampton	0-8	Epsom	0-3	Thirsk	0-1
Doncaster	0-7	Yarmouth	0-3		
Leicester	0-7	Ascot	0-2		

WINNING HORSES

	Age	Races Run	1st	2nd	3rd	Unpl	Win £
Cheveux Mitchell	5	15	2	0	1	12	13,743
Misdemeanours Girl	4	21	3	2	0	16	9,996
Grog	3	12	3	3	2	4	8,065
Aradanza	2	9	2	2	1	4	6,095
Silca-Cisa	3	8	1	3	0	4	5,692
Pleasure Ahead	5	3	2	0	0	1	4,452
Clifton Charlie	4	11	1	1	0	9	2,805
Felt Lucky	2	6	1	0	0	5	2,783
Latest Flame	2	7	1	2	0	4	2,700
Mr Butch	2	11	1	2	3	5	2,700
Sunley Silks	3	4	1	0	1	2	2,693
Mighty Miss Magpie	2	12	1	0	3	8	2,616
Star Goddess	3	4	1	0	0	3	2,595
Double Flutter	3	5	1	0	2	2	2,364
George Roper	2	9	1	2	2	4	1,932
Canadian Capers	3	10	1	0	3	6	1,926
Marchwell Lad	2	5	1	0	0	4	1,725
Miss Doody	3	11	1	2	1	7	1,459
Knobbleeneeze	2	8	1	1	0	6	1,193

WINNING OWNERS

	Races Won	Value £		Races Won	Value £
Chitty Ltd	2	13,743	M Channon	1	2,783
M G Michaels	3	9,996	Miss Juliet E Reed	1	2,700
Mrs D Hanson	3	8,065	G Herridge	1	2,700
Mighty Quinn Racing (II) Ltd	3	7,068	Sunley Holdings Plc	1	2,693
Mrs P Lewis	2	6,095	Peter Taplin	1	1,926
Aldridge Racing Limited	1	5,692	C C Buckley	1	1,725
John W Mitchell	2	5,169	Vincent Herridge	1	1,459
K Higson	2	4,527	Anthony Andrews	1	1,193

Favourites	8-19	42.1%	+ 7.28	Total winning prize-money			£77,533

Longest winning sequence		2	Average SP of winner		5.8/1
Longest losing sequence		55	Return on stakes invested		-38.3%

1991 Form	22-235	9.4%	- 55.25	1990 Form	16-162	9.9%	+ 2.66

D W CHAPMAN (York, North Yorks)

	No. of Horses	Races Run	1st	2nd	3rd	Unpl	Per cent	£1 Level Stake
2-y-o	4	13	1	0	0	12	7.7	+ 21.00
3-y-o	6	45	2	4	4	35	4.4	- 25.75
4-y-o+	23	206	9	10	14	173	4.4	- 79.00
Totals	33	264	12	14	18	220	4.5	- 83.75

BY MONTH

2-y-o	W-R	Per cent	£1 Level Stake	3-y-o	W-R	Per cent	£1 Level Stake
January	0-0	-	0.00	January	2-11	18.2	+ 8.25
February	0-0	-	0.00	February	0-3	-	- 3.00
March	0-2	-	- 2.00	March	0-4	-	- 4.00
April	0-0	-	0.00	April	0-1	-	- 1.00
May	0-0	-	0.00	May	0-8	-	- 8.00
June	0-0	-	0.00	June	0-2	-	- 2.00
July	0-2	-	- 2.00	July	0-4	-	- 4.00
August	1-3	33.3	+ 31.00	August	0-6	-	- 6.00
September	0-2	-	- 2.00	September	0-2	-	- 2.00
Oct/Nov	0-4	-	- 4.00	Oct/Nov	0-4	-	- 4.00

4-y-o+	W-R	Per cent	£1 Level Stake	Totals	W-R	Per cent	£1 Level Stake
January	1-29	3.4	- 8.00	January	3-40	7.5	+ 0.25
February	1-17	5.9	- 5.00	February	1-20	5.0	- 8.00
March	0-18	-	- 18.00	March	0-24	-	- 24.00
April	0-22	-	- 22.00	April	0-23	-	- 23.00
May	1-14	7.1	+ 3.00	May	1-22	4.5	- 5.00
June	1-14	7.1	- 8.50	June	1-16	6.3	- 10.50
July	1-28	3.6	- 15.00	July	1-34	2.9	- 21.00
August	2-24	8.3	+ 13.00	August	3-33	9.1	+ 38.00
September	2-21	9.5	+ 0.50	September	2-25	8.0	- 3.50
Oct/Nov	0-19	-	- 19.00	Oct/Nov	0-27	-	- 27.00

DISTANCE

2-y-o	W-R	Per cent	£1 Level Stake	3-y-o	W-R	Per cent	£1 Level Stake
5f-6f	1-9	11.1	+ 25.00	5f-6f	1-30	3.3	- 13.00
7f-8f	0-4	-	- 4.00	7f-8f	1-15	6.7	- 12.75
9f-13f	0-0	-	0.00	9f-13f	0-0	-	0.00
14f+	0-0	-	0.00	14f+	0-0	-	0.00

4-y-o+	W-R	Per cent	£1 Level Stake	Totals	W-R	Per cent	£1 Level Stake
5f-6f	5-121	4.1	- 53.00	5f-6f	7-160	4.4	- 41.00
7f-8f	2-60	3.3	- 30.00	7f-8f	3-79	3.8	- 46.75
9f-13f	2-22	9.1	+ 7.00	9f-13f	2-22	9.1	+ 7.00
14f+	0-3	-	- 3.00	14f+	0-3	-	- 3.00

TYPE OF RACE

Non-Handicaps	W-R	Per cent	£1 Level Stake	Handicaps	W-R	Per cent	£1 Level Stake
2-y-o	1-4	25.0	+ 30.00	2-y-o	0-6	-	- 6.00
3-y-o	1-11	9.1	- 8.75	3-y-o	1-28	3.6	- 11.00
4-y-o+	2-26	7.7	+ 7.00	4-y-o+	6-152	3.9	- 71.00
Selling	0-8	-	- 8.00	Selling	1-5	20.0	+ 8.00
Apprentice	0-1	-	- 1.00	Apprentice	0-19	-	- 19.00
Amat/Ladies	0-1	-	- 1.00	Amat/Ladies	0-3	-	- 3.00
Totals	4-51	7.8	+ 18.25	Totals	8-213	3.8	-102.00

COURSE GRADE

	W-R	Per cent	£1 Level Stake
Group 1	1-30	3.3	- 13.00
Group 2	4-36	11.1	+ 19.50
Group 3	1-46	2.2	- 41.50
Group 4	6-152	3.9	- 48.75

FIRST TIME OUT

	W-R	Per cent	£1 Level Stake
2-y-o	0-3	-	- 3.00
3-y-o	0-6	-	- 6.00
4-y-o+	2-23	8.7	+ 10.00
Totals	2-32	6.3	+ 1.00

JOCKEYS RIDING

	W-R	Per cent	£1 Level Stake		W-R	Per cent	£1 Level Stake
S Wood	10-175	5.7	- 33.75	K Darley	1-11	9.1	+ 2.00
N Connorton	1-2	50.0	+ 24.00				

S D Williams	0-10	M Harris	0-2	G Husband	0-1
D Moffatt	0-8	Miss R Clark	0-2	J Marshall	0-1
J Fanning	0-8	S Webster	0-2	J Weaver	0-1
O Pears	0-7	T Quinn	0-2	M Hills	0-1
G Baxter	0-6	A Tucker	0-1	Mr M Buckley	0-1
S Maloney	0-3	B Raymond	0-1	Mrs A Farrell	0-1
J Fortune	0-2	C Hawksley	0-1	P Burke	0-1
J Lowe	0-2	Claire Balding	0-1	T Williams	0-1
J Quinn	0-2	G Carter	0-1	V Halliday	0-1
L Dettori	0-2	G Coogan	0-1		
M Baird	0-2	G Forster	0-1		

COURSE RECORD

	Total W-R	Non-Handicaps 2-y-o	3-y-o+	Handicaps 2-y-o	3-y-o+	Per cent	£1 Level Stake
Southwell (AW)	4-102	0-3	3-29	0-0	1-70	3.9	- 49.75
Thirsk	2-13	0-0	0-0	0-0	2-13	15.4	+ 18.50
Leicester	1-3	0-0	0-0	0-1	1-2	33.3	+ 1.50
York	1-3	0-0	0-0	0-1	1-2	33.3	+ 14.00
Carlisle	1-9	0-0	0-1	0-0	1-8	11.1	+ 8.00
Ripon	1-10	0-0	0-1	0-0	1-9	10.0	+ 1.00
Redcar	1-13	0-0	0-0	0-0	1-13	7.7	0.00
Edinburgh	1-15	1-1	0-1	0-0	0-13	6.7	+ 19.00

Catterick	0-15	Haydock	0-7	Folkestone	0-1
Hamilton	0-13	Ayr	0-6	Newmarket	0-1
Pontefract	0-12	Lingfield (AW)	0-5	Warwick	0-1
Doncaster	0-9	Newcastle	0-4	Yarmouth	0-1
Nottingham	0-8	Wolverhampton	0-4		
Beverley	0-7	Chepstow	0-2		

WINNING HORSES

	Age	Races Run	1st	2nd	3rd	Unpl	Win £
Yours Or Mine	4	14	3	1	1	9	10,319
Dawn Success	6	16	1	0	1	14	4,136
Chaplin's Club	12	8	1	1	0	6	2,971
Sully's Choice	11	13	1	1	2	9	2,727
Sporting Spirit	2	7	1	0	0	6	2,448
Tempering	6	12	1	0	1	10	2,422
Ruth's Gamble	4	9	1	0	0	8	2,346
Runnel	3	4	1	0	1	2	2,148
Lets Go Sabo	4	5	1	0	0	4	2,050
Kalar	3	22	1	4	3	14	2,030

WINNING OWNERS

	Races Won	Value £		Races Won	Value £
Mrs J M Davenport	3	10,319	Michael Hill	1	2,422
P D Savill	2	5,317	E Stockdale	1	2,148
Mrs Jeanne Chapman	1	4,136	Bill Waddington	1	2,050
Walter Nelson	1	2,727	C C Pryor	1	2,030
Phillip Kneafsey	1	2,448			

Favourites	2-9	22.2%	- 2.25	Total winning prize-money		£33,595
Longest winning sequence			1	Average SP of winner		14.1/1
Longest losing sequence			62	Return on stakes invested		-31.5%
1991 Form	24-365	6.6%	-158.10	1989 Form	29-474	6.1%	-253.81
1990 Form	22-415	5.3%	-245.78	1988 Form	36-328	11.0%	- 11.00

P CHAPPLE-HYAM (Marlborough, Wilts)

	No. of Horses	Races Run	1st	2nd	3rd	Unpl	Per cent	£1 Level Stake
2-y-o	39	111	22	16	20	53	19.8	- 34.41
3-y-o	23	119	19	18	8	74	16.0	- 5.29
4-y-o+	4	15	0	1	1	13	-	- 15.00
Totals	66	245	41	35	29	140	16.7	- 54.70

BY MONTH

2-y-o	W-R	Per cent	£1 Level Stake	3-y-o	W-R	Per cent	£1 Level Stake
Mar/Apr	1-2	50.0	+ 1.25	Mar/Apr	4-21	19.0	+ 10.75
May	1-8	12.5	- 5.12	May	3-19	15.8	- 2.12
June	1-8	12.5	- 6.33	June	4-14	28.6	+ 11.70
July	1-9	11.1	- 7.60	July	1-9	11.1	+ 1.00
August	5-22	22.7	+ 0.68	August	5-21	23.8	+ 6.50
September	8-32	25.0	- 9.42	September	1-18	5.6	- 14.50
Oct/Nov	5-30	16.7	- 7.87	Oct/Nov	1-17	5.9	- 14.62

4-y-o+	W-R	Per cent	£1 Level Stake	Totals	W-R	Per cent	£1 Level Stake
Mar/Apr	0-1	-	- 1.00	Mar/Apr	5-24	20.8	+ 11.00
May	0-2	-	- 2.00	May	4-29	13.8	- 9.24
June	0-2	-	- 2.00	June	5-24	20.8	+ 3.37
July	0-2	-	- 2.00	July	2-20	10.0	- 8.60
August	0-2	-	- 2.00	August	10-45	22.2	+ 5.18
September	0-4	-	- 4.00	September	9-54	16.7	- 27.92
Oct/Nov	0-2	-	- 2.00	Oct/Nov	6-49	12.2	- 24.49

DISTANCE

2-y-o	W-R	Per cent	£1 Level Stake	3-y-o	W-R	Per cent	£1 Level Stake
5f-6f	10-46	21.7	- 6.57	5f-6f	0-6	-	- 6.00
7f-8f	12-65	18.5	- 27.84	7f-8f	6-33	18.2	+ 4.63
9f-13f	0-0	-	0.00	9f-13f	10-62	16.1	- 8.42
14f+	0-0	-	0.00	14f+	3-18	16.7	+ 4.50

4-y-o+	W-R	Per cent	£1 Level Stake	Totals	W-R	Per cent	£1 Level Stake
5f-6f	0-0	-	0.00	5f-6f	10-52	19.2	- 12.57
7f-8f	0-9	-	- 9.00	7f-8f	18-107	16.8	- 32.21
9f-13f	0-5	-	- 5.00	9f-13f	10-67	14.9	- 13.42
14f+	0-1	-	- 1.00	14f+	3-19	15.8	+ 3.50

TYPE OF RACE

Non-Handicaps	W-R	Per cent	£1 Level Stake	Handicaps	W-R	Per cent	£1 Level Stake
2-y-o	21-103	20.4	- 31.41	2-y-o	1-8	12.5	- 3.00
3-y-o	12-75	16.0	- 14.29	3-y-o	6-41	14.6	+ 8.50
4-y-o+	0-4	-	- 4.00	4-y-o+	0-8	-	- 8.00
Selling	0-0	-	0.00	Selling	0-0	-	0.00
Apprentice	1-1	100.0	+ 2.50	Apprentice	0-1	-	- 1.00
Amat/Ladies	0-1	-	- 1.00	Amat/Ladies	0-3	-	- 3.00
Totals	34-184	18.5	- 48.20	Totals	7-61	11.5	- 6.50

COURSE GRADE

	W-R	Per cent	£1 Level Stake
Group 1	26-135	19.3	- 9.18
Group 2	4-31	12.9	- 16.15
Group 3	3-41	7.3	- 31.75
Group 4	8-38	21.1	+ 2.38

FIRST TIME OUT

	W-R	Per cent	£1 Level Stake
2-y-o	2-38	5.3	- 33.45
3-y-o	3-23	13.0	+ 0.75
4-y-o+	0-3	-	- 3.00
Totals	5-64	7.8	- 35.70

JOCKEYS RIDING

	W-R	Per cent	£1 Level Stake		W-R	Per cent	£1 Level Stake
D Holland	8-25	32.0	+ 4.08	R Price	1-1	100.0	+ 4.00
Paul Eddery	7-57	12.3	- 21.57	J Quinn	1-1	100.0	+ 4.50
L Piggott	5-23	21.7	+ 1.26	A Munro	1-2	50.0	+ 1.25
F Norton	3-15	20.0	+ 6.20	G Duffield	1-2	50.0	0.00
J Reid	3-29	10.3	- 15.58	L Newton	1-3	33.3	+ 0.50
Pat Eddery	2-4	50.0	+ 3.75	D Harrison	1-3	33.3	- 0.12
S Whitworth	2-11	18.2	- 2.25	T Sprake	1-4	25.0	+ 6.00
S Cauthen	1-1	100.0	+ 1.88	L Dettori	1-6	16.7	+ 4.00
R Hills	1-1	100.0	+ 0.40	W Carson	1-8	12.5	- 4.00

Chapple-Hyam P

M Roberts	0-5	B Thomas	0-2	G Carter	0-1
J Weaver	0-4	C Asmussen	0-2	J Lowe	0-1
M Hills	0-4	M Tebbutt	0-2	J Williams	0-1
Mrs J Chapple-Hyam	0-4	W R Swinburn	0-2	Mr J Durkan	0-1
A Clark	0-3	B Crossley	0-1	P Robinson	0-1
K Fallon	0-3	D Carson	0-1	R Cochrane	0-1
M Birch	0-3	D McKeown	0-1	R Perham	0-1
W Ryan	0-3	G Andrew	0-1	W Newnes	0-1

COURSE RECORD

	Total	Non-Handicaps		Handicaps		Per	£1 Level
	W-R	2-y-o	3-y-o+	2-y-o	3-y-o+	cent	Stake
Ayr	7-18	5-11	1-2	0-0	1-5	38.9	+ 7.05
Newmarket	6-24	0-11	5-11	0-0	1-2	25.0	+ 3.01
Newbury	5-17	2-10	2-5	0-0	1-2	29.4	+ 13.05
York	4-15	2-6	1-5	0-0	1-4	26.7	+ 9.13
Folkestone	3-7	3-3	0-0	0-0	0-4	42.9	+ 4.50
Warwick	3-18	0-4	0-6	1-2	2-6	16.7	+ 2.50
Goodwood	2-13	2-7	0-2	0-0	0-4	15.4	− 6.42
Carlisle	1-2	1-1	0-1	0-0	0-0	50.0	+ 0.88
Epsom	1-3	0-0	1-2	0-0	0-1	33.3	+ 6.00
Salisbury	1-3	1-2	0-0	0-0	0-1	33.3	− 0.25
Ripon	1-4	1-2	0-1	0-0	0-1	25.0	+ 4.00
Catterick	1-5	1-1	0-2	0-1	0-1	20.0	+ 0.50
Chester	1-6	1-2	0-4	0-0	0-0	16.7	− 3.90
Haydock	1-6	0-2	1-2	0-0	0-2	16.7	− 2.00
Bath	1-9	1-4	0-2	0-0	0-3	11.1	− 6.50
Pontefract	1-9	1-5	0-2	0-2	0-0	11.1	− 5.75
Thirsk	1-9	0-2	1-3	0-0	0-4	11.1	− 7.00
Chepstow	1-10	0-3	1-5	0-0	0-2	10.0	− 6.50

Doncaster	0-19	Hamilton	0-3	Southwell (AW)	0-2
Ascot	0-14	Kempton	0-3	Wolverhampton	0-2
Redcar	0-7	Brighton	0-2	Sandown	0-1
Beverley	0-6	Lingfield (AW)	0-2		
Nottingham	0-4	Newcastle	0-2		

WINNING HORSES

		Races					Win
	Age	Run	1st	2nd	3rd	Unpl	£
Rodrigo De Triano	3	6	3	0	0	3	494,764
Dr Devious	3	3	1	1	0	1	355,000
Rain Brother	2	4	3	0	1	0	16,782
Feminine Wiles	3	6	1	2	0	3	10,965
King Olaf	3	4	2	0	0	2	10,325
Ecliptic	3	4	2	0	0	2	9,832
Fyfield Flyer	2	7	2	3	1	1	9,792
Wootton Rivers	2	5	2	0	1	2	7,579
Arctic Splendour	3	9	2	1	1	5	7,029
Encore Une Fois	3	7	2	0	1	4	6,855
Antester	2	4	2	0	1	1	5,575
Juniper Berry	3	10	2	3	0	5	5,419

Lyford Cay	2	3	1	2	0	0	5,010
Abury	2	4	1	0	1	2	4,013
River Defences	3	4	1	0	1	2	3,875
Chaddleworth	2	1	1	0	0	0	3,818
Lacerta	2	1	1	0	0	0	2,924
Crested Wave	2	2	1	0	0	1	2,868
Express Mariecurie	2	6	1	1	1	3	2,763
Legendary	3	5	1	0	1	3	2,762
Toledo Queen	2	3	1	0	1	1	2,752
Newton's Law	2	4	1	0	0	3	2,637
Eleusis	2	5	1	1	1	2	2,553
Lamu Lady	2	3	1	0	0	2	2,532
Nico Mike	2	3	1	1	1	0	2,469
Suez Canal	3	9	1	6	0	2	2,445
Guilty Secret	3	7	1	1	2	3	2,406
Burbage	2	2	1	0	0	1	2,070
Rocket To The Moon	2	8	1	1	3	3	1,688

WINNING OWNERS

	Races Won	Value £		Races Won	Value £
R E Sangster	31	602,354	Express Marie Curie Racing	1	2,763
Sidney H Craig	1	355,000	Mrs Jane Chapple-Hyam	1	1,688
Luciano Gaucci	7	27,694			

Favourites	14-45	31.1%	- 13.54	Total winning prize-money	£989,499
Longest winning sequence			2	Average SP of winner	3.6/1
Longest losing sequence			16	Return on stakes invested	-22.3%
1991 Form	27-112	24.1%	+ 20.35		

G F H CHARLES-JONES (Wantage, Oxon)

	No. of Horses	Races Run	1st	2nd	3rd	Unpl	Per cent	£1 Level Stake
2-y-o	0	0	0	0	0	0	-	0.00
3-y-o	4	6	1	0	0	5	16.7	+ 28.00
4-y-o+	1	2	0	0	0	2	-	- 2.00
Totals	5	8	1	0	0	7	12.5	+ 26.00

Jan	Feb	Mar	Apr	May	Jun	Jul	Aug	Sep	Oct/Nov
0-0	0-0	0-0	0-0	0-2	0-0	0-0	1-5	0-1	0-0

		£1 Level				£1 Level
Winning Jockey	W-R	Stake	Winning Course	W-R		Stake
P McCabe	1-2	+ 32.00	Brighton	1-1		+ 33.00

		Races					Win
Winning Horse	Age	Run	1st	2nd	3rd	Unpl	£
Shirl	3	3	1	0	0	2	2,553

Favourites	0-0	Total winning prize-money	£2,553

R CHARLTON (Beckhampton, Wilts)

	No. of Horses	Races Run	1st	2nd	3rd	Unpl	Per cent	£1 Level Stake
2-y-o	21	42	11	8	5	18	26.2	+ 10.43
3-y-o	21	92	24	18	15	35	26.1	+ 22.43
4-y-o+	5	33	8	5	4	16	24.2	+ 31.75
Totals	47	167	43	31	24	69	25.7	+ 64.61

BY MONTH

2-y-o	W-R	Per cent	£1 Level Stake	3-y-o	W-R	Per cent	£1 Level Stake
Mar/Apr	0-0	-	0.00	Mar/Apr	2-13	15.4	- 6.00
May	0-0	-	0.00	May	5-18	27.8	- 1.73
June	1-4	25.0	- 1.50	June	7-14	50.0	+ 17.22
July	1-2	50.0	- 0.60	July	3-15	20.0	- 4.06
August	1-7	14.3	+ 6.00	August	2-7	28.6	+ 6.00
September	8-16	50.0	+ 19.53	September	3-12	25.0	+ 5.00
Oct/Nov	0-13	-	- 13.00	Oct/Nov	2-13	15.4	+ 6.00

4-y-o+	W-R	Per cent	£1 Level Stake	Totals	W-R	Per cent	£1 Level Stake
Mar/Apr	1-3	33.3	+ 2.00	Mar/Apr	3-16	18.8	- 4.00
May	1-5	20.0	- 0.50	May	6-23	26.1	- 2.23
June	0-5	-	- 5.00	June	8-23	34.8	+ 10.72
July	3-9	33.3	+ 9.25	July	7-26	26.9	+ 4.59
August	0-3	-	- 3.00	August	3-17	17.6	+ 9.00
September	2-5	40.0	+ 15.00	September	13-33	39.4	+ 39.53
Oct/Nov	1-3	33.3	+ 14.00	Oct/Nov	3-29	10.3	+ 7.00

DISTANCE

2-y-o	W-R	Per cent	£1 Level Stake	3-y-o	W-R	Per cent	£1 Level Stake
5f-6f	5-17	29.4	+ 4.80	5f-6f	1-8	12.5	0.00
7f-8f	6-25	24.0	+ 5.63	7f-8f	8-32	25.0	- 1.08
9f-13f	0-0	-	0.00	9f-13f	11-41	26.8	+ 19.50
14f+	0-0	-	0.00	14f+	4-11	36.4	+ 4.01

4-y-o+	W-R	Per cent	£1 Level Stake	Totals	W-R	Per cent	£1 Level Stake
5f-6f	2-10	20.0	+ 16.00	5f-6f	8-35	22.9	+ 20.80
7f-8f	3-10	30.0	+ 15.50	7f-8f	17-67	25.4	+ 20.05
9f-13f	3-13	23.1	+ 0.25	9f-13f	14-54	25.9	+ 19.75
14f+	0-0	-	0.00	14f+	4-11	36.4	+ 4.01

TYPE OF RACE

Non-Handicaps	W-R	Per cent	£1 Level Stake	Handicaps	W-R	Per cent	£1 Level Stake
2-y-o	11-36	30.6	+ 16.43	2-y-o	0-5	-	- 5.00
3-y-o	13-50	26.0	+ 10.71	3-y-o	11-38	28.9	+ 15.72
4-y-o+	0-5	-	- 5.00	4-y-o+	8-28	28.6	+ 36.75
Selling	0-1	-	- 1.00	Selling	0-0	-	0.00
Apprentice	0-0	-	0.00	Apprentice	0-4	-	- 4.00
Amat/Ladies	0-0	-	0.00	Amat/Ladies	0-0	-	0.00
Totals	24-92	26.1	+ 21.14	Totals	19-75	25.3	+ 43.47

COURSE GRADE

	W-R	Per cent	£1 Level Stake
Group 1	24-105	22.9	+ 43.65
Group 2	4-23	17.4	- 4.70
Group 3	8-22	36.4	+ 10.97
Group 4	7-17	41.2	+ 14.69

FIRST TIME OUT

	W-R	Per cent	£1 Level Stake
2-y-o	6-21	28.6	+ 19.50
3-y-o	3-21	14.3	- 10.75
4-y-o+	1-5	20.0	0.00
Totals	10-47	21.3	+ 8.75

JOCKEYS RIDING

	W-R	Per cent	£1 Level Stake		W-R	Per cent	£1 Level Stake
Pat Eddery	21-54	38.9	+ 37.76	S Cauthen	1-2	50.0	+ 4.00
Paul Eddery	4-21	19.0	0.00	G Carter	1-2	50.0	+ 5.00
M Hills	3-9	33.3	- 0.40	D Holland	1-3	33.3	+ 1.00
T Quinn	3-10	30.0	+ 13.25	L Dettori	1-6	16.7	0.00
D Harrison	2-4	50.0	+ 9.50	T Sprake	1-6	16.7	+ 7.00
R Cochrane	2-8	25.0	+ 5.50	W Ryan	1-7	14.3	- 2.00
J Reid	1-1	100.0	+ 16.00	S Raymont	1-12	8.3	- 10.00

W R Swinburn	0-4	A McGlone	0-2	J Weaver	0-1
Dale Gibson	0-3	B Doyle	0-1	M Roberts	0-1
Rhona Gent	0-3	J Fanning	0-1	R Price	0-1
W Carson	0-3	J Lloyd	0-1	T Rogers	0-1

COURSE RECORD

	Total W-R	Non-Handicaps 2-y-o	3-y-o+	Handicaps 2-y-o	3-y-o+	Per cent	£1 Level Stake
Nottingham	4-7	1-3	2-3	0-0	1-1	57.1	+ 12.32
Haydock	4-12	1-1	1-5	0-0	2-6	33.3	+ 1.25
Bath	3-5	1-1	2-4	0-0	0-0	60.0	+ 2.65
Doncaster	3-6	1-2	0-1	0-1	2-2	50.0	+ 21.50
Goodwood	3-9	0-1	1-2	0-0	2-6	33.3	+ 6.00
Warwick	3-9	0-0	1-5	0-0	2-4	33.3	+ 0.18
Kempton	3-15	2-4	1-7	0-0	0-4	20.0	+ 2.40
Newbury	3-19	0-6	0-2	0-1	3-10	15.8	- 9.25
Ayr	2-2	1-1	0-0	0-0	1-1	100.0	+ 12.50

Charlton R

Folkestone	2-2	0-0	1-1	0-0	1-1	100.0	+ 12.29
Lingfield	2-4	0-0	1-2	0-0	1-2	50.0	+ 4.80
Wolverhampton	2-5	1-2	1-3	0-0	0-0	40.0	+ 3.22
Ascot	2-8	1-1	0-0	0-0	1-7	25.0	+ 8.25
Newmarket	2-19	1-7	0-3	0-1	1-8	10.5	+ 5.00
Newcastle	1-1	0-0	1-1	0-0	0-0	100.0	+ 5.00
Chester	1-4	0-0	0-2	0-0	1-2	25.0	+ 0.50
Windsor	1-4	0-0	0-1	0-1	1-2	25.0	+ 2.00
York	1-8	1-1	0-2	0-1	0-4	12.5	− 3.00
Salisbury	1-9	0-4	1-4	0-0	0-1	11.1	− 4.00

Sandown	0-6	Brighton	0-2	Lingfield (AW)	0-1
Leicester	0-4	Beverley	0-1		
Redcar	0-4	Chepstow	0-1		

WINNING HORSES

	Age	Races Run	1st	2nd	3rd	Unpl	Win £
Matador	5	5	3	0	1	1	30,911
White Shadow	2	5	2	2	0	1	21,992
Consigliere	4	6	1	2	1	2	21,525
Source Of Light	3	5	2	1	1	1	20,477
Eclipsing	4	7	2	1	2	2	19,392
Garden District	3	6	4	2	0	0	17,887
Storm Dove	3	6	2	2	1	1	17,110
Inchinor	2	3	2	1	0	0	15,628
Torrey Canyon	3	4	1	0	2	1	14,313
Green Lane (Ire)	3	9	4	0	1	4	12,345
Inchcailloch	3	5	2	0	1	2	10,217
Arboretum	3	6	2	1	0	3	7,362
Everglades	4	7	2	0	0	5	7,026
Kusamba	2	2	1	0	0	1	5,163
Athens Belle	2	1	1	0	0	0	4,760
Bagalino	2	3	1	0	1	1	3,915
Pluck	2	3	1	1	0	1	2,840
River Delta	2	1	1	0	0	0	2,616
Frontier Flight	2	1	1	0	0	0	2,553
Morocco	3	10	1	3	1	5	2,363
Cantanta	3	5	1	1	1	2	2,265
Jezebel Monroe	3	4	1	1	1	1	2,246
Gushing	3	2	1	0	0	1	2,070
Sea Dune	3	3	1	1	1	0	1,932
River Anchor	3	4	1	0	0	3	1,744
Pelargonia	3	4	1	2	1	0	1,518
In Case	2	4	1	1	0	2	1,478

WINNING OWNERS

	Races Won	Value £		Races Won	Value £
K Abdulla	18	132,964	Lord Derby	1	2,840
Sir Philip Oppenheimer	4	25,844	Dr Carlos E Stelling	1	2,553
Terry Ellis	1	21,525	Martin Myers	1	2,363
Jeremy Tree	2	19,392	Mrs Amanda Skiffington	1	2,070
Lord Weinstock	5	17,105	Jocelyn Hambro	1	1,932
S S Niarchos	2	7,408	R S Dawes	1	1,744
Mrs J De Rothschild	2	7,362	Christopher Heath	1	1,518
Miss Sophie Oppenheimer	2	7,026			

Favourites	20-46	43.5%	+ 10.86	Total winning prize-money			£253,646
Longest winning sequence			4	Average SP of winner			4.4/1
Longest losing sequence			10	Return on stakes invested			38.7%
1991 Form	26-180	14.4%	- 57.48	1990 Form	37-159	23.3%	+ 19.55

L J CODD (Nantwich, Cheshire)

	No. of Horses	Races Run	1st	2nd	3rd	Unpl	Per cent	£1 Level Stake
2-y-o	1	1	0	0	0	1	-	- 1.00
3-y-o	5	20	0	0	1	19	-	- 20.00
4-y-o+	8	35	1	0	3	31	2.9	- 29.50
Totals	14	56	1	0	4	51	1.8	- 50.50

Jan	Feb	Mar	Apr	May	Jun	Jul	Aug	Sep	Oct/Nov
0-0	0-1	0-3	0-4	0-11	0-12	0-2	0-11	1-6	0-6

Winning Jockey	W-R	£1 Level Stake	Winning Course	W-R	£1 Level Stake
G Duffield	1-1	+ 4.50	Haydock	1-7	- 1.50

Winning Horse	Age	Races Run	1st	2nd	3rd	Unpl	Win £
Petraco	4	17	1	0	3	13	3,436

Favourites	0-3			Total winning prize-money		£3,436

1991 Form	3-48	6.3%	- 31.00	1989 Form	3-26	11.5%	+ 2.00
1990 Form	0-20						

P F I COLE (Whatcombe, Oxon)

	No. of Horses	Races Run	1st	2nd	3rd	Unpl	Per cent	£1 Level Stake
2-y-o	59	173	39	25	26	83	22.5	+ 3.25
3-y-o	41	185	33	29	31	92	17.8	- 41.68
4-y-o+	19	92	13	12	6	61	14.1	- 24.68
Totals	119	450	85	66	63	236	18.9	- 63.11

BY MONTH

2-y-o	W-R	Per cent	£1 Level Stake	3-y-o	W-R	Per cent	£1 Level Stake
January	0-0	-	0.00	January	1-2	50.0	- 0.43
February	0-0	-	0.00	February	0-1	-	- 1.00
March	0-0	-	0.00	March	0-1	-	- 1.00
April	1-9	11.1	+ 1.00	April	3-36	8.3	- 25.87
May	3-10	30.0	+ 1.13	May	2-28	7.1	- 23.00
June	14-28	50.0	+ 25.92	June	10-38	26.3	- 1.88
July	6-29	20.7	- 14.64	July	9-27	33.3	+ 2.84
August	7-32	21.9	+ 0.49	August	7-19	36.8	+ 15.66
September	4-34	11.8	- 5.50	September	0-18	-	- 18.00
Oct/Nov	4-31	12.9	- 5.15	Oct/Nov	1-15	6.7	+ 11.00

4-y-o+	W-R	Per cent	£1 Level Stake	Totals	W-R	Per cent	£1 Level Stake
January	0-1	-	- 1.00	January	1-3	33.3	- 1.43
February	0-0	-	0.00	February	0-1	-	- 1.00
March	0-1	-	- 1.00	March	0-2	-	- 2.00
April	0-12	-	- 12.00	April	4-57	7.0	- 36.87
May	2-18	11.1	- 13.00	May	7-56	12.5	- 34.87
June	2-14	14.3	- 7.56	June	26-80	32.5	+ 16.48
July	3-15	20.0	+ 8.38	July	18-71	25.4	- 3.42
August	4-16	25.0	+ 1.00	August	18-67	26.9	+ 17.15
September	1-8	12.5	+ 5.00	September	5-60	8.3	- 18.50
Oct/Nov	1-7	14.3	- 4.50	Oct/Nov	6-53	11.3	+ 1.35

DISTANCE

2-y-o	W-R	Per cent	£1 Level Stake	3-y-o	W-R	Per cent	£1 Level Stake
5f-6f	23-85	27.1	+ 26.13	5f-6f	0-9	-	- 9.00
7f-8f	15-83	18.1	- 19.98	7f-8f	14-63	22.2	- 2.16
9f-13f	1-5	20.0	- 2.90	9f-13f	14-90	15.6	- 28.18
14f+	0-0	-	0.00	14f+	5-23	21.7	- 2.34

4-y-o+	W-R	Per cent	£1 Level Stake	Totals	W-R	Per cent	£1 Level Stake
5f-6f	0-2	-	- 2.00	5f-6f	23-96	24.0	+ 15.13
7f-8f	0-7	-	- 7.00	7f-8f	29-153	19.0	- 29.14
9f-13f	6-48	12.5	- 23.12	9f-13f	21-143	14.7	- 54.20
14f+	7-35	20.0	+ 7.44	14f+	12-58	20.7	+ 5.10

TYPE OF RACE

Non-Handicaps	W-R	Per cent	£1 Level Stake	Handicaps	W-R	Per cent	£1 Level Stake
2-y-o	36-146	24.7	+ 2.25	2-y-o	2-17	11.8	+ 4.00
3-y-o	19-108	17.6	- 27.90	3-y-o	8-60	13.3	- 22.17
4-y-o+	2-26	7.7	- 14.00	4-y-o+	7-48	14.6	- 11.37
Selling	5-20	25.0	+ 0.19	Selling	0-2	-	- 2.00
Apprentice	4-10	40.0	- 0.61	Apprentice	1-7	14.3	+ 1.50
Amat/Ladies	0-3	-	- 3.00	Amat/Ladies	1-3	33.3	+ 10.00
Totals	66-313	21.1	- 43.07	Totals	19-137	13.9	- 20.04

COURSE GRADE

	W-R	Per cent	£1 Level Stake
Group 1	31-193	16.1	- 11.11
Group 2	14-72	19.4	- 14.06
Group 3	22-109	20.2	- 17.74
Group 4	18-76	23.7	- 20.20

FIRST TIME OUT

	W-R	Per cent	£1 Level Stake
2-y-o	16-59	27.1	+ 26.34
3-y-o	3-41	7.3	- 29.37
4-y-o+	1-19	5.3	- 16.00
Totals	20-119	16.8	- 19.03

JOCKEYS RIDING

	W-R	Per cent	£1 Level Stake		W-R	Per cent	£1 Level Stake
A Munro	30-132	22.7	- 17.67	S Cauthen	1-1	100.0	+ 1.75
T Quinn	30-187	16.0	- 53.08	J Quinn	1-4	25.0	0.00
J D Smith	7-30	23.3	+ 7.39	Pat Eddery	1-4	25.0	+ 2.00
M Roberts	4-5	80.0	+ 3.99	D Biggs	1-5	20.0	+ 3.50
C Rutter	3-28	10.7	- 15.93	G Baxter	1-6	16.7	+ 1.00
T G McLaughlin	2-5	40.0	+ 16.00	Miss M Clark	1-6	16.7	+ 7.00
L Dettori	1-1	100.0	+ 2.50	A Clark	1-8	12.5	- 6.56
B Raymond	1-1	100.0	+ 12.00				

Paul Eddery	0-5	G Bardwell	0-1	P Turner	0-1
W Carson	0-4	G Hind	0-1	R Cochrane	0-1
F Norton	0-2	J Fanning	0-1	S Drowne	0-1
A Tucker	0-1	J Reid	0-1	S O'Gorman	0-1
B Crossley	0-1	Mr M Armytage	0-1	W Ryan	0-1
D Harrison	0-1	N Kennedy	0-1		
D McKeown	0-1	P McCormick	0-1		

COURSE RECORD

	Total W-R	Non-Handicaps 2-y-o	Non-Handicaps 3-y-o+	Handicaps 2-y-o	Handicaps 3-y-o+	Per cent	£1 Level Stake
Lingfield (AW)	9-25	1-6	4-12	0-0	4-7	36.0	- 5.36
Newmarket	8-34	3-12	3-10	1-5	1-7	23.5	+ 7.63
Nottingham	7-22	4-9	2-7	0-1	1-5	31.8	- 6.54
York	6-17	5-9	1-7	0-0	0-1	35.3	+ 6.28
Bath	6-31	1-9	2-9	0-0	3-13	19.4	- 10.11
Salisbury	5-17	4-8	1-6	0-0	0-3	29.4	+ 14.46

Cole P F I

Leicester	4-12	4-9	0-2	0-1	0-0	33.3	+ 15.00
Chepstow	4-19	3-9	0-7	0-0	1-3	21.1	+ 7.00
Warwick	4-19	0-5	3-8	0-2	1-4	21.1	- 3.38
Brighton	4-21	1-5	2-11	0-0	1-5	19.0	- 10.37
Sandown	4-25	2-6	1-7	0-3	1-9	16.0	+ 2.00
Goodwood	4-27	1-7	1-11	0-0	2-9	14.8	- 5.37
Newbury	3-29	2-10	1-8	0-2	0-9	10.3	+ 7.00
Catterick	2-5	0-2	2-3	0-0	0-0	40.0	- 1.46
Haydock	2-7	0-2	2-4	0-0	0-1	28.6	+ 3.00
Epsom	2-13	1-2	0-6	0-0	1-5	15.4	- 5.75
Folkestone	2-14	1-2	0-7	1-2	0-3	14.3	- 3.00
Lingfield	2-17	0-6	2-7	0-0	0-4	11.8	- 10.67
Southwell (AW)	1-2	1-2	0-0	0-0	0-0	50.0	+ 4.00
Beverley	1-3	0-1	1-2	0-0	0-0	33.3	- 1.09
Thirsk	1-3	1-1	0-1	0-0	0-1	33.3	- 1.89
Redcar	1-4	1-2	0-2	0-0	0-0	25.0	+ 2.50
Chester	1-10	1-4	0-3	0-1	0-2	10.0	- 8.09
Kempton	1-14	0-3	0-1	0-1	1-9	7.1	- 1.00
Ascot	1-21	0-9	1-7	0-0	0-5	4.8	- 18.90

Windsor	0-15	Doncaster	0-5	Pontefract	0-2
Wolverhampton	0-11	Yarmouth	0-5	Newcastle	0-1

WINNING HORSES

		Races					Win
	Age	Run	1st	2nd	3rd	Unpl	£
Splendent	2	4	3	0	1	0	70,380
Ruby Tiger	5	2	1	0	0	1	50,980
Up Anchor	3	5	3	0	0	2	26,733
Half A Tick	4	3	1	0	0	2	17,600
Perfect Halo	2	2	2	0	0	0	17,123
Woodchat	2	3	2	0	1	0	16,825
Bardolph	5	11	2	3	1	5	14,208
Profusion	3	6	2	1	1	2	12,574
Yenoora	3	8	4	1	2	1	10,069
Bright Generation	2	3	2	0	0	1	9,695
Grand Master	3	6	3	1	1	1	9,267
Speaker's House	3	2	2	0	0	0	8,985
Lindon Lime	2	2	2	0	0	0	8,711
Green's Bid	2	5	1	2	1	1	8,415
Ardisia	3	7	3	1	1	2	8,172
Tioman Island	2	5	2	2	0	1	7,917
Monarda	5	8	3	0	1	4	7,789
Power Of Polly	2	2	2	0	0	0	7,768
Red Leader	2	9	2	1	2	4	7,414
Lord Vivienne	3	7	2	0	1	4	7,106
Hero's Light	3	4	1	0	2	1	4,905
The Last Empress	4	3	2	0	0	1	4,857
Maribella	2	5	2	0	0	3	4,540
Lord President	2	4	1	1	1	1	4,386
Glenstal Priory	5	6	2	0	0	4	3,776
Firm Pledge	2	3	1	1	1	0	3,688
Prevene	2	5	1	1	1	2	3,655

Dilum	3	4	1	0	0	3	3,608
Empire Blue	9	9	1	1	0	7	3,553
First Century	3	6	1	1	1	3	3,184
Heathfield	2	2	1	1	0	0	3,184
Instant Affair	2	2	1	0	0	1	3,106
Revere	2	1	1	0	0	0	2,858
Comme D'Habitude	2	2	1	0	0	1	2,812
Known Approach	2	4	1	2	0	1	2,807
Brightside	2	2	1	0	0	1	2,783
Confronter	3	11	2	3	2	4	2,723
Soviet Express	2	2	1	0	0	1	2,679
Moorish	2	3	1	0	0	2	2,637
Fret	2	3	1	1	0	1	2,559
Star Manager	2	2	1	0	0	1	2,553
Cap Camarat	3	3	1	0	0	2	2,532
Alderney Prince	2	5	1	2	1	1	2,465
Zilfi	2	2	1	0	0	1	2,422
Desert Peace	3	6	1	2	3	0	2,385
Desert Zone	3	3	1	0	1	1	2,363
Salisong	3	10	1	1	0	8	2,320
Break My Heart	2	3	1	0	0	2	2,285
Alternation	3	10	1	4	0	5	2,128
Fusion (USA)	3	5	1	1	2	1	2,070
Frescade	2	3	1	0	1	1	2,070
Chief Of Staff	3	5	1	2	0	2	2,069
Secretary Of State	6	4	1	0	0	3	2,050
Just Speculation	2	1	1	0	0	0	1,730
Last Conquest	3	5	1	0	2	2	1,725
Rock Song	3	7	1	0	0	6	1,674
Five Islands	2	2	1	0	0	1	1,618

WINNING OWNERS

	Races Won	Value £		Races Won	Value £
Fahd Salman	42	235,562	George Johnson	2	4,540
Mrs Philip Blacker	1	50,980	Norman Hill Plant Hire Ltd	2	3,776
Reg Hester	8	22,032	Lord Donoughmore	1	3,184
C J Wates	1	17,600	Athos Christodoulou	1	3,106
Sir George Meyrick	3	17,392	Christopher Heath	1	2,807
Richard Green (Fine Paintings)	2	11,968	Faisal Salman	1	2,783
M Arbib	3	11,538	Brook Land	1	2,679
H H Sultan Ahmad Shah	2	7,917	Mrs Martyn Arbib	1	2,320
G J Beck	2	7,768	Ray Taylor	1	2,128
Generous Racing Club	2	7,414	W H Ponsonby	1	2,050
Yahya Nasib	3	5,108	Stephen Crown	1	1,674
Christopher Wright	2	4,542	Lord Portman	1	1,618

Favourites	41-101	40.6%	- 6.53	Total winning prize-money		£432,485
Longest winning sequence			4	Average SP of winner		3.6/1
Longest losing sequence			37	Return on stakes invested		-13.8%
1991 Form	73-392	18.6%	- 31.18	1989 Form	51-403	12.7%	-116.41
1990 Form	53-394	13.5%	- 60.48	1988 Form	43-406	10.6%	-172.49

H J COLLINGRIDGE (Newmarket)

	No. of Horses	Races Run	1st	2nd	3rd	Unpl	Per cent	£1 Level Stake
2-y-o	3	6	0	1	0	5	-	- 6.00
3-y-o	8	51	5	4	3	39	9.8	- 11.62
4-y-o+	13	70	5	2	9	54	7.1	- 16.50
Totals	24	127	10	7	12	98	7.9	- 34.12

BY MONTH

2-y-o	W-R	Per cent	£1 Level Stake	3-y-o	W-R	Per cent	£1 Level Stake
January	0-0	-	0.00	January	0-2	-	- 2.00
February	0-0	-	0.00	February	0-2	-	- 2.00
March	0-0	-	0.00	March	0-2	-	- 2.00
April	0-0	-	0.00	April	0-6	-	- 6.00
May	0-0	-	0.00	May	0-5	-	- 5.00
June	0-0	-	0.00	June	0-6	-	- 6.00
July	0-0	-	0.00	July	2-8	25.0	+ 7.88
August	0-0	-	0.00	August	1-6	16.7	+ 3.50
September	0-0	-	0.00	September	0-5	-	- 5.00
Oct/Nov	0-6	-	- 6.00	Oct/Nov	2-9	22.2	+ 5.00

4-y-o+	W-R	Per cent	£1 Level Stake	Totals	W-R	Per cent	£1 Level Stake
January	0-4	-	- 4.00	January	0-6	-	- 6.00
February	1-4	25.0	+ 0.50	February	1-6	16.7	- 1.50
March	0-2	-	- 2.00	March	0-4	-	- 4.00
April	0-5	-	- 5.00	April	0-11	-	- 11.00
May	1-6	16.7	0.00	May	1-11	9.1	- 5.00
June	0-11	-	- 11.00	June	0-17	-	- 17.00
July	2-9	22.2	+ 17.00	July	4-17	23.5	+ 24.88
August	0-4	-	- 4.00	August	1-10	10.0	- 0.50
September	1-10	10.0	+ 7.00	September	1-15	6.7	+ 2.00
Oct/Nov	0-15	-	- 15.00	Oct/Nov	2-30	6.7	- 16.00

DISTANCE

2-y-o	W-R	Per cent	£1 Level Stake	3-y-o	W-R	Per cent	£1 Level Stake
5f-6f	0-0	-	0.00	5f-6f	1-6	16.7	+ 5.00
7f-8f	0-6	-	- 6.00	7f-8f	4-30	13.3	- 1.62
9f-13f	0-0	-	0.00	9f-13f	0-14	-	- 14.00
14f+	0-0	-	0.00	14f+	0-1	-	- 1.00

4-y-o+	W-R	Per cent	£1 Level Stake	Totals	W-R	Per cent	£1 Level Stake
5f-6f	0-5	-	- 5.00	5f-6f	1-11	9.1	0.00
7f-8f	2-24	8.3	+ 6.00	7f-8f	6-60	10.0	- 1.62
9f-13f	3-34	8.8	- 10.50	9f-13f	3-48	6.3	- 24.50
14f+	0-7	-	- 7.00	14f+	0-8	-	- 8.00

TYPE OF RACE

Non-Handicaps	W-R	Per cent	£1 Level Stake	Handicaps	W-R	Per cent	£1 Level Stake
2-y-o	0-6	-	- 6.00	2-y-o	0-0	-	0.00
3-y-o	1-13	7.7	- 10.00	3-y-o	4-34	11.8	+ 2.38
4-y-o+	0-7	-	- 7.00	4-y-o+	4-47	8.5	- 10.50
Selling	0-2	-	- 2.00	Selling	0-4	-	- 4.00
Apprentice	0-0	-	0.00	Apprentice	0-8	-	- 8.00
Amat/Ladies	0-0	-	0.00	Amat/Ladies	1-6	16.7	+ 11.00
Totals	1-28	3.6	- 25.00	Totals	9-99	9.1	- 9.12

COURSE GRADE

	W-R	Per cent	£1 Level Stake
Group 1	2-40	5.0	- 21.00
Group 2	2-15	13.3	+ 13.00
Group 3	4-44	9.1	- 5.62
Group 4	2-28	7.1	- 20.50

FIRST TIME OUT

	W-R	Per cent	£1 Level Stake
2-y-o	0-3	-	- 3.00
3-y-o	0-7	-	- 7.00
4-y-o+	0-13	-	- 13.00
Totals	0-23	-	- 23.00

JOCKEYS RIDING

	W-R	Per cent	£1 Level Stake		W-R	Per cent	£1 Level Stake
J Quinn	5-68	7.4	- 22.00	Mr P Close	1-6	16.7	+ 11.00
V Smith	2-18	11.1	+ 4.50	C Hawksley	1-19	5.3	- 14.50
M Roberts	1-5	20.0	- 2.12				

N Howe	0-3	Dale Gibson	0-1	Paul Eddery	0-1
B Doyle	0-1	N Adams	0-1	T Wilson	0-1
C Rutter	0-1	N Kennedy	0-1	W Ryan	0-1

COURSE RECORD

	Total W-R	Non-Handicaps 2-y-o	Non-Handicaps 3-y-o+	Handicaps 2-y-o	Handicaps 3-y-o+	Per cent	£1 Level Stake
Yarmouth	2-11	0-1	0-0	0-0	2-10	18.2	+ 11.50
Edinburgh	1-1	0-0	1-1	0-0	0-0	100.0	+ 2.00
Redcar	1-1	0-0	0-0	0-0	1-1	100.0	+ 16.00
Beverley	1-3	0-0	0-1	0-0	1-2	33.3	- 0.12
Lingfield	1-6	0-0	0-1	0-0	1-5	16.7	+ 5.00
Newmarket	1-6	0-0	0-0	0-0	1-6	16.7	+ 7.00
Pontefract	1-7	0-0	0-1	0-0	1-6	14.3	+ 6.00
Doncaster	1-8	0-1	0-1	0-0	1-6	12.5	- 2.00
Southwell (AW)	1-12	0-0	0-5	0-0	1-7	8.3	- 7.50

Collingridge H J

Leicester	0-11	Ripon	0-3	Windsor	0-2
Goodwood	0-8	Wolverhampton	0-3	Chepstow	0-1
Nottingham	0-8	Ascot	0-2	Hamilton	0-1
Kempton	0-7	Brighton	0-2	Newcastle	0-1
Folkestone	0-5	Haydock	0-2	Thirsk	0-1
Lingfield (AW)	0-5	Salisbury	0-2	York	0-1
Sandown	0-5	Warwick	0-2		

WINNING HORSES

	Age	Races Run	1st	2nd	3rd	Unpl	Win £
Buzzards Bellbuoy	3	12	2	2	0	8	6,394
Kelly's Kite	4	11	2	0	0	9	5,411
Westfield Moves	4	7	2	0	1	4	4,905
Taylors Prince	5	12	1	2	3	6	3,028
Bright Paragon	3	5	1	1	0	3	3,028
Cappahoosh	3	11	1	0	2	8	2,976
Ballyranter	3	9	1	1	1	6	1,501

WINNING OWNERS

	Races Won	Value £		Races Won	Value £
H J Collingridge	4	11,118	Mrs P A L Butler	1	2,976
N H Gardner	2	6,394	A G Wakley	1	2,226
D C G Cooper	1	3,028	Graeme Short	1	1,501

Favourites	1-6	16.7%	- 3.12		Total winning prize-money			£27,242
Longest winning sequence			1		Average SP of winner			8.3/1
Longest losing sequence			26		Return on stakes invested			-26.9%
1991 Form	9-139	6.5%	- 6.50		1989 Form	12-175	6.9%	- 12.00
1990 Form	7-158	4.4%	-100.75		1988 Form	7-98	7.1%	+ 12.00

D J S COSGROVE (Newmarket)

	No. of Horses	Races Run	1st	2nd	3rd	Unpl	Per cent	£1 Level Stake
2-y-o	3	14	2	4	1	7	14.3	+ 1.00
3-y-o	3	12	0	1	2	9	-	- 12.00
4-y-o+	6	20	1	1	3	15	5.0	- 12.00
Totals	12	46	3	6	6	31	6.5	- 23.00

Jan	Feb	Mar	Apr	May	Jun	Jul	Aug	Sep	Oct/Nov
0-0	0-0	0-0	0-1	1-3	0-10	1-9	0-12	0-4	1-7

Winning Jockeys	W-R	£1 Level Stake		W-R	£1 Level Stake
D Harrison	2-12	+ 3.00	J Lowe	1-2	+ 6.00

Winning Courses	W-R	£1 Level Stake		W-R	£1 Level Stake
Leicester	1-1	+ 3.00	Pontefract	1-2	+ 9.00
Lingfield	1-2	+ 6.00			

Winning Horses	Age	Races Run	1st	2nd	3rd	Unpl	Win £
My Bonus	2	10	2	4	1	3	4,660
Tiger Shoot	5	8	1	0	2	5	3,240

Favourites	0-3		Total winning prize-money		£7,900

L G COTTRELL (Cullompton, Devon)

	No. of Horses	Races Run	1st	2nd	3rd	Unpl	Per cent	£1 Level Stake
2-y-o	3	11	0	0	0	11	-	- 11.00
3-y-o	5	29	3	4	3	19	10.3	- 13.25
4-y-o+	7	58	5	6	8	39	8.6	- 14.17
Totals	15	98	8	10	11	69	8.2	- 38.42

Jan	Feb	Mar	Apr	May	Jun	Jul	Aug	Sep	Oct/Nov
0-0	0-0	0-0	0-4	1-17	3-20	2-17	1-16	0-15	1-9

Winning Jockeys	W-R	£1 Level Stake		W-R	£1 Level Stake
A Munro	2-12	+ 2.33	Mr D Salter	1-2	+ 5.50
N Carlisle	2-21	- 0.25	D Harrison	1-5	- 0.50
D Holland	1-2	+ 6.00	T Rogers	1-24	- 19.50

Winning Courses	W-R	£1 Level Stake		W-R	£1 Level Stake
Folkestone	2-5	+ 6.25	Lingfield (AW)	1-5	- 0.50
Goodwood	2-6	+ 8.33	Brighton	1-7	- 2.50
Warwick	1-4	+ 13.00	Chepstow	1-13	- 5.00

Winning Horses	Age	Races Run	1st	2nd	3rd	Unpl	Win £
Cape Pigeon	7	12	2	2	1	7	8,727
Pride Of Britain	3	8	2	2	0	4	5,028
Jess Rebec	4	5	1	0	1	3	3,255
Old Comrades	5	14	1	2	4	7	2,950
Wakil	3	3	1	1	1	0	2,742
Premier Prince	6	7	1	1	0	5	1,725

Favourites	2-9	22.2%	- 0.92	Total winning prize-money		£24,427

1991 Form	10-83	12.0%	+ 4.00	1989 Form	12-219	5.5%	-114.50
1990 Form	4-125	3.2%	- 97.00	1988 Form	19-258	7.4%	- 66.62

C G COX (Wootton Bassett, Wilts)

	No. of Horses	Races Run	1st	2nd	3rd	Unpl	Per cent	£1 Level Stake
2-y-o	4	22	0	3	1	18	-	- 22.00
3-y-o	3	13	1	1	2	9	7.7	+ 0.60
4-y-o+	6	27	2	2	4	19	7.4	- 5.00
Totals	13	62	3	6	7	46	4.8	- 26.40

Jan	Feb	Mar	Apr	May	Jun	Jul	Aug	Sep	Oct/Nov
0-0	0-0	0-0	0-6	0-5	0-8	0-15	2-14	1-8	0-6

Winning Jockeys	W-R	£1 Level Stake			W-R	£1 Level Stake
D Wright	2-7	+ 23.60	M Roberts		1-1	+ 4.00

Winning Courses						
Chepstow	1-3	+ 14.00	Pontefract		1-8	- 3.00
Wolverhampton	1-3	+ 10.60				

Winning Horses		Age	Races Run	1st	2nd	3rd	Unpl	Win £
Spanish Love		6	7	1	0	2	4	3,567
Ushba		4	6	1	0	0	5	3,210
Call To The Bar		3	9	1	0	2	6	2,721

Favourites	0-1		Total winning prize-money		£9,498

T CRAIG (Dunbar, Lothian)

	No. of Horses	Races Run	1st	2nd	3rd	Unpl	Per cent	£1 Level Stake
2-y-o	1	3	0	0	0	3	-	- 3.00
3-y-o	2	2	0	0	0	2	-	- 2.00
4-y-o+	11	42	1	0	2	39	2.4	- 39.62
Totals	14	47	1	0	2	44	2.1	- 44.62

Jan	Feb	Mar	Apr	May	Jun	Jul	Aug	Sep	Oct/Nov
0-0	0-0	0-0	0-3	0-5	1-14	0-4	0-7	0-10	0-4

Winning Jockey	W-R	£1 Level Stake	Winning Course		W-R	£1 Level Stake
D Moffatt	1-10	- 7.62	Edinburgh		1-21	- 18.62

Winning Horse		Age	Races Run	1st	2nd	3rd	Unpl	Win £
Valley Of Time		4	6	1	0	1	4	2,169

Favourites	1-1	100.0%	+ 1.38	Total winning prize-money		£2,169

1991 Form	1-21	4.8%	- 4.00	1989 Form	4-62	6.5%	+ 23.50
1990 Form	1-66	1.5%	- 61.67	1988 Form	1-42	2.4%	- 31.00

L M CUMANI (Newmarket)

	No. of Horses	Races Run	1st	2nd	3rd	Unpl	Per cent	£1 Level Stake
2-y-o	33	82	17	15	14	36	20.7	- 3.39
3-y-o	40	163	34	22	26	81	20.9	- 26.54
4-y-o+	12	47	3	10	3	31	6.4	- 39.82
Totals	85	292	54	47	43	148	18.5	- 69.75

BY MONTH

2-y-o	W-R	Per cent	£1 Level Stake	3-y-o	W-R	Per cent	£1 Level Stake
Mar/Apr	0-0	-	0.00	Mar/Apr	3-18	16.7	+ 8.50
May	1-3	33.3	- 0.12	May	2-18	11.1	- 14.17
June	1-4	25.0	- 2.20	June	5-16	31.3	- 2.27
July	2-10	20.0	- 5.08	July	6-25	24.0	+ 8.42
August	4-12	33.3	+ 2.94	August	8-29	27.6	- 9.13
September	3-17	17.6	+ 2.38	September	3-29	10.3	- 16.59
Oct/Nov	6-36	16.7	- 1.31	Oct/Nov	7-28	25.0	- 1.30

4-y-o+	W-R	Per cent	£1 Level Stake	Totals	W-R	Per cent	£1 Level Stake
Mar/Apr	1-7	14.3	- 4.62	Mar/Apr	4-25	16.0	+ 3.88
May	0-8	-	- 8.00	May	3-29	10.3	- 22.29
June	0-5	-	- 5.00	June	6-25	24.0	- 9.47
July	1-8	12.5	- 6.95	July	9-43	20.9	- 3.61
August	1-7	14.3	- 3.25	August	13-48	27.1	- 9.44
September	0-9	-	- 9.00	September	6-55	10.9	- 23.21
Oct/Nov	0-3	-	- 3.00	Oct/Nov	13-67	19.4	- 5.61

DISTANCE

2-y-o	W-R	Per cent	£1 Level Stake	3-y-o	W-R	Per cent	£1 Level Stake
5f-6f	7-30	23.3	+ 2.43	5f-6f	0-6	-	- 6.00
7f-8f	10-52	19.2	- 5.82	7f-8f	7-43	16.3	- 23.71
9f-13f	0-0	-	0.00	9f-13f	26-108	24.1	+ 1.17
14f+	0-0	-	0.00	14f+	1-6	16.7	+ 2.00

4-y-o+	W-R	Per cent	£1 Level Stake	Totals	W-R	Per cent	£1 Level Stake
5f-6f	0-0	-	0.00	5f-6f	7-36	19.4	- 3.57
7f-8f	1-17	5.9	- 13.25	7f-8f	18-112	16.1	- 42.78
9f-13f	1-22	4.5	- 20.95	9f-13f	27-130	20.8	- 19.78
14f+	1-8	12.5	- 5.62	14f+	2-14	14.3	- 3.62

Cumani L M

TYPE OF RACE

Non-Handicaps	W-R	Per cent	£1 Level Stake	Handicaps	W-R	Per cent	£1 Level Stake
2-y-o	17-77	22.1	+ 1.61	2-y-o	0-5	-	- 5.00
3-y-o	27-111	24.3	- 16.44	3-y-o	5-44	11.4	- 6.00
4-y-o+	2-17	11.8	- 13.57	4-y-o+	1-29	3.4	- 25.25
Selling	1-1	100.0	+ 1.10	Selling	0-0	-	0.00
Apprentice	0-5	-	- 5.00	Apprentice	0-2	-	- 2.00
Amat/Ladies	1-1	100.0	+ 0.80	Amat/Ladies	0-0	-	0.00
Totals	48-212	22.6	- 31.50	Totals	6-80	7.5	- 38.25

COURSE GRADE

	W-R	Per cent	£1 Level Stake
Group 1	28-175	16.0	- 58.76
Group 2	11-40	27.5	+ 9.34
Group 3	11-59	18.6	- 14.33
Group 4	4-18	22.2	- 6.00

FIRST TIME OUT

	W-R	Per cent	£1 Level Stake
2-y-o	5-33	15.2	+ 8.17
3-y-o	6-40	15.0	- 21.42
4-y-o+	1-12	8.3	- 9.62
Totals	12-85	14.1	- 22.87

JOCKEYS RIDING

	W-R	Per cent	£1 Level Stake		W-R	Per cent	£1 Level Stake
L Dettori	42-212	19.8	- 47.39	J Quinn	1-1	100.0	+ 0.83
J Weaver	4-28	14.3	- 0.33	Mrs S Cumani	1-1	100.0	+ 0.80
J Fortune	3-32	9.4	- 21.92	A Munro	1-2	50.0	+ 9.00
R Cochrane	2-4	50.0	+ 1.26				

J Harris	0-4		M Roberts	0-2		D Holland	0-1
S Cauthen	0-3		B Raymond	0-1		P Robinson	0-1

COURSE RECORD

	Total W-R	Non-Handicaps 2-y-o	Non-Handicaps 3-y-o+	Handicaps 2-y-o	Handicaps 3-y-o+	Per cent	£1 Level Stake
Newmarket	12-69	4-28	6-25	0-1	2-15	17.4	- 9.29
Brighton	6-14	4-4	1-5	0-1	1-4	42.9	+ 8.01
Yarmouth	5-23	3-10	2-10	0-0	0-3	21.7	- 0.67
Newbury	4-12	1-2	1-2	0-1	2-7	33.3	- 3.33
York	3-16	0-2	2-7	0-0	1-7	18.8	- 4.82
Newcastle	2-3	1-1	1-1	0-0	0-1	66.7	+ 3.57
Folkestone	2-4	0-2	2-2	0-0	0-0	50.0	+ 5.10
Salisbury	2-5	0-1	2-4	0-0	0-0	40.0	+ 12.38
Windsor	2-10	0-0	2-7	0-1	0-2	20.0	- 4.87
Doncaster	2-11	0-1	2-5	0-0	0-5	18.2	- 7.26
Ascot	2-23	1-5	1-8	0-0	0-10	8.7	- 10.38
Ayr	1-2	1-1	0-1	0-0	0-0	50.0	+ 1.25
Lingfield	1-2	1-1	0-1	0-0	0-0	50.0	+ 0.88
Edinburgh	1-3	0-0	1-2	0-0	0-1	33.3	- 1.67

Pontefract	1-3	0-0	1-3	0-0	0-0	33.3	+ 3.00
Ripon	1-3	0-0	1-2	0-0	0-1	33.3	- 1.43
Warwick	1-3	0-0	1-2	0-0	0-1	33.3	- 1.43
Beverley	1-4	0-0	1-3	0-0	0-1	25.0	+ 0.33
Bath	1-5	0-0	1-3	0-0	0-2	20.0	- 2.62
Kempton	1-8	0-0	1-5	0-0	0-3	12.5	- 4.50
Leicester	1-9	1-2	0-6	0-0	0-1	11.1	- 4.50
Goodwood	1-10	0-2	1-5	0-0	0-3	10.0	- 3.00
Redcar	1-13	0-6	1-4	0-0	0-3	7.7	- 7.50

Sandown	0-11	Nottingham	0-3	Carlisle	0-2
Haydock	0-10	Thirsk	0-3	Chepstow	0-1
Catterick	0-3	Wolverhampton	0-3	Hamilton	0-1

WINNING HORSES

		Races					Win
	Age	Run	1st	2nd	3rd	Unpl	£
Bonny Scot	3	8	2	1	2	3	66,572
Cunning	3	5	4	0	0	1	47,910
Red Slippers	3	4	2	0	0	2	43,384
Duke Of Eurolink	3	8	3	3	0	2	33,030
Inner City	3	7	3	2	2	0	20,565
Barathea	2	2	2	0	0	0	12,668
Only Royale	3	4	3	1	0	0	9,543
Fermoy	3	3	2	0	1	0	9,213
Queen's View	2	2	1	1	0	0	9,081
Calling Collect	3	3	1	0	1	1	8,976
Criquette	2	2	1	1	0	0	8,805
Dress Sense	3	7	2	2	0	3	8,515
Chief Minister	3	4	2	0	0	2	7,883
Lost Soldier	2	4	2	0	1	1	6,566
Sheriffmuir	3	4	2	0	0	2	5,002
Adam Smith	4	3	1	2	0	0	4,575
Le Corsaire	4	5	1	0	1	3	4,338
Masad	3	3	1	0	0	2	4,056
Field Of Honour	4	9	1	0	0	8	3,883
Woodenville	2	4	1	1	1	1	3,818
Fortensky	2	4	1	1	1	1	3,366
Coneybury	2	3	1	0	1	1	2,784
Many A Quest	3	5	1	0	2	2	2,658
Declassified	2	5	1	2	1	1	2,616
Euridice	3	7	1	1	4	1	2,574
Kahellan	2	3	1	0	0	2	2,543
Freewheel	3	1	1	0	0	0	2,406
Retender	3	8	1	1	2	4	2,238
Fitzcarraldo	2	5	1	1	3	0	2,196
Esbooain	3	7	1	1	2	3	2,070
Fern	3	4	1	0	1	2	2,070
Jallaaf	2	6	1	1	2	2	2,070
Wild Princess	2	2	1	1	0	0	2,070
Shintillo	2	3	1	0	0	2	2,070
Lille Hammer	2	1	1	0	0	0	2,070
Alycida	3	7	1	1	0	5	1,932
Palm Chat	2	5	1	0	3	1	1,467

WINNING OWNERS

	Races Won	Value £		Races Won	Value £
Sheikh Mohammed	20	124,924	Sheikh Ahmed Al Maktoum	2	4,140
Lord Weinstock	2	66,572	Mrs G Zanocchio	1	4,056
Fittocks Stud Ltd	5	49,980	Lord Portsmouth	1	3,883
Eurolink Computer Services Ltd	3	33,030	R E Sangster	1	2,784
Gerald Leigh	2	12,171	Studcrown Ltd	1	2,574
G Sainaghi	3	9,543	Sultan Mohammed	1	2,543
Miss G Gatto-Roissard	1	8,976	W S Farish III	1	2,406
David Thompson	2	7,883	L Gatto-Roissard	1	2,238
Richard L Duchossois	2	6,476	Baron Edouard De Rothschild	1	2,070
Edward P Evans	2	4,686	F Franzi	1	2,070
Lord White Of Hull	1	4,575			

Favourites	34-88	38.6%	- 13.58	Total winning prize-money			£357,579
Longest winning sequence			3	Average SP of winner			3.1/1
Longest losing sequence			22	Return on stakes invested			-23.7%
1991 Form	72-334	21.6%	- 63.91	1989 Form	88-330	26.7%	- 23.72
1990 Form	108-405	26.7%	+ 16.83	1988 Form	73-277	26.4%	- 36.86

P D CUNDELL (Newbury, Berks)

	No. of Horses	Races Run	1st	2nd	3rd	Unpl	Per cent	£1 Level Stake
2-y-o	0	0	0	0	0	0	-	0.00
3-y-o	5	27	1	0	0	26	3.7	- 10.00
4-y-o+	2	10	0	0	2	8	-	- 10.00
Totals	7	37	1	0	2	34	2.7	- 20.00

Jan	Feb	Mar	Apr	May	Jun	Jul	Aug	Sep	Oct/Nov
0-0	0-0	0-1	1-7	0-6	0-2	0-8	0-9	0-3	0-1

Winning Jockey	W-R	£1 Level Stake	Winning Course	W-R	£1 Level Stake
D Gibbs	1-4	+ 13.00	Salisbury	1-4	+ 13.00

Winning Horse	Age	Races Run	1st	2nd	3rd	Unpl	Win £
Aragona	3	7	1	0	0	6	2,481

Favourites	0-0			Total winning prize-money			£2,481
1991 Form	1-16	6.3%	+ 18.00	1989 Form	1-48	2.1%	- 33.00
1990 Form	0-22			1988 Form	5-108	4.6%	- 65.43

K O CUNNINGHAM-BROWN (Stockbridge, Hants)

	No. of Horses	Races Run	1st	2nd	3rd	Unpl	Per cent	£1 Level Stake
2-y-o	5	11	0	0	0	11	-	- 11.00
3-y-o	8	39	4	3	2	30	10.3	+ 15.00
4-y-o+	13	75	14	3	6	52	18.7	+114.33
Totals	26	125	18	6	8	93	14.4	+118.33

BY MONTH

2-y-o	W-R	Per cent	£1 Level Stake	3-y-o	W-R	Per cent	£1 Level Stake
January	0-0	-	0.00	January	0-0	-	0.00
February	0-0	-	0.00	February	0-0	-	0.00
March	0-0	-	0.00	March	0-0	-	0.00
April	0-0	-	0.00	April	0-2	-	- 2.00
May	0-0	-	0.00	May	0-2	-	- 2.00
June	0-3	-	- 3.00	June	1-6	16.7	+ 15.00
July	0-2	-	- 2.00	July	1-7	14.3	+ 14.00
August	0-2	-	- 2.00	August	2-7	28.6	+ 5.00
September	0-2	-	- 2.00	September	0-12	-	- 12.00
Oct/Nov	0-2	-	- 2.00	Oct/Nov	0-3	-	- 3.00

4-y-o+	W-R	Per cent	£1 Level Stake	Totals	W-R	Per cent	£1 Level Stake
January	3-6	50.0	+ 44.50	January	3-6	50.0	+ 44.50
February	3-13	23.1	+ 1.25	February	3-13	23.1	+ 1.25
March	2-6	33.3	+ 14.25	March	2-6	33.3	+ 14.25
April	0-5	-	- 5.00	April	0-7	-	- 7.00
May	1-7	14.3	+ 14.00	May	1-9	11.1	+ 12.00
June	1-9	11.1	+ 42.00	June	2-18	11.1	+ 54.00
July	2-11	18.2	+ 4.33	July	3-20	15.0	+ 16.33
August	1-9	11.1	- 3.00	August	3-18	16.7	0.00
September	1-5	20.0	+ 6.00	September	1-19	5.3	- 8.00
Oct/Nov	0-4	-	- 4.00	Oct/Nov	0-9	-	- 9.00

DISTANCE

2-y-o	W-R	Per cent	£1 Level Stake	3-y-o	W-R	Per cent	£1 Level Stake
5f-6f	0-7	-	- 7.00	5f-6f	0-1	-	- 1.00
7f-8f	0-4	-	- 4.00	7f-8f	4-34	11.8	+ 20.00
9f-13f	0-0	-	0.00	9f-13f	0-4	-	- 4.00
14f+	0-0	-	0.00	14f+	0-0	-	0.00

4-y-o+	W-R	Per cent	£1 Level Stake	Totals	W-R	Per cent	£1 Level Stake
5f-6f	3-15	20.0	+ 51.33	5f-6f	3-23	13.0	+ 43.33
7f-8f	2-25	8.0	- 8.00	7f-8f	6-63	9.5	+ 8.00
9f-13f	9-34	26.5	+ 72.00	9f-13f	9-38	23.7	+ 68.00
14f+	0-1	-	- 1.00	14f+	0-1	-	- 1.00

TYPE OF RACE

Non-Handicaps	W-R	Per cent	£1 Level Stake	Handicaps	W-R	Per cent	£1 Level Stake
2-y-o	0-9	-	- 9.00	2-y-o	0-0	-	0.00
3-y-o	1-11	9.1	+ 10.00	3-y-o	2-17	11.8	+ 11.50
4-y-o+	0-5	-	- 5.00	4-y-o+	13-61	21.3	+111.33
Selling	0-2	-	- 2.00	Selling	0-4	-	- 4.00
Apprentice	1-4	25.0	+ 13.00	Apprentice	1-11	9.1	- 6.50
Amat/Ladies	0-0	-	0.00	Amat/Ladies	0-1	-	- 1.00
Totals	2-31	6.5	+ 7.00	Totals	16-94	17.0	+111.33

COURSE GRADE

	W-R	Per cent	£1 Level Stake
Group 1	0-18	-	- 18.00
Group 2	3-34	8.8	+ 2.33
Group 3	5-29	17.2	+ 79.50
Group 4	10-44	22.7	+ 54.50

FIRST TIME OUT

	W-R	Per cent	£1 Level Stake
2-y-o	0-4	-	- 4.00
3-y-o	0-4	-	- 4.00
4-y-o+	2-12	16.7	+ 39.00
Totals	2-20	10.0	+ 31.00

JOCKEYS RIDING

	W-R	Per cent	£1 Level Stake		W-R	Per cent	£1 Level Stake
D Biggs	4-18	22.2	+ 30.50	N Varley	1-2	50.0	+ 5.50
S Whitworth	3-15	20.0	+ 4.50	Pat Eddery	1-2	50.0	+ 9.00
N Carlisle	2-9	22.2	+ 48.00	S Davies	1-3	33.3	+ 14.00
D Holland	2-10	20.0	+ 15.33	M Bressington	1-3	33.3	+ 1.50
G Bardwell	2-12	16.7	+ 30.00	S Dawson	1-8	12.5	+ 3.00

F Norton	0-4	B Thomas	0-1	Miss M Juster	0-1
T Quinn	0-4	Debbie Biggs	0-1	N Adams	0-1
W Newnes	0-4	J Hunter	0-1	P Turner	0-1
A Munro	0-2	J Quinn	0-1	Paul Eddery	0-1
B Doyle	0-2	J Wilkinson	0-1	R Fox	0-1
J Reid	0-2	K L Tsui	0-1	R Perham	0-1
J Williams	0-2	L Dettori	0-1	R Price	0-1
S D Williams	0-2	L Piggott	0-1	T Rogers	0-1
A McGlone	0-1	M Hills	0-1	W Aldwinckle	0-1
B Russell	0-1	M Roberts	0-1		

COURSE RECORD

	Total W-R	Non-Handicaps 2-y-o	3-y-o+	Handicaps 2-y-o	3-y-o+	Per cent	£1 Level Stake
Lingfield (AW)	8-33	0-1	1-8	0-0	7-24	24.2	+ 52.00
Bath	2-10	0-0	0-1	0-0	2-9	20.0	+ 15.50
Chester	1-1	0-0	0-0	0-0	1-1	100.0	+ 20.00
Warwick	1-1	0-0	0-0	0-0	1-1	100.0	+ 6.50
Leicester	1-4	0-1	0-1	0-0	1-2	25.0	+ 7.00

Chepstow	1-5	0-0	0-0	0-0	1-5	20.0	+ 46.00
Folkestone	1-6	0-1	0-1	0-0	1-4	16.7	0.00
Lingfield	1-6	0-1	0-0	0-0	1-5	16.7	- 1.67
Windsor	1-7	0-2	1-2	0-0	0-3	14.3	+ 14.00
Brighton	1-10	0-1	0-0	0-0	1-9	10.0	+ 1.00

Salisbury	0-17	Sandown	0-2	Epsom	0-1
Kempton	0-7	Southwell (AW)	0-2	Newbury	0-1
Goodwood	0-5	Wolverhampton	0-2	Newmarket	0-1
Nottingham	0-2	Ascot	0-1	Pontefract	0-1

WINNING HORSES

	Age	Races Run	1st	2nd	3rd	Unpl	Win £
Modesto	4	17	6	1	3	7	19,597
Kirriemuir	4	12	3	0	1	8	7,627
Emaura	3	8	2	1	1	4	5,111
El Dominio	4	10	2	1	0	7	4,444
Jolto	3	5	1	1	0	3	2,931
Waverley Star	7	3	1	0	0	2	2,490
With Gusto	5	4	1	0	0	3	2,108
Lamore Ritorna	3	12	1	1	1	9	1,582
Maria Cappucini	4	7	1	0	0	6	1,456

WINNING OWNERS

	Races Won	Value £		Races Won	Value £
D Bass	10	27,747	Mrs G M Gooderham	1	2,931
R N Short	3	7,627	S Pederson	1	2,490
M D Brunton	3	6,553			

Favourites	3-8	37.5%	+ 8.75	Total winning prize-money	£47,347

Longest winning sequence		2	Average SP of winner	12.5/1
Longest losing sequence		15	Return on stakes invested	94.7%

1991 Form	2-68	2.9%	- 30.00	1989 Form	7-107	6.5%	- 74.50
1990 Form	4-98	4.1%	- 43.00	1988 Form	0-20		

R CURTIS (Epsom, Surrey)

	No. of Horses	Races Run	1st	2nd	3rd	Unpl	Per cent	£1 Level Stake
2-y-o	3	8	0	0	0	8	-	- 8.00
3-y-o	2	5	1	0	1	3	20.0	+ 4.00
4-y-o+	16	46	2	2	3	39	4.3	- 34.50
Totals	21	59	3	2	4	50	5.1	- 38.50

Curtis R

Jan	Feb	Mar	Apr	May	Jun	Jul	Aug	Sep	Oct/Nov
0-0	0-0	0-0	0-5	0-4	2-17	1-10	0-4	0-7	0-12

Winning Jockeys		W-R	£1 Level Stake					W-R	£1 Level Stake
N Day		2-7	+ 4.50		B Doyle			1-1	+ 8.00

Winning Courses		W-R	£1 Level Stake					W-R	£1 Level Stake
Bath		1-1	+ 8.00		Pontefract			1-3	- 0.50
Leicester		1-3	+ 6.00						

Winning Horses	Age	Races Run	1st	2nd	3rd	Unpl	Win £
I'm Electric	6	8	2	2	2	2	5,232
Tajigrey	3	4	1	0	1	2	1,996

Favourites	1-1	100.0%	+ 1.50	Total winning prize-money			£7,228

1991 Form	3-57	5.3%	- 2.50	1989 Form	3-73	4.1%	+ 49.00
1990 Form	4-66	6.1%	- 30.37	1988 Form	3-80	3.8%	- 55.50

C A CYZER (Horsham, West Sussex)

	No. of Horses	Races Run	1st	2nd	3rd	Unpl	Per cent	£1 Level Stake
2-y-o	10	37	1	5	6	25	2.7	- 22.00
3-y-o	9	64	11	3	5	45	17.2	+ 65.50
4-y-o+	10	98	15	15	9	59	15.3	+ 39.25
Totals	29	199	27	23	20	129	13.6	+ 82.75

BY MONTH

2-y-o	W-R	Per cent	£1 Level Stake	3-y-o	W-R	Per cent	£1 Level Stake
January	0-0	-	0.00	January	0-0	-	0.00
February	0-0	-	0.00	February	0-0	-	0.00
March	0-0	-	0.00	March	0-2	-	- 2.00
April	0-1	-	- 1.00	April	0-6	-	- 6.00
May	0-1	-	- 1.00	May	1-8	12.5	+ 1.00
June	0-3	-	- 3.00	June	1-16	6.3	+ 5.00
July	0-6	-	- 6.00	July	3-15	20.0	+ 8.00
August	0-7	-	- 7.00	August	3-9	33.3	+ 41.50
September	1-9	11.1	+ 6.00	September	1-5	20.0	+ 3.00
Oct/Nov	0-10	-	- 10.00	Oct/Nov	2-3	66.7	+ 15.00

4-y-o+	W-R	Per cent	£1 Level Stake	Totals	W-R	Per cent	£1 Level Stake
January	0-0	-	0.00	January	0-0	-	0.00
February	0-1	-	- 1.00	February	0-1	-	- 1.00
March	2-11	18.2	- 3.00	March	2-13	15.4	- 5.00
April	2-10	20.0	+ 33.00	April	2-17	11.8	+ 26.00
May	3-11	27.3	+ 15.50	May	4-20	20.0	+ 15.50
June	0-14	-	- 14.00	June	1-33	3.0	- 12.00
July	3-19	15.8	+ 4.00	July	6-40	15.0	+ 6.00
August	2-18	11.1	- 2.00	August	5-34	14.7	+ 32.50
September	2-10	20.0	+ 7.00	September	4-24	16.7	+ 16.00
Oct/Nov	1-4	25.0	- 0.25	Oct/Nov	3-17	17.6	+ 4.75

DISTANCE

2-y-o	W-R	Per cent	£1 Level Stake	3-y-o	W-R	Per cent	£1 Level Stake
5f-6f	0-19	-	- 19.00	5f-6f	3-12	25.0	+ 24.00
7f-8f	1-18	5.6	- 3.00	7f-8f	0-14	-	- 14.00
9f-13f	0-0	-	0.00	9f-13f	8-31	25.8	+ 62.50
14f+	0-0	-	0.00	14f+	0-7	-	- 7.00

4-y-o+	W-R	Per cent	£1 Level Stake	Totals	W-R	Per cent	£1 Level Stake
5f-6f	1-5	20.0	+ 5.00	5f-6f	4-36	11.1	+ 10.00
7f-8f	0-10	-	- 10.00	7f-8f	1-42	2.4	- 27.00
9f-13f	10-68	14.7	+ 23.50	9f-13f	18-99	18.2	+ 86.00
14f+	4-15	26.7	+ 20.75	14f+	4-22	18.2	+ 13.75

TYPE OF RACE

Non-Handicaps	W-R	Per cent	£1 Level Stake	Handicaps	W-R	Per cent	£1 Level Stake
2-y-o	0-32	-	- 32.00	2-y-o	1-5	20.0	+ 10.00
3-y-o	2-22	9.1	+ 13.00	3-y-o	7-30	23.3	+ 36.00
4-y-o+	1-20	5.0	- 9.00	4-y-o+	12-66	18.2	+ 26.75
Selling	1-6	16.7	+ 20.00	Selling	3-10	30.0	+ 26.00
Apprentice	0-4	-	- 4.00	Apprentice	0-2	-	- 2.00
Amat/Ladies	0-0	-	0.00	Amat/Ladies	0-2	-	- 2.00
Totals	4-84	4.8	- 12.00	Totals	23-115	20.0	+ 94.75

COURSE GRADE

	W-R	Per cent	£1 Level Stake
Group 1	11-67	16.4	+ 54.25
Group 2	3-32	9.4	- 8.00
Group 3	1-26	3.8	- 5.00
Group 4	12-74	16.2	+ 41.50

FIRST TIME OUT

	W-R	Per cent	£1 Level Stake
2-y-o	0-10	-	- 10.00
3-y-o	0-9	-	- 9.00
4-y-o+	0-10	-	- 10.00
Totals	0-29	-	- 29.00

JOCKEYS RIDING

	W-R	Per cent	£1 Level Stake		W-R	Per cent	£1 Level Stake
D Biggs	8-52	15.4	+ 35.50	T Williams	1-1	100.0	+ 8.00
G Carter	6-32	18.8	+ 60.00	G Duffield	1-4	25.0	+ 1.00
M Roberts	4-13	30.8	+ 13.25	K Fallon	1-6	16.7	+ 4.00
T Quinn	4-14	28.6	+ 14.00	T G McLaughlin	1-22	4.5	− 7.00
R Cochrane	1-1	100.0	+ 8.00				

A Morris	0-14	W Carson	0-2	L Dettori	0-1
D McKeown	0-5	W Newnes	0-2	N Adams	0-1
J Quinn	0-5	A Tucker	0-1	N Carlisle	0-1
A Munro	0-3	D Harrison	0-1	P Robinson	0-1
W Ryan	0-3	G Bardwell	0-1	Pat Eddery	0-1
F Norton	0-2	J Reid	0-1	R Perham	0-1
J Fortune	0-2	J Williams	0-1	Samantha Benney	0-1
Miss M Cornelius	0-2	L Charnock	0-1	W R Swinburn	0-1

COURSE RECORD

	Total W-R	Non-Handicaps 2-y-o	3-y-o+	Handicaps 2-y-o	3-y-o+	Per cent	£1 Level Stake
Lingfield (AW)	5-33	0-3	0-12	0-0	5-18	15.2	− 6.50
Folkestone	4-14	0-1	0-2	0-0	4-11	28.6	+ 24.00
Newmarket	4-17	0-7	2-3	0-2	2-5	23.5	+ 37.00
Ascot	2-5	0-1	0-0	0-0	2-4	40.0	+ 4.75
Goodwood	2-10	0-2	0-2	0-0	2-6	20.0	+ 14.00
Sandown	2-12	0-1	0-4	0-0	2-7	16.7	+ 4.50
York	1-5	0-0	0-1	0-0	1-4	20.0	+ 12.00
Salisbury	1-6	0-1	1-3	0-0	0-2	16.7	+ 5.00
Windsor	1-7	0-1	0-2	0-0	1-4	14.3	+ 14.00
Wolverhampton	1-7	0-0	0-5	1-1	0-1	14.3	+ 8.00
Warwick	1-8	0-2	1-2	0-1	0-3	12.5	+ 18.00
Lingfield	1-10	0-1	0-2	0-1	1-6	10.0	− 3.00
Southwell (AW)	1-12	0-0	0-2	0-0	1-10	8.3	− 2.00
Brighton	1-13	0-0	0-3	0-0	1-10	7.7	− 7.00

Kempton	0-9	Leicester	0-4	Haydock	0-1
Nottingham	0-8	Ripon	0-3	Newcastle	0-1
Newbury	0-7	Bath	0-1		
Yarmouth	0-5	Beverley	0-1		

WINNING HORSES

	Age	Races Run	1st	2nd	3rd	Unpl	Win £
Bold Resolution	4	14	5	2	0	7	29,695
Master Planner	3	14	3	1	1	9	25,456
Day Of History	3	13	3	0	1	9	9,592
Temple Knight	3	8	2	1	0	5	8,750
Ideal Candidate	3	9	3	1	2	3	6,849
Dazzle The Crowd	4	9	3	1	1	4	6,334
Smiling Chief	4	12	2	3	2	5	6,017

Molly Splash	5	16	2	3	2	9	4,276
Art Form	5	3	1	0	0	2	4,045
Rising Tempo	4	17	1	5	2	9	3,716
Formal Affair	2	7	1	1	4	1	2,910
One Magic Moment	4	11	1	0	0	10	1,245

WINNING OWNERS

	Races Won	Value £		Races Won	Value £
R M Cyzer	25	100,134	S Wingfield Digby	2	8,750

Favourites	5-17	29.4%	+ 6.25	Total winning prize-money	£108,884
Longest winning sequence			2	Average SP of winner	9.4/1
Longest losing sequence			31	Return on stakes invested	41.6%
1991 Form	20-217	9.2%	- 79.48	1989 Form	14-148	9.5%	- 1.75
1990 Form	9-165	5.5%	- 70.50				

A R DAVISON (Caterham, Surrey)

	No. of Horses	Races Run	1st	2nd	3rd	Unpl	Per cent	£1 Level Stake
2-y-o	1	1	0	0	0	1	-	- 1.00
3-y-o	1	3	0	1	0	2	-	- 3.00
4-y-o+	7	20	1	1	2	16	5.0	- 11.50
Totals	9	24	1	2	2	19	4.2	- 15.50

Jan	Feb	Mar	Apr	May	Jun	Jul	Aug	Sep	Oct/Nov
0-0	0-0	0-0	0-6	0-1	0-5	0-6	1-3	0-3	0-0

Winning Jockey	W-R	£1 Level Stake	Winning Course	W-R	£1 Level Stake
J Lloyd	1-1	+ 7.50	Salisbury	1-6	+ 2.50

Winning Horse	Age	Races Run	1st	2nd	3rd	Unpl	Win £
Face North	4	6	1	1	0	4	2,950

Favourites	0-1	Total winning prize-money	£2,950

1991 Form	0-40	1989 Form	0-8	
1990 Form	0-26	1988 Form	2-24	8.3%	- 6.50

MRS J C DAWE (Bridgwater, Somerset)

	No. of Horses	Races Run	1st	2nd	3rd	Unpl	Per cent	£1 Level Stake
2-y-o	1	4	0	0	0	4	-	- 4.00
3-y-o	1	1	0	0	0	1	-	- 1.00
4-y-o+	5	42	2	1	7	32	4.8	- 21.00
Totals	7	47	2	1	7	37	4.3	- 26.00

Jan	Feb	Mar	Apr	May	Jun	Jul	Aug	Sep	Oct/Nov
0-0	0-4	0-6	0-4	1-6	0-6	0-6	0-3	0-9	1-3

Winning Jockeys	W-R	£1 Level Stake				W-R	£1 Level Stake
T Sprake	1-2	+ 9.00		A Tucker		1-8	+ 2.00

Winning Courses	W-R	£1 Level Stake				W-R	£1 Level Stake
Warwick	1-2	+ 9.00		Lingfield (AW)		1-8	+ 2.00

Winning Horses	Age	Races Run	1st	2nd	3rd	Unpl	Win £
John O'Dreams	7	11	1	0	2	8	2,910
Sareen Express	4	22	1	1	5	15	2,584

Favourites	0-0		Total winning prize-money	£5,494

R DICKIN (Newent, Glos)

	No. of Horses	Races Run	1st	2nd	3rd	Unpl	Per cent	£1 Level Stake
2-y-o	2	5	1	0	0	4	20.0	+ 46.00
3-y-o	4	21	0	4	1	16	-	- 21.00
4-y-o+	3	16	2	0	3	11	12.5	- 1.50
Totals	9	42	3	4	4	31	7.1	+ 23.50

Jan	Feb	Mar	Apr	May	Jun	Jul	Aug	Sep	Oct/Nov
0-0	0-0	0-0	0-1	0-3	0-8	0-9	2-8	0-4	1-9

Winning Jockeys	W-R	£1 Level Stake			W-R	£1 Level Stake
D Meredith	2-5	+ 9.50		S Dawson	1-9	+ 42.00

Winning Courses	W-R	£1 Level Stake			W-R	£1 Level Stake
Goodwood	1-2	+ 4.50		Pontefract	1-7	+ 1.00
Leicester	1-2	+ 49.00				

Winning Horses	Age	Races Run	1st	2nd	3rd	Unpl	Win £
Ballasecret	4	9	2	0	2	5	6,660
Kadastrof	2	3	1	0	0	2	2,070

Favourites	0-3			Total winning prize-money			£8,730

1991 Form	5-46	10.9%	- 2.75	1989 Form	0-33
1990 Form	1-28	3.6%	- 2.00	1988 Form	0-16

M DIXON (Epsom, Surrey)

	No. of Horses	Races Run	1st	2nd	3rd	Unpl	Per cent	£1 Level Stake
2-y-o	3	11	0	0	0	11	-	- 11.00
3-y-o	5	15	0	0	0	15	-	- 15.00
4-y-o+	7	44	4	4	4	32	9.1	+ 5.50
Totals	15	70	4	4	4	58	5.7	- 20.50

Jan	Feb	Mar	Apr	May	Jun	Jul	Aug	Sep	Oct/Nov
0-4	0-5	0-2	1-2	1-6	0-8	1-13	1-13	0-8	0-9

Winning Jockeys	W-R	£1 Level Stake			W-R	£1 Level Stake
Dale Gibson	2-24	- 7.50	A Tucker		1-9	+ 12.00
M Perrett	1-4	+ 8.00				

Winning Courses	W-R	£1 Level Stake		W-R	£1 Level Stake
Wolverhampton	1-1	+ 12.00	Folkestone	1-7	+ 5.00
Brighton	1-6	+ 15.00	Lingfield (AW)	1-17	- 13.50

Winning Horses	Age	Races Run	1st	2nd	3rd	Unpl	Win £
Prosequendo	5	11	3	2	1	5	7,499
Dr Zeva	6	8	1	1	1	5	2,344

Favourites	1-5	20.0%	- 1.50	Total winning prize-money			£9,843

1991 Form	0-1

M DODS (Darlington, Co Durham)

	No. of Horses	Races Run	1st	2nd	3rd	Unpl	Per cent	£1 Level Stake
2-y-o	1	4	0	0	0	4	-	- 4.00
3-y-o	3	16	1	0	2	13	6.3	- 10.05
4-y-o+	10	46	6	1	4	35	13.0	+ 19.60
Totals	14	66	7	1	6	52	10.6	+ 5.55

Dods M

Jan	Feb	Mar	Apr	May	Jun	Jul	Aug	Sep	Oct/Nov
0-1	0-0	0-0	1-7	2-9	1-9	1-12	1-13	1-9	0-6

Winning Jockeys		W-R	£1 Level Stake					W-R	£1 Level Stake
K Fallon		4-18	+ 19.60		P Burke			1-3	+ 10.00
J Lowe		2-18	+ 2.95						

Winning Courses									
Pontefract		2-5	+ 17.50		Catterick			1-7	+ 8.00
Edinburgh		2-10	+ 5.10		Redcar			1-9	+ 4.00
Doncaster		1-2	+ 3.95						

Winning Horses		Age	Races Run	1st	2nd	3rd	Unpl		Win £
Blue Grit		6	18	4	1	2	11		11,810
Young George		5	12	2	0	1	9		6,369
Ned's Bonanza		3	10	1	0	2	7		2,364

Favourites	1-4	25.0%	- 1.90	Total winning prize-money					£20,543

1991 Form	3-40	7.5%	- 26.50	1990 Form	0-5

J DOOLER (Goole, South Humberside)

	No. of Horses	Races Run	1st	2nd	3rd	Unpl	Per cent	£1 Level Stake
2-y-o	0	0	0	0	0	0	-	0.00
3-y-o	2	5	0	0	0	5	-	- 5.00
4-y-o+	7	17	1	0	1	15	5.9	- 10.50
Totals	9	22	1	0	1	20	4.5	- 15.50

Jan	Feb	Mar	Apr	May	Jun	Jul	Aug	Sep	Oct/Nov
0-0	0-1	0-1	0-0	0-1	0-3	1-6	0-5	0-3	0-2

Winning Jockey	W-R	£1 Level Stake	Winning Course		W-R	£1 Level Stake
G Bardwell	1-1	+ 5.50	Beverley		1-4	+ 2.50

Winning Horse	Age	Races Run	1st	2nd	3rd	Unpl	Win £
Escape Talk	5	8	1	0	1	6	2,805

Favourites	0-0	Total winning prize-money		£2,805

1991 Form	0-16	1989 Form	0-6
1990 Form	0-35		

S DOW (Epsom, Surrey)

	No. of Horses	Races Run	1st	2nd	3rd	Unpl	Per cent	£1 Level Stake
2-y-o	14	63	2	4	3	54	3.2	- 50.50
3-y-o	6	40	2	1	5	32	5.0	- 33.75
4-y-o+	16	81	10	11	3	57	12.3	+ 9.88
Totals	36	184	14	16	11	143	7.6	- 74.37

BY MONTH

2-y-o	W-R	Per cent	£1 Level Stake	3-y-o	W-R	Per cent	£1 Level Stake
January	0-0	-	0.00	January	0-2	-	- 2.00
February	0-0	-	0.00	February	1-5	20.0	- 2.75
March	0-0	-	0.00	March	0-6	-	- 6.00
April	0-1	-	- 1.00	April	0-2	-	- 2.00
May	0-3	-	- 3.00	May	1-6	16.7	- 2.00
June	1-17	5.9	- 11.50	June	0-10	-	- 10.00
July	0-10	-	- 10.00	July	0-6	-	- 6.00
August	0-9	-	- 9.00	August	0-1	-	- 1.00
September	0-11	-	- 11.00	September	0-2	-	- 2.00
Oct/Nov	1-12	8.3	- 5.00	Oct/Nov	0-0	-	0.00

4-y-o+	W-R	Per cent	£1 Level Stake	Totals	W-R	Per cent	£1 Level Stake
January	0-10	-	- 10.00	January	0-12	-	- 12.00
February	1-8	12.5	+ 0.50	February	2-13	15.4	- 2.25
March	2-10	20.0	+ 26.50	March	2-16	12.5	+ 20.50
April	0-5	-	- 5.00	April	0-8	-	- 8.00
May	1-6	16.7	+ 0.50	May	2-15	13.3	- 4.50
June	3-11	27.3	+ 7.38	June	4-38	10.5	- 14.12
July	1-12	8.3	- 3.00	July	1-28	3.6	- 19.00
August	1-10	10.0	- 3.00	August	1-20	5.0	- 13.00
September	0-7	-	- 7.00	September	0-20	-	- 20.00
Oct/Nov	1-2	50.0	+ 3.00	Oct/Nov	2-14	14.3	- 2.00

DISTANCE

2-y-o	W-R	Per cent	£1 Level Stake	3-y-o	W-R	Per cent	£1 Level Stake
5f-6f	2-42	4.8	- 29.50	5f-6f	0-9	-	- 9.00
7f-8f	0-19	-	- 19.00	7f-8f	2-25	8.0	- 18.75
9f-13f	0-2	-	- 2.00	9f-13f	0-6	-	- 6.00
14f+	0-0	-	0.00	14f+	0-0	-	0.00

4-y-o+	W-R	Per cent	£1 Level Stake	Totals	W-R	Per cent	£1 Level Stake
5f-6f	4-22	18.2	+ 29.50	5f-6f	6-73	8.2	- 9.00
7f-8f	3-33	9.1	- 12.50	7f-8f	5-77	6.5	- 50.25
9f-13f	3-19	15.8	- 0.12	9f-13f	3-27	11.1	- 8.12
14f+	0-7	-	- 7.00	14f+	0-7	-	- 7.00

TYPE OF RACE

Non-Handicaps	W-R	Per cent	£1 Level Stake	Handicaps	W-R	Per cent	£1 Level Stake
2-y-o	2-48	4.2	- 35.50	2-y-o	0-7	-	- 7.00
3-y-o	1-19	5.3	- 16.75	3-y-o	0-10	-	- 10.00
4-y-o+	2-9	22.2	- 2.00	4-y-o+	8-62	12.9	+ 21.88
Selling	1-11	9.1	- 7.00	Selling	0-3	-	- 3.00
Apprentice	0-1	-	- 1.00	Apprentice	0-8	-	- 8.00
Amat/Ladies	0-1	-	- 1.00	Amat/Ladies	0-5	-	- 5.00
Totals	6-89	6.7	- 63.25	Totals	8-95	8.4	- 11.12

COURSE GRADE

	W-R	Per cent	£1 Level Stake
Group 1	2-50	4.0	- 38.50
Group 2	3-48	6.3	- 28.50
Group 3	1-16	6.3	- 9.00
Group 4	8-70	11.4	+ 1.63

FIRST TIME OUT

	W-R	Per cent	£1 Level Stake
2-y-o	0-14	-	- 14.00
3-y-o	0-5	-	- 5.00
4-y-o+	1-15	6.7	- 4.00
Totals	1-34	2.9	- 23.00

JOCKEYS RIDING

	W-R	Per cent	£1 Level Stake		W-R	Per cent	£1 Level Stake
T Quinn	7-43	16.3	+ 20.50	J Quinn	1-9	11.1	0.00
L Piggott	2-7	28.6	+ 6.88	J Williams	1-11	9.1	- 2.50
Miss M Juster	1-1	100.0	+ 6.00	F Norton	1-11	9.1	- 8.75
B Rouse	1-8	12.5	- 2.50				

M Jermy	0-13	A Munro	0-3	A Garth	0-1
A Martinez	0-11	G Baxter	0-3	D McKeown	0-1
W Newnes	0-8	G Duffield	0-3	J Lloyd	0-1
G Carter	0-6	M Perrett	0-3	J Reid	0-1
Mr T Cuff	0-6	R Cochrane	0-3	L Dettori	0-1
Paul Eddery	0-5	C Rutter	0-2	N Day	0-1
W Ryan	0-5	D Biggs	0-2	N Kennedy	0-1
M Roberts	0-4	Dale Gibson	0-2	R Perham	0-1
W Carson	0-4	P Robinson	0-2	W R Swinburn	0-1

COURSE RECORD

	Total W-R	Non-Handicaps 2-y-o	Non-Handicaps 3-y-o+	Handicaps 2-y-o	Handicaps 3-y-o+	Per cent	£1 Level Stake
Folkestone	4-20	1-4	0-1	0-1	3-14	20.0	+ 33.38
Lingfield (AW)	4-38	0-3	2-10	0-0	2-25	10.5	- 19.75
Lingfield	2-24	0-11	0-5	0-0	2-8	8.3	- 8.50
Leicester	1-5	1-3	0-1	0-1	0-0	20.0	+ 2.00
Newmarket	1-6	0-2	0-0	0-1	1-3	16.7	+ 1.00
Goodwood	1-11	0-5	1-2	0-1	0-3	9.1	- 6.50
Brighton	1-16	0-4	1-4	0-1	0-7	6.3	- 12.00

Epsom	0-12	Southwell (AW)	0-4	Newbury	0-2
Kempton	0-11	Warwick	0-4	Redcar	0-2
Windsor	0-7	Wolverhampton	0-4	Bath	0-1
Salisbury	0-6	Ascot	0-2	Doncaster	0-1
Sandown	0-5	Chepstow	0-2	Nottingham	0-1

WINNING HORSES

		Races					Win
	Age	Run	1st	2nd	3rd	Unpl	£
Across The Bay	5	19	3	4	0	12	7,674
Dodgy	5	8	2	1	1	4	6,529
Snow Blizzard	4	6	3	0	0	3	5,904
Young Ern	2	7	2	1	1	3	5,300
Up The Punjab	3	11	2	0	3	6	4,550
Murmuring	6	8	1	1	0	6	2,324
Very Dicey	4	4	1	1	1	1	2,285

WINNING OWNERS

	Races Won	Value £		Races Won	Value £
J A Redmond	6	16,528	Ray Hawthorn	2	4,550
M F Kentish	5	11,204	Mrs G R Smith	1	2,285

Favourites	5-18	27.8%	- 1.37	Total winning prize-money		£34,567

Longest winning sequence		2	Average SP of winner	6.8/1
Longest losing sequence		42	Return on stakes invested	-40.4%

1991 Form	17-213	8.0%	- 31.92	1989 Form	7-116	6.0%	- 64.00
1990 Form	5-188	2.7%	-163.54	1988 Form	6-82	7.3%	- 20.27

J L DUNLOP (Arundel, West Sussex)

	No. of Horses	Races Run	1st	2nd	3rd	Unpl	Per cent	£1 Level Stake
2-y-o	48	145	21	15	9	100	14.5	- 72.24
3-y-o	56	301	48	42	36	175	15.9	- 66.46
4-y-o+	12	56	6	8	7	35	10.7	- 25.54
Totals	116	502	75	65	52	310	14.9	-164.24

BY MONTH

2-y-o	W-R	Per cent	£1 Level Stake	3-y-o	W-R	Per cent	£1 Level Stake
Mar/Apr	0-0	-	0.00	Mar/Apr	3-42	7.1	- 30.38
May	1-1	100.0	+ 3.00	May	9-43	20.9	- 3.62
June	1-6	16.7	- 4.17	June	15-51	29.4	+ 26.50
July	5-24	20.8	- 13.32	July	8-41	19.5	- 16.40
August	6-35	17.1	- 10.25	August	5-37	13.5	- 2.65
September	7-45	15.6	- 16.00	September	6-46	13.0	- 12.29
Oct/Nov	1-34	2.9	- 31.50	Oct/Nov	2-41	4.9	- 27.62

4-y-o+	W-R	Per cent	£1 Level Stake	Totals	W-R	Per cent	£1 Level Stake
Mar/Apr	0-12	-	- 12.00	Mar/Apr	3-54	5.6	- 42.38
May	1-11	9.1	- 4.50	May	11-55	20.0	- 5.12
June	2-6	33.3	+ 2.08	June	18-63	28.6	+ 24.41
July	2-9	22.2	- 2.12	July	15-74	20.3	- 31.84
August	0-5	-	- 5.00	August	11-77	14.3	- 17.90
September	1-7	14.3	+ 2.00	September	14-98	14.3	- 26.29
Oct/Nov	0-6	-	- 6.00	Oct/Nov	3-81	3.7	- 65.12

DISTANCE

2-y-o	W-R	Per cent	£1 Level Stake	3-y-o	W-R	Per cent	£1 Level Stake
5f-6f	8-38	21.1	- 8.79	5f-6f	0-19	-	- 19.00
7f-8f	13-106	12.3	- 62.45	7f-8f	8-70	11.4	- 32.06
9f-13f	0-1	-	- 1.00	9f-13f	31-160	19.4	- 2.80
14f+	0-0	-	0.00	14f+	9-52	17.3	- 12.60

4-y-o+	W-R	Per cent	£1 Level Stake	Totals	W-R	Per cent	£1 Level Stake
5f-6f	0-0	-	0.00	5f-6f	8-57	14.0	- 27.79
7f-8f	3-8	37.5	+ 11.83	7f-8f	24-184	13.0	- 82.68
9f-13f	2-33	6.1	- 25.25	9f-13f	33-194	17.0	- 29.05
14f+	1-15	6.7	- 12.12	14f+	10-67	14.9	- 24.72

TYPE OF RACE

Non-Handicaps	W-R	Per cent	£1 Level Stake	Handicaps	W-R	Per cent	£1 Level Stake
2-y-o	17-123	13.8	- 64.49	2-y-o	4-19	21.1	- 4.75
3-y-o	25-148	16.9	- 45.55	3-y-o	21-149	14.1	- 39.21
4-y-o+	3-14	21.4	+ 3.33	4-y-o+	3-42	7.1	- 28.87
Selling	0-1	-	- 1.00	Selling	0-2	-	- 2.00
Apprentice	0-0	-	0.00	Apprentice	0-1	-	- 1.00
Amat/Ladies	1-1	100.0	+ 0.30	Amat/Ladies	1-2	50.0	+ 19.00
Totals	46-287	16.0	- 107.41	Totals	29-215	13.5	- 56.83

COURSE GRADE

	W-R	Per cent	£1 Level Stake
Group 1	30-254	11.8	- 90.81
Group 2	19-101	18.8	- 17.89
Group 3	13-83	15.7	- 42.48
Group 4	13-64	20.3	- 13.06

FIRST TIME OUT

	W-R	Per cent	£1 Level Stake
2-y-o	4-48	8.3	- 27.25
3-y-o	2-56	3.6	- 47.38
4-y-o+	0-12	-	- 12.00
Totals	6-116	5.2	- 86.63

JOCKEYS RIDING

	W-R	Per cent	£1 Level Stake		W-R	Per cent	£1 Level Stake
W Carson	31-144	21.5	- 27.11	L Piggott	2-10	20.0	+ 2.50
J Reid	8-50	16.0	- 18.12	B Raymond	2-11	18.2	- 4.88
M Roberts	4-14	28.6	+ 7.26	L Dettori	2-22	9.1	- 15.50
G Duffield	4-18	22.2	+ 1.00	B Crossley	1-1	100.0	+ 14.00
Pat Eddery	4-18	22.2	- 5.73	W Newnes	1-7	14.3	- 0.50
T Quinn	4-50	8.0	- 24.75	A Clark	1-9	11.1	- 6.00
W Ryan	3-15	20.0	+ 0.25	A Munro	1-9	11.1	- 7.09
G Carter	3-20	15.0	- 2.62	R Hills	1-11	9.1	- 9.00
Miss E Houghton	2-3	66.7	+ 19.30	A McGlone	1-22	4.5	- 19.25

M Hills	0-6	J Carroll	0-3	R P Elliott	0-2
S Cauthen	0-6	M Birch	0-3	C Rutter	0-1
W R Swinburn	0-6	N Carlisle	0-3	D McKeown	0-1
J Lowe	0-5	T Williams	0-3	G Baxter	0-1
P Robinson	0-5	J Williams	0-2	G Hind	0-1
B Rouse	0-4	N Adams	0-2	J Fortune	0-1
Kate Ahern	0-4	Paul Eddery	0-2	N Day	0-1
D Holland	0-3	R Cochrane	0-2	Robin Gray	0-1

COURSE RECORD

	Total W-R	Non-Handicaps 2-y-o	Non-Handicaps 3-y-o+	Handicaps 2-y-o	Handicaps 3-y-o+	Per cent	£1 Level Stake
Brighton	7-26	1-6	2-8	0-2	4-10	26.9	+ 0.61
Wolverhampton	6-21	2-6	0-2	0-0	4-13	28.6	+ 7.75
Haydock	5-25	1-5	2-10	0-0	2-10	20.0	+ 9.13
Nottingham	5-26	3-12	1-4	1-2	0-8	19.2	- 4.00
Salisbury	5-26	1-8	2-6	0-0	2-12	19.2	+ 10.00
Goodwood	5-37	1-12	2-8	1-2	1-15	13.5	- 9.65
Newmarket	5-45	0-13	5-18	0-1	0-13	11.1	- 25.50
Carlisle	4-6	1-2	2-2	0-0	1-2	66.7	+ 11.62
Kempton	4-29	0-7	3-11	0-0	1-11	13.8	- 0.50
Redcar	3-15	0-1	1-5	1-1	1-8	20.0	- 5.50
Leicester	3-18	1-5	2-8	0-2	0-3	16.7	- 11.30
Ascot	3-20	1-7	2-7	0-1	0-5	15.0	- 3.92
Lingfield	3-22	0-8	1-4	0-1	2-9	13.6	- 14.00
Ayr	2-3	1-1	0-0	0-0	1-2	66.7	+ 1.88
Beverley	2-7	1-2	0-1	0-1	1-3	28.6	- 2.61
Folkestone	2-13	0-1	2-4	0-0	0-8	15.4	- 10.26
Epsom	1-1	0-0	0-0	1-1	0-0	100.0	+ 4.50

Dunlop J L

Thirsk	1-4	0-1	0-2	0-0	1-1	25.0	−	1.00
Yarmouth	1-5	0-0	1-4	0-0	0-1	20.0	−	3.20
Newcastle	1-7	0-3	0-2	0-0	1-2	14.3	−	2.50
Bath	1-9	1-1	0-2	0-0	0-6	11.1	−	6.37
Chepstow	1-9	0-2	1-3	0-0	0-4	11.1	−	6.00
York	1-15	0-0	0-5	0-1	1-9	6.7	−	11.25
Warwick	1-16	1-1	0-9	0-2	0-4	6.3	−	14.17
Doncaster	1-18	0-3	0-5	0-1	1-9	5.6	−	7.00
Sandown	1-20	0-6	0-8	0-0	1-6	5.0	−	17.00
Newbury	1-34	1-8	0-16	0-0	0-10	2.9	−	29.00

Windsor	0-7	Ripon	0-5	Lingfield (AW)	0-3
Catterick	0-5	Chester	0-3	Pontefract	0-2

WINNING HORSES

	Age	Races Run	1st	2nd	3rd	Unpl	Win £
Lahib	4	5	2	2	0	1	263,312
Rain Rider	3	6	4	1	0	1	25,958
Oumaldaaya	3	3	1	0	0	2	13,840
Thawakib	2	3	2	0	0	1	13,682
Captain Horatius	3	2	1	0	0	1	10,770
Cloud Of Dust	3	4	1	1	0	2	9,910
Top Royal	3	10	3	2	2	3	9,015
Futurballa	2	6	3	0	1	2	9,002
Ventiquattrofogli	2	4	3	1	0	0	8,774
Lucky Guest	5	10	1	1	0	8	8,460
Spring	3	4	2	1	0	1	8,321
Delve	3	6	2	1	0	3	7,783
Spectacular Dawn	3	9	3	1	1	4	7,462
Eurolink Thunder	2	3	2	0	0	1	7,127
Farat	4	8	1	1	2	4	6,970
Visto Si Stampi	2	3	2	0	0	1	6,517
Katiba	2	4	2	0	0	2	5,957
Prince Mercury	3	10	2	2	1	5	5,807
Persian Fantasy	3	7	2	4	0	1	5,590
Mahasin	3	5	2	0	0	3	5,507
Thamestar	3	7	2	1	0	4	5,446
Galactic Miss	3	6	2	3	0	1	5,435
Rajai	3	9	2	1	1	5	5,430
Timurid	3	9	2	1	0	6	4,532
Rainridge	3	5	2	0	1	2	4,191
Talb	3	7	1	2	2	2	3,785
Lobinda	3	5	1	0	0	4	3,720
Pizza Connection	2	5	2	2	0	1	3,714
Inan	3	9	1	1	1	6	3,546
Bold Stroke	3	5	1	1	0	3	3,465
Southwold Air	3	9	1	0	1	7	3,314
Dawning Street	4	2	1	0	0	1	3,158
Arman's Sax	2	2	1	0	0	1	3,106

Azzilfi	2	2	1	1	0	0	2,880
Eagle Feather	4	5	1	1	2	1	2,637
Carelaman	2	4	1	1	1	1	2,574
Silvernesian	3	4	1	1	0	2	2,532
Severine	3	6	1	1	2	2	2,511
Ma Bella Luna	3	4	1	0	2	1	2,369
Sky Train	3	8	1	0	1	6	2,148
Mrs West	2	4	1	0	0	3	2,145
Agincourt Song	3	9	1	4	1	3	2,070
Barahin	3	5	1	1	2	1	2,070
Wufud	2	6	1	2	0	3	1,932
Forelino	3	6	1	1	0	4	1,814
Beauchamp Grace	3	5	1	0	2	2	1,548
Three Wells	3	10	1	2	2	5	1,214
Fortune Star	3	5	1	0	1	3	1,171

WINNING OWNERS

	Races Won	Value £		Races Won	Value £
Hamdan Al-Maktoum	15	319,061	Cyril Humphris	3	5,702
Gerecon Italia	12	33,644	J E Nash	2	5,446
Mrs E M H Ogden White	4	25,958	J L Dunlop	2	5,006
Windflower O'seas Holdings Inc	4	17,208	Raymond Tooth	1	4,464
P G Goulandris	7	15,228	Lord Chelsea	2	4,218
D R Hunnisett	1	10,770	Hesmonds Stud	1	3,720
Miss Peggy Kwoh	1	9,910	Tom Wilson	1	3,465
Aubrey Ison	3	9,015	Sir Robin McAlpine	1	3,319
Lord Halifax	2	8,321	Lady Cohen	1	3,314
Peter S Winfield	3	7,462	Prince A A Faisal	1	2,880
Eurolink Computer Services Ltd	2	7,127	Miss K Rausing	1	2,511
Lady Swaythling	1	6,970	S Khaled	1	2,145
Duke Of Marlborough	2	5,807	E Penser	1	1,548

Favourites	43-112	38.4%	+ 12.26	Total winning prize-money			£524,218
Longest winning sequence			3	Average SP of winner			3.5/1
Longest losing sequence			67	Return on stakes invested			-32.7%
1991 Form	58-366	15.8%	- 64.77	1989 Form	66-456	14.5%	- 89.29
1990 Form	78-444	17.6%	- 50.88	1988 Form	66-582	11.3%	- 102.23

M H EASTERBY (Malton, North Yorks)

	No. of Horses	Races Run	1st	2nd	3rd	Unpl	Per cent	£1 Level Stake
2-y-o	31	134	14	14	12	94	10.4	- 30.83
3-y-o	17	104	11	13	11	69	10.6	- 64.61
4-y-o+	22	141	13	21	15	92	9.2	- 42.25
Totals	70	379	38	48	38	255	10.0	-137.69

BY MONTH

2-y-o	W-R	Per cent	£1 Level Stake	3-y-o	W-R	Per cent	£1 Level Stake
Mar/Apr	1-9	11.1	- 2.00	Mar/Apr	1-14	7.1	- 6.50
May	0-17	-	- 17.00	May	0-15	-	- 15.00
June	2-25	8.0	- 17.25	June	1-15	6.7	- 11.50
July	1-15	6.7	- 13.33	July	3-17	17.6	- 3.95
August	5-27	18.5	+ 15.75	August	5-16	31.3	+ 1.84
September	1-20	5.0	- 16.00	September	1-12	8.3	- 10.50
Oct/Nov	4-21	19.0	+ 23.00	Oct/Nov	0-15	-	- 15.00

4-y-o+	W-R	Per cent	£1 Level Stake	Totals	W-R	Per cent	£1 Level Stake
Mar/Apr	1-18	5.6	- 4.00	Mar/Apr	3-41	7.3	- 12.50
May	1-21	4.8	- 13.50	May	1-53	1.9	- 45.50
June	2-26	7.7	- 11.50	June	5-66	7.6	- 40.25
July	1-29	3.4	- 24.50	July	5-61	8.2	- 41.78
August	3-15	20.0	+ 3.25	August	13-58	22.4	+ 20.84
September	2-17	11.8	+ 3.00	September	4-49	8.2	- 23.50
Oct/Nov	3-15	20.0	+ 9.00	Oct/Nov	7-51	13.7	+ 17.00

DISTANCE

2-y-o	W-R	Per cent	£1 Level Stake	3-y-o	W-R	Per cent	£1 Level Stake
5f-6f	7-79	8.9	- 50.25	5f-6f	0-15	-	- 15.00
7f-8f	6-54	11.1	+ 15.42	7f-8f	10-68	14.7	- 30.11
9f-13f	1-1	100.0	+ 4.00	9f-13f	1-19	5.3	- 17.50
14f+	0-0	-	0.00	14f+	0-2	-	- 2.00

4-y-o+	W-R	Per cent	£1 Level Stake	Totals	W-R	Per cent	£1 Level Stake
5f-6f	1-33	3.0	- 28.50	5f-6f	8-127	6.3	- 93.75
7f-8f	7-58	12.1	- 9.50	7f-8f	23-180	12.8	- 24.19
9f-13f	5-43	11.6	+ 2.75	9f-13f	7-63	11.1	- 10.75
14f+	0-7	-	- 7.00	14f+	0-9	-	- 9.00

TYPE OF RACE

Non-Handicaps	W-R	Per cent	£1 Level Stake	Handicaps	W-R	Per cent	£1 Level Stake
2-y-o	7-79	8.9	- 41.83	2-y-o	3-22	13.6	+ 8.25
3-y-o	4-25	16.0	- 17.54	3-y-o	4-61	6.6	- 43.67
4-y-o+	1-13	7.7	- 7.50	4-y-o+	12-119	10.1	- 25.75
Selling	4-33	12.1	- 21.15	Selling	1-11	9.1	+ 15.00
Apprentice	0-1	-	- 1.00	Apprentice	1-7	14.3	+ 2.00
Amat/Ladies	1-2	50.0	+ 1.50	Amat/Ladies	0-6	-	- 6.00
Totals	17-153	11.1	- 87.52	Totals	21-226	9.3	- 50.17

COURSE GRADE

	W-R	Per cent	£1 Level Stake
Group 1	17-156	10.9	- 31.92
Group 2	11-109	10.1	- 37.84
Group 3	4-60	6.7	- 29.90
Group 4	6-54	11.1	- 38.03

FIRST TIME OUT

	W-R	Per cent	£1 Level Stake
2-y-o	2-30	6.7	- 21.50
3-y-o	0-17	-	- 17.00
4-y-o+	2-22	9.1	- 4.50
Totals	4-69	5.8	- 43.00

JOCKEYS RIDING

	W-R	Per cent	£1 Level Stake		W-R	Per cent	£1 Level Stake
M Birch	17-192	8.9	- 98.36	O Pears	1-1	100.0	+ 8.00
K Darley	8-40	20.0	- 3.33	J Williams	1-2	50.0	+ 24.00
S Maloney	8-103	7.8	- 52.50	Mrs Sarah Easterby	1-7	14.3	- 3.50
J Quinn	2-3	66.7	+ 19.00				

T Lucas	0-6	D Biggs	0-1	Miss A Harwood	0-1
G Carter	0-4	D McKeown	0-1	Mr R Dyer	0-1
F Norton	0-2	G Hind	0-1	Pat Eddery	0-1
J Lowe	0-2	J Marshall	0-1	S Dawson	0-1
L Piggott	0-2	K Fallon	0-1	W Ryan	0-1
N Connorton	0-2	L Newton	0-1		
B Raymond	0-1	M Roberts	0-1		

COURSE RECORD

	Total W-R	Non-Handicaps 2-y-o	Non-Handicaps 3-y-o+	Handicaps 2-y-o	Handicaps 3-y-o+	Per cent	£1 Level Stake
Redcar	5-35	3-14	2-4	0-2	0-15	14.3	- 12.59
Ayr	4-15	0-2	0-2	1-2	3-9	26.7	+ 8.75
Haydock	4-29	1-7	1-2	0-2	2-18	13.8	- 6.00
Beverley	3-28	1-11	1-1	0-1	1-15	10.7	- 10.90
Ripon	3-40	1-14	0-4	0-2	2-20	7.5	- 20.75
York	3-41	1-3	0-3	0-3	2-32	7.3	- 23.00
Edinburgh	2-5	1-2	0-1	0-0	1-2	40.0	+ 0.17
Carlisle	2-13	1-3	1-4	0-0	0-6	15.4	- 8.00
Doncaster	2-24	0-4	1-3	1-3	0-14	8.3	- 5.50

Easterby M H

Newcastle	2-25	0-7	0-2	0-1	2-15	8.0	- 17.17
Thirsk	2-25	0-10	0-4	0-2	2-9	8.0	- 8.50
Folkestone	1-1	1-1	0-0	0-0	0-0	100.0	+ 3.00
Sandown	1-4	0-0	0-0	1-2	0-2	25.0	+ 22.00
Hamilton	1-5	0-1	0-0	1-2	0-2	20.0	+ 8.00
Ascot	1-6	0-0	0-0	0-0	1-6	16.7	+ 1.00
Chester	1-7	0-2	0-2	0-1	1-2	14.3	+ 6.00
Catterick	1-25	0-10	1-4	0-2	0-9	4.0	- 23.20

Pontefract	0-19	Newmarket	0-4	Newbury	0-2
Southwell (AW)	0-7	Kempton	0-2	Warwick	0-2
Nottingham	0-6	Leicester	0-2	Wolverhampton	0-1
Goodwood	0-4	Lingfield	0-2		

WINNING HORSES

		Races					Win
	Age	Run	1st	2nd	3rd	Unpl	£
Forever Diamonds	5	9	3	4	0	2	17,815
Tell No Lies	5	9	2	2	1	4	17,251
Mhemeanles	2	8	3	0	1	4	11,692
First Option	2	10	4	4	0	2	10,222
Cumbrian Challenge	3	8	2	1	1	4	10,062
Gymcrak Premiere	4	11	1	3	0	7	9,240
Norton Challenger	5	8	1	1	0	6	9,219
Bold Angel	5	4	2	0	1	1	8,131
Thornton Gate	3	10	3	1	0	6	7,731
St Ninian	6	10	1	0	1	8	7,635
Patience Please	3	11	2	4	1	4	5,228
Westholme	4	11	1	1	1	8	4,825
Who's That Lady	3	5	1	0	1	3	3,558
Gymcrak Tiger	2	4	1	1	1	1	3,392
Playful Poet	5	5	1	1	0	3	3,355
Sarsta Grai	4	4	1	0	0	3	2,881
Bonarme	2	4	1	0	0	3	2,679
Gymcrak Tycoon	3	7	1	1	0	5	2,637
Yeveed	2	8	1	1	1	5	2,570
Northern Chief	2	5	1	0	0	4	2,469
Norstano	2	8	1	1	0	6	2,363
Harpoon Louie	2	5	1	2	0	2	2,360
Fanfan	2	9	1	1	1	6	2,344
Ernestan	3	7	1	2	0	4	2,259
Canon Kyle	3	7	1	1	1	4	2,217

WINNING OWNERS

	Races Won	Value £		Races Won	Value £
Mrs J B Russell	3	17,815	Maj J S Linley	1	9,219
Mrs A Johnstone	2	17,251	I Bray	2	5,228
P D Savill	6	14,926	Jonathan Gill	1	3,558
A M Wragg	4	12,753	Gymcrak Th'bred Racing IV Plc	1	3,392
T H Bennett	4	12,556	Peter C Bourke	1	3,355
Gymcrak Th'bred Racing III Plc	2	11,877	T K Kindon	1	2,881
Les Ford	3	11,692	M H Easterby	1	2,679
Cumbrian Industrials Ltd	2	10,062	Mrs Marjorie Graham	1	2,570
Lady Murless	2	9,852	T C Chiang	1	2,469

Favourites	14-53	26.4%	- 13.44	Total winning prize-money			£154,133
Longest winning sequence			4	Average SP of winner			5.4/1
Longest losing sequence			38	Return on stakes invested			-36.3%
1991 Form	58-531	10.9%	-187.51	1989 Form	57-494	11.5%	-202.88
1990 Form	61-562	10.9%	-230.30	1988 Form	64-499	12.8%	-140.97

M W EASTERBY (Sherriff Hutton, North Yorks)

	No. of Horses	Races Run	1st	2nd	3rd	Unpl	Per cent	£1 Level Stake
2-y-o	20	74	1	4	6	63	1.4	- 65.00
3-y-o	8	25	1	0	0	24	4.0	+ 1.00
4-y-o+	9	51	10	5	7	29	19.6	+ 18.50
Totals	37	150	12	9	13	116	8.0	- 45.50

BY MONTH

2-y-o	W-R	Per cent	£1 Level Stake	3-y-o	W-R	Per cent	£1 Level Stake
January	0-0	-	0.00	January	0-1	-	- 1.00
February	0-0	-	0.00	February	0-0	-	0.00
March	0-1	-	- 1.00	March	0-1	-	- 1.00
April	0-2	-	- 2.00	April	1-6	16.7	+ 20.00
May	0-9	-	- 9.00	May	0-1	-	- 1.00
June	0-9	-	- 9.00	June	0-3	-	- 3.00
July	0-18	-	- 18.00	July	0-8	-	- 8.00
August	0-15	-	- 15.00	August	0-2	-	- 2.00
September	1-15	6.7	- 6.00	September	0-1	-	- 1.00
Oct/Nov	0-5	-	- 5.00	Oct/Nov	0-2	-	- 2.00

Easterby M W

4-y-o+	W-R	Per cent	£1 Level Stake		Totals	W-R	Per cent	£1 Level Stake
January	0-0	-		0.00	January	0-1	-	- 1.00
February	0-0	-		0.00	February	0-0	-	0.00
March	1-3	33.3	+	8.00	March	1-5	20.0	+ 6.00
April	2-13	15.4	-	1.50	April	3-21	14.3	+ 16.50
May	3-8	37.5	+	9.00	May	3-18	16.7	- 1.00
June	0-3	-	-	3.00	June	0-15	-	- 15.00
July	2-10	20.0	-	0.50	July	2-36	5.6	- 26.50
August	0-3	-	-	3.00	August	0-20	-	- 20.00
September	2-8	25.0	+	12.50	September	3-24	12.5	+ 5.50
Oct/Nov	0-3	-	-	3.00	Oct/Nov	0-10	-	- 10.00

DISTANCE

2-y-o	W-R	Per cent	£1 Level Stake		3-y-o	W-R	Per cent	£1 Level Stake
5f-6f	1-46	2.2	-	37.00	5f-6f	0-3	-	- 3.00
7f-8f	0-27	-	-	27.00	7f-8f	1-18	5.6	+ 8.00
9f-13f	0-1	-	-	1.00	9f-13f	0-4	-	- 4.00
14f+	0-0	-		0.00	14f+	0-0	-	0.00

4-y-o+	W-R	Per cent	£1 Level Stake		Totals	W-R	Per cent	£1 Level Stake
5f-6f	9-28	32.1	+	36.00	5f-6f	10-77	13.0	- 4.00
7f-8f	0-18	-	-	18.00	7f-8f	1-63	1.6	- 37.00
9f-13f	1-2	50.0	+	3.50	9f-13f	1-7	14.3	- 1.50
14f+	0-3	-	-	3.00	14f+	0-3	-	- 3.00

TYPE OF RACE

Non-Handicaps	W-R	Per cent	£1 Level Stake		Handicaps	W-R	Per cent	£1 Level Stake
2-y-o	1-39	2.6	-	30.00	2-y-o	0-5	-	- 5.00
3-y-o	0-1	-	-	1.00	3-y-o	1-16	6.3	+ 10.00
4-y-o+	0-5	-	-	5.00	4-y-o+	6-39	15.4	+ 9.50
Selling	0-28	-	-	28.00	Selling	0-10	-	- 10.00
Apprentice	0-0	-		0.00	Apprentice	4-7	57.1	+ 14.00
Amat/Ladies	0-0	-		0.00	Amat/Ladies	0-0	-	0.00
Totals	1-73	1.4	-	64.00	Totals	11-77	14.3	+ 18.50

COURSE GRADE

	W-R	Per cent	£1 Level Stake
Group 1	3-16	18.8	+ 15.00
Group 2	1-45	2.2	- 19.00
Group 3	2-39	5.1	- 30.50
Group 4	6-50	12.0	- 11.00

FIRST TIME OUT

	W-R	Per cent	£1 Level Stake
2-y-o	0-19	-	- 19.00
3-y-o	1-8	12.5	+ 18.00
4-y-o+	1-9	11.1	+ 2.00
Totals	2-36	5.6	+ 1.00

132

JOCKEYS RIDING

	W-R	Per cent	£1 Level Stake		W-R	Per cent	£1 Level Stake
T Lucas	5-94	5.3	- 54.00	J Lowe	1-2	50.0	+ 24.00
J Marshall	4-16	25.0	+ 5.00	K Darley	1-14	7.1	- 7.50
M Birch	1-2	50.0	+ 9.00				

L Charnock	0-4	Antoinette Armes	0-1	J Fanning	0-1
P Johnson	0-3	B Doyle	0-1	O Pears	0-1
C Dwyer	0-2	D Nicholls	0-1	R P Elliott	0-1
S Maloney	0-2	D Wright	0-1	T Quinn	0-1
A Clark	0-1	G Duffield	0-1	W Ryan	0-1

COURSE RECORD

	Total W-R	Non-Handicaps 2-y-o	3-y-o+	Handicaps 2-y-o	3-y-o+	Per cent	£1 Level Stake
Carlisle	2-4	0-2	0-0	0-0	2-2	50.0	+ 6.50
Hamilton	2-4	0-1	0-1	0-0	2-2	50.0	+ 4.50
Doncaster	2-5	0-1	0-0	0-0	2-4	40.0	+ 17.00
Catterick	2-18	0-5	0-2	0-1	2-10	11.1	- 5.50
Ayr	1-3	1-1	0-0	0-1	0-1	33.3	+ 6.00
Wolverhampton	1-3	0-0	0-1	0-0	1-2	33.3	+ 8.00
Edinburgh	1-5	0-3	0-0	0-0	1-2	20.0	0.00
Ripon	1-14	0-5	0-0	0-2	1-7	7.1	+ 12.00

Southwell (AW)	0-18	Nottingham	0-6	Newcastle	0-1
Beverley	0-17	Haydock	0-4	Newmarket	0-1
Redcar	0-16	York	0-2	Warwick	0-1
Thirsk	0-15	Folkestone	0-1		
Pontefract	0-11	Leicester	0-1		

WINNING HORSES

	Age	Races Run	1st	2nd	3rd	Unpl	Win £
Penny Hasset	4	14	6	2	1	5	14,038
Catherines Well	9	12	3	1	4	4	10,070
Tolls Choice	3	3	1	0	0	2	3,097
Benzoe	2	7	1	1	3	2	2,710
Blanc Seing	5	5	1	0	1	3	2,700

WINNING OWNERS

	Races Won	Value £		Races Won	Value £
Mrs Anne Henson	6	14,038	T A Hughes	1	3,097
K Hodgson	1	5,127	Tony Fawcett	1	2,710
Robert Cox	2	4,943	J R Chester	1	2,700

| Favourites | 2-14 | 14.3% | - 4.00 | Total winning prize-money | | | £32,615 |

| Longest winning sequence | | | 1 | Average SP of winner | | | 7.7/1 |
| Longest losing sequence | | | 40 | Return on stakes invested | | | -30.3% |

| 1991 Form | 14-258 | 5.4% | -182.09 | 1989 Form | 19-271 | 7.0% | -145.29 |
| 1990 Form | 25-286 | 8.7% | - 94.71 | 1988 Form | 25-308 | 8.1% | -153.10 |

M W ECKLEY (Ludlow, Salop)

	No. of Horses	Races Run	1st	2nd	3rd	Unpl	Per cent	£1 Level Stake
2-y-o	1	3	0	0	0	3	-	- 3.00
3-y-o	1	2	0	0	0	2	-	- 2.00
4-y-o+	1	6	1	0	0	5	16.7	+ 5.00
Totals	3	11	1	0	0	10	9.1	0.00

Jan	Feb	Mar	Apr	May	Jun	Jul	Aug	Sep	Oct/Nov
0-0	0-0	0-1	1-1	0-3	0-3	0-1	0-1	0-1	0-0

Winning Jockey	W-R	£1 Level Stake	Winning Course	W-R	£1 Level Stake
D Moffatt	1-2	+ 9.00	Redcar	1-1	+ 10.00

Winning Horse	Age	Races Run	1st	2nd	3rd	Unpl	Win £
Rag Time Belle	6	6	1	0	0	5	2,402

| Favourites | 0-0 | | Total winning prize-money | | | £2,402 |

| 1991 Form | 2-12 | 16.7% | + 14.00 | 1989 Form | 1-15 | 6.7% | + 2.00 |
| 1990 Form | 1-7 | 14.3% | + 6.00 | 1988 Form | 4-53 | 7.5% | - 3.50 |

G H EDEN (Newmarket)

	No. of Horses	Races Run	1st	2nd	3rd	Unpl	Per cent	£1 Level Stake
2-y-o	4	7	0	0	0	7	-	- 7.00
3-y-o	5	22	1	4	4	13	4.5	- 20.50
4-y-o+	7	38	4	3	4	27	10.5	- 13.50
Totals	16	67	5	7	8	47	7.5	- 41.00

Jan	Feb	Mar	Apr	May	Jun	Jul	Aug	Sep	Oct/Nov
0-2	1-4	0-1	0-7	0-14	0-6	1-11	2-6	0-5	1-11

Winning Jockeys	W-R	£1 Level Stake				W-R	£1 Level Stake
W Carson	2-5	+ 5.50	P Turner			1-4	- 1.50
G Duffield	1-1	+ 7.00	A Munro			1-7	- 2.00

Winning Courses							
Edinburgh	1-1	+ 7.00	Lingfield (AW)			1-5	- 2.50
Haydock	1-2	- 0.50	Newmarket			1-8	- 3.00
Goodwood	1-5	+ 4.00					

Winning Horses		Age	Races Run	1st	2nd	3rd	Unpl	Win £
So Rhythmical		8	13	2	3	2	6	15,953
Galaxy Express		4	7	2	0	1	4	4,262
Artistic Reef		3	5	1	2	2	0	3,085

Favourites	2-6	33.3%	+ 0.50	Total winning prize-money			£23,299
1991 Form	4-70	5.7%	- 10.75	1990 Form	2-78	2.6%	- 65.50

J A C EDWARDS (Ross-on-Wye, H'ford & Worcs)

	No. of Horses	Races Run	1st	2nd	3rd	Unpl	Per cent	£1 Level Stake
2-y-o	0	0	0	0	0	0	-	0.00
3-y-o	0	0	0	0	0	0	-	0.00
4-y-o+	i	5	1	2	1	1	20.0	+ 16.00
Totals	1	5	1	2	1	1	20.0	+ 16.00

Jan	Feb	Mar	Apr	May	Jun	Jul	Aug	Sep	Oct/Nov
0-0	0-0	0-0	0-0	0-0	1-2	0-1	0-2	0-0	0-0

Winning Jockey		W-R	£1 Level Stake	Winning Course		W-R	£1 Level Stake
D Harrison		1-1	+ 20.00	Chepstow		1-1	+ 20.00

Winning Horse		Age	Races Run	1st	2nd	3rd	Unpl	Win £
Muizenberg		5	5	1	2	1	1	2,338

Favourites	0-0		Total winning prize-money			£2,338

1991 Form	0-29		1989 Form	1-30	3.3%	- 24.50
1990 Form	0-13		1988 Form	6-87	6.9%	- 53.06

M W ELLERBY (Pickering, North Yorks)

	No. of Horses	Races Run	1st	2nd	3rd	Unpl	Per cent	£1 Level Stake
2-y-o	2	10	1	0	1	8	10.0	+ 16.00
3-y-o	9	32	1	0	0	31	3.1	+ 2.00
4-y-o+	0	0	0	0	0	0	-	0.00
Totals	11	42	2	0	1	39	4.8	+ 18.00

Jan	Feb	Mar	Apr	May	Jun	Jul	Aug	Sep	Oct/Nov
0-0	0-0	0-0	0-6	1-9	0-9	0-8	1-6	0-4	0-0

Winning Jockeys	W-R	£1 Level Stake			W-R	£1 Level Stake
P Burke	1-8	+ 26.00	S Morris		1-31	- 5.00

Winning Courses						
Thirsk	1-2	+ 32.00	Beverley		1-7	+ 19.00

Winning Horses	Age	Races Run	1st	2nd	3rd	Unpl	Win £
Whisperdales	2	6	1	0	1	4	2,595
Cledeschamps	3	8	1	0	0	7	1,800

Favourites	0-0		Total winning prize-money			£4,395

1991 Form	0-43		1989 Form	1-27	3.7%	- 24.25
1990 Form	0-26		1988 Form	0-34		

B ELLISON (Malton, North Yorks)

	No. of Horses	Races Run	1st	2nd	3rd	Unpl	Per cent	£1 Level Stake
2-y-o	1	7	0	0	0	7	-	- 7.00
3-y-o	3	7	0	0	0	7	-	- 7.00
4-y-o+	9	65	4	3	6	52	6.2	- 38.50
Totals	13	79	4	3	6	66	5.1	- 52.50

Jan	Feb	Mar	Apr	May	Jun	Jul	Aug	Sep	Oct/Nov
1-3	2-5	0-6	0-9	0-12	0-14	1-15	0-6	0-9	0-0

Winning Jockeys	W-R	£1 Level Stake			W-R	£1 Level Stake
N Carlisle	2-16	- 0.50	J Fortune		1-8	- 1.00
M Hills	1-6	- 2.00				

Winning Courses						
Southwell (AW)	3-13	+ 9.50	Lingfield (AW)		1-5	- 1.00

Winning Horses		Age	Races Run	1st	2nd	3rd	Unpl	Win £
Meeson Times		4	11	2	0	3	6	4,609
Jovial Kate		5	17	2	3	0	12	3,370

Favourites	1-4	25.0%	0.00	Total winning prize-money				£7,979

1991 Form	3-51	5.9%	- 1.50	1990 Form	0-6

C C ELSEY (Lambourn, Berks)

	No. of Horses	Races Run	1st	2nd	3rd	Unpl	Per cent	£1 Level Stake
2-y-o	5	10	0	1	3	6	-	- 10.00
3-y-o	7	41	1	8	4	28	2.4	- 37.75
4-y-o+	4	43	5	4	7	27	11.6	- 12.07
Totals	16	94	6	13	14	61	6.4	- 59.82

Jan	Feb	Mar	Apr	May	Jun	Jul	Aug	Sep	Oct/Nov
2-5	2-7	0-5	0-6	0-6	0-7	1-17	1-22	0-8	0-11

Winning Jockeys	W-R	£1 Level Stake			W-R	£1 Level Stake
M Roberts	2-3	+ 9.25	T Rogers		2-24	- 6.00
W Newnes	2-11	- 7.07				

Winning Courses	W-R	£1 Level Stake			W-R	£1 Level Stake
Southwell (AW)	2-6	+ 12.00	Nottingham		1-3	+ 0.25
Lingfield (AW)	2-21	- 17.07	Sandown		1-6	+ 3.00

Winning Horses	Age	Races Run	1st	2nd	3rd	Unpl	Win £
Rapporteur	6	10	2	2	2	4	4,808
Kissavos	6	17	2	1	3	11	4,668
Intricacy	4	13	1	1	2	9	2,921
Ghostly Glow	3	8	1	2	2	3	1,674

Favourites	2-8	25.0%	- 4.07	Total winning prize-money			£14,071

1991 Form	7-121	5.8%	- 70.00	1989 Form	3-60	5.0%	- 32.00
1990 Form	8-98	8.2%	- 36.27				

C W C ELSEY (Malton, North Yorks)

	No. of Horses	Races Run	1st	2nd	3rd	Unpl	Per cent	£1 Level Stake
2-y-o	6	25	2	1	6	16	8.0	- 14.50
3-y-o	7	43	4	2	5	32	9.3	- 9.57
4-y-o+	10	30	3	4	2	21	10.0	+ 0.50
Totals	23	98	9	7	13	69	9.2	- 23.57

Jan	Feb	Mar	Apr	May	Jun	Jul	Aug	Sep	Oct/Nov
0-0	0-3	1-9	1-13	2-13	3-13	0-9	0-9	1-14	1-15

Winning Jockeys	W-R	£1 Level Stake			W-R	£1 Level Stake
S Maloney	4-21	- 4.57	N Kennedy		1-4	+ 2.50
J Carroll	2-12	+ 14.00	L Dettori		1-8	+ 9.00
B Raymond	1-4	+ 4.50				

Winning Courses	W-R	£1 Level Stake			W-R	£1 Level Stake
Yarmouth	1-2	+ 2.00	Hamilton		1-5	- 0.67
York	1-3	+ 5.50	Leicester		1-5	+ 12.00
Pontefract	1-4	+ 2.50	Redcar		1-5	+ 16.00
Ayr	1-5	0.00	Newcastle		1-11	- 5.00
Edinburgh	1-5	- 2.90				

Winning Horses	Age	Races Run	1st	2nd	3rd	Unpl	Win £
Linpac West	6	7	2	1	0	4	14,619
Philgun	3	14	3	0	3	8	7,225
Pennine Star	4	8	1	1	0	6	3,714
Royal Folly	2	4	1	0	3	0	2,469
Spark	2	4	1	0	2	1	2,072
Best Gun	3	6	1	0	0	5	1,932

Favourites	2-6	33.3%	+ 0.43	Total winning prize-money			£32,030

1991 Form	4-88	4.5%	- 61.00	1989 Form	10-114	8.8%	- 35.25
1990 Form	9-140	6.4%	- 77.04	1988 Form	10-137	7.3%	- 49.87

D R C ELSWORTH (Whitsbury, Hants)

	No. of Horses	Races Run	1st	2nd	3rd	Unpl	Per cent	£1 Level Stake
2-y-o	29	101	12	11	9	69	11.9	+ 5.55
3-y-o	33	127	11	20	17	79	8.7	- 65.06
4-y-o+	21	90	8	8	7	67	8.9	+ 2.50
Totals	83	318	31	39	33	215	9.7	- 57.01

BY MONTH

2-y-o	W-R	Per cent	£1 Level Stake	3-y-o	W-R	Per cent	£1 Level Stake
January	0-0	-	0.00	January	0-2	-	- 2.00
February	0-0	-	0.00	February	0-3	-	- 3.00
March	0-0	-	0.00	March	0-0	-	0.00
April	0-3	-	- 3.00	April	1-12	8.3	- 2.00
May	0-2	-	- 2.00	May	0-20	-	- 20.00
June	1-5	20.0	- 2.25	June	3-25	12.0	- 9.42
July	1-8	12.5	+ 3.00	July	4-19	21.1	+ 3.73
August	2-23	8.7	- 16.75	August	0-24	-	- 24.00
September	1-28	3.6	- 21.50	September	2-12	16.7	- 2.70
Oct/Nov	7-32	21.9	+ 48.05	Oct/Nov	1-10	10.0	- 5.67

4-y-o+	W-R	Per cent	£1 Level Stake	Totals	W-R	Per cent	£1 Level Stake
January	0-1	-	- 1.00	January	0-3	-	- 3.00
February	0-2	-	- 2.00	February	0-5	-	- 5.00
March	1-3	33.3	- 0.25	March	1-3	33.3	- 0.25
April	0-8	-	- 8.00	April	1-23	4.3	- 13.00
May	2-12	16.7	+ 42.00	May	2-34	5.9	+ 20.00
June	3-13	23.1	+ 10.25	June	7-43	16.3	- 1.42
July	0-10	-	- 10.00	July	5-37	13.5	- 3.27
August	1-12	8.3	- 6.00	August	3-59	5.1	- 46.75
September	0-16	-	- 16.00	September	3-56	5.4	- 40.20
Oct/Nov	1-13	7.7	- 6.50	Oct/Nov	9-55	16.4	+ 35.88

DISTANCE

2-y-o	W-R	Per cent	£1 Level Stake	3-y-o	W-R	Per cent	£1 Level Stake
5f-6f	7-55	12.7	- 11.75	5f-6f	1-17	5.9	- 7.00
7f-8f	5-45	11.1	+ 18.30	7f-8f	3-53	5.7	- 40.70
9f-13f	0-1	-	- 1.00	9f-13f	7-56	12.5	- 16.36
14f+	0-0	-	0.00	14f+	0-1	-	- 1.00

4-y-o+	W-R	Per cent	£1 Level Stake	Totals	W-R	Per cent	£1 Level Stake
5f-6f	0-6	-	- 6.00	5f-6f	8-78	10.3	- 24.75
7f-8f	2-22	9.1	- 4.50	7f-8f	10-120	8.3	- 26.90
9f-13f	6-52	11.5	+ 23.00	9f-13f	13-109	11.9	+ 5.64
14f+	0-10	-	- 10.00	14f+	0-11	-	- 11.00

TYPE OF RACE

Non-Handicaps	W-R	Per cent	£1 Level Stake	Handicaps	W-R	Per cent	£1 Level Stake
2-y-o	9-89	10.1	- 18.45	2-y-o	3-9	33.3	+ 27.00
3-y-o	7-76	9.2	- 42.64	3-y-o	3-42	7.1	- 17.75
4-y-o+	2-18	11.1	+ 26.75	4-y-o+	3-63	4.8	- 28.50
Selling	0-8	-	- 8.00	Selling	0-1	-	- 1.00
Apprentice	1-2	50.0	+ 0.75	Apprentice	1-6	16.7	- 1.50
Amat/Ladies	0-1	-	- 1.00	Amat/Ladies	2-3	66.7	+ 7.33
Totals	19-194	9.8	- 42.59	Totals	12-124	9.7	- 14.42

Elsworth D R C

COURSE GRADE

	W-R	Per cent	£1 Level Stake
Group 1	18-207	8.7	- 13.11
Group 2	2-47	4.3	- 34.25
Group 3	7-40	17.5	+ 4.75
Group 4	4-24	16.7	- 14.40

FIRST TIME OUT

	W-R	Per cent	£1 Level Stake
2-y-o	4-29	13.8	+ 24.00
3-y-o	1-31	3.2	- 21.00
4-y-o+	1-19	5.3	+ 22.00
Totals	6-79	7.6	+ 25.00

JOCKEYS RIDING

	W-R	Per cent	£1 Level Stake		W-R	Per cent	£1 Level Stake
J Williams	13-113	11.5	- 8.90	Mr C Vigors	1-1	100.0	+ 3.33
W Carson	3-23	13.0	- 3.52	G Bardwell	1-1	100.0	+ 8.00
J Hunter	3-25	12.0	+ 1.50	Ross Berry	1-3	33.3	+ 1.50
R Cochrane	2-21	9.5	+ 31.00	L Dettori	1-4	25.0	+ 3.00
T Quinn	2-25	8.0	- 14.17	B Doyle	1-14	7.1	- 7.50
Mr S Swiers	1-1	100.0	+ 5.00	S Cauthen	1-35	2.9	- 31.75
Y Okabe	1-1	100.0	+ 6.50				

B Rouse	0-8	A Munro	0-1	L Piggott	0-1
C Asmussen	0-7	A Procter	0-1	M Roberts	0-1
D Holland	0-4	A Shoults	0-1	M Tebbutt	0-1
S Whitworth	0-4	A Tucker	0-1	Mr F Schafer	0-1
W Newnes	0-3	D Harrison	0-1	Mr R Alner	0-1
N Kennedy	0-2	G Carter	0-1	P Robinson	0-1
Paul Eddery	0-2	G Duffield	0-1	Pat Eddery	0-1
R Hills	0-2	J Fortune	0-1	W R Swinburn	0-1
S Dawson	0-2	J Reid	0-1		

COURSE RECORD

	Total W-R	Non-Handicaps 2-y-o	3-y-o+	Handicaps 2-y-o	3-y-o+	Per cent	£1 Level Stake
Epsom	4-15	0-2	1-8	0-0	3-5	26.7	+ 15.23
Newmarket	3-27	0-5	2-9	1-2	0-11	11.1	+ 37.00
Ascot	3-28	2-8	0-6	0-1	1-13	10.7	+ 0.33
Newbury	3-33	1-11	0-7	1-3	1-12	9.1	+ 6.50
Goodwood	3-38	1-11	1-9	0-1	1-17	7.9	- 18.00
Lingfield (AW)	2-9	1-2	1-5	0-0	0-2	22.2	- 4.45
Bath	2-10	1-3	0-3	0-0	1-4	20.0	+ 6.00
Windsor	2-14	0-4	1-6	0-0	1-4	14.3	- 5.25
Kempton	2-29	0-10	2-10	0-0	0-9	6.9	- 17.17
Salisbury	2-34	1-13	1-8	0-0	0-13	5.9	- 21.25
Yarmouth	1-2	1-2	0-0	0-0	0-0	50.0	+ 4.50
Pontefract	1-3	0-1	0-0	1-1	0-1	33.3	+ 4.00
Warwick	1-4	1-1	0-2	0-0	0-1	25.0	- 0.75
Chepstow	1-7	0-3	0-2	0-0	1-2	14.3	- 0.50
Folkestone	1-7	0-2	1-5	0-0	0-0	14.3	- 5.20

Sandown	0-22	Southwell (AW)	0-4	Beverley	0-1
York	0-11	Brighton	0-2	Leicester	0-1
Lingfield	0-9	Nottingham	0-2		
Doncaster	0-4	Redcar	0-2		

WINNING HORSES

	Age	Races Run	1st	2nd	3rd	Unpl	Win £
Party Cited	3	5	3	1	1	0	36,096
Sapience	6	8	1	3	1	3	34,254
Hashar	4	5	1	0	0	4	13,550
Statajack	4	10	2	1	2	5	11,539
Rapid Success	2	3	1	0	1	1	10,770
Law Commission	2	6	1	1	1	3	8,675
Rustic Craft	2	1	1	0	0	0	8,460
Pontevecchio Moda	2	6	2	2	0	2	7,276
Ivor's Flutter	3	9	2	2	2	3	6,336
Camden's Ransom	5	15	2	1	0	12	6,146
Hamsah	2	8	2	2	0	4	5,730
Midwinter Dream	2	5	1	1	0	3	4,338
Shrewd Partner	3	8	1	1	2	4	3,948
Arusha	2	1	1	0	0	0	3,915
Crystado	3	3	1	1	0	1	3,655
Bright Spells	2	4	1	2	0	1	3,496
Hideyoshi	3	3	1	0	1	1	2,832
Amazing Baby	2	3	1	0	0	2	2,756
Milzig	3	8	1	3	1	3	2,721
Regal Racer	3	7	1	1	1	4	2,540
Riviera Rainbow	4	4	1	1	0	2	2,128
Thames Glow	3	5	1	1	0	3	2,070
Pelorus	7	9	1	2	1	5	1,725
Aberdeen Heather	2	11	1	0	2	8	1,214

WINNING OWNERS

	Races Won	Value £		Races Won	Value £
Raymond Tooth	5	48,686	W I M Perry	2	6,336
W H O'Gorman	1	34,254	Bob Cullen	2	6,146
Yoshiki Akazawa	3	17,549	A Foustok	1	3,655
W J Brown	1	13,550	C J Harper	1	3,496
Mrs M E Slade	2	11,539	Mrs J E Ohlsson	1	2,721
Sheikh Ahmed Al Maktoum	3	8,486	Sir Clement Freud	1	2,128
D R C Elsworth	1	8,460	A C Morgan	1	2,070
Walter Mariti	2	7,276	George Ennor	1	1,725
J C Smith	2	6,877	Major H S Cayzer	1	1,214

Favourites	10-34	29.4%	- 4.34	Total winning prize-money	£186,168
Longest winning sequence			2	Average SP of winner	7.4/1
Longest losing sequence			43	Return on stakes invested	-17.9%
1991 Form	40-354	11.3%	- 93.91	1989 Form 35-202 17.3%	+ 34.24
1990 Form	44-335	13.1%	+ 11.79	1988 Form 28-281 10.0%	-104.31

J ETHERINGTON (Malton, North Yorks)

	No. of Horses	Races Run	1st	2nd	3rd	Unpl	Per cent	£1 Level Stake
2-y-o	8	46	4	3	5	34	8.7	- 1.75
3-y-o	12	96	11	20	10	55	11.5	- 38.33
4-y-o+	1	4	0	0	0	4	-	- 4.00
Totals	21	146	15	23	15	93	10.3	- 44.08

BY MONTH

2-y-o	W-R	Per cent	£1 Level Stake	3-y-o	W-R	Per cent	£1 Level Stake
Mar/Apr	2-2	100.0	+ 22.25	Mar/Apr	2-9	22.2	+ 1.00
May	1-4	25.0	+ 1.00	May	1-15	6.7	- 13.33
June	0-5	-	- 5.00	June	0-21	-	- 21.00
July	1-5	20.0	+ 10.00	July	0-11	-	- 11.00
August	0-10	-	- 10.00	August	4-13	30.8	+ 2.15
September	0-14	-	- 14.00	September	1-13	7.7	- 9.75
Oct/Nov	0-6	-	- 6.00	Oct/Nov	3-14	21.4	+ 4.60

4-y-o+	W-R	Per cent	£1 Level Stake	Totals	W-R	Per cent	£1 Level Stake
Mar/Apr	0-0	-	0.00	Mar/Apr	4-11	36.4	+ 23.25
May	0-1	-	- 1.00	May	2-20	10.0	- 13.33
June	0-0	-	0.00	June	0-26	-	- 26.00
July	0-0	-	0.00	July	1-16	6.3	- 1.00
August	0-3	-	- 3.00	August	4-26	15.4	- 10.85
September	0-0	-	0.00	September	1-27	3.7	- 23.75
Oct/Nov	0-0	-	0.00	Oct/Nov	3-20	15.0	- 1.40

DISTANCE

2-y-o	W-R	Per cent	£1 Level Stake	3-y-o	W-R	Per cent	£1 Level Stake
5f-6f	4-21	19.0	+ 23.25	5f-6f	1-9	11.1	- 7.33
7f-8f	0-23	-	- 23.00	7f-8f	2-33	6.1	- 14.00
9f-13f	0-2	-	- 2.00	9f-13f	7-47	14.9	- 11.40
14f+	0-0	-	0.00	14f+	1-7	14.3	- 5.60

4-y-o+	W-R	Per cent	£1 Level Stake	Totals	W-R	Per cent	£1 Level Stake
5f-6f	0-1	-	- 1.00	5f-6f	5-31	16.1	+ 14.92
7f-8f	0-3	-	- 3.00	7f-8f	2-59	3.4	- 40.00
9f-13f	0-0	-	0.00	9f-13f	7-49	14.3	- 13.40
14f+	0-0	-	0.00	14f+	1-7	14.3	- 5.60

TYPE OF RACE

Non-Handicaps	W-R	Per cent	£1 Level Stake	Handicaps	W-R	Per cent	£1 Level Stake
2-y-o	3-25	12.0	+ 4.25	2-y-o	1-14	7.1	+ 1.00
3-y-o	5-21	23.8	- 5.23	3-y-o	4-55	7.3	- 18.00
4-y-o+	0-1	-	- 1.00	4-y-o+	0-2	-	- 2.00
Selling	2-19	10.5	- 14.10	Selling	0-6	-	- 6.00
Apprentice	0-1	-	- 1.00	Apprentice	0-2	-	- 2.00
Amat/Ladies	0-0	-	0.00	Amat/Ladies	0-0	-	0.00
Totals	10-67	14.9	- 17.08	Totals	5-79	6.3	- 27.00

COURSE GRADE

	W-R	Per cent	£1 Level Stake
Group 1	2-38	5.3	- 2.00
Group 2	4-29	13.8	- 9.25
Group 3	4-42	9.5	- 11.75
Group 4	5-37	13.5	- 21.08

FIRST TIME OUT

	W-R	Per cent	£1 Level Stake
2-y-o	3-8	37.5	+ 21.25
3-y-o	2-12	16.7	+ 7.00
4-y-o+	0-1	-	- 1.00
Totals	5-21	23.8	+ 27.25

JOCKEYS RIDING

	W-R	Per cent	£1 Level Stake		W-R	Per cent	£1 Level Stake
G Duffield	4-8	50.0	+ 3.60	M Birch	1-1	100.0	+ 5.00
T Lucas	4-18	22.2	+ 18.25	J Carroll	1-7	14.3	+ 8.00
J Weaver	2-17	11.8	+ 2.00	N Connorton	1-21	4.8	- 10.00
K Darley	2-22	9.1	- 18.93				

F Norton	0-9	Pat Eddery	0-2	J Fanning	0-1
J Lowe	0-8	R Cochrane	0-2	J Quinn	0-1
K Fallon	0-5	Antoinette Armes	0-1	J Reid	0-1
L Charnock	0-3	B Raymond	0-1	K Rutter	0-1
L Dettori	0-3	C Rutter	0-1	M Roberts	0-1
M Hills	0-2	D Harrison	0-1	M Wood	0-1
N Day	0-2	G Carter	0-1	N Kennedy	0-1
P Robinson	0-2	G Hind	0-1	W Ryan	0-1

COURSE RECORD

	Total W-R	Non-Handicaps 2-y-o	Non-Handicaps 3-y-o+	Handicaps 2-y-o	Handicaps 3-y-o+	Per cent	£1 Level Stake
Hamilton	2-3	0-0	1-1	0-0	1-2	66.7	+ 11.25
Edinburgh	2-6	0-0	2-2	0-0	0-4	33.3	- 3.00
Ripon	2-7	0-1	1-3	0-0	1-3	28.6	+ 3.50
Newcastle	2-8	1-3	0-1	1-3	0-1	25.0	+ 28.00
Carlisle	2-10	1-3	0-0	0-0	1-7	20.0	+ 1.25
Beverley	2-17	1-5	0-4	0-1	1-7	11.8	- 1.00
Warwick	1-4	0-0	1-3	0-0	0-1	25.0	- 2.33
Redcar	1-10	0-3	1-3	0-1	0-3	10.0	- 4.00
Thirsk	1-12	0-2	1-5	0-3	0-2	8.3	- 8.75

Etherington J

Doncaster	0-9	Nottingham	0-6	Ascot	0-1
Haydock	0-9	York	0-6	Folkestone	0-1
Pontefract	0-9	Catterick	0-5	Newmarket	0-1
Southwell (AW)	0-8	Ayr	0-4	Yarmouth	0-1
Leicester	0-6	Wolverhampton	0-3		

WINNING HORSES

		Races					Win
	Age	Run	1st	2nd	3rd	Unpl	£
Salu	3	16	4	3	4	5	8,683
Tarnside Rosal	2	8	2	0	2	4	6,025
Spray Of Orchids	3	13	2	3	3	5	5,875
Whitley Gorse	2	5	1	1	0	3	2,783
Doyce	3	11	1	1	1	8	2,532
Stingray City	3	10	1	7	0	2	2,403
Trafalgar Boy	3	8	1	1	1	5	2,383
Aegaen Lady	3	13	1	3	0	9	2,343
Razaroo	2	5	1	0	1	3	2,324
Haunting Rhapsody	3	3	1	1	0	1	1,380

WINNING OWNERS

	Races Won	Value £		Races Won	Value £
W N Lumley	4	8,683	P D Savill	1	2,403
Mrs Ann Lockhart	2	6,025	W L Armitage	1	2,383
T A Stephenson	2	5,875	Ron Watkins	1	2,343
Mrs G Liversidge	1	2,783	J R Rowbottom	1	2,324
Lord Matthews	1	2,532	David Wosskow	1	1,380

Favourites	5-11	45.5%	+ 0.17	Total winning prize-money	£36,729

Longest winning sequence	2	Average SP of winner	5.8/1
Longest losing sequence	43	Return on stakes invested	-30.2%

1991 Form	9-193	4.7%	- 87.71	1989 Form	18-180	10.0%	- 30.00
1990 Form	17-201	8.5%	- 98.77	1988 Form	11-190	5.8%	-121.20

J M P EUSTACE (Newmarket)

	No. of Horses	Races Run	1st	2nd	3rd	Unpl	Per cent	£1 Level Stake
2-y-o	9	40	1	6	5	28	2.5	- 38.00
3-y-o	5	29	2	1	0	26	6.9	- 13.00
4-y-o+	2	22	4	5	1	12	18.2	- 8.00
Totals	16	91	7	12	6	66	7.7	- 59.00

Jan	Feb	Mar	Apr	May	Jun	Jul	Aug	Sep	Oct/Nov
0-0	0-0	0-0	0-10	2-13	0-12	4-19	1-17	0-13	0-7

Winning Jockeys	W-R	£1 Level Stake				W-R	£1 Level Stake
M Tebbutt	4-39	- 27.50					
R Cochrane	2-16	0.00	Antoinette Armes			1-4	+ 0.50

Winning Courses	W-R	£1 Level Stake		W-R	£1 Level Stake
Yarmouth	2-7	- 1.00	Ayr	1-3	- 0.75
Hamilton	1-1	+ 2.25	Newbury	1-3	+ 8.00
Thirsk	1-2	+ 2.50	Goodwood	1-5	0.00

Winning Horses	Age	Races Run	1st	2nd	3rd	Unpl	Win £
Philidor	3	7	2	0	0	5	11,485
Briggsmaid	4	12	3	3	1	5	8,282
Expo Mondial	2	8	1	1	1	5	3,231
Checkpoint Charlie	7	10	1	2	0	7	2,870

Favourites	3-7	42.9%	+ 2.25	Total winning prize-money			£25,868
1991 Form	10-118	8.5%	- 59.82	1990 Form	6-78	7.7%	- 3.00

P D EVANS (Welshpool, Powys)

	No. of Horses	Races Run	1st	2nd	3rd	Unpl	Per cent	£1 Level Stake
2-y-o	2	6	1	0	1	4	16.7	+ 1.00
3-y-o	4	12	0	0	0	12	-	- 12.00
4-y-o+	11	68	5	6	4	53	7.4	+ 0.50
Totals	17	86	6	6	5	69	7.0	- 10.50

Jan	Feb	Mar	Apr	May	Jun	Jul	Aug	Sep	Oct/Nov
0-4	0-3	0-2	1-12	1-6	1-13	2-17	0-11	1-9	0-9

Winning Jockeys	W-R	£1 Level Stake		W-R	£1 Level Stake
B Raymond	1-2	+ 6.00	A Munro	1-6	+ 1.50
L Dettori	1-4	+ 3.00	Mr W McLaughlin	1-7	+ 6.00
Hayley Williams	1-5	+ 4.00	L Newton	1-10	+ 21.00

Winning Courses	W-R	£1 Level Stake		W-R	£1 Level Stake
Wolverhampton	2-28	- 12.00	Windsor	1-2	+ 6.00
Goodwood	1-1	+ 12.00	Nottingham	1-8	- 0.50
Beverley	1-2	+ 29.00			

Evans P D

Winning Horses		Age	Races Run	1st	2nd	3rd	Unpl	Win £
Shaffaaf		4	12	2	5	1	4	4,421
Luckifosome		2	5	1	0	1	3	2,363
Rednet		5	6	1	0	0	5	2,344
Lillah Darak		4	2	1	0	0	1	1,932
Sanawi		5	13	1	0	2	10	1,618

Favourites	0-4				Total winning prize-money			£12,678

1991 Form	3-55	5.5%	- 22.50	1989 Form	0-17
1990 Form	0-33				

J L EYRE (Dewsbury, West Yorks)

	No. of Horses	Races Run	1st	2nd	3rd	Unpl	Per cent	£1 Level Stake
2-y-o	1	2	0	0	0	2	-	- 2.00
3-y-o	1	1	0	0	0	1	-	- 1.00
4-y-o+	4	17	1	1	1	14	5.9	- 12.50
Totals	6	20	1	1	1	17	5.0	- 15.50

Jan	Feb	Mar	Apr	May	Jun	Jul	Aug	Sep	Oct/Nov
0-0	0-0	0-0	0-0	0-0	0-0	1-6	0-5	0-6	0-3

Winning Jockey	W-R	£1 Level Stake	Winning Course	W-R	£1 Level Stake
O Pears	1-10	- 5.50	Edinburgh	1-1	+ 3.50

Winning Horse	Age	Races Run	1st	2nd	3rd	Unpl	Win £
Bidweaya	5	8	1	1	1	5	2,482

Favourites	0-0	Total winning prize-money	£2,482

T FAIRHURST (Middleham, North Yorks)

	No. of Horses	Races Run	1st	2nd	3rd	Unpl	Per cent	£1 Level Stake
2-y-o	13	68	2	5	6	55	2.9	- 51.75
3-y-o	8	58	3	6	6	43	5.2	- 8.00
4-y-o+	13	76	3	2	6	65	3.9	- 60.62
Totals	34	202	8	13	18	163	4.0	-120.37

Jan	Feb	Mar	Apr	May	Jun	Jul	Aug	Sep	Oct/Nov
0-4	1-9	2-13	0-18	1-25	2-35	0-23	1-25	1-32	0-18

Winning Jockey	W-R	£1 Level Stake				W-R	£1 Level Stake
J Fanning	8-179	- 97.37					

Winning Courses							
Catterick	2-19	+ 18.25	Ripon			1-9	+ 4.00
Southwell (AW)	2-24	- 14.62	Edinburgh			1-16	- 7.00
Hamilton	1-7	0.00	Thirsk			1-17	- 11.00

Winning Horses	Age	Races Run	1st	2nd	3rd	Unpl	Win £
Celestine	3	4	2	0	0	2	4,258
Barrys Gamble	6	8	1	0	0	7	2,798
Blue Radiance	2	6	1	1	2	2	2,344
Bright Gem	2	9	1	2	1	5	2,301
Spanish Performer	3	11	1	2	0	8	2,243
Brisas	5	14	1	1	1	11	2,128
Super Benz	6	15	1	1	1	12	2,069

Favourites	1-8	12.5%	- 5.12	Total winning prize-money			£18,141

1991 Form	15-236	6.4%	- 31.50	1989 Form	11-201	5.5%	- 90.25
1990 Form	12-259	4.6%	-162.25	1988 Form	10-205	4.9%	-122.20

J R FANSHAWE (Newmarket)

	No. of Horses	Races Run	1st	2nd	3rd	Unpl	Per cent	£1 Level Stake
2-y-o	22	61	2	7	6	46	3.3	- 56.54
3-y-o	28	156	21	13	23	99	13.5	+ 2.84
4-y-o+	6	30	5	2	4	19	16.7	+ 6.00
Totals	56	247	28	22	33	164	11.3	- 47.70

BY MONTH

2-y-o	W-R	Per cent	£1 Level Stake	3-y-o	W-R	Per cent	£1 Level Stake
January	0-0	-	0.00	January	0-0	-	0.00
February	0-0	-	0.00	February	1-1	100.0	+ 4.00
March	0-0	-	0.00	March	0-1	-	- 1.00
April	0-1	-	- 1.00	April	2-17	11.8	+ 9.00
May	0-1	-	- 1.00	May	3-17	17.6	- 0.90
June	0-6	-	- 6.00	June	2-31	6.5	- 16.27
July	0-7	-	- 7.00	July	5-30	16.7	- 2.99
August	0-13	-	- 13.00	August	3-21	14.3	- 1.50
September	1-15	6.7	- 13.17	September	2-19	10.5	- 4.50
Oct/Nov	1-18	5.6	- 15.37	Oct/Nov	3-19	15.8	+ 17.00

Fanshawe J R

4-y-o+	W-R	Per cent	£1 Level Stake	Totals	W-R	Per cent	£1 Level Stake
January	0-0	-	0.00	January	0-0	-	0.00
February	0-0	-	0.00	February	1-1	100.0	+ 4.00
March	0-1	-	- 1.00	March	0-2	-	- 2.00
April	1-6	16.7	+ 2.00	April	3-24	12.5	+ 10.00
May	1-3	33.3	+ 8.00	May	4-21	19.0	+ 6.10
June	2-4	50.0	+ 7.00	June	4-41	9.8	- 15.27
July	0-1	-	- 1.00	July	5-38	13.2	- 10.99
August	0-4	-	- 4.00	August	3-38	7.9	- 18.50
September	1-3	33.3	+ 3.00	September	4-37	10.8	- 14.67
Oct/Nov	0-8	-	- 8.00	Oct/Nov	4-45	8.9	- 6.37

DISTANCE

2-y-o	W-R	Per cent	£1 Level Stake	3-y-o	W-R	Per cent	£1 Level Stake
5f-6f	2-27	7.4	- 22.54	5f-6f	3-13	23.1	+ 9.50
7f-8f	0-33	-	- 33.00	7f-8f	5-36	13.9	+ 10.60
9f-13f	0-1	-	- 1.00	9f-13f	11-89	12.4	- 13.76
14f+	0-0	-	0.00	14f+	2-18	11.1	- 3.50

4-y-o+	W-R	Per cent	£1 Level Stake	Totals	W-R	Per cent	£1 Level Stake
5f-6f	0-0	-	0.00	5f-6f	5-40	12.5	- 13.04
7f-8f	0-8	-	- 8.00	7f-8f	5-77	6.5	- 30.40
9f-13f	5-20	25.0	+ 16.00	9f-13f	16-110	14.5	+ 1.24
14f+	0-2	-	- 2.00	14f+	2-20	10.0	- 5.50

TYPE OF RACE

Non-Handicaps	W-R	Per cent	£1 Level Stake	Handicaps	W-R	Per cent	£1 Level Stake
2-y-o	2-52	3.8	- 47.54	2-y-o	0-4	-	- 4.00
3-y-o	12-70	17.1	+ 5.96	3-y-o	7-78	9.0	- 11.00
4-y-o+	1-10	10.0	- 4.00	4-y-o+	4-20	20.0	+ 10.00
Selling	0-3	-	- 3.00	Selling	0-2	-	- 2.00
Apprentice	1-2	50.0	+ 0.88	Apprentice	1-5	20.0	+ 8.00
Amat/Ladies	0-1	-	- 1.00	Amat/Ladies	0-0	-	0.00
Totals	16-138	11.6	- 48.70	Totals	12-109	11.0	+ 1.00

COURSE GRADE

	W-R	Per cent	£1 Level Stake
Group 1	13-127	10.2	- 52.06
Group 2	4-37	10.8	- 1.00
Group 3	5-57	8.8	- 23.77
Group 4	6-26	23.1	+ 29.13

FIRST TIME OUT

	W-R	Per cent	£1 Level Stake
2-y-o	0-22	-	- 22.00
3-y-o	4-27	14.8	+ 6.10
4-y-o+	1-6	16.7	+ 5.00
Totals	5-55	9.1	- 10.90

JOCKEYS RIDING

	W-R	Per cent	£1 Level Stake		W-R	Per cent	£1 Level Stake
G Duffield	8-49	16.3	+ 27.63	L Dettori	2-9	22.2	+ 4.00
N Varley	5-26	19.2	+ 20.38	T Quinn	1-2	50.0	+ 1.50
W R Swinburn	4-44	9.1	- 32.44	R Hills	1-2	50.0	+ 9.00
G Carter	4-61	6.6	- 42.27	K Darley	1-7	14.3	- 2.50
M Roberts	2-5	40.0	+ 9.00				

S Cauthen	0-6	J Lowe	0-2	Mr J Fanshawe	0-1
G Bardwell	0-5	M Hills	0-2	P Robinson	0-1
A Munro	0-4	N Carlisle	0-2	Paul Eddery	0-1
Pat Eddery	0-4	N Day	0-2	R Cochrane	0-1
B Rouse	0-3	C Asmussen	0-1	W Carson	0-1
B Raymond	0-2	D McKeown	0-1		
D Holland	0-2	David Eddery	0-1		

COURSE RECORD

	Total W-R	Non-Handicaps 2-y-o	Non-Handicaps 3-y-o+	Handicaps 2-y-o	Handicaps 3-y-o+	Per cent	£1 Level Stake
Newmarket	6-39	0-4	2-13	0-1	4-21	15.4	+ 1.48
Kempton	3-14	1-4	1-5	0-1	1-4	21.4	+ 1.83
Beverley	2-5	0-0	2-4	0-0	0-1	40.0	+ 8.50
Haydock	2-10	1-3	1-4	0-0	0-3	20.0	- 2.87
Sandown	2-16	0-0	1-8	0-1	1-7	12.5	- 4.50
Carlisle	1-1	0-0	1-1	0-0	0-0	100.0	+ 4.50
Edinburgh	1-1	0-0	1-1	0-0	0-0	100.0	+ 0.13
Southwell (AW)	1-2	0-0	1-1	0-0	0-1	50.0	+ 3.00
Warwick	1-4	0-2	1-1	0-1	0-0	25.0	+ 17.00
Ripon	1-6	0-0	1-1	0-0	0-5	16.7	+ 7.00
Thirsk	1-6	0-2	1-3	0-0	0-1	16.7	- 1.00
Salisbury	1-7	0-1	0-4	0-0	1-2	14.3	0.00
Folkestone	1-8	0-4	0-0	0-0	1-4	12.5	+ 7.00
Redcar	1-9	0-5	0-2	0-0	1-2	11.1	+ 2.00
Wolverhampton	1-9	0-2	0-0	0-1	1-6	11.1	- 1.50
Leicester	1-11	0-5	0-2	0-0	1-4	9.1	+ 1.00
Yarmouth	1-11	0-2	0-3	0-0	1-6	9.1	- 5.00
Nottingham	1-13	0-7	1-4	0-0	0-2	7.7	- 11.27

Doncaster	0-12	Newbury	0-6	Chester	0-3
Ascot	0-8	Pontefract	0-6	Lingfield	0-3
York	0-8	Goodwood	0-5	Ayr	0-1
Epsom	0-7	Bath	0-4	Catterick	0-1
Windsor	0-7	Brighton	0-3	Newcastle	0-1

WINNING HORSES

	Age	Races Run	1st	2nd	3rd	Unpl	Win £
Rose Alto	4	7	2	0	1	4	26,394
Splice	3	10	2	0	0	8	24,751
Mohican Girl	4	4	1	0	1	2	8,894
Barford Lad	5	10	2	1	1	6	8,746
Anne Bonny	3	7	2	2	2	1	7,458

Fanshawe J R

Swan Heights	3	9	2	0	0	7	6,016
Valley Of Fire	3	6	2	0	1	3	5,890
Native Idol	3	5	2	0	0	3	5,358
Wilkins	3	6	2	1	1	2	4,966
Storm Dust	3	9	2	0	1	6	4,364
Mithl Al Hawa	2	4	1	2	0	1	2,805
My Sovereign	3	6	1	0	1	4	2,774
Vayavaig	2	3	1	0	1	1	2,742
Kanvass	3	8	1	1	0	6	2,427
Legal Embrace	3	4	1	0	2	1	2,322
Sir Mark Sykes	3	4	1	0	0	3	2,265
Remany	3	6	1	1	0	4	2,215
Whirl	3	7	1	1	2	3	1,660
Bustinetta	3	9	1	2	3	3	1,506

WINNING OWNERS

	Races Won	Value £		Races Won	Value £
T & J Vestey	2	26,394	John R Sims	2	4,364
Cheveley Park Stud	2	24,751	B E Nielsen	2	4,280
David Thompson	4	12,816	Mohamed Suhail	1	2,805
A R G Cane	1	8,894	Dexa'Tex Ltd	1	2,742
Mrs Christine Handscombe	2	8,746	Mrs Jacqueline Slaytor	1	2,322
Sheikh Mohammed	3	8,317	Lord White Of Hull	1	2,265
Peter Wetzel	2	6,016	A C Hall	1	2,215
Lord Vestey	2	4,966	Lord Halifax	1	1,660

Favourites	8-26	30.8%	- 4.20	Total winning prize-money			£123,553
Longest winning sequence			3	Average SP of winner			6.1/1
Longest losing sequence			28	Return on stakes invested			-19.3%
1991 Form	22-152	14.5%	+ 7.14	1990 Form	18-113	15.9%	+ 58.96

P J FEILDEN (Newmarket)

	No. of Horses	Races Run	1st	2nd	3rd	Unpl	Per cent	£1 Level Stake
2-y-o	0	0	0	0	0	0	-	0.00
3-y-o	4	13	1	1	0	11	7.7	- 10.12
4-y-o+	6	47	4	10	11	22	8.5	- 19.93
Totals	10	60	5	11	11	33	8.3	- 30.05

Jan	Feb	Mar	Apr	May	Jun	Jul	Aug	Sep	Oct/Nov
0-7	0-2	1-3	0-1	1-9	0-7	0-9	0-8	2-8	1-6

Winning Jockeys	W-R	£1 Level Stake			W-R	£1 Level Stake
Miss J Feilden	2-15	+ 3.50	A Shoults		1-5	- 2.12
M Roberts	1-2	+ 5.00	B Raymond		1-6	- 4.43

Winning Courses	W-R	£1 Level Stake			W-R	£1 Level Stake
Haydock	1-1	+ 0.57	Wolverhampton		1-4	+ 3.00
Chepstow	1-2	+ 9.00	Lingfield (AW)		1-8	- 5.12
Catterick	1-4	+ 3.50				

Winning Horses	Age	Races Run	1st	2nd	3rd	Unpl	Win £
Carrolls Marc	4	17	2	3	5	7	5,190
Bill Moon	6	14	1	4	5	4	2,679
Easy Line	9	9	1	3	1	4	2,532
Granite Boy	3	4	1	1	0	2	2,108

Favourites	2-9	22.2%	- 4.55	Total winning prize-money			£12,509

1991 Form	5-53	9.4%	- 27.00	1989 Form	7-128	5.5%	- 53.50
1990 Form	6-60	10.0%	- 3.00	1988 Form	1-27	3.7%	- 21.50

P S FELGATE (Melton Mowbray, Leics)

	No. of Horses	Races Run	1st	2nd	3rd	Unpl	Per cent	£1 Level Stake
2-y-o	4	20	3	3	1	13	15.0	- 10.92
3-y-o	4	23	1	0	1	21	4.3	- 14.00
4-y-o+	4	40	6	5	1	28	15.0	+ 0.88
Totals	12	83	10	8	3	62	12.0	- 24.04

BY MONTH

2-y-o	W-R	Per cent	£1 Level Stake	3-y-o	W-R	Per cent	£1 Level Stake
Mar/Apr	0-1	-	- 1.00	Mar/Apr	0-5	-	- 5.00
May	1-2	50.0	+ 0.75	May	1-2	50.0	+ 7.00
June	0-2	-	- 2.00	June	0-3	-	- 3.00
July	2-7	28.6	- 0.67	July	0-1	-	- 1.00
August	0-4	-	- 4.00	August	0-5	-	- 5.00
September	0-3	-	- 3.00	September	0-1	-	- 1.00
Oct/Nov	0-1	-	- 1.00	Oct/Nov	0-6	-	- 6.00

4-y-o+	W-R	Per cent	£1 Level Stake	Totals	W-R	Per cent	£1 Level Stake
Mar/Apr	2-9	22.2	+ 0.88	Mar/Apr	2-15	13.3	- 5.12
May	0-7	-	- 7.00	May	2-11	18.2	+ 0.75
June	2-6	33.3	+ 10.00	June	2-11	18.2	+ 5.00
July	1-7	14.3	- 1.00	July	3-15	20.0	- 2.67
August	0-5	-	- 5.00	August	0-14	-	- 14.00
September	0-3	-	- 3.00	September	0-7	-	- 7.00
Oct/Nov	1-3	33.3	+ 8.00	Oct/Nov	1-10	10.0	+ 1.00

Felgate P S

DISTANCE

2-y-o	W-R	Per cent	£1 Level Stake	3-y-o	W-R	Per cent	£1 Level Stake
5f-6f	3-18	16.7	- 8.92	5f-6f	0-15	-	- 15.00
7f-8f	0-2	-	- 2.00	7f-8f	1-6	16.7	+ 3.00
9f-13f	0-0	-	0.00	9f-13f	0-2	-	- 2.00
14f+	0-0	-	0.00	14f+	0-0	-	0.00

4-y-o+	W-R	Per cent	£1 Level Stake	Totals	W-R	Per cent	£1 Level Stake
5f-6f	5-29	17.2	+ 0.88	5f-6f	8-62	12.9	- 23.04
7f-8f	1-11	9.1	0.00	7f-8f	2-19	10.5	+ 1.00
9f-13f	0-0	-	0.00	9f-13f	0-2	-	- 2.00
14f+	0-0	-	0.00	14f+	0-0	-	0.00

TYPE OF RACE

Non-Handicaps	W-R	Per cent	£1 Level Stake	Handicaps	W-R	Per cent	£1 Level Stake
2-y-o	2-14	14.3	- 9.92	2-y-o	1-5	20.0	0.00
3-y-o	0-2	-	- 2.00	3-y-o	0-10	-	- 10.00
4-y-o+	0-2	-	- 2.00	4-y-o+	6-36	16.7	+ 4.88
Selling	1-9	11.1	0.00	Selling	0-2	-	- 2.00
Apprentice	0-0	-	0.00	Apprentice	0-3	-	- 3.00
Amat/Ladies	0-0	-	0.00	Amat/Ladies	0-0	-	0.00
Totals	3-27	11.1	- 13.92	Totals	7-56	12.5	- 10.12

COURSE GRADE

	W-R	Per cent	£1 Level Stake
Group 1	1-7	14.3	- 4.62
Group 2	0-11	-	- 11.00
Group 3	6-46	13.0	- 11.92
Group 4	3-19	15.8	+ 3.50

FIRST TIME OUT

	W-R	Per cent	£1 Level Stake
2-y-o	0-4	-	- 4.00
3-y-o	0-4	-	- 4.00
4-y-o+	0-4	-	- 4.00
Totals	0-12	-	- 12.00

JOCKEYS RIDING

	W-R	Per cent	£1 Level Stake		W-R	Per cent	£1 Level Stake
K Darley	2-8	25.0	- 1.67	M Roberts	1-3	33.3	+ 2.50
J Lowe	2-16	12.5	- 4.62	J Fanning	1-5	20.0	+ 6.00
W Ryan	2-17	11.8	- 6.00	J Williams	1-5	20.0	+ 6.00
N Connorton	1-1	100.0	+ 1.75				

F Norton	0-5	R Price	0-2	K Fallon	0-1
T Quinn	0-4	A Tucker	0-1	L Dettori	0-1
A Mackay	0-2	D Harrison	0-1	Mrs M Morris	0-1
C Hodgson	0-2	D Meredith	0-1	N Kennedy	0-1
D Toole	0-2	G Hind	0-1		
N Adams	0-2	J Quinn	0-1		

COURSE RECORD

	Total	Non-Handicaps		Handicaps		Per	£1 Level
	W-R	2-y-o	3-y-o+	2-y-o	3-y-o+	cent	Stake
Hamilton	3-6	2-2	0-1	1-1	0-2	50.0	+ 3.08
Wolverhampton	2-8	0-3	0-1	0-0	2-4	25.0	+ 3.50
Leicester	2-9	0-1	0-1	0-1	2-6	22.2	+ 7.00
Folkestone	1-1	0-0	0-0	0-0	1-1	100.0	+ 10.00
Newcastle	1-1	0-0	0-0	0-0	1-1	100.0	+ 1.38
Beverley	1-3	0-0	1-2	0-0	0-1	33.3	+ 6.00

Nottingham	0-12	Yarmouth	0-3	Doncaster	0-1
Thirsk	0-6	Catterick	0-2	Haydock	0-1
Warwick	0-5	Newmarket	0-2	Lingfield (AW)	0-1
Windsor	0-5	Ripon	0-2	Southwell (AW)	0-1
Bath	0-4	Ayr	0-1	York	0-1
Pontefract	0-3	Carlisle	0-1		
Redcar	0-3	Chepstow	0-1		

WINNING HORSES

		Races					Win
	Age	Run	1st	2nd	3rd	Unpl	£
Second Colours	2	14	3	3	1	7	7,578
Bernstein Bette	6	11	2	0	1	8	5,715
No Quarter Given	7	10	2	1	0	7	4,414
Hotfoot Hannah	4	8	2	1	0	5	3,409
Katie's Dream	3	5	1	0	0	4	2,598

WINNING OWNERS

	Races Won	Value £		Races Won	Value £
P D Savill	3	7,578	John S Martin	2	3,409
John Ford	2	5,715	P O'Malley	1	2,598
P S Felgate	2	4,414			

Favourites	4-12	33.3%	- 0.54	Total winning prize-money			£23,714
Longest winning sequence			3	Average SP of winner			4.9/1
Longest losing sequence			29	Return on stakes invested			-29.0%
1991 Form	6-97	6.2%	- 46.37	1989 Form	12-152	7.9%	- 20.00
1990 Form	10-156	6.4%	- 79.25	1988 Form	17-175	9.7%	+ 18.13

M J FETHERSTON-GODLEY (East Ilsley, Berks)

	No. of Horses	Races Run	1st	2nd	3rd	Unpl	Per cent	£1 Level Stake
2-y-o	4	22	1	0	0	21	4.5	- 11.00
3-y-o	4	23	1	1	2	19	4.3	- 14.00
4-y-o+	6	51	5	3	3	40	9.8	+ 1.00
Totals	14	96	7	4	5	80	7.3	- 24.00

Jan	Feb	Mar	Apr	May	Jun	Jul	Aug	Sep	Oct/Nov
0-4	0-4	0-0	0-9	1-13	0-12	0-11	0-10	1-12	5-21

Winning Jockeys	W-R	£1 Level Stake		W-R	£1 Level Stake
M Roberts	3-8	+ 14.00	L Dettori	1-6	+ 5.00
F Norton	1-3	+ 10.00	D Harrison	1-16	- 3.00
D Holland	1-3	+ 10.00			

Winning Courses					
York	2-3	+ 15.50	Leicester	1-7	+ 4.00
Doncaster	2-4	+ 16.50	Kempton	1-8	+ 5.00
Nottingham	1-4	+ 5.00			

Winning Horses	Age	Races Run	1st	2nd	3rd	Unpl	Win £
Highland Magic	4	16	3	2	2	9	13,429
Takenhall	7	14	2	0	0	12	12,233
Trepidation	2	9	1	0	0	8	2,805
Judge And Jury	3	12	1	1	1	9	2,322

Favourites	0-4	Total winning prize-money	£30,789

1991 Form	13-151	8.6%	- 74.79	1989 Form	2-115	1.7%	- 91.00
1990 Form	7-123	5.7%	- 72.59	1988 Form	10-137	7.3%	- 55.25

J FFITCH-HEYES (Lewes, East Sussex)

	No. of Horses	Races Run	1st	2nd	3rd	Unpl	Per cent	£1 Level Stake
2-y-o	0	0	0	0	0	0	-	0.00
3-y-o	3	20	1	2	2	15	5.0	- 5.00
4-y-o+	6	36	2	4	4	26	5.6	- 7.00
Totals	9	56	3	6	6	41	5.4	- 12.00

Jan	Feb	Mar	Apr	May	Jun	Jul	Aug	Sep	Oct/Nov
0-6	0-0	0-3	2-6	0-9	0-4	0-9	0-9	1-8	0-2

		£1 Level					£1 Level
Winning Jockeys		W-R	Stake			W-R	Stake
A Mackay		2-17	+ 15.00	T Williams		1-9	+ 3.00

Winning Courses							
Bath		1-4	+ 11.00	Brighton		1-22	- 5.00
Goodwood		1-7	+ 5.00				

			Races				Win
Winning Horses		Age	Run	1st	2nd	3rd	Unpl	£
Assignment		6	13	1	2	3	7	15,530
Marzocco		4	12	1	2	1	8	2,598
Savalaro		3	13	1	2	2	8	2,355

| Favourites | 0-1 | | | Total winning prize-money | | | £20,483 |

| 1991 Form | 2-71 | 2.8% | - 64.00 | 1989 Form | 0-23 | |
| 1990 Form | 1-22 | 4.5% | - 16.00 | 1988 Form | 0-17 | |

J G FITZGERALD (Malton, North Yorks)

	No. of Horses	Races Run	1st	2nd	3rd	Unpl	Per cent	£1 Level Stake
2-y-o	13	50	3	7	5	35	6.0	- 19.67
3-y-o	14	48	1	5	2	40	2.1	- 42.50
4-y-o+	13	46	3	4	7	32	6.5	- 18.50
Totals	40	144	7	16	14	107	4.9	- 80.67

Jan	Feb	Mar	Apr	May	Jun	Jul	Aug	Sep	Oct/Nov
0-4	1-3	1-4	0-4	1-20	1-24	1-29	0-17	1-22	1-17

		£1 Level				£1 Level
Winning Jockeys	W-R	Stake			W-R	Stake
K Fallon	5-77	- 31.17	M Hunt		1-16	- 6.00
T Lucas	1-9	- 1.50				

Winning Courses						
Southwell (AW)	3-29	+ 2.33	Haydock		1-6	+ 4.00
Edinburgh	1-4	+ 1.50	Beverley		1-14	- 6.50
Newmarket	1-4	+ 5.00				

		Races				Win
Winning Horses	Age	Run	1st	2nd	3rd	Unpl	£
Abergele	2	5	2	1	1	1	12,711
Nijmegen	4	6	1	1	2	2	3,553
Dari Sound	4	7	1	0	2	4	2,500
Saladan Knight	7	10	1	2	1	6	2,461
Sweet Lips	3	1	1	0	0	0	2,138
Mohican Brave	2	6	1	1	0	4	1,203

| Favourites | 0-6 | | | Total winning prize-money | | | £24,566 |

| 1991 Form | 12-176 | 6.8% | - 98.25 | 1989 Form | 22-162 | 13.6% | - 4.97 |
| 1990 Form | 21-206 | 10.2% | - 24.70 | 1988 Form | 20-151 | 13.2% | - 4.52 |

J A GLOVER (Worksop, Notts)

	No. of Horses	Races Run	1st	2nd	3rd	Unpl	Per cent	£1 Level Stake
2-y-o	4	16	1	0	2	13	6.3	- 6.00
3-y-o	10	84	9	11	12	52	10.7	- 0.50
4-y-o+	12	76	15	11	4	46	19.7	+ 26.75
Totals	26	176	25	22	18	111	14.2	+ 20.25

BY MONTH

2-y-o	W-R	Per cent	£1 Level Stake	3-y-o	W-R	Per cent	£1 Level Stake
January	0-0	-	0.00	January	0-2	-	- 2.00
February	0-0	-	0.00	February	0-2	-	- 2.00
March	0-0	-	0.00	March	0-4	-	- 4.00
April	0-1	-	- 1.00	April	0-8	-	- 8.00
May	0-1	-	- 1.00	May	2-11	18.2	+ 3.00
June	1-4	25.0	+ 6.00	June	2-16	12.5	- 8.00
July	0-2	-	- 2.00	July	1-12	8.3	- 7.50
August	0-3	-	- 3.00	August	0-11	-	- 11.00
September	0-2	-	- 2.00	September	3-8	37.5	+ 23.00
Oct/Nov	0-3	-	- 3.00	Oct/Nov	1-10	10.0	+ 16.00

4-y-o+	W-R	Per cent	£1 Level Stake	Totals	W-R	Per cent	£1 Level Stake
January	2-13	15.4	- 6.25	January	2-15	13.3	- 8.25
February	0-2	-	- 2.00	February	0-4	-	- 4.00
March	0-5	-	- 5.00	March	0-9	-	- 9.00
April	0-8	-	- 8.00	April	0-17	-	- 17.00
May	2-5	40.0	+ 14.00	May	4-17	23.5	+ 16.00
June	3-11	27.3	+ 5.50	June	6-31	19.4	+ 3.50
July	3-11	27.3	+ 17.00	July	4-25	16.0	+ 7.50
August	2-8	25.0	+ 11.00	August	2-22	9.1	- 3.00
September	2-5	40.0	+ 3.00	September	5-15	33.3	+ 24.00
Oct/Nov	1-8	12.5	- 2.50	Oct/Nov	2-21	9.5	+ 10.50

DISTANCE

2-y-o	W-R	Per cent	£1 Level Stake	3-y-o	W-R	Per cent	£1 Level Stake
5f-6f	1-6	16.7	+ 4.00	5f-6f	2-25	8.0	- 16.50
7f-8f	0-9	-	- 9.00	7f-8f	2-19	10.5	+ 20.00
9f-13f	0-1	-	- 1.00	9f-13f	5-38	13.2	- 2.00
14f+	0-0	-	0.00	14f+	0-2	-	- 2.00

4-y-o+	W-R	Per cent	£1 Level Stake	Totals	W-R	Per cent	£1 Level Stake
5f-6f	2-19	10.5	- 8.00	5f-6f	5-50	10.0	- 20.50
7f-8f	7-31	22.6	+ 24.25	7f-8f	9-59	15.3	+ 35.25
9f-13f	5-17	29.4	+ 13.50	9f-13f	10-56	17.9	+ 10.50
14f+	1-9	11.1	- 3.00	14f+	1-11	9.1	- 5.00

TYPE OF RACE

Non-Handicaps	W-R	Per cent	£1 Level Stake	Handicaps	W-R	Per cent	£1 Level Stake
2-y-o	1-8	12.5	+ 2.00	2-y-o	0-4	-	- 4.00
3-y-o	0-13	-	- 13.00	3-y-o	5-45	11.1	+ 11.50
4-y-o+	2-10	20.0	- 3.50	4-y-o+	13-57	22.8	+ 39.25
Selling	1-12	8.3	- 10.00	Selling	0-10	-	- 10.00
Apprentice	0-1	-	- 1.00	Apprentice	3-14	21.4	+ 11.00
Amat/Ladies	0-1	-	- 1.00	Amat/Ladies	0-1	-	- 1.00
Totals	4-45	8.9	- 26.50	Totals	21-131	16.0	+ 46.75

COURSE GRADE

	W-R	Per cent	£1 Level Stake
Group 1	8-40	20.0	+ 17.50
Group 2	1-11	9.1	- 2.00
Group 3	8-61	13.1	+ 10.00
Group 4	8-64	12.5	- 5.25

FIRST TIME OUT

	W-R	Per cent	£1 Level Stake
2-y-o	0-4	-	- 4.00
3-y-o	0-9	-	- 9.00
4-y-o+	1-11	9.1	- 7.25
Totals	1-24	4.2	- 20.25

JOCKEYS RIDING

	W-R	Per cent	£1 Level Stake		W-R	Per cent	£1 Level Stake
S D Williams	9-49	18.4	+ 27.75	D Nicholls	2-7	28.6	- 0.50
J Fortune	4-30	13.3	- 13.00	F Norton	2-11	18.2	+ 4.50
D McKeown	3-11	27.3	+ 10.00	S Sanders	1-1	100.0	+ 8.00
N Carlisle	3-16	18.8	+ 8.50	S Maloney	1-8	12.5	+ 18.00

J Quinn	0-10	B Crossley	0-1	L Charnock	0-1
C Hawksley	0-6	C Rutter	0-1	M Birch	0-1
A Munro	0-3	Claire Balding	0-1	Miss A Billot	0-1
D Holland	0-3	D Biggs	0-1	Mr S Astaire	0-1
G Carter	0-3	G Duffield	0-1	N Connorton	0-1
Dale Gibson	0-2	G Hind	0-1	O Pears	0-1
M Hunt	0-2	G Mitchell	0-1	W Ryan	0-1

COURSE RECORD

	Total W-R	Non-Handicaps 2-y-o	3-y-o+	Handicaps 2-y-o	3-y-o+	Per cent	£1 Level Stake
Pontefract	5-23	1-3	1-2	0-1	3-17	21.7	+ 12.00
Southwell (AW)	4-42	0-3	0-9	0-0	4-30	9.5	- 25.25
Haydock	3-10	0-0	2-4	0-1	1-5	30.0	+ 6.50
Wolverhampton	2-8	0-0	0-1	0-0	2-7	25.0	+ 2.50
Beverley	2-10	0-1	0-0	0-1	2-8	20.0	+ 9.00

Glover J A

Newmarket	2-10	0-0	0-0	0-0	2-10	20.0	+ 4.50
Ascot	1-2	0-0	0-0	0-0	1-2	50.0	+ 3.50
Newcastle	1-2	0-0	0-0	0-0	1-2	50.0	+ 4.00
York	1-2	0-0	0-0	0-0	1-2	50.0	+ 13.00
Redcar	1-6	0-0	0-1	0-0	1-5	16.7	+ 3.00
Warwick	1-6	0-0	0-1	0-0	1-5	16.7	− 0.50
Catterick	1-7	0-1	0-3	0-0	1-3	14.3	+ 19.00
Leicester	1-11	0-2	0-3	0-0	1-6	9.1	+ 6.00

Nottingham	0-14	Yarmouth	0-2	Sandown	0-1
Doncaster	0-13	Carlisle	0-1		
Ripon	0-5	Hamilton	0-1		

WINNING HORSES

		Races					Win
	Age	Run	1st	2nd	3rd	Unpl	£
Rambo's Hall	7	7	4	1	0	2	82,302
Doulab's Image	5	17	6	2	1	8	40,268
Cold Shower	3	14	5	3	1	5	18,256
Samain	5	11	3	2	1	5	7,449
Fighter Squadron	3	17	2	4	5	6	4,749
Arc Lamp	6	15	2	2	1	10	3,351
Abeloni	3	4	1	0	0	3	3,346
Miss Hyde	3	9	1	0	2	6	2,511
Atherton Green	2	7	1	0	2	4	2,469

WINNING OWNERS

	Races Won	Value £		Races Won	Value £
B Dixon	4	82,302	A F Budge (Equine) Limited	1	3,346
Claremont Management Services	13	63,273	Hyde Sporting Promotions	1	2,511
Countrywide Classics Ltd	3	7,449	Atherton and Green	1	2,469
B Bruce	2	3,351			

Favourites	10-24	41.7%	+ 16.75	Total winning prize-money			£164,701

Longest winning sequence		2	Average SP of winner	6.9/1
Longest losing sequence		49	Return on stakes invested	11.5%

1991 Form	4-103	3.9%	− 51.00	1989 Form	3-103	2.9%	− 65.50
1990 Form	5-84	6.0%	− 16.50	1988 Form	12-101	11.9%	− 1.50

J H M GOSDEN (Newmarket)

	No. of Horses	Races Run	1st	2nd	3rd	Unpl	Per cent	£1 Level Stake
2-y-o	45	99	29	16	14	40	29.3	+ 7.61
3-y-o	69	321	64	43	45	169	19.9	- 32.12
4-y-o+	20	91	19	23	11	38	20.9	+ 38.41
Totals	134	511	112	82	70	247	21.9	+ 13.90

BY MONTH

2-y-o	W-R	Per cent	£1 Level Stake	3-y-o	W-R	Per cent	£1 Level Stake
January	0-0	-	0.00	January	0-0	-	0.00
February	0-0	-	0.00	February	0-0	-	0.00
March	0-0	-	0.00	March	1-3	33.3	+ 8.00
April	0-0	-	0.00	April	4-28	14.3	- 14.37
May	0-3	-	- 3.00	May	8-36	22.2	+ 13.37
June	1-6	16.7	- 4.83	June	17-52	32.7	+ 7.37
July	4-13	30.8	- 3.12	July	8-58	13.8	- 10.90
August	4-16	25.0	+ 3.20	August	7-36	19.4	- 9.73
September	8-18	44.4	+ 13.25	September	14-53	26.4	+ 2.08
Oct/Nov	12-43	27.9	+ 2.11	Oct/Nov	5-55	9.1	- 27.94

4-y-o+	W-R	Per cent	£1 Level Stake	Totals	W-R	Per cent	£1 Level Stake
January	1-2	50.0	+ 0.50	January	1-2	50.0	+ 0.50
February	0-1	-	- 1.00	February	0-1	-	- 1.00
March	0-0	-	0.00	March	1-3	33.3	+ 8.00
April	3-16	18.8	0.00	April	7-44	15.9	- 14.37
May	3-12	25.0	+ 3.33	May	11-51	21.6	+ 13.70
June	2-10	20.0	+ 3.00	June	20-68	29.4	+ 5.54
July	4-14	28.6	+ 2.58	July	16-85	18.8	- 11.44
August	4-9	44.4	+ 26.00	August	15-61	24.6	+ 19.47
September	1-11	9.1	+ 15.00	September	23-82	28.0	+ 30.33
Oct/Nov	1-16	6.3	- 11.00	Oct/Nov	18-114	15.8	- 36.83

DISTANCE

2-y-o	W-R	Per cent	£1 Level Stake	3-y-o	W-R	Per cent	£1 Level Stake
5f-6f	6-38	15.8	- 18.90	5f-6f	13-33	39.4	+ 7.91
7f-8f	23-61	37.7	+ 26.51	7f-8f	16-112	14.3	- 35.60
9f-13f	0-0	-	0.00	9f-13f	31-154	20.1	- 3.93
14f+	0-0	-	0.00	14f+	4-22	18.2	- 0.50

4-y-o+	W-R	Per cent	£1 Level Stake	Totals	W-R	Per cent	£1 Level Stake
5f-6f	0-5	-	- 5.00	5f-6f	19-76	25.0	- 15.99
7f-8f	7-34	20.6	+ 13.58	7f-8f	46-207	22.2	+ 4.49
9f-13f	7-39	17.9	+ 19.83	9f-13f	38-193	19.7	+ 15.90
14f+	5-13	38.5	+ 10.00	14f+	9-35	25.7	+ 9.50

TYPE OF RACE

Non-Handicaps	W–R	Per cent	£1 Level Stake	Handicaps	W–R	Per cent	£1 Level Stake
2-y-o	27–93	29.0	+ 3.61	2-y-o	1–5	20.0	0.00
3-y-o	39–199	19.6	- 39.19	3-y-o	24–113	21.2	+ 14.94
4-y-o+	9–37	24.3	+ 28.08	4-y-o+	11–52	21.2	+ 17.33
Selling	0–1	–	- 1.00	Selling	0–0	–	0.00
Apprentice	1–4	25.0	- 2.87	Apprentice	0–5	–	- 5.00
Amat/Ladies	0–1	–	- 1.00	Amat/Ladies	0–1	–	- 1.00
Totals	76–335	22.7	- 12.37	Totals	36–176	20.5	+ 26.27

COURSE GRADE

	W–R	Per cent	£1 Level Stake
Group 1	70–336	20.8	+ 39.33
Group 2	14–74	18.9	- 26.44
Group 3	18–72	25.0	+ 2.46
Group 4	10–29	34.5	- 1.45

FIRST TIME OUT

	W–R	Per cent	£1 Level Stake
2-y-o	10–45	22.2	- 1.60
3-y-o	10–69	14.5	- 7.74
4-y-o+	4–20	20.0	+ 0.83
Totals	24–134	17.9	- 8.51

JOCKEYS RIDING

	W–R	Per cent	£1 Level Stake		W–R	Per cent	£1 Level Stake
S Cauthen	37–152	24.3	+ 8.77	W R Swinburn	2–11	18.2	- 5.55
Pat Eddery	18–49	36.7	+ 22.40	A McGlone	2–11	18.2	- 0.75
R Cochrane	15–80	18.8	- 13.46	Mrs L Pearce	1–1	100.0	+ 3.33
G Hind	7–41	17.1	- 9.60	N Day	1–2	50.0	+ 5.00
D Holland	6–22	27.3	+ 33.66	L Piggott	1–2	50.0	+ 1.00
W Carson	5–41	12.2	- 2.38	J Weaver	1–2	50.0	+ 5.00
Paul Eddery	4–18	22.2	- 8.12	S Wynne	1–2	50.0	- 0.87
G Duffield	3–6	50.0	+ 12.50	M Roberts	1–4	25.0	- 0.25
J Carroll	3–11	27.3	- 2.68	B Raymond	1–7	14.3	- 5.60
M Hills	3–15	20.0	+ 5.50				

L Dettori	0–7	W Ryan	0–3	D Harrison		0–1
D Dunnachie	0–4	G Carter	0–2	F Arrowsmith		0–1
P Robinson	0–4	J Williams	0–2	N Carlisle		0–1
J Reid	0–3	Mr J Durkan	0–2			
S Davies	0–3	B Crossley	0–1			

COURSE RECORD

	Total W–R	Non-Handicaps 2-y-o	3-y-o+	Handicaps 2-y-o	3-y-o+	Per cent	£1 Level Stake
Newmarket	15–101	1–18	7–45	0–1	7–37	14.9	- 14.59
Doncaster	10–37	5–13	2–12	0–0	3–12	27.0	+ 6.05
Newbury	8–24	3–7	2–8	0–0	3–9	33.3	+ 6.53
York	8–32	1–5	3–11	0–1	4–15	25.0	+ 4.13
Haydock	7–21	2–5	3–11	0–0	2–5	33.3	+ 18.50

Kempton	6-26	1-2	3-16	0-1	2-7	23.1	+	3.62
Ascot	6-31	1-5	4-10	0-0	1-16	19.4	+	1.71
Chester	5-12	2-3	1-2	0-0	2-7	41.7	+	12.88
Yarmouth	5-18	2-3	2-10	0-0	1-5	27.8	+	0.78
Catterick	4-8	1-2	3-5	0-0	0-1	50.0	+	2.90
Goodwood	4-23	0-4	1-9	1-1	2-9	17.4	+	23.75
Nottingham	3-8	0-0	2-5	0-0	1-3	37.5	+	3.50
Brighton	3-15	0-0	2-11	0-0	1-4	20.0	-	7.87
Windsor	3-15	0-0	2-12	0-1	1-2	20.0	-	0.50
Sandown	3-18	0-1	2-9	0-0	1-8	16.7	-	0.37
Thirsk	2-3	0-0	2-2	0-0	0-1	66.7	+	1.65
Wolverhampton	2-3	1-1	0-1	0-0	1-1	66.7	+	4.17
Chepstow	2-4	1-2	1-1	0-0	0-1	50.0	+	1.48
Edinburgh	2-4	1-2	1-1	0-0	0-1	50.0	+	1.25
Pontefract	2-10	0-1	1-8	0-0	1-1	20.0		0.00
Leicester	2-14	2-5	0-6	0-0	0-3	14.3	-	10.80
Lingfield	2-15	1-6	1-7	0-0	0-2	13.3	-	8.67
Redcar	2-16	1-5	1-8	0-0	0-3	12.5	-	11.43
Beverley	1-3	0-0	1-3	0-0	0-0	33.3	+	8.00
Southwell (AW)	1-3	0-0	0-1	0-0	1-2	33.3	-	0.50
Ayr	1-4	1-2	0-0	0-0	0-2	25.0	-	0.50
Warwick	1-5	0-0	1-5	0-0	0-0	20.0	-	3.27
Newcastle	1-6	0-0	0-4	0-0	1-2	16.7	+	1.00
Epsom	1-13	0-0	1-7	0-0	0-6	7.7	-	10.50

Ripon	0-9	Folkestone	0-3	Lingfield (AW)	0-1
Salisbury	0-4	Carlisle	0-2		

WINNING HORSES

		Races					Win
	Age	Run	1st	2nd	3rd	Unpl	£
Wolfhound	3	6	2	0	2	2	49,626
Witness Box	5	6	2	3	0	1	49,144
Landowner	3	9	4	1	1	3	42,496
Daru	3	7	5	1	0	1	35,941
Pollen Count	3	4	2	0	0	2	35,614
Turgenev	3	9	3	2	0	4	33,183
Marillette	2	8	4	1	1	2	29,648
Beggarman Thief	2	4	2	0	0	2	28,070
Badawi	4	11	3	3	2	3	21,622
Toussaud	3	5	3	1	1	0	21,556
Deprecator	4	12	2	3	2	5	19,520
Brier Creek	3	12	4	1	3	4	19,219
Taos	2	3	3	0	0	0	18,951
Knifebox	4	4	1	0	1	2	18,350
Western Approach	3	5	3	0	0	2	17,030
Susurration	5	6	2	1	2	1	14,339
Kasmayo	3	3	2	1	0	0	13,619
Zalon	3	7	2	0	0	5	12,526
Pembroke	2	2	2	0	0	0	11,973
Mashaallah	4	3	1	1	1	0	11,355
What Katy Did	3	2	2	0	0	0	10,557

Gosden J H M

Emperor Jones	2	3	2	0	1	0	9,952
Red Bishop	4	4	1	3	0	0	9,000
Specificity	4	4	1	1	0	2	8,894
Lord Chickney	3	2	1	0	0	1	8,538
Mesleh	5	2	1	1	0	0	8,025
Charlo	4	5	1	1	0	3	7,375
Sharling	3	7	1	0	1	5	7,304
King's Signet	3	6	2	0	0	4	7,251
Scrutineer	3	9	2	2	2	3	7,159
Sastago	3	7	1	1	0	5	7,148
Scarlatine	3	5	1	1	0	3	6,732
Sahel	4	6	1	2	1	2	5,900
Combative	3	7	2	2	1	2	5,793
Avice Caro	3	7	2	0	2	3	4,856
Cape Weaver	2	3	1	1	1	0	4,797
Kinematic	4	7	1	2	1	3	4,695
Kansk	4	7	1	0	1	5	4,464
Sonus	3	5	1	3	0	1	4,425
Catrail	2	1	1	0	0	0	4,347
Ribbonwood	2	3	1	1	0	1	4,338
Icy South	2	5	1	0	2	2	4,078
Dawaahi	3	5	1	0	0	4	3,785
Lemon's Mill	3	5	1	0	2	2	3,688
True Hero	2	2	1	0	0	1	3,496
Tinners Way	2	1	1	0	0	0	3,224
Azilian	2	1	1	0	0	0	3,199
Redisham	3	3	1	1	0	1	3,002
Bonjour	2	4	1	0	0	3	2,881
Fair Maid Of Kent	2	2	1	0	0	1	2,807
Specified	2	2	1	1	0	0	2,784
Cachou	3	8	1	2	3	2	2,763
Bezique	2	3	1	0	1	1	2,700
Set Table	3	9	1	2	0	6	2,637
Anna Of Saxony	3	6	1	2	1	2	2,616
Wild Applause	3	6	1	0	1	4	2,616
Jumaira Star	3	6	1	0	0	5	2,616
Draft Board	3	6	1	1	1	3	2,616
Ivory Palm	2	1	1	0	0	0	2,595
Stepanov	2	3	1	0	1	1	2,511
Woodhaunter	2	4	1	2	1	0	2,459
Majjra	3	3	1	0	0	2	2,385
Key Suspect	3	4	1	0	2	1	2,385
Coniston Water	3	3	1	0	0	2	2,364
Ansillo	2	2	1	0	0	1	2,295
Silica	3	7	1	2	0	4	2,070
Laughsome	3	5	1	1	1	2	2,070
Half Term	2	1	1	0	0	0	2,070
Fiala	4	3	1	1	0	1	2,069
Jumaira Shark	3	7	1	0	2	4	1,892
North Russia	3	4	1	2	0	1	1,702
Vratislav	3	2	1	1	0	0	1,532
So Smug	3	7	1	1	1	4	1,506
La Kermesse	3	8	1	0	2	5	1,109

WINNING OWNERS

	Races Won	Value £		Races Won	Value £
Sheikh Mohammed	72	502,657	Ali Saeed	1	9,000
K Abdulla	17	76,769	C M Watt	1	7,304
Sheikh Ahmed Al Maktoum	7	41,292	Saeed Manana	1	4,078
Landon Knight	3	30,455	R E Sangster	1	2,616
Pin Oak Stable	3	23,232	C A B St George	1	2,069
Ms Rachel D S Hood	2	19,520	Mrs Elizabeth Moran	1	1,506
Lord Derby	2	9,348			

Favourites	59-158	37.3%	+ 3.16	Total winning prize-money			£729,846
Longest winning sequence			4	Average SP of winner			3.8/1
Longest losing sequence			25	Return on stakes invested			4.5%
1991 Form	86-384	22.4%	- 7.12	1989 Form	28-144	19.4%	- 14.66
1990 Form	87-354	24.6%	+ 12.87	1988 Form	0-0		

N A GRAHAM (Newmarket)

	No. of Horses	Races Run	1st	2nd	3rd	Unpl	Per cent	£1 Level Stake
2-y-o	5	19	2	3	0	14	10.5	- 14.71
3-y-o	10	49	2	6	7	34	4.1	- 34.50
4-y-o+	4	18	2	0	2	14	11.1	+ 5.00
Totals	19	86	6	9	9	62	7.0	- 44.21

Jan	Feb	Mar	Apr	May	Jun	Jul	Aug	Sep	Oct/Nov
0-1	0-2	0-0	1-7	0-9	1-13	3-15	1-13	0-10	0-16

Winning Jockeys	W-R	£1 Level Stake			W-R	£1 Level Stake
M Roberts	4-11	+ 13.79	R Cochrane		1-18	- 7.00
S Cauthen	1-3	+ 3.00				

Winning Courses		£1 Level Stake				
Ascot	1-2	+ 15.00	Sandown		1-5	+ 1.00
Southwell (AW)	1-2	- 0.09	Lingfield (AW)		1-8	- 5.62
Wolverhampton	1-3	+ 8.00	Leicester		1-10	- 6.50

Winning Horses	Age	Races Run	1st	2nd	3rd	Unpl	Win £
Gay Glint	5	7	2	0	0	5	14,596
Foolish Heart	2	4	2	2	0	0	3,771
Karamoja	3	8	1	1	2	4	2,324
Free Mover	3	4	1	0	2	1	1,646

Favourites	1-9	11.1%	- 7.09	Total winning prize-money			£22,337
1991 Form	7-81	8.6%	- 24.56	1989 Form	0-0		
1990 Form	6-73	8.2%	- 38.50	1988 Form	11-71	15.5%	- 32.60

B GUBBY (Bagshot, Surrey)

	No. of Horses	Races Run	1st	2nd	3rd	Unpl	Per cent	£1 Level Stake
2-y-o	4	13	0	0	1	12	-	- 13.00
3-y-o	2	10	0	0	0	10	-	- 10.00
4-y-o+	7	47	2	4	3	38	4.3	- 13.00
Totals	13	70	2	4	4	60	2.9	- 36.00

Jan	Feb	Mar	Apr	May	Jun	Jul	Aug	Sep	Oct/Nov
0-3	0-5	0-3	0-8	0-11	1-16	1-11	0-10	0-3	0-0

Winning Jockeys	W-R	£1 Level Stake			W-R	£1 Level Stake
Mr P Daw	1-1	+ 7.00	C Avery		1-6	+ 20.00

Winning Courses						
Goodwood	1-12	+ 14.00	Lingfield (AW)		1-14	- 6.00

Winning Horses	Age	Races Run	1st	2nd	3rd	Unpl	Win £
Belfort Ruler	5	14	1	1	1	11	6,212
USA Dollar	5	14	1	2	1	10	1,660

Favourites	0-3	Total winning prize-money	£7,872

1991 Form	0-52			1989 Form	0-39		
1990 Form	7-49	14.3%	+ 74.50	1988 Form	1-30	3.3%	- 15.00

R GUEST (Newmarket)

	No. of Horses	Races Run	1st	2nd	3rd	Unpl	Per cent	£1 Level Stake
2-y-o	5	13	3	0	1	9	23.1	+ 4.50
3-y-o	8	42	3	4	5	30	7.1	- 28.25
4-y-o+	5	27	6	2	0	19	22.2	+ 32.25
Totals	18	82	12	6	6	58	14.6	+ 8.50

BY MONTH

2-y-o	W-R	Per cent	£1 Level Stake	3-y-o	W-R	Per cent	£1 Level Stake
January	0-0	-	0.00	January	1-1	100.0	+ 4.50
February	0-0	-	0.00	February	0-1	-	- 1.00
March	0-0	-	0.00	March	0-1	-	- 1.00
April	0-0	-	0.00	April	0-3	-	- 3.00
May	0-0	-	0.00	May	0-6	-	- 6.00
June	0-0	-	0.00	June	0-11	-	- 11.00
July	2-4	50.0	+ 10.50	July	2-11	18.2	- 2.75
August	1-2	50.0	+ 1.00	August	0-1	-	- 1.00
September	0-2	-	- 2.00	September	0-5	-	- 5.00
Oct/Nov	0-5	-	- 5.00	Oct/Nov	0-2	-	- 2.00

4-y-o+	W-R	Per cent	£1 Level Stake	Totals	W-R	Per cent	£1 Level Stake
January	0-0	-	0.00	January	1-1	100.0	+ 4.50
February	1-2	50.0	+ 0.75	February	1-3	33.3	- 0.25
March	0-1	-	- 1.00	March	0-2	-	- 2.00
April	0-2	-	- 2.00	April	0-5	-	- 5.00
May	1-5	20.0	+ 10.00	May	1-11	9.1	+ 4.00
June	1-4	25.0	+ 6.00	June	1-15	6.7	- 5.00
July	1-3	33.3	+ 2.50	July	5-18	27.8	+ 10.25
August	0-2	-	- 2.00	August	1-5	20.0	- 2.00
September	2-4	50.0	+ 22.00	September	2-11	18.2	+ 15.00
Oct/Nov	0-4	-	- 4.00	Oct/Nov	0-11	-	- 11.00

DISTANCE

2-y-o	W-R	Per cent	£1 Level Stake	3-y-o	W-R	Per cent	£1 Level Stake
5f-6f	3-6	50.0	+ 11.50	5f-6f	0-9	-	- 9.00
7f-8f	0-7	-	- 7.00	7f-8f	2-19	10.5	- 8.00
9f-13f	0-0	-	0.00	9f-13f	1-12	8.3	- 9.25
14f+	0-0	-	0.00	14f+	0-2	-	- 2.00

4-y-o+	W-R	Per cent	£1 Level Stake	Totals	W-R	Per cent	£1 Level Stake
5f-6f	0-2	-	- 2.00	5f-6f	3-17	17.6	+ 0.50
7f-8f	6-14	42.9	+ 45.25	7f-8f	8-40	20.0	+ 30.25
9f-13f	0-11	-	- 11.00	9f-13f	1-23	4.3	- 20.25
14f+	0-0	-	0.00	14f+	0-2	-	- 2.00

TYPE OF RACE

Non-Handicaps	W-R	Per cent	£1 Level Stake	Handicaps	W-R	Per cent	£1 Level Stake
2-y-o	3-13	23.1	+ 4.50	2-y-o	0-0	-	0.00
3-y-o	1-17	5.9	- 11.50	3-y-o	1-15	6.7	- 9.50
4-y-o+	2-4	50.0	+ 11.75	4-y-o+	3-18	16.7	+ 10.50
Selling	2-7	28.6	+ 10.75	Selling	0-0	-	0.00
Apprentice	0-3	-	- 3.00	Apprentice	0-5	-	- 5.00
Amat/Ladies	0-0	-	0.00	Amat/Ladies	0-0	-	0.00
Totals	8-44	18.2	+ 12.50	Totals	4-38	10.5	- 4.00

COURSE GRADE

	W-R	Per cent	£1 Level Stake
Group 1	3-19	15.8	+ 5.00
Group 2	2-14	14.3	- 1.00
Group 3	2-22	9.1	- 10.25
Group 4	5-27	18.5	+ 14.75

FIRST TIME OUT

	W-R	Per cent	£1 Level Stake
2-y-o	2-5	40.0	+ 7.00
3-y-o	1-8	12.5	- 2.50
4-y-o+	2-5	40.0	+ 12.75
Totals	5-18	27.8	+ 17.25

JOCKEYS RIDING

	W-R	Per cent	£1 Level Stake		W-R	Per cent	£1 Level Stake
N Day	2-5	40.0	+ 3.25	S Eiffert	2-11	18.2	+ 17.00
M Roberts	2-6	33.3	+ 8.50	J Weaver	1-1	100.0	+ 4.50
D Harrison	2-6	33.3	+ 10.00	Pat Eddery	1-2	50.0	+ 8.00
C Hawksley	2-11	18.2	- 2.75				

G Baxter	0-7	P Robinson	0-2	L Dettori		0-1
J Quinn	0-4	R Cochrane	0-2	S Cauthen		0-1
L Piggott	0-4	W Newnes	0-2	S Davies		0-1
M Hills	0-3	W Woods	0-2	W Carson		0-1
Antoinette Armes	0-2	D Biggs	0-1	Wally Swinburn		0-1
Dale Gibson	0-2	F Norton	0-1			
J Lowe	0-2	J Reid	0-1			

COURSE RECORD

	Total W-R	Non-Handicaps 2-y-o	Non-Handicaps 3-y-o+	Handicaps 2-y-o	Handicaps 3-y-o+	Per cent	£1 Level Stake
Lingfield (AW)	2-7	0-0	1-2	0-0	1-5	28.6	+ 1.25
Southwell (AW)	2-9	0-0	2-6	0-0	0-3	22.2	+ 19.00
Catterick	1-1	0-0	0-0	0-0	1-1	100.0	+ 4.50
Salisbury	1-1	1-1	0-0	0-0	0-0	100.0	+ 2.00
Windsor	1-1	1-1	0-0	0-0	0-0	100.0	+ 8.00
Goodwood	1-2	1-1	0-1	0-0	0-0	50.0	+ 3.50
Doncaster	1-4	0-2	0-0	0-0	1-2	25.0	+ 9.00
Brighton	1-7	0-0	0-2	0-0	1-5	14.3	+ 3.00
Newmarket	1-10	0-1	1-6	0-0	0-3	10.0	- 4.50
Yarmouth	1-13	0-4	1-5	0-0	0-4	7.7	- 10.25

Folkestone	0-5	Redcar	0-2	Pontefract	0-1
Edinburgh	0-4	Beverley	0-1	Ripon	0-1
Leicester	0-4	Chester	0-1	Thirsk	0-1
Kempton	0-2	Epsom	0-1	Warwick	0-1
Nottingham	0-2	Lingfield	0-1		

WINNING HORSES

	Age	Races Run	1st	2nd	3rd	Unpl	Win £
Indian Slave	4	8	3	1	0	4	21,882
Millyant	2	3	2	0	0	1	21,672
By Arrangement	3	8	2	1	2	3	5,173
Gallery Artist	4	7	2	0	0	5	4,635
Exclusively Yours	2	2	1	0	0	1	3,077
Level Up	3	3	1	0	1	1	2,187
Sauvignon	4	6	1	0	0	5	2,108

WINNING OWNERS

	Races Won	Value £		Races Won	Value £
R Axford	3	21,882	Rae Guest	2	4,635
Bradmill Ltd	2	21,672	Christopher P J Brown	2	4,295
C J Mills	2	5,173	Mrs Lesley Mills	1	3,077

Favourites	3-8	37.5%	+ 3.00	Total winning prize-money			£60,734

Longest winning sequence			3	Average SP of winner			6.5/1
Longest losing sequence			18	Return on stakes invested			10.4%

1991 Form	5-92	5.4%	- 60.87	1989 Form	7-99	7.1%	- 24.50
1990 Form	7-151	4.6%	-110.95				

W J HAGGAS (Newmarket)

	No. of Horses	Races Run	1st	2nd	3rd	Unpl	Per cent	£1 Level Stake
2-y-o	11	38	5	3	5	25	13.2	- 11.87
3-y-o	12	48	6	9	5	28	12.5	- 20.37
4-y-o+	8	42	1	2	3	36	2.4	- 25.00
Totals	31	128	12	14	13	89	9.4	- 57.24

BY MONTH

2-y-o	W-R	Per cent	£1 Level Stake	3-y-o	W-R	Per cent	£1 Level Stake
January	0-0	-	0.00	January	1-4	25.0	- 1.75
February	0-0	-	0.00	February	0-2	-	- 2.00
March	0-0	-	0.00	March	0-0	-	0.00
April	1-1	100.0	+ 0.80	April	1-8	12.5	- 5.50
May	0-4	-	- 4.00	May	1-11	9.1	- 8.00
June	0-1	-	- 1.00	June	1-7	14.3	+ 1.00
July	2-2	100.0	+ 12.83	July	0-7	-	- 7.00
August	1-10	10.0	- 6.50	August	0-5	-	- 5.00
September	1-9	11.1	- 3.00	September	2-3	66.7	+ 8.88
Oct/Nov	0-11	-	- 11.00	Oct/Nov	0-1	-	- 1.00

4-y-o+	W-R	Per cent	£1 Level Stake	Totals	W-R	Per cent	£1 Level Stake
January	0-2	-	- 2.00	January	1-6	16.7	- 3.75
February	0-2	-	- 2.00	February	0-4	-	- 4.00
March	1-5	20.0	+ 12.00	March	1-5	20.0	+ 12.00
April	0-6	-	- 6.00	April	2-15	13.3	- 10.70
May	0-5	-	- 5.00	May	1-20	5.0	- 17.00
June	0-4	-	- 4.00	June	1-12	8.3	- 4.00
July	0-8	-	- 8.00	July	2-17	11.8	- 2.17
August	0-3	-	- 3.00	August	1-18	5.6	- 14.50
September	0-3	-	- 3.00	September	3-15	20.0	+ 2.88
Oct/Nov	0-4	-	- 4.00	Oct/Nov	0-16	-	- 16.00

DISTANCE

2-y-o	W-R	Per cent	£1 Level Stake	3-y-o	W-R	Per cent	£1 Level Stake
5f-6f	4-21	19.0	+ 1.63	5f-6f	0-3	-	- 3.00
7f-8f	1-17	5.9	- 13.50	7f-8f	6-32	18.8	- 4.37
9f-13f	0-0	-	0.00	9f-13f	0-13	-	- 13.00
14f+	0-0	-	0.00	14f+	0-0	-	0.00

4-y-o+	W-R	Per cent	£1 Level Stake	Totals	W-R	Per cent	£1 Level Stake
5f-6f	0-6	-	- 6.00	5f-6f	4-30	13.3	- 7.37
7f-8f	1-18	5.6	- 1.00	7f-8f	8-67	11.9	- 18.87
9f-13f	0-14	-	- 14.00	9f-13f	0-27	-	- 27.00
14f+	0-4	-	- 4.00	14f+	0-4	-	- 4.00

TYPE OF RACE

Non-Handicaps	W-R	Per cent	£1 Level Stake	Handicaps	W-R	Per cent	£1 Level Stake
2-y-o	4-24	16.7	- 1.37	2-y-o	1-11	9.1	- 7.50
3-y-o	4-22	18.2	- 11.37	3-y-o	1-21	4.8	- 13.00
4-y-o+	0-8	-	- 8.00	4-y-o+	1-31	3.2	- 14.00
Selling	0-4	-	- 4.00	Selling	0-1	-	- 1.00
Apprentice	0-1	-	- 1.00	Apprentice	1-5	20.0	+ 4.00
Amat/Ladies	0-0	-	0.00	Amat/Ladies	0-0	-	0.00
Totals	8-59	13.6	- 25.74	Totals	4-69	5.8	- 31.50

COURSE GRADE

	W-R	Per cent	£1 Level Stake
Group 1	4-62	6.5	- 17.00
Group 2	3-23	13.0	- 11.37
Group 3	2-19	10.5	- 13.00
Group 4	3-24	12.5	- 15.87

FIRST TIME OUT

	W-R	Per cent	£1 Level Stake
2-y-o	1-11	9.1	- 9.20
3-y-o	1-12	8.3	- 9.50
4-y-o+	1-8	12.5	+ 9.00
Totals	3-31	9.7	- 9.70

JOCKEYS RIDING

	W-R	Per cent	£1 Level Stake		W-R	Per cent	£1 Level Stake
M Hills	4-28	14.3	- 4.70	J Quinn	2-16	12.5	+ 4.00
G Duffield	2-6	33.3	+ 0.38	M Roberts	1-6	16.7	- 4.17
Sally R-Howes	2-7	28.6	+ 10.00	N Day	1-32	3.1	- 29.75

L Piggott	0-5	Antoinette Armes	0-1	Ron Hillis	0-1
Pat Eddery	0-5	D Holland	0-1	S Cauthen	0-1
B Rouse	0-3	Emma O'Gorman	0-1	W Carson	0-1
R Hills	0-3	F Norton	0-1	W Newnes	0-1
C Rutter	0-2	J Carroll	0-1	W Ryan	0-1
J Williams	0-2	J Weaver	0-1		
A Munro	0-1	K Darley	0-1		

COURSE RECORD

	Total W-R	Non-Handicaps 2-y-o	3-y-o+	Handicaps 2-y-o	3-y-o+	Per cent	£1 Level Stake
Ripon	2-4	2-3	0-1	0-0	0-0	50.0	- 0.37
Sandown	2-6	1-2	0-0	0-0	1-4	33.3	+ 9.00
Carlisle	1-1	0-0	1-1	0-0	0-0	100.0	+ 1.88
Hamilton	1-1	0-0	1-1	0-0	0-0	100.0	+ 1.50
Doncaster	1-2	0-0	0-1	0-0	1-1	50.0	+ 15.00
Epsom	1-3	1-1	0-1	0-0	0-1	33.3	+ 10.00
Warwick	1-3	0-0	1-3	0-0	0-0	33.3	0.00
Yarmouth	1-10	0-4	0-3	1-2	0-1	10.0	- 6.50
Chester	1-11	0-1	0-2	0-1	1-7	9.1	- 3.00
Southwell (AW)	1-12	0-1	1-3	0-0	0-8	8.3	- 9.75

Newmarket	0-20	Lingfield	0-4	Windsor	0-2
Ascot	0-6	Brighton	0-2	Chepstow	0-1
Lingfield (AW)	0-6	Haydock	0-2	Edinburgh	0-1
Newbury	0-6	Leicester	0-2	Pontefract	0-1
York	0-6	Newcastle	0-2	Wolverhampton	0-1
Goodwood	0-5	Nottingham	0-2		
Kempton	0-4	Thirsk	0-2		

WINNING HORSES

	Age	Races Run	1st	2nd	3rd	Unpl	Win £
High Low	4	8	1	1	0	6	45,533
Hand On Heart	3	12	4	3	2	3	10,027
Awestruck	2	7	2	1	1	3	6,208
By Hand	3	10	1	3	1	5	2,999
Jobie	2	2	1	0	0	1	2,863
Huffa	2	3	1	0	1	1	2,415
St James's Antigua	3	2	1	0	0	1	2,148
Premium	2	7	1	0	1	5	1,548

WINNING OWNERS

	Races Won	Value £		Races Won	Value £
B Haggas	2	47,948	J A Redmond	1	2,863
Mrs M M Haggas	5	13,026	Sheikh Amin Dahlawi	1	2,148
Mrs David Thompson	2	6,208	Kennet Valley Th'breds Ltd	1	1,548

Favourites	6-16	37.5%	- 0.74	Total winning prize-money			£73,740
Longest winning sequence			1	Average SP of winner			4.9/1
Longest losing sequence			19	Return on stakes invested			-44.7%
1991 Form	27-136	19.9%	+ 37.00	1989 Form	16-153	10.5%	- 66.04
1990 Form	21-141	14.9%	- 20.68	1988 Form	14-132	10.6%	- 67.75

W W HAIGH (Malton, North Yorks)

	No. of Horses	Races Run	1st	2nd	3rd	Unpl	Per cent	£1 Level Stake
2-y-o	4	13	0	0	2	11	-	- 13.00
3-y-o	7	32	2	1	4	25	6.3	- 24.87
4-y-o+	9	47	6	6	6	29	12.8	+ 9.50
Totals	20	92	8	7	12	65	8.7	- 28.37

Jan	Feb	Mar	Apr	May	Jun	Jul	Aug	Sep	Oct/Nov
0-4	0-4	2-5	0-4	2-14	2-15	2-13	0-15	0-8	0-10

Winning Jockeys	W-R	£1 Level Stake		W-R	£1 Level Stake
A Culhane	3-15	+ 17.50	D McKeown	2-28	- 17.50
F Norton	2-10	+ 8.00	G Duffield	1-2	+ 0.63

Winning Courses	W-R	£1 Level Stake		W-R	£1 Level Stake
Southwell (AW)	3-15	+ 9.00	Newcastle	1-5	- 0.50
Beverley	3-17	+ 10.63	Ripon	1-6	+ 1.50

Winning Horses	Age	Races Run	1st	2nd	3rd	Unpl	Win £
Major Mouse	4	7	3	0	0	4	12,846
Round By The River	3	6	2	1	0	3	4,970
Swinging Lady	4	13	2	3	0	8	4,708
Steppey Lane	7	5	1	0	2	2	2,108

Favourites	1-4	25.0%	- 1.37	Total winning prize-money	£24,632

1991 Form	7-80	8.8%	- 48.29	1989 Form	3-65	4.6%	- 16.00
1990 Form	5-87	5.7%	- 19.00	1988 Form	3-88	3.4%	- 54.12

MISS S E HALL (Middleham, North Yorks)

	No. of Horses	Races Run	1st	2nd	3rd	Unpl	Per cent	£1 Level Stake
2-y-o	11	48	5	4	5	34	10.4	+ 6.90
3-y-o	4	15	2	1	1	11	13.3	- 5.62
4-y-o+	5	21	2	0	1	18	9.5	- 10.80
Totals	20	84	9	5	7	63	10.7	- 9.52

Jan	Feb	Mar	Apr	May	Jun	Jul	Aug	Sep	Oct/Nov
0-0	0-0	0-4	0-8	1-4	2-11	3-15	2-15	1-22	0-5

Winning Jockeys	W-R	£1 Level Stake			W-R	£1 Level Stake
N Connorton	6-34	+ 18.98	G Hind		1-4	+ 8.00
N Kennedy	1-3	0.00	O Pears		1-5	+ 1.50

Winning Courses	W-R	£1 Level Stake			W-R	£1 Level Stake
Ripon	3-10	+ 4.70	Catterick		1-3	- 0.12
Redcar	2-16	- 2.60	Carlisle		1-6	+ 0.50
Hamilton	1-2	+ 1.00	Ayr		1-8	+ 26.00

Winning Horses	Age	Races Run	1st	2nd	3rd	Unpl	Win £
Silverlocks	2	6	2	1	0	3	6,499
Royal Girl	5	9	2	0	0	7	4,377
Tancred Grange	3	7	1	0	0	6	2,736
Royal Diva	2	5	1	0	1	3	2,685
Make Mine A Double	2	7	1	0	1	5	2,285
Crept Out	3	5	1	1	1	2	2,259
Amerigue	2	8	1	2	1	4	1,674

Favourites	4-9	44.4%	+ 0.48	Total winning prize-money			£22,514

1991 Form	6-88	6.8%	- 39.17	1989 Form	6-81	7.4%	- 32.75
1990 Form	12-133	9.0%	- 46.35	1988 Form	7-90	7.8%	- 13.75

G A HAM (Axbridge, Somerset)

	No. of Horses	Races Run	1st	2nd	3rd	Unpl	Per cent	£1 Level Stake
2-y-o	0	0	0	0	0	0	-	0.00
3-y-o	2	10	0	0	0	10	-	- 10.00
4-y-o+	9	23	1	1	0	21	4.3	- 15.00
Totals	11	33	1	1	0	31	3.0	- 25.00

Jan	Feb	Mar	Apr	May	Jun	Jul	Aug	Sep	Oct/Nov
0-0	0-0	0-2	0-3	0-4	0-2	0-11	1-6	0-5	0-0

Winning Jockey	W-R	£1 Level Stake	Winning Course	W-R	£1 Level Stake
D Harrison	1-3	+ 5.00	Redcar	1-1	+ 7.00

Winning Horse	Age	Races Run	1st	2nd	3rd	Unpl	Win £
Premier Princess	6	6	1	1	0	4	2,924

Favourites	0-2		Total winning prize-money	£2,924

1991 Form	1-21	4.8%	+ 5.00	1990 Form	0-7

M D HAMMOND (Middleham, North Yorks)

	No. of Horses	Races Run	1st	2nd	3rd	Unpl	Per cent	£1 Level Stake
2-y-o	0	0	0	0	0	0	-	0.00
3-y-o	1	2	0	1	0	1	-	- 2.00
4-y-o+	18	55	9	3	1	42	16.4	- 0.49
Totals	19	57	9	4	1	43	15.8	- 2.49

Jan	Feb	Mar	Apr	May	Jun	Jul	Aug	Sep	Oct/Nov
0-1	0-1	0-1	0-4	0-4	1-6	2-8	4-13	0-15	2-4

Winning Jockeys	W-R	£1 Level Stake			W-R	£1 Level Stake
G Duffield	2-4	+ 5.00		K Darley	1-2	+ 7.00
A Lakeman	2-7	+ 3.75		J Carroll	1-8	+ 7.00
J Weaver	1-1	+ 1.38		D McKeown	1-9	- 6.62
Mrs L Pearce	1-1	+ 5.00				

Winning Courses						
Edinburgh	3-5	+ 17.38		Thirsk	1-3	+ 1.00
Redcar	2-6	+ 3.75		Hamilton	1-5	- 2.62
Catterick	1-2	+ 7.00		Ripon	1-6	+ 1.00

Winning Horses	Age	Races Run	1st	2nd	3rd	Unpl	Win £
Flashy's Son	4	10	4	2	0	4	10,710
Explosive Speed	4	4	2	0	0	2	5,868
Heliopsis	4	6	2	0	1	3	5,785
Routing	4	10	1	1	0	8	2,295

Favourites	3-6	50.0%	+ 6.13	Total winning prize-money			£24,658
1991 Form	1-42	2.4%	- 31.00	1990 Form	5-25	20.0%	+ 15.50

B HANBURY (Newmarket)

	No. of Horses	Races Run	1st	2nd	3rd	Unpl	Per cent	£1 Level Stake
2-y-o	19	68	10	11	11	36	14.7	- 38.04
3-y-o	37	197	20	29	27	121	10.2	- 40.57
4-y-o+	7	43	9	4	4	26	20.9	+ 13.13
Totals	63	308	39	44	42	183	12.7	- 65.48

BY MONTH

2-y-o	W-R	Per cent	£1 Level Stake	3-y-o	W-R	Per cent	£1 Level Stake
January	0-0	-	0.00	January	0-0	-	0.00
February	0-0	-	0.00	February	0-1	-	- 1.00
March	0-0	-	0.00	March	0-5	-	- 5.00
April	0-3	-	- 3.00	April	2-25	8.0	+ 1.00
May	1-5	20.0	- 1.00	May	4-29	13.8	+ 3.50
June	1-7	14.3	- 2.67	June	2-31	6.5	- 19.80
July	3-14	21.4	- 5.75	July	1-26	3.8	- 22.75
August	1-10	10.0	- 6.75	August	3-28	10.7	- 5.50
September	1-15	6.7	- 13.60	September	5-34	14.7	- 3.02
Oct/Nov	3-14	21.4	- 5.27	Oct/Nov	3-18	16.7	+ 12.00

4-y-o+	W-R	Per cent	£1 Level Stake	Totals	W-R	Per cent	£1 Level Stake
January	0-0	-	0.00	January	0-0	-	0.00
February	0-0	-	0.00	February	0-1	-	- 1.00
March	0-4	-	- 4.00	March	0-9	-	- 9.00
April	1-5	20.0	- 2.25	April	3-33	9.1	- 4.25
May	2-7	28.6	- 1.37	May	7-41	17.1	+ 1.13
June	1-3	33.3	+ 3.00	June	4-41	9.8	- 19.47
July	0-4	-	- 4.00	July	4-44	9.1	- 32.50
August	2-9	22.2	+ 3.00	August	6-47	12.8	- 9.25
September	3-7	42.9	+ 22.75	September	9-56	16.1	+ 6.13
Oct/Nov	0-4	-	- 4.00	Oct/Nov	6-36	16.7	+ 2.73

DISTANCE

2-y-o	W-R	Per cent	£1 Level Stake	3-y-o	W-R	Per cent	£1 Level Stake
5f-6f	3-23	13.0	- 13.62	5f-6f	1-12	8.3	- 6.50
7f-8f	7-45	15.6	- 24.42	7f-8f	14-99	14.1	+ 4.83
9f-13f	0-0	-	0.00	9f-13f	3-81	3.7	- 57.90
14f+	0-0	-	0.00	14f+	2-5	40.0	+ 19.00

4-y-o+	W-R	Per cent	£1 Level Stake	Totals	W-R	Per cent	£1 Level Stake
5f-6f	1-2	50.0	+ 0.75	5f-6f	5-37	13.5	- 19.37
7f-8f	3-15	20.0	+ 14.88	7f-8f	24-159	15.1	- 4.71
9f-13f	5-25	20.0	- 1.50	9f-13f	8-106	7.5	- 59.40
14f+	0-1	-	- 1.00	14f+	2-6	33.3	+ 18.00

TYPE OF RACE

Non-Handicaps	W-R	Per cent	£1 Level Stake	Handicaps	W-R	Per cent	£1 Level Stake
2-y-o	9-55	16.4	- 27.54	2-y-o	0-9	-	- 9.00
3-y-o	11-101	10.9	- 13.57	3-y-o	8-81	9.9	- 21.00
4-y-o+	1-5	20.0	- 2.25	4-y-o+	7-32	21.9	+ 15.88
Selling	1-13	7.7	- 10.50	Selling	0-2	-	- 2.00
Apprentice	1-5	20.0	+ 4.00	Apprentice	0-3	-	- 3.00
Amat/Ladies	0-0	-	0.00	Amat/Ladies	1-2	50.0	+ 3.50
Totals	23-179	12.8	- 49.86	Totals	16-129	12.4	- 15.62

173

Hanbury B

COURSE GRADE

	W-R	Per cent	£1 Level Stake
Group 1	15-152	9.9	- 37.42
Group 2	6-39	15.4	- 5.95
Group 3	13-78	16.7	- 18.19
Group 4	5-39	12.8	- 3.92

FIRST TIME OUT

	W-R	Per cent	£1 Level Stake
2-y-o	1-19	5.3	- 16.12
3-y-o	2-37	5.4	- 19.00
4-y-o+	0-7	-	- 7.00
Totals	3-63	4.8	- 42.12

JOCKEYS RIDING

	W-R	Per cent	£1 Level Stake
B Raymond	15-96	15.6	- 16.32
W Ryan	5-27	18.5	+ 2.25
W R Swinburn	4-45	8.9	- 20.92
L Dettori	3-7	42.9	+ 12.88
M Roberts	2-7	28.6	- 1.12
L Piggott	2-9	22.2	+ 2.25
V Bray	2-27	7.4	- 1.00

	W-R	Per cent	£1 Level Stake
J Lloyd	1-1	100.0	+ 6.50
F Grasso-Caprioli	1-1	100.0	+ 4.50
J Reid	1-2	50.0	+ 4.00
M Hills	1-3	33.3	+ 12.00
R Cochrane	1-5	20.0	+ 1.00
N Carlisle	1-9	11.1	- 2.50

A Shoults	0-9	A McGlone	0-1	N Adams	0-1
D Harrison	0-7	B Crossley	0-1	N Kennedy	0-1
G Baxter	0-5	B Rouse	0-1	P Turner	0-1
G Duffield	0-5	Dale Gibson	0-1	Pat Eddery	0-1
D McKeown	0-4	E Johnson	0-1	Paul Eddery	0-1
C Hawksley	0-3	G Hind	0-1	R Fox	0-1
W Carson	0-3	J Carroll	0-1	R Havlin	0-1
A Munro	0-2	J Fortune	0-1	S Cauthen	0-1
J Fanning	0-2	J Lowe	0-1	S Whitworth	0-1
M Birch	0-2	J Quinn	0-1	T Williams	0-1
P Robinson	0-2	M Wigham	0-1	W Woods	0-1
R Hills	0-2	Mr M Armytage	0-1		

COURSE RECORD

	Total W-R	Non-Handicaps 2-y-o	Non-Handicaps 3-y-o+	Handicaps 2-y-o	Handicaps 3-y-o+	Per cent	£1 Level Stake
Hamilton	4-17	0-1	3-8	0-0	1-8	23.5	- 4.94
Pontefract	3-12	0-1	1-5	0-0	2-6	25.0	- 1.75
York	3-13	2-3	0-3	0-0	1-7	23.1	+ 1.08
Wolverhampton	3-15	2-6	0-2	0-2	1-5	20.0	+ 8.83
Redcar	2-8	1-2	1-2	0-0	0-4	25.0	+ 7.00
Doncaster	2-9	0-1	1-3	0-1	1-4	22.2	+ 23.00
Leicester	2-11	0-4	0-4	0-0	2-3	18.2	- 2.25
Newbury	2-11	1-3	1-3	0-0	0-5	18.2	- 1.50
Goodwood	2-13	0-1	0-3	0-0	2-9	15.4	+ 0.50
Newmarket	2-39	0-14	1-17	0-1	1-7	5.1	- 17.00
Warwick	1-3	0-0	1-3	0-0	0-0	33.3	+ 6.00
Windsor	1-3	0-0	0-1	0-0	1-2	33.3	+ 0.25
Edinburgh	1-4	1-1	0-2	0-0	0-1	25.0	- 1.75
Lingfield	1-4	0-0	0-1	0-1	1-2	25.0	+ 2.00
Salisbury	1-4	0-0	0-2	0-0	1-2	25.0	+ 3.65

Kempton	1-7	0-1	1-5	0-0	0-1	14.3	+ 0.50
Brighton	1-8	0-1	1-3	0-0	0-4	12.5	- 5.00
Nottingham	1-8	0-2	1-3	0-2	0-1	12.5	+ 5.00
Thirsk	1-8	1-2	0-4	0-0	0-2	12.5	- 6.60
Newcastle	1-11	0-2	1-8	0-0	0-1	9.1	- 2.00
Yarmouth	1-11	0-3	0-2	0-1	1-5	9.1	- 4.50
Beverley	1-13	0-2	0-5	0-0	1-6	7.7	- 7.00
Sandown	1-14	1-2	0-3	0-1	0-8	7.1	- 10.75
Haydock	1-18	1-2	0-9	0-0	0-7	5.6	- 14.25

Ascot	0-9	Folkestone	0-4	Epsom	0-2
Catterick	0-7	Carlisle	0-3	Southwell (AW)	0-2
Ayr	0-6	Chepstow	0-3	Lingfield (AW)	0-1
Ripon	0-5	Chester	0-2		

WINNING HORSES

		Races					Win
	Age	Run	1st	2nd	3rd	Unpl	£
White Crown	2	6	3	1	1	1	30,169
Surrey Dancer	4	12	4	1	1	6	12,304
Jahangir	3	11	2	1	0	8	10,557
Tik Fa	3	7	2	1	2	2	9,438
En Attendant	4	8	2	0	1	5	9,068
Owner's Dream	3	7	2	1	1	3	8,040
Stani	3	6	2	0	0	4	7,329
Lahoob	3	6	2	1	0	3	5,598
Ikteshaf	4	9	2	1	2	4	5,451
Soviet Secret	2	1	1	0	0	0	4,542
Bin Ajwaad	2	3	1	2	0	0	4,347
Moonlight Quest	4	5	1	1	0	3	3,132
Mashakel (USA)	3	7	1	0	1	5	3,028
Bold Boss	3	10	1	3	2	4	2,701
Oak Apple	3	6	1	2	0	3	2,679
Millfit	3	6	1	0	0	5	2,598
Neieb	3	7	1	1	2	3	2,532
Dixieland Melody	2	2	1	1	0	0	2,511
Massiba	3	5	1	0	2	2	2,448
Blue Blazer	2	6	1	1	1	3	2,427
Clear Honey	2	5	1	0	0	4	2,392
Sovereign Page	3	10	1	1	0	8	2,072
Teslemi	3	4	1	0	0	3	2,072
Alyafill	3	8	1	4	1	2	2,070
Rafah	3	8	1	3	1	3	1,932
Hawayah	2	4	1	0	2	1	1,918
Minshaar	2	3	1	0	1	1	1,319

WINNING OWNERS

	Races Won	Value £		Races Won	Value £
Saeed Suhail	8	43,860	Hilal Salem	2	4,530
B Hanbury	6	19,089	A Merza	1	4,347
Cronk Thoroughbred Racing Ltd	4	12,304	Mrs John Lamb	1	3,132
Abdullah Ali	3	11,508	O Zawawi	1	2,701
J R Ali	2	10,557	Z Kashiwagi	1	2,679
Muttar Salem	4	9,466	McHalapar Syndicate	1	2,427
Bernard Newton	2	9,068	Nasser Abdullah	1	2,392
Hamad Ali	1	4,542	Mrs J M Beeby	1	2,072

Favourites	10-31	32.3%	- 3.02	Total winning prize-money		£144,672
Longest winning sequence			2	Average SP of winner		5.2/1
Longest losing sequence			31	Return on stakes invested		-21.1%
1991 Form	36-302	11.9%	- 45.68	1989 Form	42-225	18.7%	+ 32.78
1990 Form	36-274	13.1%	- 51.86	1988 Form	40-298	13.4%	+ 9.64

R HANNON (East Everleigh, Wilts)

	No. of Horses	Races Run	1st	2nd	3rd	Unpl	Per cent	£1 Level Stake
2-y-o	102	485	73	56	62	294	15.1	- 155.40
3-y-o	70	440	55	49	43	293	12.5	- 89.75
4-y-o+	26	182	19	25	21	117	10.4	- 66.44
Totals	198	1107	147	130	126	704	13.3	- 311.59

BY MONTH

2-y-o	W-R	Per cent	£1 Level Stake	3-y-o	W-R	Per cent	£1 Level Stake
Mar/Apr	5-30	16.7	+ 9.50	Mar/Apr	10-80	12.5	- 34.29
May	15-47	31.9	- 6.18	May	16-85	18.8	+ 3.11
June	7-45	15.6	- 21.58	June	6-66	9.1	- 32.49
July	13-92	14.1	- 31.09	July	9-61	14.8	- 22.46
August	17-90	18.9	- 20.62	August	9-53	17.0	+ 33.50
September	6-94	6.4	- 54.59	September	2-54	3.7	- 29.00
Oct/Nov	10-87	11.5	- 26.84	Oct/Nov	3-41	7.3	- 11.50

4-y-o+	W-R	Per cent	£1 Level Stake	Totals	W-R	Per cent	£1 Level Stake
Mar/Apr	3-28	10.7	+ 4.75	Mar/Apr	18-138	13.0	- 20.04
May	6-32	18.8	+ 1.95	May	37-164	22.6	- 1.12
June	1-28	3.6	- 24.00	June	14-139	10.1	- 78.07
July	3-32	9.4	- 5.75	July	25-185	13.5	- 59.30
August	3-19	15.8	- 9.64	August	29-162	17.9	+ 3.24
September	3-24	12.5	- 7.75	September	11-172	6.4	- 91.34
Oct/Nov	0-19	-	- 19.00	Oct/Nov	13-147	8.8	- 57.34

DISTANCE

2-y-o	W-R	Per cent	£1 Level Stake	3-y-o	W-R	Per cent	£1 Level Stake
5f-6f	60-318	18.9	- 71.71	5f-6f	18-117	15.4	- 1.52
7f-8f	13-163	8.0	- 79.69	7f-8f	27-211	12.8	- 58.23
9f-13f	0-4	-	- 4.00	9f-13f	10-108	9.3	- 29.50
14f+	0-0	-	0.00	14f+	0-4	-	- 4.00

4-y-o+	W-R	Per cent	£1 Level Stake	Totals	W-R	Per cent	£1 Level Stake
5f-6f	5-36	13.9	+ 1.57	5f-6f	83-471	17.6	- 71.66
7f-8f	5-85	5.9	- 66.89	7f-8f	45-459	9.8	-204.81
9f-13f	9-55	16.4	+ 4.88	9f-13f	19-167	11.4	- 28.62
14f+	0-6	-	- 6.00	14f+	0-10	-	- 10.00

TYPE OF RACE

Non-Handicaps	W-R	Per cent	£1 Level Stake	Handicaps	W-R	Per cent	£1 Level Stake
2-y-o	61-370	16.5	-121.63	2-y-o	8-91	8.8	- 31.50
3-y-o	32-171	18.7	- 8.98	3-y-o	22-231	9.5	- 46.52
4-y-o+	12-48	25.0	+ 12.54	4-y-o+	7-121	5.8	- 70.25
Selling	3-29	10.3	- 9.00	Selling	0-3	-	- 3.00
Apprentice	1-5	20.0	+ 1.00	Apprentice	0-25	-	- 25.00
Amat/Ladies	1-4	25.0	- 0.25	Amat/Ladies	0-9	-	- 9.00
Totals	110-627	17.5	-126.32	Totals	37-480	7.7	-185.27

COURSE GRADE

	W-R	Per cent	£1 Level Stake
Group 1	72-663	10.9	-236.46
Group 2	34-178	19.1	- 31.99
Group 3	29-185	15.7	- 20.88
Group 4	12-81	14.8	- 22.26

FIRST TIME OUT

	W-R	Per cent	£1 Level Stake
2-y-o	8-101	7.9	- 37.30
3-y-o	7-66	10.6	- 28.29
4-y-o+	3-24	12.5	- 11.43
Totals	18-191	9.4	- 77.02

JOCKEYS RIDING

	W-R	Per cent	£1 Level Stake		W-R	Per cent	£1 Level Stake
M Roberts	29-137	21.2	- 19.56	W R Swinburn	3-20	15.0	- 2.08
J Reid	22-126	17.5	- 11.34	R Hills	3-28	10.7	- 10.50
W Carson	15-69	21.7	- 16.25	M Hills	2-6	33.3	- 0.85
Pat Eddery	12-67	17.9	- 21.38	M J Kinane	2-16	12.5	+ 3.50
R Perham	11-129	8.5	- 52.25	R Cochrane	2-16	12.5	+ 7.50
B Raymond	9-89	10.1	- 20.50	N Day	1-1	100.0	+ 7.00
K Darley	6-25	24.0	- 7.53	D McKeown	1-2	50.0	+ 5.00
A McGlone	6-57	10.5	- 16.30	G Duffield	1-6	16.7	- 1.00
J Lloyd	5-29	17.2	+ 25.00	Paul Eddery	1-7	14.3	- 5.00
L Piggott	5-35	14.3	- 0.46	Mrs J Boggis	1-9	11.1	- 5.25
B Rouse	5-55	9.1	- 18.50	N Carlisle	1-11	9.1	- 7.50
L Dettori	3-11	27.3	+ 6.66	Mark Denaro	1-13	7.7	- 7.00

S Raymont	0-26	G Hind	0-4	D Harrison	0-2
D Gibbs	0-11	N Adams	0-4	D Holland	0-2
A Whelan	0-10	A Munro	0-3	J Quinn	0-2
P Robinson	0-10	D Biggs	0-3	B Doyle	0-1
G Bardwell	0-9	Dale Gibson	0-3	D Moffatt	0-1
T Quinn	0-9	Mr R Hannon	0-3	J Jones	0-1
T Williams	0-9	S Cauthen	0-3	J Williams	0-1
G Carter	0-7	Wendy Jones	0-3	M R Hunt	0-1
S Whitworth	0-5	A Clark	0-2	M Wigham	0-1
D O'Neill	0-4	B Crossley	0-2	Miss S Dalton	0-1

COURSE RECORD

	Total	Non-Handicaps		Handicaps		Per	£1 Level
	W-R	2-y-o	3-y-o+	2-y-o	3-y-o+	cent	Stake
Windsor	14-52	7-21	1-5	2-6	4-20	26.9	+ 48.61
Newmarket	13-128	6-39	5-30	0-15	2-44	10.2	- 30.93
Brighton	11-39	4-9	5-12	0-3	2-15	28.2	+ 4.42
Goodwood	11-84	4-32	3-17	0-5	4-30	13.1	- 16.48
Doncaster	10-65	6-20	1-15	1-7	2-23	15.4	- 19.08
Salisbury	10-74	4-27	4-15	0-1	2-31	13.5	- 27.44
Newbury	8-100	3-42	1-17	2-10	2-31	8.0	- 60.28
Ascot	7-58	4-18	2-9	1-6	0-25	12.1	- 2.87
Sandown	7-68	3-21	3-15	0-3	1-29	10.3	- 36.88
Folkestone	6-25	1-9	4-6	0-2	1-8	24.0	+ 10.98
Lingfield	6-35	2-11	3-8	0-2	1-14	17.1	- 10.54
Leicester	6-44	3-23	2-8	0-3	1-10	13.6	- 10.50
Kempton	6-54	2-16	2-14	1-4	1-20	11.1	- 16.17
Chester	5-19	3-9	1-4	1-2	0-4	26.3	+ 1.57
Bath	4-29	3-12	1-9	0-1	0-7	13.8	- 17.40
York	4-46	2-17	2-7	0-3	0-19	8.7	- 29.94
Epsom	3-31	0-5	1-10	0-2	2-14	9.7	- 5.50
Newcastle	2-5	1-1	0-0	0-1	1-3	40.0	+ 2.17
Wolverhampton	2-18	0-7	2-4	0-2	0-5	11.1	- 10.12
Nottingham	2-26	1-15	0-3	0-2	1-6	7.7	- 19.25
Warwick	2-28	0-6	0-11	0-3	2-8	7.1	- 22.37
Chepstow	2-29	0-7	2-8	0-4	0-10	6.9	- 21.09
Catterick	1-3	1-1	0-0	0-1	0-1	33.3	+ 0.75
Redcar	1-4	1-4	0-0	0-0	0-0	25.0	+ 3.00
Thirsk	1-4	1-2	0-1	0-0	0-1	25.0	0.00
Southwell (AW)	1-4	1-4	0-0	0-0	0-0	25.0	+ 1.50
Yarmouth	1-5	0-1	1-1	0-1	0-2	20.0	- 1.25
Haydock	1-17	1-4	0-7	0-2	0-4	5.9	- 13.50

Ayr	0-7	Lingfield (AW)	0-3	Ripon	0-3

WINNING HORSES

	Age	Races Run	1st	2nd	3rd	Unpl	Win £
Lyric Fantasy	2	6	5	1	0	0	185,605
Pips Pride	2	8	3	1	2	2	97,818
Mr Brooks	5	4	1	3	0	0	92,620
Beyton	3	5	2	0	1	2	73,815
Shalford	4	7	3	0	0	4	72,867
Niche	2	7	4	0	1	2	66,807
Son Pardo	2	7	4	0	0	3	64,159
Assessor	3	5	1	0	2	2	35,740
My Memoirs	3	3	1	0	1	1	23,378
Central City	3	8	2	1	1	4	21,086
Night Melody	2	14	6	2	3	3	16,478
Brigante Di Cielo	2	6	2	1	1	2	14,042
After The Last	2	8	3	0	1	4	13,555
Right Win	2	6	2	3	0	1	13,275
Lucky Lindy	3	5	1	1	0	3	12,794
Venture Capitalist	3	13	3	3	2	5	12,015
Brigg Fair	2	6	2	0	1	3	11,245
Notley	5	8	1	2	1	4	11,160
Sovereign Rock	3	12	3	2	0	7	10,552
Lady Debra Darley	3	10	3	2	2	3	9,654
Cradle Days	3	9	3	3	0	3	9,484
Sky Hunter	3	6	2	1	1	2	9,307
Rocality	3	8	2	0	1	5	8,701
Rockover	2	6	1	2	1	2	8,220
Scottish Bambi	4	9	3	0	0	6	7,991
In The Picture	3	8	3	1	1	3	7,615
Revelation	2	4	1	1	0	2	7,505
Grand Vitesse	3	8	2	0	0	6	7,504
Geisway	2	7	2	3	0	2	7,229
Elle Shaped	2	7	2	0	0	5	7,180
Arabellajill	3	10	2	0	2	6	6,963
Abingdon Flyer	4	10	3	1	3	3	6,123
Knight Of Mercy	6	10	1	0	2	7	6,056
Risk Zone	3	14	2	3	2	7	5,964
Temple Fortune	3	7	2	1	0	4	5,855
River Falls	3	9	1	1	0	7	5,796
Our Occasion	3	5	2	0	1	2	5,674
Petal Girl	3	7	2	2	1	2	5,663
Prince Rodney	3	6	2	1	0	3	5,567
Surprise Offer	2	8	2	1	3	2	5,549
Milagro	3	7	1	0	0	6	5,385
Miss Nosey Parker	3	7	1	0	1	5	5,299
Port Lucaya	2	8	2	1	3	2	5,253
Defenceless	2	9	2	2	1	4	4,895

Nicki-J	2	4	2	0	0	2	4,818
Lake Pleasant	2	3	1	0	1	1	4,503
True Story	2	8	2	1	0	5	4,332
Fortune Cay	2	5	2	1	0	2	4,329
Holly Golightly	2	5	1	1	2	1	4,273
Risk Me's Girl	2	9	2	1	1	5	4,189
Normanton Park	2	2	1	0	0	1	3,818
Port Sunlight	4	3	1	0	1	1	3,785
Redenham	2	3	1	1	0	1	3,655
Hopeful Bid	3	9	1	0	1	7	3,590
Rain Splash	2	8	1	1	0	6	3,558
Jackpot Star	2	5	1	1	0	3	3,522
Heavenly Risk	2	5	1	1	0	3	3,262
Seal Indigo	4	12	1	2	0	9	3,200
Dream Carrier	4	12	1	2	0	9	3,171
Forthwith	2	2	1	0	0	1	3,150
Kaloochi	2	7	1	0	0	6	3,132
Absonal	5	11	1	0	1	9	2,973
Striking Image	3	8	1	0	0	7	2,881
Southern Memories	2	5	1	0	0	4	2,783
Easy Access	2	6	1	1	1	3	2,783
Delta Downs	2	5	1	0	1	3	2,723
Anaheim	2	5	1	0	1	3	2,700
Primo Figlio	2	5	1	1	1	2	2,658
Brockton Dancer	2	10	1	1	2	6	2,637
Kandy Secret	3	7	1	0	2	4	2,630
Princely Favour	2	8	1	2	1	4	2,532
Tango Time	4	1	1	0	0	0	2,469
Prince Manki	2	6	1	1	0	4	2,469
Kentucky Starlet	3	9	1	0	0	8	2,448
Gotcha	3	10	1	2	0	7	2,406
Durneltor	4	12	1	4	1	6	2,385
Crusade	2	7	1	2	1	3	2,326
Power Lake	3	6	1	0	1	4	2,322
Systematic	3	7	1	0	1	5	2,322
Do Run Run	3	4	1	1	1	1	2,320
The Karaoke King	3	13	1	1	3	8	2,072
Efra	3	12	1	0	1	10	2,070
Chance To Dream	3	6	1	0	1	4	2,070
Pistol River	2	3	1	1	0	1	2,070
Regalsett	2	6	1	0	1	4	1,992
Top Pet	2	6	1	1	0	4	1,988
Courageous Knight	3	7	1	1	1	4	1,932
Sabo's Express	2	6	1	1	1	3	1,814
Michelozzo	6	2	1	0	0	1	1,646

WINNING OWNERS

	Races Won	Value £		Races Won	Value £
Lord Carnavon	11	257,961	Mrs C J Powell	2	6,666
D F Cock	6	157,842	J A Nichols	3	6,123
Mrs V S Grant	3	97,818	M W Grant	1	6,056
Paul Green	1	92,620	Simon Ellis Ltd	2	5,674
N T C Racing Ltd	5	67,681	John L Moore	2	5,663
A F Budge (Equine) Limited	13	61,553	G A Bosley	2	5,567
B E Nielsen	2	39,395	T S M Cunningham	1	5,299
Amity Finance Ltd	1	23,378	Derek Joseph	2	4,818
G Howard-Spink	3	18,652	Mrs A Valentine	2	4,373
P D Savill	6	16,478	Guy Hart	2	4,332
Roldvale Ltd	6	15,883	Victor Behrens	1	4,273
P J Christey	2	14,042	N Capon	1	3,590
Roger Barby	3	13,555	R A Bernard	1	3,558
Conal Kavanagh	2	13,275	Mrs J Reglar	1	3,171
D K Harris	3	12,015	Lord Of Lewknor	1	3,132
John Norman	2	11,245	Capt R W Hornall	1	2,973
Edward St George	5	11,228	Jim Horgan	1	2,783
P A Howell	3	10,552	Mrs D A La Trobe	1	2,637
Mrs M R T Rimell	3	9,654	C S Chiles	1	2,630
T A Johnsey	3	9,484	C M Hamer	1	2,532
L H J Ward	3	9,005	R J Shannon	1	2,469
G Mizel	2	8,701	W F Hawkings	1	2,448
D B Gallop	1	8,220	David Seale	1	2,406
William J Kelly	3	7,991	Kennet Valley Th'breds Ltd	1	2,326
N Ahamad	3	7,677	Mrs F Cooney & Mrs A Turner	1	2,322
Mrs Diana Attwood	3	7,615	Mrs Henry Lopes	1	2,320
J G Davis	1	7,505	P F Boggis	1	2,072
Robert Whitworth	2	7,504	Paul Jubert	1	2,070
Mrs D Hammerson	2	7,455	G Z Mizel	1	1,992
J E Marsden	2	7,180	T E Bucknall	1	1,932
Mrs J Cash	2	6,963	Miss W M Jones	1	1,814

Favourites	64-169	37.9%	- 12.76	Total winning prize-money		£1,150,144
Longest winning sequence			4	Average SP of winner		4.4/1
Longest losing sequence			53	Return on stakes invested		-28.1%
1991 Form	126-958	13.2%	- 149.42	1989 Form	55-603	9.1% - 198.78
1990 Form	73-796	9.2%	- 192.68	1988 Form	43-591	7.3% - 211.76

J HANSON (Wetherby, West Yorks)

	No. of Horses	Races Run	1st	2nd	3rd	Unpl	Per cent	£1 Level Stake
2-y-o	4	13	1	1	1	10	7.7	- 10.50
3-y-o	0	0	0	0	0	0	-	0.00
4-y-o+	0	0	0	0	0	0	-	0.00
Totals	4	13	1	1	1	10	7.7	- 10.50

Hanson J

Jan	Feb	Mar	Apr	May	Jun	Jul	Aug	Sep	Oct/Nov
0-0	0-0	0-0	0-0	0-0	0-0	0-0	0-4	1-7	0-2

Winning Jockey		W-R	£1 Level Stake		Winning Course		W-R	£1 Level Stake
E Johnson		1-12	- 9.50		Redcar		1-4	- 1.50

Winning Horse		Age	Races Run	1st	2nd	3rd	Unpl	Win £
Blow Dry		2	4	1	1	0	2	2,832

Favourites	1-3	33.3%	- 0.50	Total winning prize-money		£2,832

1991 Form	0-0			1989 Form	2-19	10.5%	- 13.93
1990 Form	0-0			1988 Form	1-13	7.7%	- 2.00

J L HARRIS (Melton Mowbray, Leics)

	No. of Horses	Races Run	1st	2nd	3rd	Unpl	Per cent	£1 Level Stake
2-y-o	2	10	2	1	0	7	20.0	+ 16.00
3-y-o	8	40	2	2	6	30	5.0	- 26.25
4-y-o+	15	69	5	2	2	60	7.2	- 31.50
Totals	25	119	9	5	8	97	7.6	- 41.75

Jan	Feb	Mar	Apr	May	Jun	Jul	Aug	Sep	Oct/Nov
2-9	2-4	0-4	1-12	0-8	0-16	4-27	0-18	0-13	0-8

Winning Jockeys	W-R	£1 Level Stake			W-R	£1 Level Stake
R Cochrane	3-9	+ 5.50	G Baxter		1-3	+ 12.00
P Robinson	2-6	+ 7.75	J Williams		1-4	+ 7.00
S D Williams	1-1	+ 11.00	F Norton		1-5	+ 6.00

Winning Courses						
Lingfield (AW)	3-6	+ 8.50	York		1-2	+ 9.00
Southwell (AW)	2-28	- 2.00	Leicester		1-8	+ 3.00
Redcar	1-2	+ 10.00	Nottingham		1-12	- 9.25

Winning Horses		Age	Races Run	1st	2nd	3rd	Unpl	Win £
Sir Tasker		4	13	5	0	1	7	11,658
Meadmore Magic		2	5	2	1	0	2	7,772
Legend Dulac		3	7	2	0	0	5	3,414

Favourites	2-4	50.0%	+ 1.75	Total winning prize-money		£22,843

1991 Form	8-128	6.3%	- 35.75	1989 Form	0-25
1990 Form	6-51	11.8%	+ 26.50	1988 Form	0-61

P W HARRIS (Berkhamsted, Herts)

	No. of Horses	Races Run	1st	2nd	3rd	Unpl	Per cent	£1 Level Stake
2-y-o	12	27	1	0	2	24	3.7	- 21.50
3-y-o	17	95	5	7	13	70	5.3	- 23.50
4-y-o+	4	30	7	5	3	15	23.3	+ 45.00
Totals	33	152	13	12	18	109	8.6	0.00

BY MONTH

2-y-o	W-R	Per cent	£1 Level Stake	3-y-o	W-R	Per cent	£1 Level Stake
January	0-0	-	0.00	January	0-0	-	0.00
February	0-0	-	0.00	February	0-0	-	0.00
March	0-0	-	0.00	March	1-2	50.0	+ 9.00
April	0-0	-	0.00	April	0-11	-	- 11.00
May	0-0	-	0.00	May	0-18	-	- 18.00
June	0-0	-	0.00	June	0-13	-	- 13.00
July	0-3	-	- 3.00	July	1-16	6.3	+ 18.00
August	0-6	-	- 6.00	August	1-13	7.7	- 3.00
September	0-6	-	- 6.00	September	1-12	8.3	- 8.50
Oct/Nov	1-12	8.3	- 6.50	Oct/Nov	1-10	10.0	+ 3.00

4-y-o+	W-R	Per cent	£1 Level Stake	Totals	W-R	Per cent	£1 Level Stake
January	0-0	-	0.00	January	0-0	-	0.00
February	0-0	-	0.00	February	0-0	-	0.00
March	0-2	-	- 2.00	March	1-4	25.0	+ 7.00
April	1-4	25.0	+ 2.00	April	1-15	6.7	- 9.00
May	0-2	-	- 2.00	May	0-20	-	- 20.00
June	0-3	-	- 3.00	June	0-16	-	- 16.00
July	3-5	60.0	+ 33.00	July	4-24	16.7	+ 48.00
August	2-6	33.3	+ 15.00	August	3-25	12.0	+ 6.00
September	1-5	20.0	+ 5.00	September	2-23	8.7	- 9.50
Oct/Nov	0-3	-	- 3.00	Oct/Nov	2-25	8.0	- 6.50

DISTANCE

2-y-o	W-R	Per cent	£1 Level Stake	3-y-o	W-R	Per cent	£1 Level Stake
5f-6f	1-15	6.7	- 9.50	5f-6f	0-11	-	- 11.00
7f-8f	0-12	-	- 12.00	7f-8f	2-50	4.0	- 5.00
9f-13f	0-0	-	0.00	9f-13f	3-32	9.4	- 5.50
14f+	0-0	-	0.00	14f+	0-2	-	- 2.00

4-y-o+	W-R	Per cent	£1 Level Stake	Totals	W-R	Per cent	£1 Level Stake
5f-6f	0-0	-	0.00	5f-6f	1-26	3.8	- 20.50
7f-8f	0-1	-	- 1.00	7f-8f	2-63	3.2	- 18.00
9f-13f	7-29	24.1	+ 46.00	9f-13f	10-61	16.4	+ 40.50
14f+	0-0	-	0.00	14f+	0-2	-	- 2.00

TYPE OF RACE

Non-Handicaps	W-R	Per cent	£1 Level Stake	Handicaps	W-R	Per cent	£1 Level Stake
2-y-o	1-26	3.8	- 20.50	2-y-o	0-1	-	- 1.00
3-y-o	3-44	6.8	+ 4.50	3-y-o	2-51	3.9	- 28.00
4-y-o+	0-2	-	- 2.00	4-y-o+	7-26	26.9	+ 49.00
Selling	0-0	-	0.00	Selling	0-0	-	0.00
Apprentice	0-0	-	0.00	Apprentice	0-2	-	- 2.00
Amat/Ladies	0-0	-	0.00	Amat/Ladies	0-0	-	0.00
Totals	4-72	5.6	- 18.00	Totals	9-80	11.3	+ 18.00

COURSE GRADE

	W-R	Per cent	£1 Level Stake
Group 1	5-56	8.9	+ 7.00
Group 2	5-31	16.1	+ 31.00
Group 3	2-45	4.4	- 29.00
Group 4	1-20	5.0	- 9.00

FIRST TIME OUT

	W-R	Per cent	£1 Level Stake
2-y-o	0-12	-	- 12.00
3-y-o	1-17	5.9	- 6.00
4-y-o+	0-4	-	- 4.00
Totals	1-33	3.0	- 22.00

JOCKEYS RIDING

	W-R	Per cent	£1 Level Stake		W-R	Per cent	£1 Level Stake
Paul Eddery	5-43	11.6	+ 23.50	M Birch	1-3	33.3	+ 7.00
W R Swinburn	3-10	30.0	+ 15.50	G Hind	1-9	11.1	+ 17.00
J Fortune	1-2	50.0	+ 5.50	S Whitworth	1-18	5.6	- 12.50
G Duffield	1-3	33.3	+ 8.00				

	W-R			W-R			W-R
W Ryan	0-11	T Quinn	0-2	M Roberts	0-1
F Norton	0-7	A Clark	0-1	M Wigham	0-1
A Tucker	0-6	A Mackay	0-1	N Howe	0-1
J Quinn	0-6	A Munro	0-1	P Robinson	0-1
N Adams	0-6	B Rouse	0-1	R Fox	0-1
W Newnes	0-6	C Rutter	0-1	R Hills	0-1
R Cochrane	0-4	D Harrison	0-1	T Williams	0-1
G Carter	0-2	G Bardwell	0-1		

COURSE RECORD

	Total W-R	Non-Handicaps 2-y-o	3-y-o+	Handicaps 2-y-o	3-y-o+	Per cent	£1 Level Stake
Redcar	2-4	0-0	0-1	0-0	2-3	50.0	+ 19.00
Lingfield	2-10	1-3	0-3	0-0	1-4	20.0	+ 21.50
Ripon	1-3	0-2	0-0	0-0	1-1	33.3	+ 4.50
Beverley	1-4	0-1	0-0	0-0	1-3	25.0	+ 2.00
Newmarket	1-4	0-0	0-1	0-0	1-3	25.0	+ 2.00
Folkestone	1-6	0-3	1-1	0-0	0-2	16.7	+ 5.00

Newbury	1 - 7	0 - 2	0 - 1	0 - 1	1 - 3	14.3	- 2.50
York	1 - 7	0 - 2	0 - 2	0 - 0	1 - 3	14.3	+ 8.00
Haydock	1 - 8	0 - 3	1 - 2	0 - 0	0 - 3	12.5	- 4.50
Leicester	1 - 8	0 - 1	0 - 3	0 - 0	1 - 4	12.5	+ 2.00
Kempton	1 - 13	0 - 0	1 - 11	0 - 0	0 - 2	7.7	+ 21.00

Windsor	0 - 10	Wolverhampton	0 - 5	Ascot	0 - 1
Goodwood	0 - 8	Doncaster	0 - 4	Carlisle	0 - 1
Nottingham	0 - 8	Brighton	0 - 3	Catterick	0 - 1
Salisbury	0 - 8	Sandown	0 - 3	Chepstow	0 - 1
Yarmouth	0 - 7	Thirsk	0 - 3	Epsom	0 - 1
Pontefract	0 - 5	Bath	0 - 2		
Warwick	0 - 5	Lingfield (AW)	0 - 2		

WINNING HORSES

	Age	Races Run	1st	2nd	3rd	Unpl	Win £
Opera Ghost	6	9	2	1	1	5	17,028
Vallance	4	9	3	2	1	3	14,286
Supertop	4	10	2	2	1	5	6,349
Unforgiving Minute	3	8	2	4	1	1	6,170
Hester Stanhope	3	9	1	1	0	7	3,002
Agnes Flemming	3	7	1	0	1	5	2,856
Most Eminent	2	3	1	0	0	2	2,532
Thinking Twice	3	9	1	0	3	5	2,226

WINNING OWNERS

	Races Won	Value £		Races Won	Value £
Mrs P W Harris	10	45,568	Twelve Of The Best	1	2,532
Mrs G A Godfrey	2	6,349			

Favourites	2-6	33.3%	+ 2.00	Total winning prize-money			£54,449
Longest winning sequence			2	Average SP of winner			10.7/1
Longest losing sequence			43	Return on stakes invested			0.0%
1991 Form	3-74	4.1%	- 50.50	1989 Form	2-37	5.4%	- 16.75
1990 Form	8-69	11.6%	+ 3.25	1988 Form	0-27		

A HARRISON (Middleham, North Yorks)

	No. of Horses	Races Run	1st	2nd	3rd	Unpl	Per cent	£1 Level Stake
2-y-o	2	9	0	1	0	8	-	- 9.00
3-y-o	2	24	1	9	4	10	4.2	- 17.50
4-y-o+	7	34	2	3	2	27	5.9	- 28.25
Totals	11	67	3	13	6	45	4.5	- 54.75

Jan	Feb	Mar	Apr	May	Jun	Jul	Aug	Sep	Oct/Nov
0-1	0-0	0-3	0-6	0-10	2-11	0-10	1-8	0-8	0-10

Winning Jockeys	W-R	£1 Level Stake			W-R	£1 Level Stake
W R Swinburn	1-5	- 2.25	K Fallon		1-23	- 20.00
D Harrison	1-6	+ 0.50				

Winning Courses	W-R	£1 Level Stake			W-R	£1 Level Stake
Wolverhampton	1-1	+ 1.75	Edinburgh		1-7	- 4.00
Beverley	1-6	+ 0.50				

Winning Horses	Age	Races Run	1st	2nd	3rd	Unpl	Win £
Plain Fact	7	4	2	1	0	1	4,308
Kadari	3	17	1	7	2	7	3,548

Favourites	1-5	20.0%	- 2.25	Total winning prize-money		£7,856

1991 Form	4-103	3.9%	- 78.50	1990 Form	7-50	14.0%	- 12.12

G HARWOOD (Pulborough, West Sussex)

	No. of Horses	Races Run	1st	2nd	3rd	Unpl	Per cent	£1 Level Stake
2-y-o	20	61	9	13	7	32	14.8	- 29.11
3-y-o	22	120	14	11	18	77	11.7	- 48.13
4-y-o+	11	50	4	1	6	39	8.0	- 22.97
Totals	53	231	27	25	31	148	11.7	-100.21

BY MONTH

2-y-o	W-R	Per cent	£1 Level Stake	3-y-o	W-R	Per cent	£1 Level Stake
January	0-0	-	0.00	January	0-0	-	0.00
February	0-0	-	0.00	February	0-0	-	0.00
March	0-0	-	0.00	March	0-0	-	0.00
April	0-0	-	0.00	April	0-3	-	- 3.00
May	1-3	33.3	+ 1.33	May	3-18	16.7	+ 0.25
June	3-7	42.9	+ 3.43	June	5-18	27.8	- 0.38
July	2-8	25.0	+ 0.50	July	3-22	13.6	- 10.58
August	2-7	28.6	- 0.75	August	2-24	8.3	- 2.67
September	0-4	-	- 4.00	September	0-17	-	- 17.00
Oct/Nov	1-32	3.1	- 29.62	Oct/Nov	1-18	5.6	- 14.75

4-y-o+	W-R	Per cent	£1 Level Stake	Totals	W-R	Per cent	£1 Level Stake
January	0-0	-	0.00	January	0-0	-	0.00
February	0-1	-	- 1.00	February	0-1	-	- 1.00
March	0-1	-	- 1.00	March	0-1	-	- 1.00
April	0-7	-	- 7.00	April	0-10	-	- 10.00
May	0-5	-	- 5.00	May	4-26	15.4	- 3.42
June	1-8	12.5	- 6.97	June	9-33	27.3	- 3.92
July	1-10	10.0	- 4.00	July	6-40	15.0	- 14.08
August	0-4	-	- 4.00	August	4-35	11.4	- 7.42
September	0-6	-	- 6.00	September	0-27	-	- 27.00
Oct/Nov	2-8	25.0	+ 12.00	Oct/Nov	4-58	6.9	- 32.37

DISTANCE

2-y-o	W-R	Per cent	£1 Level Stake	3-y-o	W-R	Per cent	£1 Level Stake
5f-6f	5-18	27.8	- 2.49	5f-6f	1-7	14.3	- 5.00
7f-8f	4-42	9.5	- 25.62	7f-8f	4-33	12.1	- 13.63
9f-13f	0-1	-	- 1.00	9f-13f	7-65	10.8	- 22.08
14f+	0-0	-	0.00	14f+	2-15	13.3	- 7.42

4-y-o+	W-R	Per cent	£1 Level Stake	Totals	W-R	Per cent	£1 Level Stake
5f-6f	0-0	-	0.00	5f-6f	6-25	24.0	- 7.49
7f-8f	2-19	10.5	- 4.00	7f-8f	10-94	10.6	- 43.25
9f-13f	2-27	7.4	- 14.97	9f-13f	9-93	9.7	- 38.05
14f+	0-4	-	- 4.00	14f+	2-19	10.5	- 11.42

TYPE OF RACE

Non-Handicaps	W-R	Per cent	£1 Level Stake	Handicaps	W-R	Per cent	£1 Level Stake
2-y-o	9-52	17.3	- 20.11	2-y-o	0-8	-	- 8.00
3-y-o	8-51	15.7	- 11.38	3-y-o	6-62	9.7	- 29.75
4-y-o+	1-14	7.1	- 12.97	4-y-o+	3-27	11.1	- 1.00
Selling	0-0	-	0.00	Selling	0-0	-	0.00
Apprentice	0-0	-	0.00	Apprentice	0-11	-	- 11.00
Amat/Ladies	0-3	-	- 3.00	Amat/Ladies	0-3	-	- 3.00
Totals	18-120	15.0	- 47.46	Totals	9-111	8.1	- 52.75

Harwood G

COURSE GRADE

	W-R	Per cent	£1 Level Stake
Group 1	4-124	3.2	- 94.50
Group 2	10-38	26.3	+ 2.53
Group 3	7-44	15.9	- 23.42
Group 4	6-25	24.0	+ 15.18

FIRST TIME OUT

	W-R	Per cent	£1 Level Stake
2-y-o	4-20	20.0	- 5.37
3-y-o	2-22	9.1	- 17.75
4-y-o+	1-11	9.1	- 9.97
Totals	7-53	13.2	- 33.09

JOCKEYS RIDING

	W-R	Per cent	£1 Level Stake		W-R	Per cent	£1 Level Stake
A Clark	9-85	10.6	- 18.55	Pat Eddery	2-13	15.4	- 9.20
M Roberts	3-11	27.3	- 2.87	G Duffield	1-2	50.0	- 0.97
T Quinn	2-9	22.2	- 3.37	M Hills	1-5	20.0	- 2.25
K Darley	2-9	22.2	+ 4.50	P Houghton	1-6	16.7	+ 5.00
S Cauthen	2-12	16.7	- 6.00	W Carson	1-6	16.7	- 2.50
J Reid	2-12	16.7	- 5.25	R Cochrane	1-11	9.1	- 8.75

Gaye Harwood	0-10	L Piggott	0-2	K Fallon	0-1
M Perrett	0-9	B Doyle	0-1	L Dettori	0-1
Miss A Harwood	0-6	D McKeown	0-1	R Hills	0-1
J Jones	0-4	G Carter	0-1	W R Swinburn	0-1
Paul Eddery	0-3	G Starkey	0-1	W Ryan	0-1
A McGlone	0-2	J Carroll	0-1	W Woods	0-1
B Raymond	0-2	J Quinn	0-1		

COURSE RECORD

	Total W-R	Non-Handicaps 2-y-o	3-y-o+	Handicaps 2-y-o	3-y-o+	Per cent	£1 Level Stake
Salisbury	4-11	1-3	0-0	0-0	3-8	36.4	+ 5.00
Folkestone	4-13	2-4	1-5	0-0	1-4	30.8	+ 19.18
Pontefract	3-6	1-3	1-1	0-0	1-2	50.0	+ 1.50
Lingfield	3-13	1-3	1-2	0-1	1-7	23.1	+ 0.25
Brighton	2-7	0-0	2-5	0-0	0-2	28.6	+ 3.25
Bath	2-8	1-1	1-4	0-0	0-3	25.0	- 2.00
Sandown	2-8	1-2	0-2	0-0	1-4	25.0	+ 4.50
Thirsk	1-2	0-0	1-1	0-0	0-1	50.0	- 0.97
Newcastle	1-3	0-0	0-1	0-0	1-2	33.3	+ 6.00
Nottingham	1-3	0-1	1-2	0-0	0-0	33.3	+ 1.33
Wolverhampton	1-3	1-2	0-0	0-0	0-1	33.3	+ 3.00
Warwick	1-6	0-2	1-3	0-0	0-1	16.7	- 4.00
Windsor	1-6	1-1	0-3	0-0	0-2	16.7	- 3.25
Goodwood	1-40	0-8	0-10	0-2	1-20	2.5	- 32.00

Newmarket	0-28	Beverley	0-4	Lingfield (AW)	0-2
Ascot	0-17	York	0-4	Redcar	0-2
Newbury	0-9	Doncaster	0-3	Ayr	0-1
Kempton	0-8	Yarmouth	0-3	Haydock	0-1
Chepstow	0-7	Chester	0-2	Ripon	0-1
Leicester	0-7	Epsom	0-2	Southwell (AW)	0-1

WINNING HORSES

	Age	Races Run	1st	2nd	3rd	Unpl	Win £
Baluga	3	11	4	1	0	6	14,453
Thourios	3	7	1	1	0	5	11,160
Little Too Much	2	6	2	1	0	3	8,808
Lucky Noire	4	18	3	0	2	13	7,724
Kayvee	3	10	1	0	1	8	5,775
Realities	2	5	2	1	0	2	5,685
Puritan	3	8	2	2	2	2	5,164
Darbonne	2	5	1	0	1	3	3,101
Duke Of Paducah	5	2	1	0	0	1	3,067
Satin Dancer	2	4	1	1	0	2	2,947
Semillon	2	5	1	2	1	1	2,490
Trooping	3	12	1	1	2	8	2,427
So Factual	2	3	1	2	0	0	2,343
Debacle	3	6	1	0	0	5	2,070
Regal Aura	2	7	1	1	2	3	2,040
Young Freeman	3	6	1	0	1	4	1,932
Simonov	3	7	1	1	1	4	1,932
Chatterer	3	2	1	0	0	1	1,718
Storm Crossing	3	4	1	2	0	1	1,380

WINNING OWNERS

	Races Won	Value £		Races Won	Value £
J C Thompson	4	14,453	Simon Karmel	2	5,685
J Garcia-Roady	3	11,875	P D Savill	1	2,947
Athos Christodoulou	1	11,160	Nigel Grandfield	1	2,427
Sheikh Mohammed	4	9,983	David Saxby	1	2,070
K Abdulla	4	8,145	Skytraders Racing	1	2,040
Mrs Carol Harrison	3	7,724	R A Kirstein	1	1,932
J H Richmond-Watson	1	5,775			

Favourites	11-36	30.6%	- 6.87	Total winning prize-money			£86,215
Longest winning sequence			2	Average SP of winner			3.8/1
Longest losing sequence			73	Return on stakes invested			-43.4%
1991 Form	55-326	16.9%	- 47.76	1989 Form	109-410	26.6%	+ 26.79
1990 Form	69-396	17.4%	- 46.87	1988 Form	73-306	23.9%	- 40.44

P C HASLAM (Middleham, North Yorks)

	No. of Horses	Races Run	1st	2nd	3rd	Unpl	Per cent	£1 Level Stake
2-y-o	9	24	2	0	2	20	8.3	- 20.18
3-y-o	13	79	11	7	10	51	13.9	- 32.86
4-y-o+	14	102	16	11	13	62	15.7	- 15.26
Totals	36	205	29	18	25	133	14.1	- 68.30

BY MONTH

2-y-o	W-R	Per cent	£1 Level Stake	3-y-o	W-R	Per cent	£1 Level Stake
January	0-0	-	0.00	January	1-4	25.0	+ 1.00
February	0-0	-	0.00	February	0-0	-	0.00
March	0-0	-	0.00	March	0-2	-	- 2.00
April	0-1	-	- 1.00	April	0-10	-	- 10.00
May	1-6	16.7	- 3.75	May	1-13	7.7	- 4.50
June	1-3	33.3	- 1.43	June	1-15	6.7	- 13.09
July	0-2	-	- 2.00	July	6-15	40.0	+ 5.23
August	0-4	-	- 4.00	August	2-11	18.2	- 0.50
September	0-3	-	- 3.00	September	0-6	-	- 6.00
Oct/Nov	0-5	-	- 5.00	Oct/Nov	0-3	-	- 3.00

4-y-o+	W-R	Per cent	£1 Level Stake	Totals	W-R	Per cent	£1 Level Stake
January	2-15	13.3	- 3.67	January	3-19	15.8	- 2.67
February	0-3	-	- 3.00	February	0-3	-	- 3.00
March	1-6	16.7	+ 11.00	March	1-8	12.5	+ 9.00
April	2-13	15.4	0.00	April	2-24	8.3	- 11.00
May	1-12	8.3	- 7.50	May	3-31	9.7	- 15.75
June	4-14	28.6	+ 9.00	June	6-32	18.8	- 5.52
July	4-19	21.1	- 7.71	July	10-36	27.8	- 4.48
August	2-10	20.0	- 3.38	August	4-25	16.0	- 7.88
September	0-5	-	- 5.00	September	0-14	-	- 14.00
Oct/Nov	0-5	-	- 5.00	Oct/Nov	0-13	-	- 13.00

DISTANCE

2-y-o	W-R	Per cent	£1 Level Stake	3-y-o	W-R	Per cent	£1 Level Stake
5f-6f	2-19	10.5	- 15.18	5f-6f	0-16	-	- 16.00
7f-8f	0-5	-	- 5.00	7f-8f	7-34	20.6	- 6.61
9f-13f	0-0	-	0.00	9f-13f	4-28	14.3	- 9.25
14f+	0-0	-	0.00	14f+	0-1	-	- 1.00

4-y-o+	W-R	Per cent	£1 Level Stake	Totals	W-R	Per cent	£1 Level Stake
5f-6f	4-26	15.4	+ 4.50	5f-6f	6-61	9.8	- 26.68
7f-8f	7-40	17.5	- 10.30	7f-8f	14-79	17.7	- 21.91
9f-13f	3-24	12.5	- 5.37	9f-13f	7-52	13.5	- 14.62
14f+	2-12	16.7	- 4.09	14f+	2-13	15.4	- 5.09

TYPE OF RACE

Non-Handicaps	W-R	Per cent	£1 Level Stake	Handicaps	W-R	Per cent	£1 Level Stake
2-y-o	2-15	13.3	- 11.18	2-y-o	0-1	-	- 1.00
3-y-o	3-15	20.0	- 4.84	3-y-o	5-48	10.4	- 27.52
4-y-o+	3-15	20.0	+ 1.33	4-y-o+	11-67	16.4	- 1.71
Selling	3-14	21.4	- 2.88	Selling	0-15	-	- 15.00
Apprentice	0-1	-	- 1.00	Apprentice	2-11	18.2	- 1.50
Amat/Ladies	0-0	-	0.00	Amat/Ladies	0-3	-	- 3.00
Totals	11-60	18.3	- 18.57	Totals	18-145	12.4	- 49.73

COURSE GRADE

	W-R	Per cent	£1 Level Stake
Group 1	5-34	14.7	- 14.14
Group 2	7-53	13.2	- 21.88
Group 3	8-60	13.3	- 27.43
Group 4	9-58	15.5	- 4.85

FIRST TIME OUT

	W-R	Per cent	£1 Level Stake
2-y-o	0-8	-	- 8.00
3-y-o	1-13	7.7	- 8.00
4-y-o+	1-14	7.1	- 9.67
Totals	2-35	5.7	- 25.67

JOCKEYS RIDING

	W-R	Per cent	£1 Level Stake		W-R	Per cent	£1 Level Stake
K Darley	10-35	28.6	+ 6.86	J Fanning	2-28	7.1	- 18.67
J Weaver	5-17	29.4	+ 4.16	Dale Gibson	2-28	7.1	- 21.09
D McKeown	3-30	10.0	- 5.43	M Roberts	1-1	100.0	+ 1.25
Nicola Howarth	2-14	14.3	- 4.50	D Harrison	1-1	100.0	+ 0.62
L Piggott	2-17	11.8	- 4.50	R Cochrane	1-6	16.7	+ 1.00

E Johnson	0-7	D Moffatt	0-1	R P Elliott	0-1
N Kennedy	0-5	E Husband	0-1	S Maloney	0-1
L Charnock	0-2	J Lowe	0-1	T Lucas	0-1
Miss A Billot	0-2	M Denaro	0-1	Tracey Lynagh	0-1
B Raymond	0-1	Miss J Feilden	0-1		
D Holland	0-1	N Connorton	0-1		

COURSE RECORD

	Total W-R	Non-Handicaps 2-y-o	3-y-o+	Handicaps 2-y-o	3-y-o+	Per cent	£1 Level Stake
Hamilton	5-25	0-1	3-8	0-0	2-16	20.0	+ 0.25
Ayr	4-8	0-0	0-1	0-0	4-7	50.0	+ 2.86
Edinburgh	4-14	0-1	1-3	0-0	3-10	28.6	+ 0.82
Redcar	3-19	0-0	2-7	0-1	1-11	15.8	- 9.88
Ripon	3-24	0-1	0-4	0-1	3-18	12.5	- 6.50
Catterick	2-7	0-1	0-0	0-0	2-6	28.6	+ 15.00
Southwell (AW)	2-18	0-0	2-7	0-0	0-11	11.1	- 8.67

191

Haslam P C

Beverley	2-21	2-5	0-4	0-0	0-12	9.5	- 17.18
Yarmouth	1-6	0-1	1-1	0-0	0-4	16.7	- 2.50
York	1-7	0-3	0-2	0-0	1-2	14.3	+ 2.00
Thirsk	1-8	0-1	0-0	0-0	1-7	12.5	- 3.50
Lingfield (AW)	1-12	0-1	0-2	0-0	1-9	8.3	- 5.00

Doncaster	0-7	Haydock	0-3	Warwick	0-2
Pontefract	0-7	Ascot	0-2	Nottingham	0-1
Carlisle	0-5	Chester	0-2		
Newmarket	0-5	Newcastle	0-2		

WINNING HORSES

	Age	Races Run	1st	2nd	3rd	Unpl	Win £
Furiella	4	17	4	3	3	7	11,383
Ringland	4	13	3	2	3	5	10,872
Talented Ting	3	8	4	0	2	2	8,088
Inseyab	4	13	3	1	3	6	7,850
Rose Gem	3	8	3	1	0	4	6,145
Bold Melody	3	6	2	0	0	4	5,224
Purchased By Phone	2	2	2	0	0	0	4,648
Magic Secret	4	9	2	1	1	5	4,524
Fen Princess	4	9	2	1	1	5	4,502
Pickles	4	7	1	1	1	4	2,801
Reel Of Tulloch	3	16	1	2	1	12	2,318
General John	3	2	1	0	0	1	2,167
Saint Bene't	4	10	1	0	0	9	1,932

WINNING OWNERS

	Races Won	Value £		Races Won	Value £
S A B Dinsmore	7	20,021	Martin Wickens	4	8,088
Mrs P Haslam	5	13,074	Mrs M E F Haslam	3	6,145
W J Hall	4	11,383	Lord Scarsdale	2	4,485
Hambleton Th'Breds Plc	4	9,257			

Favourites	15-37	40.5%	+ 5.12	Total winning prize-money			£72,454
Longest winning sequence			3	Average SP of winner			3.7/1
Longest losing sequence			36	Return on stakes invested			-33.3%
1991 Form	14-145	9.7%	- 56.76	1989 Form	0-0		
1990 Form	0-0			1988 Form	22-247	8.9%	-125.86

M J HAYNES (Epsom, Surrey)

	No. of Horses	Races Run	1st	2nd	3rd	Unpl	Per cent	£1 Level Stake
2-y-o	5	22	2	2	3	15	9.1	0.00
3-y-o	6	32	0	6	4	22	-	- 32.00
4-y-o+	9	46	2	3	4	37	4.3	- 18.00
Totals	20	100	4	11	11	74	4.0	- 50.00

Jan	Feb	Mar	Apr	May	Jun	Jul	Aug	Sep	Oct/Nov
0-5	0-4	0-4	0-16	1-12	1-18	1-21	0-7	0-4	1-9

Winning Jockeys	W-R	£1 Level Stake			W-R	£1 Level Stake
N Howe	1-1	+ 10.00	S Cauthen		1-9	+ 4.00
C Asmussen	1-2	+ 9.00	D Toole		1-17	- 2.00

Winning Courses	W-R	£1 Level Stake			W-R	£1 Level Stake
Salisbury	1-2	+ 9.00	Nottingham		1-6	+ 9.00
Doncaster	1-5	+ 6.00	Lingfield		1-13	0.00

Winning Horses	Age	Races Run	1st	2nd	3rd	Unpl	Win £
Ansellman	2	10	2	2	2	4	9,468
Bold Lez	5	10	1	1	1	7	6,056
Caroles Clown	6	8	1	0	2	5	2,532

Favourites	0-3		Total winning prize-money		£18,056

1991 Form	9-122	7.4%	+ 6.83	1989 Form	6-111	5.4%	- 64.50
1990 Form	9-134	6.7%	- 52.00	1988 Form	11-161	6.8%	- 37.62

M J HEATON-ELLIS (Wroughton, Wilts)

	No. of Horses	Races Run	1st	2nd	3rd	Unpl	Per cent	£1 Level Stake
2-y-o	17	48	2	4	4	38	4.2	- 41.25
3-y-o	17	72	6	2	5	59	8.3	- 11.75
4-y-o+	4	13	0	2	2	9	-	- 13.00
Totals	38	133	8	8	11	106	6.0	- 66.00

Jan	Feb	Mar	Apr	May	Jun	Jul	Aug	Sep	Oct/Nov
0-0	0-0	0-2	0-12	0-9	1-14	3-28	2-17	0-23	2-28

Winning Jockeys	W-R	£1 Level Stake				W-R	£1 Level Stake
W Newnes	2-16	+ 8.25		Ruth Coulter		1-5	+ 2.50
G Duffield	1-2	+ 0.25		B Raymond		1-7	- 0.50
Pat Eddery	1-3	+ 3.00		D Holland		1-7	+ 10.00
R Cochrane	1-4	- 0.50					

Winning Courses							
Windsor	3-15	+ 20.00		York		1-3	+ 3.00
Warwick	2-9	- 2.25		Folkestone		1-13	+ 4.00
Haydock	1-2	+ 0.25					

Winning Horses		Age	Races Run	1st	2nd	3rd	Unpl	Win £
Reported		3	4	1	1	1	1	11,843
Massiba		3	7	2	0	0	5	5,550
Santana Lady		3	8	2	0	1	5	5,333
Mullitover		2	3	1	1	0	1	2,783
Florac		2	4	1	0	0	3	2,285
April City		3	3	1	0	0	2	1,245

Favourites	1-4	25.0%	- 1.75	Total winning prize-money			£29,037

1991 Form	0-6

W R HERN (Lambourn, Berks)

	No. of Horses	Races Run	1st	2nd	3rd	Unpl	Per cent	£1 Level Stake
2-y-o	13	20	3	0	3	14	15.0	- 0.12
3-y-o	24	95	12	10	12	61	12.6	- 28.89
4-y-o+	3	9	2	2	0	5	22.2	+ 4.10
Totals	40	124	17	12	15	80	13.7	- 24.91

BY MONTH

2-y-o	W-R	Per cent	£1 Level Stake	3-y-o	W-R	Per cent	£1 Level Stake
Mar/Apr	0-0	-	0.00	Mar/Apr	0-10	-	- 10.00
May	0-0	-	0.00	May	1-17	5.9	- 15.00
June	0-0	-	0.00	June	0-7	-	- 7.00
July	1-2	50.0	+ 0.88	July	2-11	18.2	- 2.62
August	0-2	-	- 2.00	August	6-20	30.0	+ 15.50
September	0-7	-	- 7.00	September	1-15	6.7	0.00
Oct/Nov	2-9	22.2	+ 8.00	Oct/Nov	2-15	13.3	- 9.77

4-y-o+	W-R	Per cent	£1 Level Stake	Totals	W-R	Per cent	£1 Level Stake
Mar/Apr	0-0	-	0.00	Mar/Apr	0-10	-	- 10.00
May	0-0	-	0.00	May	1-17	5.9	- 15.00
June	1-1	100.0	+ 10.00	June	1-8	12.5	+ 3.00
July	0-4	-	- 4.00	July	3-17	17.6	- 5.74
August	1-1	100.0	+ 1.10	August	7-23	30.4	+ 14.60
September	0-2	-	- 2.00	September	1-24	4.2	- 9.00
Oct/Nov	0-1	-	- 1.00	Oct/Nov	4-25	16.0	- 2.77

DISTANCE

2-y-o	W-R	Per cent	£1 Level Stake	3-y-o	W-R	Per cent	£1 Level Stake
5f-6f	1-4	25.0	- 1.12	5f-6f	2-11	18.2	- 5.75
7f-8f	2-16	12.5	+ 1.00	7f-8f	2-19	10.5	- 12.12
9f-13f	0-0	-	0.00	9f-13f	7-56	12.5	- 17.02
14f+	0-0	-	0.00	14f+	1-9	11.1	+ 6.00

4-y-o+	W-R	Per cent	£1 Level Stake	Totals	W-R	Per cent	£1 Level Stake
5f-6f	0-0	-	0.00	5f-6f	3-15	20.0	- 6.87
7f-8f	0-1	-	- 1.00	7f-8f	4-36	11.1	- 12.12
9f-13f	2-8	25.0	+ 5.10	9f-13f	9-64	14.1	- 11.92
14f+	0-0	-	0.00	14f+	1-9	11.1	+ 6.00

TYPE OF RACE

Non-Handicaps	W-R	Per cent	£1 Level Stake	Handicaps	W-R	Per cent	£1 Level Stake
2-y-o	3-20	15.0	- 0.12	2-y-o	0-0	-	0.00
3-y-o	8-53	15.1	- 22.52	3-y-o	4-42	9.5	- 6.37
4-y-o+	2-5	40.0	+ 8.10	4-y-o+	0-4	-	- 4.00
Selling	0-0	-	0.00	Selling	0-0	-	0.00
Apprentice	0-0	-	0.00	Apprentice	0-0	-	0.00
Amat/Ladies	0-0	-	0.00	Amat/Ladies	0-0	-	0.00
Totals	13-78	16.7	- 14.54	Totals	4-46	8.7	- 10.37

COURSE GRADE

	W-R	Per cent	£1 Level Stake
Group 1	6-55	10.9	+ 5.88
Group 2	4-24	16.7	- 3.90
Group 3	7-39	17.9	- 20.89
Group 4	0-6	-	- 6.00

FIRST TIME OUT

	W-R	Per cent	£1 Level Stake
2-y-o	3-13	23.1	+ 6.88
3-y-o	2-24	8.3	- 16.25
4-y-o+	1-3	33.3	+ 8.00
Totals	6-40	15.0	- 1.37

JOCKEYS RIDING

	W-R	Per cent	£1 Level Stake		W-R	Per cent	£1 Level Stake
W Carson	12-60	20.0	+ 10.86	S Cauthen	1-7	14.3	- 5.00
R Hills	2-10	20.0	- 0.50	J Williams	1-7	14.3	+ 8.00
B Raymond	1-2	50.0	- 0.27				

B Procter	0-7	M Hills	0-3	L Piggott		0-1
W Ryan	0-6	A Clark	0-2	M Roberts		0-1
A Munro	0-5	R Cochrane	0-2	S Dawson		0-1
J Reid	0-4	B Rouse	0-1			
W R Swinburn	0-4	G Carter	0-1			

COURSE RECORD

	Total W-R	Non-Handicaps 2-y-o	3-y-o+	Handicaps 2-y-o	3-y-o+	Per cent	£1 Level Stake
Bath	2-8	0-0	1-5	0-0	1-3	25.0	- 2.75
Kempton	2-10	0-3	0-3	0-0	2-4	20.0	+ 20.00
Newmarket	2-19	1-7	1-7	0-0	0-5	10.5	+ 3.00
Beverley	1-1	0-0	0-0	0-0	1-1	100.0	+ 1.38
Lingfield	1-2	1-1	0-0	0-0	0-1	50.0	+ 4.00
Brighton	1-4	0-0	1-2	0-0	0-2	25.0	+ 3.50
Chepstow	1-4	0-0	1-3	0-0	0-1	25.0	- 2.27
Goodwood	1-4	1-1	0-1	0-0	0-2	25.0	- 1.12
Pontefract	1-4	0-0	1-3	0-0	0-1	25.0	- 0.50
Chester	1-6	0-0	1-6	0-0	0-0	16.7	- 3.90
Leicester	1-6	0-2	1-2	0-0	0-2	16.7	- 2.75
Windsor	1-7	0-0	1-4	0-0	0-3	14.3	- 5.00
Newbury	1-8	0-0	1-6	0-0	0-2	12.5	- 2.00
Salisbury	1-8	0-1	1-2	0-0	0-5	12.5	- 3.50

Doncaster	0-6	Folkestone	0-2	Ripon		0-2
Nottingham	0-5	Haydock	0-2	Warwick		0-2
Sandown	0-5	Lingfield (AW)	0-2	York		0-1
Yarmouth	0-4	Redcar	0-2			

WINNING HORSES

	Age	Races Run	1st	2nd	3rd	Unpl	Win £
Jahafil	4	4	2	2	0	0	25,985
Mack The Knife	3	6	2	0	1	3	6,424
Liyakah	2	3	1	0	1	1	6,264
Bashayer	2	1	1	0	0	0	5,010
Wesaam	3	9	1	1	1	6	3,905
Top Spin	3	4	1	1	0	2	3,641
Tafrah	3	4	1	0	0	3	3,200
Quadrireme	3	7	1	1	0	5	3,158
Moon Spin	3	7	1	0	1	5	2,921
Faez	2	1	1	0	0	0	2,700

Sweet Jaffa	3	4	1	0	0	3	2,574
Iftakhaar	3	6	1	0	3	2	2,553
Desert Dagger	3	3	1	0	1	1	2,390
Elhasha	3	3	1	1	0	1	2,259
Busman	3	5	1	0	0	4	2,070

WINNING OWNERS

	Races Won	Value £		Races Won	Value £
Hamdan Al-Maktoum	9	51,876	Mrs W R Hern	1	2,921
Sir John Astor	2	6,424	Mrs C A Waters	1	2,574
Mrs Hugh Dalgety	1	3,641	Sheikh Ahmed Al Maktoum	1	2,390
R D Hollingsworth	1	3,158	Lord Weinstock	1	2,070

Favourites	7-17	41.2%	- 0.66	Total winning prize-money			£75,054
Longest winning sequence			2	Average SP of winner			4.8/1
Longest losing sequence			21	Return on stakes invested			-20.1%
1991 Form	23-138	16.7%	- 27.87	1989 Form	45-228	19.7%	- 72.98
1990 Form	30-152	19.7%	- 45.58	1988 Form	30-126	23.8%	- 7.74

LADY HERRIES (Littlehampton, West Sussex)

	No. of Horses	Races Run	1st	2nd	3rd	Unpl	Per cent	£1 Level Stake
2-y-o	5	19	2	1	2	14	10.5	- 13.50
3-y-o	2	16	1	1	4	10	6.3	+ 10.00
4-y-o+	8	40	3	7	6	24	7.5	- 13.50
Totals	15	75	6	9	12	48	8.0	- 17.00

Jan	Feb	Mar	Apr	May	Jun	Jul	Aug	Sep	Oct/Nov
0-0	0-1	0-0	1-6	2-11	1-13	1-10	0-12	1-10	0-12

Winning Jockeys	W-R	£1 Level Stake		W-R	£1 Level Stake
S Whitworth	1-2	+ 24.00	W Ryan	1-7	- 2.50
W R Swinburn	1-2	+ 5.00	L Dettori	1-9	+ 6.00
G Carter	1-2	+ 0.50	J Williams	1-19	- 16.00

Winning Courses	W-R	£1 Level Stake		W-R	£1 Level Stake
Beverley	1-3	+ 4.00	Salisbury	1-5	- 2.00
Kempton	1-4	+ 11.00	Newmarket	1-6	- 1.50
Newbury	1-4	+ 22.00	Goodwood	1-10	- 7.50

Herries Lady

Winning Horses	Age	Races Run	1st	2nd	3rd	Unpl	Win £
Castle Courageous	5	8	1	0	3	4	6,160
Amaze	3	9	1	1	2	5	4,175
Aitch N'Bee	9	9	1	3	1	4	3,728
Polar Storm	2	5	1	0	0	4	2,898
Petavious	7	4	1	1	1	1	2,637
Cissbury Ring	2	4	1	1	1	1	2,058

Favourites	2-12	16.7%	- 6.50	Total winning prize-money			£21,656
1991 Form	14-99	14.1%	- 6.18	1989 Form	9-76	11.8%	- 30.46
1990 Form	4-60	6.7%	- 30.70	1988 Form	6-41	14.6%	+ 12.25

J HETHERTON (Malton, North Yorks)

	No. of Horses	Races Run	1st	2nd	3rd	Unpl	Per cent	£1 Level Stake
2-y-o	0	0	0	0	0	0	-	0.00
3-y-o	2	6	1	1	1	3	16.7	- 3.25
4-y-o+	1	2	0	1	0	1	-	- 2.00
Totals	3	8	1	2	1	4	12.5	- 5.25

Jan	Feb	Mar	Apr	May	Jun	Jul	Aug	Sep	Oct/Nov
1-8	0-0	0-0	0-0	0-0	0-0	0-0	0-0	0-0	0-0

Winning Jockey		W-R	£1 Level Stake	Winning Course		W-R	£1 Level Stake
W Newnes		1-4	- 1.25	Southwell (AW)		1-6	- 3.25

Winning Horse		Age	Races Run	1st	2nd	3rd	Unpl	Win £
Meltonby		3	4	1	1	1	1	2,167

Favourites	1-3	33.3%	- 0.25	Total winning prize-money			£2,167
1991 Form	10-91	11.0%	- 20.42	1989 Form	2-38	5.3%	- 25.50
1990 Form	4-49	8.2%	- 27.37				

A HIDE (Newmarket)

	No. of Horses	Races Run	1st	2nd	3rd	Unpl	Per cent	£1 Level Stake
2-y-o	6	14	0	1	0	13	-	- 14.00
3-y-o	10	29	1	2	1	25	3.4	- 27.00
4-y-o+	5	34	4	0	2	28	11.8	+ 5.00
Totals	21	77	5	3	3	66	6.5	- 36.00

Jan	Feb	Mar	Apr	May	Jun	Jul	Aug	Sep	Oct/Nov
0-4	0-0	0-1	0-13	0-6	1-14	1-9	2-10	1-11	0-9

Winning Jockeys	W-R	£1 Level Stake			W-R	£1 Level Stake
N Varley	2-6	+ 13.00	Miss L Hide		1-5	+ 4.00
W Newnes	1-5	+ 6.00	W Ryan		1-9	- 7.00

Winning Courses						
Brighton	1-3	+ 8.00	Redcar		1-6	+ 3.00
Lingfield	1-4	+ 2.00	Yarmouth		1-6	+ 7.00
Ripon	1-4	- 2.00				

Winning Horses	Age	Races Run	1st	2nd	3rd	Unpl	Win £
Night Transaction	5	13	3	0	1	9	9,019
Asian Punter	3	7	1	1	0	5	2,976
Scenic Dancer	4	10	1	0	0	9	2,427

Favourites	1-1	100.0%	+ 1.00	Total winning prize-money			£14,422

1991 Form	15-163	9.2%	- 7.92	1989 Form	11-126	8.7%	- 22.75
1990 Form	10-94	10.6%	+ 1.00	1988 Form	8-104	7.7%	- 1.25

C J HILL (Barnstaple, Devon)

	No. of Horses	Races Run	1st	2nd	3rd	Unpl	Per cent	£1 Level Stake
2-y-o	6	23	1	1	0	21	4.3	- 20.50
3-y-o	3	19	1	1	0	17	5.3	- 7.00
4-y-o+	30	139	11	8	7	113	7.9	- 46.17
Totals	39	181	13	10	7	151	7.2	- 73.67

BY MONTH

2-y-o	W-R	Per cent	£1 Level Stake	3-y-o	W-R	Per cent	£1 Level Stake
January	0-0	-	0.00	January	0-1	-	- 1.00
February	0-0	-	0.00	February	1-4	25.0	+ 8.00
March	0-0	-	0.00	March	0-0	-	0.00
April	0-3	-	- 3.00	April	0-2	-	- 2.00
May	0-2	-	- 2.00	May	0-0	-	0.00
June	0-4	-	- 4.00	June	0-3	-	- 3.00
July	0-5	-	- 5.00	July	0-1	-	- 1.00
August	1-3	33.3	- 0.50	August	0-4	-	- 4.00
September	0-5	-	- 5.00	September	0-2	-	- 2.00
Oct/Nov	0-1	-	- 1.00	Oct/Nov	0-2	-	- 2.00

Hill C J

4-y-o+	W-R	Per cent	£1 Level Stake	Totals	W-R	Per cent	£1 Level Stake
January	0-15	-	- 15.00	January	0-16	-	- 16.00
February	2-13	15.4	+ 16.00	February	3-17	17.6	+ 24.00
March	0-6	-	- 6.00	March	0-6	-	- 6.00
April	0-14	-	- 14.00	April	0-19	-	- 19.00
May	1-16	6.3	- 10.00	May	1-18	5.6	- 12.00
June	2-22	9.1	0.00	June	2-29	6.9	- 7.00
July	0-16	-	- 16.00	July	0-22	-	- 22.00
August	2-18	11.1	- 3.50	August	3-25	12.0	- 8.00
September	4-14	28.6	+ 7.33	September	4-21	19.0	+ 0.33
Oct/Nov	0-5	-	- 5.00	Oct/Nov	0-8	-	- 8.00

DISTANCE

2-y-o	W-R	Per cent	£1 Level Stake	3-y-o	W-R	Per cent	£1 Level Stake
5f-6f	1-18	5.6	- 15.50	5f-6f	1-11	9.1	+ 1.00
7f-8f	0-4	-	- 4.00	7f-8f	0-6	-	- 6.00
9f-13f	0-1	-	- 1.00	9f-13f	0-2	-	- 2.00
14f+	0-0	-	0.00	14f+	0-0	-	0.00

4-y-o+	W-R	Per cent	£1 Level Stake	Totals	W-R	Per cent	£1 Level Stake
5f-6f	1-49	2.0	- 43.00	5f-6f	3-78	3.8	- 57.50
7f-8f	6-64	9.4	- 18.17	7f-8f	6-74	8.1	- 28.17
9f-13f	4-24	16.7	+ 17.00	9f-13f	4-27	14.8	+ 14.00
14f+	0-2	-	- 2.00	14f+	0-2	-	- 2.00

TYPE OF RACE

Non-Handicaps	W-R	Per cent	£1 Level Stake	Handicaps	W-R	Per cent	£1 Level Stake
2-y-o	0-14	-	- 14.00	2-y-o	0-1	-	- 1.00
3-y-o	0-6	-	- 6.00	3-y-o	1-6	16.7	+ 6.00
4-y-o+	0-14	-	- 14.00	4-y-o+	7-104	6.7	- 40.00
Selling	1-17	5.9	- 14.50	Selling	3-7	42.9	+ 16.33
Apprentice	0-0	-	0.00	Apprentice	1-12	8.3	- 6.50
Amat/Ladies	0-0	-	0.00	Amat/Ladies	0-0	-	0.00
Totals	1-51	2.0	- 48.50	Totals	12-130	9.2	- 25.17

COURSE GRADE / FIRST TIME OUT

	W-R	Per cent	£1 Level Stake		W-R	Per cent	£1 Level Stake
Group 1	1-11	9.1	- 2.00	2-y-o	0-6	-	- 6.00
Group 2	3-34	8.8	- 20.00	3-y-o	0-3	-	- 3.00
Group 3	5-60	8.3	- 25.67	4-y-o+	0-28	-	- 28.00
Group 4	4-76	5.3	- 26.00				
				Totals	0-37	-	- 37.00

JOCKEYS RIDING

	W-R	Per cent	£1 Level Stake		W-R	Per cent	£1 Level Stake
J Weaver	2-4	50.0	+ 14.50	P McCabe	1-1	100.0	+ 4.50
W Carson	2-6	33.3	+ 4.33	G Duffield	1-2	50.0	+ 0.50
D Biggs	2-19	10.5	+ 1.00	A Clark	1-4	25.0	+ 5.00
N Adams	2-63	3.2	- 48.00	F Norton	1-7	14.3	- 1.50
T Quinn	1-1	100.0	+ 20.00				

T Williams	0-7	J Reid	0-3	G Carter	0-1
D Holland	0-6	Paul Eddery	0-3	J Carroll	0-1
D Harrison	0-5	B Doyle	0-2	Pat Eddery	0-1
J Quinn	0-5	N Kennedy	0-2	R Cochrane	0-1
A Mackay	0-4	P Bowe	0-2	R Street	0-1
A Tucker	0-4	R Price	0-2	S Dawson	0-1
B Russell	0-4	S Whitworth	0-2	S Maloney	0-1
G Bardwell	0-4	A Dicks	0-1	T Rogers	0-1
A Proud	0-3	A Garth	0-1	T Wilson	0-1
G Hind	0-3	G Baxter	0-1	W Ryan	0-1

COURSE RECORD

	Total W-R	Non-Handicaps 2-y-o	3-y-o+	Handicaps 2-y-o	3-y-o+	Per cent	£1 Level Stake
Bath	3-21	0-5	0-3	0-0	3-13	14.3	- 5.67
Southwell (AW)	3-39	0-3	0-11	0-0	3-25	7.7	- 10.00
Brighton	2-15	1-1	0-1	0-0	1-13	13.3	- 7.00
Goodwood	1-1	0-0	0-0	0-0	1-1	100.0	+ 8.00
Yarmouth	1-4	0-1	0-0	0-0	1-3	25.0	+ 9.00
Lingfield	1-10	0-3	0-0	0-0	1-7	10.0	- 4.00
Chepstow	1-11	0-0	0-2	0-0	1-9	9.1	- 5.00
Lingfield (AW)	1-17	0-1	0-3	0-0	1-13	5.9	+ 4.00

Leicester	0-9	Folkestone	0-5	Ascot	0-1
Salisbury	0-9	Pontefract	0-5	Epsom	0-1
Wolverhampton	0-8	Kempton	0-4	Haydock	0-1
Warwick	0-7	Windsor	0-4	Newmarket	0-1
Nottingham	0-6	Doncaster	0-2		

WINNING HORSES

	Age	Races Run	1st	2nd	3rd	Unpl	Win £
Darakah	5	14	3	0	0	11	11,436
Atlantic Way	4	9	2	1	3	3	4,877
Seaside Minstrel	4	5	1	2	0	2	2,740
Top One	7	7	1	0	0	6	2,677
Tendresse	4	4	1	2	0	1	2,637
Nikki Noo Noo	2	6	1	1	0	4	2,469
Gilbert's Girl	5	2	1	0	0	1	2,324
Mushy Boff	4	10	1	0	1	8	2,304
Grand Time	3	10	1	1	0	8	2,167
Klairover	5	7	1	0	1	5	1,786

Hill C J

		Races Won	Value £			Races Won	Value £
C John Hill		12	33,093	A G Newcombe		1	2,324

Favourites	2-22	9.1%	- 12.17	Total winning prize-money			£35,417
Longest winning sequence			2	Average SP of winner			7.3/1
Longest losing sequence			42	Return on stakes invested			-40.7%
1991 Form	16-221	7.2%	-106.00	1989 Form	3-111	2.7%	- 88.50
1990 Form	11-125	8.8%	- 56.33	1988 Form	5-64	7.8%	+ 2.50

S M HILLEN (Corse Lawn, Glos)

	No. of Horses	Races Run	1st	2nd	3rd	Unpl	Per cent	£1 Level Stake
2-y-o	4	6	1	0	0	5	16.7	+ 20.00
3-y-o	2	4	0	1	0	3	-	- 4.00
4-y-o+	0	0	0	0	0	0	-	0.00
Totals	6	10	1	1	0	8	10.0	+ 16.00

Jan	Feb	Mar	Apr	May	Jun	Jul	Aug	Sep	Oct/Nov
0-0	0-0	0-0	0-0	0-0	0-0	0-0	0-0	1-6	0-4

Winning Jockey	W-R	£1 Level Stake	Winning Course	W-R	£1 Level Stake
J Lowe	1-8	+ 18.00	Catterick	1-2	+ 24.00

Winning Horse	Age	Races Run	1st	2nd	3rd	Unpl	Win £
Dr Lechter	2	2	1	0	0	1	2,881

Favourites	0-0				Total winning prize-money	£2,881

B W HILLS (Lambourn, Berks)

	No. of Horses	Races Run	1st	2nd	3rd	Unpl	Per cent	£1 Level Stake
2-y-o	54	148	26	23	17	82	17.6	- 18.20
3-y-o	53	207	28	23	29	127	13.5	- 57.22
4-y-o+	13	63	7	5	3	48	11.1	- 24.97
Totals	120	418	61	51	49	257	14.6	-100.39

BY MONTH

2-y-o	W-R	Per cent	£1 Level Stake	3-y-o	W-R	Per cent	£1 Level Stake
Mar/Apr	1-6	16.7	- 4.00	Mar/Apr	3-38	7.9	- 22.50
May	2-18	11.1	- 13.12	May	5-31	16.1	- 6.75
June	0-0	-	0.00	June	0-13	-	- 13.00
July	1-8	12.5	- 4.50	July	4-23	17.4	+ 1.36
August	2-29	6.9	- 17.50	August	5-30	16.7	- 0.09
September	9-44	20.5	- 3.91	September	6-37	16.2	- 11.49
Oct/Nov	11-43	25.6	+ 16.83	Oct/Nov	5-35	14.3	- 3.13

4-y-o+	W-R	Per cent	£1 Level Stake	Totals	W-R	Per cent	£1 Level Stake
Mar/Apr	2-10	20.0	+ 10.00	Mar/Apr	6-54	11.1	- 16.50
May	0-13	-	- 13.00	May	7-62	11.3	- 32.87
June	0-6	-	- 6.00	June	0-19	-	- 19.00
July	1-10	10.0	- 2.00	July	6-41	14.6	- 5.14
August	1-4	25.0	- 2.17	August	8-63	12.7	- 19.76
September	1-7	14.3	- 5.47	September	16-88	18.2	- 20.87
Oct/Nov	2-13	15.4	- 4.33	Oct/Nov	18-91	19.8	+ 9.37

DISTANCE

2-y-o	W-R	Per cent	£1 Level Stake	3-y-o	W-R	Per cent	£1 Level Stake
5f-6f	12-71	16.9	- 20.20	5f-6f	0-9	-	- 9.00
7f-8f	13-75	17.3	- 3.50	7f-8f	6-60	10.0	- 17.75
9f-13f	1-2	50.0	+ 5.50	9f-13f	15-106	14.2	- 36.97
14f+	0-0	-	0.00	14f+	7-32	21.9	+ 6.50

4-y-o+	W-R	Per cent	£1 Level Stake	Totals	W-R	Per cent	£1 Level Stake
5f-6f	0-1	-	- 1.00	5f-6f	12-81	14.8	- 30.20
7f-8f	0-16	-	- 16.00	7f-8f	19-151	12.6	- 37.25
9f-13f	2-24	8.3	- 6.00	9f-13f	18-132	13.6	- 37.47
14f+	5-22	22.7	- 1.97	14f+	12-54	22.2	+ 4.53

TYPE OF RACE

Non-Handicaps	W-R	Per cent	£1 Level Stake	Handicaps	W-R	Per cent	£1 Level Stake
2-y-o	21-130	16.2	- 32.03	2-y-o	4-13	30.8	+ 14.50
3-y-o	20-132	15.2	- 23.22	3-y-o	5-65	7.7	- 36.50
4-y-o+	5-30	16.7	- 6.97	4-y-o+	2-26	7.7	- 11.00
Selling	1-7	14.3	- 2.67	Selling	0-2	-	- 2.00
Apprentice	1-2	50.0	- 0.38	Apprentice	0-7	-	- 7.00
Amat/Ladies	1-1	100.0	+ 1.88	Amat/Ladies	1-3	33.3	+ 5.00
Totals	49-302	16.2	- 63.39	Totals	12-116	10.3	- 37.00

COURSE GRADE

	W-R	Per cent	£1 Level Stake
Group 1	27-240	11.3	- 112.32
Group 2	10-62	16.1	+ 3.41
Group 3	15-80	18.8	- 7.21
Group 4	9-36	25.0	+ 15.73

FIRST TIME OUT

	W-R	Per cent	£1 Level Stake
2-y-o	5-53	9.4	- 18.00
3-y-o	6-52	11.5	- 16.12
4-y-o+	2-13	15.4	+ 5.00
Totals	13-118	11.0	- 29.12

JOCKEYS RIDING

	W-R	Per cent	£1 Level Stake		W-R	Per cent	£1 Level Stake
D Holland	21-146	14.4	- 29.06	S Mulvey	1-1	100.0	+ 0.62
Pat Eddery	12-50	24.0	+ 12.21	K L Tsui	1-2	50.0	+ 3.50
M Hills	5-46	10.9	- 31.06	R Cochrane	1-2	50.0	- 0.09
W Carson	4-26	15.4	- 8.12	D Wright	1-2	50.0	+ 6.00
S Cauthen	3-25	12.0	- 9.62	Dale Gibson	1-5	20.0	+ 3.00
Miss E Houghton	2-3	66.7	+ 7.88	R Hills	1-6	16.7	+ 1.00
A Munro	2-4	50.0	+ 7.10	J Reid	1-9	11.1	- 3.50
T Quinn	2-5	40.0	+ 8.00	J Williams	1-10	10.0	- 4.00
T Sprake	1-1	100.0	+ 1.75	Paul Eddery	1-11	9.1	- 2.00

D Harrison	0-8	D Biggs	0-2	K Darley		0-1
G Baxter	0-6	J Tate	0-2	M Birch		0-1
G Duffield	0-6	P Robinson	0-2	M Perrett		0-1
R Street	0-6	W Ryan	0-2	N Adams		0-1
C Munday	0-4	B Raymond	0-1	S Busfield		0-1
D Lee	0-4	B Rouse	0-1	S Lanigan		0-1
E Johnson	0-4	D McKeown	0-1	W R Swinburn		0-1
J Lowe	0-3	Emile Faurie	0-1			
S McCarthy	0-3	J Carroll	0-1			

COURSE RECORD

	Total W-R	Non-Handicaps 2-y-o	Non-Handicaps 3-y-o+	Handicaps 2-y-o	Handicaps 3-y-o+	Per cent	£1 Level Stake
Newmarket	10-75	5-23	4-29	0-2	1-21	13.3	- 28.00
Chester	7-18	3-5	2-8	1-1	1-4	38.9	+ 29.41
Doncaster	6-29	3-9	3-13	0-2	0-5	20.7	- 2.59
Catterick	5-10	1-2	3-6	0-0	1-2	50.0	+ 25.12
Bath	4-19	0-3	3-12	1-1	0-3	21.1	- 4.12
Yarmouth	3-8	1-4	1-2	0-0	1-2	37.5	+ 11.00
Lingfield	3-9	2-7	0-1	1-1	0-0	33.3	+ 9.00
Sandown	3-15	1-2	1-8	1-2	0-3	20.0	- 2.12
Ayr	2-5	0-0	1-2	0-0	1-3	40.0	+ 0.63
Beverley	2-6	2-3	0-2	0-0	0-1	33.3	+ 2.25
Lingfield (AW)	2-6	0-1	1-2	0-0	1-3	33.3	+ 1.25
Chepstow	2-8	0-0	2-5	0-0	0-3	25.0	+ 3.75
Nottingham	2-12	1-4	0-4	0-0	1-4	16.7	- 0.50
Newbury	2-31	1-14	1-9	0-0	0-8	6.5	- 19.90
Wolverhampton	1-2	0-0	1-1	0-1	0-0	50.0	+ 6.00
Pontefract	1-4	1-1	0-1	0-1	0-1	25.0	- 2.09

						Hills	B W
Ascot	1-7	0-0	1-5	0-1	0-1	14.3	+ 6.00
Haydock	1-10	1-3	0-4	0-0	0-3	10.0	- 8.17
Warwick	1-13	0-2	1-7	0-0	0-4	7.7	- 11.64
Leicester	1-14	0-9	0-1	0-0	1-4	7.1	- 8.50
Goodwood	1-19	0-5	1-6	0-2	0-6	5.3	- 11.00
York	1-21	0-7	1-8	0-1	0-5	4.8	- 19.17

Kempton	0-17	Windsor	0-9	Ripon	0-2
Salisbury	0-12	Redcar	0-8	Southwell (AW)	0-2
Newcastle	0-10	Thirsk	0-4	Epsom	0-1
Brighton	0-9	Folkestone	0-3		

WINNING HORSES

	Age	Races Run	1st	2nd	3rd	Unpl	Win £
Further Flight	6	6	4	0	0	2	86,252
Aquamarine	3	3	1	0	0	2	21,996
Yawl	2	3	2	0	1	0	19,672
Sure Sharp	5	4	1	1	0	2	18,990
Well Beyond	3	4	2	0	0	2	14,216
Lost Reputation	3	5	3	0	1	1	12,624
Marius	2	7	3	0	0	4	10,964
Bandoline	3	8	3	0	1	4	8,244
Magnified	3	4	1	1	0	2	7,635
Hung Parliament	2	10	2	2	3	3	7,353
The Seer	2	6	2	1	2	1	7,132
Yildiz	3	8	2	3	1	2	6,082
Northern Bird	2	8	2	0	1	5	5,585
Close Friend	4	5	1	0	0	4	5,481
Antiguan Flyer	3	5	2	1	0	2	4,838
Soaking	2	3	1	1	0	1	4,760
Nicer	2	4	1	1	0	2	4,620
Blues Traveller	2	3	1	0	1	1	4,370
Colorific	3	3	1	0	0	2	4,308
Dime Bag	3	7	2	0	1	4	3,875
Guv's Joy	2	1	1	0	0	0	3,860
Touch Silver	2	5	1	0	0	4	3,688
Factual	2	3	1	0	1	1	3,688
Pamzig	2	1	1	0	0	0	3,641
Claybank	3	7	1	2	0	4	3,590
Mystery Play	3	6	1	0	2	3	3,548
Kimberley Boy	2	3	1	0	0	2	3,522
Carbon Steel	2	4	1	1	0	2	3,465
Ajanta	2	4	1	0	1	2	3,216
Zimzalabim	2	5	1	1	0	3	3,184
Tychonic	2	2	1	0	0	1	3,028
Mark's Club	2	4	1	0	1	2	3,027
Mrs Barton	4	8	1	1	0	6	2,937
Urgent Request	2	3	1	1	0	1	2,925
Snow Board	3	3	1	0	1	1	2,679
Taahhub	2	2	1	1	0	0	2,637

Hills B W

Dazzling Fire	3	5	1	0	3	1	2,443
Touch Paper	3	6	1	1	0	4	2,427
Highland Fantasy	3	5	1	0	0	4	2,385
Besotted	3	4	1	2	1	0	2,250
Quadrant	3	6	1	1	0	4	2,238
Scandalmonger	3	6	1	0	2	3	1,730
Two And Sixpence	3	6	1	1	1	3	1,660
Resounding Success	3	4	1	1	1	1	1,380

WINNING OWNERS

	Races Won	Value £		Races Won	Value £
S Wingfield Digby	4	86,252	Mrs J M Corbett	1	4,620
K Abdulla	13	72,858	Alan Lamont	1	3,860
Sheikh Mohammed	6	33,209	John Leat	1	3,688
R D Hollingsworth	3	21,910	D F Smurfit	1	3,590
R E Sangster	5	15,734	Mrs Angie Silver	1	3,522
Mrs Leonard Simpson	3	10,964	R A N Bonnycastle	1	3,027
Wafic Said	2	9,851	A L R Morton	1	2,937
W J Gredley	2	7,353	J Hanson	1	2,679
A R B Aspinall	2	7,132	Hamdan Al-Maktoum	1	2,637
Howard Kaskel	2	7,106	N N Browne	1	2,443
K Al-Said	3	7,059	A B Weller	1	2,385
S Mino	2	6,082	D J Deer	1	1,660
John E Bradley	2	5,585			

Favourites	27-80	33.8%	- 9.39	Total winning prize-money			£328,141
Longest winning sequence			3	Average SP of winner			4.2/1
Longest losing sequence			34	Return on stakes invested			-24.0%
1991 Form	99-491	20.2%	+ 7.81	1989 Form	73-463	15.8%	-156.28
1990 Form	113-579	19.5%	- 52.11	1988 Form	93-521	17.9%	- 38.49

J W HILLS (Lambourn, Berks)

	No. of Horses	Races Run	1st	2nd	3rd	Unpl	Per cent	£1 Level Stake
2-y-o	12	41	3	5	6	27	7.3	- 17.00
3-y-o	17	99	12	14	17	56	12.1	- 34.95
4-y-o+	8	72	7	10	11	44	9.7	- 14.84
Totals	37	212	22	29	34	127	10.4	- 66.79

BY MONTH

2-y-o	W-R	Per cent	£1 Level Stake	3-y-o	W-R	Per cent	£1 Level Stake
Mar/Apr	0-0	-	0.00	Mar/Apr	0-11	-	- 8.00
May	0-0	-	0.00	May	4-21	19.0	- 4.75
June	0-4	-	- 4.00	June	2-15	13.3	+ 1.00
July	1-5	20.0	0.00	July	2-15	13.3	- 12.20
August	1-7	14.3	+ 2.00	August	0-14	-	- 14.00
September	1-10	10.0	0.00	September	2-12	16.7	+ 7.00
Oct/Nov	0-15	-	- 15.00	Oct/Nov	2-11	18.2	- 1.00

4-y-o+	W-R	Per cent	£1 Level Stake	Totals	W-R	Per cent	£1 Level Stake
Mar/Apr	0-5	-	- 5.00	Mar/Apr	0-16	-	- 13.00
May	0-6	-	- 6.00	May	4-27	14.8	- 10.75
June	3-5	60.0	+ 15.83	June	5-24	20.8	+ 12.83
July	0-13	-	- 13.00	July	3-33	9.1	- 25.20
August	1-16	6.3	- 1.00	August	2-37	5.4	- 13.00
September	1-14	7.1	- 5.00	September	4-36	11.1	+ 2.00
Oct/Nov	2-13	15.4	- 0.67	Oct/Nov	4-39	10.3	- 16.67

DISTANCE

2-y-o	W-R	Per cent	£1 Level Stake	3-y-o	W-R	Per cent	£1 Level Stake
5f-6f	1-26	3.8	- 21.00	5f-6f	0-1	-	- 1.00
7f-8f	2-15	13.3	+ 4.00	7f-8f	5-42	11.9	- 12.56
9f-13f	0-0	-	0.00	9f-13f	6-45	13.3	- 11.75
14f+	0-0	-	0.00	14f+	1-11	9.1	- 9.64

4-y-o+	W-R	Per cent	£1 Level Stake	Totals	W-R	Per cent	£1 Level Stake
5f-6f	1-9	11.1	- 4.67	5f-6f	2-36	5.6	- 26.67
7f-8f	2-30	6.7	- 7.00	7f-8f	9-87	10.3	- 15.56
9f-13f	4-31	12.9	- 1.17	9f-13f	10-76	13.2	- 12.92
14f+	0-2	-	- 2.00	14f+	1-13	7.7	- 11.64

TYPE OF RACE

Non-Handicaps	W-R	Per cent	£1 Level Stake	Handicaps	W-R	Per cent	£1 Level Stake
2-y-o	1-31	3.2	- 26.00	2-y-o	1-8	12.5	+ 1.00
3-y-o	5-42	11.9	- 26.20	3-y-o	5-50	10.0	- 10.75
4-y-o+	1-2	50.0	+ 6.00	4-y-o+	6-60	10.0	- 10.84
Selling	0-2	-	- 2.00	Selling	2-5	40.0	+ 10.00
Apprentice	1-3	33.3	+ 1.00	Apprentice	0-7	-	- 7.00
Amat/Ladies	0-0	-	0.00	Amat/Ladies	0-2	-	- 2.00
Totals	8-80	10.0	- 47.20	Totals	14-132	10.6	- 19.59

COURSE GRADE

	W-R	Per cent	£1 Level Stake
Group 1	6-105	5.7	- 54.50
Group 2	6-28	21.4	+ 5.02
Group 3	6-55	10.9	- 9.00
Group 4	4-24	16.7	- 8.31

FIRST TIME OUT

	W-R	Per cent	£1 Level Stake
2-y-o	0-11	-	- 11.00
3-y-o	0-17	-	- 17.00
4-y-o+	0-7	-	- 7.00
Totals	0-35	-	- 35.00

JOCKEYS RIDING

	W-R	Per cent	£1 Level Stake		W-R	Per cent	£1 Level Stake
M Hills	9-53	17.0	+ 2.91	D Holland	2-10	20.0	+ 5.00
R Hills	6-60	10.0	- 19.20	J Weaver	1-2	50.0	+ 6.00
D Harrison	4-18	22.2	+ 7.50				

W Newnes	0-11	Mr C Vigors	0-2	J Reid	0-1
S Dawson	0-9	Paul Eddery	0-2	K Rutter	0-1
S Whitworth	0-5	S Cauthen	0-2	L Piggott	0-1
J Williams	0-3	W R Swinburn	0-2	M Roberts	0-1
N Carlisle	0-3	Antoinette Armes	0-1	N Kennedy	0-1
W Carson	0-3	Emma O'Gorman	0-1	P Robinson	0-1
B Rouse	0-2	G Carter	0-1	R Perham	0-1
Dale Gibson	0-2	G Duffield	0-1	T Quinn	0-1
F Norton	0-2	J D Smith	0-1	T Williams	0-1
G Baxter	0-2	J Fortune	0-1	W Ryan	0-1
M Henry	0-2	J Lowe	0-1		

COURSE RECORD

	Total W-R	Non-Handicaps 2-y-o	Non-Handicaps 3-y-o+	Handicaps 2-y-o	Handicaps 3-y-o+	Per cent	£1 Level Stake
Redcar	3-8	0-1	0-1	0-0	3-6	37.5	+ 11.33
Lingfield	2-2	0-0	0-0	1-1	1-1	100.0	+ 10.25
Warwick	2-10	0-0	1-4	0-0	1-6	20.0	- 3.64
Goodwood	2-21	0-1	1-5	0-0	1-15	9.5	- 7.00
Beverley	1-1	0-0	0-0	1-1	0-0	100.0	+ 9.00
Lingfield (AW)	1-1	0-0	0-0	0-0	1-1	100.0	+ 3.33
Thirsk	1-2	0-0	1-1	0-0	0-1	50.0	- 0.56
Wolverhampton	1-3	1-2	0-0	0-0	0-1	33.3	+ 2.00
Doncaster	1-6	0-1	0-0	0-1	1-4	16.7	+ 9.00
Epsom	1-6	0-0	0-1	0-0	1-5	16.7	+ 1.50
Nottingham	1-6	0-2	1-1	0-0	0-3	16.7	- 2.00
Chepstow	1-8	0-3	1-2	0-0	0-3	12.5	0.00
Leicester	1-8	0-2	1-3	0-0	0-3	12.5	- 4.00
Windsor	1-8	0-4	0-1	0-1	1-2	12.5	+ 7.00
Yarmouth	1-8	0-2	1-2	0-0	0-4	12.5	- 3.00
York	1-8	0-1	0-0	0-0	1-7	12.5	- 3.00
Newbury	1-12	0-3	0-2	0-0	1-7	8.3	- 3.00

Newmarket	0-19	Catterick	0-5	Hamilton	0-2
Bath	0-14	Chester	0-4	Ripon	0-2
Kempton	0-11	Salisbury	0-4	Ayr	0-1
Ascot	0-10	Haydock	0-3	Newcastle	0-1
Sandown	0-7	Southwell (AW)	0-3		
Brighton	0-6	Folkestone	0-2		

WINNING HORSES

		Races					Win
	Age	Run	1st	2nd	3rd	Unpl	£
Castoret	6	12	2	2	3	5	32,389
Jade Vale	3	10	3	0	2	5	8,956
Edge Of Darkness	3	9	2	1	3	3	6,769
Nashville Blues	3	8	2	3	1	2	6,566
Gilderdale	10	14	2	0	3	9	5,105
Glide Path	3	9	2	2	1	4	5,085
Salbyng	4	11	1	3	2	5	3,980
Eternal Flame	4	10	1	4	1	4	2,930
Scales Of Justice	6	7	1	0	0	6	2,889
Fairy Story	2	6	1	1	1	3	2,658
Teddy's Play	3	5	1	2	0	2	2,636
Edgeaway	3	9	1	1	1	6	2,364
Tempelhof	3	5	1	1	1	2	2,233
Special One	2	4	1	1	1	1	2,070
Hotel California	2	5	1	0	1	3	1,884

WINNING OWNERS

	Races Won	Value £		Races Won	Value £
Lady D'Avigdor-Goldsmid	2	32,389	Mrs P Jubert	1	3,980
Mrs S Bosher	5	15,699	Cliffe Rowlands	1	2,930
Christopher Wright	3	7,409	The Fairy Story Partnership	1	2,658
Major Brijendra Singh	2	6,592	The Thoroughbred Exchange	1	2,364
Abbott Racing Partners	2	5,105	R E Sangster	1	2,233
The Jampot Partnership	2	5,085	Mrs Christine Shove	1	2,070

Favourites	6-29	20.7%	- 9.95	Total winning prize-money			£88,512
Longest winning sequence			3	Average SP of winner			5.6/1
Longest losing sequence			29	Return on stakes invested			-31.5%
1991 Form	20-191	10.5%	- 24.75	1989 Form	16-183	8.7%	- 72.07
1990 Form	28-202	13.9%	+ 20.72	1988 Form	14-164	8.5%	- 82.15

P J HOBBS (Minehead, Somerset)

	No. of Horses	Races Run	1st	2nd	3rd	Unpl	Per cent	£1 Level Stake
2-y-o	0	0	0	0	0	0	-	0.00
3-y-o	1	1	0	0	0	1	-	- 1.00
4-y-o+	11	22	2	0	0	20	9.1	- 6.00
Totals	12	23	2	0	0	21	8.7	- 7.00

Jan	Feb	Mar	Apr	May	Jun	Jul	Aug	Sep	Oct/Nov
0-1	0-0	0-0	0-0	2-5	0-7	0-3	0-4	0-1	0-2

Winning Jockeys	W-R	£1 Level Stake		W-R	£1 Level Stake
J Carroll	1-3	+ 3.00	Mrs S Hobbs	1-4	+ 6.00

Winning Courses	W-R	£1 Level Stake		W-R	£1 Level Stake
Beverley	1-1	+ 5.00	Haydock	1-1	+ 9.00

Winning Horses	Age	Races Run	1st	2nd	3rd	Unpl	Win £
Aswamedh	4	2	1	0	0	1	3,052
Row Ree	4	3	1	0	0	2	2,344

Favourites	0-0	Total winning prize-money	£5,396

1991 Form	0-11	1989 Form	0-4
1990 Form	0-8	1988 Form	0-13

R J HODGES (Charlton Adam, Somerset)

	No. of Horses	Races Run	1st	2nd	3rd	Unpl	Per cent	£1 Level Stake
2-y-o	4	17	3	1	0	13	17.6	+ 30.20
3-y-o	17	86	1	5	4	76	1.2	- 76.00
4-y-o+	37	263	17	22	31	193	6.5	-117.16
Totals	58	366	21	28	35	282	5.7	-162.96

BY MONTH

2-y-o	W-R	Per cent	£1 Level Stake	3-y-o	W-R	Per cent	£1 Level Stake
January	0-0	-	0.00	January	0-0	-	0.00
February	0-0	-	0.00	February	0-0	-	0.00
March	0-0	-	0.00	March	0-3	-	- 3.00
April	1-1	100.0	+ 33.00	April	0-10	-	- 10.00
May	0-1	-	- 1.00	May	0-14	-	- 14.00
June	0-2	-	- 2.00	June	0-15	-	- 15.00
July	1-3	33.3	+ 8.00	July	0-12	-	- 12.00
August	0-4	-	- 4.00	August	1-16	6.3	- 6.00
September	1-3	33.3	- 0.80	September	0-10	-	- 10.00
Oct/Nov	0-3	-	- 3.00	Oct/Nov	0-6	-	- 6.00

4-y-o+	W-R	Per cent	£1 Level Stake	Totals	W-R	Per cent	£1 Level Stake
January	0-3	-	- 3.00	January	0-3	-	- 3.00
February	0-6	-	- 6.00	February	0-6	-	- 6.00
March	0-4	-	- 4.00	March	0-7	-	- 7.00
April	1-33	3.0	- 12.00	April	2-44	4.5	+ 11.00
May	3-38	7.9	- 19.37	May	3-53	5.7	- 34.37
June	3-45	6.7	- 27.62	June	3-62	4.8	- 44.62
July	2-29	6.9	- 13.67	July	3-44	6.8	- 17.67
August	4-50	8.0	- 20.50	August	5-70	7.1	- 30.50
September	1-33	3.0	- 12.00	September	2-46	4.3	- 22.80
Oct/Nov	3-22	13.6	+ 1.00	Oct/Nov	3-31	9.7	- 8.00

DISTANCE

2-y-o	W-R	Per cent	£1 Level Stake	3-y-o	W-R	Per cent	£1 Level Stake
5f-6f	3-13	23.1	+ 34.20	5f-6f	1-20	5.0	- 10.00
7f-8f	0-4	-	- 4.00	7f-8f	0-40	-	- 40.00
9f-13f	0-0	-	0.00	9f-13f	0-23	-	- 23.00
14f+	0-0	-	0.00	14f+	0-3	-	- 3.00

4-y-o+	W-R	Per cent	£1 Level Stake	Totals	W-R	Per cent	£1 Level Stake
5f-6f	13-155	8.4	- 43.99	5f-6f	17-188	9.0	- 19.79
7f-8f	2-54	3.7	- 44.50	7f-8f	2-98	2.0	- 88.50
9f-13f	1-46	2.2	- 41.67	9f-13f	1-69	1.4	- 64.67
14f+	1-8	12.5	+ 13.00	14f+	1-11	9.1	+ 10.00

TYPE OF RACE

Non-Handicaps	W-R	Per cent	£1 Level Stake	Handicaps	W-R	Per cent	£1 Level Stake
2-y-o	2-7	28.6	+ 29.20	2-y-o	0-5	-	- 5.00
3-y-o	0-17	-	- 17.00	3-y-o	1-46	2.2	- 36.00
4-y-o+	0-12	-	- 12.00	4-y-o+	15-207	7.2	- 77.49
Selling	1-28	3.6	- 17.00	Selling	0-13	-	- 13.00
Apprentice	0-1	-	- 1.00	Apprentice	2-23	8.7	- 6.67
Amat/Ladies	0-1	-	- 1.00	Amat/Ladies	0-6	-	- 6.00
Totals	3-66	4.5	- 18.80	Totals	18-300	6.0	-144.16

COURSE GRADE

	W-R	Per cent	£1 Level Stake
Group 1	6-72	8.3	- 5.50
Group 2	3-95	3.2	- 80.25
Group 3	10-141	7.1	- 29.41
Group 4	2-58	3.4	- 47.80

FIRST TIME OUT

	W-R	Per cent	£1 Level Stake
2-y-o	1-4	25.0	+ 30.00
3-y-o	0-15	-	- 15.00
4-y-o+	1-35	2.9	- 14.00
Totals	2-54	3.7	+ 1.00

JOCKEYS RIDING

	W-R	Per cent	£1 Level Stake		W-R	Per cent	£1 Level Stake
T Sprake	7-96	7.3	+ 0.88	D Biggs	1-9	11.1	+ 3.00
S Drowne	4-48	8.3	- 29.97	Pat Eddery	1-9	11.1	- 3.50
R Cochrane	2-29	6.9	- 12.50	J Quinn	1-19	5.3	- 9.00
N Kennedy	1-3	33.3	+ 3.00	F Norton	1-20	5.0	- 9.00
M Hills	1-6	16.7	+ 15.00	W Carson	1-26	3.8	- 22.25
Paul Eddery	1-7	14.3	- 4.62				

A Dicks	0-8	A Munro	0-1	N Carlisle		0-1
M Roberts	0-8	A Tucker	0-1	N Gwilliams		0-1
T Quinn	0-8	B Crossley	0-1	P Bowe		0-1
T Thompson	0-7	B Raymond	0-1	R Street		0-1
D Holland	0-6	B Thomas	0-1	R Waterfield		0-1
N Adams	0-6	D Carson	0-1	S Cauthen		0-1
Dale Gibson	0-5	Dana Mellor	0-1	S Mulvey		0-1
Mrs S J Hembrow	0-5	G Bardwell	0-1	S Whitworth		0-1
C Hawksley	0-4	G Forster	0-1	T G McLaughlin		0-1
A McGlone	0-2	G Hind	0-1	T Williams		0-1
C Avery	0-2	J Fortune	0-1	W Hollick		0-1
J Williams	0-2	J Reid	0-1			
L Piggott	0-2	M Humphries	0-1			
R Perham	0-2	Mr O Frei	0-1			
A Garth	0-1	Mr T Piper	0-1			

COURSE RECORD

	Total W-R	Non-Handicaps 2-y-o	Non-Handicaps 3-y-o+	Handicaps 2-y-o	Handicaps 3-y-o+	Per cent	£1 Level Stake
Bath	4-42	1-2	0-12	0-0	3-28	9.5	+ 8.71
Nottingham	3-18	0-0	0-0	0-1	3-17	16.7	+ 23.00
Chepstow	2-36	0-1	0-5	0-1	2-29	5.6	- 27.12
Ayr	1-2	0-0	0-0	0-0	1-2	50.0	+ 19.00
Ascot	1-3	0-0	0-0	0-0	1-3	33.3	+ 7.00
Epsom	1-5	0-0	0-0	0-0	1-5	20.0	+ 1.00
Newmarket	1-7	0-0	0-1	0-0	1-6	14.3	- 1.50
Kempton	1-11	0-0	0-1	0-0	1-10	9.1	+ 1.00
Lingfield (AW)	1-14	0-1	0-3	0-0	1-10	7.1	- 6.00
Wolverhampton	1-18	1-1	0-7	0-0	0-10	5.6	- 15.80
Goodwood	1-21	0-1	0-0	0-0	1-20	4.8	- 9.00
Lingfield	1-23	0-2	0-2	0-1	1-18	4.3	- 15.50
Windsor	1-23	1-2	0-7	0-0	0-14	4.3	- 12.00
Salisbury	1-34	0-1	0-1	0-1	1-31	2.9	- 30.25
Brighton	1-35	0-0	0-4	0-0	1-31	2.9	- 31.50

Folkestone	0-12	Pontefract	0-7	Chester	0-2
Warwick	0-10	Yarmouth	0-6	Hamilton	0-2
Sandown	0-8	Doncaster	0-4	Haydock	0-1
Leicester	0-7	Catterick	0-3	Ripon	0-1
Newbury	0-7	York	0-3	Southwell (AW)	0-1

WINNING HORSES

	Age	Races Run	1st	2nd	3rd	Unpl	Win £
Ashtina	7	17	3	1	3	10	30,151
How's Yer Father	6	17	3	3	2	9	18,739
Fivesevenfiveo	4	15	2	3	2	8	5,809
Harry's Coming	8	14	2	1	1	10	5,542
Hard To Figure	6	16	1	2	4	9	3,420
Esthal	2	3	1	1	0	1	3,028
Dickens Lane	5	13	1	0	2	10	3,002
Jeremiahs Boy	2	2	1	0	0	1	2,930
Mister Jolson	3	5	1	1	1	2	2,856
Lady Electric	6	3	1	1	1	0	2,657
Beatle Song	4	12	1	0	0	11	2,532
Amethystine	6	12	1	1	1	9	2,532
Now Boarding	5	9	1	1	2	5	2,192
Scarlet Princess	4	9	1	0	1	7	2,093
Hy Wilma	2	6	1	0	0	5	1,532

WINNING OWNERS

	Races Won	Value £		Races Won	Value £
Ms S A Joyner	3	30,151	J Barber	1	2,930
Unity Farm Holiday Centre Ltd	4	21,766	A J Coombes	1	2,657
J W Mursell	3	8,808	Miss R Dobson	1	2,532
George W Baker	2	5,809	Miss M E Gibbon	1	2,192
Mrs D A Wetherall	2	5,542	D J F Phillips	1	2,093
Bull & Bear Racing	1	3,002	R J Hodges	1	1,532

Favourites	6-29	20.7%	- 8.79	Total winning prize-money £89,013
Longest winning sequence			1	Average SP of winner 8.7/1
Longest losing sequence			42	Return on stakes invested -44.5%
1991 Form	27-287	9.4%	- 93.74	1989 Form 12-123 9.8% - 13.87
1990 Form	25-245	10.2%	- 76.57	1988 Form 8-97 8.2% - 12.93

K W HOGG (Isle of Man)

	No. of Horses	Races Run	1st	2nd	3rd	Unpl	Per cent	£1 Level Stake
2-y-o	1	12	1	3	1	7	8.3	- 4.00
3-y-o	1	12	0	0	1	11	-	- 12.00
4-y-o+	3	19	3	1	1	14	15.8	+ 24.00
Totals	5	43	4	4	3	32	9.3	+ 8.00

Jan	Feb	Mar	Apr	May	Jun	Jul	Aug	Sep	Oct/Nov
0-0	0-0	0-4	0-3	0-5	0-8	1-6	3-11	0-6	0-0

Hogg K W

Winning Jockeys	W-R	£1 Level Stake			W-R	£1 Level Stake
J Corrigan	2-11	+ 11.00	A Garth		1-9	+ 12.00
W Ryan	1-5	+ 3.00				

Winning Courses	W-R	£1 Level Stake			W-R	£1 Level Stake
Beverley	2-11	+ 8.00	Leicester		1-9	+ 12.00
Ripon	1-4	+ 7.00				

Winning Horses	Age	Races Run	1st	2nd	3rd	Unpl	Win £
Kinoko	4	11	3	1	1	6	10,588
Costa Verde	2	12	1	3	1	7	3,652

Favourites	0-0		Total winning prize-money	£14,240

W HOLDEN (Newmarket)

	No. of Horses	Races Run	1st	2nd	3rd	Unpl	Per cent	£1 Level Stake
2-y-o	1	2	0	0	0	2	-	- 2.00
3-y-o	3	8	0	0	0	8	-	- 8.00
4-y-o+	6	20	2	2	2	14	10.0	- 7.00
Totals	10	30	2	2	2	24	6.7	- 17.00

Jan	Feb	Mar	Apr	May	Jun	Jul	Aug	Sep	Oct/Nov
0-3	0-4	0-5	0-1	1-2	1-4	0-2	0-3	0-3	0-3

Winning Jockey	W-R	£1 Level Stake			W-R	£1 Level Stake
T Williams	2-3	+ 10.00				

Winning Courses	W-R	£1 Level Stake			W-R	£1 Level Stake
Kempton	1-1	+ 6.00	Brighton		1-3	+ 3.00

Winning Horse	Age	Races Run	1st	2nd	3rd	Unpl	Win £
Kawwas	7	7	2	1	0	4	5,945

Favourites	1-2	50.0%	+ 4.00	Total winning prize-money	£5,945

1991 Form	3-67	4.5%	- 24.05	1989 Form	3-60	5.0%	- 23.50
1990 Form	1-31	3.2%	- 27.50	1988 Form	4-50	8.0%	- 18.50

R J HOLDER (Bristol, Avon)

	No. of Horses	Races Run	1st	2nd	3rd	Unpl	Per cent	£1 Level Stake
2-y-o	14	63	2	4	3	54	3.2	- 45.00
3-y-o	12	74	3	6	6	59	4.1	- 56.50
4-y-o+	20	112	6	6	10	90	5.4	- 46.00
Totals	46	249	11	16	19	203	4.4	-147.50

BY MONTH

2-y-o	W-R	Per cent	£1 Level Stake	3-y-o	W-R	Per cent	£1 Level Stake
Mar/Apr	0-4	-	- 3.00	Mar/Apr	0-14	-	- 12.00
May	0-9	-	- 9.00	May	0-16	-	- 16.00
June	1-11	9.1	- 8.00	June	0-11	-	- 11.00
July	0-9	-	- 9.00	July	0-6	-	- 6.00
August	0-12	-	- 12.00	August	0-7	-	- 7.00
September	1-10	10.0	+ 5.00	September	2-13	15.4	+ 1.00
Oct/Nov	0-8	-	- 8.00	Oct/Nov	1-7	14.3	- 3.50

4-y-o+	W-R	Per cent	£1 Level Stake	Totals	W-R	Per cent	£1 Level Stake
Mar/Apr	1-19	5.3	+ 3.00	Mar/Apr	1-37	2.7	- 12.00
May	0-19	-	- 19.00	May	0-44	-	- 44.00
June	1-26	3.8	- 20.00	June	2-48	4.2	- 39.00
July	4-20	20.0	+ 23.00	July	4-35	11.4	+ 8.00
August	0-11	-	- 11.00	August	0-30	-	- 30.00
September	0-12	-	- 12.00	September	3-35	8.6	- 6.00
Oct/Nov	0-5	-	- 5.00	Oct/Nov	1-20	5.0	- 16.50

DISTANCE

2-y-o	W-R	Per cent	£1 Level Stake	3-y-o	W-R	Per cent	£1 Level Stake
5f-6f	0-30	-	- 30.00	5f-6f	3-29	10.3	- 11.50
7f-8f	2-32	6.3	- 14.00	7f-8f	0-21	-	- 21.00
9f-13f	0-1	-	- 1.00	9f-13f	0-20	-	- 20.00
14f+	0-0	-	0.00	14f+	0-4	-	- 4.00

4-y-o+	W-R	Per cent	£1 Level Stake	Totals	W-R	Per cent	£1 Level Stake
5f-6f	3-33	9.1	+ 3.00	5f-6f	6-92	6.5	- 38.50
7f-8f	1-28	3.6	- 21.00	7f-8f	3-81	3.7	- 56.00
9f-13f	1-36	2.8	- 19.00	9f-13f	1-57	1.8	- 40.00
14f+	1-15	6.7	- 9.00	14f+	1-19	5.3	- 13.00

TYPE OF RACE

Non-Handicaps	W-R	Per cent	£1 Level Stake	Handicaps	W-R	Per cent	£1 Level Stake
2-y-o	0-38	-	- 38.00	2-y-o	0-12	-	- 12.00
3-y-o	1-20	5.0	- 13.00	3-y-o	2-37	5.4	- 26.50
4-y-o+	0-11	-	- 11.00	4-y-o+	6-86	7.0	- 20.00
Selling	1-22	4.5	- 19.00	Selling	1-11	9.1	+ 4.00
Apprentice	0-0	-	0.00	Apprentice	0-10	-	- 10.00
Amat/Ladies	0-2	-	- 2.00	Amat/Ladies	0-0	-	0.00
Totals	2-93	2.2	- 83.00	Totals	9-156	5.8	- 64.50

COURSE GRADE

	W-R	Per cent	£1 Level Stake
Group 1	1-46	2.2	- 29.00
Group 2	3-49	6.1	- 24.00
Group 3	7-97	7.2	- 37.50
Group 4	0-57	-	- 57.00

FIRST TIME OUT

	W-R	Per cent	£1 Level Stake
2-y-o	0-14	-	- 14.00
3-y-o	0-12	-	- 12.00
4-y-o+	1-20	5.0	- 3.00
Totals	1-46	2.2	- 29.00

JOCKEYS RIDING

	W-R	Per cent	£1 Level Stake		W-R	Per cent	£1 Level Stake
J Williams	7-53	13.2	+ 6.50	L Dettori	1-5	20.0	+ 12.00
P Robinson	1-2	50.0	+ 13.00	N Adams	1-65	1.5	- 62.00
M Roberts	1-5	20.0	+ 2.00				

S Drowne	0-35	C Hawksley	0-3	L Piggott		0-1
A Dicks	0-18	F Norton	0-3	M Hills		0-1
A Tucker	0-7	G Carter	0-3	Mr R Farrant		0-1
J Quinn	0-6	Paul Eddery	0-2	Mrs E Mellor		0-1
A Munro	0-5	A Proud	0-1	Pat Eddery		0-1
G Duffield	0-5	D Biggs	0-1	R Hills		0-1
D Holland	0-4	D Moffatt	0-1	R Price		0-1
J Lowe	0-4	Dale Gibson	0-1	Robyn Fullelove		0-1
R Fox	0-4	J Dennis	0-1	S Cauthen		0-1
R Waterfield	0-4	J Reid	0-1	W R Swinburn		0-1

COURSE RECORD

	Total W-R	Non-Handicaps 2-y-o	3-y-o+	Handicaps 2-y-o	3-y-o+	Per cent	£1 Level Stake
Chepstow	3-25	0-3	1-4	0-2	2-16	12.0	- 7.50
Bath	3-34	0-10	0-5	0-3	3-16	8.8	- 7.00
Salisbury	2-30	0-6	0-4	0-1	2-19	6.7	- 8.00
Ascot	1-3	0-0	0-0	0-0	1-3	33.3	+ 14.00
Brighton	1-9	1-1	0-2	0-1	0-5	11.1	- 6.00
Leicester	1-10	0-4	0-2	1-2	0-2	10.0	+ 5.00

Wolverhampton	0-33	Newmarket	0-5	Epsom	0-2
Warwick	0-17	Beverley	0-4	Pontefract	0-2
Windsor	0-12	Folkestone	0-4	Catterick	0-1
Nottingham	0-10	Haydock	0-4	Chester	0-1
Goodwood	0-7	Kempton	0-4	Lingfield (AW)	0-1
Lingfield	0-7	Sandown	0-4	Redcar	0-1
Doncaster	0-5	York	0-4	Ripon	0-1
Newbury	0-5	Ayr	0-3	Southwell (AW)	0-1

WINNING HORSES

		Races					Win
	Age	Run	1st	2nd	3rd	Unpl	£
Bertie Wooster	9	12	1	1	1	9	10,598
Blue Topaze	4	9	2	0	4	3	7,443
Paper Dance	4	7	1	1	1	4	4,175
Teanarco	4	13	1	2	1	9	3,418
Jigsaw Boy	3	8	1	1	1	5	3,290
Easy Purchase	5	5	1	0	0	4	2,902
General Chase	2	8	1	0	1	6	2,763
Sir Joey	3	5	1	1	0	3	2,448
Neither Nor	3	6	1	0	2	3	2,406
Homemaker	2	9	1	3	0	5	2,108

WINNING OWNERS

	Races Won	Value £		Races Won	Value £
Miss Amanda J Rawding	1	10,598	Ian Purchase	1	2,902
M S Saunders	2	7,443	Mrs Marigold West	1	2,763
M Dallimore	1	4,175	Mrs A G Sims	1	2,448
B K Symonds	1	3,418	D Tylden-Wright	1	2,406
All Eight Club	1	3,290	R J Glenn	1	2,108

Favourites	2-9	22.2%	- 1.50	Total winning prize-money			£41,550
Longest winning sequence			2	Average SP of winner			8.2/1
Longest losing sequence			69	Return on stakes invested			-59.2%
1991 Form	18-271	6.6%	- 97.25	1989 Form	17-204	8.3%	- 59.42
1990 Form	16-224	7.1%	-121.37	1988 Form	8-178	4.5%	-118.50

R HOLLINSHEAD (Upper Longdon, Staffs)

	No. of Horses	Races Run	1st	2nd	3rd	Unpl	Per cent	£1 Level Stake
2-y-o	27	148	12	21	21	94	8.1	- 44.20
3-y-o	26	238	24	33	31	150	10.1	- 74.55
4-y-o+	24	186	19	13	23	131	10.2	+ 7.11
Totals	77	572	55	67	75	375	9.6	-111.64

BY MONTH

2-y-o	W-R	Per cent	£1 Level Stake	3-y-o	W-R	Per cent	£1 Level Stake
January	0-0	-	0.00	January	2-10	20.0	+ 5.00
February	0-0	-	0.00	February	3-10	30.0	+ 3.23
March	0-3	-	- 3.00	March	2-17	11.8	- 10.50
April	0-9	-	- 9.00	April	2-28	7.1	- 17.17
May	0-13	-	- 13.00	May	3-28	10.7	+ 10.00
June	2-18	11.1	- 12.25	June	2-25	8.0	- 10.00
July	1-17	5.9	- 12.00	July	5-32	15.6	+ 0.29
August	5-28	17.9	+ 14.55	August	4-23	17.4	+ 4.10
September	0-25	-	- 25.00	September	0-34	-	- 34.00
Oct/Nov	4-35	11.4	+ 15.50	Oct/Nov	1-31	3.2	- 25.50

4-y-o+	W-R	Per cent	£1 Level Stake	Totals	W-R	Per cent	£1 Level Stake
January	0-3	-	- 3.00	January	2-13	15.4	+ 2.00
February	0-2	-	- 2.00	February	3-12	25.0	+ 1.23
March	0-11	-	- 11.00	March	2-31	6.5	- 24.50
April	2-19	10.5	+ 18.00	April	4-56	7.1	- 8.17
May	2-26	7.7	- 12.50	May	5-67	7.5	- 15.50
June	5-28	17.9	+ 23.63	June	9-71	12.7	+ 1.38
July	6-32	18.8	+ 5.75	July	12-81	14.8	- 5.96
August	3-26	11.5	+ 1.23	August	12-77	15.6	+ 19.88
September	0-20	-	- 20.00	September	0-79	-	- 79.00
Oct/Nov	1-19	5.3	+ 7.00	Oct/Nov	6-85	7.1	- 3.00

DISTANCE

2-y-o	W-R	Per cent	£1 Level Stake	3-y-o	W-R	Per cent	£1 Level Stake
5f-6f	9-95	9.5	- 26.70	5f-6f	3-26	11.5	- 7.90
7f-8f	3-51	5.9	- 15.50	7f-8f	9-91	9.9	- 41.64
9f-13f	0-2	-	- 2.00	9f-13f	12-103	11.7	- 7.01
14f+	0-0	-	0.00	14f+	0-18	-	- 18.00

4-y-o+	W-R	Per cent	£1 Level Stake	Totals	W-R	Per cent	£1 Level Stake
5f-6f	4-59	6.8	- 10.50	5f-6f	16-180	8.9	- 45.10
7f-8f	5-43	11.6	+ 10.75	7f-8f	17-185	9.2	- 46.39
9f-13f	6-57	10.5	+ 7.50	9f-13f	18-162	11.1	- 1.51
14f+	4-27	14.8	- 0.64	14f+	4-45	8.9	- 18.64

TYPE OF RACE

Non-Handicaps	W-R	Per cent	£1 Level Stake	Handicaps	W-R	Per cent	£1 Level Stake
2-y-o	10-119	8.4	- 39.20	2-y-o	2-27	7.4	- 3.00
3-y-o	12-107	11.2	- 38.54	3-y-o	7-88	8.0	- 31.17
4-y-o+	1-20	5.0	- 18.27	4-y-o+	16-138	11.6	+ 18.38
Selling	4-27	14.8	+ 10.16	Selling	1-11	9.1	+ 10.00
Apprentice	1-11	9.1	- 5.00	Apprentice	1-22	4.5	- 13.00
Amat/Ladies	0-0	-	0.00	Amat/Ladies	0-2	-	- 2.00
Totals	28-284	9.9	- 90.85	Totals	27-288	9.4	- 20.79

COURSE GRADE

	W-R	Per cent	£1 Level Stake
Group 1	13-151	8.6	- 16.44
Group 2	10-101	9.9	- 11.87
Group 3	14-172	8.1	- 63.27
Group 4	18-148	12.2	- 20.06

FIRST TIME OUT

	W-R	Per cent	£1 Level Stake
2-y-o	0-26	-	- 26.00
3-y-o	2-25	8.0	- 7.00
4-y-o+	2-23	8.7	- 3.00
Totals	4-74	5.4	- 36.00

JOCKEYS RIDING

	W-R	Per cent	£1 Level Stake		W-R	Per cent	£1 Level Stake
W Ryan	23-195	11.8	- 38.43	N Carlisle	1-4	25.0	+ 7.00
A Garth	6-89	6.7	- 28.37	L Piggott	1-5	20.0	- 0.50
M Humphries	5-44	11.4	+ 8.75	W R Swinburn	1-5	20.0	- 2.50
L Dettori	3-20	15.0	- 1.00	J Dennis	1-11	9.1	- 5.00
K Darley	3-30	10.0	+ 8.50	R Cochrane	1-12	8.3	- 1.00
S Perks	2-12	16.7	- 6.34	D Carson	1-12	8.3	- 1.00
S Wynne	2-16	12.5	+ 11.00	E Husband	1-13	7.7	- 1.00
N Connorton	1-1	100.0	+ 2.25	W Carson	1-18	5.6	- 1.00
A Cruz	1-1	100.0	+ 16.00	Paul Eddery	1-25	4.0	- 20.00

A Culhane	0-9	Mrs G Rees	0-3	G Hind	0-1
A Munro	0-9	Carl Llewellyn	0-2	G Parkin	0-1
R Hills	0-6	T Lucas	0-2	J Carroll	0-1
Pat Eddery	0-4	C Rutter	0-1	J Quinn	0-1
B Raymond	0-3	D Holland	0-1	M Hills	0-1
G Duffield	0-3	Dale Gibson	0-1	P Bowe	0-1
J Fordham	0-3	F Savage	0-1	T Williams	0-1
M Birch	0-3	G Carter	0-1		

COURSE RECORD

	Total W-R	Non-Handicaps 2-y-o	3-y-o+	Handicaps 2-y-o	3-y-o+	Per cent	£1 Level Stake
Southwell (AW)	13-61	1-5	7-29	0-0	5-27	21.3	+ 8.44
Pontefract	8-53	2-11	2-15	0-2	4-25	15.1	- 16.52
Haydock	7-41	2-9	2-9	0-3	3-20	17.1	+ 23.10

Hollinshead R

Chester	4-32	1-11	1-3	0-2	2-16	12.5	+	5.50
Doncaster	4-51	0-14	2-13	0-4	2-20	7.8	-	12.54
Redcar	3-24	1-5	0-4	0-0	2-15	12.5	+	7.30
Beverley	3-30	1-7	0-2	0-0	2-21	10.0	+	3.25
Wolverhampton	3-51	0-9	2-22	0-1	1-19	5.9	-	27.50
Ripon	2-26	0-6	0-9	0-0	2-11	7.7	-	11.67
Chepstow	1-6	0-0	0-2	0-0	1-4	16.7	+	15.00
Warwick	1-12	0-1	0-3	0-0	1-8	8.3	+	14.00
York	1-12	0-2	0-4	1-1	0-5	8.3	+	3.00
Catterick	1-13	0-2	0-6	1-1	0-4	7.7	-	4.00
Newmarket	1-19	1-2	0-3	0-5	0-9	5.3	-	2.00
Thirsk	1-19	0-4	1-7	0-1	0-7	5.3	-	13.00
Leicester	1-38	1-10	0-12	0-4	0-12	2.6	-	33.00
Nottingham	1-41	0-12	1-13	0-2	0-14	2.4	-	28.00

Newcastle	0-14	Ascot		0-3	Kempton	0-2
Carlisle	0-11	Bath		0-2	Hamilton	0-1
Newbury	0-7	Goodwood		0-2	Windsor	0-1

WINNING HORSES

	Age	Races Run	1st	2nd	3rd	Unpl	Win £
Nominator	2	18	4	8	3	3	21,508
Mad Militant	3	14	5	0	2	7	18,412
Bit Of A Lark	4	7	2	0	1	4	14,500
Eastleigh	3	21	2	3	1	15	9,689
Sinclair Lad	4	17	3	2	3	9	9,671
Tyrian Purple	4	16	4	5	1	6	9,632
Birchwood Sun	2	11	2	3	0	6	8,965
Firefighter	3	16	4	6	1	5	8,863
Silver Samurai	3	19	3	6	7	3	8,687
Iron Baron	3	18	3	1	4	10	7,449
Heathyards Boy	2	4	2	0	0	2	6,326
Castlerea Lad	3	12	2	0	0	10	5,575
Farsi	4	10	2	2	2	4	5,172
Friendlypersuasion	4	14	1	0	1	12	3,600
Eager Deva	5	10	1	0	1	8	3,525
Dodger Dickins	5	4	1	0	0	3	3,322
The Sharp Bidder	2	10	1	2	1	6	3,262
Metal Boys	5	14	1	3	1	9	3,054
Heathyards Gem	2	10	1	0	4	5	2,848
Famous Beauty	5	10	1	0	3	6	2,637
Daytona Beach	2	5	1	3	1	0	2,481
Gay Ming	3	12	1	3	2	6	2,442
Nipotina	6	10	1	0	0	9	2,441
Be My Everything	3	10	1	1	2	6	2,364
Rousitto	4	10	1	0	2	7	2,265
Grubby	3	13	1	3	1	8	2,196
Brotherlyaffection	3	10	1	0	2	7	2,050
Ferdia	3	6	1	1	0	4	2,050
Master Sinclair	2	9	1	0	0	8	1,576
Miss Sarajane	8	8	1	0	0	7	1,245

WINNING OWNERS

	Races Won	Value £		Races Won	Value £
Mrs B Facchino	16	45,775	Mrs Robert Heathcote	1	3,262
J D Graham	4	21,508	North Staffs Racing Club	1	3,054
R E Mason	2	14,500	Mrs B L Morgan	1	2,848
J E Bigg	3	12,326	P D Savill	1	2,481
Sinclair Developments Ltd	4	11,247	H S Yates	1	2,442
Rykneld Th'bred Co Ltd	4	9,632	Miss Sarah Hollinshead	1	2,441
B Swain	2	8,965	Mrs G E Maloney	1	2,265
Dickins Ltd	2	6,922	Mrs A Mutch	1	2,196
L A Morgan	2	6,326	Noel Sweeney	1	2,050
Mrs Tess Graham	2	5,575	Mrs R Hollinshead	1	2,050
J F Bower	2	5,172	J Smyth	1	1,245
Mrs E G Faulkner	1	3,525			

Favourites	13-43	30.2%	- 11.97	Total winning prize-money	£177,805
Longest winning sequence			3	Average SP of winner	7.4/1
Longest losing sequence			91	Return on stakes invested	-19.5%
1991 Form	31-549	5.6%	-264.91	1989 Form	30-518	5.8%	-260.62
1990 Form	41-549	7.5%	-221.15	1988 Form	33-535	6.2%	-312.70

L J HOLT (Basingstoke, Hants)

	No. of Horses	Races Run	1st	2nd	3rd	Unpl	Per cent	£1 Level Stake
2-y-o	9	34	2	0	4	28	5.9	- 16.00
3-y-o	8	50	4	2	5	39	8.0	- 23.25
4-y-o+	7	61	4	8	6	43	6.6	- 23.50
Totals	24	145	10	10	15	110	6.9	- 62.75

BY MONTH

2-y-o	W-R	Per cent	£1 Level Stake	3-y-o	W-R	Per cent	£1 Level Stake
January	0-0	–	0.00	January	0-0	–	0.00
February	0-0	–	0.00	February	0-1	–	- 1.00
March	0-1	–	- 1.00	March	1-3	33.3	+ 1.00
April	1-1	100.0	+ 14.00	April	0-4	–	- 4.00
May	0-5	–	- 5.00	May	0-3	–	- 3.00
June	1-8	12.5	- 5.00	June	3-10	30.0	+ 12.75
July	0-2	–	- 2.00	July	0-8	–	- 8.00
August	0-5	–	- 5.00	August	0-7	–	- 7.00
September	0-6	–	- 6.00	September	0-6	–	- 6.00
Oct/Nov	0-6	–	- 6.00	Oct/Nov	0-8	–	- 8.00

4-y-o+	W-R	Per cent	£1 Level Stake	Totals	W-R	Per cent	£1 Level Stake
January	0-0	-	0.00	January	0-0	-	0.00
February	0-0	-	0.00	February	0-1	-	- 1.00
March	0-3	-	- 3.00	March	1-7	14.3	- 3.00
April	0-10	-	- 10.00	April	1-15	6.7	0.00
May	0-11	-	- 11.00	May	0-19	-	- 19.00
June	3-16	18.8	+ 16.00	June	7-34	20.6	+ 23.75
July	0-9	-	- 9.00	July	0-19	-	- 19.00
August	1-6	16.7	- 0.50	August	1-18	5.6	- 12.50
September	0-5	-	- 5.00	September	0-17	-	- 17.00
Oct/Nov	0-1	-	- 1.00	Oct/Nov	0-15	-	- 15.00

DISTANCE

2-y-o	W-R	Per cent	£1 Level Stake	3-y-o	W-R	Per cent	£1 Level Stake
5f-6f	2-33	6.1	- 15.00	5f-6f	2-28	7.1	- 9.00
7f-8f	0-1	-	- 1.00	7f-8f	2-20	10.0	- 12.25
9f-13f	0-0	-	0.00	9f-13f	0-2	-	- 2.00
14f+	0-0	-	0.00	14f+	0-0	-	0.00

4-y-o+	W-R	Per cent	£1 Level Stake	Totals	W-R	Per cent	£1 Level Stake
5f-6f	4-44	9.1	- 6.50	5f-6f	8-105	7.6	- 30.50
7f-8f	0-8	-	- 8.00	7f-8f	2-29	6.9	- 21.25
9f-13f	0-8	-	- 8.00	9f-13f	0-10	-	- 10.00
14f+	0-1	-	- 1.00	14f+	0-1	-	- 1.00

TYPE OF RACE

Non-Handicaps	W-R	Per cent	£1 Level Stake	Handicaps	W-R	Per cent	£1 Level Stake
2-y-o	2-27	7.4	- 9.00	2-y-o	0-7	-	- 7.00
3-y-o	1-18	5.6	- 14.00	3-y-o	3-29	10.3	- 6.25
4-y-o+	0-4	-	- 4.00	4-y-o+	3-50	6.0	- 17.00
Selling	0-1	-	- 1.00	Selling	0-3	-	- 3.00
Apprentice	0-1	-	- 1.00	Apprentice	1-5	20.0	- 0.50
Amat/Ladies	0-0	-	0.00	Amat/Ladies	0-0	-	0.00
Totals	3-51	5.9	- 29.00	Totals	7-94	7.4	- 33.75

COURSE GRADE

	W-R	Per cent	£1 Level Stake
Group 1	4-50	8.0	- 22.25
Group 2	3-36	8.3	- 13.00
Group 3	1-29	3.4	- 22.50
Group 4	2-30	6.7	- 5.00

FIRST TIME OUT

	W-R	Per cent	£1 Level Stake
2-y-o	0-8	-	- 8.00
3-y-o	1-8	12.5	- 4.00
4-y-o+	0-7	-	- 7.00
Totals	1-23	4.3	- 19.00

JOCKEYS RIDING

	W-R	Per cent	£1 Level Stake			W-R	Per cent	£1 Level Stake
J Reid	8-50	16.0	+ 6.75	C Avery		1-22	4.5	- 17.50
W Newnes	1-5	20.0	+ 16.00					

	W-R					W-R
N Adams	0-20	W Carson	0-2	J Quinn		0-1
A McGlone	0-18	A Garth	0-1	M Perrett		0-1
A Munro	0-8	B Rouse	0-1	P V Gilson		0-1
L Dettori	0-5	C Hawksley	0-1	Ron Hillis		0-1
M Roberts	0-4	Dale Gibson	0-1			
M Hills	0-2	G Duffield	0-1			

COURSE RECORD

	Total W-R	Non-Handicaps 2-y-o	3-y-o+	Handicaps 2-y-o	3-y-o+	Per cent	£1 Level Stake
Goodwood	3-16	0-2	0-2	0-1	3-11	18.8	- 3.25
Wolverhampton	1-5	0-0	1-1	0-0	0-4	20.0	- 1.00
Epsom	1-6	0-2	0-0	0-0	1-4	16.7	+ 9.00
Warwick	1-7	0-0	0-2	0-0	1-5	14.3	+ 14.00
Lingfield	1-11	1-3	0-2	0-0	0-6	9.1	+ 4.00
Salisbury	1-11	1-4	0-0	0-0	0-7	9.1	- 8.00
Windsor	1-11	0-5	0-1	0-0	1-5	9.1	- 4.50
Brighton	1-13	0-0	0-3	0-0	1-10	7.7	- 8.00

Folkestone	0-14	Ascot		0-3	Ayr		0-1
Kempton	0-10	Bath		0-3	Chepstow		0-1
Leicester	0-8	Doncaster		0-3	Thirsk		0-1
Nottingham	0-5	Newbury		0-3	Yarmouth		0-1
Lingfield (AW)	0-4	Newmarket		0-2			
Sandown	0-4	York		0-2			

WINNING HORSES

	Age	Races Run	1st	2nd	3rd	Unpl	Win £
Paddy Chalk	6	10	2	2	1	5	8,652
Alltruthenight	3	11	1	1	1	8	4,923
Court Minstrel	3	10	2	0	1	7	4,534
Chatterberry	2	4	1	0	0	3	2,611
Polity Prince	2	3	1	0	0	2	2,383
Rays Mead	4	10	1	1	2	6	2,324
Uccello	3	7	1	1	2	3	2,206
Coppermill Lad	9	13	1	3	1	8	1,918

WINNING OWNERS

	Races Won	Value £		Races Won	Value £
Mrs R G Wellman	2	8,652	Mrs S Khan	1	2,383
G Steinberg	1	4,923	Miss D M Green	1	2,324
G W Knight	2	4,534	K F Khan	1	2,206
David Hicks	1	2,611	L J Holt	1	1,918

Favourites	3-17	17.6%	- 2.00	Total winning prize-money		£29,550

Longest winning sequence	2	Average SP of winner	7.2/1
Longest losing sequence	49	Return on stakes invested	-43.3%

1991 Form	4-160	2.5%	-131.12	1989 Form	13-140	9.3%	- 19.75
1990 Form	6-178	3.4%	-102.75	1988 Form	6-154	3.9%	- 89.50

C A HORGAN (Billingbear, Berks)

	No. of Horses	Races Run	1st	2nd	3rd	Unpl	Per cent	£1 Level Stake
2-y-o	3	9	0	0	1	8	-	- 9.00
3-y-o	7	44	4	1	2	37	9.1	+ 17.00
4-y-o+	8	32	1	4	6	21	3.1	- 25.00
Totals	18	85	5	5	9	66	5.9	- 17.00

Jan	Feb	Mar	Apr	May	Jun	Jul	Aug	Sep	Oct/Nov
0-0	0-0	0-3	1-8	0-7	1-5	2-21	0-19	1-14	0-8

Winning Jockeys	W-R	£1 Level Stake			W-R	£1 Level Stake
C Asmussen	1-1	+ 6.00			1-5	+ 8.00
D Holland	1-3	+ 31.00	S Dawson		1-27	- 20.00
R Hills	1-4	+ 3.00	A McGlone			

Winning Courses						
Newbury	1-5	+ 2.00	Leicester		1-6	+ 1.00
Newmarket	1-5	+ 2.00	Goodwood		1-9	+ 25.00
Wolverhampton	1-5	+ 8.00				

Winning Horses	Age	Races Run	1st	2nd	3rd	Unpl	Win £
Risk Master	3	8	2	0	1	5	11,583
Mango Manila	7	6	1	0	1	4	7,895
Tiffany's Case	3	9	2	1	0	6	5,749

Favourites	1-7	14.3%	0.00	Total winning prize-money		£25,227

1991 Form	4-105	3.8%	- 57.62	1989 Form	9-97	9.3%	- 37.80
1990 Form	3-69	4.3%	- 26.50	1988 Form	6-124	4.8%	- 91.00

R F JOHNSON HOUGHTON (Didcot, Oxon)

	No. of Horses	Races Run	1st	2nd	3rd	Unpl	Per cent	£1 Level Stake
2-y-o	11	62	5	4	9	44	8.1	- 17.92
3-y-o	10	60	5	3	9	43	8.3	- 39.65
4-y-o+	1	3	0	0	1	2	-	- 3.00
Totals	22	125	10	7	19	89	8.0	- 60.57

BY MONTH

2-y-o	W-R	Per cent	£1 Level Stake	3-y-o	W-R	Per cent	£1 Level Stake
Mar/Apr	0-0	-	0.00	Mar/Apr	0-5	-	- 5.00
May	1-9	11.1	- 4.67	May	0-10	-	- 10.00
June	0-6	-	- 6.00	June	0-12	-	- 12.00
July	3-8	37.5	+ 16.75	July	4-11	36.4	+ 1.85
August	0-15	-	- 15.00	August	0-10	-	- 10.00
September	0-12	-	- 12.00	September	1-8	12.5	- 0.50
Oct/Nov	1-12	8.3	+ 3.00	Oct/Nov	0-4	-	- 4.00

4-y-o+	W-R	Per cent	£1 Level Stake	Totals	W-R	Per cent	£1 Level Stake
Mar/Apr	0-1	-	- 1.00	Mar/Apr	0-6	-	- 6.00
May	0-2	-	- 2.00	May	1-21	4.8	- 16.67
June	0-0	-	0.00	June	0-18	-	- 18.00
July	0-0	-	0.00	July	7-19	36.8	+ 18.60
August	0-0	-	0.00	August	0-25	-	- 25.00
September	0-0	-	0.00	September	1-20	5.0	- 12.50
Oct/Nov	0-0	-	0.00	Oct/Nov	1-16	6.3	- 1.00

DISTANCE

2-y-o	W-R	Per cent	£1 Level Stake	3-y-o	W-R	Per cent	£1 Level Stake
5f-6f	3-31	9.7	- 7.92	5f-6f	0-5	-	- 5.00
7f-8f	2-31	6.5	- 10.00	7f-8f	0-8	-	- 8.00
9f-13f	0-0	-	0.00	9f-13f	1-28	3.6	- 23.50
14f+	0-0	-	0.00	14f+	4-19	21.1	- 3.15

4-y-o+	W-R	Per cent	£1 Level Stake	Totals	W-R	Per cent	£1 Level Stake
5f-6f	0-0	-	0.00	5f-6f	3-36	8.3	- 12.92
7f-8f	0-2	-	- 2.00	7f-8f	2-41	4.9	- 20.00
9f-13f	0-1	-	- 1.00	9f-13f	1-29	3.4	- 24.50
14f+	0-0	-	0.00	14f+	4-19	21.1	- 3.15

TYPE OF RACE

Non-Handicaps	W-R	Per cent	£1 Level Stake	Handicaps	W-R	Per cent	£1 Level Stake
2-y-o	2-38	5.3	- 29.67	2-y-o	2-17	11.8	+ 1.75
3-y-o	3-12	25.0	- 3.65	3-y-o	2-44	4.5	- 32.00
4-y-o+	0-1	-	- 1.00	4-y-o+	0-2	-	- 2.00
Selling	1-8	12.5	+ 9.00	Selling	0-0	-	0.00
Apprentice	0-1	-	- 1.00	Apprentice	0-0	-	0.00
Amat/Ladies	0-1	-	- 1.00	Amat/Ladies	0-1	-	- 1.00
Totals	6-61	9.8	- 27.32	Totals	4-64	6.3	- 33.25

COURSE GRADE

	W–R	Per cent	£1 Level Stake
Group 1	3-50	6.0	− 28.25
Group 2	1-15	6.7	− 10.67
Group 3	1-37	2.7	− 32.50
Group 4	5-23	21.7	+ 10.85

FIRST TIME OUT

	W–R	Per cent	£1 Level Stake
2-y-o	0-11	-	− 11.00
3-y-o	0-10	-	− 10.00
4-y-o+	0-1	-	− 1.00
Totals	0-22	-	− 22.00

JOCKEYS RIDING

	W–R	Per cent	£1 Level Stake
D Harrison	2-8	25.0	+ 0.08
G Duffield	1-3	33.3	+ 4.50
M Roberts	1-4	25.0	+ 0.50
J Lowe	1-4	25.0	+ 11.00
D Holland	1-6	16.7	+ 11.00
W Ryan	1-6	16.7	− 3.00
R Hills	1-7	14.3	− 3.00
A Munro	1-7	14.3	− 3.75
T Quinn	1-8	12.5	− 5.90

J Reid	0-15	Paul Eddery	0-2	Miss E Houghton	0-1
S Whitworth	0-10	T Sprake	0-2	Mr G J Houghton	0-1
R Cochrane	0-6	A Clark	0-1	P Robinson	0-1
M Hills	0-4	Antoinette Armes	0-1	Pat Eddery	0-1
W Carson	0-4	B Doyle	0-1	R Price	0-1
B Raymond	0-3	F Norton	0-1	S Cauthen	0-1
J Lloyd	0-3	G Bardwell	0-1	W Newnes	0-1
K Darley	0-3	G Carter	0-1	W R Swinburn	0-1
J Weaver	0-2	J Williams	0-1		
M Birch	0-2	L Dettori	0-1		

COURSE RECORD

	Total W–R	Non-Handicaps 2-y-o	Non-Handicaps 3-y-o+	Handicaps 2-y-o	Handicaps 3-y-o+	Per cent	£1 Level Stake
Catterick	2-5	1-3	1-1	0-0	0-1	40.0	+ 1.10
Wolverhampton	2-8	1-4	0-1	0-0	1-3	25.0	+ 16.50
Newcastle	1-1	0-0	1-1	0-0	0-0	100.0	+ 2.00
Ascot	1-3	0-0	0-0	1-3	0-0	33.3	+ 0.75
Pontefract	1-3	0-0	0-1	0-0	1-2	33.3	+ 1.50
Salisbury	1-3	1-1	0-1	0-0	0-1	33.3	+ 1.33
Warwick	1-3	0-2	1-1	0-0	0-0	33.3	+ 0.25
Newmarket	1-11	0-2	0-2	1-3	0-4	9.1	+ 4.00

Bath	0-9	Leicester	0-4	Chester	0-2
Newbury	0-8	Sandown	0-4	Lingfield (AW)	0-2
Windsor	0-8	Brighton	0-3	Thirsk	0-2
Nottingham	0-7	Chepstow	0-3	Redcar	0-1
Kempton	0-6	Doncaster	0-3	Ripon	0-1
Epsom	0-5	Haydock	0-3	Southwell (AW)	0-1
Goodwood	0-5	Lingfield	0-3	Yarmouth	0-1
Folkestone	0-4	Beverley	0-2	York	0-1

WINNING HORSES

	Age	Races Run	1st	2nd	3rd	Unpl	Win £
No Reservations	2	11	2	3	3	3	9,232
Heavenly Waters	3	11	2	3	1	5	4,623
Melodys Daughter	2	6	1	0	1	4	4,342
Maestroso	3	10	1	0	1	8	2,763
Water Diviner	2	9	1	0	0	8	2,574
Ellafitzetty	3	4	1	0	0	3	2,406
Credit Squeeze	2	8	1	0	1	6	2,301
Bar Billiards	3	9	1	0	3	5	2,196

WINNING OWNERS

	Races Won	Value £		Races Won	Value £
C W Sumner and Jim Short	2	9,232	R F Johnson Houghton	1	2,574
R Crutchley	2	4,623	A P Hamilton	1	2,406
Lord Leverhulme	1	4,342	R C Naylor	1	2,301
Mrs Trisha Dunbar	1	2,763	Mrs E W Richards	1	2,196

Favourites	1-9	11.1%	- 6.90	Total winning prize-money		£30,437
Longest winning sequence			2	Average SP of winner		5.4/1
Longest losing sequence			30	Return on stakes invested		-48.5%
1991 Form	13-171	7.6%	- 57.07	1989 Form	24-211	11.4%	- 82.46
1990 Form	25-191	13.1%	- 31.02	1988 Form	36-235	15.3%	+ 27.45

P HOWLING (Guildford, Surrey)

	No. of Horses	Races Run	1st	2nd	3rd	Unpl	Per cent	£1 Level Stake
2-y-o	9	31	0	0	1	30	-	- 31.00
3-y-o	3	13	0	0	0	13	-	- 13.00
4-y-o+	13	122	2	4	7	109	1.6	-112.37
Totals	25	166	2	4	8	152	1.2	-156.37

Jan	Feb	Mar	Apr	May	Jun	Jul	Aug	Sep	Oct/Nov
0-6	0-7	0-11	0-11	0-29	0-27	1-14	0-19	1-24	0-18

Winning Jockeys	W-R	£1 Level Stake		W-R	£1 Level Stake
M Roberts	1-3	+ 3.50	W Newnes	1-11	- 7.87

Winning Course		
Yarmouth	2-14	- 4.37

Winning Horses	Age	Races Run	1st	2nd	3rd	Unpl	Win £
Joe Sugden	8	13	1	1	1	10	3,114
Ski Captain	8	13	1	2	2	8	2,820

Favourites	1-4	25.0%	- 0.87	Total winning prize-money			£5,934

1991 Form	6-185	3.2%	-110.50	1989 Form	5-165	3.0%	-121.00
1990 Form	6-185	3.2%	-102.50	1988 Form	9-174	5.2%	-104.00

LORD HUNTINGDON (West Ilsley, Berks)

	No. of Horses	Races Run	1st	2nd	3rd	Unpl	Per cent	£1 Level Stake
2-y-o	21	74	11	5	14	44	14.9	- 34.89
3-y-o	36	168	26	19	14	109	15.5	+ 15.37
4-y-o+	15	69	18	8	8	35	26.1	+ 28.16
Totals	72	311	55	32	36	188	17.7	+ 8.64

BY MONTH

2-y-o	W-R	Per cent	£1 Level Stake	3-y-o	W-R	Per cent	£1 Level Stake
January	0-0	-	0.00	January	1-1	100.0	+ 1.38
February	0-0	-	0.00	February	1-3	33.3	+ 1.00
March	0-0	-	0.00	March	0-8	-	- 8.00
April	0-0	-	0.00	April	5-14	35.7	+ 19.21
May	0-5	-	- 5.00	May	3-15	20.0	+ 5.50
June	2-9	22.2	- 4.75	June	3-20	15.0	+ 5.50
July	4-10	40.0	+ 5.58	July	2-16	12.5	- 4.35
August	2-13	15.4	- 4.60	August	2-24	8.3	- 15.00
September	3-23	13.0	- 12.12	September	5-34	14.7	+ 6.50
Oct/Nov	0-14	-	- 14.00	Oct/Nov	4-33	12.1	+ 3.63

4-y-o+	W-R	Per cent	£1 Level Stake	Totals	W-R	Per cent	£1 Level Stake
January	0-0	-	0.00	January	1-1	100.0	+ 1.38
February	0-2	-	- 2.00	February	1-5	20.0	- 1.00
March	1-5	20.0	+ 3.00	March	1-13	7.7	- 5.00
April	3-8	37.5	+ 5.46	April	8-22	36.4	+ 24.67
May	5-9	55.6	+ 8.95	May	8-29	27.6	+ 9.45
June	5-7	71.4	+ 26.75	June	10-36	27.8	+ 27.50
July	1-8	12.5	- 2.50	July	7-34	20.6	- 1.27
August	2-8	25.0	+ 2.50	August	6-45	13.3	- 17.10
September	1-9	11.1	- 1.00	September	9-66	13.6	- 6.62
Oct/Nov	0-13	-	- 13.00	Oct/Nov	4-60	6.7	- 23.37

DISTANCE

2-y-o	W-R	Per cent	£1 Level Stake	3-y-o	W-R	Per cent	£1 Level Stake
5f-6f	7-35	20.0	- 6.67	5f-6f	3-13	23.1	+ 20.65
7f-8f	4-39	10.3	- 28.22	7f-8f	10-60	16.7	- 6.28
9f-13f	0-0	-	0.00	9f-13f	12-88	13.6	- 5.00
14f+	0-0	-	0.00	14f+	1-7	14.3	+ 6.00

4-y-o+	W-R	Per cent	£1 Level Stake	Totals	W-R	Per cent	£1 Level Stake
5f-6f	0-2	-	- 2.00	5f-6f	10-50	20.0	+ 11.98
7f-8f	8-39	20.5	+ 17.63	7f-8f	22-138	15.9	- 16.87
9f-13f	6-17	35.3	+ 11.45	9f-13f	18-105	17.1	+ 6.45
14f+	4-11	36.4	+ 1.08	14f+	5-18	27.8	+ 7.08

TYPE OF RACE

Non-Handicaps	W-R	Per cent	£1 Level Stake	Handicaps	W-R	Per cent	£1 Level Stake
2-y-o	7-56	12.5	- 36.22	2-y-o	3-16	18.8	- 1.67
3-y-o	18-88	20.5	+ 32.71	3-y-o	7-70	10.0	- 13.34
4-y-o+	4-12	33.3	+ 1.88	4-y-o+	13-53	24.5	+ 28.45
Selling	1-3	33.3	+ 2.00	Selling	0-1	-	- 1.00
Apprentice	0-2	-	- 2.00	Apprentice	2-7	28.6	+ 0.83
Amat/Ladies	0-1	-	- 1.00	Amat/Ladies	0-2	-	- 2.00
Totals	30-162	18.5	- 2.63	Totals	25-149	16.8	+ 11.27

COURSE GRADE   FIRST TIME OUT

	W-R	Per cent	£1 Level Stake		W-R	Per cent	£1 Level Stake
Group 1	29-183	15.8	- 0.15	2-y-o	1-21	4.8	- 17.00
Group 2	8-42	19.0	- 5.37	3-y-o	11-35	31.4	+ 42.71
Group 3	11-50	22.0	+ 10.15	4-y-o+	5-15	33.3	+ 25.13
Group 4	7-36	19.4	+ 4.01				
				Totals	17-71	23.9	+ 50.84

JOCKEYS RIDING

	W-R	Per cent	£1 Level Stake		W-R	Per cent	£1 Level Stake
A Munro	10-63	15.9	+ 8.38	L Dettori	4-21	19.0	- 5.75
M Roberts	9-30	30.0	+ 24.03	W Ryan	3-8	37.5	+ 9.38
W R Swinburn	8-34	23.5	+ 2.97	D McKeown	3-26	11.5	- 4.25
D Harrison	6-56	10.7	- 15.54	S Cauthen	2-11	18.2	- 6.75
Pat Eddery	4-7	57.1	+ 6.09	A Proud	1-1	100.0	+ 3.50
J Reid	4-9	44.4	+ 24.58	K Fallon	1-3	33.3	+ 4.00

B Raymond	0-10	D Salt	0-1	Mr L Maynard	0-1
L Piggott	0-8	J Carroll	0-1	N Carlisle	0-1
Dale Gibson	0-6	J Lowe	0-1	P Robinson	0-1
R Hills	0-3	J Wilkinson	0-1	Princess Royal	0-1
A Tucker	0-1	J Williams	0-1	T Quinn	0-1
D Biggs	0-1	M J Kinane	0-1		
D Holland	0-1	Miss J Allison	0-1		

COURSE RECORD

	Total W-R	Non-Handicaps 2-y-o	Non-Handicaps 3-y-o+	Handicaps 2-y-o	Handicaps 3-y-o+	Per cent	£1 Level Stake
Ascot	6-26	0-1	3-7	0-1	3-17	23.1	+ 14.08
Sandown	5-23	1-7	2-9	0-0	2-7	21.7	- 1.62
Windsor	4-14	2-5	1-5	0-0	1-4	28.6	+ 5.52
Southwell (AW)	4-18	0-0	3-13	0-0	1-5	22.2	0.00
Newbury	4-35	0-9	1-7	0-1	3-18	11.4	- 10.00
Haydock	3-15	1-3	0-6	0-0	2-6	20.0	+ 4.38
Newcastle	2-2	0-0	0-0	1-1	1-1	100.0	+ 8.75
Pontefract	2-3	0-0	1-2	0-0	1-1	66.7	+ 10.00
Epsom	2-5	1-2	1-1	0-1	0-1	40.0	+ 14.63
Bath	2-8	0-1	0-3	1-1	1-3	25.0	+ 1.00
Brighton	2-9	1-2	0-4	0-0	1-3	22.2	- 4.60
Lingfield	2-10	0-4	1-2	1-1	0-3	20.0	- 1.34
Goodwood	2-11	0-1	2-4	0-2	0-4	18.2	+ 3.50
Salisbury	2-14	0-1	1-5	0-0	1-8	14.3	- 9.18
Kempton	2-18	1-5	0-5	0-1	1-7	11.1	- 12.37
Thirsk	1-2	0-1	1-1	0-0	0-0	50.0	+ 1.75
Chepstow	1-4	0-0	1-2	0-0	0-2	25.0	+ 7.00
Nottingham	1-4	0-2	0-0	0-0	1-2	25.0	- 1.37
Redcar	1-4	0-0	0-1	0-0	1-3	25.0	+ 11.00
Wolverhampton	1-4	0-0	1-1	0-1	0-2	25.0	- 1.37
Warwick	1-5	0-1	1-4	0-0	0-0	20.0	+ 12.00
Lingfield (AW)	1-5	0-0	1-4	0-0	0-1	20.0	- 2.62
York	1-9	0-2	1-3	0-0	0-4	11.1	- 3.50
Doncaster	1-12	0-1	0-2	0-1	1-8	8.3	- 4.00
Leicester	1-12	1-4	0-5	0-0	0-3	8.3	- 7.00
Newmarket	1-27	0-1	0-5	0-4	1-17	3.7	- 14.00
Folkestone	0-4	Ripon		0-2	Chester		0-1
Hamilton	0-3	Yarmouth		0-2			

WINNING HORSES

	Age	Races Run	1st	2nd	3rd	Unpl	Win £
Drum Taps	6	2	2	0	0	0	137,745
Colour Sergeant	4	4	2	0	0	2	47,037
Montpelier Boy	4	8	1	1	2	4	18,238
Irek	3	7	2	0	1	4	13,340
Sharp Prod	2	6	3	0	2	1	12,595
Piquant	5	11	2	2	1	6	11,527

Talent	4	7	3	1	0	3	10,749
Whitechapel	4	8	3	0	1	4	10,728
Arbusha	3	2	1	0	0	1	9,672
Last Embrace	3	3	2	0	0	1	9,584
Top Register	3	4	1	0	0	3	9,503
Penny Drops	3	5	3	1	0	1	8,877
Discord	6	3	3	0	0	0	7,977
Bangles	2	8	2	1	2	3	7,190
Trumpet	3	5	2	0	1	2	6,677
Her Honour	3	2	2	0	0	0	6,245
Rosina Mae	3	7	1	2	0	4	5,436
Ingenuity	3	8	2	0	0	6	5,167
Larrikin	3	3	1	0	0	2	4,659
Erlking	2	5	1	1	0	3	3,384
Majestic Image	6	4	1	1	0	2	3,215
Mossy Rose	6	9	1	1	2	5	2,973
Diskette	2	3	1	0	0	2	2,700
Commanche Gold	2	2	1	0	1	0	2,700
Greek Chime	3	6	1	0	1	4	2,553
Cottonwood	3	6	1	0	0	5	2,511
Belle Isis	3	3	1	0	0	2	2,469
Scottish Peak	2	2	1	0	0	1	2,427
Empire Pool	2	5	1	0	0	4	2,343
Handsome Gent	3	7	1	2	1	3	2,324
Warm Spell	2	2	1	0	0	1	2,226
Money Spinner	3	3	1	0	0	2	2,206
Sand Table	3	7	1	0	2	4	2,167
Welsh Mill	3	5	1	3	1	0	1,861
Shirley's Train	3	8	1	0	0	7	1,725
Spencer's Revenge	3	4	1	0	1	2	1,660

WINNING OWNERS

	Races Won	Value £		Races Won	Value £
Yoshio Asakawa	3	140,825	Jocelyn Hambro	2	6,245
The Queen	20	118,532	Greenland Park Ltd	1	5,436
Sir Michael Sandberg	1	18,238	Mrs Evan Williams	2	4,897
Sheikh Mohammed	2	13,340	Maverick Productions Ltd	1	4,659
Stanley J Sharp	4	11,850	M L Oberstein	2	4,425
Henryk De Kwiatkowski	1	9,672	Lady Newman	1	3,384
E J Loder	2	9,584	Lord Huntingdon	1	3,215
Lord Weinstock	4	9,541	K H Fischer	1	2,324
Lord Carnavon	3	7,206	Lord Derby	1	2,167
J Rose	2	7,190	Lord Crawshaw	1	1,660

Favourites	20-65	30.8%	- 8.47	Total winning prize-money			£384,388

Longest winning sequence			3
Longest losing sequence			21

Average SP of winner   4.8/1
Return on stakes invested   2.8%

1991 Form	36-254	14.2%	+ 91.26	1989 Form	26-171	15.2%	- 42.55
1990 Form	20-197	10.2%	- 53.59	1988 Form	31-184	16.8%	+ 55.98

D E INCISA (Coverham, North Yorks)

	No. of Horses	Races Run	1st	2nd	3rd	Unpl	Per cent	£1 Level Stake
2-y-o	2	15	0	0	1	14	-	- 15.00
3-y-o	2	19	0	0	3	16	-	- 19.00
4-y-o+	5	38	1	3	2	32	2.6	- 25.00
Totals	9	72	1	3	6	62	1.4	- 59.00

Jan	Feb	Mar	Apr	May	Jun	Jul	Aug	Sep	Oct/Nov
0-0	0-0	0-3	0-10	0-12	1-9	0-11	0-8	0-13	0-6

Winning Jockey	W-R	£1 Level Stake	Winning Course	W-R	£1 Level Stake
Claire Balding	1-28	- 15.00	Ripon	1-12	+ 1.00

Winning Horse	Age	Races Run	1st	2nd	3rd	Unpl	Win £
Filicaia	6	13	1	2	1	9	5,434

Favourites	0-1		Total winning prize-money	£5,434

1991 Form	4-73	5.5%	- 26.50	1989 Form	0-67		
1990 Form	2-67	3.0%	- 24.00	1988 Form	2-69	2.9%	- 53.75

R INGRAM (Epsom, Surrey)

	No. of Horses	Races Run	1st	2nd	3rd	Unpl	Per cent	£1 Level Stake
2-y-o	3	15	0	1	2	12	-	- 15.00
3-y-o	1	5	0	0	0	5	-	- 5.00
4-y-o+	4	8	1	0	2	5	12.5	+ 26.00
Totals	8	28	1	1	4	22	3.6	+ 6.00

Jan	Feb	Mar	Apr	May	Jun	Jul	Aug	Sep	Oct/Nov
0-0	0-0	0-1	0-1	0-2	0-4	0-1	0-4	1-9	0-6

Winning Jockey	W-R	£1 Level Stake	Winning Course	W-R	£1 Level Stake
C Dwyer	1-5	+ 29.00	Lingfield (AW)	1-4	+ 30.00

Winning Horse	Age	Races Run	1st	2nd	3rd	Unpl	Win £
Jo N Jack	4	2	1	0	0	1	2,490

Favourites	0-0	Total winning prize-money	£2,490

1991 Form	2-27	7.4%	- 4.00

K T IVORY (Radlett, Herts)

	No. of Horses	Races Run	1st	2nd	3rd	Unpl	Per cent	£1 Level Stake
2-y-o	3	11	0	2	0	9	-	- 11.00
3-y-o	3	23	2	0	3	18	8.7	+ 3.00
4-y-o+	9	57	7	4	4	42	12.3	+ 21.23
Totals	15	91	9	6	7	69	9.9	+ 13.23

Jan	Feb	Mar	Apr	May	Jun	Jul	Aug	Sep	Oct/Nov
0-0	0-2	1-7	1-13	1-12	1-12	3-13	2-15	0-12	0-5

Winning Jockeys	W-R	£1 Level Stake				W-R	£1 Level Stake
G Bardwell	8-53	+ 49.13		C Scally		1-7	- 4.90

Winning Courses						
Yarmouth	4-15	+ 3.23		Southwell (AW)	1-4	+ 17.00
Bath	1-1	+ 6.00		Warwick	1-5	+ 21.00
Salisbury	1-4	+ 17.00		Newmarket	1-8	+ 3.00

Winning Horses	Age	Races Run	1st	2nd	3rd	Unpl	Win £
Spring High	5	15	5	3	3	4	14,550
Myfontaine	5	7	2	0	1	4	11,114
Roly Wallace	3	12	1	0	2	9	3,101
Scala Milano	3	5	1	0	0	4	2,217

Favourites	2-5	40.0%	+ 0.23	Total winning prize-money		£30,981

1991 Form	5-148	3.4%	- 97.00	1989 Form	7-145	4.8%	- 54.37
1990 Form	7-128	5.5%	- 46.00	1988 Form	7-231	3.0%	-151.50

C JAMES (Newbury, Berks)

	No. of Horses	Races Run	1st	2nd	3rd	Unpl	Per cent	£1 Level Stake
2-y-o	6	26	3	2	1	20	11.5	+ 13.75
3-y-o	4	25	1	1	2	21	4.0	- 8.00
4-y-o+	2	4	0	0	0	4	-	- 4.00
Totals	12	55	4	3	3	45	7.3	+ 1.75

Jan	Feb	Mar	Apr	May	Jun	Jul	Aug	Sep	Oct/Nov
0-0	0-0	0-0	0-2	1-3	1-11	0-11	2-10	0-12	0-6

James C

Winning Jockeys	W-R	£1 Level Stake		W-R	£1 Level Stake
G Baxter	2-9	+ 20.75	Dale Gibson	1-9	+ 8.00
J Quinn	1-9	+ 1.00			

Winning Courses	W-R	£1 Level Stake		W-R	£1 Level Stake
Bath	1-2	+ 8.00	Lingfield (AW)	1-4	+ 22.00
Nottingham	1-3	+ 0.75	Salisbury	1-9	+ 8.00

Winning Horses	Age	Races Run	1st	2nd	3rd	Unpl	Win £
Grey Charmer	3	13	1	0	1	11	3,003
Stroika	2	7	1	0	0	6	2,658
Moon Over Miami	2	4	1	1	0	2	1,814
Regent's Lady	2	5	1	1	0	3	1,632

Favourites	0-2		Total winning prize-money		£9,107

1991 Form	3-56	5.4%	- 37.25	1989 Form	1-37	2.7%	- 33.00
1990 Form	1-45	2.2%	- 40.00	1988 Form	6-28	21.4%	+ 10.88

A P JARVIS (Aston Upthorpe, Oxon)

	No. of Horses	Races Run	1st	2nd	3rd	Unpl	Per cent	£1 Level Stake
2-y-o	10	45	1	2	2	40	2.2	- 28.00
3-y-o	3	11	0	0	1	10	-	- 11.00
4-y-o+	4	15	1	0	1	13	6.7	0.00
Totals	17	71	2	2	4	63	2.8	- 39.00

Jan	Feb	Mar	Apr	May	Jun	Jul	Aug	Sep	Oct/Nov
0-3	0-0	0-1	0-0	0-4	0-6	0-11	0-14	1-17	1-15

Winning Jockeys	W-R	£1 Level Stake		W-R	£1 Level Stake
T Quinn	1-5	+ 10.00	D Wright	1-16	+ 1.00

Winning Courses	W-R	£1 Level Stake		W-R	£1 Level Stake
Chepstow	1-4	+ 13.00	Brighton	1-5	+ 10.00

Winning Horses	Age	Races Run	1st	2nd	3rd	Unpl	Win £
Genuine Lady	4	8	1	0	1	6	2,805
Another Jade	2	7	1	0	0	6	2,574

Favourites	0-1		Total winning prize-money		£5,379

1991 Form	1-11	9.1%	- 2.00

M A JARVIS (Newmarket)

	No. of Horses	Races Run	1st	2nd	3rd	Unpl	Per cent	£1 Level Stake
2-y-o	12	33	6	1	4	22	18.2	+ 8.63
3-y-o	19	100	11	10	8	71	11.0	- 28.67
4-y-o+	7	50	8	7	4	31	16.0	- 12.90
Totals	38	183	25	18	16	124	13.7	- 32.94

BY MONTH

2-y-o	W-R	Per cent	£1 Level Stake	3-y-o	W-R	Per cent	£1 Level Stake
January	0-0	-	0.00	January	0-0	-	0.00
February	0-0	-	0.00	February	0-0	-	0.00
March	0-0	-	0.00	March	0-0	-	0.00
April	0-0	-	0.00	April	4-13	30.8	+ 33.50
May	1-3	33.3	+ 8.00	May	1-17	5.9	- 12.67
June	1-2	50.0	+ 11.00	June	5-24	20.8	- 4.50
July	1-3	33.3	+ 1.00	July	1-17	5.9	- 16.00
August	2-5	40.0	+ 4.63	August	0-7	-	- 7.00
September	1-8	12.5	- 4.00	September	0-12	-	- 12.00
Oct/Nov	0-12	-	- 12.00	Oct/Nov	0-10	-	- 10.00

4-y-o+	W-R	Per cent	£1 Level Stake	Totals	W-R	Per cent	£1 Level Stake
January	0-1	-	- 1.00	January	0-1	-	- 1.00
February	0-1	-	- 1.00	February	0-1	-	- 1.00
March	0-0	-	0.00	March	0-0	-	0.00
April	0-5	-	- 5.00	April	4-18	22.2	+ 28.50
May	1-4	25.0	+ 5.00	May	3-24	12.5	+ 0.33
June	2-10	20.0	- 4.20	June	8-36	22.2	+ 2.30
July	3-7	42.9	+ 0.30	July	5-27	18.5	- 14.70
August	1-11	9.1	- 5.00	August	3-23	13.0	- 7.37
September	1-6	16.7	+ 3.00	September	2-26	7.7	- 13.00
Oct/Nov	0-5	-	- 5.00	Oct/Nov	0-27	-	- 27.00

DISTANCE

2-y-o	W-R	Per cent	£1 Level Stake	3-y-o	W-R	Per cent	£1 Level Stake
5f-6f	4-17	23.5	+ 13.63	5f-6f	0-4	-	- 4.00
7f-8f	2-15	13.3	- 4.00	7f-8f	2-29	6.9	- 18.50
9f-13f	0-1	-	- 1.00	9f-13f	8-59	13.6	- 0.67
14f+	0-0	-	0.00	14f+	1-8	12.5	- 5.50

4-y-o+	W-R	Per cent	£1 Level Stake	Totals	W-R	Per cent	£1 Level Stake
5f-6f	0-0	-	0.00	5f-6f	4-21	19.0	+ 9.63
7f-8f	3-25	12.0	- 13.20	7f-8f	7-69	10.1	- 35.70
9f-13f	5-25	20.0	+ 0.30	9f-13f	13-85	15.3	- 1.37
14f+	0-0	-	0.00	14f+	1-8	12.5	- 5.50

TYPE OF RACE

Non-Handicaps	W-R	Per cent	£1 Level Stake	Handicaps	W-R	Per cent	£1 Level Stake
2-y-o	6-28	21.4	+ 13.63	2-y-o	0-4	-	- 4.00
3-y-o	4-38	10.5	+ 5.50	3-y-o	6-48	12.5	- 22.67
4-y-o+	2-12	16.7	- 1.20	4-y-o+	3-25	12.0	- 13.50
Selling	2-9	22.2	- 3.20	Selling	1-6	16.7	+ 3.00
Apprentice	1-3	33.3	- 0.50	Apprentice	0-10	-	- 10.00
Amat/Ladies	0-0	-	0.00	Amat/Ladies	0-0	-	0.00
Totals	15-90	16.7	+ 14.23	Totals	10-93	10.8	- 47.17

COURSE GRADE

	W-R	Per cent	£1 Level Stake
Group 1	11-77	14.3	- 15.37
Group 2	3-23	13.0	- 7.50
Group 3	5-56	8.9	- 19.50
Group 4	6-27	22.2	+ 9.43

FIRST TIME OUT

	W-R	Per cent	£1 Level Stake
2-y-o	2-12	16.7	+ 6.00
3-y-o	3-18	16.7	+ 24.50
4-y-o+	0-7	-	- 7.00
Totals	5-37	13.5	+ 23.50

JOCKEYS RIDING

	W-R	Per cent	£1 Level Stake		W-R	Per cent	£1 Level Stake
K Rutter	8-37	21.6	+ 12.80	W R Swinburn	1-1	100.0	0.00
R Cochrane	2-4	50.0	+ 11.00	N Day	1-2	50.0	+ 4.00
M Hills	2-7	28.6	+ 12.33	S Cauthen	1-4	25.0	+ 3.00
W Ryan	2-7	28.6	+ 1.50	J Quinn	1-6	16.7	- 5.00
L Dettori	2-10	20.0	- 2.00	P Robinson	1-11	9.1	- 8.37
M Roberts	1-1	100.0	+ 0.80	A Munro	1-15	6.7	+ 6.00
Pat Eddery	1-1	100.0	+ 4.00	G Crealock	1-27	3.7	- 23.00

B Raymond	0-26	L Piggott	0-2	G Carter	0-1
G Duffield	0-4	C Hawksley	0-1	J Lowe	0-1
Paul Eddery	0-4	D Biggs	0-1	J Williams	0-1
W Carson	0-3	F Arrowsmith	0-1	N Gwilliams	0-1
J Carroll	0-2	G Bardwell	0-1	T Lucas	0-1

COURSE RECORD

	Total W-R	Non-Handicaps 2-y-o	Non-Handicaps 3-y-o+	Handicaps 2-y-o	Handicaps 3-y-o+	Per cent	£1 Level Stake
Wolverhampton	3-5	2-2	0-1	0-0	1-2	60.0	+ 16.63
Sandown	2-4	1-1	1-1	0-0	0-2	50.0	+ 7.00
Southwell (AW)	2-5	1-1	1-4	0-0	0-0	40.0	+ 8.00
Doncaster	2-8	0-2	0-1	0-1	2-4	25.0	- 6.00
Leicester	2-10	0-0	1-4	0-0	1-6	20.0	+ 2.50
Haydock	2-13	0-3	0-3	0-0	2-7	15.4	- 4.67
Newmarket	2-21	0-4	2-6	0-2	0-9	9.5	+ 2.50
Salisbury	1-4	0-0	0-1	0-0	1-3	25.0	+ 0.50

York	1-4	1-1	0-2	0-0	0-1	25.0	0.00
Goodwood	1-5	0-0	1-1	0-0	0-4	20.0	- 3.20
Hamilton	1-5	0-0	1-2	0-0	0-3	20.0	+ 10.00
Lingfield	1-5	0-1	0-2	0-0	1-2	20.0	- 0.50
Chepstow	1-6	0-1	1-4	0-1	0-0	16.7	- 2.00
Warwick	1-6	0-1	1-4	0-0	0-1	16.7	- 4.20
Kempton	1-7	1-2	0-1	0-0	0-4	14.3	+ 4.00
Brighton	1-8	0-1	0-4	0-0	1-3	12.5	- 1.50
Windsor	1-8	0-0	0-4	0-0	1-4	12.5	- 3.00

Yarmouth	0-9	Newbury	0-5	Epsom	0-2
Pontefract	0-7	Catterick	0-4	Folkestone	0-2
Nottingham	0-6	Redcar	0-4	Ripon	0-2
Ascot	0-5	Carlisle	0-3	Edinburgh	0-1
Beverley	0-5	Newcastle	0-3	Lingfield (AW)	0-1

WINNING HORSES

	Age	Races Run	1st	2nd	3rd	Unpl	Win £
Savoyard	4	8	1	0	1	6	10,035
New Capricorn	2	4	2	0	0	2	8,496
Bentico	3	11	2	1	1	7	8,336
Magnificent	3	7	2	0	0	5	7,080
Misty View	3	7	2	1	0	4	6,643
Misty Goddess	4	10	3	2	0	5	6,535
Sayh	3	7	2	0	1	4	5,494
Rival Bid	4	7	2	2	1	2	5,104
Skipper To Bilge	5	9	2	0	1	6	4,110
Courtline Jester	3	5	1	1	0	3	3,948
Aberlady	2	7	2	1	1	3	3,546
Sharjah	2	3	1	0	2	0	3,540
Hidden Light	3	6	1	2	1	2	2,820
Iolite	2	4	1	0	0	3	2,553
Lady Lydia	3	2	1	0	0	1	1,932

WINNING OWNERS

	Races Won	Value £		Races Won	Value £
Lady Butt	1	10,035	David Altham	2	5,104
Sheikh Ahmed Al Maktoum	3	9,034	Mrs J R Collins	2	4,110
K G Powter	3	8,575	Jerry Sung	1	3,948
Kamal Bhatia	2	8,496	M Sinclair	2	3,546
Mark Christofi	2	8,336	Lord Harrington	1	2,820
Mrs P L Yong	2	7,080	R P Marchant	1	2,553
J R Good	3	6,535			

Favourites	7-22	31.8%	+ 1.23	
Longest winning sequence			3	
Longest losing sequence			40	

Total winning prize-money			£80,171
Average SP of winner			5.7/1
Return on stakes invested			-8.2%

1991 Form	24-249	9.6%	- 55.22	1989 Form	28-270	10.4%	-119.08
1990 Form	28-258	10.9%	- 70.12	1988 Form	31-228	13.6%	- 66.54

W JARVIS (Newmarket)

	No. of Horses	Races Run	1st	2nd	3rd	Unpl	Per cent	£1 Level Stake
2-y-o	13	38	3	5	4	26	7.9	- 25.20
3-y-o	20	81	12	12	10	47	14.8	- 12.13
4-y-o+	9	61	6	7	5	43	9.8	- 31.62
Totals	42	180	21	24	19	116	11.7	- 68.95

BY MONTH

2-y-o	W-R	Per cent	£1 Level Stake	3-y-o	W-R	Per cent	£1 Level Stake
January	0-0	-	0.00	January	1-4	25.0	+ 1.50
February	0-0	-	0.00	February	2-3	66.7	+ 4.63
March	0-0	-	0.00	March	0-1	-	- 1.00
April	0-2	-	- 2.00	April	0-10	-	- 10.00
May	2-3	66.7	+ 8.00	May	1-9	11.1	- 1.50
June	0-7	-	- 7.00	June	2-13	15.4	- 6.93
July	0-2	-	- 2.00	July	2-9	22.2	+ 8.50
August	1-5	20.0	- 3.20	August	1-8	12.5	- 5.90
September	0-7	-	- 7.00	September	3-12	25.0	+ 10.57
Oct/Nov	0-12	-	- 12.00	Oct/Nov	0-12	-	- 12.00

4-y-o+	W-R	Per cent	£1 Level Stake	Totals	W-R	Per cent	£1 Level Stake
January	0-2	-	- 2.00	January	1-6	16.7	- 0.50
February	0-0	-	0.00	February	2-3	66.7	+ 4.63
March	0-0	-	0.00	March	0-1	-	- 1.00
April	0-4	-	- 4.00	April	0-16	-	- 16.00
May	2-7	28.6	- 1.62	May	5-19	26.3	+ 4.88
June	3-14	21.4	+ 2.50	June	5-34	14.7	- 11.43
July	1-9	11.1	- 1.50	July	3-20	15.0	+ 5.00
August	0-6	-	- 6.00	August	2-19	10.5	- 15.10
September	0-11	-	- 11.00	September	3-30	10.0	- 7.43
Oct/Nov	0-8	-	- 8.00	Oct/Nov	0-32	-	- 32.00

DISTANCE

2-y-o	W-R	Per cent	£1 Level Stake	3-y-o	W-R	Per cent	£1 Level Stake
5f-6f	3-25	12.0	- 12.20	5f-6f	0-6	-	- 6.00
7f-8f	0-13	-	- 13.00	7f-8f	6-34	17.6	+ 7.10
9f-13f	0-0	-	0.00	9f-13f	6-37	16.2	- 9.23
14f+	0-0	-	0.00	14f+	0-4	-	- 4.00

4-y-o+	W-R	Per cent	£1 Level Stake	Totals	W-R	Per cent	£1 Level Stake
5f-6f	1-14	7.1	- 11.62	5f-6f	4-45	8.9	- 29.82
7f-8f	2-16	12.5	- 0.50	7f-8f	8-63	12.7	- 6.40
9f-13f	2-21	9.5	- 12.50	9f-13f	8-58	13.8	- 21.73
14f+	1-10	10.0	- 7.00	14f+	1-14	7.1	- 11.00

TYPE OF RACE

Non-Handicaps	W-R	Per cent	£1 Level Stake	Handicaps	W-R	Per cent	£1 Level Stake
2-y-o	3-33	9.1	- 20.20	2-y-o	0-4	-	- 4.00
3-y-o	7-49	14.3	- 16.26	3-y-o	5-29	17.2	+ 7.13
4-y-o+	1-14	7.1	- 11.62	4-y-o+	4-42	9.5	- 19.50
Selling	0-2	-	- 2.00	Selling	0-1	-	- 1.00
Apprentice	0-1	-	- 1.00	Apprentice	0-2	-	- 2.00
Amat/Ladies	1-1	100.0	+ 3.50	Amat/Ladies	0-2	-	- 2.00
Totals	12-100	12.0	- 47.58	Totals	9-80	11.3	- 21.37

COURSE GRADE

	W-R	Per cent	£1 Level Stake
Group 1	10-95	10.5	- 22.00
Group 2	5-15	33.3	+ 1.75
Group 3	1-45	2.2	- 42.90
Group 4	5-25	20.0	- 5.80

FIRST TIME OUT

	W-R	Per cent	£1 Level Stake
2-y-o	1-12	8.3	- 9.00
3-y-o	1-20	5.0	- 8.00
4-y-o+	0-9	-	- 9.00
Totals	2-41	4.9	- 26.00

JOCKEYS RIDING

	W-R	Per cent	£1 Level Stake		W-R	Per cent	£1 Level Stake
M Tebbutt	6-46	13.0	- 27.68	Pat Eddery	1-2	50.0	+ 2.00
J Carroll	3-9	33.3	+ 15.50	Mrs L Pearce	1-2	50.0	+ 2.50
N Day	3-11	27.3	+ 12.10	F Norton	1-3	33.3	+ 2.00
Emma O'Gorman	2-3	66.7	+ 5.13	S Cauthen	1-6	16.7	- 3.00
J Reid	2-11	18.2	+ 2.00	A Munro	1-17	5.9	- 9.50

R Cochrane	0-11	M Roberts	0-3	J Fortune	0-1
W Carson	0-9	G Milligan	0-2	K Darley	0-1
B Raymond	0-8	L Dettori	0-2	K Rutter	0-1
P Robinson	0-7	L Piggott	0-2	Miss A Rutherford	0-1
S Davies	0-4	W R Swinburn	0-2	N Carlisle	0-1
D Holland	0-3	D Harrison	0-1	O Pears	0-1
J Weaver	0-3	G Duffield	0-1	Paul Eddery	0-1
M Hills	0-3	G Hind	0-1	T Quinn	0-1

COURSE RECORD

	Total W-R	Non-Handicaps 2-y-o	Non-Handicaps 3-y-o+	Handicaps 2-y-o	Handicaps 3-y-o+	Per cent	£1 Level Stake
Haydock	3-8	0-1	1-2	0-0	2-5	37.5	+ 14.50
Lingfield (AW)	3-8	0-0	1-4	0-0	2-4	37.5	+ 5.13
Thirsk	2-2	2-2	0-0	0-0	0-0	100.0	+ 9.00
Newbury	2-7	0-0	0-0	0-2	2-5	28.6	+ 7.00
Edinburgh	1-1	0-0	1-1	0-0	0-0	100.0	+ 0.57
Lingfield	1-2	0-0	1-1	0-0	0-1	50.0	+ 0.38
Ripon	1-3	1-1	0-2	0-0	0-0	33.3	- 1.20

Jarvis W

Catterick	1-4	0-0	1-3	0-0	0-1	25.0	+	0.50
Ayr	1-5	0-1	1-1	0-0	0-3	20.0	+	0.50
Kempton	1-5	0-0	0-2	0-0	1-3	20.0	+	6.00
Redcar	1-5	0-2	1-2	0-0	0-1	20.0	-	3.43
Newcastle	1-6	0-0	0-2	0-0	1-4	16.7	+	2.00
Sandown	1-8	0-2	0-2	0-0	1-4	12.5	-	0.50
Nottingham	1-10	0-3	1-5	0-0	0-2	10.0	-	7.90
York	1-12	0-4	1-5	0-0	0-3	8.3	-	7.50

Newmarket	0-23	Ascot	0-3	Hamilton	0-2
Yarmouth	0-13	Folkestone	0-3	Warwick	0-2
Beverley	0-9	Leicester	0-3	Windsor	0-2
Goodwood	0-8	Pontefract	0-3	Bath	0-1
Doncaster	0-6	Southwell (AW)	0-3	Brighton	0-1
Epsom	0-4	Chepstow	0-2		
Wolverhampton	0-4	Chester	0-2		

WINNING HORSES

		Races					Win
	Age	Run	1st	2nd	3rd	Unpl	£
Sharpitor	3	5	2	0	3	0	33,305
Lap Of Luxury	3	7	3	1	1	2	20,665
Sea Goddess	4	9	3	2	0	4	16,834
Superbrave	6	7	1	0	1	5	7,180
Rosa Why	3	4	3	0	1	0	6,713
Lord Olivier	2	10	2	3	1	4	4,864
Dovale	4	8	1	1	1	5	3,215
Leif The Lucky	3	5	1	1	0	3	2,783
Petite Epaulette	2	6	1	0	1	4	2,543
Briggs Lad	3	7	1	1	1	4	2,445
Kirsten	3	6	1	1	1	3	2,070
Cutleaf	3	3	1	0	1	1	1,876
Love Returned	5	12	1	0	2	9	1,632

WINNING OWNERS

	Races Won	Value £		Races Won	Value £
Henry Lopes	2	33,305	Mrs E G Lambton	1	3,215
Lord Howard De Walden	5	20,781	The Singular Six Partnership	1	2,783
I C Hill-Wood	3	20,665	Mrs F G Allen	1	2,543
Willie W Robertson	1	7,180	F W Briggs	1	2,445
Jerry Sung	3	6,713	J M Ratcliffe	1	1,632
Miss V R Jarvis	2	4,864			

Favourites	6-17	35.3%	- 2.96	Total winning prize-money			£106,125
Longest winning sequence			2	Average SP of winner			4.3/1
Longest losing sequence			34	Return on stakes invested			-38.3%
1991 Form	29-208	13.9%	- 43.94	1989 Form	32-218	14.7%	- 18.25
1990 Form	31-239	13.0%	- 69.91	1988 Form	26-186	14.0%	- 12.52

J R JENKINS (Royston, Herts)

	No. of Horses	Races Run	1st	2nd	3rd	Unpl	Per cent	£1 Level Stake
2-y-o	10	43	2	3	2	36	4.7	- 35.00
3-y-o	3	10	0	1	0	9	-	- 10.00
4-y-o+	24	90	10	4	5	71	11.1	+ 16.00
Totals	37	143	12	8	7	116	8.4	- 29.00

BY MONTH

2-y-o	W-R	Per cent	£1 Level Stake	3-y-o	W-R	Per cent	£1 Level Stake
January	0-0	-	0.00	January	0-0	-	0.00
February	0-0	-	0.00	February	0-0	-	0.00
March	0-3	-	- 3.00	March	0-0	-	0.00
April	0-9	-	- 9.00	April	0-3	-	- 3.00
May	0-9	-	- 9.00	May	0-2	-	- 2.00
June	1-6	16.7	- 3.50	June	0-1	-	- 1.00
July	1-8	12.5	- 2.50	July	0-2	-	- 2.00
August	0-4	-	- 4.00	August	0-1	-	- 1.00
September	0-1	-	- 1.00	September	0-0	-	0.00
Oct/Nov	0-3	-	- 3.00	Oct/Nov	0-1	-	- 1.00

4-y-o+	W-R	Per cent	£1 Level Stake	Totals	W-R	Per cent	£1 Level Stake
January	1-4	25.0	+ 1.00	January	1-4	25.0	+ 1.00
February	0-3	-	- 3.00	February	0-3	-	- 3.00
March	2-6	33.3	+ 11.50	March	2-9	22.2	+ 8.50
April	2-18	11.1	+ 2.50	April	2-30	6.7	- 9.50
May	2-13	15.4	+ 23.00	May	2-24	8.3	+ 12.00
June	1-12	8.3	- 4.00	June	2-19	10.5	- 8.50
July	2-16	12.5	+ 3.00	July	3-26	11.5	- 1.50
August	0-4	-	- 4.00	August	0-9	-	- 9.00
September	0-10	-	- 10.00	September	0-11	-	- 11.00
Oct/Nov	0-4	-	- 4.00	Oct/Nov	0-8	-	- 8.00

DISTANCE

2-y-o	W-R	Per cent	£1 Level Stake	3-y-o	W-R	Per cent	£1 Level Stake
5f-6f	2-39	5.1	- 31.00	5f-6f	0-0	-	0.00
7f-8f	0-4	-	- 4.00	7f-8f	0-3	-	- 3.00
9f-13f	0-0	-	0.00	9f-13f	0-7	-	- 7.00
14f+	0-0	-	0.00	14f+	0-0	-	0.00

4-y-o+	W-R	Per cent	£1 Level Stake	Totals	W-R	Per cent	£1 Level Stake
5f-6f	0-0	-	0.00	5f-6f	2-39	5.1	- 31.00
7f-8f	2-11	18.2	+ 10.00	7f-8f	2-18	11.1	+ 3.00
9f-13f	4-49	8.2	- 2.00	9f-13f	4-56	7.1	- 9.00
14f+	4-30	13.3	+ 8.00	14f+	4-30	13.3	+ 8.00

TYPE OF RACE

Non-Handicaps	W-R	Per cent	£1 Level Stake	Handicaps	W-R	Per cent	£1 Level Stake
2-y-o	2-25	8.0	- 17.00	2-y-o	0-6	-	- 6.00
3-y-o	0-2	-	- 2.00	3-y-o	0-2	-	- 2.00
4-y-o+	2-19	10.5	- 8.50	4-y-o+	8-63	12.7	+ 32.50
Selling	0-18	-	- 18.00	Selling	0-4	-	- 4.00
Apprentice	0-1	-	- 1.00	Apprentice	0-2	-	- 2.00
Amat/Ladies	0-0	-	0.00	Amat/Ladies	0-1	-	- 1.00
Totals	4-65	6.2	- 46.50	Totals	8-78	10.3	+ 17.50

COURSE GRADE

	W-R	Per cent	£1 Level Stake
Group 1	6-39	15.4	+ 14.50
Group 2	1-28	3.6	- 25.50
Group 3	1-35	2.9	- 29.00
Group 4	4-41	9.8	+ 11.00

FIRST TIME OUT

	W-R	Per cent	£1 Level Stake
2-y-o	0-9	-	- 9.00
3-y-o	0-2	-	- 2.00
4-y-o+	5-24	20.8	+ 26.50
Totals	5-35	14.3	+ 15.50

JOCKEYS RIDING

	W-R	Per cent	£1 Level Stake		W-R	Per cent	£1 Level Stake
S Whitworth	6-52	11.5	+ 14.00	W Newnes	1-4	25.0	+ 11.00
Pat Eddery	3-9	33.3	+ 16.00	G Baxter	1-21	4.8	- 18.50
R Cochrane	1-1	100.0	+ 4.50				

N Carlisle	0-6	R Price	0-2	L Charnock	0-1
M Roberts	0-5	S Dawson	0-2	M Denaro	0-1
D Harrison	0-4	A Clark	0-1	M J Kinane	0-1
J Williams	0-4	A Munro	0-1	Miss A Rutherford	0-1
C Addington	0-3	A Tucker	0-1	N Adams	0-1
L Dettori	0-3	C Rutter	0-1	N Day	0-1
W Carson	0-3	D Carson	0-1	S Maloney	0-1
W Ryan	0-3	G Bardwell	0-1	T Quinn	0-1
E Johnson	0-2	G Duffield	0-1	T Williams	0-1
J Fortune	0-2	K Darley	0-1		

COURSE RECORD

	Total W-R	Non-Handicaps 2-y-o	Non-Handicaps 3-y-o+	Handicaps 2-y-o	Handicaps 3-y-o+	Per cent	£1 Level Stake
Epsom	2-6	1-1	0-1	0-0	1-4	33.3	+ 7.50
Southwell (AW)	2-8	0-1	0-2	0-0	2-5	25.0	+ 10.00
Kempton	2-9	0-2	0-2	0-0	2-5	22.2	+ 13.50
Newbury	1-2	0-0	0-0	0-0	1-2	50.0	+ 11.00
Doncaster	1-4	0-1	1-1	0-0	0-2	25.0	+ 0.50
Chester	1-5	1-2	0-0	0-1	0-2	20.0	- 2.50
Wolverhampton	1-6	0-2	0-1	0-0	1-3	16.7	+ 7.00
Warwick	1-11	0-3	0-2	0-0	1-6	9.1	+ 10.00
Windsor	1-19	0-8	1-9	0-0	0-2	5.3	- 13.00

Brighton	0-15	Yarmouth	0-4	Hamilton	0-1
Folkestone	0-12	Goodwood	0-3	Haydock	0-1
Newmarket	0-6	Pontefract	0-3	Redcar	0-1
Nottingham	0-6	Ascot	0-2	Ripon	0-1
Sandown	0-5	Salisbury	0-2	York	0-1
Lingfield	0-4	Bath	0-1		
Lingfield (AW)	0-4	Beverley	0-1		

WINNING HORSES

	Age	Races Run	1st	2nd	3rd	Unpl	Win £
Star Quest	5	5	2	0	0	3	9,626
Vanroy	8	12	2	2	1	7	5,217
Go South	8	13	1	0	1	11	3,980
Gin And Orange	6	2	1	0	0	1	3,574
Stormy Heights	2	8	1	2	1	4	3,418
Kaytak	5	5	1	0	0	4	3,314
Solid	4	5	1	0	1	3	2,736
Glowing Dancer	2	5	1	1	0	3	2,343
Qualitair Blazer	5	4	1	0	2	1	2,108
Moot Point	4	7	1	0	0	6	1,245

WINNING OWNERS

	Races Won	Value £		Races Won	Value £
A Escudero	4	13,214	Miss Elizabeth Colver	1	3,418
Derek Garrad	2	5,217	T J Myles & Co Contractors Ltd	1	3,314
Rex Joachim	1	3,980	J McBarron	1	2,736
Paul Walker	1	3,574	Brooke (Enfield Wash) Ltd	1	2,108

Favourites	1-5	20.0%	- 2.50	Total winning prize-money		£37,560
Longest winning sequence			1	Average SP of winner		8.5/1
Longest losing sequence			33	Return on stakes invested		-20.3%
1991 Form	12-152	7.9%	- 27.87	1989 Form	10-209	4.8%	- 94.50
1990 Form	13-239	5.4%	-137.84	1988 Form	15-220	6.8%	- 98.79

M S JOHNSTON (Middleham, North Yorks)

	No. of Horses	Races Run	1st	2nd	3rd	Unpl	Per cent	£1 Level Stake
2-y-o	24	121	13	11	9	88	10.7	- 48.67
3-y-o	16	135	28	19	9	79	20.7	+ 46.54
4-y-o+	11	128	9	16	18	85	7.0	0.00
Totals	51	384	50	46	36	252	13.0	- 2.13

BY MONTH

2-y-o	W-R	Per cent	£1 Level Stake	3-y-o	W-R	Per cent	£1 Level Stake
January	0-0	-	0.00	January	0-0	-	0.00
February	0-0	-	0.00	February	1-3	33.3	+ 14.00
March	0-3	-	- 3.00	March	2-6	33.3	+ 4.80
April	0-13	-	- 13.00	April	5-15	33.3	+ 22.87
May	2-11	18.2	- 0.25	May	3-17	17.6	+ 0.50
June	2-12	16.7	- 4.25	June	7-20	35.0	+ 9.82
July	6-17	35.3	+ 15.83	July	1-12	8.3	- 6.50
August	1-16	6.3	- 12.00	August	2-21	9.5	- 3.00
September	1-21	4.8	- 15.00	September	1-23	4.3	- 20.00
Oct/Nov	1-28	3.6	- 17.00	Oct/Nov	6-18	33.3	+ 24.05

4-y-o+	W-R	Per cent	£1 Level Stake	Totals	W-R	Per cent	£1 Level Stake
January	0-3	-	- 3.00	January	0-3	-	- 3.00
February	0-6	-	- 6.00	February	1-9	11.1	+ 8.00
March	1-9	11.1	- 5.00	March	3-18	16.7	- 3.20
April	0-9	-	- 9.00	April	5-37	13.5	+ 0.87
May	1-20	5.0	- 5.00	May	6-48	12.5	- 4.75
June	2-26	7.7	+ 29.50	June	11-58	19.0	+ 35.07
July	1-16	6.3	- 13.50	July	8-45	17.8	- 4.17
August	1-9	11.1	+ 8.00	August	4-46	8.7	- 7.00
September	2-14	14.3	+ 7.00	September	4-58	6.9	- 28.00
Oct/Nov	1-16	6.3	- 3.00	Oct/Nov	8-62	12.9	+ 4.05

DISTANCE

2-y-o	W-R	Per cent	£1 Level Stake	3-y-o	W-R	Per cent	£1 Level Stake
5f-6f	11-90	12.2	- 35.17	5f-6f	20-77	26.0	+ 20.29
7f-8f	2-31	6.5	- 13.50	7f-8f	5-36	13.9	+ 27.00
9f-13f	0-0	-	0.00	9f-13f	2-19	10.5	- 4.75
14f+	0-0	-	0.00	14f+	1-3	33.3	+ 4.00

4-y-o+	W-R	Per cent	£1 Level Stake	Totals	W-R	Per cent	£1 Level Stake
5f-6f	3-65	4.6	- 42.00	5f-6f	34-232	14.7	- 56.88
7f-8f	0-15	-	- 15.00	7f-8f	7-82	8.5	- 1.50
9f-13f	5-38	13.2	+ 50.00	9f-13f	7-57	12.3	+ 45.25
14f+	1-10	10.0	+ 7.00	14f+	2-13	15.4	+ 11.00

TYPE OF RACE

Non-Handicaps	W-R	Per cent	£1 Level Stake	Handicaps	W-R	Per cent	£1 Level Stake
2-y-o	11-68	16.2	- 12.67	2-y-o	1-30	3.3	- 26.00
3-y-o	9-33	27.3	+ 10.54	3-y-o	18-93	19.4	+ 36.00
4-y-o+	0-6	-	- 6.00	4-y-o+	8-109	7.3	+ 13.00
Selling	2-25	8.0	- 6.00	Selling	1-9	11.1	0.00
Apprentice	0-4	-	- 4.00	Apprentice	0-7	-	- 7.00
Amat/Ladies	0-0	-	0.00	Amat/Ladies	0-0	-	0.00
Totals	22-136	16.2	- 18.13	Totals	28-248	11.3	+ 16.00

<table>
<tr><th colspan="4">COURSE GRADE</th><th colspan="4">FIRST TIME OUT</th></tr>
<tr><th></th><th>W-R</th><th>Per cent</th><th>£1 Level Stake</th><th></th><th>W-R</th><th>Per cent</th><th>£1 Level Stake</th></tr>
<tr><td>Group 1</td><td>17-137</td><td>12.4</td><td>- 1.12</td><td>2-y-o</td><td>1-23</td><td>4.3</td><td>- 20.25</td></tr>
<tr><td>Group 2</td><td>4-67</td><td>6.0</td><td>- 31.00</td><td>3-y-o</td><td>4-12</td><td>33.3</td><td>+ 27.80</td></tr>
<tr><td>Group 3</td><td>18-101</td><td>17.8</td><td>- 9.95</td><td>4-y-o+</td><td>1-10</td><td>10.0</td><td>+ 5.00</td></tr>
<tr><td>Group 4</td><td>11-79</td><td>13.9</td><td>+ 39.94</td><td></td><td></td><td></td><td></td></tr>
<tr><td></td><td></td><td></td><td></td><td>Totals</td><td>6-45</td><td>13.3</td><td>+ 12.55</td></tr>
</table>

JOCKEYS RIDING

	W-R	Per cent	£1 Level Stake		W-R	Per cent	£1 Level Stake
D McKeown	27-160	16.9	+ 7.95	G Duffield	2-6	33.3	- 0.50
R P Elliott	9-93	9.7	+ 1.25	M Baird	2-21	9.5	+ 34.50
M Roberts	6-19	31.6	+ 14.87	N Adams	1-3	33.3	+ 6.00
J Reid	2-2	100.0	+ 10.80	J Lowe	1-19	5.3	- 16.00

J Fanning	0-10	A Culhane	0-1	L Dettori	0-1
J Carroll	0-4	A McGlone	0-1	M Humphries	0-1
L Newton	0-4	A Munro	0-1	N Carlisle	0-1
Paul Eddery	0-4	D Biggs	0-1	N Varley	0-1
T Quinn	0-4	D Holland	0-1	P Burke	0-1
B Raymond	0-3	D Wright	0-1	Pat Eddery	0-1
C Hawksley	0-3	Dale Gibson	0-1	R Hills	0-1
F Norton	0-3	G Bardwell	0-1	S Dawson	0-1
J Weaver	0-2	H Bastiman	0-1	S Wood	0-1
N Gwilliams	0-2	J Williams	0-1	T Williams	0-1
A Clark	0-1	K Darley	0-1		

COURSE RECORD

	Total W-R	Non-Handicaps 2-y-o	Non-Handicaps 3-y-o+	Handicaps 2-y-o	Handicaps 3-y-o+	Per cent	£1 Level Stake
Hamilton	8-38	3-10	2-8	0-1	3-19	21.1	+ 0.63
Carlisle	4-16	0-1	2-4	0-0	2-11	25.0	+ 48.19
Lingfield (AW)	4-18	1-2	0-3	0-0	3-13	22.2	+ 14.00
Pontefract	4-27	1-9	1-5	0-2	2-11	14.8	- 5.00
Ascot	3-7	1-2	0-2	0-0	2-3	42.9	+ 19.83
Beverley	3-15	1-6	1-1	0-2	1-6	20.0	- 1.38
Ayr	3-17	1-1	0-1	0-3	2-12	17.6	- 3.25
York	3-19	1-4	0-1	0-1	2-13	15.8	+ 8.50
Thirsk	2-17	0-4	1-3	0-1	1-9	11.8	- 3.00
Newcastle	2-19	0-6	1-3	0-0	1-10	10.5	- 10.70
Newmarket	2-29	0-2	0-0	0-6	2-21	6.9	+ 2.50
Windsor	1-1	0-0	0-0	1-1	0-0	100.0	+ 3.00
Kempton	1-2	0-0	0-0	0-0	1-2	50.0	+ 1.50
Chepstow	1-3	0-0	0-0	0-1	1-2	33.3	+ 8.00
Sandown	1-5	1-1	0-1	0-0	0-3	20.0	- 1.50
Wolverhampton	1-5	0-2	0-0	0-0	1-3	20.0	- 2.00
Haydock	1-6	0-0	0-0	0-0	1-6	16.7	+ 9.00

Johnston M S

Nottingham	1-8	0-3	1-2	0-0	0-3	12.5	- 6.20
Catterick	1-11	1-1	0-2	0-1	0-7	9.1	- 8.25
Ripon	1-14	0-4	0-1	0-1	1-8	7.1	- 5.00
Southwell (AW)	1-15	0-0	1-5	0-0	0-10	6.7	+ 2.00
Doncaster	1-21	0-4	0-1	0-3	1-13	4.8	- 15.00
Redcar	1-28	1-12	0-3	0-7	0-6	3.6	- 15.00

Edinburgh	0-11	Newbury		0-4	Brighton	0-1
Bath	0-6	Epsom		0-3	Chester	0-1
Goodwood	0-5	Leicester		0-3	Folkestone	0-1
Lingfield	0-5	Warwick		0-2	Salisbury	0-1

WINNING HORSES

		Races					Win
	Age	Run	1st	2nd	3rd	Unpl	£
Quick Ransom	4	11	4	3	1	3	143,675
Marina Park	2	6	3	2	0	1	31,891
Taufan Blu	3	12	3	0	2	7	27,112
Branston Abby	3	9	5	1	0	3	16,961
Double Blue	3	15	5	4	1	5	13,208
Educated Pet	3	25	6	3	0	16	12,503
Bold County	2	9	3	1	1	4	7,485
Akura	3	11	3	1	1	6	6,230
Fair Flyer	3	4	2	0	0	2	5,849
Beware Of Agents	3	7	1	1	1	4	5,481
Hinari Video	7	31	2	2	7	20	4,672
Luks Akura	4	21	2	2	1	16	3,964
Sweet Romeo	2	4	1	0	0	3	2,853
Boy Martin	3	15	2	3	1	9	2,751
Stardust Express	2	13	1	1	1	10	2,574
Pretonic	4	19	1	3	6	9	2,511
Arctic Guest	2	8	1	1	0	6	2,511
Pine Ridge Lad	2	4	1	0	0	3	2,448
Milngavie	2	6	1	0	0	5	2,427
Just Baileys	2	9	1	0	1	7	2,320
Straw Thatch	3	11	1	3	2	5	2,108
Field Of Vision	2	10	1	1	1	7	1,492

WINNING OWNERS

	Races Won	Value £		Races Won	Value £
J S Morrison	4	143,675	Mark Johnston Racing Ltd	2	4,217
Laharna Ltd	5	34,642	Luks Ind Co (UK) Ltd	2	3,964
Hambleton Lodge Equine Ltd	3	27,112	Mrs R A Johnson	1	2,574
J David Abell	5	16,961	L G McMullan	1	2,544
Billy Morgan	8	16,644	R Jenkinson	1	2,448
R W Huggins	6	14,700	A S Robertson	1	2,427
The Fairyhouse 1992 Partnership	5	12,849	G R Bailey Ltd (Horse Feed)	1	2,320
Brian Yeardley Continental Ltd	2	7,992	David McKenzie	1	2,108
William Provan Hunter	2	5,849			

Favourites	17-61	27.9%	- 11.71	Total winning prize-money			£303,026

Longest winning sequence			3	Average SP of winner			6.6/1
Longest losing sequence			23	Return on stakes invested			-0.6%

1991 Form	31-287	10.8%	-116.01	1989 Form	15-122	12.3%	+ 27.58
1990 Form	28-261	10.7%	- 4.63	1988 Form	5-89	5.6%	- 14.50

A W JONES (Oswestry, Salop)

	No. of Horses	Races Run	1st	2nd	3rd	Unpl	Per cent	£1 Level Stake
2-y-o	0	0	0	0	0	0	-	0.00
3-y-o	1	6	0	0	0	6	-	- 6.00
4-y-o+	6	37	1	5	8	23	2.7	- 28.00
Totals	7	43	1	5	8	29	2.3	- 34.00

Jan	Feb	Mar	Apr	May	Jun	Jul	Aug	Sep	Oct/Nov
0-0	0-1	0-1	0-5	1-6	0-6	0-8	0-6	0-4	0-6

		W-R	£1 Level Stake				W-R	£1 Level Stake
Winning Jockey				Winning Course				
Miss I D W Jones		1-10	- 1.00	Wolverhampton			1-6	+ 3.00

		Age	Races Run	1st	2nd	3rd	Unpl	Win £
Winning Horse								
Thundering		7	10	1	1	3	5	1,361

Favourites	0-0			Total winning prize-money			£1,361

1991 Form	0-10			1989 Form	1-44	2.3%	- 27.00
1990 Form	1-31	3.2%	+ 3.00	1988 Form	0-51		

BOB JONES (Newmarket)

	No. of Horses	Races Run	1st	2nd	3rd	Unpl	Per cent	£1 Level Stake
2-y-o	6	18	0	0	1	17	-	- 18.00
3-y-o	6	51	8	5	2	36	15.7	+ 4.75
4-y-o+	5	27	1	1	5	20	3.7	- 20.50
Totals	17	96	9	6	8	73	9.4	- 33.75

Jan	Feb	Mar	Apr	May	Jun	Jul	Aug	Sep	Oct/Nov
0-0	0-1	1-4	0-9	1-12	1-12	3-15	2-12	1-11	0-20

		£1 Level					£1 Level
Winning Jockeys	W-R	Stake			W-R	Stake
N Day	6-31	+ 13.25	N Connorton		1-5	+ 1.50
V Smith	2-24	- 12.50				

Winning Courses						
Haydock	3-7	+ 10.50	Redcar	1-7	- 0.50
Thirsk	1-1	+ 1.25	Nottingham	1-9	- 2.50
Folkestone	1-2	+ 13.00	Southwell (AW)	1-9	- 4.00
Lingfield	1-3	+ 6.50			

			Races					Win
Winning Horses		Age	Run	1st	2nd	3rd	Unpl	£
Jack Button		3	14	5	2	1	6	14,529
Sword Master		3	11	1	3	0	7	2,988
Watch Me Go		3	13	1	0	1	11	2,976
Lookingforararainbow		4	10	1	1	3	5	2,618
Sirtelimar		3	6	1	0	0	5	1,151

Favourites	1-5	20.0%	+ 1.50	Total winning prize-money		£24,262
1991 Form	4-52	7.7%	- 4.00			

D HAYDN JONES (Pontypridd, Mid-Glamorgan)

	No. of Horses	Races Run	1st	2nd	3rd	Unpl	Per cent	£1 Level Stake
2-y-o	10	52	1	2	6	43	1.9	- 35.00
3-y-o	5	37	1	2	3	31	2.7	- 16.00
4-y-o+	7	51	3	6	4	38	5.9	- 19.50
Totals	22	140	5	10	13	112	3.6	- 70.50

Jan	Feb	Mar	Apr	May	Jun	Jul	Aug	Sep	Oct/Nov
0-4	2-6	1-7	0-11	1-18	1-23	0-22	0-24	0-14	0-11

		£1 Level				£1 Level
Winning Jockeys	W-R	Stake			W-R	Stake
R Cochrane	1-2	+ 15.00	W Ryan		1-4	+ 9.00
J Fanning	1-3	+ 4.50	J Williams		1-20	- 9.00
D Holland	1-4	+ 17.00				

Winning Courses					
Lingfield (AW)	2-12	+ 6.50	Southwell (AW)	1-24	- 11.00
Pontefract	1-5	+ 12.00	Wolverhampton	1-28	- 7.00

			Races					Win
Winning Horses		Age	Run	1st	2nd	3rd	Unpl	£
Quinzii Martin		4	15	2	1	3	9	5,125
Lowrianna		2	8	1	1	0	6	2,783
Rocky Bay		3	7	1	0	0	6	2,677
Premier Dance		5	11	1	1	1	8	2,324

Favourites	0-6			Total winning prize-money			£12,908
1991 Form	2-131	1.5%	- 109.50	1989 Form	3-97	3.1%	- 67.75
1990 Form	7-159	4.4%	- 114.62	1988 Form	6-140	4.3%	- 76.62

H THOMSON JONES (Newmarket)

	No. of Horses	Races Run	1st	2nd	3rd	Unpl	Per cent	£1 Level Stake
2-y-o	19	63	12	13	12	26	19.0	- 23.22
3-y-o	23	107	14	20	9	64	13.1	- 0.81
4-y-o+	4	18	1	1	2	14	5.6	- 9.50
Totals	46	188	27	34	23	104	14.4	- 33.53

BY MONTH

2-y-o	W-R	Per cent	£1 Level Stake	3-y-o	W-R	Per cent	£1 Level Stake
January	0-0	-	0.00	January	1-1	100.0	+ 1.10
February	0-0	-	0.00	February	0-1	-	- 1.00
March	0-0	-	0.00	March	0-2	-	- 2.00
April	0-0	-	0.00	April	1-15	6.7	- 12.00
May	0-1	-	- 1.00	May	1-16	6.3	- 10.00
June	4-10	40.0	+ 7.00	June	4-18	22.2	+ 2.21
July	3-11	27.3	- 2.74	July	1-14	7.1	- 10.75
August	3-13	23.1	- 6.05	August	3-11	27.3	+ 7.63
September	1-17	5.9	- 15.43	September	1-11	9.1	+ 4.00
Oct/Nov	1-11	9.1	- 5.00	Oct/Nov	2-18	11.1	+ 20.00

4-y-o+	W-R	Per cent	£1 Level Stake	Totals	W-R	Per cent	£1 Level Stake
January	0-0	-	0.00	January	1-1	100.0	+ 1.10
February	0-0	-	0.00	February	0-1	-	- 1.00
March	0-1	-	- 1.00	March	0-3	-	- 3.00
April	0-3	-	- 3.00	April	1-18	5.6	- 15.00
May	0-4	-	- 4.00	May	1-21	4.8	- 15.00
June	0-4	-	- 4.00	June	8-32	25.0	+ 5.21
July	1-1	100.0	+ 7.50	July	5-26	19.2	- 5.99
August	0-2	-	- 2.00	August	6-26	23.1	- 0.42
September	0-2	-	- 2.00	September	2-30	6.7	- 13.43
Oct/Nov	0-1	-	- 1.00	Oct/Nov	3-30	10.0	+ 14.00

DISTANCE

2-y-o	W-R	Per cent	£1 Level Stake	3-y-o	W-R	Per cent	£1 Level Stake
5f-6f	8-29	27.6	+ 0.95	5f-6f	6-38	15.8	+ 14.88
7f-8f	4-34	11.8	- 24.17	7f-8f	2-31	6.5	- 9.67
9f-13f	0-0	-	0.00	9f-13f	5-33	15.2	- 6.52
14f+	0-0	-	0.00	14f+	1-5	20.0	+ 0.50

4-y-o+	W-R	Per cent	£1 Level Stake	Totals	W-R	Per cent	£1 Level Stake
5f-6f	0-0	-	0.00	5f-6f	14-67	20.9	+ 15.83
7f-8f	0-1	-	- 1.00	7f-8f	6-66	9.1	- 34.84
9f-13f	1-10	10.0	- 1.50	9f-13f	6-43	14.0	- 8.02
14f+	0-7	-	- 7.00	14f+	1-12	8.3	- 6.50

TYPE OF RACE

Non-Handicaps	W-R	Per cent	£1 Level Stake	Handicaps	W-R	Per cent	£1 Level Stake
2-y-o	12-55	21.8	- 15.22	2-y-o	0-8	-	- 8.00
3-y-o	7-44	15.9	- 14.69	3-y-o	7-60	11.7	+ 16.88
4-y-o+	0-0	-	0.00	4-y-o+	1-17	5.9	- 8.50
Selling	0-1	-	- 1.00	Selling	0-0	-	0.00
Apprentice	0-1	-	- 1.00	Apprentice	0-0	-	0.00
Amat/Ladies	0-1	-	- 1.00	Amat/Ladies	0-1	-	- 1.00
Totals	19-102	18.6	- 32.91	Totals	8-86	9.3	- 0.62

COURSE GRADE

	W-R	Per cent	£1 Level Stake
Group 1	14-106	13.2	- 12.41
Group 2	5-30	16.7	- 11.92
Group 3	5-33	15.2	+ 3.75
Group 4	3-19	15.8	- 12.95

FIRST TIME OUT

	W-R	Per cent	£1 Level Stake
2-y-o	4-19	21.1	- 4.25
3-y-o	3-23	13.0	- 15.27
4-y-o+	0-4	-	- 4.00
Totals	7-46	15.2	- 23.52

JOCKEYS RIDING

	W-R	Per cent	£1 Level Stake		W-R	Per cent	£1 Level Stake
R Hills	22-140	15.7	- 34.78	M Hills	1-3	33.3	+ 18.00
N Carlisle	2-25	8.0	- 14.00	W Carson	1-6	16.7	- 3.75
W Ryan	1-3	33.3	+ 12.00				

M Birch	0-3	G Duffield	0-1	Mr M Whitaker		0-1
Pat Eddery	0-2	G Forster	0-1	Stan Mellor		0-1
A Munro	0-1	Mr G Haine	0-1			

COURSE RECORD

	Total W-R	Non-Handicaps 2-y-o	3-y-o+	Handicaps 2-y-o	3-y-o+	Per cent	£1 Level Stake
Doncaster	3-10	2-4	1-2	0-0	0-4	30.0	+ 8.00
Brighton	2-2	1-1	1-1	0-0	0-0	100.0	+ 2.20
Bath	2-3	1-2	1-1	0-0	0-0	66.7	+ 10.50
Epsom	2-5	0-1	1-1	0-0	1-3	40.0	+ 7.33
Redcar	2-7	0-1	1-1	0-2	1-3	28.6	+ 3.63
Kempton	2-10	1-2	0-4	0-0	1-4	20.0	- 2.25
Yarmouth	2-12	2-6	0-5	0-0	0-1	16.7	- 5.75
Haydock	2-13	1-4	0-5	0-1	1-3	15.4	+ 4.50
Ascot	2-15	1-9	0-1	0-0	1-5	13.3	- 3.50
Chepstow	1-2	0-0	0-0	0-0	1-2	50.0	+ 15.00
Lingfield (AW)	1-2	0-0	1-1	0-0	0-1	50.0	+ 0.10
Carlisle	1-3	0-2	0-0	0-0	1-1	33.3	- 0.62

Ayr	1-5	1-4	0-0	0-0	0-1	20.0	- 2.37
Wolverhampton	1-5	1-2	0-1	0-0	0-2	20.0	- 3.43
Thirsk	1-6	0-1	1-3	0-0	0-2	16.7	- 2.75
Goodwood	1-7	0-3	0-1	0-1	1-2	14.3	+ 14.00
Newmarket	1-18	1-3	0-2	0-0	0-13	5.6	- 15.12

Chester	0-9	Folkestone	0-4	Warwick	0-3
York	0-9	Nottingham	0-4	Beverley	0-2
Sandown	0-6	Salisbury	0-4	Catterick	0-2
Newbury	0-5	Leicester	0-3	Ripon	0-2
Pontefract	0-5	Newcastle	0-3	Windsor	0-2

WINNING HORSES

	Age	Races Run	1st	2nd	3rd	Unpl	Win £
Zaahi	3	4	1	2	0	1	19,293
Humam	2	4	2	1	1	0	17,868
Hazm	3	8	2	1	1	4	8,794
Libk	4	8	1	1	0	6	7,375
Wathik	2	4	2	1	0	1	7,221
Belated	3	10	2	3	2	3	6,184
Mathaayl	3	8	2	1	2	3	5,907
Elsals	3	4	2	0	0	2	5,506
Mujid	3	6	1	2	0	3	3,319
Dalalah	2	5	1	0	2	2	3,054
Binkhaldoun	3	3	1	1	0	1	2,898
Mootawel	3	7	1	0	1	5	2,820
Yakin	2	4	1	2	0	1	2,805
Abtaal	2	4	1	1	1	1	2,763
Shahaamh	3	6	1	2	1	2	2,756
Ihtiraz	2	6	1	3	0	2	2,427
Ajfan	2	3	1	1	1	0	2,385
Ibraz	2	3	1	1	1	0	2,301
Dahliz	2	6	1	2	0	3	2,253
Noble Singer	3	2	1	1	0	0	2,187
Tahasun	2	3	1	0	1	1	1,520

WINNING OWNERS

	Races Won	Value £		Races Won	Value £
Hamdan Al-Maktoum	23	100,444	Maktoum Al Maktoum	1	2,820
Mrs H T Jones	2	6,184	W J Gredley	1	2,187

Favourites	12-36	33.3%	- 5.78	Total winning prize-money			£111,634
Longest winning sequence			3	Average SP of winner			4.7/1
Longest losing sequence			33	Return on stakes invested			-17.8%
1991 Form	37-190	19.5%	+ 25.39	1989 Form	37-189	19.6%	- 25.69
1990 Form	34-209	16.3%	- 13.92	1988 Form	41-269	15.2%	- 25.45

T THOMSON JONES (Upper Lambourn, Berks)

	No. of Horses	Races Run	1st	2nd	3rd	Unpl	Per cent	£1 Level Stake
2-y-o	5	20	0	2	2	16	-	- 20.00
3-y-o	10	38	3	4	3	28	7.9	- 2.00
4-y-o+	5	28	2	2	0	24	7.1	- 20.00
Totals	20	86	5	8	5	68	5.8	- 42.00

Jan	Feb	Mar	Apr	May	Jun	Jul	Aug	Sep	Oct/Nov
0-3	1-5	1-4	0-2	0-2	0-7	2-22	1-16	0-16	0-9

Winning Jockeys	W-R	£1 Level Stake				W-R	£1 Level Stake
D Biggs	2-4	+ 4.00		T Quinn		1-3	+ 23.00
S Cauthen	1-1	+ 5.00		W Carson		1-5	- 1.00

Winning Courses	W-R	£1 Level Stake				W-R	£1 Level Stake
Southwell (AW)	2-9	- 1.00		Warwick		1-3	+ 3.00
Beverley	1-3	+ 1.00		Folkestone		1-6	+ 20.00

Winning Horses	Age	Races Run	1st	2nd	3rd	Unpl	Win £
Horizon	4	12	2	2	0	8	4,354
Blazon Of Troy	3	3	1	0	0	2	2,070
Arfey	3	5	1	1	0	3	1,478
Honey Seeker	3	2	1	0	0	1	1,380

Favourites	1-3	33.3%	- 1.00	Total winning prize-money			£9,282
1991 Form	7-106	6.6%	- 38.50	1989 Form	7-50	14.0%	+ 20.00
1990 Form	8-131	6.1%	- 84.11				

MRS J JORDAN (Lambourn, Berks)

	No. of Horses	Races Run	1st	2nd	3rd	Unpl	Per cent	£1 Level Stake
2-y-o	2	6	0	0	0	6	-	- 6.00
3-y-o	4	13	0	0	0	13	-	- 13.00
4-y-o+	2	16	1	0	2	13	6.3	- 1.00
Totals	8	35	1	0	2	32	2.9	- 20.00

Jan	Feb	Mar	Apr	May	Jun	Jul	Aug	Sep	Oct/Nov
0-0	0-0	0-8	0-2	0-7	0-6	1-4	0-6	0-1	0-1

Winning Jockey	W-R	£1 Level Stake	Winning Course	W-R	£1 Level Stake
Kim McDonnell	1-8	+ 7.00	Redcar	1-10	+ 5.00

Winning Horse	Age	Races Run	1st	2nd	3rd	Unpl	Win £
Doctor's Remedy	6	14	1	0	2	11	3,200

Favourites	0-1			Total winning prize-money	£3,200
1991 Form	3-60	5.0%	- 45.25		

P A KELLEWAY (Newmarket)

	No. of Horses	Races Run	1st	2nd	3rd	Unpl	Per cent	£1 Level Stake
2-y-o	18	63	4	9	7	43	6.3	- 6.37
3-y-o	11	67	8	6	5	48	11.9	- 24.05
4-y-o+	8	40	4	6	4	26	10.0	- 19.30
Totals	37	170	16	21	16	117	9.4	- 49.72

BY MONTH

2-y-o	W-R	Per cent	£1 Level Stake	3-y-o	W-R	Per cent	£1 Level Stake
January	0-0	-	0.00	January	1-2	50.0	+ 7.00
February	0-0	-	0.00	February	1-3	33.3	+ 7.00
March	0-3	-	- 3.00	March	0-2	-	- 2.00
April	0-2	-	- 2.00	April	0-10	-	- 10.00
May	0-9	-	- 9.00	May	1-9	11.1	- 5.00
June	2-10	20.0	- 0.37	June	1-8	12.5	- 5.25
July	0-6	-	- 6.00	July	2-10	20.0	- 1.30
August	1-7	14.3	+ 6.00	August	1-10	10.0	- 7.50
September	1-12	8.3	+ 22.00	September	1-7	14.3	- 1.00
Oct/Nov	0-14	-	- 14.00	Oct/Nov	0-6	-	- 6.00

4-y-o+	W-R	Per cent	£1 Level Stake	Totals	W-R	Per cent	£1 Level Stake
January	0-9	-	- 9.00	January	1-11	9.1	- 2.00
February	0-3	-	- 3.00	February	1-6	16.7	+ 4.00
March	1-7	14.3	+ 5.00	March	1-12	8.3	0.00
April	0-4	-	- 4.00	April	0-16	-	- 16.00
May	0-5	-	- 5.00	May	1-23	4.3	- 19.00
June	0-3	-	- 3.00	June	3-21	14.3	- 8.62
July	0-1	-	- 1.00	July	2-17	11.8	- 8.30
August	1-3	33.3	- 0.80	August	3-20	15.0	- 2.30
September	1-2	50.0	+ 0.75	September	3-21	14.3	+ 21.75
Oct/Nov	1-3	33.3	+ 0.75	Oct/Nov	1-23	4.3	- 19.25

DISTANCE

2-y-o	W-R	Per cent	£1 Level Stake	3-y-o	W-R	Per cent	£1 Level Stake
5f-6f	2-39	5.1	- 29.37	5f-6f	5-16	31.3	+ 5.45
7f-8f	2-23	8.7	+ 24.00	7f-8f	1-14	7.1	- 11.50
9f-13f	0-1	-	- 1.00	9f-13f	2-34	5.9	- 15.00
14f+	0-0	-	0.00	14f+	0-3	-	- 3.00

4-y-o+	W-R	Per cent	£1 Level Stake	Totals	W-R	Per cent	£1 Level Stake
5f-6f	0-0	-	0.00	5f-6f	7-55	12.7	- 23.92
7f-8f	1-7	14.3	+ 5.00	7f-8f	4-44	9.1	+ 17.50
9f-13f	3-22	13.6	- 13.30	9f-13f	5-57	8.8	- 29.30
14f+	0-11	-	- 11.00	14f+	0-14	-	- 14.00

TYPE OF RACE

Non-Handicaps	W-R	Per cent	£1 Level Stake	Handicaps	W-R	Per cent	£1 Level Stake
2-y-o	2-49	4.1	- 39.37	2-y-o	1-3	33.3	+ 10.00
3-y-o	5-43	11.6	- 20.55	3-y-o	2-18	11.1	- 1.50
4-y-o+	3-16	18.8	+ 2.50	4-y-o+	0-22	-	- 22.00
Selling	2-15	13.3	+ 23.00	Selling	0-1	-	- 1.00
Apprentice	1-1	100.0	+ 1.20	Apprentice	0-0	-	0.00
Amat/Ladies	0-2	-	- 2.00	Amat/Ladies	0-0	-	0.00
Totals	13-126	10.3	- 35.22	Totals	3-44	6.8	- 14.50

COURSE GRADE

	W-R	Per cent	£1 Level Stake
Group 1	4-70	5.7	- 46.17
Group 2	3-17	17.6	- 5.80
Group 3	5-35	14.3	+ 16.50
Group 4	4-48	8.3	- 14.25

FIRST TIME OUT

	W-R	Per cent	£1 Level Stake
2-y-o	0-18	-	- 18.00
3-y-o	1-10	10.0	- 1.00
4-y-o+	0-6	-	- 6.00
Totals	1-34	2.9	- 25.00

JOCKEYS RIDING

	W-R	Per cent	£1 Level Stake		W-R	Per cent	£1 Level Stake
W Carson	2-3	66.7	+ 3.50	Gay Kelleway	2-27	7.4	+ 9.50
Pat Eddery	2-5	40.0	- 0.05	A Bates	1-3	33.3	- 0.80
D Biggs	2-8	25.0	+ 17.00	A Munro	1-5	20.0	+ 1.00
G Bardwell	2-13	15.4	+ 6.00	K Darley	1-5	20.0	+ 1.50
P Robinson	2-24	8.3	- 13.00	M Roberts	1-11	9.1	- 8.37

W Newnes	0-7	G Hind	0-2	J Fanning	0-1
T Quinn	0-6	J Quinn	0-2	J Reid	0-1
B Raymond	0-5	K Fallon	0-2	J Weaver	0-1
C Asmussen	0-5	Miss S Kelleway	0-2	J Williams	0-1
J Carroll	0-4	Paul Eddery	0-2	L Dettori	0-1
C Rutter	0-3	W Ryan	0-2	L Piggott	0-1
D Holland	0-3	W Woods	0-2	M Hills	0-1
G Duffield	0-3	A Clark	0-1	N Adams	0-1
A McGlone	0-2	B Doyle	0-1	S Cauthen	0-1
G Carter	0-2	F Norton	0-1		

COURSE RECORD

	Total W-R	Non-Handicaps 2-y-o	3-y-o+	Handicaps 2-y-o	3-y-o+	Per cent	£1 Level Stake
Nottingham	3-6	1-3	2-3	0-0	0-0	50.0	+ 34.50
Sandown	2-9	0-4	1-4	1-1	0-0	22.2	+ 10.00
Lingfield (AW)	2-25	0-3	1-7	0-0	1-15	8.0	- 6.00
Epsom	1-2	1-1	0-1	0-0	0-0	50.0	+ 0.63
Newcastle	1-2	0-0	1-1	0-0	0-1	50.0	+ 0.20

Thirsk	1-2	0-0	0-1	0-0	1-1	50.0	+	4.50
Hamilton	1-3	1-1	0-1	0-1	0-0	33.3	+	4.00
Lingfield	1-4	0-0	1-2	0-0	0-2	25.0	-	1.80
Brighton	1-5	0-2	1-2	0-0	0-1	20.0	-	2.50
Leicester	1-7	0-3	1-3	0-1	0-0	14.3	-	3.00
Folkestone	1-8	0-4	1-3	0-0	0-1	12.5	-	5.25
Southwell (AW)	1-10	0-2	1-4	0-0	0-4	10.0	+	2.00

Newmarket	0-20	Haydock	0-5	Chester		0-2
Goodwood	0-9	Newbury	0-4	Wolverhampton		0-2
Ascot	0-8	Pontefract	0-3	Chepstow		0-1
Doncaster	0-8	Redcar	0-3	Edinburgh		0-1
Beverley	0-7	York	0-3	Salisbury		0-1
Yarmouth	0-7	Catterick	0-2	Windsor		0-1

WINNING HORSES

	Age	Races Run	1st	2nd	3rd	Unpl	Win £
Marcus Thorpe	4	8	3	0	1	4	8,289
Our Rita	3	8	3	1	0	4	7,829
Iommelli	2	6	2	1	0	3	6,820
Miss Bluebird	3	6	2	0	0	4	5,162
Slight Risk	3	10	2	3	0	5	4,491
John Rose	3	6	1	1	1	3	2,984
Always Risky	2	7	1	2	0	4	2,826
Kay's Dilemma	4	5	1	1	0	3	2,324
Dailysportdutch	2	2	1	0	0	1	1,932

WINNING OWNERS

	Races Won	Value £		Races Won	Value £
G Mazza	5	15,109	Lewis H Norris	1	2,984
P A Kelleway	3	7,988	Alexander Pereira	1	2,324
T Brady	3	7,829	Roldvale Ltd	1	1,932
Mrs G E Kelleway	2	4,491			

Favourites	4-12	33.3%	- 0.97	Total winning prize-money			£42,656

Longest winning sequence		2	Average SP of winner	6.5/1
Longest losing sequence		44	Return on stakes invested	-29.2%

1991 Form	13-156	8.3%	- 56.92	1989 Form	13-138	9.4%	- 50.38
1990 Form	8-170	4.7%	-123.20	1988 Form	16-177	9.0%	- 56.00

S E KETTLEWELL (Middleham, North Yorks)

	No. of Horses	Races Run	1st	2nd	3rd	Unpl	Per cent	£1 Level Stake
2-y-o	2	8	0	0	0	8	-	- 8.00
3-y-o	3	12	2	0	0	10	16.7	+ 12.00
4-y-o+	4	16	3	1	0	12	18.8	+ 5.00
Totals	9	36	5	1	0	30	13.9	+ 9.00

Jan	Feb	Mar	Apr	May	Jun	Jul	Aug	Sep	Oct/Nov
0-1	0-0	0-0	0-3	1-3	1-4	1-3	2-6	0-7	0-9

Winning Jockeys	W-R	£1 Level Stake		W-R	£1 Level Stake
J Fortune	2-10	+ 5.00	G Carter	1-2	+ 4.00
M Humphries	1-1	+ 2.00	Mrs D Kettlewell	1-4	+ 17.00

Winning Courses	W-R	£1 Level Stake		W-R	£1 Level Stake
Nottingham	1-1	+ 2.00	Hamilton	1-3	+ 18.00
Ripon	1-1	+ 5.00	Newcastle	1-4	+ 7.00
Ayr	1-3	+ 1.00			

Winning Horses	Age	Races Run	1st	2nd	3rd	Unpl	Win £
Mbulwa	6	11	3	1	0	7	10,789
Just Bob	3	10	2	0	0	8	3,962

Favourites	3-3	100.0%	+ 10.00	Total winning prize-money	£14,751

1991 Form	2-17	11.8%	+ 3.00	1989 Form	0-20
1990 Form	1-17	5.9%	+ 4.00	1988 Form	0-27

J S KING (Swindon, Wilts)

	No. of Horses	Races Run	1st	2nd	3rd	Unpl	Per cent	£1 Level Stake
2-y-o	0	0	0	0	0	0	-	0.00
3-y-o	0	0	0	0	0	0	-	0.00
4-y-o+	5	21	5	1	1	14	23.8	+ 6.75
Totals	5	21	5	1	1	14	23.8	+ 6.75

Jan	Feb	Mar	Apr	May	Jun	Jul	Aug	Sep	Oct/Nov
0-0	0-0	0-0	0-1	0-6	2-5	2-3	1-2	0-2	0-2

Winning Jockeys	W-R	£1 Level Stake		W-R	£1 Level Stake
T Quinn	3-3	+ 14.75	Paul Eddery	1-2	+ 2.00
Mrs L Pearce	1-2	+ 4.00			

Winning Courses	W-R	£1 Level Stake		W-R	£1 Level Stake
Bath	3-4	+ 14.00	Lingfield	1-3	+ 0.75
Salisbury	1-2	+ 4.00			

Winning Horses	Age	Races Run	1st	2nd	3rd	Unpl	Win £
Chucklestone	9	10	4	0	1	5	11,336
Marchman	7	3	1	1	0	1	3,444

Favourites	0-0			Total winning prize-money			£14,780

1991 Form	0-19			1989 Form	4-36	11.1%	+ 4.00
1990 Form	2-25	8.0%	- 11.50	1988 Form	0-47		

MRS A L M KING (Stratford-upon-Avon, Warwicks)

	No. of Horses	Races Run	1st	2nd	3rd	Unpl	Per cent	£1 Level Stake
2-y-o	0	0	0	0	0	0	-	0.00
3-y-o	2	12	1	0	1	10	8.3	+ 89.00
4-y-o+	4	18	0	2	1	15	-	- 18.00
Totals	6	30	1	2	2	25	3.3	+ 71.00

Jan	Feb	Mar	Apr	May	Jun	Jul	Aug	Sep	Oct/Nov
0-0	0-0	0-0	0-4	0-6	0-4	1-6	0-6	0-2	0-2

Winning Jockey	W-R	£1 Level Stake	Winning Course	W-R	£1 Level Stake
A Garth	1-5	+ 96.00	Pontefract	1-7	+ 94.00

Winning Horse	Age	Races Run	1st	2nd	3rd	Unpl	Win £
Followmegirls	3	7	1	0	1	5	2,385

Favourites	0-1			Total winning prize-money			£2,385

1991 Form	3-22	13.6%	+ 32.00	1989 Form	0-0		
1990 Form	1-12	8.3%	+ 1.00	1988 Form	0-11		

MISS H C KNIGHT (Wantage, Oxon)

	No. of Horses	Races Run	1st	2nd	3rd	Unpl	Per cent	£1 Level Stake
2-y-o	0	0	0	0	0	0	-	0.00
3-y-o	2	12	1	2	0	9	8.3	+ 5.00
4-y-o+	2	7	0	1	0	6	-	- 7.00
Totals	4	19	1	3	0	15	5.3	- 2.00

Jan	Feb	Mar	Apr	May	Jun	Jul	Aug	Sep	Oct/Nov
0-0	0-0	0-0	0-2	0-1	0-3	1-8	0-2	0-0	0-3

		£1 Level					£1 Level
Winning Jockey	W-R	Stake	Winning Course		W-R	Stake
M Roberts	1-2	+ 15.00	Leicester		1-4	+ 13.00

		Races					Win
Winning Horse	Age	Run	1st	2nd	3rd	Unpl	£
Karen Louise	3	6	1	0	0	5	1,646

Favourites	0-2		Total winning prize-money		£1,646

1991 Form	1-19	5.3%	+ 32.00	1990 Form	0-6

MRS A KNIGHT (Cullompton, Devon)

	No. of Horses	Races Run	1st	2nd	3rd	Unpl	Per cent	£1 Level Stake
2-y-o	1	1	0	0	0	1	-	- 1.00
3-y-o	4	19	1	0	1	17	5.3	+ 2.00
4-y-o+	13	100	11	13	10	66	11.0	+ 24.75
Totals	18	120	12	13	11	84	10.0	+ 25.75

BY MONTH

2-y-o	W-R	Per cent	£1 Level Stake	3-y-o	W-R	Per cent	£1 Level Stake
January	0-0	-	0.00	January	0-0	-	0.00
February	0-0	-	0.00	February	0-0	-	0.00
March	0-0	-	0.00	March	0-1	-	- 1.00
April	0-0	-	0.00	April	0-1	-	- 1.00
May	0-0	-	0.00	May	0-3	-	- 3.00
June	0-0	-	0.00	June	0-4	-	- 4.00
July	0-0	-	0.00	July	0-4	-	- 4.00
August	0-0	-	0.00	August	1-1	100.0	+ 20.00
September	0-1	-	- 1.00	September	0-2	-	- 2.00
Oct/Nov	0-0	-	0.00	Oct/Nov	0-3	-	- 3.00

4-y-o+	W-R	Per cent	£1 Level Stake	Totals	W-R	Per cent	£1 Level Stake
January	0-13	-	- 13.00	January	0-13	-	- 13.00
February	4-12	33.3	+ 65.50	February	4-12	33.3	+ 65.50
March	1-11	9.1	- 5.00	March	1-12	8.3	- 6.00
April	0-4	-	- 4.00	April	0-5	-	- 5.00
May	3-11	27.3	+ 18.00	May	3-14	21.4	+ 15.00
June	1-13	7.7	- 10.25	June	1-17	5.9	- 14.25
July	1-8	12.5	- 2.00	July	1-12	8.3	- 6.00
August	1-8	12.5	- 4.50	August	2-9	22.2	+ 15.50
September	0-11	-	- 11.00	September	0-14	-	- 14.00
Oct/Nov	0-9	-	- 9.00	Oct/Nov	0-12	-	- 12.00

DISTANCE

2-y-o	W-R	Per cent	£1 Level Stake	3-y-o	W-R	Per cent	£1 Level Stake
5f-6f	0-0	-	0.00	5f-6f	1-5	20.0	+ 16.00
7f-8f	0-1	-	- 1.00	7f-8f	0-11	-	- 11.00
9f-13f	0-0	-	0.00	9f-13f	0-3	-	- 3.00
14f+	0-0	-	0.00	14f+	0-0	-	0.00

4-y-o+	W-R	Per cent	£1 Level Stake	Totals	W-R	Per cent	£1 Level Stake
5f-6f	1-11	9.1	+ 40.00	5f-6f	2-16	12.5	+ 56.00
7f-8f	1-32	3.1	- 22.00	7f-8f	1-44	2.3	- 34.00
9f-13f	3-36	8.3	- 20.50	9f-13f	3-39	7.7	- 23.50
14f+	6-21	28.6	+ 27.25	14f+	6-21	28.6	+ 27.25

TYPE OF RACE

Non-Handicaps	W-R	Per cent	£1 Level Stake	Handicaps	W-R	Per cent	£1 Level Stake
2-y-o	0-1	-	- 1.00	2-y-o	0-0	-	0.00
3-y-o	0-6	-	- 6.00	3-y-o	0-9	-	- 9.00
4-y-o+	0-16	-	- 16.00	4-y-o+	9-69	13.0	+ 1.25
Selling	1-7	14.3	+ 14.00	Selling	0-2	-	- 2.00
Apprentice	0-1	-	- 1.00	Apprentice	1-3	33.3	+ 0.50
Amat/Ladies	0-0	-	0.00	Amat/Ladies	1-6	16.7	+ 45.00
Totals	1-31	3.2	- 10.00	Totals	11-89	12.4	+ 35.75

COURSE GRADE

	W-R	Per cent	£1 Level Stake
Group 1	2-22	9.1	+ 4.00
Group 2	2-23	8.7	- 13.50
Group 3	2-25	8.0	- 1.00
Group 4	6-50	12.0	+ 36.25

FIRST TIME OUT

	W-R	Per cent	£1 Level Stake
2-y-o	0-0	-	0.00
3-y-o	0-2	-	- 2.00
4-y-o+	0-13	-	- 13.00
Totals	0-15	-	- 15.00

JOCKEYS RIDING

	W-R	Per cent	£1 Level Stake		W-R	Per cent	£1 Level Stake
F Norton	5-34	14.7	+ 3.75	Mr D Salter	1-4	25.0	+ 47.00
D Biggs	3-16	18.8	+ 10.50	S Whitworth	1-8	12.5	- 2.00
J Quinn	2-16	12.5	+ 8.50				

D Harrison	0-12	B Doyle	0-1	Miss A Billot	0-1		
O Pears	0-5	Dale Gibson	0-1	Miss E Folkes	0-1		
C Hodgson	0-2	G Parkin	0-1	N Kennedy	0-1		
G Bardwell	0-2	J Fanning	0-1	R Price	0-1		
K Rutter	0-2	J Lowe	0-1	T Sprake	0-1		
N Carlisle	0-2	J Williams	0-1	W Ryan	0-1		
S Wynne	0-2	L Newton	0-1				
Alex Greaves	0-1	L Piggott	0-1				

COURSE RECORD

	Total W-R	Non-Handicaps 2-y-o	3-y-o+	Handicaps 2-y-o	3-y-o+	Per cent	£1 Level Stake
Lingfield (AW)	4-28	0-0	0-10	0-0	4-18	14.3	+ 42.50
Salisbury	2-11	0-0	0-1	0-0	2-10	18.2	- 1.50
Sandown	1-2	0-0	0-0	0-0	1-2	50.0	+ 15.00
Windsor	1-3	0-0	1-2	0-0	0-1	33.3	+ 18.00
Warwick	1-4	0-0	0-2	0-0	1-2	25.0	- 1.25
Beverley	1-5	0-0	0-0	0-0	1-5	20.0	- 2.00
Kempton	1-6	0-0	0-1	0-0	1-5	16.7	+ 3.00
Southwell (AW)	1-15	0-0	0-4	0-0	1-11	6.7	- 2.00

Chester	0-6	Bath	0-4	Nottingham	0-2
Haydock	0-6	Doncaster	0-3	Brighton	0-1
Chepstow	0-5	Wolverhampton	0-3	Pontefract	0-1
Leicester	0-5	Ascot	0-2	York	0-1
Lingfield	0-5	Newmarket	0-2		

WINNING HORSES

	Age	Races Run	1st	2nd	3rd	Unpl	Win £
Aude La Belle	4	16	5	2	3	6	21,840
Caspian Beluga	4	13	3	3	1	6	8,526
Predictable	6	11	1	0	1	9	2,888
Broom Isle	4	12	1	5	4	2	2,709
Easy Does It	3	6	1	0	1	4	2,658
Courting Newmarket	4	13	1	1	0	11	2,206

WINNING OWNERS

	Races Won	Value £		Races Won	Value £
Mrs Val Rapkins	5	21,840	Derek V Bolt	1	2,658
L J Hawkings	4	11,414	Geo Taylor	1	2,206
Vivian Guy	1	2,709			

Favourites	1-8	12.5%	- 5.00	Total winning prize-money	£40,827

Longest winning sequence	2	Average SP of winner	11.1/1
Longest losing sequence	29	Return on stakes invested	21.5%

1991 Form	4-50	8.0%	- 12.00	1989 Form	0-13
1990 Form	0-9			1988 Form	0-22

D R LAING (Lambourn, Berks)

	No. of Horses	Races Run	1st	2nd	3rd	Unpl	Per cent	£1 Level Stake
2-y-o	7	42	0	4	2	36	-	- 42.00
3-y-o	5	41	5	3	4	29	12.2	+ 18.00
4-y-o+	6	40	3	4	5	28	7.5	- 4.50
Totals	18	123	8	11	11	93	6.5	- 28.50

Jan	Feb	Mar	Apr	May	Jun	Jul	Aug	Sep	Oct/Nov
0-3	0-0	0-1	0-6	1-15	1-18	1-19	1-20	2-24	2-17

Winning Jockeys	W-R	£1 Level Stake		W-R	£1 Level Stake
T Williams	3-68	- 44.00	A Tucker	2-17	- 2.00
Kim McDonnell	2-9	+ 17.50	J Williams	1-3	+ 26.00

Winning Courses					
Bath	2-13	0.00	Haydock	1-3	+ 18.00
Salisbury	2-13	- 2.50	Nottingham	1-6	+ 3.00
Redcar	1-2	+ 27.00	Wolverhampton	1-6	+ 6.00

Winning Horses	Age	Races Run	1st	2nd	3rd	Unpl	Win £
My Ruby Ring	5	19	3	1	4	11	9,428
Bells Of Longwick	3	15	3	3	1	8	7,870
City Line	3	7	1	0	2	4	2,469
Broadway Ruckus	3	5	1	0	0	4	2,448

Favourites	1-5	20.0%	0.00	Total winning prize-money		£22,215

1991 Form	4-100	4.0%	- 73.50	1989 Form	0-0		
1990 Form	0-0			1988 Form	19-254	7.5%	- 49.75

A N LEE (Newmarket)

	No. of Horses	Races Run	1st	2nd	3rd	Unpl	Per cent	£1 Level Stake
2-y-o	1	2	0	0	0	2	-	- 2.00
3-y-o	8	32	2	1	3	26	6.3	- 12.00
4-y-o+	0	0	0	0	0	0	-	0.00
Totals	9	34	2	1	3	28	5.9	- 14.00

Jan	Feb	Mar	Apr	May	Jun	Jul	Aug	Sep	Oct/Nov
0-0	0-0	0-1	1-7	0-4	1-7	0-2	0-9	0-2	0-2

Winning Jockey	W-R	£1 Level Stake				W-R	£1 Level Stake
J Quinn	2-17	+ 3.00					

Winning Courses							
Nottingham	1-1	+ 10.00		Leicester		1-5	+ 4.00

Winning Horse	Age	Races Run	1st	2nd	3rd	Unpl	Win £
Elizabethan Air	3	8	2	1	2	3	6,082

Favourites	0-0			Total winning prize-money			£6,082

1991 Form	4-64	6.3%	+ 1.41	1989 Form	8-76	10.5%	- 8.00
1990 Form	7-76	9.2%	- 36.50	1988 Form	2-46	4.3%	- 27.00

F H LEE (Wilmslow, Cheshire)

	No. of Horses	Races Run	1st	2nd	3rd	Unpl	Per cent	£1 Level Stake
2-y-o	13	68	5	10	6	47	7.4	- 33.50
3-y-o	11	59	5	5	4	45	8.5	- 22.25
4-y-o+	18	168	16	17	17	118	9.5	- 18.25
Totals	42	295	26	32	27	210	8.8	- 74.00

BY MONTH

2-y-o	W-R	Per cent	£1 Level Stake	3-y-o	W-R	Per cent	£1 Level Stake
January	0-0	-	0.00	January	0-0	-	0.00
February	0-0	-	0.00	February	0-0	-	0.00
March	0-0	-	0.00	March	0-1	-	- 1.00
April	0-4	-	- 4.00	April	1-9	11.1	- 3.00
May	0-5	-	- 5.00	May	0-9	-	- 9.00
June	1-7	14.3	- 3.00	June	1-5	20.0	+ 3.00
July	2-9	22.2	+ 4.50	July	1-8	12.5	- 4.00
August	2-14	14.3	+ 3.00	August	0-6	-	- 6.00
September	0-12	-	- 12.00	September	1-9	11.1	- 3.25
Oct/Nov	0-17	-	- 17.00	Oct/Nov	1-12	8.3	+ 1.00

4-y-o+	W-R	Per cent	£1 Level Stake	Totals	W-R	Per cent	£1 Level Stake
January	0-0	-	0.00	January	0-0	-	0.00
February	0-2	-	- 2.00	February	0-2	-	- 2.00
March	1-7	14.3	+ 6.00	March	1-8	12.5	+ 5.00
April	1-17	5.9	- 10.50	April	2-30	6.7	- 17.50
May	3-22	13.6	+ 11.50	May	3-36	8.3	- 2.50
June	4-24	16.7	0.00	June	6-36	16.7	0.00
July	4-25	16.0	+ 23.00	July	7-42	16.7	+ 23.50
August	3-24	12.5	+ 0.75	August	5-44	11.4	- 2.25
September	0-24	-	- 24.00	September	1-45	2.2	- 39.25
Oct/Nov	0-23	-	- 23.00	Oct/Nov	1-52	1.9	- 39.00

DISTANCE

2-y-o	W-R	Per cent	£1 Level Stake	3-y-o	W-R	Per cent	£1 Level Stake
5f-6f	3-43	7.0	- 28.00	5f-6f	2-22	9.1	- 5.00
7f-8f	2-25	8.0	- 5.50	7f-8f	2-19	10.5	- 7.25
9f-13f	0-0	-	0.00	9f-13f	1-18	5.6	- 10.00
14f+	0-0	-	0.00	14f+	0-0	-	0.00

4-y-o+	W-R	Per cent	£1 Level Stake	Totals	W-R	Per cent	£1 Level Stake
5f-6f	7-50	14.0	- 5.00	5f-6f	12-115	10.4	- 38.00
7f-8f	2-46	4.3	- 21.00	7f-8f	6-90	6.7	- 33.75
9f-13f	6-52	11.5	+ 21.25	9f-13f	7-70	10.0	+ 11.25
14f+	1-20	5.0	- 13.50	14f+	1-20	5.0	- 13.50

TYPE OF RACE

Non-Handicaps	W-R	Per cent	£1 Level Stake	Handicaps	W-R	Per cent	£1 Level Stake
2-y-o	1-42	2.4	- 38.00	2-y-o	3-25	12.0	+ 1.50
3-y-o	1-17	5.9	- 11.00	3-y-o	3-33	9.1	- 8.00
4-y-o+	0-13	-	- 13.00	4-y-o+	14-119	11.8	+ 0.75
Selling	1-5	20.0	- 1.00	Selling	1-12	8.3	- 6.25
Apprentice	0-1	-	- 1.00	Apprentice	1-19	5.3	- 2.00
Amat/Ladies	0-0	-	0.00	Amat/Ladies	1-9	11.1	+ 4.00
Totals	3-78	3.8	- 64.00	Totals	23-217	10.6	- 10.00

COURSE GRADE

	W-R	Per cent	£1 Level Stake
Group 1	14-143	9.8	- 36.25
Group 2	5-68	7.4	- 30.00
Group 3	5-59	8.5	- 19.75
Group 4	2-25	8.0	+ 12.00

FIRST TIME OUT

	W-R	Per cent	£1 Level Stake
2-y-o	0-13	-	- 13.00
3-y-o	1-11	9.1	- 5.00
4-y-o+	1-18	5.6	- 5.00
Totals	2-42	4.8	- 23.00

JOCKEYS RIDING

	W-R	Per cent	£1 Level Stake		W-R	Per cent	£1 Level Stake
N Kennedy	9-94	9.6	- 27.50	W R Swinburn	1-2	50.0	+ 8.00
R Lappin	5-40	12.5	+ 12.00	Mrs G Rees	1-4	25.0	+ 9.00
Paul Eddery	3-23	13.0	+ 6.50	M Hills	1-4	25.0	+ 2.00
B Raymond	2-8	25.0	+ 5.50	P Robinson	1-4	25.0	- 0.25
D McKeown	2-16	12.5	- 2.25	W Carson	1-9	11.1	+ 4.00

Lee F H

A Culhane	0-10	S Maloney	0-2	J Williams	0-1
G Carter	0-9	S Webster	0-2	L Charnock	0-1
M Roberts	0-9	A Tucker	0-1	M Birch	0-1
W Ryan	0-6	Alex Greaves	0-1	M Tebbutt	0-1
A Munro	0-5	C Hawksley	0-1	Miss A Billot	0-1
D Biggs	0-3	D Carson	0-1	Miss D Pomeroy	0-1
G Duffield	0-3	D Holland	0-1	Miss I D W Jones	0-1
L Dettori	0-3	F Norton	0-1	Miss J Winter	0-1
Pat Eddery	0-3	G Bardwell	0-1	Miss K Burgess	0-1
D Wright	0-2	G Forster	0-1	N Adams	0-1
K Fallon	0-2	G Hind	0-1	O Pears	0-1
N Carlisle	0-2	G Parkin	0-1	S Wood	0-1
N Connorton	0-2	J Fortune	0-1	T Sprake	0-1
R Cochrane	0-2	J Marshall	0-1	T Williams	0-1

COURSE RECORD

	Total W-R	Non-Handicaps		Handicaps		Per cent	£1 Level Stake
		2-y-o	3-y-o+	2-y-o	3-y-o+		
Doncaster	4-29	0-3	0-1	0-6	4-19	13.8	+ 17.50
Ayr	4-30	0-5	0-1	1-2	3-22	13.3	- 8.50
Southwell (AW)	2-11	0-0	0-4	0-0	2-7	18.2	+ 26.00
Nottingham	2-12	0-2	1-4	0-0	1-6	16.7	+ 7.00
Chester	2-13	0-2	0-2	0-1	2-8	15.4	+ 1.50
Thirsk	2-18	1-4	0-4	0-1	1-9	11.1	- 7.50
York	2-18	1-5	0-0	0-3	1-10	11.1	- 7.50
Haydock	2-33	0-9	0-1	0-2	2-21	6.1	- 20.25
Epsom	1-1	0-0	0-0	0-0	1-1	100.0	+ 1.50
Beverley	1-10	0-1	0-2	1-2	0-5	10.0	- 3.50
Newcastle	1-11	0-1	0-0	1-1	0-9	9.1	+ 2.00
Hamilton	1-12	0-2	0-0	0-0	1-10	8.3	- 4.00
Pontefract	1-20	0-1	0-3	0-3	1-13	5.0	- 14.25
Redcar	1-23	0-1	0-3	0-1	1-18	4.3	- 10.00

Ripon	0-13	Ascot	0-4	Edinburgh	0-2
Goodwood	0-8	Carlisle	0-4	Sandown	0-2
Newmarket	0-7	Leicester	0-4	Bath	0-1
Warwick	0-6	Catterick	0-2	Lingfield	0-1

WINNING HORSES

		Races					Win
	Age	Run	1st	2nd	3rd	Unpl	£
Crystal Jack	4	12	4	1	0	7	18,221
Beau Venture	4	13	2	2	2	7	11,654
Bold Seven	2	12	2	3	2	5	10,615
I Perceive	5	11	3	1	0	7	8,599
Sir Norman Holt	3	14	2	0	1	11	5,812
Umbubuzi	2	9	2	0	1	6	5,570
Sir Arthur Hobbs	5	15	2	1	1	11	5,404
Coolaba Prince	3	10	2	4	0	4	5,404
Must Be Magical	4	13	2	0	0	11	3,777

Sigama	6	12	1	4	1	6	3,525
Killy	3	7	1	0	0	6	3,290
Argyle Cavalier	2	8	1	1	0	6	3,184
Aahsaylad	6	9	1	2	1	5	3,028
Young Jason	9	13	1	0	2	10	2,679

WINNING OWNERS

	Races Won	Value £		Races Won	Value £
F H Lee	7	22,991	John Hardman	2	5,404
Mrs B Facchino	4	18,221	P J Cosgrove	2	5,404
Mrs A L Stacey	2	11,654	Peter Barr	1	3,290
Mrs Gillian Lee	2	6,204	E H Jones (Paints) Ltd	1	3,184
D Holt	2	5,812	M Stapleton	1	3,028
Semi-Chem Bargain Centres	2	5,570			

Favourites	7-24	29.2%	+ 5.50	Total winning prize-money		£90,760

Longest winning sequence		2	Average SP of winner	7.5/1
Longest losing sequence		54	Return on stakes invested	-25.1%

1991 Form	30-285	10.5%	- 11.12	1989 Form	27-221	12.2%	- 30.46
1990 Form	25-256	9.8%	- 49.25	1988 Form	8-150	5.3%	- 12.84

R LEE (Presteigne, Powys)

	No. of Horses	Races Run	1st	2nd	3rd	Unpl	Per cent	£1 Level Stake
2-y-o	0	0	0	0	0	0	-	0.00
3-y-o	0	0	0	0	0	0	-	0.00
4-y-o+	12	63	3	6	8	46	4.8	- 40.50
Totals	12	63	3	6	8	46	4.8	- 40.50

Jan	Feb	Mar	Apr	May	Jun	Jul	Aug	Sep	Oct/Nov
0-0	0-0	0-0	0-5	0-13	2-10	0-10	1-6	0-9	0-10

Winning Jockeys	W-R	£1 Level Stake			W-R	£1 Level Stake
Pat Eddery	2-7	+ 10.50	W Carson		1-5	0.00

Winning Courses						
Kempton	2-7	+ 4.50	Newbury		1-3	+ 8.00

Winning Horses	Age	Races Run	1st	2nd	3rd	Unpl	Win £
Darussalam	5	15	2	1	2	10	6,446
Good For A Loan	5	8	1	1	2	4	3,340

Favourites	1-5	20.0%	0.00	Total winning prize-money		£9,786
1991 Form	2-13	15.4%	+ 6.00	1989 Form	0-1	
1990 Form	0-5			1988 Form	0-1	

J P LEIGH (Gainsborough, Lincs)

	No. of Horses	Races Run	1st	2nd	3rd	Unpl	Per cent	£1 Level Stake
2-y-o	4	14	0	2	1	11	-	- 14.00
3-y-o	3	15	1	1	2	11	6.7	- 6.00
4-y-o+	8	49	0	9	2	38	-	- 49.00
Totals	15	78	1	12	5	60	1.3	- 69.00

Jan	Feb	Mar	Apr	May	Jun	Jul	Aug	Sep	Oct/Nov
0-4	0-5	0-8	0-10	1-11	0-10	0-9	0-3	0-7	0-11

Winning Jockey	W-R	£1 Level Stake	Winning Course	W-R	£1 Level Stake
J Weaver	1-13	- 4.00	Beverley	1-13	- 4.00

Winning Horse	Age	Races Run	1st	2nd	3rd	Unpl	Win £
Scottish Park	3	8	1	1	0	6	2,206

Favourites	0-2			Total winning prize-money			£2,206
1991 Form	5-54	9.3%	- 12.00	1989 Form	1-48	2.1%	- 22.00
1990 Form	4-57	7.0%	- 17.50	1988 Form	3-61	4.9%	- 24.50

G LEWIS (Epsom, Surrey)

	No. of Horses	Races Run	1st	2nd	3rd	Unpl	Per cent	£1 Level Stake
2-y-o	32	152	16	11	21	104	10.5	- 17.96
3-y-o	19	152	24	11	15	102	15.8	+ 30.72
4-y-o+	6	48	14	7	0	27	29.2	+ 43.88
Totals	57	352	54	29	36	233	15.3	+ 56.64

BY MONTH

2-y-o	W-R	Per cent	£1 Level Stake	3-y-o	W-R	Per cent	£1 Level Stake
Mar/Apr	1-12	8.3	- 6.00	Mar/Apr	2-22	9.1	- 3.00
May	3-15	20.0	+ 8.23	May	6-25	24.0	+ 23.00
June	1-26	3.8	- 5.00	June	4-29	13.8	- 13.75
July	4-19	21.1	- 8.32	July	5-28	17.9	+ 12.57
August	2-28	7.1	- 8.00	August	2-23	8.7	+ 7.00
September	3-32	9.4	- 12.87	September	2-15	13.3	+ 2.00
Oct/Nov	2-20	10.0	+ 14.00	Oct/Nov	3-10	30.0	+ 5.90

4-y-o+	W-R	Per cent	£1 Level Stake	Totals	W-R	Per cent	£1 Level Stake
Mar/Apr	0-6	-	- 6.00	Mar/Apr	3-40	7.5	- 15.00
May	0-7	-	- 7.00	May	9-47	19.1	+ 24.23
June	1-8	12.5	- 2.00	June	6-63	9.5	- 20.75
July	4-8	50.0	+ 11.38	July	13-55	23.6	+ 15.63
August	5-9	55.6	+ 12.50	August	9-60	15.0	+ 11.50
September	2-4	50.0	+ 10.00	September	7-51	13.7	- 0.87
Oct/Nov	2-6	33.3	+ 25.00	Oct/Nov	7-36	19.4	+ 44.90

DISTANCE

2-y-o	W-R	Per cent	£1 Level Stake	3-y-o	W-R	Per cent	£1 Level Stake
5f-6f	14-119	11.8	- 1.46	5f-6f	4-41	9.8	- 16.75
7f-8f	2-32	6.3	- 15.50	7f-8f	8-58	13.8	+ 20.25
9f-13f	0-1	-	- 1.00	9f-13f	11-44	25.0	+ 30.22
14f+	0-0	-	0.00	14f+	1-9	11.1	- 3.00

4-y-o+	W-R	Per cent	£1 Level Stake	Totals	W-R	Per cent	£1 Level Stake
5f-6f	1-5	20.0	+ 1.00	5f-6f	19-165	11.5	- 17.21
7f-8f	6-20	30.0	+ 27.17	7f-8f	16-110	14.5	+ 31.92
9f-13f	7-21	33.3	+ 17.71	9f-13f	18-66	27.3	+ 46.93
14f+	0-2	-	- 2.00	14f+	1-11	9.1	- 5.00

TYPE OF RACE

Non-Handicaps	W-R	Per cent	£1 Level Stake	Handicaps	W-R	Per cent	£1 Level Stake
2-y-o	11-105	10.5	- 13.96	2-y-o	2-27	7.4	- 10.50
3-y-o	8-50	16.0	- 18.18	3-y-o	11-81	13.6	+ 35.00
4-y-o+	3-8	37.5	- 0.50	4-y-o+	7-35	20.0	+ 20.38
Selling	5-27	18.5	+ 9.90	Selling	1-8	12.5	+ 5.00
Apprentice	0-0	-	0.00	Apprentice	6-11	54.5	+ 29.50
Amat/Ladies	0-0	-	0.00	Amat/Ladies	0-0	-	0.00
Totals	27-190	14.2	- 22.74	Totals	27-162	16.7	+ 79.38

COURSE GRADE

	W-R	Per cent	£1 Level Stake
Group 1	25-147	17.0	+ 72.51
Group 2	8-73	11.0	- 13.19
Group 3	12-84	14.3	- 14.28
Group 4	9-48	18.8	+ 11.60

FIRST TIME OUT

	W-R	Per cent	£1 Level Stake
2-y-o	1-30	3.3	- 15.00
3-y-o	1-18	5.6	+ 3.00
4-y-o+	0-6	-	- 6.00
Totals	2-54	3.7	- 18.00

267

JOCKEYS RIDING

	W-R	Per cent	£1 Level Stake		W-R	Per cent	£1 Level Stake
Paul Eddery	15-124	12.1	- 37.02	A Garth	1-1	100.0	+ 14.00
D Harrison	10-44	22.7	+ 19.15	G Carter	1-3	33.3	+ 3.50
B Russell	9-21	42.9	+ 47.50	C Hawksley	1-6	16.7	+ 13.00
B Rouse	9-49	18.4	+ 53.17	D Biggs	1-7	14.3	- 2.00
J Reid	5-11	45.5	+ 13.71	Pat Eddery	1-9	11.1	- 6.37
S Cauthen	1-1	100.0	+ 14.00				

R Berry	0-10	G Bardwell	0-2	G Duffield	0-1
F Norton	0-8	K Darley	0-2	J Fanning	0-1
A Clark	0-7	P Robinson	0-2	J Lowe	0-1
A Tucker	0-5	Amanda Bowen	0-1	N Day	0-1
M Hills	0-5	Antoinette Armes	0-1	N Gwilliams	0-1
A McGlone	0-3	B Doyle	0-1	N Howe	0-1
J Quinn	0-3	C Teague	0-1	R Perham	0-1
N Adams	0-3	D McKeown	0-1	R Price	0-1
W Carson	0-3	D Wright	0-1	W Hood	0-1
B Raymond	0-2	Dale Gibson	0-1	W Newnes	0-1
D Holland	0-2	G Baxter	0-1	W Ryan	0-1

COURSE RECORD

	Total W-R	Non-Handicaps 2-y-o	Non-Handicaps 3-y-o+	Handicaps 2-y-o	Handicaps 3-y-o+	Per cent	£1 Level Stake
Goodwood	7-24	2-9	2-2	0-4	3-9	29.2	+ 38.63
Warwick	4-10	2-3	0-3	0-1	2-3	40.0	+ 16.60
Epsom	4-26	0-5	2-8	0-1	2-12	15.4	- 2.42
Chepstow	3-10	0-1	1-4	0-1	2-4	30.0	+ 1.07
Wolverhampton	3-10	1-3	1-1	0-1	1-5	30.0	+ 6.50
Nottingham	3-13	0-5	2-3	0-0	1-5	23.1	+ 9.00
Bath	3-15	0-6	2-5	0-0	1-4	20.0	- 2.75
Kempton	3-21	2-7	0-4	0-2	1-8	14.3	+ 8.13
Brighton	3-23	0-6	1-5	1-2	1-10	13.0	+ 4.67
Newmarket	3-23	1-8	0-3	0-2	2-10	13.0	+ 23.00
Lingfield	3-26	1-10	0-4	0-1	2-11	11.5	+ 2.50
York	2-4	0-1	0-0	1-1	1-2	50.0	+ 12.00
Leicester	2-11	1-8	1-1	0-1	0-1	18.2	+ 8.40
Newbury	2-12	1-7	0-1	0-1	1-3	16.7	- 0.33
Ascot	2-14	0-3	0-2	0-2	2-7	14.3	- 0.50
Sandown	2-18	0-7	1-3	0-2	1-6	11.1	- 1.00
Folkestone	2-20	0-4	0-7	0-2	2-7	10.0	- 3.50
Chester	1-2	1-1	0-0	0-0	0-1	50.0	- 0.09
Salisbury	1-18	1-6	0-4	0-1	0-7	5.6	- 16.27
Windsor	1-21	1-11	0-2	0-2	0-6	4.8	- 16.00

Yarmouth	0-11	Doncaster	0-2	Pontefract	0-1
Lingfield (AW)	0-6	Newcastle	0-2	Thirsk	0-1
Redcar	0-3	Southwell (AW)	0-2		
Beverley	0-2	Haydock	0-1		

WINNING HORSES

	Age	Races Run	1st	2nd	3rd	Unpl	Win £
Orthorhombus	3	13	2	0	0	11	29,862
Plan Ahead	3	14	8	1	3	2	28,541
Silver Wizard	2	7	4	1	1	1	24,412
Neptune's Pet	4	12	4	2	0	6	18,068
Loki	4	13	5	2	0	6	17,264
Rocky Waters	3	5	3	0	0	2	14,968
Silver Wisp	3	5	1	0	2	2	14,118
Surrey Racing	4	14	4	3	0	7	12,505
Devilry	2	5	2	0	2	1	9,922
Zuno Warrior	2	6	2	2	1	1	8,446
Dare To Dream	3	12	3	0	1	8	7,241
Lady Sabo	3	14	2	0	3	9	5,483
Bar Billiards	3	1	1	0	0	0	4,347
Awesome Risk	2	13	2	0	7	4	4,344
Formal Invitation	3	14	2	0	2	10	4,283
Karinga Bay	5	2	1	0	0	1	3,660
Mr Nevermind	2	10	1	2	0	7	3,574
Rich Midas	2	9	1	0	2	6	3,548
Coniston Lake	3	12	1	1	1	9	3,288
Risk Proof	2	4	1	0	0	3	2,868
Coy Boy	2	3	1	0	0	2	2,511
Sadler's Way	3	8	1	2	0	5	1,380
Jarena	2	6	1	0	2	3	1,380
Toff Sundae	2	7	1	1	1	4	1,245

WINNING OWNERS

	Races Won	Value £		Races Won	Value £
Mrs Shirley Robins	8	45,770	Roldvale Ltd	4	8,457
K Higson	10	37,995	Vic Fatah	2	8,446
M J E Thornhill	2	29,862	A J Richards	2	5,727
Planflow (Leasing) Ltd	8	28,541	Cronk Thoroughbred Racing Ltd	2	5,483
K B Symonds and Partners	4	18,068	Mrs N Lewis	2	4,283
Lady McIndoe	2	9,922	Mrs Sally Van Tooren	1	3,548
Michael H Watt	2	8,729	Nigel H Morris	1	2,511
T K Laidlaw	3	8,535	Miss V McNeill	1	1,380

Favourites	15–51	29.4%	– 11.51	Total winning prize-money			£227,256
Longest winning sequence			3	Average SP of winner			6.6/1
Longest losing sequence			20	Return on stakes invested			16.1%
1991 Form	41–355	11.5%	– 42.89	1989 Form	23–304	7.6%	– 132.25
1990 Form	26–285	9.1%	– 118.86	1988 Form	32–260	12.3%	– 19.09

D R LODER (Newmarket)

	No. of Horses	Races Run	1st	2nd	3rd	Unpl	Per cent	£1 Level Stake
2-y-o	2	3	0	0	2	1	-	- 3.00
3-y-o	2	4	0	0	0	4	-	- 4.00
4-y-o+	2	4	1	0	0	3	25.0	+ 17.00
Totals	6	11	1	0	2	8	9.1	+ 10.00

Jan	Feb	Mar	Apr	May	Jun	Jul	Aug	Sep	Oct/Nov
0-0	0-0	0-0	0-0	0-0	0-0	0-0	0-0	0-0	1-11

Winning Jockey	W-R	£1 Level Stake	Winning Course	W-R	£1 Level Stake
L Dettori	1-1	+ 20.00	Newmarket	1-4	+ 17.00

Winning Horse	Age	Races Run	1st	2nd	3rd	Unpl	Win £
Lupescu	4	1	1	0	0	0	9,300

Favourites	0-0	Total winning prize-money	£9,300

MRS N MACAULEY (Melton Mowbray, Leics)

	No. of Horses	Races Run	1st	2nd	3rd	Unpl	Per cent	£1 Level Stake
2-y-o	7	31	1	1	3	26	3.2	- 24.00
3-y-o	9	64	4	2	5	53	6.3	- 41.77
4-y-o+	17	111	5	7	6	93	4.5	- 59.87
Totals	33	206	10	10	14	172	4.9	- 125.64

BY MONTH

2-y-o	W-R	Per cent	£1 Level Stake	3-y-o	W-R	Per cent	£1 Level Stake
January	0-0	-	0.00	January	2-3	66.7	+ 1.73
February	0-0	-	0.00	February	0-3	-	- 3.00
March	0-0	-	0.00	March	1-4	25.0	+ 0.50
April	0-0	-	0.00	April	0-5	-	- 5.00
May	0-0	-	0.00	May	0-5	-	- 5.00
June	0-6	-	- 6.00	June	0-9	-	- 9.00
July	1-9	11.1	- 2.00	July	0-12	-	- 12.00
August	0-4	-	- 4.00	August	1-12	8.3	+ 1.00
September	0-9	-	- 9.00	September	0-9	-	- 9.00
Oct/Nov	0-3	-	- 3.00	Oct/Nov	0-2	-	- 2.00

4-y-o+	W-R	Per cent	£1 Level Stake	Totals	W-R	Per cent	£1 Level Stake
January	0-15	-	- 15.00	January	2-18	11.1	- 13.27
February	1-9	11.1	+ 2.00	February	1-12	8.3	- 1.00
March	1-9	11.1	+ 12.00	March	2-13	15.4	+ 12.50
April	0-7	-	- 7.00	April	0-12	-	- 12.00
May	1-6	16.7	+ 7.00	May	1-11	9.1	+ 2.00
June	0-20	-	- 20.00	June	0-35	-	- 35.00
July	2-20	10.0	- 13.87	July	3-41	7.3	- 27.87
August	0-12	-	- 12.00	August	1-28	3.6	- 15.00
September	0-10	-	- 10.00	September	0-28	-	- 28.00
Oct/Nov	0-3	-	- 3.00	Oct/Nov	0-8	-	- 8.00

DISTANCE

2-y-o	W-R	Per cent	£1 Level Stake	3-y-o	W-R	Per cent	£1 Level Stake
5f-6f	0-27	-	- 27.00	5f-6f	4-34	11.8	- 11.77
7f-8f	1-4	25.0	+ 3.00	7f-8f	0-14	-	- 14.00
9f-13f	0-0	-	0.00	9f-13f	0-9	-	- 9.00
14f+	0-0	-	0.00	14f+	0-7	-	- 7.00

4-y-o+	W-R	Per cent	£1 Level Stake	Totals	W-R	Per cent	£1 Level Stake
5f-6f	3-57	5.3	- 21.50	5f-6f	7-118	5.9	- 60.27
7f-8f	2-43	4.7	- 27.37	7f-8f	3-61	4.9	- 38.37
9f-13f	0-6	-	- 6.00	9f-13f	0-15	-	- 15.00
14f+	0-5	-	- 5.00	14f+	0-12	-	- 12.00

TYPE OF RACE

Non-Handicaps	W-R	Per cent	£1 Level Stake	Handicaps	W-R	Per cent	£1 Level Stake
2-y-o	0-17	-	- 17.00	2-y-o	0-1	-	- 1.00
3-y-o	2-24	8.3	- 19.27	3-y-o	1-28	3.6	- 23.50
4-y-o+	2-20	10.0	- 6.37	4-y-o+	3-80	3.8	- 42.50
Selling	1-25	4.0	- 18.00	Selling	0-3	-	- 3.00
Apprentice	0-1	-	- 1.00	Apprentice	1-7	14.3	+ 6.00
Amat/Ladies	0-0	-	0.00	Amat/Ladies	0-0	-	0.00
Totals	5-87	5.7	- 61.64	Totals	5-119	4.2	- 64.00

COURSE GRADE

	W-R	Per cent	£1 Level Stake
Group 1	0-29	-	- 29.00
Group 2	1-26	3.8	- 13.00
Group 3	2-65	3.1	- 55.37
Group 4	7-86	8.1	- 28.27

FIRST TIME OUT

	W-R	Per cent	£1 Level Stake
2-y-o	0-7	-	- 7.00
3-y-o	1-8	12.5	- 5.37
4-y-o+	0-16	-	- 16.00
Totals	1-31	3.2	- 28.37

JOCKEYS RIDING

	W-R	Per cent	£1 Level Stake		W-R	Per cent	£1 Level Stake
M Roberts	2-6	33.3	+ 3.63	F Norton	1-6	16.7	+ 15.00
N Day	2-35	5.7	- 30.27	Madeleine Smith	1-9	11.1	+ 2.00
M Humphries	1-3	33.3	+ 10.00	D Biggs	1-20	5.0	- 7.00
P Robinson	1-5	20.0	- 1.50	S D Williams	1-21	4.8	- 16.50

D McKeown	0-14	A Munro	0-2	G King	0-1
N Adams	0-11	D Holland	0-2	J McLaughlin	0-1
N Carlisle	0-11	L Charnock	0-2	J Reid	0-1
L Dettori	0-9	M Hills	0-2	J Williams	0-1
T Sprake	0-8	S Wynne	0-2	M Harris	0-1
B Crossley	0-6	W Wharton	0-2	R Hills	0-1
B Raymond	0-4	A Clark	0-1	S Keightley	0-1
J Quinn	0-4	Dale Gibson	0-1	S O'Gorman	0-1
C Rutter	0-3	Emma O'Gorman	0-1	S Whitworth	0-1
M Tebbutt	0-3	G Forster	0-1		
A McGlone	0-2	G Hind	0-1		

COURSE RECORD

	Total W-R	Non-Handicaps 2-y-o	3-y-o+	Handicaps 2-y-o	3-y-o+	Per cent	£1 Level Stake
Southwell (AW)	6-61	0-3	2-22	0-0	4-36	9.8	- 5.90
Yarmouth	2-24	1-10	1-2	0-0	0-12	8.3	- 14.37
Thirsk	1-7	0-0	0-1	0-0	1-6	14.3	+ 6.00
Lingfield (AW)	1-9	0-1	1-3	0-0	0-5	11.1	- 6.37

Nottingham	0-18	Pontefract	0-4	Folkestone	0-1
Wolverhampton	0-13	Bath	0-3	Goodwood	0-1
Doncaster	0-9	Ripon	0-3	Kempton	0-1
Redcar	0-8	Ascot	0-2	Newbury	0-1
Leicester	0-7	Chepstow	0-2	Newcastle	0-1
Lingfield	0-6	Epsom	0-2	Salisbury	0-1
Beverley	0-5	Warwick	0-2	Sandown	0-1
Haydock	0-5	Windsor	0-2	York	0-1
Newmarket	0-5	Brighton	0-1		

WINNING HORSES

	Age	Races Run	1st	2nd	3rd	Unpl	Win £
Creche	3	11	3	1	0	7	6,678
Lady Of The Fen	4	9	1	0	0	8	6,108
Brown Fairy	4	10	1	0	1	8	3,753
Annabelle Royale	6	15	1	2	0	12	3,330
The Dream Maker	3	11	1	0	1	9	2,532
Red Ballet	2	8	1	1	0	6	2,448
Maid Welcome	5	6	1	0	0	5	2,246
Drummer's Dream	4	11	1	1	0	9	2,175

WINNING OWNERS

	Races Won	Value £		Races Won	Value £
P Mingay	1	6,108	Donald Cooper	1	2,448
Mrs N Macauley	2	4,432	Stephen Roots	1	2,246
Mrs Carole Biggs	1	3,753	Brian Pollins	1	2,246
P W Saunders	1	3,330	Mrs Gail Orbell	1	2,175
Robert Dixon	1	2,532			

Favourites	3-12	25.0%	- 2.77	Total winning prize-money		£29,269
Longest winning sequence			1	Average SP of winner		7.0/1
Longest losing sequence			50	Return on stakes invested		-61.0%
1991 Form	21-307	6.8%	-105.60	1989 Form	14-241	5.8%	-123.17
1990 Form	24-271	8.9%	- 66.10	1988 Form	6-190	3.2%	-105.00

J MACKIE (Church Broughton, Derbys)

	No. of Horses	Races Run	1st	2nd	3rd	Unpl	Per cent	£1 Level Stake
2-y-o	0	0	0	0	0	0	-	0.00
3-y-o	3	14	0	0	1	13	-	- 14.00
4-y-o+	10	39	3	3	2	31	7.7	- 16.50
Totals	13	53	3	3	3	44	5.7	- 30.50

Jan	Feb	Mar	Apr	May	Jun	Jul	Aug	Sep	Oct/Nov
0-0	0-0	0-0	0-4	1-6	1-7	0-14	0-10	1-8	0-4

Winning Jockeys	W-R	£1 Level Stake			W-R	£1 Level Stake
W Carson	1-1	+ 4.50	G Carter		1-5	+ 8.00
Pat Eddery	1-2	+ 2.00				

Winning Courses	W-R	£1 Level Stake			W-R	£1 Level Stake
Kempton	1-1	+ 12.00	Leicester		1-3	+ 2.50
Newcastle	1-1	+ 3.00				

Winning Horse	Age	Races Run	1st	2nd	3rd	Unpl	Win £
Daisy Girl	6	6	3	0	1	2	19,030

Favourites	1-3	33.3%	+ 2.50	Total winning prize-money		£19,030
1991 Form	3-61	4.9%	- 30.00	1989 Form	6-120	5.0%	- 64.75
1990 Form	8-73	11.0%	+ 16.00	1988 Form	9-73	12.3%	+ 8.50

273

P J MAKIN (Marlborough, Wilts)

	No. of Horses	Races Run	1st	2nd	3rd	Unpl	Per cent	£1 Level Stake
2-y-o	4	16	0	1	2	13	-	- 16.00
3-y-o	18	87	7	16	11	53	8.0	- 28.59
4-y-o+	12	47	3	5	6	33	6.4	- 12.50
Totals	34	150	10	22	19	99	6.7	- 57.09

BY MONTH

2-y-o	W-R	Per cent	£1 Level Stake	3-y-o	W-R	Per cent	£1 Level Stake
January	0-0	-	0.00	January	0-0	-	0.00
February	0-0	-	0.00	February	0-0	-	0.00
March	0-0	-	0.00	March	0-0	-	0.00
April	0-0	-	0.00	April	1-11	9.1	- 2.00
May	0-2	-	- 2.00	May	0-12	-	- 12.00
June	0-3	-	- 3.00	June	1-8	12.5	- 3.50
July	0-2	-	- 2.00	July	4-17	23.5	+ 22.91
August	0-3	-	- 3.00	August	0-12	-	- 12.00
September	0-3	-	- 3.00	September	0-15	-	- 15.00
Oct/Nov	0-3	-	- 3.00	Oct/Nov	1-12	8.3	- 7.00

4-y-o+	W-R	Per cent	£1 Level Stake	Totals	W-R	Per cent	£1 Level Stake
January	0-0	-	0.00	January	0-0	-	0.00
February	0-1	-	- 1.00	February	0-1	-	- 1.00
March	0-3	-	- 3.00	March	0-3	-	- 3.00
April	0-7	-	- 7.00	April	1-18	5.6	- 9.00
May	2-9	22.2	+ 4.50	May	2-23	8.7	- 9.50
June	0-8	-	- 8.00	June	1-19	5.3	- 14.50
July	0-3	-	- 3.00	July	4-22	18.2	+ 17.91
August	0-3	-	- 3.00	August	0-18	-	- 18.00
September	1-5	20.0	+ 16.00	September	1-23	4.3	- 2.00
Oct/Nov	0-8	-	- 8.00	Oct/Nov	1-23	4.3	- 18.00

DISTANCE

2-y-o	W-R	Per cent	£1 Level Stake	3-y-o	W-R	Per cent	£1 Level Stake
5f-6f	0-13	-	- 13.00	5f-6f	2-14	14.3	- 7.09
7f-8f	0-3	-	- 3.00	7f-8f	2-43	4.7	- 27.50
9f-13f	0-0	-	0.00	9f-13f	3-29	10.3	+ 7.00
14f+	0-0	-	0.00	14f+	0-1	-	- 1.00

4-y-o+	W-R	Per cent	£1 Level Stake	Totals	W-R	Per cent	£1 Level Stake
5f-6f	1-13	7.7	+ 8.00	5f-6f	3-40	7.5	- 12.09
7f-8f	1-17	5.9	- 8.00	7f-8f	3-63	4.8	- 38.50
9f-13f	1-15	6.7	- 10.50	9f-13f	4-44	9.1	- 3.50
14f+	0-2	-	- 2.00	14f+	0-3	-	- 3.00

TYPE OF RACE

Non-Handicaps	W-R	Per cent	£1 Level Stake	Handicaps	W-R	Per cent	£1 Level Stake
2-y-o	0-14	-	- 14.00	2-y-o	0-2	-	- 2.00
3-y-o	4-32	12.5	+ 5.91	3-y-o	3-46	6.5	- 25.50
4-y-o+	0-9	-	- 9.00	4-y-o+	3-30	10.0	+ 4.50
Selling	0-4	-	- 4.00	Selling	0-4.	-	- 4.00
Apprentice	0-2	-	- 2.00	Apprentice	0-7	-	- 7.00
Amat/Ladies	0-0	-	0.00	Amat/Ladies	0-0	-	0.00
Totals	4-61	6.6	- 23.09	Totals	6-89	6.7	- 34.00

COURSE GRADE

	W-R	Per cent	£1 Level Stake
Group 1	3-63	4.8	- 16.00
Group 2	2-29	6.9	- 11.00
Group 3	3-33	9.1	- 14.59
Group 4	2-25	8.0	- 15.50

FIRST TIME OUT

	W-R	Per cent	£1 Level Stake
2-y-o	0-4	-	- 4.00
3-y-o	1-18	5.6	- 9.00
4-y-o+	1-12	8.3	- 3.00
Totals	2-34	5.9	- 16.00

JOCKEYS RIDING

	W-R	Per cent	£1 Level Stake		W-R	Per cent	£1 Level Stake
T Quinn	4-21	19.0	+ 20.00	J Reid	1-6	16.7	+ 9.00
T Sprake	2-33	6.1	- 23.50	L Dettori	1-13	7.7	- 8.50
M Roberts	1-4	25.0	- 2.09	W R Swinburn	1-17	5.9	+ 4.00

B Raymond	0-10	C Asmussen	0-2	G Duffield	0-1
A Munro	0-9	D Middleton	0-2	R Cochrane	0-1
Pat Eddery	0-6	W Ryan	0-2	R Hills	0-1
C Webb	0-4	C Rutter	0-1	R Perham	0-1
W Newnes	0-4	D Holland	0-1	S Dawson	0-1
L Piggott	0-3	Dale Gibson	0-1	S Whitworth	0-1
S Cauthen	0-3	G Carter	0-1	W Carson	0-1

COURSE RECORD

	Total W-R	Non-Handicaps 2-y-o	Non-Handicaps 3-y-o+	Handicaps 2-y-o	Handicaps 3-y-o+	Per cent	£1 Level Stake
Leicester	2-9	0-0	1-2	0-0	1-7	22.2	+ 7.50
Ripon	1-1	0-0	1-1	0-0	0-0	100.0	+ 8.00
Epsom	1-2	0-0	1-1	0-0	0-1	50.0	+ 13.00
Edinburgh	1-3	0-0	0-2	0-0	1-1	33.3	+ 2.00
Lingfield (AW)	1-3	0-1	0-1	0-0	1-1	33.3	+ 1.50
Ascot	1-7	0-1	0-1	0-0	1-5	14.3	+ 14.00
Sandown	1-8	0-2	0-3	0-0	1-3	12.5	+ 3.00
Windsor	1-8	0-1	1-5	0-0	0-2	12.5	- 6.09
Lingfield	1-9	0-2	0-3	0-0	1-4	11.1	0.00

Makin P J

Salisbury	0-13	Brighton	0-6	Southwell (AW)	0-4
Goodwood	0-11	Newbury	0-6	Haydock	0-3
Kempton	0-9	Nottingham	0-5	Chepstow	0-2
Newmarket	0-8	Warwick	0-5	Yarmouth	0-2
Bath	0-7	Wolverhampton	0-5	York	0-2
Doncaster	0-7	Folkestone	0-4	Catterick	0-1

WINNING HORSES

	Age	Races Run	1st	2nd	3rd	Unpl	Win £
Spaniards Close	4	5	1	1	0	3	17,090
Noble Pet	3	7	1	2	1	3	7,263
Fen Dance	3	4	1	1	1	1	4,240
Deer Hunt	3	3	1	2	0	0	2,481
La Reine Rouge	4	5	1	2	1	1	2,427
Storm Drum	3	8	1	0	1	6	2,322
Tea Dust	4	3	1	0	0	2	2,103
Little Saboteur	3	7	1	2	0	4	1,924
Addicted To Love	3	7	1	2	1	3	1,618
Wandering Stranger	3	4	1	0	2	1	1,544

WINNING OWNERS

	Races Won	Value £		Races Won	Value £
Avon Industries Ltd	1	17,090	R P Marchant	1	2,103
A W Schiff	1	7,263	Mrs W D Blackwood	1	1,924
D M Ahier	2	6,667	Mascalls Stud	1	1,618
Mrs P J Makin	1	2,481	Barrie C Whitehouse	1	1,544
A R C Hobbs	1	2,322			

Favourites	3-21	14.3%	- 10.09	Total winning prize-money			£43,012
Longest winning sequence			2	Average SP of winner			8.3/1
Longest losing sequence			39	Return on stakes invested			-38.1%
1991 Form	23-200	11.5%	- 44.46	1989 Form	29-186	15.6%	+ 23.75
1990 Form	27-146	18.5%	- 28.65	1988 Form	24-227	10.6%	+ 7.70

D MARKS (Upper Lambourn, Berks)

	No. of Horses	Races Run	1st	2nd	3rd	Unpl	Per cent	£1 Level Stake
2-y-o	1	6	0	0	0	6	-	- 6.00
3-y-o	4	32	6	4	2	20	18.8	+ 23.00
4-y-o+	5	33	2	3	1	27	6.1	- 25.25
Totals	10	71	8	7	3	53	11.3	- 8.25

Jan	Feb	Mar	Apr	May	Jun	Jul	Aug	Sep	Oct/Nov
0-2	0-4	0-3	0-5	1-9	2-8	1-7	0-12	2-9	2-12

Winning Jockeys		W-R	£1 Level Stake					W-R	£1 Level Stake
S Dawson		4-12	+ 31.00		J Reid			1-1	+ 2.25
T Quinn		2-4	+ 8.00		M Hills			1-3	+ 1.50

Winning Courses		W-R	£1 Level Stake					W-R	£1 Level Stake
Wolverhampton		2-9	+ 3.50		Nottingham			1-3	+ 6.50
Bath		1-1	+ 5.00		Warwick			1-5	+ 16.00
Yarmouth		1-1	+ 3.50		Lingfield (AW)			1-13	- 7.00
Goodwood		1-3	+ 0.25						

Winning Horses	Age	Races Run	1st	2nd	3rd	Unpl	Win £
Child Star	3	11	3	2	0	6	6,929
High Post	3	10	2	0	1	7	5,330
Rainbow Fleet	4	6	2	1	0	3	5,015
Crackling	3	8	1	2	1	4	2,889

Favourites	4-6	66.7%	+ 14.75	Total winning prize-money			£20,163

1991 Form	0-41			1989 Form	2-26	7.7%	+ 4.00
1990 Form	1-32	3.1%	+ 19.00	1988 Form	1-36	2.8%	- 29.00

M MCCORMACK (Wantage, Oxon)

	No. of Horses	Races Run	1st	2nd	3rd	Unpl	Per cent	£1 Level Stake
2-y-o	8	30	0	6	0	24	-	- 30.00
3-y-o	10	68	8	10	9	41	11.8	- 15.35
4-y-o+	10	70	8	6	6	50	11.4	- 17.62
Totals	28	168	16	22	15	115	9.5	- 62.97

BY MONTH

2-y-o	W-R	Per cent	£1 Level Stake	3-y-o	W-R	Per cent	£1 Level Stake
January	0-0	-	0.00	January	0-2	-	- 2.00
February	0-0	-	0.00	February	1-3	33.3	+ 5.50
March	0-0	-	0.00	March	0-6	-	- 6.00
April	0-2	-	- 2.00	April	1-6	16.7	- 2.75
May	0-5	-	- 5.00	May	3-12	25.0	+ 2.90
June	0-6	-	- 6.00	June	2-9	22.2	+ 7.00
July	0-7	-	- 7.00	July	0-7	-	- 7.00
August	0-7	-	- 7.00	August	1-7	14.3	+ 3.00
September	0-1	-	- 1.00	September	0-10	-	- 10.00
Oct/Nov	0-2	-	- 2.00	Oct/Nov	0-6	-	- 6.00

McCormack M

4-y-o+	W-R	Per cent	£1 Level Stake	Totals	W-R	Per cent	£1 Level Stake
January	0-1	-	- 1.00	January	0-3	-	- 3.00
February	0-3	-	- 3.00	February	1-6	16.7	+ 2.50
March	0-5	-	- 5.00	March	0-11	-	- 11.00
April	1-7	14.3	+ 1.00	April	2-15	13.3	- 3.75
May	1-14	7.1	- 10.00	May	4-31	12.9	- 12.10
June	3-11	27.3	+ 11.75	June	5-26	19.2	+ 12.75
July	1-8	12.5	- 1.00	July	1-22	4.5	- 15.00
August	0-7	-	- 7.00	August	1-21	4.8	- 11.00
September	0-5	-	- 5.00	September	0-16	-	- 16.00
Oct/Nov	2-9	22.2	+ 1.63	Oct/Nov	2-17	11.8	- 6.37

DISTANCE

2-y-o	W-R	Per cent	£1 Level Stake	3-y-o	W-R	Per cent	£1 Level Stake
5f-6f	0-26	-	- 26.00	5f-6f	4-27	14.8	- 0.25
7f-8f	0-4	-	- 4.00	7f-8f	4-36	11.1	- 10.10
9f-13f	0-0	-	0.00	9f-13f	0-5	-	- 5.00
14f+	0-0	-	0.00	14f+	0-0	-	0.00

4-y-o+	W-R	Per cent	£1 Level Stake	Totals	W-R	Per cent	£1 Level Stake
5f-6f	5-41	12.2	- 8.62	5f-6f	9-94	9.6	- 34.87
7f-8f	3-28	10.7	- 8.00	7f-8f	7-68	10.3	- 22.10
9f-13f	0-1	-	- 1.00	9f-13f	0-6	-	- 6.00
14f+	0-0	-	0.00	14f+	0-0	-	0.00

TYPE OF RACE

Non-Handicaps	W-R	Per cent	£1 Level Stake	Handicaps	W-R	Per cent	£1 Level Stake
2-y-o	0-25	-	- 25.00	2-y-o	0-2	-	- 2.00
3-y-o	6-34	17.6	+ 0.65	3-y-o	2-24	8.3	- 6.00
4-y-o+	3-26	11.5	- 12.37	4-y-o+	5-32	15.6	+ 6.75
Selling	0-10	-	- 10.00	Selling	0-5	-	- 5.00
Apprentice	0-3	-	- 3.00	Apprentice	0-4	-	- 4.00
Amat/Ladies	0-2	-	- 2.00	Amat/Ladies	0-1	-	- 1.00
Totals	9-100	9.0	- 51.72	Totals	7-68	10.3	- 11.25

COURSE GRADE

	W-R	Per cent	£1 Level Stake
Group 1	8-72	11.1	- 7.75
Group 2	2-24	8.3	- 12.75
Group 3	2-35	5.7	- 24.37
Group 4	4-37	10.8	- 18.10

FIRST TIME OUT

	W-R	Per cent	£1 Level Stake
2-y-o	0-8	-	- 8.00
3-y-o	1-10	10.0	- 6.75
4-y-o+	0-9	-	- 9.00
Totals	1-27	3.7	- 23.75

278

JOCKEYS RIDING

	W-R	Per cent	£1 Level Stake			W-R	Per cent	£1 Level Stake
J Reid	9-67	13.4	- 23.47	S Cauthen		1-4	25.0	+ 11.00
W Newnes	3-28	10.7	- 7.50	A Clark		1-18	5.6	- 10.00
M Roberts	2-2	100.0	+ 16.00					

C Rutter	0-6	T Quinn	0-2	L Piggott	0-1
M Birch	0-3	A Garth	0-1	P Bowe	0-1
M Perrett	0-3	A Munro	0-1	P V Gilson	0-1
Miss S Farrant	0-3	B Thomas	0-1	Pat Eddery	0-1
R Street	0-3	C Asmussen	0-1	Paul Eddery	0-1
A Shoults	0-2	E Husband	0-1	S Davies	0-1
G Baxter	0-2	G Duffield	0-1	S Drowne	0-1
J Fortune	0-2	H Bastiman	0-1	S Mulvey	0-1
J Quinn	0-2	J Hunter	0-1	W Carson	0-1
R Cochrane	0-2	J Weaver	0-1	W R Swinburn	0-1

COURSE RECORD

	Total W-R	Non-Handicaps 2-y-o	3-y-o+	Handicaps 2-y-o	3-y-o+	Per cent	£1 Level Stake
Thirsk	2-4	0-0	1-2	0-0	1-2	50.0	+ 7.25
Epsom	2-6	0-0	1-2	0-0	1-4	33.3	+ 18.00
Wolverhampton	2-8	0-2	1-4	0-0	1-2	25.0	- 1.60
Haydock	1-2	0-0	1-2	0-0	0-0	50.0	+ 3.50
Carlisle	1-3	0-0	1-2	0-0	0-1	33.3	+ 1.00
Pontefract	1-4	0-0	0-2	0-0	1-2	25.0	+ 4.00
Lingfield (AW)	1-4	0-0	1-1	0-0	0-3	25.0	+ 4.50
Ascot	1-6	0-1	1-3	0-0	0-2	16.7	+ 1.00
Newbury	1-7	0-3	1-1	0-0	0-3	14.3	0.00
Chepstow	1-8	0-2	1-5	0-0	0-1	12.5	- 5.37
Kempton	1-8	0-2	0-3	0-0	1-3	12.5	0.00
Newmarket	1-10	0-2	0-4	0-1	1-3	10.0	0.00
Goodwood	1-14	0-3	0-4	0-1	1-6	7.1	- 11.25

Folkestone	0-10	Windsor	0-5	Catterick	0-2
Doncaster	0-9	Lingfield	0-4	Chester	0-2
Bath	0-8	Nottingham	0-4	York	0-2
Brighton	0-7	Salisbury	0-4	Ayr	0-1
Leicester	0-5	Sandown	0-4	Beverley	0-1
Southwell (AW)	0-5	Newcastle	0-3		
Warwick	0-5	Ripon	0-3		

WINNING HORSES

	Age	Races Run	1st	2nd	3rd	Unpl	Win £
Prince Ferdinand	3	8	4	3	0	1	59,954
Montendre	5	10	2	0	1	7	15,069
Inherent Magic	3	15	2	4	4	5	11,014
Poets Cove	4	8	1	1	0	6	5,842

McCormack M

Just A Step	6	12	2	0	0	10	5,187
The Noble Oak	4	21	2	3	4	12	2,907
Good For The Roses	6	2	1	1	0	0	2,847
Hugging	3	12	1	3	1	7	2,364
Walkonthemoon	3	11	1	0	2	8	2,108

WINNING OWNERS

	Races Won	Value £		Races Won	Value £
Miss J Winch	4	59,954	Mrs M E Cooke	2	5,187
David Mort	2	15,069	Brian North	2	4,472
Orchid Racing & Bloodstock Ltd	3	13,861	M McCormack	2	2,907
P R Cruden	1	5,842			

Favourites	5-18	27.8%	- 1.72	Total winning prize-money			£107,292
Longest winning sequence			2	Average SP of winner			5.6/1
Longest losing sequence			25	Return on stakes invested			-37.5%
1991 Form	16-145	11.0%	- 22.50	1989 Form	12-106	11.3%	- 12.75
1990 Form	5-152	3.3%	-116.25	1988 Form	4-129	3.1%	-109.62

M MCCOURT (Wantage, Oxon)

	No. of Horses	Races Run	1st	2nd	3rd	Unpl	Per cent	£1 Level Stake
2-y-o	1	1	0	0	0	1	-	- 1.00
3-y-o	0	0	0	0	0	0	-	0.00
4-y-o+	2	15	3	1	0	11	20.0	+ 5.00
Totals	3	16	3	1	0	12	18.8	+ 4.00

Jan	Feb	Mar	Apr	May	Jun	Jul	Aug	Sep	Oct/Nov
0-1	0-1	0-0	1-1	2-2	0-2	0-2	0-3	0-3	0-1

Winning Jockey	W-R	£1 Level Stake		W-R	£1 Level Stake
T Quinn	3-8	+ 12.00			

Winning Courses					
Bath	2-6	+ 10.00	Kempton	1-2	+ 2.00

Winning Horse	Age	Races Run	1st	2nd	3rd	Unpl	Win £
Cee-En-Cee	8	14	3	1	0	10	9,098

Favourites	1-4	25.0%	0.00	Total winning prize-money		£9,098
1991 Form	1-38	2.6%	- 31.00	1989 Form	3-40	7.5%	- 11.50
1990 Form	2-43	4.7%	- 19.00	1988 Form	1-72	1.4%	- 61.00

P M MCENTEE (Windsor, Berks)

	No. of Horses	Races Run	1st	2nd	3rd	Unpl	Per cent	£1 Level Stake
2-y-o	5	15	1	1	1	12	6.7	- 10.00
3-y-o	1	1	0	0	0	1	-	- 1.00
4-y-o+	1	1	0	0	0	1	-	- 1.00
Totals	7	17	1	1	1	14	5.9	- 12.00

Jan	Feb	Mar	Apr	May	Jun	Jul	Aug	Sep	Oct/Nov
0-0	0-1	0-0	0-0	0-1	0-0	0-0	0-5	0-4	1-6

Winning Jockey	W-R	£1 Level Stake	Winning Course	W-R	£1 Level Stake
J Weaver	1-2	+ 3.00	Doncaster	1-2	+ 3.00

Winning Horse	Age	Races Run	1st	2nd	3rd	Unpl	Win £
Royal Deed	2	6	1	1	1	3	2,898

Favourites	0-0	Total winning prize-money	£2,898

B A MCMAHON (Tamworth, Staffs)

	No. of Horses	Races Run	1st	2nd	3rd	Unpl	Per cent	£1 Level Stake
2-y-o	9	50	4	5	6	35	8.0	- 25.17
3-y-o	16	110	9	11	11	79	8.2	- 59.60
4-y-o+	21	136	17	21	9	89	12.5	+ 6.25
Totals	46	296	30	37	26	203	10.1	- 78.52

BY MONTH

2-y-o	W-R	Per cent	£1 Level Stake	3-y-o	W-R	Per cent	£1 Level Stake
January	0-0	-	0.00	January	0-0	-	0.00
February	0-0	-	0.00	February	0-0	-	0.00
March	0-0	-	0.00	March	0-6	-	- 6.00
April	0-2	-	- 2.00	April	3-15	20.0	+ 10.00
May	0-8	-	- 8.00	May	2-16	12.5	- 10.43
June	0-9	-	- 9.00	June	0-17	-	- 17.00
July	2-8	25.0	- 0.17	July	2-18	11.1	- 8.67
August	0-9	-	- 9.00	August	0-9	-	- 9.00
September	2-7	28.6	+ 10.00	September	0-12	-	- 12.00
Oct/Nov	0-7	-	- 7.00	Oct/Nov	2-17	11.8	- 6.50

McMahon B A

4-y-o+	W-R	Per cent	£1 Level Stake	Totals	W-R	Per cent	£1 Level Stake
January	0-8	-	- 8.00	January	0-8	-	- 8.00
February	0-4	-	- 4.00	February	0-4	-	- 4.00
March	0-5	-	- 5.00	March	0-11	-	- 11.00
April	4-10	40.0	+ 30.50	April	7-27	25.9	+ 38.50
May	1-10	10.0	0.00	May	3-34	8.8	- 18.43
June	3-20	15.0	- 5.50	June	3-46	6.5	- 31.50
July	4-23	17.4	+ 10.25	July	8-49	16.3	+ 1.41
August	1-22	4.5	- 15.00	August	1-40	2.5	- 33.00
September	4-18	22.2	+ 19.00	September	6-37	16.2	+ 17.00
Oct/Nov	0-16	-	- 16.00	Oct/Nov	2-40	5.0	- 29.50

DISTANCE

2-y-o	W-R	Per cent	£1 Level Stake	3-y-o	W-R	Per cent	£1 Level Stake
5f-6f	2-40	5.0	- 24.67	5f-6f	8-59	13.6	- 13.60
7f-8f	2-10	20.0	- 0.50	7f-8f	0-21	-	- 21.00
9f-13f	0-0	-	0.00	9f-13f	1-29	3.4	- 24.00
14f+	0-0	-	0.00	14f+	0-1	-	- 1.00

4-y-o+	W-R	Per cent	£1 Level Stake	Totals	W-R	Per cent	£1 Level Stake
5f-6f	8-52	15.4	+ 9.75	5f-6f	18-151	11.9	- 28.52
7f-8f	5-36	13.9	+ 22.50	7f-8f	7-67	10.4	+ 1.00
9f-13f	4-31	12.9	- 9.00	9f-13f	5-60	8.3	- 33.00
14f+	0-17	-	- 17.00	14f+	0-18	-	- 18.00

TYPE OF RACE

Non-Handicaps	W-R	Per cent	£1 Level Stake	Handicaps	W-R	Per cent	£1 Level Stake
2-y-o	2-37	5.4	- 26.67	2-y-o	1-5	20.0	+ 6.00
3-y-o	5-50	10.0	- 24.93	3-y-o	2-39	5.1	- 27.67
4-y-o+	3-28	10.7	- 12.50	4-y-o+	12-90	13.3	+ 9.25
Selling	1-18	5.6	- 14.50	Selling	0-3	-	- 3.00
Apprentice	2-10	20.0	+ 5.50	Apprentice	2-15	13.3	+ 11.00
Amat/Ladies	0-0	-	0.00	Amat/Ladies	0-1	-	- 1.00
Totals	13-143	9.1	- 73.10	Totals	17-153	11.1	- 5.42

COURSE GRADE

	W-R	Per cent	£1 Level Stake
Group 1	8-89	9.0	- 19.67
Group 2	5-33	15.2	+ 17.90
Group 3	10-90	11.1	- 31.00
Group 4	7-84	8.3	- 45.75

FIRST TIME OUT

	W-R	Per cent	£1 Level Stake
2-y-o	0-9	-	- 9.00
3-y-o	1-16	6.3	- 13.00
4-y-o+	3-21	14.3	+ 25.00
Totals	4-46	8.7	+ 3.00

282

JOCKEYS RIDING

	W-R	Per cent	£1 Level Stake		W-R	Per cent	£1 Level Stake
T Quinn	13-49	26.5	+ 43.41	G Duffield	1-7	14.3	- 5.43
S Sanders	9-66	13.6	+ 20.50	L Dettori	1-10	10.0	- 6.00
B Raymond	2-19	10.5	0.00	J Lowe	1-12	8.3	- 9.00
K Fallon	1-2	50.0	+ 1.50	M Birch	1-15	6.7	- 11.00
D McKeown	1-6	16.7	- 2.50				

J Bramhill	0-21	W Ryan	0-4	D Holland	0-1	
J Fortune	0-19	G Carter	0-3	J Quinn	0-1	
A Munro	0-8	M Roberts	0-3	J Williams	0-1	
W Carson	0-6	N Carlisle	0-3	L Charnock	0-1	
G Hind	0-4	A Culhane	0-2	Mr N Skelton	0-1	
J Reid	0-4	C Hawksley	0-2	S D Williams	0-1	
K Darley	0-4	G Bardwell	0-2	T Williams	0-1	
M Hills	0-4	K Rutter	0-2	W Newnes	0-1	
R Cochrane	0-4	P Robinson	0-2			
S Maloney	0-4	D Biggs	0-1			

COURSE RECORD

	Total W-R	Non-Handicaps 2-y-o	Non-Handicaps 3-y-o+	Handicaps 2-y-o	Handicaps 3-y-o+	Per cent	£1 Level Stake
Pontefract	6-32	0-3	3-15	0-0	3-14	18.8	+ 10.00
Haydock	4-29	2-7	0-11	1-1	1-10	13.8	+ 0.33
Warwick	3-12	0-1	0-5	0-0	3-6	25.0	+ 6.50
Thirsk	2-5	0-0	1-2	0-0	1-3	40.0	+ 11.57
York	2-12	0-1	0-3	0-0	2-8	16.7	+ 5.00
Chester	2-15	0-1	0-2	0-0	2-12	13.3	+ 10.33
Nottingham	2-25	0-3	2-9	0-0	0-13	8.0	- 15.50
Wolverhampton	2-35	0-8	1-6	0-0	1-21	5.7	- 24.50
Kempton	1-2	0-0	1-1	0-0	0-1	50.0	+ 4.00
Catterick	1-3	0-0	0-1	0-0	1-2	33.3	- 0.75
Ascot	1-9	0-2	0-1	0-1	1-5	11.1	+ 8.00
Ripon	1-10	0-1	1-3	0-0	0-6	10.0	- 1.00
Beverley	1-14	1-2	0-4	0-0	0-8	7.1	- 10.50
Leicester	1-16	0-2	1-9	0-0	0-5	6.3	- 12.00
Southwell (AW)	1-24	0-1	0-9	0-0	1-14	4.2	- 17.00

Doncaster	0-19	Ayr	0-2	Folkestone	0-1	
Carlisle	0-9	Epsom	0-2	Salisbury	0-1	
Newmarket	0-6	Redcar	0-2	Sandown	0-1	
Goodwood	0-4	Yarmouth	0-2			
Newbury	0-3	Bath	0-1			

WINNING HORSES

	Age	Races Run	1st	2nd	3rd	Unpl	Win £
Band On The Run	5	7	2	0	0	5	35,983
Bunty Boo	3	10	3	2	1	4	13,535
Breezy Day	6	18	4	2	0	12	11,297

McMahon B A

Samson-Agonistes	6	11	4	2	0	5	9,942
Katy's Lad	5	12	2	2	0	8	6,179
Absolutely Nuts	3	11	2	2	1	6	5,013
The Old Chapel	3	8	2	0	0	6	4,923
Kinlacey	5	7	2	0	2	3	4,905
Look Who's Here	2	7	1	1	1	4	3,948
Causley	7	12	1	6	3	2	3,817
Shadows Of Silver	4	2	1	1	0	0	2,658
Viva Darling	3	8	1	2	2	3	2,511
Admirals Realm	3	7	1	1	2	3	2,427
Beauman	2	3	1	0	1	1	2,427
Wentbridge Lad	2	6	1	0	0	5	2,128
Persian Revival	2	10	1	1	1	7	1,646
Access Cruise	5	7	1	0	0	6	1,214

WINNING OWNERS

	Races Won	Value £		Races Won	Value £
D J Allen	2	35,983	S L Edwards	1	3,948
Mrs R C Mayall	4	16,193	Henry Pearce	1	3,817
Mrs J McMahon	4	11,297	Anthony Laurence Macias	1	2,511
J B Wilcox	4	9,942	Mrs B Facchino	1	2,427
J W Butler	2	6,179	P W Leslie	1	2,427
J W Hall	2	5,013	G Charlesworth	1	2,128
R A Holdings Ltd	2	4,923	Michael Sturgess	1	1,646
Michael G T Stokes	2	4,905	M Hindes-Randle	1	1,214

Favourites	6-27	22.2%	- 8.68	Total winning prize-money	£114,550
Longest winning sequence			3	Average SP of winner	6.2/1
Longest losing sequence			37	Return on stakes invested	-26.5%
1991 Form	14-277	5.1%	-150.37	1989 Form	21-195	10.8%	+ 16.56
1990 Form	22-275	8.0%	- 55.74	1988 Form	20-244	8.2%	- 26.37

B J MCMATH (Newmarket)

		No. of Horses	Races Run	1st	2nd	3rd	Unpl	Per cent	£1 Level Stake
2-y-o		4	16	0	0	0	16	-	- 16.00
3-y-o		5	9	1	0	0	8	11.1	- 3.50
4-y-o+		2	9	0	0	0	9	-	- 9.00
Totals		11	34	1	0	0	33	2.9	- 28.50

Jan	Feb	Mar	Apr	May	Jun	Jul	Aug	Sep	Oct/Nov
0-0	0-0	0-1	0-1	0-4	0-2	0-5	0-10	1-5	0-6

Winning Jockey	W-R	£1 Level Stake	Winning Course	W-R	£1 Level Stake
E Johnson	1-16	- 10.50	Leicester	1-5	+ 0.50

Winning Horse	Age	Races Run	1st	2nd	3rd	Unpl	Win £
Telephus	3	4	1	0	0	3	2,574

Favourites	0-0		Total winning prize-money		£2,574

1991 Form	0-32		1990 Form	0-14

B R MILLMAN (Cullompton, Devon)

	No. of Horses	Races Run	1st	2nd	3rd	Unpl	Per cent	£1 Level Stake
2-y-o	4	20	3	3	3	11	15.0	+ 62.00
3-y-o	7	31	1	1	0	29	3.2	- 22.00
4-y-o+	6	56	3	4	4	45	5.4	- 25.00
Totals	17	107	7	8	7	85	6.5	+ 15.00

Jan	Feb	Mar	Apr	May	Jun	Jul	Aug	Sep	Oct/Nov
0-0	0-0	0-2	1-18	0-10	3-11	0-18	2-16	1-19	0-13

Winning Jockeys	W-R	£1 Level Stake		W-R	£1 Level Stake
J Williams	3-18	+ 75.00	J Weaver	1-5	+ 3.50
G Baxter	2-25	- 10.00	A Mackay	1-12	- 6.50

Winning Courses					
Chepstow	2-10	+ 74.00	Epsom	1-5	+ 4.00
Haydock	1-3	+ 2.50	Bath	1-10	- 6.00
Windsor	1-4	+ 7.00	Salisbury	1-15	- 6.50

Winning Horses	Age	Races Run	1st	2nd	3rd	Unpl	Win £
Marine Diver	6	12	1	2	1	8	7,310
Royal Seaton	3	10	1	1	0	8	6,970
Simply Sooty	2	10	2	3	3	2	6,375
Baysham	6	13	1	0	0	12	3,392
World Express	2	6	1	0	0	5	2,725
Royal Dartmouth	7	12	1	2	1	8	2,390

Favourites	1-8	12.5%	- 2.50	Total winning prize-money		£29,162

1991 Form	9-178	5.1%	- 84.92	1990 Form	12-153	7.8%	- 37.25

P MITCHELL (Epsom, Surrey)

	No. of Horses	Races Run	1st	2nd	3rd	Unpl	Per cent	£1 Level Stake
2-y-o	6	32	3	4	5	20	9.4	+ 1.00
3-y-o	9	44	1	1	7	35	2.3	- 40.75
4-y-o+	6	28	0	2	2	24	-	- 28.00
Totals	21	104	4	7	14	79	3.8	- 67.75

Jan	Feb	Mar	Apr	May	Jun	Jul	Aug	Sep	Oct/Nov
0-0	0-1	0-4	0-7	1-14	0-15	1-20	1-18	1-14	0-11

Winning Jockeys	W-R	£1 Level Stake				W-R	£1 Level Stake
S O'Gorman	2-27	+ 1.00					
Pat Eddery	1-2	+ 3.00	L Piggott			1-4	- 0.75

Winning Courses	W-R	£1 Level Stake				W-R	£1 Level Stake
Lingfield	2-14	+ 6.25	Goodwood			1-9	+ 2.00
Folkestone	1-6	- 1.00					

Winning Horses	Age	Races Run	1st	2nd	3rd	Unpl	Win £
Kyrenia Game	2	8	2	1	1	4	5,849
Flight Lieutenant	3	5	1	0	1	3	2,427
Second Chance	2	14	1	2	3	8	2,406

Favourites	0-4		Total winning prize-money		£10,682

1991 Form	8-149	5.4%	- 63.00	1989 Form	15-169	8.9%	- 62.35
1990 Form	13-210	6.2%	-118.42	1988 Form	12-188	6.4%	- 92.16

PAT MITCHELL (Newmarket)

	No. of Horses	Races Run	1st	2nd	3rd	Unpl	Per cent	£1 Level Stake
2-y-o	6	23	1	0	0	22	4.3	- 2.00
3-y-o	6	56	6	3	0	47	10.7	+ 1.75
4-y-o+	7	46	2	2	2	40	4.3	- 25.25
Totals	19	125	9	5	2	109	7.2	- 25.50

Jan	Feb	Mar	Apr	May	Jun	Jul	Aug	Sep	Oct/Nov
0-7	0-5	0-10	0-12	2-22	3-23	2-14	1-6	0-11	1-15

Winning Jockeys	W-R	£1 Level Stake			W-R	£1 Level Stake
D Biggs	5-23	+ 13.75	A Munro		1-4	+ 17.00
S O'Gorman	3-35	+ 6.75				

Winning Courses	W-R	£1 Level Stake			W-R	£1 Level Stake
Nottingham	3-12	+ 31.00	Doncaster		1-6	- 2.25
Kempton	2-7	+ 15.00	Sandown		1-6	0.00
Thirsk	1-2	+ 19.00	Lingfield		1-25	- 21.25

Winning Horses		Age	Races Run	1st	2nd	3rd	Unpl	Win £
Miss Pin Up		3	16	5	1	0	10	12,499
Tauber		8	15	2	1	2	10	5,970
Peerage Prince		3	14	1	1	0	12	2,805
Nitouche		2	6	1	0	0	5	2,383

Favourites	3-7	42.9%	+ 6.75	Total winning prize-money				£23,656

1991 Form	5-130	3.8%	- 86.00	1989 Form	6-104	5.8%	- 24.00
1990 Form	11-215	5.1%	- 62.17	1988 Form	2-130	1.5%	- 100.00

D MOFFATT (Cartmel, Cumbria)

	No. of Horses	Races Run	1st	2nd	3rd	Unpl	Per cent	£1 Level Stake
2-y-o	6	21	3	4	3	11	14.3	+ 12.00
3-y-o	2	7	0	0	0	7	-	- 7.00
4-y-o+	11	38	2	4	3	29	5.3	- 17.50
Totals	19	66	5	8	6	47	7.6	- 12.50

Jan	Feb	Mar	Apr	May	Jun	Jul	Aug	Sep	Oct/Nov
1-2	0-6	0-5	2-5	1-8	0-5	0-6	1-8	0-6	0-15

Winning Jockeys	W-R	£1 Level Stake			W-R	£1 Level Stake
D Moffatt	3-45	- 13.50	J Fortune		2-6	+ 16.00

Winning Courses						
Hamilton	3-18	+ 23.00	Southwell (AW)		1-8	- 4.50
Thirsk	1-2	+ 7.00				

Winning Horses	Age	Races Run	1st	2nd	3rd	Unpl	Win £
Key To My Heart	2	8	2	2	1	3	5,037
Hamilton Lady	4	9	1	1	2	5	2,318
Bridge Player	5	10	1	3	0	6	2,304
Purchased By Phone	2	1	1	0	0	0	2,128

Favourites	1-4	25.0%	- 0.50	Total winning prize-money		£11,787

1991 Form	7-94	7.4%	- 26.50	1989 Form	2-36	5.6%	- 2.00
1990 Form	1-34	2.9%	- 27.50	1988 Form	0-44		

A MOORE (Brighton, East Sussex)

	No. of Horses	Races Run	1st	2nd	3rd	Unpl	Per cent	£1 Level Stake
2-y-o	4	15	0	0	0	15	-	- 15.00
3-y-o	5	17	0	0	0	17	-	- 17.00
4-y-o+	17	75	5	3	2	65	6.7	+ 7.00
Totals	26	107	5	3	2	97	4.7	- 25.00

Jan	Feb	Mar	Apr	May	Jun	Jul	Aug	Sep	Oct/Nov
0-6	2-13	1-8	0-14	0-13	0-6	0-8	1-10	1-11	0-18

Winning Jockeys	W-R	£1 Level Stake			W-R	£1 Level Stake
N Adams	3-29	+ 32.00	B Rouse		2-28	- 7.00

Winning Courses	W-R	£1 Level Stake			W-R	£1 Level Stake
Lingfield (AW)	3-31	+ 30.00	Brighton		1-27	- 14.00
Bath	1-3	+ 5.00				

Winning Horses	Age	Races Run	1st	2nd	3rd	Unpl	Win £
Precious Air	4	13	2	1	0	10	5,592
Invocation	5	11	2	0	1	8	4,432
Present Times	6	3	1	0	1	1	2,187

Favourites	0-2	Total winning prize-money	£12,211

1991 Form	1-92	1.1%	- 79.00	1989 Form	4-51	7.8%	+ 3.88
1990 Form	3-80	3.8%	- 52.25	1988 Form	0-34		

G M MOORE (Middleham, North Yorks)

	No. of Horses	Races Run	1st	2nd	3rd	Unpl	Per cent	£1 Level Stake
2-y-o	8	48	5	4	6	33	10.4	- 24.10
3-y-o	4	18	4	1	3	10	22.2	+ 12.33
4-y-o+	15	42	1	5	1	35	2.4	- 31.00
Totals	27	108	10	10	10	78	9.3	- 42.77

BY MONTH

2-y-o	W-R	Per cent	£1 Level Stake	3-y-o	W-R	Per cent	£1 Level Stake
Mar/Apr	2-7	28.6	+ 4.10	Mar/Apr	1-1	100.0	+ 7.00
May	1-8	12.5	- 4.00	May	0-2	-	- 2.00
June	1-9	11.1	- 7.20	June	0-1	-	- 1.00
July	0-12	-	- 12.00	July	1-3	33.3	- 1.17
August	1-10	10.0	- 2.00	August	1-4	25.0	+ 1.50
September	0-2	-	- 2.00	September	1-3	33.3	+ 12.00
Oct/Nov	0-0	-	0.00	Oct/Nov	0-4	-	- 4.00

4-y-o+	W-R	Per cent	£1 Level Stake	Totals	W-R	Per cent	£1 Level Stake
Mar/Apr	0-7	-	- 4.00	Mar/Apr	3-15	20.0	+ 7.10
May	0-9	-	- 9.00	May	1-19	5.3	- 15.00
June	1-6	16.7	+ 5.00	June	2-16	12.5	- 3.20
July	0-2	-	- 2.00	July	1-17	5.9	- 15.17
August	0-3	-	- 3.00	August	2-17	11.8	- 3.50
September	0-10	-	- 10.00	September	1-15	6.7	0.00
Oct/Nov	0-5	-	- 5.00	Oct/Nov	0-9	-	- 9.00

DISTANCE

2-y-o	W-R	Per cent	£1 Level Stake	3-y-o	W-R	Per cent	£1 Level Stake
5f-6f	5-46	10.9	- 22.10	5f-6f	0-0	-	0.00
7f-8f	0-2	-	- 2.00	7f-8f	3-10	30.0	+ 14.83
9f-13f	0-0	-	0.00	9f-13f	1-7	14.3	- 1.50
14f+	0-0	-	0.00	14f+	0-1	-	- 1.00

4-y-o+	W-R	Per cent	£1 Level Stake	Totals	W-R	Per cent	£1 Level Stake
5f-6f	0-1	-	- 1.00	5f-6f	5-47	10.6	- 23.10
7f-8f	0-11	-	- 11.00	7f-8f	3-23	13.0	+ 1.83
9f-13f	0-15	-	- 15.00	9f-13f	1-22	4.5	- 16.50
14f+	1-15	6.7	- 4.00	14f+	1-16	6.3	- 5.00

TYPE OF RACE

Non-Handicaps	W-R	Per cent	£1 Level Stake	Handicaps	W-R	Per cent	£1 Level Stake
2-y-o	2-30	6.7	- 19.90	2-y-o	1-4	25.0	+ 4.00
3-y-o	2-7	28.6	+ 2.83	3-y-o	2-10	20.0	+ 10.50
4-y-o+	0-7	-	- 7.00	4-y-o+	1-33	3.0	- 22.00
Selling	2-13	15.4	- 7.20	Selling	0-3	-	- 3.00
Apprentice	0-0	-	0.00	Apprentice	0-1	-	- 1.00
Amat/Ladies	0-0	-	0.00	Amat/Ladies	0-0	-	0.00
Totals	6-57	10.5	- 31.27	Totals	4-51	7.8	- 11.50

COURSE GRADE

	W-R	Per cent	£1 Level Stake
Group 1	3-38	7.9	- 4.00
Group 2	1-24	4.2	- 20.00
Group 3	3-22	13.6	- 10.10
Group 4	3-24	12.5	- 8.67

FIRST TIME OUT

	W-R	Per cent	£1 Level Stake
2-y-o	0-8	-	- 8.00
3-y-o	1-4	25.0	+ 4.00
4-y-o+	0-15	-	- 15.00
Totals	1-27	3.7	- 19.00

JOCKEYS RIDING

	W-R	Per cent	£1 Level Stake		W-R	Per cent	£1 Level Stake
K Fallon	5-31	16.1	- 4.10	J Fanning	1-6	16.7	+ 9.00
W Newnes	3-11	27.3	+ 4.33	J Carroll	1-8	12.5	0.00

D McKeown	0-11	M Hills	0-2	N Carlisle	0-1
J Weaver	0-7	N Adams	0-2	N Connorton	0-1
J Lowe	0-5	O Pears	0-2	Paul Eddery	0-1
P Burke	0-5	D Harrison	0-1	R Cochrane	0-1
J Quinn	0-3	K Darley	0-1	S Sanders	0-1
S Maloney	0-3	K Rutter	0-1	W Carson	0-1
A Culhane	0-2	Lisa Cropp	0-1		

COURSE RECORD

	Total W-R	Non-Handicaps 2-y-o	Non-Handicaps 3-y-o+	Handicaps 2-y-o	Handicaps 3-y-o+	Per cent	£1 Level Stake
Southwell (AW)	3-12	0-5	1-4	1-1	1-2	25.0	+ 3.33
Haydock	2-7	0-0	0-0	0-0	2-7	28.6	+ 19.00
Pontefract	2-10	2-3	0-2	0-0	0-5	20.0	+ 0.10
Thirsk	1-4	1-4	0-0	0-0	0-0	25.0	0.00
Beverley	1-6	1-4	0-0	0-0	0-2	16.7	- 4.20
Newcastle	1-13	0-3	1-1	0-1	0-8	7.7	- 5.00

Redcar	0-11	Carlisle	0-5	Goodwood	0-1
Ripon	0-9	Doncaster	0-5	Leicester	0-1
Catterick	0-6	Hamilton	0-3	Newmarket	0-1
York	0-6	Nottingham	0-2		
Ayr	0-5	Edinburgh	0-1		

WINNING HORSES

	Age	Races Run	1st	2nd	3rd	Unpl	Win £
Cool Luke	3	8	2	0	1	5	10,032
Isotonic	2	11	3	1	3	4	5,467
Coconut Johnny	2	8	2	1	1	4	4,609
Highflying	6	4	1	0	0	3	3,818
Take By Storm	3	6	2	1	1	2	2,821

WINNING OWNERS

	Races Won	Value £		Races Won	Value £
B Batey	3	13,850	Crestmart Ltd	2	4,609
J Burgess	3	5,467	Miss V Foster	2	2,821

Favourites	4-7	57.1%	+ 2.73	Total winning prize-money		£26,746
Longest winning sequence			2	Average SP of winner		5.5/1
Longest losing sequence			21	Return on stakes invested		-39.6%

1991 Form	7-126	5.6%	- 36.50	1989 Form	18-183	9.8%	+ 4.25
1990 Form	10-154	6.5%	- 95.17	1988 Form	12-168	7.1%	- 88.50

J S MOORE (Andover, Hants)

	No. of Horses	Races Run	1st	2nd	3rd	Unpl	Per cent	£1 Level Stake
2-y-o	7	44	2	2	5	35	4.5	- 24.00
3-y-o	2	5	0	0	0	5	-	- 5.00
4-y-o+	6	17	0	3	0	14	-	- 17.00
Totals	15	66	2	5	5	54	3.0	- 46.00

Jan	Feb	Mar	Apr	May	Jun	Jul	Aug	Sep	Oct/Nov
0-0	0-0	0-3	0-5	0-6	0-12	1-15	0-14	0-6	1-5

Winning Jockeys	W-R	£1 Level Stake			W-R	£1 Level Stake
A Clark	1-2	+ 9.00	J Quinn		1-5	+ 4.00

Winning Courses	W-R	£1 Level Stake			W-R	£1 Level Stake
Lingfield (AW)	1-4	+ 7.00	Folkestone		1-5	+ 4.00

Winning Horses	Age	Races Run	1st	2nd	3rd	Unpl	Win £
Wealthywoo	2	10	1	0	2	7	2,660
Risky Number	2	11	1	2	1	7	2,574

Favourites	0-2	Total winning prize-money	£5,234

1991 Form	1-33	3.0%	- 20.00	1990 Form	0-8

B C MORGAN (Burton-on-Trent, Staffs)

	No. of Horses	Races Run	1st	2nd	3rd	Unpl	Per cent	£1 Level Stake
2-y-o	1	1	0	0	0	1	-	- 1.00
3-y-o	4	39	2	2	1	34	5.1	- 9.00
4-y-o+	5	26	1	0	5	20	3.8	- 20.00
Totals	10	66	3	2	6	55	4.5	- 30.00

Jan	Feb	Mar	Apr	May	Jun	Jul	Aug	Sep	Oct/Nov
0-0	0-0	1-2	0-11	0-7	1-6	0-6	0-7	1-16	0-11

Winning Jockeys	W-R	£1 Level Stake			W-R	£1 Level Stake
M Roberts	1-2	+ 11.00	P Robinson		1-3	+ 14.00
S Cauthen	1-3	+ 3.00				

Winning Courses	W-R	£1 Level Stake			W-R	£1 Level Stake
Newcastle	1-2	+ 4.00	Beverley		1-6	+ 7.00
Ayr	1-3	+ 14.00				

Morgan B C

Winning Horses	Age	Races Run	1st	2nd	3rd	Unpl	Win £
We're All Game	3	8	1	1	1	5	2,853
Don't Run Me Over	3	15	1	1	0	13	2,774
Needwood Muppet	5	6	1	0	3	2	2,469

Favourites	0-4			Total winning prize-money			£8,096

1991 Form	0-39			1989 Form	3-72	4.2%	- 34.25
1990 Form	2-67	3.0%	- 51.50	1988 Form	6-126	4.8%	- 40.25

D MORLEY (Newmarket)

	No. of Horses	Races Run	1st	2nd	3rd	Unpl	Per cent	£1 Level Stake
2-y-o	11	31	8	1	1	21	25.8	+ 37.05
3-y-o	10	80	9	16	15	40	11.3	- 27.12
4-y-o+	6	38	2	3	6	27	5.3	- 26.00
Totals	27	149	19	20	22	88	12.8	- 16.07

BY MONTH

2-y-o	W-R	Per cent	£1 Level Stake	3-y-o	W-R	Per cent	£1 Level Stake
January	0-0	-	0.00	January	0-0	-	0.00
February	0-0	-	0.00	February	0-0	-	0.00
March	0-0	-	0.00	March	0-2	-	- 2.00
April	0-0	-	0.00	April	0-10	-	- 10.00
May	0-1	-	- 1.00	May	2-10	20.0	- 5.75
June	0-2	-	- 2.00	June	3-11	27.3	+ 9.00
July	3-3	100.0	+ 26.30	July	1-11	9.1	- 8.37
August	1-5	20.0	+ 0.50	August	3-13	23.1	+ 13.00
September	2-6	33.3	+ 3.25	September	0-9	-	- 9.00
Oct/Nov	2-14	14.3	+ 10.00	Oct/Nov	0-14	-	- 14.00

4-y-o+	W-R	Per cent	£1 Level Stake	Totals	W-R	Per cent	£1 Level Stake
January	0-1	-	- 1.00	January	0-1	-	- 1.00
February	0-0	-	0.00	February	0-0	-	0.00
March	0-2	-	- 2.00	March	0-4	-	- 4.00
April	0-6	-	- 6.00	April	0-16	-	- 16.00
May	0-3	-	- 3.00	May	2-14	14.3	- 9.75
June	1-7	14.3	- 3.00	June	4-20	20.0	+ 4.00
July	0-8	-	- 8.00	July	4-22	18.2	+ 9.93
August	0-4	-	- 4.00	August	4-22	18.2	+ 9.50
September	1-4	25.0	+ 4.00	September	3-19	15.8	- 1.75
Oct/Nov	0-3	-	- 3.00	Oct/Nov	2-31	6.5	- 7.00

DISTANCE

2-y-o	W–R	Per cent	£1 Level Stake	3-y-o	W–R	Per cent	£1 Level Stake
5f-6f	4-12	33.3	+ 19.55	5f-6f	1-2	50.0	+ 0.63
7f-8f	4-19	21.1	+ 17.50	7f-8f	4-29	13.8	- 14.75
9f-13f	0-0	-	0.00	9f-13f	4-46	8.7	- 10.00
14f+	0-0	-	0.00	14f+	0-3	-	- 3.00

4-y-o+	W–R	Per cent	£1 Level Stake	Totals	W–R	Per cent	£1 Level Stake
5f-6f	0-0	-	0.00	5f-6f	5-14	35.7	+ 20.18
7f-8f	0-3	-	- 3.00	7f-8f	8-51	15.7	- 0.25
9f-13f	0-6	-	- 6.00	9f-13f	4-52	7.7	- 16.00
14f+	2-29	6.9	- 17.00	14f+	2-32	6.3	- 20.00

TYPE OF RACE

Non-Handicaps	W–R	Per cent	£1 Level Stake	Handicaps	W–R	Per cent	£1 Level Stake
2-y-o	6-20	30.0	+ 40.25	2-y-o	1-9	11.1	- 3.50
3-y-o	2-18	11.1	- 8.75	3-y-o	5-50	10.0	- 11.00
4-y-o+	0-3	-	- 3.00	4-y-o+	2-31	6.5	- 19.00
Selling	1-2	50.0	+ 0.30	Selling	0-0	-	0.00
Apprentice	1-5	20.0	- 3.00	Apprentice	1-10	10.0	- 7.37
Amat/Ladies	0-0	-	0.00	Amat/Ladies	0-1	-	- 1.00
Totals	10-48	20.8	+ 25.80	Totals	9-101	8.9	- 41.87

COURSE GRADE

	W–R	Per cent	£1 Level Stake
Group 1	2-40	5.0	- 30.50
Group 2	7-35	20.0	+ 16.75
Group 3	7-55	12.7	- 0.32
Group 4	3-19	15.8	- 2.00

FIRST TIME OUT

	W–R	Per cent	£1 Level Stake
2-y-o	2-11	18.2	+ 1.50
3-y-o	0-10	-	- 10.00
4-y-o+	0-6	-	- 6.00
Totals	2-27	7.4	- 14.50

JOCKEYS RIDING

	W–R	Per cent	£1 Level Stake		W–R	Per cent	£1 Level Stake
Paul Eddery	5-18	27.8	+ 18.50	M Birch	2-20	10.0	- 3.00
W Ryan	3-12	25.0	+ 16.50	G Hind	1-3	33.3	- 0.75
M Hills	2-6	33.3	+ 20.50	P Robinson	1-4	25.0	+ 2.00
W Carson	2-16	12.5	- 6.75	W R Swinburn	1-5	20.0	- 2.70
E Bentley	2-19	10.5	- 14.37				

B Raymond	0-8	G Duffield	0-3	O Pears		0-1
M Tebbutt	0-8	J Fortune	0-2	S Whitworth		0-1
L Dettori	0-5	A Munro	0-1	S Wood		0-1
K Darley	0-4	J Quinn	0-1	W Newnes		0-1
M Roberts	0-4	Miss L Peate	0-1			
R Hills	0-4	N Day	0-1			

Morley D

COURSE RECORD

	Total	Non-Handicaps		Handicaps		Per	£1 Level
	W-R	2-y-o	3-y-o+	2-y-o	3-y-o+	cent	Stake
Yarmouth	3-15	2-5	0-1	0-0	1-9	20.0	+ 10.93
Lingfield	2-5	1-1	1-1	0-0	0-3	40.0	+ 3.50
Ripon	2-7	0-1	0-1	0-0	2-5	28.6	+ 10.00
Beverley	2-11	1-1	0-1	0-0	1-9	18.2	+ 5.00
Redcar	2-11	2-2	0-4	0-0	0-5	18.2	+ 13.00
Nottingham	2-17	1-4	0-3	0-1	1-9	11.8	- 4.25
Wolverhampton	1-4	0-0	0-1	0-0	1-3	25.0	+ 1.50
Catterick	1-5	0-0	1-2	0-0	0-3	20.0	+ 2.00
Folkestone	1-5	0-1	0-2	0-0	1-2	20.0	- 0.50
Thirsk	1-7	0-1	1-1	0-0	0-5	14.3	- 4.75
Doncaster	1-9	0-2	0-0	0-1	1-6	11.1	- 5.00
Newmarket	1-9	0-3	0-2	1-1	0-3	11.1	- 3.50

Leicester	0-6	Brighton	0-3	Lingfield (AW)	0-2
Newcastle	0-6	Pontefract	0-3	Warwick	0-2
Haydock	0-5	Chester	0-2	Bath	0-1
Ascot	0-4	Hamilton	0-2	Carlisle	0-1
York	0-4	Kempton	0-2	Newbury	0-1

WINNING HORSES

	Age	Races Run	1st	2nd	3rd	Unpl	Win £
Tajdif	2	6	2	0	0	4	17,399
Milanese	3	13	2	2	2	7	5,979
Merton Mill	5	12	2	1	2	7	4,998
Morsun	3	12	2	3	3	4	3,760
Much Sought After	3	11	1	4	2	4	3,494
Daaris	3	6	2	2	1	1	3,421
Burooj	2	2	1	0	0	1	2,925
Qaffal	2	3	1	0	0	2	2,881
Ribhi	2	4	1	1	1	1	2,881
Tomos	2	2	1	0	0	1	2,763
Cubist	2	3	1	0	0	2	2,700
Skullcap	2	3	1	0	0	2	2,246
Don't Forsake Me	3	10	1	0	1	8	2,165
Maji	3	12	1	3	3	5	1,161

WINNING OWNERS

	Races Won	Value £		Races Won	Value £
Hamdan Al-Maktoum	7	29,505	Saif Ali	1	2,763
Lord Clinton	3	7,162	Lord Hartington	1	2,700
Sir William McAlpine	2	5,979	Christopher Spence	1	2,246
John B Sunley	2	3,760	Saeed Manana	1	1,161
The MSA Partnership	1	3,494			

Favourites	6-19	31.6%	- 1.57	Total winning prize-money			£58,770
Longest winning sequence			2	Average SP of winner			6.0/1
Longest losing sequence			27	Return on stakes invested			-10.8%
1991 Form	20-181	11.0%	- 45.07	1989 Form	26-193	13.5%	- 6.59
1990 Form	24-238	10.1%	-102.01	1988 Form	30-228	13.2%	+ 57.59

D MORRIS (Newmarket)

	No. of Horses	Races Run	1st	2nd	3rd	Unpl	Per cent	£1 Level Stake
2-y-o	4	18	1	3	1	13	5.6	- 10.00
3-y-o	5	21	3	1	2	15	14.3	+ 15.00
4-y-o+	9	53	4	6	1	42	7.5	- 20.75
Totals	18	92	8	10	4	70	8.7	- 15.75

Jan	Feb	Mar	Apr	May	Jun	Jul	Aug	Sep	Oct/Nov
0-0	1-3	1-6	0-3	0-3	2-13	2-20	0-9	2-17	0-18

Winning Jockeys	W-R	£1 Level Stake			W-R	£1 Level Stake
M Tebbutt	4-23	+ 22.00		R Cochrane	1-2	+ 10.00
S Davies	3-38	- 18.75				

Winning Courses						
Yarmouth	3-22	+ 12.00		Leicester	1-4	+ 9.00
Lingfield (AW)	2-4	+ 4.25		Salisbury	1-4	+ 9.00
Doncaster	1-4	+ 4.00				

Winning Horses	Age	Races Run	1st	2nd	3rd	Unpl	Win £
Pytchley Night	5	4	2	0	0	2	13,301
Queen Of Shannon	4	7	2	1	0	4	12,182
Norman Warrior	3	6	1	0	0	5	2,500
Saifan	3	6	1	0	1	4	2,469
Amadeus Aes	3	4	1	1	0	2	2,364
Silent Expression	2	5	1	0	1	3	1,660

Favourites	1-5	20.0%	0.00	Total winning prize-money		£34,476
1991 Form	6-88	6.8%	- 37.50	1990 Form	2-54	3.7%	- 23.00

295

M MOUBARAK (Newmarket)

	No. of Horses	Races Run	1st	2nd	3rd	Unpl	Per cent	£1 Level Stake
2-y-o	15	38	5	9	5	19	13.2	- 22.75
3-y-o	15	61	8	9	7	37	13.1	- 5.62
4-y-o+	6	26	5	4	3	14	19.2	+ 7.75
Totals	36	125	18	22	15	70	14.4	- 20.62

BY MONTH

2-y-o	W-R	Per cent	£1 Level Stake	3-y-o	W-R	Per cent	£1 Level Stake
Mar/Apr	0-0	-	0.00	Mar/Apr	3-13	23.1	- 7.00
May	0-0	-	0.00	May	0-0	-	0.00
June	2-5	40.0	- 1.17	June	0-11	-	- 11.00
July	1-14	7.1	- 12.33	July	4-20	20.0	+ 6.18
August	1-12	8.3	- 8.75	August	1-13	7.7	0.00
September	1-7	14.3	- 0.50	September	0-4	-	- 4.00
Oct/Nov	0-0	-	0.00	Oct/Nov	0-0	-	0.00

4-y-o+	W-R	Per cent	£1 Level Stake	Totals	W-R	Per cent	£1 Level Stake
Mar/Apr	0-7	-	- 5.00	Mar/Apr	3-20	15.0	- 12.00
May	0-0	-	0.00	May	0-0	-	0.00
June	1-3	33.3	+ 3.50	June	3-19	15.8	- 8.67
July	3-8	37.5	+ 16.25	July	8-42	19.0	+ 10.10
August	1-6	16.7	- 3.00	August	3-31	9.7	- 11.75
September	0-2	-	- 2.00	September	1-13	7.7	- 6.50
Oct/Nov	0-0	-	0.00	Oct/Nov	0-0	-	0.00

DISTANCE

2-y-o	W-R	Per cent	£1 Level Stake	3-y-o	W-R	Per cent	£1 Level Stake
5f-6f	5-30	16.7	- 14.75	5f-6f	2-7	28.6	+ 14.00
7f-8f	0-8	-	- 8.00	7f-8f	4-30	13.3	- 4.30
9f-13f	0-0	-	0.00	9f-13f	2-22	9.1	- 13.32
14f+	0-0	-	0.00	14f+	0-2	-	- 2.00

4-y-o+	W-R	Per cent	£1 Level Stake	Totals	W-R	Per cent	£1 Level Stake
5f-6f	0-1	-	- 1.00	5f-6f	7-38	18.4	- 1.75
7f-8f	5-16	31.3	+ 17.75	7f-8f	9-54	16.7	+ 5.45
9f-13f	0-7	-	- 7.00	9f-13f	2-29	6.9	- 20.32
14f+	0-2	-	- 2.00	14f+	0-4	-	- 4.00

TYPE OF RACE

Non-Handicaps	W-R	Per cent	£1 Level Stake	Handicaps	W-R	Per cent	£1 Level Stake
2-y-o	5-35	14.3	- 19.75	2-y-o	0-3	-	- 3.00
3-y-o	5-28	17.9	- 0.12	3-y-o	3-30	10.0	- 2.50
4-y-o+	0-4	-	- 4.00	4-y-o+	3-20	15.0	+ 1.75
Selling	0-0	-	0.00	Selling	0-0	-	0.00
Apprentice	0-0	-	0.00	Apprentice	2-2	100.0	+ 10.00
Amat/Ladies	0-1	-	- 1.00	Amat/Ladies	0-2	-	- 2.00
Totals	10-68	14.7	- 24.87	Totals	8-57	14.0	+ 4.25

COURSE GRADE

	W-R	Per cent	£1 Level Stake
Group 1	10-74	13.5	- 4.80
Group 2	3-19	15.8	- 9.59
Group 3	4-25	16.0	- 14.23
Group 4	1-7	14.3	+ 8.00

FIRST TIME OUT

	W-R	Per cent	£1 Level Stake
2-y-o	4-14	28.6	- 5.25
3-y-o	4-15	26.7	+ 8.70
4-y-o+	0-6	-	- 6.00
Totals	8-35	22.9	- 2.55

JOCKEYS RIDING

	W-R	Per cent	£1 Level Stake		W-R	Per cent	£1 Level Stake
L Dettori	9-60	15.0	- 3.78	C Hawksley	1-2	50.0	+ 4.50
T Quinn	3-9	33.3	+ 4.23	W R Swinburn	1-2	50.0	+ 1.75
S Davies	2-6	33.3	+ 2.50	J Weaver	1-9	11.1	+ 6.00
Julie Krone	1-1	100.0	+ 0.18				

G Baxter	0-6	D Holland	0-2	Icky Fustok	0-1
W Carson	0-4	Miss I Foustok	0-2	J Fortune	0-1
A Cruz	0-3	P Robinson	0-2	Pat Eddery	0-1
G Carter	0-3	D Harrison	0-1	R Cochrane	0-1
G Duffield	0-3	Donna Hayman	0-1	R Hills	0-1
A Munro	0-2	F Norton	0-1	W Ryan	0-1

COURSE RECORD

	Total W-R	Non-Handicaps 2-y-o	Non-Handicaps 3-y-o+	Handicaps 2-y-o	Handicaps 3-y-o+	Per cent	£1 Level Stake
Newmarket	3-17	0-2	1-6	0-0	2-9	17.6	+ 13.50
Pontefract	2-4	1-2	0-1	0-0	1-1	50.0	+ 1.10
Beverley	2-7	1-1	1-2	0-0	0-4	28.6	- 1.33
Ascot	2-8	0-1	1-2	0-0	1-5	25.0	+ 5.00
Doncaster	2-10	0-1	1-5	0-0	1-4	20.0	+ 2.20
Redcar	1-1	0-0	1-1	0-0	0-0	100.0	+ 0.18
Lingfield (AW)	1-1	0-0	0-0	0-0	1-1	100.0	+ 14.00
Brighton	1-4	0-0	0-1	0-0	1-3	25.0	+ 2.50
Sandown	1-4	0-1	0-2	0-0	1-1	25.0	- 0.25
Ripon	1-6	1-3	0-0	0-0	0-3	16.7	- 4.27
Newbury	1-8	1-2	0-1	0-0	0-5	12.5	- 1.50
Goodwood	1-9	1-4	0-0	0-1	0-4	11.1	- 5.75

Moubarak M

Kempton	0-6	Yarmouth	0-4	Folkestone	0-1
Thirsk	0-5	Catterick	0-2	Newcastle	0-1
York	0-5	Epsom	0-2	Salisbury	0-1
Chepstow	0-4	Lingfield	0-2	Warwick	0-1
Haydock	0-4	Nottingham	0-2		
Windsor	0-4	Wolverhampton	0-2		

WINNING HORSES

	Age	Races Run	1st	2nd	3rd	Unpl	Win £
Forest Wind	2	3	2	1	0	0	36,928
Big Leap	3	7	2	2	1	2	24,725
Rose Indien	3	7	2	1	0	4	13,717
Starlight Flyer	5	5	1	1	1	2	10,455
Norfolkiev	6	7	2	1	0	4	10,231
Fast Manouvre	3	2	1	0	1	0	10,052
State Dancer	5	7	2	1	2	2	7,419
Majestic Hawk	2	5	1	0	0	4	2,616
Alasib	2	3	1	0	1	1	2,611
Forest Tiger	3	4	1	0	0	3	2,427
Brightness	3	5	1	0	0	4	1,932
Al Karnak	3	7	1	1	3	2	1,590
Classic Story	2	3	1	0	1	1	1,548

WINNING OWNER

	Races Won	Value £
Ecurie Fustok	18	126,251

Favourites	8-25	32.0%	- 6.12	Total winning prize-money			£126,251
Longest winning sequence			2	Average SP of winner			4.8/1
Longest losing sequence			21	Return on stakes invested			-16.5%
1991 Form	18-128	14.1%	- 10.67	1989 Form	1-44	2.3%	- 40.00
1990 Form	18-101	17.8%	+ 3.18	1988 Form	1-23	4.3%	- 17.00

M P MUGGERIDGE (Marlborough, Wilts)

	No. of Horses	Races Run	1st	2nd	3rd	Unpl	Per cent	£1 Level Stake
2-y-o	3	7	1	0	0	6	14.3	+ 6.00
3-y-o	1	13	1	1	2	9	7.7	+ 4.00
4-y-o+	6	23	0	1	0	22	-	- 23.00
Totals	10	43	2	2	2	37	4.7	- 13.00

Jan	Feb	Mar	Apr	May	Jun	Jul	Aug	Sep	Oct/Nov
0-3	0-3	0-3	0-4	0-3	0-3	0-7	0-6	2-6	0-5

Winning Jockeys		W-R	£1 Level Stake				W-R	£1 Level Stake
A Munro		1-3	+ 14.00		B Rouse		1-3	+ 10.00
Winning Courses								
Lingfield (AW)		1-7	+ 6.00		Brighton		1-8	+ 9.00

Winning Horses	Age	Races Run	1st	2nd	3rd	Unpl	Win £
Duty Sergeant	3	13	1	1	2	9	2,805
Pat Poindestres	2	4	1	0	0	3	2,679

Favourites	0-1			Total winning prize-money			£5,484
1991 Form	3-55	5.5%	+ 48.88	1990 Form	1-42	2.4%	- 25.00

W R MUIR (Lambourn, Berks)

	No. of Horses	Races Run	1st	2nd	3rd	Unpl	Per cent	£1 Level Stake
2-y-o	13	46	1	4	1	40	2.2	- 37.00
3-y-o	8	50	3	4	4	39	6.0	- 4.75
4-y-o+	11	58	3	6	9	40	5.2	- 37.50
Totals	32	154	7	14	14	119	4.5	- 79.25

Jan	Feb	Mar	Apr	May	Jun	Jul	Aug	Sep	Oct/Nov
0-0	0-0	0-6	2-12	0-19	1-16	0-32	2-22	2-29	0-18

Winning Jockeys	W-R	£1 Level Stake			W-R	£1 Level Stake
F Norton	2-3	+ 42.00	W Carson		1-5	+ 3.00
S Whitworth	2-54	- 45.25	M Roberts		1-9	- 5.00
W Woods	1-1	+ 8.00				

Winning Courses						
Brighton	2-13	- 1.75	Newmarket		1-9	+ 25.00
Haydock	1-2	+ 3.50	Sandown		1-9	+ 2.00
Folkestone	1-6	- 2.00	Kempton		1-13	- 4.00

Winning Horses	Age	Races Run	1st	2nd	3rd	Unpl	Win £
Rose Elegance	3	6	2	0	1	3	8,300
Hello My Darling	4	4	1	0	0	3	4,328
Saffaah	5	4	1	1	2	0	3,785
Pair Of Jacks	2	7	1	1	0	5	2,595
Sure Lord	3	8	1	2	1	4	2,364
Zeboim	6	7	1	0	4	2	1,828

Favourites	1-6	16.7%	- 2.00	Total winning prize-money		£23,200
1991 Form	13-97	13.4%	- 9.08			

P G MURPHY (Bristol, Avon)

	No. of Horses	Races Run	1st	2nd	3rd	Unpl	Per cent	£1 Level Stake
2-y-o	2	3	0	0	0	3	-	- 3.00
3-y-o	6	6	3	1	1	1	50.0	+ 24.00
4-y-o+	0	0	0	0	0	0	-	0.00
Totals	8	9	3	1	1	4	33.3	+ 21.00

Jan	Feb	Mar	Apr	May	Jun	Jul	Aug	Sep	Oct/Nov
0-0	0-0	0-0	0-0	0-0	0-0	0-0	0-0	0-0	3-9

Winning Jockeys	W-R	£1 Level Stake			W-R	£1 Level Stake
S Drowne	2-3	+ 21.00	J Williams		1-2	+ 4.00

Winning Courses						
Leicester	2-3	+ 16.00	Doncaster		1-1	+ 10.00

Winning Horses	Age	Races Run	1st	2nd	3rd	Unpl	Win £
Mexican Dancer	3	1	1	0	0	0	2,784
Jigsaw Boy	3	1	1	0	0	0	2,721
Ceatharlach	3	1	1	0	0	0	2,658

Favourites	0-2		Total winning prize-money	£8,163

W J MUSSON (Newmarket)

	No. of Horses	Races Run	1st	2nd	3rd	Unpl	Per cent	£1 Level Stake
2-y-o	4	11	0	0	1	10	-	- 11.00
3-y-o	6	41	2	8	1	30	4.9	- 28.00
4-y-o+	12	71	4	7	4	56	5.6	- 40.75
Totals	22	123	6	15	6	96	4.9	- 79.75

Jan	Feb	Mar	Apr	May	Jun	Jul	Aug	Sep	Oct/Nov
1-9	0-5	0-5	0-12	0-10	0-13	2-18	1-13	2-16	0-22

Winning Jockeys	W-R	£1 Level Stake			W-R	£1 Level Stake
J Reid	2-10	+ 1.50	D McCabe		1-9	0.00
Mrs J Musson	1-2	+ 1.25	P Bowe		1-19	- 4.00
Pat Eddery	1-2	+ 2.50				

Winning Courses	W-R	£1 Level Stake			W-R	£1 Level Stake
Ayr	1-1	+ 2.25	Leicester		1-9	- 5.00
Folkestone	1-7	+ 2.00	Windsor		1-12	- 4.50
Southwell (AW)	1-7	+ 8.00	Newmarket		1-16	- 11.50

Winning Horses	Age	Races Run	1st	2nd	3rd	Unpl	Win £
Swift Silver	5	10	2	2	1	5	5,635
Rise Up Singing	4	9	1	0	0	8	3,623
Bit On The Side	3	9	1	2	0	6	3,420
Broughton's Tango	3	9	1	1	1	6	2,490
Foolish Touch	10	20	1	5	1	13	2,285

Favourites	2-13	15.4%	- 5.75	Total winning prize-money			£17,452

1991 Form	9-114	7.9%	- 51.25	1989 Form	6-131	4.6%	- 103.37
1990 Form	4-154	2.6%	- 134.00	1988 Form	10-132	7.6%	- 62.50

M P NAUGHTON (Richmond, North Yorks)

	No. of Horses	Races Run	1st	2nd	3rd	Unpl	Per cent	£1 Level Stake
2-y-o	1	1	0	0	0	1	-	- 1.00
3-y-o	6	34	7	5	2	20	20.6	+ 6.33
4-y-o+	32	307	25	18	35	229	8.1	- 112.74
Totals	39	342	32	23	37	250	9.4	- 107.41

BY MONTH

2-y-o	W-R	Per cent	£1 Level Stake	3-y-o	W-R	Per cent	£1 Level Stake
January	0-0	-	0.00	January	0-0	-	0.00
February	0-0	-	0.00	February	0-0	-	0.00
March	0-0	-	0.00	March	0-1	-	- 1.00
April	0-1	-	- 1.00	April	0-2	-	- 2.00
May	0-0	-	0.00	May	1-5	20.0	+ 12.00
June	0-0	-	0.00	June	3-8	37.5	+ 5.75
July	0-0	-	0.00	July	2-4	50.0	- 0.42
August	0-0	-	0.00	August	1-5	20.0	+ 1.00
September	0-0	-	0.00	September	0-4	-	- 4.00
Oct/Nov	0-0	-	0.00	Oct/Nov	0-5	-	- 5.00

4-y-o+	W-R	Per cent	£1 Level Stake	Totals	W-R	Per cent	£1 Level Stake
January	3-21	14.3	+ 11.00	January	3-21	14.3	+ 11.00
February	0-12	-	- 12.00	February	0-12	-	- 12.00
March	1-10	10.0	0.00	March	1-11	9.1	- 1.00
April	0-21	-	- 21.00	April	0-24	-	- 24.00
May	2-43	4.7	- 27.00	May	3-48	6.3	- 15.00
June	5-42	11.9	- 23.50	June	8-50	16.0	- 17.75
July	8-55	14.5	- 23.24	July	10-59	16.9	- 23.66
August	3-36	8.3	+ 16.00	August	4-41	9.8	+ 17.00
September	2-35	5.7	- 9.00	September	2-39	5.1	- 13.00
Oct/Nov	1-32	3.1	- 24.00	Oct/Nov	1-37	2.7	- 29.00

DISTANCE

	W-R	Per cent	£1 Level Stake		W-R	Per cent	£1 Level Stake
2-y-o				3-y-o			
5f-6f	0-1	-	- 1.00	5f-6f	6-20	30.0	+ 14.33
7f-8f	0-0	-	0.00	7f-8f	0-7	-	- 7.00
9f-13f	0-0	-	0.00	9f-13f	0-2	-	- 2.00
14f+	0-0	-	0.00	14f+	1-5	20.0	+ 1.00
		Per cent	£1 Level Stake			Per cent	£1 Level Stake
4-y-o+	W-R			Totals	W-R		
5f-6f	13-127	10.2	- 45.87	5f-6f	19-148	12.8	- 32.54
7f-8f	0-74	-	- 74.00	7f-8f	0-81	-	- 81.00
9f-13f	11-89	12.4	+ 14.13	9f-13f	11-91	12.1	+ 12.13
14f+	1-17	5.9	- 7.00	14f+	2-22	9.1	- 6.00

TYPE OF RACE

	W-R	Per cent	£1 Level Stake		W-R	Per cent	£1 Level Stake
Non-Handicaps	0-1	-	- 1.00	Handicaps	0-0	-	0.00
2-y-o	0-1	-	- 1.00	2-y-o	0-0	-	0.00
3-y-o	1-5	20.0	+ 12.00	3-y-o	5-26	19.2	- 7.67
4-y-o+	4-39	10.3	- 12.25	4-y-o+	17-215	7.9	- 71.49
Selling	0-12	-	- 12.00	Selling	1-11	9.1	- 4.00
Apprentice	0-1	-	- 1.00	Apprentice	2-16	12.5	- 2.00
Amat/Ladies	0-1	-	- 1.00	Amat/Ladies	2-15	13.3	- 7.00
Totals	5-59	8.5	- 15.25	Totals	27-283	9.5	- 92.16

COURSE GRADE

	W-R	Per cent	£1 Level Stake
Group 1	6-99	6.1	- 70.34
Group 2	4-81	4.9	- 56.50
Group 3	8-58	13.8	+ 10.00
Group 4	14-104	13.5	+ 9.43

FIRST TIME OUT

	W-R	Per cent	£1 Level Stake
2-y-o	0-1	-	- 1.00
3-y-o	0-1	-	- 1.00
4-y-o+	0-31	-	- 31.00
Totals	0-33	-	- 33.00

JOCKEYS RIDING

	W-R	Per cent	£1 Level Stake		W-R	Per cent	£1 Level Stake
J Weaver	8-57	14.0	- 25.57	A Dobbin	1-3	33.3	+ 6.00
K Fallon	7-26	26.9	+ 42.75	K Darley	1-4	25.0	+ 2.00
M Roberts	4-19	21.1	- 1.34	A Munro	1-9	11.1	- 6.25
B Doyle	3-29	10.3	+ 3.00	Miss P Robson	1-9	11.1	- 6.50
Jaki Houston	2-51	3.9	- 24.00	N Connorton	1-11	9.1	+ 6.00
C Munday	1-2	50.0	+ 3.00	L Charnock	1-17	5.9	- 7.00
Mr R D Green	1-2	50.0	+ 3.50				

G Hind	0-23	D Nicholls	0-2	J Fortune	0-1
D Harrison	0-11	O Pears	0-2	J Reid	0-1
D Holland	0-8	Paul Eddery	0-2	Julie Krone	0-1
J Fanning	0-8	R Cochrane	0-2	L Piggott	0-1
S Wynne	0-7	R Price	0-2	M Hills	0-1
D McKeown	0-5	S Webster	0-2	Miss A Bycroft	0-1
Mr R Greene	0-4	A Garth	0-1	Mrs A Farrell	0-1
G Carter	0-3	Antoinette Armes	0-1	S Maloney	0-1
A McGlone	0-2	Carol Davison	0-1	Susanne Berneklint	0-1
C Hawksley	0-2	D Biggs	0-1	T Quinn	0-1
D Carson	0-2	G Duffield	0-1	W Carson	0-1

COURSE RECORD

	Total W-R	Non-Handicaps 2-y-o	3-y-o+	Handicaps 2-y-o	3-y-o+	Per cent	£1 Level Stake
Hamilton	6-32	0-0	1-8	0-0	5-24	18.8	+ 23.25
Edinburgh	5-28	0-0	0-6	0-0	5-22	17.9	+ 19.38
Catterick	4-25	0-0	0-6	0-0	4-19	16.0	- 6.45
Sandown	3-9	0-0	1-1	0-0	2-8	33.3	+ 1.91
Redcar	3-35	0-0	1-3	0-0	2-32	8.6	- 18.50
Lingfield (AW)	2-13	0-0	1-3	0-0	1-10	15.4	+ 8.00
Ayr	2-18	0-0	0-5	0-0	2-13	11.1	- 9.25
Southwell (AW)	2-31	0-0	0-11	0-0	2-20	6.5	- 10.00
Leicester	1-3	0-0	0-0	0-0	1-3	33.3	+ 0.75
Carlisle	1-5	0-0	0-0	0-0	1-5	20.0	+ 0.50
Beverley	1-11	0-0	0-2	0-0	1-9	9.1	- 2.00
Newcastle	1-16	0-0	1-1	0-0	0-15	6.3	- 7.00
Ripon	1-17	0-1	0-0	0-0	1-16	5.9	- 9.00

Thirsk	0-27	Pontefract	0-9	Wolverhampton	0-2
Haydock	0-19	Doncaster	0-8	Ascot	0-1
York	0-15	Nottingham	0-3	Epsom	0-1
Newmarket	0-11	Chester	0-2	Kempton	0-1

WINNING HORSES

	Age	Races Run	1st	2nd	3rd	Unpl	Win £
Carlingford	6	13	5	0	1	7	11,963
Optical	3	8	3	1	1	3	7,734
Finjan	5	8	3	2	0	3	7,556
Invigilate	3	13	3	3	0	7	7,101
Arabat	5	10	2	0	1	7	5,623
J P Morgan	4	18	2	0	4	12	5,474
Prince Belfort	4	14	2	0	1	11	5,108
Best Effort	6	14	2	1	2	9	4,230
Pallium	4	13	1	0	2	10	3,561
Jubran	6	9	1	1	1	6	3,494
Rolling The Bones	3	5	1	0	0	4	2,801

North Of Watford	7	7	1	1	1	4	2,758
Absolution	8	14	1	1	2	10	2,723
Rock Opera	4	11	1	1	2	7	2,477
Lord Advocate	4	19	1	5	1	12	2,383
Mississippi Beat	5	8	1	1	0	6	2,363
Frescobaldo	6	3	1	1	1	0	2,226
Flying Down To Rio	4	16	1	0	2	13	1,814

WINNING OWNERS

	Races Won	Value £		Races Won	Value £
Mrs H H Wane	14	35,178	Mrs Carole Sykes	2	5,108
Raymond Miquel	4	9,704	Mrs Elke Scullion	1	3,494
W J Kelly	3	7,758	Philip Davies	1	2,477
Mrs R Olivier	3	7,556	Michael O'Grady	1	2,363
M F Hyman	2	5,524	M P Naughton	1	2,226

Favourites	11-38	28.9%	- 7.41	Total winning prize-money			£81,388
Longest winning sequence			3	Average SP of winner			6.3/1
Longest losing sequence			53	Return on stakes invested			-31.4%
1991 Form	21-201	10.4%	- 42.52	1989 Form	19-164	11.6%	- 7.75
1990 Form	12-219	5.5%	-102.17	1988 Form	8-108	7.4%	- 15.00

T J NAUGHTON (Epsom, Surrey)

	No. of Horses	Races Run	1st	2nd	3rd	Unpl	Per cent	£1 Level Stake
2-y-o	9	28	1	3	1	23	3.6	+ 6.00
3-y-o	8	33	5	3	3	22	15.2	+ 10.75
4-y-o+	6	52	3	4	8	37	5.8	- 2.00
Totals	23	113	9	10	12	82	8.0	+ 14.75

Jan	Feb	Mar	Apr	May	Jun	Jul	Aug	Sep	Oct/Nov
0-3	0-6	0-0	1-7	1-10	1-20	0-19	2-20	3-14	1-14

Winning Jockeys	W-R	£1 Level Stake		W-R	£1 Level Stake
G Carter	4-33	+ 27.50	J Fanning	1-5	+ 16.00
D Biggs	2-5	+ 11.25	D Holland	1-14	+ 7.00
Paul Eddery	1-4	+ 5.00			

Winning Courses					
Folkestone	3-19	+ 28.50	Goodwood	1-9	- 5.75
Wolverhampton	1-2	+ 11.00	Lingfield	1-12	+ 9.00
Sandown	1-5	+ 8.00	Lingfield (AW)	1-14	+ 7.00
Epsom	1-9	0.00			

			Races					Win
Winning Horses		Age	Run	1st	2nd	3rd	Unpl	£
Ideal Candidate		3	7	3	2	0	2	10,207
Ain'tlifelikethat		5	14	2	2	3	7	5,101
Clare Kerry Lass		3	4	1	1	0	2	3,019
Allmosa		3	9	1	0	3	5	2,679
Fabriana		2	1	1	0	0	0	2,070
Catalani		7	11	1	1	4	5	1,730
Favourites	1-9	11.1%	- 5.75	Total winning prize-money				£24,805
1991 Form	6-88	6.8%	- 39.25					

C R NELSON (Upper Lambourn, Berks)

		No. of Horses	Races Run	1st	2nd	3rd	Unpl	Per cent	£1 Level Stake
2-y-o		1	2	0	0	0	2	-	- 2.00
3-y-o		12	55	5	4	4	42	9.1	- 7.75
4-y-o+		6	31	2	6	2	21	6.5	- 19.50
Totals		19	88	7	10	6	65	8.0	- 29.25

Jan	Feb	Mar	Apr	May	Jun	Jul	Aug	Sep	Oct/Nov
0-2	1-5	0-2	0-14	1-10	2-22	2-17	0-0	0-11	1-5

Winning Jockeys	W-R	£1 Level Stake		W-R	£1 Level Stake
N Adams	4-13	+ 29.75	Miss J Winter	1-2	+ 2.00
J Lowe	1-1	+ 3.50	Paul Eddery	1-4	+ 3.50

Winning Courses	W-R	£1 Level Stake		W-R	£1 Level Stake
Southwell (AW)	3-7	+ 8.75	Salisbury	1-5	+ 21.00
Lingfield (AW)	2-11	+ 0.50	Bath	1-6	- 0.50

		Races					Win
Winning Horses	Age	Run	1st	2nd	3rd	Unpl	£
Thunderbird One	3	5	2	0	1	2	5,196
Awesome Power	6	10	2	5	1	2	5,000
Cool Society	3	6	1	0	0	5	2,826
Themeda	3	7	1	0	0	6	2,265
Whitehall	3	9	1	1	1	6	2,167

Favourites	2-5	40.0%	+ 2.25	Total winning prize-money			£17,454
1991 Form	11-115	9.6%	- 28.18	1989 Form	19-143	13.3%	- 47.41
1990 Form	30-189	15.9%	+ 37.07	1988 Form	22-184	12.0%	- 35.03

D NICHOLSON (Temple Guiting, Glos)

	No. of Horses	Races Run	1st	2nd	3rd	Unpl	Per cent	£1 Level Stake
2-y-o	0	0	0	0	0	0	-	0.00
3-y-o	2	7	1	0	1	5	14.3	+ 60.00
4-y-o+	0	0	0	0	0	0	-	0.00
Totals	2	7	1	0	1	5	14.3	+ 60.00

Jan	Feb	Mar	Apr	May	Jun	Jul	Aug	Sep	Oct/Nov
0-0	0-0	0-0	0-0	0-1	1-2	0-2	0-1	0-1	0-0

Winning Jockey	W-R	£1 Level Stake	Winning Course	W-R	£1 Level Stake
J Williams	1-4	+ 63.00	Leicester	1-3	+ 64.00

Winning Horse	Age	Races Run	1st	2nd	3rd	Unpl	Win £
Clurican	3	4	1	0	1	2	2,040

Favourites	0-0	Total winning prize-money	£2,040

1991 Form	0-8	1989 Form	0-0
1990 Form	0-5	1988 Form	0-5

S G NORTON (Barnsley, South Yorks)

	No. of Horses	Races Run	1st	2nd	3rd	Unpl	Per cent	£1 Level Stake
2-y-o	12	55	4	11	6	34	7.3	- 36.31
3-y-o	11	83	9	8	9	57	10.8	- 26.00
4-y-o+	10	43	12	3	3	25	27.9	+ 41.88
Totals	33	181	25	22	18	116	13.8	- 20.43

BY MONTH

2-y-o	W-R	Per cent	£1 Level Stake	3-y-o	W-R	Per cent	£1 Level Stake
January	0-0	-	0.00	January	0-0	-	0.00
February	0-0	-	0.00	February	0-0	-	0.00
March	0-0	-	0.00	March	2-10	20.0	- 0.50
April	0-1	-	- 1.00	April	1-14	7.1	- 5.00
May	0-6	-	- 6.00	May	1-14	7.1	- 10.75
June	0-8	-	- 8.00	June	2-15	13.3	- 6.75
July	1-10	10.0	+ 1.00	July	1-10	10.0	- 5.00
August	2-7	28.6	- 2.56	August	0-3	-	- 3.00
September	1-8	12.5	- 4.75	September	2-9	22.2	+ 13.00
Oct/Nov	0-15	-	- 15.00	Oct/Nov	0-8	-	- 8.00

4-y-o+	W-R	Per cent	£1 Level Stake	Totals	W-R	Per cent	£1 Level Stake
January	0-0	-	0.00	January	0-0	-	0.00
February	0-1	-	- 1.00	February	0-1	-	- 1.00
March	2-3	66.7	+ 16.00	March	4-13	30.8	+ 15.50
April	1-4	25.0	+ 1.50	April	2-19	10.5	- 4.50
May	0-8	-	- 8.00	May	1-28	3.6	- 24.75
June	3-12	25.0	+ 0.88	June	5-35	14.3	- 13.87
July	1-4	25.0	- 3.00	July	3-24	12.5	- 7.00
August	3-4	75.0	+ 22.50	August	5-14	35.7	+ 16.94
September	1-3	33.3	+ 2.00	September	4-20	20.0	+ 10.25
Oct/Nov	1-4	25.0	+ 11.00	Oct/Nov	1-27	3.7	- 12.00

DISTANCE

2-y-o	W-R	Per cent	£1 Level Stake	3-y-o	W-R	Per cent	£1 Level Stake
5f-6f	3-32	9.4	- 16.56	5f-6f	0-16	-	- 16.00
7f-8f	1-21	4.8	- 17.75	7f-8f	5-28	17.9	+ 14.00
9f-13f	0-2	-	- 2.00	9f-13f	4-26	15.4	- 11.00
14f+	0-0	-	0.00	14f+	0-13	-	- 13.00

4-y-o+	W-R	Per cent	£1 Level Stake	Totals	W-R	Per cent	£1 Level Stake
5f-6f	0-3	-	- 3.00	5f-6f	3-51	5.9	- 35.56
7f-8f	0-5	-	- 5.00	7f-8f	6-54	11.1	- 8.75
9f-13f	8-21	38.1	+ 46.50	9f-13f	12-49	24.5	+ 33.50
14f+	4-14	28.6	+ 3.38	14f+	4-27	14.8	- 9.62

TYPE OF RACE

Non-Handicaps	W-R	Per cent	£1 Level Stake	Handicaps	W-R	Per cent	£1 Level Stake
2-y-o	4-38	10.5	- 19.31	2-y-o	0-13	-	- 13.00
3-y-o	4-25	16.0	+ 3.50	3-y-o	4-44	9.1	- 19.00
4-y-o+	0-2	-	- 2.00	4-y-o+	10-34	29.4	+ 20.88
Selling	0-12	-	- 12.00	Selling	0-2	-	- 2.00
Apprentice	0-2	-	- 2.00	Apprentice	3-6	50.0	+ 27.50
Amat/Ladies	0-1	-	- 1.00	Amat/Ladies	0-2	-	- 2.00
Totals	8-80	10.0	- 32.81	Totals	17-101	16.8	+ 12.38

COURSE GRADE

	W-R	Per cent	£1 Level Stake
Group 1	6-48	12.5	+ 0.50
Group 2	3-38	7.9	- 9.75
Group 3	5-41	12.2	- 20.81
Group 4	11-54	20.4	+ 9.63

FIRST TIME OUT

	W-R	Per cent	£1 Level Stake
2-y-o	1-12	8.3	- 9.00
3-y-o	1-11	9.1	- 5.00
4-y-o+	2-9	22.2	+ 10.00
Totals	4-32	12.5	- 4.00

JOCKEYS RIDING

	W-R	Per cent	£1 Level Stake		W-R	Per cent	£1 Level Stake
O Pears	11-67	16.4	+ 8.38	M Roberts	1-2	50.0	- 0.50
K Darley	5-22	22.7	+ 4.50	G Parkin	1-2	50.0	+ 13.00
N Connorton	2-7	28.6	+ 15.00	L Piggott	1-3	33.3	+ 2.00
J Fortune	2-12	16.7	- 5.06	D Nicholls	1-6	16.7	- 2.75
S D Williams	1-1	100.0	+ 4.00				

L Charnock	0-13	A Garth	0-1	M Humphries	0-1
F Norton	0-10	B Crossley	0-1	Mr S Lyons	0-1
S Maloney	0-6	D Moffatt	0-1	Mr S Swiers	0-1
C Hawksley	0-5	Dale Gibson	0-1	Mrs J Crossley	0-1
A Proud	0-4	J Fanning	0-1	N Carlisle	0-1
B Raymond	0-2	J Lowe	0-1	R Cochrane	0-1
J Quinn	0-2	K L Tsui	0-1	W Carson	0-1
M Wood	0-2	M Hills	0-1		

COURSE RECORD

	Total W-R	Non-Handicaps 2-y-o	3-y-o+	Handicaps 2-y-o	3-y-o+	Per cent	£1 Level Stake
Southwell (AW)	7-26	1-8	2-6	0-0	4-12	26.9	+ 11.50
Haydock	3-12	0-2	0-1	0-1	3-8	25.0	+ 9.50
Chester	3-14	0-4	0-1	0-1	3-8	21.4	+ 14.25
Pontefract	3-16	2-5	0-4	0-1	1-6	18.8	- 4.56
Catterick	2-12	0-2	0-3	0-2	2-5	16.7	- 0.37
Nottingham	1-4	0-2	0-0	0-0	1-2	25.0	+ 1.50
Carlisle	1-5	0-1	1-3	0-0	0-1	20.0	+ 6.00
Newcastle	1-5	0-1	1-1	0-1	0-2	20.0	+ 6.00
Wolverhampton	1-5	0-0	0-1	0-0	1-4	20.0	- 1.50
Hamilton	1-9	1-2	0-4	0-0	0-3	11.1	- 5.75
York	1-9	0-2	0-1	0-1	1-5	11.1	- 8.00
Doncaster	1-15	0-4	0-1	0-3	1-7	6.7	0.00

Redcar	0-12	Thirsk	0-4	Goodwood	0-1
Beverley	0-11	Newmarket	0-3	Lingfield (AW)	0-1
Ripon	0-8	Ascot	0-2	Yarmouth	0-1
Edinburgh	0-5	Ayr	0-1		

WINNING HORSES

	Age	Races Run	1st	2nd	3rd	Unpl	Win £
Mr Confusion	4	5	5	0	0	0	59,035
Our Aisling	4	8	3	1	0	4	15,888
Eriny	3	9	3	0	1	5	5,706
Lord Hastie	4	11	2	2	1	6	5,203
Stoproveritate	3	13	2	1	1	9	4,672
Five To Seven	3	11	2	2	2	5	4,628
Shabanaz	7	2	1	0	0	1	3,933
Salman	6	5	1	0	0	4	3,003
Goodbye Millie	2	7	1	1	0	5	2,685

Cure The King	2	6	1	2	0	3	2,678
Celestial Key	2	5	1	0	0	4	2,513
Debsy Do	3	12	1	3	2	6	2,322
Northern Kingdom	3	7	1	2	1	3	1,725
Astrac Trio	2	5	1	0	0	4	1,182

WINNING OWNERS

	Races Won	Value £		Races Won	Value £
R Fenwick-Gibson	5	59,035	Peter Hayes	1	3,933
A K Smeaton	3	15,888	G Corbett	1	2,685
R W Cousins	3	5,706	P D Savill	1	2,678
S G Norton	2	5,325	M J Brodrick	1	2,513
Mrs Joy Bendall	2	5,203	P A Deal	1	1,725
John D Clark	2	4,672	T L Beecroft	1	1,182
The Five To Seven Partnership	2	4,628			

Favourites	7-21	33.3%	+ 0.07	Total winning prize-money		£115,173
Longest winning sequence			2	Average SP of winner		5.7/1
Longest losing sequence			25	Return on stakes invested		-8.0%
1991 Form	19-153	12.4%	- 7.27	1989 Form	11-254	4.3%	-196.52
1990 Form	20-199	10.1%	- 39.25	1988 Form	33-466	7.1%	-205.81

W A O'GORMAN (Newmarket)

	No. of Horses	Races Run	1st	2nd	3rd	Unpl	Per cent	£1 Level Stake
2-y-o	11	35	4	7	3	21	11.4	- 23.54
3-y-o	12	68	7	12	10	39	10.3	- 39.41
4-y-o+	10	63	10	14	9	30	15.9	- 23.51
Totals	33	166	21	33	22	90	12.7	- 86.46

BY MONTH

2-y-o	W-R	Per cent	£1 Level Stake	3-y-o	W-R	Per cent	£1 Level Stake
January	0-0	-	0.00	January	0-10	-	- 10.00
February	0-0	-	0.00	February	0-13	-	- 13.00
March	0-0	-	0.00	March	6-11	54.5	+ 16.23
April	0-2	-	- 2.00	April	0-4	-	- 4.00
May	0-4	-	- 4.00	May	0-7	-	- 7.00
June	1-5	20.0	- 3.71	June	1-7	14.3	- 5.64
July	2-8	25.0	- 3.83	July	0-7	-	- 7.00
August	0-3	-	- 3.00	August	0-2	-	- 2.00
September	0-2	-	- 2.00	September	0-2	-	- 2.00
Oct/Nov	1-11	9.1	- 5.00	Oct/Nov	0-5	-	- 5.00

O'Gorman W A

4-y-o+	W-R	Per cent	£1 Level Stake		Totals	W-R	Per cent	£1 Level Stake
January	4-13	30.8	+	2.75	January	4-23	17.4	-	7.25
February	1-12	8.3	-	9.62	February	1-25	4.0	-	22.62
March	2-7	28.6	-	2.77	March	8-18	44.4	+	13.46
April	0-4	-	-	4.00	April	0-10	-	-	10.00
May	0-4	-	-	4.00	May	0-15	-	-	15.00
June	2-5	40.0	+	9.50	June	4-17	23.5	+	0.15
July	0-2	-	-	2.00	July	2-17	11.8	-	12.83
August	0-4	-	-	4.00	August	0-9	-	-	9.00
September	0-5	-	-	5.00	September	0-9	-	-	9.00
Oct/Nov	1-7	14.3	-	4.37	Oct/Nov	2-23	8.7	-	14.37

DISTANCE

2-y-o	W-R	Per cent	£1 Level Stake		3-y-o	W-R	Per cent	£1 Level Stake	
5f-6f	4-32	12.5	-	20.54	5f-6f	3-28	10.7	-	15.77
7f-8f	0-3	-	-	3.00	7f-8f	4-36	11.1	-	19.64
9f-13f	0-0	-		0.00	9f-13f	0-4	-	-	4.00
14f+	0-0	-		0.00	14f+	0-0	-		0.00

4-y-o+	W-R	Per cent	£1 Level Stake		Totals	W-R	Per cent	£1 Level Stake	
5f-6f	5-18	27.8	+	8.25	5f-6f	12-78	15.4	-	28.06
7f-8f	5-43	11.6	-	29.76	7f-8f	9-82	11.0	-	52.40
9f-13f	0-2	-	-	2.00	9f-13f	0-6	-	-	6.00
14f+	0-0	-		0.00	14f+	0-0	-		0.00

TYPE OF RACE

Non-Handicaps	W-R	Per cent	£1 Level Stake		Handicaps	W-R	Per cent	£1 Level Stake	
2-y-o	4-29	13.8	-	17.54	2-y-o	0-3	-	-	3.00
3-y-o	5-28	17.9	-	9.41	3-y-o	2-38	5.3	-	28.00
4-y-o+	7-22	31.8	-	3.26	4-y-o+	2-37	5.4	-	22.25
Selling	0-4	-	-	4.00	Selling	0-0	-		0.00
Apprentice	0-1	-	-	1.00	Apprentice	1-4	25.0	+	2.00
Amat/Ladies	0-0	-		0.00	Amat/Ladies	0-0	-		0.00
Totals	16-84	19.0	-	35.21	Totals	5-82	6.1	-	51.25

COURSE GRADE					FIRST TIME OUT				
	W-R	Per cent	£1 Level Stake			W-R	Per cent	£1 Level Stake	
Group 1	0-31	-	-	31.00	2-y-o	0-11	-	-	11.00
Group 2	1-6	16.7	-	4.60	3-y-o	0-12	-	-	12.00
Group 3	3-26	11.5	-	12.04	4-y-o+	1-9	11.1	-	6.00
Group 4	17-103	16.5	-	38.82					
					Totals	1-32	3.1	-	29.00

JOCKEYS RIDING

	W-R	Per cent	£1 Level Stake		W-R	Per cent	£1 Level Stake
Emma O'Gorman	17-124	13.7	- 50.18	D Holland	1-6	16.7	- 4.33
G Carter	1-3	33.3	- 1.64	R Cochrane	1-7	14.3	- 5.60
Pat Eddery	1-4	25.0	- 2.71				

A Munro	0-6	D Biggs	0-1	M Hills	0-1
L Dettori	0-3	D McKeown	0-1	N Adams	0-1
B Doyle	0-2	D Nicholls	0-1	Paul Eddery	0-1
J Fortune	0-2	G Duffield	0-1		
C Rutter	0-1	J Williams	0-1		

COURSE RECORD

	Total W-R	Non-Handicaps 2-y-o	3-y-o+	Handicaps 2-y-o	3-y-o+	Per cent	£1 Level Stake
Lingfield (AW)	11-48	0-4	7-19	0-0	4-25	22.9	- 6.05
Southwell (AW)	5-48	1-3	4-22	0-0	0-23	10.4	- 31.77
Bath	1-2	0-0	0-0	0-0	1-2	50.0	+ 9.00
Brighton	1-2	0-0	1-1	0-0	0-1	50.0	- 0.60
Catterick	1-2	1-2	0-0	0-0	0-0	50.0	+ 4.00
Nottingham	1-2	1-2	0-0	0-0	0-0	50.0	- 0.33
Windsor	1-3	1-2	0-0	0-0	0-1	33.3	- 1.71

Newmarket	0-18	Kempton	0-3	Goodwood	0-1
Yarmouth	0-8	Redcar	0-2	Newbury	0-1
Leicester	0-6	Sandown	0-2	Salisbury	0-1
Newcastle	0-4	Warwick	0-2	Thirsk	0-1
Pontefract	0-4	Beverley	0-1	York	0-1
Folkestone	0-3	Doncaster	0-1		

WINNING HORSES

	Age	Races Run	1st	2nd	3rd	Unpl	Win £
African Chimes	5	15	7	2	0	6	20,063
Appealing Times	3	12	3	1	2	6	8,161
Sally's Son	6	12	2	4	2	4	4,819
Joyofracing	2	8	2	3	1	2	4,353
Saseedo	2	4	1	1	0	2	2,532
Penang Star	2	4	1	1	1	1	2,454
Lord Naskra	3	5	1	0	1	3	2,187
Blake End	3	5	1	2	0	2	1,932
Badawiah	3	9	1	1	0	7	1,932
Tara's Delight	5	8	1	1	1	5	1,721
Cellito	3	10	1	3	0	6	895

WINNING OWNERS

	Races Won	Value £		Races Won	Value £
D G Wheatley	7	20,063	Curley O'Gorman	1	2,187
Times Of Wigan	3	8,161	Tamdown Ltd	1	1,932
N S Yong	3	6,807	Maclaine Racing	1	1,721
W A O'Gorman	2	4,819	R A Meadows	1	895
S Fustok	2	4,464			

Favourites	11-37	29.7%	- 12.54	Total winning prize-money			£51,050
Longest winning sequence			2	Average SP of winner			2.8/1
Longest losing sequence			33	Return on stakes invested			-52.1%
1991 Form	29-232	12.5%	- 95.24	1989 Form	10-78	12.8%	- 26.58
1990 Form	51-209	24.4%	+ 25.24	1988 Form	24-133	18.0%	- 7.05

F J O'MAHONY (Lingfield, Surrey)

	No. of Horses	Races Run	1st	2nd	3rd	Unpl	Per cent	£1 Level Stake
2-y-o	0	0	0	0	0	0	-	0.00
3-y-o	0	0	0	0	0	0	-	0.00
4-y-o+	2	20	3	5	1	11	15.0	- 10.17
Totals	2	20	3	5	1	11	15.0	- 10.17

Jan	Feb	Mar	Apr	May	Jun	Jul	Aug	Sep	Oct/Nov
0-0	0-4	0-1	0-0	0-3	0-2	2-3	1-2	0-2	0-3

Winning Jockeys	W-R	£1 Level Stake		W-R	£1 Level Stake
W R Swinburn	2-5	+ 0.50	W Carson	1-2	+ 2.33

Winning Courses	W-R	£1 Level Stake		W-R	£1 Level Stake
Newbury	1-1	+ 3.33	Newmarket	1-4	+ 0.50
Doncaster	1-2	- 1.00			

Winning Horse	Age	Races Run	1st	2nd	3rd	Unpl	Win £
Mull House	5	12	3	4	0	5	14,875

Favourites	1-2	50.0%	+ 2.33	Total winning prize-money		£14,875

1991 Form	0-3		1990 Form	0-8

J J O'NEILL (Penrith, Cumbria)

	No. of Horses	Races Run	1st	2nd	3rd	Unpl	Per cent	£1 Level Stake
2-y-o	6	20	1	1	3	15	5.0	- 10.50
3-y-o	4	9	0	0	0	9	-	- 9.00
4-y-o+	15	33	0	0	1	32	-	- 33.00
Totals	25	62	1	1	4	56	1.6	- 52.50

Jan	Feb	Mar	Apr	May	Jun	Jul	Aug	Sep	Oct/Nov
0-0	0-0	0-2	0-12	0-9	0-3	0-3	0-11	0-16	1-6

		W-R	£1 Level Stake			W-R	£1 Level Stake
Winning Jockey				Winning Course			
Pat Eddery		1-1	+ 8.50	Doncaster		1-3	+ 6.50

	Age	Races Run	1st	2nd	3rd	Unpl	Win £
Winning Horse							
Reasons For Love	2	6	1	0	2	3	2,742

Favourites	0-4	Total winning prize-money	£2,742

1991 Form	2-68	2.9%	- 56.00	1989 Form	0-51		
1990 Form	8-37	21.6%	+ 2.00	1988 Form	1-35	2.9%	- 24.00

M O'NEILL (Lydiate, Merseyside)

	No. of Horses	Races Run	1st	2nd	3rd	Unpl	Per cent	£1 Level Stake
2-y-o	1	1	0	0	0	1	-	- 1.00
3-y-o	6	27	0	2	4	21	-	- 27.00
4-y-o+	8	40	2	1	4	33	5.0	- 2.00
Totals	15	68	2	3	8	55	2.9	- 30.00

Jan	Feb	Mar	Apr	May	Jun	Jul	Aug	Sep	Oct/Nov
1-3	0-1	0-5	1-16	0-19	0-10	0-9	0-5	0-0	0-0

		W-R	£1 Level Stake			W-R	£1 Level Stake
Winning Jockeys							
S Maloney		1-6	+ 15.00	J Fortune		1-24	- 7.00
Winning Courses							
Southwell (AW)		1-4	+ 17.00	Thirsk		1-6	+ 11.00

	Age	Races Run	1st	2nd	3rd	Unpl	Win £
Winning Horses							
Lombard Ships	5	8	1	0	0	7	2,500
Cleo Modena	4	2	1	0	0	1	2,226

Favourites	0-1	Total winning prize-money	£4,726

1991 Form	13-144	9.0%	- 12.25	1989 Form	9-150	6.0%	- 19.50
1990 Form	12-166	7.2%	- 31.25				

R J O'SULLIVAN (Bognor Regis, West Sussex)

	No. of Horses	Races Run	1st	2nd	3rd	Unpl	Per cent	£1 Level Stake
2-y-o	0	0	0	0	0	0	-	0.00
3-y-o	0	0	0	0	0	0	-	0.00
4-y-o+	13	64	3	7	11	43	4.7	- 1.00
Totals	13	64	3	7	11	43	4.7	- 1.00

Jan	Feb	Mar	Apr	May	Jun	Jul	Aug	Sep	Oct/Nov
1-3	0-3	1-9	0-7	1-7	0-6	0-10	0-9	0-4	0-6

Winning Jockeys	W-R	£1 Level Stake			W-R	£1 Level Stake
J Quinn	1-5	+ 46.00	D Biggs		1-18	- 14.00
R Cochrane	1-6	+ 2.00				

Winning Courses						
Brighton	1-6	+ 45.00	Lingfield (AW)		1-15	- 11.00
Goodwood	1-10	- 2.00				

Winning Horses	Age	Races Run	1st	2nd	3rd	Unpl	Win £
El Volador	5	10	2	3	2	3	6,110
Sparkler Gebe	6	5	1	1	0	3	2,259

Favourites	1-7	14.3%	- 3.00	Total winning prize-money		£8,369

1991 Form	11-103	10.7%	+ 22.00	1989 Form	7-49	14.3%	- 9.00
1990 Form	6-68	8.8%	- 6.50	1988 Form	0-6		

J A B OLD (Wroughton, Wilts)

	No. of Horses	Races Run	1st	2nd	3rd	Unpl	Per cent	£1 Level Stake
2-y-o	0	0	0	0	0	0	-	0.00
3-y-o	0	0	0	0	0	0	-	0.00
4-y-o+	6	14	3	1	2	8	21.4	+ 28.08
Totals	6	14	3	1	2	8	21.4	+ 28.08

Jan	Feb	Mar	Apr	May	Jun	Jul	Aug	Sep	Oct/Nov
0-0	0-1	0-4	2-6	1-2	0-1	0-0	0-0	0-0	0-0

Winning Jockeys	W-R	£1 Level Stake			W-R	£1 Level Stake
L Dettori	2-4	+ 33.75	R Fox		1-5	- 0.67

Winning Courses						
Ascot	1-1	+ 33.00	Sandown		1-2	+ 2.33
Wolverhampton	1-1	+ 2.75				

Winning Horses	Age	Races Run	1st	2nd	3rd	Unpl	Win £
Al Mutahm	4	4	2	1	0	1	32,488
Wick Pound	6	2	1	0	1	0	3,113

Favourites	2-5	40.0%	+ 3.08	Total winning prize-money			£35,601

1991 Form	1-20	5.0%	+ 6.00	1989 Form	0-9		
1990 Form	1-13	7.7%	- 9.00	1988 Form	1-13	7.7%	- 7.00

B PALLING (Cowbridge, South Glamorgan)

	No. of Horses	Races Run	1st	2nd	3rd	Unpl	Per cent	£1 Level Stake
2-y-o	8	32	3	0	4	25	9.4	- 1.00
3-y-o	7	44	3	2	3	36	6.8	- 9.25
4-y-o+	4	15	1	0	1	13	6.7	- 7.50
Totals	19	91	7	2	8	74	7.7	- 17.75

Jan	Feb	Mar	Apr	May	Jun	Jul	Aug	Sep	Oct/Nov
0-2	0-2	0-2	2-9	2-10	0-12	1-12	1-12	0-14	1-16

Winning Jockeys	W-R	£1 Level Stake			W-R	£1 Level Stake
S Davies	2-30	+ 2.00		G Carter	1-3	+ 4.00
A Garth	1-1	+ 10.00		W Ryan	1-9	- 1.50
Paul Eddery	1-2	+ 11.00		R Hills	1-10	- 7.25

Winning Courses						
Windsor	2-6	+ 26.00		Nottingham	1-4	+ 7.00
Beverley	1-2	+ 0.75		Salisbury	1-6	+ 1.00
Sandown	1-3	+ 4.50		Leicester	1-9	+ 4.00

Winning Horses	Age	Races Run	1st	2nd	3rd	Unpl	Win £
Carranita	2	9	3	0	0	6	7,502
Eiras Mood	3	5	1	2	0	2	2,868
Jimlil	4	8	1	0	1	6	2,863
Haroldon	3	7	1	0	0	6	2,285
Sally Fast	3	9	1	0	0	8	1,507

Favourites	1-2	50.0%	+ 0.75	Total winning prize-money			£17,024

1991 Form	1-79	1.3%	- 72.00	1989 Form	4-69	5.8%	- 1.00
1990 Form	4-101	4.0%	- 47.62	1988 Form	1-48	2.1%	- 22.00

C PARKER (Lockerbie, Dumfries)

	No. of Horses	Races Run	1st	2nd	3rd	Unpl	Per cent	£1 Level Stake
2-y-o	0	0	0	0	0	0	-	0.00
3-y-o	2	3	1	0	0	2	33.3	+ 0.75
4-y-o+	1	1	0	0	0	1	-	- 1.00
Totals	3	4	1	0	0	3	25.0	- 0.25

Jan	Feb	Mar	Apr	May	Jun	Jul	Aug	Sep	Oct/Nov
0-0	0-0	0-0	0-0	1-1	0-0	0-0	0-0	0-0	0-3

Winning Jockey	W-R	£1 Level Stake	Winning Course	W-R	£1 Level Stake
J Carroll	1-2	+ 1.75	Hamilton	1-2	+ 1.75

Winning Horse	Age	Races Run	1st	2nd	3rd	Unpl	Win £
Trump	3	1	1	0	0	0	2,148

Favourites	1-1	100.0%	+ 2.75	Total winning prize-money	£2,148

1991 Form	0-6		1989 Form	0-4
1990 Form	0-15		1988 Form	0-1

J PARKES (Malton, North Yorks)

	No. of Horses	Races Run	1st	2nd	3rd	Unpl	Per cent	£1 Level Stake
2-y-o	0	0	0	0	0	0	-	0.00
3-y-o	2	5	0	0	0	5	-	- 5.00
4-y-o+	12	85	4	11	10	60	4.7	- 63.00
Totals	14	90	4	11	10	65	4.4	- 68.00

Jan	Feb	Mar	Apr	May	Jun	Jul	Aug	Sep	Oct/Nov
0-0	0-0	0-4	0-11	1-13	0-9	1-23	1-12	0-10	1-8

Winning Jockeys	W-R	£1 Level Stake		W-R	£1 Level Stake
M Roberts	3-4	+ 9.50	N Carlisle	1-19	- 10.50

Winning Courses					
Nottingham	1-1	+ 4.50	York	1-3	+ 4.00
Haydock	1-3	+ 5.50	Doncaster	1-4	- 3.00

Winning Horse	Age	Races Run	1st	2nd	3rd	Unpl	Win £
Drum Sergeant	5	19	4	2	2	11	19,782

Favourites	1-6	16.7%	- 0.50	Total winning prize-money	£19,782

1991 Form	3-95	3.2%	- 45.00	1989 Form	6-69	8.7%	+ 24.75
1990 Form	2-90	2.2%	- 35.00	1988 Form	1-26	3.8%	- 5.00

MRS H PARROTT (Coombe Hill, Glos)

	No. of Horses	Races Run	1st	2nd	3rd	Unpl	Per cent	£1 Level Stake
2-y-o	0	0	0	0	0	0	-	0.00
3-y-o	0	0	0	0	0	0	-	0.00
4-y-o+	1	4	1	0	1	2	25.0	+ 7.00
Totals	1	4	1	0	1	2	25.0	+ 7.00

Jan	Feb	Mar	Apr	May	Jun	Jul	Aug	Sep	Oct/Nov
0-0	0-0	0-0	0-0	0-0	0-0	0-0	0-1	1-3	0-0

Winning Jockey	W-R	£1 Level Stake	Winning Course	W-R	£1 Level Stake
M Wigham	1-1	+ 10.00	Nottingham	1-1	+ 10.00

Winning Horse	Age	Races Run	1st	2nd	3rd	Unpl	Win £
Mahong	4	4	1	0	1	2	3,057

Favourites	0-0	Total winning prize-money		£3,057

1991 Form	0-0	1990 Form	0-1

J W PAYNE (Newmarket)

	No. of Horses	Races Run	1st	2nd	3rd	Unpl	Per cent	£1 Level Stake
2-y-o	9	43	2	5	1	35	4.7	- 36.90
3-y-o	5	31	2	2	6	21	6.5	- 17.50
4-y-o+	3	27	5	1	2	19	18.5	+ 11.00
Totals	17	101	9	8	9	75	8.9	- 43.40

Jan	Feb	Mar	Apr	May	Jun	Jul	Aug	Sep	Oct/Nov
0-0	0-0	0-2	0-6	3-15	0-13	5-20	1-13	0-16	0-16

Winning Jockeys	W-R	£1 Level Stake		W-R	£1 Level Stake
A Munro	3-29	- 15.90	J Quinn	2-8	+ 6.00
G Duffield	2-6	+ 11.00	R Cochrane	2-22	- 8.50

Winning Courses					
Yarmouth	2-11	+ 7.00	Goodwood	1-2	+ 2.00
Lingfield	2-13	- 0.50	Warwick	1-4	- 1.90
Newcastle	1-1	+ 5.00	Sandown	1-6	+ 1.00
Thirsk	1-1	+ 7.00			

			Races					Win
Winning Horses		Age	Run	1st	2nd	3rd	Unpl	£
Casteddu		3	7	1	0	3	3	16,435
Medaille D'Or		4	9	2	0	1	6	13,062
Coral Flutter		5	11	3	1	1	6	8,347
Bourbon Jack		2	8	2	0	0	6	6,024
Lifetime Fame		3	9	1	0	2	6	1,380
Favourites	3-10	30.0%	+ 1.10	Total winning prize-money				£45,247
1991 Form	12-82	14.6%	+ 26.83	1989 Form	5-113	4.4%		- 84.75
1990 Form	4-88	4.5%	- 67.50	1988 Form	9-89	10.1%		- 9.25

J PEARCE (Newmarket)

	No. of Horses	Races Run	1st	2nd	3rd	Unpl	Per cent	£1 Level Stake
2-y-o	5	12	1	1	1	9	8.3	- 6.00
3-y-o	11	67	6	7	9	45	9.0	- 7.45
4-y-o+	12	73	12	9	9	43	16.4	- 17.61
Totals	28	152	19	17	19	97	12.5	- 31.06

BY MONTH

2-y-o	W-R	Per cent	£1 Level Stake	3-y-o	W-R	Per cent	£1 Level Stake
January	0-0	-	0.00	January	0-0	-	0.00
February	0-0	-	0.00	February	0-0	-	0.00
March	0-0	-	0.00	March	0-1	-	- 1.00
April	0-0	-	0.00	April	0-6	-	- 6.00
May	0-0	-	0.00	May	0-11	-	- 11.00
June	0-0	-	0.00	June	0-7	-	- 7.00
July	0-4	-	- 4.00	July	1-11	9.1	- 9.20
August	0-1	-	- 1.00	August	4-13	30.8	+ 35.75
September	1-1	100.0	+ 5.00	September	1-10	10.0	- 1.00
Oct/Nov	0-6	-	- 6.00	Oct/Nov	0-8	-	- 8.00
4-y-o+	W-R	Per cent	£1 Level Stake	Totals	W-R	Per cent	£1 Level Stake
January	2-4	50.0	+ 3.38	January	2-4	50.0	+ 3.38
February	1-11	9.1	- 8.00	February	1-11	9.1	- 8.00
March	1-7	14.3	- 4.12	March	1-8	12.5	- 5.12
April	0-9	-	- 9.00	April	0-15	-	- 15.00
May	2-6	33.3	+ 7.00	May	2-17	11.8	- 4.00
June	2-9	22.2	- 0.87	June	2-16	12.5	- 7.87
July	2-10	20.0	+ 0.50	July	3-25	12.0	- 12.70
August	1-4	25.0	+ 0.50	August	5-18	27.8	+ 35.25
September	1-7	14.3	- 1.00	September	3-18	16.7	+ 3.00
Oct/Nov	0-6	-	- 6.00	Oct/Nov	0-20	-	- 20.00

DISTANCE

	W-R	Per cent	£1 Level Stake		W-R	Per cent	£1 Level Stake
2-y-o				3-y-o			
5f-6f	1-7	14.3	- 1.00	5f-6f	0-11	-	- 11.00
7f-8f	0-5	-	- 5.00	7f-8f	2-19	10.5	- 10.25
9f-13f	0-0	-	0.00	9f-13f	4-34	11.8	+ 16.80
14f+	0-0	-	0.00	14f+	0-3	-	- 3.00
4-y-o+				Totals			
5f-6f	0-9	-	- 9.00	5f-6f	1-27	3.7	- 21.00
7f-8f	4-16	25.0	+ 6.00	7f-8f	6-40	15.0	- 9.25
9f-13f	8-45	17.8	- 11.61	9f-13f	12-79	15.2	+ 5.19
14f+	0-3	-	- 3.00	14f+	0-6	-	- 6.00

TYPE OF RACE

Non-Handicaps	W-R	Per cent	£1 Level Stake	Handicaps	W-R	Per cent	£1 Level Stake
2-y-o	1-10	10.0	- 4.00	2-y-o	0-1	-	- 1.00
3-y-o	4-26	15.4	+ 25.75	3-y-o	0-21	-	- 21.00
4-y-o+	5-14	35.7	+ 4.76	4-y-o+	0-22	-	- 22.00
Selling	3-20	15.0	- 3.50	Selling	1-13	7.7	- 11.20
Apprentice	0-1	-	- 1.00	Apprentice	0-4	-	- 4.00
Amat/Ladies	1-2	50.0	+ 5.00	Amat/Ladies	4-18	22.2	+ 1.13
Totals	14-73	19.2	+ 27.01	Totals	5-79	6.3	- 58.07

COURSE GRADE

	W-R	Per cent	£1 Level Stake
Group 1	3-36	8.3	- 18.50
Group 2	1-21	4.8	- 15.00
Group 3	6-50	12.0	+ 11.30
Group 4	9-45	20.0	- 8.86

FIRST TIME OUT

	W-R	Per cent	£1 Level Stake
2-y-o	0-5	-	- 5.00
3-y-o	1-9	11.1	+ 25.00
4-y-o+	3-11	27.3	+ 3.38
Totals	4-25	16.0	+ 23.38

JOCKEYS RIDING

	W-R	Per cent	£1 Level Stake		W-R	Per cent	£1 Level Stake
R Price	9-80	11.3	- 9.44	K Darley	1-4	25.0	- 1.25
Mrs L Pearce	5-21	23.8	+ 5.13	C Hawksley	1-5	20.0	0.00
R Cochrane	1-1	100.0	+ 3.50	Dale Gibson	1-6	16.7	0.00
M Birch	1-2	50.0	+ 4.00				

D Wright	0-4	P Robinson	0-2	M Roberts	0-1
G Bardwell	0-4	Pat Eddery	0-2	M Tebbutt	0-1
W Carson	0-4	D Biggs	0-1	P Turner	0-1
W Newnes	0-3	F Arrowsmith	0-1	R Perham	0-1
G Carter	0-2	J McLaughlin	0-1	S Cauthen	0-1
G Duffield	0-2	L Piggott	0-1	T Quinn	0-1

COURSE RECORD

	Total W-R	Non-Handicaps 2-y-o	Non-Handicaps 3-y-o+	Handicaps 2-y-o	Handicaps 3-y-o+	Per cent	£1 Level Stake
Beverley	3-10	0-1	0-1	0-0	3-8	30.0	+ 2.30
Lingfield (AW)	3-12	0-0	3-5	0-0	0-7	25.0	- 1.12
Folkestone	2-9	0-0	1-5	0-0	1-4	22.2	- 1.87
Yarmouth	2-16	1-1	1-7	0-0	0-8	12.5	+ 24.00
Newbury	1-1	0-0	0-0	0-0	1-1	100.0	+ 5.00
Newcastle	1-1	0-0	1-1	0-0	0-0	100.0	+ 5.00
Thirsk	1-3	0-0	1-2	0-0	0-1	33.3	+ 3.00
Wolverhampton	1-4	0-0	1-4	0-0	0-0	25.0	+ 2.00
Edinburgh	1-6	0-1	1-3	0-0	0-2	16.7	- 3.25
Southwell (AW)	1-6	0-0	1-4	0-0	0-2	16.7	- 3.62
Doncaster	1-7	0-1	1-2	0-0	0-4	14.3	- 1.50
Warwick	1-7	0-0	1-3	0-0	0-4	14.3	0.00
Leicester	1-8	0-1	1-6	0-0	0-1	12.5	+ 1.00

Newmarket	0-12	Haydock	0-4	Chester		0-1
Redcar	0-8	Nottingham	0-4	Kempton		0-1
Windsor	0-7	Salisbury	0-3	Ripon		0-1
Brighton	0-5	Sandown	0-3	York		0-1
Pontefract	0-5	Epsom	0-2			
Goodwood	0-4	Catterick	0-1			

WINNING HORSES

	Age	Races Run	1st	2nd	3rd	Unpl	Win £
Kirby Opportunity	4	12	5	3	1	3	9,645
Lots Of Luck	9	9	3	2	0	4	8,506
Big Pat	3	13	3	2	5	3	6,696
Brilliant	4	8	2	3	0	3	5,040
Super Summit	3	8	2	1	1	4	4,781
Racing Telegraph	2	6	1	1	1	3	3,106
Irish Stamp	3	4	1	1	0	2	2,448
Aragon Court	4	9	1	0	2	6	2,427
Hand Painted	8	1	1	0	0	0	2,206

WINNING OWNERS

	Races Won	Value £		Races Won	Value £
Burton Park Country Club	6	15,202	D J Maden	2	4,781
Peter Bradley	5	9,645	Cliff Woof	1	3,106
Arthur Old	2	5,040	Mrs Margaret Baxter	1	2,206
Jeff Pearce	2	4,875			

Favourites	7-32	21.9%	- 8.19	Total winning prize-money			£44,856

Longest winning sequence		2
Longest losing sequence		27

Average SP of winner		5.4/1
Return on stakes invested		-20.4%

1991 Form	11-152	7.2%	- 92.25	1989 Form	5-72	6.9%	+ 24.00
1990 Form	13-119	10.9%	- 32.00	1988 Form	3-49	6.1%	- 30.37

W J PEARCE (Hambleton, North Yorks)

	No. of Horses	Races Run	1st	2nd	3rd	Unpl	Per cent	£1 Level Stake
2-y-o	11	28	1	3	3	21	3.6	- 22.00
3-y-o	13	38	3	2	6	27	7.9	- 29.84
4-y-o+	17	71	9	14	8	40	12.7	- 25.70
Totals	41	137	13	19	17	88	9.5	- 77.54

BY MONTH

2-y-o	W-R	Per cent	£1 Level Stake	3-y-o	W-R	Per cent	£1 Level Stake
January	0-0	-	0.00	January	1-2	50.0	+ 1.50
February	0-0	-	0.00	February	0-2	-	- 2.00
March	0-1	-	- 1.00	March	0-1	-	- 1.00
April	0-7	-	- 7.00	April	1-13	7.7	- 10.25
May	1-15	6.7	- 9.00	May	1-11	9.1	- 9.09
June	0-5	-	- 5.00	June	0-9	-	- 9.00
July	0-0	-	0.00	July	0-0	-	0.00
August	0-0	-	0.00	August	0-0	-	0.00
September	0-0	-	0.00	September	0-0	-	0.00
Oct/Nov	0-0	-	0.00	Oct/Nov	0-0	-	0.00

4-y-o+	W-R	Per cent	£1 Level Stake	Totals	W-R	Per cent	£1 Level Stake
January	3-10	30.0	+ 1.80	January	4-12	33.3	+ 3.30
February	3-13	23.1	+ 3.00	February	3-15	20.0	+ 1.00
March	0-8	-	- 8.00	March	0-10	-	- 10.00
April	1-13	7.7	- 8.00	April	2-33	6.1	- 25.25
May	0-20	-	- 20.00	May	2-46	4.3	- 38.09
June	2-7	28.6	+ 5.50	June	2-21	9.5	- 8.50
July	0-0	-	0.00	July	0-0	-	0.00
August	0-0	-	0.00	August	0-0	-	0.00
September	0-0	-	0.00	September	0-0	-	0.00
Oct/Nov	0-0	-	0.00	Oct/Nov	0-0	-	0.00

DISTANCE

2-y-o	W-R	Per cent	£1 Level Stake	3-y-o	W-R	Per cent	£1 Level Stake
5f-6f	1-28	3.6	- 22.00	5f-6f	2-10	20.0	- 5.34
7f-8f	0-0	-	0.00	7f-8f	1-16	6.3	- 12.50
9f-13f	0-0	-	0.00	9f-13f	0-12	-	- 12.00
14f+	0-0	-	0.00	14f+	0-0	-	0.00

4-y-o+	W-R	Per cent	£1 Level Stake	Totals	W-R	Per cent	£1 Level Stake
5f-6f	3-22	13.6	- 3.00	5f-6f	6-60	10.0	- 30.34
7f-8f	3-33	9.1	- 21.20	7f-8f	4-49	8.2	- 33.70
9f-13f	1-8	12.5	- 3.00	9f-13f	1-20	5.0	- 15.00
14f+	2-8	25.0	+ 1.50	14f+	2-8	25.0	+ 1.50

TYPE OF RACE

Non-Handicaps	W-R	Per cent	£1 Level Stake	Handicaps	W-R	Per cent	£1 Level Stake
2-y-o	0-23	-	- 23.00	2-y-o	0-0	-	0.00
3-y-o	2-8	25.0	- 3.34	3-y-o	1-26	3.8	- 22.50
4-y-o+	1-22	4.5	- 20.20	4-y-o+	8-41	19.5	+ 2.50
Selling	1-11	9.1	- 5.00	Selling	0-3	-	- 3.00
Apprentice	0-0	-	0.00	Apprentice	0-1	-	- 1.00
Amat/Ladies	0-0	-	0.00	Amat/Ladies	0-2	-	- 2.00
Totals	4-64	6.3	- 51.54	Totals	9-73	12.3	- 26.00

COURSE GRADE

	W-R	Per cent	£1 Level Stake
Group 1	2-13	15.4	- 0.50
Group 2	0-30	-	- 30.00
Group 3	1-38	2.6	- 32.00
Group 4	10-56	17.9	- 15.04

FIRST TIME OUT

	W-R	Per cent	£1 Level Stake
2-y-o	0-11	-	- 11.00
3-y-o	2-12	16.7	- 5.75
4-y-o+	2-17	11.8	- 7.20
Totals	4-40	10.0	- 23.95

JOCKEYS RIDING

	W-R	Per cent	£1 Level Stake		W-R	Per cent	£1 Level Stake
D Nicholls	8-87	9.2	- 52.34	R Cochrane	1-1	100.0	+ 6.50
L Charnock	3-22	13.6	- 6.50	G Husband	1-3	33.3	- 1.20

S Webster	0-9	B Doyle	0-1	J Fanning		0-1
Mr D Durrant	0-2	F Norton	0-1	P Turner		0-1
N Connorton	0-2	G Duffield	0-1	T Lucas		0-1
S Maloney	0-2	G Parkin	0-1			
A Culhane	0-1	J Carroll	0-1			

COURSE RECORD

	Total W-R	Non-Handicaps 2-y-o	Non-Handicaps 3-y-o+	Handicaps 2-y-o	Handicaps 3-y-o+	Per cent	£1 Level Stake
Southwell (AW)	5-24	0-1	1-10	0-0	4-13	20.8	- 4.20
Lingfield (AW)	2-14	0-0	0-7	0-0	2-7	14.3	- 2.50
Epsom	1-2	0-0	0-0	0-0	1-2	50.0	+ 5.50
Sandown	1-2	0-0	0-1	0-0	1-1	50.0	+ 3.00
Carlisle	1-3	0-1	1-1	0-0	0-1	33.3	- 1.09
Edinburgh	1-6	0-0	1-3	0-0	0-3	16.7	- 3.25
Nottingham	1-7	1-1	0-1	0-0	0-5	14.3	- 1.00
Catterick	1-9	0-0	0-3	0-0	1-6	11.1	- 4.00

Hamilton	0-19	Beverley	0-6	Haydock	0-1
Redcar	0-11	Pontefract	0-6	Newmarket	0-1
Thirsk	0-11	Newcastle	0-4		
Ripon	0-8	York	0-3		

WINNING HORSES

	Age	Races Run	1st	2nd	3rd	Unpl	Win £
Viceroy	5	3	1	0	1	1	14,330
Malenoir	4	9	2	2	1	4	5,286
Martini Executive	4	6	2	1	1	2	4,570
Toshiba Comet	5	9	2	2	0	5	4,413
Father Hayes	4	4	1	0	0	3	3,113
A Bridge Too Far	2	4	1	0	1	2	2,481
Act Of Union	3	4	1	1	1	1	2,385
Jefferson Davis	3	4	1	0	3	0	2,280
Bold Habit	7	6	1	2	1	2	2,265
Stonewall Jackson	3	2	1	0	0	1	1,501

WINNING OWNERS

	Races Won	Value £		Races Won	Value £
Franco Gamma	1	14,330	R J Pearce	1	3,113
John Purcell	2	5,286	The Royal Partnership	1	2,481
Roger Jelley	2	4,570	Derek Atkinson	1	2,385
Mike Clynes Associates Ltd	2	4,413	Roger Sterry	1	2,265
The Confederacy Ltd	2	3,781			

Favourites	6-15	40.0%	+ 1.96	Total winning prize-money			£42,623
Longest winning sequence			2	Average SP of winner			3.6/1
Longest losing sequence			50	Return on stakes invested			-56.6%
1991 Form	29-291	10.0%	- 22.25	1989 Form	24-314	7.6%	-111.05
1990 Form	21-298	7.0%	-112.24	1988 Form	18-215	8.4%	- 55.52

MISS L A PERRATT (Ayr, Strathclyde)

	No. of Horses	Races Run	1st	2nd	3rd	Unpl	Per cent	£1 Level Stake
2-y-o	10	43	2	4	4	33	4.7	- 20.95
3-y-o	7	42	2	7	6	27	4.8	- 32.50
4-y-o+	13	75	6	11	2	56	8.0	- 15.50
Totals	30	160	10	22	12	116	6.3	- 68.95

BY MONTH

2-y-o	W-R	Per cent	£1 Level Stake	3-y-o	W-R	Per cent	£1 Level Stake
Mar/Apr	0-2	-	- 2.00	Mar/Apr	0-4	-	- 4.00
May	0-5	-	- 5.00	May	0-10	-	- 10.00
June	0-3	-	- 3.00	June	1-6	16.7	0.00
July	2-11	18.2	+ 11.05	July	1-11	9.1	- 7.50
August	0-9	-	- 9.00	August	0-6	-	- 6.00
September	0-8	-	- 8.00	September	0-5	-	- 5.00
Oct/Nov	0-5	-	- 5.00	Oct/Nov	0-0	-	0.00

Perratt Miss L A

4-y-o+	W-R	Per cent	£1 Level Stake	Totals	W-R	Per cent	£1 Level Stake
Mar/Apr	0-7	-	- 7.00	Mar/Apr	0-13	-	- 13.00
May	3-18	16.7	+ 17.00	May	3-33	9.1	+ 2.00
June	1-14	7.1	- 7.50	June	2-23	8.7	- 10.50
July	1-11	9.1	+ 2.00	July	4-33	12.1	+ 5.55
August	0-10	-	- 10.00	August	0-25	-	- 25.00
September	1-11	9.1	- 6.00	September	1-24	4.2	- 19.00
Oct/Nov	0-4	-	- 4.00	Oct/Nov	0-9	-	- 9.00

DISTANCE

2-y-o	W-R	Per cent	£1 Level Stake	3-y-o	W-R	Per cent	£1 Level Stake
5f-6f	1-25	4.0	- 8.00	5f-6f	0-9	-	- 9.00
7f-8f	1-18	5.6	- 12.95	7f-8f	2-23	8.7	- 13.50
9f-13f	0-0	-	0.00	9f-13f	0-10	-	- 10.00
14f+	0-0	-	0.00	14f+	0-0	-	0.00

4-y-o+	W-R	Per cent	£1 Level Stake	Totals	W-R	Per cent	£1 Level Stake
5f-6f	3-28	10.7	+ 2.00	5f-6f	4-62	6.5	- 15.00
7f-8f	0-12	-	- 12.00	7f-8f	3-53	5.7	- 38.45
9f-13f	2-22	9.1	- 5.50	9f-13f	2-32	6.3	- 15.50
14f+	1-13	7.7	0.00	14f+	1-13	7.7	0.00

TYPE OF RACE

Non-Handicaps	W-R	Per cent	£1 Level Stake	Handicaps	W-R	Per cent	£1 Level Stake
2-y-o	1-31	3.2	- 14.00	2-y-o	0-4	-	- 4.00
3-y-o	1-19	5.3	- 15.50	3-y-o	1-18	5.6	- 12.00
4-y-o+	1-10	10.0	- 5.00	4-y-o+	3-49	6.1	- 22.00
Selling	2-11	18.2	+ 15.05	Selling	0-6	-	- 6.00
Apprentice	0-1	-	- 1.00	Apprentice	0-3	-	- 3.00
Amat/Ladies	1-4	25.0	+ 2.50	Amat/Ladies	0-4	-	- 4.00
Totals	6-76	7.9	- 17.95	Totals	4-84	4.8	- 51.00

COURSE GRADE

	W-R	Per cent	£1 Level Stake
Group 1	2-50	4.0	- 40.50
Group 2	0-18	-	- 18.00
Group 3	5-53	9.4	- 6.50
Group 4	3-39	7.7	- 3.95

FIRST TIME OUT

	W-R	Per cent	£1 Level Stake
2-y-o	0-9	-	- 9.00
3-y-o	0-5	-	- 5.00
4-y-o+	1-13	7.7	+ 8.00
Totals	1-27	3.7	- 6.00

JOCKEYS RIDING

	W-R	Per cent	£1 Level Stake		W-R	Per cent	£1 Level Stake
J Fanning	3-49	6.1	- 25.95	R Cochrane	1-2	50.0	+ 4.00
Dale Gibson	2-15	13.3	- 1.50	Miss L Perratt	1-4	25.0	+ 2.50
R Havlin	2-28	7.1	- 3.00	Claire Balding	1-7	14.3	+ 10.00

G Duffield	0-7	Mr M Lightbody	0-2	M Hills	0-1
N Kennedy	0-7	C Dwyer	0-1	Miss L Robertson	0-1
J Carroll	0-5	C Hodgson	0-1	Mr R Hale	0-1
N Connorton	0-5	D Carson	0-1	N Carlisle	0-1
A McGlone	0-3	D Harrison	0-1	S Cauthen	0-1
S Wood	0-3	D Moffatt	0-1	S Maloney	0-1
B Raymond	0-2	J Scotland	0-1	W Carson	0-1
J Lowe	0-2	J Weaver	0-1	W R Swinburn	0-1
J Marshall	0-2	L Charnock	0-1	W Ryan	0-1

COURSE RECORD

	Total W-R	Non-Handicaps 2-y-o	Non-Handicaps 3-y-o+	Handicaps 2-y-o	Handicaps 3-y-o+	Per cent	£1 Level Stake
Hamilton	5-47	0-6	3-11	0-1	2-29	10.6	- 0.50
Edinburgh	3-33	2-9	0-6	0-0	1-18	9.1	+ 2.05
Epsom	1-2	0-0	0-1	0-0	1-1	50.0	+ 4.00
Ayr	1-38	0-8	1-13	0-2	0-15	2.6	- 34.50

Redcar	0-8	Carlisle	0-3	Newmarket	0-2
Haydock	0-7	Catterick	0-3	Newcastle	0-1
Ripon	0-5	Beverley	0-2	Nottingham	0-1
Thirsk	0-5	Leicester	0-2	Pontefract	0-1

WINNING HORSES

	Age	Races Run	1st	2nd	3rd	Unpl	Win £
Petite-D-Argent	3	4	1	2	0	1	7,100
Francis Ann	4	10	2	1	0	7	4,696
Shadideen	4	7	1	2	0	4	2,427
Diet	6	15	1	3	1	10	2,383
Alpha Helix	9	14	1	1	0	12	2,370
Princess Maxine	3	8	1	3	1	3	2,285
Persuasive	5	3	1	0	0	2	1,861
Selvole	2	11	1	0	1	9	1,355
Lucky Owl	2	6	1	1	0	4	1,318

WINNING OWNERS

	Races Won	Value £		Races Won	Value £
Daniel A Couper	1	7,100	J Fox	1	2,285
Miss L A Perratt	2	4,675	W G McHarg	1	1,861
Mrs M Gray	1	2,448	John Muir	1	1,355
Mrs M S J Clydesdale	1	2,383	William Provan Hunter	1	1,318
J W M M Richard	1	2,370			

Favourites	2-10	20.0%	- 2.50	Total winning prize-money	£25,794

Longest winning sequence			1	Average SP of winner	8.1/1
Longest losing sequence			30	Return on stakes invested	-43.1%

1991 Form	6-73	8.2%	+ 8.50

MRS L PIGGOTT (Newmarket)

	No. of Horses	Races Run	1st	2nd	3rd	Unpl	Per cent	£1 Level Stake
2-y-o	9	38	2	4	5	27	5.3	- 33.25
3-y-o	4	22	3	4	3	12	13.6	- 4.75
4-y-o+	7	49	5	5	5	34	10.2	- 21.50
Totals	20	109	10	13	13	73	9.2	- 59.50

BY MONTH

2-y-o	W-R	Per cent	£1 Level Stake	3-y-o	W-R	Per cent	£1 Level Stake
January	0-0	-	0.00	January	1-2	50.0	+ 0.25
February	0-0	-	0.00	February	0-1	-	- 1.00
March	0-0	-	0.00	March	0-0	-	0.00
April	0-0	-	0.00	April	0-1	-	- 1.00
May	0-0	-	0.00	May	0-1	-	- 1.00
June	0-3	-	- 3.00	June	0-2	-	- 2.00
July	1-8	12.5	- 5.75	July	0-5	-	- 5.00
August	1-9	11.1	- 6.50	August	1-9	11.1	0.00
September	0-10	-	- 10.00	September	1-1	100.0	+ 5.00
Oct/Nov	0-8	-	- 8.00	Oct/Nov	0-0	-	0.00

4-y-o+	W-R	Per cent	£1 Level Stake	Totals	W-R	Per cent	£1 Level Stake
January	0-0	-	0.00	January	1-2	50.0	+ 0.25
February	0-0	-	0.00	February	0-1	-	- 1.00
March	0-2	-	- 2.00	March	0-2	-	- 2.00
April	0-6	-	- 6.00	April	0-7	-	- 7.00
May	0-8	-	- 8.00	May	0-9	-	- 9.00
June	2-9	22.2	+ 0.25	June	2-14	14.3	- 4.75
July	1-7	14.3	- 3.50	July	2-20	10.0	- 14.25
August	2-7	28.6	+ 7.75	August	4-25	16.0	+ 1.25
September	0-6	-	- 6.00	September	1-17	5.9	- 11.00
Oct/Nov	0-4	-	- 4.00	Oct/Nov	0-12	-	- 12.00

DISTANCE

2-y-o	W-R	Per cent	£1 Level Stake	3-y-o	W-R	Per cent	£1 Level Stake
5f-6f	1-18	5.6	- 15.50	5f-6f	1-4	25.0	- 1.75
7f-8f	1-19	5.3	- 16.75	7f-8f	2-17	11.8	- 2.00
9f-13f	0-1	-	- 1.00	9f-13f	0-1	-	- 1.00
14f+	0-0	-	0.00	14f+	0-0	-	0.00

4-y-o+	W-R	Per cent	£1 Level Stake	Totals	W-R	Per cent	£1 Level Stake
5f-6f	2-16	12.5	- 1.25	5f-6f	4-38	10.5	- 18.50
7f-8f	2-14	14.3	- 6.75	7f-8f	5-50	10.0	- 25.50
9f-13f	1-19	5.3	- 13.50	9f-13f	1-21	4.8	- 15.50
14f+	0-0	-	0.00	14f+	0-0	-	0.00

TYPE OF RACE

Non-Handicaps	W-R	Per cent	£1 Level Stake	Handicaps	W-R	Per cent	£1 Level Stake
2-y-o	1-26	3.8	- 23.50	2-y-o	0-8	-	- 8.00
3-y-o	2-9	22.2	+ 2.25	3-y-o	1-10	10.0	- 4.00
4-y-o+	0-7	-	- 7.00	4-y-o+	3-38	7.9	- 19.75
Selling	2-4	50.0	+ 2.00	Selling	0-1	-	- 1.00
Apprentice	0-2	-	- 2.00	Apprentice	0-3	-	- 3.00
Amat/Ladies	0-0	-	0.00	Amat/Ladies	1-1	100.0	+ 4.50
Totals	5-48	10.4	- 28.25	Totals	5-61	8.2	- 31.25

COURSE GRADE

	W-R	Per cent	£1 Level Stake
Group 1	1-34	2.9	- 28.50
Group 2	2-13	15.4	+ 0.50
Group 3	3-38	7.9	- 28.50
Group 4	4-24	16.7	- 3.00

FIRST TIME OUT

	W-R	Per cent	£1 Level Stake
2-y-o	0-9	-	- 9.00
3-y-o	2-4	50.0	+ 7.25
4-y-o+	0-6	-	- 6.00
Totals	2-19	10.5	- 7.75

JOCKEYS RIDING

	W-R	Per cent	£1 Level Stake		W-R	Per cent	£1 Level Stake
L Piggott	7-60	11.7	- 27.25	L Dettori	1-3	33.3	+ 6.00
Mrs V Leng	1-1	100.0	+ 4.50	J Williams	1-5	20.0	- 2.75

	W-R				W-R
G Milligan	0-16	B Raymond	0-1	P Robinson	0-1
J Quinn	0-4	D Harrison	0-1	Paul Eddery	0-1
R Cochrane	0-4	F Norton	0-1	S Dawson	0-1
M Tebbutt	0-3	G Duffield	0-1	W Newnes	0-1
W Aldwinckle	0-2	J Reid	0-1		
A Munro	0-1	Mrs J Crossley	0-1		

Piggott Mrs L

COURSE RECORD

	Total W–R	Non-Handicaps 2-y-o	3-y-o+	Handicaps 2-y-o	3-y-o+	Per cent	£1 Level Stake
Lingfield (AW)	3-10	0-0	2-3	0-0	1-7	30.0	+ 7.25
Yarmouth	3-18	1-7	0-0	0-1	2-10	16.7	- 8.50
Brighton	2-11	1-4	0-1	0-1	1-5	18.2	+ 2.50
Folkestone	1-6	0-1	1-1	0-0	0-4	16.7	- 2.25
Kempton	1-8	0-0	0-2	0-0	1-6	12.5	- 2.50

Newmarket	0-14	Pontefract	0-5	Lingfield	0-1
Doncaster	0-6	Windsor	0-4	Newbury	0-1
Leicester	0-6	Ascot	0-2	Salisbury	0-1
Warwick	0-6	Wolverhampton	0-2	Sandown	0-1
Nottingham	0-5	York	0-2		

WINNING HORSES

	Age	Races Run	1st	2nd	3rd	Unpl	Win £
Shining Jewel	5	16	3	0	3	10	7,479
Albert The Bold	3	2	2	0	0	0	5,180
Liffey River	4	14	2	1	1	10	4,969
Troon	2	8	1	2	0	5	2,611
Myasha	3	8	1	1	2	4	2,246
Miss Fayruz	2	8	1	0	0	7	1,548

WINNING OWNERS

	Races Won	Value £		Races Won	Value £
D W Rolt	3	7,479	Tony Hirschfeld	1	2,611
Miss J Semple	2	5,180	J D Ashenheim	1	2,246
Mrs Heather Hirschfield	2	4,969	K Philipp	1	1,548

Favourites	5-16	31.3%	- 1.75	Total winning prize-money			£24,032

Longest winning sequence		1	Average SP of winner	4.0/1
Longest losing sequence		26	Return on stakes invested	-54.6%

1991 Form	15-179	8.4%	- 86.87	1989 Form	34-209	16.3%	- 32.64
1990 Form	13-193	6.7%	-122.70	1988 Form	17-170	10.0%	- 14.30

M C PIPE (Wellington, Somerset)

	No. of Horses	Races Run	1st	2nd	3rd	Unpl	Per cent	£1 Level Stake
2-y-o	0	0	0	0	0	0	-	0.00
3-y-o	6	16	3	0	1	12	18.8	+ 17.50
4-y-o+	17	77	12	7	8	50	15.6	- 33.92
Totals	23	93	15	7	9	62	16.1	- 16.42

BY MONTH

2-y-o	W-R	Per cent	£1 Level Stake	3-y-o	W-R	Per cent	£1 Level Stake
January	0-0	-	0.00	January	0-0	-	0.00
February	0-0	-	0.00	February	0-0	-	0.00
March	0-0	-	0.00	March	0-0	-	0.00
April	0-0	-	0.00	April	0-0	-	0.00
May	0-0	-	0.00	May	0-0	-	0.00
June	0-0	-	0.00	June	0-0	-	0.00
July	0-0	-	0.00	July	0-0	-	0.00
August	0-0	-	0.00	August	1-5	20.0	+ 12.00
September	0-0	-	0.00	September	1-6	16.7	+ 1.50
Oct/Nov	0-0	-	0.00	Oct/Nov	1-5	20.0	+ 4.00

4-y-o+	W-R	Per cent	£1 Level Stake	Totals	W-R	Per cent	£1 Level Stake
January	0-0	-	0.00	January	0-0	-	0.00
February	0-3	-	- 3.00	February	0-3	-	- 3.00
March	0-2	-	- 2.00	March	0-2	-	- 2.00
April	0-10	-	- 10.00	April	0-10	-	- 10.00
May	1-13	7.7	- 10.62	May	1-13	7.7	- 10.62
June	1-13	7.7	- 10.00	June	1-13	7.7	- 10.00
July	7-16	43.8	+ 11.67	July	7-16	43.8	+ 11.67
August	1-10	10.0	- 8.20	August	2-15	13.3	+ 3.80
September	2-5	40.0	+ 3.23	September	3-11	27.3	+ 4.73
Oct/Nov	0-5	-	- 5.00	Oct/Nov	1-10	10.0	- 1.00

DISTANCE

2-y-o	W-R	Per cent	£1 Level Stake	3-y-o	W-R	Per cent	£1 Level Stake
5f-6f	0-0	-	0.00	5f-6f	0-0	-	0.00
7f-8f	0-0	-	0.00	7f-8f	1-6	16.7	+ 1.50
9f-13f	0-0	-	0.00	9f-13f	2-8	25.0	+ 18.00
14f+	0-0	-	0.00	14f+	0-2	-	- 2.00

4-y-o+	W-R	Per cent	£1 Level Stake	Totals	W-R	Per cent	£1 Level Stake
5f-6f	0-5	-	- 5.00	5f-6f	0-5	-	- 5.00
7f-8f	0-5	-	- 5.00	7f-8f	1-11	9.1	- 3.50
9f-13f	11-49	22.4	- 10.92	9f-13f	13-57	22.8	+ 7.08
14f+	1-18	5.6	- 13.00	14f+	1-20	5.0	- 15.00

TYPE OF RACE

Non-Handicaps	W-R	Per cent	£1 Level Stake	Handicaps	W-R	Per cent	£1 Level Stake
2-y-o	0-0	-	0.00	2-y-o	0-0	-	0.00
3-y-o	0-5	-	- 5.00	3-y-o	2-2	100.0	+ 24.00
4-y-o+	5-30	16.7	- 7.14	4-y-o+	3-29	10.3	- 16.87
Selling	0-7	-	- 7.00	Selling	0-5	-	- 5.00
Apprentice	1-3	33.3	- 1.00	Apprentice	1-8	12.5	- 0.50
Amat/Ladies	3-3	100.0	+ 3.09	Amat/Ladies	0-1	-	- 1.00
Totals	9-48	18.8	- 17.05	Totals	6-45	13.3	+ 0.63

Pipe M C

<table>
<tr><th colspan="4">COURSE GRADE</th><th colspan="4">FIRST TIME OUT</th></tr>
<tr><th></th><th>W-R</th><th>Per cent</th><th>£1 Level Stake</th><th></th><th>W-R</th><th>Per cent</th><th>£1 Level Stake</th></tr>
<tr><td>Group 1</td><td>4-35</td><td>11.4</td><td>- 17.29</td><td>2-y-o</td><td>0-0</td><td>-</td><td>0.00</td></tr>
<tr><td>Group 2</td><td>3-14</td><td>21.4</td><td>+ 7.38</td><td>3-y-o</td><td>1-3</td><td>33.3</td><td>+ 14.00</td></tr>
<tr><td>Group 3</td><td>5-23</td><td>21.7</td><td>+ 3.76</td><td>4-y-o+</td><td>1-15</td><td>6.7</td><td>- 12.00</td></tr>
<tr><td>Group 4</td><td>3-21</td><td>14.3</td><td>- 10.27</td><td></td><td></td><td></td><td></td></tr>
<tr><td></td><td></td><td></td><td></td><td>Totals</td><td>2-18</td><td>11.1</td><td>+ 2.00</td></tr>
</table>

JOCKEYS RIDING

<table>
<tr><th></th><th>W-R</th><th>Per cent</th><th>£1 Level Stake</th><th></th><th>W-R</th><th>Per cent</th><th>£1 Level Stake</th></tr>
<tr><td>M Roberts</td><td>7-17</td><td>41.2</td><td>+ 5.99</td><td>L Dettori</td><td>1-2</td><td>50.0</td><td>+ 7.00</td></tr>
<tr><td>Mrs L Pearce</td><td>3-4</td><td>75.0</td><td>+ 2.09</td><td>S Davies</td><td>1-3</td><td>33.3</td><td>+ 4.50</td></tr>
<tr><td>B Doyle</td><td>1-1</td><td>100.0</td><td>+ 16.00</td><td>E Husband</td><td>1-5</td><td>20.0</td><td>- 3.00</td></tr>
<tr><td>G Baxter</td><td>1-2</td><td>50.0</td><td>+ 10.00</td><td></td><td></td><td></td><td></td></tr>
</table>

<table>
<tr><td>L Piggott</td><td>0-6</td><td>A Clark</td><td>0-1</td><td>M Hills</td><td>0-1</td></tr>
<tr><td>D Holland</td><td>0-5</td><td>A McGlone</td><td>0-1</td><td>N Gwilliams</td><td>0-1</td></tr>
<tr><td>B Crossley</td><td>0-4</td><td>B Raymond</td><td>0-1</td><td>N Varley</td><td>0-1</td></tr>
<tr><td>J Williams</td><td>0-4</td><td>D Biggs</td><td>0-1</td><td>Pat Eddery</td><td>0-1</td></tr>
<tr><td>Paul Eddery</td><td>0-4</td><td>D McKeown</td><td>0-1</td><td>S Dawson</td><td>0-1</td></tr>
<tr><td>R Hills</td><td>0-4</td><td>F Norton</td><td>0-1</td><td>S Drowne</td><td>0-1</td></tr>
<tr><td>A Munro</td><td>0-2</td><td>G Bardwell</td><td>0-1</td><td>S Wood</td><td>0-1</td></tr>
<tr><td>D Harrison</td><td>0-2</td><td>J Quinn</td><td>0-1</td><td>S Wynne</td><td>0-1</td></tr>
<tr><td>K Rutter</td><td>0-2</td><td>J Reid</td><td>0-1</td><td>T Williams</td><td>0-1</td></tr>
<tr><td>P Shanahan</td><td>0-2</td><td>J Tate</td><td>0-1</td><td>W O'Connor</td><td>0-1</td></tr>
<tr><td>S Cauthen</td><td>0-2</td><td>L Charnock</td><td>0-1</td><td>W R Swinburn</td><td>0-1</td></tr>
</table>

COURSE RECORD

<table>
<tr><th></th><th>Total W-R</th><th colspan="2">Non-Handicaps</th><th colspan="2">Handicaps</th><th>Per cent</th><th>£1 Level Stake</th></tr>
<tr><th></th><th></th><th>2-y-o</th><th>3-y-o+</th><th>2-y-o</th><th>3-y-o+</th><th></th><th></th></tr>
<tr><td>Bath</td><td>2-4</td><td>0-0</td><td>1-2</td><td>0-0</td><td>1-2</td><td>50.0</td><td>+ 14.50</td></tr>
<tr><td>Chepstow</td><td>2-5</td><td>0-0</td><td>0-2</td><td>0-0</td><td>2-3</td><td>40.0</td><td>+ 0.63</td></tr>
<tr><td>Lingfield (AW)</td><td>1-2</td><td>0-0</td><td>1-2</td><td>0-0</td><td>0-0</td><td>50.0</td><td>- 0.50</td></tr>
<tr><td>Brighton</td><td>1-3</td><td>0-0</td><td>1-1</td><td>0-0</td><td>0-2</td><td>33.3</td><td>- 1.00</td></tr>
<tr><td>Doncaster</td><td>1-3</td><td>0-0</td><td>1-1</td><td>0-0</td><td>0-2</td><td>33.3</td><td>- 1.09</td></tr>
<tr><td>Lingfield</td><td>1-3</td><td>0-0</td><td>1-2</td><td>0-0</td><td>0-1</td><td>33.3</td><td>- 0.62</td></tr>
<tr><td>Sandown</td><td>1-3</td><td>0-0</td><td>1-2</td><td>0-0</td><td>0-1</td><td>33.3</td><td>- 1.20</td></tr>
<tr><td>York</td><td>1-3</td><td>0-0</td><td>1-3</td><td>0-0</td><td>0-0</td><td>33.3</td><td>+ 2.00</td></tr>
<tr><td>Salisbury</td><td>1-4</td><td>0-0</td><td>0-3</td><td>0-0</td><td>1-1</td><td>25.0</td><td>+ 13.00</td></tr>
<tr><td>Newmarket</td><td>1-5</td><td>0-0</td><td>0-3</td><td>0-0</td><td>1-2</td><td>20.0</td><td>+ 4.00</td></tr>
<tr><td>Leicester</td><td>1-6</td><td>0-0</td><td>1-3</td><td>0-0</td><td>0-3</td><td>16.7</td><td>- 3.37</td></tr>
<tr><td>Wolverhampton</td><td>1-6</td><td>0-0</td><td>1-4</td><td>0-0</td><td>0-2</td><td>16.7</td><td>- 4.27</td></tr>
<tr><td>Southwell (AW)</td><td>1-6</td><td>0-0</td><td>0-3</td><td>0-0</td><td>1-3</td><td>16.7</td><td>+ 1.50</td></tr>
</table>

<table>
<tr><td>Warwick</td><td>0-7</td><td>Epsom</td><td>0-2</td><td>Newcastle</td><td>0-1</td></tr>
<tr><td>Ascot</td><td>0-6</td><td>Haydock</td><td>0-2</td><td>Nottingham</td><td>0-1</td></tr>
<tr><td>Goodwood</td><td>0-6</td><td>Newbury</td><td>0-2</td><td>Yarmouth</td><td>0-1</td></tr>
<tr><td>Windsor</td><td>0-6</td><td>Ayr</td><td>0-1</td><td></td><td></td></tr>
<tr><td>Chester</td><td>0-4</td><td>Kempton</td><td>0-1</td><td></td><td></td></tr>
</table>

WINNING HORSES

	Age	Races Run	1st	2nd	3rd	Unpl	Win £
Tyrone Bridge	6	6	1	0	1	4	9,219
Pharly Story	4	10	3	1	1	5	7,090
Bighayir	5	6	3	1	0	2	6,348
Flying Speed	4	7	2	0	1	4	5,910
Princess Moodyshoe	4	5	2	1	1	1	5,813
Her Honour	3	1	1	0	0	0	4,628
C U Coral	3	2	1	0	0	1	3,132
Tyrone Flyer	3	3	1	0	1	1	2,553
Diamond Cut	4	2	1	0	0	1	2,070

WINNING OWNERS

		Races Won	Value £			Races Won	Value £
A J Lomas		6	13,437	F Barr		3	7,980
Mrs Alison C Farrant		3	10,441	D E McDowell		1	3,132
Paul Green		1	9,219	J Naughton		1	2,553
Favourites	9-22	40.9%	- 2.42	Total winning prize-money			£46,761
Longest winning sequence			3	Average SP of winner			4.1/1
Longest losing sequence			27	Return on stakes invested			-17.7%
1991 Form	17-97	17.5%	- 2.15	1989 Form	2-23	8.7%	- 6.00
1990 Form	10-50	20.0%	+ 2.28	1988 Form	5-46	10.9%	+ 12.32

A W POTTS (Barton-on-Humber, South Humberside)

	No. of Horses	Races Run	1st	2nd	3rd	Unpl	Per cent	£1 Level Stake
2-y-o	2	9	0	0	0	9	-	- 9.00
3-y-o	3	17	1	0	0	16	5.9	- 6.00
4-y-o+	3	7	0	0	0	7	-	- 7.00
Totals	8	33	1	0	0	32	3.0	- 22.00

Jan	Feb	Mar	Apr	May	Jun	Jul	Aug	Sep	Oct/Nov
0-1	0-1	0-0	1-3	0-0	0-7	0-5	0-7	0-6	0-3

Winning Jockey		W-R	£1 Level Stake	Winning Course		W-R	£1 Level Stake
A Proud		1-9	+ 2.00	Ripon		1-3	+ 8.00

Winning Horse		Age	Races Run	1st	2nd	3rd	Unpl	Win £
Futures Gift		3	10	1	0	0	9	2,442

Favourites	0-0		Total winning prize-money		£2,442
1991 Form	0-35		1989 Form	0-17	
1990 Form	0-37		1988 Form	0-18	

SIR MARK PRESCOTT (Newmarket)

	No. of Horses	Races Run	1st	2nd	3rd	Unpl	Per cent	£1 Level Stake
2-y-o	25	93	13	12	9	59	14.0	- 16.95
3-y-o	22	123	28	17	15	63	22.8	+ 5.77
4-y-o+	8	50	8	6	9	27	16.0	- 24.59
Totals	55	266	49	35	33	149	18.4	- 35.77

BY MONTH

2-y-o	W-R	Per cent	£1 Level Stake	3-y-o	W-R	Per cent	£1 Level Stake
January	0-0	-	0.00	January	0-1	-	- 1.00
February	0-0	-	0.00	February	0-2	-	- 2.00
March	0-0	-	0.00	March	1-5	20.0	- 2.25
April	0-0	-	0.00	April	3-18	16.7	- 7.37
May	1-1	100.0	+ 3.50	May	6-22	27.3	+ 6.00
June	2-13	15.4	- 4.00	June	5-23	21.7	+ 3.83
July	3-13	23.1	- 5.95	July	10-27	37.0	+ 25.86
August	3-14	21.4	+ 19.50	August	1-13	7.7	- 10.75
September	1-19	5.3	- 12.50	September	2-7	28.6	- 1.55
Oct/Nov	3-33	9.1	- 17.50	Oct/Nov	0-5	-	- 5.00

4-y-o+	W-R	Per cent	£1 Level Stake	Totals	W-R	Per cent	£1 Level Stake
January	0-0	-	0.00	January	0-1	-	- 1.00
February	0-0	-	0.00	February	0-2	-	- 2.00
March	0-2	-	- 2.00	March	1-7	14.3	- 4.25
April	3-12	25.0	- 3.62	April	6-30	20.0	- 10.99
May	1-9	11.1	- 7.87	May	8-32	25.0	+ 1.63
June	1-8	12.5	- 4.50	June	8-44	18.2	- 4.67
July	0-8	-	- 8.00	July	13-48	27.1	+ 11.91
August	2-4	50.0	+ 6.83	August	6-31	19.4	+ 15.58
September	0-5	-	- 5.00	September	3-31	9.7	- 19.05
Oct/Nov	1-2	50.0	- 0.43	Oct/Nov	4-40	10.0	- 22.93

DISTANCE

2-y-o	W-R	Per cent	£1 Level Stake	3-y-o	W-R	Per cent	£1 Level Stake
5f-6f	7-39	17.9	- 10.20	5f-6f	1-7	14.3	- 4.25
7f-8f	6-54	11.1	- 6.75	7f-8f	10-43	23.3	- 5.19
9f-13f	0-0	-	0.00	9f-13f	15-64	23.4	+ 11.96
14f+	0-0	-	0.00	14f+	2-9	22.2	+ 3.25

4-y-o+	W-R	Per cent	£1 Level Stake	Totals	W-R	Per cent	£1 Level Stake
5f-6f	2-16	12.5	- 11.62	5f-6f	10-62	16.1	- 26.07
7f-8f	3-17	17.6	- 4.60	7f-8f	19-114	16.7	- 16.54
9f-13f	1-8	12.5	- 5.50	9f-13f	16-72	22.2	+ 6.46
14f+	2-9	22.2	- 2.87	14f+	4-18	22.2	+ 0.38

TYPE OF RACE

	W-R	Per cent	£1 Level Stake		W-R	Per cent	£1 Level Stake
Non-Handicaps				Handicaps			
2-y-o	10-69	14.5	- 11.95	2-y-o	2-19	10.5	- 4.50
3-y-o	11-33	33.3	+ 7.73	3-y-o	13-80	16.3	- 9.29
4-y-o+	3-6	50.0	+ 0.20	4-y-o+	4-36	11.1	- 19.29
Selling	2-10	20.0	- 2.87	Selling	2-5	40.0	+ 7.50
Apprentice	2-4	50.0	+ 0.70	Apprentice	0-3	-	- 3.00
Amat/Ladies	0-1	-	- 1.00	Amat/Ladies	0-0	-	0.00
Totals	28-123	22.8	- 7.19	Totals	21-143	14.7	- 28.58

COURSE GRADE

	W-R	Per cent	£1 Level Stake
Group 1	6-58	10.3	- 36.55
Group 2	16-61	26.2	+ 1.04
Group 3	11-60	18.3	+ 7.02
Group 4	16-87	18.4	- 7.28

FIRST TIME OUT

	W-R	Per cent	£1 Level Stake
2-y-o	3-25	12.0	- 9.50
3-y-o	3-22	13.6	- 11.42
4-y-o+	0-8	-	- 8.00
Totals	6-55	10.9	- 28.92

JOCKEYS RIDING

	W-R	Per cent	£1 Level Stake		W-R	Per cent	£1 Level Stake
G Duffield	38-191	19.9	- 2.35	J Weaver	1-1	100.0	+ 1.20
K Rutter	2-6	33.3	+ 0.83	J Carroll	1-1	100.0	+ 2.00
M Roberts	2-7	28.6	+ 2.00	J Lowe	1-6	16.7	- 3.37
C Nutter	2-23	8.7	- 10.50	A Munro	1-11	9.1	- 7.25
T Quinn	1-1	100.0	+ 0.67				

D Biggs	0-3		D Harrison	0-1	Mrs E Mellor		0-1
M Birch	0-3		E Bentley	0-1	R Cochrane		0-1
J Fanning	0-2		J Quinn	0-1	R Hills		0-1
B Doyle	0-1		L Charnock	0-1	Tom O'Ryan		0-1
C Munday	0-1		M Hills	0-1			

COURSE RECORD

	Total W-R	Non-Handicaps 2-y-o	Non-Handicaps 3-y-o+	Handicaps 2-y-o	Handicaps 3-y-o+	Per cent	£1 Level Stake
Redcar	5-11	0-2	3-3	0-0	2-6	45.5	+ 6.71
Thirsk	4-9	1-3	1-2	1-2	1-2	44.4	+ 10.25
Southwell (AW)	4-23	0-6	3-10	0-1	1-6	17.4	- 2.42
Carlisle	3-8	2-3	0-1	0-0	1-4	37.5	+ 14.00
Nottingham	3-8	0-3	0-0	0-0	3-5	37.5	+ 15.13
Catterick	3-10	1-4	2-4	0-0	0-2	30.0	- 0.99
Brighton	3-17	0-3	1-2	0-1	2-11	17.6	- 8.50
Ripon	2-4	0-0	0-0	0-0	2-4	50.0	+ 4.08
Chepstow	2-5	0-0	2-3	0-1	0-1	40.0	- 2.03
Haydock	2-7	1-3	0-0	0-0	1-4	28.6	- 2.25
Warwick	2-8	1-2	0-2	0-0	1-4	25.0	- 0.87

Edinburgh	2-9	1-4	0-1	0-0	1-4	22.2	+	4.00
Newcastle	2-9	0-1	0-1	0-1	2-6	22.2	+	1.00
Ascot	1-3	0-0	1-1	0-0	0-2	33.3	-	0.80
Bath	1-3	1-1	0-0	0-1	0-1	33.3	-	1.33
Kempton	1-3	0-0	1-1	0-0	0-2	33.3	+	1.50
Windsor	1-4	1-1	0-1	0-1	0-1	25.0	+	0.50
Salisbury	1-6	0-2	0-0	0-0	1-4	16.7	+	0.50
Pontefract	1-7	0-1	0-0	0-2	1-4	14.3	-	4.50
Folkestone	1-8	1-5	0-1	0-0	0-2	12.5	-	3.50
Yarmouth	1-8	1-5	0-1	0-1	0-1	12.5	+	13.00
Hamilton	1-10	0-2	1-4	0-0	0-4	10.0	-	6.75
Leicester	1-11	0-6	0-0	1-1	0-4	9.1	-	3.00
Lingfield	1-11	0-5	1-1	0-2	0-3	9.1	-	9.00
Lingfield (AW)	1-16	0-2	1-5	0-0	0-9	6.3	-	12.50

Newmarket	0-9	Wolverhampton	0-5	Epsom	0-3
Doncaster	0-7	Beverley	0-4	Goodwood	0-2
Ayr	0-6	Sandown	0-4		
Newbury	0-5	Chester	0-3		

WINNING HORSES

	Age	Races Run	1st	2nd	3rd	Unpl	Win £
Two Left Feet	5	13	4	0	3	6	17,629
Battle Colours	3	9	3	0	4	2	12,778
Mrs Fisher	3	6	3	1	1	1	7,677
Area Girl	2	9	3	1	1	4	6,187
Wishing Cap	2	8	2	1	2	3	5,817
Khazar	3	7	2	1	0	4	5,404
Benevolent	2	8	2	0	2	4	5,295
Quantity Surveyor	3	5	2	0	0	3	4,925
Pie Hatch	3	8	2	0	2	4	4,752
Plain Fact	7	5	2	0	2	1	4,556
Lady St Lawrence	3	4	2	1	0	1	4,432
Great Max	3	6	2	2	0	2	4,426
Moving Out	4	9	1	1	1	6	3,553
Simply Amiss	2	7	2	0	0	5	3,253
Tronchetto	3	3	1	0	0	2	2,422
Mr Ziegfeld	3	9	1	0	1	7	2,364
Desert Mist	3	5	1	0	0	4	2,346
Prince Of Darkness	3	6	1	0	0	5	2,324
Ponsardin	3	8	1	2	2	3	2,280
Dune River	3	6	1	3	0	2	2,259
Mystic Memory	3	3	1	1	1	0	2,259
Perforate	3	9	1	2	1	5	2,128
Trump	3	4	1	1	1	1	2,070
Wintering	2	1	1	0	0	0	2,058
Tales Of Wisdom	3	7	1	2	0	4	2,051
Just You Dare	2	3	1	0	0	2	1,903
Sure Haven	3	5	1	1	0	3	1,725
Ripsnorter	3	7	1	0	1	5	1,716
Doulabella	2	2	1	0	0	1	1,702
Seama	2	2	1	1	0	0	1,595
Serious Time	4	6	1	2	1	2	1,277

WINNING OWNERS

	Races Won	Value £		Races Won	Value £
P W W Molins	4	17,629	Miss Elizabeth Aldous	2	4,752
W E Sturt	6	13,023	Hesmonds Stud	2	4,432
Garth Insoll	3	12,778	Lord Derby	1	2,422
Fahd Salman	5	12,494	Capt J Macdonald-Buchanan	1	2,364
Mrs David Thompson	4	7,733	Mrs C R Philipson	1	2,346
G D Waters	3	7,677	Pin Oak Stable	1	2,324
Sir Mark Prescott	3	6,554	P G Goulandris	1	2,259
Pinnacle Racing Stable	2	5,817	Mrs P G Goulandris	1	2,259
Saeed Manana	2	5,404	B Haggas	1	1,716
Neil Greig	3	4,978	G Moore	1	1,277
Lady Fairhaven	2	4,925			

Favourites	24-65	36.9%	+ 1.57	Total winning prize-money			£125,163
Longest winning sequence			3	Average SP of winner			3.7/1
Longest losing sequence			21	Return on stakes invested			-13.4%
1991 Form	48-238	20.2%	+ 14.32	1989 Form	40-247	16.2%	- 54.45
1990 Form	48-265	18.1%	- 35.55	1988 Form	34-234	14.5%	- 59.50

R J PRICE (Leominster, H'ford & Worcs)

	No. of Horses	Races Run	1st	2nd	3rd	Unpl	Per cent	£1 Level Stake
2-y-o	0	0	0	0	0	0	-	0.00
3-y-o	2	6	0	0	1	5	-	- 6.00
4-y-o+	4	10	2	2	0	6	20.0	+ 12.00
Totals	6	16	2	2	1	11	12.5	+ 6.00

Jan	Feb	Mar	Apr	May	Jun	Jul	Aug	Sep	Oct/Nov
0-0	0-0	0-0	1-3	1-4	0-2	0-0	0-3	0-4	0-0

Winning Jockeys	W-R	£1 Level Stake			W-R	£1 Level Stake
S Davies	1-2	+ 3.00	T Sprake		1-3	+ 14.00

Winning Courses	W-R	£1 Level Stake			W-R	£1 Level Stake
Bath	1-2	+ 3.00	Wolverhampton		1-3	+ 14.00

Winning Horse	Age	Races Run	1st	2nd	3rd	Unpl	Win £
Zealous Kitten	4	4	2	0	0	2	5,393

Favourites	0-0		Total winning prize-money	£5,393

G A PRITCHARD-GORDON (Newmarket)

	No. of Horses	Races Run	1st	2nd	3rd	Unpl	Per cent	£1 Level Stake
2-y-o	15	71	6	8	5	52	8.5	- 5.17
3-y-o	12	71	8	16	10	37	11.3	- 36.50
4-y-o+	9	37	3	1	5	28	8.1	- 18.25
Totals	36	179	17	25	20	117	9.5	- 59.92

BY MONTH

2-y-o	W-R	Per cent	£1 Level Stake	3-y-o	W-R	Per cent	£1 Level Stake
January	0-0	-	0.00	January	0-0	-	0.00
February	0-0	-	0.00	February	0-0	-	0.00
March	0-0	-	0.00	March	0-0	-	0.00
April	0-5	-	- 5.00	April	0-9	-	- 9.00
May	0-13	-	- 13.00	May	1-9	11.1	+ 3.00
June	2-12	16.7	+ 26.33	June	2-16	12.5	- 9.00
July	2-12	16.7	- 0.50	July	3-14	21.4	- 3.50
August	1-7	14.3	- 3.00	August	1-8	12.5	- 5.00
September	1-9	11.1	+ 3.00	September	1-6	16.7	- 4.00
Oct/Nov	0-13	-	- 13.00	Oct/Nov	0-9	-	- 9.00

4-y-o+	W-R	Per cent	£1 Level Stake	Totals	W-R	Per cent	£1 Level Stake
January	0-2	-	- 2.00	January	0-2	-	- 2.00
February	0-0	-	0.00	February	0-0	-	0.00
March	0-2	-	- 2.00	March	0-2	-	- 2.00
April	0-3	-	- 3.00	April	0-17	-	- 17.00
May	0-3	-	- 3.00	May	1-25	4.0	- 13.00
June	0-6	-	- 6.00	June	4-34	11.8	+ 11.33
July	0-3	-	- 3.00	July	5-29	17.2	- 7.00
August	2-4	50.0	+ 6.75	August	4-19	21.1	- 1.25
September	0-7	-	- 7.00	September	2-22	9.1	- 8.00
Oct/Nov	1-7	14.3	+ 1.00	Oct/Nov	1-29	3.4	- 21.00

DISTANCE

2-y-o	W-R	Per cent	£1 Level Stake	3-y-o	W-R	Per cent	£1 Level Stake
5f-6f	5-54	9.3	- 0.17	5f-6f	1-11	9.1	- 9.00
7f-8f	1-17	5.9	- 5.00	7f-8f	2-25	8.0	- 18.25
9f-13f	0-0	-	0.00	9f-13f	0-21	-	- 21.00
14f+	0-0	-	0.00	14f+	5-14	35.7	+ 11.75

4-y-o+	W-R	Per cent	£1 Level Stake	Totals	W-R	Per cent	£1 Level Stake
5f-6f	0-0	-	0.00	5f-6f	6-65	9.2	- 9.17
7f-8f	1-13	7.7	- 5.00	7f-8f	4-55	7.3	- 28.25
9f-13f	2-18	11.1	- 7.25	9f-13f	2-39	5.1	- 28.25
14f+	0-6	-	- 6.00	14f+	5-20	25.0	+ 5.75

TYPE OF RACE

Non-Handicaps	W-R	Per cent	£1 Level Stake	Handicaps	W-R	Per cent	£1 Level Stake
2-y-o	0-42	-	- 42.00	2-y-o	3-17	17.6	+ 8.00
3-y-o	3-30	10.0	- 21.75	3-y-o	4-34	11.8	- 11.50
4-y-o+	0-3	-	- 3.00	4-y-o+	3-25	12.0	- 6.25
Selling	3-14	21.4	+ 26.83	Selling	0-0	-	0.00
Apprentice	1-1	100.0	+ 2.75	Apprentice	0-6	-	- 6.00
Amat/Ladies	0-1	-	- 1.00	Amat/Ladies	0-6	-	- 6.00
Totals	7-91	7.7	- 38.17	Totals	10-88	11.4	- 21.75

COURSE GRADE

	W-R	Per cent	£1 Level Stake
Group 1	3-87	3.4	- 72.75
Group 2	4-25	16.0	- 7.75
Group 3	5-30	16.7	+ 28.75
Group 4	5-37	13.5	- 8.17

FIRST TIME OUT

	W-R	Per cent	£1 Level Stake
2-y-o	0-15	-	- 15.00
3-y-o	0-12	-	- 12.00
4-y-o+	0-9	-	- 9.00
Totals	0-36	-	- 36.00

JOCKEYS RIDING

	W-R	Per cent	£1 Level Stake		W-R	Per cent	£1 Level Stake
D Harrison	4-25	16.0	+ 3.75	L Dettori	2-8	25.0	- 3.25
G Carter	3-27	11.1	+ 21.75	N Day	2-9	22.2	+ 1.75
P Robinson	2-6	33.3	+ 1.33	R Cochrane	1-9	11.1	- 4.00
G Duffield	2-8	25.0	- 2.25	W Hood	1-19	5.3	- 11.00

	W-R			W-R			W-R
N Carlisle	0-9	P Turner	0-2	M Roberts			0-1
B Doyle	0-6	A Clark	0-1	Miss C Preston			0-1
W Ryan	0-6	A Tucker	0-1	Miss L S-Sackville			0-1
A McGlone	0-5	Antoinette Armes	0-1	R Fox			0-1
Mr P P-Gordon	0-5	D Biggs	0-1	R Hills			0-1
A Munro	0-3	D Holland	0-1	R Perham			0-1
F Norton	0-3	J Fanning	0-1	S Cauthen			0-1
W Carson	0-3	J Lowe	0-1	S Maloney			0-1
W R Swinburn	0-3	J Reid	0-1	S Whitworth			0-1
J Quinn	0-2	J Weaver	0-1				
K Fallon	0-2	K Darley	0-1				

COURSE RECORD

	Total W-R	Non-Handicaps 2-y-o	Non-Handicaps 3-y-o+	Handicaps 2-y-o	Handicaps 3-y-o+	Per cent	£1 Level Stake
Yarmouth	4-13	1-7	0-1	1-1	2-4	30.8	+ 42.75
Redcar	3-12	0-3	0-0	1-1	2-8	25.0	+ 2.75
Wolverhampton	2-6	0-2	0-1	0-0	2-3	33.3	+ 9.75
Folkestone	2-12	1-2	0-3	0-2	1-5	16.7	- 2.67

Pritchard-Gordon G A

Beverley	1-1	0-0	1-1	0-0	0-0	100.0	+	2.00
York	1-4	0-1	1-2	0-0	0-1	25.0	-	0.75
Lingfield (AW)	1-4	0-1	1-1	0-0	0-2	25.0	-	0.25
Kempton	1-7	0-2	1-2	0-0	0-3	14.3	-	5.00
Lingfield	1-7	1-4	0-0	0-1	0-2	14.3	-	4.50
Goodwood	1-13	0-5	0-2	1-2	0-4	7.7	-	4.00

Newmarket	0-29	Newbury	0-4	Salisbury		0-2
Doncaster	0-11	Nottingham	0-4	Windsor		0-2
Southwell (AW)	0-11	Pontefract	0-4	Ascot		0-1
Leicester	0-6	Ayr	0-2	Brighton		0-1
Sandown	0-6	Catterick	0-2	Ripon		0-1
Haydock	0-5	Chester	0-2			
Newcastle	0-5	Edinburgh	0-2			

WINNING HORSES

		Races					Win
	Age	Run	1st	2nd	3rd	Unpl	£
Zany Zanna	2	13	4	2	1	6	16,225
Farmer's Pet	3	10	3	3	0	4	7,630
Newton Point	3	9	2	0	3	4	6,687
Trundley Wood	2	7	1	1	0	5	6,160
Shadow Bird	5	10	2	1	2	5	4,570
La Bamba	6	12	1	0	1	10	3,470
Harvest Girl	3	9	1	2	0	6	3,231
King's Guest	3	9	1	4	2	2	2,685
Burishki	2	8	1	1	1	5	2,324
Missy-S	3	11	1	2	2	6	1,618

WINNING OWNERS

	Races Won	Value £		Races Won	Value £
Giles W Pritchard-Gordon	6	21,780	A G Don	2	4,570
D R Midwwod	3	7,630	Miss M C Macrae	1	3,470
A M Ennever	2	6,687	Lord Cadogan	1	2,685
Mrs E H Vestey	1	6,160	Mrs Stephanie Goodman	1	1,618

Favourites	8-26	30.8%	+	4.00	Total winning prize-money			£54,599

Longest winning sequence			2
Longest losing sequence			26

Average SP of winner			6.0/1
Return on stakes invested			-33.5%

1991 Form	14-223	6.3%	- 94.26	1989 Form	16-223	7.2%	- 108.95
1990 Form	18-201	9.0%	- 74.95	1988 Form	20-250	8.0%	- 102.89

MRS J RAMSDEN (Thirsk, North Yorks)

	No. of Horses	Races Run	1st	2nd	3rd	Unpl	Per cent	£1 Level Stake
2-y-o	10	35	2	2	3	28	5.7	- 16.00
3-y-o	20	116	11	12	14	79	9.5	+ 2.75
4-y-o+	18	94	11	13	7	63	11.7	- 44.37
Totals	48	245	24	27	24	170	9.8	- 57.62

BY MONTH

2-y-o	W-R	Per cent	£1 Level Stake	3-y-o	W-R	Per cent	£1 Level Stake
January	0-0	-	0.00	January	0-0	-	0.00
February	0-0	-	0.00	February	1-1	100.0	+ 16.00
March	0-0	-	0.00	March	1-13	7.7	- 3.00
April	0-2	-	- 2.00	April	0-25	-	- 25.00
May	0-2	-	- 2.00	May	0-22	-	- 22.00
June	0-3	-	- 3.00	June	2-15	13.3	+ 5.00
July	0-4	-	- 4.00	July	1-6	16.7	+ 2.00
August	1-6	16.7	+ 9.00	August	2-12	16.7	+ 10.00
September	1-9	11.1	- 5.00	September	2-11	18.2	- 2.75
Oct/Nov	0-9	-	- 9.00	Oct/Nov	2-11	18.2	+ 22.50

4-y-o+	W-R	Per cent	£1 Level Stake	Totals	W-R	Per cent	£1 Level Stake
January	0-0	-	0.00	January	0-0	-	0.00
February	0-1	-	- 1.00	February	1-2	50.0	+ 15.00
March	1-9	11.1	- 1.50	March	2-22	9.1	- 4.50
April	3-21	14.3	- 12.12	April	3-48	6.3	- 39.12
May	2-18	11.1	- 10.00	May	2-42	4.8	- 34.00
June	1-9	11.1	- 1.00	June	3-27	11.1	+ 1.00
July	0-7	-	- 7.00	July	1-17	5.9	- 9.00
August	3-10	30.0	+ 3.75	August	6-28	21.4	+ 22.75
September	1-9	11.1	- 5.50	September	4-29	13.8	- 13.25
Oct/Nov	0-10	-	- 10.00	Oct/Nov	2-30	6.7	+ 3.50

DISTANCE

2-y-o	W-R	Per cent	£1 Level Stake	3-y-o	W-R	Per cent	£1 Level Stake
5f-6f	1-19	5.3	- 4.00	5f-6f	3-23	13.0	+ 19.00
7f-8f	1-16	6.3	- 12.00	7f-8f	7-56	12.5	+ 17.75
9f-13f	0-0	-	0.00	9f-13f	1-35	2.9	- 32.00
14f+	0-0	-	0.00	14f+	0-2	-	- 2.00

4-y-o+	W-R	Per cent	£1 Level Stake	Totals	W-R	Per cent	£1 Level Stake
5f-6f	0-5	-	- 5.00	5f-6f	4-47	8.5	+ 10.00
7f-8f	5-34	14.7	- 9.75	7f-8f	13-106	12.3	- 4.00
9f-13f	5-43	11.6	- 21.12	9f-13f	6-78	7.7	- 53.12
14f+	1-12	8.3	- 8.50	14f+	1-14	7.1	- 10.50

TYPE OF RACE

Non-Handicaps	W-R	Per cent	£1 Level Stake	Handicaps	W-R	Per cent	£1 Level Stake
2-y-o	1-23	4.3	- 8.00	2-y-o	1-9	11.1	- 5.00
3-y-o	4-29	13.8	+ 8.00	3-y-o	7-73	9.6	+ 8.75
4-y-o+	0-2	-	- 2.00	4-y-o+	6-74	8.1	- 45.37
Selling	0-8	-	- 8.00	Selling	1-7	14.3	- 4.00
Apprentice	0-1	-	- 1.00	Apprentice	4-13	30.8	+ 5.00
Amat/Ladies	0-0	-	0.00	Amat/Ladies	0-6	-	- 6.00
Totals	5-63	7.9	- 11.00	Totals	19-182	10.4	- 46.62

COURSE GRADE

	W-R	Per cent	£1 Level Stake
Group 1	10-97	10.3	- 20.50
Group 2	5-38	13.2	+ 2.00
Group 3	7-71	9.9	- 20.12
Group 4	2-39	5.1	- 19.00

FIRST TIME OUT

	W-R	Per cent	£1 Level Stake
2-y-o	0-9	-	- 9.00
3-y-o	1-17	5.9	0.00
4-y-o+	2-14	14.3	- 3.25
Totals	3-40	7.5	- 12.25

JOCKEYS RIDING

	W-R	Per cent	£1 Level Stake		W-R	Per cent	£1 Level Stake
G Baxter	6-29	20.7	+ 31.00	S Davies	1-4	25.0	+ 2.50
J Weaver	3-24	12.5	- 9.25	J Lowe	1-6	16.7	+ 1.50
R Havlin	2-6	33.3	+ 0.50	M Roberts	1-6	16.7	- 2.50
M Birch	2-16	12.5	- 3.00	D Holland	1-6	16.7	+ 3.00
P Robinson	1-2	50.0	+ 1.00	K Darley	1-9	11.1	- 7.75
R Burke	1-2	50.0	+ 24.00	K Fallon	1-11	9.1	- 4.00
M Hills	1-3	33.3	+ 14.00	A Munro	1-12	8.3	- 2.00
N Carlisle	1-3	33.3	- 0.62				

T Lucas	0-30	S Wood	0-3	M Tebbutt	0-1
P Burke	0-12	B Crossley	0-2	Miss D Pomeroy	0-1
D McKeown	0-7	B Raymond	0-2	Miss T Bracegirdle	0-1
A Mackay	0-5	J Reid	0-2	N Kennedy	0-1
D Harrison	0-5	N Connorton	0-2	P Bowe	0-1
J Fanning	0-4	Dale Gibson	0-1	R Hills	0-1
Mr R Hale	0-4	G Carter	0-1	R Lappin	0-1
D Biggs	0-3	G Duffield	0-1	R Price	0-1
F Norton	0-3	G Hind	0-1	T Quinn	0-1
J Carroll	0-3	L Charnock	0-1	T Williams	0-1
J Tate	0-3	L Dettori	0-1		

COURSE RECORD

	Total W-R	Non-Handicaps 2-y-o	Non-Handicaps 3-y-o+	Handicaps 2-y-o	Handicaps 3-y-o+	Per cent	£1 Level Stake
Ayr	3-9	0-0	2-2	0-0	1-7	33.3	+ 4.50
Newmarket	3-11	0-0	0-0	0-2	3-9	27.3	+ 29.00
Thirsk	3-16	1-3	0-1	0-0	2-12	18.8	+ 12.00

Pontefract	3-26	0-2	0-5	0-1	3-18	11.5	- 10.75
Hamilton	2-15	0-1	0-5	0-0	2-9	13.3	- 9.37
Nottingham	2-16	0-1	0-2	0-1	2-12	12.5	+ 14.00
Haydock	2-24	0-3	0-1	0-1	2-19	8.3	- 18.50
Doncaster	2-27	0-1	1-5	0-2	1-19	7.4	- 9.50
Southwell (AW)	1-4	0-0	1-1	0-0	0-3	25.0	+ 13.00
Redcar	1-7	0-2	0-0	1-1	0-4	14.3	- 3.00
Edinburgh	1-10	0-1	0-2	0-0	1-7	10.0	- 7.00
Ripon	1-13	0-2	0-3	0-0	1-8	7.7	- 5.00

Newcastle	0-15	York		0-7	Chester	0-2
Catterick	0-14	Carlisle		0-6	Sandown	0-1
Beverley	0-7	Wolverhampton		0-5		
Leicester	0-7	Ascot		0-3		

WINNING HORSES

	Age	Races Run	1st	2nd	3rd	Unpl	Win £
Daros	3	4	2	1	0	1	16,755
Hob Green	3	9	3	1	0	5	15,276
Vague Dancer	6	10	3	0	0	7	10,037
Sillars Stalker	4	7	3	2	0	2	8,608
King Of Chance	4	6	2	1	0	3	7,018
Tahitian	3	15	2	4	0	9	5,409
Houlston's Will	3	10	2	1	1	6	5,172
Doc Cottrill	2	6	1	0	1	4	3,834
Halston Prince	5	4	1	0	0	3	3,080
Double Feature	3	13	1	1	3	8	3,048
Latin Leader	2	4	1	0	0	3	2,784
Cool Enough	11	15	1	2	1	11	2,390
Admirals Seat	4	6	1	0	1	4	2,385
Breakdancer	3	6	1	1	0	4	2,232

WINNING OWNERS

	Races Won	Value £		Races Won	Value £
K E Wheldon	10	42,163	Mark Houlston (Decorators)	2	5,172
Mrs A E Sigsworth	3	15,276	Mrs J R Ramsden	1	2,390
David Thompson	3	9,802	Nicholas De Savary	1	2,385
Sillars Civil Engineering	3	8,608	R C Moody	1	2,232

Favourites	10-34	29.4%	- 0.62	Total winning prize-money			£88,026

Longest winning sequence		2	Average SP of winner		6.8/1
Longest losing sequence		34	Return on stakes invested		-23.3%

1991 Form	38-294	12.9%	- 123.50	1989 Form	32-249	12.9%	- 53.95
1990 Form	26-239	10.9%	- 104.32	1988 Form	14-123	11.4%	+ 20.25

A S REID (Thurleigh, Beds)

	No. of Horses	Races Run	1st	2nd	3rd	Unpl	Per cent	£1 Level Stake
2-y-o	0	0	0	0	0	0	-	0.00
3-y-o	4	18	0	0	0	18	-	- 18.00
4-y-o+	11	28	1	1	2	24	3.6	- 21.00
Totals	15	46	1	1	2	42	2.2	- 39.00

Jan	Feb	Mar	Apr	May	Jun	Jul	Aug	Sep	Oct/Nov
0-2	0-5	0-5	1-15	0-4	0-6	0-3	0-0	0-2	0-4

Winning Jockey		W-R	£1 Level Stake	Winning Course		W-R	£1 Level Stake
P McCabe		1-16	- 9.00	Brighton		1-2	+ 5.00

Winning Horse	Age	Races Run	1st	2nd	3rd	Unpl	Win £
Daisy Grey	4	7	1	1	0	5	2,520

Favourites	0-1	Total winning prize-money	£2,520

1991 Form	0-14

MRS G R REVELEY (Lingdale, Co Cleveland)

	No. of Horses	Races Run	1st	2nd	3rd	Unpl	Per cent	£1 Level Stake
2-y-o	13	51	6	6	6	33	11.8	- 21.00
3-y-o	25	121	24	10	10	77	19.8	- 14.36
4-y-o+	30	154	38	19	28	69	24.7	+ 32.49
Totals	68	326	68	35	44	179	20.9	- 2.87

BY MONTH

2-y-o	W-R	Per cent	£1 Level Stake	3-y-o	W-R	Per cent	£1 Level Stake
January	0-0	-	0.00	January	0-1	-	- 1.00
February	0-0	-	0.00	February	0-0	-	0.00
March	1-3	33.3	- 1.00	March	0-1	-	- 1.00
April	1-6	16.7	- 3.62	April	0-8	-	- 8.00
May	2-7	28.6	- 4.38	May	4-15	26.7	+ 5.63
June	0-4	-	- 4.00	June	0-19	-	- 19.00
July	0-5	-	- 5.00	July	9-26	34.6	+ 14.98
August	2-14	14.3	+ 9.00	August	4-17	23.5	- 7.55
September	0-3	-	- 3.00	September	4-13	30.8	+ 7.33
Oct/Nov	0-9	-	- 9.00	Oct/Nov	3-21	14.3	- 5.75

4-y-o+	W-R	Per cent	£1 Level Stake	Totals	W-R	Per cent	£1 Level Stake
January	0-0	-	0.00	January	0-1	-	- 1.00
February	0-0	-	0.00	February	0-0	-	0.00
March	0-3	-	- 3.00	March	1-7	14.3	- 5.00
April	2-13	15.4	- 3.50	April	3-27	11.1	- 15.12
May	3-18	16.7	- 0.50	May	9-40	22.5	+ 0.75
June	8-24	33.3	+ 4.49	June	8-47	17.0	- 18.51
July	9-34	26.5	- 3.13	July	18-65	27.7	+ 6.85
August	4-27	14.8	- 3.50	August	10-58	17.2	- 2.05
September	7-20	35.0	+ 32.38	September	11-36	30.6	+ 36.71
Oct/Nov	5-15	33.3	+ 9.25	Oct/Nov	8-45	17.8	- 5.50

DISTANCE

2-y-o	W-R	Per cent	£1 Level Stake	3-y-o	W-R	Per cent	£1 Level Stake
5f-6f	5-22	22.7	- 9.00	5f-6f	1-14	7.1	- 11.80
7f-8f	1-29	3.4	- 12.00	7f-8f	8-35	22.9	+ 4.87
9f-13f	0-0	-	0.00	9f-13f	13-61	21.3	- 6.00
14f+	0-0	-	0.00	14f+	2-11	18.2	- 1.43

4-y-o+	W-R	Per cent	£1 Level Stake	Totals	W-R	Per cent	£1 Level Stake
5f-6f	0-3	-	- 3.00	5f-6f	6-39	15.4	- 23.80
7f-8f	9-44	20.5	+ 20.50	7f-8f	18-108	16.7	+ 13.37
9f-13f	20-81	24.7	+ 6.93	9f-13f	33-142	23.2	+ 0.93
14f+	9-26	34.6	+ 8.06	14f+	11-37	29.7	+ 6.63

TYPE OF RACE

Non-Handicaps	W-R	Per cent	£1 Level Stake	Handicaps	W-R	Per cent	£1 Level Stake
2-y-o	3-34	8.8	- 24.33	2-y-o	1-11	9.1	+ 6.00
3-y-o	7-31	22.6	- 9.84	3-y-o	11-68	16.2	- 7.75
4-y-o+	5-26	19.2	- 12.64	4-y-o+	24-105	22.9	+ 21.88
Selling	8-18	44.4	+ 9.41	Selling	0-7	-	- 7.00
Apprentice	1-2	50.0	- 0.43	Apprentice	6-18	33.3	+ 15.33
Amat/Ladies	0-0	-	0.00	Amat/Ladies	2-6	33.3	+ 6.50
Totals	24-111	21.6	- 37.83	Totals	44-215	20.5	+ 34.96

COURSE GRADE

	W-R	Per cent	£1 Level Stake
Group 1	20-96	20.8	+ 9.41
Group 2	14-103	13.6	- 31.79
Group 3	23-85	27.1	+ 9.91
Group 4	11-42	26.2	+ 9.60

FIRST TIME OUT

	W-R	Per cent	£1 Level Stake
2-y-o	1-12	8.3	- 6.00
3-y-o	2-22	9.1	- 12.80
4-y-o+	1-25	4.0	- 21.00
Totals	4-59	6.8	- 39.80

343

JOCKEYS RIDING

	W-R	Per cent	£1 Level Stake		W-R	Per cent	£1 Level Stake
K Darley	27-102	26.5	+ 13.90	Mr J Durkan	1-1	100.0	+ 3.00
D Moffatt	12-49	24.5	+ 14.71	M J Kinane	1-1	100.0	+ 11.00
J Lowe	11-70	15.7	- 11.25	F Norton	1-2	50.0	+ 0.50
J Fanning	6-16	37.5	+ 10.29	Mr M Buckley	1-2	50.0	+ 6.50
Claire Balding	2-5	40.0	+ 10.50	J Fortune	1-3	33.3	- 1.71
M Birch	2-10	20.0	- 4.00	M Roberts	1-3	33.3	- 1.56
Jaki Houston	1-1	100.0	+ 3.00	D McKeown	1-3	33.3	+ 0.25

K Fallon	0-8	B Raymond	0-2	G Baxter	0-1
Dale Gibson	0-7	G Hind	0-2	G Forster	0-1
S Copp	0-5	L Piggott	0-2	L Charnock	0-1
G Duffield	0-4	Miss M Juster	0-2	Mr N Wilson	0-1
J Weaver	0-3	N Kennedy	0-2	S Wynne	0-1
L Dettori	0-3	R Cochrane	0-2	W Carson	0-1
M Hills	0-3	S Maloney	0-2	W Ryan	0-1
N Carlisle	0-3	D Harrison	0-1		

COURSE RECORD

	Total W-R	Non-Handicaps 2-y-o	Non-Handicaps 3-y-o+	Handicaps 2-y-o	Handicaps 3-y-o+	Per cent	£1 Level Stake
Redcar	12-70	1-11	2-11	0-3	9-45	17.1	- 11.79
Hamilton	10-39	1-6	5-15	0-0	4-18	25.6	- 5.61
Pontefract	8-25	0-3	2-4	1-3	5-15	32.0	+ 23.75
Catterick	7-14	0-1	4-7	0-0	3-6	50.0	+ 16.90
Newcastle	6-21	0-3	0-3	0-1	6-14	28.6	+ 2.00
Beverley	4-12	2-4	0-0	0-1	2-7	33.3	- 0.67
Ayr	4-15	0-2	2-6	0-0	2-7	26.7	+ 4.33
Doncaster	4-22	0-3	0-1	0-1	4-17	18.2	- 1.25
Carlisle	3-12	0-0	1-4	0-0	2-8	25.0	+ 7.41
Haydock	2-11	0-0	0-5	0-0	2-6	18.2	+ 1.83
York	2-12	0-1	0-0	0-0	2-11	16.7	+ 1.00
Ascot	1-3	0-0	0-0	0-0	1-3	33.3	+ 9.00
Yarmouth	1-3	0-0	1-2	0-0	0-1	33.3	- .1.56
Thirsk	1-11	0-3	0-1	0-0	1-7	9.1	0.00
Newmarket	1-12	0-0	1-1	0-2	0-9	8.3	- 7.50
Edinburgh	1-13	1-2	0-4	0-0	0-7	7.7	- 11.71
Ripon	1-18	0-0	1-5	0-0	0-13	5.6	- 16.00

Chester	0-4	Nottingham	0-3	Southwell (AW)	0-1
Leicester	0-3	Wolverhampton	0-2		

WINNING HORSES

	Age	Races Run	1st	2nd	3rd	Unpl	Win £
Sharpalto	5	15	4	1	1	9	61,336
Mellottie	7	5	2	1	0	2	32,613
Amazing Feat	3	8	4	0	1	3	17,896
Majed	4	6	3	0	1	2	10,830
Azureus	4	8	3	1	1	3	10,408
Grouse-N-Heather	3	8	5	0	0	3	10,355

Express Gift	3	6	3	0	0	3	10,330
Broctune Grey	8	7	4	1	1	1	10,192
Sweet Mignonette	4	7	4	0	2	1	9,860
Northern Graduate	3	8	3	3	0	2	9,062
Sunderland Echo	3	6	3	1	0	2	7,984
Corn Lily	6	5	2	0	0	3	7,528
Shadow Jury	2	6	3	2	1	0	6,927
Kagram Queen	4	6	3	0	1	2	6,580
My Desire	4	6	2	0	1	3	5,597
Jazilah	4	4	2	1	1	0	5,518
Kayartis	3	5	2	0	0	3	4,667
Sarawat	4	5	1	0	2	2	3,787
Kiss In The Dark	2	8	1	1	2	4	3,418
Imhotep	5	3	1	0	0	2	3,036
Bold Amusement	2	1	1	0	0	0	2,654
Batabanoo	3	11	1	2	3	5	2,595
Ambuscade	6	3	1	1	1	0	2,574
Bonus Point	2	7	1	0	0	6	2,508
Henbury Hall	4	9	1	3	1	4	2,469
Tarda	5	9	1	1	1	6	2,448
Danza Heights	6	5	1	1	0	3	2,406
Brodessa	6	4	1	1	2	0	2,363
Grey Power	5	9	1	1	3	4	2,343
Persian Fleece	3	5	1	2	1	1	2,290
Able Lassie	4	9	1	1	4	3	2,259
Tees Gazette Girl	3	6	1	0	0	5	1,618
White Willow	3	4	1	0	0	3	1,478

WINNING OWNERS

	Races Won	Value £		Races Won	Value £
T J Prew	2	54,351	Mrs M A Spensley	2	5,597
P D Savill	12	38,988	Mrs J M Allen	2	4,667
Mrs J G Fulton	2	32,613	R Meredith	1	3,418
Robbie Cameron	6	12,614	David Bell	1	2,654
Laurel (Leisure) Ltd	3	10,830	Mrs Lynne Firth	1	2,574
J C Murdoch	3	10,408	Mrs M E Gray	1	2,469
H Young	3	10,330	Mrs Dorothy Horner	1	2,448
D Playforth	4	10,192	Mrs M Williams	1	2,406
M J Ogden	4	9,860	R W S Jevon	1	2,363
Mrs E A Kettlewell	4	9,616	J P S Racing	1	2,343
S Aitken	3	9,305	Miss S Hainey	1	2,290
Northeast Press Ltd	3	7,984	North Eastern Evening Gazette	1	1,618
Mrs Susan McDonald	2	7,528	Mrs H North	1	1,478
Millprew Bloodstock	2	6,985			

Favourites	32-69	46.4%	+ 13.51	Total winning prize-money			£267,927
Longest winning sequence			4	Average SP of winner			3.8/1
Longest losing sequence			17	Return on stakes invested			-0.9%
1991 Form	34-226	15.0%	- 56.47	1989 Form	15-131	11.5%	- 39.37
1990 Form	15-146	10.3%	+ 1.42	1988 Form	12-187	6.4%	- 87.75

B S ROTHWELL (Catwick, North Humberside)

	No. of Horses	Races Run	1st	2nd	3rd	Unpl	Per cent	£1 Level Stake
2-y-o	9	47	3	7	2	35	6.4	- 18.00
3-y-o	1	4	0	0	0	4	-	- 4.00
4-y-o+	2	6	0	2	0	4	-	- 6.00
Totals	12	57	3	9	2	43	5.3	- 28.00

Jan	Feb	Mar	Apr	May	Jun	Jul	Aug	Sep	Oct/Nov
0-0	0-0	0-1	0-4	0-2	0-10	2-14	1-10	0-10	0-6

Winning Jockeys	W-R	£1 Level Stake				W-R	£1 Level Stake
D Harrison	1-2	+ 4.00		D Holland		1-8	- 2.00
S Wood	1-5	+ 12.00					

Winning Courses	W-R	£1 Level Stake				W-R	£1 Level Stake
Chester	2-4	+ 8.00		Beverley		1-15	+ 2.00

Winning Horses	Age	Races Run	1st	2nd	3rd	Unpl	Win £
Riston Lady	2	9	2	4	0	3	8,373
Persian Fountain	2	4	1	0	0	3	2,128

Favourites	0-0	Total winning prize-money	£10,501

1991 Form   0-5

R ROWE (Pulborough, West Sussex)

	No. of Horses	Races Run	1st	2nd	3rd	Unpl	Per cent	£1 Level Stake
2-y-o	0	0	0	0	0	0	-	· 0.00
3-y-o	0	0	0	0	0	0	-	0.00
4-y-o+	3	12	1	0	2	9	8.3	- 5.50
Totals	3	12	1	0	2	9	8.3	- 5.50

Jan	Feb	Mar	Apr	May	Jun	Jul	Aug	Sep	Oct/Nov
0-0	0-0	0-0	0-0	0-0	0-4	0-4	0-1	1-3	0-0

Winning Jockey	W-R	£1 Level Stake	Winning Course	W-R	£1 Level Stake
G Baxter	1-4	+ 2.50	Salisbury	1-2	+ 4.50

Winning Horse	Age	Races Run	1st	2nd	3rd	Unpl	Win £
L'Uomo Classics	5	5	1	0	1	3	3,915

Favourites	0-0	Total winning prize-money	£3,915

346

M J RYAN (Newmarket)

	No. of Horses	Races Run	1st	2nd	3rd	Unpl	Per cent	£1 Level Stake
2-y-o	6	24	0	2	0	22	-	- 24.00
3-y-o	5	49	10	3	4	32	20.4	+ 23.50
4-y-o+	12	99	12	16	20	51	12.1	- 28.24
Totals	23	172	22	21	24	105	12.8	- 28.74

BY MONTH

2-y-o	W-R	Per cent	£1 Level Stake	3-y-o	W-R	Per cent	£1 Level Stake
January	0-0	-	0.00	January	0-0	-	0.00
February	0-0	-	0.00	February	0-0	-	0.00
March	0-0	-	0.00	March	0-1	-	- 1.00
April	0-0	-	0.00	April	1-2	50.0	+ 3.50
May	0-0	-	0.00	May	0-6	-	- 6.00
June	0-1	-	- 1.00	June	1-8	12.5	+ 9.00
July	0-5	-	- 5.00	July	4-9	44.4	+ 20.00
August	0-1	-	- 1.00	August	3-7	42.9	+ 10.25
September	0-5	-	- 5.00	September	1-7	14.3	- 3.25
Oct/Nov	0-12	-	- 12.00	Oct/Nov	0-9	-	- 9.00

4-y-o+	W-R	Per cent	£1 Level Stake	Totals	W-R	Per cent	£1 Level Stake
January	4-15	26.7	+ 2.63	January	4-15	26.7	+ 2.63
February	1-6	16.7	- 1.50	February	1-6	16.7	- 1.50
March	0-9	-	- 9.00	March	0-10	-	- 10.00
April	2-12	16.7	+ 3.50	April	3-14	21.4	+ 7.00
May	1-12	8.3	- 9.37	May	1-18	5.6	- 15.37
June	1-14	7.1	- 1.00	June	2-23	8.7	+ 7.00
July	0-7	-	- 7.00	July	4-21	19.0	+ 8.00
August	1-6	16.7	+ 2.00	August	4-14	28.6	+ 11.25
September	1-9	11.1	- 2.50	September	2-21	9.5	- 10.75
Oct/Nov	1-9	11.1	- 6.00	Oct/Nov	1-30	3.3	- 27.00

DISTANCE

2-y-o	W-R	Per cent	£1 Level Stake	3-y-o	W-R	Per cent	£1 Level Stake
5f-6f	0-15	-	- 15.00	5f-6f	3-16	18.8	+ 1.50
7f-8f	0-9	-	- 9.00	7f-8f	5-19	26.3	+ 15.25
9f-13f	0-0	-	0.00	9f-13f	1-12	8.3	+ 5.00
14f+	0-0	-	0.00	14f+	1-2	50.0	+ 1.75

4-y-o+	W-R	Per cent	£1 Level Stake	Totals	W-R	Per cent	£1 Level Stake
5f-6f	0-0	-	0.00	5f-6f	3-31	9.7	- 13.50
7f-8f	6-41	14.6	- 5.87	7f-8f	11-69	15.9	+ 0.38
9f-13f	5-51	9.8	- 23.37	9f-13f	6-63	9.5	- 18.37
14f+	1-7	14.3	+ 1.00	14f+	2-9	22.2	+ 2.75

Ryan M J

TYPE OF RACE

Non-Handicaps	W-R	Per cent	£1 Level Stake	Handicaps	W-R	Per cent	£1 Level Stake
2-y-o	0-14	-	- 14.00	2-y-o	0-10	-	- 10.00
3-y-o	0-1	-	- 1.00	3-y-o	10-48	20.8	+ 24.50
4-y-o+	5-14	35.7	+ 4.26	4-y-o+	5-77	6.5	- 45.50
Selling	0-1	-	- 1.00	Selling	1-3	33.3	+ 10.00
Apprentice	0-0	-	0.00	Apprentice	1-3	33.3	+ 5.00
Amat/Ladies	0-0	-	0.00	Amat/Ladies	0-1	-	- 1.00
Totals	5-30	16.7	- 11.74	Totals	17-142	12.0	- 17.00

COURSE GRADE

	W-R	Per cent	£1 Level Stake
Group 1	3-50	6.0	- 17.50
Group 2	2-15	13.3	- 7.25
Group 3	8-61	13.1	- 11.87
Group 4	9-46	19.6	+ 7.88

FIRST TIME OUT

	W-R	Per cent	£1 Level Stake
2-y-o	0-5	-	- 5.00
3-y-o	0-5	-	- 5.00
4-y-o+	2-12	16.7	+ 4.00
Totals	2-22	9.1	- 6.00

JOCKEYS RIDING

	W-R	Per cent	£1 Level Stake		W-R	Per cent	£1 Level Stake
D Biggs	17-99	17.2	+ 0.26	A Munro	1-3	33.3	+ 2.50
A Tucker	1-2	50.0	+ 13.00	L Dettori	1-5	20.0	+ 6.00
W Carson	1-3	33.3	+ 1.50	P McCabe	1-7	14.3	+ 1.00

P Robinson	0-12	M Tebbutt	0-3	C Hawksley	0-1
R Cochrane	0-8	G Duffield	0-2	G Hind	0-1
G Bardwell	0-6	J Weaver	0-2	J McLaughlin	0-1
N Day	0-5	A Clark	0-1	Mrs L Pearce	0-1
G Carter	0-4	A Mackay	0-1	Paul Eddery	0-1
M Roberts	0-3	B Raymond	0-1		

COURSE RECORD

	Total W-R	Non-Handicaps 2-y-o	Non-Handicaps 3-y-o+	Handicaps 2-y-o	Handicaps 3-y-o+	Per cent	£1 Level Stake
Southwell (AW)	5-10	0-0	1-1	0-0	4-9	50.0	+ 26.58
Yarmouth	3-27	0-6	0-4	0-1	3-16	11.1	- 7.50
Brighton	2-7	0-0	0-0	0-0	2-7	28.6	+ 0.75
Folkestone	2-13	0-3	1-1	0-3	1-6	15.4	- 2.00
Lingfield (AW)	2-17	0-0	1-3	0-0	1-14	11.8	- 10.70
Kempton	2-18	0-1	1-1	0-0	1-16	11.1	- 0.50
Hamilton	1-3	0-0	1-1	0-0	0-2	33.3	- 0.37
Pontefract	1-3	0-0	0-0	0-1	1-2	33.3	+ 10.00
Windsor	1-3	0-0	0-0	0-0	1-3	33.3	+ 2.50
Bath	1-4	0-0	0-0	0-0	1-4	25.0	+ 1.00
Sandown	1-5	0-0	0-1	0-0	1-4	20.0	+ 10.00
Leicester	1-14	0-2	0-0	0-0	1-12	7.1	- 10.50

Newmarket	0-7	Haydock	0-3	Chepstow	0-1
Goodwood	0-6	Newcastle	0-3	Chester	0-1
Lingfield	0-4	Ascot	0-2	Redcar	0-1
Nottingham	0-4	Beverley	0-2	Salisbury	0-1
Wolverhampton	0-4	Newbury	0-2	Thirsk	0-1
Doncaster	0-3	Warwick	0-2	York	0-1

WINNING HORSES

		Races					Win
	Age	Run	1st	2nd	3rd	Unpl	£
Truthful Image	3	16	3	0	1	12	8,537
Kingchip Boy	3	11	3	1	0	7	8,403
Sharp Top	4	21	3	5	4	9	7,667
Super Sally	5	8	3	2	2	1	7,372
Roca Murada	3	14	2	2	3	7	5,572
Tara's Delight	5	4	2	1	1	0	4,374
Shakinski	3	7	2	0	0	5	3,767
Western Dynasty	6	13	1	2	2	8	3,496
Langtry Lady	6	13	1	1	1	10	2,742
Crown Reserve	4	7	1	0	1	5	2,579
Joli's Great	4	9	1	1	4	3	2,427

WINNING OWNERS

	Races Won	Value £		Races Won	Value £
Mrs Margaret Baxter	3	8,537	N H Tampkins	2	3,767
Four Jays Racing Partnership	3	8,403	M F Kentish	1	3,496
Malpass Bros Ltd	3	7,667	Mrs L Seale	1	2,861
Tim Corby	2	5,572	Mrs Teresa Baron	1	2,742
Leonard Seale	2	4,511	F A J Cosgrove	1	2,579
W G Dixon	2	4,374	Enterprise Markets Ltd	1	2,427

Favourites	8-23	34.8%	+ 7.43	Total winning prize-money			£56,934
Longest winning sequence			3	Average SP of winner			5.5/1
Longest losing sequence			24	Return on stakes invested			-16.7%
1991 Form	23-234	9.8%	- 63.50	1989 Form	13-200	6.5%	- 30.49
1990 Form	32-233	13.7%	- 0.16	1988 Form	22-272	8.1%	- 156.80

MISS B SANDERS (Epsom, Surrey)

	No. of Horses	Races Run	1st	2nd	3rd	Unpl	Per cent	£1 Level Stake
2-y-o	4	13	0	0	0	13	-	- 13.00
3-y-o	4	22	1	0	1	20	4.5	- 5.00
4-y-o+	10	41	3	3	2	33	7.3	- 20.00
Totals	18	76	4	3	3	66	5.3	- 38.00

Jan	Feb	Mar	Apr	May	Jun	Jul	Aug	Sep	Oct/Nov
0-2	0-4	0-1	0-6	0-4	1-13	3-12	0-10	0-16	0-8

Winning Jockeys	W-R	£1 Level Stake				W-R	£1 Level Stake
M Roberts	2-6	+ 4.00		Antoinette Armes		1-4	+ 7.00
M Jermy	1-1	+ 16.00					

Winning Courses	W-R	£1 Level Stake				W-R	£1 Level Stake
Newmarket	1-3	+ 2.00		Windsor		1-7	+ 10.00
Epsom	1-6	- 1.00		Lingfield		1-15	- 4.00

Winning Horses	Age	Races Run	1st	2nd	3rd	Unpl	Win £
Running Glimpse	4	11	2	3	1	5	8,061
Dutch Czarina	4	4	1	0	0	3	2,226
Smudgemupum	3	13	1	0	0	12	1,544

Favourites	1-2	50.0%	+ 3.00	Total winning prize-money			£11,831

1991 Form	7-84	8.3%	- 21.00	1989 Form	7-76	9.2%	- 29.70
1990 Form	4-71	5.6%	- 35.50	1988 Form	14-105	13.3%	- 4.17

DR J D SCARGILL (Newmarket)

	No. of Horses	Races Run	1st	2nd	3rd	Unpl	Per cent	£1 Level Stake
2-y-o	9	39	3	2	4	30	7.7	+ 0.91
3-y-o	7	29	3	0	3	23	10.3	0.00
4-y-o+	9	45	3	5	5	32	6.7	- 30.25
Totals	25	113	9	7	12	85	8.0	- 29.34

Jan	Feb	Mar	Apr	May	Jun	Jul	Aug	Sep	Oct/Nov
1-9	2-9	0-5	1-8	1-9	1-17	0-16	1-18	1-11	1-11

Winning Jockeys	W-R	£1 Level Stake			W-R	£1 Level Stake
J Quinn	3-34	+ 11.25	L Piggott		1-2	+ 2.00
R Cochrane	2-6	+ 2.91	K Rutter		1-6	- 2.50
J Fanning	2-8	+ 14.00				

Winning Courses	W-R	£1 Level Stake			W-R	£1 Level Stake
Lingfield (AW)	3-19	- 1.00	Salisbury		1-4	+ 30.00
Hamilton	1-2	+ 11.00	Newcastle		1-5	+ 2.00
Nottingham	1-3	+ 1.00	Pontefract		1-6	- 0.25
Folkestone	1-4	- 2.09				

Winning Horses	Age	Races Run	1st	2nd	3rd	Unpl	Win £
Snowy River	2	5	2	1	1	1	5,631
Jawani	4	8	2	1	2	3	5,018
Our Rita	3	4	1	0	1	2	2,950
Caps Ninety-Two	2	9	1	0	1	7	2,807
Merseyside Man	6	6	1	2	0	3	2,285
A Nymph Too Far	3	11	1	0	2	8	2,187
Abigails Boy	3	4	1	0	0	3	2,187

Favourites	2-5	40.0%	+ 2.41	Total winning prize-money			£23,065

1991 Form	7-172	4.1%	- 141.87	1989 Form	8-107	7.5%	- 69.95
1990 Form	18-185	9.7%	- 37.56	1988 Form	9-67	13.4%	+ 17.63

A A SCOTT (Newmarket)

	No. of Horses	Races Run	1st	2nd	3rd	Unpl	Per cent	£1 Level Stake
2-y-o	36	105	11	16	7	71	10.5	- 37.02
3-y-o	34	202	23	21	19	139	11.4	- 99.18
4-y-o+	3	8	2	2	1	3	25.0	- .0.25
Totals	73	315	36	39	27	213	11.4	-136.45

BY MONTH

2-y-o	W-R	Per cent	£1 Level Stake	3-y-o	W-R	Per cent	£1 Level Stake
Mar/Apr	1-3	33.3	+ 8.00	Mar/Apr	1-24	4.2	- 11.00
May	0-4	-	- 4.00	May	4-32	12.5	- 17.05
June	3-10	30.0	+ 9.25	June	7-37	18.9	- 14.73
July	1-27	3.7	- 25.27	July	5-34	14.7	- 16.15
August	1-18	5.6	- 16.00	August	5-37	13.5	- 4.75
September	1-20	5.0	- 3.00	September	1-27	3.7	- 22.50
Oct/Nov	4-23	17.4	- 6.00	Oct/Nov	0-11	-	- 11.00

Scott A A

4-y-o+	W-R	Per cent	£1 Level Stake	Totals	W-R	Per cent	£1 Level Stake
Mar/Apr	0-1	-	- 1.00	Mar/Apr	2-28	7.1	- 4.00
May	0-1	-	- 1.00	May	4-37	10.8	- 22.05
June	1-3	33.3	+ 1.50	June	11-50	22.0	- 3.98
July	0-2	-	- 2.00	July	6-63	9.5	- 43.42
August	0-0	-	0.00	August	6-55	10.9	- 20.75
September	1-1	100.0	+ 2.25	September	3-48	6.3	- 23.25
Oct/Nov	0-0	-	0.00	Oct/Nov	4-34	11.8	- 17.00

DISTANCE

2-y-o	W-R	Per cent	£1 Level Stake	3-y-o	W-R	Per cent	£1 Level Stake
5f-6f	6-49	12.2	- 13.52	5f-6f	1-16	6.3	- 14.00
7f-8f	4-55	7.3	- 25.00	7f-8f	18-98	18.4	- 16.31
9f-13f	1-1	100.0	+ 1.50	9f-13f	4-82	4.9	- 62.87
14f+	0-0	-	0.00	14f+	0-6	-	- 6.00

4-y-o+	W-R	Per cent	£1 Level Stake	Totals	W-R	Per cent	£1 Level Stake
5f-6f	2-3	66.7	+ 4.75	5f-6f	9-68	13.2	- 22.77
7f-8f	0-2	-	- 2.00	7f-8f	22-155	14.2	- 43.31
9f-13f	0-3	-	- 3.00	9f-13f	5-86	5.8	- 64.37
14f+	0-0	-	0.00	14f+	0-6	-	- 6.00

TYPE OF RACE

Non-Handicaps	W-R	Per cent	£1 Level Stake	Handicaps	W-R	Per cent	£1 Level Stake
2-y-o	10-89	11.2	- 38.02	2-y-o	1-16	6.3	+ 1.00
3-y-o	10-76	13.2	- 37.45	3-y-o	12-102	11.8	- 40.98
4-y-o+	2-7	28.6	+ 0.75	4-y-o+	0-0	-	0.00
Selling	0-0	-	0.00	Selling	0-0	-	0.00
Apprentice	1-4	25.0	- 0.75	Apprentice	0-11	-	- 11.00
Amat/Ladies	0-2	-	- 2.00	Amat/Ladies	0-8	-	- 8.00
Totals	23-178	12.9	- 77.47	Totals	13-137	9.5	- 58.98

COURSE GRADE / FIRST TIME OUT

	W-R	Per cent	£1 Level Stake		W-R	Per cent	£1 Level Stake
Group 1	14-132	10.6	- 62.99	2-y-o	5-36	13.9	- 4.25
Group 2	4-54	7.4	- 28.50	3-y-o	2-34	5.9	- 18.50
Group 3	10-89	11.2	- 33.02	4-y-o+	1-3	33.3	+ 1.50
Group 4	8-40	20.0	- 11.94	Totals	8-73	11.0	- 21.25

JOCKEYS RIDING

	W-R	Per cent	£1 Level Stake			W-R	Per cent	£1 Level Stake
W R Swinburn	12-69	17.4	- 20.51	S Cauthen		3-7	42.9	+ 1.50
J Fortune	7-59	11.9	- 28.02	R Hills		2-7	28.6	+ 13.50
B Raymond	6-86	7.0	- 49.68	L Dettori		1-1	100.0	+ 3.50
W Carson	4-12	33.3	+ 14.01	J Tate		1-9	11.1	- 5.75

L Newton	0-9	S Dawson	0-2	J Fanning	0-1
Miss T Bracegirdle	0-9	A Clark	0-1	J Mercer	0-1
G Hind	0-5	A Culhane	0-1	M Humphries	0-1
Dale Gibson	0-3	A McGlone	0-1	Mr T Denne	0-1
G King	0-3	C Rutter	0-1	N Carlisle	0-1
Hazel Milligan	0-3	D Harrison	0-1	N Day	0-1
M Hills	0-3	D Holland	0-1	N Kennedy	0-1
W Newnes	0-3	D McKeown	0-1	S Wood	0-1
A Munro	0-2	E Bentley	0-1	W Ryan	0-1
F Norton	0-2	E Husband	0-1		
G Carter	0-2	J Carroll	0-1		

COURSE RECORD

	Total W-R	Non-Handicaps 2-y-o	Non-Handicaps 3-y-o+	Handicaps 2-y-o	Handicaps 3-y-o+	Per cent	£1 Level Stake
Newmarket	4-30	3-14	1-9	0-3	0-4	13.3	- 3.00
Beverley	3-9	1-2	0-1	0-0	2-6	33.3	+ 6.50
Warwick	3-10	1-1	0-3	0-0	2-6	30.0	+ 2.01
Catterick	2-5	0-1	1-2	0-0	1-2	40.0	+ 1.07
Redcar	2-6	0-0	1-1	0-0	1-5	33.3	+ 13.00
Salisbury	2-7	0-0	2-2	0-0	0-5	28.6	- 0.50
Goodwood	2-13	0-2	2-4	0-1	0-6	15.4	- 5.00
Haydock	2-13	0-3	2-5	0-0	0-5	15.4	- 7.75
Doncaster	2-15	0-8	0-2	0-2	2-3	13.3	- 8.99
Newbury	2-15	2-6	0-4	0-1	0-4	13.3	- 0.75
Nottingham	2-16	1-4	1-5	0-0	0-7	12.5	- 10.25
Yarmouth	2-19	0-8	0-4	1-1	1-6	10.5	+ .2.00
Carlisle	1-3	0-0	1-3	0-0	0-0	33.3	- 1.27
Folkestone	1-5	0-1	0-1	0-0	1-3	20.0	- 0.50
Newcastle	1-5	0-0	0-3	0-0	1-2	20.0	- 1.00
Southwell (AW)	1-6	0-1	1-2	0-0	0-3	16.7	- 2.25
Windsor	1-11	1-4	0-3	0-0	0-4	9.1	- 9.27
Ascot	1-13	0-6	1-3	0-0	0-4	7.7	- 8.50
Leicester	1-13	1-4	0-5	0-0	0-4	7.7	- 9.50
Pontefract	1-17	0-0	0-7	0-2	1-8	5.9	- 8.50

Ripon	0-16	Kempton	0-7	Edinburgh	0-1
Sandown	0-14	York	0-6	Epsom	0-1
Thirsk	0-12	Bath	0-4	Lingfield (AW)	0-1
Wolverhampton	0-9	Brighton	0-4		
Lingfield	0-8	Chester	0-1		

WINNING HORSES

	Age	Races Run	1st	2nd	3rd	Unpl	Win £
Sheikh Albadou	4	4	2	0	1	1	131,963
Thewaari	3	13	3	1	2	7	8,943
Waseela	3	11	3	1	0	7	7,471
Alkarif	3	8	3	1	1	3	7,114
Rock Symphony	2	4	1	1	0	2	7,050
Bayaireg	3	9	2	0	2	5	6,446
Muhayaa	3	4	1	0	1	2	5,618
Hawa Layaam	3	9	2	1	0	6	4,926
Hadaad	3	5	1	0	0	4	3,915
Hawl	2	8	1	1	1	5	3,883
Yajeed	2	3	1	0	0	2	3,753
Na-Ayim	2	1	1	0	0	0	3,288
Kharaj	2	3	1	2	0	0	3,132
Siwaayib	2	1	1	0	0	0	3,126
Hazaaf	3	9	1	1	0	7	3,054
Amirati	2	3	1	0	0	2	3,002
Fraam	3	2	1	0	0	1	2,954
Anaxagoras	2	4	1	1	0	2	2,758
Hameem	3	8	1	2	1	4	2,385
Zawaahy	3	8	1	3	2	2	2,304
Turtle Beach	3	5	1	1	0	3	2,285
Bletchley Park	3	5	1	0	0	4	2,196
Janaat	3	4	1	0	1	2	2,145
Manaarah	2	4	1	2	0	1	2,070
Kamaatera	2	4	1	1	0	2	1,969
Weeheby	3	12	1	2	2	7	1,932
Munnasib	2	1	1	0	0	0	000

WINNING OWNERS

	Races Won	Value £		Races Won	Value £
Hilal Salem	2	131,963	A Merza	1	3,753
Maktoum Al Maktoum	15	41,129	Abigail Ltd	1	2,758
Hamdan Al-Maktoum	6	17,417	Juma Humaid	1	2,646
Sheikh Ahmed Al Maktoum	4	9,541	Mrs P D Rossdale	1	2,285
Saeed Suhail	3	8,943	Paul Moorhouse	1	2,196
Sir Anthony Page-Wood	1	7,050			

Favourites	21-49	42.9%	+ 15.05	Total winning prize-money			£229,680
Longest winning sequence			2	Average SP of winner			4.0/1
Longest losing sequence			27	Return on stakes invested			-43.3%
1991 Form	23-225	10.2%	-104.93	1989 Form	24-132	18.2%	- 15.56
1990 Form	29-194	14.9%	- 78.07				

D SHAW (Ashington, West Sussex)

	No. of Horses	Races Run	1st	2nd	3rd	Unpl	Per cent	£1 Level Stake
2-y-o	1	1	0	0	0	1	-	- 1.00
3-y-o	2	6	0	0	0	6	-	- 6.00
4-y-o+	7	46	2	1	2	41	4.3	+ 20.00
Totals	10	53	2	1	2	48	3.8	+ 13.00

Jan	Feb	Mar	Apr	May	Jun	Jul	Aug	Sep	Oct/Nov
0-0	0-0	1-2	0-7	0-7	0-9	0-6	0-0	1-9	0-13

Winning Jockeys	W-R	£1 Level Stake		W-R	£1 Level Stake
B Raymond	1-1	+ 14.00	G Carter	1-14	+ 37.00

Winning Courses					
Doncaster	1-4	+ 47.00	Lingfield	1-6	+ 9.00

Winning Horses	Age	Races Run	1st	2nd	3rd	Unpl	Win £
Coleridge	4	11	1	0	0	10	6,400
Fascination Waltz	5	11	1	1	0	9	3,473

Favourites	0-2	Total winning prize-money	£9,873

MISS L C SIDDALL (Tadcaster, North Yorks)

	No. of Horses	Races Run	1st	2nd	3rd	Unpl	Per cent	£1 Level Stake
2-y-o	4	13	0	0	0	13	-	- 13.00
3-y-o	11	60	2	2	4	52	3.3	- 43.00
4-y-o+	5	34	2	2	3	27	5.9	- 6.00
Totals	20	107	4	4	7	92	3.7	- 62.00

Jan	Feb	Mar	Apr	May	Jun	Jul	Aug	Sep	Oct/Nov
0-1	0-0	0-1	0-6	1-12	1-11	2-21	0-20	0-22	0-13

Winning Jockeys	W-R	£1 Level Stake		W-R	£1 Level Stake
F Norton	2-10	+ 18.00	D Harrison	1-7	+ 4.00
Pat Eddery	1-6	0.00			

Winning Courses					
Sandown	2-6	+ 11.00	Ripon	1-10	+ 7.00
Doncaster	1-8	+ 3.00			

Winning Horses	Age	Races Run	1st	2nd	3rd	Unpl	Win £
Euro Festival	3	12	2	1	4	5	6,531
Miss Aragon	4	12	1	2	2	7	2,950
Quiet Victory	5	13	1	0	1	11	1,646

Favourites	1-5	20.0%	+ 1.00	Total winning prize-money			£11,127
1991 Form	2-64	3.1%	- 54.67	1989 Form	8-103	7.8%	- 25.25
1990 Form	4-98	4.1%	- 61.25	1988 Form	9-119	7.6%	- 17.06

R SIMPSON (Foxhill, Wilts)

	No. of Horses	Races Run	1st	2nd	3rd	Unpl	Per cent	£1 Level Stake
2-y-o	3	13	2	1	1	9	15.4	+ 1.00
3-y-o	6	56	5	12	3	36	8.9	- 40.32
4-y-o+	9	51	4	4	5	38	7.8	- 8.00
Totals	18	120	11	17	9	83	9.2	- 47.32

BY MONTH

2-y-o	W-R	Per cent	£1 Level Stake	3-y-o	W-R	Per cent	£1 Level Stake
January	0-0	-	0.00	January	0-3	-	- 3.00
February	0-0	-	0.00	February	0-1	-	- 1.00
March	0-0	-	0.00	March	0-0	-	0.00
April	0-1	-	- 1.00	April	1-9	11.1	- 5.50
May	0-0	-	0.00	May	1-8	12.5	- 4.50
June	0-0	-	0.00	June	0-6	-	- 6.00
July	0-1	-	- 1.00	July	1-13	7.7	- 10.90
August	0-3	-	- 3.00	August	1-7	14.3	- 4.75
September	0-4	-	- 4.00	September	1-7	14.3	- 2.67
Oct/Nov	2-4	50.0	+ 10.00	Oct/Nov	0-2	-	- 2.00

4-y-o+	W-R	Per cent	£1 Level Stake	Totals	W-R	Per cent	£1 Level Stake
January	0-4	-	- 4.00	January	0-7	-	- 7.00
February	0-0	-	0.00	February	0-1	-	- 1.00
March	0-2	-	- 2.00	March	0-2	-	- 2.00
April	2-6	33.3	+ 22.00	April	3-16	18.8	+ 15.50
May	0-1	-	- 1.00	May	1-9	11.1	- 5.50
June	0-9	-	- 9.00	June	0-15	-	- 15.00
July	2-10	20.0	+ 5.00	July	3-24	12.5	- 6.90
August	0-7	-	- 7.00	August	1-17	5.9	- 14.75
September	0-6	-	- 6.00	September	1-17	5.9	- 12.67
Oct/Nov	0-6	-	- 6.00	Oct/Nov	2-12	16.7	+ 2.00

DISTANCE

2-y-o	W-R	Per cent	£1 Level Stake	3-y-o	W-R	Per cent	£1 Level Stake
5f-6f	1-4	25.0	+ 3.00	5f-6f	2-20	10.0	- 15.65
7f-8f	1-9	11.1	- 2.00	7f-8f	0-16	-	- 16.00
9f-13f	0-0	-	0.00	9f-13f	3-16	18.8	- 4.67
14f+	0-0	-	0.00	14f+	0-4	-	- 4.00

4-y-o+	W-R	Per cent	£1 Level Stake	Totals	W-R	Per cent	£1 Level Stake
5f-6f	3-20	15.0	+ 17.00	5f-6f	6-44	13.6	+ 4.35
7f-8f	1-17	5.9	- 11.00	7f-8f	2-42	4.8	- 29.00
9f-13f	0-5	-	- 5.00	9f-13f	3-21	14.3	- 9.67
14f+	0-9	-	- 9.00	14f+	0-13	-	- 13.00

TYPE OF RACE

Non-Handicaps	W-R	Per cent	£1 Level Stake	Handicaps	W-R	Per cent	£1 Level Stake
2-y-o	1-7	14.3	0.00	2-y-o	1-5	20.0	+ 2.00
3-y-o	4-38	10.5	- 25.82	3-y-o	0-13	-	- 13.00
4-y-o+	0-4	-	- 4.00	4-y-o+	4-45	8.9	- 2.00
Selling	1-4	25.0	- 0.50	Selling	0-1	-	- 1.00
Apprentice	0-2	-	- 2.00	Apprentice	0-1	-	- 1.00
Amat/Ladies	0-0	-	0.00	Amat/Ladies	0-0	-	0.00
Totals	6-55	10.9	- 32.32	Totals	5-65	7.7	- 15.00

COURSE GRADE

	W-R	Per cent	£1 Level Stake
Group 1	9-68	13.2	- 5.82
Group 2	0-14	-	- 14.00
Group 3	1-16	6.3	- 12.50
Group 4	1-22	4.5	- 15.00

FIRST TIME OUT

	W-R	Per cent	£1 Level Stake
2-y-o	0-2	-	- 2.00
3-y-o	0-5	-	- 5.00
4-y-o+	0-7	-	- 7.00
Totals	0-14	-	- 14.00

JOCKEYS RIDING

	W-R	Per cent	£1 Level Stake		W-R	Per cent	£1 Level Stake
A Tucker	5-60	8.3	- 38.15	L Dettori	1-2	50.0	+ 1.50
W Ryan	3-15	20.0	+ 22.00	J Reid	1-4	25.0	+ 2.00
B Doyle	1-1	100.0	+ 3.33				

	W-R		W-R		W-R
S Whitworth	0-10	A Munro	0-1	G Carter	0-1
G Duffield	0-5	C Hawksley	0-1	Pat Eddery	0-1
A Mackay	0-3	D Biggs	0-1	R Price	0-1
B Rouse	0-3	D Gibbs	0-1	S Dawson	0-1
M Wigham	0-3	D Holland	0-1	T Sprake	0-1
T Quinn	0-2	G Bardwell	0-1	W Carson	0-1

COURSE RECORD

	Total	Non-Handicaps		Handicaps		Per	£1 Level
	W-R	2-y-o	3-y-o+	2-y-o	3-y-o+	cent	Stake
Sandown	4-14	0-1	2-3	0-0	2-10	28.6	+ 6.35
Goodwood	3-18	0-0	2-6	1-2	0-10	16.7	- 3.17
Edinburgh	1-1	1-1	0-0	0-0	0-0	100.0	+ 6.00
Nottingham	1-3	0-0	1-3	0-0	0-0	33.3	+ 0.50
Epsom	1-6	0-0	0-1	0-0	1-5	16.7	0.00
Kempton	1-9	0-0	0-3	0-0	1-6	11.1	+ 12.00

Lingfield (AW)	0-10	Haydock	0-3	Newmarket	0-2
Brighton	0-8	Lingfield	0-3	Redcar	0-2
Newbury	0-8	Warwick	0-3	Wolverhampton	0-2
Ascot	0-4	Windsor	0-3	Newcastle	0-1
Chepstow	0-4	Catterick	0-2	Pontefract	0-1
Folkestone	0-4	Doncaster	0-2	Ripon	0-1
Bath	0-3	Leicester	0-2	York	0-1

WINNING HORSES

		Races					Win
	Age	Run	1st	2nd	3rd	Unpl	£
Olifantsfontein	4	15	3	1	1	10	10,438
Lyn's Return	3	18	3	2	1	12	6,774
Walk In The Park	3	17	2	5	1	9	5,015
Warm Spell	2	5	1	1	0	3	4,273
Helios	4	13	1	2	2	8	3,850
Walk The Beat	2	2	1	0	0	1	2,211

WINNING OWNERS

	Races Won	Value £		Races Won	Value £
Trevor Painting	3	10,438	K Higson	1	4,273
Rod Simpson	3	6,774	Mrs Christine Painting	1	3,850
M J Lewin	2	5,015	The Country Life Partnership	1	2,211

Favourites	5-16	31.3%	+ 2.35	Total winning prize-money	£32,560

Longest winning sequence	1	Average SP of winner	5.6/1
Longest losing sequence	25	Return on stakes invested	-39.4%

1991 Form	5-104	4.8%	- 44.67	1989 Form	7-117	6.0%	- 33.87
1990 Form	6-96	6.3%	- 23.50	1988 Form	8-97	8.2%	- 56.62

B SMART (Lambourn, Berks)

		No. of Horses	Races Run	1st	2nd	3rd	Unpl	Per cent	£1 Level Stake
2-y-o		2	6	1	0	0	5	16.7	+ 3.00
3-y-o		2	7	0	0	1	6	-	- 7.00
4-y-o+		2	8	1	0	0	7	12.5	- 3.67
Totals		6	21	2	0	1	18	9.5	- 7.67

Jan	Feb	Mar	Apr	May	Jun	Jul	Aug	Sep	Oct/Nov
0-0	0-1	0-0	0-1	0-1	0-2	1-4	0-4	1-3	0-5

Winning Jockeys	W-R	£1 Level Stake			W-R	£1 Level Stake
S Davies	1-1	+ 3.33	Dale Gibson		1-7	+ 2.00

Winning Courses	W-R	£1 Level Stake			W-R	£1 Level Stake
Kempton	1-1	+ 3.33	Bath		1-2	+ 7.00

Winning Horses	Age	Races Run	1st	2nd	3rd	Unpl	Win £
Sharp Dream	4	7	1	0	0	6	2,721
Sharp Gazelle	2	4	1	0	0	3	1,590

Favourites	1-1	100.0%	+ 3.33	Total winning prize-money		£4,311

1991 Form	0-5			1989 Form	0-13
1990 Form	0-5			1988 Form	0-5

A SMITH (Beverley, North Humberside)

		No. of Horses	Races Run	1st	2nd	3rd	Unpl	Per cent	£1 Level Stake
2-y-o		1	4	0	0	0	4	-	- ·4.00
3-y-o		6	31	1	4	3	23	3.2	- 25.00
4-y-o+		4	27	2	4	2	19	7.4	- 5.50
Totals		11	62	3	8	5	46	4.8	- 34.50

Jan	Feb	Mar	Apr	May	Jun	Jul	Aug	Sep	Oct/Nov
0-1	0-0	0-2	0-6	0-8	0-10	0-12	0-10	2-9	1-4

Winning Jockey	W-R	£1 Level Stake			W-R	£1 Level Stake
S Webster	3-29	- 1.50				

Winning Courses	W-R	£1 Level Stake			W-R	£1 Level Stake
Carlisle	1-2	+ 10.00	Southwell (AW)		1-7	- 1.00
Edinburgh	1-2	+ 7.50				

Smith A

Winning Horses	Age	Races Run	1st	2nd	3rd	Unpl	Win £
Supreme Desire	4	11	2	2	1	6	4,407
Auction King	3	12	1	3	2	6	2,070

Favourites	1-1	100.0%	+ 5.00	Total winning prize-money			£6,477

1991 Form	1-113	0.9%	-101.00	1989 Form	1-41	2.4%	- 26.00
1990 Form	1-28	3.6%	- 20.00	1988 Form	3-54	5.6%	- 21.00

D J G MURRAY SMITH (Upper Lambourn, Berks)

	No. of Horses	Races Run	1st	2nd	3rd	Unpl	Per cent	£1 Level Stake
2-y-o	2	8	1	1	1	5	12.5	- 5.00
3-y-o	1	2	0	0	0	2	-	- 2.00
4-y-o+	4	24	1	6	2	15	4.2	- 18.50
Totals	7	34	2	7	3	22	5.9	- 25.50

Jan	Feb	Mar	Apr	May	Jun	Jul	Aug	Sep	Oct/Nov
0-3	0-1	0-1	0-1	0-4	0-8	2-6	0-2	0-5	0-3

Winning Jockeys	W-R	£1 Level Stake			W-R	£1 Level Stake
M Roberts	1-1	+ 4.50	J Reid		1-2	+ 1.00

Winning Courses						
Newbury	1-3	0.00	Southwell (AW)		1-3	+ 2.50

Winning Horses	Age	Races Run	1st	2nd	3rd	Unpl	Win £
Norfolk Hero	2	2	1	0	1	0	3,850
Idir Linn	4	11	1	3	1	6	1,256

Favourites	1-4	25.0%	- 1.00	Total winning prize-money			£5,106

1991 Form	7-76	9.2%	- 12.00	1989 Form	8-76	10.5%	- 19.50
1990 Form	9-100	9.0%	- 40.69	1988 Form	9-85	10.6%	+ 37.00

DENYS SMITH (Bishop Auckland, Co Durham)

	No. of Horses	Races Run	1st	2nd	3rd	Unpl	Per cent	£1 Level Stake
2-y-o	4	24	3	2	6	13	12.5	+ 9.50
3-y-o	13	60	2	5	8	45	3.3	- 56.01
4-y-o+	8	60	9	8	9	34	15.0	+ 5.92
Totals	25	144	14	15	23	92	9.7	- 40.59

BY MONTH

2-y-o	W-R	Per cent	£1 Level Stake	3-y-o	W-R	Per cent	£1 Level Stake
January	0-0	-	0.00	January	0-0	-	0.00
February	0-0	-	0.00	February	0-0	-	0.00
March	0-0	-	0.00	March	0-1	-	- 1.00
April	0-0	-	0.00	April	0-2	-	- 2.00
May	1-2	50.0	0.00	May	0-11	-	- 11.00
June	0-2	-	- 2.00	June	0-5	-	- 5.00
July	2-6	33.3	+ 25.50	July	2-11	18.2	- 7.01
August	0-7	-	- 7.00	August	0-14	-	- 14.00
September	0-4	-	- 4.00	September	0-9	-	- 9.00
Oct/Nov	0-3	-	- 3.00	Oct/Nov	0-7	-	- 7.00

4-y-o+	W-R	Per cent	£1 Level Stake	Totals	W-R	Per cent	£1 Level Stake
January	0-1	-	- 1.00	January	0-1	-	- 1.00
February	0-2	-	- 2.00	February	0-2	-	- 2.00
March	0-2	-	- 2.00	March	0-3	-	- 3.00
April	0-6	-	- 6.00	April	0-8	-	- 8.00
May	1-8	12.5	- 0.50	May	2-21	9.5	- 11.50
June	4-8	50.0	+ 8.00	June	4-15	26.7	+ 1.00
July	2-8	25.0	- 3.58	July	6-25	24.0	+ 14.91
August	0-10	-	- 10.00	August	0-31	-	- 31.00
September	1-8	12.5	+ 13.00	September	1-21	4.8	0.00
Oct/Nov	1-7	14.3	+ 10.00	Oct/Nov	1-17	5.9	0.00

DISTANCE

2-y-o	W-R	Per cent	£1 Level Stake	3-y-o	W-R	Per cent	£1 Level Stake
5f-6f	3-16	18.8	+ 17.50	5f-6f	1-9	11.1	- 7.64
7f-8f	0-8	-	- 8.00	7f-8f	0-20	-	- 20.00
9f-13f	0-0	-	0.00	9f-13f	0-29	-	- 29.00
14f+	0-0	-	0.00	14f+	1-2	50.0	+ 0.63

4-y-o+	W-R	Per cent	£1 Level Stake	Totals	W-R	Per cent	£1 Level Stake
5f-6f	5-20	25.0	+ 15.17	5f-6f	9-45	20.0	+ 25.03
7f-8f	4-21	19.0	+ 9.75	7f-8f	4-49	8.2	- 18.25
9f-13f	0-16	-	- 16.00	9f-13f	0-45	-	- 45.00
14f+	0-3	-	- 3.00	14f+	1-5	20.0	- 2.37

TYPE OF RACE

Non-Handicaps	W-R	Per cent	£1 Level Stake	Handicaps	W-R	Per cent	£1 Level Stake
2-y-o	2-18	11.1	+ 10.00	2-y-o	1-6	16.7	- 0.50
3-y-o	1-12	8.3	- 10.64	3-y-o	1-32	3.1	- 29.37
4-y-o+	0-2	-	- 2.00	4-y-o+	9-52	17.3	+ 13.92
Selling	0-2	-	- 2.00	Selling	0-5	-	- 5.00
Apprentice	0-0	-	0.00	Apprentice	0-8	-	- 8.00
Amat/Ladies	0-1	-	- 1.00	Amat/Ladies	0-6	-	- 6.00
Totals	3-35	8.6	- 5.64	Totals	11-109	10.1	- 34.95

COURSE GRADE

	W-R	Per cent	£1 Level Stake
Group 1	1-40	2.5	- 23.00
Group 2	5-38	13.2	- 0.33
Group 3	3-33	9.1	- 21.25
Group 4	5-33	15.2	+ 3.99

FIRST TIME OUT

	W-R	Per cent	£1 Level Stake
2-y-o	1-4	25.0	+ 22.00
3-y-o	0-11	-	- 11.00
4-y-o+	0-8	-	- 8.00
Totals	1-23	4.3	+ 3.00

JOCKEYS RIDING

	W-R	Per cent	£1 Level Stake
K Fallon	11-63	17.5	+ 12.41
D Holland	2-4	50.0	+ 3.00

	W-R	Per cent	£1 Level Stake
C Teague	1-28	3.6	- 7.00

L Charnock	0-9	Dale Gibson	0-3	J Carroll	0-1
N Connorton	0-9	G Forster	0-3	J Fortune	0-1
Miss M Carson	0-8	J Fanning	0-2	J Williams	0-1
J Lowe	0-5	A Munro	0-1	M Roberts	0-1
B Raymond	0-4	B Rouse	0-1		

COURSE RECORD

	Total W-R	Non-Handicaps 2-y-o	Non-Handicaps 3-y-o+	Handicaps 2-y-o	Handicaps 3-y-o+	Per cent	£1 Level Stake
Redcar	4-17	1-3	0-1	0-0	3-13	23.5	+ 15.17
Carlisle	2-7	0-0	0-2	0-0	2-5	28.6	0.00
Edinburgh	2-12	1-2	0-1	0-0	1-9	16.7	+ 16.63
Pontefract	2-12	0-2	0-2	0-0	2-8	16.7	- 3.00
York	1-5	0-1	0-0	0-1	1-3	20.0	+ 12.00
Catterick	1-7	0-0	1-2	0-1	0-4	14.3	- 5.64
Thirsk	1-9	0-2	0-2	1-1	0-4	11.1	- 3.50
Hamilton	1-14	0-0	0-3	0-0	1-11	7.1	- 11.25

Ayr	0-13	Southwell (AW)	0-7	Newmarket	0-1
Ripon	0-11	Beverley	0-6	Nottingham	0-1
Newcastle	0-9	Haydock	0-5		
Doncaster	0-7	Chester	0-1		

WINNING HORSES

	Age	Races Run	1st	2nd	3rd	Unpl	Win £
Densben	8	17	5	3	4	5	26,243
Spanish Verdict	5	19	4	3	2	10	10,709
Grinnell	2	6	2	0	1	3	5,429
Willshe Gan	2	11	1	2	4	4	2,285
Desert Mist	3	2	1	0	0	1	1,632
Lift Boy	3	11	1	2	1	7	1,257

WINNING OWNERS

	Races Won	Value £		Races Won	Value £
Mrs Janet M Pike	5	26,243	Hamish Alexander	1	2,285
Cox & Allen (Kendal) Ltd	4	10,709	Albury Racing Ltd	1	1,632
David McCune	2	5,429	J A Bianchi	1	1,257

Favourites	7-11	63.6%	+ 6.91	Total winning prize-money		£47,554
Longest winning sequence			2	Average SP of winner		6.4/1
Longest losing sequence			48	Return on stakes invested		-28.2%
1991 Form	9-207	4.3%	-144.25	1989 Form	16-214	7.5%	-104.15
1990 Form	8-215	3.7%	-172.13	1988 Form	14-283	4.9%	-115.12

J P SMITH (Rugeley, Staffs)

	No. of Horses	Races Run	1st	2nd	3rd	Unpl	Per cent	£1 Level Stake
2-y-o	0	0	0	0	0	0	-	0.00
3-y-o	1	3	0	0	0	3	-	- 3.00
4-y-o+	6	23	2	2	2	17	8.7	+ 37.00
Totals	7	26	2	2	2	20	7.7	+ 34.00

Jan	Feb	Mar	Apr	May	Jun	Jul	Aug	Sep	Oct/Nov
0-1	0-0	0-0	0-0	0-2	0-6	2-6	0-5	0-4	0-2

		£1 Level				£1 Level
Winning Jockey	W-R	Stake			W-R	Stake
A Garth	2-7	+ 53.00				.

Winning Courses						
Nottingham	1-6	+ 45.00		Wolverhampton	1-7	+ 2.00

			Races					Win
Winning Horses		Age	Run	1st	2nd	3rd	Unpl	£
My Swan Song		7	5	1	0	1	3	1,872
Irish Groom		5	8	1	2	1	4	1,413

Favourites	0-0			Total winning prize-money		£3,285
1991 Form	0-28			1989 Form	1-36	2.8%	- 28.00
1990 Form	0-71			1988 Form	0-41		

J L SPEARING (Alcester, Warwicks)

	No. of Horses	Races Run	1st	2nd	3rd	Unpl	Per cent	£1 Level Stake
2-y-o	9	34	1	2	0	31	2.9	- 8.00
3-y-o	7	40	4	1	6	29	10.0	- 15.29
4-y-o+	16	125	9	18	7	91	7.2	- 69.00
Totals	32	199	14	21	13	151	7.0	- 92.29

BY MONTH

2-y-o	W-R	Per cent	£1 Level Stake	3-y-o	W-R	Per cent	£1 Level Stake
January	0-0	-	0.00	January	0-2	-	- 2.00
February	0-0	-	0.00	February	2-5	40.0	+ 10.33
March	0-0	-	0.00	March	0-3	-	- 3.00
April	0-0	-	0.00	April	0-1	-	- 1.00
May	0-2	-	- 2.00	May	0-5	-	- 5.00
June	0-3	-	- 3.00	June	0-6	-	- 6.00
July	0-8	-	- 8.00	July	1-6	16.7	- 3.62
August	1-5	20.0	+ 21.00	August	1-4	25.0	+ 3.00
September	0-8	-	- 8.00	September	0-5	-	- 5.00
Oct/Nov	0-8	-	- 8.00	Oct/Nov	0-3	-	- 3.00

4-y-o+	W-R	Per cent	£1 Level Stake	Totals	W-R	Per cent	£1 Level Stake
January	0-4	-	- 4.00	January	0-6	-	- 6.00
February	0-3	-	- 3.00	February	2-8	25.0	+ 7.33
March	0-3	-	- 3.00	March	0-6	-	- 6.00
April	0-14	-	- 14.00	April	0-15	-	- 15.00
May	3-18	16.7	+ 4.50	May	3-25	12.0	- 2.50
June	1-19	5.3	- 8.00	June	1-28	3.6	- 17.00
July	3-19	15.8	- 5.00	July	4-33	12.1	- 16.62
August	1-16	6.3	- 10.50	August	3-25	12.0	+ 13.50
September	0-17	-	- 17.00	September	0-30	-	- 30.00
Oct/Nov	1-12	8.3	- 9.00	Oct/Nov	1-23	4.3	- 20.00

DISTANCE

2-y-o	W-R	Per cent	£1 Level Stake	3-y-o	W-R	Per cent	£1 Level Stake
5f-6f	1-16	6.3	+ 10.00	5f-6f	4-23	17.4	+ 1.71
7f-8f	0-16	-	- 16.00	7f-8f	0-9	-	- 9.00
9f-13f	0-2	-	- 2.00	9f-13f	0-8	-	- 8.00
14f+	0-0	-	0.00	14f+	0-0	-	0.00

4-y-o+	W-R	Per cent	£1 Level Stake	Totals	W-R	Per cent	£1 Level Stake
5f-6f	4-59	6.8	- 29.50	5f-6f	9-98	9.2	- 17.79
7f-8f	5-33	15.2	- 6.50	7f-8f	5-58	8.6	- 31.50
9f-13f	0-27	-	- 27.00	9f-13f	0-37	-	- 37.00
14f+	0-6	-	- 6.00	14f+	0-6	-	- 6.00

TYPE OF RACE

Non-Handicaps	W-R	Per cent	£1 Level Stake	Handicaps	W-R	Per cent	£1 Level Stake
2-y-o	0-21	-	- 21.00	2-y-o	1-3	33.3	+ 23.00
3-y-o	2-14	14.3	+ 1.33	3-y-o	1-22	4.5	- 19.62
4-y-o+	0-5	-	- 5.00	4-y-o+	7-101	6.9	- 58.50
Selling	0-8	-	- 8.00	Selling	2-8	25.0	+ 5.50
Apprentice	0-0	-	0.00	Apprentice	1-9	11.1	- 2.00
Amat/Ladies	0-1	-	- 1.00	Amat/Ladies	0-7	-	- 7.00
Totals	2-49	4.1	- 33.67	Totals	12-150	8.0	- 58.62

COURSE GRADE

	W-R	Per cent	£1 Level Stake
Group 1	2-42	4.8	- 26.00
Group 2	1-21	4.8	- 12.00
Group 3	0-53	-	- 53.00
Group 4	11-83	13.3	- 1.29

FIRST TIME OUT

	W-R	Per cent	£1 Level Stake
2-y-o	0-8	-	- 8.00
3-y-o	1-7	14.3	+ 4.00
4-y-o+	0-16	-	- 16.00
Totals	1-31	3.2	- 20.00

JOCKEYS RIDING

	W-R	Per cent	£1 Level Stake		W-R	Per cent	£1 Level Stake
K Darley	4-18	22.2	+ 3.00	M Humphries	1-6	16.7	+ 1.00
D Nicholls	2-7	28.6	+ 8.33	D McKeown	1-7	14.3	- 2.00
A Garth	2-18	11.1	- 8.00	C Hawksley	1-8	12.5	+ 18.00
G Hind	2-36	5.6	- 22.62	N Howe	1-10	10.0	- 1.00

J Lowe	0-11	Miss C Spearing	0-3	D Carson	0-1
R Fox	0-10	Alex Greaves	0-2	D Wright	0-1
J Williams	0-7	Emma O'Gorman	0-2	Donna Hayman	0-1
M Roberts	0-7	L Dettori	0-2	P Roberts	0-1
Miss T Spearing	0-7	Paul Eddery	0-2	P Robinson	0-1
G Bardwell	0-5	W Newnes	0-2	R Cochrane	0-1
A Mackay	0-4	A Clark	0-1	S Sanders	0-1
E Husband	0-4	B Crossley	0-1	S Wood	0-1
J Fanning	0-4	B Raymond	0-1	S Wynne	0-1
G Duffield	0-3	C Rutter	0-1	W Carson	0-1

COURSE RECORD

	Total W-R	Non-Handicaps 2-y-o	Non-Handicaps 3-y-o+	Handicaps 2-y-o	Handicaps 3-y-o+	Per cent	£1 Level Stake
Edinburgh	5-18	0-4	0-2	0-0	5-12	27.8	+ 4.88
Wolverhampton	3-20	0-4	0-1	1-3	2-12	15.0	+ 16.00
Lingfield (AW)	2-16	0-0	2-7	0-0	0-9	12.5	- 0.67
York	1-5	0-0	0-0	0-0	1-5	20.0	+ 6.00
Brighton	1-6	0-0	0-0	0-0	1-6	16.7	+ 3.00
Carlisle	1-7	0-1	0-1	0-0	1-5	14.3	+ 0.50
Haydock	1-8	0-0	0-0	0-1	1-7	12.5	- 3.00

Warwick	0-14	Folkestone	0-4	Catterick	0-2
Beverley	0-13	Newmarket	0-4	Hamilton	0-2
Doncaster	0-11	Salisbury	0-4	Newcastle	0-2
Pontefract	0-11	Sandown	0-4	Ripon	0-2
Nottingham	0-10	Chepstow	0-3	Southwell (AW)	0-2
Redcar	0-8	Kempton	0-3	Lingfield	0-1
Leicester	0-7	Newbury	0-3	Windsor	0-1
Bath	0-6	Ayr	0-2		

WINNING HORSES

	Age	Races Run	1st	2nd	3rd	Unpl	Win £
Dominuet	7	13	1	3	1	8	11,063
Lawnswood Junior	5	16	4	5	2	5	8,802
Miss Vaxette	3	13	2	1	4	6	4,321
Summer Express	3	5	2	0	0	3	4,276
Iron King	6	23	2	2	1	18	4,003
Glenscar	6	5	1	1	0	3	2,637
Lucedeo	8	13	1	1	0	11	2,322
Magic Orb	2	6	1	0	0	5	1,744

WINNING OWNERS

	Races Won	Value £		Races Won	Value £
Graham Treglown	6	13,077	Stephen Borsberry	1	2,637
Mrs Robert Heathcote	1	11,063	Non-Stop Promotions	1	2,322
Vax Appliances Ltd	2	4,321	M Olden	1	1,744
Tom Coleman	2	4,003			

Favourites	4-12	33.3%	+ 3.88	Total winning prize-money		£39,166
Longest winning sequence			2	Average SP of winner		6.6/1
Longest losing sequence			52	Return on stakes invested		-46.4%
1991 Form	12-177	6.8%	- 64.75	1989 Form	8-145	5.5%	-100.87
1990 Form	13-176	7.4%	-103.37	1988 Form	3-104	2.9%	- 85.00

R C SPICER (Spalding, Lincs)

	No. of Horses	Races Run	1st	2nd	3rd	Unpl	Per cent	£1 Level Stake
2-y-o	0	0	0	0	0	0	-	0.00
3-y-o	4	12	1	0	2	9	8.3	+ 22.00
4-y-o+	5	12	2	1	2	7	16.7	+ 20.00
Totals	9	24	3	1	4	16	12.5	+ 42.00

Jan	Feb	Mar	Apr	May	Jun	Jul	Aug	Sep	Oct/Nov
0-0	0-0	0-0	0-1	0-0	0-0	0-0	0-2	1-7	2-14

Winning Jockeys	W-R	£1 Level Stake				W-R	£1 Level Stake
A Garth	2-5	+ 46.00	D Harrison			1-5	+ 10.00

Winning Courses					
Goodwood	1-1	+ 14.00	Pontefract		1-2	+ 15.00
Folkestone	1-2	+ 32.00			

Winning Horses	Age	Races Run	1st	2nd	3rd	Unpl	Win £
Modest Hope	5	2	1	0	1	0	2,742
Broad Appeal	4	7	1	1	1	4	2,658
Rural Lad	3	2	1	0	0	1	2,637

Favourites	0-2	Total winning prize-money	£8,037

W A STEPHENSON (Bishop Auckland, Co Durham)

	No. of Horses	Races Run	1st	2nd	3rd	Unpl	Per cent	£1 Level Stake
2-y-o	1	2	0	0	1	1	-	- 2.00
3-y-o	1	6	0	0	0	6	-	- 6.00
4-y-o+	2	12	1	0	2	9	8.3	- 4.00
Totals	4	20	1	0	3	16	5.0	- 12.00

Jan	Feb	Mar	Apr	May	Jun	Jul	Aug	Sep	Oct/Nov
0-0	0-0	0-0	0-0	0-1	1-5	0-6	0-2	0-1	0-5

Winning Jockey	W-R	£1 Level Stake		W-R	£1 Level Stake
M Birch	1-3	+ 5.00	Winning Course	1-3	+ 5.00
			Hamilton		

Winning Horse	Age	Races Run	1st	2nd	3rd	Unpl	Win £
Silver Haze	8	5	1	0	1	3	3,003

Favourites	0-1	Total winning prize-money	£3,003

1991 Form	0-16	1989 Form	0-11
1990 Form	0-16	1988 Form	0-31

A C STEWART (Newmarket)

	No. of Horses	Races Run	1st	2nd	3rd	Unpl	Per cent	£1 Level Stake
2-y-o	8	12	1	1	1	9	8.3	- 9.62
3-y-o	29	92	17	10	10	55	18.5	- 15.58
4-y-o+	4	24	3	2	4	15	12.5	- 6.00
Totals	41	128	21	13	15	79	16.4	- 31.20

BY MONTH

2-y-o	W-R	Per cent	£1 Level Stake	3-y-o	W-R	Per cent	£1 Level Stake
Mar/Apr	0-0	-	0.00	Mar/Apr	1-8	12.5	- 1.00
May	0-0	-	0.00	May	0-5	-	- 5.00
June	0-0	-	0.00	June	0-0	-	0.00
July	0-0	-	0.00	July	1-1	100.0	+ 4.00
August	0-1	-	- 1.00	August	9-27	33.3	+ 2.82
September	0-6	-	- 6.00	September	4-26	15.4	+ 3.50
Oct/Nov	1-5	20.0	- 2.62	Oct/Nov	2-25	8.0	- 19.90

4-y-o+	W-R	Per cent	£1 Level Stake	Totals	W-R	Per cent	£1 Level Stake
Mar/Apr	3-5	60.0	+ 13.00	Mar/Apr	4-13	30.8	+ 12.00
May	0-2	-	- 2.00	May	0-7	-	- 7.00
June	0-2	-	- 2.00	June	0-2	-	- 2.00
July	0-5	-	- 5.00	July	1-6	16.7	- 1.00
August	0-5	-	- 5.00	August	9-33	27.3	- 3.18
September	0-2	-	- 2.00	September	4-34	11.8	- 4.50
Oct/Nov	0-3	-	- 3.00	Oct/Nov	3-33	9.1	- 25.52

DISTANCE

2-y-o	W-R	Per cent	£1 Level Stake	3-y-o	W-R	Per cent	£1 Level Stake
5f-6f	1-2	50.0	+ 0.38	5f-6f	0-1	-	- 1.00
7f-8f	0-10	-	- 10.00	7f-8f	8-26	30.8	+ 4.74
9f-13f	0-0	-	0.00	9f-13f	9-63	14.3	- 17.32
14f+	0-0	-	0.00	14f+	0-2	-	- 2.00

4-y-o+	W-R	Per cent	£1 Level Stake	Totals	W-R	Per cent	£1 Level Stake
5f-6f	0-0	-	0.00	5f-6f	1-3	33.3	- 0.62
7f-8f	1-6	16.7	+ 5.00	7f-8f	9-42	21.4	- 0.26
9f-13f	2-13	15.4	- 6.00	9f-13f	11-76	14.5	- 23.32
14f+	0-5	-	- 5.00	14f+	0-7	-	- 7.00

TYPE OF RACE

Non-Handicaps	W-R	Per cent	£1 Level Stake	Handicaps	W-R	Per cent	£1 Level Stake
2-y-o	1-12	8.3	- 9.62	2-y-o	0-0	-	0.00
3-y-o	13-62	21.0	- 10.58	3-y-o	4-26	15.4	- 1.00
4-y-o+	0-4	-	- 4.00	4-y-o+	3-19	15.8	- 1.00
Selling	0-1	-	- 1.00	Selling	0-0	-	0.00
Apprentice	0-2	-	- 2.00	Apprentice	0-1	-	- 1.00
Amat/Ladies	0-0	-	0.00	Amat/Ladies	0-1	-	- 1.00
Totals	14-81	17.3	- 27.20	Totals	7-47	14.9	- 4.00

COURSE GRADE

	W-R	Per cent	£1 Level Stake
Group 1	12-70	17.1	- 18.62
Group 2	4-20	20.0	+ 4.60
Group 3	3-26	11.5	- 18.56
Group 4	2-12	16.7	+ 1.38

FIRST TIME OUT

	W-R	Per cent	£1 Level Stake
2-y-o	0-8	-	- 8.00
3-y-o	6-29	20.7	- 5.70
4-y-o+	1-4	25.0	+ 0.50
Totals	7-41	17.1	- 13.20

JOCKEYS RIDING

	W-R	Per cent	£1 Level Stake			W-R	Per cent	£1 Level Stake
M Roberts	19-87	21.8	- 11.20	S Whitworth		1-4	25.0	+ 7.00
Brough Scott	1-1	100.0	+ 9.00					

R Hills	0-8	W Ryan	0-3	G Crealock	0-1
A McGlone	0-4	A Clark	0-2	J Quinn	0-1
E Forletta	0-4	K Darley	0-2	Mr V Lukanuik	0-1
M Birch	0-3	F Norton	0-1	Pat Eddery	0-1
W Carson	0-3	G Carter	0-1	R Cochrane	0-1

COURSE RECORD

	Total W-R	Non-Handicaps 2-y-o	3-y-o+	Handicaps 2-y-o	3-y-o+	Per cent	£1 Level Stake
Sandown	3-9	0-0	2-4	0-0	1-5	33.3	+ 3.58
Newmarket	3-21	0-1	2-9	0-0	1-11	14.3	- 8.00
Ascot	2-4	0-0	0-1	0-0	2-3	50.0	+ 9.50
Windsor	2-4	0-0	2-3	0-0	0-1	50.0	+ 0.44
Epsom	2-5	0-0	2-4	0-0	0-1	40.0	+ 1.80
Folkestone	2-7	1-1	1-6	0-0	0-0	28.6	+ 6.38
Chester	1-2	0-0	1-2	0-0	0-0	50.0	+ 0.10
Salisbury	1-2	0-0	0-0	0-0	1-2	50.0	+ 9.00
Kempton	1-3	0-0	0-2	0-0	1-1	33.3	- 0.50
Brighton	1-5	0-1	1-4	0-0	0-0	20.0	+ 2.00
Pontefract	1-5	0-0	1-4	0-0	0-1	20.0	- 2.00
Ripon	1-5	0-0	0-3	0-0	1-2	20.0	- 0.50
York	1-11	0-0	1-6	0-0	0-5	9.1	- 8.00

Stewart A C

Doncaster	0-7	Redcar	0-3	Catterick	0-1
Nottingham	0-5	Wolverhampton	0-3	Edinburgh	0-1
Leicester	0-4	Yarmouth	0-3	Goodwood	0-1
Newbury	0-4	Lingfield	0-2	Hamilton	0-1
Beverley	0-3	Ayr	0-1	Newcastle	0-1
Haydock	0-3	Bath	0-1	Thirsk	0-1

WINNING HORSES

	Age	Races Run	1st	2nd	3rd	Unpl	Win £
Jdaayel	3	5	3	2	0	0	15,990
Revif	4	5	2	0	0	3	15,487
Mamdooh	3	5	2	0	0	3	14,880
Shuailaan	3	5	2	1	0	2	12,710
Amwag	3	2	2	0	0	0	12,185
Jasoorah	3	5	2	1	0	2	9,185
Little Rousillon	4	7	1	0	1	5	3,340
Blue Marine	3	3	1	1	0	1	2,685
Anghaam	3	5	1	0	1	3	2,570
Kitaab	3	6	2	0	0	4	2,520
Almuhtarama	3	4	1	1	0	2	2,511
Barik	2	3	1	0	0	2	2,180
Kasisi	3	4	1	0	0	3	1,576

WINNING OWNERS

	Races Won	Value £		Races Won	Value £
Hamdan Al-Maktoum	11	50,325	Fayzad Thoroughbred Ltd	1	3,340
Sheikh Ahmed Al Maktoum	5	24,406	The Snailwell Stud Co Ltd	1	2,685
S Corman Ltd	2	15,487	Mrs H R Stack	1	1,576

Favourites	9-31	29.0%	- 6.28	Total winning prize-money			£97,818
Longest winning sequence			3	Average SP of winner			3.6/1
Longest losing sequence			23	Return on stakes invested			-24.4%
1991 Form	29-194	14.9%	- 2.19	1989 Form	30-200	15.0%	- 75.03
1990 Form	40-234	17.1%	- 81.52	1988 Form	40-194	20.6%	- 37.68

W STOREY (Consett, Co Durham)

	No. of Horses	Races Run	1st	2nd	3rd	Unpl	Per cent	£1 Level Stake
2-y-o	0	0	0	0	0	0	-	0.00
3-y-o	5	17	1	3	2	11	5.9	- 12.50
4-y-o+	7	34	1	3	2	28	2.9	- 8.00
Totals	12	51	2	6	4	39	3.9	- 20.50

Jan	Feb	Mar	Apr	May	Jun	Jul	Aug	Sep	Oct/Nov
0-0	0-0	0-2	0-3	1-11	0-14	1-16	0-2	0-0	0-3

			£1 Level					£1 Level
Winning Jockeys		W-R	Stake				W-R	Stake
J Fanning		1-9	+ 17.00		S Webster		1-19	- 14.50

Winning Courses		W-R	Stake				W-R	Stake
Edinburgh		1-9	- 4.50		Catterick		1-12	+ 14.00

		Races					Win
Winning Horses	Age	Run	1st	2nd	3rd	Unpl	£
Sexy Mover	5	6	1	2	0	3	2,807
Boring	3	5	1	1	1	2	2,264

Favourites	0-2	Total winning prize-money	£5,071

1991 Form	2-35	5.7%	- 16.50	1989 Form	0-15
1990 Form	0-49			1988 Form	0-26

M R STOUTE (Newmarket)

	No. of Horses	Races Run	1st	2nd	3rd	Unpl	Per cent	£1 Level Stake
2-y-o	60	146	24	21	19	82	16.4	- 48.00
3-y-o	56	230	38	33	23	136	16.5	- 56.27
4-y-o+	15	73	12	8	9	44	16.4	- 24.83
Totals	131	449	74	62	51	262	16.5	-129.10

BY MONTH

2-y-o	W-R	Per cent	£1 Level Stake	3-y-o	W-R	Per cent	£1 Level Stake
Mar/Apr	0-1	-	- 1.00	Mar/Apr	5-39	12.8	- 22.47
May	1-2	50.0	+ 7.00	May	13-46	28.3	+ 1.66
June	3-12	25.0	- 6.65	June	6-36	16.7	- 12.16
July	4-17	23.5	- 9.83	July	6-36	16.7	- 17.74
August	7-31	22.6	- 9.54	August	3-34	8.8	- 12.14
September	4-25	16.0	+ 1.73	September	2-22	9.1	- 12.75
Oct/Nov	5-58	8.6	- 29.71	Oct/Nov	3-17	17.6	+ 12.00

4-y-o+	W-R	Per cent	£1 Level Stake	Totals	W-R	Per cent	£1 Level Stake
Mar/Apr	1-8	12.5	- 4.75	Mar/Apr	6-48	12.5	- 28.22
May	5-14	35.7	+ 11.32	May	19-62	30.6	+ 19.98
June	3-14	21.4	- 7.22	June	12-62	19.4	- 26.03
July	2-14	14.3	- 4.43	July	12-67	17.9	- 32.00
August	0-10	-	- 10.00	August	10-75	13.3	- 31.68
September	1-7	14.3	- 3.75	September	7-54	13.0	- 14.77
Oct/Nov	0-6	-	- 6.00	Oct/Nov	8-81	9.9	- 23.71

DISTANCE

2-y-o	W-R	Per cent	£1 Level Stake	3-y-o	W-R	Per cent	£1 Level Stake
5f-6f	15-53	28.3	+ 14.00	5f-6f	0-4	-	- 4.00
7f-8f	9-91	9.9	- 60.00	7f-8f	17-84	20.2	- 7.27
9f-13f	0-2	-	- 2.00	9f-13f	19-127	15.0	- 39.25
14f+	0-0	-	0.00	14f+	2-15	13.3	- 5.75

4-y-o+	W-R	Per cent	£1 Level Stake	Totals	W-R	Per cent	£1 Level Stake
5f-6f	1-3	33.3	+ 12.00	5f-6f	16-60	26.7	+ 22.00
7f-8f	1-15	6.7	- 12.37	7f-8f	27-190	14.2	- 79.64
9f-13f	8-38	21.1	- 19.79	9f-13f	27-167	16.2	- 61.04
14f+	2-17	11.8	- 4.67	14f+	4-32	12.5	- 10.42

TYPE OF RACE

Non-Handicaps	W-R	Per cent	£1 Level Stake	Handicaps	W-R	Per cent	£1 Level Stake
2-y-o	22-128	17.2	- 48.00	2-y-o	2-15	13.3	+ 3.00
3-y-o	33-153	21.6	+ 6.12	3-y-o	4-70	5.7	- 56.75
4-y-o+	10-35	28.6	+ 2.17	4-y-o+	2-36	5.6	- 25.00
Selling	0-3	-	- 3.00	Selling	0-1	-	- 1.00
Apprentice	1-1	100.0	+ 0.36	Apprentice	0-3	-	- 3.00
Amat/Ladies	0-1	-	- 1.00	Amat/Ladies	0-3	-	- 3.00
Totals	66-321	20.6	- 43.35	Totals	8-128	6.3	- 85.75

COURSE GRADE

	W-R	Per cent	£1 Level Stake
Group 1	45-290	15.5	- 53.29
Group 2	11-51	21.6	- 20.28
Group 3	12-72	16.7	- 35.89
Group 4	6-36	16.7	- 19.64

FIRST TIME OUT

	W-R	Per cent	£1 Level Stake
2-y-o	9-60	15.0	- 16.43
3-y-o	9-56	16.1	+ 2.91
4-y-o+	2-15	13.3	- 9.12
Totals	20-131	15.3	- 22.64

JOCKEYS RIDING

	W-R	Per cent	£1 Level Stake		W-R	Per cent	£1 Level Stake
Pat Eddery	17-74	23.0	+ 18.82	M Roberts	2-11	18.2	+ 2.75
W R Swinburn	14-87	16.1	- 29.88	W Ryan	2-12	16.7	- 7.12
S Cauthen	12-52	23.1	- 16.35	C Dwyer	1-3	33.3	+ 3.00
P D'Arcy	5-23	21.7	- 4.88	K Darley	1-3	33.3	- 0.75
D Holland	4-14	28.6	+ 5.80	C Asmussen	1-3	33.3	+ 1.00
M Birch	3-11	27.3	- 2.58	K Pattinson	1-4	25.0	- 2.64
W Carson	3-15	20.0	- 7.34	L Dettori	1-6	16.7	- 3.25
Paul Eddery	3-20	15.0	- 3.77	R Cochrane	1-16	6.3	- 9.00
G Duffield	2-11	18.2	+ 10.00	B Raymond	1-18	5.6	- 16.91

J Jones	0-19	G Carter	0-2	J Fortune	0-1
F Norton	0-7	J Carroll	0-2	J Lloyd	0-1
A Munro	0-6	T Quinn	0-2	J Lowe	0-1
J Reid	0-6	W Newnes	0-2	L Piggott	0-1
Miss M Juster	0-4	B Rouse	0-1	M Hills	0-1
P Robinson	0-4	D Harrison	0-1	R Perham	0-1
R Hills	0-3	Dale Gibson	0-1		

COURSE RECORD

	Total	Non-Handicaps		Handicaps		Per	£1 Level
	W-R	2-y-o	3-y-o+	2-y-o	3-y-o+	cent	Stake
Newmarket	8-64	4-30	3-23	1-4	0-7	12.5	- 11.58
Yarmouth	6-20	2-10	3-7	0-0	1-3	30.0	- 1.41
Sandown	6-36	1-4	4-20	0-2	1-10	16.7	+ 1.01
Doncaster	5-22	1-8	3-8	1-2	0-4	22.7	+ 8.35
Newbury	5-27	1-6	4-14	0-2	0-5	18.5	+ 8.42
York	5-30	0-3	4-13	0-1	1-13	16.7	- 10.42
Newcastle	4-9	2-3	2-3	0-0	0-3	44.4	- 1.53
Chester	4-12	1-2	2-2	0-0	1-8	33.3	- 3.45
Haydock	4-12	0-3	4-8	0-0	0-1	33.3	+ 4.80
Ascot	4-39	2-11	2-15	0-1	0-12	10.3	- 18.59
Goodwood	3-18	1-5	1-4	0-1	1-8	16.7	- 3.00
Pontefract	2-4	1-2	1-1	0-0	0-1	50.0	- 1.08
Catterick	2-7	1-1	1-6	0-0	0-0	28.6	- 2.91
Beverley	2-8	0-0	2-4	0-0	0-4	25.0	- 3.70
Lingfield	2-8	0-2	2-3	0-1	0-2	25.0	+ 0.57
Ripon	2-8	1-2	1-3	0-0	0-3	25.0	- 2.31
Salisbury	2-8	0-3	1-4	0-0	1-1	25.0	- 2.34
Carlisle	1-2	0-0	1-2	0-0	0-0	50.0	- 0.80
Southwell (AW)	1-4	0-0	1-2	0-0	0-2	25.0	- 0.50
Folkestone	1-5	0-1	1-4	0-0	0-0	20.0	+ 1.00
Redcar	1-6	1-3	0-0	0-0	0-3	16.7	- 3.75
Windsor	1-8	1-3	0-2	0-0	0-3	12.5	- 6.70
Wolverhampton	1-8	1-4	0-2	0-0	0-2	12.5	- 6.43
Epsom	1-13	0-0	1-10	0-0	0-3	7.7	- 10.75
Leicester	1-16	1-9	0-6	0-0	0-1	6.3	- 7.00

Kempton	0-17	Bath	0-4	Edinburgh	0-2
Nottingham	0-8	Ayr	0-3	Chepstow	0-1
Warwick	0-7	Brighton	0-3	Lingfield (AW)	0-1
Thirsk	0-6	Hamilton	0-3		

WINNING HORSES

		Races					Win
	Age	Run	1st	2nd	3rd	Unpl	£
Saddlers' Hall	4	5	4	1	0	0	179,323
Rock Hopper	5	7	2	1	1	3	108,427
Alnasr Alwasheek	3	5	2	0	0	3	92,355
Desert Secret	2	4	1	1	0	2	66,609
Niodini	3	8	2	4	0	2	45,273

Opera House	4	6	2	1	2	1	44,051
Falsoola	2	6	3	0	1	2	37,297
Snaadee	5	3	1	0	0	2	37,260
Hazaam	3	6	4	1	1	0	28,744
Mizaaya	3	7	3	0	0	4	27,208
Mojave	3	4	1	1	0	2	19,613
Blush Rambler	2	4	2	2	0	0	14,181
Mystic Goddess	2	6	2	1	2	1	11,291
Dancing Bloom	2	2	1	1	0	0	9,688
Perfect Circle	3	7	1	2	0	4	9,463
Zinaad	3	2	1	0	1	0	9,219
Desert Shot	2	3	2	0	0	1	8,704
Polish Blue	3	9	2	2	2	3	8,233
Lyphantastic	3	2	2	0	0	0	6,357
Viardot	3	5	2	1	0	2	5,429
Logan's Luck	2	2	1	0	0	1	4,854
Gulf Sailor	4	6	2	1	0	3	4,830
Shaiba	2	2	1	1	0	0	4,347
Zarani Sidi Anna	2	1	1	0	0	0	4,273
Serious	2	1	1	0	0	0	4,240
Highland Dress	3	3	1	0	0	2	4,078
Greek Gold	3	5	1	1	0	3	3,818
Dahyah	2	2	1	0	0	1	3,670
Alessandrina	3	6	1	0	0	5	3,590
Ajzem	3	3	1	0	1	1	3,460
Jungle Dancer	4	9	1	3	2	3	3,301
Almamzar	2	2	1	0	0	1	2,898
Born To Dance	3	3	1	0	0	2	2,856
Greenlet	2	6	1	2	0	3	2,777
Ezzoud	3	3	1	1	1	0	2,714
Iviza	2	3	1	0	1	1	2,700
Cezanne	3	4	1	1	0	2	2,595
Funoon	3	4	1	0	1	2	2,427
Drought	3	4	1	1	0	2	2,427
West Stow	3	9	1	2	1	5	2,383
Azhar	2	4	1	1	0	2	2,343
Garp	2	5	1	0	0	4	2,301
Fit On Time	3	4	1	2	0	1	2,301
Asaasy	3	5	1	2	0	2	2,285
Sun Seeker	3	3	1	0	1	1	2,285
Colyan	2	4	1	1	1	1	2,208
Bineyah	3	5	1	1	0	3	2,072
Wrets	3	6	1	2	0	3	2,070
Desired Guest	3	4	1	0	0	3	2,050
Chain Dance	2	5	1	1	1	2	1,970
Ustka	3	4	1	0	1	2	1,856
Cultured	3	7	1	1	1	4	1,604
Shebl	2	8	1	2	1	4	1,308

WINNING OWNERS

	Races Won	Value £		Races Won	Value £
Maktoum Al Maktoum	17	278,327	Lord White Of Hull	2	5,509
Lord Weinstock	9	199,943	P D Savill	1	4,854
Sheikh Mohammed	20	189,507	J M Greetham	2	4,397
Sheikh Ahmed Al Maktoum	6	103,251	Malcolm Parrish	1	3,590
Sultan Mohammed	1	19,613	Khalifa Sultan	1	2,301
Cheveley Park Stud	3	14,147	Miss H Al Maktoum	1	2,301
Hanson Leigh Racing	1	9,463	Mrs V Hue-Williams	1	2,050
Mana Al Maktoum	2	8,233	James Wigan	1	1,856
Miss Sandra H Payson	2	6,357	Mrs David Thompson	1	1,604
Mrs Denis Haynes	2	6,310			

Favourites	44-102	43.1% - 3.48	Total winning prize-money		£863,611
Longest winning sequence		2	Average SP of winner		3.3/1
Longest losing sequence		39	Return on stakes invested		-28.8%
1991 Form	83-413	20.1% - 57.70	1989 Form	117-498	23.5% - 67.47
1990 Form	78-428	18.2% -116.07	1988 Form	99-448	22.1% - 10.26

A P STRINGER (Thirsk, North Yorks)

	No. of Horses	Races Run	1st	2nd	3rd	Unpl	Per cent	£1 Level Stake
2-y-o	4	16	1	0	0	15	6.3	+ 35.00
3-y-o	4	12	0	0	2	10	-	- 12.00
4-y-o+	9	43	5	5	4	29	11.6	+ 13.50
Totals	17	71	6	5	6	54	8.5	+ 36.50

Jan	Feb	Mar	Apr	May	Jun	Jul	Aug	Sep	Oct/Nov
0-3	1-4	0-5	0-5	0-10	0-8	3-13	0-9	0-5	2-9

Winning Jockeys	W-R	£1 Level Stake			W-R	£1 Level Stake
S Maloney	3-16	+ 3.50	S Wood		1-2	+ 49.00
R Cochrane	1-1	+ 10.00	J Quinn		1-7	+ 19.00

Winning Courses						
Ayr	2-3	+ 10.50	Newcastle		1-5	+ 6.00
Redcar	1-3	+ 48.00	Southwell (AW)		1-8	+ 18.00
York	1-3	+ 3.00				

Winning Horses	Age	Races Run	1st	2nd	3rd	Unpl	Win £
Golden Chip	4	13	3	3	1	6	12,175
Nellie's Gamble	2	9	1	0	0	8	3,120
The Goofer	5	3	1	0	1	1	2,900
Heir Of Excitement	7	2	1	0	0	1	2,579

Favourites	0-1		Total winning prize-money		£20,774
1991 Form	4-84	4.8% - 39.00	1989 Form	2-51	3.9% - 12.00
1990 Form	5-77	6.5% - 10.50			

J SUTCLIFFE (Epsom, Surrey)

	No. of Horses	Races Run	1st	2nd	3rd	Unpl	Per cent	£1 Level Stake
2-y-o	6	24	1	1	4	18	4.2	- 21.00
3-y-o	10	66	5	3	7	51	7.6	- 43.50
4-y-o+	7	38	8	3	2	25	21.1	+ 5.51
Totals	23	128	14	7	13	94	10.9	- 58.99

BY MONTH

2-y-o	W-R	Per cent	£1 Level Stake	3-y-o	W-R	Per cent	£1 Level Stake
January	0-0	-	0.00	January	0-0	-	0.00
February	0-0	-	0.00	February	0-0	-	0.00
March	0-0	-	0.00	March	0-0	-	0.00
April	0-0	-	0.00	April	0-3	-	- 3.00
May	0-2	-	- 2.00	May	0-7	-	- 7.00
June	0-7	-	- 7.00	June	0-13	-	- 13.00
July	1-5	20.0	- 2.00	July	0-9	-	- 9.00
August	0-5	-	- 5.00	August	3-13	23.1	- 1.00
September	0-2	-	- 2.00	September	2-12	16.7	- 1.50
Oct/Nov	0-3	-	- 3.00	Oct/Nov	0-9	-	- 9.00

4-y-o+	W-R	Per cent	£1 Level Stake	Totals	W-R	Per cent	£1 Level Stake
January	0-1	-	- 1.00	January	0-1	-	- 1.00
February	0-0	-	0.00	February	0-0	-	0.00
March	0-0	-	0.00	March	0-0	-	0.00
April	0-5	-	- 5.00	April	0-8	-	- 8.00
May	2-9	22.2	+ 3.00	May	2-18	11.1	- 6.00
June	3-6	50.0	+ 8.88	June	3-26	11.5	- 11.12
July	2-5	40.0	- 1.37	July	3-19	15.8	- 12.37
August	0-3	-	- 3.00	August	3-21	14.3	- 9.00
September	0-5	-	- 5.00	September	2-19	10.5	- 8.50
Oct/Nov	1-4	25.0	+ 9.00	Oct/Nov	1-16	6.3	- 3.00

DISTANCE

2-y-o	W-R	Per cent	£1 Level Stake	3-y-o	W-R	Per cent	£1 Level Stake
5f-6f	1-22	4.5	- 19.00	5f-6f	0-19	-	- 19.00
7f-8f	0-2	-	- 2.00	7f-8f	0-35	-	- 35.00
9f-13f	0-0	-	0.00	9f-13f	5-12	41.7	+ 10.50
14f+	0-0	-	0.00	14f+	0-0	-	0.00

4-y-o+	W-R	Per cent	£1 Level Stake	Totals	W-R	Per cent	£1 Level Stake
5f-6f	2-7	28.6	- 3.37	5f-6f	3-48	6.3	- 41.37
7f-8f	6-30	20.0	+ 9.88	7f-8f	6-67	9.0	- 27.12
9f-13f	0-0	-	0.00	9f-13f	5-12	41.7	+ 10.50
14f+	0-1	-	- 1.00	14f+	0-1	-	- 1.00

TYPE OF RACE

Non-Handicaps	W-R	Per cent	£1 Level Stake	Handicaps	W-R	Per cent	£1 Level Stake
2-y-o	0-13	-	- 13.00	2-y-o	0-5	-	- 5.00
3-y-o	0-11	-	- 11.00	3-y-o	3-44	6.8	- 30.75
4-y-o+	2-4	50.0	- 0.37	4-y-o+	6-33	18.2	+ 6.88
Selling	2-13	15.4	- 4.00	Selling	1-3	33.3	+ 0.25
Apprentice	0-0	-	0.00	Apprentice	0-2	-	- 2.00
Amat/Ladies	0-0	-	0.00	Amat/Ladies	0-0	-	0.00
Totals	4-41	9.8	- 28.37	Totals	10-87	11.5	- 30.62

COURSE GRADE

	W-R	Per cent	£1 Level Stake
Group 1	8-45	17.8	- 5.24
Group 2	3-29	10.3	- 10.50
Group 3	3-35	8.6	- 24.25
Group 4	0-19	-	- 19.00

FIRST TIME OUT

	W-R	Per cent	£1 Level Stake
2-y-o	0-6	-	- 6.00
3-y-o	0-8	-	- 8.00
4-y-o+	0-7	-	- 7.00
Totals	0-21	-	- 21.00

JOCKEYS RIDING

	W-R	Per cent	£1 Level Stake		W-R	Per cent	£1 Level Stake
M Roberts	5-15	33.3	+ 2.01	Pat Eddery	1-3	33.3	+ 3.00
B Rouse	3-58	5.2	- 48.25	N Adams	1-4	25.0	+ 3.00
W R Swinburn	1-2	50.0	+ 7.00	A Tucker	1-6	16.7	- 3.25
W Carson	1-2	50.0	+ 11.00	J Tate	1-6	16.7	- 1.50

B Crossley	0-4	R Hills	0-2	D McKeown	0-1
A Munro	0-3	S Whitworth	0-2	Dale Gibson	0-1
D Harrison	0-3	T Quinn	0-2	G Baxter	0-1
W Newnes	0-3	C Rutter	0-1	L Dettori	0-1
P Robinson	0-2	D Biggs	0-1	T G McLaughlin	0-1
Paul Eddery	0-2	D Holland	0-1	W Ryan	0-1

COURSE RECORD

	Total W-R	Non-Handicaps 2-y-o	Non-Handicaps 3-y-o+	Handicaps 2-y-o	Handicaps 3-y-o+	Per cent	£1 Level Stake
Goodwood	2-4	0-0	0-0	0-0	2-4	50.0	+ 6.25
Sandown	2-6	0-3	0-0	0-0	2-3	33.3	+ 3.88
Newmarket	2-11	0-0	0-1	0-0	2-10	18.2	+ 5.00
Salisbury	2-12	0-1	0-3	0-0	2-8	16.7	+ 0.50
Doncaster	1-4	0-0	1-1	0-0	0-3	25.0	- 3.00
Nottingham	1-4	0-0	0-0	0-0	1-4	25.0	- 0.75
Chepstow	1-5	0-0	0-0	0-1	1-4	20.0	- 0.50
Leicester	1-9	1-2	0-2	0-2	0-3	11.1	- 6.00
Kempton	1-11	0-1	1-4	0-0	0-6	9.1	- 8.37
Brighton	1-12	0-1	1-2	0-0	0-9	8.3	- 6.00

Sutcliffe J

Folkestone	0-15	Lingfield	0-5	Ascot	0-2
Windsor	0-11	Yarmouth	0-5	Newbury	0-2
Epsom	0-5	Lingfield (AW)	0-4	Bath	0-1

WINNING HORSES

		Races					Win
	Age	Run	1st	2nd	3rd	Unpl	£
Saafend	4	11	2	1	1	7	32,640
Bo Knows Best	3	10	4	1	0	5	13,399
Jaldi	4	10	3	2	0	5	9,895
A Prayer For Wings	8	4	2	0	0	2	8,184
Superoo	6	10	1	0	0	9	3,720
Chummy's Child	3	4	1	0	0	3	2,280
No Extras	2	10	1	1	4	4	1,544

WINNING OWNERS

	Races Won	Value £		Races Won	Value £
J B R Leisure Ltd	2	32,640	Mrs P A Garner	1	3,720
John Sutcliffe	4	13,399	C Gaventa	1	2,280
Albert Finney	3	9,895	K Higson	1	1,544
S Powell	2	8,184			

Favourites	7-20	35.0%	+ 2.51	Total winning prize-money			£71,663
Longest winning sequence			2	Average SP of winner			4.6/1
Longest losing sequence			18	Return on stakes invested			-39.1%
1991 Form	3-103	2.9%	- 82.00	1989 Form	18-127	14.2%	- 19.92
1990 Form	17-153	11.1%	- 46.91	1988 Form	12-114	10.5%	- 59.74

D T THOM (Exning, Suffolk)

	No. of Horses	Races Run	1st	2nd	3rd	Unpl	Per cent	£1 Level Stake
2-y-o	4	35	1	2	3	29	2.9	- 14.00
3-y-o	5	41	1	1	7	32	2.4	- 37.75
4-y-o+	4	56	5	3	7	41	8.9	- 18.00
Totals	13	132	7	6	17	102	5.3	- 69.75

Jan	Feb	Mar	Apr	May	Jun	Jul	Aug	Sep	Oct/Nov
1-8	1-8	0-5	0-15	1-9	1-12	0-17	1-20	1-19	1-19

Winning Jockeys	W-R	£1 Level Stake			W-R	£1 Level Stake
Miss I D W Jones	2-6	+ 7.50	P Bowe		1-4	+ 3.50
S Cauthen	1-1	+ 8.00	J Williams		1-6	- 2.75
F Arrowsmith	1-3	+ 5.00	D Biggs		1-13	+ 8.00

Winning Courses	W-R	£1 Level Stake		W-R	£1 Level Stake
Yarmouth	4-14	+ 31.50	Lingfield (AW)	1-12	- 8.75
Lingfield	1-1	+ 6.00	Southwell (AW)	1-15	- 8.50

Winning Horses	Age	Races Run	1st	2nd	3rd	Unpl	Win £
Ballerina Bay	4	22	4	1	2	15	10,407
Cuddly Date	2	9	1	1	0	7	2,679
Yes	4	16	1	2	4	9	2,187
Doesyoudoes	3	12	1	0	1	10	2,050

Favourites	1-7	14.3%	- 0.50	Total winning prize-money		£17,322

1991 Form	3-104	2.9%	- 55.00	1989 Form	6-133	4.5%	- 28.00
1990 Form	11-130	8.5%	- 21.63	1988 Form	10-179	5.6%	-103.62

RONALD THOMPSON (Doncaster, South Yorks)

	No. of Horses	Races Run	1st	2nd	3rd	Unpl	Per cent	£1 Level Stake
2-y-o	6	16	0	2	0	14	-	- 16.00
3-y-o	3	32	3	6	2	21	9.4	- 3.12
4-y-o+	2	2	0	0	0	2	-	- 2.00
Totals	11	50	3	8	2	37	6.0	- 21.12

Jan	Feb	Mar	Apr	May	Jun	Jul	Aug	Sep	Oct/Nov
0-3	0-0	0-0	1-8	0-10	0-8	1-9	0-4	0-5	1-3

Winning Jockeys	W-R	£1 Level Stake		W-R	£1 Level Stake
M Denaro	1-2	+ 0.88	R P Elliott	1-13	- 8.00
A Mackay	1-3	+ 18.00			

Winning Courses	W-R	£1 Level Stake		W-R	£1 Level Stake
Haydock	1-2	+ 3.00	Hamilton	1-8	+ 13.00
Ripon	1-2	+ 0.88			

Winning Horses	Age	Races Run	1st	2nd	3rd	Unpl	Win £
Ready To Draw	3	13	2	5	1	5	4,568
Our John	3	9	1	1	0	7	2,280

Favourites	1-8	12.5%	- 5.12	Total winning prize-money		£6,848

1991 Form	4-75	5.3%	- 23.00	1989 Form	5-121	4.1%	- 72.00
1990 Form	7-123	5.7%	- 46.00	1988 Form	7-129	5.4%	- 54.75

C W THORNTON (Middleham, North Yorks)

	No. of Horses	Races Run	1st	2nd	3rd	Unpl	Per cent	£1 Level Stake
2-y-o	6	22	1	0	2	19	4.5	- 17.00
3-y-o	12	60	1	3	6	50	1.7	- 55.00
4-y-o+	4	12	0	0	0	12	-	- 12.00
Totals	22	94	2	3	8	81	2.1	- 84.00

Jan	Feb	Mar	Apr	May	Jun	Jul	Aug	Sep	Oct/Nov
0-0	0-0	0-0	0-7	1-12	0-11	1-28	0-11	0-21	0-4

Winning Jockeys	W-R	£1 Level Stake			W-R	£1 Level Stake
G Duffield	1-5	0.00	G Hind		1-17	- 12.00

Winning Courses	W-R	£1 Level Stake			W-R	£1 Level Stake
Carlisle	1-5	0.00	Thirsk		1-8	- 3.00

Winning Horses	Age	Races Run	1st	2nd	3rd	Unpl	Win £
Any Dream Would Do	3	3	1	0	0	2	2,469
Contract Elite	2	8	1	0	1	6	2,324

Favourites	0-4			Total winning prize-money		£4,793

1991 Form	9-102	8.8%	- 54.17	1989 Form	12-172	7.0%	- 35.17
1990 Form	12-146	8.2%	- 47.06	1988 Form	15-142	10.6%	- 24.12

C TINKLER (Malton, North Yorks)

	No. of Horses	Races Run	1st	2nd	3rd	Unpl	Per cent	£1 Level Stake
2-y-o	13	69	0	6	5	58	-	- 69.00
3-y-o	5	18	0	0	0	18	-	- 18.00
4-y-o+	8	43	4	5	2	32	9.3	+ 10.50
Totals	26	130	4	11	7	108	3.1	- 76.50

Jan	Feb	Mar	Apr	May	Jun	Jul	Aug	Sep	Oct/Nov
0-0	1-2	0-6	0-15	1-19	0-12	0-21	0-28	1-13	1-14

Winning Jockeys	W-R	£1 Level Stake			W-R	£1 Level Stake
P Burke	2-8	+ 15.50	M Birch		1-47	- 34.00
J Weaver	1-3	+ 14.00				

Winning Courses	W-R	£1 Level Stake			W-R	£1 Level Stake
Southwell (AW)	1-4	+ 9.00	Edinburgh		1-7	- 0.50
Nottingham	1-6	+ 11.00	Doncaster		1-10	+ 7.00

Winning Horses	Age	Races Run	1st	2nd	3rd	Unpl	Win £
John Shaw	4	4	2	0	0	2	4,386
American Hero	4	6	1	1	0	4	3,052
Battle Standard	5	1	1	0	0	0	2,285

Favourites	0-10			Total winning prize-money			£9,723

| 1991 Form | 15-188 | 8.0% | - 69.09 | 1989 Form | 35-322 | 10.9% | - 120.83 |
| 1990 Form | 28-284 | 9.9% | - 135.39 | 1988 Form | 24-274 | 8.8% | - 134.13 |

N TINKLER (Malton, North Yorks)

	No. of Horses	Races Run	1st	2nd	3rd	Unpl	Per cent	£1 Level Stake
2-y-o	16	52	3	6	2	41	5.8	- 39.25
3-y-o	11	34	1	3	0	30	2.9	- 26.50
4-y-o+	21	58	5	2	8	43	8.6	- 19.17
Totals	48	144	9	11	10	114	6.3	- 84.92

Jan	Feb	Mar	Apr	May	Jun	Jul	Aug	Sep	Oct/Nov
1-6	1-6	0-14	1-15	1-13	2-14	0-26	3-14	0-15	0-21

Winning Jockeys	W-R	£1 Level Stake		W-R	£1 Level Stake
L Charnock	2-35	- 24.17	G Duffield	1-3	+ 1.50
Kim Tinkler	2-37	- 19.00	M Birch	1-6	- 3.25
Mrs A Farrell	1-1	+ 9.00	K Darley	1-9	- 3.50
W Newnes	1-2	+ 5.50			

Winning Courses					
Southwell (AW)	2-24	- 6.00	Redcar	1-8	- 3.50
Yarmouth	1-1	+ 1.75	Newcastle	1-9	- 4.67
Nottingham	1-2	+ 4.50	Ripon	1-10	- .4.50
Beverley	1-6	+ 4.00	Haydock	1-11	- 3.50

Winning Horses	Age	Races Run	1st	2nd	3rd	Unpl	Win £
Vain Prince	5	4	3	0	1	0	9,009
Trevorsninepoints	2	4	2	2	0	0	4,540
Sonderise	3	10	1	1	0	8	3,623
Peperonata	2	2	1	1	0	0	2,415
Le Temeraire	6	8	1	1	3	3	2,383
Question Of Degree	6	4	1	0	1	2	2,128

Favourites	3-9	33.3%	+ 4.58	Total winning prize-money			£24,098

| 1991 Form | 13-197 | 6.6% | - 110.64 | 1989 Form | 24-291 | 8.2% | - 146.14 |
| 1990 Form | 17-300 | 5.7% | - 231.34 | 1988 Form | 24-319 | 7.5% | - 163.25 |

J A R TOLLER (Newmarket)

	No. of Horses	Races Run	1st	2nd	3rd	Unpl	Per cent	£1 Level Stake
2-y-o	2	5	0	0	0	5	-	- 5.00
3-y-o	7	39	8	6	3	22	20.5	- 0.94
4-y-o+	3	14	1	3	1	9	7.1	- 7.50
Totals	12	58	9	9	4	36	15.5	- 13.44

Jan	Feb	Mar	Apr	May	Jun	Jul	Aug	Sep	Oct/Nov
0-0	0-0	0-0	0-7	0-7	5-11	1-11	2-8	0-7	1-7

Winning Jockeys	W-R	£1 Level Stake			W-R	£1 Level Stake
M Roberts	3-7	+ 11.50	G Duffield		1-3	+ 0.25
P Robinson	2-4	- 1.19	J Weaver		1-5	+ 0.50
R Hills	1-1	+ 1.50	Dale Gibson		1-13	- 1.00

Winning Courses						
Carlisle	1-1	+ 0.08	Ascot		1-3	+ 5.50
Catterick	1-1	+ 11.00	Newbury		1-3	+ 2.50
Hamilton	1-1	+ 0.73	Lingfield		1-6	- 3.50
Thirsk	1-1	+ 2.25	Yarmouth		1-9	- 2.50
Pontefract	1-2	+ 1.50				

Winning Horses	Age	Races Run	1st	2nd	3rd	Unpl	Win £
Calpella	3	7	2	0	0	5	14,130
Nagida	3	12	2	3	2	5	5,950
Wellington Rock	3	4	2	0	1	1	4,418
Sugemar	6	10	1	3	1	5	3,028
Nellie Dean	3	6	1	2	0	3	2,490
Turret Gates	3	6	1	1	0	4	2,343

Favourites	3-8	37.5%	- 2.69	Total winning prize-money			£32,359
1991 Form	4-66	6.1%	- 42.12	1989 Form	7-65	10.8%	+ 49.25
1990 Form	7-84	8.3%	- 46.75	1988 Form	6-93	6.5%	- 58.00

M H TOMPKINS (Newmarket)

	No. of Horses	Races Run	1st	2nd	3rd	Unpl	Per cent	£1 Level Stake
2-y-o	27	129	17	5	14	93	13.2	+ 11.78
3-y-o	23	110	12	16	10	72	10.9	- 65.93
4-y-o+	25	127	13	11	15	88	10.2	- 28.20
Totals	75	366	42	32	39	253	11.5	- 82.35

BY MONTH

2-y-o	W-R	Per cent	£1 Level Stake	3-y-o	W-R	Per cent	£1 Level Stake
January	0-0	-	0.00	January	0-2	-	- 2.00
February	0-0	-	0.00	February	0-0	-	0.00
March	0-0	-	0.00	March	1-1	100.0	+ 5.50
April	0-5	-	- 5.00	April	0-8	-	- 8.00
May	4-12	33.3	+ 24.94	May	3-20	15.0	- 6.75
June	2-18	11.1	- 11.87	June	4-20	20.0	- 6.60
July	2-22	9.1	- 17.54	July	2-19	10.5	- 15.08
August	2-20	10.0	- 7.00	August	0-9	-	- 9.00
September	2-27	7.4	+ 1.50	September	2-15	13.3	- 8.00
Oct/Nov	5-25	20.0	+ 26.75	Oct/Nov	0-16	-	- 16.00

4-y-o+	W-R	Per cent	£1 Level Stake	Totals	W-R	Per cent	£1 Level Stake
January	1-7	14.3	+ 4.00	January	1-9	11.1	+ 2.00
February	0-7	-	- 7.00	February	0-7	-	- 7.00
March	0-8	-	- 8.00	March	1-9	11.1	- 2.50
April	1-9	11.1	- 2.00	April	1-22	4.5	- 15.00
May	3-9	33.3	+ 19.50	May	10-41	24.4	+ 37.69
June	0-12	-	- 12.00	June	6-50	12.0	- 30.47
July	2-15	13.3	- 5.00	July	6-56	10.7	- 37.62
August	2-16	12.5	+ 8.00	August	4-45	8.9	- 8.00
September	1-21	4.8	- 19.20	September	5-63	7.9	- 25.70
Oct/Nov	3-23	13.0	- 6.50	Oct/Nov	8-64	12.5	+ 4.25

DISTANCE

2-y-o	W-R	Per cent	£1 Level Stake	3-y-o	W-R	Per cent	£1 Level Stake
5f-6f	11-75	14.7	- 4.92	5f-6f	2-17	11.8	- 2.00
7f-8f	5-49	10.2	+ 6.70	7f-8f	2-25	8.0	- 20.85
9f-13f	1-5	20.0	+ 10.00	9f-13f	5-57	8.8	- 40.50
14f+	0-0	-	0.00	14f+	3-11	27.3	- 2.58

4-y-o+	W-R	Per cent	£1 Level Stake	Totals	W-R	Per cent	£1 Level Stake
5f-6f	0-10	-	- 10.00	5f-6f	13-102	12.7	- 16.92
7f-8f	3-46	6.5	- 17.50	7f-8f	10-120	8.3	- 31.65
9f-13f	10-62	16.1	+ 8.30	9f-13f	16-124	12.9	- 22.20
14f+	0-9	-	- 9.00	14f+	3-20	15.0	- 11.58

TYPE OF RACE

Non-Handicaps	W-R	Per cent	£1 Level Stake	Handicaps	W-R	Per cent	£1 Level Stake
2-y-o	12-70	17.1	+ 37.77	2-y-o	3-28	10.7	+ 0.55
3-y-o	7-43	16.3	- 25.93	3-y-o	5-52	9.6	- 25.00
4-y-o+	4-27	14.8	- 4.70	4-y-o+	5-72	6.9	- 29.50
Selling	2-36	5.6	- 31.54	Selling	0-9	-	- 9.00
Apprentice	0-5	-	- 5.00	Apprentice	4-16	25.0	+ 18.00
Amat/Ladies	0-1	-	- 1.00	Amat/Ladies	0-7	-	- 7.00
Totals	25-182	13.7	- 30.40	Totals	17-184	9.2	- 51.95

COURSE GRADE

	W-R	Per cent	£1 Level Stake
Group 1	10-131	7.6	- 45.20
Group 2	4-33	12.1	- 1.00
Group 3	15-119	12.6	- 26.03
Group 4	13-83	15.7	- 10.12

FIRST TIME OUT

	W-R	Per cent	£1 Level Stake
2-y-o	2-26	7.7	- 5.50
3-y-o	3-21	14.3	- 8.50
4-y-o+	3-24	12.5	+ 17.00
Totals	8-71	11.3	+ 3.00

JOCKEYS RIDING

	W-R	Per cent	£1 Level Stake
P Robinson	30-209	14.4	- 12.90
S Mulvey	5-55	9.1	- 24.65
R Cochrane	2-10	20.0	+ 3.20
C Hodgson	2-25	8.0	- 11.50
Pat Eddery	1-1	100.0	+ 11.00
K Darley	1-6	16.7	- 2.50
M Godsafe	1-8	12.5	+ 7.00

R Hills	0-11	M Humphries	0-2	L Dettori	0-1
Dale Gibson	0-9	Mr M Jenkins	0-2	Mr M Armytage	0-1
G Duffield	0-5	Mr P P-Gordon	0-2	Mrs L Pearce	0-1
A Mackay	0-4	D Harrison	0-1	N Day	0-1
M Birch	0-4	G Bardwell	0-1	N Kennedy	0-1
David Williams	0-2	J Reid	0-1		
Georgina Oxley	0-2	Julie Krone	0-1		

COURSE RECORD

	Total W-R	Non-Handicaps 2-y-o	Non-Handicaps 3-y-o+	Handicaps 2-y-o	Handicaps 3-y-o+	Per cent	£1 Level Stake
Beverley	4-19	0-6	1-3	0-1	3-9	21.1	+ 5.90
Haydock	4-21	1-2	1-9	0-3	2-7	19.0	+ 0.30
Pontefract	4-25	2-7	1-7	1-2	0-9	16.0	+ 4.44
Yarmouth	4-29	2-15	1-5	0-2	1-7	13.8	- 21.12
Carlisle	3-9	1-1	2-4	0-0	0-4	33.3	+ 4.00
Folkestone	3-15	1-6	1-4	1-1	0-4	20.0	+ 4.18
Newmarket	3-27	1-6	0-4	0-4	2-13	11.1	+ 1.50
Edinburgh	2-5	1-1	1-2	0-0	0-2	40.0	- 0.80
Hamilton	2-7	1-1	1-1	0-1	0-4	28.6	+ 8.75
Catterick	2-8	0-2	1-3	0-1	1-2	25.0	+ 3.25
Doncaster	2-17	1-2	0-2	0-2	1-11	11.8	+ 15.50
Chester	1-2	0-0	0-0	0-0	1-2	50.0	+ 6.50
Lingfield	1-4	0-2	0-0	0-1	1-1	25.0	+ 11.00
Ripon	1-6	1-2	0-2	0-1	0-1	16.7	0.00
Nottingham	1-8	1-3	0-3	0-0	0-2	12.5	+ 7.00
Wolverhampton	1-8	0-3	1-3	0-1	0-1	12.5	- 5.75
Warwick	1-10	0-3	0-3	1-1	0-3	10.0	+ 2.00
Ayr	1-13	0-3	0-3	0-1	1-6	7.7	- 9.50
Redcar	1-13	1-7	0-2	0-0	0-4	7.7	- 10.50
Southwell (AW)	1-23	0-4	0-10	0-0	1-9	4.3	- 12.00

Leicester	0-20	Windsor	0-8	Chepstow	0-2
York	0-13	Brighton	0-7	Newcastle	0-2
Ascot	0-10	Lingfield (AW)	0-5	Bath	0-1
Goodwood	0-10	Newbury	0-5	Epsom	0-1
Kempton	0-8	Sandown	0-4	Salisbury	0-1

WINNING HORSES

		Races					Win
	Age	Run	1st	2nd	3rd	Unpl	£
Star Family Friend	2	6	3	0	1	2	14,225
Highbrook	4	9	3	1	0	5	14,136
Bob's Return	2	4	2	0	0	2	11,823
Cindora	3	8	2	0	0	6	10,602
Light Hand	6	9	3	2	1	3	8,037
Cov Tel Lady	3	10	3	2	2	3	7,778
Guv'Nors Gift	2	9	3	2	1	3	7,363
Sudbury	2	4	2	0	1	1	5,953
Overpower	8	11	2	1	3	5	5,284
Walsham Witch	2	7	2	0	0	5	4,892
Metternich	7	6	2	0	2	2	4,726
Billy Blazer	3	7	1	1	1	4	4,221
Jungle Knife	6	2	1	0	0	1	4,078
Tykeyvor	2	4	1	0	1	2	3,883
Cliburnel News	2	8	2	0	0	6	3,503
Grove Daffodil	2	3	1	0	1	1	3,371
Canny Chronicle	4	3	1	0	0	2	3,021
Moor Lodge	3	6	1	1	0	4	2,954
Don't Smile	3	9	1	2	0	6	2,574
Alle-Roy	4	3	1	0	1	1	2,304
Forest Dew	3	6	1	1	0	4	2,187
Ballymoneyboy	3	3	1	0	0	2	2,167
Eden's Close	3	11	1	0	2	8	2,092
Full Sight	3	3	1	0	0	2	2,089
Formaestre	2	8	1	0	0	7	1,932

WINNING OWNERS

	Races Won	Value £		Races Won	Value £
Nick Cook	4	18,214	P D Savill	1	4,221
Sheffield Newspapers Ltd	3	14,225	H Key	1	3,883
Mrs G A E Smith	2	11,823	East Lancs Newspapers Readers	2	3,503
Mark Tompkins Racing	2	10,602	P H Betts (Holdings) Ltd	1	3,371
John A Furze	3	8,037	Newcastle Evening Chronicle	1	3,021
Coventry Newspapers Ltd	3	7,778	M H Tompkins	1	2,304
The Tompkins Team	3	7,363	Ecurie Fustok	1	2,187
John Wimbs	2	5,953	Mrs Anne Coughlan	1	2,167
B Schmidt-Bodner	2	5,528	Mrs M Barwell	1	2,092
M P Bowring	2	5,284	J A Fuller	1	2,089
J H Ellis	2	4,892	Saracen Racing	1	1,932
Ian Lochhead	2	4,726			

Favourites	15-47	31.9%	- 13.65	Total winning prize-money		£135,194

Longest winning sequence		2	Average SP of winner		5.8/1
Longest losing sequence		51	Return on stakes invested		-22.5%

1991 Form	42-411	10.2%	-115.54	1989 Form	44-366	12.0%	-104.18
1990 Form	46-435	10.6%	-161.69	1988 Form	16-317	5.0%	-166.50

D R TUCKER (Cullompton, Devon)

	No. of Horses	Races Run	1st	2nd	3rd	Unpl	Per cent	£1 Level Stake
2-y-o	2	5	0	0	0	5	-	- 5.00
3-y-o	3	13	0	1	1	11	-	- 13.00
4-y-o+	7	48	1	0	2	45	2.1	- 31.00
Totals	12	66	1	1	3	61	1.5	- 49.00

Jan	Feb	Mar	Apr	May	Jun	Jul	Aug	Sep	Oct/Nov
0-5	0-7	0-5	0-12	0-9	0-4	0-8	0-8	0-4	1-4

Winning Jockey	W-R	£1 Level Stake	Winning Course	W-R	£1 Level Stake
P McCabe	1-2	+ 15.00	Folkestone	1-3	+ 14.00

Winning Horse	Age	Races Run	1st	2nd	3rd	Unpl	Win £
Goody Four Shoes	4	13	1	0	0	12	1,329

Favourites	0-1		Total winning prize-money	£1,329

1991 Form	0-26	1989 Form	0-15
1990 Form	0-15	1988 Form	0-25

W G M TURNER (Sherborne, Dorset)

	No. of Horses	Races Run	1st	2nd	3rd	Unpl	Per cent	£1 Level Stake
2-y-o	16	69	6	4	9	50	8.7	0.00
3-y-o	2	14	5	1	2	6	35.7	+ 23.88
4-y-o+	10	26	0	1	1	24	-	- 26.00
Totals	28	109	11	6	12	80	10.1	- 2.12

BY MONTH

2-y-o	W-R	Per cent	£1 Level Stake	3-y-o	W-R	Per cent	£1 Level Stake
January	0-0	-	0.00	January	0-0	-	0.00
February	0-0	-	0.00	February	0-0	-	0.00
March	1-4	25.0	+ 13.00	March	0-2	-	- 2.00
April	0-16	-	- 16.00	April	1-1	100.0	+ 4.50
May	1-20	5.0	- 12.00	May	1-4	25.0	+ 7.00
June	1-8	12.5	- 3.00	June	2-3	66.7	+ 8.38
July	1-7	14.3	+ 14.00	July	0-0	-	0.00
August	1-6	16.7	+ 2.00	August	0-1	-	- 1.00
September	1-5	20.0	+ 5.00	September	1-3	33.3	+ 7.00
Oct/Nov	0-3	-	- 3.00	Oct/Nov	0-0	-	0.00

4-y-o+	W-R	Per cent	£1 Level Stake	Totals	W-R	Per cent	£1 Level Stake
January	0-1	-	- 1.00	January	0-1	-	- 1.00
February	0-0	-	0.00	February	0-0	-	0.00
March	0-3	-	- 3.00	March	1-9	11.1	+ 8.00
April	0-3	-	- 3.00	April	1-20	5.0	- 14.50
May	0-5	-	- 5.00	May	2-29	6.9	- 10.00
June	0-2	-	- 2.00	June	3-13	23.1	+ 3.38
July	0-5	-	- 5.00	July	1-12	8.3	+ 9.00
August	0-5	-	- 5.00	August	1-12	8.3	- 4.00
September	0-2	-	- 2.00	September	2-10	20.0	+ 10.00
Oct/Nov	0-0	-	0.00	Oct/Nov	0-3	-	- 3.00

DISTANCE

2-y-o	W-R	Per cent	£1 Level Stake	3-y-o	W-R	Per cent	£1 Level Stake
5f-6f	6-60	10.0	+ 9.00	5f-6f	5-11	45.5	+ 26.88
7f-8f	0-9	-	- 9.00	7f-8f	0-3	-	- 3.00
9f-13f	0-0	-	0.00	9f-13f	0-0	-	0.00
14f+	0-0	-	0.00	14f+	0-0	-	0.00

4-y-o+	W-R	Per cent	£1 Level Stake	Totals	W-R	Per cent	£1 Level Stake
5f-6f	0-1	-	- 1.00	5f-6f	11-72	15.3	+ 34.88
7f-8f	0-9	-	- 9.00	7f-8f	0-21	-	- 21.00
9f-13f	0-15	-	- 15.00	9f-13f	0-15	-	- 15.00
14f+	0-1	-	- 1.00	14f+	0-1	-	- 1.00

TYPE OF RACE

Non-Handicaps	W-R	Per cent	£1 Level Stake	Handicaps	W-R	Per cent	£1 Level Stake
2-y-o	2-38	5.3	0.00	2-y-o	2-6	33.3	+ 12.00
3-y-o	2-5	40.0	+ 11.50	3-y-o	2-6	33.3	+ 5.38
4-y-o+	0-10	-	- 10.00	4-y-o+	0-2	-	- 2.00
Selling	2-26	7.7	- 13.00	Selling	1-6	16.7	+ 4.00
Apprentice	0-2	-	- 2.00	Apprentice	0-1	-	- 1.00
Amat/Ladies	0-1	-	- 1.00	Amat/Ladies	0-6	-	- 6.00
Totals	6-82	7.3	- 14.50	Totals	5-27	18.5	+ 12.38

COURSE GRADE

	W-R	Per cent	£1 Level Stake
Group 1	1-12	8.3	- 2.00
Group 2	5-20	25.0	+ 30.38
Group 3	4-47	8.5	- 5.50
Group 4	1-30	3.3	- 25.00

FIRST TIME OUT

	W-R	Per cent	£1 Level Stake
2-y-o	2-16	12.5	+ 22.00
3-y-o	0-1	-	- 1.00
4-y-o+	0-9	-	- 9.00
Totals	2-26	7.7	+ 12.00

JOCKEYS RIDING

	W-R	Per cent	£1 Level Stake
T Sprake	8-65	12.3	+ 12.88
D Biggs	2-7	28.6	+ 12.00
A Tucker	1-1	100.0	+ 9.00

	W-R			W-R
Mrs J Gault	0-4	A Clark	0-1	Julie Goult	0-1
P Burke	0-4	A Garth	0-1	P McCabe	0-1
T Wilson	0-3	B Crossley	0-1	P Turner	0-1
D Moffatt	0-2	F Norton	0-1	R Hills	0-1
K Rutter	0-2	G Bardwell	0-1	S Drowne	0-1
Mrs C Price	0-2	G Baxter	0-1	S Mulvey	0-1
R Price	0-2	J Fanning	0-1	T G McLaughlin	0-1
W Newnes	0-2	J Lowe	0-1		

COURSE RECORD

	Total W-R	Non-Handicaps 2-y-o	3-y-o+	Handicaps 2-y-o	3-y-o+	Per cent	£1 Level Stake
Brighton	3-12	2-7	0-3	0-0	1-2	25.0	+ 27.00
Ascot	1-1	0-0	0-0	1-1	0-0	100.0	+ 9.00
Ripon	1-1	0-0	0-0	0-0	1-1	100.0	+ 1.88
Nottingham	1-4	0-3	1-1	0-0	0-0	25.0	+ 1.50
Salisbury	1-4	0-2	0-0	0-0	1-2	25.0	+ 4.50
Beverley	1-5	1-4	0-1	0-0	0-0	20.0	+ 12.00
Pontefract	1-5	0-4	1-1	0-0	0-0	20.0	+ 6.00
Windsor	1-5	0-1	0-3	1-1	0-0	20.0	+ 3.00
Wolverhampton	1-11	1-8	0-1	0-1	0-1	9.1	- 6.00

Hamilton	0-10	Goodwood	0-3	Haydock	0-1
Bath	0-8	Lingfield (AW)	0-3	Kempton	0-1
Warwick	0-8	Edinburgh	0-2	Lingfield	0-1
Leicester	0-6	Newcastle	0-2	Redcar	0-1
Chepstow	0-4	Southwell (AW)	0-2	Thirsk	0-1
Doncaster	0-3	Catterick	0-1		
Folkestone	0-3	Epsom	0-1		

WINNING HORSES

	Age	Races Run	1st	2nd	3rd	Unpl	Win £
Yours By Right	2	3	3	0	0	0	14,196
Fangio	3	11	4	1	2	4	10,220
Not So Generous	2	7	2	1	2	2	3,589
Rockbourne	3	3	1	0	0	2	2,574
Calisar	2	8	1	2	1	4	2,383

WINNING OWNERS

	Races Won	Value £		Races Won	Value £
John Turner	3	14,196	J W Aplin	1	2,574
Simon Swift	4	10,220	A Poole	1	2,383
E Goody	2	3,589			

Favourites	1-1	100.0%	+ 1.88	Total winning prize-money			£32,961
Longest winning sequence			2	Average SP of winner			8.7/1
Longest losing sequence			20	Return on stakes invested			-1.9%
1991 Form	2-61	3.3%	- 38.50	1989 Form	6-59	10.2%	- 19.67
1990 Form	2-88	2.3%	- 62.50	1988 Form	3-39	7.7%	- 15.00

M D I USHER (East Garston, Berks)

	No. of Horses	Races Run	1st	2nd	3rd	Unpl	Per cent	£1 Level Stake
2-y-o	9	35	1	1	1	32	2.9	- 30.00
3-y-o	6	35	1	2	4	28	2.9	- 18.00
4-y-o+	9	47	1	1	5	40	2.1	- 26.00
Totals	24	117	3	4	10	100	2.6	- 74.00

Jan	Feb	Mar	Apr	May	Jun	Jul	Aug	Sep	Oct/Nov
0-6	0-0	0-1	0-13	1-15	0-14	1-21	1-18	0-16	0-13

Winning Jockeys	W-R	£1 Level Stake		W-R	£1 Level Stake
M Wigham	2-24	+ 2.00	D Harrison	1-9	+ 8.00

Winning Courses	W-R	£1 Level Stake		W-R	£1 Level Stake
Southwell (AW)	1-7	- 2.00	Brighton	1-16	+ 5.00
Newbury	1-10	+ 7.00			

Winning Horses	Age	Races Run	1st	2nd	3rd	Unpl	Win £
Louisville Belle	3	9	1	0	1	7	8,344
Caromish	5	10	1	0	2	7	2,322
Shades Of Croft	2	10	1	1	1	7	1,224

Favourites	0-3			Total winning prize-money			£11,890
1991 Form	4-166	2.4%	-141.68	1989 Form	14-212	6.6%	-108.59
1990 Form	12-289	4.2%	-101.62	1988 Form	8-251	3.2%	-152.12

R VOORSPUY (Polegate, East Sussex)

	No. of Horses	Races Run	1st	2nd	3rd	Unpl	Per cent	£1 Level Stake
2-y-o	5	23	0	0	2	21	-	- 23.00
3-y-o	3	17	0	1	0	16	-	- 17.00
4-y-o+	6	22	2	1	0	19	9.1	- 4.50
Totals	14	62	2	2	2	56	3.2	- 44.50

Jan	Feb	Mar	Apr	May	Jun	Jul	Aug	Sep	Oct/Nov
0-1	0-0	0-2	1-10	0-8	1-14	0-9	0-6	0-5	0-7

Winning Jockeys	W-R	£1 Level Stake				W-R	£1 Level Stake
Paul Eddery	1-3	+ 4.50		S Dawson		1-41	- 31.00

Winning Course							
Pontefract	2-3	+ 14.50					

Winning Horse	Age	Races Run	1st	2nd	3rd	Unpl	Win £
Patroclus	7	7	2	0	0	5	5,001

Favourites	0-1			Total winning prize-money			£5,001
1991 Form	5-58	8.6%	+ 36.50	1989 Form	0-42		
1990 Form	1-50	2.0%	- 29.00	1988 Form	2-53	3.8%	- 40.00

J S WAINWRIGHT (Malton, North Yorks)

	No. of Horses	Races Run	1st	2nd	3rd	Unpl	Per cent	£1 Level Stake
2-y-o	9	36	1	0	4	31	2.8	- 15.00
3-y-o	3	14	0	0	2	12	-	- 14.00
4-y-o+	5	22	0	1	0	21	-	- 22.00
Totals	17	72	1	1	6	64	1.4	- 51.00

Jan	Feb	Mar	Apr	May	Jun	Jul	Aug	Sep	Oct/Nov
0-5	0-3	0-6	0-4	0-6	1-11	0-14	0-14	0-6	0-3

Winning Jockey	W-R	£1 Level Stake	Winning Course	W-R	£1 Level Stake
G Baxter	1-3	+ 18.00	Ayr	1-1	+ 20.00

Winning Horse	Age	Races Run	1st	2nd	3rd	Unpl	Win £
Shadow Jury	2	9	1	0	3	5	2,264

Favourites	0-1		Total winning prize-money	£2,264

1991 Form	5-137	3.6%	- 61.50	1989 Form	4-131	3.1%	- 75.17
1990 Form	3-141	2.1%	-105.00	1988 Form	2-124	1.6%	- 95.00

C F WALL (Newmarket)

	No. of Horses	Races Run	1st	2nd	3rd	Unpl	Per cent	£1 Level Stake
2-y-o	13	33	0	1	3	29	-	- 33.00
3-y-o	20	108	7	15	14	72	6.5	- 44.80
4-y-o+	2	8	0	1	0	7	-	- 8.00
Totals	35	149	7	17	17	108	4.7	- 85.80

Jan	Feb	Mar	Apr	May	Jun	Jul	Aug	Sep	Oct/Nov
0-0	1-2	0-4	1-13	1-23	1-19	1-19	0-18	1-23	1-28

Winning Jockeys	W-R	£1 Level Stake		W-R	£1 Level Stake
N Day	2-43	- 25.50	R Cochrane	1-6	+ 2.50
S Cauthen	1-1	+ 1.20	W R Swinburn	1-6	- 1.00
J Lowe	1-5	+ 12.00	N Carlisle	1-18	- 5.00

Winning Courses					
Thirsk	1-3	+ 10.00	Sandown	1-8	+ 0.50
Haydock	1-4	+ 1.00	Wolverhampton	1-8	- 5.80
Southwell (AW)	1-5	+ 7.00	Newmarket	1-14	+ 3.00
Lingfield	1-6	- 0.50			.

Winning Horses	Age	Races Run	1st	2nd	3rd	Unpl	Win £
Walimu	3	8	3	0	2	3	10,645
Ships Lantern	3	7	2	1	1	3	5,889
Admirals Secret	3	4	1	2	0	1	2,206
Hardliner	3	3	1	0	0	2	1,646

Favourites	1-12	8.3%	- 9.80	Total winning prize-money	£20,386

1991 Form	7-135	5.2%	- 83.77	1989 Form	9-117	7.7%	- 33.27
1990 Form	15-159	9.4%	- 70.56	1988 Form	13-112	11.6%	- 9.50

P T WALWYN (Lambourn, Berks)

	No. of Horses	Races Run	1st	2nd	3rd	Unpl	Per cent	£1 Level Stake
2-y-o	19	52	3	6	6	37	5.8	- 29.00
3-y-o	21	138	18	21	14	85	13.0	- 2.10
4-y-o+	6	37	1	7	3	26	2.7	- 32.50
Totals	46	227	22	34	23	148	9.7	- 63.60

BY MONTH

2-y-o	W-R	Per cent	£1 Level Stake	3-y-o	W-R	Per cent	£1 Level Stake
January	0-0	-	0.00	January	0-1	-	- 1.00
February	0-0	-	0.00	February	0-1	-	- 1.00
March	0-0	-	0.00	March	1-1	100.0	+ 1.00
April	0-0	-	0.00	April	5-19	26.3	+ 11.17
May	0-1	-	- 1.00	May	5-23	21.7	+ 11.73
June	0-1	-	- 1.00	June	1-18	5.6	- 3.00
July	1-4	25.0	0.00	July	3-18	16.7	+ 5.00
August	0-10	-	- 10.00	August	1-17	5.9	- 11.00
September	1-13	7.7	- 7.00	September	0-22	-	- 22.00
Oct/Nov	1-23	4.3	- 10.00	Oct/Nov	2-18	11.1	+ 7.00

4-y-o+	W-R	Per cent	£1 Level Stake	Totals	W-R	Per cent	£1 Level Stake
January	0-1	-	- 1.00	January	0-2	-	- 2.00
February	0-3	-	- 3.00	February	0-4	-	- 4.00
March	0-2	-	- 2.00	March	1-3	33.3	- 1.00
April	0-6	-	- 6.00	April	5-25	20.0	+ 5.17
May	0-7	-	- 7.00	May	5-31	16.1	+ 3.73
June	1-5	20.0	- 0.50	June	2-24	8.3	- 4.50
July	0-5	-	- 5.00	July	4-27	14.8	0.00
August	0-2	-	- 2.00	August	1-29	3.4	- 23.00
September	0-5	-	- 5.00	September	1-40	2.5	- 34.00
Oct/Nov	0-1	-	- 1.00	Oct/Nov	3-42	7.1	- 4.00

DISTANCE

2-y-o	W-R	Per cent	£1 Level Stake	3-y-o	W-R	Per cent	£1 Level Stake
5f-6f	0-24	-	- 24.00	5f-6f	2-14	14.3	+ 16.00
7f-8f	3-28	10.7	- 5.00	7f-8f	7-61	11.5	- 38.10
9f-13f	0-0	-	0.00	9f-13f	7-55	12.7	+ 9.00
14f+	0-0	-	0.00	14f+	2-8	25.0	+ 11.00

4-y-o+	W-R	Per cent	£1 Level Stake	Totals	W-R	Per cent	£1 Level Stake
5f-6f	0-2	-	- 2.00	5f-6f	2-40	5.0	- 10.00
7f-8f	0-6	-	- 6.00	7f-8f	10-95	10.5	- 49.10
9f-13f	1-19	5.3	- 14.50	9f-13f	8-74	10.8	- 5.50
14f+	0-10	-	- 10.00	14f+	2-18	11.1	+ 1.00

TYPE OF RACE

Non-Handicaps	W-R	Per cent	£1 Level Stake	Handicaps	W-R	Per cent	£1 Level Stake
2-y-o	2-47	4.3	- 30.00	2-y-o	1-5	20.0	+ 1.00
3-y-o	12-64	18.8	+ 17.23	3-y-o	5-65	7.7	- 12.00
4-y-o+	0-15	-	- 15.00	4-y-o+	1-19	5.3	- 14.50
Selling	0-0	-	0.00	Selling	0-1	-	- 1.00
Apprentice	1-2	50.0	- 0.33	Apprentice	0-1	-	- 1.00
Amat/Ladies	0-1	-	- 1.00	Amat/Ladies	0-7	-	- 7.00
Totals	15-129	11.6	- 29.10	Totals	7-98	7.1	- 34.50

COURSE GRADE

	W-R	Per cent	£1 Level Stake
Group 1	11-136	8.1	- 49.17
Group 2	0-27	-	- 27.00
Group 3	8-39	20.5	+ 31.90
Group 4	3-25	12.0	- 19.33

FIRST TIME OUT

	W-R	Per cent	£1 Level Stake
2-y-o	0-19	-	- 19.00
3-y-o	4-19	21.1	+ 26.00
4-y-o+	0-6	-	- 6.00
Totals	4-44	9.1	+ 1.00

JOCKEYS RIDING

	W-R	Per cent	£1 Level Stake		W-R	Per cent	£1 Level Stake
W Carson	9-75	12.0	- 3.50	M Birch	1-4	25.0	+ 8.00
Pat Eddery	2-9	22.2	+ 2.33	A Mackay	1-5	20.0	- 0.50
A Munro	2-15	13.3	- 3.60	P Robinson	1-5	20.0	- 1.00
E Husband	1-1	100.0	+ 0.67	T Quinn	1-6	16.7	+ 3.00
R Fox	1-1	100.0	+ 14.00	G Carter	1-9	11.1	- 1.00
W R Swinburn	1-2	50.0	+ 11.00	R Cochrane	1-26	3.8	- 24.00

R Hills	0-12	N Howe	0-3	L Charnock	0-1
L Dettori	0-9	B Raymond	0-2	Lord Oaksey	0-1
D Biggs	0-7	G Duffield	0-2	Miss J Winter	0-1
D Holland	0-5	J Reid	0-2	Miss T Bracegirdle	0-1
G Baxter	0-4	M Roberts	0-2	Mr J Durkan	0-1
A Tucker	0-3	Rose Nugent	0-2	Paul Eddery	0-1
B Rouse	0-3	S Cauthen	0-2	W Ryan	0-1
Miss A Turner	0-3	K Rutter	0-1		

COURSE RECORD

	Total W-R	Non-Handicaps 2-y-o	3-y-o+	Handicaps 2-y-o	3-y-o+	Per cent	£1 Level Stake
Chepstow	3-6	0-1	1-2	0-0	2-3	50.0	+ 14.90
Kempton	3-15	0-2	1-8	0-0	2-5	20.0	+ 8.00
Newmarket	3-19	0-4	3-7	0-0	0-8	15.8	+ 12.33
Leicester	2-10	1-4	1-3	0-1	0-2	20.0	+ 11.00
Sandown	2-16	0-0	2-8	0-0	0-8	12.5	- 2.50
Newbury	2-20	0-4	0-7	1-1	1-8	10.0	- 5.00

Beverley	1-4	0-1	1-1	0-0	0-2	25.0	+	8.00
Warwick	1-4	0-1	1-3	0-0	0-0	25.0	-	2.00
Nottingham	1-5	0-2	1-1	0-0	0-2	20.0	-	1.00
Lingfield (AW)	1-6	0-0	1-3	0-0	0-3	16.7	-	4.00
Folkestone	1-7	0-3	1-2	0-0	0-2	14.3	-	5.33
Bath	1-8	0-4	0-0	0-0	1-4	12.5	+	5.00
Ascot	1-18	1-6	0-5	0-1	0-6	5.6	-	14.00

Doncaster	0-14	Wolverhampton	0-5	Pontefract		0-2
Goodwood	0-12	Epsom	0-4	Thirsk		0-2
York	0-11	Ayr	0-3	Newcastle		0-1
Salisbury	0-9	Haydock	0-3	Redcar		0-1
Brighton	0-8	Southwell (AW)	0-3	Ripon		0-1
Lingfield	0-6	Windsor	0-3	Yarmouth		0-1

WINNING HORSES

		Races					Win
	Age	Run	1st	2nd	3rd	Unpl	£
Hamas	3	11	3	4	1	3	15,391
Spikenard	3	8	3	0	1	4	10,785
Salatin	2	3	1	1	0	1	9,688
Muhit	3	9	2	1	2	4	5,710
Fengari	3	8	2	3	0	3	5,423
Shamam	2	5	1	1	1	2	5,192
Dyab	2	2	1	0	0	1	3,371
Samurai Gold	4	11	1	4	1	5	3,028
Iywaan	3	4	1	1	0	2	2,950
Ghalyoon	3	5	1	0	0	4	2,819
Gong	3	9	1	1	0	7	2,777
Kabayil	3	10	1	1	1	7	2,658
Winter Lightning	3	3	1	0	0	2	2,490
Ahbab	3	10	1	1	3	5	2,383
Majboor	3	8	1	2	1	4	2,304
Queen Warrior	3	8	1	2	1	4	000

WINNING OWNERS

	Races Won	Value £		Races Won	Value £
Hamdan Al-Maktoum	13	52,466	A D G Oldrey	1	2,777
Lord Howard De Walden	3	10,785	Mrs R B Kennard	1	2,490
Fairly Stable	2	5,423	Christopher Spence	1	000
I Karageorgis	1	3,028			

Favourites	5-18	27.8%	- 9.60	Total winning prize-money			£76,968
Longest winning sequence			3	Average SP of winner			6.4/1
Longest losing sequence			48	Return on stakes invested			-28.0%
1991 Form	24-262	9.2%	-101.99	1989 Form	36-327	11.0%	- 96.72
1990 Form	48-312	15.4%	+ 36.45	1988 Form	30-299	10.0%	-112.20

MRS BARBARA WARING (Chippenham, Wilts)

	No. of Horses	Races Run	1st	2nd	3rd	Unpl	Per cent	£1 Level Stake
2-y-o	2	7	0	0	1	6	-	- 7.00
3-y-o	5	21	0	0	0	21	-	- 21.00
4-y-o+	12	71	3	3	1	64	4.2	- 40.75
Totals	19	99	3	3	2	91	3.0	- 68.75

Jan	Feb	Mar	Apr	May	Jun	Jul	Aug	Sep	Oct/Nov
0-0	0-5	0-1	0-10	0-14	0-10	2-14	0-15	1-12	0-18

Winning Jockeys	W-R	£1 Level Stake				W-R	£1 Level Stake
J Lowe	1-4	- 0.25		N Howe		1-83	- 62.00
C Hawksley	1-7	- 1.50					

Winning Courses	W-R	£1 Level Stake				W-R	£1 Level Stake
Doncaster	1-5	- 1.25		Warwick		1-7	- 1.50
Lingfield	1-6	+ 15.00					

Winning Horses	Age	Races Run	1st	2nd	3rd	Unpl	Win £
Smilingatstrangers	4	12	2	2	0	8	5,357
Janiski	9	6	1	0	0	5	2,385

Favourites	1-1	100.0%	+ 2.75	Total winning prize-money			£7,742

1991 Form	6-111	5.4%	- 35.00	1989 Form	1-34	2.9%	0.00
1990 Form	5-83	6.0%	+ 20.25	1988 Form	2-36	5.6%	- 10.00

J W WATTS (Richmond, North Yorks)

	No. of Horses	Races Run	1st	2nd	3rd	Unpl	Per cent	£1 Level Stake
2-y-o	16	53	6	11	9	27	11.3	- 8.50
3-y-o	11	57	6	8	5	38	10.5	+ 1.75
4-y-o+	5	52	5	7	6	34	9.6	- 1.00
Totals	32	162	17	26	20	99	10.5	- 7.75

BY MONTH

2-y-o	W-R	Per cent	£1 Level Stake	3-y-o	W-R	Per cent	£1 Level Stake
Mar/Apr	0-2	-	- 2.00	Mar/Apr	0-6	-	- 6.00
May	1-5	20.0	+ 3.00	May	2-13	15.4	+ 11.25
June	2-7	28.6	+ 6.50	June	2-14	14.3	+ 4.00
July	2-7	28.6	+ 3.00	July	1-11	9.1	- 3.50
August	0-4	-	- 4.00	August	0-2	-	- 2.00
September	1-15	6.7	- 2.00	September	0-7	-	- 7.00
Oct/Nov	0-13	-	- 13.00	Oct/Nov	1-4	25.0	+ 5.00

Watts J W

4-y-o+	W-R	Per cent	£1 Level Stake	Totals	W-R	Per cent	£1 Level Stake
Mar/Apr	2-11	18.2	+ 6.00	Mar/Apr	2-19	10.5	- 2.00
May	2-7	28.6	+ 15.00	May	5-25	20.0	+ 29.25
June	0-8	-	- 8.00	June	4-29	13.8	+ 2.50
July	0-8	-	- 8.00	July	3-26	11.5	- 8.50
August	0-3	-	- 3.00	August	0-9	-	- 9.00
September	0-9	-	- 9.00	September	1-31	3.2	- 18.00
Oct/Nov	1-6	16.7	+ 1.00	Oct/Nov	2-23	8.7	- 7.00

DISTANCE

2-y-o	W-R	Per cent	£1 Level Stake	3-y-o	W-R	Per cent	£1 Level Stake
5f-6f	4-35	11.4	- 5.50	5f-6f	2-11	18.2	+ 6.50
7f-8f	2-18	11.1	- 3.00	7f-8f	1-16	6.3	- 8.00
9f-13f	0-0	-	0.00	9f-13f	2-21	9.5	- 8.75
14f+	0-0	-	0.00	14f+	1-9	11.1	+ 12.00

4-y-o+	W-R	Per cent	£1 Level Stake	Totals	W-R	Per cent	£1 Level Stake
5f-6f	0-0	-	0.00	5f-6f	6-46	13.0	+ 1.00
7f-8f	3-33	9.1	- 6.00	7f-8f	6-67	9.0	- 17.00
9f-13f	1-9	11.1	+ 2.00	9f-13f	3-30	10.0	- 6.75
14f+	1-10	10.0	+ 3.00	14f+	2-19	10.5	+ 15.00

TYPE OF RACE

Non-Handicaps	W-R	Per cent	£1 Level Stake	Handicaps	W-R	Per cent	£1 Level Stake
2-y-o	6-41	14.6	+ 3.50	2-y-o	0-10	-	- 10.00
3-y-o	0-13	-	- 13.00	3-y-o	5-41	12.2	+ 8.75
4-y-o+	0-1	-	- 1.00	4-y-o+	5-48	10.4	+ 3.00
Selling	0-2	-	- 2.00	Selling	0-1	-	- 1.00
Apprentice	0-1	-	- 1.00	Apprentice	1-3	33.3	+ 6.00
Amat/Ladies	0-0	-	0.00	Amat/Ladies	0-1	-	- 1.00
Totals	6-58	10.3	- 13.50	Totals	11-104	10.6	+ 5.75

COURSE GRADE

	W-R	Per cent	£1 Level Stake
Group 1	7-83	8.4	- 25.50
Group 2	4-43	9.3	+ 6.00
Group 3	4-22	18.2	+ 6.75
Group 4	2-14	14.3	+ 5.00

FIRST TIME OUT

	W-R	Per cent	£1 Level Stake
2-y-o	3-16	18.8	+ 13.00
3-y-o	0-11	-	- 11.00
4-y-o+	2-5	40.0	+ 17.00
Totals	5-32	15.6	+ 19.00

JOCKEYS RIDING

	W-R	Per cent	£1 Level Stake		W-R	Per cent	£1 Level Stake
B Raymond	3-7	42.9	+ 12.75	G Hind	1-3	33.3	+ 8.00
N Connorton	3-22	13.6	+ 12.00	L Piggott	1-3	33.3	+ 5.00
G Duffield	2-28	7.1	- 12.00	P Robinson	1-3	33.3	+ 5.00
J Lowe	2-38	5.3	- 20.50	Pat Eddery	1-5	20.0	+ 3.00
S Davies	1-2	50.0	+ 7.00	W Ryan	1-7	14.3	- 5.00
G Bardwell	1-3	33.3	+ 18.00				

S Cauthen	0-10	J Reid	0-2	D McKeown	0-1
W R Swinburn	0-5	M Roberts	0-2	F Norton	0-1
D Holland	0-3	R Fox	0-2	G Baxter	0-1
E Husband	0-3	W Carson	0-2	Miss L S-Sackville	0-1
M Birch	0-3	A Mercer	0-1	N Adams	0-1
J Fanning	0-2	D Harrison	0-1		

COURSE RECORD

	Total W-R	Non-Handicaps 2-y-o	Non-Handicaps 3-y-o+	Handicaps 2-y-o	Handicaps 3-y-o+	Per cent	£1 Level Stake
Beverley	2-6	1-3	0-0	0-0	1-3	33.3	+ 8.50
Pontefract	2-9	0-1	0-0	0-1	2-7	22.2	+ 5.25
Ayr	2-12	1-3	0-1	0-0	1-8	16.7	+ 8.50
Ripon	2-13	1-3	0-1	0-0	1-9	15.4	+ 8.00
Carlisle	1-3	0-1	0-0	0-0	1-2	33.3	+ 5.00
Wolverhampton	1-3	0-0	0-0	0-0	1-3	33.3	+ 8.00
Ascot	1-5	1-2	0-1	0-0	0-2	20.0	+ 3.00
Chester	1-7	0-1	0-0	0-1	1-5	14.3	0.00
York	1-10	0-5	0-1	0-1	1-3	10.0	- 1.00
Newcastle	1-11	0-1	0-3	0-1	1-6	9.1	- 1.00
Redcar	1-15	0-9	0-2	0-0	1-4	6.7	+ 6.00
Haydock	1-16	1-4	0-2	0-1	0-9	6.3	- 8.00
Doncaster	1-21	1-3	0-1	0-2	0-15	4.8	- 19.00

Thirsk	0-8	Goodwood	0-3	Newbury	0-2
Catterick	0-7	Newmarket	0-3	Southwell (AW)	0-1
Nottingham	0-4	Leicester	0-2	Windsor	0-1

WINNING HORSES

	Age	Races Run	1st	2nd	3rd	Unpl	Win £
Big Hand	3	5	2	1	0	2	23,003
Satank	2	4	1	1	2	0	15,790
Jervia	2	6	2	1	0	3	9,906
Good Hand	6	10	1	1	1	7	7,375
Habeta	6	14	2	1	1	10	6,212
Bigwheel Bill	3	8	1	2	1	4	6,056
Sagebrush Roller	4	12	1	4	1	6	5,426
Colway Rock	2	3	1	0	2	0	2,724

Watts J W

Stapleton	3	8	1	2	0	5	2,679
Tricycle	3	4	1	0	0	3	2,608
Storiths	2	4	1	1	1	1	2,465
Great Lord	3	8	1	0	1	6	2,422
Execution Only	4	9	1	1	2	5	2,402
Chevrotain	2	4	1	3	0	0	1,758

WINNING OWNERS

	Races Won	Value £		Races Won	Value £
Mrs M M Haggas	3	30,378	A K Collins	1	5,426
Sheikh Mohammed	5	16,765	R Coleman	1	2,724
R E Sangster	1	15,790	Duke Of Sutherland	1	2,608
R D Bickenson	2	6,212	Mrs M Irwin	1	2,465
Gerald Cooper	1	6,056	Jeremy J Thompson	1	2,402

Favourites	2-20	10.0%	- 14.75	Total winning prize-money		£90,826
Longest winning sequence			2	Average SP of winner		8.1/1
Longest losing sequence			38	Return on stakes invested		-4.8%
1991 Form	14-192	7.3%	-136.44	1989 Form	25-221	11.3%	- 25.83
1990 Form	27-228	11.8%	- 74.77	1988 Form	23-246	9.3%	-122.84

E WEYMES (Middleham, North Yorks)

	No. of Horses	Races Run	1st	2nd	3rd	Unpl	Per cent	£1 Level Stake
2-y-o	6	23	4	3	1	15	17.4	- 6.50
3-y-o	5	39	8	2	3	26	20.5	- 0.21
4-y-o+	1	16	0	3	1	12	-	- 16.00
Totals	12	78	12	8	5	53	15.4	- 22.71

BY MONTH

2-y-o	W-R	Per cent	£1 Level Stake	3-y-o	W-R	Per cent	£1 Level Stake
Mar/Apr	0-1	-	- 1.00	Mar/Apr	1-6	16.7	- 4.00
May	0-2	-	- 2.00	May	1-7	14.3	- 2.00
June	1-5	20.0	- 1.50	June	4-6	66.7	+ 7.04
July	1-3	33.3	+ 2.50	July	1-6	16.7	+ 0.50
August	0-1	-	- 1.00	August	0-5	-	- 5.00
September	1-7	14.3	- 1.50	September	0-6	-	- 6.00
Oct/Nov	1-4	25.0	- 2.00	Oct/Nov	1-3	33.3	+ 0.25

4-y-o+	W-R	Per cent	£1 Level Stake	Totals	W-R	Per cent	£1 Level Stake
Mar/Apr	0-3	-	- 2.00	Mar/Apr	1-10	10.0	- 7.00
May	0-2	-	- 2.00	May	1-11	9.1	- 6.00
June	0-3	-	- 3.00	June	5-14	35.7	+ 2.54
July	0-3	-	- 3.00	July	2-12	16.7	0.00
August	0-2	-	- 2.00	August	0-8	-	- 8.00
September	0-2	-	- 2.00	September	1-15	6.7	- 9.50
Oct/Nov	0-1	-	- 1.00	Oct/Nov	2-8	25.0	- 2.75

DISTANCE

2-y-o	W-R	Per cent	£1 Level Stake	3-y-o	W-R	Per cent	£1 Level Stake
5f-6f	1-13	7.7	- 9.50	5f-6f	0-1	-	- 1.00
7f-8f	3-10	30.0	+ 3.00	7f-8f	4-23	17.4	- 0.87
9f-13f	0-0	-	0.00	9f-13f	4-15	26.7	+ 1.66
14f+	0-0	-	0.00	14f+	0-0	-	0.00

4-y-o+	W-R	Per cent	£1 Level Stake	Totals	W-R	Per cent	£1 Level Stake
5f-6f	0-0	-	0.00	5f-6f	1-14	7.1	- 10.50
7f-8f	0-0	-	0.00	7f-8f	7-33	21.2	+ 2.13
9f-13f	0-15	-	- 15.00	9f-13f	4-30	13.3	- 13.34
14f+	0-1	-	- 1.00	14f+	0-1	-	- 1.00

TYPE OF RACE

Non-Handicaps	W-R	Per cent	£1 Level Stake	Handicaps	W-R	Per cent	£1 Level Stake
2-y-o	4-21	19.0	- 4.50	2-y-o	0-2	-	- 2.00
3-y-o	0-11	-	- 11.00	3-y-o	7-20	35.0	+ 7.79
4-y-o+	0-0	-	0.00	4-y-o+	0-9	-	- 9.00
Selling	1-7	14.3	+ 4.00	Selling	0-4	-	- 4.00
Apprentice	0-0	-	0.00	Apprentice	0-1	-	- 1.00
Amat/Ladies	0-1	-	- 1.00	Amat/Ladies	0-2	-	- 2.00
Totals	5-40	12.5	- 12.50	Totals	7-38	18.4	- 10.21

COURSE GRADE

	W-R	Per cent	£1 Level Stake
Group 1	5-17	29.4	+ 3.25
Group 2	1-16	6.3	- 10.50
Group 3	1-11	9.1	- 9.09
Group 4	5-34	14.7	- 6.37

FIRST TIME OUT

	W-R	Per cent	£1 Level Stake
2-y-o	0-6	-	- 6.00
3-y-o	1-5	20.0	+ 6.00
4-y-o+	0-1	-	- 1.00
Totals	1-12	8.3	- 1.00

JOCKEYS RIDING

	W-R	Per cent	£1 Level Stake		W-R	Per cent	£1 Level Stake
D McKeown	3-14	21.4	- 2.34	W R Swinburn	1-1	100.0	+ 4.00
L Dettori	2-3	66.7	+ 6.33	M Roberts	1-2	50.0	0.00
W Newnes	2-4	50.0	+ 1.30	J Weaver	1-4	25.0	+ 1.50
G Hind	2-15	13.3	+ 1.50				

A Culhane	0-5	J Fortune	0-2	R Lappin		0-1
A Garth	0-5	W Woods	0-2	S Wood		0-1
Dale Gibson	0-4	G Duffield	0-1	W Carson		0-1
J Fanning	0-4	J Quinn	0-1	W Ryan		0-1
Mr J Weymes	0-3	K Fallon	0-1			
B Raymond	0-2	M Humphries	0-1			

COURSE RECORD

	Total W-R	Non-Handicaps 2-y-o	Non-Handicaps 3-y-o+	Handicaps 2-y-o	Handicaps 3-y-o+	Per cent	£1 Level Stake
York	4-5	2-2	0-0	0-1	2-2	80.0	+ 10.25
Southwell (AW)	2-8	0-0	0-3	0-0	2-5	25.0	+ 1.33
Edinburgh	2-10	1-3	0-2	0-0	1-5	20.0	- 2.70
Hamilton	1-3	0-0	0-2	0-0	1-1	33.3	- 1.09
Newcastle	1-3	0-1	0-0	0-0	1-2	33.3	+ 2.00
Redcar	1-6	1-3	0-1	0-0	0-2	16.7	- 0.50
Catterick	1-10	0-2	1-4	0-0	0-4	10.0	+ 1.00

Carlisle	0-6	Ayr		0-4	Pontefract	0-3
Ripon	0-5	Doncaster		0-4	Nottingham	0-2
Thirsk	0-5	Beverley		0-3	Haydock	0-1

WINNING HORSES

	Age	Races Run	1st	2nd	3rd	Unpl	Win £
Drummer Hicks	3	10	4	2	0	4	23,754
Great Steps	2	3	2	1	0	0	9,545
Coastal Express	3	11	3	0	1	7	7,201
Ten To Six	2	3	1	1	0	1	4,269
Emerald Ears	3	9	1	0	1	7	2,402
Peaceful Air	2	5	1	1	1	2	2,122

WINNING OWNERS

	Races Won	Value £		Races Won	Value £
Mrs N Napier	4	23,754	Mrs V Mooney	1	4,269
Norman A Blyth	2	9,545	F Town	1	2,402
Mrs R L Heaton	3	7,201	T A Scothern	1	2,122

Favourites	8-11	72.7%	+ 15.79	Total winning prize-money			£49,293
Longest winning sequence			2	Average SP of winner			3.6/1
Longest losing sequence			28	Return on stakes invested			-29.1%
1991 Form	2-68	2.9%	- 56.00	1989 Form	6-118	5.1%	- 85.75
1990 Form	5-122	4.1%	- 85.00	1988 Form	10-105	9.5%	- 43.25

J WHARTON (Melton Mowbray, Leics)

	No. of Horses	Races Run	1st	2nd	3rd	Unpl	Per cent	£1 Level Stake
2-y-o	9	38	5	1	6	26	13.2	- 10.25
3-y-o	6	27	5	0	4	18	18.5	+ 11.50
4-y-o+	16	74	7	15	11	41	9.5	+ 39.70
Totals	31	139	17	16	21	85	12.2	+ 40.95

BY MONTH

2-y-o	W-R	Per cent	£1 Level Stake	3-y-o	W-R	Per cent	£1 Level Stake
January	0-0	-	0.00	January	0-1	-	- 1.00
February	0-0	-	0.00	February	0-1	-	- 1.00
March	0-1	-	- 1.00	March	0-1	-	- 1.00
April	2-3	66.7	+ 6.50	April	0-2	-	- 2.00
May	0-7	-	- 7.00	May	1-5	20.0	+ 6.00
June	0-4	-	- 4.00	June	2-5	40.0	+ 8.00
July	2-7	28.6	+ 2.75	July	1-4	25.0	+ 6.00
August	1-3	33.3	+ 5.50	August	1-5	20.0	- 0.50
September	0-5	-	- 5.00	September	0-3	-	- 3.00
Oct/Nov	0-8	-	- 8.00	Oct/Nov	0-0	-	0.00

4-y-o+	W-R	Per cent	£1 Level Stake	Totals	W-R	Per cent	£1 Level Stake
January	0-0	-	0.00	January	0-1	-	- 1.00
February	1-5	20.0	- 1.75	February	1-6	16.7	- 2.75
March	0-5	-	- 5.00	March	0-7	-	- 7.00
April	1-6	16.7	+ 20.00	April	3-11	27.3	+ 24.50
May	3-15	20.0	+ 48.95	May	4-27	14.8	+ 47.95
June	1-17	5.9	- 11.50	June	3-26	11.5	- 7.50
July	0-11	-	- 11.00	July	3-22	13.6	- 2.25
August	0-5	-	- 5.00	August	2-13	15.4	0.00
September	0-3	-	- 3.00	September	0-11	-	- 11.00
Oct/Nov	1-7	14.3	+ 8.00	Oct/Nov	1-15	6.7	0.00

DISTANCE

	W-R	Per cent	£1 Level Stake		W-R	Per cent	£1 Level Stake
2-y-o				3-y-o			
5f-6f	4-30	13.3	- 5.00	5f-6f	4-9	44.4	+ 22.50
7f-8f	1-7	14.3	- 4.25	7f-8f	0-8	-	- 8.00
9f-13f	0-1	-	- 1.00	9f-13f	1-9	11.1	- 2.00
14f+	0-0	-	0.00	14f+	0-1	-	- 1.00
		Per cent	£1 Level Stake			Per cent	£1 Level Stake
4-y-o+	W-R			Totals	W-R		
5f-6f	3-20	15.0	- 1.55	5f-6f	11-59	18.6	+ 15.95
7f-8f	0-11	-	- 11.00	7f-8f	1-26	3.8	- 23.25
9f-13f	1-21	4.8	- 6.00	9f-13f	2-31	6.5	- 9.00
14f+	3-22	13.6	+ 58.25	14f+	3-23	13.0	+ 57.25

TYPE OF RACE

	W-R	Per cent	£1 Level Stake		W-R	Per cent	£1 Level Stake
Non-Handicaps	1-23	4.3	- 20.25	Handicaps	0-5	-	- 5.00
2-y-o	1-23	4.3	- 20.25	2-y-o	0-5	-	- 5.00
3-y-o	2-13	15.4	0.00	3-y-o	3-13	23.1	+ 12.50
4-y-o+	0-9	-	- 9.00	4-y-o+	6-60	10.0	+ 38.70
Selling	3-11	27.3	+ 7.00	Selling	2-5	40.0	+ 17.00
Apprentice	0-0	-	0.00	Apprentice	0-0	-	0.00
Amat/Ladies	0-0	-	0.00	Amat/Ladies	0-0	-	0.00
Totals	6-56	10.7	- 22.25	Totals	11-83	13.3	+ 63.20

COURSE GRADE

	W-R	Per cent	£1 Level Stake
Group 1	3-43	7.0	- 20.50
Group 2	3-15	20.0	+ 6.45
Group 3	6-48	12.5	+ 9.00
Group 4	5-33	15.2	+ 46.00

FIRST TIME OUT

	W-R	Per cent	£1 Level Stake
2-y-o	0-9	-	- 9.00
3-y-o	1-6	16.7	0.00
4-y-o+	2-16	12.5	+ 61.00
Totals	3-31	9.7	+ 52.00

JOCKEYS RIDING

	W-R	Per cent	£1 Level Stake		W-R	Per cent	£1 Level Stake
J Quinn	5-25	20.0	+ 60.75	W Carson	1-4	25.0	+ 3.00
M Birch	3-8	37.5	+ 13.50	A Shoults	1-4	25.0	+ 4.50
J Fanning	3-21	14.3	+ 13.75	W Newnes	1-5	20.0	0.00
D Holland	1-2	50.0	+ 2.50	J Williams	1-28	3.6	- 21.00
W Ryan	1-3	33.3	+ 2.95				

S D Williams	0-14	S Maloney	0-2	K Fallon	0-1
D Biggs	0-4	A Clark	0-1	N Day	0-1
P Robinson	0-4	C Rutter	0-1	N Kennedy	0-1
G Forster	0-2	Dale Gibson	0-1	R Fox	0-1
K Rutter	0-2	F Norton	0-1		
N Adams	0-2	G Baxter	0-1		

COURSE RECORD

	Total	Non-Handicaps		Handicaps		Per	£1 Level
	W-R	2-y-o	3-y-o+	2-y-o	3-y-o+	cent	Stake
Nottingham	4-15	2-7	1-1	0-0	1-7	26.7	+ 31.00
Warwick	2-4	0-0	0-0	1-2	1-2	50.0	+ 18.00
Ripon	2-6	0-0	0-2	0-0	2-4	33.3	+ 9.50
York	2-10	0-1	0-0	0-0	2-9	20.0	+ 5.50
Southwell (AW)	2-16	1-5	0-5	0-0	1-6	12.5	- 10.00
Redcar	1-3	0-0	0-0	0-0	1-3	33.3	+ 2.95
Beverley	1-10	0-3	1-4	0-0	0-3	10.0	- 4.00
Wolverhampton	1-11	0-3	0-2	0-0	1-6	9.1	+ 40.00
Leicester	1-12	1-8	0-2	0-0	0-2	8.3	- 7.00
Newmarket	1-16	0-0	0-3	0-3	1-10	6.3	- 9.00

Doncaster	0-8	Chepstow	0-2	Windsor	0-2
Pontefract	0-5	Chester	0-2	Yarmouth	0-2
Thirsk	0-3	Haydock	0-2	Ayr	0-1
Ascot	0-2	Newbury	0-2	Lingfield	0-1
Catterick	0-2	Sandown	0-2		

WINNING HORSES

	Age	Races Run	1st	2nd	3rd	Unpl	Win £
First Gold	3	13	3	0	1	9	10,554
Tongue Tied	4	6	2	1	0	3	7,206
Martina	4	9	1	3	2	3	5,796
Ruby Cooper	2	7	2	0	1	4	5,040
Another Kingdom	2	6	2	0	1	3	4,541
Branston Abby	3	2	1	0	0	1	3,460
Drinks Party	4	5	1	0	1	3	2,889
Seldom In	6	7	1	0	2	4	2,677
Creeager	10	4	1	2	0	1	2,551
Handy Lass	3	4	1	0	1	2	2,402
Unpaid Member	8	4	1	1	1	1	2,089
Walid's Princess	2	8	1	0	1	6	1,582

WINNING OWNERS

	Races Won	Value £		Races Won	Value £
J L Ashby	3	10,554	David Edge	1	2,889
J Rose	3	7,442	Mrs V Craggs	1	2,677
Mrs R T Watson	2	7,206	J M Berry	1	2,551
M J Yarrow	1	5,796	W Fletcher	1	2,089
W Wharton	2	4,541	Mrs Violet J Hannigan	1	1,582
J David Abell	1	3,460			

Favourites	4-7	57.1%	+ 10.75	Total winning prize-money			£50,788
Longest winning sequence			2	Average SP of winner			9.6/1
Longest losing sequence			21	Return on stakes invested			29.5%
1991 Form	11-119	9.2%	- 30.17	1989 Form	13-176	7.4%	- 33.00
1990 Form	15-198	7.6%	- 38.00	1988 Form	9-173	5.2%	- 43.00

E A WHEELER (Lambourn, Berks)

	No. of Horses	Races Run	1st	2nd	3rd	Unpl	Per cent	£1 Level Stake
2-y-o	1	4	0	0	0	4	-	- 4.00
3-y-o	9	49	1	1	4	43	2.0	- 46.00
4-y-o+	6	57	5	3	1	48	8.8	- 8.00
Totals	16	110	6	4	5	95	5.5	- 58.00

Jan	Feb	Mar	Apr	May	Jun	Jul	Aug	Sep	Oct/Nov
0-0	0-0	0-1	2-9	2-8	0-22	0-18	1-27	1-18	0-7

Winning Jockeys	W-R	£1 Level Stake			W-R	£1 Level Stake
D Harrison	2-24	- 7.50				
M Roberts	1-1	+ 2.00	M Tebbutt		1-5	+ 12.00
M Wigham	1-4	+ 5.00	F Norton		1-10	- 3.50

Winning Courses	W-R	£1 Level Stake			W-R	£1 Level Stake
Hamilton	1-1	+ 2.50	Newmarket		1-3	+ 10.00
Ripon	1-1	+ 16.00	Pontefract		1-4	+ 2.50
Thirsk	1-2	+ 7.00	Brighton		1-8	- 5.00

Winning Horses	Age	Races Run	1st	2nd	3rd	Unpl	Win £
Green Dollar	9	20	2	2	0	16	21,805
Pharaoh's Dancer	5	10	3	0	0	7	7,508
Batchworth Bound	3	12	1	0	3	8	2,070

Favourites	1-6	16.7%	- 2.50	Total winning prize-money			£31,383

1991 Form	8-116	6.9%	- 29.00	1989 Form	2-74	2.7%	- 55.50
1990 Form	7-126	5.6%	- 68.50	1988 Form	4-96	4.2%	- 56.00

R M WHITAKER (Wetherby, West Yorks)

	No. of Horses	Races Run	1st	2nd	3rd	Unpl	Per cent	£1 Level Stake
2-y-o	15	73	4	11	8	50	5.5	- 34.12
3-y-o	22	137	6	15	7	109	4.4	- 93.62
4-y-o+	13	78	12	8	14	44	15.4	+ 26.25
Totals	50	288	22	34	29	203	7.6	-101.49

Whitaker R M

BY MONTH

2-y-o	W-R	Per cent	£1 Level Stake	3-y-o	W-R	Per cent	£1 Level Stake
January	0-0	-	0.00	January	0-0	-	0.00
February	0-0	-	0.00	February	0-0	-	0.00
March	0-1	-	- 1.00	March	0-4	-	- 4.00
April	1-2	50.0	+ 8.00	April	0-9	-	- 9.00
May	1-6	16.7	+ 3.00	May	0-14	-	- 14.00
June	1-12	8.3	- 9.12	June	2-26	7.7	- 14.75
July	0-8	-	- 8.00	July	2-19	10.5	- 7.37
August	0-10	-	- 10.00	August	1-22	4.5	- 9.00
September	1-21	4.8	- 4.00	September	1-20	5.0	- 12.50
Oct/Nov	0-13	-	- 13.00	Oct/Nov	0-23	-	- 23.00

4-y-o+	W-R	Per cent	£1 Level Stake	Totals	W-R	Per cent	£1 Level Stake
January	0-2	-	- 2.00	January	0-2	-	- 2.00
February	0-0	-	0.00	February	0-0	-	0.00
March	0-1	-	- 1.00	March	0-6	-	- 6.00
April	0-6	-	- 6.00	April	1-17	5.9	- 7.00
May	2-14	14.3	+ 16.00	May	3-34	8.8	+ 5.00
June	4-22	18.2	+ 3.50	June	7-60	11.7	- 20.37
July	2-13	15.4	+ 0.75	July	4-40	10.0	- 14.62
August	2-10	20.0	+ 9.00	August	3-42	7.1	- 10.00
September	2-5	40.0	+ 11.00	September	4-46	8.7	- 5.50
Oct/Nov	0-5	-	- 5.00	Oct/Nov	0-41	-	- 41.00

DISTANCE

2-y-o	W-R	Per cent	£1 Level Stake	3-y-o	W-R	Per cent	£1 Level Stake
5f-6f	4-55	7.3	- 16.12	5f-6f	3-52	5.8	- 37.12
7f-8f	0-17	-	- 17.00	7f-8f	2-58	3.4	- 37.50
9f-13f	0-1	-	- 1.00	9f-13f	1-25	4.0	- 17.00
14f+	0-0	-	0.00	14f+	0-2	-	- 2.00

4-y-o+	W-R	Per cent	£1 Level Stake	Totals	W-R	Per cent	£1 Level Stake
5f-6f	0-5	-	- 5.00	5f-6f	7-112	6.3	- 58.24
7f-8f	5-36	13.9	+ 17.50	7f-8f	7-111	6.3	- 37.00
9f-13f	5-28	17.9	+ 6.25	9f-13f	6-54	11.1	- 11.75
14f+	2-9	22.2	+ 7.50	14f+	2-11	18.2	+ 5.50

TYPE OF RACE

Non-Handicaps	W-R	Per cent	£1 Level Stake	Handicaps	W-R	Per cent	£1 Level Stake
2-y-o	4-49	8.2	- 10.12	2-y-o	0-8	-	- 8.00
3-y-o	1-37	2.7	- 34.37	3-y-o	3-75	4.0	- 46.50
4-y-o+	1-3	33.3	+ 6.00	4-y-o+	9-63	14.3	+ 13.25
Selling	0-26	-	- 26.00	Selling	1-14	7.1	- 5.00
Apprentice	1-2	50.0	+ 1.25	Apprentice	1-9	11.1	- 2.00
Amat/Ladies	0-0	-	0.00	Amat/Ladies	1-2	50.0	+ 10.00
Totals	7-117	6.0	- 63.24	Totals	15-171	8.8	- 38.25

405

COURSE GRADE

	W-R	Per cent	£1 Level Stake
Group 1	5-97	5.2	- 60.12
Group 2	7-89	7.9	- 9.25
Group 3	6-60	10.0	- 21.12
Group 4	4-42	9.5	- 11.00

FIRST TIME OUT

	W-R	Per cent	£1 Level Stake
2-y-o	1-15	6.7	- 6.00
3-y-o	0-22	-	- 22.00
4-y-o+	1-13	7.7	+ 8.00
Totals	2-50	4.0	- 20.00

JOCKEYS RIDING

	W-R	Per cent	£1 Level Stake		W-R	Per cent	£1 Level Stake
A Culhane	12-162	7.4	- 56.99	G Carter	1-3	33.3	+ 10.00
J Fanning	4-17	23.5	+ 9.75	M Birch	1-4	25.0	+ 3.50
Julie Krone	1-1	100.0	+ 9.00	A Garth	1-9	11.1	- 5.75
Mr S Whitaker	1-1	100.0	+ 11.00	Dale Gibson	1-18	5.6	- 9.00

G Parkin	0-17	D McKeown	0-2	F Norton		0-1
P Burke	0-9	L Piggott	0-2	J Reid		0-1
D Wright	0-4	N Carlisle	0-2	M Humphries		0-1
N Kennedy	0-4	Paul Eddery	0-2	Mr F Hines		0-1
D Harrison	0-3	S Wood	0-2	O Pears		0-1
M Roberts	0-3	A Mackay	0-1	S Cauthen		0-1
W Carson	0-3	A Shoults	0-1	S Maloney		0-1
W R Swinburn	0-3	B Doyle	0-1	S Wynne		0-1
A Munro	0-2	B Raymond	0-1			
D Holland	0-2	E Johnson	0-1			

COURSE RECORD

	Total W-R	Non-Handicaps 2-y-o	Non-Handicaps 3-y-o+	Handicaps 2-y-o	Handicaps 3-y-o+	Per cent	£1 Level Stake
Beverley	3-24	0-4	1-6	0-2	2-12	12.5	- 7.37
Edinburgh	2-9	0-1	0-3	0-0	2-5	22.2	+ 5.50
Nottingham	2-11	0-2	0-2	0-0	2-7	18.2	+ 8.00
Ripon	2-21	2-3	0-6	0-1	0-11	9.5	+ 5.00
Thirsk	2-27	1-3	0-8	0-1	1-15	7.4	- 8.00
Redcar	2-33	0-13	0-6	0-1	2-13	6.1	- 19.25
Chester	1-5	0-0	0-0	0-0	1-5	20.0	+ 16.00
Haydock	1-9	0-2	0-0	0-1	1-6	11.1	+ 4.00
Carlisle	1-10	0-1	0-3	0-0	1-6	10.0	- 5.50
Newcastle	1-12	0-3	0-2	0-0	1-7	8.3	- 4.50
Ayr	1-13	0-4	0-3	0-1	1-5	7.7	- 8.50
Pontefract	1-15	0-4	1-4	0-0	0-7	6.7	- 11.75
Doncaster	1-16	1-2	0-1	0-1	0-12	6.3	- 13.12
Catterick	1-17	0-5	0-4	0-0	1-8	5.9	- 5.00
York	1-20	0-3	1-4	0-0	0-13	5.0	- 11.00

Newmarket	0-15	Southwell (AW)	0-2	Kempton	0-1
Leicester	0-6	Warwick	0-2	Lingfield	0-1
Goodwood	0-5	Wolverhampton	0-2	Sandown	0-1
Newbury	0-3	Ascot	0-1	Windsor	0-1
Hamilton	0-2	Bath	0-1		
Salisbury	0-2	Epsom	0-1		

WINNING HORSES

	Age	Races Run	1st	2nd	3rd	Unpl	Win £
Parliament Piece	6	6	1	0	0	5	14,020
Star Connection	4	7	1	0	1	5	10,575
Gant Bleu	5	16	3	2	3	8	9,491
First Bid	5	14	3	2	4	5	8,907
Salda	3	8	2	0	0	6	7,110
Saint Express	2	7	2	4	0	1	5,013
Beau Quest	5	7	2	1	1	3	4,636
Hotaria	2	9	1	1	1	6	3,782
Sapphirine	5	9	2	1	3	3	3,488
Breeze Away	3	4	1	0	0	3	2,775
Sison	2	2	1	0	0	1	2,630
Saddlehome	3	13	1	2	0	10	2,322
Reach For Glory	3	12	1	3	1	7	2,264
Katie-A	3	11	1	1	2	7	1,932

WINNING OWNERS

	Races Won	Value £		Races Won	Value £
G A Farndon	3	18,656	Frazer Hines	2	3,488
A F S Bridgwood	1	10,575	G F Pemberton	1	2,775
E C Alton	3	9,491	Mrs Carol A Wyatt	1	2,630
Thomlinson's	3	8,907	Hyde Sporting Promotions	1	2,322
E R Thomas	2	7,110	R M Whitaker	1	2,264
M G St Quinton	2	5,013	D J Soley	1	1,932
Mrs Julia Richmond	1	3,782			

Favourites	4-18	22.2%	+ 1.88	Total winning prize-money		£78,944
Longest winning sequence			2	Average SP of winner		7.5/1
Longest losing sequence			42	Return on stakes invested		-35.2%
1991 Form	24-286	8.4%	- 87.80	1989 Form	29-428	6.8%	-219.50
1990 Form	36-380	9.5%	- 82.40	1988 Form	49-453	10.8%	-168.81

J WHITE (Wendover, Bucks)

	No. of Horses	Races Run	1st	2nd	3rd	Unpl	Per cent	£1 Level Stake
2-y-o	7	15	0	0	1	14	-	- 15.00
3-y-o	9	29	3	3	4	19	10.3	- 20.25
4-y-o+	14	46	5	2	4	35	10.9	- 25.00
Totals	30	90	8	5	9	68	8.9	- 60.25

Jan	Feb	Mar	Apr	May	Jun	Jul	Aug	Sep	Oct/Nov
0-6	0-2	0-5	0-6	1-18	3-16	2-13	2-12	0-5	0-7

White J

Winning Jockeys	W-R	£1 Level Stake			W-R	£1 Level Stake
Dale Gibson	3-19	- 10.25	G Duffield		1-2	+ 2.00
T Quinn	2-4	+ 3.00	P Robinson		1-3	+ 1.50
T Williams	1-2	+ 3.50				

Winning Courses	W-R	£1 Level Stake			W-R	£1 Level Stake
Brighton	5-13	+ 6.25	Hamilton		1-6	- 4.50
Ayr	1-1	+ 2.50	Windsor		1-20	- 14.50

Winning Horses	Age	Races Run	1st	2nd	3rd	Unpl	Win £
Shikari's Son	5	10	4	1	1	4	12,726
Treasure Time	3	8	2	2	2	2	4,270
Cobblers Hill	3	2	1	0	1	0	2,232
Take Two	4	2	1	0	0	1	1,683

Favourites	3-4	75.0%	+ 4.50	Total winning prize-money			£20,911

1991 Form	5-106	4.7%	- 36.00	1989 Form	5-77	6.5%	- 45.67
1990 Form	2-88	2.3%	- 72.00	1988 Form	0-13		

MISS A J WHITFIELD (Lambourn, Berks)

	No. of Horses	Races Run	1st	2nd	3rd	Unpl	Per cent	£1 Level Stake
2-y-o	2	5	0	0	0	5	-	- 5.00
3-y-o	4	11	1	1	1	8	9.1	- 2.50
4-y-o+	4	32	6	3	1	22	18.8	+ 29.00
Totals	10	48	7	4	2	35	14.6	+ 21.50

Jan	Feb	Mar	Apr	May	Jun	Jul	Aug	Sep	Oct/Nov
1-5	1-2	1-7	0-6	0-2	1-7	2-7	1-3	0-6	0-3

Winning Jockeys	W-R	£1 Level Stake		W-R	£1 Level Stake
N Adams	3-15	+ 18.00	Dale Gibson	2-15	+ 5.00
A Tucker	2-8	+ 8.50			

Winning Courses	W-R	£1 Level Stake		W-R	£1 Level Stake
Southwell (AW)	4-12	+ 31.50	Salisbury	1-1	+ 7.50
Lingfield (AW)	2-11	+ 6.50			

Winning Horses	Age	Races Run	1st	2nd	3rd	Unpl	Win £
Hawaii Storm	4	15	5	2	1	7	12,178
In The Game	3	5	1	1	0	3	2,285
Super Heights	4	10	1	1	0	8	2,187

Favourites	1-2	50.0%	+ 1.50	Total winning prize-money			£16,650

1991 Form	3-74	4.1%	- 29.00	1989 Form	0-50
1990 Form	4-58	6.9%	- 12.00		

P WIGHAM (Malton, North Yorks)

	No. of Horses	Races Run	1st	2nd	3rd	Unpl	Per cent	£1 Level Stake
2-y-o	0	0	0	0	0	0	-	0.00
3-y-o	0	0	0	0	0	0	-	0.00
4-y-o+	2	20	4	2	1	13	20.0	+ 7.00
Totals	2	20	4	2	1	13	20.0	+ 7.00

Jan	Feb	Mar	Apr	May	Jun	Jul	Aug	Sep	Oct/Nov
0-0	0-0	0-0	0-3	0-3	0-2	4-6	0-3	0-1	0-2

Winning Jockeys	W-R	£1 Level Stake			W-R	£1 Level Stake
M Wigham	3-17	+ 3.50	G Carter		1-1	+ 5.50

Winning Courses	W-R	£1 Level Stake			W-R	£1 Level Stake
Beverley	3-9	+ 8.00	Ripon		1-4	+ 6.00

Winning Horses	Age	Races Run	1st	2nd	3rd	Unpl	Win £
Bold Elect	4	11	3	0	0	8	7,860
Floating Line	4	9	1	2	1	5	2,872

Favourites	0-2		Total winning prize-money	£10,732

1991 Form	1-15	6.7%	- 11.75	1989 Form	0-12
1990 Form	1-12	8.3%	+ 5.00	1988 Form	0-16

W G R WIGHTMAN (Upham, Hants)

	No. of Horses	Races Run	1st	2nd	3rd	Unpl	Per cent	£1 Level Stake
2-y-o	4	24	4	1	2	17	16.7	+ 24.00
3-y-o	4	28	5	4	1	18	17.9	+ 44.00
4-y-o+	6	54	5	4	7	38	9.3	- 0.50
Totals	14	106	14	9	10	73	13.2	+ 67.50

BY MONTH

2-y-o	W-R	Per cent	£1 Level Stake	3-y-o	W-R	Per cent	£1 Level Stake
January	0-0	-	0.00	January	0-1	-	- 1.00
February	0-0	-	0.00	February	0-0	-	0.00
March	0-0	-	0.00	March	1-3	33.3	+ 7.00
April	0-0	-	0.00	April	1-4	25.0	+ 37.00
May	0-2	-	- 2.00	May	1-4	25.0	+ 7.00
June	1-4	25.0	+ 17.00	June	0-2	-	- 2.00
July	2-5	40.0	+ 9.00	July	0-3	-	- 3.00
August	0-4	-	- 4.00	August	1-4	25.0	+ 1.00
September	1-4	25.0	+ 9.00	September	1-4	25.0	+ 1.00
Oct/Nov	0-5	-	- 5.00	Oct/Nov	0-3	-	- 3.00

Wightman W G R

4-y-o+	W-R	Per cent	£1 Level Stake		Totals	W-R	Per cent	£1 Level Stake
January	0-2	-	- 2.00		January	0-3	-	- 3.00
February	0-3	-	- 3.00		February	0-3	-	- 3.00
March	0-4	-	- 4.00		March	1-7	14.3	+ 3.00
April	0-1	-	- 1.00		April	1-5	20.0	+ 36.00
May	1-3	33.3	+ 6.00		May	2-9	22.2	+ 11.00
June	1-9	11.1	+ 12.00		June	2-15	13.3	+ 27.00
July	2-9	22.2	+ 3.50		July	4-17	23.5	+ 9.50
August	0-10	-	- 10.00		August	1-18	5.6	- 13.00
September	1-8	12.5	+ 3.00		September	3-16	18.8	+ 13.00
Oct/Nov	0-5	-	- 5.00		Oct/Nov	0-13	-	- 13.00

DISTANCE

2-y-o	W-R	Per cent	£1 Level Stake		3-y-o	W-R	Per cent	£1 Level Stake
5f-6f	4-22	18.2	+ 26.00		5f-6f	1-4	25.0	+ 6.00
7f-8f	0-2	-	- 2.00		7f-8f	0-9	-	- 9.00
9f-13f	0-0	-	0.00		9f-13f	4-15	26.7	+ 47.00
14f+	0-0	-	0.00		14f+	0-0	-	0.00

4-y-o+	W-R	Per cent	£1 Level Stake		Totals	W-R	Per cent	£1 Level Stake
5f-6f	4-34	11.8	- 1.50		5f-6f	9-60	15.0	+ 30.50
7f-8f	1-10	10.0	+ 11.00		7f-8f	1-21	4.8	0.00
9f-13f	0-10	-	- 10.00		9f-13f	4-25	16.0	+ 37.00
14f+	0-0	-	0.00		14f+	0-0	-	0.00

TYPE OF RACE

Non-Handicaps	W-R	Per cent	£1 Level Stake		Handicaps	W-R	Per cent	£1 Level Stake
2-y-o	1-16	6.3	- 3.00		2-y-o	2-7	28.6	+ 7.00
3-y-o	1-9	11.1	+ 1.00		3-y-o	4-19	21.1	+ 43.00
4-y-o+	0-5	-	- 5.00		4-y-o+	4-40	10.0	- 7.50
Selling	1-1	100.0	+ 20.00		Selling	1-3	33.3	+ 18.00
Apprentice	0-0	-	0.00		Apprentice	0-0	-	0.00
Amat/Ladies	0-1	-	- 1.00		Amat/Ladies	0-5	-	- 5.00
Totals	3-32	9.4	+ 12.00		Totals	11-74	14.9	+ 55.50

COURSE GRADE

	W-R	Per cent	£1 Level Stake
Group 1	4-35	11.4	+ 7.00
Group 2	3-31	9.7	- 4.00
Group 3	4-12	33.3	+ 32.50
Group 4	3-28	10.7	+ 32.00

FIRST TIME OUT

	W-R	Per cent	£1 Level Stake
2-y-o	0-4	-	- 4.00
3-y-o	0-4	-	- 4.00
4-y-o+	0-6	-	- 6.00
Totals	0-14	-	- 14.00

JOCKEYS RIDING

	W-R	Per cent	£1 Level Stake			W-R	Per cent	£1 Level Stake
G Bardwell	8-43	18.6	+ 63.00	G Carter		1-4	25.0	+ 17.00
J Williams	5-35	14.3	+ 11.50					

T Williams	0-4	T Rogers	0-2	Miss L Hide		0-1
W Newnes	0-4	F Norton	0-1	Paul Eddery		0-1
Mr G Kille	0-3	G Duffield	0-1	S Dawson		0-1
D Harrison	0-2	J Lowe	0-1			
Miss M Clark	0-2	M Hills	0-1			

COURSE RECORD

	Total W-R	Non-Handicaps 2-y-o	Non-Handicaps 3-y-o+	Handicaps 2-y-o	Handicaps 3-y-o+	Per cent	£1 Level Stake
Chepstow	2-6	0-0	0-2	1-1	1-3	33.3	+ 6.50
Goodwood	2-11	1-2	0-0	1-1	0-8	18.2	+ 15.00
Salisbury	2-14	1-5	0-0	0-0	1-9	14.3	+ 4.00
Southwell (AW)	1-1	0-0	0-0	0-0	1-1	100.0	+ 8.00
Haydock	1-2	0-0	0-0	0-0	1-2	50.0	+ 3.00
Windsor	1-2	0-0	0-1	0-0	1-1	50.0	+ 19.00
Bath	1-3	0-1	0-1	0-0	1-1	33.3	+ 8.00
Lingfield	1-3	0-0	0-0	0-0	1-3	33.3	+ 6.00
Kempton	1-6	0-1	0-1	0-1	1-3	16.7	+ 5.00
Folkestone	1-8	0-1	0-0	0-1	1-6	12.5	+ 33.00
Lingfield (AW)	1-16	0-0	1-4	0-0	0-12	6.3	- 6.00

Brighton	0-14	Warwick	0-3	Epsom	0-1
Newbury	0-9	Ascot	0-2	Leicester	0-1
Sandown	0-3	Doncaster	0-1		

WINNING HORSES

	Age	Races Run	1st	2nd	3rd	Unpl	Win £
Googly	3	12	4	4	1	3	12,851
Hallorina	2	9	3	0	0	6	11,143
Catherineofaragon	2	7	1	1	2	3	7,498
Martinosky	6	15	2	2	1	10	4,408
Divine Pet	7	9	1	1	2	5	3,270
Mardior	4	8	1	0	2	5	1,814
Inswinger	6	13	1	1	1	10	1,235
Great Hall	3	4	1	0	0	3	878

WINNING OWNERS

	Races Won	Value £		Races Won	Value £
Mrs J A Thomson	4	12,957	Mrs A J Taylor	1	3,270
A G Lansley	4	12,851	W G R Wightman	1	1,235
T R Mountain	1	7,498	Mrs J M Joyce	1	878
D B Clark	2	4,408			

Wightman W G R

| Favourites | 3-8 | 37.5% | + 5.50 | Total winning prize-money | | | £43,097 |

| Longest winning sequence | | 2 | Average SP of winner | | 11.4/1 |
| Longest losing sequence | | 15 | Return on stakes invested | | 63.7% |

| 1991 Form | 5-108 | 4.6% | - 78.00 | 1989 Form | 8-100 | 8.0% | - 49.50 |
| 1990 Form | 3-136 | 2.2% | -122.00 | 1988 Form | 3-79 | 3.8% | - 65.50 |

C P WILDMAN (Salisbury, Wilts)

		No. of Horses	Races Run	1st	2nd	3rd	Unpl	Per cent	£1 Level Stake
2-y-o		2	7	0	0	0	7	-	- 7.00
3-y-o		1	2	0	0	0	2	-	- 2.00
4-y-o+		3	23	3	3	3	14	13.0	- 11.25
Totals		6	32	3	3	3	23	9.4	- 20.25

Jan	Feb	Mar	Apr	May	Jun	Jul	Aug	Sep	Oct/Nov
0-3	2-5	1-2	0-4	0-4	0-3	0-5	0-3	0-3	0-0

Winning Jockeys	W-R	£1 Level Stake			W-R	£1 Level Stake
C Rutter	2-19	- 11.25	D Biggs		1-3	+ 1.00

Winning Course		
Lingfield (AW)	3-14	- 2.25

Winning Horse	Age	Races Run	1st	2nd	3rd	Unpl	Win £
Sarum	6	12	3	3	3	3	6,890

| Favourites | 2-3 | 66.7% | + 4.75 | Total winning prize-money | | | £6,890 |

| 1991 Form | 3-31 | 9.7% | - 8.00 | 1989 Form | 3-56 | 5.4% | - 15.50 |
| 1990 Form | 3-45 | 6.7% | + 6.00 | 1988 Form | 1-38 | 2.6% | - 17.00 |

C N WILLIAMS (Newmarket)

		No. of Horses	Races Run	1st	2nd	3rd	Unpl	Per cent	£1 Level Stake
2-y-o		2	16	3	1	2	10	18.8	- 7.00
3-y-o		1	2	0	0	0	2	-	- 2.00
4-y-o+		4	16	0	0	1	15	-	- 16.00
Totals		7	34	3	1	3	27	8.8	- 25.00

Jan	Feb	Mar	Apr	May	Jun	Jul	Aug	Sep	Oct/Nov
0-0	0-0	0-1	0-3	0-2	2-7	1-6	0-6	0-5	0-4

Winning Jockeys		W-R	£1 Level Stake				W-R	£1 Level Stake
J Quinn		2-9	- 2.75	T Quinn			1-1	+ 1.75

Winning Courses								
Wolverhampton		1-2	+ 1.00	Leicester			1-4	- 0.75
Lingfield		1-3	- 0.25					

Winning Horses		Age	Races Run	1st	2nd	3rd	Unpl	Win £
Strike-A-Pose		2	9	2	0	1	6	4,981
Tee Gee Jay		2	7	1	1	1	4	2,363

Favourites	3-7	42.9%	+ 2.00	Total winning prize-money				£7,344

1991 Form	2-36	5.6%	- 26.09	1989 Form	2-68	2.9%	- 39.50
1990 Form	4-60	6.7%	- 15.50	1988 Form	1-32	3.1%	- 28.25

R J R WILLIAMS (Newmarket)

	No. of Horses	Races Run	1st	2nd	3rd	Unpl	Per cent	£1 Level Stake
2-y-o	8	34	5	2	6	21	14.7	- 10.82
3-y-o	4	23	1	7	2	13	4.3	- 20.25
4-y-o+	9	76	8	7	13	48	10.5	+ 0.10
Totals	21	133	14	16	21	82	10.5	- 30.97

BY MONTH

2-y-o	W-R	Per cent	£1 Level Stake	3-y-o	W-R	Per cent	£1 Level Stake
January	0-0	-	0.00	January	0-7	-	- 7.00
February	0-0	-	0.00	February	0-3	-	- 3.00
March	0-0	-	0.00	March	0-1	-	- 1.00
April	0-2	-	- 2.00	April	0-0	-	0.00
May	2-2	100.0	+ 6.30	May	0-0	-	0.00
June	0-6	-	- 6.00	June	0-0	-	0.00
July	1-6	16.7	+ 3.00	July	0-1	-	- 1.00
August	1-6	16.7	- 2.75	August	1-5	20.0	- 2.25
September	1-7	14.3	- 4.37	September	0-3	-	- 3.00
Oct/Nov	0-5	-	- 5.00	Oct/Nov	0-3	-	- 3.00

4-y-o+	W-R	Per cent	£1 Level Stake	Totals	W-R	Per cent	£1 Level Stake
January	1-12	8.3	- 5.00	January	1-19	5.3	- 12.00
February	1-6	16.7	- 1.50	February	1-9	11.1	- 4.50
March	0-4	-	- 4.00	March	0-5	-	- 5.00
April	0-1	-	- 1.00	April	0-3	-	- 3.00
May	1-6	16.7	+ 5.00	May	3-8	37.5	+ 11.30
June	2-14	14.3	- 1.50	June	2-20	10.0	- 7.50
July	3-13	23.1	+ 28.10	July	4-20	20.0	+ 30.10
August	0-11	-	- 11.00	August	2-22	9.1	- 16.00
September	0-5	-	- 5.00	September	1-15	6.7	- 12.37
Oct/Nov	0-4	-	- 4.00	Oct/Nov	0-12	-	- 12.00

Williams R J R

DISTANCE

	W-R	Per cent	£1 Level Stake		W-R	Per cent	£1 Level Stake
2-y-o				3-y-o			
5f-6f	5-22	22.7	+ 1.18	5f-6f	0-2	-	- 2.00
7f-8f	0-10	-	- 10.00	7f-8f	1-16	6.3	- 13.25
9f-13f	0-2	-	- 2.00	9f-13f	0-4	-	- 4.00
14f+	0-0	-	0.00	14f+	0-1	-	- 1.00

	W-R	Per cent	£1 Level Stake		W-R	Per cent	£1 Level Stake
4-y-o+				Totals			
5f-6f	0-10	-	- 10.00	5f-6f	5-34	14.7	- 10.82
7f-8f	8-32	25.0	+ 44.10	7f-8f	9-58	15.5	+ 20.85
9f-13f	0-33	-	- 33.00	9f-13f	0-39	-	- 39.00
14f+	0-1	-	- 1.00	14f+	0-2	-	- 2.00

TYPE OF RACE

	W-R	Per cent	£1 Level Stake		W-R	Per cent	£1 Level Stake
Non-Handicaps				Handicaps			
2-y-o	1-20	5.0	- 11.00	2-y-o	2-6	33.3	- 0.12
3-y-o	1-16	6.3	- 13.25	3-y-o	0-5	-	- 5.00
4-y-o+	1-9	11.1	- 4.50	4-y-o+	6-54	11.1	+ 12.60
Selling	2-8	25.0	+ 0.30	Selling	0-1	-	- 1.00
Apprentice	0-1	-	- 1.00	Apprentice	1-9	11.1	- 4.00
Amat/Ladies	0-1	-	- 1.00	Amat/Ladies	0-3	-	- 3.00
Totals	5-55	9.1	- 30.45	Totals	9-78	11.5	- 0.52

COURSE GRADE

	W-R	Per cent	£1 Level Stake
Group 1	3-42	7.1	- 22.25
Group 2	3-10	30.0	+ 35.50
Group 3	5-28	17.9	- 4.52
Group 4	3-53	5.7	- 39.70

FIRST TIME OUT

	W-R	Per cent	£1 Level Stake
2-y-o	0-8	-	- 8.00
3-y-o	0-4	-	- 4.00
4-y-o+	1-9	11.1	- 2.00
Totals	1-21	4.8	- 14.00

JOCKEYS RIDING

	W-R	Per cent	£1 Level Stake		W-R	Per cent	£1 Level Stake
R Cochrane	6-30	20.0	+ 26.65	S Cauthen	1-2	50.0	+ 0.63
M Hills	2-15	13.3	- 7.75	K Darley	1-5	20.0	+ 1.00
E Hide	1-1	100.0	+ 10.00	J Quinn	1-10	10.0	- 3.00
A Clark	1-1	100.0	+ 5.50	G Mitchell	1-17	5.9	- 12.00

D Holland	0-10	C Rutter	0-1	M Birch	0-1
D Biggs	0-6	D Harrison	0-1	Miss A Giambertone	0-1
C Hodgson	0-4	D McKeown	0-1	Mrs J Crossley	0-1
R Hills	0-4	Dale Gibson	0-1	N Day	0-1
Mr S Astaire	0-3	F Norton	0-1	P Robinson	0-1
A Munro	0-2	G Carter	0-1	Pat Eddery	0-1
M Denaro	0-2	G Duffield	0-1	S D Williams	0-1
W Ryan	0-2	J Carroll	0-1	T Rogers	0-1
B Raymond	0-1	J Williams	0-1	W Newnes	0-1

COURSE RECORD

	Total W-R	Non-Handicaps 2-y-o	Non-Handicaps 3-y-o+	Handicaps 2-y-o	Handicaps 3-y-o+	Per cent	£1 Level Stake
Chepstow	2-4	0-0	0-0	1-1	1-3	50.0	+ 5.75
Southwell (AW)	2-28	0-0	1-10	0-1	1-17	7.1	- 16.50
Warwick	1-1	1-1	0-0	0-0	0-0	100.0	+ 0.80
Lingfield	1-2	1-1	0-0	0-0	0-1	50.0	+ 4.50
Ripon	1-2	0-1	0-0	0-0	1-1	50.0	+ 32.00
Thirsk	1-4	0-0	0-2	0-0	1-2	25.0	+ 1.00
Haydock	1-5	0-1	1-1	0-1	0-2	20.0	- 2.25
Leicester	1-5	0-2	0-1	1-1	0-1	20.0	- 2.37
Nottingham	1-5	1-3	0-1	0-0	0-1	20.0	+ 4.00
Newmarket	1-7	0-4	0-1	0-0	1-2	14.3	+ 4.00
Yarmouth	1-9	0-5	0-2	0-0	1-2	11.1	- 6.90
Doncaster	1-11	0-1	0-0	0-0	1-10	9.1	- 5.00

Lingfield (AW)	0-16	Ascot	0-2	Windsor	0-2
Newbury	0-4	Catterick	0-2	Ayr	0-1
Beverley	0-3	Epsom	0-2	Carlisle	0-1
Sandown	0-3	Folkestone	0-2	Chester	0-1
Wolverhampton	0-3	Kempton	0-2	Salisbury	0-1
York	0-3	Newcastle	0-2		

WINNING HORSES

	Age	Races Run	1st	2nd	3rd	Unpl	Win £
Shiro	2	5	3	0	1	1	9,041
Shaieef	4	6	3	0	0	3	7,325
Buddy's Friend	4	13	2	3	2	6	5,777
Grand Dancer	2	12	2	2	4	4	5,682
Charming Gift	5	9	2	0	1	6	4,150
On Y Va	5	11	1	0	2	8	2,304
Chequers	3	7	1	1	0	5	1,548

WINNING OWNERS

	Races Won	Value £		Races Won	Value £
Colin G R Booth	4	9,927	D A Johnson	3	7,230
Saeed Manana	3	9,041	T F Hornett	1	2,304
Terry Minahan	3	7,325			

Williams R J R

Favourites	5-18	27.8%	- 2.22	Total winning prize-money			£35,828

Longest winning sequence			1	Average SP of winner			6.3/1
Longest losing sequence			21	Return on stakes invested			-23.3%

1991 Form	20-186	10.8%	- 7.96	1989 Form	17-235	7.2%	- 25.95
1990 Form	15-171	8.8%	- 47.67	1988 Form	18-220	8.2%	- 72.00

D A WILSON (Epsom, Surrey)

	No. of Horses	Races Run	1st	2nd	3rd	Unpl	Per cent	£1 Level Stake
2-y-o	2	7	0	0	0	7	-	- 7.00
3-y-o	7	47	4	2	5	36	8.5	- 16.50
4-y-o+	10	98	5	16	9	68	5.1	- 60.25
Totals	19	152	9	18	14	111	5.9	- 83.75

Jan	Feb	Mar	Apr	May	Jun	Jul	Aug	Sep	Oct/Nov
0-2	0-0	0-1	0-8	0-11	3-19	3-32	2-33	1-21	0-25

Winning Jockeys	W-R	£1 Level Stake			W-R	£1 Level Stake
M Roberts	2-4	+ 3.25	G Duffield		1-6	+ 2.00
Miss J Allison	2-10	+ 8.00	D Harrison		1-14	- 6.50
Miss L Hide	1-4	+ 2.50	G Carter		1-21	- 10.00
M Wigham	1-4	+ 6.00				

Winning Courses						
Ripon	1-1	+ 8.00	Goodwood		1-12	- 3.00
Wolverhampton	1-2	+ 9.00	Sandown		1-12	- 4.50
Southwell (AW)	1-2	+ 8.00	Folkestone		1-13	- 9.75
Newmarket	1-7	- 3.00	Salisbury		1-14	- 7.50
Redcar	1-10	- 2.00				

Winning Horses	Age	Races Run	1st	2nd	3rd	Unpl	Win £
Bodari	3	16	2	2	3	9	10,430
Corinthian God	3	8	2	0	0	6	5,717
Cathos	7	14	2	3	1	8	5,106
Thimbalina	6	13	1	1	2	9	2,805
Profit A Prendre	8	14	1	3	2	8	2,406
Albert	5	11	1	1	0	9	2,303

Favourites	1-12	8.3%	- 8.75	Total winning prize-money			£28,767

1991 Form	11-177	6.2%	- 90.00	1989 Form	15-137	10.9%	+ 3.46
1990 Form	19-197	9.6%	- 83.54	1988 Form	7-174	4.0%	- 114.25

CAPT J WILSON (Preston, Lancs)

	No. of Horses	Races Run	1st	2nd	3rd	Unpl	Per cent	£1 Level Stake
2-y-o	4	17	0	2	3	12	-	- 17.00
3-y-o	5	46	1	7	5	33	2.2	- 25.00
4-y-o+	6	52	3	5	7	37	5.8	- 0.50
Totals	15	115	4	14	15	82	3.5	- 42.50

Jan	Feb	Mar	Apr	May	Jun	Jul	Aug	Sep	Oct/Nov
0-2	0-5	0-4	0-6	2-16	1-9	1-21	0-19	0-20	0-13

Winning Jockeys	W-R	£1 Level Stake		W-R	£1 Level Stake
G Carter	2-21	+ 19.50	J Carroll	1-10	+ 1.00
G Bardwell	1-5	+ 16.00			

Winning Courses	W-R	£1 Level		W-R	£1 Level
Ascot	1-2	+ 32.00	Ripon	1-10	- 3.50
Catterick	1-9	+ 2.00	Southwell (AW)	1-18	+ 3.00

Winning Horses	Age	Races Run	1st	2nd	3rd	Unpl	Win £
Red Rosein	6	16	2	0	3	11	39,696
Racing Raskal	5	8	1	2	2	3	2,868
Sie Amato	3	13	1	3	2	7	2,763

Favourites	0-3		Total winning prize-money		£45,327

1991 Form	12-108	11.1%	+ 15.88	1989 Form	8-132	6.1%	- 57.50
1990 Form	7-96	7.3%	- 22.67	1988 Form	11-170	6.5%	- 1.50

S P C WOODS (Newmarket)

	No. of Horses	Races Run	1st	2nd	3rd	Unpl	Per cent	£1 Level Stake
2-y-o	11	40	3	2	4	31	7.5	+ 13.00
3-y-o	8	32	5	2	3	22	15.6	- 7.00
4-y-o+	1	1	0	0	0	1	-	- 1.00
Totals	20	73	8	4	7	54	11.0	+ 5.00

Jan	Feb	Mar	Apr	May	Jun	Jul	Aug	Sep	Oct/Nov
0-0	0-0	0-0	0-0	0-0	1-7	2-22	3-15	1-12	1-17

Winning Jockeys	W-R	£1 Level Stake		W-R	£1 Level Stake
W Woods	7-60	+ 14.25	W Ryan	1-2	+ 1.75

Winning Courses	W-R	£1 Level		W-R	£1 Level
Thirsk	2-3	+ 6.25	Redcar	1-2	+ 1.75
Yarmouth	2-11	+ 3.50	Beverley	1-4	- 0.50
Haydock	1-2	+ 19.00	Nottingham	1-12	+ 14.00

Woods S P C

Winning Horses		Age	Races Run	1st	2nd	3rd	Unpl	Win £
Expansionist		3	7	4	1	0	2	10,766
Sebosan		3	2	1	0	0	1	3,590
Cosmic Star		2	2	1	0	0	1	3,080
Gangleader		2	7	1	1	1	4	3,057
Stapleford Lass		2	5	1	0	1	3	2,616
Favourites	2-5	40.0%	+ 2.00	Total winning prize-money				£23,109

G WRAGG (Newmarket)

	No. of Horses	Races Run	1st	2nd	3rd	Unpl	Per cent	£1 Level Stake
2-y-o	11	31	10	7	1	13	32.3	+ 3.88
3-y-o	24	128	27	28	18	55	21.1	- 7.13
4-y-o+	10	51	7	10	9	25	13.7	- 28.48
Totals	45	210	44	45	28	93	21.0	- 31.73

BY MONTH

2-y-o	W-R	Per cent	£1 Level Stake	3-y-o	W-R	Per cent	£1 Level Stake
January	0-0	-	0.00	January	0-0	-	0.00
February	0-0	-	0.00	February	0-0	-	0.00
March	0-0	-	0.00	March	3-6	50.0	+ 0.70
April	1-2	50.0	+ 4.00	April	3-17	17.6	- 3.17
May	2-5	40.0	- 1.86	May	3-14	21.4	+ 2.20
June	2-3	66.7	+ 4.91	June	4-15	26.7	- 0.15
July	1-4	25.0	- 1.25	July	6-18	33.3	+ 12.93
August	2-5	40.0	- 0.42	August	2-16	12.5	- 11.14
September	1-3	33.3	+ 3.50	September	4-22	18.2	+ 2.75
Oct/Nov	1-9	11.1	- 5.00	Oct/Nov	2-20	10.0	- 11.25

4-y-o+	W-R	Per cent	£1 Level Stake	Totals	W-R	Per cent	£1 Level Stake
January	1-4	25.0	+ 3.50	January	1-4	25.0	+ 3.50
February	1-4	25.0	- 0.50	February	1-4	25.0	- 0.50
March	0-1	-	- 1.00	March	3-7	42.9	- 0.30
April	1-9	11.1	- 7.17	April	5-28	17.9	- 6.34
May	1-8	12.5	- 4.75	May	6-27	22.2	- 4.41
June	2-7	28.6	- 1.56	June	8-25	32.0	+ 3.20
July	1-10	10.0	- 9.00	July	8-32	25.0	+ 2.68
August	0-4	-	- 4.00	August	4-25	16.0	- 15.56
September	0-1	-	- 1.00	September	5-26	19.2	+ 5.25
Oct/Nov	0-3	-	- 3.00	Oct/Nov	3-32	9.4	- 19.25

DISTANCE

	W-R	Per cent	£1 Level Stake		W-R	Per cent	£1 Level Stake
2-y-o				3-y-o			
5f-6f	7-20	35.0	+ 1.63	5f-6f	0-2	-	- 2.00
7f-8f	3-11	27.3	+ 2.25	7f-8f	14-50	28.0	+ 4.61
9f-13f	0-0	-	0.00	9f-13f	11-64	17.2	- 12.24
14f+	0-0	-	0.00	14f+	2-12	16.7	+ 2.50

	W-R	Per cent	£1 Level Stake		W-R	Per cent	£1 Level Stake
4-y-o+				Totals			
5f-6f	0-1	-	- 1.00	5f-6f	7-23	30.4	- 1.37
7f-8f	2-11	18.2	0.00	7f-8f	19-72	26.4	+ 6.86
9f-13f	2-31	6.5	- 27.73	9f-13f	13-95	13.7	- 39.97
14f+	3-8	37.5	+ 0.25	14f+	5-20	25.0	+ 2.75

TYPE OF RACE

	W-R	Per cent	£1 Level Stake		W-R	Per cent	£1 Level Stake
Non-Handicaps				Handicaps			
2-y-o	10-29	34.5	+ 5.88	2-y-o	0-2	-	- 2.00
3-y-o	20-77	26.0	+ 4.12	3-y-o	6-49	12.2	- 12.50
4-y-o+	5-33	15.2	- 21.48	4-y-o+	2-17	11.8	- 6.00
Selling	0-0	-	0.00	Selling	0-0	-	0.00
Apprentice	1-2	50.0	+ 1.25	Apprentice	0-1	-	- 1.00
Amat/Ladies	0-0	-	0.00	Amat/Ladies	0-0	-	0.00
Totals	36-141	25.5	- 10.23	Totals	8-69	11.6	- 21.50

COURSE GRADE

	W-R	Per cent	£1 Level Stake
Group 1	18-109	16.5	- 32.53
Group 2	5-23	21.7	- 8.00
Group 3	10-44	22.7	- 8.15
Group 4	11-34	32.4	+ 16.95

FIRST TIME OUT

	W-R	Per cent	£1 Level Stake
2-y-o	2-11	18.2	- 7.42
3-y-o	6-24	25.0	- 6.47
4-y-o+	2-10	20.0	- 0.67
Totals	10-45	22.2	- 14.56

JOCKEYS RIDING

	W-R	Per cent	£1 Level Stake		W-R	Per cent	£1 Level Stake
M Hills	13-43	30.2	+ 14.52	N Day	1-1	100.0	+ 9.00
W R Swinburn	11-49	22.4	- 20.30	W Ryan	1-1	100.0	+ 5.50
R Hills	4-16	25.0	+ 2.83	J Weaver	1-1	100.0	+ 2.25
R Cochrane	3-10	30.0	+ 7.00	Pat Eddery	1-3	33.3	- 0.90
J Reid	2-5	40.0	+ 2.58	G Duffield	1-4	25.0	+ 3.50
M Roberts	2-13	15.4	- 3.50	P Robinson	1-4	25.0	- 2.38
F Norton	2-37	5.4	- 30.03	S Cauthen	1-12	8.3	- 10.80

Paul Eddery	0-3	Bill Smith	0-1	J Carroll	0-1
N Hall	0-2	D Harrison	0-1	W Newnes	0-1
A Munro	0-1	Dale Gibson	0-1		

COURSE RECORD

	Total W-R	Non-Handicaps 2-y-o	3-y-o+	Handicaps 2-y-o	3-y-o+	Per cent	£1 Level Stake
Ascot	5-22	2-3	3-12	0-0	0-7	22.7	- 5.11
Lingfield (AW)	4-5	0-0	2-2	0-0	2-3	80.0	+ 21.50
Doncaster	4-9	2-2	1-4	0-0	1-3	44.4	+ 4.67
Yarmouth	4-11	0-5	2-3	0-0	2-3	36.4	+ 5.45
Catterick	3-10	0-0	3-10	0-0	0-0	30.0	+ 5.00
Goodwood	3-11	0-0	2-8	0-0	1-3	27.3	+ 9.10
Newmarket	3-27	0-5	2-14	0-0	1-8	11.1	- 13.64
Wolverhampton	2-3	1-1	1-2	0-0	0-0	66.7	+ 0.95
Nottingham	2-5	2-2	0-1	0-1	0-1	40.0	+ 5.00
Thirsk	2-5	0-0	2-3	0-0	0-2	40.0	+ 3.83
Haydock	2-6	1-1	1-4	0-0	0-1	33.3	- 0.55
Brighton	1-1	0-0	0-0	0-0	1-1	100.0	+ 2.50
Windsor	1-2	1-1	0-0	0-0	0-1	50.0	+ 0.38
Lingfield	1-3	1-1	0-1	0-1	0-0	33.3	- 1.53
Warwick	1-3	0-1	1-2	0-0	0-0	33.3	0.00
Ripon	1-4	0-0	1-2	0-0	0-2	25.0	- 2.80
Beverley	1-6	0-0	1-5	0-0	0-1	16.7	- 4.56
Pontefract	1-6	0-0	1-5	0-0	0-1	16.7	- 4.17
Leicester	1-8	0-3	1-3	0-0	0-2	12.5	- 4.25
Kempton	1-9	0-0	1-5	0-0	0-4	11.1	- 2.00
Southwell (AW)	1-9	0-0	1-3	0-0	0-6	11.1	- 6.50

York	0-9	Folkestone	0-3	Newcastle	0-2
Sandown	0-7	Newbury	0-3	Edinburgh	0-1
Chepstow	0-4	Redcar	0-3	Epsom	0-1
Chester	0-4	Salisbury	0-3		
Ayr	0-3	Bath	0-2		

WINNING HORSES

	Age	Races Run	1st	2nd	3rd	Unpl	Win £
Marling	3	4	2	1	0	1	184,587
Little Bean	3	7	3	2	0	2	78,204
Petardia	2	5	3	0	0	2	71,287
Jeune	3	8	3	2	2	1	47,743
Romany Rye	4	3	2	0	1	0	19,877
Young Buster	4	6	1	1	1	3	12,990
Wild Fire	3	9	2	2	1	4	11,001
Olette	3	8	3	1	0	4	9,033
Sumoto	2	1	1	0	0	0	7,310
Torchon	4	6	2	0	0	4	6,876
Upper House	3	7	3	1	0	3	6,719
Simmering	2	9	3	2	0	4	6,320
Goldsmiths' Hall	3	7	3	0	2	2	5,822
Beneficial	2	3	2	1	0	0	5,470
Dorset Duke	5	8	2	0	5	1	5,178
Waterfowl Creek	3	8	2	2	1	3	4,778

Faugeron	3	5	1	2	0	2	3,428
Pridian	3	4	1	1	0	2	2,285
Riviera Vista	3	8	1	0	0	7	2,285
Nuryandra	2	5	1	2	1	1	2,233
Romansh	3	6	1	2	2	1	2,226
Pippas Song	3	7	1	1	1	4	2,148
Ginger Flower	3	3	1	2	0	0	2,070

WINNING OWNERS

	Races Won	Value £		Races Won	Value £
E J Loder	2	184,587	Mrs G Wragg	3	6,320
Sir Philip Oppenheimer	18	141,302	J L C Pearce	2	5,712
Mollers Racing	5	86,562	G Wragg	2	5,178
Sir Robin McAlpine	7	60,089	Mrs H H Morriss	1	2,070
Sheikh Mohammed	4	8,048			

Favourites	19-54	35.2%	- 11.19	Total winning prize-money			£499,868
Longest winning sequence			4	Average SP of winner			3.3/1
Longest losing sequence			21	Return on stakes invested			-10.8%
1991 Form	51-220	23.2%	+ 27.73	1989 Form	25-199	12.6%	- 28.49
1990 Form	32-224	14.3%	+ 0.57	1988 Form	31-194	16.0%	- 6.69

N C WRIGHT (Newmarket)

	No. of Horses	Races Run	1st	2nd	3rd	Unpl	Per cent	£1 Level Stake
2-y-o	3	6	1	0	0	5	16.7	+ 20.00
3-y-o	8	25	1	1	0	23	4.0	- 20.00
4-y-o+	0	0	0	0	0	0	-	0.00
Totals	11	31	2	1	0	28	6.5	0.00

Jan	Feb	Mar	Apr	May	Jun	Jul	Aug	Sep	Oct/Nov
0-0	0-0	1-1	0-6	0-6	0-2	1-7	0-5	0-4	0-0

Winning Jockeys	W-R	£1 Level Stake		W-R	£1 Level Stake
W Ryan	1-1	+ 4.00	G Duffield	1-10	+ 16.00

Winning Courses					
Doncaster	1-1	+ 25.00	Yarmouth	1-4	+ 1.00

Winning Horses	Age	Races Run	1st	2nd	3rd	Unpl	Win £
Other One	2	2	1	0	0	1	2,832
Resplendent	3	5	1	0	0	4	2,532

Favourites	0-1	Total winning prize-money	£5,364

TRAINERS WITH NO WINNERS 1992

	No. of Horses	Races Run	2nd	3rd	Unpl
Mrs V Aconley	15	47	1	1	45
Mrs S M Austin	1	1	0	0	1
M Avison	5	18	0	1	17
K C Bailey	4	23	0	1	22
J H Baker	2	3	0	0	3
J Balding	16	73	4	6	63
Mrs P A Barker	4	15	1	2	12
R E Barr	6	21	1	1	19
L J Barratt	7	25	1	1	23
A Barrow	7	19	0	0	19
C R Barwell	3	8	0	2	6
P Beaumont	4	8	0	0	8
W Bentley	5	12	1	2	9
K Bishop	1	2	0	0	2
P A Blockley	10	40	2	0	38
J R Bosley	5	23	1	1	21
J R Bostock	8	39	2	4	33
Miss L Bower	2	4	0	0	4
Mrs S C Bradburne	2	4	0	0	4
M Bradstock	1	2	1	0	1
Mrs S Bramall	1	4	0	0	4
O Brennan	4	11	0	0	11
C P E Brooks	1	1	0	0	1
R Brotherton	5	23	1	0	22
P Burgoyne	4	16	0	0	16
B R Cambidge	6	25	1	1	23
A Chamberlain	9	14	0	1	13
R Champion	3	8	0	0	8
M C Chapman	19	63	1	0	62
M J Charles	6	17	0	0	17
W Clay	8	21	0	0	21
J K Cresswell	1	1	0	0	1
B J Curley	4	6	0	0	6
T A K Cuthbert	4	14	0	0	14
P T Dalton	2	3	0	0	3
A W Denson	8	28	0	1	27
T W Donnelly	3	6	0	0	6
Miss J S Doyle	2	5	2	0	3
R Earnshaw	7	30	0	3	27
G P Enright	2	4	0	0	4
R F Fisher	1	8	2	0	6
G Fleming	5	12	0	1	11
B Forsey	8	27	3	0	24
J C Fox	3	7	0	0	7
D R Franks	4	5	0	0	5
R G Frost	1	1	0	0	1
D R Gandolfo	2	9	1	0	8
J T Gifford	1	3	0	0	3
Paul Green	2	3	0	0	3
Mrs D Haine	1	1	0	0	1
J S Haldane	6	28	0	1	27
T B Hallett	1	1	0	0	1
P R Hedger	9	15	0	0	15

	No. of Horses	Races Run	2nd	3rd	Unpl
N J Henderson	2	3	0	0	3
R P C Hoad	5	12	0	0	12
C Holmes	3	8	0	0	8
C F C Jackson	2	3	0	0	3
A P James	5	16	0	0	16
M B James	3	8	0	1	7
J M Jefferson	6	17	0	2	15
D C Jermy	5	20	0	0	20
J H Johnson	6	14	1	3	10
A P Jones	5	29	1	3	25
G H Jones	2	3	0	0	3
P J Jones	3	7	0	0	7
T M Jones	5	11	0	0	11
F Jordan	7	20	0	1	19
Mrs P M Joynes	1	1	0	0	1
R T Juckes	3	4	1	0	3
Miss Gay Kelleway	18	72	6	4	62
G P Kelly	5	12	0	0	12
W T Kemp	2	5	0	0	5
T Kersey	11	56	1	2	53
R V King	1	1	0	0	1
R Lamb	7	20	0	0	20
M R Leach	2	3	0	0	3
P Leach	3	6	0	0	6
J E Long	4	11	0	0	11
L Lungo	6	21	2	2	17
B W Lunness	3	7	0	0	7
M J Madgwick	10	39	1	2	36
R Manning	4	5	0	0	5
R F Marvin	2	2	0	0	2
D McCain	4	12	1	2	9
J C McConnochie	2	5	0	0	5
T P McGovern	6	13	1	1	11
S Mellor	13	53	1	3	49
N Miller	1	1	0	0	1
N R Mitchell	1	2	0	0	2
P Monteith	17	59	7	2	50
K A Morgan	5	9	0	0	9
J Mulhall	1	1	0	0	1
B W Murray	10	42	1	3	38
C T Nash	2	8	1	2	5
J Norton	8	27	1	0	26
J O'Donoghue	5	11	0	0	11
R O'Leary	9	32	2	2	28
O O'Neill	9	18	0	0	18
J G M O'Shea	1	1	0	0	1
Mrs S Oliver	6	12	0	0	12
E H Owen	5	20	0	0	20
S G Payne	2	5	0	1	4
R E Peacock	10	23	0	1	22
Mrs J S Perrin	1	2	0	0	2
C L Popham	3	3	0	0	3
B Preece	3	6	0	0	6
P A Pritchard	3	5	0	0	5
Mrs J G Retter	1	3	0	0	3
G Richards	5	6	0	0	6

	No. of Horses	Races Run	2nd	3rd	Unpl
B Richmond	5	17	0	0	17
J D Roberts	7	20	1	2	17
Graeme Roe	1	7	0	0	7
D Sasse	9	47	0	1	46
M Scudamore	1	1	0	0	1
Mrs N Sharpe	1	1	0	0	1
O Sherwood	1	1	0	0	1
S Sherwood	1	1	0	0	1
C Smith	2	2	0	0	2
C A Smith	11	61	6	7	48
N A Smith	1	2	0	0	2
Mrs S J Smith	5	17	1	1	15
B Stevens	2	13	0	1	12
M Tate	2	6	0	0	6
R Thompson	10	37	1	2	34
V Thompson	2	4	0	0	4
G Thorner	2	8	0	0	8
C Trietline	1	2	0	0	2
D C Tucker	3	7	0	0	7
P F Tulk	5	30	2	2	26
A Turnell	5	11	0	0	11
N A Twiston-Davies	3	7	0	0	7
John R Upson	1	2	0	0	2
F Watson	4	6	0	0	6
R J Weaver	6	19	0	3	16
C Weedon	7	9	1	0	8
K White	8	37	0	2	35
H A T Whiting	4	9	2	2	5
B E Wilkinson	2	5	1	1	3
M J Wilkinson	3	5	0	0	5
D L Williams	7	20	0	0	20
M Williams	1	2	0	0	2
W R Williams	4	19	0	1	18
Miss S J Wilton	7	16	0	1	15
K G Wingrove	5	9	1	0	8
D J Wintle	5	6	0	0	6
R D E Woodhouse	5	8	0	1	7
S Woodman	3	7	0	0	7
F J Yardley	6	17	0	1	16
G H Yardley	2	12	0	0	12

WINNING OVERSEAS TRAINERS 1992

J S BOLGER (Ireland)

	No. of Horses	Races Run	1st	2nd	3rd	Unpl	Per cent	£1 Level Stake
2-y-o	2	2	0	0	0	2	-	- 2.00
3-y-o	11	15	2	2	2	9	13.3	- 10.20
4-y-o+	5	6	0	1	0	5	-	- 6.00
Totals	18	23	2	3	2	16	8.7	- 18.20

Jan	Feb	Mar	Apr	May	Jun	Jul	Aug	Sep	Oct/Nov
0-0	0-0	0-0	1-7	0-1	0-13	1-1	0-0	0-1	0-0

Winning Jockeys	W-R	£1 Level Stake			W-R	£1 Level Stake
S Craine	1-1	+ 0.80	C Roche		1-19	- 16.00

Winning Courses	W-R	£1 Level Stake			W-R	£1 Level Stake
Lingfield (AW)	1-1	+ 2.00	Ascot		1-14	- 12.20

Winning Horses		Age	Races Run	1st	2nd	3rd	Unpl	Win £
St Jovite		3	2	1	1	0	0	261,216
Thyer		3	3	1	0	1	1	4,308

Favourites	1-2	50.0%	- 0.20	Total winning prize-money	£265,524

1991 Form	2-20	10.0%	+ 40.00	1989 Form	0-2
1990 Form	1-5	20.0%	+ 1.00	1988 Form	0-4

J G COOGAN (Ireland)

	No. of Horses	Races Run	1st	2nd	3rd	Unpl	Per cent	£1 Level Stake
2-y-o	1	1	1	0	0	0	100.0	+ 5.50
3-y-o	0	0	0	0	0	0	-	0.00
4-y-o+	0	0	0	0	0	0	-	0.00
Totals	1	1	1	0	0	0	100.0	+ 5.50

Jan	Feb	Mar	Apr	May	Jun	Jul	Aug	Sep	Oct/Nov
0-0	0-0	0-0	0-0	0-0	0-0	0-0	0-0	0-0	1-1

Winning Jockey	W-R	£1 Level Stake	Winning Course		W-R	£1 Level Stake
B Coogan	1-1	+ 5.50	Ascot		1-1	+ 5.50

Winning Horse		Age	Races Run	1st	2nd	3rd	Unpl	Win £
Up And At 'Em		2	1	1	0	0	0	22,140

Favourites	0-0		Total winning prize-money	£22,140

A FABRE (France)

	No. of Horses	Races Run	1st	2nd	3rd	Unpl	Per cent	£1 Level Stake
2-y-o	2	2	2	0	0	0	100.0	+ 3.41
3-y-o	6	9	1	2	0	6	11.1	- 5.75
4-y-o+	8	9	1	1	1	6	11.1	- 1.20
Totals	16	20	4	3	1	12	20.0	- 3.54

Jan	Feb	Mar	Apr	May	Jun	Jul	Aug	Sep	Oct/Nov
0-0	0-0	0-0	1-3	1-5	0-7	0-1	0-1	0-0	2-3

Winning Jockeys	W-R	£1 Level Stake			W-R	£1 Level Stake
S Cauthen	2-5	+ 1.75	Pat Eddery		1-8	- 6.09
T Jarnet	1-5	+ 2.80				

Winning Courses		£1 Level Stake			W-R	£1 Level Stake
Newmarket	3-8	+ 5.21	Newbury		1-1	+ 2.25

Winning Horses	Age	Races Run	1st	2nd	3rd	Unpl	Win £
Zafonic	2	1	1	0	0	0	95,052
Zieten	2	1	1	0	0	0	62,949
Lion Cavern	3	1	1	0	0	0	18,558
Monde Bleu	4	2	1	0	0	1	15,654

Favourites	1-6	16.7%	- 4.09	Total winning prize-money			£192,212
1991 Form	5-12	41.7%	+ 15.94	1989 Form	1-6	16.7%	- 1.50
1990 Form	2-7	28.6%	- 1.49	1988 Form	2-6	33.3%	- 0.87

J E HAMMOND (France)

	No. of Horses	Races Run	1st	2nd	3rd	Unpl	Per cent	£1 Level Stake
2-y-o	0	0	0	0	0	0	-	0.00
3-y-o	1	1	0	0	0	1	-	- 1.00
4-y-o+	3	4	1	0	0	3	25.0	+ 3.00
Totals	4	5	1	0	0	4	20.0	+ 2.00

Jan	Feb	Mar	Apr	May	Jun	Jul	Aug	Sep	Oct/Nov
0-0	0-0	0-0	1-1	0-0	0-2	0-1	0-0	0-1	0-0

Winning Jockey	W-R	£1 Level Stake	Winning Course		W-R	£1 Level Stake
C Asmussen	1-3	+ 4.00	Sandown		1-1	+ 6.00

Winning Horse	Age	Races Run	1st	2nd	3rd	Unpl	Win £
Dear Doctor	5	1	1	0	0	0	23,328

Favourites	0-1			Total winning prize-money		£23,328
1991 Form	2-6	33.3%	+ 5.50	1990 Form	0-1	

MRS C HEAD (France)

	No. of Horses	Races Run	1st	2nd	3rd	Unpl	Per cent	£1 Level Stake
2-y-o	0	0	0	0	0	0	-	0.00
3-y-o	1	1	1	0	0	0	100.0	+ 5.00
4-y-o+	0	0	0	0	0	0	-	0.00
Totals	1	1	1	0	0	0	100.0	+ 5.00

Jan	Feb	Mar	Apr	May	Jun	Jul	Aug	Sep	Oct/Nov
0-0	0-0	0-0	1-1	0-0	0-0	0-0	0-0	0-0	0-0

Winning Jockey	W-R	£1 Level Stake	Winning Course	W-R	£1 Level Stake
W R Swinburn	1-1	+ 5.00	Newmarket	1-1	+ 5.00

Winning Horse		Age	Races Run	1st	2nd	3rd	Unpl	Win £
Hatoof		3	1	1	0	0	0	111,387

Favourites	0-0			Total winning prize-money		£111,387

1991 Form	0-1			1989 Form	0-0		
1990 Form	0-2			1988 Form	1-4	25.0%	- 2.20

M KAUNTZE (Ireland)

	No. of Horses	Races Run	1st	2nd	3rd	Unpl	Per cent	£1 Level Stake
2-y-o	2	2	0	2	0	0	-	- 2.00
3-y-o	1	1	0	0	0	1	-	- 1.00
4-y-o+	2	4	1	0	1	2	25.0	+ 0.50
Totals	5	7	1	2	1	3	14.3	- 2.50

Jan	Feb	Mar	Apr	May	Jun	Jul	Aug	Sep	Oct/Nov
0-0	0-0	0-0	0-0	0-1	0-1	1-1	0-1	0-3	0-0

Winning Jockey	W-R	£1 Level Stake	Winning Course	W-R	£1 Level Stake
W O'Connor	1-5	- 0.50	Sandown	1-1	+ 3.50

Winning Horse		Age	Races Run	1st	2nd	3rd	Unpl	Win £
Kooyonga		4	3	1	0	1	1	152,356

Favourites	1-3	33.3%	+ 1.50	Total winning prize-money		£152,356

1991 Form	1-3	33.3%	+ 1.00	1989 Form	0-1		
1990 Form	2-3	66.7%	+ 7.25	1988 Form	0-3		

D K WELD (Ireland)

	No. of Horses	Races Run	1st	2nd	3rd	Unpl	Per cent	£1 Level Stake
2-y-o	0	0	0	0	0	0	-	0.00
3-y-o	2	3	1	1	0	1	33.3	+ 23.00
4-y-o+	6	6	1	0	0	5	16.7	0.00
Totals	8	9	2	1	0	6	22.2	+ 23.00

Jan	Feb	Mar	Apr	May	Jun	Jul	Aug	Sep	Oct/Nov
0-0	0-0	0-0	0-0	0-0	1-4	0-1	0-1	0-2	1-1

Winning Jockeys	W-R	£1 Level Stake				W-R	£1 Level Stake
W R Swinburn	1-1	+ 5.00	M J Kinane			1-7	+ 19.00

Winning Courses							
Newmarket	1-1	+ 5.00	Ascot			1-6	+ 20.00

Winning Horses	Age	Races Run	1st	2nd	3rd	Unpl	Win £
Brief Truce	3	2	1	1	0	0	118,188
Vintage Crop	5	1	1	0	0	0	48,120

Favourites	1-1	100.0%	+ 5.00	Total winning prize-money		£166,308
1991 Form	0-2			1989 Form	0-5	
1990 Form	0-2			1988 Form	0-3	

OVERSEAS TRAINERS WITH NO WINNERS 1992

	No. of Horses	Races Run	2nd	3rd	Unpl
E Bartholomew (Fra)	1	1	0	0	1
Mme Bollack-Badel (Fra)	1	1	0	0	1
F Boutin (Fra)	5	5	0	1	4
Victor Bowens (Ire)	1	1	0	0	1
J Burns (Ire)	2	2	0	0	2
L Camici (Ita)	1	1	0	0	1
C Collins (Ire)	1	1	0	0	1
F Dunne (Ire)	1	1	0	0	1
E Lellouche (Fra)	1	1	0	0	1
N Meade (Ire)	1	1	0	0	1
J E Mulhern (Ire)	1	1	0	0	1
D J Murphy (Ire)	1	1	0	0	1
M V O'Brien (Ire)	3	3	0	0	3
P O'Leary (Ire)	1	2	0	1	1
M O'Toole (Ire)	1	1	0	0	1
J Pease (Fra)	2	2	0	2	0
Ovidio Pessi (Ita)	1	1	0	0	1
P Prendergast (Ire)	1	1	0	0	1
B Schutz (Ger)	1	1	0	0	1
D Smaga (Fra)	1	1	0	0	1
A Spanu (Fra)	1	1	0	0	1
T Stack (Ire)	5	6	0	0	6
D Vella (Can)	1	1	0	1	0

COURSE SECTION

ASCOT (Group 1)

Leading Trainers 1988-92

	Total W-R	Non-handicaps 2-y-o	Non-handicaps 3-y-o+	Handicaps 2-y-o	Handicaps 3-y-o+	Per cent	£1 Level Stake
M R Stoute	27-174	9-40	13-72	1-4	4-58	15.5	- 33.66
H R A Cecil	26-106	7-25	15-65	0-0	4-16	24.5	+ 43.60
G Harwood	25-139	2-23	16-54	0-5	7-57	18.0	+ 30.36
L M Cumani	22-118	9-25	9-48	0-0	4-45	18.6	- 12.99
J L Dunlop	17-117	4-26	9-48	0-4	4-39	14.5	+ 29.82
D R C Elsworth	16-115	8-29	2-38	0-2	6-46	13.9	+ 79.08
Lord Huntingdon	15-63	0-2	5-17	1-2	9-42	23.8	+ 88.67
J H M Gosden	15-70	2-11	8-24	0-0	5-35	21.4	+ 5.03
R Hannon	14-175	6-50	3-29	2-17	3-79	8.0	+ 65.13
P F I Cole	12-84	7-32	3-24	0-4	2-24	14.3	- 32.87
H Thomson Jones	11-63	8-28	1-16	1-1	1-18	17.5	+ 7.56
C E Brittain	11-237	2-57	3-79	1-4	5-97	4.6	-117.50
R Akehurst	9-60	0-1	1-5	0-1	8-53	15.0	+ 23.50
G Wragg	9-63	3-11	4-33	0-0	2-19	14.3	- 6.36
A C Stewart	8-38	1-3	3-12	0-2	4-21	21.1	+ 6.53
I A Balding	7-103	0-19	1-24	0-1	6-59	6.8	- 2.50
B W Hills	7-112	4-25	2-48	0-2	1-37	6.3	- 55.29
W R Hern	6-30	1-8	2-14	0-0	3-8	20.0	+ 6.22
G Lewis	6-58	0-13	0-11	1-6	5-28	10.3	+ 7.00
M S Johnston	5-23	1-4	1-5	0-0	3-14	21.7	+ 25.83
W A O'Gorman	5-24	2-8	0-3	0-2	3-11	20.8	+ 28.00
B Hanbury	5-41	1-8	2-12	0-1	2-20	12.2	+ 22.38

Leading Jockeys

	Total W-R	Per cent	£1 Level Stake	Best Trainer	W-R	Per cent	£1 Level Stake
Pat Eddery	54-265	20.4	+ 71.93	G Harwood	10-24	41.7	+ 20.73
S Cauthen	42-244	17.2	- 20.77	H R A Cecil	19-62	30.6	+ 15.71
W Carson	35-263	13.3	- 42.57	J L Dunlop	12-58	20.7	+ 20.33
M Roberts	29-243	11.9	- 41.67	C E Brittain	8-112	7.1	- 41.50
L Dettori	24-163	14.7	+ 57.02	L M Cumani	16-77	20.8	+ 5.27
W R Swinburn	23-173	13.3	- 30.36	M R Stoute	13-81	16.0	- 27.50
R Cochrane	17-168	10.1	+ 30.10	L M Cumani	4-22	18.2	- 3.90
A Munro	13-100	13.0	- 16.14	P F I Cole	7-25	28.0	- 3.97
R Hills	12-80	15.0	- 1.44	H Thomson Jones	11-49	22.4	+ 21.56
T Quinn	9-117	7.7	- 42.25	P F I Cole	3-38	7.9	- 23.00
J Reid	9-157	5.7	- 32.17	M McCormack	2-12	16.7	+ 5.00
C Asmussen	6-45	13.3	+ 27.00	W A O'Gorman	2-3	66.7	+ 35.00

How the Favourites Fared

Non-handicaps	W-R	Per cent	£1 Level Stake	Handicaps	W-R	Per cent	£1 Level Stake
2-y-o	45-107	42.1	+ 2.70	2-y-o	0-11	-	- 11.00
3-y-o	21-57	36.8	- 5.30	3-y-o	7-29	24.1	- 1.15
Weight-for-age	37-83	44.6	+ 2.92	All-aged	20-122	16.4	- 37.60
Totals	103-247	41.7	+ 0.32	Totals	27-162	16.7	- 49.75
All favs	130-409	31.8	- 49.43				

Leading Trainers by Month at Ascot

March/Apr

	Total W-R	Non-handicaps 2-y-o	3-y-o+	Handicaps 2-y-o	3-y-o+	Per cent	£1 Level Stake
Lord Huntingdon	3-7	0-0	2-3	0-0	1-4	42.9	+ 3.83
J L Dunlop	2-4	0-0	2-4	0-0	0-0	50.0	+ 7.75
H R A Cecil	2-5	0-0	2-5	0-0	0-0	40.0	+ 23.38
A Bailey	1-1	0-0	0-0	0-0	1-1	100.0	+ 7.00
B A McMahon	1-1	0-0	0-0	0-0	1-1	100.0	+ 16.00

May

	Total W-R	Non-handicaps 2-y-o	3-y-o+	Handicaps 2-y-o	3-y-o+	Per cent	£1 Level Stake
P F I Cole	3-6	1-1	1-3	0-0	1-2	50.0	+ 7.60
M R Stoute	2-5	0-0	2-5	0-0	0-0	40.0	+ 5.50
J Berry	1-1	1-1	0-0	0-0	0-0	100.0	+ 2.00
B Hanbury	1-1	0-0	1-1	0-0	0-0	100.0	+ 1.00
M S Johnston	1-1	0-0	1-1	0-0	0-0	100.0	+ 10.00

June

	Total W-R	Non-handicaps 2-y-o	3-y-o+	Handicaps 2-y-o	3-y-o+	Per cent	£1 Level Stake
H R A Cecil	14-50	2-4	9-38	0-0	3-8	28.0	+ 35.22
G Harwood	12-65	0-6	9-32	0-0	3-27	18.5	+ 32.86
J L Dunlop	9-48	1-4	5-26	0-0	3-18	18.8	+ 49.21
M R Stoute	8-62	0-7	7-40	0-0	1-15	12.9	- 23.72
R Hannon	8-78	3-22	2-17	0-0	3-39	10.3	+100.38

July

	Total W-R	Non-handicaps 2-y-o	3-y-o+	Handicaps 2-y-o	3-y-o+	Per cent	£1 Level Stake
M R Stoute	4-28	2-7	1-10	0-0	1-11	14.3	- 8.65
H Thomson Jones	3-5	2-3	0-1	0-0	1-1	60.0	+ 12.60
W R Hern	3-8	1-2	1-4	0-0	1-2	37.5	+ 5.72
J H M Gosden	3-10	0-0	2-5	0-0	1-5	30.0	+ 1.96
H R A Cecil	3-11	2-5	1-5	0-0	0-1	27.3	+ 3.63

September

	Total W-R	Non-handicaps 2-y-o	3-y-o+	Handicaps 2-y-o	3-y-o+	Per cent	£1 Level Stake
L M Cumani	13-49	8-19	2-8	0-0	3-22	26.5	+ 21.04
M R Stoute	10-49	6-17	3-8	0-2	1-22	20.4	+ 1.71
G Harwood	7-28	1-6	4-7	0-1	2-14	25.0	+ 15.00
M H Tompkins	4-12	0-0	0-0	1-2	3-10	33.3	+ 15.00
A C Stewart	4-15	0-1	0-1	0-1	4-12	26.7	+ 14.50

Oct/Nov

	Total W-R	Non-handicaps 2-y-o	3-y-o+	Handicaps 2-y-o	3-y-o+	Per cent	£1 Level Stake
J H M Gosden	5-16	1-5	1-5	0-0	3-6	31.3	+ 3.41
L M Cumani	5-17	1-4	4-11	0-0	0-2	29.4	- 3.38
D R C Elsworth	5-22	2-8	0-6	0-2	3-6	22.7	+ 32.33
R Akehurst	4-11	0-0	1-1	0-1	3-9	36.4	+ 27.00
M H Easterby	3-7	0-1	1-1	0-1	2-4	42.9	+ 13.50

AYR (Group 1)

Leading Trainers 1988-92

	Total W-R	Non-handicaps 2-y-o	3-y-o+	Handicaps 2-y-o	3-y-o+	Per cent	£1 Level Stake
J Berry	32-219	12-70	9-39	2-26	9-84	14.6	+ 2.37
Mrs J Ramsden	20-68	2-5	3-9	2-6	13-48	29.4	+ 51.96
M H Easterby	18-124	4-21	3-16	1-12	10-75	14.5	- 49.81
B W Hills	17-44	4-12	9-19	0-0	4-13	38.6	+ 13.02
M Brittain	13-153	0-23	3-18	1-16	9-96	8.5	+ 22.50
P Chapple-Hyam	12-27	7-14	2-4	1-1	2-8	44.4	+ 27.58
J W Watts	12-85	5-18	2-10	0-9	5-48	14.1	- 19.93
M P Naughton	11-86	0-2	1-25	0-0	10-59	12.8	- 17.25
F H Lee	11-99	1-18	0-11	1-6	9-64	11.1	- 23.88
R M Whitaker	10-136	2-26	2-25	0-9	6-76	7.4	- 31.63
M H Tompkins	9-91	0-13	4-18	1-12	4-48	9.9	- 21.00
M W Easterby	8-51	2-7	0-5	0-8	6-31	15.7	+ 8.08
N Tinkler	8-119	0-21	4-32	2-11	2-55	6.7	- 62.56
J L Dunlop	7-18	3-6	2-5	0-0	2-7	38.9	- 0.74
H Thomson Jones	7-27	3-11	3-6	0-0	1-10	25.9	+ 4.54
Mrs G R Reveley	7-45	0-6	4-13	0-1	3-25	15.6	- 10.42
T D Barron	7-48	0-6	0-6	3-10	4-26	14.6	- 15.42
C B B Booth	7-54	2-11	2-12	0-3	3-28	13.0	- 18.00
M S Johnston	7-54	2-11	1-8	0-5	4-30	13.0	- 1.75
A Bailey	7-55	1-15	1-9	1-9	4-22	12.7	- 24.97
Sir M Prescott	6-27	2-7	2-8	1-3	1-9	22.2	- 1.90
C Tinkler	6-48	2-10	1-11	0-11	3-16	12.5	- 17.88

Leading Jockeys

	Total W-R	Per cent	£1 Level Stake	Best Trainer	W-R	Per cent	£1 Level Stake
K Darley	29-183	15.8	- 53.01	Mrs G R Reveley	4-14	28.6	+ 7.83
M Birch	24-147	16.3	- 17.59	M H Easterby	10-60	16.7	- 27.09
D McKeown	22-156	14.1	- 33.03	Mrs J Ramsden	5-14	35.7	+ 15.58
J Carroll	19-161	11.8	- 66.93	J Berry	17-113	15.0	- 32.43
M Hills	18-76	23.7	+ 16.07	B W Hills	10-22	45.5	+ 9.91
K Fallon	15-137	10.9	- 47.63	M P Naughton	7-31	22.6	+ 7.75
G Duffield	14-112	12.5	- 38.61	Sir M Prescott	4-19	21.1	+ 1.23
N Connorton	13-103	12.6	+ 15.66	J W Watts	7-24	29.2	+ 15.83
A Munro	12-74	16.2	+ 47.86	M Brittain	5-39	12.8	+ 50.00
G Carter	11-53	20.8	+ 3.71	J Berry	3-9	33.3	+ 0.08
M Roberts	10-45	22.2	+ 16.38	Mrs J Ramsden	1-1	100.0	+ 2.50
R Hills	10-49	20.4	- 14.05	H Thomson Jones	5-18	27.8	- 6.45

How the Favourites Fared

Non-handicaps	W-R	Per cent	£1 Level Stake	Handicaps	W-R	Per cent	£1 Level Stake
2-y-o	43-98	43.9	- 9.47	2-y-o	7-27	25.9	- 8.61
3-y-o	19-48	39.6	- 4.83	3-y-o	16-49	32.7	- 0.53
Weight-for-age	32-72	44.4	+ 5.50	All-aged	57-163	35.0	+ 18.83
Totals	94-218	43.1	- 8.80	Totals	80-239	33.5	+ 9.69
All favs	174-457	38.1	+ 0.89				

Leading Trainers by Month at Ayr

March/Apr

	Total W-R	Non-handicaps 2-y-o	3-y-o+	Handicaps 2-y-o	3-y-o+	Per cent	£1 Level Stake
J Berry	6-23	1-2	2-10	0-0	3-11	26.1	+ 8.80
M Brittain	4-29	0-3	2-7	0-0	2-19	13.8	+ 18.25
Mrs J Ramsden	3-8	0-0	1-2	0-0	2-6	37.5	+ 5.75
M H Easterby	3-13	0-2	1-3	0-0	2-8	23.1	- 5.05
B W Hills	2-2	0-0	2-2	0-0	0-0	100.0	+ 4.12

June

	Total W-R	Non-handicaps 2-y-o	3-y-o+	Handicaps 2-y-o	3-y-o+	Per cent	£1 Level Stake
M H Easterby	4-13	2-5	1-1	0-0	1-7	30.8	- 3.46
F H Lee	4-16	1-5	0-1	0-0	3-10	25.0	+ 12.00
J Berry	4-28	2-14	1-3	0-0	1-11	14.3	- 4.50
P Chapple-Hyam	3-7	0-1	1-2	0-0	2-4	42.9	+ 11.70
C Tinkler	3-8	0-1	1-2	0-0	2-5	37.5	+ 2.75

July

	Total W-R	Non-handicaps 2-y-o	3-y-o+	Handicaps 2-y-o	3-y-o+	Per cent	£1 Level Stake
J Berry	10-54	4-19	3-12	0-3	3-20	18.5	- 18.55
J W Watts	6-19	1-2	2-4	0-2	3-11	31.6	- 0.93
F H Lee	6-35	0-5	0-3	1-3	5-24	17.1	- 0.88
Mrs J Ramsden	5-14	1-1	0-2	0-0	4-11	35.7	+ 6.21
A Bailey	5-18	0-3	1-4	1-2	3-9	27.8	+ 1.28

August

	Total W-R	Non-handicaps 2-y-o	3-y-o+	Handicaps 2-y-o	3-y-o+	Per cent	£1 Level Stake
J Berry	4-14	1-3	3-6	0-2	0-3	28.6	+ 28.08
M H Easterby	3-7	1-1	0-2	1-1	1-3	42.9	+ 2.87
J Etherington	2-2	1-1	1-1	0-0	0-0	100.0	+ 9.50
Lord Huntingdon	2-3	1-1	0-0	1-1	0-1	66.7	+ 1.50
B W Hills	2-4	1-2	0-0	0-0	1-2	50.0	+ 0.62

September

	Total W-R	Non-handicaps 2-y-o	3-y-o+	Handicaps 2-y-o	3-y-o+	Per cent	£1 Level Stake
B W Hills	9-26	3-9	5-10	0-0	1-7	34.6	+ 5.79
Mrs J Ramsden	8-27	1-4	1-1	1-4	5-18	29.6	+ 23.50
M H Tompkins	8-57	0-9	3-10	1-9	4-29	14.0	+ 8.00
P Chapple-Hyam	6-10	4-5	1-2	1-1	0-2	60.0	+ 19.70
J L Dunlop	5-14	2-4	2-5	0-0	1-5	35.7	- 1.62

Oct/Nov

	Total W-R	Non-handicaps 2-y-o	3-y-o+	Handicaps 2-y-o	3-y-o+	Per cent	£1 Level Stake
N Tinkler	3-20	0-3	1-7	2-3	0-7	15.0	+ 17.00
J Berry	3-24	3-13	0-4	0-2	0-5	12.5	- 18.08
M W Easterby	2-4	1-1	0-0	0-1	1-2	50.0	+ 20.50
C B B Booth	2-6	0-2	1-2	0-1	1-1	33.3	+ 5.50
Sir M Prescott	2-6	1-3	0-1	1-2	0-0	33.3	+ 9.50

BATH (Group 3)

Leading Trainers 1988-92

	Total W-R	Non-handicaps 2-y-o	3-y-o+	Handicaps 2-y-o	3-y-o+	Per cent	£1 Level Stake
B W Hills	23-87	4-16	12-39	1-2	6-30	26.4	+ 0.83
R Hannon	20-119	7-39	6-32	2-5	5-43	16.8	- 14.40
I A Balding	18-132	2-29	3-44	0-3	13-56	13.6	- 18.44
G Harwood	14-51	1-7	9-21	0-2	4-21	27.5	- 1.18
R J Hodges	14-119	2-10	0-23	0-2	12-84	11.8	- 4.42
P F I Cole	13-112	2-23	5-36	0-4	6-49	11.6	- 44.00
G Lewis	12-53	1-16	3-13	1-4	7-20	22.6	+ 14.13
C J Hill	11-100	1-21	1-24	1-1	8-54	11.0	- 29.42
W R Hern	9-34	1-3	3-16	1-1	4-14	26.5	+ 5.88
J Berry	9-53	7-23	2-9	0-4	0-17	17.0	+ 0.13
D R C Elsworth	9-53	1-12	2-18	0-2	6-21	17.0	+ 2.50
R Akehurst	8-41	0-4	2-5	0-0	6-32	19.5	+ 34.58
J L Dunlop	8-59	1-9	3-21	0-2	4-27	13.6	- 28.26
J S King	6-19	0-2	0-2	0-0	6-15	31.6	+ 23.50
D W P Arbuthnot	6-42	3-11	0-13	0-1	3-17	14.3	+ 36.60
H Candy	6-47	0-6	3-13	0-1	3-27	12.8	+ 1.37
P T Walwyn	6-55	2-14	1-16	0-2	3-23	10.9	- 19.34
R Charlton	5-12	3-5	2-7	0-0	0-0	41.7	+ 4.40
M McCourt	5-16	0-0	0-2	0-0	5-14	31.3	+ 29.00
R F J Houghton	5-36	0-7	4-11	0-1	1-17	13.9	- 1.55
L G Cottrell	5-68	0-12	0-13	0-1	5-42	7.4	- 28.75
H R A Cecil	4-5	2-2	1-2	0-0	1-1	80.0	+ 9.75

Leading Jockeys

	Total W-R	Per cent	£1 Level Stake	Best Trainer	W-R	Per cent	£1 Level Stake
Pat Eddery	27-93	29.0	+ 2.75	B W Hills	8-16	50.0	+ 4.73
J Reid	24-127	18.9	+ 26.09	I A Balding	4-19	21.1	+ 8.10
W Carson	22-96	22.9	- 0.92	W R Hern	7-14	50.0	+ 20.63
J Williams	21-202	10.4	- 12.99	D R C Elsworth	5-18	27.8	+ 16.00
T Quinn	20-132	15.2	+ 3.11	P F I Cole	9-64	14.1	- 9.66
G Duffield	12-52	23.1	+ 27.71	R Boss	2-2	100.0	+ 13.38
A Munro	12-71	16.9	- 10.40	M Brittain	3-6	50.0	+ 7.00
M Roberts	10-55	18.2	+ 12.41	Lord Huntingdon	2-3	66.7	+ 13.00
A Clark	9-79	11.4	- 18.05	G Harwood	4-20	20.0	- 4.80
N Adams	9-211	4.3	-136.25	R J Hodges	2-6	33.3	+ 6.25
Paul Eddery	8-56	14.3	- 31.72	G Lewis	2-14	14.3	- 8.25
D Holland	8-73	11.0	- 20.98	B W Hills	4-24	16.7	- 2.58

How the Favourites Fared

Non-handicaps	W-R	Per cent	£1 Level Stake	Handicaps	W-R	Per cent	£1 Level Stake
2-y-o	29-81	35.8	- 12.13	2-y-o	6-12	50.0	+ 8.75
3-y-o	41-87	47.1	+ 5.67	3-y-o	25-55	45.5	+ 16.04
Weight-for-age	3-12	25.0	- 2.87	All-aged	31-119	26.1	- 17.79
Totals	73-180	40.6	- 9.33	Totals	62-186	33.3	+ 7.00
All favs	135-366	36.9	- 2.33				

Leading Trainers by Month at Bath

March/Apr	Total W-R	Non-handicaps 2-y-o	3-y-o+	Handicaps 2-y-o	3-y-o+	Per cent	£1 Level Stake
W R Hern	2-2	0-0	1-1	0-0	1-1	100.0	+ 4.38
Dr J D Scargill	2-4	1-2	1-1	0-0	0-1	50.0	+ 13.50
P F I Cole	2-15	0-3	1-9	0-0	1-3	13.3	- 5.50
M McCourt	1-1	0-0	0-0	0-0	1-1	100.0	+ 14.00
P Hayward	1-1	0-0	0-0	0-0	1-1	100.0	+ 14.00

May	Total W-R	Non-handicaps 2-y-o	3-y-o+	Handicaps 2-y-o	3-y-o+	Per cent	£1 Level Stake
G Harwood	7-13	1-1	5-10	0-0	1-2	53.8	+ 12.03
B W Hills	6-20	0-0	2-12	0-0	4-8	30.0	- 2.40
H Candy	3-8	0-0	0-3	0-0	3-5	37.5	+ 24.50
W R Hern	3-9	0-0	2-6	0-0	1-3	33.3	+ 2.25
J Berry	3-12	3-8	0-1	0-0	0-3	25.0	+ 7.00

June	Total W-R	Non-handicaps 2-y-o	3-y-o+	Handicaps 2-y-o	3-y-o+	Per cent	£1 Level Stake
R Akehurst	5-10	0-0	2-3	0-0	3-7	50.0	+ 44.58
R J Hodges	5-24	1-3	0-5	0-0	4-16	20.8	+ 9.63
P F I Cole	3-15	0-4	2-6	0-0	1-5	20.0	+ 2.90
R Hannon	3-16	2-5	1-9	0-0	0-2	18.8	+ 4.91
W A O'Gorman	2-4	1-2	0-0	0-0	1-2	50.0	+ 11.00

July	Total W-R	Non-handicaps 2-y-o	3-y-o+	Handicaps 2-y-o	3-y-o+	Per cent	£1 Level Stake
B W Hills	8-15	2-2	5-9	0-0	1-4	53.3	+ 10.48
R Hannon	6-26	1-10	2-2	0-0	3-14	23.1	+ 1.33
G Harwood	5-14	0-0	3-6	0-0	2-8	35.7	+ 2.17
R J Hodges	5-29	0-1	0-6	0-0	5-22	17.2	- 7.04
I A Balding	5-31	1-8	1-8	0-0	3-15	16.1	- 2.29

August	Total W-R	Non-handicaps 2-y-o	3-y-o+	Handicaps 2-y-o	3-y-o+	Per cent	£1 Level Stake
R Hannon	4-11	1-2	2-5	0-1	1-3	36.4	+ 2.82
G Lewis	3-5	0-1	1-1	1-1	1-2	60.0	+ 7.25
I A Balding	3-14	0-2	1-3	0-2	2-7	21.4	+ 6.50
M C Pipe	2-3	0-0	2-3	0-0	0-0	66.7	+ 14.10
B W Hills	2-6	1-2	0-1	1-1	0-2	33.3	+ 2.75

September	Total W-R	Non-handicaps 2-y-o	3-y-o+	Handicaps 2-y-o	3-y-o+	Per cent	£1 Level Stake
I A Balding	4-15	1-5	0-4	0-1	3-5	26.7	+ 7.35
C J Hill	4-19	0-3	0-2	0-0	4-14	21.1	+ 6.33
R Hannon	4-21	1-7	0-4	2-4	1-6	19.0	+ 8.53
M McCourt	3-4	0-0	0-0	0-0	3-4	75.0	+ 25.00
H Candy	3-13	0-2	3-5	0-1	0-5	23.1	+ 2.87

Oct/Nov	Total W-R	Non-handicaps 2-y-o	3-y-o+	Handicaps 2-y-o	3-y-o+	Per cent	£1 Level Stake
H Thomson Jones	2-2	2-2	0-0	0-0	0-0	100.0	+ 8.00
P J Makin	2-3	0-0	0-0	0-0	2-3	66.7	+ 1.66
W Jarvis	2-3	0-1	1-1	0-0	1-1	66.7	+ 7.00
W R Hern	2-4	1-2	0-0	0-0	1-2	50.0	+ 2.00
C J Hill	2-6	0-0	0-3	1-1	1-2	33.3	+ 4.25

435

BEVERLEY (Group 3)

Leading Trainers 1988-92

	Total W-R	Non-handicaps 2-y-o	3-y-o+	Handicaps 2-y-o	3-y-o+	Per cent	£1 Level Stake
M H Easterby	26-204	12-73	3-30	1-11	10-90	12.7	- 73.34
J Berry	22-164	15-100	2-32	1-7	4-25	13.4	- 39.13
H R A Cecil	18-44	2-5	12-32	0-0	4-7	40.9	- 0.96
R Hollinshead	17-148	4-29	4-36	0-0	9-83	11.5	- 46.70
I A Balding	15-44	4-7	2-14	0-0	9-23	34.1	+ 7.94
M Brittain	15-196	6-68	2-31	1-5	6-92	7.7	- 38.38
M R Stoute	14-54	1-5	13-39	0-0	0-10	25.9	- 17.83
T D Barron	14-122	1-27	1-12	2-9	10-74	11.5	- 32.65
Mrs G R Reveley	12-68	4-12	0-4	0-3	8-49	17.6	+ 4.42
R M Whitaker	12-156	4-28	2-29	0-4	6-95	7.7	- 61.88
L M Cumani	11-19	0-0	11-18	0-0	0-1	57.9	+ 12.48
B W Hills	10-35	2-5	6-19	0-0	2-11	28.6	+ 3.40
D Morley	10-61	1-6	3-16	0-0	6-39	16.4	- 2.04
C E Brittain	9-49	1-5	6-25	0-0	2-19	18.4	+ 5.33
S G Norton	9-80	1-15	2-22	0-1	6-42	11.3	- 6.53
P F I Cole	8-24	1-4	6-16	0-1	1-3	33.3	- 1.40
M H Tompkins	8-60	0-22	4-12	0-3	4-23	13.3	- 14.02
J L Spearing	8-68	0-7	0-9	0-1	8-51	11.8	- 17.25
F H Lee	8-72	1-10	1-11	1-4	5-47	11.1	- 16.75
J G FitzGerald	8-99	1-30	4-29	1-1	2-39	8.1	- 26.50
M S Johnston	7-47	2-17	3-8	0-2	2-20	14.9	+ 8.95
T Fairhurst	7-111	4-46	1-16	1-6	1-43	6.3	- 39.20

Leading Jockeys

	Total W-R	Per cent	£1 Level Stake	Best Trainer	W-R	Per cent	£1 Level Stake
M Birch	29-247	11.7	- 76.35	M H Easterby	14-102	13.7	- 35.64
K Darley	27-202	13.4	- 36.21	M H Easterby	5-17	29.4	+ 1.64
J Lowe	21-220	9.5	- 54.37	Mrs G R Reveley	6-23	26.1	+ 28.33
W R Swinburn	18-79	22.8	+ 1.21	M R Stoute	8-28	28.6	- 6.29
M Roberts	17-89	19.1	- 2.01	C E Brittain	4-12	33.3	+ 9.83
W Ryan	17-97	17.5	- 22.79	H R A Cecil	9-22	40.9	- 0.14
D McKeown	17-193	8.8	-117.63	D Morley	2-2	100.0	+ 5.25
A Culhane	16-143	11.2	- 44.37	R Hollinshead	6-35	17.1	- 7.00
J Carroll	15-120	12.5	- 31.03	J Berry	13-88	14.8	- 22.03
B Raymond	13-79	16.5	- 12.88	A A Scott	2-4	50.0	+ 3.91
N Connorton	13-117	11.1	- 11.75	M J Camacho	4-29	13.8	- 5.25
G Duffield	13-119	10.9	- 65.16	J R Fanshawe	2-3	66.7	+ 8.00

How the Favourites Fared

Non-handicaps	W-R	Per cent	£1 Level Stake	Handicaps	W-R	Per cent	£1 Level Stake
2-y-o	58-137	42.3	- 15.03	2-y-o	4-15	26.7	- 1.12
3-y-o	32-70	45.7	+ 6.73	3-y-o	13-55	23.6	- 20.68
Weight-for-age	49-92	53.3	+ 0.25	All-aged	57-208	27.4	- 32.62
Totals	139-299	46.5	- 8.05	Totals	74-278	26.6	- 54.42
All favs	213-577	36.9	- 62.47				

Leading Trainers by Month at Beverley

March/Apr	Total W-R	Non-handicaps 2-y-o	3-y-o+	Handicaps 2-y-o	3-y-o+	Per cent	£1 Level Stake
R Hollinshead	5-21	2-5	0-8	0-0	3-8	23.8	+ 3.70
J Berry	5-29	3-16	1-4	0-0	1-9	17.2	- 9.10
C E Brittain	4-11	0-0	2-7	0-0	2-4	36.4	+ 22.08
P F I Cole	3-5	0-0	3-5	0-0	0-0	60.0	+ 3.03
M R Channon	3-5	0-0	1-2	0-0	2-3	60.0	+ 18.50

May	Total W-R	Non-handicaps 2-y-o	3-y-o+	Handicaps 2-y-o	3-y-o+	Per cent	£1 Level Stake
M R Stoute	6-17	0-0	6-16	0-0	0-1	35.3	- 2.23
S G Norton	5-18	1-2	1-7	0-0	3-9	27.8	+ 19.48
M Brittain	5-53	2-23	1-12	0-0	2-18	9.4	- 7.50
J Berry	4-32	4-26	0-6	0-0	0-0	12.5	- 15.25
M H Easterby	4-47	2-19	0-11	0-0	2-17	8.5	- 23.00

June	Total W-R	Non-handicaps 2-y-o	3-y-o+	Handicaps 2-y-o	3-y-o+	Per cent	£1 Level Stake
M H Easterby	8-30	6-12	0-0	0-0	2-18	26.7	+ 4.47
L M Cumani	5-7	0-0	5-7	0-0	0-0	71.4	+ 4.13
H R A Cecil	4-6	0-0	2-4	0-0	2-2	66.7	+ 4.90
P F I Cole	3-9	0-1	2-5	0-0	1-3	33.3	- 1.84
A A Scott	3-9	3-4	0-1	0-0	0-4	33.3	- 0.26

July	Total W-R	Non-handicaps 2-y-o	3-y-o+	Handicaps 2-y-o	3-y-o+	Per cent	£1 Level Stake
J Berry	7-28	6-18	0-4	0-0	1-6	25.0	+ 11.97
M H Easterby	6-56	2-19	0-6	0-5	4-26	10.7	- 20.83
I A Balding	5-14	0-1	0-1	0-0	5-12	35.7	+ 7.25
M R Stoute	5-14	0-1	5-6	0-0	0-7	35.7	- 0.30
Mrs G R Reveley	5-16	1-1	0-0	0-1	4-14	31.3	+ 14.33

August	Total W-R	Non-handicaps 2-y-o	3-y-o+	Handicaps 2-y-o	3-y-o+	Per cent	£1 Level Stake
I A Balding	4-4	1-1	0-0	0-0	3-3	100.0	+ 7.75
H R A Cecil	4-8	1-1	3-6	0-0	0-1	50.0	+ 2.28
R M Whitaker	4-22	2-5	0-2	0-1	2-14	18.2	+ 5.00
R Hollinshead	4-27	1-4	2-7	0-0	1-16	14.8	+ 3.50
B W Hills	3-9	1-2	2-5	0-0	0-2	33.3	+ 0.32

September	Total W-R	Non-handicaps 2-y-o	3-y-o+	Handicaps 2-y-o	3-y-o+	Per cent	£1 Level Stake
I A Balding	3-4	3-4	0-0	0-0	0-0	75.0	+ 3.37
H Thomson Jones	3-4	3-3	0-1	0-0	0-0	75.0	+ 7.13
W Jarvis	3-5	2-3	1-2	0-0	0-0	60.0	+ 0.97
B W Hills	3-6	1-1	2-4	0-0	0-1	50.0	+ 5.75
M H Easterby	3-15	1-4	1-2	1-4	0-5	20.0	- 5.33

BRIGHTON (Group 2)

Leading Trainers 1988-92

	Total W-R	Non-handicaps 2-y-o	3-y-o+	Handicaps 2-y-o	3-y-o+	Per cent	£1 Level Stake
R Hannon	40-217	18-61	11-55	3-10	8-91	18.4	- 13.92
L M Cumani	26-50	10-12	13-26	1-2	2-10	52.0	+ 27.29
G Harwood	19-66	1-11	16-43	1-2	1-10	28.8	+ 3.87
Sir M Prescott	18-71	1-13	3-11	0-3	14-44	25.4	+ 7.85
R Akehurst	18-103	0-3	8-25	1-2	9-73	17.5	- 0.92
J L Dunlop	17-84	6-25	6-32	0-5	5-22	20.2	- 4.26
P F I Cole	15-116	4-28	8-39	1-5	2-44	12.9	- 61.85
R J Hodges	15-124	0-0	0-19	0-1	15-104	12.1	- 46.83
M J Ryan	13-53	3-6	0-7	0-0	10-40	24.5	+ 21.75
H R A Cecil	9-22	2-3	7-18	0-0	0-1	40.9	- 0.60
H Thomson Jones	9-29	2-7	4-14	0-0	3-8	31.0	+ 28.48
J H M Gosden	9-32	1-2	7-26	0-0	1-4	28.1	- 11.19
W Carter	9-69	2-9	0-14	0-1	7-45	13.0	- 21.25
R Boss	8-25	1-4	1-4	0-1	6-16	32.0	+ 29.03
A C Stewart	8-28	2-5	5-19	0-0	1-4	28.6	+ 4.20
M A Jarvis	8-40	0-6	4-14	0-2	4-18	20.0	+ 4.00
J Berry	7-23	4-11	0-1	1-4	2-7	30.4	+ 2.92
E A Wheeler	7-42	0-4	1-9	0-0	6-29	16.7	- 1.50
N A Callaghan	7-48	1-12	1-8	1-3	4-25	14.6	- 24.14
I A Balding	7-55	1-8	3-18	0-4	3-25	12.7	- 6.38
S Dow	7-66	1-9	1-12	0-1	5-44	10.6	- 4.00
G Lewis	7-79	1-16	1-21	2-3	3-39	8.9	- 18.83

Leading Jockeys

	Total W-R	Per cent	£1 Level Stake	Best Trainer	W-R	Per cent	£1 Level Stake
W Carson	50-204	24.5	+ 20.59	J L Dunlop	11-40	27.5	+ 11.83
J Reid	34-204	16.7	- 3.35	R Hannon	6-12	50.0	+ 34.93
T Quinn	32-205	15.6	+ 9.54	P F I Cole	9-71	12.7	- 33.71
B Rouse	27-208	13.0	- 35.75	R Hannon	11-91	12.1	- 27.05
R Cochrane	25-128	19.5	- 17.79	G Harwood	6-21	28.6	- 7.53
L Dettori	23-80	28.8	- 6.36	L M Cumani	17-31	54.8	+ 26.57
Pat Eddery	22-120	18.3	- 22.48	J H M Gosden	3-5	60.0	+ 1.38
M Roberts	21-111	18.9	- 11.14	A C Stewart	6-21	28.6	+ 1.44
G Duffield	18-109	16.5	- 23.52	Sir M Prescott	14-59	23.7	+ 4.48
J Williams	15-161	9.3	- 40.09	G B Balding	6-16	37.5	+ 27.63
A Munro	14-79	17.7	- 9.05	P F I Cole	3-10	30.0	- 1.62
T Williams	14-159	8.8	- 12.42	D R Laing	5-26	19.2	+ 37.25

How the Favourites Fared

Non-handicaps	W-R	Per cent	£1 Level Stake	Handicaps	W-R	Per cent	£1 Level Stake
2-y-o	49-102	48.0	+ 0.93	2-y-o	3-14	21.4	- 1.25
3-y-o	36-77	46.8	+ 0.59	3-y-o	15-63	23.8	- 21.19
Weight-for-age	41-91	45.1	- 8.36	All-aged	47-198	23.7	- 52.76
Totals	126-270	46.7	- 6.84	Totals	65-275	23.6	- 75.20
All favs	191-545	35.0	- 82.04				

Leading Trainers by Month at Brighton

March/Apr	Total W-R	Non-handicaps 2-y-o	3-y-o+	Handicaps 2-y-o	3-y-o+	Per cent	£1 Level Stake
R Hannon	6-42	2-6	3-20	0-0	1-16	14.3	- 8.17
G Harwood	5-7	0-0	5-6	0-0	0-1	71.4	+ 17.17
R J Hodges	5-22	0-0	0-6	0-0	5-16	22.7	+ 10.50
Sir M Prescott	4-10	0-0	2-4	0-0	2-6	40.0	+ 0.88
P F I Cole	4-18	0-1	4-12	0-0	0-5	22.2	- 1.59

May	Total W-R	Non-handicaps 2-y-o	3-y-o+	Handicaps 2-y-o	3-y-o+	Per cent	£1 Level Stake
R Hannon	10-44	5-9	3-14	0-0	2-21	22.7	- 7.40
S Dow	5-14	1-3	1-4	0-0	3-7	35.7	+ 11.00
H R A Cecil	4-7	0-0	4-6	0-0	0-1	57.1	+ 1.67
G Harwood	4-12	0-1	4-11	0-0	0-0	33.3	+ 1.97
M J Ryan	4-12	1-2	0-0	0-0	3-10	33.3	+ 14.88

June	Total W-R	Non-handicaps 2-y-o	3-y-o+	Handicaps 2-y-o	3-y-o+	Per cent	£1 Level Stake
R Hannon	5-39	2-14	2-8	0-0	1-17	12.8	- 14.48
P F I Cole	4-22	2-4	1-8	0-0	1-10	18.2	- 4.63
G B Balding	3-5	0-0	1-2	0-0	2-3	60.0	+ 18.38
C R Nelson	3-5	2-4	0-0	0-0	1-1	60.0	+ 10.00
J L Dunlop	3-8	0-2	2-4	0-0	1-2	37.5	+ 13.58

July	Total W-R	Non-handicaps 2-y-o	3-y-o+	Handicaps 2-y-o	3-y-o+	Per cent	£1 Level Stake
J L Dunlop	4-10	2-3	1-2	0-0	1-5	40.0	- 0.43
R Boss	3-5	1-1	0-0	0-0	2-4	60.0	+ 20.91
J White	3-6	0-1	0-1	0-0	3-4	50.0	+ 7.00
R Hannon	3-12	0-3	1-2	0-0	2-7	25.0	+ 15.00
A C Stewart	2-2	0-0	2-2	0-0	0-0	100.0	+ 2.61

August	Total W-R	Non-handicaps 2-y-o	3-y-o+	Handicaps 2-y-o	3-y-o+	Per cent	£1 Level Stake
Sir M Prescott	8-23	1-6	0-2	0-1	7-14	34.8	+ 13.95
R Hannon	8-46	3-15	2-10	2-4	1-17	17.4	+ 5.34
L M Cumani	7-11	2-2	3-5	0-0	2-4	63.6	+ 12.23
R Akehurst	7-19	0-0	3-7	1-1	3-11	36.8	+ 27.50
D R Laing	4-11	0-1	2-4	0-0	2-6	36.4	+ 49.00

September	Total W-R	Non-handicaps 2-y-o	3-y-o+	Handicaps 2-y-o	3-y-o+	Per cent	£1 Level Stake
L M Cumani	7-15	4-5	3-6	0-1	0-3	46.7	+ 11.03
R Hannon	6-17	5-9	0-1	0-2	1-5	35.3	+ 4.58
R W Armstrong	3-4	1-1	1-1	0-0	1-2	75.0	+ 42.50
J L Dunlop	3-12	2-6	1-3	0-1	0-2	25.0	- 0.34
Sir M Prescott	3-12	0-3	0-0	0-1	3-8	25.0	+ 9.00

Oct/Nov	Total W-R	Non-handicaps 2-y-o	3-y-o+	Handicaps 2-y-o	3-y-o+	Per cent	£1 Level Stake
L M Cumani	7-8	4-4	2-3	1-1	0-0	87.5	+ 7.61
G Harwood	2-4	0-0	0-1	1-2	1-1	50.0	+ 7.33
G Wragg	2-5	1-1	1-4	0-0	0-0	40.0	+ 1.50
A Turnell	2-5	0-1	0-0	0-0	2-4	40.0	+ 6.00
R Hannon	2-17	1-5	0-0	1-4	0-8	11.8	- 8.80

CARLISLE (Group 4)

Leading Trainers 1988-92

	Total W-R	Non-handicaps 2-y-o	3-y-o+	Handicaps 2-y-o	3-y-o+	Per cent	£1 Level Stake
J Berry	25-113	14-58	6-31	0-1	5-23	22.1	+ 37.75
J W Watts	11-45	1-7	3-17	0-0	7-21	24.4	+ 43.58
S G Norton	11-67	2-21	6-25	0-0	3-21	16.4	+ 11.00
M H Easterby	11-74	5-24	2-21	0-0	4-29	14.9	- 21.05
M H Tompkins	10-42	3-8	4-12	0-2	3-20	23.8	- 0.05
R Hollinshead	10-113	3-22	3-33	0-1	4-57	8.8	- 24.38
Sir M Prescott	9-53	3-13	3-18	0-0	3-22	17.0	- 6.80
M S Johnston	8-38	1-6	2-11	0-0	5-21	21.1	+ 55.69
N Tinkler	8-46	3-19	3-11	0-0	2-16	17.4	- 0.77
Denys Smith	8-62	1-12	3-14	0-1	4-35	12.9	- 1.00
R M Whitaker	7-37	2-5	3-12	0-1	2-19	18.9	+ 22.50
Mrs G R Reveley	6-43	0-3	1-14	0-0	5-26	14.0	- 6.84
T Fairhurst	6-52	1-13	2-15	0-0	3-24	11.5	+ 11.75
M Brittain	6-57	1-12	0-12	0-0	5-33	10.5	- 9.50
C W Thornton	5-44	2-11	0-15	0-0	3-18	11.4	- 20.88
J L Dunlop	4-6	1-2	2-2	0-0	1-2	66.7	+ 11.62
M R Stoute	4-15	0-2	4-13	0-0	0-0	26.7	- 7.51
E J Alston	4-33	0-10	0-5	0-0	4-18	12.1	+ 8.50
G M Moore	4-34	0-6	1-13	0-0	3-15	11.8	- 13.50
T D Barron	4-45	0-12	2-9	0-2	2-22	8.9	- 15.50
J Etherington	4-48	2-18	1-13	0-0	1-17	8.3	- 13.65
J G FitzGerald	3-7	2-2	0-1	0-0	1-4	42.9	+ 14.50

Leading Jockeys

	Total W-R	Per cent	£1 Level Stake	Best Trainer	W-R	Per cent	£1 Level Stake
D McKeown	23-121	19.0	+ 34.28	M S Johnston	4-12	33.3	+ 7.19
G Duffield	18-127	14.2	- 22.92	Sir M Prescott	9-48	18.8	+ 1.70
K Darley	17-125	13.6	- 34.76	J Berry	4-10	40.0	+ 8.75
J Carroll	16-120	13.3	- 42.25	J Berry	16-84	19.0	- 6.25
M Birch	15-117	12.8	- 27.27	M H Easterby	8-50	16.0	- 3.50
A Culhane	12-62	19.4	+ 33.75	R M Whitaker	5-19	26.3	+ 27.50
D Nicholls	10-71	14.1	- 7.86	B Beasley	1-1	100.0	+ 0.73
S Perks	8-52	15.4	- 6.24	R Hollinshead	5-32	15.6	- 0.62
B Raymond	7-44	15.9	- 8.95	B A McMahon	2-6	33.3	+ 10.00
K Fallon	7-66	10.6	- 3.50	E J Alston	2-4	50.0	+ 22.50
J Lowe	7-115	6.1	- 41.25	S G Norton	3-28	10.7	+ 7.25
P Robinson	6-14	42.9	+ 14.08	M H Tompkins	3-9	33.3	+ 4.00

How the Favourites Fared

Non-handicaps	W-R	Per cent	£1 Level Stake	Handicaps	W-R	Per cent	£1 Level Stake
2-y-o	15-60	25.0	- 23.95	2-y-o	0-1	-	- 1.00
3-y-o	33-60	55.0	+ 14.38	3-y-o	9-38	23.7	- 12.74
Weight-for-age	14-35	40.0	+ 2.85	All-aged	22-86	25.6	- 12.86
Totals	62-155	40.0	- 6.72	Totals	31-125	24.8	- 26.60
All favs	93-280	33.2	- 33.32				

Leading Trainers by Month at Carlisle

March/Apr	Total W-R	Non-handicaps 2-y-o	3-y-o+	Handicaps 2-y-o	3-y-o+	Per cent	£1 Level Stake
J Berry	6-21	4-7	2-10	0-0	0-4	28.6	+ 1.00
M H Easterby	4-14	1-2	1-7	0-0	2-5	28.6	+ 13.50
M R Stoute	3-5	0-0	3-5	0-0	0-0	60.0	+ 0.83
J W Watts	3-15	0-1	2-8	0-0	1-6	20.0	+ 14.33
S G Norton	3-16	0-3	3-10	0-0	0-3	18.8	+ 23.00

May	Total W-R	Non-handicaps 2-y-o	3-y-o+	Handicaps 2-y-o	3-y-o+	Per cent	£1 Level Stake
M H Tompkins	5-19	1-4	1-6	0-0	3-9	26.3	+ 3.35
J Berry	5-27	3-16	2-8	0-0	0-3	18.5	+ 22.75
M S Johnston	4-13	1-2	1-5	0-0	2-6	30.8	+ 18.50
Sir M Prescott	4-18	1-3	1-7	0-0	2-8	22.2	+ 5.00
F H Lee	3-10	0-1	0-0	0-0	3-9	30.0	+ 3.38

June	Total W-R	Non-handicaps 2-y-o	3-y-o+	Handicaps 2-y-o	3-y-o+	Per cent	£1 Level Stake
J Berry	9-42	4-22	1-10	0-0	4-10	21.4	+ 6.50
Denys Smith	6-27	1-5	2-5	0-0	3-17	22.2	+ 20.00
J W Watts	5-16	0-2	1-6	0-0	4-8	31.3	+ 26.50
S G Norton	5-28	1-8	2-8	0-0	2-12	17.9	- 8.75
R Hollinshead	5-45	1-7	2-12	0-0	2-26	11.1	- 0.75

July	Total W-R	Non-handicaps 2-y-o	3-y-o+	Handicaps 2-y-o	3-y-o+	Per cent	£1 Level Stake
J Berry	3-9	1-3	1-2	0-0	1-4	33.3	+ 5.50
J L Dunlop	2-2	1-1	0-0	0-0	1-1	100.0	+ 3.00
O Brennan	1-1	0-0	0-0	0-0	1-1	100.0	+ 3.50
C R Nelson	1-1	0-0	1-1	0-0	0-0	100.0	+ 1.75
J A Glover	1-1	1-1	0-0	0-0	0-0	100.0	+ 2.25

September	Total W-R	Non-handicaps 2-y-o	3-y-o+	Handicaps 2-y-o	3-y-o+	Per cent	£1 Level Stake
J G FitzGerald	2-2	2-2	0-0	0-0	0-0	100.0	+ 8.50
J Berry	2-13	2-10	0-1	0-0	0-2	15.4	+ 3.00
B R Cambidge	1-1	0-0	0-0	0-0	1-1	100.0	+ 3.50
D Morley	1-1	0-0	1-1	0-0	0-0	100.0	+ 1.10
A Smith	1-1	0-0	0-0	0-0	1-1	100.0	+ 11.00

Oct/Nov	Total W-R	Non-handicaps 2-y-o	3-y-o+	Handicaps 2-y-o	3-y-o+	Per cent	£1 Level Stake
H Thomson Jones	2-3	1-1	1-1	0-0	0-1	66.7	- 0.19
S R Bowring	1-1	0-0	0-0	0-0	1-1	100.0	+ 8.00
J G FitzGerald	1-2	0-0	0-0	0-0	1-2	50.0	+ 9.00
B W Hills	1-2	1-1	0-0	0-0	0-1	50.0	+ 3.50
R O'Leary	1-3	0-2	0-0	1-1	0-0	33.3	+ 7.00

CATTERICK (Group 4)

Leading Trainers 1988-92

	Total W-R	Non-handicaps 2-y-o	3-y-o+	Handicaps 2-y-o	3-y-o+	Per cent	£1 Level Stake
J Berry	32-186	23-103	6-27	1-13	2-43	17.2	- 20.59
T D Barron	24-138	6-33	3-19	2-10	13-76	17.4	+ 10.11
B W Hills	17-48	1-5	15-37	0-0	1-6	35.4	+ 23.53
M H Easterby	17-150	5-54	4-28	2-6	6-62	11.3	- 84.11
R M Whitaker	15-107	2-25	3-28	0-3	10-51	14.0	- 17.37
Sir M Prescott	13-53	7-22	4-14	0-1	2-16	24.5	- 3.70
H R A Cecil	11-21	1-1	10-20	0-0	0-0	52.4	+ 11.58
M R Stoute	10-32	2-5	8-26	0-1	0-0	31.3	+ 2.66
M W Easterby	9-89	4-34	0-13	0-5	5-37	10.1	- 26.77
N A Callaghan	8-19	5-6	2-9	1-1	0-3	42.1	+ 24.75
J H M Gosden	8-21	1-2	6-15	0-1	1-3	38.1	+ 13.31
L M Cumani	8-22	0-3	8-18	0-0	0-1	36.4	- 8.92
Mrs G R Reveley	8-41	0-8	4-11	0-1	4-21	19.5	- 6.10
D Morley	8-66	0-8	2-21	0-1	6-36	12.1	- 30.75
G Wragg	7-25	1-2	5-21	0-0	1-2	28.0	+ 20.00
M H Tompkins	7-31	5-13	1-6	0-3	1-9	22.6	+ 6.48
M P Naughton	7-62	0-3	0-13	0-0	7-46	11.3	- 15.96
R J R Williams	6-16	2-3	2-8	0-0	2-5	37.5	+ 15.62
P F I Cole	6-28	3-11	2-12	0-0	1-5	21.4	- 13.04
Capt J Wilson	6-53	1-9	0-5	0-2	5-37	11.3	+ 49.38
S G Norton	6-65	0-21	2-26	0-3	4-15	9.2	- 33.38
Mrs J Ramsden	6-84	2-20	0-8	0-3	4-53	7.1	- 54.63

Leading Jockeys

	Total W-R	Per cent	£1 Level Stake	Best Trainer	W-R	Per cent	£1 Level Stake
M Birch	28-192	14.6	- 52.76	M H Easterby	11-80	13.8	- 40.26
J Carroll	27-162	16.7	- 31.74	J Berry	21-118	17.8	- 27.49
K Darley	27-193	14.0	- 56.06	M W Easterby	6-26	23.1	+ 18.73
G Duffield	21-148	14.2	- 46.12	Sir M Prescott	10-42	23.8	- 5.82
D McKeown	14-144	9.7	- 87.98	R M Whitaker	4-10	40.0	+ 6.83
J Lowe	14-165	8.5	- 46.37	Sir M Prescott	3-4	75.0	+ 9.13
J Fortune	12-81	14.8	+ 28.30	L M Cumani	3-6	50.0	- 0.95
N Connorton	11-81	13.6	- 30.98	R M Whitaker	3-4	75.0	+ 11.10
Alex Greaves	10-55	18.2	+ 18.88	T D Barron	10-53	18.9	+ 20.88
J Fanning	10-94	10.6	- 0.26	T D Barron	3-7	42.9	+ 10.00
M Hills	9-34	26.5	+ 16.02	B W Hills	3-8	37.5	+ 3.88
W Ryan	9-54	16.7	- 15.95	H R A Cecil	7-11	63.6	+ 12.17

How the Favourites Fared

Non-handicaps	W-R	Per cent	£1 Level Stake	Handicaps	W-R	Per cent	£1 Level Stake
2-y-o	45-126	35.7	- 35.34	2-y-o	4-12	33.3	- 2.12
3-y-o	42-88	47.7	- 5.97	3-y-o	17-47	36.2	+ 4.76
Weight-for-age	26-55	47.3	- 6.28	All-aged	36-130	27.7	- 28.24
Totals	113-269	42.0	- 47.59	Totals	57-189	30.2	- 25.60
All favs	170-458	37.1	- 73.19				

442

Leading Trainers by Month at Catterick

March/Apr

	Total W-R	Non-handicaps 2-y-o	3-y-o+	Handicaps 2-y-o	3-y-o+	Per cent	£1 Level Stake
J Berry	10-38	7-16	2-6	0-0	1-16	26.3	+ 3.32
T D Barron	8-32	0-8	0-6	0-0	8-18	25.0	+ 1.16
G Wragg	2-3	0-0	2-3	0-0	0-0	66.7	+ 4.50
M Bell	2-5	0-2	2-3	0-0	0-0	40.0	+ 9.25
S G Norton	2-6	0-0	1-5	0-0	1-1	33.3	+ 6.50

May

	Total W-R	Non-handicaps 2-y-o	3-y-o+	Handicaps 2-y-o	3-y-o+	Per cent	£1 Level Stake
J Berry	4-10	4-7	0-2	0-0	0-1	40.0	+ 11.00
N A Callaghan	2-3	1-1	1-2	0-0	0-0	66.7	+ 18.50
M R Stoute	2-3	0-0	2-3	0-0	0-0	66.7	+ 3.33
R M Whitaker	2-9	0-1	1-4	0-0	1-4	22.2	+ 2.50
T D Barron	2-12	1-2	0-1	0-0	1-9	16.7	- 3.80

June

	Total W-R	Non-handicaps 2-y-o	3-y-o+	Handicaps 2-y-o	3-y-o+	Per cent	£1 Level Stake
P F I Cole	5-14	2-4	2-6	0-0	1-4	35.7	- 0.04
J Berry	5-25	3-12	2-7	0-0	0-6	20.0	- 5.47
B W Hills	4-8	0-0	4-8	0-0	0-0	50.0	+ 8.10
L M Cumani	3-3	0-0	3-3	0-0	0-0	100.0	+ 1.69
S G Norton	3-7	0-2	1-2	0-0	2-3	42.9	+ 7.13

July

	Total W-R	Non-handicaps 2-y-o	3-y-o+	Handicaps 2-y-o	3-y-o+	Per cent	£1 Level Stake
M H Easterby	11-56	3-18	3-11	0-0	5-27	19.6	- 18.03
J Berry	7-42	5-29	2-8	0-0	0-5	16.7	- 14.19
B W Hills	6-11	0-0	6-11	0-0	0-0	54.5	+ 17.19
L M Cumani	5-9	0-0	5-9	0-0	0-0	55.6	- 0.61
Sir M Prescott	5-14	3-5	1-5	0-0	1-4	35.7	- 1.18

August

	Total W-R	Non-handicaps 2-y-o	3-y-o+	Handicaps 2-y-o	3-y-o+	Per cent	£1 Level Stake
N Tinkler	3-3	0-0	3-3	0-0	0-0	100.0	+ 1.06
Sir M Prescott	3-11	2-6	1-1	0-1	0-3	27.3	- 1.15
R M Whitaker	3-12	0-3	0-3	0-1	3-5	25.0	+ 19.10
T D Barron	3-14	1-4	0-1	1-2	1-7	21.4	+ 13.00
N A Callaghan	2-3	1-1	0-1	1-1	0-0	66.7	+ 3.00

September

	Total W-R	Non-handicaps 2-y-o	3-y-o+	Handicaps 2-y-o	3-y-o+	Per cent	£1 Level Stake
H Thomson Jones	2-2	0-0	2-2	0-0	0-0	100.0	+ 7.50
E J Alston	2-3	0-0	0-0	1-1	1-2	66.7	+ 20.00
J H M Gosden	2-3	0-0	2-2	0-1	0-0	66.7	+ 5.25
R J R Williams	2-4	0-0	2-4	0-0	0-0	50.0	+ 12.00
Mrs G R Reveley	2-4	0-0	0-0	0-1	2-3	50.0	+ 2.38

Oct/Nov

	Total W-R	Non-handicaps 2-y-o	3-y-o+	Handicaps 2-y-o	3-y-o+	Per cent	£1 Level Stake
H R A Cecil	5-8	1-1	4-7	0-0	0-0	62.5	+ 8.50
T D Barron	5-20	2-8	1-1	0-2	2-9	25.0	+ 20.88
J Berry	4-35	4-24	0-1	0-3	0-7	11.4	- 9.25
R W Armstrong	3-6	1-3	1-2	0-0	1-1	50.0	+ 15.41
J H M Gosden	3-9	1-2	2-6	0-0	0-1	33.3	- 2.19

CHEPSTOW (Group 3)

Leading Trainers 1988-92

	Total W-R	Non-handicaps 2-y-o	3-y-o+	Handicaps 2-y-o	3-y-o+	Per cent	£1 Level Stake
R Hannon	16-141	5-53	4-28	1-10	6-50	11.3	- 42.59
R J Hodges	14-106	0-4	1-18	0-1	13-83	13.2	+ 1.96
P F I Cole	12-76	6-30	2-22	0-1	4-23	15.8	- 11.25
L M Cumani	10-20	0-0	9-16	1-1	0-3	50.0	+ 1.47
I A Balding	10-50	2-17	3-14	0-1	5-18	20.0	+ 36.98
B W Hills	9-50	1-8	7-26	0-2	1-14	18.0	+ 13.30
H R A Cecil	8-17	1-3	4-10	0-0	3-4	47.1	+ 11.73
H Candy	8-48	1-5	3-16	0-1	4-26	16.7	+ 30.00
H Thomson Jones	7-20	1-4	2-8	1-1	3-7	35.0	+ 31.90
R F J Houghton	6-27	3-8	2-11	0-1	1-7	22.2	+ 14.50
J Berry	6-28	2-10	3-11	0-2	1-5	21.4	- 0.17
M C Pipe	6-28	0-3	0-9	0-0	6-16	21.4	+ 37.13
G Lewis	6-39	0-4	2-10	1-6	3-19	15.4	- 15.13
J L Dunlop	6-53	1-22	3-14	0-0	2-17	11.3	- 20.58
Lord Huntingdon	5-21	0-3	4-11	0-0	1-7	23.8	+ 14.75
M A Jarvis	5-29	1-7	3-11	0-1	1-10	17.2	- 2.43
P J Makin	5-31	1-5	0-13	0-1	4-12	16.1	+ 12.50
D Murray Smith	5-32	1-10	2-9	0-0	2-13	15.6	+ 12.00
P T Walwyn	5-35	0-13	2-13	0-1	3-8	14.3	- 6.27
G Harwood	5-37	2-13	2-12	0-0	1-12	13.5	- 22.87
R Hollinshead	5-42	1-5	0-11	0-2	4-24	11.9	+ 15.00
C J Hill	5-73	1-8	1-23	0-0	3-42	6.8	- 47.25

Leading Jockeys

	Total W-R	Per cent	£1 Level Stake	Best Trainer	W-R	Per cent	£1 Level Stake
J Williams	14-148	9.5	+ 48.83	B R Millman	2-7	28.6	+ 77.00
J Reid	13-97	13.4	- 22.32	J L Dunlop	2-4	50.0	+ 0.18
M Roberts	12-37	32.4	+ 24.52	M C Pipe	3-3	100.0	+ 8.13
T Sprake	10-55	18.2	+ 29.88	R J Hodges	7-30	23.3	+ 19.13
L Dettori	9-35	25.7	- 6.65	L M Cumani	7-11	63.6	+ 6.10
W Carson	9-54	16.7	- 18.06	M R Stoute	2-2	100.0	+ 1.06
T Quinn	9-90	10.0	- 27.84	P F I Cole	4-35	11.4	- 14.75
Pat Eddery	8-39	20.5	- 6.92	R Lee	1-1	100.0	+ 7.00
T Williams	8-117	6.8	- 46.62	D R Laing	2-20	10.0	- 10.50
A Clark	7-73	9.6	- 30.59	J L Dunlop	2-5	40.0	+ 9.00
C Rutter	7-89	7.9	- 43.50	H Candy	3-14	21.4	+ 13.00
R Wernham	6-26	23.1	+ 33.00	D Murray Smith	5-19	26.3	+ 25.00

How the Favourites Fared

Non-handicaps	W-R	Per cent	£1 Level Stake	Handicaps	W-R	Per cent	£1 Level Stake
2-y-o	14-58	24.1	- 23.71	2-y-o	4-12	33.3	+ 2.50
3-y-o	29-57	50.9	- 0.65	3-y-o	7-22	31.8	+ 2.21
Weight-for-age	30-52	57.7	+ 6.42	All-aged	38-116	32.8	+ 17.78
Totals	73-167	43.7	- 17.94	Totals	49-150	32.7	+ 22.49
All favs	122-317	38.5	+ 4.55				

Leading Trainers by Month at Chepstow

May	Total	Non-handicaps		Handicaps		Per	£1 Level
	W-R	2-y-o	3-y-o+	2-y-o	3-y-o+	cent	Stake
R J Hodges	5-17	0-0	0-0	0-0	5-17	29.4	+ 12.13
H Thomson Jones	2-4	0-0	2-3	0-0	0-1	50.0	- 0.10
R F J Houghton	2-5	1-2	1-3	0-0	0-0	40.0	+ 5.00
J L Dunlop	2-7	0-0	2-6	0-0	0-1	28.6	- 2.83
C J Hill	2-20	0-2	1-5	0-0	1-13	10.0	- 8.50

June	Total	Non-handicaps		Handicaps		Per	£1 Level
	W-R	2-y-o	3-y-o+	2-y-o	3-y-o+	cent	Stake
J Berry	4-8	1-4	3-4	0-0	0-0	50.0	+ 0.92
P F I Cole	4-17	3-6	0-4	0-0	1-7	23.5	+ 0.50
P T Walwyn	3-9	0-3	0-1	0-0	3-5	33.3	+ 16.50
D A Wilson	3-10	0-0	0-2	0-0	3-8	30.0	+ 16.50
D Murray Smith	3-10	1-3	0-1	0-0	2-6	30.0	+ 11.00

July	Total	Non-handicaps		Handicaps		Per	£1 Level
	W-R	2-y-o	3-y-o+	2-y-o	3-y-o+	cent	Stake
R Hannon	6-26	2-7	2-9	1-2	1-8	23.1	- 3.09
R J Hodges	5-25	0-1	0-6	0-0	5-18	20.0	+ 17.33
H R A Cecil	4-7	0-0	4-7	0-0	0-0	57.1	- 1.52
L M Cumani	4-8	0-0	4-8	0-0	0-0	50.0	+ 2.03
P F I Cole	4-16	1-2	0-8	0-0	3-6	25.0	+ 10.25

August	Total	Non-handicaps		Handicaps		Per	£1 Level
	W-R	2-y-o	3-y-o+	2-y-o	3-y-o+	cent	Stake
L M Cumani	4-5	0-0	3-3	1-1	0-1	80.0	+ 3.99
I A Balding	4-13	2-8	1-1	0-0	1-4	30.8	+ 36.73
G Harwood	2-6	2-4	0-1	0-0	0-1	33.3	+ 0.41
M R Stoute	2-7	2-3	0-1	0-1	0-2	28.6	+ 5.62
B R Millman	2-7	1-1	0-1	0-1	1-4	28.6	+ 72.00

September	Total	Non-handicaps		Handicaps		Per	£1 Level
	W-R	2-y-o	3-y-o+	2-y-o	3-y-o+	cent	Stake
P J Makin	3-7	1-1	0-3	0-0	2-3	42.9	+ 29.75
B W Hills	2-3	0-0	2-2	0-1	0-0	66.7	+ 1.82
W Carter	2-4	2-2	0-0	0-0	0-2	50.0	+164.00
L M Cumani	2-5	0-0	2-5	0-0	0-0	40.0	- 2.55
I A Balding	2-9	0-2	1-4	0-0	1-3	22.2	- 0.25

Oct/Nov	Total	Non-handicaps		Handicaps		Per	£1 Level
	W-R	2-y-o	3-y-o+	2-y-o	3-y-o+	cent	Stake
J H M Gosden	3-9	1-5	1-1	0-0	1-3	33.3	+ 6.25
B W Hills	3-13	1-5	1-3	0-0	1-5	23.1	+ 28.75
M A Jarvis	3-13	1-5	1-4	0-1	1-3	23.1	+ 8.00
R Hannon	3-46	1-21	1-11	0-2	1-12	6.5	- 16.00
H R A Cecil	2-5	1-1	0-2	0-0	1-2	40.0	+ 7.50

CHESTER (Group 2)

Leading Trainers 1988-92

	Total W-R	Non-handicaps 2-y-o	3-y-o+	Handicaps 2-y-o	3-y-o+	Per cent	£1 Level Stake
B W Hills	25-78	6-15	13-40	1-2	5-21	32.1	+ 31.59
M R Stoute	13-44	5-7	6-18	0-1	2-18	29.5	- 7.87
S G Norton	12-61	4-22	1-11	1-3	6-25	19.7	+ 33.32
J H M Gosden	11-38	3-5	3-14	0-0	5-19	28.9	+ 12.73
B Hanbury	10-34	3-8	4-7	0-2	3-17	29.4	+ 13.58
A Bailey	10-53	1-13	4-10	0-2	5-28	18.9	+ 54.67
C E Brittain	10-71	5-20	3-20	0-2	2-29	14.1	+ 2.62
J Berry	10-104	6-37	1-7	0-7	3-53	9.6	- 26.13
H R A Cecil	9-29	3-6	5-16	0-0	1-7	31.0	- 4.35
R Hannon	8-35	4-13	1-6	2-6	1-10	22.9	- 5.81
F H Lee	8-46	2-12	0-4	0-3	6-27	17.4	+ 14.50
B A McMahon	8-63	0-12	0-6	0-4	8-41	12.7	+ 23.96
R Hollinshead	8-124	4-37	2-21	0-6	2-60	6.5	- 47.75
M H Easterby	6-66	2-20	0-5	0-7	4-34	9.1	- 20.25
G Wragg	5-28	0-3	4-16	0-1	1-8	17.9	- 4.50
R M Whitaker	5-32	0-4	0-0	0-1	5-27	15.6	+ 16.00
P F I Cole	5-39	5-15	0-13	0-1	0-10	12.8	- 25.47
P A Kelleway	4-11	1-2	2-5	0-0	1-4	36.4	+ 25.75
G Lewis	4-13	3-5	0-0	0-1	1-7	30.8	+ 0.41
W R Hern	4-22	0-2	3-17	1-1	0-2	18.2	- 11.48
A C Stewart	3-7	0-0	2-4	0-0	1-3	42.9	+ 4.48
J D Bethell	3-11	0-0	0-0	0-0	3-11	27.3	+ 9.38

Leading Jockeys

	Total W-R	Per cent	£1 Level Stake		Best Trainer	W-R	Per cent	£1 Level Stake
Pat Eddery	22-75	29.3	+ 5.10		B W Hills	6-13	46.2	+ 4.58
M Roberts	15-76	19.7	+ 11.64		C E Brittain	5-30	16.7	+ 20.75
M Hills	13-72	18.1	- 5.59		B W Hills	8-33	24.2	- 8.59
W R Swinburn	13-74	17.6	- 22.99		M R Stoute	6-27	22.2	- 13.06
A Munro	13-78	16.7	- 16.39		C E Brittain	2-4	50.0	+ 0.20
W Carson	13-81	16.0	- 5.49		W R Hern	4-18	22.2	- 7.49
S Cauthen	10-45	22.2	- 15.84		H R A Cecil	4-11	36.4	- 2.68
J Lowe	10-61	16.4	+ 13.13		S G Norton	4-12	33.3	+ 14.50
Paul Eddery	9-52	17.3	- 5.61		G Lewis	3-6	50.0	+ 4.66
D Holland	8-38	21.1	+ 16.50		B W Hills	5-12	41.7	+ 24.50
G Carter	8-63	12.7	0.00		J Berry	2-11	18.2	+ 12.00
T Quinn	7-33	21.2	- 4.67		P F I Cole	3-19	15.8	- 10.25

How the Favourites Fared

Non-handicaps	W-R	Per cent	£1 Level Stake	Handicaps	W-R	Per cent	£1 Level Stake
2-y-o	34-75	45.3	- 6.03	2-y-o	4-13	30.8	- 2.62
3-y-o	22-47	46.8	- 0.39	3-y-o	11-33	33.3	+ 6.13
Weight-for-age	7-18	38.9	- 4.70	All-aged	18-88	20.5	- 19.98
Totals	63-140	45.0	- 11.12	Totals	33-134	24.6	- 16.47
All favs	96-274	35.0	- 27.59				

Leading Trainers by Month at Chester

May	Total W-R	Non-handicaps 2-y-o	3-y-o+	Handicaps 2-y-o	3-y-o+	Per cent	£1 Level Stake
B W Hills	9-36	0-2	7-25	0-0	2-9	25.0	+ 2.85
H R A Cecil	5-12	0-0	5-11	0-0	0-1	41.7	+ 1.84
J H M Gosden	5-13	0-0	1-7	0-0	4-6	38.5	+ 16.00
M R Stoute	5-19	0-0	4-13	0-0	1-6	26.3	- 7.46
J Berry	5-31	4-12	0-1	0-0	1-18	16.1	- 4.75

June	Total W-R	Non-handicaps 2-y-o	3-y-o+	Handicaps 2-y-o	3-y-o+	Per cent	£1 Level Stake
P F I Cole	3-4	3-3	0-0	0-0	0-1	75.0	+ 4.66
B W Hills	3-4	1-1	1-1	0-0	1-2	75.0	+ 1.27
B A McMahon	3-10	0-4	0-1	0-0	3-5	30.0	+ 4.63
S G Norton	3-10	2-4	0-3	0-0	1-3	30.0	+ 5.25
A Bailey	2-4	0-2	2-2	0-0	0-0	50.0	+ 2.67

July	Total W-R	Non-handicaps 2-y-o	3-y-o+	Handicaps 2-y-o	3-y-o+	Per cent	£1 Level Stake
G Lewis	4-6	3-3	0-0	0-0	1-3	66.7	+ 7.41
J H M Gosden	4-7	2-2	2-3	0-0	0-2	57.1	+ 6.13
A Bailey	4-12	1-5	1-1	0-0	2-6	33.3	+ 27.50
R M Whitaker	3-5	0-0	0-0	0-0	3-5	60.0	+ 11.00
S G Norton	3-11	2-5	0-3	0-0	1-3	27.3	+ 9.57

August	Total W-R	Non-handicaps 2-y-o	3-y-o+	Handicaps 2-y-o	3-y-o+	Per cent	£1 Level Stake
B W Hills	6-15	2-6	3-6	0-1	1-2	40.0	+ 5.97
S G Norton	3-10	0-3	0-0	0-2	3-5	30.0	+ 28.00
R Hollinshead	3-18	1-4	1-2	0-2	1-10	16.7	+ 22.00
G Wragg	2-5	0-0	2-2	0-1	0-2	40.0	+ 3.50
R Hannon	2-6	0-2	0-1	2-3	0-0	33.3	- 1.13

September	Total W-R	Non-handicaps 2-y-o	3-y-o+	Handicaps 2-y-o	3-y-o+	Per cent	£1 Level Stake
M R Stoute	3-7	2-2	1-3	0-0	0-2	42.9	+ 5.23
B Hanbury	2-4	2-2	0-0	0-1	0-1	50.0	+ 4.00
W R Hern	2-5	0-1	1-2	1-1	0-1	40.0	+ 2.08
G Wragg	1-1	0-0	1-1	0-0	0-0	100.0	+ 1.00
Mrs L Piggott	1-1	0-0	1-1	0-0	0-0	100.0	+ 7.50

Oct/Nov	Total W-R	Non-handicaps 2-y-o	3-y-o+	Handicaps 2-y-o	3-y-o+	Per cent	£1 Level Stake
B W Hills	6-14	3-5	1-2	1-1	1-6	42.9	+ 28.00
C E Brittain	3-15	3-6	0-1	0-2	0-6	20.0	- 4.80
M R Stoute	2-6	2-3	0-0	0-1	0-2	33.3	- 0.83
J W Watts	2-6	0-1	0-0	1-1	1-4	33.3	+ 6.50
M J Camacho	2-8	1-1	0-1	0-1	1-5	25.0	+ 1.63

DONCASTER (Group 1)

Leading Trainers 1988-92

	Total W-R	Non-handicaps 2-y-o	3-y-o+	Handicaps 2-y-o	3-y-o+	Per cent	£1 Level Stake
H R A Cecil	34-93	15-26	18-55	0-0	1-12	36.6	+ 19.59
B W Hills	25-126	5-37	16-53	0-4	4-32	19.8	- 13.28
J H M Gosden	22-78	9-24	6-24	0-1	7-29	28.2	+ 33.15
R Hannon	20-168	9-46	4-37	3-23	4-62	11.9	- 49.50
M R Stoute	18-89	8-34	6-32	2-5	2-18	20.2	+ 0.12
L M Cumani	15-67	0-11	9-32	0-1	6-23	22.4	- 10.24
J Berry	15-114	10-61	2-13	0-9	3-31	13.2	- 3.36
Mrs J Ramsden	14-132	2-21	3-17	3-9	6-85	10.6	- 44.81
M H Easterby	12-158	2-40	2-15	2-10	6-93	7.6	- 61.50
J L Dunlop	9-73	1-11	2-26	1-4	5-32	12.3	- 8.58
M S Johnston	9-89	2-21	1-11	0-10	6-47	10.1	+ 5.50
C E Brittain	9-144	0-29	4-44	1-8	4-63	6.3	- 57.29
R Hollinshead	9-210	1-52	2-42	0-14	6-102	4.3	-110.04
R W Armstrong	8-42	4-10	1-10	0-3	3-19	19.0	+ 12.11
G Wragg	8-47	2-5	1-22	0-0	5-20	17.0	- 6.33
M A Jarvis	8-53	1-13	2-11	1-5	4-24	15.1	- 23.05
F H Lee	8-87	1-12	0-7	0-14	7-54	9.2	- 10.38
A C Stewart	7-46	1-8	2-13	0-1	4-24	15.2	- 5.50
Mrs G R Reveley	7-52	0-8	0-5	0-3	7-36	13.5	- 5.25
I A Balding	7-55	1-9	2-16	0-2	4-28	12.7	+ 6.03
R M Whitaker	7-88	2-11	2-11	0-7	3-59	8.0	- 22.50
M W Easterby	7-99	3-37	1-11	0-10	3-41	7.1	- 37.03

Leading Jockeys

	Total W-R	Per cent	£1 Level Stake	Best Trainer	W-R	Per cent	£1 Level Stake
Pat Eddery	42-195	21.5	- 5.88	J H M Gosden	6-11	54.5	+ 9.43
W Carson	30-226	13.3	- 79.61	N A Graham	5-15	33.3	+ 8.13
S Cauthen	27-131	20.6	- 29.18	H R A Cecil	11-20	55.0	+ 7.85
M Roberts	27-196	13.8	- 35.96	A C Stewart	6-28	21.4	+ 7.50
B Raymond	25-167	15.0	+ 57.25	B Hanbury	4-15	26.7	+ 55.50
R Cochrane	23-151	15.2	+ 5.92	L M Cumani	6-11	54.5	+ 16.20
K Darley	19-161	11.8	- 22.43	Mrs G R Reveley	3-12	25.0	+ 1.25
W Ryan	18-133	13.5	- 35.97	H R A Cecil	10-32	31.3	+ 5.77
M Hills	17-136	12.5	- 5.59	B W Hills	9-62	14.5	- 9.09
A Munro	16-138	11.6	+ 19.33	Mrs J Ramsden	3-23	13.0	+ 3.00
J Lowe	15-223	6.7	- 99.55	Mrs G R Reveley	4-21	19.0	+ 12.50
W R Swinburn	14-144	9.7	- 86.29	M R Stoute	6-35	17.1	- 9.47

How the Favourites Fared

Non-handicaps	W-R	Per cent	£1 Level Stake	Handicaps	W-R	Per cent	£1 Level Stake
2-y-o	61-146	41.8	- 12.85	2-y-o	9-26	34.6	+ 11.50
3-y-o	18-63	28.6	- 24.20	3-y-o	16-64	25.0	- 10.86
Weight-for-age	37-86	43.0	- 1.66	All-aged	58-192	30.2	+ 11.99
Totals	116-295	39.3	- 38.71	Totals	83-282	29.4	+ 12.63
All favs	199-577	34.5	- 26.08				

Leading Trainers by Month at Doncaster

March/Apr	Total W-R	Non-handicaps 2-y-o	3-y-o+	Handicaps 2-y-o	3-y-o+	Per cent	£1 Level Stake
J Berry	8-32	4-16	2-2	0-0	2-14	25.0	+ 45.73
B W Hills	6-20	1-3	5-14	0-0	0-3	30.0	+ 6.03
C E Brittain	4-39	0-0	2-20	0-0	2-19	10.3	- 5.04
W A O'Gorman	3-10	2-4	1-5	0-0	0-1	30.0	+ 4.00
Mrs J Ramsden	3-32	0-0	1-8	0-0	2-24	9.4	- 8.50

May	Total W-R	Non-handicaps 2-y-o	3-y-o+	Handicaps 2-y-o	3-y-o+	Per cent	£1 Level Stake
H R A Cecil	8-16	2-2	6-14	0-0	0-0	50.0	+ 4.37
M R Stoute	5-11	1-1	2-6	0-0	2-4	45.5	+ 13.83
B W Hills	5-13	1-3	4-6	0-0	0-4	38.5	+ 5.54
F H Lee	4-20	1-3	0-1	0-0	3-16	20.0	+ 16.00
M W Easterby	4-22	2-10	0-2	0-0	2-10	18.2	+ 10.48

June	Total W-R	Non-handicaps 2-y-o	3-y-o+	Handicaps 2-y-o	3-y-o+	Per cent	£1 Level Stake
G Wragg	4-5	0-0	0-1	0-0	4-4	80.0	+ 22.50
Mrs L Piggott	4-14	2-3	0-6	0-0	2-5	28.6	- 0.90
J H M Gosden	3-5	0-1	2-3	0-0	1-1	60.0	+ 1.80
C W C Elsey	3-7	0-1	0-1	0-0	3-5	42.9	+ 12.13
A C Stewart	3-7	0-0	1-3	0-0	2-4	42.9	+ 5.50

July	Total W-R	Non-handicaps 2-y-o	3-y-o+	Handicaps 2-y-o	3-y-o+	Per cent	£1 Level Stake
H R A Cecil	5-8	3-3	1-4	0-0	1-1	62.5	+ 2.50
L M Cumani	4-6	0-0	2-3	0-0	2-3	66.7	+ 4.61
R Hannon	4-11	3-6	0-1	0-0	1-4	36.4	- 0.75
R Hollinshead	4-27	1-8	1-4	0-0	2-15	14.8	- 6.67
Mrs G R Reveley	3-7	0-2	0-0	0-0	3-5	42.9	+ 16.00

September	Total W-R	Non-handicaps 2-y-o	3-y-o+	Handicaps 2-y-o	3-y-o+	Per cent	£1 Level Stake
H R A Cecil	12-35	5-10	7-20	0-0	0-5	34.3	+ 3.12
R Hannon	9-64	1-18	3-10	2-13	3-23	14.1	+ 2.25
M R Stoute	8-44	4-14	2-15	2-5	0-10	18.2	- 6.18
J H M Gosden	7-25	3-5	2-10	0-0	2-10	28.0	+ 13.83
B W Hills	6-54	1-15	2-18	0-3	3-18	11.1	- 17.47

Oct/Nov	Total W-R	Non-handicaps 2-y-o	3-y-o+	Handicaps 2-y-o	3-y-o+	Per cent	£1 Level Stake
J H M Gosden	10-35	5-15	2-6	0-1	3-13	28.6	+ 27.02
H R A Cecil	7-23	5-10	2-8	0-0	0-5	30.4	+ 10.50
J L Dunlop	5-27	1-7	1-5	0-3	3-12	18.5	+ 6.68
M R Stoute	4-22	3-17	1-4	0-0	0-1	18.2	- 6.54
B W Hills	4-25	2-14	1-6	0-1	1-4	16.0	- 0.50

EDINBURGH (Group 4)

Leading Trainers 1988-92

	Total W-R	Non-handicaps 2-y-o	Non-handicaps 3-y-o+	Handicaps 2-y-o	Handicaps 3-y-o+	Per cent	£1 Level Stake
J Berry	34-154	21-71	8-31	1-8	4-44	22.1	- 11.38
Sir M Prescott	20-77	5-22	8-27	1-3	6-25	26.0	+ 7.85
M P Naughton	16-96	0-2	2-30	0-0	14-64	16.7	+ 72.98
Mrs G R Reveley	11-73	3-12	0-10	0-1	8-50	15.1	- 10.25
D W Chapman	10-127	1-6	0-19	1-3	8-99	7.9	+ 2.00
M H Tompkins	9-21	3-6	2-7	0-1	4-7	42.9	+ 16.65
C Tinkler	9-41	3-11	1-5	0-2	5-23	22.0	+ 10.67
J G FitzGerald	9-43	2-9	2-13	0-2	5-19	20.9	+ 2.08
S G Norton	8-71	3-25	4-25	1-5	0-16	11.3	+ 5.00
J H M Gosden	7-21	2-7	4-11	0-0	1-3	33.3	- 1.73
M J Camacho	7-25	0-4	2-7	1-3	4-11	28.0	+ 8.23
R M Whitaker	7-62	1-9	0-15	1-3	5-35	11.3	- 20.33
T D Barron	7-73	0-16	0-10	2-7	5-40	9.6	- 11.17
F H Lee	6-41	1-9	0-2	0-2	5-28	14.6	- 2.09
M H Easterby	6-43	2-13	2-9	0-1	2-20	14.0	- 25.75
J L Spearing	6-43	1-9	0-7	0-0	5-27	14.0	- 16.63
Denys Smith	6-93	2-21	2-18	0-1	2-53	6.5	- 29.38
B W Hills	5-14	0-2	4-9	0-0	1-3	35.7	+ 0.10
N A Callaghan	5-16	3-5	1-3	0-2	1-6	31.3	+ 34.00
B Hanbury	5-18	1-4	4-11	0-0	0-3	27.8	+ 15.91
P C Haslam	5-18	0-1	1-3	0-0	4-14	27.8	+ 3.32
J W Watts	5-29	1-6	2-10	0-0	2-13	17.2	- 8.30

Leading Jockeys

	Total W-R	Per cent	£1 Level Stake	Best Trainer	W-R	Per cent	£1 Level Stake
G Duffield	32-172	18.6	- 23.58	Sir M Prescott	17-67	25.4	+ 10.11
J Carroll	30-135	22.2	+ 4.27	J Berry	22-83	26.5	- 17.73
K Fallon	23-158	14.6	+ 42.27	J G FitzGerald	7-27	25.9	+ 2.46
K Darley	22-128	17.2	+ 47.70	J Berry	5-14	35.7	+ 11.38
D McKeown	15-160	9.4	- 93.58	J Berry	2-6	33.3	- 0.50
N Connorton	14-100	14.0	+ 31.68	M J Camacho	5-16	31.3	+ 3.48
L Charnock	13-163	8.0	- 47.25	Denys Smith	3-35	8.6	- 4.50
P Burke	10-79	12.7	+ 8.08	C Tinkler	5-15	33.3	+ 15.33
J Fanning	10-98	10.2	+ 40.05	Miss L A Perrat	3-16	18.8	+ 15.05
S Webster	10-106	9.4	+ 5.00	F H Lee	2-6	33.3	+ 10.50
A Munro	9-50	18.0	+ 1.75	N A Callaghan	2-2	100.0	+ 7.00
J Lowe	9-192	4.7	- 144.95	Mrs G R Reveley	4-31	12.9	- 7.70

How the Favourites Fared

Non-handicaps	W-R	Per cent	£1 Level Stake	Handicaps	W-R	Per cent	£1 Level Stake
2-y-o	36-90	40.0	- 18.17	2-y-o	6-9	66.7	+ 11.45
3-y-o	21-39	53.8	+ 4.56	3-y-o	4-20	20.0	- 9.70
Weight-for-age	28-66	42.4	- 4.83	All-aged	47-150	31.3	+ 5.71
Totals	85-195	43.6	- 18.44	Totals	57-179	31.8	+ 7.46
All favs	142-374	38.0	- 10.98				

Leading Trainers by Month at Edinburgh

March/Apr	Total W-R	Non-handicaps 2-y-o	3-y-o+	Handicaps 2-y-o	3-y-o+	Per cent	£1 Level Stake
Sir M Prescott	5-9	0-0	4-5	0-0	1-4	55.6	+ 9.50
J Berry	4-13	3-5	1-5	0-0	0-3	30.8	+ 0.49
J H M Gosden	2-2	0-0	2-2	0-0	0-0	100.0	+ 1.87
M Brittain	2-14	1-4	0-4	0-0	1-6	14.3	- 7.50
M J Camacho	1-1	0-0	0-0	0-0	1-1	100.0	+ 1.38

May	Total W-R	Non-handicaps 2-y-o	3-y-o+	Handicaps 2-y-o	3-y-o+	Per cent	£1 Level Stake
J Berry	5-16	2-5	1-4	0-0	2-7	31.3	+ 15.50
J W Watts	2-2	1-1	1-1	0-0	0-0	100.0	+ 1.20
M Dods	2-2	0-0	0-0	0-0	2-2	100.0	+ 13.10
J G FitzGerald	2-6	0-0	1-3	0-0	1-3	33.3	+ 4.50
M Brittain	2-7	0-2	1-2	0-0	1-3	28.6	+ 17.75

June	Total W-R	Non-handicaps 2-y-o	3-y-o+	Handicaps 2-y-o	3-y-o+	Per cent	£1 Level Stake
J Berry	12-40	7-19	4-9	0-0	1-12	30.0	+ 0.01
Sir M Prescott	6-18	2-3	2-6	0-0	2-9	33.3	+ 7.38
Mrs G R Reveley	6-18	1-2	0-3	0-0	5-13	33.3	+ 24.00
B W Hills	4-9	0-0	3-7	0-0	1-2	44.4	+ 2.60
R M Whitaker	4-18	1-1	0-4	0-0	3-13	22.2	+ 11.60

July	Total W-R	Non-handicaps 2-y-o	3-y-o+	Handicaps 2-y-o	3-y-o+	Per cent	£1 Level Stake
J Berry	7-37	5-19	1-7	1-2	0-9	18.9	- 4.91
M P Naughton	6-20	0-0	1-7	0-0	5-13	30.0	+ 1.88
Sir M Prescott	5-19	0-3	2-8	0-0	3-8	26.3	+ 3.23
F H Lee	3-7	1-2	0-0	0-0	2-5	42.9	+ 3.66
M H Tompkins	3-8	1-3	1-3	0-0	1-2	37.5	+ 8.12

August	Total W-R	Non-handicaps 2-y-o	3-y-o+	Handicaps 2-y-o	3-y-o+	Per cent	£1 Level Stake
M H Easterby	2-4	1-2	0-0	0-0	1-2	50.0	+ 1.33
J Berry	2-6	2-5	0-0	0-0	0-1	33.3	- 1.94
J Etherington	1-1	0-0	1-1	0-0	0-0	100.0	+ 0.40
A N Lee	1-1	0-0	0-0	0-0	1-1	100.0	+ 1.25
N A Graham	1-1	0-0	1-1	0-0	0-0	100.0	+ 0.44

September	Total W-R	Non-handicaps 2-y-o	3-y-o+	Handicaps 2-y-o	3-y-o+	Per cent	£1 Level Stake
M P Naughton	2-7	0-0	0-1	0-0	2-6	28.6	+ 12.50
T D Barron	2-9	0-1	0-0	1-3	1-5	22.2	+ 8.33
Mrs G R Reveley	2-10	1-2	0-1	0-1	1-6	20.0	+ 2.67
N A Callaghan	1-1	1-1	0-0	0-0	0-0	100.0	+ 2.50
W W Haigh	1-1	1-1	0-0	0-0	0-0	100.0	+ 16.00

Oct/Nov	Total W-R	Non-handicaps 2-y-o	3-y-o+	Handicaps 2-y-o	3-y-o+	Per cent	£1 Level Stake
C Tinkler	4-14	0-4	1-2	0-1	3-7	28.6	+ 19.00
Sir M Prescott	4-20	3-13	0-2	1-3	0-2	20.0	- 1.25
M S Johnston	3-15	2-8	0-0	0-0	1-7	20.0	+ 3.50
S G Norton	3-25	1-13	2-5	0-4	0-3	12.0	- 2.00
D W Chapman	3-27	0-1	0-2	1-3	2-21	11.1	+ 10.00

EPSOM (Group 1)

Leading Trainers 1988-92

	Total W-R	Non-handicaps 2-y-o	3-y-o+	Handicaps 2-y-o	3-y-o+	Per cent	£1 Level Stake
R Hannon	12-115	3-28	2-31	1-4	6-52	10.4	- 31.88
P F I Cole	10-62	2-11	2-24	0-0	6-27	16.1	+ 0.58
G Lewis	10-89	3-20	2-17	0-1	5-51	11.2	- 21.92
J Berry	9-36	5-17	1-3	0-0	3-16	25.0	+ 2.03
R Akehurst	9-64	1-6	1-8	0-0	7-50	14.1	+ 5.75
M R Stoute	8-54	1-3	4-31	0-0	3-20	14.8	- 29.46
L M Cumani	7-28	0-0	3-14	0-0	4-14	25.0	+ 8.33
A C Stewart	6-22	0-0	5-13	0-0	1-9	27.3	- 2.17
H R A Cecil	6-24	0-3	5-19	0-0	1-2	25.0	+ 2.08
D R C Elsworth	6-45	0-4	2-23	0-0	4-18	13.3	+ 4.73
C E Brittain	6-62	2-6	2-28	0-2	2-26	9.7	+ 1.00
H Thomson Jones	5-27	0-1	2-8	0-0	3-18	18.5	+ 4.83
B Hanbury	5-30	0-1	2-10	0-1	3-18	16.7	+ 17.00
P T Walwyn	5-33	0-1	1-9	0-0	4-23	15.2	+ 25.50
M McCormack	4-12	0-0	1-2	0-0	3-10	33.3	+ 31.50
J L Dunlop	4-24	1-2	2-9	1-2	0-11	16.7	- 8.63
L G Cottrell	4-39	0-1	0-4	0-0	4-34	10.3	- 7.00
Lord Huntingdon	3-13	1-3	1-3	0-1	1-6	23.1	+ 10.38
H Candy	3-15	0-0	0-4	0-0	3-11	20.0	+ 3.50
B R Millman	3-21	0-2	0-3	0-0	3-16	14.3	0.00
I A Balding	3-27	1-2	1-10	0-1	1-14	11.1	- 1.50
P A Kelleway	3-30	2-5	1-16	0-2	0-7	10.0	- 19.79

Leading Jockeys

	Total W-R	Per cent	£1 Level Stake	Best Trainer	W-R	Per cent	£1 Level Stake
M Roberts	22-136	16.2	+ 21.97	A C Stewart	6-20	30.0	- 0.16
W Carson	19-109	17.4	+ 11.24	J L Dunlop	3-13	23.1	- 3.12
Pat Eddery	18-130	13.8	- 21.46	J Berry	5-17	29.4	- 1.96
R Cochrane	16-81	19.8	+ 20.21	L M Cumani	5-12	41.7	+ 17.08
S Cauthen	13-89	14.6	- 10.64	H R A Cecil	5-9	55.6	+ 9.08
J Reid	11-85	12.9	+ 15.08	M McCormack	2-6	33.3	+ 12.50
T Quinn	10-73	13.7	- 3.00	P F I Cole	6-41	14.6	- 0.25
R Hills	6-43	14.0	- 6.17	H Thomson Jones	4-23	17.4	- 0.17
A Munro	6-45	13.3	+ 31.00	P F I Cole	2-6	33.3	+ 8.00
B Rouse	6-74	8.1	- 39.88	R Hannon	3-33	9.1	- 18.38
W R Swinburn	6-75	8.0	- 50.65	M R Stoute	4-33	12.1	- 23.15
C Asmussen	5-15	33.3	+ 27.13	J Berry	1-1	100.0	+ 7.00

How the Favourites Fared

Non-handicaps	W-R	Per cent	£1 Level Stake	Handicaps	W-R	Per cent	£1 Level Stake
2-y-o	11-34	32.4	- 6.14	2-y-o	1-3	33.3	+ 2.50
3-y-o	21-54	38.9	- 3.53	3-y-o	8-42	19.0	- 11.12
Weight-for-age	7-13	53.8	+ 5.14	All-aged	10-65	15.4	- 31.15
Totals	39-101	38.6	- 4.53	Totals	19-110	17.3	- 39.77
All favs	58-211	27.5	- 44.30				

Leading Trainers by Month at Epsom

March/Apr	Total W-R	Non-handicaps 2-y-o	3-y-o+	Handicaps 2-y-o	3-y-o+	Per cent	£1 Level Stake
H R A Cecil	3-5	0-0	3-5	0-0	0-0	60.0	+ 3.83
J Berry	3-7	2-3	0-0	0-0	1-4	42.9	+ 3.13
P F I Cole	3-16	0-0	0-5	0-0	3-11	18.8	+ 8.50
G Lewis	3-17	2-3	0-2	0-0	1-12	17.6	+ 2.00
M McCormack	2-4	0-0	0-0	0-0	2-4	50.0	+ 15.50

June	Total W-R	Non-handicaps 2-y-o	3-y-o+	Handicaps 2-y-o	3-y-o+	Per cent	£1 Level Stake
L M Cumani	6-26	0-0	2-12	0-0	4-14	23.1	+ 6.58
M R Stoute	6-45	0-1	3-26	0-0	3-18	13.3	- 24.65
C E Brittain	6-48	2-5	2-21	0-0	2-22	12.5	+ 15.00
R Hannon	6-74	3-20	1-21	0-0	2-33	8.1	- 47.38
J Berry	5-23	3-13	0-1	0-0	2-9	21.7	+ 3.41

July	Total W-R	Non-handicaps 2-y-o	3-y-o+	Handicaps 2-y-o	3-y-o+	Per cent	£1 Level Stake
G Lewis	2-5	0-0	0-2	0-0	2-3	40.0	+ 14.50
D R C Elsworth	1-1	0-0	1-1	0-0	0-0	100.0	+ 0.73
P J Makin	1-1	0-0	1-1	0-0	0-0	100.0	+ 14.00
A C Stewart	1-1	0-0	1-1	0-0	0-0	100.0	+ 4.00
Miss B Sanders	1-1	0-0	0-0	0-0	1-1	100.0	+ 4.00

August	Total W-R	Non-handicaps 2-y-o	3-y-o+	Handicaps 2-y-o	3-y-o+	Per cent	£1 Level Stake
P F I Cole	3-10	1-3	1-3	0-0	1-4	30.0	+ 1.83
A C Stewart	2-4	0-0	2-2	0-0	0-2	50.0	- 0.95
R Akehurst	2-12	1-3	0-0	0-0	1-9	16.7	- 2.50
R Hannon	2-13	0-2	0-5	1-2	1-4	15.4	+ 1.50
L M Cumani	1-1	0-0	1-1	0-0	0-0	100.0	+ 2.75

September	Total W-R	Non-handicaps 2-y-o	3-y-o+	Handicaps 2-y-o	3-y-o+	Per cent	£1 Level Stake
H Candy	1-1	0-0	0-0	0-0	1-1	100.0	+ 5.00
J L Dunlop	1-1	0-0	0-0	1-1	0-0	100.0	+ 4.50
D R C Elsworth	1-1	0-0	0-0	0-0	1-1	100.0	+ 6.50
J Berry	1-2	0-0	1-1	0-0	0-1	50.0	- 0.50
Lord Huntingdon	1-2	0-0	1-1	0-1	0-0	50.0	+ 15.00

FOLKESTONE (Group 4)

Leading Trainers 1988-92

	Total W-R	Non-handicaps 2-y-o	Non-handicaps 3-y-o+	Handicaps 2-y-o	Handicaps 3-y-o+	Per cent	£1 Level Stake
G Harwood	25-67	6-13	15-38	0-0	4-16	37.3	+ 38.00
R Hannon	16-140	3-46	6-25	1-9	6-60	11.4	- 31.08
P F I Cole	13-66	4-9	3-23	1-4	5-30	19.7	- 6.38
Mrs L Piggott	12-56	0-4	9-27	0-1	3-24	21.4	+ 7.38
N A Callaghan	10-42	1-6	3-12	2-7	4-17	23.8	+ 14.73
R Akehurst	9-78	2-10	3-21	0-2	4-45	11.5	+ 7.63
L G Cottrell	8-37	1-7	1-5	0-1	6-24	21.6	+ 33.25
D R C Elsworth	8-45	1-13	3-20	1-1	3-11	17.8	+ 2.43
M R Stoute	7-30	2-10	5-19	0-0	0-1	23.3	- 1.68
D Morley	7-51	2-9	4-20	0-1	1-21	13.7	+ 9.63
W Carter	7-66	3-17	2-17	0-4	2-28	10.6	- 12.88
B Hanbury	6-21	0-1	5-14	1-1	0-5	28.6	+ 14.50
A C Stewart	6-21	2-4	3-15	0-0	1-2	28.6	+ 10.50
L M Cumani	6-23	1-5	5-15	0-0	0-3	26.1	- 0.32
J Berry	6-31	3-17	3-7	0-5	0-2	19.4	- 14.38
C A Cyzer	6-33	0-2	1-13	0-0	5-18	18.2	+ 37.00
P T Walwyn	6-44	1-17	4-16	0-1	1-10	13.6	- 9.20
J L Dunlop	6-54	2-11	3-22	1-1	0-20	11.1	- 42.90
M J Ryan	6-59	1-9	2-6	0-5	3-39	10.2	- 19.13
S Dow	6-64	1-10	1-16	0-2	4-36	9.4	+ 55.38
M J Haynes	6-66	1-11	2-15	0-5	3-35	9.1	+ 8.50
D A Wilson	6-71	0-5	0-12	0-0	6-54	8.5	- 31.17

Leading Jockeys

	Total W-R	Per cent	£1 Level Stake	Best Trainer	W-R	Per cent	£1 Level Stake
Pat Eddery	35-129	27.1	- 23.76	G Harwood	6-7	85.7	+ 3.13
R Cochrane	30-150	20.0	- 25.71	G Harwood	9-18	50.0	+ 17.63
T Quinn	21-151	13.9	+ 37.51	P F I Cole	9-40	22.5	+ 0.63
Paul Eddery	17-111	15.3	+ 31.05	P Chapple-Hyam	3-4	75.0	+ 21.50
B Rouse	16-215	7.4	-118.35	R Hannon	5-63	7.9	- 42.56
W Newnes	15-148	10.1	- 20.87	Miss B Sanders	3-13	23.1	+ 10.00
M Roberts	14-82	17.1	- 6.03	A C Stewart	5-10	50.0	+ 13.01
S Whitworth	13-156	8.3	- 47.76	P D Cundell	1-1	100.0	+ 0.57
J Reid	12-124	9.7	- 52.75	R F J Houghton	3-9	33.3	+ 25.00
G Carter	10-99	10.1	- 4.25	C A Cyzer	3-4	75.0	+ 26.00
J Williams	10-126	7.9	- 50.46	G B Balding	3-17	17.6	- 2.52
W R Swinburn	9-44	20.5	+ 10.45	M R Stoute	4-11	36.4	+ 4.95

How the Favourites Fared

Non-handicaps	W-R	Per cent	£1 Level Stake	Handicaps	W-R	Per cent	£1 Level Stake
2-y-o	39-97	40.2	- 8.46	2-y-o	7-19	36.8	+ 2.25
3-y-o	38-80	47.5	- 0.70	3-y-o	13-34	38.2	+ 3.66
Weight-for-age	33-65	50.8	+ 18.26	All-aged	35-152	23.0	- 36.91
Totals	110-242	45.5	+ 9.10	Totals	55-205	26.8	- 31.00
All favs	165-447	36.9	- 21.90				

Leading Trainers by Month at Folkestone

March/Apr	Total W-R	Non-handicaps 2-y-o	3-y-o+	Handicaps 2-y-o	3-y-o+	Per cent	£1 Level Stake
Mrs L Piggott	6-16	0-0	3-9	0-0	3-7	37.5	+ 21.00
N A Callaghan	4-11	0-1	1-4	0-0	3-6	36.4	+ 10.10
R Hannon	4-28	1-6	3-8	0-0	0-14	14.3	- 16.31
P T Walwyn	3-5	0-0	3-5	0-0	0-0	60.0	+ 2.70
D R C Elsworth	3-6	0-0	1-3	0-0	2-3	50.0	+ 10.88

May	Total W-R	Non-handicaps 2-y-o	3-y-o+	Handicaps 2-y-o	3-y-o+	Per cent	£1 Level Stake
G Harwood	4-4	0-0	3-3	0-0	1-1	100.0	+ 7.18
W A O'Gorman	3-4	3-3	0-1	0-0	0-0	75.0	+ 1.63
J Berry	2-2	1-1	1-1	0-0	0-0	100.0	+ 2.12
N A Callaghan	2-4	0-1	2-3	0-0	0-0	50.0	+ 7.50
J T Gifford	1-1	0-0	0-0	0-0	1-1	100.0	+ 5.50

June	Total W-R	Non-handicaps 2-y-o	3-y-o+	Handicaps 2-y-o	3-y-o+	Per cent	£1 Level Stake
G Harwood	3-5	1-1	2-4	0-0	0-0	60.0	+ 1.24
S Dow	3-6	1-1	0-1	0-0	2-4	50.0	+ 13.38
W G M Turner	2-4	0-2	1-1	0-0	1-1	50.0	+ 17.00
J L Dunlop	2-6	1-2	1-2	0-0	0-2	33.3	- 2.94
P S Felgate	1-1	0-0	0-0	0-0	1-1	100.0	+ 10.00

July	Total W-R	Non-handicaps 2-y-o	3-y-o+	Handicaps 2-y-o	3-y-o+	Per cent	£1 Level Stake
P F I Cole	5-15	0-1	2-4	0-0	3-10	33.3	+ 10.50
W Carter	4-11	3-6	0-0	0-0	1-5	36.4	+ 24.50
C A Cyzer	3-4	0-0	0-0	0-0	3-4	75.0	+ 30.00
B W Hills	3-5	0-0	2-3	0-0	1-2	60.0	+ 2.76
N A Callaghan	3-13	1-2	0-2	1-3	1-6	23.1	- 1.88

August	Total W-R	Non-handicaps 2-y-o	3-y-o+	Handicaps 2-y-o	3-y-o+	Per cent	£1 Level Stake
G Harwood	4-12	1-1	2-7	0-0	1-4	33.3	+ 19.50
L G Cottrell	3-11	0-1	0-2	0-0	3-8	27.3	+ 4.75
W Carter	3-11	0-2	2-4	0-0	1-5	27.3	+ 6.63
J Pearce	2-2	0-0	2-2	0-0	0-0	100.0	+ 8.00
R Curtis	2-4	0-1	0-0	0-0	2-3	50.0	+ 10.50

September	Total W-R	Non-handicaps 2-y-o	3-y-o+	Handicaps 2-y-o	3-y-o+	Per cent	£1 Level Stake
G Harwood	4-14	0-3	3-8	0-0	1-3	28.6	+ 13.50
R Akehurst	3-17	2-4	1-3	0-0	0-10	17.6	+ 32.88
A C Stewart	2-3	0-0	2-2	0-0	0-1	66.7	+ 12.00
Mrs J Cecil	2-3	2-2	0-1	0-0	0-0	66.7	+ 5.83
M Blanshard	2-4	1-1	0-0	0-0	1-3	50.0	+ 30.00

Oct/Nov	Total W-R	Non-handicaps 2-y-o	3-y-o+	Handicaps 2-y-o	3-y-o+	Per cent	£1 Level Stake
G Harwood	7-19	4-8	2-5	0-0	1-6	36.8	+ 4.74
M J Ryan	4-26	1-7	2-2	0-4	1-13	15.4	- 0.63
R Hannon	4-37	2-18	0-2	0-5	2-12	10.8	- 2.00
B Hanbury	3-5	0-1	3-3	0-0	0-1	60.0	+ 10.00
L M Cumani	3-9	0-2	3-5	0-0	0-2	33.3	+ 2.85

GOODWOOD (Group 1)

Leading Trainers 1988-92

	Total W-R	Non-handicaps 2-y-o	3-y-o+	Handicaps 2-y-o	3-y-o+	Per cent	£1 Level Stake
J L Dunlop	29-201	10-77	9-47	3-12	7-65	14.4	- 40.24
R Hannon	26-281	8-101	7-58	1-26	10-96	9.3	- 77.94
H R A Cecil	25-73	11-16	12-41	0-1	2-15	34.2	+ 16.07
D R C Elsworth	25-171	9-42	4-54	0-1	12-74	14.6	- 38.06
I A Balding	23-132	4-32	8-41	2-5	9-54	17.4	+ 60.30
G Harwood	19-163	5-31	9-62	0-6	5-64	11.7	- 78.29
L M Cumani	18-89	2-10	13-51	0-0	3-28	20.2	- 6.61
B W Hills	18-111	5-34	12-42	0-5	1-30	16.2	- 7.83
M R Stoute	17-90	4-20	9-35	0-4	4-31	18.9	- 7.92
P F I Cole	15-99	4-34	5-30	0-3	6-32	15.2	- 17.60
G Lewis	14-100	4-35	4-19	0-10	6-36	14.0	+ 19.73
J H M Gosden	11-59	3-12	3-23	1-2	4-22	18.6	+ 6.50
R Akehurst	11-93	0-8	2-14	1-5	8-66	11.8	- 12.17
Lord Huntingdon	10-46	2-8	5-17	0-2	3-19	21.7	+ 40.00
J Berry	10-71	6-27	0-9	3-14	1-21	14.1	- 16.41
W R Hern	9-39	5-10	3-16	0-2	1-11	23.1	- 3.89
R F J Houghton	9-59	2-10	4-17	0-4	3-28	15.3	- 13.94
J W Hills	9-60	0-9	4-17	0-1	5-33	15.0	- 5.88
P T Walwyn	9-90	1-16	3-33	0-3	5-38	10.0	- 14.75
P J Makin	8-64	0-10	4-23	0-0	4-31	12.5	- 3.83
C E Brittain	8-105	4-17	3-46	0-4	1-38	7.6	- 38.92
Mrs L Piggott	7-26	0-4	2-7	0-2	5-13	26.9	+ 21.50

Leading Jockeys

	Total W-R	Per cent	£1 Level Stake	Best Trainer	W-R	Per cent	£1 Level Stake
Pat Eddery	57-273	20.9	- 40.39	G Harwood	6-22	27.3	- 1.49
W Carson	52-280	18.6	- 49.03	J L Dunlop	15-72	20.8	- 21.22
S Cauthen	37-186	19.9	- 22.53	H R A Cecil	15-34	44.1	+ 4.28
J Reid	34-198	17.2	- 3.10	R Hannon	4-15	26.7	+ 11.73
R Cochrane	32-228	14.0	+ 7.05	I A Balding	10-29	34.5	+ 55.30
M Roberts	27-204	13.2	- 41.93	A C Stewart	6-24	25.0	+ 5.75
M Hills	22-107	20.6	+ 75.58	B W Hills	12-50	24.0	+ 24.58
L Dettori	19-126	15.1	- 45.54	L M Cumani	14-50	28.0	+ 6.64
A Munro	18-87	20.7	+ 29.06	Lord Huntingdon	4-9	44.4	+ 43.25
T Quinn	15-162	9.3	- 54.12	P F I Cole	8-54	14.8	+ 4.75
D Holland	14-60	23.3	+113.63	C A Horgan	1-1	100.0	+ 33.00
W R Swinburn	14-117	12.0	- 55.67	M R Stoute	10-39	25.6	- 1.92

How the Favourites Fared

Non-handicaps	W-R	Per cent	£1 Level Stake	Handicaps	W-R	Per cent	£1 Level Stake
2-y-o	71-139	51.1	+ 19.90	2-y-o	8-30	26.7	+ 0.88
3-y-o	33-94	35.1	- 8.85	3-y-o	22-74	29.7	- 2.86
Weight-for-age	26-77	33.8	- 13.71	All-aged	41-164	25.0	- 18.67
Totals	130-310	41.9	- 2.66	Totals	71-268	26.5	- 20.65
All favs	201-578	34.8	- 23.31				

Leading Trainers by Month at Goodwood

May	Total W-R	Non-handicaps 2-y-o	3-y-o+	Handicaps 2-y-o	3-y-o+	Per cent	£1 Level Stake
R Hannon	8-53	1-17	3-17	0-0	4-19	15.1	- 2.46
I A Balding	5-25	1-1	3-18	0-0	1-6	20.0	+ 32.50
D R C Elsworth	5-41	2-5	2-24	0-0	1-12	12.2	- 10.44
H R A Cecil	4-9	0-0	4-9	0-0	0-0	44.4	+ 4.00
P T Walwyn	4-20	0-2	3-12	0-0	1-6	20.0	+ 16.75

June	Total W-R	Non-handicaps 2-y-o	3-y-o+	Handicaps 2-y-o	3-y-o+	Per cent	£1 Level Stake
J L Dunlop	10-46	4-14	3-12	0-0	3-20	21.7	- 8.31
D A Wilson	5-16	0-2	0-0	0-0	5-14	31.3	+ 12.21
R Hannon	5-60	3-22	1-17	0-0	1-21	8.3	- 42.95
H R A Cecil	4-7	2-3	2-3	0-0	0-1	57.1	+ 0.48
J Berry	4-10	4-7	0-0	0-0	0-3	40.0	+ 1.59

July	Total W-R	Non-handicaps 2-y-o	3-y-o+	Handicaps 2-y-o	3-y-o+	Per cent	£1 Level Stake
M R Stoute	7-31	1-6	4-9	0-0	2-16	22.6	+ 5.75
G Harwood	7-39	2-7	4-14	0-1	1-17	17.9	- 8.57
H R A Cecil	6-21	4-4	1-8	0-0	1-9	28.6	- 5.05
B W Hills	6-37	2-15	3-9	0-2	1-11	16.2	+ 7.00
R Hannon	6-59	2-20	0-6	1-9	3-24	10.2	+ 13.50

August	Total W-R	Non-handicaps 2-y-o	3-y-o+	Handicaps 2-y-o	3-y-o+	Per cent	£1 Level Stake
I A Balding	7-29	0-5	2-9	2-2	3-13	24.1	+ 2.00
H R A Cecil	6-24	3-5	3-16	0-0	0-3	25.0	- 9.61
B W Hills	6-33	0-10	6-11	0-2	0-10	18.2	+ 3.83
D R C Elsworth	6-35	3-8	1-9	0-0	2-18	17.1	- 9.88
J L Dunlop	6-38	2-19	2-7	1-1	1-11	15.8	- 11.93

September	Total W-R	Non-handicaps 2-y-o	3-y-o+	Handicaps 2-y-o	3-y-o+	Per cent	£1 Level Stake
G Harwood	4-33	0-8	3-13	0-1	1-11	12.1	- 13.09
J L Dunlop	4-37	1-20	1-6	0-3	2-8	10.8	- 1.00
B W Hills	3-5	1-1	2-3	0-0	0-1	60.0	+ 6.83
A C Stewart	3-8	1-2	2-4	0-0	0-2	37.5	+ 3.25
R Akehurst	3-9	0-0	0-2	1-1	2-6	33.3	+ 13.33

Oct/Nov	Total W-R	Non-handicaps 2-y-o	3-y-o+	Handicaps 2-y-o	3-y-o+	Per cent	£1 Level Stake
D R C Elsworth	5-20	2-10	0-2	0-0	3-8	25.0	- 1.90
J L Dunlop	5-26	1-10	2-7	2-5	0-4	19.2	+ 16.75
H Thomson Jones	4-10	1-2	1-3	0-0	2-5	40.0	+ 20.83
R Hannon	4-34	2-14	1-6	0-5	1-9	11.8	+ 10.25
H R A Cecil	3-5	0-0	2-3	0-1	1-1	60.0	+ 22.50

HAMILTON (Group 3)

Leading Trainers 1988-92

	Total W-R	Non-handicaps 2-y-o	3-y-o+	Handicaps 2-y-o	3-y-o+	Per cent	£1 Level Stake
J Berry	51-262	24-98	11-63	4-23	12-78	19.5	- 44.42
Mrs G R Reveley	18-89	2-16	6-28	0-1	10-44	20.2	- 11.87
M S Johnston	18-114	3-20	5-32	0-3	10-59	15.8	+ 9.35
P C Haslam	17-121	2-16	6-29	0-7	9-69	14.0	- 18.36
C Tinkler	14-107	4-38	4-23	1-10	5-36	13.1	- 39.55
Mrs J Ramsden	13-56	1-7	2-13	1-3	9-33	23.2	+ 35.53
B Hanbury	12-37	2-5	6-18	1-1	3-13	32.4	+ 16.18
M H Easterby	12-74	5-14	2-15	1-10	4-35	16.2	+ 7.59
M H Tompkins	11-69	4-14	5-12	0-8	2-35	15.9	- 9.37
Sir M Prescott	10-60	4-13	4-23	0-5	2-19	16.7	- 32.52
S G Norton	10-79	4-18	6-26	0-3	0-32	12.7	- 12.38
M P Naughton	9-87	0-1	2-35	0-0	7-51	10.3	- 15.00
M A Jarvis	8-31	1-5	5-12	0-2	2-12	25.8	+ 10.99
Miss L A Perratt	8-65	0-13	3-11	1-5	4-36	12.3	+ 34.50
R M Whitaker	7-62	1-9	1-16	1-6	4-31	11.3	- 20.00
N Tinkler	7-94	0-17	5-31	0-6	2-40	7.4	- 64.23
Lord Huntingdon	6-17	1-3	3-6	0-2	2-6	35.3	+ 17.91
N A Callaghan	6-47	2-17	2-10	0-2	2-18	12.8	- 23.38
G M Moore	6-55	0-4	0-11	0-1	6-39	10.9	+ 18.83
D Moffatt	6-62	2-8	1-14	0-2	3-38	9.7	+ 21.50
T D Barron	6-63	2-12	0-9	2-6	2-36	9.5	- 34.19
Denys Smith	6-69	0-7	4-23	0-1	2-38	8.7	- 27.25

Leading Jockeys

	Total W-R	Per cent	£1 Level Stake	Best Trainer	W-R	Per cent	£1 Level Stake
J Carroll	44-227	19.4	- 36.78	J Berry	35-148	23.6	- 18.76
D McKeown	42-234	17.9	+ 11.08	R M Whitaker	5-17	29.4	+ 3.00
K Darley	38-255	14.9	- 83.92	Mrs G R Reveley	6-18	33.3	+ 4.17
G Duffield	25-214	11.7	-121.44	Sir M Prescott	7-49	14.3	- 29.67
J Lowe	23-237	9.7	- 56.87	Mrs G R Reveley	5-33	15.2	- 1.75
D Nicholls	21-177	11.9	- 8.79	N Tinkler	2-2	100.0	+ 13.75
B Raymond	18-78	23.1	+ 20.06	B Hanbury	9-19	47.4	+ 19.31
M Birch	18-172	10.5	- 83.02	C Tinkler	9-52	17.3	- 4.25
K Fallon	18-182	9.9	- 46.25	M P Naughton	5-34	14.7	- 6.50
J Fanning	15-106	14.2	+ 4.43	Miss L A Perrat	3-21	14.3	+ 20.00
J Fortune	12-125	9.6	- 10.59	Capt J Wilson	3-6	50.0	+ 22.00
N Connorton	11-103	10.7	+ 10.15	M J Camacho	5-23	21.7	+ 40.50

How the Favourites Fared

Non-handicaps	W-R	Per cent	£1 Level Stake	Handicaps	W-R	Per cent	£1 Level Stake
2-y-o	42-106	39.6	- 15.15	2-y-o	6-25	24.0	- 3.91
3-y-o	40-89	44.9	- 0.37	3-y-o	24-52	46.2	+ 12.66
Weight-for-age	22-65	33.8	- 12.42	All-aged	53-194	27.3	- 18.99
Totals	104-260	40.0	- 27.94	Totals	83-271	30.6	- 10.24
All favs	187-531	35.2	- 38.18				

Leading Trainers by Month at Hamilton

March/Apr

	Total W-R	Non-handicaps 2-y-o	3-y-o+	Handicaps 2-y-o	3-y-o+	Per cent	£1 Level Stake
J Berry	6-30	3-11	0-5	0-0	3-14	20.0	+ 5.35
Mrs J Ramsden	4-16	0-0	0-4	0-0	4-12	25.0	- 0.38
D Moffatt	3-9	2-3	1-2	0-0	0-4	33.3	+ 36.00
D Burchell	3-9	0-0	2-5	0-0	1-4	33.3	+ 8.75
P C Haslam	3-12	0-1	1-3	0-0	2-8	25.0	+ 5.50

May

	Total W-R	Non-handicaps 2-y-o	3-y-o+	Handicaps 2-y-o	3-y-o+	Per cent	£1 Level Stake
J Berry	14-55	9-22	2-17	0-0	3-16	25.5	+ 6.82
Sir M Prescott	4-13	1-1	2-7	0-0	1-5	30.8	- 1.25
M H Tompkins	4-18	1-4	3-4	0-0	0-10	22.2	+ 14.00
M S Johnston	4-26	0-3	3-12	0-0	1-11	15.4	0.00
P J Makin	3-3	0-0	3-3	0-0	0-0	100.0	+ 6.35

June

	Total W-R	Non-handicaps 2-y-o	3-y-o+	Handicaps 2-y-o	3-y-o+	Per cent	£1 Level Stake
J Berry	6-38	3-15	2-10	0-0	1-13	15.8	- 14.00
S G Norton	5-14	1-4	4-4	0-0	0-6	35.7	+ 11.38
M S Johnston	5-20	1-4	1-4	0-0	3-12	25.0	- 0.88
Sir M Prescott	3-10	1-2	1-3	0-0	1-5	30.0	- 4.07
M H Easterby	3-14	2-6	0-4	0-0	1-4	21.4	- 6.07

July

	Total W-R	Non-handicaps 2-y-o	3-y-o+	Handicaps 2-y-o	3-y-o+	Per cent	£1 Level Stake
J Berry	16-63	7-33	2-9	2-7	5-14	25.4	- 7.74
Mrs G R Reveley	10-35	1-6	5-15	0-0	4-14	28.6	+ 5.76
C Tinkler	8-24	3-10	2-6	0-1	3-7	33.3	+ 7.20
P C Haslam	5-27	0-6	2-6	0-1	3-14	18.5	+ 2.75
M S Johnston	4-23	2-5	0-4	0-1	2-13	17.4	- 6.77

August

	Total W-R	Non-handicaps 2-y-o	3-y-o+	Handicaps 2-y-o	3-y-o+	Per cent	£1 Level Stake
J Berry	4-16	1-3	3-7	0-0	0-6	25.0	- 7.60
N Tinkler	2-5	0-0	2-3	0-0	0-2	40.0	- 0.35
M S Johnston	2-6	0-1	0-0	0-0	2-5	33.3	+ 22.00
Mrs G R Reveley	2-9	1-4	0-2	0-0	1-3	22.2	+ 3.00
I A Balding	1-1	0-0	0-0	0-0	1-1	100.0	+ 2.75

September

	Total W-R	Non-handicaps 2-y-o	3-y-o+	Handicaps 2-y-o	3-y-o+	Per cent	£1 Level Stake
B Hanbury	9-17	2-4	5-8	1-1	1-4	52.9	+ 24.71
M A Jarvis	3-10	0-3	2-2	0-2	1-3	30.0	+ 7.00
C Tinkler	3-24	0-8	1-2	1-7	1-7	12.5	- 5.50
P C Haslam	3-33	0-1	2-11	0-5	1-16	9.1	+ 0.50
C W C Elsey	2-6	1-2	0-1	0-2	1-1	33.3	+ 17.00

Oct/Nov

	Total W-R	Non-handicaps 2-y-o	3-y-o+	Handicaps 2-y-o	3-y-o+	Per cent	£1 Level Stake
Mrs J Ramsden	3-9	0-1	1-2	1-3	1-3	33.3	+ 14.50
J Berry	3-18	1-6	2-4	0-4	0-4	16.7	- 5.25
Lord Huntingdon	2-2	0-0	1-1	0-0	1-1	100.0	+ 20.00
R Akehurst	2-4	0-0	0-0	0-0	2-4	50.0	+ 11.00
Miss S E Hall	2-4	1-1	0-0	0-1	1-2	50.0	+ 22.00

HAYDOCK (Group 1)

Leading Trainers 1988-92

	Total W-R	Non-handicaps 2-y-o	3-y-o+	Handicaps 2-y-o	3-y-o+	Per cent	£1 Level Stake
H R A Cecil	21-60	9-13	9-33	0-0	3-14	35.0	+ 10.21
B W Hills	20-98	5-19	11-42	0-2	4-35	20.4	- 17.40
J H M Gosden	18-57	3-8	10-35	0-0	5-14	31.6	+ 54.57
J Berry	18-216	8-81	5-53	3-32	2-50	8.3	-119.28
H Thomson Jones	16-65	8-18	4-20	0-1	4-26	24.6	+ 21.08
J L Dunlop	16-86	5-25	4-23	0-0	7-38	18.6	+ 8.71
M H Easterby	16-173	7-41	2-18	1-17	6-97	9.2	- 85.75
L M Cumani	15-74	3-11	7-33	0-0	5-30	20.3	+ 6.76
R Hollinshead	14-202	4-51	3-47	1-14	6-90	6.9	- 50.90
M R Stoute	13-79	0-11	9-40	0-2	4-26	16.5	- 31.99
R Boss	12-37	2-12	3-12	1-1	6-12	32.4	+ 26.50
J W Watts	12-86	1-12	1-14	1-3	9-57	14.0	- 16.43
B Hanbury	11-68	2-17	5-28	0-0	4-23	16.2	+ 12.75
M H Tompkins	11-95	2-11	2-29	2-14	5-41	11.6	- 20.90
F H Lee	11-135	2-32	1-17	1-7	7-79	8.1	- 42.50
Mrs J Ramsden	10-94	2-14	2-7	1-7	5-66	10.6	- 48.25
C E Brittain	9-85	2-14	4-35	1-5	2-31	10.6	- 15.08
R Charlton	8-31	2-3	3-12	0-0	3-16	25.8	- 2.24
R Hannon	8-53	3-14	2-16	1-3	2-20	15.1	+ 12.00
B A McMahon	8-138	2-22	2-45	1-2	3-69	5.8	- 36.67
G Wragg	7-25	1-1	4-18	0-0	2-6	28.0	+ 14.80
M J Camacho	7-44	0-2	2-13	1-5	4-24	15.9	+ 40.50

Leading Jockeys

	Total W-R	Per cent	£1 Level Stake		Best Trainer	W-R	Per cent	£1 Level Stake
Pat Eddery	37-147	25.2	+ 5.67		B W Hills	6-16	37.5	+ 5.07
W Ryan	22-144	15.3	- 9.10		H R A Cecil	10-27	37.0	+ 8.55
J Reid	20-78	25.6	+ 22.67		J L Dunlop	4-8	50.0	+ 12.75
M Hills	20-103	19.4	- 1.02		B W Hills	11-47	23.4	- 6.30
D McKeown	20-156	12.8	- 31.83		J W Watts	5-21	23.8	+ 4.69
M Birch	19-166	11.4	- 47.27		M H Easterby	12-91	13.2	- 28.75
B Raymond	18-148	12.2	- 41.88		B Hanbury	4-20	20.0	- 3.25
W Carson	17-107	15.9	- 38.41		W R Hern	4-19	21.1	- 4.75
J Carroll	17-169	10.1	- 46.51		J Berry	12-123	9.8	- 74.51
L Dettori	16-90	17.8	+ 8.57		L M Cumani	6-31	19.4	+ 1.32
M Roberts	15-111	13.5	- 25.77		A C Stewart	4-18	22.2	- 5.90
R Hills	15-127	11.8	- 55.84		H Thomson Jones	12-50	24.0	- 5.41

How the Favourites Fared

Non-handicaps	W-R	Per cent	£1 Level Stake	Handicaps	W-R	Per cent	£1 Level Stake
2-y-o	54-119	45.4	- 2.22	2-y-o	3-27	11.1	- 16.25
3-y-o	41-103	39.8	- 11.39	3-y-o	11-51	21.6	- 14.24
Weight-for-age	21-69	30.4	- 20.02	All-aged	53-192	27.6	- 21.84
Totals	116-291	39.9	- 33.63	Totals	67-270	24.8	- 52.33
All favs	183-561	32.6	- 85.96				

Leading Trainers by Month at Haydock

March/Apr	Total W-R	Non-handicaps 2-y-o	3-y-o+	Handicaps 2-y-o	3-y-o+	Per cent	£1 Level Stake
M H Easterby	3-12	3-3	0-3	0-0	0-6	25.0	+ 2.25
R Charlton	2-2	0-0	2-2	0-0	0-0	100.0	+ 1.91
B Hanbury	2-4	0-1	2-3	0-0	0-0	50.0	+ 4.25
R Boss	2-7	0-1	1-4	0-0	1-2	28.6	+ 2.75
Mrs J Ramsden	2-7	0-0	0-0	0-0	2-7	28.6	- 0.25

May	Total W-R	Non-handicaps 2-y-o	3-y-o+	Handicaps 2-y-o	3-y-o+	Per cent	£1 Level Stake
M R Stoute	8-18	0-0	6-12	0-0	2-6	44.4	+ 6.16
B W Hills	6-18	2-3	4-11	0-0	0-4	33.3	- 0.37
H Thomson Jones	5-13	3-4	1-4	0-0	1-5	38.5	+ 3.24
J Berry	4-29	2-11	1-10	0-0	1-8	13.8	+ 0.25
P F I Cole	3-6	1-1	2-3	0-0	0-2	50.0	+ 8.00

June	Total W-R	Non-handicaps 2-y-o	3-y-o+	Handicaps 2-y-o	3-y-o+	Per cent	£1 Level Stake
B Hanbury	4-9	0-1	2-3	0-0	2-5	44.4	+ 37.00
B W Hills	4-12	0-1	3-6	0-0	1-5	33.3	+ 2.25
R Hollinshead	3-21	0-2	1-4	0-0	2-15	14.3	+ 7.00
M H Easterby	3-30	0-10	1-2	0-0	2-18	10.0	- 12.50
R F J Houghton	2-3	0-0	0-1	0-0	2-2	66.7	+ 11.25

July	Total W-R	Non-handicaps 2-y-o	3-y-o+	Handicaps 2-y-o	3-y-o+	Per cent	£1 Level Stake
M H Easterby	5-22	3-9	1-3	0-0	1-10	22.7	0.00
J L Dunlop	4-9	0-0	2-5	0-0	2-4	44.4	+ 9.00
H R A Cecil	4-10	1-1	2-6	0-0	1-3	40.0	+ 10.53
L M Cumani	4-12	1-2	3-8	0-0	0-2	33.3	+ 20.30
J H M Gosden	3-5	0-0	3-5	0-0	0-0	60.0	+ 11.50

August	Total W-R	Non-handicaps 2-y-o	3-y-o+	Handicaps 2-y-o	3-y-o+	Per cent	£1 Level Stake
F H Lee	6-32	1-8	0-2	1-3	4-19	18.8	+ 10.00
H R A Cecil	5-8	2-2	3-6	0-0	0-0	62.5	- 0.41
J W Watts	5-11	0-2	1-2	1-1	3-6	45.5	+ 19.94
R Hollinshead	4-28	2-7	1-5	0-3	1-13	14.3	+ 1.10
J Berry	4-37	2-13	2-9	0-7	0-8	10.8	- 28.26

September	Total W-R	Non-handicaps 2-y-o	3-y-o+	Handicaps 2-y-o	3-y-o+	Per cent	£1 Level Stake
J H M Gosden	8-22	1-2	4-15	0-0	3-5	36.4	+ 39.50
H R A Cecil	6-17	3-6	2-6	0-0	1-5	35.3	+ 11.77
H Thomson Jones	5-13	1-2	2-4	0-1	2-6	38.5	+ 37.50
R Charlton	5-14	2-3	1-7	0-0	2-4	35.7	+ 7.10
L M Cumani	5-21	1-4	2-7	0-0	2-10	23.8	+ 0.19

Oct/Nov	Total W-R	Non-handicaps 2-y-o	3-y-o+	Handicaps 2-y-o	3-y-o+	Per cent	£1 Level Stake
H R A Cecil	4-6	3-3	0-0	0-0	1-3	66.7	+ 2.32
S G Norton	4-17	0-1	0-2	0-2	4-12	23.5	+ 38.00
L M Cumani	3-9	1-3	0-2	0-0	2-4	33.3	+ 9.90
C E Brittain	3-14	1-6	0-3	0-2	2-3	21.4	+ 20.00
J L Dunlop	3-19	2-13	1-1	0-0	0-5	15.8	+ 1.25

KEMPTON (Group 1)

Leading Trainers 1988-92

	Total	Non-handicaps		Handicaps		Per	£1 Level
	W-R	2-y-o	3-y-o+	2-y-o	3-y-o+	cent	Stake
R Hannon	20-235	9-70	3-52	2-12	6-101	8.5	-100.67
D R C Elsworth	17-125	4-23	9-56	0-1	4-45	13.6	- 1.67
B W Hills	13-76	3-23	5-35	0-0	5-18	17.1	+ 27.41
J H M Gosden	13-77	1-4	9-54	0-1	3-18	16.9	- 19.38
M R Stoute	13-78	3-16	4-44	1-1	5-17	16.7	- 20.29
P T Walwyn	13-80	1-10	6-36	0-0	6-34	16.3	+ 22.24
C E Brittain	13-120	1-15	4-47	1-4	7-54	10.8	- 1.00
G Harwood	12-78	3-10	6-32	1-3	2-33	15.4	- 31.41
M J Ryan	11-60	2-5	4-11	0-0	5-44	18.3	+ 47.00
G Lewis	11-86	4-20	1-15	0-3	6-48	12.8	- 7.46
I A Balding	11-101	1-16	6-40	0-2	4-43	10.9	+ 5.00
L M Cumani	10-53	1-6	7-30	0-0	2-17	18.9	- 9.60
H Candy	10-76	0-5	4-33	0-1	6-37	13.2	+ 99.00
J L Dunlop	10-109	3-29	5-44	0-0	2-36	9.2	- 27.00
H R A Cecil	9-35	1-3	8-25	0-0	0-7	25.7	+ 4.52
A A Scott	9-40	1-4	2-16	0-1	6-19	22.5	+ 17.08
R Charlton	9-42	3-8	6-20	0-0	0-14	21.4	+ 16.65
P F I Cole	9-86	1-15	1-32	1-3	6-36	10.5	- 34.80
G Wragg	8-39	0-1	6-25	0-0	2-13	20.5	+ 6.33
B Hanbury	8-47	1-5	6-18	0-1	1-23	17.0	+ 3.82
Lord Huntingdon	8-66	1-9	2-27	0-1	5-29	12.1	- 12.13
W R Hern	7-36	0-7	3-15	0-0	4-14	19.4	+ 14.28

Leading Jockeys

	Total W-R	Per cent	£1 Level Stake	Best Trainer	W-R	Per cent	£1 Level Stake
Pat Eddery	52-218	23.9	+ 37.12	R Charlton	6-25	24.0	+ 7.15
W Carson	35-239	14.6	- 37.25	W R Hern	4-19	21.1	+ 2.28
S Cauthen	25-139	18.0	+ 13.27	J H M Gosden	7-14	50.0	+ 19.12
R Cochrane	24-188	12.8	- 37.43	L M Cumani	7-17	41.2	+ 16.40
M Roberts	22-178	12.4	- 16.29	C E Brittain	7-52	13.5	+ 8.50
W R Swinburn	17-164	10.4	- 51.78	M R Stoute	6-45	13.3	- 9.99
A Munro	15-104	14.4	+ 39.58	G Wragg	2-3	66.7	+ 7.75
T Quinn	14-150	9.3	- 63.72	P F I Cole	5-59	8.5	- 37.05
J Reid	13-157	8.3	- 30.25	R Hannon	2-5	40.0	+ 3.50
L Dettori	12-138	8.7	- 41.00	L M Cumani	3-30	10.0	- 20.00
B Raymond	11-113	9.7	- 60.92	B Hanbury	2-16	12.5	- 10.90
W Newnes	11-128	8.6	- 31.20	Miss B Sanders	2-14	14.3	- 5.70

How the Favourites Fared

Non-handicaps	W-R	Per cent	£1 Level Stake	Handicaps	W-R	Per cent	£1 Level Stake
2-y-o	26-71	36.6	- 10.19	2-y-o	5-11	45.5	+ 9.00
3-y-o	40-103	38.8	- 9.73	3-y-o	18-56	32.1	+ 7.31
Weight-for-age	14-38	36.8	- 0.66	All-aged	35-155	22.6	- 26.08
Totals	80-212	37.7	- 20.58	Totals	58-222	26.1	- 9.77
All favs	138-434	31.8	- 30.35				

Leading Trainers by Month at Kempton

March/Apr

	Total W-R	Non-handicaps 2-y-o	3-y-o+	Handicaps 2-y-o	3-y-o+	Per cent	£1 Level Stake
R Hannon	7-75	5-23	2-17	0-0	0-35	9.3	- 41.92
C E Brittain	6-41	0-0	2-21	0-0	4-20	14.6	+ 27.13
M J Ryan	5-17	0-0	2-5	0-0	3-12	29.4	+ 36.50
P T Walwyn	5-21	0-0	2-6	0-0	3-15	23.8	+ 29.36
J H M Gosden	4-11	0-0	3-7	0-0	1-4	36.4	+ 9.00

May

	Total W-R	Non-handicaps 2-y-o	3-y-o+	Handicaps 2-y-o	3-y-o+	Per cent	£1 Level Stake
D R C Elsworth	5-19	1-3	3-11	0-0	1-5	26.3	+ 6.99
B W Hills	4-12	0-1	2-8	0-0	2-3	33.3	+ 36.50
M A Jarvis	4-12	1-3	1-4	0-0	2-5	33.3	+ 15.63
P F I Cole	4-26	1-2	0-13	0-0	3-11	15.4	- 8.30
H R A Cecil	3-8	0-0	3-6	0-0	0-2	37.5	+ 3.25

June

	Total W-R	Non-handicaps 2-y-o	3-y-o+	Handicaps 2-y-o	3-y-o+	Per cent	£1 Level Stake
D R C Elsworth	5-28	0-2	4-16	0-0	1-10	17.9	+ 9.83
Lord Huntingdon	3-10	0-0	1-7	0-0	2-3	30.0	+ 5.25
A A Scott	3-10	1-1	1-7	0-0	1-2	30.0	+ 3.75
J Sutcliffe	3-11	0-3	0-0	0-0	3-8	27.3	+ 4.25
P T Walwyn	3-12	0-0	3-10	0-0	0-2	25.0	+ 8.88

July

	Total W-R	Non-handicaps 2-y-o	3-y-o+	Handicaps 2-y-o	3-y-o+	Per cent	£1 Level Stake
G Harwood	4-11	0-0	3-6	0-0	1-5	36.4	+ 7.24
H Candy	3-6	0-1	1-2	0-0	2-3	50.0	+ 53.00
B W Hills	3-8	1-2	1-5	0-0	1-1	37.5	+ 11.88
P T Walwyn	3-10	1-2	0-5	0-0	2-3	30.0	+ 8.00
M R Stoute	3-11	0-1	1-6	0-0	2-4	27.3	0.00

August

	Total W-R	Non-handicaps 2-y-o	3-y-o+	Handicaps 2-y-o	3-y-o+	Per cent	£1 Level Stake
R Hannon	4-15	2-5	0-1	1-5	1-4	26.7	+ 8.00
C E Brittain	3-6	0-0	1-1	1-2	1-3	50.0	+ 17.00
W R Hern	2-4	0-2	0-0	0-0	2-2	50.0	+ 16.00
B W Hills	2-9	1-7	1-1	0-0	0-1	22.2	- 3.30
R Lee	1-1	0-0	0-0	0-0	1-1	100.0	+ 4.00

September

	Total W-R	Non-handicaps 2-y-o	3-y-o+	Handicaps 2-y-o	3-y-o+	Per cent	£1 Level Stake
G Wragg	6-12	0-1	4-6	0-0	2-5	50.0	+ 23.00
M R Stoute	5-21	3-12	0-6	1-1	1-2	23.8	- 3.32
G Harwood	5-23	2-6	1-5	1-1	1-11	21.7	- 1.72
L M Cumani	5-24	1-6	3-8	0-0	1-10	20.8	+ 4.50
R Charlton	4-19	2-6	2-6	0-0	0-7	21.1	+ 1.00

LEICESTER (Group 3)

Leading Trainers 1988-92

	Total W-R	Non-handicaps 2-y-o	3-y-o+	Handicaps 2-y-o	3-y-o+	Per cent	£1 Level Stake
H R A Cecil	27-97	13-41	14-51	0-0	0-5	27.8	- 22.85
M R Stoute	25-104	15-62	8-30	0-1	2-11	24.0	- 19.61
J H M Gosden	17-62	8-27	6-23	0-1	3-11	27.4	- 6.08
G Wragg	12-60	3-21	8-27	0-1	1-11	20.0	+ 16.17
R Hannon	12-130	6-65	2-23	2-12	2-30	9.2	- 61.75
G Harwood	11-52	3-19	4-20	1-2	3-11	21.2	+ 6.35
P F I Cole	11-94	5-36	5-37	0-6	1-15	11.7	- 33.63
J L Dunlop	10-98	4-40	4-34	1-4	1-20	10.2	- 59.30
R F J Houghton	9-52	3-19	5-19	0-2	1-12	17.3	+ 3.68
M A Jarvis	9-58	1-16	5-24	1-3	2-15	15.5	- 3.71
B Hanbury	9-67	4-30	3-26	0-0	2-11	13.4	- 17.01
J Berry	8-67	5-43	2-8	1-10	0-6	11.9	- 24.39
C E Brittain	8-73	2-29	5-26	1-4	0-14	11.0	- 24.71
G Lewis	7-42	4-17	2-6	0-4	1-15	16.7	+ 15.48
W R Hern	7-48	1-18	4-18	0-0	2-12	14.6	- 20.20
A C Stewart	7-52	2-19	4-23	0-0	1-10	13.5	- 17.45
B W Hills	7-77	4-47	1-16	0-1	2-13	9.1	- 33.76
M Brittain	7-94	0-27	1-13	1-8	5-46	7.4	- 16.00
L M Cumani	6-36	4-8	2-25	0-0	0-3	16.7	- 20.29
W A O'Gorman	6-37	2-19	2-9	2-4	0-5	16.2	- 11.67
P T Walwyn	6-56	1-23	4-21	0-1	1-11	10.7	+ 1.25
B A McMahon	6-85	2-19	3-33	0-4	1-29	7.1	- 25.50

Leading Jockeys

	Total W-R	Per cent	£1 Level Stake	Best Trainer	W-R	Per cent	£1 Level Stake
S Cauthen	27-105	25.7	- 9.05	H R A Cecil	14-28	50.0	+ 7.25
W R Swinburn	27-135	20.0	- 34.84	M R Stoute	16-49	32.7	- 0.64
M Roberts	27-207	13.0	- 60.02	C E Brittain	6-35	17.1	- 0.21
W Carson	26-167	15.6	- 49.92	J H M Gosden	5-10	50.0	- 0.97
W Ryan	22-170	12.9	- 61.25	H R A Cecil	11-41	26.8	- 5.96
R Cochrane	21-161	13.0	- 50.30	G Harwood	5-20	25.0	+ 2.48
Paul Eddery	20-142	14.1	+ 1.30	Mrs J Cecil	3-8	37.5	+ 6.13
T Quinn	20-146	13.7	- 2.71	P F I Cole	10-57	17.5	+ 1.88
Pat Eddery	19-111	17.1	- 35.75	J H M Gosden	3-4	75.0	+ 9.33
G Carter	19-202	9.4	- 49.69	G Wragg	5-27	18.5	- 1.48
L Dettori	18-117	15.4	+ 16.98	L M Cumani	3-23	13.0	- 12.37
B Raymond	15-155	9.7	- 61.20	M A Jarvis	4-26	15.4	- 6.70

How the Favourites Fared

Non-handicaps	W-R	Per cent	£1 Level Stake	Handicaps	W-R	Per cent	£1 Level Stake
2-y-o	73-160	45.6	+ 12.30	2-y-o	8-26	30.8	- 1.45
3-y-o	60-141	42.6	- 14.45	3-y-o	13-50	26.0	- 1.55
Weight-for-age	7-27	25.9	- 10.70	All-aged	19-94	20.2	- 19.54
Totals	140-328	42.7	- 12.85	Totals	40-170	23.5	- 22.54
All favs	180-498	36.1	- 35.39				

Leading Trainers by Month at Leicester

March/Apr	Total W–R	Non-handicaps 2-y-o	3-y-o+	Handicaps 2-y-o	3-y-o+	Per cent	£1 Level Stake
M R Stoute	5-13	0-0	5-13	0-0	0-0	38.5	− 1.73
B Hanbury	3-8	0-0	2-5	0-0	1-3	37.5	+ 0.12
H R A Cecil	3-9	0-0	3-9	0-0	0-0	33.3	− 3.19
M Bell	3-12	2-6	0-3	0-0	1-3	25.0	+ 4.50
J Berry	3-15	3-14	0-0	0-0	0-1	20.0	− 5.60

May	Total W–R	Non-handicaps 2-y-o	3-y-o+	Handicaps 2-y-o	3-y-o+	Per cent	£1 Level Stake
M R Stoute	7-16	2-4	3-8	0-0	2-4	43.8	+ 4.69
J Berry	3-11	2-7	1-4	0-0	0-0	27.3	+ 15.30
C E Brittain	2-3	1-1	1-2	0-0	0-0	66.7	+ 6.83
M A Jarvis	2-7	0-1	1-2	0-0	1-4	28.6	+ 4.63
H Thomson Jones	2-7	1-1	1-3	0-0	0-3	28.6	− 3.09

June	Total W–R	Non-handicaps 2-y-o	3-y-o+	Handicaps 2-y-o	3-y-o+	Per cent	£1 Level Stake
J H M Gosden	4-9	2-4	2-3	0-0	0-2	44.4	− 0.15
N A Callaghan	2-5	1-2	1-2	0-0	0-1	40.0	+ 0.35
R Charlton	2-5	0-2	1-1	0-0	1-2	40.0	+ 1.00
P S Felgate	2-7	0-1	0-2	0-0	2-4	28.6	+ 5.50
Mrs L Piggott	2-7	0-1	0-1	0-0	2-5	28.6	+ 9.50

July	Total W–R	Non-handicaps 2-y-o	3-y-o+	Handicaps 2-y-o	3-y-o+	Per cent	£1 Level Stake
H R A Cecil	7-13	1-2	6-10	0-0	0-1	53.8	+ 1.45
M J Ryan	4-19	0-8	1-3	0-0	3-8	21.1	+ 8.25
G Wragg	3-4	1-1	2-3	0-0	0-0	75.0	+ 30.00
C Tinkler	3-9	2-6	1-2	0-0	0-1	33.3	+ 3.25
B A McMahon	3-20	2-4	1-8	0-2	0-6	15.0	+ 1.50

August	Total W–R	Non-handicaps 2-y-o	3-y-o+	Handicaps 2-y-o	3-y-o+	Per cent	£1 Level Stake
Mrs L Piggott	3-5	0-0	3-5	0-0	0-0	60.0	+ 21.00
W R Hern	3-7	0-4	2-2	0-0	1-1	42.9	+ 5.50
R Hannon	3-10	1-3	0-2	1-2	1-3	30.0	+ 4.00
H R A Cecil	2-2	2-2	0-0	0-0	0-0	100.0	+ 1.98
G Harwood	2-3	0-0	1-1	1-1	0-1	66.7	+ 4.88

September	Total W–R	Non-handicaps 2-y-o	3-y-o+	Handicaps 2-y-o	3-y-o+	Per cent	£1 Level Stake
H R A Cecil	5-10	3-5	2-4	0-0	0-1	50.0	+ 7.41
J H M Gosden	4-11	2-5	0-2	0-0	2-4	36.4	+ 5.20
J L Dunlop	4-19	3-14	0-1	0-1	1-3	21.1	− 8.03
A Hide	3-8	1-3	1-2	0-0	1-3	37.5	+ 26.50
R F J Houghton	3-9	2-5	1-2	0-1	0-1	33.3	+ 21.75

Oct/Nov	Total W–R	Non-handicaps 2-y-o	3-y-o+	Handicaps 2-y-o	3-y-o+	Per cent	£1 Level Stake
M R Stoute	11-44	11-43	0-1	0-0	0-0	25.0	− 0.57
H R A Cecil	8-46	7-31	1-13	0-0	0-2	17.4	− 20.80
R Hannon	7-39	4-26	1-2	1-5	1-6	17.9	+ 2.25
G Harwood	6-24	3-15	1-5	0-1	2-3	25.0	+ 12.10
J H M Gosden	5-23	3-15	2-6	0-0	0-2	21.7	− 2.18

LINGFIELD TURF (Group 2)

Leading Trainers 1988-92

	Total W-R	Non-handicaps 2-y-o	3-y-o+	Handicaps 2-y-o	3-y-o+	Per cent	£1 Level Stake
G Harwood	22-79	6-19	11-33	1-4	4-23	27.8	+ 2.05
J L Dunlop	22-122	6-43	8-34	0-3	8-42	18.0	+ 29.64
P F I Cole	19-90	5-29	8-32	1-4	5-25	21.1	+ 8.74
R Akehurst	17-174	1-25	0-31	0-3	16-115	9.8	- 28.25
R Hannon	16-182	5-55	7-36	0-16	4-75	8.8	-101.80
L M Cumani	15-34	1-3	14-28	0-0	0-3	44.1	+ 9.77
B W Hills	13-50	4-15	3-16	1-1	5-18	26.0	+ 10.66
H R A Cecil	12-45	4-14	7-27	0-0	1-4	26.7	- 20.81
P Mitchell	12-108	2-22	3-22	2-7	5-57	11.1	- 2.63
N A Callaghan	10-37	1-8	1-7	1-2	7-20	27.0	+ 18.54
M R Stoute	10-55	4-19	6-24	0-1	0-11	18.2	- 22.15
C E Brittain	10-80	1-15	3-26	0-1	6-38	12.5	- 15.13
Sir M Prescott	9-42	0-17	4-10	0-2	5-13	21.4	- 12.63
Pat Mitchell	9-95	2-24	0-18	0-5	7-48	9.5	- 18.92
A C Stewart	8-17	0-4	2-6	0-0	6-7	47.1	+ 15.49
P J Makin	8-49	0-9	2-13	0-0	6-27	16.3	+ 0.25
C J Benstead	8-76	1-13	1-17	0-1	6-45	10.5	- 10.50
G Lewis	8-102	2-33	2-19	0-6	4-44	7.8	- 45.25
R Boss	7-31	4-9	0-3	1-2	2-17	22.6	+ 21.50
J H M Gosden	7-43	3-16	4-20	0-0	0-7	16.3	- 24.22
P T Walwyn	7-53	1-11	4-18	0-1	2-23	13.2	- 26.18
J W Hills	6-20	0-4	2-5	1-1	3-10	30.0	+ 16.00

Leading Jockeys

	Total W-R	Per cent	£1 Level Stake	Best Trainer	W-R	Per cent	£1 Level Stake
W Carson	30-129	23.3	- 1.61	J L Dunlop	11-32	34.4	+ 12.50
J Reid	29-154	18.8	- 22.26	P J Makin	4-10	40.0	+ 13.75
M Roberts	27-165	16.4	+ 3.26	A C Stewart	7-11	63.6	+ 17.75
Pat Eddery	26-115	22.6	- 3.19	G Harwood	4-9	44.4	- 1.21
S Cauthen	25-97	25.8	- 7.15	H R A Cecil	7-19	36.8	- 8.03
R Cochrane	25-134	18.7	+ 26.67	L M Cumani	5-9	55.6	+ 8.14
T Quinn	25-191	13.1	- 19.13	P F I Cole	14-59	23.7	+ 2.24
L Dettori	18-79	22.8	+ 6.56	L M Cumani	5-11	45.5	+ 1.50
B Raymond	18-108	16.7	- 1.99	M A Jarvis	4-21	19.0	- 0.37
S Whitworth	14-156	9.0	- 60.12	P Mitchell	3-16	18.8	- 6.37
B Rouse	14-228	6.1	-113.25	R Hannon	3-69	4.3	- 55.00
M Hills	13-77	16.9	- 11.55	J W Hills	3-6	50.0	+ 12.75

How the Favourites Fared

Non-handicaps	W-R	Per cent	£1 Level Stake	Handicaps	W-R	Per cent	£1 Level Stake
2-y-o	41-117	35.0	- 23.94	2-y-o	7-19	36.8	+ 4.74
3-y-o	39-88	44.3	+ 0.22	3-y-o	18-50	36.0	+ 3.63
Weight-for-age	34-65	52.3	+ 0.81	All-aged	55-206	26.7	- 36.76
Totals	114-270	42.2	- 22.91	Totals	80-275	29.1	- 28.39
All favs	194-545	35.6	- 51.30				

Leading Trainers by Month at Lingfield

March/Apr	Total W-R	Non-handicaps 2-y-o	3-y-o+	Handicaps 2-y-o	3-y-o+	Per cent	£1 Level Stake
L J Holt	2-6	1-2	0-0	0-0	1-4	33.3	+ 15.50
R Boss	1-1	0-0	0-0	0-0	1-1	100.0	+ 6.00
Lord Huntingdon	1-1	0-0	1-1	0-0	0-0	100.0	+ 3.33
K R Burke	1-1	0-0	0-0	0-0	1-1	100.0	+ 5.50
M Blanshard	1-2	0-0	1-1	0-0	0-1	50.0	+ 6.00

May	Total W-R	Non-handicaps 2-y-o	3-y-o+	Handicaps 2-y-o	3-y-o+	Per cent	£1 Level Stake
H R A Cecil	6-16	2-3	4-12	0-0	0-1	37.5	− 3.63
R Hannon	6-41	1-11	5-11	0-0	0-19	14.6	− 25.88
L M Cumani	5-11	1-1	4-9	0-0	0-1	45.5	+ 5.77
N A Callaghan	5-17	1-5	1-2	0-0	3-10	29.4	+ 9.38
M R Stoute	5-19	0-1	5-17	0-0	0-1	26.3	− 3.51

June	Total W-R	Non-handicaps 2-y-o	3-y-o+	Handicaps 2-y-o	3-y-o+	Per cent	£1 Level Stake
P F I Cole	6-13	2-4	2-5	0-0	2-4	46.2	+ 22.41
G Harwood	6-18	1-2	4-12	0-0	1-4	33.3	+ 12.18
J L Dunlop	5-18	1-2	2-7	0-0	2-9	27.8	− 5.25
R Hannon	5-32	2-6	1-9	0-0	2-17	15.6	− 11.67
R Charlton	4-5	0-0	3-4	0-0	1-1	80.0	+ 14.43

July	Total W-R	Non-handicaps 2-y-o	3-y-o+	Handicaps 2-y-o	3-y-o+	Per cent	£1 Level Stake
G Harwood	7-14	2-2	3-4	0-0	2-8	50.0	+ 16.69
L M Cumani	4-7	0-0	4-6	0-0	0-1	57.1	+ 1.67
P F I Cole	4-15	1-3	2-4	0-1	1-7	26.7	− 3.25
J L Dunlop	4-24	0-4	0-5	0-1	4-14	16.7	+ 19.19
R Akehurst	4-32	0-3	0-4	0-1	4-24	12.5	+ 14.00

August	Total W-R	Non-handicaps 2-y-o	3-y-o+	Handicaps 2-y-o	3-y-o+	Per cent	£1 Level Stake
G Harwood	6-12	2-3	2-2	1-2	1-5	50.0	+ 1.94
P F I Cole	4-14	0-4	3-4	1-2	0-4	28.6	+ 1.83
P J Makin	4-14	0-0	1-4	0-0	3-10	28.6	+ 8.75
P Mitchell	4-14	1-4	0-1	2-3	1-6	28.6	+ 40.50
W Jarvis	3-8	1-2	1-3	0-0	1-3	37.5	+ 7.80

September	Total W-R	Non-handicaps 2-y-o	3-y-o+	Handicaps 2-y-o	3-y-o+	Per cent	£1 Level Stake
B W Hills	5-7	3-5	1-1	0-0	1-1	71.4	+ 21.00
J L Dunlop	3-29	2-22	1-2	0-0	0-5	10.3	+ 2.80
G Blum	2-2	1-1	1-1	0-0	0-0	100.0	+ 21.50
N A Callaghan	2-2	0-0	0-0	0-0	2-2	100.0	+ 9.33
R Bastiman	2-2	0-0	0-0	0-0	2-2	100.0	+ 11.00

Oct/Nov	Total W-R	Non-handicaps 2-y-o	3-y-o+	Handicaps 2-y-o	3-y-o+	Per cent	£1 Level Stake
J L Dunlop	6-23	1-10	5-8	0-2	0-3	26.1	+ 16.15
R Akehurst	4-21	1-5	0-2	0-1	3-13	19.0	+ 21.00
M R Stoute	3-13	3-10	0-1	0-1	0-1	23.1	− 7.55
R Hannon	3-25	2-7	0-4	0-3	1-11	12.0	− 5.00
C E Brittain	2-3	0-1	0-0	0-0	2-2	66.7	+ 14.00

LINGFIELD (AW)

Leading Trainers 1989-92

	Total W-R	Non-handicaps 2-y-o	3-y-o+	Handicaps 2-y-o	3-y-o+	Per cent	£1 Level Stake
W A O'Gorman	26-108	2-9	12-39	2-2	10-58	24.1	+ 21.66
B W Hills	18-53	1-7	9-17	0-1	8-28	34.0	- 4.99
P F I Cole	18-89	3-22	9-27	1-3	5-37	20.2	- 26.54
C A Cyzer	15-82	0-7	6-31	0-0	9-44	18.3	+ 0.20
Sir M Prescott	14-58	4-18	4-15	0-1	6-24	24.1	- 9.83
P Mitchell	12-98	0-7	1-20	0-4	11-67	12.2	- 3.42
C C Elsey	11-78	0-9	1-14	0-0	10-55	14.1	- 18.57
R J O'Sullivan	11-84	0-0	2-10	0-0	9-74	13.1	- 12.25
M S Johnston	10-54	2-5	1-11	0-1	7-37	18.5	+ 5.25
D Murray Smith	10-68	1-5	2-19	0-2	7-42	14.7	- 3.69
K O C-Brown	10-69	0-1	1-20	0-0	9-48	14.5	+ 28.00
N A Callaghan	9-47	4-8	2-13	2-8	1-18	19.1	+ 12.00
S Dow	9-109	1-7	3-36	1-3	4-63	8.3	- 51.75
J Berry	8-25	5-14	1-4	0-0	2-7	32.0	+ 1.97
R Boss	8-26	4-9	3-6	1-3	0-8	30.8	+ 16.04
Mrs L Piggott	8-48	2-9	3-16	0-3	3-20	16.7	+ 7.50
C P Wildman	8-56	0-4	1-11	0-0	7-41	14.3	+ 8.75
M J Ryan	8-63	1-5	2-13	0-0	5-45	12.7	- 9.45
J D Bethell	8-67	2-5	3-16	0-4	3-42	11.9	+ 32.38
G Wragg	7-17	0-1	2-3	0-1	5-12	41.2	+ 26.00
G B Balding	7-29	0-1	2-6	0-1	5-21	24.1	- 4.84
D R C Elsworth	7-36	5-11	1-12	1-1	0-12	19.4	- 13.95

Leading Jockeys

	Total W-R	Per cent	£1 Level Stake	Best Trainer	W-R	Per cent	£1 Level Stake
T Quinn	37-197	18.8	- 23.73	P F I Cole	7-50	14.0	- 30.76
J Williams	36-245	14.7	- 25.42	D R C Elsworth	6-21	28.6	- 1.70
G Duffield	27-138	19.6	- 10.62	Sir M Prescott	12-41	29.3	- 3.50
Emma O'Gorman	24-97	24.7	+ 40.85	W A O'Gorman	20-75	26.7	+ 33.22
D Biggs	21-157	13.4	- 16.45	R J O'Sullivan	7-35	20.0	+ 21.00
G Carter	19-153	12.4	- 66.16	J H M Gosden	3-5	60.0	+ 8.57
N Adams	19-253	7.5	- 28.75	D Burchell	3-5	60.0	+ 14.00
D McKeown	18-93	19.4	+ 37.84	J D Bethell	3-4	75.0	+ 56.00
W Newnes	15-134	11.2	- 54.57	C C Elsey	5-22	22.7	- 0.07
N Day	14-70	20.0	+ 24.81	R Boss	4-10	40.0	+ 3.05
M Hills	14-97	14.4	- 44.94	B W Hills	6-22	27.3	- 7.52
S O'Gorman	13-79	16.5	+ 61.83	P Mitchell	6-35	17.1	+ 2.83

How the Favourites Fared

Non-handicaps	W-R	Per cent	£1 Level Stake	Handicaps	W-R	Per cent	£1 Level Stake
2-y-o	23-64	35.9	- 7.42	2-y-o	4-10	40.0	+ 3.25
3-y-o	37-82	45.1	- 4.61	3-y-o	15-38	39.5	- 5.33
Weight-for-age	44-105	41.9	+ 5.05	All-aged	77-267	28.8	- 30.29
Totals	104-251	41.4	- 6.98	Totals	96-315	30.5	- 32.37
All favs	200-566	35.3	- 39.35				

Leading Trainers by Month at Lingfield (AW)

January	Total W-R	Non-handicaps 2-y-o	3-y-o+	Handicaps 2-y-o	3-y-o+	Per cent	£1 Level Stake
W A O'Gorman	7-21	0-0	3-11	0-0	4-10	33.3	+ 6.75
M S Johnston	4-14	0-0	1-5	0-0	3-9	28.6	+ 6.25

February	Total W-R	Non-handicaps 2-y-o	3-y-o+	Handicaps 2-y-o	3-y-o+	Per cent	£1 Level Stake
Dr J D Scargill	6-18	0-0	1-5	0-0	5-13	33.3	+ 16.73
Mrs A Knight	4-11	0-0	0-1	0-0	4-10	36.4	+ 59.50

March	Total W-R	Non-handicaps 2-y-o	3-y-o+	Handicaps 2-y-o	3-y-o+	Per cent	£1 Level Stake
W A O'Gorman	5-19	0-0	2-8	0-0	3-11	26.3	+ 5.83
P Mitchell	4-12	0-0	0-3	0-0	4-9	33.3	+ 16.50

April	Total W-R	Non-handicaps 2-y-o	3-y-o+	Handicaps 2-y-o	3-y-o+	Per cent	£1 Level Stake
Sir M Prescott	4-6	0-0	2-2	0-0	2-4	66.7	+ 3.60
N A Callaghan	2-2	1-1	1-1	0-0	0-0	100.0	+ 10.25

May	Total W-R	Non-handicaps 2-y-o	3-y-o+	Handicaps 2-y-o	3-y-o+	Per cent	£1 Level Stake
M C Pipe	1-1	0-0	1-1	0-0	0-0	100.0	+ 6.00
R Charlton	1-1	0-0	1-1	0-0	0-0	100.0	+ 2.00

June	Total W-R	Non-handicaps 2-y-o	3-y-o+	Handicaps 2-y-o	3-y-o+	Per cent	£1 Level Stake
J Berry	2-2	1-1	0-0	0-0	1-1	100.0	+ 5.50
P A Kelleway	2-3	0-0	1-2	0-0	1-1	66.7	+ 11.50

July	Total W-R	Non-handicaps 2-y-o	3-y-o+	Handicaps 2-y-o	3-y-o+	Per cent	£1 Level Stake
P F I Cole	3-4	0-0	2-3	0-0	1-1	75.0	+ 0.83
B W Hills	2-2	0-0	2-2	0-0	0-0	100.0	+ 3.79

August	Total W-R	Non-handicaps 2-y-o	3-y-o+	Handicaps 2-y-o	3-y-o+	Per cent	£1 Level Stake
C A Cyzer	4-12	0-3	0-0	0-0	4-9	33.3	+ 14.50
P F I Cole	3-5	1-3	1-1	0-0	1-1	60.0	+ 0.67

September	Total W-R	Non-handicaps 2-y-o	3-y-o+	Handicaps 2-y-o	3-y-o+	Per cent	£1 Level Stake
B W Hills	2-3	0-0	1-2	0-0	1-1	66.7	+ 7.50
G Lewis	1-1	0-0	1-1	0-0	0-0	100.0	+ 14.00

October	Total W-R	Non-handicaps 2-y-o	3-y-o+	Handicaps 2-y-o	3-y-o+	Per cent	£1 Level Stake
D W Chapman	1-1	0-0	1-1	0-0	0-0	100.0	+ 2.00
G Wragg	1-1	0-0	1-1	0-0	0-0	100.0	+ 4.50

November	Total W-R	Non-handicaps 2-y-o	3-y-o+	Handicaps 2-y-o	3-y-o+	Per cent	£1 Level Stake
R Boss	6-13	4-8	1-1	1-2	0-2	46.2	+ 20.88
B W Hills	6-22	1-3	2-3	0-1	3-15	27.3	- 5.00

December	Total W-R	Non-handicaps 2-y-o	3-y-o+	Handicaps 2-y-o	3-y-o+	Per cent	£1 Level Stake
J D Bethell	6-20	2-4	2-5	0-1	2-10	30.0	+ 63.38
D R C Elsworth	5-10	4-5	0-0	1-1	0-4	50.0	+ 7.50

NEWBURY (Group 1)

Leading Trainers 1988-92

	Total W-R	Non-handicaps 2-y-o	3-y-o+	Handicaps 2-y-o	3-y-o+	Per cent	£1 Level Stake
H R A Cecil	34-97	6-14	24-68	0-0	4-15	35.1	+ 41.92
R Hannon	30-357	12-164	4-51	3-25	11-117	8.4	-119.28
M R Stoute	26-127	5-30	12-55	1-3	8-39	20.5	+ 29.92
B W Hills	21-185	9-67	6-68	0-1	6-49	11.4	- 38.91
I A Balding	21-212	8-79	3-49	1-3	9-81	9.9	- 46.85
J H M Gosden	16-79	4-18	6-32	0-0	6-29	20.3	+ 13.63
P T Walwyn	16-141	4-33	3-52	1-2	8-54	11.3	- 15.25
P F I Cole	16-142	6-48	5-40	1-4	4-50	11.3	- 20.77
L M Cumani	13-75	4-10	6-34	0-2	3-29	17.3	- 29.94
C E Brittain	13-154	2-41	6-53	1-8	4-52	8.4	- 40.67
Lord Huntingdon	12-107	0-21	3-24	2-5	7-57	11.2	- 6.25
J L Dunlop	11-182	5-50	3-78	0-2	3-52	6.0	-116.75
W R Hern	10-85	5-19	4-48	0-0	1-18	11.8	- 37.15
D R C Elsworth	10-140	2-42	1-44	1-5	6-49	7.1	- 45.67
P Chapple-Hyam	8-26	5-19	2-5	0-0	1-2	30.8	+ 25.04
R Charlton	8-62	1-19	3-19	0-2	4-22	12.9	- 6.75
R W Armstrong	7-32	2-7	2-12	0-0	3-13	21.9	+ 20.50
G Harwood	7-80	2-17	2-30	0-1	3-32	8.8	- 32.13
J Berry	6-48	5-21	1-11	0-5	0-11	12.5	- 8.83
A C Stewart	6-52	0-5	1-23	0-1	5-23	11.5	- 17.05
B Hanbury	6-67	1-21	4-24	0-0	1-22	9.0	- 37.88
R F J Houghton	6-78	1-20	1-20	0-4	4-34	7.7	- 31.00

Leading Jockeys

	Total W-R	Per cent	£1 Level Stake	Best Trainer	W-R	Per cent	£1 Level Stake
Pat Eddery	55-280	19.6	+ 17.77	H R A Cecil	6-14	42.9	+ 12.28
S Cauthen	43-200	21.5	+ 16.27	H R A Cecil	20-47	42.6	+ 25.37
W Carson	42-276	15.2	- 41.95	W R Hern	9-61	14.8	- 21.15
M Roberts	37-253	14.6	+ 17.98	C E Brittain	10-74	13.5	+ 21.83
R Cochrane	23-206	11.2	- 60.55	I A Balding	8-30	26.7	+ 20.95
T Quinn	22-183	12.0	- 42.89	P F I Cole	13-91	14.3	- 27.77
W R Swinburn	21-197	10.7	- 80.80	M R Stoute	13-73	17.8	+ 4.25
L Dettori	20-142	14.1	+ 21.50	L M Cumani	7-35	20.0	- 7.50
J Reid	17-184	9.2	- 64.11	R F J Houghton	3-21	14.3	- 2.00
M Hills	10-131	7.6	- 72.09	B W Hills	9-82	11.0	- 25.00
B Raymond	10-176	5.7	- 53.50	R Hannon	4-36	11.1	+ 24.00
W Newnes	9-139	6.5	- 59.49	J A R Toller	2-8	25.0	+ 6.00

How the Favourites Fared

Non-handicaps	W-R	Per cent	£1 Level Stake	Handicaps	W-R	Per cent	£1 Level Stake
2-y-o	57-130	43.8	+ 3.72	2-y-o	4-17	23.5	- 2.25
3-y-o	25-80	31.3	- 18.99	3-y-o	19-79	24.1	- 19.39
Weight-for-age	19-58	32.8	- 6.62	All-aged	28-106	26.4	+ 2.15
Totals	101-268	37.7	- 21.89	Totals	51-202	25.2	- 19.49
All favs	152-470	32.3	- 41.38				

Leading Trainers by Month at Newbury

March/Apr	Total W-R	Non-handicaps 2-y-o	3-y-o+	Handicaps 2-y-o	3-y-o+	Per cent	£1 Level Stake
H R A Cecil	10-26	0-0	9-24	0-0	1-2	38.5	+ 21.53
B W Hills	4-35	1-2	2-27	0-0	1-6	11.4	+ 1.00
R Hannon	4-48	2-14	2-17	0-0	0-17	8.3	+ 6.50
P T Walwyn	3-23	0-0	2-20	0-0	1-3	13.0	+ 9.50
P F I Cole	3-29	1-4	1-16	0-0	1-9	10.3	- 17.25

May	Total W-R	Non-handicaps 2-y-o	3-y-o+	Handicaps 2-y-o	3-y-o+	Per cent	£1 Level Stake
I A Balding	6-17	1-5	2-5	0-0	3-7	35.3	+ 40.00
M R Stoute	6-19	0-0	4-13	0-0	2-6	31.6	+ 10.50
H R A Cecil	5-21	0-0	4-17	0-0	1-4	23.8	+ 4.82
P T Walwyn	4-20	1-1	0-6	0-0	3-13	20.0	+ 21.00
P F I Cole	4-26	2-8	2-9	0-0	0-9	15.4	- 7.27

June	Total W-R	Non-handicaps 2-y-o	3-y-o+	Handicaps 2-y-o	3-y-o+	Per cent	£1 Level Stake
H R A Cecil	6-14	1-2	5-12	0-0	0-0	42.9	+ 5.01
R Hannon	6-68	3-35	0-8	0-0	3-25	8.8	+ 1.65
M R Stoute	4-16	0-2	3-7	0-0	1-7	25.0	+ 6.67
Lord Huntingdon	4-17	0-3	2-6	0-0	2-8	23.5	+ 19.50
D R C Elsworth	4-18	0-4	1-4	0-0	3-10	22.2	+ 2.83

July	Total W-R	Non-handicaps 2-y-o	3-y-o+	Handicaps 2-y-o	3-y-o+	Per cent	£1 Level Stake
L M Cumani	6-10	0-0	4-5	0-0	2-5	60.0	+ 14.58
H R A Cecil	5-10	0-1	4-6	0-0	1-3	50.0	+ 5.59
W R Hern	3-16	2-4	1-10	0-0	0-2	18.8	+ 0.50
B W Hills	3-19	1-6	1-4	0-0	1-9	15.8	+ 4.00
I A Balding	3-36	1-11	1-10	0-0	1-15	8.3	- 22.05

August	Total W-R	Non-handicaps 2-y-o	3-y-o+	Handicaps 2-y-o	3-y-o+	Per cent	£1 Level Stake
R Hannon	6-50	1-24	1-5	1-2	3-19	12.0	- 13.50
B W Hills	5-27	2-14	2-8	0-0	1-5	18.5	+ 2.88
H R A Cecil	4-8	2-3	1-3	0-0	1-2	50.0	+ 4.69
M R Stoute	4-20	0-7	1-5	0-0	3-8	20.0	+ 12.50
C E Brittain	4-25	0-7	4-11	0-0	0-7	16.0	+ 17.50

September	Total W-R	Non-handicaps 2-y-o	3-y-o+	Handicaps 2-y-o	3-y-o+	Per cent	£1 Level Stake
R Hannon	6-51	1-23	0-3	2-11	3-14	11.8	- 15.25
J H M Gosden	5-15	1-6	2-2	0-0	2-7	33.3	+ 3.75
M R Stoute	4-21	2-9	1-4	1-1	0-7	19.0	+ 0.25
B W Hills	4-24	2-15	0-0	0-1	2-8	16.7	+ 6.10
J L Dunlop	4-26	3-15	0-2	0-2	1-7	15.4	+ 11.50

Oct/Nov	Total W-R	Non-handicaps 2-y-o	3-y-o+	Handicaps 2-y-o	3-y-o+	Per cent	£1 Level Stake
M R Stoute	5-22	3-10	1-6	0-2	1-4	22.7	+ 15.25
P F I Cole	4-15	0-5	1-2	1-2	2-6	26.7	+ 48.00
G B Balding	4-20	0-4	0-0	1-3	3-13	20.0	+ 44.50
L M Cumani	4-21	3-3	1-8	0-2	0-8	19.0	- 9.13
J H M Gosden	4-22	2-7	0-8	0-0	2-7	18.2	+ 9.08

NEWCASTLE (Group 1)

Leading Trainers 1988-92

	Total W-R	Non-handicaps 2-y-o	3-y-o+	Handicaps 2-y-o	3-y-o+	Per cent	£1 Level Stake
J Berry	20-110	11-49	3-13	0-6	6-42	18.2	- 33.98
H R A Cecil	14-34	5-7	8-22	0-1	1-4	41.2	- 9.08
M H Easterby	14-140	1-33	2-15	0-6	11-86	10.0	- 71.67
M R Stoute	12-41	4-10	6-20	0-1	2-10	29.3	- 22.09
B W Hills	12-45	4-10	5-22	0-1	3-12	26.7	- 3.01
J W Watts	11-77	2-19	2-13	0-1	7-44	14.3	- 22.33
L M Cumani	9-20	2-4	5-11	0-1	2-4	45.0	+ 2.65
B Hanbury	9-33	3-8	3-15	0-0	3-10	27.3	+ 26.88
M J Camacho	9-37	1-9	4-8	0-1	4-19	24.3	+ 35.70
Mrs G R Reveley	9-67	0-7	0-8	0-4	9-48	13.4	- 35.20
Mrs J Ramsden	9-72	0-18	1-7	0-4	8-43	12.5	- 9.62
M W Easterby	8-68	4-28	1-9	0-7	3-24	11.8	- 32.82
Sir M Prescott	7-26	2-5	0-3	1-3	4-15	26.9	+ 8.96
D Morley	7-35	3-8	1-10	0-1	3-16	20.0	- 0.07
J Etherington	7-62	4-18	0-14	1-5	2-25	11.3	+ 24.00
S G Norton	6-42	3-15	2-11	1-3	0-13	14.3	+ 0.48
F H Lee	6-50	0-8	0-4	2-4	4-34	12.0	- 11.00
T D Barron	6-61	2-16	1-5	1-6	2-34	9.8	- 10.50
R M Whitaker	6-78	1-18	0-9	1-3	4-48	7.7	- 44.00
R W Armstrong	5-9	1-3	3-4	0-0	1-2	55.6	+ 10.20
B Beasley	5-10	2-4	0-0	0-1	3-5	50.0	+ 42.50
G Harwood	5-16	0-1	2-7	0-0	3-8	31.3	+ 6.80

Leading Jockeys

	Total W-R	Per cent	£1 Level Stake	Best Trainer	W-R	Per cent	£1 Level Stake
M Birch	25-165	15.2	- 18.27	M H Easterby	9-87	10.3	- 44.04
W Carson	21-52	40.4	+ 36.25	W R Hern	3-3	100.0	+ 8.07
Pat Eddery	18-40	45.0	+ 11.45	M R Stoute	4-6	66.7	- 0.40
J Carroll	18-105	17.1	+ 1.70	J Berry	13-62	21.0	- 7.80
D McKeown	18-140	12.9	- 41.76	J W Watts	7-26	26.9	- 0.81
J Lowe	14-151	9.3	- 48.99	Mrs G R Reveley	4-29	13.8	- 12.75
S Cauthen	13-30	43.3	- 0.01	H R A Cecil	6-10	60.0	- 1.21
R Cochrane	13-51	25.5	- 0.43	L M Cumani	3-3	100.0	+ 2.52
K Darley	13-128	10.2	- 76.04	J Berry	2-6	33.3	0.00
G Duffield	11-63	17.5	- 2.62	Sir M Prescott	5-19	26.3	+ 6.21
K Fallon	9-104	8.7	- 33.00	J G FitzGerald	2-19	10.5	- 6.00
N Connorton	8-71	11.3	- 14.80	M J Camacho	5-20	25.0	+ 7.20

How the Favourites Fared

Non-handicaps	W-R	Per cent	£1 Level Stake	Handicaps	W-R	Per cent	£1 Level Stake
2-y-o	44-77	57.1	+ 18.43	2-y-o	2-12	16.7	- 5.27
3-y-o	13-38	34.2	- 11.93	3-y-o	14-43	32.6	- 0.44
Weight-for-age	28-52	53.8	- 4.17	All-aged	44-121	36.4	+ 16.76
Totals	85-167	50.9	+ 2.33	Totals	60-176	34.1	+ 11.05
All favs	145-343	42.3	+ 13.38				

Leading Trainers by Month at Newcastle

March/Apr	Total W-R	Non-handicaps 2-y-o	3-y-o+	Handicaps 2-y-o	3-y-o+	Per cent	£1 Level Stake
J Berry	6-25	4-10	1-6	0-0	1-9	24.0	- 0.18
M J Camacho	5-10	0-0	2-4	0-0	3-6	50.0	+ 41.00
J W Watts	5-18	0-0	2-9	0-0	3-9	27.8	+ 3.30
Mrs J Ramsden	5-22	0-1	1-6	0-0	4-15	22.7	+ 18.63
H R A Cecil	2-4	0-0	2-4	0-0	0-0	50.0	- 0.13

May	Total W-R	Non-handicaps 2-y-o	3-y-o+	Handicaps 2-y-o	3-y-o+	Per cent	£1 Level Stake
J Berry	3-3	1-1	1-1	0-0	1-1	100.0	+ 6.21
W W Haigh	1-1	0-0	1-1	0-0	0-0	100.0	+ 3.50
R Hannon	1-1	1-1	0-0	0-0	0-0	100.0	+ 0.67
M R Stoute	1-1	0-0	1-1	0-0	0-0	100.0	+ 0.17
J A Glover	1-1	0-0	0-0	0-0	1-1	100.0	+ 5.00

June	Total W-R	Non-handicaps 2-y-o	3-y-o+	Handicaps 2-y-o	3-y-o+	Per cent	£1 Level Stake
H R A Cecil	6-6	2-2	4-4	0-0	0-0	100.0	+ 2.84
M H Easterby	4-34	0-9	1-4	0-0	3-21	11.8	- 14.13
M R Stoute	3-7	1-1	1-3	0-0	1-3	42.9	- 2.57
J Etherington	3-15	1-4	0-2	0-0	2-9	20.0	+ 9.00
J W Watts	3-16	2-7	0-0	0-0	1-9	18.8	- 1.38

July	Total W-R	Non-handicaps 2-y-o	3-y-o+	Handicaps 2-y-o	3-y-o+	Per cent	£1 Level Stake
J Berry	5-18	4-10	0-0	0-1	1-7	27.8	- 5.21
G Harwood	4-5	0-0	2-3	0-0	2-2	80.0	+ 8.80
M R Stoute	4-12	2-2	2-7	0-0	0-3	33.3	- 5.88
M H Easterby	4-27	0-7	1-3	0-0	3-17	14.8	- 8.63
H R A Cecil	3-5	0-0	2-3	0-0	1-2	60.0	+ 0.08

August	Total W-R	Non-handicaps 2-y-o	3-y-o+	Handicaps 2-y-o	3-y-o+	Per cent	£1 Level Stake
B W Hills	5-15	1-4	2-6	0-0	2-5	33.3	+ 5.21
L M Cumani	3-3	0-0	3-3	0-0	0-0	100.0	+ 4.56
B Hanbury	3-11	1-2	1-6	0-0	1-3	27.3	+ 8.25
F H Lee	3-13	0-1	0-1	2-4	1-7	23.1	+ 10.00
T D Barron	3-19	0-2	1-2	1-5	1-10	15.8	+ 8.00

September	Total W-R	Non-handicaps 2-y-o	3-y-o+	Handicaps 2-y-o	3-y-o+	Per cent	£1 Level Stake
H R A Cecil	1-1	1-1	0-0	0-0	0-0	100.0	+ 3.50
S G Norton	1-1	0-0	1-1	0-0	0-0	100.0	+ 10.00
M Bell	1-1	1-1	0-0	0-0	0-0	100.0	+ 0.62
J Berry	1-2	0-1	0-0	0-0	1-1	50.0	+ 3.50
J L Dunlop	1-3	0-2	0-0	0-0	1-1	33.3	+ 1.50

Oct/Nov	Total W-R	Non-handicaps 2-y-o	3-y-o+	Handicaps 2-y-o	3-y-o+	Per cent	£1 Level Stake
D Morley	6-15	3-6	1-4	0-0	2-5	40.0	+ 15.60
R W Armstrong	4-8	1-3	2-3	0-0	1-2	50.0	+ 8.20
J H M Gosden	3-9	0-3	3-5	0-0	0-1	33.3	- 4.98
M J Camacho	3-10	0-2	2-4	0-0	1-4	30.0	+ 2.70
L M Cumani	3-10	2-4	1-3	0-1	0-2	30.0	- 1.98

NEWMARKET (Group 1)

Leading Trainers 1988-92

	Total W-R	Non-handicaps 2-y-o	3-y-o+	Handicaps 2-y-o	3-y-o+	Per cent	£1 Level Stake
H R A Cecil	77-362	32-122	38-180	0-2	7-58	21.3	- 73.47
M R Stoute	59-308	26-136	27-119	1-11	5-42	19.2	- 10.01
L M Cumani	58-340	14-101	34-159	1-5	9-75	17.1	- 73.02
B W Hills	49-366	16-111	14-135	1-9	18-111	13.4	- 43.79
R Hannon	43-399	18-136	12-84	7-49	6-130	10.8	- 32.33
C E Brittain	35-450	11-133	11-161	2-16	11-140	7.8	-102.77
J H M Gosden	31-185	2-38	19-85	0-4	10-58	16.8	- 13.87
J L Dunlop	26-244	3-65	15-97	0-2	8-80	10.7	-105.54
W R Hern	24-95	8-28	13-47	0-0	3-20	25.3	+ 4.29
G Wragg	23-179	5-46	11-81	1-4	6-48	12.8	- 33.19
G Harwood	18-205	7-60	7-78	0-2	4-65	8.8	- 82.54
P F I Cole	17-108	8-37	5-37	1-10	3-24	15.7	+ 40.13
M A Jarvis	17-169	2-57	8-40	1-9	6-63	10.1	- 27.45
A A Scott	14-125	7-56	7-46	0-7	0-16	11.2	- 45.18
A C Stewart	13-123	3-19	5-49	0-1	5-54	10.6	- 17.53
G Lewis	12-79	3-23	3-16	2-11	4-29	15.2	+ 38.00
J Berry	12-97	4-28	3-21	1-18	4-30	12.4	- 15.06
P T Walwyn	12-144	3-29	6-57	0-2	3-56	8.3	- 59.18
W Jarvis	12-162	3-55	5-52	0-7	4-48	7.4	- 27.20
N A Callaghan	12-216	5-92	4-46	0-18	3-60	5.6	-104.67
J R Fanshawe	11-68	2-16	4-23	1-2	4-27	16.2	+ 16.98
M Bell	11-97	2-29	3-20	3-13	3-35	11.3	- 26.13

Leading Jockeys

	Total W-R	Per cent	£1 Level Stake	Best Trainer	W-R	Per cent	£1 Level Stake
W Carson	88-557	15.8	- 59.70	W R Hern	23-76	30.3	+ 21.30
S Cauthen	81-464	17.5	-134.50	H R A Cecil	44-149	29.5	- 11.43
Pat Eddery	81-492	16.5	-124.89	H R A Cecil	14-40	35.0	+ 1.20
M Roberts	73-570	12.8	- 30.01	C E Brittain	26-194	13.4	+ 43.50
W R Swinburn	59-410	14.4	-121.96	M R Stoute	31-152	20.4	- 28.48
L Dettori	54-379	14.2	- 33.19	L M Cumani	30-178	16.9	- 41.77
R Cochrane	51-413	12.3	+ 5.57	L M Cumani	16-77	20.8	- 0.80
M Hills	41-292	14.0	+114.76	B W Hills	21-131	16.0	+ 39.38
B Raymond	39-447	8.7	-166.63	B Hanbury	7-82	8.5	- 28.26
Paul Eddery	27-288	9.4	-101.50	G Lewis	8-38	21.1	+ 29.50
J Reid	23-242	9.5	- 7.50	C E Brittain	2-4	50.0	+ 24.00
R Hills	20-253	7.9	- 79.14	H Thomson Jones	6-78	7.7	- 54.14

How the Favourites Fared

Non-handicaps	W-R	Per cent	£1 Level Stake	Handicaps	W-R	Per cent	£1 Level Stake
2-y-o	107-259	41.3	- 10.16	2-y-o	12-52	23.1	+ 3.26
3-y-o	93-210	44.3	+ 19.40	3-y-o	24-115	20.9	- 26.03
Weight-for-age	60-149	40.3	- 14.33	All-aged	45-207	21.7	- 49.17
Totals	260-618	42.1	- 5.09	Totals	81-374	21.7	- 71.94
All favs	341-992	34.4	- 77.03				

Leading Trainers by Month at Newmarket

March/Apr	Total W-R	Non-handicaps 2-y-o	3-y-o+	Handicaps 2-y-o	3-y-o+	Per cent	£1 Level Stake
H R A Cecil	10-56	0-0	9-48	0-0	1-8	17.9	- 19.40
C E Brittain	9-68	0-4	6-41	0-0	3-23	13.2	+ 53.75
L M Cumani	8-56	0-0	8-44	0-0	0-12	14.3	- 28.00
M R Stoute	7-36	0-0	7-32	0-0	0-4	19.4	- 13.95
B W Hills	7-69	0-3	1-49	0-0	6-17	10.1	- 6.00

May	Total W-R	Non-handicaps 2-y-o	3-y-o+	Handicaps 2-y-o	3-y-o+	Per cent	£1 Level Stake
M R Stoute	9-36	1-3	7-29	0-0	1-4	25.0	- 10.93
L M Cumani	8-43	0-0	7-35	0-0	1-8	18.6	+ 9.79
C E Brittain	8-63	2-10	3-38	0-0	3-15	12.7	+ 11.75
H R A Cecil	7-53	0-2	6-45	0-0	1-6	13.2	- 36.32
J Berry	6-27	4-10	2-9	0-0	0-8	22.2	- 7.06

June	Total W-R	Non-handicaps 2-y-o	3-y-o+	Handicaps 2-y-o	3-y-o+	Per cent	£1 Level Stake
J H M Gosden	5-13	0-1	4-9	0-0	1-3	38.5	+ 13.11
L M Cumani	4-14	1-2	3-10	0-0	0-2	28.6	- 4.67
H R A Cecil	4-19	2-3	2-14	0-0	0-2	21.1	- 8.38
J R Fanshawe	3-7	0-0	1-3	0-0	2-4	42.9	+ 22.00
P F I Cole	3-8	1-1	1-4	0-0	1-3	37.5	+ 5.50

July	Total W-R	Non-handicaps 2-y-o	3-y-o+	Handicaps 2-y-o	3-y-o+	Per cent	£1 Level Stake
H R A Cecil	24-70	12-26	9-30	0-0	3-14	34.3	- 6.93
R Hannon	16-88	9-37	4-15	1-3	2-33	18.2	+ 12.42
M R Stoute	10-44	4-21	3-14	0-0	3-9	22.7	- 0.76
L M Cumani	8-49	1-7	5-25	0-0	2-17	16.3	- 8.56
B W Hills	8-55	2-16	3-16	0-0	3-23	14.5	- 4.25

August	Total W-R	Non-handicaps 2-y-o	3-y-o+	Handicaps 2-y-o	3-y-o+	Per cent	£1 Level Stake
M R Stoute	11-45	9-25	1-7	1-2	0-11	24.4	+ 6.55
R Hannon	10-57	3-20	2-10	4-13	1-14	17.5	+ 36.25
H R A Cecil	7-32	4-11	2-11	0-1	1-9	21.9	- 12.00
L M Cumani	7-38	3-14	2-12	0-1	2-11	18.4	- 15.50
A C Stewart	6-20	2-6	2-7	0-0	2-7	30.0	+ 7.88

September	Total W-R	Non-handicaps 2-y-o	3-y-o+	Handicaps 2-y-o	3-y-o+	Per cent	£1 Level Stake
H R A Cecil	3-15	3-9	0-3	0-0	0-3	20.0	- 6.30
B W Hills	2-13	1-3	1-2	0-2	0-6	15.4	+ 10.00
M J Camacho	1-1	0-0	1-1	0-0	0-0	100.0	+ 6.00
Sir M Prescott	1-1	0-0	1-1	0-0	0-0	100.0	+ 6.00
C W Thornton	1-1	0-0	1-1	0-0	0-0	100.0	+ 6.00

Oct/Nov	Total W-R	Non-handicaps 2-y-o	3-y-o+	Handicaps 2-y-o	3-y-o+	Per cent	£1 Level Stake
B W Hills	24-153	10-68	6-32	1-7	7-46	15.7	+ 1.58
H R A Cecil	22-117	11-71	10-29	0-1	1-16	18.8	+ 15.87
L M Cumani	22-131	8-72	9-31	1-4	4-24	16.8	- 19.59
M R Stoute	20-126	11-74	8-33	0-7	1-12	15.9	+ 24.25
J H M Gosden	8-71	0-22	6-23	0-2	2-24	11.3	- 32.18

NOTTINGHAM (Group 3)

Leading Trainers 1988-92

	Total W-R	Non-handicaps 2-y-o	3-y-o+	Handicaps 2-y-o	3-y-o+	Per cent	£1 Level Stake
H R A Cecil	28-78	10-26	18-52	0-0	0-0	35.9	+ 3.85
J L Dunlop	23-128	6-37	7-47	2-10	8-34	18.0	+ 8.09
P F I Cole	16-86	7-27	4-25	2-12	3-22	18.6	- 6.91
D Morley	16-95	2-20	3-22	1-2	10-51	16.8	+ 28.13
M R Stoute	15-59	7-27	7-23	1-6	0-3	25.4	+ 12.03
J Berry	13-92	8-55	4-22	0-12	1-3	14.1	- 43.78
C Tinkler	10-64	4-22	0-10	0-4	6-28	15.6	+ 14.13
B A McMahon	10-117	2-19	3-30	0-4	5-64	8.5	- 18.50
L M Cumani	9-34	4-11	5-21	0-0	0-2	26.5	- 9.26
R J Hodges	9-58	0-3	1-7	0-1	8-47	15.5	+ 58.00
J H M Gosden	8-32	2-6	5-19	0-1	1-6	25.0	- 11.00
P T Walwyn	8-39	4-14	4-11	0-3	0-11	20.5	- 3.50
G Lewis	8-54	0-8	3-11	0-4	5-31	14.8	+ 4.75
B W Hills	8-63	5-26	1-24	1-5	1-8	12.7	- 22.22
R Hollinshead	8-193	2-48	3-62	0-12	3-71	4.1	-104.50
R Charlton	7-17	2-9	4-7	0-0	1-1	41.2	+ 9.32
N A Callaghan	7-45	1-15	4-13	1-5	1-12	15.6	- 6.90
F H Lee	7-49	1-9	2-9	0-0	4-31	14.3	+ 97.00
R J R Williams	7-52	1-8	3-16	0-4	3-24	13.5	+ 15.25
M J Ryan	7-71	0-7	3-16	0-5	4-43	9.9	- 21.13
J Wharton	7-79	2-28	3-16	0-3	2-32	8.9	- 12.00
G Harwood	6-20	1-5	5-13	0-0	0-2	30.0	+ 4.61

Leading Jockeys

	Total W-R	Per cent	£1 Level Stake	Best Trainer	W-R	Per cent	£1 Level Stake
W Carson	40-212	18.9	+ 32.39	J L Dunlop	10-48	20.8	+ 11.55
Pat Eddery	38-152	25.0	+ 8.31	R Charlton	6-8	75.0	+ 11.82
S Cauthen	34-117	29.1	+ 16.94	H R A Cecil	16-35	45.7	+ 9.29
M Roberts	22-189	11.6	- 44.49	D Morley	3-11	27.3	+ 4.25
W R Swinburn	21-132	15.9	+ 0.17	M R Stoute	11-38	28.9	+ 12.79
L Dettori	18-104	17.3	- 16.78	L M Cumani	4-17	23.5	- 3.33
R Cochrane	16-127	12.6	- 39.20	L M Cumani	3-10	30.0	- 2.33
W Ryan	16-153	10.5	- 69.49	H R A Cecil	9-29	31.0	- 5.74
G Carter	16-167	9.6	- 46.77	G Wragg	3-16	18.8	- 7.50
T Quinn	14-98	14.3	- 17.89	P F I Cole	8-43	18.6	- 2.12
M Birch	13-99	13.1	+ 21.13	C Tinkler	6-24	25.0	+ 16.13
A Munro	10-130	7.7	- 60.54	P F I Cole	5-13	38.5	+ 9.46

How the Favourites Fared

Non-handicaps	W-R	Per cent	£1 Level Stake	Handicaps	W-R	Per cent	£1 Level Stake
2-y-o	56-147	38.1	- 23.83	2-y-o	7-25	28.0	- 7.66
3-y-o	54-139	38.8	- 17.85	3-y-o	16-59	27.1	- 2.87
Weight-for-age	13-33	39.4	- 2.33	All-aged	40-149	26.8	- 7.12
Totals	123-319	38.6	- 44.01	Totals	63-233	27.0	- 17.65
All favs	186-552	33.7	- 61.66				

Leading Trainers by Month at Nottingham

March/Apr	Total	Non-handicaps		Handicaps		Per	£1 Level
	W-R	2-y-o	3-y-o+	2-y-o	3-y-o+	cent	Stake
H R A Cecil	8-16	0-0	8-16	0-0	0-0	50.0	+ 4.73
J Berry	5-16	2-7	3-9	0-0	0-0	31.3	+ 1.65
J W Hills	3-7	0-0	2-4	0-0	1-3	42.9	+ 26.75
Lord Huntingdon	3-9	0-0	2-7	0-0	1-2	33.3	+ 17.50
N A Callaghan	3-12	0-2	2-7	0-0	1-3	25.0	+ 6.10

May	Total	Non-handicaps		Handicaps		Per	£1 Level
	W-R	2-y-o	3-y-o+	2-y-o	3-y-o+	cent	Stake
H R A Cecil	5-9	2-2	3-7	0-0	0-0	55.6	+ 3.57
J L Dunlop	3-11	0-0	2-7	0-0	1-4	27.3	+ 12.75
M W Eckley	2-3	0-0	0-0	0-0	2-3	66.7	+ 39.00
J H M Gosden	2-5	0-0	1-4	0-0	1-1	40.0	+ 2.50
G A P-Gordon	2-9	0-2	1-3	0-0	1-4	22.2	+ 8.50

June	Total	Non-handicaps		Handicaps		Per	£1 Level
	W-R	2-y-o	3-y-o+	2-y-o	3-y-o+	cent	Stake
J H M Gosden	4-4	2-2	2-2	0-0	0-0	100.0	+ 4.00
M R Stoute	4-9	1-1	3-8	0-0	0-0	44.4	+ 5.17
R J Hodges	4-12	0-0	0-0	0-0	4-12	33.3	+ 43.00
B A McMahon	4-26	1-6	0-7	0-0	3-13	15.4	+ 26.50
H R A Cecil	3-10	1-1	2-9	0-0	0-0	30.0	- 3.38

July	Total	Non-handicaps		Handicaps		Per	£1 Level
	W-R	2-y-o	3-y-o+	2-y-o	3-y-o+	cent	Stake
J L Dunlop	5-13	2-4	2-4	0-0	1-5	38.5	+ 11.92
Sir M Prescott	3-7	1-2	0-0	0-0	2-5	42.9	+ 11.13
H R A Cecil	3-9	1-2	2-7	0-0	0-0	33.3	- 4.21
G Lewis	3-10	0-1	1-3	0-0	2-6	30.0	+ 5.50
B A McMahon	3-11	1-3	1-2	0-0	1-6	27.3	+ 17.00

August	Total	Non-handicaps		Handicaps		Per	£1 Level
	W-R	2-y-o	3-y-o+	2-y-o	3-y-o+	cent	Stake
H R A Cecil	3-4	2-3	1-1	0-0	0-0	75.0	+ 8.93
J L Dunlop	3-9	1-3	1-3	1-1	0-2	33.3	+ 19.50
D Morley	3-10	0-2	0-1	0-0	3-7	30.0	+ 12.00
G Harwood	2-3	0-0	2-3	0-0	0-0	66.7	+ 6.33
N Tinkler	2-5	0-2	1-2	0-0	1-1	40.0	+ 3.50

September	Total	Non-handicaps		Handicaps		Per	£1 Level
	W-R	2-y-o	3-y-o+	2-y-o	3-y-o+	cent	Stake
D Morley	8-27	1-7	2-4	1-2	4-14	29.6	+ 40.25
P F I Cole	5-27	2-11	1-4	1-7	1-5	18.5	+ 5.63
J L Dunlop	5-33	2-16	0-4	1-6	2-7	15.2	- 2.20
L M Cumani	4-8	3-6	1-2	0-0	0-0	50.0	+ 6.17
P A Kelleway	3-8	2-6	1-2	0-0	0-0	37.5	+ 41.75

Oct/Nov	Total	Non-handicaps		Handicaps		Per	£1 Level
	W-R	2-y-o	3-y-o+	2-y-o	3-y-o+	cent	Stake
P F I Cole	5-21	3-12	1-2	1-5	0-2	23.8	+ 10.85
H R A Cecil	4-14	3-10	1-4	0-0	0-0	28.6	+ 3.05
A A Scott	3-5	1-2	0-0	1-1	1-2	60.0	+ 18.00
B W Hills	3-10	2-2	0-4	1-3	0-1	30.0	+ 9.66
J L Dunlop	3-22	1-13	0-2	0-3	2-4	13.6	- 14.00

PONTEFRACT (Group 3)

Leading Trainers 1988-92

	Total W-R	Non-handicaps 2-y-o	3-y-o+	Handicaps 2-y-o	3-y-o+	Per cent	£1 Level Stake
R Hollinshead	27-200	7-38	5-46	0-6	15-110	13.5	- 73.86
J Berry	18-126	13-70	2-17	0-7	3-32	14.3	- 34.03
Mrs J Ramsden	18-128	1-13	0-13	0-5	17-97	14.1	- 41.83
M H Tompkins	15-93	5-22	6-29	1-6	3-36	16.1	- 9.41
H R A Cecil	13-31	0-2	13-29	0-0	0-0	41.9	+ 1.68
B A McMahon	13-112	0-8	4-39	0-0	9-65	11.6	- 8.50
Mrs G R Reveley	12-62	1-11	2-12	2-5	7-34	19.4	+ 19.25
T D Barron	9-79	2-11	0-2	1-6	6-60	11.4	+ 3.50
M H Easterby	9-125	2-40	3-19	1-12	3-54	7.2	- 70.13
G Harwood	8-22	1-4	4-13	2-2	1-3	36.4	- 0.09
G Wragg	8-33	0-4	8-24	0-2	0-3	24.2	+ 8.92
M S Johnston	8-48	3-12	2-10	1-3	2-23	16.7	+ 21.25
M R Stoute	7-22	3-6	3-13	0-1	1-2	31.8	+ 0.91
B W Hills	7-31	1-6	4-10	0-4	2-11	22.6	+ 4.10
I A Balding	7-32	3-5	2-12	0-3	2-12	21.9	+ 5.75
Denys Smith	7-72	1-15	0-11	0-2	6-44	9.7	- 16.50
L M Cumani	6-17	1-2	5-15	0-0	0-0	35.3	- 0.85
G M Moore	6-46	2-6	2-13	0-0	2-27	13.0	- 6.40
J W Watts	6-50	0-11	1-9	0-3	5-27	12.0	- 22.40
J Etherington	6-57	3-23	2-11	1-9	0-14	10.5	- 23.83
F H Lee	6-75	1-8	0-11	0-4	5-52	8.0	- 12.92
D W Chapman	6-89	0-2	0-4	0-5	6-78	6.7	+ 23.75

Leading Jockeys

	Total W-R	Per cent	£1 Level Stake	Best Trainer	W-R	Per cent	£1 Level Stake
K Darley	25-173	14.5	- 34.08	Mrs G R Reveley	4-11	36.4	+ 14.50
D McKeown	21-180	11.7	- 73.22	Mrs J Ramsden	6-29	20.7	- 8.91
M Roberts	18-85	21.2	+ 13.11	A C Stewart	3-16	18.8	- 9.48
B Raymond	16-106	15.1	- 15.85	B Hanbury	4-16	25.0	- 3.95
K Fallon	16-116	13.8	+ 64.85	J J O'Neill	3-8	37.5	+ 2.75
M Birch	15-179	8.4	- 86.27	M H Easterby	5-66	7.6	- 34.12
G Carter	14-107	13.1	- 29.88	G Wragg	5-17	29.4	+ 12.25
J Carroll	14-124	11.3	- 53.52	J Berry	13-82	15.9	- 14.65
W Ryan	13-82	15.9	- 44.94	H R A Cecil	5-16	31.3	- 2.43
L Dettori	12-51	23.5	+ 16.05	L M Cumani	5-11	45.5	+ 2.95
A Munro	12-95	12.6	- 24.77	W A O'Gorman	3-7	42.9	+ 2.48
J Lowe	12-191	6.3	- 64.00	Mrs G R Reveley	2-23	8.7	- 9.50

How the Favourites Fared

Non-handicaps	W-R	Per cent	£1 Level Stake	Handicaps	W-R	Per cent	£1 Level Stake
2-y-o	50-102	49.0	+ 18.85	2-y-o	6-18	33.3	+ 3.23
3-y-o	33-78	42.3	- 1.90	3-y-o	14-37	37.8	+ 3.06
Weight-for-age	20-52	38.5	- 4.50	All-aged	49-184	26.6	- 32.25
Totals	103-232	44.4	+ 12.45	Totals	69-239	28.9	- 25.96
All favs	172-471	36.5	- 13.51				

Leading Trainers by Month at Pontefract

March/Apr	Total W-R	Non-handicaps 2-y-o	3-y-o+	Handicaps 2-y-o	3-y-o+	Per cent	£1 Level Stake
H R A Cecil	6-8	0-0	6-8	0-0	0-0	75.0	+ 9.55
J Berry	6-25	4-13	1-4	0-0	1-8	24.0	+ 0.35
R Hollinshead	6-35	0-8	0-6	0-0	6-21	17.1	+ 6.54
Mrs J Ramsden	5-23	0-1	0-4	0-0	5-18	21.7	- 6.63
L M Cumani	3-5	0-0	3-5	0-0	0-0	60.0	+ 4.45

May	Total W-R	Non-handicaps 2-y-o	3-y-o+	Handicaps 2-y-o	3-y-o+	Per cent	£1 Level Stake
G Wragg	4-6	0-0	4-5	0-0	0-1	66.7	+ 15.83
J Berry	4-12	3-6	0-3	0-0	1-3	33.3	+ 10.88
Miss S E Hall	3-5	0-0	2-3	0-0	1-2	60.0	+ 25.00
J W Watts	3-8	0-0	0-3	0-0	3-5	37.5	+ 8.35
M H Tompkins	3-11	1-1	2-8	0-0	0-2	27.3	+ 15.44

June	Total W-R	Non-handicaps 2-y-o	3-y-o+	Handicaps 2-y-o	3-y-o+	Per cent	£1 Level Stake
Mrs J Ramsden	5-17	1-3	0-1	0-0	4-13	29.4	+ 13.21
R Hollinshead	5-28	3-9	0-4	0-0	2-15	17.9	- 15.86
J A Glover	3-11	1-2	1-2	0-0	1-7	27.3	+ 6.50
Denys Smith	3-12	0-3	0-3	0-0	3-6	25.0	+ 5.00
T D Barron	3-14	2-4	0-1	0-0	1-9	21.4	+ 10.50

July	Total W-R	Non-handicaps 2-y-o	3-y-o+	Handicaps 2-y-o	3-y-o+	Per cent	£1 Level Stake
R Hollinshead	6-27	2-5	0-6	0-0	4-16	22.2	+ 0.99
C F Wall	3-4	3-4	0-0	0-0	0-0	75.0	+ 12.32
B W Hills	3-6	0-1	2-3	0-0	1-2	50.0	+ 3.19
Sir M Prescott	3-6	1-1	2-2	0-0	0-3	50.0	+ 5.00
Mrs J Ramsden	3-23	0-3	0-3	0-0	3-17	13.0	- 8.67

August	Total W-R	Non-handicaps 2-y-o	3-y-o+	Handicaps 2-y-o	3-y-o+	Per cent	£1 Level Stake
Mrs G R Reveley	5-9	0-0	2-2	1-2	2-5	55.6	+ 31.50
M H Tompkins	4-16	2-6	0-0	1-2	1-8	25.0	- 0.40
R Hollinshead	4-29	1-6	2-8	0-0	1-15	13.8	- 15.27
I A Balding	3-7	2-2	0-0	0-1	1-4	42.9	+ 10.00
S G Norton	3-12	2-6	0-0	1-3	0-3	25.0	- 5.06

September	Total W-R	Non-handicaps 2-y-o	3-y-o+	Handicaps 2-y-o	3-y-o+	Per cent	£1 Level Stake
B A McMahon	4-13	0-1	1-2	0-0	3-10	30.8	+ 21.00
J D Bethell	3-9	0-1	0-0	0-0	3-8	33.3	+ 8.50
G A P-Gordon	2-3	0-0	0-0	0-0	2-3	66.7	+ 12.00
Mrs G R Reveley	2-8	0-1	0-1	1-1	1-5	25.0	+ 2.00
Denys Smith	2-11	0-2	0-0	0-1	2-8	18.2	+ 17.00

Oct/Nov	Total W-R	Non-handicaps 2-y-o	3-y-o+	Handicaps 2-y-o	3-y-o+	Per cent	£1 Level Stake
M S Johnston	5-10	1-1	2-2	1-3	1-4	50.0	+ 49.25
G Harwood	4-11	0-3	2-5	1-1	1-2	36.4	+ 3.50
R Hollinshead	4-35	1-2	2-12	0-5	1-16	11.4	- 16.75
M McCormack	2-3	0-0	1-2	0-0	1-1	66.7	+ 8.13
J L Dunlop	2-4	0-0	0-0	0-1	2-3	50.0	+ 3.80

REDCAR (Group 2)

Leading Trainers 1988-92

	Total W-R	Non-handicaps 2-y-o	3-y-o+	Handicaps 2-y-o	3-y-o+	Per cent	£1 Level Stake
M H Easterby	28-204	12-82	3-18	7-21	6-83	13.7	- 55.35
Mrs G R Reveley	27-213	5-39	4-32	1-8	17-134	12.7	- 60.62
H Thomson Jones	22-77	7-22	7-24	1-3	7-28	28.6	+ 20.65
L M Cumani	21-69	1-16	13-28	0-1	7-24	30.4	- 3.72
R M Whitaker	19-231	4-64	5-32	1-12	9-123	8.2	- 89.50
H R A Cecil	16-43	5-7	9-28	0-0	2-8	37.2	+ 2.65
J Berry	16-160	10-86	1-12	1-22	4-40	10.0	- 73.84
G Harwood	13-43	3-10	8-20	0-1	2-12	30.2	+ 9.83
J W Hills	13-48	1-9	5-13	0-0	7-26	27.1	+ 25.27
W Carter	12-46	0-12	1-2	1-6	10-26	26.1	+ 79.00
M R Stoute	12-47	3-17	8-14	0-3	1-13	25.5	- 11.84
J G FitzGerald	12-72	1-23	0-10	1-5	10-34	16.7	- 13.90
R Hollinshead	11-127	2-25	3-28	1-6	5-68	8.7	- 48.54
J L Dunlop	10-40	2-10	2-9	1-2	5-19	25.0	- 6.20
Sir M Prescott	9-43	1-16	4-7	1-2	3-18	20.9	- 7.67
J H M Gosden	9-52	6-16	2-21	0-2	1-13	17.3	- 27.63
B W Hills	8-46	1-12	5-22	0-0	2-12	17.4	- 21.83
D W Chapman	8-112	0-8	2-6	0-2	6-96	7.1	- 61.88
Denys Smith	8-124	3-24	1-10	0-4	4-86	6.5	- 69.58
C Tinkler	8-127	6-69	0-10	1-10	1-38	6.3	- 92.17
M Bell	7-23	5-11	0-0	0-4	2-8	30.4	+ 10.93
M A Jarvis	7-30	3-11	1-4	0-1	3-14	23.3	- 3.67

Leading Jockeys

	Total W-R	Per cent	£1 Level Stake	Best Trainer	W-R	Per cent	£1 Level Stake
R Hills	30-135	22.2	+ 0.06	H Thomson Jones	20-59	33.9	+ 25.17
M Birch	30-230	13.0	- 77.90	M H Easterby	16-99	16.2	- 13.54
K Darley	29-254	11.4	- 94.76	Mrs G R Reveley	9-30	30.0	+ 7.91
W Ryan	28-117	23.9	+ 59.91	H R A Cecil	13-31	41.9	+ 8.26
D McKeown	24-200	12.0	- 65.95	R M Whitaker	7-37	18.9	+ 3.00
G Duffield	22-161	13.7	- 42.91	Sir M Prescott	8-37	21.6	- 12.66
K Fallon	21-177	11.9	- 47.85	J G FitzGerald	8-33	24.2	+ 3.10
L Dettori	18-78	23.1	+ 2.98	L M Cumani	9-31	29.0	+ 3.48
J Lowe	18-264	6.8	-149.90	Mrs G R Reveley	9-79	11.4	- 25.78
R Cochrane	17-73	23.3	+ 22.39	L M Cumani	7-16	43.8	+ 5.56
M Hills	15-59	25.4	+ 5.62	J W Hills	7-13	53.8	+ 27.83
Paul Eddery	14-74	18.9	+ 19.45	G Lewis	2-4	50.0	+ 7.50

How the Favourites Fared

Non-handicaps	W-R	Per cent	£1 Level Stake	Handicaps	W-R	Per cent	£1 Level Stake
2-y-o	72-152	47.4	+ 15.41	2-y-o	10-31	32.3	- 4.71
3-y-o	27-56	48.2	- 0.25	3-y-o	24-69	34.8	- 1.30
Weight-for-age	43-77	55.8	+ 8.71	All-aged	72-211	34.1	+ 33.93
Totals	142-285	49.8	+ 23.87	Totals	106-311	34.1	+ 27.92
All favs	248-596	41.6	+ 51.79				

Leading Trainers by Month at Redcar

March/Apr	Total W-R	Non-handicaps 2-y-o	3-y-o+	Handicaps 2-y-o	3-y-o+	Per cent	£1 Level Stake
Mrs G R Reveley	2-5	1-1	0-1	0-0	1-3	40.0	+ 1.38
L M Cumani	1-1	0-0	1-1	0-0	0-0	100.0	+ 4.50
M W Eckley	1-1	0-0	0-0	0-0	1-1	100.0	+ 10.00
J L Harris	1-1	0-0	0-0	0-0	1-1	100.0	+ 11.00
M Dods	1-2	0-0	0-0	0-0	1-2	50.0	+ 11.00

May	Total W-R	Non-handicaps 2-y-o	3-y-o+	Handicaps 2-y-o	3-y-o+	Per cent	£1 Level Stake
M R Stoute	6-9	0-0	6-7	0-0	0-2	66.7	+ 8.21
Mrs G R Reveley	5-18	0-2	0-3	0-0	5-13	27.8	- 1.00
M H Easterby	5-42	4-14	0-7	0-0	1-21	11.9	- 18.42
L M Cumani	3-4	0-0	2-3	0-0	1-1	75.0	+ 3.00
W Carter	3-11	0-0	0-1	0-0	3-10	27.3	+ 2.00

June	Total W-R	Non-handicaps 2-y-o	3-y-o+	Handicaps 2-y-o	3-y-o+	Per cent	£1 Level Stake
L M Cumani	6-6	0-0	2-2	0-0	4-4	100.0	+ 9.68
J Berry	5-25	2-14	1-5	0-0	2-6	20.0	+ 19.40
C Tinkler	4-21	4-15	0-3	0-0	0-3	19.0	- 3.75
B W Hills	3-3	0-0	3-3	0-0	0-0	100.0	+ 6.60
M J Ryan	3-7	1-2	0-0	0-0	2-5	42.9	+ 5.94

July	Total W-R	Non-handicaps 2-y-o	3-y-o+	Handicaps 2-y-o	3-y-o+	Per cent	£1 Level Stake
R M Whitaker	8-37	4-12	0-0	0-0	4-25	21.6	+ 20.05
Mrs G R Reveley	8-46	4-11	0-2	0-0	4-33	17.4	+ 6.95
J G FitzGerald	5-14	0-5	0-1	0-0	5-8	35.7	+ 8.50
L M Cumani	4-13	0-1	3-6	0-0	1-6	30.8	- 2.40
J Berry	4-19	3-13	0-0	0-0	1-6	21.1	- 6.72

August	Total W-R	Non-handicaps 2-y-o	3-y-o+	Handicaps 2-y-o	3-y-o+	Per cent	£1 Level Stake
M H Easterby	13-39	3-15	2-3	6-13	2-8	33.3	+ 20.64
H Thomson Jones	6-13	2-3	2-5	0-0	2-5	46.2	+ 5.89
R Hollinshead	4-22	1-3	1-10	0-0	2-9	18.2	- 5.70
Sir M Prescott	3-5	1-1	1-1	1-1	0-2	60.0	+ 1.50
H R A Cecil	3-7	1-1	1-2	0-0	1-4	42.9	- 1.70

September	Total W-R	Non-handicaps 2-y-o	3-y-o+	Handicaps 2-y-o	3-y-o+	Per cent	£1 Level Stake
H Thomson Jones	5-12	2-4	1-2	1-3	1-3	41.7	+ 13.95
W Carter	5-15	0-5	0-0	0-2	5-8	33.3	+ 78.50
M H Easterby	3-22	1-8	1-1	0-6	1-7	13.6	- 1.50
Mrs G R Reveley	3-25	0-4	0-5	1-4	2-12	12.0	- 3.00
J Berry	3-26	3-11	0-0	0-9	0-6	11.5	- 16.25

Oct/Nov	Total W-R	Non-handicaps 2-y-o	3-y-o+	Handicaps 2-y-o	3-y-o+	Per cent	£1 Level Stake
G Harwood	8-25	3-9	3-8	0-1	2-7	32.0	+ 14.28
H R A Cecil	6-13	3-4	3-7	0-0	0-2	46.2	+ 8.73
J L Dunlop	5-23	2-7	0-5	0-1	3-10	21.7	- 8.45
H Thomson Jones	5-29	2-13	2-7	0-0	1-9	17.2	- 6.99
J H M Gosden	4-26	4-9	0-9	0-2	0-6	15.4	- 15.00

RIPON (Group 2)

Leading Trainers 1988-92

	Total W-R	Non-handicaps 2-y-o	Non-handicaps 3-y-o+	Handicaps 2-y-o	Handicaps 3-y-o+	Per cent	£1 Level Stake
H R A Cecil	23-47	3-6	19-36	0-0	1-5	48.9	+ 3.67
J Berry	21-121	17-68	1-13	2-11	1-29	17.4	- 42.95
M H Easterby	21-221	9-66	3-24	0-8	9-123	9.5	-126.25
M R Stoute	10-36	1-3	6-19	0-0	3-14	27.8	+ 5.44
B W Hills	10-38	2-5	5-19	0-0	3-14	26.3	- 0.80
D W Chapman	10-97	1-9	1-11	0-3	8-74	10.3	+ 6.50
R W Armstrong	9-28	2-5	1-6	0-0	6-17	32.1	+ 36.77
L M Cumani	9-31	2-3	6-23	0-0	1-5	29.0	- 10.84
R M Whitaker	9-120	3-26	3-27	0-3	3-64	7.5	- 52.70
M Brittain	9-135	0-32	0-14	2-8	7-81	6.7	- 29.50
D Morley	8-38	0-3	1-12	0-1	7-22	21.1	+ 14.05
J Etherington	8-61	3-22	3-13	0-1	2-25	13.1	- 6.29
J W Watts	7-73	3-19	0-14	0-0	4-40	9.6	- 18.00
T D Barron	7-95	3-21	0-8	1-3	3-63	7.4	- 1.80
M W Easterby	7-114	0-51	1-12	0-4	6-47	6.1	- 49.75
A C Stewart	6-22	1-3	3-12	0-0	2-7	27.3	- 3.01
M J Camacho	6-44	1-17	1-13	0-0	4-14	13.6	- 5.38
Mrs G R Reveley	6-56	0-4	1-12	0-2	5-38	10.7	- 19.67
R Hollinshead	6-110	1-22	0-26	0-1	5-61	5.5	- 58.17
G Harwood	5-12	0-0	3-6	0-0	2-6	41.7	+ 4.10
J L Dunlop	5-16	1-6	1-1	0-1	3-8	31.3	- 5.08
J H M Gosden	5-26	0-3	4-16	0-0	1-7	19.2	- 9.55

Leading Jockeys

	Total W-R	Per cent	£1 Level Stake	Best Trainer	W-R	Per cent	£1 Level Stake
M Birch	29-210	13.8	- 56.26	M H Easterby	15-113	13.3	- 47.86
K Darley	23-157	14.6	- 38.58	M H Easterby	5-19	26.3	+ 3.62
W Ryan	16-89	18.0	- 43.75	H R A Cecil	10-25	40.0	- 7.96
D McKeown	16-174	9.2	- 75.70	J W Watts	5-21	23.8	+ 13.00
Pat Eddery	13-31	41.9	+ 12.26	B W Hills	2-3	66.7	+ 5.53
J Carroll	13-101	12.9	- 57.29	J Berry	13-60	21.7	- 16.29
M Roberts	12-56	21.4	+ 6.08	A C Stewart	5-11	45.5	+ 5.00
Paul Eddery	12-69	17.4	+ 14.55	D Morley	2-3	66.7	+ 14.00
J Lowe	12-174	6.9	- 80.92	Mrs G R Reveley	5-28	17.9	+ 6.33
N Connorton	11-104	10.6	- 29.67	M J Camacho	6-23	26.1	+ 15.63
G Duffield	10-93	10.8	- 32.10	J L Dunlop	2-4	50.0	+ 1.32
A Culhane	9-107	8.4	- 46.20	R M Whitaker	5-47	10.6	- 6.95

How the Favourites Fared

Non-handicaps	W-R	Per cent	£1 Level Stake	Handicaps	W-R	Per cent	£1 Level Stake
2-y-o	39-95	41.1	- 17.99	2-y-o	1-8	12.5	- 4.87
3-y-o	35-63	55.6	+ 3.02	3-y-o	16-56	28.6	- 6.30
Weight-for-age	20-40	50.0	+ 9.08	All-aged	42-137	30.7	+ 13.63
Totals	94-198	47.5	- 5.89	Totals	59-201	29.4	+ 2.46
All favs	153-399	38.3	- 3.43				

Leading Trainers by Month at Ripon

March/Apr

	Total W-R	Non-handicaps 2-y-o	3-y-o+	Handicaps 2-y-o	3-y-o+	Per cent	£1 Level Stake
H R A Cecil	6-12	0-0	6-12	0-0	0-0	50.0	+ 1.94
J Berry	6-30	5-19	0-6	0-0	1-5	20.0	− 6.08
J H M Gosden	3-5	0-0	2-3	0-0	1-2	60.0	+ 0.95
B A McMahon	3-9	0-1	3-5	0-0	0-3	33.3	+ 7.75
J W Watts	3-22	0-2	0-7	0-0	3-13	13.6	+ 12.00

May

	Total W-R	Non-handicaps 2-y-o	3-y-o+	Handicaps 2-y-o	3-y-o+	Per cent	£1 Level Stake
A C Stewart	4-4	0-0	3-3	0-0	1-1	100.0	+ 6.99
H R A Cecil	2-3	0-0	1-2	0-0	1-1	66.7	+ 0.74
A Smith	2-3	1-1	0-1	0-0	1-1	66.7	+ 21.00
Mrs L Piggott	2-3	0-0	0-0	0-0	2-3	66.7	+ 2.25
R M Whitaker	2-11	1-3	1-1	0-0	0-7	18.2	+ 2.80

June

	Total W-R	Non-handicaps 2-y-o	3-y-o+	Handicaps 2-y-o	3-y-o+	Per cent	£1 Level Stake
H R A Cecil	5-9	1-3	4-6	0-0	0-0	55.6	+ 2.62
J L Dunlop	4-8	0-2	1-1	0-0	3-5	50.0	+ 1.42
J Pearce	3-7	1-1	0-1	0-0	2-5	42.9	+ 10.25
M R Stoute	3-9	0-0	2-5	0-0	1-4	33.3	+ 10.33
R Hollinshead	3-22	1-4	0-2	0-0	2-16	13.6	− 2.50

July

	Total W-R	Non-handicaps 2-y-o	3-y-o+	Handicaps 2-y-o	3-y-o+	Per cent	£1 Level Stake
L M Cumani	3-6	1-1	2-5	0-0	0-0	50.0	+ 0.72
B W Hills	3-10	0-1	1-4	0-0	2-5	30.0	+ 2.07
J Berry	3-12	3-8	0-1	0-0	0-3	25.0	− 4.53
M H Easterby	3-30	1-7	1-1	0-0	1-22	10.0	− 13.88
C E Brittain	2-2	0-0	1-1	0-0	1-1	100.0	+ 7.25

August

	Total W-R	Non-handicaps 2-y-o	3-y-o+	Handicaps 2-y-o	3-y-o+	Per cent	£1 Level Stake
J Berry	9-46	6-20	1-3	2-11	0-12	19.6	− 3.68
M H Easterby	9-76	3-19	1-5	0-8	5-44	11.8	− 38.00
B W Hills	7-18	2-3	4-9	0-0	1-6	38.9	+ 7.13
H R A Cecil	6-15	2-3	4-10	0-0	0-2	40.0	+ 0.08
J Etherington	6-24	1-9	3-6	0-1	2-8	25.0	+ 17.21

September

	Total W-R	Non-handicaps 2-y-o	3-y-o+	Handicaps 2-y-o	3-y-o+	Per cent	£1 Level Stake
D W Chapman	3-5	1-1	0-0	0-0	2-4	60.0	+ 44.00
H R A Cecil	2-3	0-0	2-2	0-0	0-1	66.7	+ 0.20
W R Hern	1-1	0-0	1-1	0-0	0-0	100.0	+ 0.53
M R Channon	1-1	0-0	1-1	0-0	0-0	100.0	+ 8.00
P A Kelleway	1-2	0-1	1-1	0-0	0-0	50.0	+ 7.00

SALISBURY (Group 2)

Leading Trainers 1988-92

	Total W-R	Non-handicaps 2-y-o	3-y-o+	Handicaps 2-y-o	3-y-o+	Per cent	£1 Level Stake
R Hannon	34-303	16-130	8-46	0-7	10-120	11.2	- 123.52
G Harwood	29-93	11-33	6-17	2-2	10-41	31.2	+ 18.03
D R C Elsworth	19-167	6-44	4-45	0-0	9-78	11.4	- 66.75
P F I Cole	17-98	10-43	1-23	0-1	6-31	17.3	- 1.43
I A Balding	15-134	4-46	5-36	0-0	6-52	11.2	- 29.63
J L Dunlop	11-110	4-34	3-38	1-2	3-36	10.0	- 29.95
L M Cumani	8-28	1-5	6-17	0-0	1-6	28.6	+ 4.71
R Akehurst	8-63	3-14	0-17	0-0	5-32	12.7	- 6.25
J H M Gosden	7-22	2-6	5-14	0-0	0-2	31.8	+ 13.80
Lord Huntingdon	7-45	1-12	4-18	0-0	2-15	15.6	- 22.13
G Lewis	7-74	6-32	0-10	0-2	1-30	9.5	- 18.02
H Candy	7-84	2-20	1-22	0-0	4-42	8.3	+ 16.00
M R Stoute	6-24	2-12	2-8	0-0	2-4	25.0	- 9.83
R F J Houghton	6-26	2-7	2-6	0-0	2-13	23.1	+ 8.17
K O C-Brown	6-48	1-12	3-6	0-1	2-29	12.5	+ 22.50
J Sutcliffe	6-49	0-6	1-11	0-1	5-31	12.2	- 14.29
W R Hern	6-54	2-21	3-15	0-0	1-18	11.1	- 30.40
C J Benstead	6-66	0-2	0-6	0-1	6-57	9.1	- 23.50
R Charlton	5-31	0-10	3-16	0-0	2-5	16.1	- 12.13
D R Laing	5-40	1-17	0-10	0-0	4-13	12.5	- 8.50
G B Balding	5-122	1-29	2-19	0-1	2-73	4.1	- 79.25
A A Scott	4-13	1-2	3-4	0-0	0-7	30.8	- 1.50

Leading Jockeys

	Total W-R	Per cent	£1 Level Stake	Best Trainer	W-R	Per cent	£1 Level Stake
Pat Eddery	29-134	21.6	- 4.21	K O C-Brown	3-3	100.0	+ 3.50
W Carson	26-149	17.4	- 46.85	J L Dunlop	5-28	17.9	- 4.25
R Cochrane	21-143	14.7	- 48.68	G Harwood	10-31	32.3	- 5.06
S Cauthen	20-79	25.3	+ 34.82	D R C Elsworth	5-31	16.1	- 13.25
J Reid	20-139	14.4	- 22.87	R Hannon	3-9	33.3	+ 1.78
B Rouse	20-199	10.1	- 97.20	R Hannon	13-87	14.9	- 16.00
J Williams	19-213	8.9	- 59.24	D R C Elsworth	8-45	17.8	+ 4.26
W R Swinburn	15-63	23.8	+ 16.97	J R Fanshawe	3-4	75.0	+ 18.50
A Munro	13-59	22.0	+ 18.33	M Brittain	2-2	100.0	+ 10.00
T Quinn	13-115	11.3	- 43.02	P F I Cole	8-52	15.4	- 9.85
M Roberts	12-77	15.6	- 1.54	G Harwood	2-3	66.7	+ 2.50
C Rutter	9-132	6.8	- 25.30	H Candy	4-42	9.5	+ 21.00

How the Favourites Fared

Non-handicaps	W-R	Per cent	£1 Level Stake	Handicaps	W-R	Per cent	£1 Level Stake
2-y-o	51-120	42.5	- 8.54	2-y-o	3-6	50.0	+ 0.02
3-y-o	26-77	33.8	- 18.05	3-y-o	13-45	28.9	- 2.49
Weight-for-age	7-8	87.5	+ 4.68	All-aged	35-145	24.1	- 15.66
Totals	84-205	41.0	- 21.91	Totals	51-196	26.0	- 18.13
All favs	135-401	33.7	- 40.04				

Leading Trainers by Month at Salisbury

March/Apr

	Total W-R	Non-handicaps 2-y-o	3-y-o+	Handicaps 2-y-o	3-y-o+	Per cent	£1 Level Stake
L M Cumani	2-3	0-0	2-3	0-0	0-0	66.7	+ 14.38
A C Stewart	1-1	0-0	0-0	0-0	1-1	100.0	+ 10.00
P D Cundell	1-2	0-0	0-0	0-0	1-2	50.0	+ 15.00
G B Balding	1-3	0-0	1-2	0-0	0-1	33.3	+ 12.00
D R C Elsworth	1-3	0-0	1-2	0-0	0-1	33.3	+ 7.00

May

	Total W-R	Non-handicaps 2-y-o	3-y-o+	Handicaps 2-y-o	3-y-o+	Per cent	£1 Level Stake
R Hannon	12-77	4-22	3-17	0-0	5-38	15.6	- 24.90
G Harwood	6-15	0-1	5-10	0-0	1-4	40.0	+ 3.82
D R C Elsworth	5-34	2-6	1-14	0-0	2-14	14.7	- 12.13
R F J Houghton	3-8	1-1	2-5	0-0	0-2	37.5	+ 13.33
M McCormack	3-18	2-6	0-6	0-0	1-6	16.7	- 4.63

June

	Total W-R	Non-handicaps 2-y-o	3-y-o+	Handicaps 2-y-o	3-y-o+	Per cent	£1 Level Stake
I A Balding	6-35	2-13	2-6	0-0	2-16	17.1	- 6.33
P F I Cole	5-20	3-10	0-0	0-0	2-10	25.0	- 3.38
R Hannon	5-60	1-31	2-9	0-0	2-20	8.3	- 24.13
J Sutcliffe	4-7	0-0	0-1	0-0	4-6	57.1	+ 16.21
G Harwood	4-11	1-4	0-1	0-0	3-6	36.4	+ 0.50

July

	Total W-R	Non-handicaps 2-y-o	3-y-o+	Handicaps 2-y-o	3-y-o+	Per cent	£1 Level Stake
G Harwood	6-13	3-7	0-0	0-0	3-6	46.2	+ 17.10
P F I Cole	4-12	2-7	0-0	0-0	2-5	33.3	+ 13.50
R Hannon	4-29	3-15	1-1	0-0	0-13	13.8	- 15.20
I A Balding	2-14	1-6	0-0	0-0	1-8	14.3	+ 1.33
W J Haggas	1-1	0-0	0-0	0-0	1-1	100.0	+ 4.00

August

	Total W-R	Non-handicaps 2-y-o	3-y-o+	Handicaps 2-y-o	3-y-o+	Per cent	£1 Level Stake
R Hannon	7-66	6-27	1-10	0-7	0-22	10.6	- 47.80
G Harwood	5-28	1-7	1-4	2-2	1-15	17.9	- 10.54
D R C Elsworth	5-42	0-8	1-15	0-0	4-19	11.9	- 17.50
J D Bethell	3-6	1-1	0-0	0-0	2-5	50.0	+ 17.00
R Akehurst	3-12	1-1	0-4	0-0	2-7	25.0	+ 7.25

September

	Total W-R	Non-handicaps 2-y-o	3-y-o+	Handicaps 2-y-o	3-y-o+	Per cent	£1 Level Stake
G Harwood	4-8	3-5	0-0	0-0	1-3	50.0	+ 8.75
J L Dunlop	3-20	2-13	0-0	0-0	1-7	15.0	- 3.25
M R Stoute	2-7	2-6	0-0	0-0	0-1	28.6	- 4.11
R Akehurst	2-9	2-4	0-0	0-0	0-5	22.2	+ 1.50
D R Laing	2-9	0-6	0-0	0-0	2-3	22.2	+ 5.00

Oct/Nov

	Total W-R	Non-handicaps 2-y-o	3-y-o+	Handicaps 2-y-o	3-y-o+	Per cent	£1 Level Stake
D R C Elsworth	4-18	2-8	0-4	0-0	2-6	22.2	+ 12.00
G Harwood	4-18	3-9	0-2	0-0	1-7	22.2	- 1.60
R Hannon	4-34	1-17	1-4	0-0	2-13	11.8	+ 3.50
J H M Gosden	3-6	2-5	1-1	0-0	0-0	50.0	+ 15.75
R F J Houghton	2-5	1-2	0-1	0-0	1-2	40.0	+ 4.33

SANDOWN (Group 1)

Leading Trainers 1988-92

	Total W-R	Non-handicaps 2-y-o	3-y-o+	Handicaps 2-y-o	3-y-o+	Per cent	£1 Level Stake
M R Stoute	27-158	7-21	12-73	0-3	8-61	17.1	- 36.38
R Hannon	25-239	7-79	4-44	0-16	14-100	10.5	- 67.90
G Harwood	21-95	4-17	7-40	1-3	9-35	22.1	+ 4.30
H R A Cecil	20-75	7-14	13-53	0-0	0-8	26.7	- 16.16
I A Balding	16-94	5-18	3-32	1-2	7-42	17.0	- 1.90
L M Cumani	15-58	0-4	12-42	0-0	3-12	25.9	+ 11.82
B W Hills	15-83	5-19	7-44	1-3	2-17	18.1	+ 20.60
R Akehurst	14-117	0-4	1-21	0-4	13-88	12.0	- 33.79
C E Brittain	14-166	1-37	8-58	0-6	5-65	8.4	- 18.93
P F I Cole	13-101	4-27	2-23	2-9	5-42	12.9	- 25.17
J L Dunlop	12-123	4-29	5-40	0-1	3-53	9.8	- 8.13
Lord Huntingdon	10-66	2-14	2-15	0-2	6-35	15.2	- 9.38
R W Armstrong	9-55	4-10	3-18	0-1	2-26	16.4	+ 22.78
J Sutcliffe	9-57	0-10	1-4	1-1	7-42	15.8	+ 6.21
J H M Gosden	8-44	2-4	3-21	0-0	3-19	18.2	- 12.08
W R Hern	8-46	3-8	5-27	0-0	0-11	17.4	- 15.62
C R Nelson	8-59	3-12	1-18	0-1	4-28	13.6	- 4.84
H Thomson Jones	7-27	2-3	2-4	0-0	3-20	25.9	+ 25.75
Sir M Prescott	7-31	1-1	4-9	0-4	2-17	22.6	+ 16.50
P J Makin	7-39	0-6	2-15	0-0	5-18	17.9	- 0.38
W Jarvis	7-41	1-4	0-9	2-4	4-24	17.1	+ 31.50
D R C Elsworth	7-130	1-20	2-60	0-3	4-47	5.4	- 96.03

Leading Jockeys

	Total W-R	Per cent	£1 Level Stake	Best Trainer	W-R	Per cent	£1 Level Stake
Pat Eddery	53-283	18.7	- 43.25	B W Hills	5-13	38.5	+ 15.35
S Cauthen	43-234	18.4	- 51.49	H R A Cecil	14-37	37.8	- 0.36
M Roberts	35-233	15.0	- 16.75	C E Brittain	7-64	10.9	- 2.75
W Carson	34-257	13.2	- 49.28	W R Hern	5-32	15.6	- 11.45
R Cochrane	30-163	18.4	+ 32.63	L M Cumani	6-14	42.9	+ 4.97
W R Swinburn	27-191	14.1	- 74.32	M R Stoute	15-75	20.0	- 15.41
T Quinn	21-146	14.4	+ 7.83	P F I Cole	11-54	20.4	+ 9.83
J Reid	14-156	9.0	- 65.59	C R Nelson	2-21	9.5	- 12.59
R Hills	13-90	14.4	+ 49.33	H Thomson Jones	6-22	27.3	+ 15.75
M Hills	12-90	13.3	- 15.62	B W Hills	5-27	18.5	+ 10.75
L Dettori	12-100	12.0	- 23.92	L M Cumani	4-35	11.4	- 9.75
G Duffield	10-76	13.2	+ 53.50	Sir M Prescott	6-26	23.1	+ 18.50

How the Favourites Fared

Non-handicaps	W-R	Per cent	£1 Level Stake	Handicaps	W-R	Per cent	£1 Level Stake
2-y-o	48-99	48.5	+ 7.29	2-y-o	3-22	13.6	- 15.12
3-y-o	37-93	39.8	- 7.57	3-y-o	26-90	28.9	- 4.57
Weight-for-age	27-72	37.5	- 4.34	All-aged	44-147	29.9	- 6.82
Totals	112-264	42.4	- 4.62	Totals	73-259	28.2	- 26.51
All favs	185-523	35.4	- 31.13				

Leading Trainers by Month at Sandown

March/Apr	Total W-R	Non-handicaps 2-y-o	3-y-o+	Handicaps 2-y-o	3-y-o+	Per cent	£1 Level Stake
H R A Cecil	6-13	0-0	6-13	0-0	0-0	46.2	+ 4.84
L M Cumani	5-14	0-0	4-12	0-0	1-2	35.7	+ 3.06
C E Brittain	5-29	1-3	3-17	0-0	1-9	17.2	+ 19.50
J L Dunlop	4-16	0-0	2-8	0-0	2-8	25.0	+ 32.75
B W Hills	3-18	1-4	2-13	0-0	0-1	16.7	+ 16.60

May	Total W-R	Non-handicaps 2-y-o	3-y-o+	Handicaps 2-y-o	3-y-o+	Per cent	£1 Level Stake
M R Stoute	11-42	1-3	8-29	0-0	2-10	26.2	+ 17.69
R Hannon	8-37	3-10	1-8	0-0	4-19	21.6	+ 14.97
G Harwood	5-15	0-0	3-11	0-0	2-4	33.3	+ 4.33
Lord Huntingdon	4-9	1-1	2-6	0-0	1-2	44.4	+ 15.00
L M Cumani	4-13	0-1	4-11	0-0	0-1	30.8	+ 6.51

June	Total W-R	Non-handicaps 2-y-o	3-y-o+	Handicaps 2-y-o	3-y-o+	Per cent	£1 Level Stake
R Hannon	5-25	0-7	2-5	0-0	3-13	20.0	+ 11.75
M R Stoute	4-14	2-2	0-4	0-0	2-8	28.6	- 2.22
R Akehurst	4-15	0-0	0-2	0-0	4-13	26.7	+ 3.83
L M Cumani	2-4	0-0	2-4	0-0	0-0	50.0	+ 6.75
M P Naughton	2-4	0-0	1-1	0-0	1-3	50.0	+ 5.00

July	Total W-R	Non-handicaps 2-y-o	3-y-o+	Handicaps 2-y-o	3-y-o+	Per cent	£1 Level Stake
I A Balding	10-35	4-11	1-8	0-0	5-16	28.6	+ 19.13
G Harwood	8-40	3-11	2-13	0-0	3-16	20.0	- 1.78
R Akehurst	8-43	0-4	1-6	0-0	7-33	18.6	+ 13.25
R Hannon	7-79	1-30	1-16	0-0	5-33	8.9	- 40.38
P F I Cole	6-30	2-9	1-7	0-0	3-14	20.0	+ 5.33

August	Total W-R	Non-handicaps 2-y-o	3-y-o+	Handicaps 2-y-o	3-y-o+	Per cent	£1 Level Stake
J R Fanshawe	3-8	1-1	1-4	0-1	1-2	37.5	+ 15.38
B W Hills	3-14	0-2	1-8	0-1	2-3	21.4	+ 3.25
H R A Cecil	3-16	3-6	0-7	0-0	0-3	18.8	- 10.47
G Harwood	3-17	1-4	0-6	1-2	1-5	17.6	- 2.88
M R Stoute	3-24	0-3	3-11	0-1	0-9	12.5	- 12.50

September	Total W-R	Non-handicaps 2-y-o	3-y-o+	Handicaps 2-y-o	3-y-o+	Per cent	£1 Level Stake
R W Armstrong	4-7	2-4	0-0	0-0	2-3	57.1	+ 51.38
H Thomson Jones	3-7	2-2	0-0	0-0	1-5	42.9	+ 9.00
J Sutcliffe	3-7	0-0	1-1	1-1	1-5	42.9	+ 7.00
C F Wall	3-7	1-1	0-1	1-1	1-4	42.9	+ 12.60
M H Easterby	3-8	0-0	2-3	0-3	1-2	37.5	+ 8.25

SOUTHWELL (AW)

Leading Trainers 1989-92

	Total W-R	Non-handicaps 2-y-o	3-y-o+	Handicaps 2-y-o	3-y-o+	Per cent	£1 Level Stake
T D Barron	52-215	7-25	24-78	2-7	19-105	24.2	+ 2.85
D W Chapman	28-338	3-24	8-93	2-16	15-205	8.3	-133.74
W A O'Gorman	26-134	14-35	7-41	1-7	4-51	19.4	- 10.92
J Berry	25-136	13-70	2-22	1-7	9-37	18.4	- 4.97
R Hollinshead	23-236	1-34	11-94	1-11	10-97	9.7	- 97.69
Sir M Prescott	16-86	3-38	8-21	0-2	5-25	18.6	- 17.89
C N Allen	15-122	2-24	6-27	1-7	6-64	12.3	- 14.23
M Brittain	14-180	2-29	9-42	0-7	3-102	7.8	- 75.50
Mrs N Macauley	14-181	2-21	3-67	1-6	8-87	7.7	- 50.00
C R Nelson	13-39	2-7	8-19	0-0	3-13	33.3	+ 21.66
Lord Huntingdon	12-45	1-4	9-27	0-1	2-13	26.7	+ 14.39
M J Ryan	11-64	0-4	3-13	0-3	8-44	17.2	+ 18.33
S G Norton	11-71	2-18	3-14	1-9	5-30	15.5	- 1.00
M Bell	10-54	6-17	1-17	0-2	3-18	18.5	+ 11.35
J G FitzGerald	10-82	2-15	1-25	0-2	7-40	12.2	+ 7.38
M W Easterby	10-89	6-41	1-8	3-11	0-29	11.2	- 23.05
C Tinkler	9-61	1-3	1-15	1-2	6-41	14.8	- 1.63
J A Glover	9-103	0-11	0-18	0-3	9-71	8.7	- 12.75
Lady Herries	8-21	0-0	4-8	0-0	4-13	38.1	+ 18.23
J H M Gosden	8-26	1-3	6-17	0-0	1-6	30.8	+ 7.48
J L Dunlop	8-33	0-5	0-7	0-0	8-21	24.2	+ 6.53
W W Haigh	8-48	0-1	3-21	0-0	5-26	16.7	+ 18.86

Leading Jockeys

	Total W-R	Per cent	£1 Level Stake	Best Trainer	W-R	Per cent	£1 Level Stake
Alex Greaves	52-192	27.1	+ 55.50	T D Barron	47-162	29.0	+ 18.85
G Duffield	32-226	14.2	- 56.26	Sir M Prescott	13-65	20.0	- 13.39
G Carter	29-208	13.9	- 35.94	J Berry	7-22	31.8	+ 22.66
Emma O'Gorman	22-138	15.9	- 41.95	W A O'Gorman	21-101	20.8	- 12.45
S Wood	20-290	6.9	-154.43	D W Chapman	15-196	7.7	- 85.56
G Bardwell	19-208	9.1	+ 0.50	J F Bottomley	5-28	17.9	+ 21.50
J Fanning	17-164	10.4	- 8.21	T Fairhurst	8-66	12.1	+ 22.88
D McKeown	17-207	8.2	- 75.45	W W Haigh	5-10	50.0	+ 21.86
D Nicholls	16-109	14.7	- 34.79	D W Chapman	5-20	25.0	- 2.17
D Biggs	15-108	13.9	+ 35.58	M J Ryan	6-14	42.9	+ 25.58
W Ryan	14-86	16.3	+ 11.23	R Hollinshead	8-34	23.5	+ 10.23
N Day	14-94	14.9	+ 10.28	Lady Herries	4-5	80.0	+ 9.43

How the Favourites Fared

Non-handicaps	W-R	Per cent	£1 Level Stake	Handicaps	W-R	Per cent	£1 Level Stake
2-y-o	44-113	38.9	- 9.87	2-y-o	8-24	33.3	+ 8.00
3-y-o	43-100	43.0	- 7.93	3-y-o	21-63	33.3	- 8.08
Weight-for-age	57-145	39.3	- 14.03	All-aged	78-276	28.3	- 44.86
Totals	144-358	40.2	- 31.83	Totals	107-363	29.5	- 44.94
All favs	251-721	34.8	- 76.77				

Leading Trainers by Month at Southwell (AW)

January	Total W-R	Non-handicaps 2-y-o	3-y-o+	Handicaps 2-y-o	3-y-o+	Per cent	£1 Level Stake
T D Barron	20-69	0-0	13-34	0-0	7-35	29.0	+ 1.40
D W Chapman	9-84	0-0	3-30	0-0	6-54	10.7	- 22.43
R Hollinshead	8-51	0-0	3-24	0-0	5-27	15.7	- 7.38

February	Total W-R	Non-handicaps 2-y-o	3-y-o+	Handicaps 2-y-o	3-y-o+	Per cent	£1 Level Stake
T D Barron	12-42	0-0	4-15	0-0	8-27	28.6	+ 3.65
C N Allen	5-22	0-0	3-8	0-0	2-14	22.7	+ 6.60
M Brittain	4-26	0-0	4-12	0-0	0-14	15.4	+ 8.25

March	Total W-R	Non-handicaps 2-y-o	3-y-o+	Handicaps 2-y-o	3-y-o+	Per cent	£1 Level Stake
W A O'Gorman	5-12	0-0	4-7	0-0	1-5	41.7	+ 5.14
C R Nelson	2-2	0-0	2-2	0-0	0-0	100.0	+ 2.88
W W Haigh	2-4	0-0	1-2	0-0	1-2	50.0	+ 8.00

May	Total W-R	Non-handicaps 2-y-o	3-y-o+	Handicaps 2-y-o	3-y-o+	Per cent	£1 Level Stake
Sir M Prescott	3-8	1-1	2-4	0-0	0-3	37.5	+ 3.35
B W Hills	2-3	0-0	2-3	0-0	0-0	66.7	+ 1.31
Lord Huntingdon	2-4	0-0	1-2	0-0	1-2	50.0	+ 5.50

June	Total W-R	Non-handicaps 2-y-o	3-y-o+	Handicaps 2-y-o	3-y-o+	Per cent	£1 Level Stake
J Berry	9-25	6-18	0-2	0-0	3-5	36.0	+ 23.91
S R Bowring	3-11	0-0	0-0	0-0	3-11	27.3	+ 9.50
R Hollinshead	3-15	1-4	0-2	0-0	2-9	20.0	+ 6.25

July	Total W-R	Non-handicaps 2-y-o	3-y-o+	Handicaps 2-y-o	3-y-o+	Per cent	£1 Level Stake
W A O'Gorman	6-15	6-10	0-1	0-0	0-4	40.0	+ 20.80
J Berry	6-36	5-28	0-0	0-0	1-8	16.7	- 16.38
G Wragg	3-4	0-0	3-3	0-0	0-1	75.0	+ 1.30

August	Total W-R	Non-handicaps 2-y-o	3-y-o+	Handicaps 2-y-o	3-y-o+	Per cent	£1 Level Stake
M W Easterby	6-25	3-13	1-1	2-3	0-8	24.0	+ 10.20
M Bell	4-10	3-4	0-1	0-1	1-4	40.0	+ 19.75
C A Cyzer	4-14	0-4	1-4	0-0	3-6	28.6	+ 32.00

September	Total W-R	Non-handicaps 2-y-o	3-y-o+	Handicaps 2-y-o	3-y-o+	Per cent	£1 Level Stake
P J Makin	2-2	0-0	0-0	0-0	2-2	100.0	+ 11.50
M A Jarvis	2-3	1-2	1-1	0-0	0-0	66.7	+ 10.00
W J Haggas	2-4	2-3	0-1	0-0	0-0	50.0	+ 4.83

November	Total W-R	Non-handicaps 2-y-o	3-y-o+	Handicaps 2-y-o	3-y-o+	Per cent	£1 Level Stake
W A O'Gorman	6-16	4-5	0-4	1-3	1-4	37.5	+ 20.25
D W Chapman	5-36	0-3	2-10	1-7	2-16	13.9	- 18.97
T D Barron	4-19	1-2	2-8	0-3	1-6	21.1	+ 3.75

December	Total W-R	Non-handicaps 2-y-o	3-y-o+	Handicaps 2-y-o	3-y-o+	Per cent	£1 Level Stake
T D Barron	12-36	5-10	3-11	2-3	2-12	33.3	+ 22.05
D W Chapman	7-54	3-8	2-14	1-9	1-23	13.0	- 3.43
J G FitzGerald	3-12	0-2	0-2	0-1	3-7	25.0	+ 15.75

Leading Trainers 1988-92

	Total W-R	Non-handicaps 2-y-o	3-y-o+	Handicaps 2-y-o	3-y-o+	Per cent	£1 Level Stake
M H Easterby	29-202	8-64	5-45	2-14	14-79	14.4	- 19.34
R M Whitaker	18-135	6-27	5-41	1-6	6-61	13.3	- 40.63
J Berry	18-147	7-70	6-28	2-11	3-38	12.2	- 75.02
R Hollinshead	12-99	3-17	4-34	0-4	5-44	12.1	- 10.63
T D Barron	12-133	3-26	1-16	2-6	6-85	9.0	- 43.88
H R A Cecil	10-28	1-4	8-21	0-1	1-2	35.7	- 9.31
D W Chapman	9-94	0-1	0-13	0-0	9-80	9.6	+ 27.50
F H Lee	8-52	1-12	1-8	1-5	5-27	15.4	- 2.67
G Harwood	7-14	0-1	6-8	0-0	1-5	50.0	- 0.41
B W Hills	7-26	1-5	5-15	0-0	1-6	26.9	- 2.06
Sir M Prescott	7-34	3-9	1-9	2-4	1-12	20.6	+ 7.08
Denys Smith	7-75	2-19	2-13	1-1	2-42	9.3	- 27.13
J L Dunlop	6-13	0-2	1-4	1-1	4-6	46.2	+ 7.50
G Wragg	6-14	1-2	4-8	0-0	1-4	42.9	+ 13.51
A A Scott	6-25	1-4	5-10	0-2	0-9	24.0	- 2.93
H Thomson Jones	6-27	3-8	2-12	0-0	1-7	22.2	- 8.66
C Tinkler	6-61	1-22	1-10	1-4	3-25	9.8	- 19.75
N Tinkler	6-72	1-22	5-25	0-2	0-23	8.3	- 29.76
M P Naughton	6-76	0-0	2-23	0-0	4-53	7.9	- 14.13
M Brittain	6-107	3-31	0-17	0-3	3-56	5.6	- 17.17
M W Easterby	6-137	2-57	3-34	0-4	1-42	4.4	-111.38
W J Haggas	5-14	1-1	1-5	0-1	3-7	35.7	+ 11.10

Leading Jockeys

	Total W-R	Per cent	£1 Level Stake	Best Trainer	W-R	Per cent	£1 Level Stake
M Birch	31-199	15.6	- 27.31	M H Easterby	21-102	20.6	+ 11.76
G Duffield	25-132	18.9	- 26.13	Sir M Prescott	7-31	22.6	+ 10.08
D McKeown	19-149	12.8	- 42.62	R M Whitaker	5-15	33.3	+ 4.13
K Darley	13-173	7.5	-106.90	M H Easterby	3-23	13.0	- 7.35
R Hills	12-46	26.1	- 3.50	H Thomson Jones	6-17	35.3	+ 1.34
G Carter	12-55	21.8	+ 21.43	G Wragg	4-8	50.0	+ 10.68
A Culhane	12-104	11.5	- 3.50	R Hollinshead	5-26	19.2	+ 25.50
K Fallon	10-100	10.0	+ 17.00	J G FitzGerald	3-22	13.6	+ 5.00
W Newnes	9-37	24.3	- 1.44	M McCormack	2-3	66.7	+ 10.50
S Perks	9-65	13.8	- 21.79	R Hollinshead	5-25	20.0	- 7.12
A Munro	9-65	13.8	+ 39.61	M Brittain	5-32	15.6	+ 53.50
J Carroll	9-99	9.1	- 50.83	J Berry	6-72	8.3	- 43.08

How the Favourites Fared

Non-handicaps	W-R	Per cent	£1 Level Stake	Handicaps	W-R	Per cent	£1 Level Stake
2-y-o	33-89	37.1	- 13.54	2-y-o	10-21	47.6	+ 3.42
3-y-o	46-99	46.5	- 6.14	3-y-o	9-25	36.0	+ 4.86
Weight-for-age	21-36	58.3	+ 7.80	All-aged	32-131	24.4	- 30.37
Totals	100-224	44.6	- 11.88	Totals	51-177	28.8	- 22.09
All favs	151-401	37.7	- 33.97				

Leading Trainers by Month at Thirsk

March/Apr	Total W-R	Non-handicaps 2-y-o	3-y-o+	Handicaps 2-y-o	3-y-o+	Per cent	£1 Level Stake
M H Easterby	8-56	2-9	3-23	0-0	3-24	14.3	- 14.15
G Wragg	4-7	0-0	3-5	0-0	1-2	57.1	+ 14.38
J Berry	4-31	2-11	1-12	0-0	1-8	12.9	- 13.75
G Harwood	3-3	0-0	3-3	0-0	0-0	100.0	+ 5.00
M McCormack	3-6	0-0	2-4	0-0	1-2	50.0	+ 10.75

May	Total W-R	Non-handicaps 2-y-o	3-y-o+	Handicaps 2-y-o	3-y-o+	Per cent	£1 Level Stake
M H Easterby	12-68	2-24	2-10	0-0	8-34	17.6	+ 19.33
R M Whitaker	7-42	3-9	2-12	0-0	2-21	16.7	- 1.75
R Hollinshead	5-36	1-7	2-12	0-0	2-17	13.9	+ 12.38
J Berry	5-40	3-24	0-4	0-0	2-12	12.5	- 15.40
T D Barron	5-45	2-12	1-5	0-0	2-28	11.1	- 12.38

June	Total W-R	Non-handicaps 2-y-o	3-y-o+	Handicaps 2-y-o	3-y-o+	Per cent	£1 Level Stake
J L Dunlop	2-2	0-0	0-0	0-0	2-2	100.0	+ 2.53
F H Lee	2-4	1-1	0-0	0-0	1-3	50.0	+ 2.50
M H Easterby	2-9	1-5	0-0	0-0	1-4	22.2	- 1.25
J L Harris	1-1	1-1	0-0	0-0	0-0	100.0	+ 3.50
G Harwood	1-1	0-0	1-1	0-0	0-0	100.0	+ 0.03

July	Total W-R	Non-handicaps 2-y-o	3-y-o+	Handicaps 2-y-o	3-y-o+	Per cent	£1 Level Stake
J Berry	5-21	1-9	2-4	2-4	0-4	23.8	- 2.83
M H Easterby	4-14	1-4	0-4	1-2	2-4	28.6	+ 4.63
Denys Smith	3-12	0-3	1-2	1-1	1-6	25.0	+ 3.12
W J Haggas	2-2	1-1	0-0	0-0	1-1	100.0	+ 2.88
S P C Woods	2-2	1-1	1-1	0-0	0-0	100.0	+ 7.25

August	Total W-R	Non-handicaps 2-y-o	3-y-o+	Handicaps 2-y-o	3-y-o+	Per cent	£1 Level Stake
Sir M Prescott	5-12	3-5	0-0	2-3	0-4	41.7	+ 22.33
D W Chapman	5-24	0-1	0-1	0-0	5-22	20.8	+ 47.00
T D Barron	5-25	1-4	0-1	2-3	2-17	20.0	+ 5.50
H R A Cecil	4-8	0-1	3-5	0-0	1-2	50.0	- 0.54
R M Whitaker	4-24	0-2	1-7	1-3	2-12	16.7	- 7.50

September	Total W-R	Non-handicaps 2-y-o	3-y-o+	Handicaps 2-y-o	3-y-o+	Per cent	£1 Level Stake
R M Whitaker	3-22	1-6	1-8	0-3	1-5	13.6	- 7.50
R W Armstrong	2-3	1-2	0-0	0-0	1-1	66.7	+ 5.38
H R A Cecil	2-3	1-1	1-1	0-1	0-0	66.7	+ 0.45
B W Hills	2-4	1-2	1-1	0-0	0-1	50.0	+ 2.41
J G FitzGerald	2-5	0-1	0-0	0-0	2-4	40.0	+ 15.50

Oct/Nov	Total W-R	Non-handicaps 2-y-o	3-y-o+	Handicaps 2-y-o	3-y-o+	Per cent	£1 Level Stake
B Hanbury	2-2	0-0	1-1	0-0	1-1	100.0	+ 5.00
J L Dunlop	1-1	0-0	0-0	1-1	0-0	100.0	+ 8.00
M P Naughton	1-1	0-0	0-0	0-0	1-1	100.0	+ 5.50
J Wharton	1-1	1-1	0-0	0-0	0-0	100.0	+ 33.00
R Hannon	1-2	1-1	0-1	0-0	0-0	50.0	+ 3.50

WARWICK (Group 4)

Leading Trainers 1988-92

	Total W-R	Non-handicaps 2-y-o	Non-handicaps 3-y-o+	Handicaps 2-y-o	Handicaps 3-y-o+	Per cent	£1 Level Stake
J Berry	22-110	8-57	3-13	3-16	8-24	20.0	+ 36.98
H R A Cecil	15-45	4-5	10-37	0-1	1-2	33.3	- 5.78
J L Dunlop	11-57	2-5	7-24	1-6	1-22	19.3	+ 5.65
I A Balding	10-61	2-8	6-28	0-3	2-22	16.4	- 22.50
B W Hills	9-56	1-10	5-29	1-2	2-15	16.1	- 27.89
G Lewis	9-58	6-16	1-17	0-4	2-21	15.5	+ 28.98
B A McMahon	9-58	1-8	1-14	0-2	7-34	15.5	+ 38.71
J W Hills	8-46	1-9	3-16	0-1	4-20	17.4	- 11.80
P F I Cole	7-81	2-18	3-30	0-7	2-26	8.6	- 48.38
W R Hern	6-14	0-3	5-6	0-1	1-4	42.9	+ 8.85
G Price	6-22	0-0	1-4	0-0	5-18	27.3	+ 41.60
R Charlton	6-22	0-1	3-13	1-1	2-7	27.3	+ 2.30
P Chapple-Hyam	6-26	1-7	2-9	1-2	2-8	23.1	+ 15.57
M R Stoute	6-35	3-11	2-17	0-0	1-7	17.1	- 12.87
G Harwood	6-37	2-11	4-17	0-1	0-8	16.2	- 16.18
H Candy	6-53	0-5	3-24	0-3	3-21	11.3	- 23.25
A Bailey	5-23	3-6	0-5	1-5	1-7	21.7	+ 15.25
J H M Gosden	5-23	0-2	5-18	0-0	0-3	21.7	- 1.02
R F J Houghton	5-29	0-5	3-11	1-2	1-11	17.2	- 1.13
P T Walwyn	5-29	1-6	4-16	0-0	0-7	17.2	- 13.33
W Carter	5-40	2-10	0-7	0-1	3-22	12.5	- 2.00
Miss L Siddall	4-11	0-0	0-0	0-0	4-11	36.4	+ 15.75

Leading Jockeys

	Total W-R	Per cent	£1 Level Stake	Best Trainer	W-R	Per cent	£1 Level Stake
W Carson	28-117	23.9	- 1.06	W R Hern	4-7	57.1	+ 14.80
Pat Eddery	21-74	28.4	+ 13.90	R Charlton	4-9	44.4	+ 6.01
J Williams	19-169	11.2	+ 50.10	G Price	6-14	42.9	+ 49.60
W Ryan	13-82	15.9	- 14.92	H R A Cecil	10-20	50.0	+ 7.58
T Quinn	13-93	14.0	- 7.67	B A McMahon	4-7	57.1	+ 15.83
S Cauthen	12-45	26.7	- 2.73	H R A Cecil	5-11	45.5	+ 4.14
R Cochrane	12-62	19.4	- 8.22	M H Tompkins	2-3	66.7	+ 3.75
M Roberts	11-51	21.6	+ 9.08	A C Stewart	3-5	60.0	+ 2.70
Paul Eddery	11-85	12.9	+ 1.38	G Lewis	7-26	26.9	+ 42.48
J Carroll	10-37	27.0	+ 28.10	J Berry	10-34	29.4	+ 31.10
J Reid	10-82	12.2	- 10.62	T Casey	2-2	100.0	+ 10.00
J Quinn	10-104	9.6	- 22.75	P Chapple-Hyam	1-1	100.0	+ 4.50

How the Favourites Fared

Non-handicaps	W-R	Per cent	£1 Level Stake	Handicaps	W-R	Per cent	£1 Level Stake
2-y-o	27-87	31.0	- 26.20	2-y-o	7-25	28.0	- 7.32
3-y-o	43-91	47.3	- 3.16	3-y-o	15-47	31.9	- 1.91
Weight-for-age	17-35	48.6	+ 9.94	All-aged	24-123	19.5	- 45.01
Totals	87-213	40.8	- 19.42	Totals	46-195	23.6	- 54.24
All favs	133-408	32.6	- 73.66				

Leading Trainers by Month at Warwick

March/Apr	Total W-R	Non-handicaps 2-y-o	3-y-o+	Handicaps 2-y-o	3-y-o+	Per cent	£1 Level Stake
J Berry	5-24	2-12	2-5	0-0	1-7	20.8	+ 12.00
B A McMahon	4-12	1-3	0-3	0-0	3-6	33.3	+ 24.00
K T Ivory	3-12	0-1	0-2	0-0	3-9	25.0	+ 42.50
G Price	3-12	0-0	1-2	0-0	2-10	25.0	+ 22.10
J H M Gosden	3-12	0-0	3-10	0-0	0-2	25.0	− 1.25

May	Total W-R	Non-handicaps 2-y-o	3-y-o+	Handicaps 2-y-o	3-y-o+	Per cent	£1 Level Stake
J Berry	5-18	5-14	0-2	0-0	0-2	27.8	+ 16.75
G Price	3-4	0-0	0-0	0-0	3-4	75.0	+ 25.50
J W Hills	3-11	0-0	2-7	0-0	1-4	27.3	+ 0.25
Mrs L Piggott	3-12	0-0	0-5	0-0	3-7	25.0	+ 17.00
Miss L Siddall	2-3	0-0	0-0	0-0	2-3	66.7	+ 8.75

June	Total W-R	Non-handicaps 2-y-o	3-y-o+	Handicaps 2-y-o	3-y-o+	Per cent	£1 Level Stake
R Charlton	2-3	0-0	1-1	0-0	1-2	66.7	+ 2.00
W R Hern	2-4	0-0	2-3	0-0	0-1	50.0	+ 2.00
Miss L Siddall	2-5	0-0	0-0	0-0	2-5	40.0	+ 10.00
I A Balding	2-6	0-0	1-4	0-0	1-2	33.3	− 1.52
G Blum	2-7	0-2	0-0	0-0	2-5	28.6	+ 21.00

July	Total W-R	Non-handicaps 2-y-o	3-y-o+	Handicaps 2-y-o	3-y-o+	Per cent	£1 Level Stake
J Berry	7-32	0-14	0-2	2-8	5-8	21.9	+ 3.73
B W Hills	6-19	1-2	4-10	1-1	0-6	31.6	− 3.55
H R A Cecil	5-10	0-0	5-10	0-0	0-0	50.0	− 1.39
I A Balding	3-7	1-2	2-4	0-0	0-1	42.9	+ 5.45
G Lewis	3-7	3-5	0-1	0-1	0-0	42.9	+ 3.48

August	Total W-R	Non-handicaps 2-y-o	3-y-o+	Handicaps 2-y-o	3-y-o+	Per cent	£1 Level Stake
H Candy	3-14	0-2	3-8	0-1	0-3	21.4	+ 3.00
P T Walwyn	2-4	1-1	1-2	0-0	0-1	50.0	+ 5.50
P Chapple-Hyam	2-4	0-1	0-1	1-1	1-1	50.0	+ 6.50
J Etherington	2-8	1-2	0-2	0-1	1-3	25.0	+ 4.63
K O C-Brown	1-1	0-0	0-0	0-0	1-1	100.0	+ 6.50

Oct/Nov	Total W-R	Non-handicaps 2-y-o	3-y-o+	Handicaps 2-y-o	3-y-o+	Per cent	£1 Level Stake
J L Dunlop	5-16	1-2	3-7	0-3	1-4	31.3	− 2.15
H R A Cecil	4-10	3-4	1-5	0-1	0-0	40.0	+ 5.57
M R Stoute	3-13	2-9	1-1	0-0	0-3	23.1	− 3.50
J Berry	3-14	1-6	0-0	1-5	1-3	21.4	+ 15.00
G Harwood	3-17	2-10	1-3	0-1	0-3	17.6	− 12.56

WINDSOR (Group 3)

Leading Trainers 1988-92

	Total W-R	Non-handicaps 2-y-o	3-y-o+	Handicaps 2-y-o	3-y-o+	Per cent	£1 Level Stake
R Hannon	27-205	14-78	2-32	4-25	7-70	13.2	- 32.71
L M Cumani	13-39	0-0	11-29	0-1	2-9	33.3	- 9.48
G Harwood	12-40	2-2	5-22	1-1	4-15	30.0	+ 12.10
D R C Elsworth	12-82	2-22	8-33	0-2	2-25	14.6	+ 34.63
P F I Cole	12-88	6-26	1-33	0-1	5-28	13.6	- 5.75
H R A Cecil	10-37	0-5	6-25	0-0	4-7	27.0	- 4.42
A C Stewart	9-35	1-4	6-19	1-2	1-10	25.7	- 9.95
J Berry	9-47	5-26	1-4	3-10	0-7	19.1	- 11.40
M R Stoute	9-48	2-11	2-18	0-0	5-19	18.8	- 11.60
R Akehurst	9-89	2-16	1-26	1-5	5-42	10.1	+ 26.38
W R Hern	8-48	1-4	5-30	0-0	2-14	16.7	- 27.79
I A Balding	8-51	1-9	2-18	0-1	5-23	15.7	- 15.31
Lord Huntingdon	7-38	3-11	3-17	0-0	1-10	18.4	- 6.32
P T Walwyn	7-47	1-10	2-16	0-0	4-21	14.9	- 7.25
P J Makin	7-50	1-10	5-20	0-0	1-20	14.0	- 13.76
N A Callaghan	7-56	1-8	0-7	0-4	6-37	12.5	- 20.50
C R Nelson	6-27	2-4	0-10	0-1	4-12	22.2	+ 8.50
J H M Gosden	6-33	2-2	3-23	0-2	1-6	18.2	- 8.84
C J Benstead	6-59	0-8	0-12	0-0	6-39	10.2	- 6.50
J White	6-74	1-12	2-33	0-1	3-28	8.1	- 24.17
G Lewis	6-87	2-29	1-16	2-6	1-36	6.9	- 55.42
W A O'Gorman	5-29	5-20	0-1	0-2	0-6	17.2	- 15.89

Leading Jockeys

	Total W-R	Per cent	£1 Level Stake	Best Trainer	W-R	Per cent	£1 Level Stake
Pat Eddery	50-224	22.3	- 58.84	H R A Cecil	5-8	62.5	+ 3.46
M Roberts	22-122	18.0	- 33.64	A C Stewart	8-33	24.2	- 15.95
R Cochrane	21-151	13.9	- 11.32	L M Cumani	4-14	28.6	- 5.79
W Carson	21-172	12.2	- 90.83	W R Hern	8-37	21.6	- 16.79
J Reid	20-155	12.9	- 18.25	C R Nelson	6-16	37.5	+ 19.50
S Cauthen	16-77	20.8	- 1.37	H R A Cecil	5-18	27.8	+ 3.13
W R Swinburn	15-92	16.3	- 29.08	M R Stoute	6-28	21.4	- 2.23
T Quinn	15-142	10.6	+ 6.75	P F I Cole	7-54	13.0	+ 3.75
L Dettori	14-85	16.5	- 40.00	L M Cumani	9-25	36.0	- 4.40
B Raymond	12-87	13.8	- 32.24	R Hannon	2-5	40.0	+ 2.88
A McGlone	8-110	7.3	- 42.99	M D I Usher	2-20	10.0	- 13.37
B Rouse	7-155	4.5	-102.54	R Hannon	2-47	4.3	- 36.50

How the Favourites Fared

Non-handicaps	W-R	Per cent	£1 Level Stake	Handicaps	W-R	Per cent	£1 Level Stake
2-y-o	43-102	42.2	+ 0.17	2-y-o	11-30	36.7	- 0.51
3-y-o	31-55	56.4	+ 7.55	3-y-o	21-66	31.8	- 5.11
Weight-for-age	19-57	33.3	- 7.86	All-aged	23-87	26.4	- 11.32
Totals	93-214	43.5	- 0.14	Totals	55-183	30.1	- 16.94
All favs	148-397	37.3	- 17.08				

Leading Trainers by Month at Windsor

March/Apr	Total W-R	Non-handicaps 2-y-o	3-y-o+	Handicaps 2-y-o	3-y-o+	Per cent	£1 Level Stake
R Hannon	5-11	4-6	1-3	0-0	0-2	45.5	+ 19.75
H R A Cecil	2-2	0-0	2-2	0-0	0-0	100.0	+ 4.13
H Candy	2-3	0-0	0-1	0-0	2-2	66.7	+ 27.00
M J Madgwick	1-1	0-0	1-1	0-0	0-0	100.0	+ 6.00
M J Ryan	1-1	0-0	0-0	0-0	1-1	100.0	+ 4.50

May	Total W-R	Non-handicaps 2-y-o	3-y-o+	Handicaps 2-y-o	3-y-o+	Per cent	£1 Level Stake
R Hannon	5-21	2-9	0-1	0-0	3-11	23.8	+ 17.17
W G R Wightman	2-3	0-0	0-1	0-0	2-2	66.7	+ 10.50
W J Musson	2-5	2-2	0-1	0-0	0-2	40.0	+ 0.38
Miss B Sanders	2-5	0-0	0-1	0-0	2-4	40.0	+ 15.00
A C Stewart	2-6	0-0	1-4	0-0	1-2	33.3	- 0.38

June	Total W-R	Non-handicaps 2-y-o	3-y-o+	Handicaps 2-y-o	3-y-o+	Per cent	£1 Level Stake
N A Callaghan	5-18	1-4	0-0	0-0	4-14	27.8	+ 10.50
L M Cumani	4-7	0-0	2-5	0-0	2-2	57.1	+ 4.35
Lord Huntingdon	4-9	2-4	2-4	0-0	0-1	44.4	+ 6.78
R Hannon	4-38	3-16	0-2	0-0	1-20	10.5	- 20.06
P F I Cole	3-19	0-4	0-4	0-0	3-11	15.8	+ 5.25

July	Total W-R	Non-handicaps 2-y-o	3-y-o+	Handicaps 2-y-o	3-y-o+	Per cent	£1 Level Stake
D R C Elsworth	9-34	2-9	6-14	0-0	1-11	26.5	+ 70.75
R Hannon	7-70	3-28	0-11	2-9	2-22	10.0	- 28.83
R Akehurst	6-39	1-8	1-9	1-2	3-20	15.4	+ 29.00
W R Hern	5-13	1-1	2-7	0-0	2-5	38.5	- 2.29
G Harwood	4-9	0-0	2-3	0-0	2-6	44.4	+ 13.14

August	Total W-R	Non-handicaps 2-y-o	3-y-o+	Handicaps 2-y-o	3-y-o+	Per cent	£1 Level Stake
G Harwood	7-23	2-2	2-12	1-1	2-8	30.4	+ 1.96
J Berry	6-17	2-4	1-3	3-9	0-1	35.3	+ 7.50
R Hannon	6-65	2-19	1-15	2-16	1-15	9.2	- 20.75
A C Stewart	5-18	0-2	4-9	1-2	0-5	27.8	- 1.94
L M Cumani	5-19	0-0	5-15	0-1	0-3	26.3	- 8.89

WOLVERHAMPTON (Group 4)

Leading Trainers 1988-92

	Total W-R	Non-handicaps 2-y-o	3-y-o+	Handicaps 2-y-o	3-y-o+	Per cent	£1 Level Stake
J Berry	20-155	8-78	1-15	7-32	4-30	12.9	- 20.08
J L Dunlop	18-68	4-20	5-18	0-0	9-30	26.5	+ 0.37
H R A Cecil	15-46	3-11	12-34	0-0	0-1	32.6	- 4.16
L M Cumani	12-28	4-8	7-17	0-0	1-3	42.9	+ 23.04
R Boss	11-41	2-8	4-12	0-6	5-15	26.8	+ 11.00
R Hollinshead	11-201	0-40	7-69	1-11	3-81	5.5	- 93.00
G Harwood	10-26	3-8	5-11	0-0	2-7	38.5	+ 7.25
B W Hills	10-28	5-11	4-7	0-2	1-8	35.7	+ 16.86
B Hanbury	10-40	4-12	3-14	0-2	3-12	25.0	+ 23.98
M A Jarvis	9-36	4-9	1-12	0-2	4-13	25.0	+ 36.13
B A McMahon	9-133	2-34	3-24	1-8	3-67	6.8	- 32.50
M R Stoute	8-38	4-16	3-15	0-0	1-7	21.1	- 14.90
J L Spearing	8-57	0-11	0-8	2-6	6-32	14.0	+ 14.00
J H M Gosden	7-14	3-4	3-8	0-0	1-2	50.0	+ 6.37
W Jarvis	7-25	3-9	3-9	1-1	0-6	28.0	+ 19.94
C E Brittain	7-51	1-13	1-20	0-0	5-18	13.7	+ 37.00
G Wragg	6-17	2-2	4-11	0-0	0-4	35.3	+ 6.58
D Morley	6-27	1-6	1-9	1-1	3-11	22.2	+ 28.25
G Lewis	6-42	1-8	2-8	0-6	3-20	14.3	+ 0.50
J Wharton	6-57	1-14	1-18	0-1	4-24	10.5	+ 34.50
R Charlton	5-15	3-5	2-6	0-0	0-4	33.3	- 0.81
Lord Huntingdon	5-19	2-3	2-8	0-4	1-4	26.3	+ 41.13

Leading Jockeys

	Total W-R	Per cent	£1 Level Stake	Best Trainer	W-R	Per cent	£1 Level Stake
Pat Eddery	38-125	30.4	- 14.43	H R A Cecil	4-6	66.7	- 0.67
M Roberts	27-157	17.2	+ 4.19	A C Stewart	5-24	20.8	- 9.62
W Carson	22-113	19.5	- 34.71	J L Dunlop	5-17	29.4	+ 3.21
G Carter	20-110	18.2	+ 31.76	J Berry	4-15	26.7	+ 8.25
R Cochrane	18-128	14.1	- 44.44	L M Cumani	8-13	61.5	+ 7.29
S Cauthen	17-56	30.4	+ 4.05	H R A Cecil	5-11	45.5	+ 5.02
J Reid	16-99	16.2	- 13.12	C R Nelson	3-6	50.0	+ 14.50
W Ryan	15-137	10.9	- 28.51	H R A Cecil	5-21	23.8	- 3.51
W R Swinburn	14-60	23.3	+ 18.48	M R Stoute	6-16	37.5	+ 3.73
B Raymond	12-88	13.6	- 17.32	B Hanbury	4-12	33.3	+ 4.55
L Dettori	11-64	17.2	- 1.24	L M Cumani	2-8	25.0	+ 3.75
G Duffield	11-98	11.2	- 8.00	Sir M Prescott	4-25	16.0	+ 11.75

How the Favourites Fared

Non-handicaps	W-R	Per cent	£1 Level Stake	Handicaps	W-R	Per cent	£1 Level Stake
2-y-o	51-122	41.8	- 18.22	2-y-o	2-29	6.9	- 23.25
3-y-o	46-85	54.1	+ 3.72	3-y-o	18-68	26.5	- 12.94
Weight-for-age	17-48	35.4	- 0.06	All-aged	32-110	29.1	- 7.66
Totals	114-255	44.7	- 14.56	Totals	52-207	25.1	- 43.85
All favs	166-462	35.9	- 58.41				

Leading Trainers by Month at Wolverhampton

March/Apr	Total W-R	Non-handicaps 2-y-o	Non-handicaps 3-y-o+	Handicaps 2-y-o	Handicaps 3-y-o+	Per cent	£1 Level Stake
H R A Cecil	5-10	0-0	5-10	0-0	0-0	50.0	- 0.58
R J Hodges	3-16	1-1	0-5	0-0	2-10	18.8	- 6.38
R Hollinshead	3-35	0-5	2-17	0-0	1-13	8.6	- 10.50
W A O'Gorman	2-2	2-2	0-0	0-0	0-0	100.0	+ 2.15
P A Kelleway	2-5	0-0	2-5	0-0	0-0	40.0	+ 6.75

May	Total W-R	Non-handicaps 2-y-o	Non-handicaps 3-y-o+	Handicaps 2-y-o	Handicaps 3-y-o+	Per cent	£1 Level Stake
L M Cumani	4-8	0-0	4-7	0-0	0-1	50.0	- 1.00
R Hollinshead	4-39	0-9	4-15	0-0	0-15	10.3	+ 14.00
R Boss	3-5	1-1	1-3	0-0	1-1	60.0	+ 2.67
B Hanbury	3-8	1-2	2-5	0-0	0-1	37.5	+ 6.35
H R A Cecil	3-10	0-0	3-10	0-0	0-0	30.0	+ 5.91

June	Total W-R	Non-handicaps 2-y-o	Non-handicaps 3-y-o+	Handicaps 2-y-o	Handicaps 3-y-o+	Per cent	£1 Level Stake
M A Jarvis	3-5	2-3	0-0	0-0	1-2	60.0	+ 16.00
R Boss	3-6	1-3	1-1	0-0	1-2	50.0	+ 7.75
J L Dunlop	3-6	0-0	1-2	0-0	2-4	50.0	+ 7.08
G Harwood	2-2	2-2	0-0	0-0	0-0	100.0	+ 6.63
Lord Huntingdon	2-2	0-0	1-1	0-0	1-1	100.0	+ 21.50

July	Total W-R	Non-handicaps 2-y-o	Non-handicaps 3-y-o+	Handicaps 2-y-o	Handicaps 3-y-o+	Per cent	£1 Level Stake
J Berry	9-29	5-21	1-2	1-1	2-5	31.0	+ 14.92
J L Dunlop	5-11	0-4	3-3	0-0	2-4	45.5	+ 4.54
R Boss	4-9	0-2	2-3	0-0	2-4	44.4	+ 12.58
P T Walwyn	3-7	3-3	0-1	0-0	0-3	42.9	+ 12.88
R F J Houghton	3-9	1-4	0-0	0-0	2-5	33.3	+ 23.50

August	Total W-R	Non-handicaps 2-y-o	Non-handicaps 3-y-o+	Handicaps 2-y-o	Handicaps 3-y-o+	Per cent	£1 Level Stake
B W Hills	5-9	2-4	3-3	0-1	0-1	55.6	+ 13.00
J L Spearing	4-14	0-2	0-2	2-5	2-5	28.6	+ 28.00
J Berry	4-30	1-13	0-0	3-14	0-3	13.3	- 3.50
M J Ryan	3-4	0-0	1-1	0-0	2-3	75.0	+ 23.00
D Morley	3-5	1-1	1-2	1-1	0-1	60.0	+ 14.25

September	Total W-R	Non-handicaps 2-y-o	Non-handicaps 3-y-o+	Handicaps 2-y-o	Handicaps 3-y-o+	Per cent	£1 Level Stake
J L Dunlop	4-11	3-5	0-1	0-0	1-5	36.4	+ 8.00
M C Pipe	3-5	0-0	2-4	0-0	1-1	60.0	+ 6.73
C E Brittain	3-8	0-3	0-0	0-0	3-5	37.5	+ 31.00
P F I Cole	3-8	3-5	0-0	0-0	0-3	37.5	- 0.63
J Berry	3-17	0-5	0-0	2-9	1-3	17.6	+ 24.00

Oct/Nov	Total W-R	Non-handicaps 2-y-o	Non-handicaps 3-y-o+	Handicaps 2-y-o	Handicaps 3-y-o+	Per cent	£1 Level Stake
L M Cumani	4-5	4-4	0-1	0-0	0-0	80.0	+ 20.33
G Harwood	4-9	1-3	3-4	0-0	0-2	44.4	- 3.17
M R Stoute	3-12	3-10	0-1	0-0	0-1	25.0	- 1.02
H Thomson Jones	2-4	2-3	0-1	0-0	0-0	50.0	+ 4.25
C E Brittain	2-6	0-2	0-1	0-0	2-3	33.3	+ 26.00

YARMOUTH (Group 3)

Leading Trainers 1988-92

	Total W-R	Non-handicaps 2-y-o	3-y-o+	Handicaps 2-y-o	3-y-o+	Per cent	£1 Level Stake
H R A Cecil	37-103	17-44	18-49	0-1	2-9	35.9	- 7.85
M R Stoute	26-99	13-48	11-32	0-2	2-17	26.3	+ 3.22
A C Stewart	17-68	5-21	7-27	0-0	5-20	25.0	+ 19.39
L M Cumani	16-104	7-37	8-51	0-1	1-15	15.4	- 43.83
G Wragg	15-91	5-38	6-32	1-2	3-19	16.5	+ 11.64
M H Tompkins	15-127	6-55	2-17	0-5	7-50	11.8	- 41.98
J H M Gosden	14-64	3-20	7-31	0-1	4-12	21.9	+ 5.38
D Morley	14-96	7-30	2-14	0-2	5-50	14.6	+ 13.43
G A P-Gordon	13-108	3-40	2-25	1-2	7-41	12.0	- 1.33
B Hanbury	12-86	6-38	3-22	0-5	3-21	14.0	- 6.59
Mrs N Macauley	12-95	1-30	1-8	0-1	10-56	12.6	+ 19.78
C E Brittain	12-122	3-34	4-34	2-4	3-50	9.8	- 41.77
W J Haggas	11-54	2-13	2-13	1-5	6-23	20.4	+ 25.21
W Jarvis	11-82	2-19	2-24	0-2	7-37	13.4	- 29.00
M J Ryan	11-137	0-30	4-29	1-4	6-74	8.0	- 65.88
B W Hills	9-32	2-11	6-15	0-0	1-6	28.1	+ 2.66
N A Callaghan	9-50	2-18	2-7	1-5	4-20	18.0	- 5.17
D T Thom	9-82	2-25	0-9	0-2	7-46	11.0	+ 55.00
Sir M Prescott	8-55	4-28	1-5	0-1	3-21	14.5	+ 2.36
H Thomson Jones	8-63	4-24	3-20	0-1	1-18	12.7	- 21.50
J Berry	7-27	7-23	0-1	0-0	0-3	25.9	+ 18.98
K T Ivory	7-65	0-13	1-11	0-1	6-40	10.8	- 18.78

Leading Jockeys

	Total W-R	Per cent	£1 Level Stake	Best Trainer	W-R	Per cent	£1 Level Stake
M Roberts	42-234	17.9	+ 32.34	A C Stewart	13-49	26.5	+ 2.81
S Cauthen	29-112	25.9	- 35.59	H R A Cecil	18-34	52.9	+ 0.09
L Dettori	24-124	19.4	- 6.88	L M Cumani	11-50	22.0	- 13.41
G Carter	24-189	12.7	+ 73.17	G Wragg	7-30	23.3	+ 35.69
W R Swinburn	22-119	18.5	+ 17.85	M R Stoute	9-35	25.7	+ 3.30
W Ryan	21-134	15.7	- 36.13	H R A Cecil	12-40	30.0	- 3.99
R Cochrane	19-124	15.3	- 15.07	L M Cumani	4-11	36.4	+ 1.58
R Hills	18-129	14.0	- 35.87	H Thomson Jones	8-41	19.5	+ 0.50
G Duffield	16-129	12.4	- 18.39	Sir M Prescott	7-32	21.9	+ 21.61
Pat Eddery	15-53	28.3	- 10.80	J Berry	2-2	100.0	+ 2.60
G Bardwell	14-131	10.7	- 17.96	K T Ivory	4-23	17.4	+ 10.13
Paul Eddery	13-128	10.2	- 63.04	Mrs J Cecil	3-11	27.3	- 1.02

How the Favourites Fared

Non-handicaps	W-R	Per cent	£1 Level Stake	Handicaps	W-R	Per cent	£1 Level Stake
2-y-o	66-152	43.4	- 17.84	2-y-o	4-18	22.2	- 7.25
3-y-o	38-76	50.0	+ 1.62	3-y-o	15-53	28.3	- 13.96
Weight-for-age	29-53	54.7	+ 15.35	All-aged	47-156	30.1	- 20.93
Totals	133-281	47.3	- 0.87	Totals	66-227	29.1	- 42.14
All favs	199-508	39.2	- 43.01				

Leading Trainers by Month at Yarmouth

June	Total W-R	Non-handicaps 2-y-o	3-y-o+	Handicaps 2-y-o	3-y-o+	Per cent	£1 Level Stake
M R Stoute	7-28	3-5	3-16	0-0	1-7	25.0	- 4.42
A C Stewart	5-13	0-1	3-9	0-0	2-3	38.5	+ 18.23
H R A Cecil	5-21	1-4	4-15	0-0	0-2	23.8	- 4.82
C E Brittain	5-31	1-4	2-11	0-0	2-16	16.1	+ 3.25
M H Tompkins	5-33	3-12	0-4	0-0	2-17	15.2	+ 4.38

July	Total W-R	Non-handicaps 2-y-o	3-y-o+	Handicaps 2-y-o	3-y-o+	Per cent	£1 Level Stake
H R A Cecil	14-23	5-6	9-17	0-0	0-0	60.9	+ 9.26
D Morley	8-30	4-8	1-7	0-0	3-15	26.7	+ 45.93
M H Tompkins	8-49	3-24	1-8	0-0	4-17	16.3	- 7.60
A C Stewart	6-18	2-5	3-7	0-0	1-6	33.3	+ 2.76
G A P-Gordon	6-31	0-9	2-10	0-0	4-12	19.4	- 9.83

August	Total W-R	Non-handicaps 2-y-o	3-y-o+	Handicaps 2-y-o	3-y-o+	Per cent	£1 Level Stake
H R A Cecil	12-23	10-16	2-6	0-0	0-1	52.2	- 0.82
M R Stoute	9-31	6-21	3-5	0-0	0-5	29.0	- 0.96
W J Haggas	7-20	2-4	1-3	1-1	3-12	35.0	+ 44.63
L M Cumani	4-24	3-12	1-10	0-0	0-2	16.7	- 10.42
M J Ryan	4-30	0-5	0-5	0-1	4-19	13.3	- 6.00

September	Total W-R	Non-handicaps 2-y-o	3-y-o+	Handicaps 2-y-o	3-y-o+	Per cent	£1 Level Stake
H R A Cecil	6-31	1-14	3-10	0-1	2-6	19.4	- 6.47
M R Stoute	5-24	2-13	2-5	0-2	1-4	20.8	+ 3.10
L M Cumani	5-35	2-17	3-13	0-1	0-4	14.3	- 17.84
B W Hills	4-13	0-5	4-6	0-0	0-2	30.8	+ 2.75
D T Thom	4-14	1-6	0-1	0-0	3-7	28.6	+ 55.00

Oct/Nov	Total W-R	Non-handicaps 2-y-o	3-y-o+	Handicaps 2-y-o	3-y-o+	Per cent	£1 Level Stake
A C Stewart	2-3	2-3	0-0	0-0	0-0	66.7	+ 19.91
J W Hills	2-5	0-2	1-2	0-0	1-1	40.0	+ 12.00
Mrs J Cecil	2-6	1-5	1-1	0-0	0-0	33.3	+ 2.25
J H M Gosden	2-8	1-5	1-3	0-0	0-0	25.0	- 1.40
N A Callaghan	1-1	0-0	0-0	0-0	1-1	100.0	+ 2.00

YORK (Group 1)

Leading Trainers 1988-92

	Total W-R	Non-handicaps 2-y-o	3-y-o+	Handicaps 2-y-o	3-y-o+	Per cent	£1 Level Stake
M R Stoute	30-133	4-17	17-56	0-3	9-57	22.6	- 8.90
H R A Cecil	28-98	3-9	17-62	1-1	7-26	28.6	+ 12.09
M H Easterby	25-210	4-31	2-14	2-18	17-147	11.9	- 31.42
J H M Gosden	23-74	5-11	9-32	0-1	9-30	31.1	+ 21.71
B W Hills	17-149	4-33	9-65	0-1	4-50	11.4	- 60.04
L M Cumani	16-85	2-7	11-49	0-2	3-27	18.8	- 12.88
R Hannon	15-120	10-46	2-9	1-12	2-53	12.5	- 17.16
C E Brittain	14-148	1-30	7-55	2-7	4-56	9.5	- 33.27
B Hanbury	12-85	6-17	1-26	0-3	5-39	14.1	- 31.58
P F I Cole	11-40	7-17	2-14	0-1	2-8	27.5	+ 2.75
J L Dunlop	11-65	5-15	3-25	0-3	3-22	16.9	- 32.25
J Berry	11-93	6-35	0-10	2-12	3-36	11.8	- 45.36
R M Whitaker	11-136	1-24	2-14	0-9	8-89	8.1	- 44.50
D R C Elsworth	10-48	3-9	4-21	0-0	3-18	20.8	+ 21.75
M H Tompkins	8-78	1-19	0-4	1-7	6-48	10.3	- 15.75
R W Armstrong	7-47	3-10	1-13	0-0	3-24	14.9	- 0.75
I A Balding	7-71	0-11	1-16	0-3	6-41	9.9	- 18.50
G Lewis	6-29	2-4	0-6	1-1	3-18	20.7	+ 18.25
Mrs G R Reveley	6-37	0-4	0-1	1-2	5-30	16.2	+ 2.50
Lord Huntingdon	6-39	1-11	2-10	0-0	3-18	15.4	+ 11.50
A A Scott	6-42	3-13	2-14	0-3	1-12	14.3	- 21.08
G Harwood	6-46	1-5	3-24	0-0	2-17	13.0	+ 0.45

Leading Jockeys

	Total W-R	Per cent	£1 Level Stake	Best Trainer	W-R	Per cent	£1 Level Stake
Pat Eddery	47-218	21.6	- 8.24	A A Scott	6-16	37.5	+ 4.92
S Cauthen	46-209	22.0	+ 30.87	H R A Cecil	18-52	34.6	+ 9.41
M Roberts	34-220	15.5	+ 42.61	C E Brittain	10-72	13.9	+ 24.50
W Carson	33-239	13.8	- 96.67	J L Dunlop	6-26	23.1	- 7.67
W R Swinburn	26-169	15.4	- 57.33	M R Stoute	18-75	24.0	- 12.46
M Birch	23-189	12.2	- 17.67	M H Easterby	17-127	13.4	- 15.67
L Dettori	18-123	14.6	- 32.35	L M Cumani	13-52	25.0	+ 7.90
Paul Eddery	15-98	15.3	+ 12.43	G Lewis	4-12	33.3	+ 20.50
M Hills	15-136	11.0	- 51.79	B W Hills	13-75	17.3	- 4.29
D McKeown	15-141	10.6	- 14.39	M S Johnston	4-12	33.3	+ 20.00
R Cochrane	14-160	8.8	- 88.58	M H Tompkins	4-20	20.0	+ 8.75
A Munro	13-135	9.6	- 46.60	P F I Cole	5-16	31.3	+ 7.90

How the Favourites Fared

Non-handicaps	W-R	Per cent	£1 Level Stake	Handicaps	W-R	Per cent	£1 Level Stake
2-y-o	53-117	45.3	+ 0.82	2-y-o	4-27	14.8	- 13.29
3-y-o	35-87	40.2	- 17.27	3-y-o	19-65	29.2	+ 13.31
Weight-for-age	19-56	33.9	- 11.57	All-aged	46-139	33.1	+ 37.84
Totals	107-260	41.2	- 28.02	Totals	69-231	29.9	+ 37.86
All favs	176-491	35.8	+ 9.84				

Leading Trainers by Month at York

May

	Total W-R	Non-handicaps 2-y-o	3-y-o+	Handicaps 2-y-o	3-y-o+	Per cent	£1 Level Stake
H R A Cecil	11-30	1-1	8-22	0-0	2-7	36.7	+ 6.78
M R Stoute	10-33	1-2	8-21	0-0	1-10	30.3	+ 1.98
M H Easterby	7-44	2-6	0-1	0-0	5-37	15.9	+ 9.75
B W Hills	5-47	0-7	3-27	0-0	2-13	10.6	- 14.50
D R C Elsworth	4-16	0-0	3-12	0-0	1-4	25.0	+ 16.00

June

	Total W-R	Non-handicaps 2-y-o	3-y-o+	Handicaps 2-y-o	3-y-o+	Per cent	£1 Level Stake
B Hanbury	5-11	2-3	1-4	0-0	2-4	45.5	+ 8.81
M H Easterby	4-34	1-5	0-3	0-0	3-26	11.8	- 14.25
A A Scott	3-5	2-2	0-1	0-0	1-2	60.0	+ 2.32
J L Dunlop	3-8	0-0	2-7	0-0	1-1	37.5	+ 1.65
I A Balding	3-11	0-0	1-4	0-0	2-7	27.3	+ 18.75

July

	Total W-R	Non-handicaps 2-y-o	3-y-o+	Handicaps 2-y-o	3-y-o+	Per cent	£1 Level Stake
J H M Gosden	4-5	0-0	3-3	0-0	1-2	80.0	+ 8.50
H R A Cecil	3-8	0-0	2-5	0-0	1-3	37.5	+ 9.25
F H Lee	3-10	1-3	0-1	0-1	2-5	30.0	+ 6.80
J Berry	3-11	2-3	0-0	1-5	0-3	27.3	- 5.01
M R Stoute	3-14	0-0	1-2	0-0	2-12	21.4	+ 3.25

August

	Total W-R	Non-handicaps 2-y-o	3-y-o+	Handicaps 2-y-o	3-y-o+	Per cent	£1 Level Stake
H R A Cecil	9-32	2-3	4-18	0-0	3-11	28.1	+ 3.98
M R Stoute	9-50	1-9	3-16	0-2	5-23	18.0	- 4.42
R Hannon	8-53	6-24	1-6	1-5	0-18	15.1	+ 10.81
R W Armstrong	5-15	3-6	1-3	0-0	1-6	33.3	+ 17.75
P F I Cole	5-17	4-8	1-8	0-0	0-1	29.4	+ 8.35

September

	Total W-R	Non-handicaps 2-y-o	3-y-o+	Handicaps 2-y-o	3-y-o+	Per cent	£1 Level Stake
L M Cumani	6-18	1-3	3-10	0-0	2-5	33.3	+ 7.44
J H M Gosden	4-15	0-1	2-10	0-0	2-4	26.7	- 0.38
M Feth-Godley	3-5	0-0	0-0	0-0	3-5	60.0	+ 19.50
C E Brittain	3-19	0-2	2-7	0-3	1-7	15.8	+ 2.00
M H Easterby	3-24	0-1	0-3	1-5	2-15	12.5	+ 19.00

Oct/Nov

	Total W-R	Non-handicaps 2-y-o	3-y-o+	Handicaps 2-y-o	3-y-o+	Per cent	£1 Level Stake
J H M Gosden	11-24	5-8	3-8	0-0	3-8	45.8	+ 14.58
M H Easterby	6-43	1-7	1-3	1-7	3-26	14.0	- 8.25
M R Stoute	4-11	1-3	2-3	0-1	1-4	36.4	+ 4.50
B Hanbury	4-22	3-4	0-1	0-2	1-15	18.2	- 9.23
R Hollinshead	3-13	1-3	0-2	1-2	1-6	23.1	+ 36.00

TRAINERS' FAVOURITES AT ASCOT 1988-92

	Total W-R	Non-handicaps 2-y-o	3-y-o+	Handicaps 2-y-o	3-y-o+	Per cent	£1 Level Stake
G Harwood	15-26	1-2	11-15	0-1	3-8	57.7	+ 20.78
H R A Cecil	14-41	6-16	7-21	0-0	1-4	34.1	- 2.50
L M Cumani	13-33	6-7	5-15	0-0	2-11	39.4	+ 1.78
M R Stoute	13-42	4-13	9-20	0-1	0-8	31.0	- 10.36
J H M Gosden	9-27	2-5	3-5	0-0	4-17	33.3	+ 5.20
P F I Cole	8-14	5-7	2-4	0-1	1-2	57.1	+ 6.63
G Wragg	5-14	3-5	1-4	0-0	1-5	35.7	+ 5.39
J L Dunlop	5-17	3-9	2-5	0-0	0-3	29.4	- 2.92
H Thomson Jones	4-9	4-8	0-0	0-0	0-1	44.4	+ 1.73
R W Armstrong	3-4	1-1	1-1	0-0	1-2	75.0	+ 6.98
B Hanbury	3-5	0-0	2-3	0-0	1-2	60.0	+ 2.38
Lord Huntingdon	3-10	0-1	1-1	0-0	2-8	30.0	- 2.67
P T Walwyn	3-11	0-2	0-3	0-0	3-6	27.3	+ 1.88
C A Cyzer	2-2	0-0	0-0	0-0	2-2	100.0	+ 7.75
W A O'Gorman	2-3	2-2	0-0	0-0	0-1	66.7	+ 2.00
M H Tompkins	2-3	0-0	0-0	0-0	2-3	66.7	+ 8.00
N A Graham	2-3	2-2	0-0	0-0	0-1	66.7	+ 0.77
A C Stewart	2-5	0-0	1-1	0-0	1-4	40.0	+ 0.03
W R Hern	2-6	0-1	1-3	0-0	1-2	33.3	- 1.78
C E Brittain	2-8	0-2	2-2	0-0	0-4	25.0	- 2.00
R Hannon	2-12	1-6	1-4	0-0	0-2	16.7	- 5.62
R Boss	1-1	1-1	0-0	0-0	0-0	100.0	+ 1.10
D Morley	1-1	1-1	0-0	0-0	0-0	100.0	+ 1.25
Mrs J Cecil	1-1	1-1	0-0	0-0	0-0	100.0	+ 2.50

TRAINERS' FAVOURITES AT AYR 1988-92

	Total W-R	Non-handicaps 2-y-o	3-y-o+	Handicaps 2-y-o	3-y-o+	Per cent	£1 Level Stake
J Berry	15-33	7-16	7-8	1-2	0-7	45.5	- 0.13
M H Easterby	12-28	4-9	3-6	1-3	4-10	42.9	- 0.31
B W Hills	10-21	2-5	5-11	0-0	3-5	47.6	+ 2.04
Mrs J Ramsden	9-28	2-2	0-3	0-1	7-22	32.1	+ 6.71
J L Dunlop	6-10	3-5	1-2	0-0	2-3	60.0	+ 4.01
J W Watts	5-13	1-2	2-4	0-3	2-4	38.5	- 0.77
L M Cumani	4-5	1-1	3-4	0-0	0-0	80.0	+ 4.46
A Bailey	4-6	1-1	1-1	0-1	2-3	66.7	+ 4.54
T D Barron	4-7	0-1	0-0	1-2	3-4	57.1	+ 6.09
M P Naughton	4-7	0-0	1-1	0-0	3-6	57.1	+ 9.75
G A Pritchard-Gordon	4-7	2-2	2-3	0-0	0-2	57.1	+ 1.54
Sir M Prescott	4-8	1-3	2-2	0-0	1-3	50.0	+ 1.61
P Chapple-Hyam	4-9	3-6	1-3	0-0	0-0	44.4	- 3.30
H Thomson Jones	4-10	3-7	1-2	0-0	0-1	40.0	- 1.20
Lord Huntingdon	3-3	1-1	1-1	1-1	0-0	100.0	+ 3.41
P C Haslam	3-5	0-0	0-1	0-0	3-4	60.0	+ 2.61
D W Chapman	3-8	0-0	0-2	1-1	2-5	37.5	+ 0.50
C Tinkler	3-8	1-1	1-4	0-0	1-3	37.5	+ 0.13
F H Lee	3-9	0-1	0-0	0-0	3-8	33.3	- 0.12
R M Whitaker	3-14	0-1	0-1	0-1	3-11	21.4	- 0.50
P F I Cole	2-2	0-0	1-1	0-0	1-1	100.0	+ 3.66
G Wragg	2-2	0-0	2-2	0-0	0-0	100.0	+ 3.55
C B B Booth	2-3	2-2	0-0	0-0	0-1	66.7	+ 3.00
M J Camacho	2-3	0-0	0-1	0-0	2-2	66.7	+ 6.75

TRAINERS' FAVOURITES AT BATH 1988-92

	Total W-R	Non-handicaps 2-y-o	3-y-o+	Handicaps 2-y-o	3-y-o+	Per cent	£1 Level Stake
B W Hills	13-23	2-5	6-7	0-1	5-10	56.5	+ 10.34
R Hannon	9-22	3-6	3-6	0-2	3-8	40.9	+ 6.26
G Harwood	8-14	0-2	6-6	0-1	2-5	57.1	+ 7.79
I A Balding	7-27	1-5	2-11	0-0	4-11	25.9	- 4.44
W R Hern	6-11	1-1	1-3	0-0	4-7	54.5	+ 5.88
P F I Cole	6-28	0-7	2-6	0-0	4-15	21.4	- 11.49
C J Hill	5-9	0-0	0-0	1-1	4-8	55.6	+ 14.08
G Lewis	5-9	0-1	2-2	1-1	2-5	55.6	+ 6.13
J L Dunlop	5-15	1-3	2-5	0-0	2-7	33.3	- 0.50
R J Hodges	5-16	0-0	0-1	0-0	5-15	31.3	+ 0.26
D R C Elsworth	4-10	0-1	1-4	0-0	3-5	40.0	+ 5.00
J Berry	4-18	3-9	1-5	0-0	0-4	22.2	- 7.37
M R Channon	3-3	1-1	1-1	0-0	1-1	100.0	+ 6.48
R Charlton	3-3	1-1	2-2	0-0	0-0	100.0	+ 4.65
H Candy	3-4	0-0	2-2	0-1	1-1	75.0	+ 4.57
R Akehurst	3-8	0-0	0-0	0-0	3-8	37.5	+ 4.83
P T Walwyn	3-12	1-2	0-2	0-1	2-7	25.0	- 2.84
M Brittain	2-2	1-1	0-0	0-0	1-1	100.0	+ 5.50
N A Graham	2-2	0-0	1-1	0-0	1-1	100.0	+ 5.50
A C Stewart	2-3	0-1	2-2	0-0	0-0	66.7	+ 3.00
L G Cottrell	2-4	0-0	0-1	0-0	2-3	50.0	+ 6.25
Sir M Prescott	2-4	1-2	1-1	0-0	0-1	50.0	- 0.33
L M Cumani	2-5	0-0	2-3	0-0	0-2	40.0	- 0.95
R F J Houghton	2-6	0-1	2-2	0-0	0-3	33.3	- 2.80

TRAINERS' FAVOURITES AT BEVERLEY 1988-92

	Total W-R	Non-handicaps 2-y-o	3-y-o+	Handicaps 2-y-o	3-y-o+	Per cent	£1 Level Stake
H R A Cecil	13-26	2-4	10-19	0-0	1-3	50.0	- 1.81
M H Easterby	12-38	7-15	3-5	1-2	1-16	31.6	- 6.83
M R Stoute	11-20	1-1	10-16	0-0	0-3	55.0	+ 3.80
J Berry	10-32	9-23	0-4	0-1	1-4	31.3	- 4.13
I A Balding	8-15	3-3	2-6	0-0	3-6	53.3	+ 2.83
L M Cumani	7-11	0-0	7-11	0-0	0-0	63.6	+ 0.65
R Hollinshead	7-18	2-4	3-4	0-0	2-10	38.9	+ 6.35
P F I Cole	6-8	0-1	5-6	0-0	1-1	75.0	+ 5.10
Mrs G R Reveley	6-13	2-2	0-0	0-0	4-11	46.2	+ 3.08
G Harwood	5-10	1-2	4-7	0-1	0-0	50.0	- 3.16
J L Spearing	5-11	0-0	0-0	0-0	5-11	45.5	+ 3.76
D Morley	5-14	0-0	2-5	0-0	3-9	35.7	+ 1.96
T D Barron	5-20	0-2	0-1	1-3	4-14	25.0	- 2.15
J L Dunlop	4-7	1-2	1-2	0-1	2-2	57.1	+ 1.40
W Jarvis	4-10	2-5	2-3	0-0	0-2	40.0	- 2.30
B W Hills	4-13	1-3	3-4	0-0	0-6	30.8	- 3.43
H Thomson Jones	3-5	2-2	0-1	0-0	1-2	60.0	+ 6.63
W A O'Gorman	3-5	2-4	1-1	0-0	0-0	60.0	+ 1.47
A A Scott	3-5	2-2	0-0	0-0	1-3	60.0	+ 3.24
C W Thornton	3-7	0-4	0-0	0-0	3-3	42.9	+ 2.00
C Tinkler	3-8	2-3	0-1	0-0	1-4	37.5	+ 1.41
M Brittain	3-8	0-0	1-1	1-1	1-6	37.5	+ 3.13
M H Tompkins	3-11	0-0	3-3	0-1	0-7	27.3	- 6.02
M W Easterby	3-14	2-5	0-2	1-1	0-6	21.4	- 5.70

TRAINERS' FAVOURITES AT BRIGHTON 1988-92

	Total W-R	Non-handicaps 2-y-o	Non-handicaps 3-y-o+	Handicaps 2-y-o	Handicaps 3-y-o+	Per cent	£1 Level Stake
R Hannon	18-54	13-20	4-9	0-1	1-24	33.3	- 8.24
L M Cumani	16-22	6-7	8-10	1-2	1-3	72.7	+ 11.09
G Harwood	13-29	0-7	12-20	0-0	1-2	44.8	- 3.86
Sir M Prescott	10-26	0-3	3-4	0-1	7-18	38.5	+ 2.98
J H M Gosden	7-10	1-1	6-9	0-0	0-0	70.0	+ 2.31
J L Dunlop	7-17	1-1	4-8	0-1	2-7	41.2	- 2.59
P F I Cole	7-23	3-7	4-11	0-0	0-5	30.4	- 7.67
R J Hodges	6-22	0-0	0-0	0-0	6-22	27.3	- 3.08
M J Ryan	5-9	1-1	0-0	0-0	4-8	55.6	+ 9.26
H R A Cecil	4-8	1-1	3-7	0-0	0-0	50.0	+ 0.27
W R Hern	3-4	0-0	2-2	0-0	1-2	75.0	+ 4.13
R F J Houghton	3-4	0-0	1-2	0-0	2-2	75.0	+ 3.26
H Thomson Jones	3-4	1-1	2-3	0-0	0-0	75.0	+ 0.49
R J R Williams	3-6	0-1	1-1	0-0	2-4	50.0	+ 3.25
W Carter	3-6	1-1	0-0	0-0	2-5	50.0	+ 4.25
M Bell	3-7	2-2	0-1	0-3	1-1	42.9	+ 0.25
J Berry	3-8	1-2	0-1	1-2	1-3	37.5	+ 1.33
R Boss	3-9	1-1	1-1	0-0	1-7	33.3	- 0.96
N A Callaghan	3-9	1-3	0-0	0-1	2-5	33.3	- 3.39
P J Makin	3-10	0-0	1-1	0-0	2-9	30.0	- 0.87
B W Hills	3-11	0-0	2-9	0-0	1-2	27.3	- 1.80
A C Stewart	3-11	2-4	1-7	0-0	0-0	27.3	- 5.56
I A Balding	3-12	0-2	2-3	0-1	1-6	25.0	- 4.38
G Lewis	3-14	0-4	1-2	1-1	1-7	21.4	- 1.83

TRAINERS' FAVOURITES AT CARLISLE 1988-92

	Total W-R	Non-handicaps 2-y-o	Non-handicaps 3-y-o+	Handicaps 2-y-o	Handicaps 3-y-o+	Per cent	£1 Level Stake
M H Easterby	6-15	3-8	1-1	0-0	2-6	40.0	+ 1.20
J Berry	5-23	2-12	2-7	0-0	1-4	21.7	- 5.25
N Tinkler	4-7	2-4	2-2	0-0	0-1	57.1	+ 2.90
M H Tompkins	4-12	2-4	1-3	0-1	1-4	33.3	- 2.54
J L Dunlop	3-4	0-0	2-2	0-0	1-2	75.0	+ 11.37
H Thomson Jones	3-6	1-2	1-2	0-0	1-2	50.0	- 0.82
M R Stoute	3-6	0-0	3-6	0-0	0-0	50.0	- 1.13
R Hollinshead	3-7	1-3	1-1	0-0	1-3	42.9	+ 1.13
Mrs G R Reveley	3-8	0-0	1-1	0-0	2-7	37.5	+ 2.66
S G Norton	3-9	2-4	0-2	0-0	1-3	33.3	+ 1.25
J W Watts	3-9	0-2	2-4	0-0	1-3	33.3	- 1.92
C R Nelson	2-2	0-0	2-2	0-0	0-0	100.0	+ 2.19
W J Haggas	2-3	0-1	2-2	0-0	0-0	66.7	+ 1.32
B W Hills	2-6	0-0	2-4	0-0	0-2	33.3	0.00
G M Moore	2-6	0-0	1-4	0-0	1-2	33.3	+ 4.00
F H Lee	2-6	0-2	0-0	0-0	2-4	33.3	+ 0.38
M S Johnston	2-7	0-0	1-3	0-0	1-4	28.6	- 1.81
Sir M Prescott	2-13	0-1	1-4	0-0	1-8	15.4	- 6.75
B R Cambidge	1-1	0-0	0-0	0-0	1-1	100.0	+ 3.50
C W C Elsey	1-1	0-0	1-1	0-0	0-0	100.0	+ 1.00
P S Felgate	1-1	0-0	0-0	0-0	1-1	100.0	+ 1.88
R E Peacock	1-1	0-0	0-0	0-0	1-1	100.0	+ 3.50
J A R Toller	1-1	0-0	1-1	0-0	0-0	100.0	+ 0.08
D A Wilson	1-1	0-0	0-0	0-0	1-1	100.0	+ 2.00

TRAINERS' FAVOURITES AT CATTERICK 1988-92

	Total W-R	Non-handicaps 2-y-o	Non-handicaps 3-y-o+	Handicaps 2-y-o	Handicaps 3-y-o+	Per cent	£1 Level Stake
J Berry	13-32	8-18	4-7	0-2	1-5	40.6	− 4.59
T D Barron	11-29	3-4	0-6	1-1	7-18	37.9	+ 5.12
M H Easterby	10-33	2-12	4-6	1-1	3-14	30.3	− 10.61
B W Hills	8-22	0-3	8-18	0-0	0-1	36.4	− 5.95
L M Cumani	7-14	0-1	7-12	0-0	0-1	50.0	− 3.03
Sir M Prescott	6-16	3-9	1-2	0-1	2-4	37.5	− 1.57
R M Whitaker	5-6	1-1	2-3	0-0	2-2	83.3	+ 4.30
Mrs G R Reveley	5-6	0-0	3-3	0-0	2-3	83.3	+ 6.90
J H M Gosden	5-8	1-1	4-6	0-1	0-0	62.5	+ 4.81
M R Stoute	5-12	2-4	3-8	0-0	0-0	41.7	− 2.26
H R A Cecil	4-7	0-0	4-7	0-0	0-0	57.1	+ 0.09
A C Stewart	4-8	1-1	3-6	0-0	0-1	50.0	− 1.94
Mrs J Ramsden	4-13	1-1	0-0	0-0	3-12	30.8	− 0.62
W A O'Gorman	3-3	3-3	0-0	0-0	0-0	100.0	+ 2.30
M J Camacho	3-4	1-1	1-1	1-1	0-1	75.0	+ 6.41
Miss S E Hall	3-5	1-2	1-2	0-0	1-1	60.0	+ 3.54
N Tinkler	3-5	0-1	2-3	0-0	1-1	60.0	− 0.58
M Bell	3-5	0-1	2-3	0-0	1-1	60.0	+ 2.83
M P Naughton	3-6	0-0	0-1	0-0	3-5	50.0	+ 3.55
D W Chapman	3-7	0-0	0-0	0-0	3-7	42.9	+ 3.23
P F I Cole	3-11	1-6	1-4	0-0	1-1	27.3	− 5.14
D Morley	3-15	0-3	0-1	0-0	3-11	20.0	− 8.50
R W Armstrong	2-2	1-1	0-0	0-0	1-1	100.0	+ 4.24
C E Brittain	2-2	1-1	1-1	0-0	0-0	100.0	+ 1.92

TRAINERS' FAVOURITES AT CHEPSTOW 1988-92

	Total W-R	Non-handicaps 2-y-o	Non-handicaps 3-y-o+	Handicaps 2-y-o	Handicaps 3-y-o+	Per cent	£1 Level Stake
L M Cumani	9-12	0-0	8-9	1-1	0-2	75.0	+ 6.22
H R A Cecil	6-9	0-1	4-5	0-0	2-3	66.7	+ 3.23
B W Hills	6-11	0-0	6-10	0-1	0-0	54.5	+ 4.80
J Berry	5-6	2-3	3-3	0-0	0-0	83.3	+ 4.84
I A Balding	5-11	1-3	2-4	0-0	2-4	45.5	+ 6.98
R J Hodges	4-10	0-0	0-0	0-0	4-10	40.0	+ 4.46
G Harwood	4-11	1-5	2-4	0-0	1-2	36.4	− 1.37
R Hannon	4-14	0-2	1-3	0-1	3-8	28.6	− 2.09
J L Dunlop	4-15	0-2	3-7	0-0	1-6	26.7	− 4.57
P F I Cole	4-17	2-8	1-4	0-1	1-4	23.5	− 6.25
M A Jarvis	3-3	1-1	2-2	0-0	0-0	100.0	+ 5.57
D A Wilson	3-7	0-0	0-0	0-0	3-7	42.9	+ 9.50
G Lewis	3-8	0-0	2-4	1-2	0-2	37.5	− 1.63
C R Nelson	2-2	0-0	2-2	0-0	0-0	100.0	+ 1.72
N Tinkler	2-2	0-0	2-2	0-0	0-0	100.0	+ 2.48
P J Makin	2-3	0-1	0-0	0-0	2-2	66.7	+ 3.75
Mrs L Piggott	2-3	1-1	1-1	0-0	0-1	66.7	+ 0.03
R Hollinshead	2-4	0-0	0-0	0-1	2-3	50.0	+ 7.50
H Thomson Jones	2-4	0-0	2-3	0-0	0-1	50.0	− 0.10
M H Tompkins	2-4	0-0	0-1	0-1	2-2	50.0	+ 2.38
P T Walwyn	2-4	0-0	2-3	0-1	0-0	50.0	− 0.77
M C Pipe	2-5	0-0	0-1	0-0	2-4	40.0	+ 0.63
Sir M Prescott	2-5	0-1	2-4	0-0	0-0	40.0	− 2.03
M R Stoute	2-8	1-1	1-5	0-0	0-2	25.0	− 4.94

TRAINERS' FAVOURITES AT CHESTER 1988-92

	Total W-R	Non-handicaps 2-y-o	3-y-o+	Handicaps 2-y-o	3-y-o+	Per cent	£1 Level Stake
B W Hills	15-34	4-8	7-14	0-1	4-11	44.1	+ 5.59
M R Stoute	9-15	4-4	4-7	0-0	1-4	60.0	+ 3.79
R Hannon	7-13	4-6	0-1	2-4	1-2	53.8	+ 5.20
H R A Cecil	6-17	3-5	3-11	0-0	0-1	35.3	- 5.34
J H M Gosden	5-12	3-4	0-3	0-0	2-5	41.7	+ 4.98
B Hanbury	3-7	0-2	3-3	0-1	0-1	42.9	+ 0.08
W R Hern	3-7	0-1	2-5	1-1	0-0	42.9	- 0.82
C E Brittain	3-8	2-3	1-2	0-0	0-3	37.5	- 2.13
P F I Cole	3-9	3-7	0-0	0-0	0-2	33.3	- 2.21
J Sutcliffe	2-2	0-0	0-0	0-0	2-2	100.0	+ 4.00
J D Bethell	2-3	0-0	0-0	0-0	2-3	66.7	+ 8.88
G Wragg	2-4	0-0	2-3	0-1	0-0	50.0	+ 1.50
A C Stewart	2-4	0-0	1-2	0-0	1-2	50.0	+ 0.48
S G Norton	2-5	1-3	0-0	0-0	1-2	40.0	- 0.18
G A Pritchard-Gordon	2-5	0-0	1-1	0-0	1-4	40.0	+ 0.75
F H Lee	2-7	0-0	0-1	0-0	2-6	28.6	+ 2.00
J Berry	2-13	2-5	0-1	0-0	0-7	15.4	- 7.25
L G Cottrell	1-1	0-0	0-0	0-0	1-1	100.0	+ 3.50
M McCormack	1-1	0-0	0-0	0-0	1-1	100.0	+ 2.25
E J Alston	1-1	0-0	0-0	0-0	1-1	100.0	+ 3.33
A M Robson	1-1	0-0	0-0	0-0	1-1	100.0	+ 3.50
S J Muldoon	1-1	1-1	0-0	0-0	0-0	100.0	+ 2.50
Mrs L Piggott	1-1	0-0	1-1	0-0	0-0	100.0	+ 2.75
B R Millman	1-1	0-0	0-0	0-0	1-1	100.0	+ 3.33

TRAINERS' FAVOURITES AT DONCASTER 1988-92

	Total W-R	Non-handicaps 2-y-o	3-y-o+	Handicaps 2-y-o	3-y-o+	Per cent	£1 Level Stake
H R A Cecil	23-44	11-17	11-20	0-0	1-7	52.3	+ 5.59
B W Hills	13-24	2-5	9-16	0-0	2-3	54.2	+ 11.35
L M Cumani	11-26	0-2	7-18	0-0	4-6	42.3	- 0.25
J H M Gosden	10-27	3-8	3-8	0-0	4-11	37.0	- 0.18
R Hannon	9-22	6-11	0-3	0-0	3-8	40.9	+ 3.50
M R Stoute	7-27	5-13	1-11	1-1	0-2	25.9	- 6.88
Mrs J Ramsden	6-21	0-3	1-1	2-4	3-13	28.6	+ 6.13
I A Balding	5-9	0-0	2-5	0-0	3-4	55.6	+ 7.04
J Berry	5-18	4-12	0-1	0-0	1-5	27.8	- 6.85
M A Jarvis	4-7	1-1	1-1	1-2	1-3	57.1	+ 4.95
R W Armstrong	4-8	3-3	0-0	0-0	1-5	50.0	+ 1.11
J L Dunlop	4-14	1-3	1-3	1-1	1-7	28.6	- 2.57
M W Easterby	3-4	3-4	0-0	0-0	0-0	75.0	+ 3.98
Sir M Prescott	3-6	0-0	1-3	0-0	2-3	50.0	+ 6.62
Mrs L Piggott	3-6	1-1	0-1	0-0	2-4	50.0	+ 5.11
D R C Elsworth	3-7	1-1	0-2	0-0	2-4	42.9	+ 9.50
W A O'Gorman	3-7	1-2	1-3	1-2	0-0	42.9	+ 5.00
A A Scott	3-7	1-2	0-1	0-0	2-4	42.9	+ 0.84
G Harwood	3-8	1-3	1-3	0-0	1-2	37.5	- 1.35
A C Stewart	3-9	0-1	1-2	0-1	2-5	33.3	+ 0.50
M H Easterby	3-23	0-3	0-0	0-0	3-20	13.0	- 10.00
W Jarvis	2-2	0-0	1-1	0-0	1-1	100.0	+ 4.70
R Akehurst	2-4	0-0	0-1	0-0	2-3	50.0	+ 4.75
H Candy	2-4	0-0	1-3	0-0	1-1	50.0	+ 4.00

TRAINERS' FAVOURITES AT EDINBURGH 1988-92

	Total W-R	Non-handicaps 2-y-o	3-y-o+	Handicaps 2-y-o	3-y-o+	Per cent	£1 Level Stake
J Berry	17-35	13-26	3-4	1-1	0-4	48.6	+ 2.90
Sir M Prescott	10-31	1-6	4-13	1-1	4-11	32.3	+ 0.98
M H Tompkins	6-8	2-2	2-3	0-0	2-3	75.0	+ 7.15
J H M Gosden	6-10	1-3	4-5	0-0	1-2	60.0	+ 5.78
M J Camacho	5-5	0-0	2-2	1-1	2-2	100.0	+ 9.23
M H Easterby	5-10	2-4	1-1	0-1	2-4	50.0	+ 2.26
B W Hills	4-6	0-0	3-4	0-0	1-2	66.7	+ 3.61
N Tinkler	4-7	1-1	2-3	0-1	1-2	57.1	+ 11.60
M P Naughton	4-8	0-1	0-1	0-0	4-6	50.0	+ 3.88
J G FitzGerald	4-9	1-3	0-0	0-0	3-6	44.4	+ 3.76
J L Spearing	3-6	0-0	0-0	0-0	3-6	50.0	+ 5.38
Mrs G R Reveley	3-8	2-2	0-1	0-0	1-5	37.5	- 2.74
C Tinkler	3-9	1-3	0-1	0-0	2-5	33.3	+ 4.00
R M Whitaker	3-11	1-2	0-3	1-1	1-5	27.3	- 2.83
J Etherington	2-2	0-0	2-2	0-0	0-0	100.0	+ 1.00
W A O'Gorman	2-2	1-1	0-0	1-1	0-0	100.0	+ 4.62
A N Lee	2-2	0-0	1-1	0-0	1-1	100.0	+ 3.13
P Calver	2-3	0-0	1-1	0-0	1-2	66.7	+ 4.75
Denys Smith	2-3	0-0	0-0	0-0	2-3	66.7	+ 4.13
W Jarvis	2-3	0-0	2-2	0-0	0-1	66.7	+ 1.20
F H Lee	2-3	1-2	0-0	0-0	1-1	66.7	+ 1.16
L M Cumani	2-4	0-0	2-3	0-0	0-1	50.0	- 0.76
E Weymes	2-4	0-0	1-1	0-0	1-3	50.0	- 0.20
M Brittain	2-4	0-0	0-1	0-0	2-3	50.0	+ 3.75

TRAINERS' FAVOURITES AT EPSOM 1988-92

	Total W-R	Non-handicaps 2-y-o	3-y-o+	Handicaps 2-y-o	3-y-o+	Per cent	£1 Level Stake
M R Stoute	7-15	1-2	4-6	0-0	2-7	46.7	+ 3.04
R Hannon	5-18	2-4	0-3	0-0	3-11	27.8	+ 4.62
A C Stewart	4-7	0-0	4-5	0-0	0-2	57.1	+ 0.84
J Berry	4-9	2-4	1-3	0-0	1-2	44.4	- 0.46
L M Cumani	3-7	0-0	1-1	0-0	2-6	42.9	+ 4.25
H R A Cecil	3-9	0-2	3-7	0-0	0-0	33.3	- 1.75
P F I Cole	3-10	0-1	1-2	0-0	2-7	30.0	+ 5.33
J L Dunlop	3-10	0-1	2-4	1-2	0-3	30.0	+ 1.38
G Lewis	3-13	1-1	2-2	0-0	0-10	23.1	- 4.42
Lord Huntingdon	2-2	1-1	0-0	0-0	1-1	100.0	+ 4.38
W R Hern	2-4	0-0	2-3	0-0	0-1	50.0	+ 0.63
C J Benstead	1-1	1-1	0-0	0-0	0-0	100.0	+ 2.50
P L Biancone (Fra)	1-1	0-0	1-1	0-0	0-0	100.0	+ 1.38
W Jarvis	1-1	0-0	1-1	0-0	0-0	100.0	+ 2.75
Lady Herries	1-1	0-0	1-1	0-0	0-0	100.0	+ 2.75
F H Lee	1-1	0-0	0-0	0-0	1-1	100.0	+ 1.50
M Bell	1-1	1-1	0-0	0-0	0-0	100.0	+ 2.75
P A Kelleway	1-2	1-1	0-0	0-1	0-0	50.0	+ 0.63
A Fabre (Fra)	1-2	0-0	1-2	0-0	0-0	50.0	+ 0.88
J H M Gosden	1-2	0-0	1-2	0-0	0-0	50.0	+ 0.50
B R Millman	1-2	0-0	0-0	0-0	1-2	50.0	+ 3.00
G Harwood	1-3	0-0	0-2	0-0	1-1	33.3	+ 0.50
Miss B Sanders	1-3	0-0	0-0	0-0	1-3	33.3	+ 1.50
J W Hills	1-3	0-0	1-1	0-0	0-2	33.3	+ 1.00

TRAINERS' FAVOURITES AT FOLKESTONE 1988-92

	Total W-R	Non-handicaps 2-y-o	3-y-o+	Handicaps 2-y-o	3-y-o+	Per cent	£1 Level Stake
G Harwood	17-34	5-10	11-21	0-0	1-3	50.0	+ 1.01
R Hannon	7-24	2-8	4-6	0-1	1-9	29.2	- 9.58
Mrs L Piggott	6-11	0-0	5-5	0-0	1-6	54.5	+ 9.55
J L Dunlop	6-16	2-3	3-6	1-1	0-6	37.5	- 4.90
D R C Elsworth	5-8	1-2	2-3	1-1	1-2	62.5	+ 9.93
J Berry	5-11	3-7	2-2	0-2	0-0	45.5	+ 1.87
P F I Cole	5-12	1-1	1-1	1-1	2-9	41.7	+ 4.38
N A Callaghan	5-14	1-3	2-8	0-0	2-3	35.7	+ 4.23
G B Balding	4-8	1-2	1-2	0-0	2-4	50.0	+ 4.98
M R Stoute	4-8	1-3	3-5	0-0	0-0	50.0	+ 1.33
B Hanbury	3-5	0-0	2-3	1-1	0-1	60.0	+ 3.50
W J Haggas	3-5	1-2	0-1	0-0	2-2	60.0	+ 3.53
J H M Gosden	3-5	0-0	3-5	0-0	0-0	60.0	+ 0.61
P T Walwyn	3-6	0-1	3-4	0-0	0-1	50.0	- 0.70
D A Wilson	3-6	0-0	0-0	0-0	3-6	50.0	+ 4.83
D Morley	3-7	0-1	3-5	0-0	0-1	42.9	+ 2.13
M H Tompkins	3-7	1-2	0-1	1-2	1-2	42.9	+ 1.13
A C Stewart	3-7	1-2	1-3	0-0	1-2	42.9	+ 1.01
M J Ryan	3-8	0-1	2-3	0-0	1-4	37.5	+ 0.38
B W Hills	3-9	1-2	2-3	0-0	0-4	33.3	- 3.83
R Akehurst	3-13	0-1	2-3	0-0	1-9	23.1	- 3.87
W G R Wightman	2-2	1-1	1-1	0-0	0-0	100.0	+ 4.25
H Candy	2-3	0-0	0-1	0-0	2-2	66.7	+ 4.25
K T Ivory	2-3	2-2	0-0	0-1	0-0	66.7	+ 3.13

TRAINERS' FAVOURITES AT GOODWOOD 1988-92

	Total W-R	Non-handicaps 2-y-o	3-y-o+	Handicaps 2-y-o	3-y-o+	Per cent	£1 Level Stake
H R A Cecil	15-29	9-10	5-14	0-1	1-4	51.7	+ 1.95
J L Dunlop	12-35	5-11	5-9	1-2	1-13	34.3	- 6.05
D R C Elsworth	10-22	4-6	1-4	0-0	5-12	45.5	+ 3.70
L M Cumani	10-29	2-4	6-19	0-0	2-6	34.5	+ 1.14
I A Balding	9-21	3-6	4-5	0-2	2-8	42.9	+ 6.05
J H M Gosden	9-24	3-4	2-8	1-2	3-10	37.5	+ 2.50
G Harwood	9-39	4-12	3-16	0-1	2-10	23.1	- 18.03
M R Stoute	6-19	3-6	2-9	0-0	1-4	31.6	- 6.17
R Hannon	6-26	2-7	3-7	0-3	1-9	23.1	- 13.18
P F I Cole	5-16	3-10	1-4	0-0	1-2	31.3	- 5.58
J Berry	5-19	4-7	0-2	0-6	1-4	26.3	- 2.74
R F J Houghton	4-4	1-1	2-2	0-0	1-1	100.0	+ 7.56
G Lewis	4-6	1-1	1-2	0-0	2-3	66.7	+ 6.67
A C Stewart	4-7	1-1	1-2	0-0	2-4	57.1	+ 10.25
P J Makin	4-9	0-0	2-4	0-0	2-5	44.4	+ 2.68
W R Hern	4-12	3-5	1-3	0-1	0-3	33.3	- 2.88
P T Walwyn	4-13	1-2	1-4	0-0	2-7	30.8	+ 4.25
R W Armstrong	3-5	3-4	0-0	0-0	0-1	60.0	+ 2.07
L J Holt	3-7	0-2	1-1	0-0	2-4	42.9	+ 7.00
Lord Huntingdon	3-7	1-3	1-1	0-0	1-3	42.9	+ 3.50
J W Hills	3-9	0-0	1-2	0-0	2-7	33.3	+ 0.13
H Thomson Jones	3-10	1-4	1-4	0-0	1-2	30.0	- 2.92
R Akehurst	3-11	0-1	1-1	0-0	2-9	27.3	- 0.75
B W Hills	3-14	1-4	2-7	0-1	0-2	21.4	- 6.75

TRAINERS' FAVOURITES AT HAMILTON 1988-92

	Total W-R	Non-handicaps 2-y-o	3-y-o+	Handicaps 2-y-o	3-y-o+	Per cent	£1 Level Stake
J Berry	26-59	11-26	7-13	1-5	7-15	44.1	+ 8.49
P C Haslam	8-16	2-3	2-6	0-0	4-7	50.0	+ 7.14
Sir M Prescott	8-20	2-3	4-10	0-1	2-6	40.0	− 0.32
Mrs G R Reveley	8-23	0-2	4-6	0-0	4-15	34.8	− 2.74
Mrs J Ramsden	7-15	0-3	2-3	0-0	5-9	46.7	+ 4.54
C Tinkler	6-22	2-5	1-5	0-2	3-10	27.3	− 4.14
M H Easterby	5-17	3-5	0-4	0-0	2-8	29.4	− 5.16
P J Makin	4-6	0-1	4-5	0-0	0-0	66.7	+ 5.08
B Hanbury	4-7	0-0	2-4	1-1	1-2	57.1	+ 6.23
M A Jarvis	4-10	0-2	3-4	0-1	1-3	40.0	+ 0.37
M H Tompkins	4-20	2-4	2-4	0-2	0-10	20.0	− 10.87
R Hollinshead	3-5	2-2	1-2	0-0	0-1	60.0	+ 3.13
N A Callaghan	3-8	1-2	1-2	0-0	1-4	37.5	− 0.87
J G FitzGerald	3-8	1-2	0-1	0-1	2-4	37.5	+ 5.75
S G Norton	3-9	0-0	3-6	0-0	0-3	33.3	+ 1.88
R M Whitaker	3-9	0-2	0-0	0-1	3-6	33.3	+ 0.25
M S Johnston	3-10	1-1	0-1	0-0	2-8	30.0	− 3.64
N Tinkler	3-12	0-1	2-6	0-0	1-5	25.0	− 4.47
P Calver	2-2	0-0	1-1	0-0	1-1	100.0	+ 4.10
J Etherington	2-2	1-1	1-1	0-0	0-0	100.0	+ 2.65
P S Felgate	2-2	2-2	0-0	0-0	0-0	100.0	+ 2.08
I A Balding	2-3	0-1	1-1	0-0	1-1	66.7	+ 7.25
R Bastiman	2-4	0-0	0-0	0-0	2-4	50.0	+ 4.50
R Akehurst	2-5	0-0	0-0	0-0	2-5	40.0	+ 4.75

TRAINERS' FAVOURITES AT HAYDOCK 1988-92

	Total W-R	Non-handicaps 2-y-o	3-y-o+	Handicaps 2-y-o	3-y-o+	Per cent	£1 Level Stake
H R A Cecil	14-33	9-13	4-16	0-0	1-4	42.4	− 3.42
B W Hills	11-31	5-7	5-14	0-1	1-9	35.5	− 9.15
L M Cumani	7-28	1-4	4-14	0-0	2-10	25.0	− 11.54
R Boss	6-9	1-1	1-1	1-1	3-6	66.7	+ 14.00
H Thomson Jones	6-11	5-9	1-1	0-0	0-1	54.5	+ 2.59
J H M Gosden	6-13	2-3	2-4	0-0	2-6	46.2	+ 8.57
M R Stoute	6-24	0-6	5-12	0-2	1-4	25.0	− 11.24
Mrs J Ramsden	6-26	1-2	1-2	0-2	4-20	23.1	− 8.25
J W Watts	5-11	0-2	1-2	0-1	4-6	45.5	+ 9.07
M H Tompkins	5-13	1-1	2-5	0-0	2-7	38.5	+ 2.10
R Charlton	5-14	1-1	2-7	0-0	2-6	35.7	− 0.74
M H Easterby	5-26	4-6	0-1	0-1	1-18	19.2	− 13.25
Sir M Prescott	4-10	1-1	2-3	0-1	1-5	40.0	0.00
G Harwood	4-15	0-1	1-7	0-0	3-7	26.7	+ 2.13
J L Dunlop	4-18	1-6	2-7	0-0	1-5	22.2	− 5.87
J Berry	4-22	3-10	1-6	0-5	0-1	18.2	− 16.03
R Hollinshead	3-8	2-3	1-2	0-0	0-3	37.5	− 1.40
A C Stewart	3-8	0-0	3-6	0-0	0-2	37.5	− 0.40
B Hanbury	3-9	1-4	0-2	0-0	2-3	33.3	+ 1.25
F H Lee	3-14	0-0	0-0	1-1	2-13	21.4	− 2.50
W A O'Gorman	2-2	0-0	0-0	0-0	2-2	100.0	+ 8.50
T Thomson Jones	2-2	0-0	0-0	0-0	2-2	100.0	+ 6.00
N A Callaghan	2-3	0-0	1-1	0-0	1-2	66.7	+ 5.00
G Wragg	2-3	1-1	1-2	0-0	0-0	66.7	+ 1.30

TRAINERS' FAVOURITES AT KEMPTON 1988-92

	Total W-R	Non-handicaps 2-y-o	3-y-o+	Handicaps 2-y-o	3-y-o+	Per cent	£1 Level Stake
J H M Gosden	7-18	0-1	6-13	0-1	1-3	38.9	+ 4.88
G Harwood	7-19	2-4	4-7	1-1	0-7	36.8	- 3.66
M R Stoute	7-21	3-4	2-12	0-0	2-5	33.3	- 4.88
P F I Cole	6-17	1-6	1-4	1-1	3-6	35.3	+ 8.70
L M Cumani	6-20	0-1	5-15	0-0	1-4	30.0	- 5.60
R Hannon	6-20	1-5	0-2	1-2	4-11	30.0	+ 1.75
B Hanbury	5-10	1-1	3-4	0-0	1-5	50.0	+ 2.32
H R A Cecil	5-13	1-2	4-9	0-0	0-2	38.5	- 1.34
D R C Elsworth	5-13	2-3	2-6	0-0	1-4	38.5	+ 1.49
R Charlton	5-13	2-2	3-7	0-0	0-4	38.5	+ 1.65
C E Brittain	4-9	1-2	2-3	0-0	1-4	44.4	+ 4.51
P T Walwyn	4-9	1-2	3-4	0-0	0-3	44.4	+ 2.74
W R Hern	4-10	0-3	3-4	0-0	1-3	40.0	+ 1.28
J Sutcliffe	4-10	0-0	2-2	0-0	2-8	40.0	+ 1.51
A A Scott	4-10	0-0	1-7	0-0	3-3	40.0	+ 4.75
B W Hills	4-12	1-3	3-7	0-0	0-2	33.3	- 1.62
G A Pritchard-Gordon	3-4	1-1	1-1	0-0	1-2	75.0	+ 2.80
Lord Huntingdon	3-6	1-1	0-2	0-0	2-3	50.0	+ 2.88
R Akehurst	3-10	0-0	0-1	0-1	3-8	30.0	+ 2.25
G Lewis	3-11	2-4	0-0	0-1	1-6	27.3	- 2.70
Miss B Sanders	2-2	0-0	0-0	0-0	2-2	100.0	+ 3.80
R F J Houghton	2-3	0-0	1-2	0-0	1-1	66.7	+ 1.00
M A Jarvis	2-4	0-1	0-0	0-0	2-3	50.0	+ 5.13
J Akehurst	2-5	0-0	0-0	1-1	1-4	40.0	+ 6.00

TRAINERS' FAVOURITES AT LEICESTER 1988-92

	Total W-R	Non-handicaps 2-y-o	3-y-o+	Handicaps 2-y-o	3-y-o+	Per cent	£1 Level Stake
H R A Cecil	20-39	10-20	10-18	0-0	0-1	51.3	+ 1.16
M R Stoute	17-41	8-19	7-17	0-0	2-5	41.5	- 10.36
J H M Gosden	10-20	6-10	2-7	0-0	2-3	50.0	+ 2.28
J L Dunlop	7-16	3-4	2-6	1-2	1-4	43.8	- 0.79
J Berry	6-12	4-9	1-1	1-1	0-1	50.0	+ 3.61
N A Callaghan	5-6	2-3	2-2	0-0	1-1	83.3	+ 12.85
L M Cumani	5-14	3-4	2-9	0-0	0-1	35.7	- 2.80
G Harwood	5-17	2-7	2-8	1-1	0-1	29.4	- 5.14
W A O'Gorman	4-4	1-1	2-2	1-1	0-0	100.0	+ 9.33
R F J Houghton	4-5	1-1	3-3	0-0	0-1	80.0	+ 4.55
B Hanbury	4-8	1-2	2-4	0-0	1-2	50.0	+ 2.25
A C Stewart	4-11	1-4	2-5	0-0	1-2	36.4	- 3.69
P F I Cole	4-12	1-2	3-9	0-1	0-0	33.3	- 2.62
R Hannon	4-13	2-6	0-3	2-3	0-1	30.8	+ 3.25
M A Jarvis	3-3	1-1	2-2	0-0	0-0	100.0	+ 5.30
H Thomson Jones	3-4	2-2	1-2	0-0	0-0	75.0	+ 2.66
C Tinkler	3-4	3-4	0-0	0-0	0-0	75.0	+ 4.75
R Charlton	3-5	0-0	2-3	0-0	1-2	60.0	+ 3.10
M C Pipe	3-6	0-0	1-1	0-0	2-5	50.0	+ 7.63
R J R Williams	3-6	2-3	0-1	1-1	0-1	50.0	+ 1.18
G Wragg	3-9	1-1	2-7	0-1	0-0	33.3	- 4.58
W R Hern	3-10	0-2	3-5	0-0	0-3	30.0	- 3.45
B W Hills	3-11	3-8	0-1	0-1	0-1	27.3	- 3.75
J Sutcliffe	2-3	0-0	0-0	0-0	2-3	66.7	+ 5.25

TRAINERS' FAVOURITES AT LINGFIELD TURF 1988-92

	Total W-R	Non-handicaps 2-y-o	Non-handicaps 3-y-o+	Handicaps 2-y-o	Handicaps 3-y-o+	Per cent	£1 Level Stake
G Harwood	16-36	4-10	7-14	1-2	4-10	44.4	+ 3.80
H R A Cecil	10-24	3-8	6-13	0-0	1-3	41.7	- 7.06
R Hannon	9-20	2-4	6-8	0-0	1-8	45.0	+ 4.38
L M Cumani	8-18	1-2	7-15	0-0	0-1	44.4	- 0.89
J L Dunlop	8-19	1-5	2-4	0-0	5-10	42.1	- 0.23
B W Hills	7-12	1-5	3-3	1-1	2-3	58.3	+ 11.16
M R Stoute	7-19	3-7	4-7	0-0	0-5	36.8	- 6.40
Sir M Prescott	6-10	0-1	4-5	0-0	2-4	60.0	+ 6.37
J H M Gosden	6-16	2-5	4-9	0-0	0-2	37.5	- 1.55
P F I Cole	5-11	2-5	1-4	0-0	2-2	45.5	+ 0.91
R W Armstrong	4-6	1-2	1-2	0-0	2-2	66.7	+ 5.21
A C Stewart	4-6	0-1	1-2	0-0	3-3	66.7	+ 3.62
M A Jarvis	4-8	0-1	1-2	0-0	3-5	50.0	+ 5.13
P Mitchell	4-11	2-2	0-0	0-1	2-8	36.4	+ 1.63
G Lewis	4-13	1-5	1-1	0-0	2-7	30.8	- 1.25
R Akehurst	4-25	0-1	0-2	0-0	4-22	16.0	- 11.25
N A Callaghan	3-6	0-1	0-0	0-0	3-5	50.0	+ 4.96
Pat Mitchell	3-6	0-0	0-0	0-0	3-6	50.0	+ 6.58
W Jarvis	3-7	0-1	1-3	0-0	2-3	42.9	+ 2.05
H Thomson Jones	3-8	1-3	2-4	0-0	0-1	37.5	- 0.33
P J Makin	3-8	0-0	1-2	0-0	2-6	37.5	+ 2.75
M J Ryan	3-8	1-1	0-1	0-0	2-6	37.5	+ 4.75
I A Balding	3-13	0-2	3-6	0-0	0-5	23.1	- 5.97
P T Walwyn	3-14	1-3	1-5	0-0	1-6	21.4	- 8.55

TRAINERS' FAVOURITES AT LINGFIELD (AW) 1989-92

	Total W-R	Non-handicaps 2-y-o	Non-handicaps 3-y-o+	Handicaps 2-y-o	Handicaps 3-y-o+	Per cent	£1 Level Stake
B W Hills	14-25	1-5	7-10	0-0	6-10	56.0	+ 4.04
P F I Cole	13-28	2-8	7-10	1-1	3-9	46.4	- 1.04
W A O'Gorman	10-38	0-2	7-20	1-1	2-15	26.3	- 10.38
Sir M Prescott	8-19	3-5	2-6	0-0	3-8	42.1	- 3.58
J Berry	5-8	2-4	1-2	0-0	2-2	62.5	+ 5.47
J Pearce	5-8	0-0	4-4	0-0	1-4	62.5	+ 10.88
R J O'Sullivan	5-16	0-0	1-1	0-0	4-15	31.3	+ 0.25
C A Cyzer	4-6	0-0	1-2	0-0	3-4	66.7	+ 7.10
Dr J D Scargill	4-7	0-0	0-1	0-0	4-6	57.1	+ 7.73
K O C-Brown	4-8	0-0	0-0	0-0	4-8	50.0	+ 11.75
M Fetherston-Godley	4-8	2-3	1-2	0-0	1-3	50.0	+ 4.58
J H M Gosden	4-8	1-1	0-1	1-2	2-4	50.0	+ 3.82
R Akehurst	4-9	0-0	2-6	0-0	2-3	44.4	+ 2.63
D Murray Smith	4-12	1-1	1-4	0-0	2-7	33.3	+ 1.48
D R C Elsworth	3-3	2-2	1-1	0-0	0-0	100.0	+ 3.55
R Boss	3-6	2-4	1-1	0-0	0-1	50.0	+ 2.55
C P Wildman	3-6	0-0	1-1	0-0	2-5	50.0	+ 4.75
P T Walwyn	3-7	0-0	3-4	0-0	0-3	42.9	- 1.09
A Bailey	3-8	0-0	0-0	0-0	3-8	37.5	+ 9.00
G B Balding	3-8	0-0	1-3	0-0	2-5	37.5	- 0.97
N A Callaghan	3-8	0-0	2-3	1-2	0-3	37.5	+ 3.00
J Akehurst	3-9	0-0	1-3	0-0	2-6	33.3	- 0.62
C E Brittain	3-11	0-0	2-7	0-0	1-4	27.3	- 5.26
M S Johnston	3-11	1-2	1-2	0-0	1-7	27.3	- 1.75

TRAINERS' FAVOURITES AT NEWBURY 1988-92

	Total W-R	Non-handicaps 2-y-o	3-y-o+	Handicaps 2-y-o	3-y-o+	Per cent	£1 Level Stake
H R A Cecil	19-45	4-11	15-29	0-0	0-5	42.2	- 2.71
M R Stoute	10-30	1-4	5-15	1-2	3-9	33.3	+ 8.42
J H M Gosden	9-23	3-6	3-10	0-0	3-7	39.1	+ 7.13
L M Cumani	9-30	4-7	3-9	0-0	2-14	30.0	- 8.02
R Hannon	8-27	4-9	1-3	2-6	1-9	29.6	- 7.28
B W Hills	6-24	4-9	1-8	0-0	1-7	25.0	- 5.90
I A Balding	5-7	3-4	0-0	0-0	2-3	71.4	+ 12.82
W R Hern	5-19	3-7	2-9	0-0	0-3	26.3	- 9.15
P T Walwyn	5-21	1-2	0-7	0-0	4-12	23.8	+ 1.50
P Chapple-Hyam	4-6	4-5	0-1	0-0	0-0	66.7	+ 4.55
J L Dunlop	4-11	1-2	2-4	0-0	1-5	36.4	- 2.99
P F I Cole	4-17	2-9	1-4	0-0	1-4	23.5	- 4.27
J Berry	3-6	3-6	0-0	0-0	0-0	50.0	+ 1.33
A A Scott	3-6	3-4	0-1	0-1	0-0	50.0	+ 6.50
A C Stewart	3-11	0-0	1-2	0-1	2-8	27.3	+ 2.45
R Charlton	3-12	0-1	1-4	0-0	2-7	25.0	- 2.25
Lord Huntingdon	3-13	0-1	0-3	1-2	2-7	23.1	+ 2.25
M H Easterby	2-4	0-0	0-0	0-0	2-4	50.0	+ 4.83
B Hanbury	2-4	0-0	1-2	0-0	1-2	50.0	+ 1.63
C R Nelson	2-4	2-4	0-0	0-0	0-0	50.0	+ 0.32
R W Armstrong	2-5	1-3	1-1	0-0	0-1	40.0	+ 0.50
R F J Houghton	2-5	0-1	0-1	0-0	2-3	40.0	+ 3.00
D R C Elsworth	2-16	0-4	0-6	0-0	2-6	12.5	- 8.00
C W C Elsey	1-1	0-0	1-1	0-0	0-0	100.0	+ 4.00

TRAINERS' FAVOURITES AT NEWCASTLE 1988-92

	Total W-R	Non-handicaps 2-y-o	3-y-o+	Handicaps 2-y-o	3-y-o+	Per cent	£1 Level Stake
H R A Cecil	12-19	4-4	7-11	0-1	1-3	63.2	- 1.22
M R Stoute	11-20	4-6	5-10	0-0	2-4	55.0	- 3.60
J Berry	9-24	7-12	1-5	0-1	1-6	37.5	- 0.43
Mrs G R Reveley	7-9	0-0	0-0	0-0	7-9	77.8	+ 13.30
L M Cumani	7-10	1-1	4-5	0-1	2-3	70.0	+ 2.64
M H Easterby	7-32	1-7	2-4	0-0	4-21	21.9	- 8.66
J W Watts	6-13	2-5	0-2	0-0	4-6	46.2	+ 2.31
B W Hills	6-14	4-5	1-6	0-0	1-3	42.9	+ 1.32
M W Easterby	5-8	3-3	0-0	0-1	2-4	62.5	+ 10.08
M J Camacho	3-4	0-0	1-2	0-0	2-2	75.0	+ 5.20
C Tinkler	3-6	3-4	0-0	0-1	0-1	50.0	+ 8.91
M Bell	3-7	3-3	0-1	0-1	0-2	42.9	- 1.71
B Hanbury	3-9	1-2	2-4	0-0	0-3	33.3	- 0.50
Mrs J Ramsden	3-12	0-1	0-1	0-1	3-9	25.0	- 2.45
W R Hern	2-2	1-1	1-1	0-0	0-0	100.0	+ 1.57
P S Felgate	2-3	0-0	0-0	0-0	2-3	66.7	+ 1.88
G Wragg	2-3	0-1	2-2	0-0	0-0	66.7	+ 1.75
A A Scott	2-3	0-0	1-2	0-0	1-1	66.7	+ 2.67
R W Armstrong	2-4	1-2	1-1	0-0	0-1	50.0	+ 1.20
R Hannon	2-4	1-2	0-0	0-0	1-2	50.0	+ 1.67
G Harwood	2-4	0-0	1-2	0-0	1-2	50.0	+ 2.80
D Morley	2-4	0-1	0-1	0-0	2-2	50.0	+ 2.43
J G FitzGerald	2-5	0-0	1-2	0-0	1-3	40.0	+ 0.88
E Weymes	2-6	0-0	0-0	0-1	2-5	33.3	+ 1.00

TRAINERS' FAVOURITES AT NEWMARKET 1988-92

	Total W-R	Non-handicaps 2-y-o	3-y-o+	Handicaps 2-y-o	3-y-o+	Per cent	£1 Level Stake
H R A Cecil	55-126	22-44	28-62	0-1	5-19	43.7	- 14.56
L M Cumani	33-72	9-17	22-38	1-3	1-14	45.8	+ 6.55
M R Stoute	31-77	14-35	15-33	0-3	2-6	40.3	- 8.58
B W Hills	16-41	4-10	7-13	0-0	5-18	39.0	+ 21.25
W R Hern	14-24	4-9	7-9	0-0	3-6	58.3	+ 10.67
J L Dunlop	13-29	3-5	8-15	0-0	2-9	44.8	+ 6.97
R Hannon	13-41	6-15	3-9	3-6	1-11	31.7	+ 3.06
J H M Gosden	13-49	1-9	8-22	0-2	4-16	26.5	- 14.69
M A Jarvis	7-21	0-4	5-6	1-1	1-10	33.3	+ 5.05
G Wragg	7-21	2-3	3-11	0-0	2-7	33.3	- 1.06
G Harwood	7-31	3-7	4-18	0-0	0-6	22.6	- 11.04
C E Brittain	6-25	3-3	2-6	1-3	0-13	24.0	- 7.02
P Chapple-Hyam	5-8	3-6	2-2	0-0	0-0	62.5	+ 5.06
J Berry	5-10	3-5	1-3	0-0	1-2	50.0	+ 6.20
A A Scott	5-11	3-4	2-5	0-0	0-2	45.5	- 0.72
P F I Cole	5-13	2-5	3-5	0-1	0-2	38.5	+ 2.75
H Thomson Jones	5-13	1-4	4-5	0-1	0-3	38.5	+ 1.11
A Fabre (Fra)	4-6	3-3	1-2	0-0	0-1	66.7	+ 4.17
J Sutcliffe	4-8	1-2	0-0	1-1	2-5	50.0	+ 12.00
Lord Huntingdon	4-15	0-0	2-5	0-1	2-9	26.7	- 2.65
W A O'Gorman	4-16	2-7	0-2	0-0	2-7	25.0	- 4.07
N A Callaghan	4-18	1-6	3-4	0-4	0-4	22.2	- 2.49
A C Stewart	4-20	1-2	2-7	0-1	1-10	20.0	- 6.27
J R Fanshawe	3-4	1-1	2-2	0-0	0-1	75.0	+ 5.48

TRAINERS' FAVOURITES AT NOTTINGHAM 1988-92

	Total W-R	Non-handicaps 2-y-o	3-y-o+	Handicaps 2-y-o	3-y-o+	Per cent	£1 Level Stake
H R A Cecil	21-48	6-10	15-38	0-0	0-0	43.8	- 7.62
J Berry	9-20	5-10	3-8	0-1	1-1	45.0	+ 6.22
P F I Cole	8-17	5-10	1-2	0-0	2-5	47.1	+ 9.36
J L Dunlop	8-30	4-13	1-4	0-2	3-11	26.7	- 8.53
M R Stoute	7-12	5-7	2-4	0-1	0-0	58.3	- 1.48
J H M Gosden	7-12	2-4	4-7	0-0	1-1	58.3	+ 8.00
L M Cumani	6-12	2-3	4-9	0-0	0-0	50.0	- 0.13
R Charlton	4-6	2-4	2-2	0-0	0-0	66.7	+ 1.32
W Jarvis	4-8	1-3	2-2	1-2	0-1	50.0	+ 2.15
D Morley	4-10	2-3	0-1	0-0	2-6	40.0	+ 2.63
M W Easterby	3-3	2-2	0-0	0-0	1-1	100.0	+ 7.28
R M Whitaker	3-3	0-0	1-1	0-0	2-2	100.0	+ 17.50
A C Stewart	3-5	1-1	1-2	0-1	1-1	60.0	+ 2.13
J Wharton	3-5	1-1	2-2	0-0	0-2	60.0	+ 7.50
H Candy	3-6	2-2	1-2	0-0	0-2	50.0	+ 4.50
M S Johnston	3-7	0-2	2-3	1-1	0-1	42.9	- 0.90
N Tinkler	3-8	0-2	1-1	0-0	2-5	37.5	+ 2.75
W R Hern	3-10	1-2	1-5	0-0	1-3	30.0	- 3.14
R Hannon	3-11	0-2	1-3	1-1	1-5	27.3	- 0.50
B W Hills	3-13	2-6	1-5	0-1	0-1	23.1	- 5.34
M J Camacho	2-2	0-0	0-0	0-0	2-2	100.0	+ 6.75
J R Fanshawe	2-2	0-0	1-1	1-1	0-0	100.0	+ 2.61
G Harwood	2-3	0-0	2-3	0-0	0-0	66.7	- 0.22
M Blanshard	2-4	0-0	0-1	0-0	2-3	50.0	+ 3.25

TRAINERS' FAVOURITES AT PONTEFRACT 1988-92

	Total W-R	Non-handicaps 2-y-o	Non-handicaps 3-y-o+	Handicaps 2-y-o	Handicaps 3-y-o+	Per cent	£1 Level Stake
R Hollinshead	14-18	6-8	2-3	0-0	6-7	77.8	+ 17.16
Mrs J Ramsden	13-33	0-2	0-2	0-1	13-28	39.4	+ 11.34
J Berry	10-24	8-10	2-9	0-0	0-5	41.7	+ 3.73
H R A Cecil	8-13	0-1	8-12	0-0	0-0	61.5	+ 5.68
G Harwood	6-10	1-1	3-7	2-2	0-0	60.0	+ 3.67
M H Tompkins	6-11	2-4	3-4	0-0	1-3	54.5	+ 6.59
M R Stoute	5-7	2-2	2-4	0-0	1-1	71.4	+ 2.42
L M Cumani	5-9	1-2	4-7	0-0	0-0	55.6	+ 1.15
J W Watts	4-10	0-1	1-1	0-0	3-8	40.0	+ 0.60
M S Johnston	3-4	1-1	1-2	0-0	1-1	75.0	+ 6.00
I A Balding	3-5	2-2	1-2	0-0	0-1	60.0	+ 1.92
J D Bethell	3-5	0-0	0-0	0-0	3-5	60.0	+ 12.50
J Etherington	3-5	2-2	1-1	0-1	0-1	60.0	+ 2.68
H Thomson Jones	3-5	1-1	2-4	0-0	0-0	60.0	+ 1.16
Sir M Prescott	3-5	1-1	1-1	0-1	1-2	60.0	+ 3.00
Mrs G R Reveley	3-8	0-0	1-1	0-0	2-7	37.5	+ 0.25
Lord Huntingdon	3-8	1-2	1-3	0-0	1-3	37.5	+ 1.18
T D Barron	3-9	1-3	0-0	1-2	1-4	33.3	+ 4.50
M H Easterby	3-11	0-4	0-0	1-1	2-6	27.3	− 2.12
C F Wall	2-2	2-2	0-0	0-0	0-0	100.0	+ 3.32
B J Curley	2-3	0-0	1-2	0-0	1-1	66.7	+ 5.10
Dr J D Scargill	2-3	2-2	0-0	0-0	0-1	66.7	+ 0.67
W J Haggas	2-4	1-1	1-1	0-0	0-2	50.0	+ 3.83
H Candy	2-5	0-0	0-1	0-0	2-4	40.0	+ 2.50

TRAINERS' FAVOURITES AT REDCAR 1988-92

	Total W-R	Non-handicaps 2-y-o	Non-handicaps 3-y-o+	Handicaps 2-y-o	Handicaps 3-y-o+	Per cent	£1 Level Stake
M H Easterby	15-35	7-12	2-4	2-6	4-13	42.9	+ 3.72
Mrs G R Reveley	12-28	3-3	2-2	0-1	7-22	42.9	+ 5.80
L M Cumani	12-30	0-6	8-9	0-0	4-15	40.0	− 5.71
H R A Cecil	11-17	4-5	6-9	0-0	1-3	64.7	+ 2.53
H Thomson Jones	10-20	4-6	4-7	0-0	2-7	50.0	+ 0.29
J Berry	9-26	5-14	1-5	1-4	2-3	34.6	− 1.83
J L Dunlop	8-13	2-3	1-2	1-1	4-7	61.5	+ 8.80
M R Stoute	8-20	3-7	4-6	0-1	1-6	40.0	− 2.71
R M Whitaker	8-22	2-8	3-5	0-0	3-9	36.4	+ 5.00
J G FitzGerald	7-7	0-0	0-0	1-1	6-6	100.0	+ 20.35
J H M Gosden	6-14	3-5	2-7	0-0	1-2	42.9	− 3.13
G Harwood	6-15	2-3	4-9	0-0	0-3	40.0	+ 0.74
M A Jarvis	5-5	2-2	1-1	0-0	2-2	100.0	+ 4.84
M H Tompkins	5-8	3-5	0-0	1-1	1-2	62.5	+ 8.86
Sir M Prescott	5-11	1-2	2-2	1-1	1-6	45.5	− 0.37
M Bell	4-4	3-3	0-0	0-0	1-1	100.0	+ 5.68
R Hollinshead	4-7	2-3	1-2	0-0	1-2	57.1	+ 2.71
M J Camacho	4-9	1-2	1-2	0-0	2-5	44.4	+ 1.88
F H Lee	4-9	0-1	0-0	0-0	4-8	44.4	+ 2.75
J W Hills	4-10	1-2	1-1	0-0	2-7	40.0	− 3.07
B W Hills	4-13	1-4	2-6	0-0	1-3	30.8	− 4.07
P C Haslam	3-3	0-0	2-2	0-0	1-1	100.0	+ 4.50
W Carter	3-4	0-0	0-0	1-2	2-2	75.0	+ 6.25
R J R Williams	3-5	0-0	0-0	0-0	3-5	60.0	+ 4.13

TRAINERS' FAVOURITES AT RIPON 1988-92

	Total W-R	Non-handicaps 2-y-o	3-y-o+	Handicaps 2-y-o	3-y-o+	Per cent	£1 Level Stake
H R A Cecil	21-34	2-4	18-26	0-0	1-4	61.8	+ 6.68
J Berry	12-30	10-22	1-4	0-2	1-2	40.0	+ 0.81
M H Easterby	12-32	4-8	2-5	0-0	6-19	37.5	+ 2.01
L M Cumani	8-13	1-1	6-10	0-0	1-2	61.5	+ 4.40
M R Stoute	5-11	1-1	2-4	0-0	2-6	45.5	+ 2.15
B W Hills	5-18	1-2	3-10	0-0	1-6	27.8	- 6.56
G Harwood	4-9	0-0 ·	2-5	0-0	2-4	44.4	+ 3.97
D Morley	3-4	0-0	1-1	0-0	2-3	75.0	+ 4.55
R W Armstrong	3-6	2-3	0-0	0-0	1-3	50.0	+ 4.77
W Jarvis	3-6	3-5	0-0	0-0	0-1	50.0	- 1.20
J L Dunlop	3-8	1-3	0-0	0-1	2-4	37.5	- 2.83
Mrs G R Reveley	3-8	0-0	1-2	0-0	2-6	37.5	+ 1.83
J H M Gosden	3-8	0-0	2-5	0-0	1-3	37.5	- 2.04
R M Whitaker	3-9	1-2	2-4	0-0	0-3	33.3	+ 1.00
R Akehurst	2-2	0-0	0-0	0-0	2-2	100.0	+ 6.50
A Hide	2-2	0-0	2-2	0-0	0-0	100.0	+ 3.25
W A O'Gorman	2-2	1-1	0-0	0-0	1-1	100.0	+ 3.25
J L Spearing	2-2	0-0	0-0	0-0	2-2	100.0	+ 3.00
Capt J Wilson	2-2	0-0	0-0	0-0	2-2	100.0	+ 11.50
M Brittain	2-2	0-0	0-0	0-0	2-2	100.0	+ 7.00
J Wharton	2-2	0-0	0-0	0-0	2-2	100.0	+ 7.00
W J Haggas	2-3	2-2	0-0	0-0	0-1	66.7	+ 0.63
Mrs L Piggott	2-3	0-0	0-0	0-0	2-3	66.7	+ 2.25
M J Camacho	2-4	0-1	1-1	0-0	1-2	50.0	+ 2.13

TRAINERS' FAVOURITES AT SALISBURY 1988-92

	Total W-R	Non-handicaps 2-y-o	3-y-o+	Handicaps 2-y-o	3-y-o+	Per cent	£1 Level Stake
G Harwood	18-36	7-17	3-6	2-2	6-11	50.0	+ 8.80
R Hannon	14-41	8-17	3-9	0-4	3-11	34.1	- 7.39
D R C Elsworth	9-29	4-11	1-5	0-0	4-13	31.0	+ 0.01
P F I Cole	8-20	6-11	0-4	0-0	2-5	40.0	+ 2.08
M R Stoute	5-10	2-6	1-2	0-0	2-2	50.0	+ 0.92
Lord Huntingdon	5-10	1-1	2-4	0-0	2-5	50.0	+ 2.87
A A Scott	4-5	1-1	3-3	0-0	0-1	80.0	+ 6.50
L M Cumani	4-11	1-2	3-7	0-0	0-2	36.4	- 3.37
G Lewis	4-15	3-6	0-1	0-0	1-8	26.7	- 3.52
I A Balding	4-20	2-6	0-3	0-0	2-11	20.0	- 6.12
K O C-Brown	3-4	1-1	2-2	0-0	0-1	75.0	+ 2.50
J H M Gosden	3-6	0-1	3-4	0-0	0-1	50.0	+ 1.80
R Charlton	3-6	0-3	2-2	0-0	1-1	50.0	+ 1.88
J L Dunlop	3-11	1-3	2-6	0-0	0-2	27.3	- 3.45
W R Hern	3-14	1-2	2-6	0-0	0-6	21.4	- 7.40
D R Laing	2-2	0-0	0-0	0-0	2-2	100.0	+ 9.00
R F J Houghton	2-3	0-0	0-1	0-0	2-2	66.7	+ 4.83
M C Pipe	2-3	0-0	0-0	0-0	2-3	66.7	+ 5.75
C J Hill	2-4	0-0	0-0	0-0	2-4	50.0	+ 7.00
L J Holt	2-4	1-1	0-0	0-0	1-3	50.0	+ 3.50
G Wragg	2-6	0-0	1-2	0-0	1-4	33.3	- 0.49
R Akehurst	2-8	1-2	0-0	0-0	1-6	25.0	- 1.25
J Sutcliffe	2-8	0-0	0-0	0-0	2-8	25.0	- 1.62
G B Balding	2-9	1-2	1-1	0-0	0-6	22.2	- 0.25

TRAINERS' FAVOURITES AT SANDOWN 1988-92

	Total W-R	Non-handicaps 2-y-o	3-y-o+	Handicaps 2-y-o	3-y-o+	Per cent	£1 Level Stake
H R A Cecil	15-35	6-9	9-23	0-0	0-3	42.9	- 3.66
M R Stoute	12-39	5-8	5-14	0-1	2-16	30.8	- 8.95
G Harwood	10-24	1-4	5-14	0-1	4-5	41.7	+ 3.44
L M Cumani	7-18	0-0	4-12	0-0	3-6	38.9	- 1.68
R Akehurst	7-19	0-1	1-2	0-2	6-14	36.8	+ 5.96
R Hannon	7-26	2-6	1-4	0-1	4-15	26.9	- 6.65
B W Hills	6-15	3-6	2-6	0-1	1-2	40.0	+ 2.36
I A Balding	6-16	3-4	1-6	0-0	2-6	37.5	+ 0.11
J H M Gosden	5-14	2-2	1-3	0-0	2-9	35.7	- 2.57
C R Nelson	5-15	2-6	1-4	0-0	2-5	33.3	+ 3.16
W R Hern	4-5	3-3	1-2	0-0	0-0	80.0	+ 1.63
J Sutcliffe	4-9	0-0	0-0	1-1	3-8	44.4	+ 4.46
R W Armstrong	4-10	2-3	1-2	0-0	1-5	40.0	+ 1.78
R Simpson	3-5	0-0	2-2	0-1	1-2	60.0	+ 6.35
W J Haggas	3-5	0-1	0-0	1-1	2-3	60.0	+ 7.38
M R Channon	3-5	1-2	0-0	0-0	2-3	60.0	+ 4.55
M H Easterby	3-7	0-0	3-6	0-1	0-0	42.9	+ 1.13
P J Makin	3-9	0-1	1-3	0-0	2-5	33.3	+ 0.13
Lord Huntingdon	3-9	0-0	1-4	0-0	2-5	33.3	+ 0.13
J Berry	3-10	0-1	3-7	0-1	0-1	30.0	- 3.36
A C Stewart	3-10	0-1	2-3	0-0	1-6	30.0	+ 0.75
C E Brittain	3-11	0-1	3-4	0-0	0-6	27.3	- 5.18
P F I Cole	3-12	1-3	1-4	1-2	0-3	25.0	- 2.00
Sir M Prescott	3-12	0-0	2-4	0-3	1-5	25.0	- 0.50

TRAINERS' FAVOURITES AT SOUTHWELL (AW) 1989-92

	Total W-R	Non-handicaps 2-y-o	3-y-o+	Handicaps 2-y-o	3-y-o+	Per cent	£1 Level Stake
T D Barron	30-70	5-5	15-34	2-2	8-29	42.9	+ 7.35
W A O'Gorman	16-43	6-11	5-15	1-3	4-14	37.2	+ 0.05
D W Chapman	12-29	0-0	5-12	1-3	6-14	41.4	+ 4.31
J Berry	10-22	7-15	0-2	1-2	2-3	45.5	+ 9.54
R Hollinshead	9-26	1-2	3-12	0-0	5-12	34.6	- 3.01
Sir M Prescott	9-26	3-10	3-6	0-2	3-8	34.6	- 2.22
C R Nelson	6-9	1-2	4-5	0-0	1-2	66.7	+ 4.16
Lady Herries	5-8	0-0	3-3	0-0	2-5	62.5	+ 4.23
C N Allen	5-11	0-2	2-2	1-1	2-6	45.5	+ 2.78
B W Hills	5-12	0-2	4-7	0-0	1-3	41.7	- 2.90
Lord Huntingdon	5-12	0-0	5-11	0-0	0-1	41.7	- 1.62
M C Pipe	4-4	0-0	3-3	0-0	1-1	100.0	+ 5.78
C Tinkler	4-7	0-0	0-0	0-0	4-7	57.1	+ 2.88
M W Easterby	4-9	3-6	0-0	1-2	0-1	44.4	+ 0.20
P F I Cole	4-11	1-4	2-5	0-0	1-2	36.4	+ 0.63
J A Glover	4-12	0-1	0-0	0-0	4-11	33.3	+ 4.25
R Akehurst	3-4	0-0	3-4	0-0	0-0	75.0	+ 3.86
J H M Gosden	3-6	0-1	2-3	0-0	1-2	50.0	+ 0.98
G Wragg	3-7	0-0	3-4	0-0	0-3	42.9	- 1.70
M J Ryan	3-8	0-0	1-1	0-1	2-6	37.5	+ 1.75
M Brittain	3-8	0-1	3-5	0-0	0-2	37.5	+ 1.25
B A McMahon	3-9	0-0	2-2	0-0	1-7	33.3	0.00
J G FitzGerald	3-10	0-0	1-2	0-0	2-8	30.0	+ 0.55
N A Callaghan	3-11	1-4	1-1	0-2	1-4	27.3	- 2.25

TRAINERS' FAVOURITES AT THIRSK 1988-92

	Total W-R	Non-handicaps 2-y-o	3-y-o+	Handicaps 2-y-o	3-y-o+	Per cent	£1 Level Stake
M H Easterby	15-39	5-15	2-5	1-4	7-15	38.5	+ 6.03
J Berry	9-32	4-17	4-6	1-3	0-6	28.1	- 12.00
H R A Cecil	8-17	1-2	6-13	0-0	1-2	47.1	- 3.30
G Harwood	6-8	0-1	5-6	0-0	1-1	75.0	+ 2.10
J L Dunlop	5-8	0-1	1-2	0-0	4-5	62.5	+ 3.50
R Hollinshead	5-9	2-2	2-4	0-0	1-3	55.6	+ 3.13
A A Scott	4-6	1-2	3-3	0-0	0-1	66.7	+ 2.32
B W Hills	4-7	0-1	3-4	0-0	1-2	57.1	+ 1.94
B Hanbury	3-4	1-2	1-1	0-0	1-1	75.0	+ 4.40
J Etherington	3-6	0-1	1-3	0-0	2-2	50.0	+ 7.25
F H Lee	3-6	0-0	1-1	0-1	2-4	50.0	+ 4.83
W J Haggas	3-6	1-1	1-2	0-0	1-3	50.0	+ 0.10
D W Chapman	3-7	0-0	0-1	0-0	3-6	42.9	+ 5.50
H Thomson Jones	3-7	2-2	1-5	0-0	0-0	42.9	- 2.66
N Tinkler	3-9	0-2	3-5	0-0	0-2	33.3	- 1.26
R M Whitaker	3-10	1-2	2-4	0-1	0-3	30.0	+ 0.25
T D Barron	3-11	2-3	0-1	1-1	0-6	27.3	- 0.87
M R Stoute	3-14	1-4	2-7	0-0	0-3	21.4	- 7.07
H Candy	2-2	0-0	2-2	0-0	0-0	100.0	+ 0.86
J H M Gosden	2-2	0-0	2-2	0-0	0-0	100.0	+ 2.65
R W Armstrong	2-3	2-2	0-0	0-0	0-1	66.7	+ 1.29
Lord Huntingdon	2-3	0-0	2-3	0-0	0-0	66.7	+ 3.13
Mrs L Piggott	2-3	0-0	2-2	0-0	0-1	66.7	+ 0.64
L M Cumani	2-5	0-0	2-5	0-0	0-0	40.0	- 1.69

TRAINERS' FAVOURITES AT WARWICK 1988-92

	Total W-R	Non-handicaps 2-y-o	3-y-o+	Handicaps 2-y-o	3-y-o+	Per cent	£1 Level Stake
H R A Cecil	9-17	3-4	6-13	0-0	0-0	52.9	- 0.53
I A Balding	7-11	2-2	4-5	0-1	1-3	63.6	+ 5.26
J L Dunlop	7-12	2-2	3-4	1-1	1-5	58.3	+ 7.30
G Harwood	5-11	2-2	3-6	0-0	0-3	45.5	- 2.18
J W Hills	5-11	1-2	3-3	0-1	1-5	45.5	+ 5.11
B W Hills	5-15	0-2	4-8	1-1	0-4	33.3	- 5.98
J Berry	5-17	1-11	0-1	2-3	2-2	29.4	- 2.77
P T Walwyn	4-6	1-1	3-5	0-0	0-0	66.7	+ 1.68
M R Stoute	4-8	3-3	1-4	0-0	0-1	50.0	- 1.37
J H M Gosden	4-10	0-1	4-8	0-0	0-1	40.0	+ 2.48
R Hollinshead	3-4	0-0	2-3	1-1	0-0	75.0	+ 5.00
L M Cumani	3-5	0-0	3-5	0-0	0-0	60.0	+ 1.24
W R Hern	3-5	0-0	3-3	0-0	0-2	60.0	+ 0.85
G Lewis	3-6	2-3	0-1	0-0	1-2	50.0	+ 4.48
B A McMahon	3-10	0-0	0-1	0-0	3-9	30.0	- 1.12
G Blum	2-2	0-0	0-0	0-0	2-2	100.0	+ 9.00
Sir M Prescott	2-2	0-0	0-0	0-0	2-2	100.0	+ 4.63
A C Stewart	2-2	0-0	2-2	0-0	0-0	100.0	+ 2.20
M A Jarvis	2-3	0-0	1-2	0-0	1-1	66.7	+ 2.80
A A Scott	2-4	0-1	0-1	0-0	2-2	50.0	+ 0.01
R Charlton	2-4	0-0	1-3	0-0	1-1	50.0	+ 0.18
J W Payne	2-5	1-2	0-0	1-3	0-0	40.0	+ 0.35
H Candy	2-6	0-0	1-1	0-2	1-3	33.3	+ 1.25
R J Hodges	2-6	0-0	1-1	0-0	1-5	33.3	+ 0.50

TRAINERS' FAVOURITES AT WINDSOR 1988-92

	Total W-R	Non-handicaps 2-y-o	3-y-o+	Handicaps 2-y-o	3-y-o+	Per cent	£1 Level Stake
L M Cumani	12-21	0-0	10-15	0-1	2-5	57.1	+ 5.03
R Hannon	10-24	6-10	1-4	2-3	1-7	41.7	+ 1.79
A C Stewart	7-10	1-2	4-4	1-1	1-3	70.0	+ 4.05
H R A Cecil	6-11	0-2	3-6	0-0	3-3	54.5	+ 4.21
G Harwood	5-8	1-1	1-3	1-1	2-3	62.5	+ 3.72
W R Hern	5-11	0-1	3-5	0-0	2-5	45.5	- 1.79
M R Stoute	5-12	2-4	0-1	0-0	3-7	41.7	+ 0.40
J Berry	5-19	1-9	1-1	3-6	0-3	26.3	- 1.00
C F Wall	4-5	3-3	1-1	0-0	0-1	80.0	+ 5.98
I A Balding	4-7	1-2	0-1	0-0	3-4	57.1	+ 4.75
A A Scott	4-7	2-4	1-1	0-0	1-2	57.1	+ 2.05
P J Makin	4-9	0-0	4-6	0-0	0-3	44.4	+ 2.91
W A O'Gorman	4-11	4-9	0-0	0-1	0-1	36.4	- 3.87
N A Callaghan	4-14	1-2	0-0	0-1	3-11	28.6	+ 1.00
P F I Cole	4-14	2-7	1-3	0-0	1-4	28.6	- 1.50
Lord Huntingdon	3-3	2-2	1-1	0-0	0-0	100.0	+ 2.54
C R Nelson	3-4	2-2	0-0	0-0	1-2	75.0	+ 4.00
D T Thom	3-4	1-1	0-1	2-2	0-0	75.0	+ 5.88
B Hanbury	3-7	0-2	2-3	0-1	1-1	42.9	+ 1.63
J White	2-4	0-0	1-3	0-0	1-1	50.0	+ 4.00
M A Jarvis	2-5	0-0	1-2	0-0	1-3	40.0	- 0.10
M Bell	2-6	0-3	0-0	0-0	2-3	33.3	+ 0.25
R Charlton	2-6	1-1	0-3	0-0	1-2	33.3	+ 2.20
R F J Houghton	2-9	0-1	2-4	0-1	0-3	22.2	- 3.25

TRAINERS' FAVOURITES AT WOLVERHAMPTON 1988-92

	Total W-R	Non-handicaps 2-y-o	3-y-o+	Handicaps 2-y-o	3-y-o+	Per cent	£1 Level Stake
H R A Cecil	11-21	3-5	8-16	0-0	0-0	52.4	- 0.91
J L Dunlop	10-18	1-2	3-5	0-0	6-11	55.6	+ 8.55
R Boss	7-11	2-3	2-2	0-1	3-5	63.6	+ 10.17
L M Cumani	7-15	1-3	6-11	0-0	0-1	46.7	- 2.79
G Harwood	6-10	2-3	4-5	0-0	0-2	60.0	- 0.49
M R Stoute	6-12	3-6	3-5	0-0	0-1	50.0	- 2.40
J H M Gosden	5-6	2-2	3-4	0-0	0-0	83.3	+ 1.37
J Berry	5-31	3-17	1-3	1-6	0-5	16.1	- 17.16
R Charlton	4-6	2-2	2-2	0-0	0-2	66.7	+ 1.19
R J Hodges	4-8	2-3	0-0	0-1	2-4	50.0	+ 3.83
B W Hills	4-10	4-6	0-1	0-1	0-2	40.0	- 2.64
W R Hern	3-3	0-0	3-3	0-0	0-0	100.0	+ 3.98
W Jarvis	3-3	1-1	2-2	0-0	0-0	100.0	+ 2.48
M C Pipe	3-4	0-0	2-3	0-0	1-1	75.0	+ 7.73
J L Spearing	3-4	0-0	0-0	0-1	3-3	75.0	+ 9.50
R Hannon	3-6	1-3	2-2	0-1	0-0	50.0	+ 4.13
B Hanbury	3-7	3-3	0-1	0-0	0-3	42.9	- 0.60
M A Jarvis	3-9	2-2	0-2	0-0	1-5	33.3	+ 1.63
P F I Cole	3-12	3-8	0-2	0-0	0-2	25.0	- 4.63
A C Stewart	3-13	1-3	1-6	0-0	1-4	23.1	- 6 25
P Calver	2-2	0-0	2-2	0-0	0-0	100.0	+ 4.00
W A O'Gorman	2-2	2-2	0-0	0-0	0-0	100.0	+ 2.15
G A Pritchard-Gordon	2-2	0-0	0-0	0-0	2-2	100.0	+ 5.00
G Wragg	2-2	1-1	1-1	0-0	0-0	100.0	+ 1.95

TRAINERS' FAVOURITES AT YARMOUTH 1988-92

	Total W-R	Non-handicaps 2-y-o	3-y-o+	Handicaps 2-y-o	3-y-o+	Per cent	£1 Level Stake
H R A Cecil	30-59	16-31	12-23	0-0	2-5	50.8	- 1.18
M R Stoute	14-25	8-13	4-8	0-0	2-4	56.0	+ 5.10
A C Stewart	12-27	3-8	5-9	0-0	4-10	44.4	+ 1.41
W J Haggas	7-11	0-0	2-3	1-2	4-6	63.6	+ 11.21
M H Tompkins	7-17	3-7	2-3	0-1	2-6	41.2	- 1.47
C E Brittain	6-11	2-3	3-4	0-0	1-4	54.5	+ 6.23
Mrs L Piggott	6-11	1-3	1-1	0-0	4-7	54.5	+ 6.17
D Morley	6-14	3-5	1-1	0-0	2-8	42.9	+ 6.43
J H M Gosden	6-14	1-2	3-7	0-0	2-5	42.9	+ 0.88
L M Cumani	6-31	3-13	2-10	0-1	1-7	19.4	- 18.43
B W Hills	5-12	2-5	3-7	0-0	0-0	41.7	+ 0.67
G Wragg	5-17	2-8	3-6	0-0	0-3	29.4	- 5.86
B Hanbury	4-11	2-5	1-2	0-1	1-3	36.4	+ 0.92
G A Pritchard-Gordon	4-11	0-2	2-3	0-0	2-6	36.4	- 0.17
N A Callaghan	4-12	1-5	1-1	1-1	1-5	33.3	- 0.50
J Berry	4-13	4-10	0-1	0-0	0-2	30.8	- 2.02
J L Dunlop	3-4	0-0	1-2	0-0	2-2	75.0	+ 4.05
P C Haslam	3-5	1-2	1-1	0-0	1-2	60.0	+ 7.25
K T Ivory	3-5	0-1	0-0	0-0	3-4	60.0	+ 4.73
Sir M Prescott	3-6	1-1	1-1	0-0	1-4	50.0	+ 3.11
W Jarvis	3-9	2-2	0-1	0-2	1-4	33.3	- 1.00
J Pearce	3-9	1-2	1-3	0-0	1-4	33.3	- 0.50
M J Ryan	3-11	0-1	0-1	0-0	3-9	27.3	+ 6.50
H Thomson Jones	3-12	2-6	1-3	0-1	0-2	25.0	- 2.50

TRAINERS' FAVOURITES AT YORK 1988-92

	Total W-R	Non-handicaps 2-y-o	3-y-o+	Handicaps 2-y-o	3-y-o+	Per cent	£1 Level Stake
M R Stoute	18-48	4-11	9-21	0-0	5-16	37.5	+ 1.79
H R A Cecil	14-41	2-4	10-29	0-0	2-8	34.1	- 12.03
J H M Gosden	12-19	1-1	4-8	0-1	7-9	63.2	+ 20.38
M H Easterby	11-42	1-4	1-2	1-4	8-32	26.2	+ 4.33
J L Dunlop	9-18	4-9	2-4	0-1	3-4	50.0	+ 5.42
P F I Cole	7-12	4-6	1-2	0-1	2-3	58.3	+ 8.26
B Hanbury	7-17	4-6	0-3	0-2	3-6	41.2	- 0.01
L M Cumani	7-24	1-3	5-15	0-1	1-5	29.2	- 10.13
B W Hills	7-25	2-8	3-9	0-0	2-8	28.0	- 0.29
J Berry	5-8	4-7	0-0	1-1	0-0	62.5	+ 1.89
R Hannon	4-5	3-4	1-1	0-0	0-0	80.0	+ 1.26
D R C Elsworth	4-9	2-2	1-4	0-0	1-3	44.4	+ 10.25
A A Scott	4-10	2-4	1-3	0-0	1-3	40.0	- 0.58
G Wragg	4-11	1-4	3-5	0-0	0-2	36.4	- 0.94
I A Balding	4-14	0-3	0-3	0-1	4-7	28.6	+ 4.50
E Weymes	3-3	2-2	0-0	0-0	1-1	100.0	+ 5.75
D W Chapman	3-6	0-0	0-1	0-0	3-5	50.0	+ 5.58
R W Armstrong	3-10	2-3	0-2	0-0	1-5	30.0	- 1.75
A C Stewart	3-11	1-2	2-3	0-0	0-6	27.3	- 4.75
P J Makin	2-3	0-0	0-0	0-0	2-3	66.7	+ 5.83
M J Ryan	2-3	1-1	0-0	0-1	1-1	66.7	+ 3.38
F H Lee	2-3	2-2	0-0	0-0	0-1	66.7	+ 2.30
C E Brittain	2-4	0-0	2-3	0-0	0-1	50.0	+ 0.73
G Lewis	2-4	2-2	0-1	0-0	0-1	50.0	+ 3.25

TOP PERCENTAGE COURSES FOR FAVOURITES 1988-92

	W-R	Per cent	£1 Level Stake		W-R	Per cent	£1 Level Stake
Newcastle	145-343	42.3	+ 13.38	Sandown	185-523	35.4	- 31.13
Redcar	248-596	41.6	+ 51.79	Lingfield (AW)	200-566	35.3	- 39.35
Yarmouth	199-508	39.2	- 43.01	Hamilton	187-531	35.2	- 38.18
Ripon	154-399	38.6	- 0.43	Brighton	191-545	35.0	- 82.04
Chepstow	122-317	38.5	+ 4.55	Chester	96-274	35.0	- 27.59
Ayr	174-457	38.1	+ 0.89	Goodwood	201-578	34.8	- 23.31
Edinburgh	142-374	38.0	- 10.98	Southwell (AW)	251-721	34.8	- 76.77
Thirsk	151-401	37.7	- 33.97	Doncaster	199-577	34.5	- 26.08
Windsor	148-397	37.3	- 17.08	Newmarket	342-992	34.5	- 74.93
Catterick	170-458	37.1	- 73.19	Nottingham	186-552	33.7	- 61.66
Bath	135-366	36.9	- 2.33	Salisbury	135-401	33.7	- 40.04
Beverley	213-577	36.9	- 62.47	Carlisle	93-280	33.2	- 33.32
Folkestone	165-447	36.9	- 21.90	Haydock	183-561	32.6	- 85.96
Pontefract	172-471	36.5	- 13.51	Warwick	133-408	32.6	- 73.66
Leicester	180-498	36.1	- 35.39	Newbury	152-470	32.3	- 41.38
Wolverhampton	166-462	35.9	- 58.41	Ascot	130-409	31.8	- 49.43
York	176-491	35.8	+ 9.84	Kempton	138-434	31.8	- 30.35
Lingfield	194-545	35.6	- 51.30	Epsom	58-211	27.5	- 44.30

FAVOURITES' PERFORMANCE BY TYPE OF RACE 1988-92

Non-h'caps	W-R	Per cent	£1 Level Stake	Handicaps	W-R	Per cent	£1 Level Stake
2-y-o	1653-3956	41.8	-274.78	2-y-o	190-687	27.7	- 66.08
3-y-o	1289-2956	43.6	-138.45	3-y-o	566-1903	29.7	-140.71
Weight/age	931-2162	43.1	- 52.60	All-aged	1495-5500	27.2	-549.80
Totals	3873-9074	42.7	-465.83	Totals	2251-8090	27.8	-756.59
All Favs	6124-17164	35.7	-1222.42				

When there is more than one favourite in a race then the £1 stake has been equally divided on each one. Only one favourite is counted for each race.

TRAINER SUMMARIES

WINNING FLAT TRAINERS 1992

	Total W-R	2-y-o	3-y-o	4-y-o+	Per cent	£1 Level Stake
R Hannon	147-1107	73-485	55-440	19-182	13.3	-311.59
J H M Gosden	112-511	29-99	64-321	19-91	21.9	+ 13.90
H R A Cecil	109-383	25-80	77-262	7-41	28.5	- 11.43
J Berry	106-788	55-431	38-262	13-95	13.5	-155.23
P F I Cole	85-450	39-173	33-185	13-92	18.9	- 63.11
J L Dunlop	75-502	21-145	48-301	6-56	14.9	-164.24
M R Stoute	74-449	24-146	38-230	12-73	16.5	-129.10
Mrs G R Reveley	68-326	6-51	24-121	38-154	20.9	- 2.87
C E Brittain	63-596	15-141	34-282	14-173	10.6	-154.44
B W Hills	61-418	26-148	28-207	7-63	14.6	-100.39
Lord Huntingdon	55-311	11-74	26-168	18-69	17.7	+ 8.64
R Hollinshead	55-572	12-148	24-238	19-186	9.6	-111.64
L M Cumani	54-292	17-82	34-163	3-47	18.5	- 69.25
G Lewis	54-352	16-152	24-152	14-48	15.3	+ 56.64
M S Johnston	50-384	13-121	28-135	9-128	13.0	- 2.13
Sir Mark Prescott	49-266	13-93	28-123	8-50	18.4	- 35.77
G Wragg	44-210	10-31	27-128	7-51	21.0	- 31.73
R Charlton	43-167	11-42	24-92	8-33	25.7	+ 64.61
M H Tompkins	42-366	17-129	12-110	13-127	11.5	- 82.35
P Chapple-Hyam	41-245	22-111	19-119	0-15	16.7	- 54.70
B Hanbury	39-308	10-68	20-197	9-43	12.7	- 64.98
M Bell	39-327	21-119	17-142	1-66	11.9	-120.01
M H Easterby	38-379	14-134	11-104	13-141	10.0	-137.69
T D Barron	37-323	11-87	13-89	13-147	11.5	- 53.70
A A Scott	36-315	11-105	23-202	2-8	11.4	-136.45
I A Balding	36-316	8-84	8-107	20-125	11.4	- 42.11
M P Naughton	32-342	0-1	7-34	25-307	9.4	-107.41
D R C Elsworth	31-318	12-101	11-127	8-90	9.7	- 57.01
B A McMahon	30-296	4-50	9-110	17-136	10.1	- 78.52
P C Haslam	29-205	2-24	11-79	16-102	14.1	- 68.30
Mrs J Cecil	28-157	4-35	24-122	0-0	17.8	+ 68.32
J R Fanshawe	28-247	2-61	21-156	5-30	11.3	- 47.70
R Akehurst	28-259	2-47	2-38	24-174	10.8	- 39.89
H Thomson Jones	27-188	12-63	14-107	1-18	14.4	- 33.53
C A Cyzer	27-199	1-37	11-64	15-98	13.6	+ 82.75
G Harwood	27-231	9-61	14-120	4-50	11.7	-100.21
M R Channon	26-285	9-122	9-106	8-57	9.1	-109.09
F H Lee	26-295	5-68	5-59	16-168	8.8	- 74.00
J A Glover	25-176	1-16	9-84	15-76	14.2	+ 20.25
S G Norton	25-181	4-55	9-83	12-43	13.8	- 20.43
M A Jarvis	25-183	6-33	11-100	8-50	13.7	- 32.94
Mrs J Ramsden	24-245	2-35	11-116	11-94	9.8	- 57.12
M J Ryan	22-172	0-24	10-49	12-99	12.8	- 28.74
J W Hills	22-212	3-41	12-99	7-72	10.4	- 66.79
P T Walwyn	22-227	3-52	18-138	1-37	9.7	- 63.60
R M Whitaker	22-288	4-73	6-137	12-78	7.6	-101.49
A C Stewart	21-128	1-12	17-92	3-24	16.4	- 31.20
W A O'Gorman	21-166	4-35	7-68	10-63	12.7	- 86.46
W Jarvis	21-180	3-38	12-81	6-61	11.7	- 68.95
H Candy	21-200	3-25	11-102	7-73	10.5	+ 11.93
R J Hodges	21-366	3-17	1-86	17-263	5.7	-162.96
M J Camacho	20-112	7-32	0-14	13-66	17.9	+ 32.76
D Morley	19-149	8-31	9-80	2-38	12.8	- 16.07
J Pearce	19-152	1-12	6-67	12-73	12.5	- 31.06

	Total W-R	2-y-o	3-y-o	4-y-o+	Per cent	£1 Level Stake
N A Callaghan	19-169	5-53	9-85	5-31	11.2	- 62.65
W Carter	19-208	6-66	5-66	8-76	9.1	- 3.75
K O C-Brown	18-125	0-11	4-39	14-75	14.4	+118.33
M Moubarak	18-125	5-38	8-61	5-26	14.4	- 20.62
W R Hern	17-124	3-20	12-95	2-9	13.7	- 24.91
J Wharton	17-139	5-38	5-27	7-74	12.2	+ 40.95
J W Watts	17-162	6-53	6-57	5-52	10.5	- 7.75
G A Pritchard-Gordon	17-179	6-71	8-71	3-37	9.5	- 59.92
M McCormack	16-168	0-30	8-68	8-70	9.5	- 62.97
P A Kelleway	16-170	4-63	8-67	4-40	9.4	- 49.72
M C Pipe	15-93	0-0	3-16	12-77	16.1	- 16.42
J Etherington	15-146	4-46	11-96	0-4	10.3	- 44.08
A Bailey	15-165	3-44	1-36	11-85	9.1	- 48.08
G B Balding	15-189	2-39	5-70	8-80	7.9	- 68.79
W G R Wightman	14-106	4-24	5-28	5-54	13.2	+ 67.50
J Sutcliffe	14-128	1-24	5-66	8-38	10.9	- 58.99
R J R Williams	14-133	5-34	1-23	8-76	10.5	- 30.97
Denys Smith	14-144	3-24	2-60	9-60	9.7	- 40.59
R W Armstrong	14-147	5-24	7-85	2-38	9.5	- 9.75
B Beasley	14-152	7-64	3-45	4-43	9.2	- 32.02
S Dow	14-184	2-63	2-40	10-81	7.6	- 74.37
J L Spearing	14-199	1-34	4-40	9-125	7.0	- 92.29
W J Pearce	13-137	1-28	3-38	9-71	9.5	- 77.54
P W Harris	13-152	1-27	5-95	7-30	8.6	0.00
C J Hill	13-181	1-23	1-19	11-139	7.2	- 73.67
E Weymes	12-78	4-23	8-39	0-16	15.4	- 22.71
R Guest	12-82	3-13	3-42	6-27	14.6	+ 8.50
Mrs A Knight	12-120	0-1	1-19	11-100	10.0	+ 25.75
W J Haggas	12-128	5-38	6-48	1-42	9.4	- 57.24
J R Jenkins	12-143	2-43	0-10	10-90	8.4	- 29.00
M W Easterby	12-150	1-74	1-25	10-51	8.0	- 45.50
D W P Arbuthnot	12-162	4-20	4-79	4-63	7.4	- 43.25
D W Chapman	12-264	1-13	2-45	9-206	4.5	- 83.25
W G M Turner	11-109	6-69	5-14	0-26	10.1	- 2.12
R Simpson	11-120	2-13	5-56	4-51	9.2	- 47.32
E J Alston	11-176	0-28	0-29	11-119	6.3	- 80.00
R J Holder	11-249	2-63	3-74	6-112	4.4	-147.50
P S Felgate	10-83	3-20	1-23	6-40	12.0	- 24.04
G M Moore	10-108	5-48	4-18	1-42	9.3	- 42.77
Mrs L Piggott	10-109	2-38	3-22	5-49	9.2	- 59.50
R Bastiman	10-121	0-8	2-32	8-81	8.3	- 31.67
R F Johnson Houghton	10-125	5-62	5-60	0-3	8.0	- 60.57
H J Collingridge	10-127	0-6	5-51	5-70	7.9	- 34.12
L J Holt	10-145	2-34	4-50	4-61	6.9	- 62.75
P J Makin	10-150	0-16	7-87	3-47	6.7	- 57.09
Miss L A Perratt	10-160	2-43	2-42	6-75	6.3	- 68.95
Mrs N Macauley	10-206	1-31	4-64	5-111	4.9	-125.64
M D Hammond	9-57	0-0	0-2	9-55	15.8	- 2.49
J A R Toller	9-58	0-5	8-39	1-14	15.5	- 13.44
S R Bowring	9-83	0-5	1-14	8-64	10.8	+ 45.90
Miss S E Hall	9-84	5-48	2-15	2-21	10.7	- 9.52
K T Ivory	9-91	0-11	2-23	7-57	9.9	+ 13.23
Bob Jones	9-96	0-18	8-51	1-27	9.4	- 33.75
C W C Elsey	9-98	2-25	4-43	3-30	9.2	- 23.57
J W Payne	9-101	2-43	2-31	5-27	8.9	- 43.40
R Boss	9-109	0-10	9-85	0-14	8.3	- 54.50

	Total W-R	2-y-o	3-y-o	4-y-o+	Per cent	£1 Level Stake
Dr J D Scargill	9-113	3-39	3-29	3-45	8.0	- 29.34
T J Naughton	9-113	1-28	5-33	3-52	8.0	+ 14.75
J L Harris	9-119	2-10	2-40	5-69	7.6	- 41.75
Pat Mitchell	9-125	1-23	6-56	2-46	7.2	- 25.50
N Tinkler	9-144	3-52	1-34	5-58	6.3	- 84.92
D A Wilson	9-152	0-7	4-47	5-98	5.9	- 83.75
D Marks	8-71	0-6	6-32	2-33	11.3	- 8.25
S P C Woods	8-73	3-40	5-32	0-1	11.0	+ 5.00
J White	8-90	0-15	3-29	5-46	8.9	- 60.25
W W Haigh	8-92	0-13	2-32	6-47	8.7	- 28.37
D Morris	8-92	1-18	3-21	4-53	8.7	- 15.75
L G Cottrell	8-98	0-11	3-29	5-58	8.2	- 38.42
C J Benstead	8-120	2-10	2-61	4-49	6.7	- 48.25
D R Laing	8-123	0-42	5-41	3-40	6.5	- 28.50
M J Heaton-Ellis	8-133	2-48	6-72	0-13	6.0	- 66.00
T Fairhurst	8-202	2-68	3-58	3-76	4.0	-120.37
Miss A J Whitfield	7-48	0-5	1-11	6-32	14.6	+ 21.50
M Dods	7-66	0-4	1-16	6-46	10.6	+ 5.55
C R Nelson	7-88	0-2	5-55	2-31	8.0	- 29.25
B Palling	7-91	3-32	3-44	1-15	7.7	- 17.75
J M P Eustace	7-91	1-40	2-29	4-22	7.7	- 59.00
M J Fetherston-Godley	7-96	1-22	1-23	5-51	7.3	- 24.00
B R Millman	7-107	3-20	1-31	3-56	6.5	+ 15.00
C N Allen	7-115	4-23	3-41	0-51	6.1	- 55.37
D T Thom	7-132	1-35	1-41	5-56	5.3	- 69.75
J G FitzGerald	7-144	3-50	1-48	3-46	4.9	- 80.67
C F Wall	7-149	0-33	7-108	0-8	4.7	- 85.80
W R Muir	7-154	1-46	3-50	3-58	4.5	- 79.25
M Blanshard	7-173	2-56	1-41	4-76	4.0	-108.25
M Brittain	7-223	3-52	0-17	4-154	3.1	-140.00
P Calver	6-70	0-14	4-43	2-13	8.6	- 18.75
A P Stringer	6-71	1-16	0-12	5-43	8.5	+ 36.50
Lady Herries	6-75	2-19	1-16	3-40	8.0	- 17.00
J Akehurst	6-84	2-12	0-21	4-51	7.1	- 50.50
N A Graham	6-86	2-19	2-49	2-18	7.0	- 44.21
P D Evans	6-86	1-6	0-12	5-68	7.0	- 10.50
C C Elsey	6-94	0-10	1-41	5-43	6.4	- 59.82
E A Wheeler	6-110	0-4	1-49	5-57	5.5	- 58.00
W J Musson	6-123	0-11	2-41	4-71	4.9	- 79.75
G C Bravery	5-17	5-10	0-6	0-1	29.4	+ 26.63
J S King	5-21	0-0	0-0	5-21	23.8	+ 6.75
M J Bolton	5-28	0-0	0-9	5-19	17.9	+ 7.00
S E Kettlewell	5-36	0-8	2-12	3-16	13.9	+ 9.00
T Casey	5-47	0-5	0-3	5-39	10.6	- 13.50
P J Feilden	5-60	0-0	1-13	4-47	8.3	- 30.05
D Moffatt	5-66	3-21	0-7	2-38	7.6	- 12.50
G H Eden	5-67	0-7	1-22	4-38	7.5	- 41.00
A Hide	5-77	0-14	1-29	4-34	6.5	- 36.00
C A Horgan	5-85	0-9	4-44	1-32	5.9	- 17.00
T Thomson Jones	5-86	0-20	3-38	2-28	5.8	- 42.00
A Moore	5-107	0-15	0-17	5-75	4.7	- 25.00
D Haydn Jones	5-140	1-52	1-37	3-51	3.6	- 70.50
P Wigham	4-20	0-0	0-0	4-20	20.0	+ 7.00
A Fabre (Fra)	4-20	2-2	1-9	1-9	20.0	- 3.54
K W Hogg	4-43	1-12	0-12	3-19	9.3	+ 8.00
J E Banks	4-49	0-4	0-13	4-32	8.2	- 28.75

	Total W-R	2-y-o	3-y-o	4-y-o+	Per cent	£1 Level Stake
I Campbell	4-50	1-6	0-20	3-24	8.0	- 36.54
C James	4-55	3-26	1-25	0-4	7.3	+ 1.75
G Blum	4-68	0-15	4-42	0-11	5.9	- 29.92
M Dixon	4-70	0-11	0-15	4-44	5.7	- 20.50
Miss B Sanders	4-76	0-13	1-22	3-41	5.3	- 38.00
B Ellison	4-79	0-7	0-7	4-65	5.1	- 52.50
J Parkes	4-90	0-0	0-5	4-85	4.4	- 68.00
M J Haynes	4-100	2-22	0-32	2-46	4.0	- 50.00
P Mitchell	4-104	3-32	1-44	0-28	3.8	- 67.75
N Bycroft	4-105	1-31	3-41	0-33	3.8	- 65.25
J D Bethell	4-106	1-18	0-29	3-59	3.8	- 71.00
Miss L C Siddall	4-107	0-13	2-60	2-34	3.7	- 62.00
Capt J Wilson	4-115	0-17	1-46	3-52	3.5	- 42.50
C Tinkler	4-130	0-69	0-18	4-43	3.1	- 76.50
P G Murphy	3-9	0-3	3-6	0-0	33.3	+ 21.00
J A B Old	3-14	0-0	0-0	3-14	21.4	+ 28.08
M McCourt	3-16	0-1	0-0	3-15	18.8	+ 4.00
F O'Mahony	3-20	0-0	0-0	3-20	15.0	- 10.17
R C Spicer	3-24	0-0	1-12	2-12	12.5	+ 42.00
C P Wildman	3-32	0-7	0-2	3-23	9.4	- 20.25
C N Williams	3-34	3-16	0-2	0-16	8.8	- 25.00
P Butler	3-39	0-22	1-7	2-10	7.7	- 12.50
R Dickin	3-42	1-5	0-21	2-16	7.1	+ 23.50
D J S Cosgrove	3-46	2-14	0-12	1-20	6.5	- 23.00
Ronald Thompson	3-50	0-16	3-32	0-2	6.0	- 21.12
J F Bottomley	3-52	1-23	0-16	2-13	5.8	- 18.50
J Mackie	3-53	0-0	0-14	3-39	5.7	- 30.50
J Ffitch-Heyes	3-56	0-0	1-20	2-36	5.4	- 12.00
B S Rothwell	3-57	3-47	0-4	0-6	5.3	- 28.00
R Curtis	3-59	0-8	1-5	2-46	5.1	- 38.50
A Smith	3-62	0-4	1-31	2-27	4.8	- 34.50
C G Cox	3-62	0-22	1-13	2-27	4.8	- 26.40
R Lee	3-63	0-0	0-0	3-63	4.8	- 40.50
R J O'Sullivan	3-64	0-0	0-0	3-64	4.7	- 1.00
B C Morgan	3-66	0-1	2-39	1-26	4.5	- 30.00
A Harrison	3-67	0-9	1-24	2-34	4.5	- 54.75
C B B Booth	3-77	1-19	1-25	1-33	3.9	- 60.75
J M Bradley	3-78	0-3	0-13	3-62	3.8	- 39.00
Mrs Barbara Waring	3-99	0-7	0-21	3-71	3.0	- 68.75
M D I Usher	3-117	1-35	1-35	1-47	2.6	- 74.00
D K Weld (Ire)	2-9	0-0	1-3	1-6	22.2	+ 23.00
P J Bevan	2-16	0-0	0-3	2-13	12.5	+ 2.00
R J Price	2-16	0-0	0-6	2-10	12.5	+ 6.00
B Smart	2-21	1-6	0-7	1-8	9.5	- 7.67
R Allan	2-23	1-5	0-4	1-14	8.7	- 5.50
J S Bolger (Ire)	2-23	0-2	2-15	0-6	8.7	- 18.20
P J Hobbs	2-23	0-0	0-1	2-22	8.7	- 7.00
M F Barraclough	2-25	0-0	2-24	0-1	8.0	- 12.00
J P Smith	2-26	0-0	0-3	2-23	7.7	+ 34.00
W M Brisbourne	2-27	0-0	0-15	2-12	7.4	- 7.00
W Holden	2-30	0-2	0-8	2-20	6.7	- 17.00
N C Wright	2-31	1-6	1-25	0-0	6.5	0.00
J M Carr	2-33	0-13	0-0	2-20	6.1	- 21.00
D J G Murray Smith	2-34	1-8	0-2	1-24	5.9	- 25.50
A N Lee	2-34	0-2	2-32	0-0	5.9	- 14.00
R J Baker	2-39	0-3	1-17	1-19	5.1	- 2.00

	Total W-R	2-y-o	3-y-o	4-y-o+	Per cent	£1 Level Stake
M W Ellerby	2-42	1-10	1-32	0-0	4.8	+ 18.00
M P Muggeridge	2-43	1-7	1-13	0-23	4.7	- 13.00
Mrs J C Dawe	2-47	0-4	0-1	2-42	4.3	- 26.00
W Storey	2-51	0-0	1-17	1-34	3.9	- 20.50
D Shaw	2-53	0-1	0-6	2-46	3.8	+ 13.00
K S Bridgwater	2-54	1-4	0-15	1-35	3.7	- 24.50
R Voorspuy	2-62	0-23	0-17	2-22	3.2	- 44.50
J S Moore	2-66	2-44	0-5	0-17	3.0	- 46.00
J J Bridger	2-68	0-22	0-28	2-18	2.9	- 48.37
M O'Neill	2-68	0-1	0-27	2-40	2.9	- 30.00
B Gubby	2-70	0-13	0-10	2-47	2.9	- 36.00
A P Jarvis	2-71	1-45	0-11	1-15	2.8	- 39.00
C W Thornton	2-94	1-22	1-60	0-12	2.1	- 84.00
P Howling	2-166	0-31	0-13	2-122	1.2	-156.37
Mrs C Head (Fra)	1-1	0-0	1-1	0-0	100.0	+ 5.00
J G Coogan (Ire)	1-1	1-1	0-0	0-0	100.0	+ 5.50
C Parker	1-4	0-0	1-3	0-1	25.0	- 0.25
Mrs H Parrott	1-4	0-0	0-0	1-4	25.0	+ 7.00
J A C Edwards	1-5	0-0	0-0	1-5	20.0	+ 16.00
J E Hammond (Fra)	1-5	0-0	0-1	1-4	20.0	+ 2.00
D Nicholson	1-7	0-0	1-7	0-0	14.3	+ 60.00
M Kauntze (Ire)	1-7	0-2	0-1	1-4	14.3	- 2.50
J Hetherton	1-8	0-0	1-6	0-2	12.5	- 5.25
G F H Charles-Jones	1-8	0-0	1-6	0-2	12.5	+ 26.00
R G Brazington	1-9	0-0	0-0	1-9	11.1	0.00
N Chamberlain	1-10	1-8	0-2	0-0	10.0	+ 16.00
S M Hillen	1-10	1-6	0-4	0-0	10.0	+ 16.00
M W Eckley	1-11	0-3	0-2	1-6	9.1	0.00
D R Loder	1-11	0-3	0-4	1-4	9.1	+ 10.00
R Rowe	1-12	0-0	0-0	1-12	8.3	- 5.50
J Hanson	1-13	1-13	0-0	0-0	7.7	- 10.50
C R Beever	1-16	0-0	0-0	1-16	6.3	- 12.00
P M McEntee	1-17	1-15	0-1	0-1	5.9	- 12.00
Miss H C Knight	1-19	0-0	1-12	0-7	5.3	- 2.00
W A Stephenson	1-20	0-2	0-6	1-12	5.0	- 12.00
J L Eyre	1-20	0-2	0-1	1-17	5.0	- 15.50
J Dooler	1-22	0-0	0-5	1-17	4.5	- 15.50
R A Bennett	1-23	0-2	0-0	1-21	4.3	- 15.50
A R Davison	1-24	0-1	0-3	1-20	4.2	- 15.50
R Ingram	1-28	0-15	0-5	1-8	3.6	+ 6.00
Mrs A L M King	1-30	0-0	1-12	0-18	3.3	+ 71.00
A W Potts	1-33	0-9	1-17	0-7	3.0	- 22.00
G A Ham	1-33	0-0	0-10	1-23	3.0	- 25.00
B J McMath	1-34	0-16	1-9	0-9	2.9	- 28.50
K R Burke	1-34	0-12	0-14	1-8	2.9	- 27.50
C D Broad	1-34	0-11	0-5	1-18	2.9	- 19.00
W L Barker	1-35	0-3	0-14	1-18	2.9	- 23.00
Mrs J Jordan	1-35	0-6	0-13	1-16	2.9	- 20.00
T H Caldwell	1-36	0-0	1-21	0-15	2.8	+ 15.00
P D Cundell	1-37	0-0	1-27	0-10	2.7	- 20.00
D Burchell	1-42	0-6	0-10	1-26	2.4	- 39.75
A W Jones	1-43	0-0	0-6	1-37	2.3	- 34.00
A S Reid	1-46	0-0	0-18	1-28	2.2	- 39.00
T Craig	1-47	0-3	0-2	1-42	2.1	- 44.62
J A Bennett	1-56	0-3	0-8	1-45	1.8	- 50.00
L J Codd	1-56	0-1	0-20	1-35	1.8	- 50.50

	Total					Per	£1 Level
	W-R	2-y-o	3-y-o	4-y-o+		cent	Stake
J J O'Neill	1-62	1-20	0-9	0-33		1.6	- 52.50
D R Tucker	1-66	0-5	0-13	1-48		1.5	- 49.00
D E Incisa	1-72	0-15	0-19	1-38		1.4	- 59.00
J S Wainwright	1-72	1-36	0-14	0-22		1.4	- 51.00
J P Leigh	1-78	0-14	1-15	0-49		1.3	- 69.00

WINNING FLAT JOCKEYS 1992

	1st	2nd	3rd	Unpl	Total Mts	Per cent	£1 Level Stake
M Roberts	206	146	113	603	1068	19.3	+ 19.63
Pat Eddery	178	118	76	359	731	24.4	+ 51.25
W Carson	125	120	107	504	856	14.6	-200.89
G Duffield	108	70	59	466	703	15.4	- 17.11
T Quinn	108	121	81	468	778	13.9	- 15.33
S Cauthen	107	85	72	293	557	19.2	-113.30
L Dettori	101	82	76	420	679	14.9	- 53.30
R Cochrane	100	96	104	479	779	12.8	-100.75
W Ryan	96	103	91	401	691	13.9	-149.24
J Reid	95	78	89	442	704	13.5	-142.39
K Darley	91	85	61	325	562	16.2	-104.33
W R Swinburn	82	86	76	279	523	15.7	-146.03
M Hills	82	72	65	351	570	14.4	- 30.89
A Munro	75	85	90	446	696	10.8	-232.90
Paul Eddery	72	66	72	440	650	11.1	-209.26
G Carter	68	59	65	425	617	11.0	+ 37.37
J Carroll	67	59	51	361	538	12.5	-164.92
D Holland	61	60	59	337	517	11.8	- 75.27
D Biggs	57	44	48	356	505	11.3	- 26.24
D McKeown	55	50	51	354	510	10.8	-136.86
B Raymond	53	61	51	429	594	8.9	-263.96
P Robinson	52	47	49	307	455	11.4	-142.13
R Hills	52	64	51	302	469	11.1	-153.00
J Williams	49	57	75	499	680	7.2	-102.89
K Fallon	44	39	51	315	449	9.8	- 97.01
J Quinn	42	47	60	573	722	5.8	-258.67
M Birch	39	47	53	341	480	8.1	-240.19
L Piggott	35	45	36	213	329	10.6	-138.15
J Lowe	33	35	52	475	595	5.5	-331.54
N Connorton	29	19	26	179	253	11.5	+ 2.24
G Bardwell	29	24	15	343	411	7.1	- 4.37
N Day	28	24	21	164	237	11.8	- 39.29
W Newnes	27	28	38	248	341	7.9	-158.68
J Fortune	25	36	35	258	354	7.1	-214.71
B Rouse	23	21	26	266	336	6.8	-133.58
T Sprake	22	20	23	182	247	8.9	- 8.99
N Carlisle	21	32	25	288	366	5.7	-170.24
S Whitworth	20	29	31	292	372	5.4	-189.00
Alex Greaves	19	27	23	109	178	10.7	- 48.20
L Charnock	19	20	24	332	395	4.8	-242.79
N Adams	19	23	31	513	586	3.2	-325.25
M Tebbutt	18	15	14	156	203	8.9	- 97.85
G Baxter	18	16	21	189	244	7.4	- 62.75
Dale Gibson	18	20	39	311	388	4.6	-250.34
D Nicholls	17	26	21	133	197	8.6	-122.78

	1st	2nd	3rd	Unpl	Total Mts	Per cent	£1 Level Stake
C Rutter	17	24	32	246	319	5.3	-202.05
A Culhane	16	28	27	188	259	6.2	-110.49
A Clark	16	19	27	206	268	6.0	-161.04
R Price	16	13	25	217	271	5.9	-147.19
A McGlone	16	17	27	222	282	5.7	-189.52
G Hind	16	20	28	219	283	5.7	-165.47
S Wood	15	14	20	239	288	5.2	- 1.25
T Williams	12	22	25	215	274	4.4	-162.00
R P Elliott	10	8	12	91	121	8.3	- 21.75
S Dawson	10	5	11	157	183	5.5	- 29.50
T Lucas	10	12	23	152	197	5.1	-113.25
S Webster	10	17	22	169	218	4.6	-117.00
W Woods	8	3	7	66	84	9.5	- 0.75
M Wigham	8	5	6	94	113	7.1	- 36.50
A Mackay	8	10	13	148	179	4.5	-100.75
J Lloyd	7	2	7	26	42	16.7	+ 28.00
P D'Arcy	5	2	3	23	33	15.2	- 14.88
R Lappin	5	2	4	35	46	10.9	+ 6.00
B Crossley	5	5	8	127	145	3.4	- 94.50
C Asmussen	4	3	4	23	34	11.8	- 5.00
M J Kinane	4	5	1	24	34	11.8	+ 23.50
V Smith	4	5	4	44	57	7.0	- 23.00
P Burke	4	8	9	147	168	2.4	- 97.50
Julie Krone	3	0	0	2	5	60.0	+ 10.18
S Morris	3	3	5	64	75	4.0	- 22.00
Jaki Houston	3	1	6	65	75	4.0	- 44.00
T Rogers	3	3	9	64	79	3.8	- 56.50
G Crealock	3	7	9	67	86	3.5	- 71.50
N Howe	3	5	2	139	149	2.0	-108.00
S Perks	2	1	1	11	15	13.3	- 9.34
C Nutter	2	2	1	21	26	7.7	- 13.50
G Oldroyd	2	2	4	19	27	7.4	- 19.75
C Dwyer	2	0	2	31	35	5.7	+ 5.00
Gay Kelleway	2	2	4	33	41	4.9	- 4.50
Kim Tinkler	2	2	4	50	58	3.4	- 40.00
E Johnson	2	4	5	62	73	2.7	- 65.00
A Proud	2	2	7	65	76	2.6	- 60.50
A Shoults	2	7	9	63	81	2.5	- 69.62
R Fox	2	11	5	92	110	1.8	- 90.67
E Hide	1	0	0	0	1	100.0	+ 10.00
B Coogan	1	0	0	0	1	100.0	+ 5.50
Y Okabe	1	0	0	0	1	100.0	+ 6.50
Brough Scott	1	0	0	0	1	100.0	+ 9.00
S Craine	1	0	0	3	4	25.0	- 2.20
A Cruz	1	0	3	0	4	25.0	+ 13.00
K L Tsui	1	0	1	4	6	16.7	- 0.50
T Jarnet	1	0	0	6	7	14.3	+ 0.80
W O'Connor	1	1	1	6	9	11.1	- 4.50
C Roche	1	2	2	15	20	5.0	- 17.00
W Hood	1	2	1	20	24	4.2	- 16.00
S Raymont	1	3	1	36	41	2.4	- 39.00
M Perrett	1	2	2	36	41	2.4	- 29.00

WINNING APPRENTICES 1992

	1st	2nd	3rd	Unpl	Total Mts	Per cent	£1 Level Stake
D Harrison	52	61	51	321	485	10.7	-102.98
J Weaver	43	57	35	203	338	12.7	- 73.41
J Fanning	42	47	51	440	580	7.2	-221.32
F Norton	34	62	43	373	512	6.6	-216.93
S Maloney	21	37	31	249	338	6.2	-167.57
Emma O'Gorman	19	26	19	79	143	13.3	- 61.05
A Tucker	19	26	23	197	265	7.2	-111.23
S Davies	18	22	14	105	159	11.3	- 32.96
D Moffatt	17	10	11	115	153	11.1	- 44.41
A Garth	17	19	21	162	219	7.8	+113.88
B Doyle	16	21	21	211	269	5.9	-125.67
O Pears	15	10	10	120	155	9.7	- 55.87
S D Williams	15	18	13	136	182	8.2	- 49.75
N Kennedy	15	19	23	183	240	6.3	- 88.50
R Perham	13	22	16	188	239	5.4	-149.75
K Rutter	11	9	11	63	94	11.7	- 33.87
S Sanders	10	11	6	58	85	11.8	+ 10.50
C Hawksley	10	10	30	222	272	3.7	-150.25
B Russell	9	0	3	22	34	26.5	+ 34.50
N Varley	8	0	5	29	42	19.0	+ 30.88
M Humphries	8	9	5	57	79	10.1	- 3.25
S Drowne	8	11	9	80	108	7.4	- 47.97
N Gwilliams	8	8	9	106	131	6.1	- 52.75
J D Smith	7	1	2	34	44	15.9	- 6.61
P Turner	7	8	10	49	74	9.5	- 43.87
J Tate	7	6	10	54	77	9.1	- 27.25
Antoinette Armes	7	4	4	72	87	8.0	- 9.50
P McCabe	6	2	2	25	35	17.1	+ 44.50
H Bastiman	6	6	3	52	67	9.0	- 24.00
S Mulvey	6	6	5	55	72	8.3	- 40.03
D Wright	6	4	5	77	92	6.5	- 9.90
J Marshall	5	8	6	48	67	7.5	- 42.75
S O'Gorman	5	9	14	116	144	3.5	- 74.25
M Harris	4	2	1	27	34	11.8	- 5.50
E Husband	4	8	5	22	39	10.3	- 15.83
R Havlin	4	2	2	52	60	6.7	- 28.50
Kim McDonnell	4	2	13	44	63	6.3	- 14.00
P Bowe	4	8	5	56	73	5.5	- 37.50
Claire Balding	4	9	11	81	105	3.8	- 59.50
E Bentley	3	5	4	11	23	13.0	- 11.87
G Mitchell	3	3	3	22	31	9.7	- 19.25
T G McLaughlin	3	2	4	27	36	8.3	0.00
J Hunter	3	3	5	26	37	8.1	- 10.50
S Wynne	3	6	7	29	45	6.7	- 16.87
V Halliday	3	6	6	30	45	6.7	+ 2.00
C Avery	3	2	5	63	73	4.1	- 25.50
G Forster	3	4	4	68	79	3.8	- 50.00
D Meredith	2	0	2	4	8	25.0	+ 6.50
Sally Radford-Howes	2	0	1	5	8	25.0	+ 9.00
A Lakeman	2	0	0	6	8	25.0	+ 2.75
J Corrigan	2	0	2	7	11	18.2	+ 11.00
F Arrowsmith	2	1	1	8	12	16.7	+ 7.00
S Eiffert	2	1	0	9	12	16.7	+ 16.00
T Ashley	2	1	1	8	12	16.7	- 4.50

	1st	2nd	3rd	Unpl	Total Mts	Per cent	£1 Level Stake
Nicola Howarth	2	3	0	13	18	11.1	− 8.50
L Carter	2	1	1	20	24	8.3	− 15.00
M Baird	2	4	1	19	26	7.7	+ 29.50
V Bray	2	5	4	17	28	7.1	− 2.00
M Denaro	2	4	3	27	36	5.6	− 28.12
C Hodgson	2	1	3	41	47	4.3	− 33.50
L Newton	2	2	4	42	50	4.0	− 15.50
G Parkin	2	4	2	51	59	3.4	− 42.80
R Burke	1	0	0	1	2	50.0	+ 24.00
M Bressington	1	1	0	1	3	33.3	+ 1.50
K Pattinson	1	0	0	3	4	25.0	− 2.64
G Husband	1	2	0	2	5	20.0	− 3.20
Ruth Coulter	1	0	1	3	5	20.0	+ 2.50
A Bates	1	0	0	4	5	20.0	− 2.80
Hayley Williams	1	0	0	4	5	20.0	+ 4.00
P Houghton	1	0	1	4	6	16.7	+ 5.00
C Scally	1	1	0	5	7	14.3	− 4.90
R Waterfield	1	1	0	8	10	10.0	+ 16.00
Madeleine Smith	1	1	0	9	11	9.1	0.00
Ross Berry	1	2	0	8	11	9.1	− 6.50
M Godsafe	1	1	3	7	12	8.3	+ 3.00
Mark Denaro	1	0	4	10	15	6.7	− 9.00
D McCabe	1	1	1	12	15	6.7	− 6.00
C Munday	1	0	1	14	16	6.3	− 11.00
M Jermy	1	1	1	13	16	6.3	+ 1.00
A Dobbin	1	2	2	12	17	5.9	− 8.00
M Hunt	1	3	2	18	24	4.2	− 14.00
D Gibbs	1	2	3	18	24	4.2	− 7.00
P Roberts	1	3	2	18	24	4.2	− 15.00
J Dennis	1	0	0	27	28	3.6	− 22.00
C Teague	1	4	5	21	31	3.2	− 10.00
D Toole	1	0	3	29	33	3.0	− 18.00
D Carson	1	1	3	31	36	2.8	− 25.00

WINNING AMATEUR RIDERS 1992

	1st	2nd	3rd	Unpl	Total Mts	Per cent	£1 Level Stake
Mrs L Pearce	13	5	3	19	40	32.5	+ 17.05
Miss E Houghton	4	0	0	4	8	50.0	+ 25.18
Miss I D W Jones	4	3	4	14	25	16.0	+ 1.50
D Salter	2	1	0	6	9	22.2	+ 49.50
Miss L Hide	2	0	0	9	11	18.2	+ 4.50
Miss J Allison	2	3	1	8	14	14.3	+ 4.00
Mrs A Farrell	2	2	1	10	15	13.3	+ 4.00
Miss J Feilden	2	2	6	7	17	11.8	+ 1.50
S Whitaker	1	0	0	0	1	100.0	+ 11.00
Mrs V Leng	1	0	0	0	1	100.0	+ 4.50
E Reitel	1	0	0	0	1	100.0	+ 2.00
P Daw	1	0	0	0	1	100.0	+ 7.00
Mrs S Cumani	1	0	0	1	2	50.0	− 0.20
Mrs J Musson	1	0	1	0	2	50.0	+ 1.25
Mrs D Arbuthnot	1	0	0	1	2	50.0	+ 15.00
R Farrant	1	0	0	1	2	50.0	+ 9.00
F Grasso-Caprioli	1	0	0	1	2	50.0	+ 3.50

	1st	2nd	3rd	Unpl	Total Mts	Per cent	£1 Level Stake
M Buckley	1	0	1	1	3	33.3	+ 5.50
C Vigors	1	0	2	0	3	33.3	+ 1.33
R D Green	1	1	0	1	3	33.3	+ 2.50
S Swiers	1	2	0	1	4	25.0	+ 2.00
Mrs S Hobbs	1	0	0	3	4	25.0	+ 6.00
Mrs D Kettlewell	1	0	0	4	5	20.0	+ 16.00
Miss J Winter	1	0	0	5	6	16.7	- 2.00
Miss L Perratt	1	0	1	4	6	16.7	+ 0.50
Miss L Eaton	1	1	0	4	6	16.7	+ 7.00
Mrs G Bell	1	0	1	4	6	16.7	+ 9.00
J Durkan	1	1	0	4	6	16.7	- 2.00
P Close	1	0	0	6	7	14.3	+ 10.00
W McLaughlin	1	0	1	5	7	14.3	+ 6.00
Miss M Clark	1	2	1	4	8	12.5	+ 5.00
Mrs Sarah Easterby	1	1	0	6	8	12.5	- 4.50
Mrs G Rees	1	0	0	8	9	11.1	+ 4.00
Mrs J Boggis	1	0	3	5	9	11.1	- 5.25
R Wilkinson	1	2	0	7	10	10.0	0.00
Miss M Juster	1	2	1	9	13	7.7	- 6.00
Miss P Robson	1	2	1	10	14	7.1	- 11.50

LEADING TRAINERS' AND OWNERS' PRIZE MONEY 1992

	Races Won	Value £		Races Won	Value £
R Hannon	147	1,150,144	Sheikh Mohammed	185	1,194,098
P Chapple-Hyam	41	989,499	Hamdan Al-Maktoum	102	692,399
C E Brittain	63	972,330	R E Sangster	47	677,228
M R Stoute	74	863,611	K Abdulla	76	620,349
H R A Cecil	109	735,088	Maktoum Al Maktoum	35	437,971
J H M Gosden	112	729,846	W J Gredley	10	417,808
J L Dunlop	75	524,218	Sidney H Craig	1	355,000
G Wragg	44	499,868	Lord Weinstock	21	295,231
I A Balding	36	499,096	Lord Carnavon	14	265,167
P F I Cole	85	432,485	Mrs Virginia Kraft	1	261,216
Lord Huntingdon	55	384,388	Fahd Salman	51	259,243
L M Cumani	54	357,579	Sheikh Ahmed Al Maktoum	34	213,184

LEADING TRAINERS FIRST TIME OUT 1988-92*

	Total W-R	2-y-o	3-y-o	4-y-o+	Per cent	£1 Level Stake
H R A Cecil	180-620	74-229	96-345	10-46	29.0	+ 41.17
M R Stoute	140-707	68-325	62-334	10-48	19.8	- 109.83
G Harwood	89-480	30-163	48-244	11-73	18.5	- 104.58
B W Hills	86-658	34-291	43-312	9-55	13.1	- 143.73
L M Cumani	84-464	21-149	49-268	14-47	18.1	- 110.93
J Berry	84-549	58-358	20-137	6-54	15.3	- 40.64
J H M Gosden	75-413	27-134	40-240	8-39	18.2	- 8.99
P F I Cole	73-537	44-236	18-213	11-88	13.6	- 176.27
H Thomson Jones	55-271	33-106	19-131	3-34	20.3	- 12.51
Lord Huntingdon	48-306	12-109	25-132	11-65	15.7	+ 88.04
J L Dunlop	46-599	24-250	16-269	6-80	7.7	- 238.95
R Hannon	46-726	25-380	18-264	3-82	6.3	- 398.12
W R Hern	43-250	19-91	20-135	4-24	17.2	- 66.83
C E Brittain	43-564	13-213	17-238	13-113	7.6	- 176.81
A C Stewart	42-292	12-83	23-177	7-32	14.4	- 65.28
D R C Elsworth	37-366	13-129	10-133	14-104	10.1	- 21.04
I A Balding	36-416	13-171	16-176	7-69	8.7	- 140.06
Sir Mark Prescott	34-266	12-128	18-107	4-31	12.8	- 93.24
G Wragg	30-242	11-79	14-130	5-33	12.4	- 75.00
P T Walwyn	30-320	7-136	19-154	4-30	9.4	- 72.97
M H Easterby	30-430	16-181	8-134	6-115	7.0	- 193.40
B Hanbury	27-333	5-130	18-172	4-31	8.1	- 141.80
R Charlton	26-146	11-58	13-72	2-16	17.8	+ 10.41
A A Scott	26-223	15-116	10-93	1-14	11.7	- 64.62
W A O'Gorman	24-162	11-85	8-53	5-24	14.8	- 64.32
M H Tompkins	24-361	3-143	9-113	12-105	6.6	- 151.95
J W Watts	23-223	9-82	7-106	7-35	10.3	- 58.81
R Hollinshead	23-419	2-147	13-144	8-128	5.5	- 108.25
C R Nelson	22-166	4-53	12-81	6-32	13.3	- 9.06
H Candy	22-248	5-72	10-115	7-61	8.9	+ 33.05
Mrs J Ramsden	20-184	4-59	8-67	8-58	10.9	- 17.09
M Bell	20-191	7-101	13-64	0-26	10.5	- 76.06
R W Armstrong	19-196	12-69	4-96	3-31	9.7	- 64.45
R Akehurst	19-268	0-42	5-76	14-150	7.1	- 83.52
R M Whitaker	19-287	6-90	5-98	8-99	6.6	- 111.62
Mrs L Piggott	18-192	3-51	12-107	3-34	9.4	- 64.31
J W Hills	17-196	5-75	7-87	5-34	8.7	+ 2.50
T D Barron	17-206	3-76	6-62	8-68	8.3	- 109.34
N A Callaghan	17-209	4-90	10-89	3-30	8.1	- 56.77
P J Makin	17-213	1-56	10-94	6-63	8.0	- 41.50
M A Jarvis	17-262	6-107	11-121	0-34	6.5	- 118.12
W Jarvis	17-277	9-121	7-117	1-39	6.1	- 122.60
M S Johnston	16-166	2-72	10-61	4-33	9.6	- 21.87
C Tinkler	16-190	9-104	1-42	6-44	8.4	- 80.91
M Brittain	16-344	4-133	8-114	4-97	4.7	- 164.25
M J Ryan	15-181	4-49	4-64	7-68	8.3	- 16.50
S G Norton	15-244	6-110	7-101	2-33	6.1	- 127.87
P Chapple-Hyam	13-98	7-64	5-30	1-4	13.3	- 15.70
A Bailey	13-130	8-43	4-49	1-38	10.0	- 43.75
J Etherington	13-167	7-72	4-68	2-27	7.8	- 34.75
W J Haggas	13-169	2-60	9-81	2-28	7.7	- 104.26
P A Kelleway	13-179	4-87	7-66	2-26	7.3	- 83.88
D Morley	13-184	6-72	6-83	1-29	7.1	- 39.12
B A McMahon	13-208	2-53	2-62	9-93	6.3	+ 29.00

	Total W-R	2-y-o	3-y-o	4-y-o+	Per cent	£1 Level Stake
R F Johnson Houghton	12-179	4-64	6-89	2-26	6.7	- 77.37
G Lewis	12-243	6-109	4-90	2-44	4.9	-118.12
J R Fanshawe	11-124	3-51	7-62	1-11	8.9	- 3.90
R J Hodges	11-181	2-25	1-41	8-115	6.1	- 68.87
J G FitzGerald	11-193	1-59	4-69	6-65	5.7	-107.18
D J G Murray Smith	10-93	3-33	5-35	2-25	10.8	+ 7.73
M J Camacho	10-116	2-40	5-45	3-31	8.6	+ 4.25
D W P Arbuthnot	10-136	2-39	2-58	6-39	7.4	- 51.00
J Wharton	10-164	3-58	3-55	4-51	6.1	+ 16.50
F H Lee	10-174	2-55	3-57	5-62	5.7	- 34.50
Mrs G R Reveley	10-198	1-47	2-52	7-99	5.1	-114.55
N Tinkler	10-230	5-80	0-49	5-101	4.3	-138.00
Mrs J Cecil	9-75	4-38	5-32	0-5	12.0	- 33.57
M C Pipe	9-87	0-4	3-16	6-67	10.3	- 17.83
R Guest	9-106	3-41	3-44	3-21	8.5	- 37.45
M McCormack	9-131	1-59	5-46	3-26	6.9	- 30.13
R Boss	9-161	6-75	3-66	0-20	5.6	-105.32
G B Balding	9-182	2-54	2-61	5-67	4.9	- 78.37
D W Chapman	9-204	0-26	1-58	8-120	4.4	- 41.37
T Thomson Jones	8-86	2-31	4-33	2-22	9.3	+ 9.00
Dr J D Scargill	8-140	2-61	4-49	2-30	5.7	- 60.00
R J R Williams	8-179	2-60	2-82	4-37	4.5	-125.00
Miss B Sanders	7-97	0-17	2-24	5-56	7.2	- 46.00
J Pearce	7-99	1-26	2-34	4-39	7.1	- 15.62
C W C Elsey	7-115	0-31	6-42	1-42	6.1	- 53.25
L J Holt	7-126	2-46	5-46	0-34	5.6	- 17.00
P Mitchell	7-140	2-48	1-43	4-49	5.0	- 85.42
T Fairhurst	7-145	2-56	1-50	4-39	4.8	- 56.25
G M Moore	7-147	0-24	2-31	5-92	4.8	- 72.00
C F Wall	7-171	4-74	3-73	0-24	4.1	- 76.00
G A Pritchard-Gordon	7-247	3-104	4-97	0-46	2.8	-193.00
D Burchell	6-69	0-5	0-10	6-54	8.7	+ 7.00
Lady Herries	6-76	0-18	2-20	4-38	7.9	+ 6.50
J A R Toller	6-83	2-19	3-43	1-21	7.2	+ 6.75
M O'Neill	6-92	1-20	1-34	4-38	6.5	- 4.50
K T Ivory	6-101	0-24	1-33	5-44	5.9	+ 8.00
Pat Mitchell	6-101	2-36	2-30	2-35	5.9	+ 28.00
M R Channon	6-111	3-46	2-38	1-27	5.4	- 37.00
P C Haslam	6-114	0-41	5-43	1-30	5.3	- 71.42
C N Allen	6-126	1-45	4-43	1-38	4.8	- 60.83
C W Thornton	6-142	4-55	1-53	1-34	4.2	- 34.00
Mrs N Macauley	6-159	2-49	4-51	0-59	3.8	-115.37
M D I Usher	6-163	2-67	2-59	2-37	3.7	- 34.00
Denys Smith	5-181	2-61	1-59	2-61	2.8	-107.00
M W Easterby	5-241	1-129	3-61	1-51	2.1	-184.00

*Five or more winners to qualify

LEADING TRAINERS SECOND TIME OUT 1988-92*

	Total W-R	2-y-o	3-y-o	4-y-o+	Per cent	£1 Level Stake
H R A Cecil	167-454	55-114	104-301	8-39	36.8	+ 9.37
L M Cumani	124-387	35-98	84-246	5-43	32.0	- 28.11
M R Stoute	119-534	44-182	65-307	10-45	22.3	-184.90
G Harwood	98-374	25-97	63-215	10-62	26.2	+ 0.01
B W Hills	94-539	39-195	50-292	5-52	17.4	-144.89
J H M Gosden	86-317	25-80	56-203	5-34	27.1	- 38.42
J L Dunlop	83-525	37-206	32-250	14-69	15.8	- 93.68
J Berry	82-519	62-337	16-132	4-50	15.8	- 95.93
R Hannon	73-678	48-353	18-253	7-72	10.8	-281.87
P F I Cole	68-450	35-183	25-192	8-75	15.1	-141.75
C E Brittain	51-484	17-159	24-219	10-106	10.5	-154.16
A C Stewart	47-225	8-44	31-152	8-29	20.9	- 42.16
I A Balding	44-353	23-124	16-163	5-66	12.5	- 93.52
P T Walwyn	40-283	18-103	17-151	5-29	14.1	- 13.69
G Wragg	39-205	10-52	23-123	6-30	19.0	- 28.85
Lord Huntingdon	38-256	10-77	16-122	12-57	14.8	- 26.51
M H Easterby	37-396	21-165	10-126	6-105	9.3	-211.77
Sir Mark Prescott	36-240	14-109	17-102	5-29	15.0	- 81.17
H Thomson Jones	35-231	20-84	11-116	4-31	15.2	- 98.19
D R C Elsworth	35-297	14-92	11-121	10-84	11.8	- 45.76
M H Tompkins	34-320	16-127	8-103	10-90	10.6	- 89.89
B Hanbury	31-278	17-98	11-150	3-30	11.2	- 68.23
R Charlton	29-118	12-35	14-68	3-15	24.6	- 16.61
W R Hern	29-182	8-48	19-116	2-18	15.9	- 80.72
J W Watts	27-203	10-70	14-98	3-35	13.3	- 19.43
W Jarvis	27-222	14-80	9-105	4-37	12.2	- 97.91
R Hollinshead	26-385	8-130	9-139	9-116	6.8	-157.55
M Bell	25-170	21-88	4-60	0-22	14.7	- 23.54
A A Scott	25-177	12-80	12-85	1-12	14.1	- 86.15
M A Jarvis	25-232	7-84	16-117	2-31	10.8	-103.50
W J Haggas	23-138	11-46	11-68	1-24	16.7	+ 40.52
G Lewis	23-229	13-99	4-87	6-43	10.0	- 79.35
R Akehurst	23-244	4-40	4-70	15-134	9.4	+ 15.09
P J Makin	22-182	5-43	10-84	7-55	12.1	+ 1.59
B A McMahon	22-187	2-48	7-61	13-78	11.8	+ 0.08
T D Barron	22-195	4-70	7-60	11-65	11.3	- 50.15
R W Armstrong	21-159	14-50	6-85	1-24	13.2	- 4.71
J W Hills	21-173	4-58	13-82	4-33	12.1	- 30.04
S G Norton	21-220	9-99	9-96	3-25	9.5	- 87.63
Mrs G R Reveley	20-181	4-45	5-50	11-86	11.0	- 46.49
P Chapple-Hyam	18-78	13-46	5-29	0-3	23.1	+ 6.58
C R Nelson	17-143	12-45	2-69	3-29	11.9	- 35.29
R F Johnson Houghton	17-155	6-51	8-83	3-21	11.0	- 29.19
R M Whitaker	17-251	6-80	4-86	7-85	6.8	-154.25
W A O'Gorman	16-127	8-60	4-45	4-22	12.6	- 76.30
R Boss	16-139	8-60	7-64	1-15	11.5	- 55.74
J G FitzGerald	16-159	5-54	5-57	6-48	10.1	- 12.42
Mrs J Ramsden	16-172	4-57	5-63	7-52	9.3	- 95.32
N A Callaghan	16-182	7-82	7-77	2-23	8.8	- 72.18
M Brittain	16-314	6-117	7-107	3-90	5.1	-160.92
M S Johnston	15-152	8-66	5-55	2-31	9.9	- 26.92
H Candy	15-207	4-44	6-109	5-54	7.2	- 86.87
M J Camacho	14-107	3-35	4-44	7-28	13.1	- 14.61
D Morley	14-169	9-63	4-78	1-28	8.3	- 29.17

	Total W-R	2-y-o	3-y-o	4-y-o+	Per cent	£1 Level Stake
R J R Williams	13-156	7-47	5-75	1-34	8.3	- 62.37
P A Kelleway	13-163	9-74	3-65	1-24	8.0	- 76.79
Mrs J Cecil	12-55	6-24	5-27	1-4	21.8	+ 51.86
Dr J D Scargill	12-122	7-53	4-44	1-25	9.8	- 73.19
Denys Smith	12-155	9-54	1-55	2-46	7.7	- 90.63
M J Ryan	12-163	2-44	5-59	5-60	7.4	- 58.46
G A Pritchard-Gordon	12-220	7-91	4-92	1-37	5.5	- 80.70
G M Moore	11-129	3-24	2-29	6-76	8.5	- 35.92
J Wharton	11-143	2-52	4-51	5-40	7.7	- 42.50
J Etherington	11-161	6-68	4-67	1-26	6.8	- 92.12
Mrs L Piggott	11-163	3-36	5-100	3-27	6.7	- 70.20
F H Lee	11-164	6-53	1-55	4-56	6.7	- 59.45
C Tinkler	11-177	9-100	1-40	1-37	6.2	-121.85
M W Easterby	11-212	6-117	2-55	3-40	5.2	-155.77
M R Channon	10-100	1-41	6-36	3-23	10.0	- 21.04
C F Wall	10-137	6-50	4-67	0-20	7.3	- 92.73
W Carter	10-148	5-54	3-53	2-41	6.8	- 27.25
M C Pipe	9-64	0-2	1-11	8-51	14.1	- 15.87
M O'Neill	9-83	2-17	4-29	3-37	10.8	+ 38.00
P Calver	9-84	1-26	2-33	6-25	10.7	- 4.40
C W C Elsey	9-102	2-27	5-39	2-36	8.8	- 23.17
J R Fanshawe	9-106	6-38	3-59	0-9	8.5	- 43.73
C N Allen	9-108	3-38	5-39	1-31	8.3	- 50.51
R J Hodges	9-147	2-21	2-31	5-95	6.1	- 60.00
G B Balding	9-166	1-50	3-58	5-58	5.4	- 96.30
Lady Herries	8-67	1-14	1-19	6-34	11.9	- 11.50
J A R Toller	8-69	1-13	4-37	3-19	11.6	- 24.02
P S Felgate	8-96	1-31	2-32	5-33	8.3	- 19.62
M J Haynes	8-98	5-26	0-36	3-36	8.2	+ 5.50
C J Hill	8-119	1-23	2-41	5-55	6.7	- 36.00
Mrs N Macauley	8-136	2-42	3-47	3-47	5.9	- 74.75
N A Graham	7-68	5-31	2-28	0-9	10.3	- 16.17
J Mackie	7-75	0-8	1-18	6-49	9.3	- 1.00
Miss B Sanders	7-80	2-12	2-24	3-44	8.8	- 28.50
A Hide	7-94	3-24	2-43	2-27	7.4	- 26.67
M J Fetherston-Godley	7-103	2-37	3-43	2-23	6.8	- 66.34
M P Naughton	7-108	0-7	2-19	5-82	6.5	- 61.29
L G Cottrell	7-117	0-22	1-32	6-63	6.0	- 63.00
M McCormack	7-123	3-55	2-45	2-23	5.7	- 85.60
T Fairhurst	7-134	2-54	1-46	4-34	5.2	- 45.62
D W Chapman	7-188	2-24	1-56	4-108	3.7	-110.62
W W Haigh	6-83	1-24	1-25	4-34	7.2	- 23.14
W J Musson	6-102	2-26	1-29	3-47	5.9	- 65.50
J Sutcliffe	6-108	4-36	1-43	1-29	5.6	- 73.62
A Bailey	6-119	3-39	0-45	3-35	5.0	- 78.42
N Tinkler	6-190	2-68	1-44	3-78	3.2	-150.87

*Six or more winners to qualify

LEADING TRAINERS BY MONTH 1988-92

January

	Total W-R	2-y-o	3-y-o	4-y-o+	Per cent	£1 Level Stake
T D Barron	21-77	0-0	11-31	10-46	27.3	- 3.60
W A O'Gorman	11-45	0-0	3-21	8-24	24.4	- 8.91
D W Chapman	10-94	0-0	4-25	6-69	10.6	- 29.42
R Hollinshead	8-51	0-0	3-19	5-32	15.7	- 7.37
D J G Murray Smith	5-16	0-0	4-8	1-8	31.3	+ 15.31
M S Johnston	5-23	0-0	1-7	4-16	21.7	- 0.25
Mrs N Macauley	5-53	0-0	5-23	0-30	9.4	- 36.37
J Berry	4-12	0-0	4-9	0-3	33.3	+ 14.50
R Akehurst	4-15	0-0	2-2	2-13	26.7	- 4.27
C Tinkler	4-15	0-0	0-0	4-15	26.7	- 5.12
C C Elsey	4-15	0-0	0-3	4-12	26.7	+ 12.33
J Wharton	4-19	0-0	2-10	2-9	21.1	+ 17.50
J L Harris	4-21	0-0	1-6	3-15	19.0	+ 11.25
J A Glover	4-23	0-0	0-2	4-21	17.4	+ 4.75
P A Kelleway	4-25	0-0	2-8	2-17	16.0	- 8.25
M J Ryan	4-28	0-0	0-3	4-25	14.3	- 10.37
A Bailey	4-35	0-0	0-9	4-26	11.4	- 6.75
C N Allen	4-36	0-0	4-24	0-12	11.1	- 2.83
J F Bottomley	3-9	0-0	0-1	3-8	33.3	+ 20.75
G B Balding	3-10	0-0	0-0	3-10	30.0	+ 2.20
N A Callaghan	3-11	0-0	2-6	1-5	27.3	+ 7.88
D T Thom	3-11	0-0	1-3	2-8	27.3	+ 7.75
D W P Arbuthnot	3-13	0-0	0-3	3-10	23.1	+ 5.50

February

	Total W-R	2-y-o	3-y-o	4-y-o+	Per cent	£1 Level Stake
T D Barron	14-53	0-0	6-22	8-31	26.4	- 1.10
C N Allen	7-39	0-0	6-26	1-13	17.9	- 5.14
Dr J D Scargill	6-21	0-0	1-4	5-17	28.6	+ 13.73
Mrs A Knight	5-15	0-0	0-0	5-15	33.3	+ 68.50
B W Hills	4-6	0-0	3-5	1-1	66.7	+ 1.93
C R Nelson	4-12	0-0	1-4	3-8	33.3	- 1.12
C P Wildman	4-17	0-0	0-3	4-14	23.5	+ 14.00
K O C-Brown	4-18	0-0	0-0	4-18	22.2	+ 5.25
M Brittain	4-26	0-0	3-12	1-14	15.4	+ 8.25
R Hollinshead	4-34	0-0	3-15	1-19	11.8	- 3.77
W A O'Gorman	4-38	0-0	2-18	2-20	10.5	- 18.62
T Thomson Jones	3-9	0-0	0-2	3-7	33.3	+ 14.00
R Akehurst	3-11	0-0	1-2	2-9	27.3	- 3.82
M J Fetherston-Godley	3-13	0-0	1-7	2-6	23.1	- 0.01
D J G Murray Smith	3-16	0-0	0-4	3-12	18.8	+ 5.50
C C Elsey	3-16	0-0	0-4	3-12	18.8	- 1.40
C J Hill	3-17	0-0	1-4	2-13	17.6	+ 24.00
D T Thom	3-18	0-0	0-5	3-13	16.7	+ 24.12
M S Johnston	3-19	0-0	1-5	2-14	15.8	+ 9.00
J Pearce	3-20	0-0	2-5	1-15	15.0	- 6.00
P Mitchell	3-21	0-0	0-6	3-15	14.3	- 8.67
S Dow	3-28	0-0	1-8	2-20	10.7	- 11.25
D W Chapman	3-59	0-0	2-13	1-46	5.1	- 39.67

March

	Total W-R	2-y-o	3-y-o	4-y-o+	Per cent	£1 Level Stake
J Berry	25-104	14-51	6-34	5-19	24.0	+ 59.09
W A O'Gorman	15-46	2-5	8-20	5-21	32.6	+ 12.70
T D Barron	13-77	0-15	3-22	10-40	16.9	+ 6.16
C E Brittain	12-84	0-0	4-43	8-41	14.3	- 5.22
M Brittain	11-143	1-28	6-56	4-59	7.7	- 53.00
B W Hills	9-28	1-3	7-18	1-7	32.1	+ 3.11
M R Channon	8-31	1-2	2-14	5-15	25.8	+ 40.00
Mrs J Ramsden	8-60	0-1	3-31	5-28	13.3	- 18.92
R Hollinshead	7-121	1-17	6-46	0-58	5.8	- 44.00
Sir Mark Prescott	6-25	0-0	5-19	1-6	24.0	- 0.35
Lord Huntingdon	6-33	0-0	3-18	3-15	18.2	+ 9.00
C Tinkler	6-41	2-10	1-10	3-21	14.6	+ 0.25
M Bell	6-41	1-8	5-22	0-11	14.6	- 5.25
S G Norton	6-44	0-0	4-27	2-17	13.6	- 4.62
M J Ryan	6-45	0-0	4-18	2-27	13.3	+ 6.00
T Fairhurst	6-47	2-17	0-13	4-17	12.8	+ 6.63
R Hannon	6-77	2-16	4-34	0-27	7.8	- 48.62
J H M Gosden	5-11	0-0	4-10	1-1	45.5	+ 18.80
P F I Cole	5-29	0-1	3-18	2-10	17.2	- 8.75
P Mitchell	5-33	1-2	0-13	4-18	15.2	+ 2.50
P A Kelleway	5-36	0-7	2-13	3-16	13.9	- 13.21
M S Johnston	5-44	0-3	3-20	2-21	11.4	- 14.20
Miss B Sanders	4-13	0-0	1-6	3-7	30.8	+ 13.50
C R Nelson	4-14	0-0	2-8	2-6	28.6	- 2.74
J G FitzGerald	4-18	0-1	1-1	3-16	22.2	+ 35.25
N A Callaghan	4-25	0-0	2-19	2-6	16.0	+ 8.20
P C Haslam	4-27	0-0	3-8	1-19	14.8	+ 0.23
G Wragg	4-27	0-0	4-21	0-6	14.8	- 18.68
M W Easterby	4-41	1-11	0-12	3-18	9.8	- 18.25
Mrs N Macauley	4-52	0-1	3-29	1-22	7.7	- 12.00
N Tinkler	4-65	2-17	0-11	2-37	6.2	- 47.50
J Etherington	3-6	0-1	1-2	2-3	50.0	+ 23.00
W W Haigh	3-11	0-0	0-1	3-10	27.3	+ 4.25
D Morley	3-11	1-1	2-6	0-4	27.3	+ 31.38
I Campbell	3-11	0-0	0-4	3-7	27.3	+ 4.88
P T Walwyn	3-12	0-0	3-8	0-4	25.0	- 6.20
M C Pipe	3-13	0-0	1-2	2-11	23.1	- 5.47
K O C-Brown	3-16	0-0	0-2	3-14	18.8	+ 7.25
J Pearce	3-16	0-0	0-3	3-13	18.8	- 2.62
R Boss	3-17	1-2	2-9	0-6	17.6	+ 7.00
D R C Elsworth	3-18	0-0	1-7	2-11	16.7	- 6.87
Mrs L Piggott	3-24	0-0	2-13	1-11	12.5	0.00
R J O'Sullivan	3-25	0-0	0-0	3-25	12.0	+ 36.00
C A Cyzer	3-26	0-0	0-9	3-17	11.5	- 9.50
M H Tompkins	3-27	0-1	3-9	0-17	11.1	- 13.75
R M Whitaker	3-29	1-3	1-14	1-12	10.3	- 3.75
R Akehurst	3-30	0-0	0-4	3-26	10.0	- 13.50
B A McMahon	3-31	1-3	1-12	1-16	9.7	+ 9.00
A Bailey	3-32	1-2	2-8	0-22	9.4	- 15.25
S Dow	3-49	1-3	0-19	2-27	6.1	- 6.00

April

	Total W-R	2-y-o	3-y-o	4-y-o+	Per cent	£1 Level Stake
H R A Cecil	77-207	0-0	66-174	11-33	37.2	+ 39.29
J Berry	71-383	40-172	23-149	8-62	18.5	- 50.16
R Hannon	40-388	19-101	16-212	5-75	10.3	- 82.39
C E Brittain	36-278	1-10	22-180	13-88	12.9	+ 71.50
M R Stoute	35-186	0-1	30-154	5-31	18.8	- 64.53
M H Easterby	34-273	11-72	14-105	9-96	12.5	- 62.96
P F I Cole	26-227	3-26	17-146	6-55	11.5	- 97.05
M Brittain	25-364	4-60	13-161	8-143	6.9	-112.50
Mrs J Ramsden	24-169	0-6	12-84	12-79	14.2	- 52.31
L M Cumani	23-122	0-0	18-99	5-23	18.9	- 35.70
B W Hills	22-230	2-12	15-181	5-37	9.6	- 56.03
R Hollinshead	22-280	3-49	8-129	11-102	7.9	- 71.92
J H M Gosden	21-104	0-0	16-74	5-30	20.2	- 13.81
P T Walwyn	21-134	0-1	14-101	7-32	15.7	+ 18.14
G Harwood	20-89	0-1	18-62	2-26	22.5	- 18.18
Sir Mark Prescott	20-104	0-1	14-78	6-25	19.2	- 21.51
J L Dunlop	20-219	0-2	15-155	5-62	9.1	- 78.85
G Wragg	18-125	1-3	13-93	4-29	14.4	- 33.29
G Lewis	18-177	6-38	5-91	7-48	10.2	- 26.12
B Hanbury	17-144	0-8	12-113	5-23	11.8	- 45.68
M J Camacho	15-59	0-3	6-32	9-24	25.4	+ 62.76
Lord Huntingdon	15-83	0-3	8-45	7-35	18.1	+ 28.92
J W Watts	15-121	0-4	10-86	5-31	12.4	- 15.36
N A Callaghan	15-135	4-29	9-78	2-28	11.1	- 37.63
R J Hodges	14-123	2-2	2-27	10-94	11.4	- 2.12
I A Balding	14-155	1-3	9-104	4-48	9.0	- 61.42
M Bell	13-101	4-26	8-53	1-22	12.9	- 29.62
B A McMahon	13-110	0-15	7-49	6-46	11.8	+ 3.75
C R Nelson	12-96	1-9	6-50	5-37	12.5	- 3.96
W R Hern	11-65	0-0	8-53	3-12	16.9	- 29.84
W A O'Gorman	11-66	8-21	3-29	0-16	16.7	- 30.44
A A Scott	11-71	1-5	10-56	0-10	15.5	+ 5.78
M McCormack	11-76	2-20	6-37	3-19	14.5	+ 16.63
G M Moore	11-80	4-11	3-19	4-50	13.8	+ 4.10
M A Jarvis	11-115	0-4	9-86	2-25	9.6	+ 8.05
M W Easterby	11-149	2-52	5-48	4-49	7.4	- 76.39
R Akehurst	10-118	0-1	1-13	9-104	8.5	- 12.50
M J Ryan	10-121	0-0	5-51	5-70	8.3	- 15.62
T D Barron	10-143	0-27	3-52	7-64	7.0	- 67.25
A C Stewart	9-66	0-0	6-57	3-9	13.6	- 9.09
H Candy	9-83	0-0	5-49	4-34	10.8	+ 41.25
M S Johnston	9-89	0-15	8-45	1-29	10.1	- 24.30
Mrs L Piggott	9-91	0-0	8-65	1-26	9.9	- 27.25
W Carter	9-118	6-25	2-55	1-38	7.6	- 3.50
Dr J D Scargill	8-64	3-15	5-36	0-13	12.5	- 6.25
J Wharton	8-82	2-22	1-31	5-29	9.8	- 8.00
R Boss	8-93	2-15	4-59	2-19	8.6	- 49.79
D R C Elsworth	8-94	1-10	1-41	6-43	8.5	- 33.12
S G Norton	8-109	0-8	7-87	1-14	7.3	- 31.00
C Tinkler	8-121	4-40	1-44	3-37	6.6	- 65.93
N Tinkler	8-177	5-48	1-65	2-64	4.5	-103.00

May

	Total W-R	2-y-o	3-y-o	4-y-o+	Per cent	£1 Level Stake
M R Stoute	98-341	7-15	76-287	15-39	28.7	+ 19.06
J Berry	93-498	68-276	16-163	9-59	18.7	+ 7.47
H R A Cecil	82-288	8-13	70-245	4-30	28.5	- 37.13
R Hannon	80-562	31-166	36-306	13-90	14.2	-164.36
B W Hills	62-349	8-46	45-242	9-61	17.8	- 74.01
L M Cumani	45-190	1-5	38-153	6-32	23.7	- 16.32
G Harwood	43-184	3-11	32-125	8-48	23.4	+ 0.01
M H Easterby	41-400	14-116	13-144	14-140	10.3	-150.34
P F I Cole	37-303	14-41	11-181	12-81	12.2	-130.64
I A Balding	35-241	3-13	18-153	14-75	14.5	+ 27.42
J L Dunlop	35-320	1-13	27-246	7-61	10.9	-119.32
J H M Gosden	32-156	0-7	29-126	3-23	20.5	- 24.11
R M Whitaker	32-267	7-40	10-109	15-118	12.0	+ 1.93
M H Tompkins	31-247	5-50	15-110	11-87	12.6	+ 21.17
Sir Mark Prescott	30-148	3-10	22-99	5-39	20.3	- 9.20
D R C Elsworth	27-208	6-22	10-113	11-73	13.0	- 15.27
C E Brittain	27-367	4-44	13-208	10-115	7.4	-113.29
P T Walwyn	26-216	3-14	19-172	4-30	12.0	- 37.86
G Lewis	26-225	8-62	15-109	3-54	11.6	- 35.86
R Hollinshead	26-366	5-77	12-154	9-135	7.1	-127.12
M Brittain	26-400	5-123	6-154	15-123	6.5	-112.42
G Wragg	25-143	5-10	14-103	6-30	17.5	- 19.38
A C Stewart	23-110	0-1	17-90	6-19	20.9	- 25.76
W Jarvis	23-132	6-22	12-79	5-31	17.4	- 3.71
H Thomson Jones	23-156	5-10	14-117	4-29	14.7	- 44.45
B Hanbury	23-169	2-21	17-125	4-23	13.6	- 20.69
N A Callaghan	23-171	3-42	16-100	4-29	13.5	+ 14.63
M S Johnston	22-127	4-22	11-60	7-45	17.3	+ 27.50
J W Watts	22-180	3-24	10-103	9-53	12.2	- 31.47
A A Scott	20-133	7-20	12-100	1-13	15.0	- 49.98
P J Makin	19-139	1-11	8-73	10-55	13.7	+ 31.73
M A Jarvis	19-153	1-14	16-106	2-33	12.4	- 59.36
C Tinkler	19-189	9-85	4-53	6-51	10.1	- 36.62
Mrs G R Reveley	18-120	3-16	5-30	10-74	15.0	- 6.00
J W Hills	18-123	0-8	9-79	9-36	14.6	+ 2.58
Lord Huntingdon	17-103	2-11	6-63	9-29	16.5	- 5.97
M Bell	17-128	7-37	10-67	0-24	13.3	- 31.17
M J Ryan	17-131	3-17	6-53	8-61	13.0	- 26.86
W R Hern	16-100	0-2	14-83	2-15	16.0	- 43.54
R F Johnson Houghton	16-133	2-20	12-97	2-16	12.0	- 20.59
Mrs J Ramsden	16-161	3-15	6-79	7-67	9.9	- 57.67
S G Norton	16-164	3-25	9-114	4-25	9.8	- 62.77
R Akehurst	16-176	0-7	3-52	13-117	9.1	- 90.67
T D Barron	16-188	7-52	2-61	7-75	8.5	- 75.57
W A O'Gorman	15-106	11-40	4-44	0-22	14.2	- 31.71
D Morley	15-133	0-5	12-92	3-36	11.3	- 29.74
R Charlton	14-73	1-2	10-55	3-16	19.2	- 5.68
R Boss	14-117	4-25	8-69	2-23	12.0	- 45.45
M McCormack	13-124	5-38	6-50	2-36	10.5	- 42.48
H Candy	13-135	1-3	4-73	8-59	9.6	+ 5.63
F H Lee	13-165	2-26	3-64	8-75	7.9	- 60.79

June

	Total W-R	2-y-o	3-y-o	4-y-o+	Per cent	£1 Level Stake
J Berry	91-549	53-322	31-173	7-54	16.6	-127.71
H R A Cecil	78-260	15-31	59-196	4-33	30.0	+ 12.95
J L Dunlop	74-339	12-53	50-221	12-65	21.8	+ 21.15
P F I Cole	68-329	29-95	30-167	9-67	20.7	- 12.39
L M Cumani	64-225	3-10	58-185	3-30	28.4	- 37.29
M R Stoute	61-318	12-34	43-244	6-40	19.2	- 98.06
R Hannon	61-602	23-212	30-288	8-102	10.1	-105.96
J H M Gosden	47-194	7-20	36-146	4-28	24.2	- 14.17
B W Hills	46-293	8-39	35-211	3-43	15.7	-115.28
G Harwood	42-223	6-25	26-146	10-52	18.8	- 22.91
M H Easterby	42-394	18-139	11-128	13-127	10.7	-202.00
C E Brittain	37-369	11-82	22-189	4-98	10.0	-137.86
I A Balding	36-272	4-43	17-154	15-75	13.2	- 22.32
B Hanbury	35-231	11-50	18-148	6-33	15.2	+ 35.20
Lord Huntingdon	31-121	7-24	14-71	10-26	25.6	+113.63
H Thomson Jones	30-167	10-27	17-114	3-26	18.0	+ 13.37
Sir Mark Prescott	30-167	7-41	17-97	6-29	18.0	- 40.58
D R C Elsworth	30-249	4-36	11-121	15-92	12.0	+ 4.54
R Hollinshead	30-355	7-79	8-143	15-133	8.5	-120.73
M A Jarvis	29-177	6-30	16-104	7-43	16.4	- 20.47
P T Walwyn	29-199	3-26	22-138	4-35	14.6	+ 30.65
R Akehurst	28-202	1-20	10-69	17-113	13.9	+ 31.04
S G Norton	28-209	7-57	15-114	6-38	13.4	- 74.30
R M Whitaker	28-254	7-42	10-100	11-112	11.0	- 87.54
A A Scott	27-159	12-42	12-100	3-17	17.0	- 47.84
M H Tompkins	25-281	7-79	10-119	8-83	8.9	-151.61
A C Stewart	24-124	0-2	16-99	8-23	19.4	- 32.00
G Lewis	23-249	6-73	11-116	6-60	9.2	- 87.87
G Wragg	22-125	3-10	16-93	3-22	17.6	- 5.16
N A Callaghan	22-174	7-50	11-93	4-31	12.6	- 49.46
J W Watts	22-175	6-28	12-104	4-43	12.6	- 41.49
B A McMahon	22-197	1-37	4-62	17-98	11.2	- 10.12
R Charlton	21-67	3-13	17-41	1-13	31.3	+ 31.11
P J Makin	21-143	2-15	11-72	8-56	14.7	- 27.57
F H Lee	21-162	3-32	7-60	11-70	13.0	+ 11.83
J Sutcliffe	20-115	1-22	10-58	9-35	17.4	- 2.98
M S Johnston	20-141	5-33	10-58	5-50	14.2	+ 40.07
W A O'Gorman	19-97	11-40	4-37	4-20	19.6	- 18.32
C R Nelson	19-113	6-28	8-55	5-30	16.8	+ 4.33
M P Naughton	19-141	0-3	4-28	15-110	13.5	+ 0.75
Mrs G R Reveley	19-149	2-21	2-43	15-85	12.8	- 53.29
W Jarvis	19-164	5-41	10-87	4-36	11.6	- 76.92
R W Armstrong	17-110	5-16	9-69	3-25	15.5	+ 5.88
W R Hern	17-117	3-17	9-81	5-19	14.5	- 38.10
D Morley	17-133	3-15	8-82	6-36	12.8	- 27.92
Mrs L Piggott	17-154	3-19	7-100	7-35	11.0	- 36.22
Denys Smith	17-198	4-41	6-82	7-75	8.6	-102.12
Mrs J Ramsden	16-160	4-34	6-68	6-58	10.0	- 62.13
T D Barron	16-181	6-39	5-61	5-81	8.8	- 67.37
G A Pritchard-Gordon	16-190	7-43	7-98	2-49	8.4	- 74.66

July

	Total W-R	2-y-o	3-y-o	4-y-o+	Per cent	£1 Level Stake
J Berry	120-634	80-400	26-154	14-80	18.9	-119.77
H R A Cecil	113-281	35-65	76-199	2-17	40.2	+ 22.77
B W Hills	80-353	16-91	57-226	7-36	22.7	- 9.54
R Hannon	79-635	39-297	31-259	9-79	12.4	-174.74
L M Cumani	75-249	5-26	63-191	7-32	30.1	+ 29.45
G Harwood	65-261	14-43	40-161	11-57	24.9	- 2.21
M R Stoute	64-333	17-73	41-230	6-30	19.2	- 72.98
P F I Cole	58-295	21-98	27-139	10-58	19.7	- 26.84
M H Easterby	56-437	20-155	19-147	17-135	12.8	-207.57
I A Balding	51-315	13-81	23-149	15-85	16.2	- 4.34
J L Dunlop	50-317	15-106	30-158	5-53	15.8	- 69.27
Sir Mark Prescott	47-198	12-58	30-107	5-33	23.7	- 11.14
Mrs G R Reveley	45-221	7-39	16-72	22-110	20.4	+ 23.18
G Lewis	40-243	13-78	15-118	12-47	16.5	- 4.16
F H Lee	38-200	7-49	18-80	13-71	19.0	+ 54.04
W R Hern	36-142	13-37	19-89	4-16	25.4	- 10.06
A C Stewart	33-137	6-19	24-98	3-20	24.1	+ 15.50
G Wragg	33-146	9-30	21-96	3-20	22.6	+ 66.66
M H Tompkins	32-285	14-116	7-88	11-81	11.2	-111.92
R M Whitaker	31-283	8-55	6-93	17-135	11.0	- 70.15
R Hollinshead	31-381	9-82	8-153	14-146	8.1	-235.20
B Hanbury	30-167	13-55	16-92	1-20	18.0	- 14.15
D R C Elsworth	30-229	6-43	19-111	5-75	13.1	+ 4.32
W Jarvis	29-151	7-39	15-83	7-29	19.2	+ 44.31
R Akehurst	29-230	2-31	9-80	18-119	12.6	- 1.00
R Boss	27-145	13-58	11-65	3-22	18.6	- 4.72
N A Callaghan	27-180	11-69	12-89	4-22	15.0	- 32.08
P T Walwyn	27-188	8-38	15-130	4-20	14.4	+ 7.83
C Tinkler	27-208	12-104	6-46	9-58	13.0	- 81.31
M P Naughton	26-150	0-5	5-24	21-121	17.3	- 14.41
B A McMahon	26-190	7-41	6-64	13-85	13.7	- 2.65
C E Brittain	26-387	11-113	11-181	4-93	6.7	-210.25
R F Johnson Houghton	25-127	8-27	12-84	5-16	19.7	+ 20.90
R W Armstrong	24-117	12-32	11-69	1-16	20.5	- 5.53
M A Jarvis	24-161	7-39	9-93	8-29	14.9	- 51.13
M W Easterby	24-242	10-121	7-68	7-53	9.9	- 86.17
D W Chapman	24-274	0-22	3-58	21-194	8.8	-103.01
P J Makin	23-127	2-21	14-74	7-32	18.1	- 5.82
G A Pritchard-Gordon	23-184	8-57	13-90	2-37	12.5	- 48.41
R J Hodges	22-162	3-18	4-35	15-109	13.6	- 10.26
H Thomson Jones	21-132	9-27	10-90	2-15	15.9	- 34.96
Mrs J Ramsden	21-135	5-35	10-50	6-50	15.6	- 39.16
D Morley	21-139	5-27	7-76	9-36	15.1	+ 6.67
Lord Huntingdon	20-123	5-29	8-62	7-32	16.3	- 14.67
M Brittain	20-366	6-120	13-139	1-107	5.5	-184.42
W J Haggas	19-86	6-18	11-47	2-21	22.1	- 2.06
W A O'Gorman	19-98	14-48	5-38	0-12	19.4	- 2.81
M J Ryan	19-145	3-34	11-52	5-59	13.1	- 25.66
R J R Williams	19-148	2-29	8-69	9-50	12.8	- 19.32
H Candy	19-162	2-20	12-84	5-58	11.7	- 24.12
M S Johnston	18-134	9-36	5-47	4-51	13.4	- 37.61
A Bailey	18-142	8-49	5-50	5-43	12.7	- 14.09
N Tinkler	18-193	5-74	7-54	6-65	9.3	-119.50
T D Barron	18-212	8-66	4-56	6-90	8.5	- 81.23

August

	Total W-R	2-y-o	3-y-o	4-y-o+	Per cent	£1 Level Stake
H R A Cecil	77-239	37-74	38-147	2-18	32.2	- 40.03
B W Hills	77-367	20-128	47-206	10-33	21.0	- 32.12
R Hannon	71-581	45-310	20-211	6-60	12.2	-113.96
J Berry	69-502	43-313	22-121	4-68	13.7	-156.84
M R Stoute	66-318	27-119	39-175	0-24	20.8	- 37.58
G Harwood	62-284	19-70	39-182	4-32	21.8	- 37.19
L M Cumani	53-223	10-40	38-156	5-27	23.8	- 52.75
M H Easterby	48-362	25-166	12-104	11-92	13.3	-114.97
P F I Cole	47-284	22-127	14-113	11-44	16.5	- 57.58
I A Balding	40-271	14-85	17-118	9-68	14.8	- 0.49
J L Dunlop	38-265	19-112	18-120	1-33	14.3	- 43.29
Sir Mark Prescott	37-171	17-74	15-66	5-31	21.6	+ 27.06
W R Hern	35-140	5-36	27-93	3-11	25.0	+ 13.23
C E Brittain	32-307	9-96	16-144	7-67	10.4	- 5.88
J H M Gosden	30-149	7-35	19-97	4-17	20.1	+ 2.01
R Hollinshead	30-341	9-88	9-124	12-129	8.8	-144.07
A C Stewart	29-150	6-33	22-99	1-18	19.3	- 37.67
G Lewis	28-236	11-103	8-84	9-49	11.9	- 56.54
M H Tompkins	27-234	12-97	8-79	7-58	11.5	-107.25
B Hanbury	25-229	6-88	14-120	5-21	10.9	- 51.46
T D Barron	24-171	11-63	5-37	8-71	14.0	+ 35.95
R Akehurst	24-190	3-30	8-76	13-84	12.6	- 5.00
R M Whitaker	24-284	5-80	8-86	11-118	8.5	-126.65
W Jarvis	23-135	10-49	11-65	2-21	17.0	- 16.66
H Thomson Jones	23-136	9-45	12-80	2-11	16.9	+ 0.12
P T Walwyn	23-192	7-64	16-112	0-16	12.0	- 63.29
D R C Elsworth	23-207	7-56	7-85	9-66	11.1	- 88.74
D W Chapman	23-259	1-21	0-66	22-172	8.9	- 26.17
H Candy	22-171	3-34	13-95	6-42	12.9	+ 20.46
Lord Huntingdon	21-159	7-40	9-75	5-44	13.2	- 29.98
F H Lee	21-180	7-53	5-57	9-70	11.7	- 13.75
Mrs G R Reveley	21-184	2-42	7-55	12-87	11.4	- 73.44
D Morley	19-137	5-43	10-62	4-32	13.9	- 2.45
M Bell	18-134	11-63	5-50	2-21	13.4	- 3.12
J Etherington	18-155	5-64	11-61	2-30	11.6	- 62.08
M W Easterby	18-196	9-113	4-50	5-33	9.2	- 73.55
P J Makin	17-112	2-19	8-54	7-39	15.2	+ 22.16
N Tinkler	17-123	1-53	8-34	8-36	13.8	- 64.88
A A Scott	17-126	9-53	7-67	1-6	13.5	- 58.46
W J Haggas	16-102	6-30	9-52	1-20	15.7	+ 14.06
Mrs L Piggott	16-111	5-28	8-59	3-24	14.4	- 5.25
R Boss	16-124	8-46	6-60	2-18	12.9	- 30.40
R W Armstrong	15-106	6-35	8-55	1-16	14.2	- 22.68
G Wragg	15-127	5-40	10-73	0-14	11.8	- 64.55
M S Johnston	15-138	5-43	6-52	4-43	10.9	- 10.70
Mrs J Ramsden	15-142	5-44	5-58	5-40	10.6	- 2.45
J W Hills	15-142	4-35	6-66	5-41	10.6	- 21.19
M A Jarvis	15-160	3-39	8-86	4-35	9.4	- 63.20
P Chapple-Hyam	14-61	8-32	6-27	0-2	23.0	+ 3.60
M J Ryan	14-102	0-17	7-45	7-40	13.7	+ 8.75
S G Norton	14-106	5-47	3-45	6-14	13.2	- 13.26
N A Callaghan	14-113	7-48	6-49	1-16	12.4	- 49.12
J W Watts	14-129	6-51	7-61	1-17	10.9	- 66.12
Mrs N Macauley	14-188	4-59	2-59	8-70	7.4	- 87.10

September

	Total W-R	2-y-o	3-y-o	4-y-o+	Per cent	£1 Level Stake
L M Cumani	66-301	26-100	37-176	3-25	21.9	- 33.44
B W Hills	64-371	27-163	34-177	3-31	17.3	- 29.88
J L Dunlop	62-390	35-194	21-147	6-49	15.9	- 50.62
H R A Cecil	60-223	27-87	31-122	2-14	26.9	- 28.28
M R Stoute	53-336	37-176	13-138	3-22	15.8	- 94.67
J H M Gosden	51-216	16-52	29-133	6-31	23.6	+ 56.69
R Hannon	47-505	24-269	12-169	11-67	9.3	-147.06
G Harwood	40-240	11-70	26-141	3-29	16.7	- 34.95
J Berry	37-463	26-270	8-124	3-69	8.0	-158.85
I A Balding	34-279	12-114	14-95	8-70	12.2	- 16.25
G Wragg	32-147	6-41	22-95	4-11	21.8	+ 52.63
H Thomson Jones	32-153	17-64	14-69	1-20	20.9	+ 30.94
M H Easterby	30-285	11-120	8-80	11-85	10.5	- 60.68
C E Brittain	30-366	12-141	15-165	3-60	8.2	-115.72
B Hanbury	28-223	11-88	13-122	4-13	12.6	- 25.74
M H Tompkins	28-282	10-123	12-77	6-82	9.9	- 93.15
P F I Cole	27-246	17-132	7-76	3-38	11.0	- 81.62
R Charlton	25-98	13-43	9-45	3-10	25.5	+ 42.76
A C Stewart	25-157	3-45	17-95	5-17	15.9	- 29.66
R M Whitaker	24-283	6-98	8-95	10-90	8.5	- 94.25
Mrs G R Reveley	23-128	4-32	6-35	13-61	18.0	+ 13.13
R W Armstrong	22-125	9-41	9-61	4-23	17.6	+ 86.09
Lord Huntingdon	22-173	5-55	11-83	6-35	12.7	+ 19.04
D Morley	20-144	5-45	13-74	2-25	13.9	+ 18.35
R Akehurst	20-175	6-31	6-60	8-84	11.4	+ 6.67
W Jarvis	19-144	7-53	10-65	2-26	13.2	- 22.38
R F Johnson Houghton	19-148	2-52	17-81	0-15	12.8	- 7.35
Mrs J Ramsden	19-156	8-57	8-55	3-44	12.2	- 49.50
W R Hern	17-114	6-40	9-65	2-9	14.9	- 44.80
W Carter	17-172	3-63	7-58	7-51	9.9	+181.73
J G FitzGerald	16-126	7-48	6-49	3-29	12.7	- 7.43
W J Haggas	15-106	6-45	8-48	1-13	14.2	- 24.79
M A Jarvis	15-159	4-62	7-68	4-29	9.4	- 57.12
D W Chapman	15-205	2-16	2-56	11-133	7.3	- 53.75
C A Cyzer	14-100	5-28	7-46	2-26	14.0	+ 32.50
M Bell	14-119	11-74	2-28	1-17	11.8	- 20.88
G Lewis	14-181	6-86	6-63	2-32	7.7	- 76.05
D R C Elsworth	14-185	6-76	6-62	2-47	7.6	- 92.17
P Chapple-Hyam	13-66	11-42	2-20	0-4	19.7	- 17.04
P J Makin	13-103	1-26	5-44	7-33	12.6	+ 8.13
J W Hills	13-147	3-50	7-59	3-38	8.8	- 18.00
H Candy	13-193	2-52	9-94	2-47	6.7	-106.65
P T Walwyn	13-209	5-74	8-112	0-23	6.2	-138.00
R Boss	12-91	7-45	4-43	1-3	13.2	- 9.12
T D Barron	12-152	9-64	0-48	3-40	7.9	- 72.29
M J Camacho	11-86	4-29	4-30	3-27	12.8	+ 34.25
G A Pritchard-Gordon	11-133	5-63	1-36	5-34	8.3	- 12.12
Sir Mark Prescott	11-157	3-77	6-53	2-27	7.0	- 85.32
B A McMahon	11-162	2-34	1-44	8-84	6.8	- 67.12
R Hollinshead	11-305	5-101	2-119	4-85	3.6	-201.00

October/November

	Total W-R	2-y-o	3-y-o	4-y-o+	Per cent	£1 Level Stake
H R A Cecil	79-348	47-184	29-151	3-13	22.7	+ 13.71
J H M Gosden	76-362	34-139	32-184	10-39	21.0	- 40.18
B W Hills	73-463	36-227	31-201	6-35	15.8	- 3.19
M R Stoute	72-396	52-279	19-96	1-21	18.2	- 31.17
L M Cumani	69-327	33-144	32-165	4-18	21.1	- 29.58
G Harwood	59-378	30-177	24-168	5-33	15.6	- 87.17
R Hannon	57-649	38-375	16-205	3-69	8.8	-187.39
J L Dunlop	56-453	20-227	31-184	5-42	12.4	-120.24
H Thomson Jones	37-220	24-115	12-89	1-16	16.8	- 15.42
D R C Elsworth	37-275	18-134	9-76	10-65	13.5	+ 22.86
Sir Mark Prescott	33-250	17-173	10-48	6-29	13.2	- 11.49
M H Tompkins	33-376	13-164	5-93	15-119	8.8	- 90.25
Lord Huntingdon	32-298	11-117	18-128	3-53	10.7	- 64.61
G Wragg	31-196	7-66	23-119	1-11	15.8	- 23.84
B Hanbury	31-216	9-83	18-114	4-19	14.4	- 7.41
P F I Cole	30-293	19-176	9-82	2-35	10.2	- 16.49
C E Brittain	30-431	11-200	15-145	4-86	7.0	-141.07
J Berry	28-384	18-235	7-101	3-48	7.3	-193.10
G Lewis	25-202	13-93	8-56	4-53	12.4	+ 58.65
M H Easterby	25-256	10-91	4-62	11-103	9.8	- 52.33
R Akehurst	24-253	1-64	11-91	12-98	9.5	- 85.25
M S Johnston	23-252	11-130	10-71	2-51	9.1	- 25.95
M A Jarvis	22-244	10-135	9-78	3-31	9.0	- 84.92
W A O'Gorman	21-127	16-72	3-38	2-17	16.5	- 5.78
R W Armstrong	21-142	11-55	8-68	2-19	14.8	- 5.96
J W Hills	21-201	3-84	10-76	8-41	10.4	- 46.54
R Hollinshead	21-446	11-193	5-149	5-104	4.7	-172.84
M J Camacho	20-129	2-43	7-46	11-40	15.5	+ 10.46
T D Barron	20-181	11-77	5-62	4-42	11.0	- 17.87
R Boss	19-134	15-84	3-38	1-12	14.2	+ 35.38
N A Callaghan	19-182	12-120	7-52	0-10	10.4	- 20.87
D Morley	19-203	6-98	9-72	4-33	9.4	- 52.02
Mrs J Cecil	17-73	8-49	9-23	0-1	23.3	+ 77.48
A C Stewart	17-206	12-59	5-123	0-24	8.3	-108.94
S G Norton	16-247	7-144	7-86	2-17	6.5	- 86.15
R F Johnson Houghton	15-173	11-89	4-78	0-6	8.7	- 73.82
P J Makin	15-193	4-67	11-90	0-36	7.8	- 73.63
W Jarvis	15-193	7-105	7-68	1-20	7.8	- 79.14
M J Ryan	15-231	3-72	5-90	7-69	6.5	- 75.12
D W Chapman	15-256	2-43	2-62	11-151	5.9	-163.21
J R Fanshawe	14-109	8-52	6-45	0-12	12.8	+ 37.51
Mrs J Ramsden	14-162	4-70	7-59	3-33	8.6	- 44.00
G B Balding	14-166	3-61	2-42	9-63	8.4	- 13.87
R J R Williams	14-199	3-72	6-88	5-39	7.0	- 43.50
P T Walwyn	14-256	7-127	6-110	1-19	5.5	-147.86
W R Hern	13-90	6-45	7-42	0-3	14.4	- 25.97
G A Pritchard-Gordon	13-181	4-107	3-43	6-31	7.2	- 83.08
H Candy	13-189	3-52	8-102	2-35	6.9	- 66.50
R Charlton	12-82	4-37	7-38	1-7	14.6	+ 2.00
Mrs G R Reveley	12-119	0-27	3-32	9-60	10.1	- 46.00
A A Scott	12-124	11-98	1-25	0-1	9.7	- 51.04
J G FitzGerald	12-139	3-58	3-40	6-41	8.6	- 41.79
A Bailey	12-140	6-57	0-26	6-57	8.6	- 6.25
R M Whitaker	12-281	2-98	1-85	9-98	4.3	-164.47

LEADING TRAINERS BY TYPE OF RACE 1988-92

2-y-o Non-Handicaps

	W-R	Per cent	£1 Level Stake		W-R	Per cent	£1 Level Stake
J Berry	231-1280	18.0	- 304.22	H R A Cecil	169-448	37.7	+ 58.37
R Hannon	167-1331	12.5	- 462.17	M R Stoute	145-640	22.7	-107.91
B W Hills	109-652	16.7	- 140.22	P F I Cole	108-584	18.5	- 75.38
J L Dunlop	87-628	13.9	- 218.65	L M Cumani	75-307	24.4	- 27.88
J H M Gosden	73-269	27.1	- 8.58	G Harwood	72-346	20.8	- 68.27
H Thomson Jones	70-265	26.4	+ 10.77	M H Easterby	67-528	12.7	-212.53
W A O'Gorman	62-258	24.0	- 39.25	D R C Elsworth	47-349	13.5	- 80.47
R Boss	46-260	17.7	+ 47.66	G Lewis	46-367	12.5	- 19.17
C E Brittain	46-588	7.8	- 333.16	A A Scott	45-272	16.5	- 85.41
Sir M Prescott	45-317	14.2	- 90.26	I A Balding	45-396	11.4	-101.25
B Hanbury	44-328	13.4	- 32.63	R W Armstrong	43-177	24.3	+ 43.28
M Bell	43-263	16.3	- 40.51	P Chapple-Hyam	40-168	23.8	- 19.79
R Hollinshead	39-532	7.3	- 283.87	W Jarvis	37-275	13.5	- 37.03
G Wragg	34-185	18.4	- 24.03	M H Tompkins	34-367	9.3	-163.67
P T Walwyn	33-322	10.2	- 123.24	W R Hern	31-168	18.5	- 55.20
R Charlton	29-116	25.0	+ 22.33	R M Whitaker	29-271	10.7	- 99.84
M S Johnston	28-233	12.0	+ 2.08	J Etherington	27-234	11.5	- 27.02
N A Callaghan	27-260	10.4	- 54.50	A C Stewart	26-143	18.2	- 14.56
M A Jarvis	26-267	9.7	- 114.07	C Tinkler	26-348	7.5	-203.76
C R Nelson	25-148	16.9	- 9.23	T D Barron	25-209	12.0	- 61.32
Lord Huntingdon	25-222	11.3	- 86.76	S G Norton	24-343	7.0	-204.26
J W Watts	22-206	10.7	- 54.91	G A P-Gordon	21-287	7.3	-120.70
R F J Houghton	20-196	10.2	- 67.00	W J Haggas	19-140	13.6	- 25.79
Mrs J Cecil	18-89	20.2	+ 22.28	D Morley	17-169	10.1	+ 18.00
W Carter	17-193	8.8	+ 97.50	P A Kelleway	17-258	6.6	-134.91
M Brittain	17-411	4.1	- 246.50	Denys Smith	16-214	7.5	-101.90
M W Easterby	16-344	4.7	- 254.87	Mrs L Piggott	15-130	11.5	- 65.38
N Tinkler	15-205	7.3	- 114.87	J R Fanshawe	14-119	11.8	- 6.92
A Bailey	14-144	9.7	- 54.63	C F Wall	14-162	8.6	- 58.10
Dr J D Scargill	14-163	8.6	- 62.79	F H Lee	14-205	6.8	- 78.95
M J Ryan	13-148	8.8	- 61.98	M R Channon	13-155	8.4	- 54.95
J G FitzGerald	13-168	7.7	- 77.55	M McCormack	13-205	6.3	-140.50
N A Graham	12-102	11.8	- 38.81	Mrs J Ramsden	12-138	8.7	- 34.42
T Fairhurst	12-220	5.5	- 62.45	J W Payne	11-132	8.3	- 86.70
L J Holt	11-151	7.3	- 48.00	H Candy	11-156	7.1	- 45.50
J W Hills	11-182	6.0	- 69.52				

3-y-o Non-Handicaps

	W-R	Per cent	£1 Level Stake		W-R	Per cent	£1 Level Stake
H R A Cecil	313-998	31.4	- 41.84	L M Cumani	221-762	29.0	- 20.79
M R Stoute	188-836	22.5	- 121.02	B W Hills	177-900	19.7	-140.25
G Harwood	141-570	24.7	- 92.92	J H M Gosden	130-596	21.8	- 80.59
J L Dunlop	103-705	14.6	- 160.96	G Wragg	92-458	20.1	- 25.03
C E Brittain	78-719	10.8	- 123.39	R Hannon	75-596	12.6	-157.32
W R Hern	73-364	20.1	- 119.37	B Hanbury	66-465	14.2	- 5.93
A C Stewart	64-389	16.5	- 125.42	P F I Cole	64-507	12.6	-216.86
J Berry	61-345	17.7	- 82.25	P T Walwyn	52-439	11.8	-116.79
H Thomson Jones	51-301	16.9	- 61.44	Lord Huntingdon	50-287	17.4	+ 51.46
I A Balding	49-435	11.3	- 124.40	Sir M Prescott	44-191	23.0	- 11.46
R Charlton	43-172	25.0	+ 30.49	W Jarvis	42-302	13.9	-102.34

	W-R	Per cent	£1 Level Stake		W-R	Per cent	£1 Level Stake
M A Jarvis	41-310	13.2	- 78.76	D R C Elsworth	39-400	9.8	-151.06
R F J Houghton	38-259	14.7	- 36.48	H Candy	33-327	10.1	- 35.69
A A Scott	32-251	12.7	- 107.55	N A Callaghan	31-193	16.1	- 0.39
J W Hills	29-212	13.7	- 31.02	J R Fanshawe	28-170	16.5	+ 42.81
S G Norton	27-251	10.8	- 50.43	W J Haggas	26-186	14.0	- 75.84
Mrs L Piggott	26-272	9.6	- 121.05	P J Makin	25-199	12.6	- 20.75
M H Easterby	25-219	11.4	- 83.24	R Hollinshead	25-455	5.5	-228.16
C R Nelson	24-188	12.8	- 90.98	P A Kelleway	24-236	10.2	- 89.76
T D Barron	21-119	17.6	- 30.26	R Boss	21-161	13.0	- 34.66
R W Armstrong	20-226	8.8	- 87.31	W A O'Gorman	19-122	15.6	- 56.75
M H Tompkins	19-205	9.3	- 108.83	G Lewis	19-212	9.0	-126.98
R M Whitaker	18-185	9.7	- 63.39	M S Johnston	17-124	13.7	- 38.71
P Chapple-Hyam	16-91	17.6	- 8.56	J A R Toller	16-113	14.2	- 17.31
D Morley	16-160	10.0	- 70.94	M Brittain	16-197	8.1	- 79.25
R J R Williams	16-201	8.0	- 1.88	Mrs J Cecil	15-72	20.8	+ 8.69
R Akehurst	15-158	9.5	- 66.42	G A P-Gordon	15-218	6.9	-130.14
M J Camacho	14-90	15.6	+ 5.80	M Bell	14-105	13.3	- 34.26
J Etherington	14-143	9.8	- 54.93	J W Watts	14-161	8.7	-100.67
B A McMahon	13-176	7.4	- 57.82	C N Allen	12-96	12.5	- 27.23
M McCormack	12-138	8.7	- 34.97	C F Wall	12-160	7.5	- 86.73
M J Ryan	11-114	9.6	- 49.74	Mrs G R Reveley	10-78	12.8	- 47.87
N A Graham	10-79	12.7	- 36.56	Mrs J Ramsden	10-89	11.2	- 20.55
R Simpson	10-109	9.2	- 19.07	Denys Smith	10-116	8.6	- 53.64
Mrs N Macauley	10-162	6.2	- 95.27				

4-y-o+ Non-Handicaps

	W-R	Per cent	£1 Level Stake		W-R	Per cent	£1 Level Stake
M R Stoute	28-127	22.0	- 32.78	H R A Cecil	23-115	20.0	- 25.07
B W Hills	22-115	19.1	- 0.19	L M Cumani	21-98	21.4	- 25.39
R Hannon	20-115	17.4	+ 14.09	J H M Gosden	19-78	24.4	+ 24.33
G Harwood	19-103	18.4	+ 17.95	Sir M Prescott	17-46	37.0	+ 5.08
C E Brittain	17-208	8.2	- 54.51	J L Dunlop	16-94	17.0	+ 27.26
A C Stewart	15-53	28.3	+ 1.17	Lord Huntingdon	13-66	19.7	+ 33.38
M C Pipe	13-69	18.8	- 9.64	M H Tompkins	13-88	14.8	+ 16.22
P F I Cole	13-91	14.3	- 31.95	R Hollinshead	13-126	10.3	- 53.92
I A Balding	12-84	14.3	- 43.01	D W Chapman	12-117	10.3	- 47.59
B Hanbury	11-45	24.4	- 4.65	T D Barron	11-46	23.9	- 1.70
W A O'Gorman	11-54	20.4	- 24.76	J Berry	11-72	15.3	- 37.61
N Tinkler	11-110	10.0	- 60.79	G Lewis	10-61	16.4	- 2.24
M J Ryan	10-66	15.2	- 19.74	G Wragg	10-77	13.0	- 3.98
D R C Elsworth	10-116	8.6	- 22.12	B A McMahon	9-89	10.1	- 29.50
R Akehurst	9-107	8.4	- 58.22	W R Hern	8-28	28.6	+ 6.58
P J Makin	8-45	17.8	- 20.54	A Bailey	8-51	15.7	- 11.83
G M Moore	8-59	13.6	+ 13.75	C R Nelson	7-41	17.1	- 9.49
R M Whitaker	7-43	16.3	+ 64.80	P A Kelleway	7-44	15.9	- 8.00
M H Easterby	7-45	15.6	- 14.37	J Pearce	7-46	15.2	- 18.24
W Jarvis	7-48	14.6	- 21.74	P T Walwyn	7-65	10.8	- 20.42
M P Naughton	7-123	5.7	- 38.37	M J Camacho	6-30	20.0	+ 7.54
N A Callaghan	6-32	18.8	+ 25.23	D Burchell	6-42	14.3	+ 51.00
J Wharton	6-47	12.8	- 4.67	G B Balding	6-48	12.5	- 17.97
Mrs G R Reveley	6-55	10.9	- 34.14	J G FitzGerald	6-63	9.5	- 33.43
P C Haslam	5-21	23.8	+ 36.33	M R Channon	5-23	21.7	+ 17.50
A A Scott	5-27	18.5	- 0.15	C A Cyzer	5-36	13.9	- 2.40
H Thomson Jones	5-41	12.2	+ 6.79	M A Jarvis	5-44	11.4	+ 2.80
M McCormack	5-57	8.8	- 28.87				

Selling Non-Handicaps

	W-R	Per cent	£1 Level Stake		W-R	Per cent	£1 Level Stake
J Berry	93-554	16.8	- 90.59	M H Easterby	31-220	14.1	-109.60
N Tinkler	28-265	10.6	-143.70	C Tinkler	26-158	16.5	- 42.83
M H Tompkins	25-183	13.7	- 57.62	M W Easterby	25-210	11.9	- 63.61
D Morley	17-105	16.2	- 6.74	Mrs G R Reveley	16-88	18.2	- 5.39
R Hollinshead	16-155	10.3	- 50.84	N A Callaghan	15-95	15.8	+ 1.48
R Hannon	15-146	10.3	- 36.00	P F I Cole	14-64	21.9	+ 25.32
J Wharton	14-103	13.6	+ 44.50	Mrs J Ramsden	13-90	14.4	- 29.28
R M Whitaker	13-155	8.4	- 94.67	Ronald Thompson	13-162	8.0	- 32.37
Sir M Prescott	12-86	14.0	- 28.79	G Lewis	12-98	12.2	- 15.02
T D Barron	12-113	10.6	- 7.74	P J Makin	11-63	17.5	+ 28.71
M Brittain	10-242	4.1	-140.67				

Apprentice Non-Handicaps

	W-R	Per cent	£1 Level Stake		W-R	Per cent	£1 Level Stake
B W Hills	11-26	42.3	- 0.60	L M Cumani	11-45	24.4	- 24.26
J H M Gosden	8-17	47.1	+ 28.74	Sir M Prescott	7-16	43.8	+ 5.87
P F I Cole	6-26	23.1	- 10.95	H R A Cecil	5-21	23.8	- 9.42
M R Stoute	4-8	50.0	+ 2.59	G Harwood	4-11	36.4	+ 10.33
B A McMahon	4-24	16.7	+ 40.50	P T Walwyn	3-8	37.5	+ 0.05
I A Balding	3-15	20.0	+ 12.50	W J Haggas	2-3	66.7	+ 2.73
C E Brittain	2-6	33.3	+ 4.30	M A Jarvis	2-6	33.3	- 1.00
Denys Smith	2-6	33.3	+ 18.00	J A R Toller	2-6	33.3	+ 27.00
M H Easterby	2-7	28.6	+ 5.50	M C Pipe	2-7	28.6	+ 2.00
G Wragg	2-8	25.0	- 1.00	J W Hills	2-8	25.0	- 2.20
R M Whitaker	2-9	22.2	- 3.65	M Bell	2-11	18.2	- 5.17
H Candy	2-12	16.7	+ 6.00	B Hanbury	2-12	16.7	+ 6.00
M H Tompkins	2-12	16.7	- 4.25	S G Norton	2-13	15.4	- 7.12
A C Stewart	2-13	15.4	- 6.50	Mrs L Piggott	2-13	15.4	+ 25.50
C A Cyzer	2-16	12.5	- 6.90	D Morley	2-18	11.1	- 14.09
R J R Williams	2-22	9.1	+ 19.00	R Hollinshead	2-32	6.3	- 5.00

Amateur Non-Handicaps

	W-R	Per cent	£1 Level Stake		W-R	Per cent	£1 Level Stake
B W Hills	7-19	36.8	+ 0.69	G Harwood	7-29	24.1	- 13.45
P T Walwyn	4-7	57.1	+ 7.00	R F J Houghton	4-9	44.4	+ 40.75
H R A Cecil	4-10	40.0	+ 2.94	M C Pipe	3-3	100.0	+ 3.09
L M Cumani	3-4	75.0	+ 3.57	J W Hills	3-5	60.0	+ 7.75
M R Stoute	3-10	30.0	+ 0.67	I A Balding	3-14	21.4	+ 32.50
R Akehurst	2-5	40.0	+ 6.25	J Berry	2-6	33.3	- 1.57
C R Nelson	2-6	33.3	- 1.65	H Thomson Jones	2-8	25.0	+ 1.67
J H M Gosden	2-8	25.0	+ 1.33	Sir M Prescott	2-10	20.0	- 6.61

2-y-o Handicaps

	W-R	Per cent	£1 Level Stake		W-R	Per cent	£1 Level Stake
R Hannon	45-347	13.0	- 4.54	J Berry	36-309	11.7	- 79.43
T D Barron	24-118	20.3	+ 50.59	M H Easterby	22-161	13.7	+ 10.58
M Bell	15-101	14.9	+ 29.38	J L Dunlop	13-72	18.1	+ 25.00
M H Tompkins	13-149	8.7	- 36.59	P F I Cole	12-86	14.0	+ 3.83
G Lewis	12-101	11.9	+ 3.33	N A Callaghan	11-85	12.9	- 23.00
C E Brittain	11-96	11.5	+ 18.00	G Harwood	10-43	23.3	- 4.40
Lord Huntingdon	10-46	21.7	+ 18.83	W A O'Gorman	9-62	14.5	- 4.00
Mrs J Ramsden	9-63	14.3	+ 1.00	S G Norton	9-87	10.3	+ 4.80
R Boss	8-44	18.2	- 1.25	B W Hills	8-53	15.1	+ 0.10
R Hollinshead	8-128	6.3	- 15.00	M J Camacho	7-28	25.0	+ 52.25
W Jarvis	7-36	19.4	+ 38.08	M R Stoute	7-55	12.7	+ 7.00
Sir M Prescott	7-60	11.7	- 22.00	F H Lee	7-71	9.9	- 10.00
D R C Elsworth	6-26	23.1	+ 23.75	W J Haggas	6-40	15.0	- 6.00
M D I Usher	6-54	11.1	- 12.12	G A P-Gordon	6-56	10.7	- 11.87
N Tinkler	6-61	9.8	- 9.00	M S Johnston	6-72	8.3	- 44.67
A Bailey	6-77	7.8	- 26.75	M W Easterby	6-96	6.3	- 49.00
M Brittain	6-134	4.5	- 97.89	J R Fanshawe	5-21	23.8	+ 12.38
W R Muir	5-24	20.8	+ 6.00	J W Payne	5-27	18.5	+ 14.25
I A Balding	5-42	11.9	- 2.25	Mrs N Macauley	5-51	9.8	- 4.50
P Mitchell	5-60	8.3	- 12.00				

3-y-o Handicaps

	W-R	Per cent	£1 Level Stake		W-R	Per cent	£1 Level Stake
J L Dunlop	90-537	16.8	- 76.10	R Hannon	81-932	8.7	- 205.64
B W Hills	74-505	14.7	- 47.63	M R Stoute	71-467	15.2	- 79.15
Sir M Prescott	56-303	18.5	+ 9.60	J H M Gosden	55-279	19.7	+ 30.09
G Harwood	50-355	14.1	- 60.19	J Berry	50-455	11.0	- 71.34
H R A Cecil	48-206	23.3	+ 13.55	L M Cumani	48-300	16.0	- 34.72
P F I Cole	44-350	12.6	- 87.29	I A Balding	44-375	11.7	- 56.21
P T Walwyn	44-414	10.6	- 35.41	M H Easterby	44-461	9.5	- 182.65
J W Watts	42-377	11.1	- 97.38	C E Brittain	42-514	8.2	- 62.25
A C Stewart	39-242	16.1	- 44.26	M S Johnston	39-246	15.9	+ 95.35
B Hanbury	38-342	11.1	- 60.03	G Lewis	37-363	10.2	- 62.50
Mrs J Ramsden	36-316	11.4	- 54.91	M J Ryan	34-279	12.2	- 26.86
R Akehurst	32-263	12.2	- 7.62	H Thomson Jones	32-293	10.9	- 14.41
G Wragg	30-222	13.5	- 5.62	D Morley	30-237	12.7	+ 1.03
F H Lee	30-277	10.8	- 13.14	N A Callaghan	29-285	10.2	- 94.04
M Brittain	29-535	5.4	- 261.67	R W Armstrong	28-192	14.6	+ 64.40
M Bell	28-236	11.9	- 31.72	M A Jarvis	28-284	9.9	- 127.87
P J Makin	27-178	15.2	- 27.91	J Sutcliffe	27-189	14.3	- 50.41
R F J Houghton	27-270	10.0	- 72.54	M H Tompkins	27-329	8.2	- 164.75
W Jarvis	26-187	13.9	- 30.12	Lord Huntingdon	24-216	11.1	+ 1.76
R Hollinshead	23-411	5.6	- 189.42	D R C Elsworth	22-195	11.3	- 37.01
W J Haggas	21-155	13.5	+ 4.81	J G FitzGerald	21-162	13.0	- 16.89
Mrs G R Reveley	20-147	13.6	- 39.75	A A Scott	20-185	10.8	- 76.40
T D Barron	20-281	7.1	- 160.67	R Charlton	19-117	16.2	- 23.15
W R Hern	19-141	13.5	- 25.12	Mrs L Piggott	19-175	10.9	- 37.50
P C Haslam	18-146	12.3	- 39.51	W A O'Gorman	18-174	10.3	- 33.08
R Boss	18-226	8.0	- 119.75	S G Norton	17-308	5.5	- 192.90
R M Whitaker	16-341	4.7	- 222.00	C W C Elsey	15-166	9.0	- 35.54
G A P-Gordon	15-205	7.3	- 97.34	D W P Arbuthnot	15-207	7.2	- 74.00
J W Hills	15-208	7.2	- 90.67	H Candy	15-210	7.1	- 42.00

	W-R	Per cent	£1 Level Stake		W-R	Per cent	£1 Level Stake
W Carter	14-228	6.1	- 58.29	C A Cyzer	13-123	10.6	+ 18.75
M R Channon	13-125	10.4	- 12.84	M W Easterby	13-179	7.3	- 70.17
J R Fanshawe	12-131	9.2	- 42.75	C W Thornton	12-147	8.2	- 51.92
H J Collingridge	12-151	7.9	- 34.62	C F Wall	12-177	6.8	- 96.32
D A Wilson	11-123	8.9	- 3.50	Mrs N Macauley	11-208	5.3	- 99.60
M P Naughton	10-83	12.0	- 32.67	M McCormack	10-101	9.9	- 25.25
J Wharton	10-104	9.6	+ 1.50	M J Camacho	10-110	9.1	+ 14.75
Dr J D Scargill	10-126	7.9	- 45.87	B A McMahon	10-163	6.1	- 95.42
J Etherington	10-184	5.4	- 90.00				

4-y-o+ Handicaps

	W-R	Per cent	£1 Level Stake		W-R	Per cent	£1 Level Stake
R Akehurst	79-609	13.0	- 50.72	D W Chapman	76-931	8.2	-285.18
M H Easterby	69-676	10.2	-244.67	Mrs G R Reveley	66-397	16.6	+ 24.07
R M Whitaker	63-604	10.4	-103.25	R J Hodges	60-576	10.4	-120.61
T D Barron	58-488	11.9	- 62.02	R Hollinshead	53-665	8.0	-214.06
M P Naughton	51-539	9.5	-122.24	B A McMahon	49-435	11.3	+ 12.97
F H Lee	43-389	11.1	- 40.16	M H Tompkins	43-412	10.4	- 78.77
I A Balding	39-285	13.7	+ 20.38	D R C Elsworth	38-296	12.8	+ 55.38
L G Cottrell	37-415	8.9	-125.92	Lord Huntingdon	34-182	18.7	+ 88.75
M J Ryan	34-336	10.1	- 29.25	C E Brittain	34-413	8.2	- 76.34
M Brittain	34-660	5.2	-181.50	Mrs J Ramsden	33-329	10.0	-161.69
J L Spearing	32-400	8.0	-171.49	R Hannon	32-403	7.9	-110.40
G B Balding	31-304	10.2	- 25.01	J Berry	31-333	9.3	- 78.15
P F I Cole	30-251	12.0	- 49.87	P S Felgate	30-271	11.1	- 15.87
C Tinkler	29-242	12.0	- 50.68	J L Dunlop	29-281	10.3	- 71.04
G Lewis	28-260	10.8	- 29.87	W Carter	28-276	10.1	- 73.00
J W Hills	27-194	13.9	+ 17.74	J A Glover	27-203	13.3	+ 28.00
Mrs N Macauley	27-349	7.7	- 96.27	M S Johnston	26-304	8.6	- 34.00
R J R Williams	25-206	12.1	- 6.40	H Candy	25-252	9.9	- 31.74
C J Benstead	25-268	9.3	- 61.25	R Bastiman	24-189	12.7	+ 24.25
Capt J Wilson	24-238	10.1	- 1.29	D Morley	23-154	14.9	- 12.75
C A Cyzer	23-173	13.3	+ 4.16	P J Makin	23-185	12.4	+ 24.25
M W Easterby	23-226	10.2	- 47.79	Denys Smith	23-325	7.1	-131.33
G M Moore	23-340	6.8	-107.17	G Harwood	22-146	15.1	+ 28.76
J Mackie	22-195	11.3	+ 32.00	J G FitzGerald	22-199	11.1	- 14.12
J W Watts	22-214	10.3	- 50.42	J D Bethell	22-230	9.6	- 43.12
P Howling	22-452	4.9	-245.87	J H M Gosden	21-107	19.6	+ 21.34
P Mitchell	21-224	9.4	- 33.17	D W P Arbuthnot	21-224	9.4	- 25.67
S G Norton	20-127	15.7	+ 8.88	P Calver	20-147	13.6	+ 32.00
A Hide	20-157	12.7	+ 59.00	Sir M Prescott	20-165	12.1	- 40.88
J Sutcliffe	20-167	12.0	- 30.41	R J O'Sullivan	20-205	9.8	+ 29.25
M J Camacho	19-128	14.8	+ 13.01	B W Hills	19-143	13.3	- 30.32
M A Jarvis	19-166	11.4	- 5.50	D A Wilson	19-363	5.2	-217.74
B Hanbury	18-111	16.2	+ 11.71	E A Wheeler	18-179	10.1	- 15.00
E J Alston	18-188	9.6	- 21.00	S Dow	18-193	9.3	- 49.39
C J Hill	18-221	8.1	- 57.58	Mrs L Piggott	17-132	12.9	- 30.49
Lady Herries	17-152	11.2	- 28.86	Miss B Sanders	17-181	9.4	- 72.17
Miss L Siddall	17-212	8.0	- 41.17	W J Musson	17-260	6.5	-138.25
T Fairhurst	17-269	6.3	-121.62	M C Pipe	16-116	13.8	- 33.05
C C Elsey	16-119	13.4	- 14.57	C R Nelson	16-122	13.1	+ 28.80
G A P-Gordon	16-151	10.6	- 33.50	Pat Mitchell	16-176	9.1	- 32.92
J Wharton	16-202	7.9	- 16.80	K T Ivory	16-213	7.5	+ 4.23
A Bailey	16-215	7.4	- 46.50	B R Millman	16-231	6.9	- 83.00

	W–R	Per cent	£1 Level Stake		W–R	Per cent	£1 Level Stake
K O C-Brown	15–113	13.3	+ 71.33	P C Haslam	15–118	12.7	− 31.98
W Jarvis	15–134	11.2	− 25.05	S R Bowring	15–172	8.7	+ 20.50
M O'Neill	15–188	8.0	+ 23.25	C A Horgan	15–196	7.7	− 54.67
N A Callaghan	14–104	13.5	− 19.90	M R Channon	14–113	12.4	+ 10.50
W W Haigh	14–160	8.8	− 37.89	N Bycroft	14–227	6.2	− 98.37
P W Harris	13–57	22.8	+ 60.50	G Wragg	13–74	17.6	+ 28.55
Mrs A Knight	13–106	12.3	+ 2.25	P T Walwyn	13–111	11.7	− 14.25
M Blanshard	13–228	5.7	− 95.00	T Casey	12–104	11.5	− 12.67
W A O'Gorman	12–116	10.3	− 30.00	R Curtis	12–140	8.6	− 14.87
W G R Wightman	12–162	7.4	− 77.00	R Simpson	12–163	7.4	− 53.62
D T Thom	12–167	7.2	− 86.88	H J Collingridge	12–203	5.9	− 35.00
W R Hern	11–54	20.4	+ 6.28	A C Stewart	11–71	15.5	− 13.55
R Boss	11–82	13.4	+ 6.50	D Murray Smith	11–84	13.1	+ 17.00
Miss S E Hall	11–121	9.1	+ 1.08	Dr J D Scargill	11–126	8.7	− 64.64
M Feth-Godley	11–146	7.5	− 70.12	C W Thornton	11–156	7.1	− 68.00
M D Hammond	10–76	13.2	− 3.24	J S King	10–80	12.5	− 4.75
L M Cumani	10–85	11.8	− 31.17	H Thomson Jones	10–86	11.6	− 21.25
M McCormack	10–99	10.1	− 14.75	R W Armstrong	10–109	9.2	− 30.75
D Morris	10–110	9.1	− 27.25	Mrs B Waring	10–148	6.8	− 34.25
M J Haynes	10–155	6.5	− 48.50	C W C Elsey	10–164	6.1	− 73.87

Selling Handicaps

	W–R	Per cent	£1 Level Stake		W–R	Per cent	£1 Level Stake
R Bastiman	11–49	22.4	+ 42.33	J Berry	11–88	12.5	+ 9.50
Mrs J Ramsden	9–50	18.0	+ 0.75	D W Chapman	9–113	8.0	− 4.00
D Morley	8–39	20.5	+ 29.21	C N Allen	7–44	15.9	+ 17.50
M H Tompkins	7–59	11.9	+ 1.00	M P Naughton	6–38	15.8	− 0.07
Sir M Prescott	6–42	14.3	+ 8.50	C A Cyzer	5–31	16.1	+ 21.00
P J Feilden	5–35	14.3	+ 21.00	M H Easterby	5–61	8.2	− 20.37
R J Hodges	5–64	7.8	− 34.75	M Brittain	5–101	5.0	− 37.25
T M Jones	4–7	57.1	+ 58.00	R J R Williams	4–18	22.2	+ 28.00
E Weymes	4–19	21.1	+ 2.25	M O'Neill	4–25	16.0	+ 23.75
Capt J Wilson	4–26	15.4	+ 27.50	E A Wheeler	4–29	13.8	+ 15.50
D A Wilson	4–33	12.1	− 6.92	I Campbell	4–34	11.8	+ 18.00
N A Callaghan	4–36	11.1	− 20.75	P J Makin	4–40	10.0	− 4.50
Mrs N Macauley	4–46	8.7	+ 20.50	C J Hill	4–52	7.7	− 18.67
M D I Usher	4–59	6.8	− 17.50	K T Ivory	4–65	6.2	− 39.00
R M Whitaker	4–66	6.1	− 29.00				

Apprentice Handicaps

	W–R	Per cent	£1 Level Stake		W–R	Per cent	£1 Level Stake
Mrs J Ramsden	11–47	23.4	+ 4.96	J Berry	11–64	17.2	+ 16.29
Mrs G R Reveley	10–55	18.2	− 5.87	D R C Elsworth	9–48	18.8	+ 9.25
R J R Williams	9–56	16.1	+ 20.84	R Hollinshead	8–104	7.7	− 51.75
G Lewis	7–36	19.4	+ 13.50	F H Lee	7–55	12.7	− 3.25
M H Tompkins	7–58	12.1	0.00	M P Naughton	7–60	11.7	− 0.50
H Candy	7–61	11.5	+ 10.50	M W Easterby	6–25	24.0	+ 6.50
D T Thom	6–25	24.0	+ 30.25	B W Hills	6–26	23.1	+ 18.75
C A Cyzer	6–31	19.4	+ 32.50	Lord Huntingdon	6–40	15.0	− 18.09

	W-R	Per cent	£1 Level Stake		Apprentice Handicaps W-R	Per cent	£1 Level Stake
C J Hill	6-49	12.2	- 5.00	I A Balding	6-65	9.2	- 25.75
R J Hodges	6-74	8.1	- 25.42	M Brittain	6-86	7.0	- 7.25
W J Haggas	5-22	22.7	+ 3.38	P C Haslam	5-28	17.9	- 2.50
P J Makin	5-31	16.1	+ 18.50	J A Glover	5-31	16.1	+ 16.00
B A McMahon	5-38	13.2	+ 42.00	A Bailey	5-58	8.6	- 21.67
R Hannon	5-96	5.2	- 42.00				

Amateur Handicaps

	W-R	Per cent	£1 Level Stake		W-R	Per cent	£1 Level Stake
D A Wilson	22-114	19.3	+ 36.75	I A Balding	14-50	28.0	+ 23.22
P F I Cole	10-31	32.3	+ 24.38	J Pearce	9-46	19.6	+ 6.88
M J Haynes	6-32	18.8	+ 49.50	G A P-Gordon	4-21	19.0	+ 8.50
G Harwood	4-34	11.8	- 10.62	A Hide	4-36	11.1	+ 12.00
P J Feilden	4-41	9.8	- 7.00	D R C Elsworth	3-18	16.7	+ 4.33
D T Thom	3-19	15.8	+ 15.50	Mrs G R Reveley	3-20	15.0	- 2.50
M P Naughton	3-29	10.3	- 8.00	Sir M Prescott	2-5	40.0	+ 5.00
L G Cottrell	2-6	33.3	+ 14.50	J W Hills	2-10	20.0	+ 2.38
G Lewis	2-11	18.2	+ 3.00	B W Hills	2-14	14.3	- 1.50
F H Lee	2-14	14.3	+ 20.00	P T Walwyn	2-17	11.8	- 4.00
M Bell	2-17	11.8	+ 8.00	A W Jones	2-19	10.5	+ 7.00
W J Musson	2-19	10.5	- 10.25	P Mitchell	2-20	10.0	- 12.50
C A Horgan	2-20	10.0	- 1.75	R M Whitaker	2-22	9.1	- 3.50
H J Collingridge	2-23	8.7	+ 45.00	E J Alston	2-25	8.0	- 4.00
G B Balding	2-35	5.7	- 16.50	J L Spearing	2-36	5.6	- 26.75
A Bailey	2-37	5.4	- 25.12	C Tinkler	2-38	5.3	- 19.50
M H Easterby	2-49	4.1	- 38.00				

LEADING TRAINERS' FAVOURITES 1988-1992

	W-R	Per cent	£1 Level Stake	% of Runners that Started Favourite	% of Winners that Started Favourite
H R A Cecil	350-748	46.8	- 44.93	40.5	61.7
M R Stoute	243-609	39.9	- 65.47	27.2	53.9
J Berry	227-619	36.7	- 34.59	17.5	42.2
L M Cumani	225-523	43.0	- 26.45	31.9	57.0
B W Hills	190-513	37.0	- 25.15	20.8	43.3
G Harwood	180-433	41.6	- 8.43	25.9	54.1
J H M Gosden	152-357	42.6	+ 46.15	25.6	48.6
J L Dunlop	152-399	38.1	+ 3.00	17.0	44.3
R Hannon	135-434	31.1	- 71.93	10.7	30.4
M H Easterby	125-402	31.1	- 42.39	16.3	45.0
P F I Cole	117-340	34.4	- 23.12	16.6	38.4
Sir M Prescott	98-274	35.8	+ 4.62	21.9	44.7
A C Stewart	89-238	37.4	- 13.87	25.1	55.6
I A Balding	77-241	32.0	- 6.13	13.6	34.8
W R Hern	74-171	43.3	- 2.83	22.3	51.0
W A O'Gorman	70-177	39.5	+ 6.93	21.6	51.9
H Thomson Jones	67-165	40.6	- 0.64	15.8	38.1
B Hanbury	63-198	31.8	- 24.57	14.1	32.6
T D Barron	63-206	30.6	- 15.65	14.0	35.8
R Hollinshead	60-152	39.5	+ 16.95	5.6	31.6
M H Tompkins	60-204	29.4	- 36.17	10.8	31.6
Mrs J Ramsden	60-209	28.7	- 9.12	18.2	45.1
A A Scott	59-141	41.8	+ 25.49	16.3	52.7
Lord Huntingdon	57-168	33.9	- 2.69	15.0	33.9
Mrs G R Reveley	53-135	39.3	+ 14.36	13.3	36.8
G Wragg	52-151	34.4	- 21.64	14.4	28.4
D R C Elsworth	51-164	31.1	- 2.66	11.0	28.7
M A Jarvis	50-134	37.3	+ 20.98	11.3	36.8
W Jarvis	47-132	35.6	- 18.18	12.8	33.8
P T Walwyn	47-165	28.5	- 38.04	11.6	29.4
C E Brittain	46-149	30.9	- 20.76	5.7	19.7
G Lewis	46-176	26.1	- 33.58	11.3	26.1
P J Makin	45-134	33.6	+ 8.21	14.7	39.8
R Akehurst	44-178	24.7	- 18.59	12.6	27.2
R W Armstrong	43-112	38.4	+ 6.28	14.6	40.2
R Charlton	41-113	36.3	- 0.79	22.3	38.7
N A Callaghan	41-136	30.1	- 1.87	12.1	29.5
R M Whitaker	41-141	29.1	+ 9.10	7.7	25.5
C R Nelson	40-96	41.7	+ 15.48	13.4	44.9
W J Haggas	38-105	36.2	+ 10.57	15.2	42.2
J W Watts	38-125	30.4	- 11.78	11.9	35.8
R F J Houghton	37-100	37.0	+ 2.99	10.7	34.3
Mrs L Piggott	37-122	30.3	- 18.09	14.2	41.6
D W Chapman	37-123	30.1	+ 0.66	6.7	30.1
C Tinkler	37-127	29.1	- 6.39	10.6	34.9
M Bell	36-121	29.8	- 27.61	12.8	29.8
R Boss	35-116	30.2	- 11.45	13.7	32.1
M W Easterby	34-120	28.3	- 9.33	9.4	35.8
D Morley	34-125	27.2	- 17.33	12.6	28.6
P C Haslam	30-81	37.0	+ 7.62	13.6	46.2
N Tinkler	30-109	27.5	- 25.00	8.7	34.5
J Sutcliffe	29-87	33.3	+ 17.28	13.9	45.3
R J Hodges	29-111	26.1	- 5.65	9.9	31.2

	W-R	Per cent	£1 Level Stake	% of Runners that Started Favourite	% of Winners that Started Favourite
G A P-Gordon	29-111	26.1	- 17.82	10.3	34.1
F H Lee	28-99	28.3	- 3.75	8.2	24.1
M J Ryan	28-106	26.4	- 5.36	9.5	25.0
M J Camacho	27-52	51.9	+ 40.10	9.2	36.0
M S Johnston	27-99	27.3	- 28.28	8.7	20.9
J G FitzGerald	25-76	32.9	+ 11.48	9.1	30.5
J Etherington	24-64	37.5	+ 3.32	7.0	34.3
R J R Williams	24-85	28.2	- 14.34	9.0	28.6
J W Hills	24-98	24.5	- 31.53	10.3	24.0
M Brittain	23-81	28.4	+ 3.36	3.3	18.4
H Candy	23-87	26.4	- 13.19	8.0	24.0
B A McMahon	23-92	25.0	- 14.56	7.1	21.5
P Chapple-Hyam	22-58	37.9	- 8.81	16.2	32.4
S G Norton	22-85	25.9	- 18.88	6.8	20.4
M C Pipe	21-53	39.6	+ 7.43	17.2	42.9
M P Naughton	21-79	26.6	- 3.41	7.6	22.8
Dr J D Scargill	19-48	39.6	+ 6.65	7.5	37.3
J R Fanshawe	18-49	36.7	+ 3.90	9.6	26.5
D A Wilson	18-63	28.6	+ 6.42	7.5	29.5
Denys Smith	17-42	40.5	+ 13.26	4.0	27.9
P A Kelleway	17-54	31.5	- 11.38	6.7	25.8
J Pearce	17-61	27.9	- 5.31	11.2	33.3
C F Wall	16-46	34.8	- 1.90	6.8	31.4
G B Balding	16-89	18.0	- 33.36	8.8	21.9
M R Channon	15-45	33.3	+ 10.69	6.6	23.4
J L Spearing	15-46	32.6	+ 4.14	5.7	30.0
M McCormack	15-53	28.3	+ 3.53	7.6	28.3
J A Glover	14-45	31.1	+ 12.75	7.9	28.6
A Bailey	14-68	20.6	- 17.92	7.6	20.3
E Weymes	13-32	40.6	+ 10.29	6.5	37.1
P Calver	13-34	38.2	+ 13.85	6.8	28.3
Miss S E Hall	13-34	38.2	+ 7.96	7.1	32.5
C A Horgan	13-43	30.2	+ 10.83	9.0	48.1
C N Allen	13-45	28.9	- 5.43	5.6	23.2
W Carter	13-56	23.2	- 5.16	5.5	16.5
Mrs J Cecil	12-43	27.9	- 7.95	17.1	25.5
L J Holt	12-52	23.1	- 1.75	6.7	30.8
Mrs N Macauley	12-54	22.2	- 9.54	4.4	16.0
G M Moore	12-54	22.2	- 11.02	7.3	21.1
J Wharton	11-30	36.7	+ 13.25	3.7	16.9
N A Graham	11-37	29.7	- 9.58	11.9	36.7
S Dow	11-40	27.5	- 3.81	5.1	22.4
C J Hill	11-49	22.4	- 2.50	7.0	22.9
C W Thornton	11-56	19.6	- 18.48	8.5	22.0
W G R Wightman	10-30	33.3	+ 10.00	5.7	30.3
R Bastiman	10-31	32.3	+ 11.58	6.7	21.7
R Simpson	10-33	30.3	+ 5.98	6.2	27.0
C A Cyzer	10-34	29.4	+ 2.67	4.7	14.3
Lady Herries	10-41	24.4	- 13.41	11.7	25.6
P Mitchell	10-48	20.8	- 18.34	5.9	19.2

TRAINER SECTION

(IRISH FLAT SEASON 1992)

J F BAILEY JNR

	No. of Horses	Races Run	1st	2nd	3rd	Unpl	Per cent	£1 Level Stake
2-y-o	2	4	0	1	1	2	-	- 4.00
3-y-o	1	9	0	0	1	8	-	- 9.00
4-y-o+	2	7	1	0	1	5	14.3	+ 14.00
Totals	5	20	1	1	3	15	5.0	+ 1.00

Mar/Apr	May	Jun	Jul	Aug	Sep	Oct/Nov
0-0	1-5	0-5	0-1	0-2	0-3	0-4

Winning Jockey	W-R	£1 Level Stake	Winning Course	W-R	£1 Level Stake
J A Heffernan	1-11	+ 10.00	Downpatrick	1-1	+ 20.00

Winning Horse	Age	Races Run	1st	2nd	3rd	Unpl	Win £
Parkal	4	2	1	0	0	1	690

Favourites	0-0	Total winning prize-money	£690

J S BOLGER

	No. of Horses	Races Run	1st	2nd	3rd	Unpl	Per cent	£1 Level Stake
2-y-o	62	192	48	41	18	85	25.0	- 58.49
3-y-o	74	349	58	50	48	193	16.6	- 45.90
4-y-o+	25	130	13	23	15	79	10.0	- 56.45
Totals	161	671	119	114	81	357	17.7	-160.84

BY MONTH

2-y-o	W-R	Per cent	£1 Level Stake	3-y-o	W-R	Per cent	£1 Level Stake
Mar/Apr	4-8	50.0	+ 1.44	Mar/Apr	17-52	32.7	+ 23.58
May	4-17	23.5	- 9.60	May	3-41	7.3	- 28.53
June	8-22	36.4	- 4.39	June	8-51	15.7	+ 5.63
July	12-21	57.1	+ 2.56	July	12-51	23.5	- 8.05
August	6-37	16.2	- 17.52	August	6-64	9.4	- 20.50
September	5-41	12.2	- 27.38	September	3-46	6.5	- 16.00
Oct/Nov	9-46	19.6	- 3.60	Oct/Nov	9-44	20.5	- 2.03

4-y-o+	W-R	Per cent	£1 Level Stake	Totals	W-R	Per cent	£1 Level Stake
Mar/Apr	3-16	18.8	+ 7.50	Mar/Apr	24-76	31.6	+ 32.52
May	3-22	13.6	- 14.12	May	10-80	12.5	- 52.25
June	2-22	9.1	- 13.00	June	18-95	18.9	- 11.76
July	3-23	13.0	- 4.33	July	27-95	28.4	- 9.82
August	0-14	-	- 14.00	August	12-115	10.4	- 52.02
September	1-15	6.7	- 7.50	September	9-102	8.8	- 50.88
Oct/Nov	1-18	5.6	- 11.00	Oct/Nov	19-108	17.6	- 16.63

DISTANCE

2-y-o	W-R	Per cent	£1 Level Stake	3-y-o	W-R	Per cent	£1 Level Stake
5f-6f	21-99	21.2	- 49.15	5f-6f	24-125	19.2	+ 0.20
7f-8f	23-81	28.4	- 7.19	7f-8f	16-91	17.6	+ 7.77
9f-13f	1-3	33.3	+ 0.50	9f-13f	15-84	17.9	- 16.17
14f+	3-9	33.3	- 2.65	14f+	3-49	6.1	- 37.70

4-y-o+	W-R	Per cent	£1 Level Stake	Totals	W-R	Per cent	£1 Level Stake
5f-6f	2-36	5.6	- 25.62	5f-6f	47-260	18.1	- 74.57
7f-8f	4-37	10.8	- 14.00	7f-8f	43-209	20.6	- 13.42
9f-13f	5-35	14.3	- 0.33	9f-13f	21-122	17.2	- 16.00
14f+	2-22	9.1	- 16.50	14f+	8-80	10.0	- 56.85

TYPE OF RACE

Non-Handicaps	W-R	Per cent	£1 Level Stake	Handicaps	W-R	Per cent	£1 Level Stake
2-y-o	46-174	26.4	- 47.79	2-y-o	2-16	12.5	- 8.70
3-y-o	39-238	16.4	- 49.98	3-y-o	16-93	17.2	+ 13.30
4-y-o+	5-39	12.8	- 13.12	4-y-o+	6-77	7.8	- 36.50
Apprentice	0-2	-	- 2.00	Apprentice	1-''	9.1	- 6.50
Amat/Ladies	4-15	26.7	- 3.55	Amat/Ladies	0-6	-	- 6.00
Totals	94-468	20.1	-116.44	Totals	25-203	12.3	- 44.40

FIRST TIME OUT

	W-R	Per cent	£1 Level Stake
2-y-o	17-61	27.9	- 20.66
3-y-o	11-73	15.1	- 17.70
4-y-o+	6-25	24.0	+ 2.05
Totals	34-159	21.4	- 36.31

JOCKEYS RIDING

	W-R	Per cent	£1 Level Stake		W-R	Per cent	£1 Level Stake
C Roche	90-344	26.2	- 7.40	Mr P Fenton	1-3	33.3	+ 2.50
K J Manning	12-108	11.1	- 46.14	Mr J A Hayes	1-4	25.0	- 2.33
J A Heffernan	6-53	11.3	- 10.00	T E Durcan	1-9	11.1	- 4.50
Miss C Hutchinson	2-5	40.0	- 0.72	B A Hunter	1-10	10.0	+ 2.00
C Everard	2-24	8.3	- 13.25	A P McCoy	1-15	6.7	+ 6.00
W J Supple	2-34	5.9	- 25.00				

D Manning	0-14	P Carberry	0-2	M Roberts	0-1
M W Martin	0-10	P P Murphy	0-2	Mr J A Nash	0-1
Mr G F Ryan	0-6	R V Skelly	0-2	R Hughes	0-1
S M Kelly	0-6	C McCormack	0-1	R M Burke	0-1
D Quirke	0-3	D Holland	0-1	S Craine	0-1
J J Stack	0-2	D J Murphy	0-1	T Murphy	0-1
Joanna Morgan	0-2	J F Egan	0-1		
Mr A P O'Brien	0-2	M Fenton	0-1		

COURSE RECORD

	Total W-R	Non-Handicaps 2-y-o	Non-Handicaps 3-y-o+	Handicaps 2-y-o	Handicaps 3-y-o+	Per cent	£1 Level Stake
The Curragh	30-189	13-51	11-80	0-6	6-52	15.9	- 38.32
Leopardstown	27-132	9-29	14-60	0-1	4-42	20.5	- 32.68
Naas	10-41	4-13	2-13	2-3	2-12	24.4	- 1.92
Tipperary	6-43	2-13	3-23	0-1	1-6	14.0	- 19.51
Roscommon	5-14	3-5	2-8	0-0	0-1	35.7	+ 2.07
Killarney	4-12	1-1	1-4	0-0	2-7	33.3	- 1.00
Tralee	4-21	1-6	2-9	0-0	1-6	19.0	- 4.00
Navan	4-23	3-7	1-12	0-0	0-4	17.4	- 10.85
Gowran Park	4-28	2-9	1-10	0-2	1-7	14.3	- 17.52
Limerick	3-13	0-1	2-8	0-0	1-4	23.1	+ 8.50
Listowel	3-19	2-5	0-9	0-1	1-4	15.8	- 4.00
Thurles	2-5	0-0	1-4	0-0	1-1	40.0	+ 25.00
Down Royal	2-5	1-3	1-2	0-0	0-0	40.0	- 1.47
Clonmel	2-7	0-0	1-4	0-0	1-3	28.6	+ 6.00
Mallow	2-15	1-4	1-8	0-0	0-3	13.3	- 8.87
Dundalk	2-15	1-4	1-8	0-0	0-3	13.3	- 9.75
Fairyhouse	2-24	1-9	1-6	0-1	0-8	8.3	- 17.25
Galway	2-37	1-7	1-11	0-1	0-18	5.4	- 33.65
Downpatrick	1-2	0-0	1-2	0-0	0-0	50.0	+ 5.50
Punchestown	1-2	1-1	0-1	0-0	0-0	50.0	+ 0.63
Bellewstown	1-5	0-1	0-1	0-0	1-3	20.0	- 2.75
Sligo	1-7	0-3	1-3	0-0	0-1	14.3	+ 3.00
Ballinrobe	1-7	0-2	0-4	0-0	1-1	14.3	- 3.00

Wexford   0-5

WINNING HORSES

	Age	Races Run	1st	2nd	3rd	Unpl	Win £
St Jovite	3	4	2	1	0	1	382,600
Park Dream	3	5	3	1	0	1	31,015
Ivory Frontier	2	5	3	0	0	2	28,170
Ballykett Prince	4	9	2	5	1	1	23,520
Tahdeed	2	3	3	0	0	0	21,145
Mining Tycoon	3	8	4	2	0	2	21,045
Basim	2	3	2	1	0	0	20,995
Nordic Fox	2	7	2	3	1	1	19,700
Arrikala	3	9	2	2	3	2	18,855

Wangola	2	6	3	1	1	1	17,595
Irish Memory	3	3	2	0	0	1	16,330
Nordic Pageant	3	4	3	0	0	1	15,525
Magic Carr	3	8	3	1	1	3	14,580
Gdansk's Honour	3	7	2	3	0	2	13,110
Perfect Impostor	2	2	2	0	0	0	12,522
Second Revolution	3	12	3	0	2	7	12,077
Nordic Oak	4	16	2	4	3	7	9,910
Direct Lady	3	10	3	1	1	5	9,839
Muir Staion	4	6	2	0	0	4	8,627
Thyer	3	3	1	1	1	0	8,625
Bint Albadou	2	5	2	1	1	1	8,382
Mr Brooks	5	1	1	0	0	0	8,282
Carressed	2	3	2	0	0	1	7,594
Layaali	3	3	2	1	0	0	7,590
Ignatius	2	2	1	0	0	1	6,900
Al Guswa	3	5	1	1	1	2	6,900
Jomel Amou	3	11	2	3	2	4	6,212
Pernilla	2	4	1	2	0	1	5,720
Persian Creek	3	8	1	1	1	5	5,670
Persian Reef	3	9	2	1	0	6	5,524
Tbaareeh	2	4	1	1	0	2	5,522
Maledetto	3	7	1	3	0	3	5,520
Alaqua	2	2	1	1	0	0	5,520
Royal Theatre	3	3	2	0	1	0	5,520
Blue Judge	2	2	1	0	1	0	5,520
Scribe	2	4	1	3	0	0	5,520
Shandon Lake	2	4	1	1	0	2	5,520
Europe	2	3	1	0	1	1	5,520
Riyoom	2	3	1	1	0	1	5,520
Alouette	2	4	1	2	1	0	5,520
St.Elias	2	1	1	0	0	0	5,520
Charette	2	1	1	0	0	0	5,520
Osvaldo	3	9	2	1	2	4	5,005
Moumayaz	2	3	1	0	0	2	4,832
Pollys Glow	3	5	1	1	0	3	4,830
Nordic Gayle	5	9	2	1	0	6	4,486
Ballykett Lady	2	2	1	1	0	0	4,485
Treasure Hope	3	1	1	0	0	0	4,140
Reliable	2	4	1	0	2	1	4,140
Tropicarr	3	6	1	0	1	4	4,140
Quick Blush	2	3	1	0	0	2	4,140
Appealing Bubbles	3	4	1	1	1	1	3,797
Gallardini	3	2	1	0	1	0	3,795
Nordic Time	3	6	1	1	1	3	3,795
Elegant King	3	3	1	0	1	1	3,795
Secret Sunday	3	7	1	1	3	2	3,702
Via Parigi	2	2	1	0	1	0	3,452
Desert Team	2	4	1	3	0	0	3,452
Bagenalstown Boy	4	1	1	0	0	0	3,452
Lord Bentley	2	2	1	1	0	0	3,452
Carrnassier	2	1	1	0	0	0	3,452
Gorgeous Dancer	3	6	1	0	2	3	3,450
Bryan Station	3	3	1	0	0	2	3,450
Barr Na Coille	3	2	1	0	0	1	3,450
Lord Noble	4	4	1	0	1	2	3,450

Short Visit	2	1	1	0	0	0	3,450
St Martha	2	1	1	0	0	0	3,450
Rondelli	2	4	1	0	0	3	3,278
Nordic Sign	3	10	1	1	0	8	2,762
Relentless Boy	2	6	1	1	0	4	2,762
Desert Wish	2	1	1	0	0	0	2,762
Staviski	2	10	1	4	2	3	2,760
Shawgatny	2	2	1	1	0	0	2,760
Kirov Premiere	2	3	1	1	1	0	2,760
Northmaid	3	6	1	0	0	5	2,245
Ferrufino	4	7	1	1	0	5	2,245
Miss Angel Too	3	6	1	1	0	4	2,245
Rodinsky	3	3	1	0	1	1	2,243
Legal Steps	3	4	1	1	0	2	2,243
Sophisticator	3	4	1	0	1	2	2,243
Almond Flower	2	6	1	1	1	3	1,725
Lyphard Abu	4	1	1	0	0	0	828

WINNING OWNERS

	Races Won	Value £		Races Won	Value £
Mrs V Kraft Payson	14	431,344	Sallyview Estates Ltd	2	5,520
Maktoum Al Maktoum	15	92,171	Miss K Rausing	1	5,520
D H W Dobson	16	90,043	Miss C M Keating	1	5,177
T F Brennan	8	40,717	T W Nicholson	1	4,830
P J P Gleeson	5	33,175	Stephen Keating	1	4,485
Patrick H Burns	3	31,015	Carlo Bascape	1	4,140
Mrs J S Bolger	9	27,819	Lady Sarah Barry	1	4,140
Miss Niamh Keating	3	26,970	Four B's Syndicate	1	3,452
Henryk De Kwiatkowski	4	24,150	Mohamed Suhail	1	3,452
Mrs Catherine Shubotham	3	22,462	Mrs Brigitte Wolff	1	3,450
Michael W J Smurfit	4	20,021	Michael H Keogh	1	3,450
M Bergl	3	12,077	F Dunne	1	3,450
Mrs D Mahony	3	9,839	Mrs Paul Butler	1	3,450
Abdullah Ali	2	9,662	Q M Syndicate	1	2,762
Hamad Ali	2	8,382	Butti Musabah	1	2,760
Paul Green	1	8,282	John L Wood	1	2,760
Mrs Barbara O'Dwyer	2	5,524	Mrs B Wolff	1	2,245
J P Hill	1	5,520	E P Spillane	1	2,243
Mrs E M H Ogden White	1	5,520	Mrs S O'Riordan	1	1,725

Favourites	62-148	41.9%	- 21.55		Total winning prize-money			£973,704
Longest winning sequence			4		Average SP of winner			3.3/1
Longest losing sequence			27		Return on stakes invested			-24.0%
1991 Form	111-622	17.8%	-124.92		1989 Form	80-444	18.0%	- 51.68
1990 Form	125-562	22.2%	- 95.72		1988 Form	38-343	11.1%	-127.06

V BOWENS

	No. of Horses	Races Run	1st	2nd	3rd	Unpl	Per cent	£1 Level Stake
2-y-o	6	21	0	0	0	21	-	- 21.00
3-y-o	5	26	4	1	1	20	15.4	+ 12.00
4-y-o+	8	38	3	4	4	27	7.9	- 7.75
Totals	19	85	7	5	5	68	8.2	- 16.75

Mar/Apr	May	Jun	Jul	Aug	Sep	Oct/Nov
2-5	0-9	1-6	1-12	1-22	2-14	0-17

Winning Jockeys	W-R	£1 Level Stake			W-R	£1 Level Stake
B Bowens	3-53	- 19.00	M Fenton		1-2	+ 0.25
A J Roche	1-1	+ 14.00	W J O'Connor		1-5	+ 4.00
P P Murphy	1-1	+ 7.00				

Winning Courses						
Down Royal	2-7	+ 8.25	Listowel		1-5	+ 5.00
Fairyhouse	1-5	+ 6.00	Leopardstown		1-16	- 1.00
Tralee	1-5	+ 3.00	The Curragh		1-16	- 7.00

Winning Horses	Age	Races Run	1st	2nd	3rd	Unpl	Win £
Mayfield Prince	3	4	2	0	0	2	6,555
Reported	3	4	1	1	0	2	5,520
Gods Express	4	11	1	2	1	7	4,142
Solar Flash	3	9	1	0	1	7	3,450
Liberated Bird	7	12	2	0	2	8	2,208

Favourites	1-2	50.0%	+ 0.25	Total winning prize-money		£21,875

1991 Form	1-52	1.9%	- 41.00	1989 Form	1-50	2.0%	- 41.00
1990 Form	2-40	5.0%	- 26.00	1988 Form	1-53	1.9%	- 50.00

LIAM BROWNE

	No. of Horses	Races Run	1st	2nd	3rd	Unpl	Per cent	£1 Level Stake
2-y-o	8	47	4	6	5	32	8.5	- 28.77
3-y-o	11	65	4	9	11	41	6.2	- 36.27
4-y-o+	5	18	0	1	2	15	-	- 18.00
Totals	24	130	8	16	18	88	6.2	- 83.04

Mar/Apr	May	Jun	Jul	Aug	Sep	Oct/Nov
1-15	1-12	1-30	3-24	2-21	0-15	0-13

Winning Jockeys	W-R	£1 Level Stake				W-R	£1 Level Stake
J J Behan	4-39	- 15.64		R Hughes		1-5	+ 6.00
J Reid	1-1	+ 1.10		S Craine		1-39	- 34.00
J P Murtagh	1-1	+ 4.50					

Winning Courses							
Down Royal	2-6	+ 7.10		Tramore		1-2	- 0.27
Naas	2-9	+ 10.00		Tralee		1-3	+ 2.50
Dundalk	1-1	+ 1.63		Limerick		1-4	+ 1.00

Winning Horses	Age	Races Run	1st	2nd	3rd	Unpl	Win £
Time It Right	3	11	1	2	1	7	4,140
Kar Or	2	7	1	0	1	5	3,452
Babushka	2	4	1	1	0	2	3,452
Lady Ounavarra	2	9	1	1	2	5	2,762
Thatcherise	3	6	1	2	2	1	2,245
Simply Marilyn	3	8	1	4	0	3	2,245
Digpast	2	7	1	2	0	4	2,070
Travel Light	3	2	1	0	0	1	828

Favourites	2-11	18.2%	- 7.17	Total winning prize-money			£21,194

1991 Form	9-128	7.0%	- 43.12	1989 Form	15-184	8.2%	- 76.92
1990 Form	13-202	6.4%	-121.25	1988 Form	26-281	9.3%	-120.47

W P BROWNE

	No. of Horses	Races Run	1st	2nd	3rd	Unpl	Per cent	£1 Level Stake
2-y-o	1	5	0	0	0	5	-	- 5.00
3-y-o	0	0	0	0	0	0	-	0.00
4-y-o+	4	13	3	3	1	6	23.1	- 1.00
Totals	5	18	3	3	1	11	16.7	- 6.00

Mar/Apr	May	Jun	Jul	Aug	Sep	Oct/Nov
0-0	0-0	0-1	0-2	3-7	0-6	0-2

Winning Jockeys	W-R	£1 Level Stake			W-R	£1 Level Stake
M J Kinane	2-6	- 2.00	R Hughes		1-1	+ 7.00

Winning Courses					
Roscommon	1-1	+ 0.50	Tramore	1-2	+ 6.00
Tralee	1-1	+ 1.50			

Winning Horses	Age	Races Run	1st	2nd	3rd	Unpl	Win £
Darcy's Thatcher	8	8	2	3	1	2	5,695
Miss Darcy	4	2	1	0	0	1	2,245

Favourites	2-4	50.0%	0.00	Total winning prize-money			£7,940

1991 Form	1-7	14.3%	- 5.33

ARTHUR BUNYAN

	No. of Horses	Races Run	1st	2nd	3rd	Unpl	Per cent	£1 Level Stake
2-y-o	1	3	0	0	0	3	-	- 3.00
3-y-o	2	14	1	1	2	10	7.1	- 12.33
4-y-o+	3	15	1	2	0	12	6.7	- 6.00
Totals	6	32	2	3	2	25	6.3	- 21.33

Mar/Apr	May	Jun	Jul	Aug	Sep	Oct/Nov
0-7	0-3	1-4	0-4	1-5	0-3	0-6

Winning Jockey	W-R	£1 Level Stake		W-R	£1 Level Stake
W J Smith	2-10	+ 0.67			

Winning Courses					
Gowran Park	1-2	+ 7.00	Tramore	1-3	- 1.33

Winning Horses	Age	Races Run	1st	2nd	3rd	Unpl	Win £
Rathbrides Joy	5	9	1	2	0	6	3,450
Tina's Charm	3	10	1	1	1	7	2,935

Favourites	1-3	33.3%	- 1.33	Total winning prize-money	£6,385

1991 Form	1-25	4.0%	- 14.00	1989 Form	0-14
1990 Form	0-4			1988 Form	0-19

J BURNS

	No. of Horses	Races Run	1st	2nd	3rd	Unpl	Per cent	£1 Level Stake
2-y-o	11	33	3	2	4	24	9.1	- 15.25
3-y-o	3	10	2	1	4	3	20.0	+ 4.00
4-y-o+	3	13	2	3	1	7	15.4	+ 7.00
Totals	17	56	7	6	9	34	12.5	- 4.25

Mar/Apr	May	Jun	Jul	Aug	Sep	Oct/Nov
0-2	1-7	0-8	2-8	3-17	1-9	0-5

Winning Jockeys	W-R	£1 Level Stake		W-R	£1 Level Stake
P Shanahan	4-21	+ 2.75	D V Smith	1-4	+ 11.00
J P Murtagh	1-3	+ 5.00	B J Walsh	1-8	- 3.00

Winning Courses					
Sligo	2-3	+ 11.00	Downpatrick	1-2	+ 13.00
Tipperary	2-8	+ 3.25	Ballinrobe	1-3	+ 2.00
Down Royal	1-2	+ 4.50			

Winning Horses	Age	Races Run	1st	2nd	3rd	Unpl	Win £
Preponderance	2	2	1	0	0	1	3,452
Last Emperor	5	7	1	1	0	5	2,945
Sovereign Grace	3	2	1	0	1	0	2,762
Kellsboro Lass	2	4	1	0	0	3	2,762
Fleur De Ciel	2	5	1	0	1	3	2,760
Felsen	3	7	1	1	3	2	2,245
Tarkhana	4	3	1	1	0	1	690

Favourites	1-1	100.0%	+ 4.00	Total winning prize-money			£17,616

1991 Form	0-0			1989 Form	0-2
1990 Form	0-0			1988 Form	0-3

J P BYRNE

	No. of Horses	Races Run	1st	2nd	3rd	Unpl	Per cent	£1 Level Stake
2-y-o	3	5	0	0	0	5	-	- 5.00
3-y-o	1	3	1	0	1	1	33.3	+ 10.00
4-y-o+	4	4	0	0	1	3	-	- 4.00
Totals	8	12	1	0	2	9	8.3	+ 1.00

Mar/Apr	May	Jun	Jul	Aug	Sep	Oct/Nov
0-1	1-2	0-2	0-1	0-0	0-3	0-3

Winning Jockey	W-R	£1 Level Stake	Winning Course	W-R	£1 Level Stake
W J Smith	1-6	+ 7.00	Navan	1-3	+ 10.00

Winning Horse	Age	Races Run	1st	2nd	3rd	Unpl	Win £
Big Chance	3	3	1	0	1	1	2,762

Favourites	0-0	Total winning prize-money	£2,762

1991 Form	1-16	6.3%	- 9.00	1989 Form	1-22	4.5%	- 19.00
1990 Form	1-12	8.3%	- 3.00	1988 Form	0-19		

J M CANTY

	No. of Horses	Races Run	1st	2nd	3rd	Unpl	Per cent	£1 Level Stake
2-y-o	6	18	0	0	0	18	-	- 18.00
3-y-o	4	20	0	4	1	15	-	- 20.00
4-y-o+	5	20	1	1	1	17	5.0	- 18.56
Totals	15	58	1	5	2	50	1.7	- 56.56

Mar/Apr	May	Jun	Jul	Aug	Sep	Oct/Nov
0-3	1-8	0-5	0-9	0-7	0-14	0-12

Winning Jockey	W-R	£1 Level Stake	Winning Course	W-R	£1 Level Stake
S Craine	1-12	- 10.56	Wexford	1-2	- 0.56

Winning Horse	Age	Races Run	1st	2nd	3rd	Unpl	Win £
Often Ahead	4	5	1	0	1	3	2,762

Favourites	1-1	100.0%	+ 0.44	Total winning prize-money		£2,762

1991 Form	3-72	4.2%	- 40.00	1989 Form	0-57		
1990 Form	6-55	10.9%	- 28.62	1988 Form	4-43	9.3%	- 9.50

PETER CASEY

	No. of Horses	Races Run	1st	2nd	3rd	Unpl	Per cent	£1 Level Stake
2-y-o	0	0	0	0	0	0	-	0.00
3-y-o	2	10	0	0	0	10	-	- 10.00
4-y-o+	6	15	1	1	3	10	6.7	- 8.00
Totals	8	25	1	1	3	20	4.0	- 18.00

Mar/Apr	May	Jun	Jul	Aug	Sep	Oct/Nov
0-1	0-2	0-2	0-4	1-10	0-4	0-2

Winning Jockey	W-R	£1 Level Stake	Winning Course	W-R	£1 Level Stake
M Fenton	1-6	+ 1.00	Downpatrick	1-3	+ 4.00

Winning Horse	Age	Races Run	1st	2nd	3rd	Unpl	Win £
Collon Beag	5	6	1	1	1	3	2,070

Favourites	0-1		Total winning prize-money		£2,070

1991 Form	3-56	5.4%	- 10.50	1989 Form	1-16	6.3%	- 5.00
1990 Form	2-35	5.7%	- 15.50	1988 Form	2-17	11.8%	+ 3.50

C CASSIDY

	No. of Horses	Races Run	1st	2nd	3rd	Unpl	Per cent	£1 Level Stake
2-y-o	0	0	0	0	0	0	-	0.00
3-y-o	2	13	1	0	1	11	7.7	- 4.00
4-y-o+	1	5	0	0	0	5	-	- 5.00
Totals	3	18	1	0	1	16	5.6	- 9.00

Mar/Apr	May	Jun	Jul	Aug	Sep	Oct/Nov
0-3	0-1	1-3	0-3	0-3	0-2	0-3

		£1 Level				£1 Level
Winning Jockey	W-R	Stake		Winning Course	W-R	Stake
D V Smith	1-11	- 2.00		Sligo	1-3	+ 6.00

		Races					Win
Winning Horse	Age	Run	1st	2nd	3rd	Unpl	£
Brackloon Boy	3	11	1	0	1	9	2,243

Favourites	0-0	Total winning prize-money	£2,243

1991 Form	0-9

C COLLINS

	No. of Horses	Races Run	1st	2nd	3rd	Unpl	Per cent	£1 Level Stake
2-y-o	18	40	6	3	4	27	15.0	- 7.58
3-y-o	18	89	8	5	4	72	9.0	- 46.50
4-y-o+	10	38	2	4	1	31	5.3	- 24.37
Totals	46	167	16	12	9	130	9.6	- 78.45

BY MONTH

2-y-o	W-R	Per cent	£1 Level Stake	3-y-o	W-R	Per cent	£1 Level Stake
Mar/Apr	1-4	25.0	+ 2.00	Mar/Apr	1-18	5.6	- 12.00
May	2-3	66.7	+ 5.67	May	1-11	9.1	- 4.00
June	0-2	-	- 2.00	June	0-8	-	- 8.00
July	0-0	-	0.00	July	1-6	16.7	+ 1.00
August	1-12	8.3	- 8.25	August	1-16	6.3	- 12.50
September	1-6	16.7	+ 5.00	September	3-12	25.0	+ 1.00
Oct/Nov	1-13	7.7	- 10.00	Oct/Nov	1-18	5.6	- 12.00

4-y-o+	W-R	Per cent	£1 Level Stake	Totals	W-R	Per cent	£1 Level Stake
Mar/Apr	0-6	-	- 6.00	Mar/Apr	2-28	7.1	- 16.00
May	0-5	-	- 5.00	May	3-19	15.8	- 3.33
June	0-4	-	- 4.00	June	0-14	-	- 14.00
July	1-10	10.0	+ 1.00	July	2-16	12.5	+ 2.00
August	1-5	20.0	- 2.37	August	3-33	9.1	- 23.12
September	0-6	-	- 6.00	September	4-24	16.7	0.00
Oct/Nov	0-2	-	- 2.00	Oct/Nov	2-33	6.1	- 24.00

DISTANCE

2-y-o	W-R	Per cent	£1 Level Stake	3-y-o	W-R	Per cent	£1 Level Stake
5f-6f	4-21	19.0	+ 1.42	5f-6f	3-37	8.1	- 20.50
7f-8f	2-17	11.8	- 7.00	7f-8f	4-37	10.8	- 16.00
9f-13f	0-0	-	0.00	9f-13f	0-10	-	- 10.00
14f+	0-2	-	- 2.00	14f+	1-5	20.0	0.00

4-y-o+	W-R	Per cent	£1 Level Stake	Totals	W-R	Per cent	£1 Level Stake
5f-6f	0-9	-	- 9.00	5f-6f	7-67	10.4	- 28.08
7f-8f	1-9	11.1	- 6.37	7f-8f	7-63	11.1	- 29.37
9f-13f	0-10	-	- 10.00	9f-13f	0-20	-	- 20.00
14f+	1-10	10.0	+ 1.00	14f+	2-17	11.8	- 1.00

TYPE OF RACE

Non-Handicaps	W-R	Per cent	£1 Level Stake	Handicaps	W-R	Per cent	£1 Level Stake
2-y-o	6-38	15.8	- 5.58	2-y-o	0-2	-	- 2.00
3-y-o	5-65	7.7	- 38.00	3-y-o	3-22	13.6	- 6.50
4-y-o+	1-4	25.0	- 1.37	4-y-o+	1-29	3.4	- 18.00
Apprentice	0-0	-	0.00	Apprentice	0-5	-	- 5.00
Amat/Ladies	0-1	-	- 1.00	Amat/Ladies	0-1	-	- 1.00
Totals	12-108	11.1	- 45.95	Totals	4-59	6.8	- 32.50

FIRST TIME OUT

	W-R	Per cent	£1 Level Stake
2-y-o	4-18	22.2	+ 4.42
3-y-o	2-18	11.1	- 5.00
4-y-o+	0-10	-	- 10.00
Totals	6-46	13.0	- 10.58

JOCKEYS RIDING

	W-R	Per cent	£1 Level Stake		W-R	Per cent	£1 Level Stake
P Shanahan	7-52	13.5	- 18.58	W J Supple	1-4	25.0	+ 1.00
P V Gilson	4-64	6.3	- 35.50	W J O'Connor	1-12	8.3	- 5.00
D G O'Shea	2-2	100.0	+ 10.00	J J Mullins	1-14	7.1	- 11.37

K J Manning	0-3	J J Behan	0-1	N G McCullagh	0-1
S Craine	0-3	L O'Shea	0-1	P Carberry	0-1
E A Leonard	0-2	Miss T Collins	0-1	R Griffiths	0-1
M Fenton	0-2	Mr J P Dempsey	0-1		
F Woods	0-1	N Byrne	0-1		

COURSE RECORD

	Total W-R	Non-Handicaps 2-y-o	3-y-o+	Handicaps 2-y-o	3-y-o+	Per cent	£1 Level Stake
The Curragh	6-52	2-12	2-18	0-1	2-21	11.5	- 22.00
Naas	2-12	2-3	0-5	0-1	0-3	16.7	- 4.33
Leopardstown	2-25	1-8	1-12	0-0	0-5	8.0	- 14.25
Limerick	1-2	0-0	1-1	0-0	0-1	50.0	+ 5.00
Tramore	1-3	0-0	1-3	0-0	0-0	33.3	- 0.37
Gowran Park	1-7	1-3	0-3	0-0	0-1	14.3	+ 4.00
Galway	1-9	0-1	0-2	0-0	1-6	11.1	+ 2.00
Tipperary	1-10	0-2	1-6	0-0	0-2	10.0	- 5.00
Tralee	1-14	0-4	0-3	0-0	1-7	7.1	- 10.50

Navan	0-9	Wexford	0-3	Down Royal	0-1
Dundalk	0-4	Ballinrobe	0-2	Listowel	0-1
Fairyhouse	0-4	Downpatrick	0-2	Roscommon	0-1
Bellewstown	0-3	Punchestown	0-2	Thurles	0-1

WINNING HORSES

	Age	Races Run	1st	2nd	3rd	Unpl	Win £
Frenchpark	2	3	2	1	0	0	20,700
Bezelle	3	4	2	0	0	2	20,125
Lavinia Fontana	3	9	3	2	1	3	18,030
Joyeus Garde	2	2	1	0	0	1	5,520
Master Tribe	2	1	1	0	0	0	5,520
Steel Head	4	5	1	0	0	4	4,485
Eurostorm	2	1	1	0	0	0	4,140
Pinta	2	1	1	0	0	0	3,450
Queens Glen	3	6	1	2	0	3	3,450
Shrewd Move	3	5	1	0	0	4	2,760
Bestbeteastwood	3	5	1	0	0	4	2,245
Fortune's Girl	4	8	1	1	0	6	2,243

WINNING OWNERS

	Races Won	Value £		Races Won	Value £
Lord Harrington	3	26,220	H Scheftel	1	4,485
James McNeil	3	23,575	Mrs G W Jennings	1	4,140
Cyril Humphris	3	18,030	A McLean	1	2,760
Edward St George	2	5,693	Mrs B J Eastwood	1	2,245
Mrs C Collins	1	5,520			

Favourites	7-17	41.2%	+ 7.80	Total winning prize-money	£92,668

Longest winning sequence	2	Average SP of winner	4.5/1
Longest losing sequence	29	Return on stakes invested	-47.0%

1991 Form	22-208	10.6%	- 73.25	1989 Form	32-287	11.1%	- 100.64
1990 Form	19-255	7.5%	- 119.27	1988 Form	33-264	12.5%	- 64.77

G M CONNOLLY

	No. of Horses	Races Run	1st	2nd	3rd	Unpl	Per cent	£1 Level Stake
2-y-o	1	4	0	0	0	4	-	- 4.00
3-y-o	4	21	1	1	2	17	4.8	- 13.00
4-y-o+	3	11	0	0	1	10	-	- 11.00
Totals	8	36	1	1	3	31	2.8	- 28.00

Mar/Apr	May	Jun	Jul	Aug	Sep	Oct/Nov
0-6	0-3	0-4	0-8	0-9	0-3	1-3

Winning Jockey	W-R	£1 Level Stake	Winning Course	W-R	£1 Level Stake
C Roche	1-4	+ 4.00	Navan	1-2	+ 6.00

Winning Horse	Age	Races Run	1st	2nd	3rd	Unpl	Win £
Moschino	3	6	1	0	1	4	3,450

Favourites	0-1	Total winning prize-money	£3,450

1991 Form	0-42

J G COOGAN

	No. of Horses	Races Run	1st	2nd	3rd	Unpl	Per cent	£1 Level Stake
2-y-o	10	46	5	5	8	28	10.9	- 21.25
3-y-o	4	14	1	2	0	11	7.1	- 11.25
4-y-o+	3	15	1	0	3	11	6.7	- 9.00
Totals	17	75	7	7	11	50	9.3	- 41.50

Mar/Apr	May	Jun	Jul	Aug	Sep	Oct/Nov
0-5	0-9	0-14	2-10	3-16	2-11	0-10

Winning Jockeys	W-R	£1 Level Stake		W-R	£1 Level Stake
B Coogan	6-44	- 16.50	J D Eddery	1-3	+ 3.00

Winning Courses					
Tipperary	2-7	+ 1.50	Leopardstown	1-4	+ 2.00
Ballinrobe	1-2	+ 1.25	Bellewstown	1-4	+ 2.00
Sligo	1-3	- 0.25	The Curragh	1-14	- 7.00

Winning Horses	Age	Races Run	1st	2nd	3rd	Unpl	Win £
Up And At'Em	2	6	3	1	1	1	21,852
Doyroy	2	8	1	0	1	6	3,450
Tombara	4	8	1	0	3	4	2,935
Cookawara	2	6	1	1	1	3	2,762
Titled Dancer	3	8	1	2	0	5	2,760

Favourites	3-6	50.0%	+ 2.50	Total winning prize-money			£33,759

1991 Form	5-67	7.5%	- 16.50	1989 Form	1-15	6.7%	- 5.00
1990 Form	1-26	3.8%	- 18.00				

MRS A M CROWLEY-O'BRIEN

	No. of Horses	Races Run	1st	2nd	3rd	Unpl	Per cent	£1 Level Stake
2-y-o	5	18	1	2	0	15	5.6	- 15.25
3-y-o	7	36	6	2	3	25	16.7	+ 3.00
4-y-o+	5	8	0	3	0	5	-	- 8.00
Totals	17	62	7	7	3	45	11.3	- 20.25

Mar/Apr	May	Jun	Jul	Aug	Sep	Oct/Nov
0-0	0-8	0-2	0-3	1-14	1-12	5-23

Winning Jockeys	W-R	£1 Level Stake		W-R	£1 Level Stake
J A Heffernan	3-20	- 8.25	J P Murtagh	1-2	+ 5.00
J F Egan	1-1	+ 2.00	W J Supple	1-15	- 8.00
R M Burke	1-1	+ 12.00			

Winning Courses					
Dundalk	1-1	+ 1.75	Navan	1-2	+ 5.00
Wexford	1-1	+ 6.00	Leopardstown	1-7	+ 6.00
Punchestown	1-1	+ 2.00	Gowran Park	1-7	- 1.50
Thurles	1-2	+ 1.50			

Winning Horses	Age	Races Run	1st	2nd	3rd	Unpl	Win £
Pharfetched	3	5	2	0	1	2	15,760
Maid Of Vision	3	6	1	0	1	4	3,450
Autumn Gorse	3	8	1	2	1	4	2,760
Amu Darya	2	4	1	0	0	3	2,760
Acrobate	3	5	1	0	0	4	2,245
Loshian	3	4	1	0	0	3	2,243

Favourites	2-4	50.0%	+ 1.75	Total winning prize-money	£29,218

1991 Form	8-56	14.3%	- 24.27

T G CURTIN

	No. of Horses	Races Run	1st	2nd	3rd	Unpl	Per cent	£1 Level Stake
2-y-o	0	0	0	0	0	0	-	0.00
3-y-o	6	30	2	1	1	26	6.7	- 20.00
4-y-o+	3	17	3	0	2	12	17.6	+ 18.00
Totals	9	47	5	1	3	38	10.6	- 2.00

Mar/Apr	May	Jun	Jul	Aug	Sep	Oct/Nov
1-3	0-7	0-7	1-7	2-12	1-6	0-5

Winning Jockeys	W-R	£1 Level Stake		W-R	£1 Level Stake
J D Eddery	1-1	+ 1.50	W J Smith	1-6	+ 9.00
M J Kinane	1-2	+ 8.00	D G O'Shea	1-12	- 4.50
Mr A J Martin	1-2	+ 8.00			

Winning Courses					
Tramore	1-3	- 0.50	Killarney	1-5	+ 10.00
Naas	1-4	+ 3.50	Tralee	1-7	+ 3.00
Listowel	1-4	+ 6.00			

Winning Horses	Age	Races Run	1st	2nd	3rd	Unpl	Win £
Desert Squaw	5	7	2	0	0	5	13,900
Floral Street	3	9	1	0	0	8	4,140
Tempted	4	5	1	0	1	3	3,452
Shakiyka	3	9	1	0	1	7	2,245

Favourites	1-2	50.0%	+ 0.50	Total winning prize-money		£23,737

1991 Form	6-42	14.3%	+ 26.00	1989 Form	10-60	16.7%	+ 26.50
1990 Form	5-56	8.9%	- 20.00	1988 Form	13-104	12.5%	- 23.70

H DE BROMHEAD

	No. of Horses	Races Run	1st	2nd	3rd	Unpl	Per cent	£1 Level Stake
2-y-o	0	0	0	0	0	0	-	0.00
3-y-o	1	11	3	1	0	7	27.3	+ 20.00
4-y-o+	1	6	0	0	0	6	-	- 6.00
Totals	2	17	3	1	0	13	17.6	+ 14.00

Mar/Apr	May	Jun	Jul	Aug	Sep	Oct/Nov
0-1	0-1	0-2	1-3	1-5	1-3	0-2

Winning Jockey	W-R	£1 Level Stake				W-R	£1 Level Stake
Joanna Morgan	3-13	+ 18.00					

Winning Courses							
Killarney	1-2	+ 15.00		Listowel		1-2	+ 3.00
Tralee	1-2	+ 7.00					

Winning Horse	Age	Races Run	1st	2nd	3rd	Unpl	Win £
Seamill	3	11	3	1	0	7	15,182

Favourites	0-0			Total winning prize-money			£15,182

1991 Form	0-5		1989 Form	0-18		
1990 Form	0-4		1988 Form	2-35	5.7%	- 20.00

F DUNNE

	No. of Horses	Races Run	1st	2nd	3rd	Unpl	Per cent	£1 Level Stake
2-y-o	6	26	0	0	2	24	-	- 26.00
3-y-o	9	59	4	5	11	39	6.8	- 24.25
4-y-o+	5	53	6	2	4	41	11.3	- 3.67
Totals	20	138	10	7	17	104	7.2	- 53.92

BY MONTH

2-y-o	W-R	Per cent	£1 Level Stake	3-y-o	W-R	Per cent	£1 Level Stake
Mar/Apr	0-0	-	0.00	Mar/Apr	0-13	-	- 13.00
May	0-1	-	- 1.00	May	0-5	-	- 5.00
June	0-4	-	- 4.00	June	0-8	-	- 8.00
July	0-11	-	- 11.00	July	0-9	-	- 9.00
August	0-9	-	- 9.00	August	2-14	14.3	+ 6.50
September	0-1	-	- 1.00	September	1-8	12.5	+ 3.00
Oct/Nov	0-0	-	0.00	Oct/Nov	1-2	50.0	+ 1.25

4-y-o+	W-R	Per cent	£1 Level Stake	Totals	W-R	Per cent	£1 Level Stake
Mar/Apr	0-2	-	- 2.00	Mar/Apr	0-15	-	- 15.00
May	0-5	-	- 5.00	May	0-11	-	- 11.00
June	3-11	27.3	+ 21.00	June	3-23	13.0	+ 9.00
July	1-12	8.3	- 7.67	July	1-32	3.1	- 27.67
August	2-13	15.4	0.00	August	4-36	11.1	- 2.50
September	0-6	-	- 6.00	September	1-15	6.7	- 4.00
Oct/Nov	0-4	-	- 4.00	Oct/Nov	1-6	16.7	- 2.75

DISTANCE

2-y-o	W-R	Per cent	£1 Level Stake	3-y-o	W-R	Per cent	£1 Level Stake
5f-6f	0-13	-	- 13.00	5f-6f	1-24	4.2	- 20.75
7f-8f	0-13	-	- 13.00	7f-8f	1-11	9.1	+ 6.00
9f-13f	0-0	-	0.00	9f-13f	2-11	18.2	+ 3.50
14f+	0-0	-	0.00	14f+	0-13	-	- 13.00

4-y-o+	W-R	Per cent	£1 Level Stake	Totals	W-R	Per cent	£1 Level Stake
5f-6f	1-16	6.3	- 1.00	5f-6f	2-53	3.8	- 34.75
7f-8f	1-7	14.3	+ 4.00	7f-8f	2-31	6.5	- 3.00
9f-13f	1-12	8.3	- 6.00	9f-13f	3-23	13.0	- 2.50
14f+	3-18	16.7	- 0.67	14f+	3-31	9.7	- 13.67

TYPE OF RACE

Non-Handicaps	W-R	Per cent	£1 Level Stake	Handicaps	W-R	Per cent	£1 Level Stake
2-y-o	0-23	-	- 23.00	2-y-o	0-3	-	- 3.00
3-y-o	2-20	10.0	+ 0.50	3-y-o	1-28	3.6	- 24.75
4-y-o+	0-8	-	- 8.00	4-y-o+	4-35	11.4	- 6.67
Apprentice	0-1	-	- 1.00	Apprentice	0-9	-	- 9.00
Amat/Ladies	3-11	27.3	+ 21.00	Amat/Ladies	0-0	-	0.00
Totals	5-63	7.9	- 10.50	Totals	5-75	6.7	- 43.42

FIRST TIME OUT

	W-R	Per cent	£1 Level Stake
2-y-o	0-6	-	- 6.00
3-y-o	0-9	-	- 9.00
4-y-o+	1-5	20.0	+ 6.00
Totals	1-20	5.0	- 9.00

JOCKEYS RIDING

	W-R	Per cent	£1 Level Stake		W-R	Per cent	£1 Level Stake
J P Murtagh	3-15	20.0	+ 15.00	J A Heffernan	1-1	100.0	+ 2.25
R M Burke	3-35	8.6	- 16.17	Miss A Gilsenan	1-5	20.0	+ 10.00
Miss A Marshall	2-6	33.3	+ 11.00				

W J O'Connor	0-19	P Carberry	0-4	J R Barry	0-1
C Everard	0-12	D G O'Shea	0-2	M J Kinane	0-1
P V Gilson	0-12	N G McCullagh	0-2	T G Hagger	0-1
W J Supple	0-9	R Hughes	0-2	W J Smith	0-1
C Roche	0-4	M Fenton	0-1		
K J Manning	0-4	J P Deegan	0-1		

COURSE RECORD

	Total W-R	Non-Handicaps 2-y-o	Non-Handicaps 3-y-o+	Handicaps 2-y-o	Handicaps 3-y-o+	Per cent	£1 Level Stake
Downpatrick	1-1	0-0	1-1	0-0	0-0	100.0	+ 2.50
Tramore	1-1	0-0	0-0	0-0	1-1	100.0	+ 5.00
Bellewstown	1-3	0-2	0-0	0-0	1-1	33.3	+ 8.00
Tipperary	1-5	0-1	0-0	0-0	1-4	20.0	+ 2.00
Down Royal	1-6	0-2	0-2	0-0	1-2	16.7	- 2.75
Fairyhouse	1-8	0-2	1-3	0-0	0-3	12.5	+ 3.00
Gowran Park	1-10	0-2	1-2	0-1	0-5	10.0	+ 5.00
Naas	1-13	0-3	0-4	0-0	1-6	7.7	- 8.67
The Curragh	1-16	0-2	1-6	0-0	0-8	6.3	- 10.00
Leopardstown	1-34	0-6	1-10	0-1	0-17	2.9	- 17.00

Dundalk	0-8	Clonmel	0-3	Ballinrobe		0-1
Roscommon	0-7	Killarney	0-3	Thurles		0-1
Galway	0-6	Navan	0-3	Wexford		0-1
Tralee	0-6	Limerick	0-2			

WINNING HORSES

	Age	Races Run	1st	2nd	3rd	Unpl	Win £
Happy Smile	4	17	2	2	2	11	11,920
Vistage	4	18	3	0	1	14	9,666
Sense Of Value	3	7	2	1	1	3	4,140
Wayward Way	3	6	1	1	1	3	3,450
Happy Rover	7	6	1	0	0	5	2,935
Happy Bliss	3	19	1	3	2	13	1,035

WINNING OWNERS

	Races Won	Value £		Races Won	Value £
Mrs E McMahon	4	15,890	F Dunne	3	7,590
Miss Therese Dunne	3	9,666			

Favourites	2-5	40.0%	+ 1.75	Total winning prize-money			£33,146
Longest winning sequence			1	Average SP of winner			7.4/1
Longest losing sequence			35	Return on stakes invested			-39.1%
1991 Form	10-139	7.2%	- 47.50	1989 Form	11-96	11.5%	+ 7.25
1990 Form	3-55	5.5%	- 39.25	1988 Form	4-86	4.7%	- 51.00

OLIVER FINNEGAN

	No. of Horses	Races Run	1st	2nd	3rd	Unpl	Per cent	£1 Level Stake
2-y-o	0	0	0	0	0	0	-	0.00
3-y-o	2	10	1	1	1	7	10.0	+ 11.00
4-y-o+	4	19	0	0	0	19	-	- 19.00
Totals	6	29	1	1	1	26	3.4	- 8.00

Mar/Apr	May	Jun	Jul	Aug	Sep	Oct/Nov
0-0	0-9	1-4	0-6	0-0	0-4	0-6

Winning Jockey	W-R	£1 Level Stake	Winning Course	W-R	£1 Level Stake
J J Behan	1-4	+ 17.00	Dundalk	1-7	+ 14.00

Winning Horse	Age	Races Run	1st	2nd	3rd	Unpl	Win £
Ardlea House	3	8	1	1	1	5	2,245

Favourites	0-0		Total winning prize-money	£2,245

1991 Form	0-11		1989 Form	0-19		
1990 Form	0-8		1988 Form	3-55	5.5%	- 35.50

F FLOOD

	No. of Horses	Races Run	1st	2nd	3rd	Unpl	Per cent	£1 Level Stake
2-y-o	1	7	0	1	2	4	-	- 7.00
3-y-o	0	0	0	0	0	0	-	0.00
4-y-o+	3	5	1	0	0	4	20.0	+ 2.00
Totals	4	12	1	1	2	8	8.3	- 5.00

Mar/Apr	May	Jun	Jul	Aug	Sep	Oct/Nov
1-2	0-0	0-2	0-0	0-3	0-3	0-2

Winning Jockey	W-R	£1 Level Stake	Winning Course	W-R	£1 Level Stake
Mr F J Flood	1-2	+ 5.00	Naas	1-1	+ 6.00

Winning Horse	Age	Races Run	1st	2nd	3rd	Unpl	Win £
Nancy Myles	7	2	1	0	0	1	3,795

Favourites	0-1		Total winning prize-money	£3,795

1991 Form	3-14	21.4%	+ 11.25	1989 Form	0-7		
1990 Form	2-7	28.6%	+ 2.40	1988 Form	2-13	15.4%	- 4.50

P J FLYNN

	No. of Horses	Races Run	1st	2nd	3rd	Unpl	Per cent	£1 Level Stake
2-y-o	9	39	2	1	2	34	5.1	- 24.00
3-y-o	12	58	9	7	7	35	15.5	- 19.25
4-y-o+	24	84	11	7	10	56	13.1	- 28.47
Totals	45	181	22	15	19	125	12.2	- 71.72

BY MONTH

2-y-o	W-R	Per cent	£1 Level Stake	3-y-o	W-R	Per cent	£1 Level Stake
Mar/Apr	0-0	-	0.00	Mar/Apr	0-5	-	- 5.00
May	0-1	-	- 1.00	May	1-9	11.1	- 2.00
June	0-5	-	- 5.00	June	1-12	8.3	- 9.00
July	0-3	-	- 3.00	July	1-4	25.0	+ 2.00
August	2-10	20.0	+ 5.00	August	4-8	50.0	+ 4.75
September	0-8	-	- 8.00	September	0-9	-	- 9.00
Oct/Nov	0-12	-	- 12.00	Oct/Nov	2-11	18.2	- 1.00

4-y-o+	W-R	Per cent	£1 Level Stake	Totals	W-R	Per cent	£1 Level Stake
Mar/Apr	0-9	-	- 9.00	Mar/Apr	0-14	-	- 14.00
May	2-16	12.5	- 5.50	May	3-26	11.5	- 8.50
June	3-14	21.4	- 3.20	June	4-31	12.9	- 17.20
July	2-12	16.7	+ 1.75	July	3-19	15.8	+ 0.75
August	1-9	11.1	+ 1.00	August	7-27	25.9	+ 10.75
September	1-13	7.7	- 7.00	September	1-30	3.3	- 24.00
Oct/Nov	2-11	18.2	- 6.52	Oct/Nov	4-34	11.8	- 19.52

DISTANCE

2-y-o	W-R	Per cent	£1 Level Stake	3-y-o	W-R	Per cent	£1 Level Stake
5f-6f	1-16	6.3	- 10.00	5f-6f	1-17	5.9	- 10.00
7f-8f	1-19	5.3	- 10.00	7f-8f	1-12	8.3	- 8.50
9f-13f	0-0	-	0.00	9f-13f	3-12	25.0	- 1.50
14f+	0-4	-	- 4.00	14f+	4-17	23.5	+ 0.75

4-y-o+	W-R	Per cent	£1 Level Stake	Totals	W-R	Per cent	£1 Level Stake
5f-6f	2-25	8.0	- 11.00	5f-6f	4-58	6.9	- 31.00
7f-8f	2-23	8.7	- 14.25	7f-8f	4-54	7.4	- 32.75
9f-13f	3-25	12.0	- 16.02	9f-13f	6-37	16.2	- 17.52
14f+	4-11	36.4	+ 12.80	14f+	8-32	25.0	+ 9.55

Flynn P J

TYPE OF RACE

Non-Handicaps	W-R	Per cent	£1 Level Stake	Handicaps	W-R	Per cent	£1 Level Stake
2-y-o	2-33	6.1	- 18.00	2-y-o	0-6	-	- 6.00
3-y-o	0-22	-	- 22.00	3-y-o	9-35	25.7	+ 3.75
4-y-o+	2-21	9.5	- 16.52	4-y-o+	7-54	13.0	- 9.70
Apprentice	0-0	-	0.00	Apprentice	1-5	20.0	- 1.00
Amat/Ladies	1-2	50.0	+ 0.75	Amat/Ladies	0-3	-	- 3.00
Totals	5-78	6.4	- 55.77	Totals	17-103	16.5	- 15.95

FIRST TIME OUT

	W-R	Per cent	£1 Level Stake
2-y-o	0-9	-	- 9.00
3-y-o	0-11	-	- 11.00
4-y-o+	1-24	4.2	- 22.27
Totals	1-44	2.3	- 42.27

JOCKEYS RIDING

	W-R	Per cent	£1 Level Stake		W-R	Per cent	£1 Level Stake
J R Barry	6-32	18.8	- 7.45	M Fenton	1-5	20.0	- 2.00
J F Egan	6-37	16.2	+ 2.25	M Duffy	1-8	12.5	- 6.27
J P Murtagh	3-13	23.1	+ 5.25	J D Eddery	1-8	12.5	- 5.75
P P Murphy	2-7	28.6	+ 3.50	P V Gilson	1-13	7.7	- 6.00
Mr E Norris	1-4	25.0	- 1.25				

E A Leonard	0-7	C Everard	0-2	K J Manning	0-1
P Shanahan	0-6	D Manning	0-2	L Piggott	0-1
D G O'Shea	0-5	R V Skelly	0-2	Mr J Butler	0-1
M C G Laurence	0-4	A Munro	0-1	Mr P Fenton	0-1
N G McCullagh	0-4	C Roche	0-1	P Braiden	0-1
S Craine	0-4	D V Smith	0-1	R Hughes	0-1
R M Burke	0-3	J F Titley	0-1	W J Smith	0-1
W J O'Connor	0-3	Joanna Morgan	0-1		

COURSE RECORD

	Total W-R	Non-Handicaps 2-y-o	3-y-o+	Handicaps 2-y-o	3-y-o+	Per cent	£1 Level Stake
Galway	4-17	0-2	2-5	0-0	2-10	23.5	+ 1.75
The Curragh	3-25	1-3	0-2	0-2	2-18	12.0	+ 0.50
Killarney	2-4	0-0	0-0	0-0	2-4	50.0	+ 0.80
Mallow	2-10	0-4	0-3	0-0	2-3	20.0	+ 2.50
Limerick	2-17	0-2	0-6	0-1	2-8	11.8	- 6.00
Thurles	1-3	0-0	1-2	0-0	0-1	33.3	- 1.27
Dundalk	1-3	0-1	0-1	0-0	1-1	33.3	+ 0.50
Clonmel	1-3	0-0	0-0	0-0	1-3	33.3	+ 1.50

Tramore	1-5	0-0	0-1	0-0	1-4	20.0	- 2.75
Wexford	1-5	0-0	0-1	0-0	1-4	20.0	+ 1.00
Sligo	1-6	0-1	0-0	0-0	1-5	16.7	- 3.75
Fairyhouse	1-6	1-1	0-2	0-1	0-2	16.7	0.00
Leopardstown	1-14	0-1	0-2	0-0	1-11	7.1	- 8.00
Gowran Park	1-17	0-6	0-8	0-1	1-2	5.9	- 12.50

Tipperary	0-9	Navan	0-6	Bellewstown	0-3
Naas	0-8	Tralee	0-6	Downpatrick	0-3
Listowel	0-6	Ballinrobe	0-4	Down Royal	0-1

WINNING HORSES

	Age	Races Run	1st	2nd	3rd	Unpl	Win £
Salmon Eile	4	9	2	2	3	2	23,782
Alalja	2	4	2	0	0	2	12,077
Tahaddi	5	5	2	0	1	2	10,525
Thatch And Gold	4	9	3	2	1	3	7,942
Beluga Girl	3	8	3	1	1	3	7,765
Al Fitzao	3	11	2	4	2	3	7,247
Cheviot Amble	4	10	1	0	3	6	6,900
Myella Prince	3	4	2	0	0	2	4,488
Alberta Rose	3	10	2	2	3	3	4,313
Prince Ole	4	4	1	0	1	2	3,452
Sanndila	4	3	1	0	0	2	3,060
Montelado	5	1	1	0	0	0	2,760

WINNING OWNERS

	Races Won	Value £		Races Won	Value £
Mrs M C O'Connor	2	23,782	Michael W J Smurfit	1	6,900
John Bernard O'Connor	2	12,077	Donal O'Sullivan	2	4,488
Strand Racing Syndicate	2	10,525	W Cotter	2	4,313
Mrs B Wolff	3	7,942	Mrs Patrick Flynn	1	3,452
Ballykisteen Stud Ltd	3	7,765	Mrs J Dermot Cantillon	1	3,060
P C J Carroll	2	7,247	F O Hannon	1	2,760

Favourites	9-21	42.9%	+ 6.53		Total winning prize-money			£94,311
Longest winning sequence			2		Average SP of winner			4.0/1
Longest losing sequence			24		Return on stakes invested			-39.6%
1991 Form	16-166	9.6%	- 49.37		1989 Form	11-92	12.0%	- 19.87
1990 Form	15-154	9.7%	- 61.27		1988 Form	7-60	11.7%	- 13.83

A GERAGHTY

	No. of Horses	Races Run	1st	2nd	3rd	Unpl	Per cent	£1 Level Stake
2-y-o	0	0	0	0	0	0	-	0.00
3-y-o	1	3	1	0	1	1	33.3	+ 10.00
4-y-o+	1	3	0	1	0	2	-	- 3.00
Totals	2	6	1	1	1	3	16.7	+ 7.00

Mar/Apr	May	Jun	Jul	Aug	Sep	Oct/Nov
0-0	1-4	0-2	0-0	0-0	0-0	0-0

Winning Jockey	W-R	£1 Level Stake	Winning Course	W-R	£1 Level Stake
W J O'Connor	1-3	+ 10.00	Naas	1-1	+ 12.00

Winning Horse	Age	Races Run	1st	2nd	3rd	Unpl	Win £
Kayfa	3	3	1	0	1	1	3,450

Favourites	0-0	Total winning prize-money	£3,450

1991 Form	0-3	1989 Form	0-1
1990 Form	0-0	1988 Form	0-16

D GILLESPIE

	No. of Horses	Races Run	1st	2nd	3rd	Unpl	Per cent	£1 Level Stake
2-y-o	13	47	3	1	2	41	6.4	- 26.90
3-y-o	22	120	7	7	14	92	5.8	- 95.70
4-y-o+	11	32	4	2	5	21	12.5	- 6.90
Totals	46	199	14	10	21	154	7.0	-129.50

BY MONTH

2-y-o	W-R	Per cent	£1 Level Stake	3-y-o	W-R	Per cent	£1 Level Stake
Mar/Apr	0-1	-	- 1.00	Mar/Apr	0-16	-	- 16.00
May	2-5	40.0	+ 13.00	May	1-18	5.6	- 15.75
June	0-5	-	- 5.00	June	2-21	9.5	- 17.20
July	0-5	-	- 5.00	July	2-19	10.5	- 15.25
August	1-9	11.1	- 6.90	August	1-16	6.3	- 5.00
September	0-9	-	- 9.00	September	1-22	4.5	- 18.50
Oct/Nov	0-13	-	- 13.00	Oct/Nov	0-8	-	- 8.00

4-y-o+	W-R	Per cent	£1 Level Stake	Totals	W-R	Per cent	£1 Level Stake
Mar/Apr	0-4	-	- 4.00	Mar/Apr	0-21	-	- 21.00
May	0-3	-	- 3.00	May	3-26	11.5	- 5.75
June	3-8	37.5	+ 14.10	June	5-34	14.7	- 8.10
July	0-8	-	- 8.00	July	2-32	6.3	- 28.25
August	1-3	33.3	0.00	August	3-28	10.7	- 11.90
September	0-3	-	- 3.00	September	1-34	2.9	- 30.50
Oct/Nov	0-3	-	- 3.00	Oct/Nov	0-24	-	- 24.00

DISTANCE

2-y-o	W-R	Per cent	£1 Level Stake	3-y-o	W-R	Per cent	£1 Level Stake
5f-6f	3-27	11.1	- 6.90	5f-6f	3-40	7.5	- 34.35
7f-8f	0-20	-	- 20.00	7f-8f	0-29	-	- 29.00
9f-13f	0-0	-	0.00	9f-13f	1-26	3.8	- 15.00
14f+	0-0	-	0.00	14f+	3-25	12.0	- 17.35

4-y-o+	W-R	Per cent	£1 Level Stake	Totals	W-R	Per cent	£1 Level Stake
5f-6f	0-5	-	- 5.00	5f-6f	6-72	8.3	- 46.25
7f-8f	0-8	-	- 8.00	7f-8f	0-57	-	- 57.00
9f-13f	4-16	25.0	+ 9.10	9f-13f	5-42	11.9	- 5.90
14f+	0-3	-	- 3.00	14f+	3-28	10.7	- 20.35

TYPE OF RACE

Non-Handicaps	W-R	Per cent	£1 Level Stake	Handicaps	W-R	Per cent	£1 Level Stake
2-y-o	2-37	5.4	- 19.00	2-y-o	1-10	10.0	- 7.90
3-y-o	2-53	3.8	- 49.85	3-y-o	3-58	5.2	- 42.25
4-y-o+	0-9	-	- 9.00	4-y-o+	0-13	-	- 13.00
Apprentice	0-0	-	0.00	Apprentice	3-10	30.0	+ 2.40
Amat/Ladies	1-2	50.0	+ 1.00	Amat/Ladies	2-7	28.6	+ 8.10
Totals	5-101	5.0	- 76.85	Totals	9-98	9.2	- 52.65

FIRST TIME OUT

	W-R	Per cent	£1 Level Stake
2-y-o	0-13	-	- 13.00
3-y-o	0-21	-	- 21.00
4-y-o+	1-11	9.1	+ 2.00
Totals	1-45	2.2	- 32.00

JOCKEYS RIDING

	W-R	Per cent	£1 Level Stake		W-R	Per cent	£1 Level Stake
D G O'Shea	3-26	11.5	- 9.25	W J Supple	2-55	3.6	- 40.10
Mr D Marnane	2-4	50.0	+ 11.10	Miss J Lewis	1-1	100.0	+ 2.00
R V Skelly	2-8	25.0	+ 0.90	P Carberry	1-6	16.7	- 3.90
S Craine	2-16	12.5	- 8.50	P Shanahan	1-11	9.1	- 9.75

D Manning	0-27	J F Egan	0-2	L O'Shea	0-1
R Hughes	0-9	Mr A E Lacy	0-2	Mr A K Wyse	0-1
J M Buckley	0-8	D Hogan	0-1	Mr D P Murphy	0-1
P P Murphy	0-5	F Berry	0-1	P Lowry	0-1
J P Murtagh	0-4	J J Behan	0-1	T Murphy	0-1
M J Kinane	0-3	Joanna Morgan	0-1		
B J Walsh	0-2	K J Manning	0-1		

COURSE RECORD

	Total W-R	Non-Handicaps 2-y-o	Non-Handicaps 3-y-o+	Handicaps 2-y-o	Handicaps 3-y-o+	Per cent	£1 Level Stake
Ballinrobe	2-8	0-0	2-5	0-0	0-3	25.0	- 4.85
Mallow	2-10	1-1	0-3	1-2	0-4	20.0	- 2.90
Tipperary	2-11	1-2	0-4	0-1	1-4	18.2	+ 4.25
Roscommon	2-12	0-2	0-4	0-0	2-6	16.7	- 2.50
Tramore	1-3	0-0	0-1	0-0	1-2	33.3	+ 8.00
Limerick	1-8	0-2	0-2	0-1	1-3	12.5	- 5.90
Gowran Park	1-9	0-4	0-2	0-1	1-2	11.1	+ 4.00
Dundalk	1-9	0-3	0-1	0-0	1-5	11.1	- 7.10
Tralee	1-9	0-2	1-3	0-0	0-4	11.1	- 6.00
Galway	1-13	0-1	0-3	0-0	1-9	7.7	- 9.50

The Curragh	0-28	Killarney	0-6	Navan	0-4
Leopardstown	0-19	Clonmel	0-5	Wexford	0-2
Naas	0-9	Fairyhouse	0-5	Downpatrick	0-1
Sligo	0-9	Listowel	0-5	Laytown	0-1
Down Royal	0-8	Bellewstown	0-4	Thurles	0-1

WINNING HORSES

	Age	Races Run	1st	2nd	3rd	Unpl	Win £
Accell	3	10	2	1	0	7	6,559
Heavenly Hope	6	4	2	0	1	1	5,695
Bally Pourri	3	10	2	0	1	7	5,007
L'Ecrivain	2	5	2	1	0	2	5,007
Legal Adviser	5	5	1	0	2	2	3,450
Royal Citizen	3	8	1	1	3	3	2,762
Angelic Sounds	2	3	1	0	0	2	2,762
Two Firsts	3	7	1	0	1	5	2,762
Valmaranda	4	6	1	0	1	4	2,762
Regina St Cyr	3	10	1	2	1	6	2,245

WINNING OWNERS

	Races Won	Value £		Races Won	Value £
Edward M Tynan	2	6,559	Frank Hardy	1	2,762
Kaniz Bloodstock Inv Ltd	2	5,695	M J G Callanan	1	2,762
Mrs A Gillespie	2	5,007	T R Smith	1	2,762
Michael H Keogh	2	5,007	Mrs J Costelloe	1	2,762
A J O'Reilly	1	3,450	Michael O'Hanlon	1	2,245

Favourites	9-20	45.0%	+ 0.50	Total winning prize-money	£39,011

Longest winning sequence			2	Average SP of winner	4.0/1
Longest losing sequence			56	Return on stakes invested	-65.1%

1991 Form	17-162	10.5%	- 62.49

J T GORMAN

	No. of Horses	Races Run	1st	2nd	3rd	Unpl	Per cent	£1 Level Stake
2-y-o	7	22	0	2	0	20	-	- 22.00
3-y-o	4	24	1	2	0	21	4.2	- 3.00
4-y-o+	6	26	0	0	3	23	-	- 26.00
Totals	17	72	1	4	3	64	1.4	- 51.00

Mar/Apr	May	Jun	Jul	Aug	Sep	Oct/Nov
1-6	0-9	0-16	0-12	0-12	0-9	0-8

Winning Jockey	W-R	£1 Level Stake	Winning Course	W-R	£1 Level Stake
R Fitzpatrick	1-28	- 7.00	The Curragh	1-16	+ 5.00

Winning Horse	Age	Races Run	1st	2nd	3rd	Unpl	Win £
Magic Don	3	6	1	0	0	5	3,105

Favourites	0-2	Total winning prize-money	£3,105

1991 Form	2-81	2.5%	- 65.00	1989 Form	0-26	
1990 Form	5-44	11.4%	+ 9.00	1988 Form	0-8	

M J GRASSICK

	No. of Horses	Races Run	1st	2nd	3rd	Unpl	Per cent	£1 Level Stake
2-y-o	12	37	2	3	2	30	5.4	- 22.00
3-y-o	14	76	12	10	9	45	15.8	+ 11.80
4-y-o+	6	21	0	1	3	17	-	- 21.00
Totals	32	134	14	14	14	92	10.4	- 31.20

BY MONTH

2-y-o	W-R	Per cent	£1 Level Stake	3-y-o	W-R	Per cent	£1 Level Stake
Mar/Apr	0-0	-	0.00	Mar/Apr	0-17	-	- 17.00
May	0-2	-	- 2.00	May	1-13	7.7	- 10.00
June	0-5	-	- 5.00	June	1-13	7.7	- 11.20
July	0-4	-	- 4.00	July	5-11	45.5	+ 27.50
August	0-5	-	- 5.00	August	2-8	25.0	+ 7.50
September	1-9	11.1	- 1.00	September	2-8	25.0	+ 8.00
Oct/Nov	1-12	8.3	- 5.00	Oct/Nov	1-6	16.7	+ 7.00

4-y-o+	W-R	Per cent	£1 Level Stake	Totals	W-R	Per cent	£1 Level Stake
Mar/Apr	0-6	-	- 6.00	Mar/Apr	0-23	-	- 23.00
May	0-3	-	- 3.00	May	1-18	5.6	- 15.00
June	0-5	-	- 5.00	June	1-23	4.3	- 21.20
July	0-3	-	- 3.00	July	5-18	27.8	+ 20.50
August	0-3	-	- 3.00	August	2-16	12.5	- 0.50
September	0-1	-	- 1.00	September	3-18	16.7	+ 6.00
Oct/Nov	0-0	-	0.00	Oct/Nov	2-18	11.1	+ 2.00

DISTANCE

2-y-o	W-R	Per cent	£1 Level Stake	3-y-o	W-R	Per cent	£1 Level Stake
5f-6f	1-19	5.3	- 11.00	5f-6f	2-20	10.0	- 10.00
7f-8f	1-15	6.7	- 8.00	7f-8f	3-23	13.0	+ 2.80
9f-13f	0-1	-	- 1.00	9f-13f	3-14	21.4	- 1.50
14f+	0-2	-	- 2.00	14f+	4-19	21.1	+ 20.50

4-y-o+	W-R	Per cent	£1 Level Stake	Totals	W-R	Per cent	£1 Level Stake
5f-6f	0-7	-	- 7.00	5f-6f	3-46	6.5	- 28.00
7f-8f	0-3	-	- 3.00	7f-8f	4-41	9.8	- 8.20
9f-13f	0-6	-	- 6.00	9f-13f	3-21	14.3	- 8.50
14f+	0-5	-	- 5.00	14f+	4-26	15.4	+ 13.50

TYPE OF RACE

Non-Handicaps	W-R	Per cent	£1 Level Stake	Handicaps	W-R	Per cent	£1 Level Stake
2-y-o	2-31	6.5	- 16.00	2-y-o	0-6	-	- 6.00
3-y-o	5-42	11.9	- 14.70	3-y-o	4-26	15.4	+ 1.50
4-y-o+	0-4	-	- 4.00	4-y-o+	0-9	-	- 9.00
Apprentice	0-0	-	0.00	Apprentice	3-14	21.4	+ 19.00
Amat/Ladies	0-1	-	- 1.00	Amat/Ladies	0-1	-	- 1.00
Totals	7-78	9.0	- 35.70	Totals	7-56	12.5	+ 4.50

FIRST TIME OUT

	W-R	Per cent	£1 Level Stake
2-y-o	1-12	8.3	- 4.00
3-y-o	1-14	7.1	- 1.00
4-y-o+	0-6	-	- 6.00
Totals	2-32	6.3	- 11.00

JOCKEYS RIDING

	W-R	Per cent	£1 Level Stake		W-R	Per cent	£1 Level Stake
R Hughes	3-28	10.7	- 10.00	J F Egan	1-3	33.3	+ 10.00
P V Gilson	2-4	50.0	+ 11.00	W J Supple	1-12	8.3	- 5.00
T J Daly	2-17	11.8	+ 3.00	D G O'Shea	1-17	5.9	- 15.20
J P Murtagh	1-1	100.0	+ 6.00	L O'Shea	1-18	5.6	- 5.00
N Byrne	1-1	100.0	+ 4.00	K J Manning	1-24	4.2	- 21.00

D Hogan	0-1	Mr R Hurley	0-1	P Shanahan	0-1
D Manning	0-1	Mr R Neylon	0-1	S Craine	0-1
M J Kinane	0-1	N G McCullagh	0-1	W J O'Connor	0-1

COURSE RECORD

	Total W-R	Non-Handicaps 2-y-o	3-y-o+	Handicaps 2-y-o	3-y-o+	Per cent	£1 Level Stake
The Curragh	3-27	1-10	0-6	0-2	2-9	11.1	+ 5.00
Down Royal	2-5	0-2	1-2	0-0	1-1	40.0	+ 2.00
Killarney	2-5	0-0	2-4	0-0	0-1	40.0	+ 9.80
Galway	2-6	0-1	0-1	0-1	2-3	33.3	+ 12.00
Gowran Park	1-3	0-0	0-0	0-1	1-2	33.3	+ 6.00
Downpatrick	1-3	0-0	1-3	0-0	0-0	33.3	+ 2.00
Wexford	1-4	0-0	1-2	0-0	0-2	25.0	- 0.50
Naas	1-9	1-2	0-4	0-1	0-2	11.1	- 2.00
Leopardstown	1-11	0-2	0-2	0-0	1-7	9.1	- 4.50

Mallow	0-8	Dundalk	0-4	Punchestown	0-2
Limerick	0-6	Fairyhouse	0-4	Tralee	0-2
Sligo	0-6	Navan	0-4	Laytown	0-1
Tipperary	0-6	Roscommon	0-4	Tramore	0-1
Ballinrobe	0-4	Listowel	0-3		
Bellewstown	0-4	Clonmel	0-2		

WINNING HORSES

		Races					Win
	Age	Run	1st	2nd	3rd	Unpl	£
Rhoman Ruby	3	10	3	2	1	4	12,903
Karoi	3	8	2	2	0	4	6,902
Honorary Prince	3	10	3	3	1	3	6,695
Danse Royale	2	2	1	0	0	1	5,520
Fromthegetgo	3	6	1	0	2	3	3,452
Knowth	3	5	1	0	1	3	3,452
Tropical Queen	3	5	1	0	0	4	3,450
Legal Flair	2	2	1	0	0	1	3,450
Kaitlin	3	7	1	2	1	3	828

WINNING OWNERS

	Races Won	Value £		Races Won	Value £
Mrs W Brannigan	3	12,903	M Sissian	3	6,695
Miss P F O'Kelly	3	12,420	J Crowley	2	4,280
T M Ward	2	6,902	P X Clarke	1	3,452

Favourites	4-9	44.4%	+ 3.30	Total winning prize-money	£46,652

Longest winning sequence		2	Average SP of winner	6.3/1
Longest losing sequence		37	Return on stakes invested	-23.3%

1991 Form	8-119	6.7%	- 61.50	1989 Form	9-149	6.0%	- 98.80
1990 Form	16-185	8.6%	- 81.70	1988 Form	20-157	12.7%	- 48.83

M HALFORD

	No. of Horses	Races Run	1st	2nd	3rd	Unpl	Per cent	£1 Level Stake
2-y-o	6	18	1	1	4	12	5.6	- 12.00
3-y-o	10	50	1	2	2	45	2.0	- 43.50
4-y-o+	6	35	3	5	3	24	8.6	- 23.67
Totals	22	103	5	8	9	81	4.9	- 79.17

Mar/Apr	May	Jun	Jul	Aug	Sep	Oct/Nov
0-10	0-15	1-18	1-23	2-22	1-11	0-4

Winning Jockeys	W-R	£1 Level Stake		W-R	£1 Level Stake
M J Kinane	2-2	+ 5.00	W J Supple	1-7	- 1.00
Mr D Marnane	1-2	+ 2.33	P V Gilson	1-40	- 33.50

Winning Courses					
Tramore	1-1	+ 3.33	Tralee	1-5	- 1.00
Sligo	1-3	+ 3.00	Galway	1-9	- 2.50
Ballinrobe	1-5	- 2.00			

Winning Horses	Age	Races Run	1st	2nd	3rd	Unpl	Win £
Nilousha	5	5	3	0	0	2	10,037
Port Princess	3	9	1	1	1	6	3,450
Funny Choice	2	4	1	0	2	1	2,935

Favourites	0-5		Total winning prize-money		£16,422

1991 Form	6-79	7.6%	- 40.75	1989 Form	7-74	9.5%	- 13.50
1990 Form	3-87	3.4%	- 64.00	1988 Form	4-106	3.8%	- 72.00

D HANLEY

	No. of Horses	Races Run	1st	2nd	3rd	Unpl	Per cent	£1 Level Stake
2-y-o	1	1	0	0	1	0	-	- 1.00
3-y-o	5	34	5	7	3	19	14.7	- 6.90
4-y-o+	0	0	0	0	0	0	-	0.00
Totals	6	35	5	7	4	19	14.3	- 7.90

Mar/Apr	May	Jun	Jul	Aug	Sep	Oct/Nov
0-2	0-4	1-3	1-9	1-3	0-6	2-8

Winning Jockeys	W-R	£1 Level Stake		W-R	£1 Level Stake
R Hughes	3-9	+ 6.00	W J Supple	2-7	+ 5.10

Winning Courses					
The Curragh	2-9	+ 0.50	Ballinrobe	1-3	+ 7.00
Tipperary	1-3	- 0.90	Galway	1-5	+ 0.50

Winning Horses	Age	Races Run	1st	2nd	3rd	Unpl	Win £
Be My Hope	3	10	3	3	1	3	10,695
Invitation Only	3	10	1	2	1	6	3,450
Call Me Jove	3	7	1	2	0	4	2,245

Favourites	2-3	66.7%	+ 9.10	Total winning prize-money		£16,390

1991 Form	3-22	13.6%	+ 1.50	1989 Form	1-8	12.5%	- 1.00
1990 Form	0-6						

J C HARLEY

	No. of Horses	Races Run	1st	2nd	3rd	Unpl	Per cent	£1 Level Stake
2-y-o	6	23	2	4	2	15	8.7	- 16.25
3-y-o	6	31	1	2	4	24	3.2	- 23.00
4-y-o+	4	25	1	3	4	17	4.0	- 10.00
Totals	16	79	4	9	10	56	5.1	- 49.25

Mar/Apr	May	Jun	Jul	Aug	Sep	Oct/Nov
0-8	1-13	0-10	2-20	0-13	1-10	0-5

Winning Jockeys	W-R	£1 Level Stake			W-R	£1 Level Stake
P V Gilson	3-26	- 4.25	C Roche		1-4	+ 4.00

Winning Courses						
Killarney	1-3	+ 12.00	Down Royal		1-7	- 4.25
Dundalk	1-6	+ 2.00	Leopardstown		1-11	- 7.00

Winning Horses	Age	Races Run	1st	2nd	3rd	Unpl	Win £
I Have To Say	2	8	2	1	1	4	4,782
Singhana	4	9	1	1	2	5	3,450
Baton	3	7	1	1	1	4	2,243

Favourites	1-4	25.0%	- 1.25	Total winning prize-money	£10,475

MRS JOHN HARRINGTON

	No. of Horses	Races Run	1st	2nd	3rd	Unpl	Per cent	£1 Level Stake
2-y-o	0	0	0	0	0	0	-	0.00
3-y-o	2	7	1	0	0	6	14.3	+ 2.00
4-y-o+	1	1	0	0	0	1	-	- 1.00
Totals	3	8	1	0	0	7	12.5	+ 1.00

Mar/Apr	May	Jun	Jul	Aug	Sep	Oct/Nov
0-3	0-0	0-0	0-1	1-2	0-2	0-0

Winning Jockey	W-R	£1 Level Stake	Winning Course	W-R	£1 Level Stake
D G O'Shea	1-2	+ 7.00	Tramore	1-1	+ 8.00

Winning Horse	Age	Races Run	1st	2nd	3rd	Unpl	Win £
Sound Performance	3	5	1	0	0	4	2,935

Favourites	0-0	Total winning prize-money	£2,935

1991 Form	0-0	1989 Form	0-1
1990 Form	0-0	1988 Form	0-11

J C HAYDEN

	No. of Horses	Races Run	1st	2nd	3rd	Unpl	Per cent	£1 Level Stake
2-y-o	5	18	1	2	3	12	5.6	- 12.50
3-y-o	4	25	4	3	1	17	16.0	- 1.25
4-y-o+	2	2	0	0	0	2	-	- 2.00
Totals	11	45	5	5	4	31	11.1	- 15.75

Mar/Apr	May	Jun	Jul	Aug	Sep	Oct/Nov
0-0	0-2	0-2	0-5	3-13	2-13	0-10

Winning Jockeys	W-R	£1 Level Stake		W-R	£1 Level Stake
W J Supple	2-17	- 4.75	M Fenton	1-6	+ 1.00
Miss C Hutchinson	1-1	+ 3.50	J F Egan	1-7	- 1.50

Winning Courses					
Limerick	1-2	+ 7.00	Leopardstown	1-5	- 0.50
Dundalk	1-3	+ 0.25	The Curragh	1-8	- 2.50
Fairyhouse	1-4	+ 3.00			

Winning Horses	Age	Races Run	1st	2nd	3rd	Unpl	Win £
Vladimir's Way	3	10	2	2	0	6	4,486
Lissadell Lady	3	9	1	0	1	7	3,797
State Of The Art	2	4	1	0	1	2	3,795
Princess Dixieland	3	1	1	0	0	0	3,450

Favourites	1-4	25.0%	- 0.75	Total winning prize-money			£15,528
1991 Form	7-65	10.8%	- 16.95	1989 Form	8-116	6.9%	- 29.50
1990 Form	5-185	2.7%	-148.00	1988 Form	5-61	8.2%	- 16.00

G T HOURIGAN

	No. of Horses	Races Run	1st	2nd	3rd	Unpl	Per cent	£1 Level Stake
2-y-o	2	8	0	3	1	4	-	- 8.00
3-y-o	2	11	1	0	0	10	9.1	+ 4.00
4-y-o+	1	2	0	0	0	2	-	- 2.00
Totals	5	21	1	3	1	16	4.8	- 6.00

Mar/Apr	May	Jun	Jul	Aug	Sep	Oct/Nov
1-4	0-4	0-2	0-3	0-3	0-2	0-3

Winning Jockey	W-R	£1 Level Stake	Winning Course	W-R	£1 Level Stake
D V Smith	1-5	+ 10.00	Down Royal	1-1	+ 14.00

Winning Horse	Age	Races Run	1st	2nd	3rd	Unpl	Win £
Sutr-Make	3	7	1	0	0	6	828

Favourites	0-0	Total winning prize-money	£828
1991 Form	0-5		

D T HUGHES

	No. of Horses	Races Run	1st	2nd	3rd	Unpl	Per cent	£1 Level Stake
2-y-o	3	3	0	0	0	3	-	- 3.00
3-y-o	2	13	1	3	0	9	7.7	0.00
4-y-o+	10	24	2	4	3	15	8.3	- 8.00
Totals	15	40	3	7	3	27	7.5	- 11.00

Mar/Apr	May	Jun	Jul	Aug	Sep	Oct/Nov
1-4	1-3	0-4	0-9	0-5	0-6	1-9

Winning Jockeys	W-R	£1 Level Stake			W-R	£1 Level Stake
P P Murphy	2-16	+ 4.00	John Tarrant		1-2	+ 7.00

Winning Courses						
Navan	2-6	+ 14.00	Fairyhouse		1-3	+ 6.00

Winning Horses	Age	Races Run	1st	2nd	3rd	Unpl	Win £
Aegean Fanfare	3	8	1	3	0	4	3,795
Lady Raheen	4	3	1	0	0	2	2,762
Adapt	8	3	1	0	0	2	000

Favourites	0-5			Total winning prize-money			£6,557
1991 Form	0-45			1989 Form	5-49	10.2%	- 9.75
1990 Form	2-65	3.1%	- 55.67	1988 Form	6-80	7.5%	- 28.50

P HUGHES

	No. of Horses	Races Run	1st	2nd	3rd	Unpl	Per cent	£1 Level Stake
2-y-o	1	3	0	0	0	3	-	- 3.00
3-y-o	1	1	0	0	0	1	-	- 1.00
4-y-o+	4	11	1	1	2	7	9.1	- 7.75
Totals	6	15	1	1	2	11	6.7	- 11.75

Mar/Apr	May	Jun	Jul	Aug	Sep	Oct/Nov
0-0	0-1	1-2	0-1	0-2	0-8	0-1

Winning Jockey	W-R	£1 Level Stake	Winning Course	W-R	£1 Level Stake
S Craine	1-3	+ 0.25	Killarney	1-1	+ 2.25

Winning Horse	Age	Races Run	1st	2nd	3rd	Unpl	Win £
Song Girl	5	4	1	1	1	1	3,452

Favourites	1-3	33.3%	+ 0.25	Total winning prize-money			£3,452
1991 Form	2-13	15.4%	- 4.33	1989 Form	2-33	6.1%	- 13.00
1990 Form	2-36	5.6%	- 12.00	1988 Form	2-21	9.5%	- 7.00

M KAUNTZE

	No. of Horses	Races Run	1st	2nd	3rd	Unpl	Per cent	£1 Level Stake
2-y-o	17	50	7	2	11	30	14.0	- 22.33
3-y-o	14	77	8	11	3	55	10.4	- 27.00
4-y-o+	3	15	1	2	4	8	6.7	- 6.00
Totals	34	142	16	15	18	93	11.3	- 55.33

BY MONTH

2-y-o	W-R	Per cent	£1 Level Stake	3-y-o	W-R	Per cent	£1 Level Stake
Mar/Apr	0-2	-	- 2.00	Mar/Apr	1-16	6.3	- 10.50
May	0-6	-	- 6.00	May	1-11	9.1	- 8.00
June	1-4	25.0	- 2.38	June	1-9	11.1	- 1.00
July	1-11	9.1	- 7.50	July	0-9	-	- 9.00
August	2-13	15.4	- 3.50	August	3-14	21.4	+ 2.50
September	1-4	25.0	+ 4.00	September	0-7	-	- 7.00
Oct/Nov	2-10	20.0	- 4.95	Oct/Nov	2-11	18.2	+ 6.00

4-y-o+	W-R	Per cent	£1 Level Stake	Totals	W-R	Per cent	£1 Level Stake
Mar/Apr	1-3	33.3	+ 6.00	Mar/Apr	2-21	9.5	- 6.50
May	0-2	-	- 2.00	May	1-19	5.3	- 16.00
June	0-4	-	- 4.00	June	2-17	11.8	- 7.38
July	0-2	-	- 2.00	July	1-22	4.5	- 18.50
August	0-1	-	- 1.00	August	5-28	17.9	- 2.00
September	0-2	-	- 2.00	September	1-13	7.7	- 5.00
Oct/Nov	0-1	-	- 1.00	Oct/Nov	4-22	18.2	+ 0.05

DISTANCE

2-y-o	W-R	Per cent	£1 Level Stake	3-y-o	W-R	Per cent	£1 Level Stake
5f-6f	3-22	13.6	- 8.88	5f-6f	6-29	20.7	+ 5.00
7f-8f	4-25	16.0	- 10.45	7f-8f	0-24	-	- 24.00
9f-13f	0-0	-	0.00	9f-13f	1-11	9.1	- 6.00
14f+	0-3	-	- 3.00	14f+	1-13	7.7	- 2.00

4-y-o+	W-R	Per cent	£1 Level Stake	Totals	W-R	Per cent	£1 Level Stake
5f-6f	1-6	16.7	+ 3.00	5f-6f	10-57	17.5	- 0.88
7f-8f	0-1	-	- 1.00	7f-8f	4-50	8.0	- 35.45
9f-13f	0-4	-	- 4.00	9f-13f	1-15	6.7	- 10.00
14f+	0-4	-	- 4.00	14f+	1-20	5.0	- 9.00

TYPE OF RACE

Non-Handicaps	W-R	Per cent	£1 Level Stake	Handicaps	W-R	Per cent	£1 Level Stake
2-y-o	5-43	11.6	- 26.58	2-y-o	2-7	28.6	+ 4.25
3-y-o	5-45	11.1	- 19.00	3-y-o	2-28	7.1	- 9.00
4-y-o+	1-10	10.0	- 1.00	4-y-o+	0-4	-	- 4.00
Apprentice	0-0	-	0.00	Apprentice	0-0	-	0.00
Amat/Ladies	1-4	25.0	+ 1.00	Amat/Ladies	0-1	-	- 1.00
Totals	12-102	11.8	- 45.58	Totals	4-40	10.0	- 9.75

FIRST TIME OUT

	W-R	Per cent	£1 Level Stake
2-y-o	3-17	17.6	- 10.08
3-y-o	1-14	7.1	- 8.50
4-y-o+	1-3	33.3	+ 6.00
Totals	5-34	14.7	- 12.58

JOCKEYS RIDING

	W-R	Per cent	£1 Level Stake		W-R	Per cent	£1 Level Stake
W J O'Connor	14-112	12.5	- 31.95	Miss S Kauntze	1-5	20.0	0.00
M J Kinane	1-1	100.0	+ 0.62				

W J Supple	0-6	A J Nolan	0-1	P Carberry	0-1
P V Gilson	0-3	A P Colgan	0-1	R M Burke	0-1
J C Barker	0-2	C F Swan	0-1	S Cauthen	0-1
M Fenton	0-2	D G O'Shea	0-1	W J Smith	0-1
R Hughes	0-2	N G McCullagh	0-1		

COURSE RECORD

	Total W-R	Non-Handicaps 2-y-o	Non-Handicaps 3-y-o+	Handicaps 2-y-o	Handicaps 3-y-o+	Per cent	£1 Level Stake
Gowran Park	3-10	2-3	0-3	1-3	0-1	30.0	- 2.95
The Curragh	3-32	1-14	2-12	0-1	0-5	9.4	- 13.50
Roscommon	2-4	0-0	2-4	0-0	0-0	50.0	+ 7.50
Tralee	1-2	1-1	0-1	0-0	0-0	50.0	+ 5.50
Listowel	1-3	0-0	0-0	1-1	0-2	33.3	+ 5.00
Punchestown	1-3	0-1	0-1	0-0	1-1	33.3	+ 8.00
Navan	1-5	0-1	1-2	0-0	0-2	20.0	- 2.00
Bellewstown	1-7	1-3	0-2	0-0	0-2	14.3	- 5.38
Naas	1-8	0-1	1-2	0-1	0-4	12.5	- 2.50
Fairyhouse	1-10	0-5	1-3	0-0	0-2	10.0	- 5.00
Leopardstown	1-32	0-8	0-18	0-0	1-6	3.1	- 24.00

Dundalk	0-7	Killarney	0-3	Laytown	0-1
Down Royal	0-5	Tipperary	0-3	Limerick	0-1
Galway	0-3	Clonmel	0-2	Thurles	0-1

WINNING HORSES

	Age	Races Run	1st	2nd	3rd	Unpl	Win £
Shrewd Idea	2	4	2	0	1	1	8,492
Domino's Ring	3	10	2	1	0	7	7,692
Key Island	3	8	3	0	0	5	7,250
Missaukee	2	6	1	0	2	3	5,520
Dowland	4	7	1	0	3	3	5,520
Colour Party	2	4	1	0	2	1	5,520
Track Twenty Nine	3	4	1	1	0	2	3,450
Flame Of Persia	2	2	1	0	0	1	3,450
Avosetta	3	7	1	3	1	2	3,450
Royal Ballerina	2	1	1	0	0	0	3,450
Gate Lodge	2	3	1	0	0	2	3,280
Marilyn	3	13	1	4	1	7	2,762

WINNING OWNERS

	Races Won	Value £		Races Won	Value £
Sheikh Mohammed	5	16,220	Tematron Racing Club	2	7,692
M Haga	2	8,970	Mrs Sonia Rogers	1	3,450
Saeed Manana	2	8,492	E Flynn	1	3,450
C S Gaisford-St Lawrence	2	8,282	Major Victor McCalmont	1	3,280

Favourites	6-18	33.3%	- 3.83	Total winning prize-money		£59,836
Longest winning sequence			2	Average SP of winner		4.4/1
Longest losing sequence			18	Return on stakes invested		-39.0%
1991 Form	19-184	10.3%	- 86.80	1989 Form	19-193	9.8%	- 93.66
1990 Form	29-226	12.8%	- 60.94	1988 Form	25-191	13.1%	- 28.45

J P KAVANAGH

	No. of Horses	Races Run	1st	2nd	3rd	Unpl	Per cent	£1 Level Stake
2-y-o	1	3	0	0	0	3	-	- 3.00
3-y-o	3	9	0	0	0	9	-	- 9.00
4-y-o+	2	10	2	0	2	6	20.0	- 2.00
Totals	6	22	2	0	2	18	9.1	- 14.00

Mar/Apr	May	Jun	Jul	Aug	Sep	Oct/Nov
0-0	0-3	2-4	0-5	0-6	0-2	0-2

Winning Jockey	W-R	£1 Level Stake			W-R	£1 Level Stake
D G O'Shea	2-9	- 1.00				

Winning Courses						
Gowran Park	1-1	+ 4.50	Clonmel		1-2	+ 0.50

593

Winning Horses	Age	Races Run	1st	2nd	3rd	Unpl	Win £
Siwana	4	5	1	0	1	3	3,452
Granados	4	5	1	0	1	3	2,245

Favourites	1-1	100.0%	+ 1.50	Total winning prize-money			£5,697

1991 Form	0-14			1989 Form	1-39	2.6%	- 31.00
1990 Form	1-41	2.4%	- 30.00	1988 Form	2-40	5.0%	- 27.60

B V KELLY

	No. of Horses	Races Run	1st	2nd	3rd	Unpl	Per cent	£1 Level Stake
2-y-o	6	28	1	2	2	23	3.6	- 24.50
3-y-o	4	20	2	0	0	18	10.0	- 2.67
4-y-o+	9	50	1	4	3	42	2.0	- 46.50
Totals	19	98	4	6	5	83	4.1	- 73.67

Mar/Apr	May	Jun	Jul	Aug	Sep	Oct/Nov
0-8	1-14	0-16	0-18	2-15	0-14	1-13

Winning Jockeys	W-R	£1 Level Stake		W-R	£1 Level Stake
C Roche	1-2	+ 1.50	J J Behan	1-9	+ 4.00
R Hughes	1-6	- 2.50	S Craine	1-14	- 9.67

Winning Courses					
Down Royal	2-13	- 6.00	The Curragh	1-8	+ 5.00
Laytown	1-1	+ 3.33			

Winning Horses	Age	Races Run	1st	2nd	3rd	Unpl	Win £
Blazing Glory	3	7	2	0	0	5	8,627
Vouvray	2	3	1	0	0	2	828
Tignes	4	12	1	3	0	8	690

Favourites	1-4	25.0%	- 0.50	Total winning prize-money			£10,145

1991 Form	9-107	8.4%	- 27.00	1989 Form	8-62	12.9%	- 13.00
1990 Form	4-76	5.3%	- 54.75	1988 Form	2-65	3.1%	- 35.50

D P KELLY

	No. of Horses	Races Run	1st	2nd	3rd	Unpl	Per cent	£1 Level Stake
2-y-o	2	15	1	3	1	10	6.7	- 2.00
3-y-o	3	9	0	0	0	9	-	- 9.00
4-y-o+	5	11	2	0	0	9	18.2	+ 21.00
Totals	10	35	3	3	1	28	8.6	+ 10.00

Mar/Apr	May	Jun	Jul	Aug	Sep	Oct/Nov
1-8	0-3	0-5	0-2	0-6	0-6	2-5

Winning Jockeys	W-R	£1 Level Stake			W-R	£1 Level Stake
Joanna Morgan	1-2	+ 11.00	K D Maher		1-7	+ 10.00
W J Supple	1-6	+ 9.00				

Winning Courses		£1 Level Stake			W-R	£1 Level Stake
The Curragh	2-11	+ 17.00	Limerick		1-2	+ 15.00

Winning Horses	Age	Races Run	1st	2nd	3rd	Unpl	Win £
Macquarie Ridge	4	3	1	0	0	2	3,105
Mrs Keppel	4	2	1	0	0	1	2,243
Cons Prince	2	8	1	1	1	5	2,070

Favourites	0-1		Total winning prize-money	£7,418
1991 Form	0-14			

V KENNEDY

	No. of Horses	Races Run	1st	2nd	3rd	Unpl	Per cent	£1 Level Stake
2-y-o	0	0	0	0	0	0	-	0.00
3-y-o	6	21	0	0	0	21	-	- 21.00
4-y-o+	5	16	1	0	0	15	6.3	- 7.00
Totals	11	37	1	0	0	36	2.7	- 28.00

Mar/Apr	May	Jun	Jul	Aug	Sep	Oct/Nov
0-4	0-9	0-5	1-7	0-6	0-2	0-4

Winning Jockey	W-R	£1 Level Stake	Winning Course	W-R	£1 Level Stake
P V Gilson	1-6	+ 3.00	Dundalk	1-2	+ 7.00

Winning Horse	Age	Races Run	1st	2nd	3rd	Unpl	Win £
Blasket Supreme	4	7	1	0	0	6	2,760

Favourites	0-1		Total winning prize-money	£2,760

1991 Form	1-67	1.5%	- 54.00	1989 Form	4-34	11.8%	+ 3.25
1990 Form	3-46	6.5%	- 10.00	1988 Form	3-48	6.3%	- 26.37

T F LACY

	No. of Horses	Races Run	1st	2nd	3rd	Unpl	Per cent	£1 Level Stake
2-y-o	7	19	0	0	1	18	-	- 19.00
3-y-o	8	41	1	1	2	37	2.4	- 38.25
4-y-o+	6	27	2	3	1	21	7.4	- 18.00
Totals	21	87	3	4	4	76	3.4	- 75.25

Mar/Apr	May	Jun	Jul	Aug	Sep	Oct/Nov
1-18	0-9	0-15	0-11	1-14	1-11	0-9

Winning Jockey	W-R	£1 Level Stake			W-R	£1 Level Stake
K J Manning	3-34	- 22.25				

Winning Courses						
Navan	1-4	- 1.25	Roscommon		1-7	- 1.00
Listowel	1-5	- 2.00				

Winning Horses	Age	Races Run	1st	2nd	3rd	Unpl	Win £
Shantalla Bay	5	8	2	3	1	2	7,075
Caurselle	3	5	1	0	1	3	3,450

Favourites	2-3	66.7%	+ 2.75	Total winning prize-money		£10,525

1991 Form	0-89			1989 Form	1-73	1.4%	- 64.00
1990 Form	2-62	3.2%	- 51.00	1988 Form	11-96	11.5%	- 27.90

AUGUSTINE LEAHY

	No. of Horses	Races Run	1st	2nd	3rd	Unpl	Per cent	£1 Level Stake
2-y-o	8	29	1	0	4	24	3.4	- 24.00
3-y-o	8	49	6	8	8	27	12.2	- 15.67
4-y-o+	9	13	1	0	1	11	7.7	- 5.00
Totals	25	91	8	8	13	62	8.8	- 44.67

Mar/Apr	May	Jun	Jul	Aug	Sep	Oct/Nov
0-5	0-7	0-14	2-14	2-22	2-18	2-11

Winning Jockeys	W-R	£1 Level Stake			W-R	£1 Level Stake
M Fenton	7-69	- 30.67	G Starkey		1-1	+ 7.00

Winning Courses					
Galway	2-8	+ 7.00	Naas	1-5	0.00
Tralee	2-11	- 0.25	Listowel	1-8	- 3.67
Ballinrobe	1-1	+ 2.25	Tipperary	1-9	- 1.00

Winning Horses		Age	Races Run	1st	2nd	3rd	Unpl	Win £
Sedov		3	9	3	1	1	4	10,044
Donnasoo		3	12	2	2	2	6	5,695
Premier Leap		3	12	1	4	4	3	5,520
Ballytigue Lord		6	2	1	0	0	1	3,452
Common Bond		2	6	1	0	3	2	2,760

Favourites	3-7	42.9%	+ 3.33	Total winning prize-money			£27,471

1991 Form	1-106	0.9%	- 91.00	1989 Form	3-65	4.6%	- 49.50
1990 Form	11-107	10.3%	- 31.50	1988 Form	3-54	5.6%	- 4.00

EDWARD LYNAM

	No. of Horses	Races Run	1st	2nd	3rd	Unpl	Per cent	£1 Level Stake
2-y-o	10	37	2	3	4	28	5.4	- 8.00
3-y-o	9	43	2	5	3	33	4.7	- 21.00
4-y-o+	2	12	1	1	2	8	8.3	- 6.50
Totals	21	92	5	9	9	69	5.4	- 35.50

Mar/Apr	May	Jun	Jul	Aug	Sep	Oct/Nov
0-12	1-14	2-13	1-12	1-16	0-16	0-9

Winning Jockeys	W-R	£1 Level Stake			W-R	£1 Level Stake
D Hogan	3-48	- 18.00	W J Smith		1-9	+ 12.00
M Fenton	1-2	+ 3.50				

Winning Courses						
Dundalk	2-6	+ 17.00	Bellewstown		1-4	+ 1.50
Killarney	1-2	+ 5.00	Tralee		1-8	+ 13.00

Winning Horses	Age	Races Run	1st	2nd	3rd	Unpl	Win £
Victory Toast	3	7	2	2	0	3	6,387
Kentucky Baby	2	12	1	1	1	9	4,142
Drumaaler	4	11	1	1	1	8	2,935
Ardgillian	2	6	1	1	0	4	2,245

Favourites	1-3	33.3%	+ 2.50	Total winning prize-money			£15,709

1991 Form	1-93	1.1%	- 87.50	1989 Form	3-79	3.8%	- 56.00
1990 Form	4-144	2.8%	-127.67	1988 Form	8-91	8.8%	- 21.25

C P MAGNIER

	No. of Horses	Races Run	1st	2nd	3rd	Unpl	Per cent	£1 Level Stake
2-y-o	0	0	0	0	0	0	-	0.00
3-y-o	4	15	2	0	0	13	13.3	- 1.00
4-y-o+	2	2	0	0	0	2	-	- 2.00
Totals	6	17	2	0	0	15	11.8	- 3.00

Mar/Apr	May	Jun	Jul	Aug	Sep	Oct/Nov
0-0	1-1	1-1	0-3	0-3	0-4	0-5

Winning Jockeys	W-R	£1 Level Stake		W-R	£1 Level Stake
S Craine	1-1	+ 4.00	M C G Laurence	1-2	+ 7.00

Winning Courses					
Navan	1-1	+ 8.00	Sligo	1-1	+ 4.00

Winning Horses	Age	Races Run	1st	2nd	3rd	Unpl	Win £
Shimeoni	3	3	1	0	0	2	2,762
Laser Sharp	3	5	1	0	0	4	2,760

Favourites	0-0	Total winning prize-money	£5,522

1991 Form	0-14	1989 Form	0-1
1990 Form	0-12		

P MARTIN

	No. of Horses	Races Run	1st	2nd	3rd	Unpl	Per cent	£1 Level Stake
2-y-o	0	0	0	0	0	0	-	0.00
3-y-o	3	21	1	2	2	16	4.8	- 16.50
4-y-o+	4	24	2	4	2	16	8.3	+ 4.00
Totals	7	45	3	6	4	32	6.7	- 12.50

Mar/Apr	May	Jun	Jul	Aug	Sep	Oct/Nov
0-2	1-7	0-10	0-8	1-8	0-7	1-3

Winning Jockeys	W-R	£1 Level Stake		W-R	£1 Level Stake
P V Gilson	1-3	+ 1.50	J P Murtagh	1-4	+ 11.00
K J Manning	1-3	+ 10.00			

Winning Courses					
Navan	1-2	+ 11.00	Dundalk	1-7	+ 8.00
Laytown	1-2	+ 2.50			

Winning Horses	Age	Races Run	1st	2nd	3rd	Unpl	Win £
Majestic Guest	4	12	2	2	0	8	5,693
Toast And Honey	3	12	1	2	2	7	1,727

Favourites	0-2			Total winning prize-money			£7,420

1991 Form	1-21	4.8%	- 4.00	1989 Form	1-40	2.5%	- 29.00
1990 Form	0-14			1988 Form	0-72		

J F C MAXWELL

	No. of Horses	Races Run	1st	2nd	3rd	Unpl	Per cent	£1 Level Stake
2-y-o	0	0	0	0	0	0	-	0.00
3-y-o	1	1	0	1	0	0	-	- 1.00
4-y-o+	4	5	1	0	0	4	20.0	- 4.00
Totals	5	6	1	1	0	4	16.7	- 5.00

Mar/Apr	May	Jun	Jul	Aug	Sep	Oct/Nov
0-0	1-3	0-0	0-1	0-1	0-0	0-1

Winning Jockey	W-R	£1 Level Stake	Winning Course	W-R	£1 Level Stake
F Berry	1-1	0.00	Downpatrick	1-3	- 2.00

Winning Horse	Age	Races Run	1st	2nd	3rd	Unpl	Win £
All For Luck	7	1	1	0	0	0	820

Favourites	0-0			Total winning prize-money			£820

1991 Form	1-2	50.0%	+ 7.00	1989 Form	0-1		
1990 Form	0-0			1988 Form	1-9	11.1%	- 7.20

T G MCCOURT

	No. of Horses	Races Run	1st	2nd	3rd	Unpl	Per cent	£1 Level Stake
2-y-o	0	0	0	0	0	0	-	0.00
3-y-o	2	12	1	1	1	9	8.3	- 1.00
4-y-o+	2	7	0	0	0	7	-	- 7.00
Totals	4	19	1	1	1	16	5.3	- 8.00

Mar/Apr	May	Jun	Jul	Aug	Sep	Oct/Nov
0-0	0-1	1-2	0-4	0-4	0-1	0-7

Winning Jockey	W-R	£1 Level Stake	Winning Course	W-R	£1 Level Stake
D O'Donoghue	1-1	+ 10.00	Ballinrobe	1-1	+ 10.00

Winning Horse	Age	Races Run	1st	2nd	3rd	Unpl	Win £
Recollection	3	7	1	0	1	5	2,245

Favourites	0-0		Total winning prize-money	£2,245

1991 Form	0-37	1989 Form	0-13
1990 Form	0-25		

M A MCCULLAGH

	No. of Horses	Races Run	1st	2nd	3rd	Unpl	Per cent	£1 Level Stake
2-y-o	0	0	0	0	0	0	-	0.00
3-y-o	1	11	3	1	1	6	27.3	+ 13.50
4-y-o+	0	0	0	0	0	0	-	0.00
Totals	1	11	3	1	1	6	27.3	+ 13.50

Mar/Apr	May	Jun	Jul	Aug	Sep	Oct/Nov
0-2	0-2	1-3	1-1	1-2	0-1	0-0

Winning Jockeys	W-R	£1 Level Stake		W-R	£1 Level Stake
N G McCullagh	2-5	+ 17.00	D M McCullagh	1-2	+ 0.50

Winning Courses					
Tramore	2-2	+ 5.50	Galway	1-1	+ 16.00

Winning Horse	Age	Races Run	1st	2nd	3rd	Unpl	Win £
Wesbest	3	11	3	1	1	6	9,282

Favourites	2-3	66.7%	+ 4.50	Total winning prize-money	£9,282

1991 Form	0-3	1989 Form	0-0
1990 Form	0-6	1988 Form	0-6

M MCDONAGH

	No. of Horses	Races Run	1st	2nd	3rd	Unpl	Per cent	£1 Level Stake
2-y-o	1	2	0	0	0	2	-	- 2.00
3-y-o	0	0	0	0	0	0	-	0.00
4-y-o+	2	3	1	0	0	2	33.3	+ 2.50
Totals	3	5	1	0	0	4	20.0	+ 0.50

Mar/Apr	May	Jun	Jul	Aug	Sep	Oct/Nov
1-1	0-0	0-0	0-1	0-1	0-2	0-0

Winning Jockey	W-R	£1 Level Stake	Winning Course	W-R	£1 Level Stake
D G O'Shea	1-1	+ 4.50	Sligo	1-1	+ 4.50

Winning Horse	Age	Races Run	1st	2nd	3rd	Unpl	Win £
Cellyph	5	1	1	0	0	0	2,243

Favourites	0-0		Total winning prize-money	£2,243

1991 Form	0-6			1989 Form	1-16	6.3%	- 12.00
1990 Form	2-13	15.4%	+ 0.75	1988 Form	0-15		

D MCDONOGH

	No. of Horses	Races Run	1st	2nd	3rd	Unpl	Per cent	£1 Level Stake
2-y-o	0	0	0	0	0	0	-	0.00
3-y-o	2	10	0	0	0	10	-	- 10.00
4-y-o+	2	16	1	1	1	13	6.3	- 10.50
Totals	4	26	1	1	1	23	3.8	- 20.50

Mar/Apr	May	Jun	Jul	Aug	Sep	Oct/Nov
0-7	0-5	0-5	0-2	0-4	0-0	1-3

Winning Jockey	W-R	£1 Level Stake	Winning Course	W-R	£1 Level Stake
J R Barry	1-1	+ 4.50	Down Royal	1-2	+ 3.50

Winning Horse	Age	Races Run	1st	2nd	3rd	Unpl	Win £
Model Dancer	4	15	1	1	1	12	690

Favourites	0-0		Total winning prize-money	£690

1991 Form	0-42			1989 Form	2-56	3.6%	- 42.00
1990 Form	1-39	2.6%	- 33.00	1988 Form	0-33		

D J MCGRATH

	No. of Horses	Races Run	1st	2nd	3rd	Unpl	Per cent	£1 Level Stake
2-y-o	0	0	0	0	0	0	-	0.00
3-y-o	0	0	0	0	0	0	-	0.00
4-y-o+	1	11	1	1	1	8	9.1	- 5.00
Totals	1	11	1	1	1	8	9.1	- 5.00

McGrath D J

Mar/Apr	May	Jun	Jul	Aug	Sep	Oct/Nov
0-0	0-0	0-1	0-2	1-3	0-3	0-2

Winning Jockey	W-R	£1 Level Stake	Winning Course	W-R	£1 Level Stake
C Everard	1-3	+ 3.00	The Curragh	1-6	0.00

Winning Horse	Age	Races Run	1st	2nd	3rd	Unpl	Win £
Grand Princess	4	11	1	1	1	8	2,760

Favourites	0-0		Total winning prize-money		£2,760

1991 Form	0-0		1989 Form	0-1		
1990 Form	0-0		1988 Form	1-1	100.0%	+ 1.00

NEIL S MCGRATH

	No. of Horses	Races Run	1st	2nd	3rd	Unpl	Per cent	£1 Level Stake
2-y-o	4	16	1	1	3	11	6.3	- 5.00
3-y-o	5	34	2	4	6	22	5.9	- 8.00
4-y-o+	1	1	0	0	0	1	-	- 1.00
Totals	10	51	3	5	9	34	5.9	- 14.00

Mar/Apr	May	Jun	Jul	Aug	Sep	Oct/Nov
0-1	0-4	1-11	0-8	0-7	2-9	0-11

Winning Jockeys	W-R	£1 Level Stake		W-R	£1 Level Stake
B Bowens	1-1	+ 14.00	R Hughes	1-19	- 8.00
S Craine	1-4	+ 7.00			

Winning Courses					
Roscommon	1-2	+ 13.00	Naas	1-8	+ 3.00
Listowel	1-4	+ 7.00			

Winning Horses	Age	Races Run	1st	2nd	3rd	Unpl	Win £
Green Glen	3	15	1	4	3	7	4,685
Pinch The Devil	2	3	1	0	0	2	2,760
Simply	3	7	1	0	1	5	2,243

Favourites	0-0		Total winning prize-money		£9,688

1991 Form	0-32			1989 Form	6-70	8.6%	- 15.75
1990 Form	3-43	7.0%	- 29.50	1988 Form	3-87	3.4%	- 57.75

J J MCLOUGHLIN

	No. of Horses	Races Run	1st	2nd	3rd	Unpl	Per cent	£1 Level Stake
2-y-o	0	0	0	0	0	0	-	0.00
3-y-o	14	120	9	14	15	82	7.5	- 76.93
4-y-o+	8	42	6	4	4	28	14.3	+ 1.75
Totals	22	162	15	18	19	110	9.3	- 75.18

BY MONTH

2-y-o	W-R	Per cent	£1 Level Stake	3-y-o	W-R	Per cent	£1 Level Stake
Mar/Apr	0-0	-	0.00	Mar/Apr	0-12	-	- 12.00
May	0-0	-	0.00	May	2-19	10.5	- 12.75
June	0-0	-	0.00	June	4-17	23.5	- 3.93
July	0-0	-	0.00	July	1-13	7.7	0.00
August	0-0	-	0.00	August	2-18	11.1	- 7.25
September	0-0	-	0.00	September	0-25	-	- 25.00
Oct/Nov	0-0	-	0.00	Oct/Nov	0-16	-	- 16.00

4-y-o+	W-R	Per cent	£1 Level Stake	Totals	W-R	Per cent	£1 Level Stake
Mar/Apr	0-5	-	- 5.00	Mar/Apr	0-17	-	- 17.00
May	1-3	33.3	+ 12.00	May	3-22	13.6	- 0.75
June	2-11	18.2	- 4.25	June	6-28	21.4	- 8.18
July	0-7	-	- 7.00	July	1-20	5.0	- 7.00
August	0-6	-	- 6.00	August	2-24	8.3	- 13.25
September	3-7	42.9	+ 15.00	September	3-32	9.4	- 10.00
Oct/Nov	0-3	-	- 3.00	Oct/Nov	0-19	-	- 19.00

DISTANCE

2-y-o	W-R	Per cent	£1 Level Stake	3-y-o	W-R	Per cent	£1 Level Stake
5f-6f	0-0	-	0.00	5f-6f	3-44	6.8	- 20.25
7f-8f	0-0	-	0.00	7f-8f	2-27	7.4	- 19.25
9f-13f	0-0	-	0.00	9f-13f	3-29	10.3	- 19.00
14f+	0-0	-	0.00	14f+	1-20	5.0	- 18.43

4-y-o+	W-R	Per cent	£1 Level Stake	Totals	W-R	Per cent	£1 Level Stake
5f-6f	1-10	10.0	+ 5.00	5f-6f	4-54	7.4	- 15.25
7f-8f	0-8	-	- 8.00	7f-8f	2-35	5.7	- 27.25
9f-13f	4-16	25.0	+ 10.50	9f-13f	7-45	15.6	- 8.50
14f+	1-8	12.5	- 5.75	14f+	2-28	7.1	- 24.18

TYPE OF RACE

Non-Handicaps	W-R	Per cent	£1 Level Stake	Handicaps	W-R	Per cent	£1 Level Stake
2-y-o	0-0	-	0.00	2-y-o	0-0	-	0.00
3-y-o	0-37	-	- 37.00	3-y-o	9-80	11.3	- 36.93
4-y-o+	1-6	16.7	- 3.75	4-y-o+	3-25	12.0	+ 0.50
Apprentice	0-0	-	0.00	Apprentice	1-6	16.7	+ 3.00
Amat/Ladies	0-5	-	- 5.00	Amat/Ladies	1-3	33.3	+ 4.00
Totals	1-48	2.1	- 45.75	Totals	14-114	12.3	- 29.43

FIRST TIME OUT

	W-R	Per cent	£1 Level Stake
2-y-o	0-0	-	0.00
3-y-o	0-14	-	- 14.00
4-y-o+	1-8	12.5	+ 7.00
Totals	1-22	4.5	- 7.00

JOCKEYS RIDING

	W-R	Per cent	£1 Level Stake		W-R	Per cent	£1 Level Stake
N G McCullagh	10-115	8.7	- 67.68	J P Murtagh	1-1	100.0	+ 3.50
J J Behan	3-9	33.3	+ 19.00	Mr J Walsh	1-2	50.0	+ 5.00

J C Barker	0-5	Miss A O'Rourke	0-2	K B Walsh	0-1
Miss C Bowden	0-4	P P Murphy	0-2	L O'Shea	0-1
N Byrne	0-3	R Fitzpatrick	0-2	M Fenton	0-1
D M McCullagh	0-2	A J Roche	0-1	P Carberry	0-1
E A Leonard	0-2	B J Walsh	0-1	R Hughes	0-1
J R Barry	0-2	B P Harding	0-1		
Joanna Morgan	0-2	D G O'Shea	0-1		

COURSE RECORD

	Total W-R	Non-Handicaps 2-y-o	Non-Handicaps 3-y-o+	Handicaps 2-y-o	Handicaps 3-y-o+	Per cent	£1 Level Stake
Clonmel	2-3	0-0	0-0	0-0	2-3	66.7	+ 7.00
Mallow	2-5	0-0	0-2	0-0	2-3	40.0	+ 1.00
Wexford	2-5	0-0	0-1	0-0	2-4	40.0	+ 14.50
Limerick	1-4	0-0	0-1	0-0	1-3	25.0	+ 3.00
Gowran Park	1-6	0-0	1-4	0-0	0-2	16.7	- 3.75
Tipperary	1-6	0-0	0-1	0-0	1-5	16.7	+ 3.00
Killarney	1-6	0-0	0-0	0-0	1-6	16.7	- 4.43
Fairyhouse	1-8	0-0	0-2	0-0	1-6	12.5	- 5.25
Roscommon	1-8	0-0	0-4	0-0	1-4	12.5	- 5.25
Naas	1-10	0-0	0-3	0-0	1-7	10.0	- 5.00
Leopardstown	1-14	0-0	0-3	0-0	1-11	7.1	- 1.00
The Curragh	1-32	0-0	0-9	0-0	1-23	3.1	- 24.00

Galway	0-11	Dundalk	0-5	Ballinrobe	0-2
Sligo	0-8	Listowel	0-5	Bellewstown	0-2
Navan	0-6	Downpatrick	0-4	Thurles	0-2
Down Royal	0-5	Laytown	0-4	Tralee	0-1

WINNING HORSES

	Age	Races Run	1st	2nd	3rd	Unpl	Win £
Robertolomy	3	14	3	1	3	7	8,976
Basie Noble	3	11	1	0	3	7	6,900
Dixie Favor	3	13	2	1	0	10	6,212
Morning Sarge	4	13	2	1	0	10	6,038
Societies Lover	3	9	2	4	2	1	4,490
Riverillon	4	7	1	0	1	5	4,140
Key Partner	5	5	1	1	0	3	2,762
Candid Lad	5	4	1	1	2	0	2,762
Noble Anchor	3	11	1	2	2	6	2,245
Top Wave	4	7	1	1	0	5	2,243

WINNING OWNER

	Races Won	Value £
John J McLoughlin	15	46,768

Favourites	8-16	50.0%	+ 7.82	Total winning prize-money			£46,768

Longest winning sequence			2	Average SP of winner			4.8/1
Longest losing sequence			29	Return on stakes invested			-46.4%

1991 Form	13-181	7.2%	- 93.50	1989 Form	10-116	8.6%	- 31.29
1990 Form	15-172	8.7%	- 42.50	1988 Form	5-56	8.9%	- 26.17

H MCMAHON

	No. of Horses	Races Run	1st	2nd	3rd	Unpl	Per cent	£1 Level Stake
2-y-o	2	7	0	0	0	7	-	- 7.00
3-y-o	4	28	2	2	1	23	7.1	- 16.50
4-y-o+	0	0	0	0	0	0	-	0.00
Totals	6	35	2	2	1	30	5.7	- 23.50

Mar/Apr	May	Jun	Jul	Aug	Sep	Oct/Nov
0-1	1-9	0-3	1-7	0-1	0-4	0-10

Winning Jockey	W-R	£1 Level Stake				W-R	£1 Level Stake
W J O'Connor	2-16	- 4.50					

Winning Courses							
Killarney	1-3	+ 4.00	Limerick			1-4	+ 0.50

Winning Horse	Age	Races Run	1st	2nd	3rd	Unpl	Win £
Thatching Craft	3	9	2	0	0	7	6,042

Favourites	0-0		Total winning prize-money	£6,042

1991 Form	0-20		1990 Form	0-8

NOEL MEADE

	No. of Horses	Races Run	1st	2nd	3rd	Unpl	Per cent	£1 Level Stake
2-y-o	16	43	4	1	0	38	9.3	- 19.50
3-y-o	10	51	4	6	6	35	7.8	- 17.75
4-y-o+	20	76	10	5	11	50	13.2	- 24.29
Totals	46	170	18	12	17	123	10.6	- 61.54

BY MONTH

2-y-o	W-R	Per cent	£1 Level Stake	3-y-o	W-R	Per cent	£1 Level Stake
Mar/Apr	0-1	-	- 1.00	Mar/Apr	1-5	20.0	- 1.50
May	0-2	-	- 2.00	May	1-9	11.1	- 5.75
June	1-7	14.3	- 2.00	June	1-5	20.0	+ 0.50
July	0-6	-	- 6.00	July	0-7	-	- 7.00
August	2-6	33.3	+ 3.50	August	0-11	-	- 11.00
September	1-14	7.1	- 5.00	September	0-4	-	- 4.00
Oct/Nov	0-7	-	- 7.00	Oct/Nov	1-10	10.0	+ 11.00

4-y-o+	W-R	Per cent	£1 Level Stake	Totals	W-R	Per cent	£1 Level Stake
Mar/Apr	0-9	-	- 9.00	Mar/Apr	1-15	6.7	- 11.50
May	3-13	23.1	+ 9.63	May	4-24	16.7	+ 1.88
June	2-13	15.4	- 5.75	June	4-25	16.0	- 7.25
July	3-17	17.6	- 1.50	July	3-30	10.0	- 14.50
August	2-10	20.0	- 3.67	August	4-27	14.8	- 11.17
September	0-8	-	- 8.00	September	1-26	3.8	- 17.00
Oct/Nov	0-6	-	- 6.00	Oct/Nov	1-23	4.3	- 2.00

DISTANCE

2-y-o	W-R	Per cent	£1 Level Stake	3-y-o	W-R	Per cent	£1 Level Stake
5f-6f	1-19	5.3	- 14.00	5f-6f	0-19	-	- 19.00
7f-8f	3-21	14.3	- 2.50	7f-8f	4-19	21.1	+ 14.25
9f-13f	0-0	-	0.00	9f-13f	0-8	-	- 8.00
14f+	0-3	-	- 3.00	14f+	0-5	-	- 5.00

4-y-o+	W-R	Per cent	£1 Level Stake	Totals	W-R	Per cent	£1 Level Stake
5f-6f	0-21	-	- 21.00	5f-6f	1-59	1.7	- 54.00
7f-8f	4-25	16.0	- 2.12	7f-8f	11-65	16.9	+ 9.63
9f-13f	6-21	28.6	+ 7.83	9f-13f	6-29	20.7	- 0.17
14f+	0-9	-	- 9.00	14f+	0-17	-	- 17.00

TYPE OF RACE

Non-Handicaps	W-R	Per cent	£1 Level Stake	Handicaps	W-R	Per cent	£1 Level Stake
2-y-o	3-36	8.3	- 16.00	2-y-o	1-7	14.3	- 3.50
3-y-o	3-24	12.5	- 11.75	3-y-o	1-26	3.8	- 5.00
4-y-o+	3-25	12.0	- 2.50	4-y-o+	3-39	7.7	- 26.04
Apprentice	0-0	-	0.00	Apprentice	1-3	33.3	- 0.25
Amat/Ladies	1-5	20.0	- 3.00	Amat/Ladies	2-5	40.0	+ 6.50
Totals	10-90	11.1	- 33.25	Totals	8-80	10.0	- 28.29

FIRST TIME OUT

	W-R	Per cent	£1 Level Stake
2-y-o	0-16	-	- 16.00
3-y-o	1-9	11.1	- 5.75
4-y-o+	0-19	-	- 19.00
Totals	1-44	2.3	- 40.75

JOCKEYS RIDING

	W-R	Per cent	£1 Level Stake		W-R	Per cent	£1 Level Stake
R Hughes	7-101	6.9	- 61.79	Joanna Morgan	2-17	11.8	- 4.50
Mr S R Murphy	4-8	50.0	+ 8.00	J P Murtagh	1-4	25.0	+ 1.00
P Carberry	3-14	21.4	+ 15.75	N G McCullagh	1-6	16.7	0.00

C F Swan	0-4	A Munro	0-1	Mr G J Harford		0-1
S Craine	0-3	A P Colgan	0-1	P P Murphy		0-1
W J Supple	0-2	J D Eddery	0-1	P V Gilson		0-1
A J Beale	0-1	Miss C E Hyde	0-1	W J Smith		0-1
A J Nolan	0-1	Mr A J Martin	0-1			

COURSE RECORD

	Total W-R	Non-Handicaps 2-y-o	3-y-o+	Handicaps 2-y-o	3-y-o+	Per cent	£1 Level Stake
Sligo	4-6	1-2	2-3	0-0	1-1	66.7	+ 8.25
Dundalk	3-10	1-3	0-2	0-0	2-5	30.0	+ 7.63
Tipperary	2-11	1-4	1-5	0-0	0-2	18.2	+ 1.00
Gowran Park	2-12	0-6	1-2	1-2	0-2	16.7	- 5.25
Galway	2-17	0-4	1-4	0-0	1-9	11.8	- 7.50
Wexford	1-2	0-0	0-0	0-0	1-2	50.0	+ 2.33
Tralee	1-5	0-0	0-1	0-0	1-4	20.0	- 0.50
Naas	1-10	0-3	1-4	0-1	0-2	10.0	- 4.50
Leopardstown	1-27	0-4	0-10	0-0	1-13	3.7	- 6.00
The Curragh	1-28	0-3	1-9	0-1	0-15	3.6	- 15.00

Navan	0-8	Punchestown	0-3	Down Royal		0-1
Listowel	0-7	Roscommon	0-3	Laytown		0-1
Fairyhouse	0-5	Ballinrobe	0-2	Mallow		0-1
Killarney	0-4	Bellewstown	0-1	Tramore		0-1
Limerick	0-4	Clonmel	0-1			

WINNING HORSES

	Age	Races Run	1st	2nd	3rd	Unpl	Win £
Beau Beauchamp	5	8	2	0	2	4	12,297
Street Rebel	4	9	1	2	2	4	11,500
Faydini	3	5	2	0	0	3	7,590
Refined Heir	4	3	1	0	0	2	3,797
Wally Wallensky	2	5	1	0	0	4	3,452
Random Prince	8	6	1	0	1	4	3,450
Kayfa	3	8	1	1	1	5	3,450
Natural Ability	7	4	1	0	0	3	2,762
Persian Power	4	5	1	1	1	2	2,762
Micks Delight	2	6	1	0	0	5	2,762
Another Coq Hardi	4	3	1	0	0	2	2,762
Kerry For August	2	4	1	0	0	3	2,760
Tymoole	4	6	1	0	1	4	2,245
Amber King	8	1	1	0	0	0	2,245
Que Cyrano	3	15	1	3	3	8	2,243
La Cenerentola	2	2	1	0	0	1	2,243

WINNING OWNERS

	Races Won	Value £		Races Won	Value £
Donal Kinsella	3	15,749	M J McCarthy	1	2,762
P Garvey	1	11,500	Mrs Catherine Howard	1	2,762
Mrs M A Brennan	2	7,590	P M Hunt	1	2,762
Vincent Loughnane	2	5,695	Anthony F O'Callaghan	1	2,760
John P Moore	1	3,797	Robert P Gogan	1	2,245
N Coburn	1	3,450	Windsor Racing Club	1	2,243
Bunker Estates Ltd	1	2,762	Mrs Maureen Hunt	1	2,243

Favourites	8-18	44.4%	+ 6.46	Total winning prize-money	£68,320
Longest winning sequence			3	Average SP of winner	5.0/1
Longest losing sequence			31	Return on stakes invested	-36.2%
1991 Form	17-207	8.2%	-123.39	1989 Form 11-188 5.9%	-122.34
1990 Form	14-209	6.7%	-129.13	1988 Form 19-213 8.9%	- 86.80

E P MITCHELL

	No. of Horses	Races Run	1st	2nd	3rd	Unpl	Per cent	£1 Level Stake
2-y-o	0	0	0	0	0	0	-	0.00
3-y-o	1	6	0	0	0	6	-	- 6.00
4-y-o+	3	6	1	0	0	5	16.7	+ 20.00
Totals	4	12	1	0	0	11	8.3	+ 14.00

Mar/Apr	May	Jun	Jul	Aug	Sep	Oct/Nov
0-5	0-1	1-3	0-1	0-2	0-0	0-0

Winning Jockey	W-R	£1 Level Stake	Winning Course	W-R	£1 Level Stake
E A Leonard	1-3	+ 23.00	Tipperary	1-2	+ 24.00

Winning Horse	Age	Races Run	1st	2nd	3rd	Unpl	Win £
Ludden Dancer	4	2	1	0	0	1	2,762

Favourites	0-0	Total winning prize-money	£2,762
1991 Form	0-27	1989 Form 0-1	
1990 Form	0-8		

A L T MOORE

	No. of Horses	Races Run	1st	2nd	3rd	Unpl	Per cent	£1 Level Stake
2-y-o	0	0	0	0	0	0	-	0.00
3-y-o	2	4	0	0	0	4	-	- 4.00
4-y-o+	7	14	1	0	3	10	7.1	- 5.00
Totals	9	18	1	0	3	14	5.6	- 9.00

Mar/Apr	May	Jun	Jul	Aug	Sep	Oct/Nov
0-2	0-0	0-0	0-4	0-5	0-4	1-3

		£1 Level				£1 Level
Winning Jockey	W-R	Stake	Winning Course		W-R	Stake
P Carberry	1-4	+ 5.00	Dundalk		1-2	+ 7.00

		Races					Win
Winning Horse	Age	Run	1st	2nd	3rd	Unpl	£
Bitofabanter	5	4	1	0	1	2	2,243

Favourites	0-2			Total winning prize-money	£2,243

1991 Form	1-18	5.6%	- 15.75	1989 Form	0-6
1990 Form	0-4			1988 Form	0-7

J MORRISON

	No. of Horses	Races Run	1st	2nd	3rd	Unpl	Per cent	£1 Level Stake
2-y-o	1	1	0	0	0	1	-	- 1.00
3-y-o	1	5	0	0	0	5	-	- 5.00
4-y-o+	2	5	1	0	0	4	20.0	+ 4.00
Totals	4	11	1	0	0	10	9.1	- 2.00

Mar/Apr	May	Jun	Jul	Aug	Sep	Oct/Nov
0-1	0-0	0-1	1-2	0-2	0-3	0-2

		£1 Level				£1 Level
Winning Jockey	W-R	Stake	Winning Course		W-R	Stake
Mr K Whelan	1-2	+ 7.00	Wexford		1-1	+ 8.00

		Races					Win
Winning Horse	Age	Run	1st	2nd	3rd	Unpl	£
Into Milk Wood	6	4	1	0	0	3	2,762

Favourites	0-2			Total winning prize-money	£2,762

1991 Form	0-10			1989 Form	0-8		
1990 Form	1-11	9.1%	- 3.00	1988 Form	3-18	16.7%	+ 6.50

J E MULHERN

	No. of Horses	Races Run	1st	2nd	3rd	Unpl	Per cent	£1 Level Stake
2-y-o	2	6	0	0	0	6	-	- 6.00
3-y-o	6	44	1	4	4	35	2.3	- 36.00
4-y-o+	5	26	3	2	2	19	11.5	+ 7.00
Totals	13	76	4	6	6	60	5.3	- 35.00

Mar/Apr	May	Jun	Jul	Aug	Sep	Oct/Nov
0-11	0-6	1-13	1-11	1-17	0-8	1-10

Winning Jockeys	W-R	£1 Level Stake			W-R	£1 Level Stake
C Everard	1-3	+ 8.00	P P Murphy		1-3	+ 10.00
J Reid	1-3	+ 6.00	R M Burke		1-18	- 10.00

Winning Courses						
Leopardstown	3-28	+ 5.00	Navan		1-3	+ 5.00

Winning Horses	Age	Races Run	1st	2nd	3rd	Unpl	Win £
Approach The Bench	4	7	2	1	0	4	25,000
The Burser	6	7	1	1	0	5	6,900
Command 'N Control	3	8	1	2	1	4	2,760

Favourites	0-0			Total winning prize-money		£34,660

1991 Form	2-50	4.0%	- 34.00	1989 Form	3-35	8.6%	- 7.00
1990 Form	4-44	9.1%	- 22.25	1988 Form	0-6		

P MULLINS

	No. of Horses	Races Run	1st	2nd	3rd	Unpl	Per cent	£1 Level Stake
2-y-o	5	22	1	0	1	20	4.5	+ 29.00
3-y-o	4	20	2	1	3	14	10.0	- 9.00
4-y-o+	9	14	0	1	4	9	-	- 14.00
Totals	18	56	3	2	8	43	5.4	+ 6.00

Mar/Apr	May	Jun	Jul	Aug	Sep	Oct/Nov
1-4	0-3	0-3	1-13	1-10	0-11	0-12

Winning Jockeys	W-R	£1 Level Stake			W-R	£1 Level Stake
J P Murtagh	2-4	+ 55.00	S Craine		1-11	- 8.00

Winning Courses						
Navan	1-1	+ 7.00	Galway		1-8	+ 43.00
Tralee	1-3	0.00				

Winning Horses	Age	Races Run	1st	2nd	3rd	Unpl	Win £
Wheatsheaf Lady	2	7	1	0	0	6	5,522
Banaiyka	3	5	1	1	1	2	3,452
Sakanda	3	9	1	0	1	7	3,450

Favourites	1-3	33.3%	0.00	Total winning prize-money		£12,424

1991 Form	1-48	2.1%	- 42.00	1989 Form	14-168	8.3%	- 88.45
1990 Form	10-147	6.8%	- 65.30	1988 Form	20-159	12.6%	- 36.60

W P MULLINS

	No. of Horses	Races Run	1st	2nd	3rd	Unpl	Per cent	£1 Level Stake
2-y-o	4	22	1	1	3	17	4.5	- 16.00
3-y-o	6	42	4	7	3	28	9.5	- 19.00
4-y-o+	7	35	2	7	4	22	5.7	- 21.75
Totals	17	99	7	15	10	67	7.1	- 56.75

Mar/Apr	May	Jun	Jul	Aug	Sep	Oct/Nov
0-4	0-10	2-20	0-18	4-16	0-17	1-14

Winning Jockeys	W-R	£1 Level Stake			W-R	£1 Level Stake
J J Behan	2-16	- 5.00	W J Supple		1-4	+ 2.00
John O'Connor	1-1	+ 1.25	N Byrne		1-7	0.00
Mr W P Mullins	1-3	+ 8.00	D G O'Shea		1-7	- 2.00

Winning Courses						
Tramore	2-6	+ 4.00	Leopardstown		1-7	- 1.00
Tralee	1-4	+ 7.00	Gowran Park		1-9	- 3.00
Naas	1-5	- 2.75	Tipperary		1-11	- 4.00

Winning Horses	Age	Races Run	1st	2nd	3rd	Unpl	Win £
Riverbeam	3	10	3	3	0	4	15,404
Future Hero	6	2	1	0	0	1	6,900
Never Back Down	2	5	1	1	1	2	2,760
Scotsman's Bay	3	15	1	2	1	11	2,243
Richmond Breeze	6	8	1	0	1	6	000

Favourites	1-1	100.0%	+ 1.25	Total winning prize-money		£27,307

1991 Form	4-59	6.8%	- 28.00	1989 Form	1-23	4.3%	- 14.00
1990 Form	4-27	14.8%	+ 2.00	1988 Form	1-7	14.3%	+ 6.00

DANIEL J MURPHY

	No. of Horses	Races Run	1st	2nd	3rd	Unpl	Per cent	£1 Level Stake
2-y-o	10	27	1	1	3	22	3.7	- 22.50
3-y-o	6	39	4	2	5	28	10.3	+ 17.00
4-y-o+	6	13	1	1	0	11	7.7	- 9.00
Totals	22	79	6	4	8	61	7.6	- 14.50

Mar/Apr	May	Jun	Jul	Aug	Sep	Oct/Nov
0-3	0-11	0-12	2-19	1-16	1-4	2-14

Winning Jockeys	W-R	£1 Level Stake			W-R	£1 Level Stake
P V Gilson	2-11	+ 6.00	W J Supple		1-1	+ 14.00
R V Skelly	2-23	+ 5.00	D Duggan		1-3	+ 1.50

Winning Courses						
Leopardstown	2-7	+ 19.00	Ballinrobe		1-3	+ 14.00
Bellewstown	1-2	+ 2.00	Tipperary		1-4	+ 9.00
Down Royal	1-3	+ 1.50				

Winning Horses	Age	Races Run	1st	2nd	3rd	Unpl	Win £
Dashing Colours	3	9	2	2	0	5	18,875
Classic Match	4	4	1	0	0	3	4,292
Prince Mark	3	6	1	0	3	2	3,452
Final Favour	3	6	1	0	0	5	2,760
True Dancer	2	3	1	0	1	1	1,725

Favourites	0-3			Total winning prize-money			£31,104

1991 Form	2-69	2.9%	- 58.00	1989 Form	0-48		
1990 Form	8-55	14.5%	- 7.18	1988 Form	1-7	14.3%	+ 14.00

J NICHOLSON

	No. of Horses	Races Run	1st	2nd	3rd	Unpl	Per cent	£1 Level Stake
2-y-o	1	4	1	1	1	1	25.0	0.00
3-y-o	0	0	0	0	0	0	-	0.00
4-y-o+	1	4	0	0	1	3	-	- 4.00
Totals	2	8	1	1	2	4	12.5	- 4.00

Mar/Apr	May	Jun	Jul	Aug	Sep	Oct/Nov
0-0	0-0	0-0	0-2	0-3	1-2	0-1

Winning Jockey	W-R	£1 Level Stake	Winning Course	W-R	£1 Level Stake
K J Manning	1-4	0.00	Galway	1-1	+ 3.00

Winning Horse	Age	Races Run	1st	2nd	3rd	Unpl	Win £
Oh Wonderful	2	4	1	1	1	1	3,452

Favourites	0-0		Total winning prize-money	£3,452

1991 Form	0-2	1989 Form	0-0
1990 Form	0-1	1988 Form	0-10

ROBERT NORRIS

	No. of Horses	Races Run	1st	2nd	3rd	Unpl	Per cent	£1 Level Stake
2-y-o	1	1	0	0	0	1	-	- 1.00
3-y-o	2	6	1	0	0	5	16.7	+ 11.00
4-y-o+	0	0	0	0	0	0	-	0.00
Totals	3	7	1	0	0	6	14.3	+ 10.00

Mar/Apr	May	Jun	Jul	Aug	Sep	Oct/Nov
0-0	0-0	0-0	0-0	0-0	0-1	1-6

Winning Jockey	W-R	£1 Level Stake	Winning Course	W-R	£1 Level Stake
W J Supple	1-3	+ 14.00	The Curragh	1-2	+ 15.00

Winning Horse	Age	Races Run	1st	2nd	3rd	Unpl	Win £
Beaumont House	3	3	1	0	0	2	3,450

Favourites	0-0	Total winning prize-money	£3,450

M V O'BRIEN

	No. of Horses	Races Run	1st	2nd	3rd	Unpl	Per cent	£1 Level Stake
2-y-o	9	17	6	1	4	6	35.3	- 1.71
3-y-o	12	36	13	5	2	16	36.1	+ 3.03
4-y-o+	0	0	0	0	0	0	-	0.00
Totals	21	53	19	6	6	22	35.8	+ 1.32

BY MONTH

2-y-o	W-R	Per cent	£1 Level Stake	3-y-o	W-R	Per cent	£1 Level Stake
Mar/Apr	0-0	-	0.00	Mar/Apr	1-4	25.0	- 2.20
May	0-0	-	0.00	May	1-6	16.7	- 4.00
June	1-1	100.0	+ 1.00	June	2-9	22.2	- 1.43
July	1-1	100.0	+ 1.25	July	2-4	50.0	+ 0.32
August	2-4	50.0	- 0.76	August	3-8	37.5	- 0.96
September	1-7	14.3	- 5.20	September	1-2	50.0	- 0.20
Oct/Nov	1-4	25.0	+ 2.00	Oct/Nov	3-3	100.0	+ 11.50

4-y-o+	W-R	Per cent	£1 Level Stake	Totals	W-R	Per cent	£1 Level Stake
Mar/Apr	0-0	-	0.00	Mar/Apr	1-4	25.0	- 2.20
May	0-0	-	0.00	May	1-6	16.7	- 4.00
June	0-0	-	0.00	June	3-10	30.0	- 0.43
July	0-0	-	0.00	July	3-5	60.0	+ 1.57
August	0-0	-	0.00	August	5-12	41.7	- 1.72
September	0-0	-	0.00	September	2-9	22.2	- 5.40
Oct/Nov	0-0	-	0.00	Oct/Nov	4-7	57.1	+ 13.50

DISTANCE

2-y-o	W-R	Per cent	£1 Level Stake	3-y-o	W-R	Per cent	£1 Level Stake
5f-6f	5-9	55.6	+ 4.29	5f-6f	5-13	38.5	+ 2.81
7f-8f	1-8	12.5	- 6.00	7f-8f	3-14	21.4	- 7.33
9f-13f	0-0	-	0.00	9f-13f	4-7	57.1	+ 7.05
14f+	0-0	-	0.00	14f+	1-2	50.0	+ 0.50

4-y-o+	W-R	Per cent	£1 Level Stake	Totals	W-R	Per cent	£1 Level Stake
5f-6f	0-0	-	0.00	5f-6f	10-22	45.5	+ 7.10
7f-8f	0-0	-	0.00	7f-8f	4-22	18.2	- 13.33
9f-13f	0-0	-	0.00	9f-13f	4-7	57.1	+ 7.05
14f+	0-0	-	0.00	14f+	1-2	50.0	+ 0.50

TYPE OF RACE

Non-Handicaps	W-R	Per cent	£1 Level Stake	Handicaps	W-R	Per cent	£1 Level Stake
2-y-o	6-17	35.3	- 1.71	2-y-o	0-0	-	0.00
3-y-o	10-31	32.3	- 2.72	3-y-o	3-5	60.0	+ 5.75
4-y-o+	0-0	-	0.00	4-y-o+	0-0	-	0.00
Apprentice	0-0	-	0.00	Apprentice	0-0	-	0.00
Amat/Ladies	0-0	-	0.00	Amat/Ladies	0-0	-	0.00
Totals	16-48	33.3	- 4.43	Totals	3-5	60.0	+ 5.75

FIRST TIME OUT

	W-R	Per cent	£1 Level Stake
2-y-o	3-9	33.3	+ 1.25
3-y-o	2-12	16.7	- 4.20
4-y-o+	0-0	-	0.00
Totals	5-21	23.8	- 2.95

JOCKEYS RIDING

	W-R	Per cent	£1 Level Stake		W-R	Per cent	£1 Level Stake
P V Gilson	9-31	29.0	- 5.44	W J O'Connor	1-1	100.0	+ 4.00
L Piggott	7-15	46.7	+ 3.38	W R Swinburn	1-3	33.3	- 0.12
W Carson	1-1	100.0	+ 1.50				

S Cauthen	0-1	W J Supple	0-1

COURSE RECORD

	Total W-R	Non-Handicaps 2-y-o	3-y-o+	Handicaps 2-y-o	3-y-o+	Per cent	£1 Level Stake
The Curragh	10-26	5-12	4-11	0-0	1-3	38.5	+ 8.67
Leopardstown	5-14	1-4	3-9	0-0	1-1	35.7	- 1.66
Naas	2-4	0-0	1-3	0-0	1-1	50.0	- 0.06
Listowel	1-1	0-0	1-1	0-0	0-0	100.0	+ 0.80
Gowran Park	1-2	0-0	1-2	0-0	0-0	50.0	- 0.43

| Tipperary | 0-3 | Fairyhouse | | 0-2 | Limerick | | 0-1 |

WINNING HORSES

	Age	Races Run	1st	2nd	3rd	Unpl	Win £
Fatherland	2	4	4	0	0	0	122,120
Andros Bay	3	5	3	2	0	0	30,590
Via Borghese	3	4	3	0	0	1	29,005
Yukon Gold	3	6	4	1	1	0	19,667
Portico	3	3	1	0	0	2	8,280
Mysterious Ways	2	1	1	0	0	0	5,520
Portrait Gallery	2	1	1	0	0	0	5,520
Lake Isle	3	2	1	1	0	0	4,140
Arcade	3	3	1	0	0	2	3,452

WINNING OWNERS

	Races Won	Value £		Races Won	Value £
Mrs M V O'Brien	8	143,512	Malcolm Parrish	3	29,005
A J O'Reilly	7	50,257	Mrs A Manning	1	5,520

Favourites	16-25	64.0%	+ 10.32	Total winning prize-money		£228,294

Longest winning sequence		3	Average SP of winner		1.9/1
Longest losing sequence		6	Return on stakes invested		2.5%

1991 Form	36-105	34.3%	+ 9.79	1989 Form	27-100	27.0%	- 9.42
1990 Form	37-119	31.1%	+ 0.64	1988 Form	33-101	32.7%	+ 7.12

N O'CALLAGHAN

	No. of Horses	Races Run	1st	2nd	3rd	Unpl	Per cent	£1 Level Stake
2-y-o	3	12	0	0	0	12	-	- 12.00
3-y-o	3	13	1	1	2	9	7.7	0.00
4-y-o+	1	6	0	2	0	4	-	- 6.00
Totals	7	31	1	3	2	25	3.2	- 18.00

Mar/Apr	May	Jun	Jul	Aug	Sep	Oct/Nov
0-2	1-16	0-4	0-4	0-5	0-0	0-0

Winning Jockey	W-R	£1 Level Stake	Winning Course	W-R	£1 Level Stake
M Fenton	1-5	+ 8.00	Down Royal	1-2	+ 11.00

Winning Horse	Age	Races Run	1st	2nd	3rd	Unpl	Win £
Castelmagner	3	3	1	0	0	2	828

Favourites	0-0			Total winning prize-money		£828

1991 Form	3-74	4.1%	- 60.75	1989 Form	3-31	9.7%	- 11.00
1990 Form	2-53	3.8%	- 34.00				

P F O'DONNELL

	No. of Horses	Races Run	1st	2nd	3rd	Unpl	Per cent	£1 Level Stake
2-y-o	0	0	0	0	0	0	-	0.00
3-y-o	2	16	0	2	5	9	-	- 16.00
4-y-o+	2	9	3	0	0	6	33.3	+ 13.00
Totals	4	25	3	2	5	15	12.0	- 3.00

Mar/Apr	May	Jun	Jul	Aug	Sep	Oct/Nov
0-1	0-2	1-2	2-6	0-7	0-5	0-2

Winning Jockey	W-R	£1 Level Stake		W-R	£1 Level Stake
T P Treacy	3-5	+ 17.00			

Winning Courses	W-R	£1 Level Stake		W-R	£1 Level Stake
Galway	1-1	+ 7.00	Clonmel	1-2	+ 4.00
Killarney	1-2	+ 6.00			

Winning Horse	Age	Races Run	1st	2nd	3rd	Unpl	Win £
Mitah	4	6	3	0	0	3	9,492

Favourites	0-1			Total winning prize-money		£9,492

1991 Form	0-9		1990 Form	0-9

R O'DONOVAN

	No. of Horses	Races Run	1st	2nd	3rd	Unpl	Per cent	£1 Level Stake
2-y-o	0	0	0	0	0	0	-	0.00
3-y-o	2	7	1	0	1	5	14.3	+ 1.00
4-y-o+	0	0	0	0	0	0	-	0.00
Totals	2	7	1	0	1	5	14.3	+ 1.00

Mar/Apr	May	Jun	Jul	Aug	Sep	Oct/Nov
0-0	0-0	0-0	0-0	0-1	1-2	0-4

Winning Jockey	W-R	£1 Level Stake	Winning Course	W-R	£1 Level Stake
R Hughes	1-3	+ 5.00	Roscommon	1-1	+ 7.00

Winning Horse	Age	Races Run	1st	2nd	3rd	Unpl	Win £
Bertone	3	5	1	0	0	4	2,243

Favourites	0-0		Total winning prize-money	£2,243

1991 Form	0-8	1989 Form	0-14
1990 Form	0-14	1988 Form	0-44

E J O'GRADY

	No. of Horses	Races Run	1st	2nd	3rd	Unpl	Per cent	£1 Level Stake
2-y-o	5	20	3	1	1	15	15.0	- 3.50
3-y-o	10	83	1	5	8	69	1.2	- 80.00
4-y-o+	3	5	1	1	0	3	20.0	- 3.10
Totals	18	108	5	7	9	87	4.6	- 86.60

Mar/Apr	May	Jun	Jul	Aug	Sep	Oct/Nov
0-18	0-7	1-8	0-14	1-25	2-18	1-18

Winning Jockeys	W-R	£1 Level Stake		W-R	£1 Level Stake
M J Kinane	2-9	- 4.60	M Fenton	1-7	0.00
R Hughes	1-7	0.00	N G McCullagh	1-36	- 33.00

Winning Courses					
Fairyhouse	1-3	- 0.50	The Curragh	1-11	- 8.00
Clonmel	1-3	- 1.10	Leopardstown	1-17	- 10.00
Limerick	1-7	0.00			

Winning Horses		Age	Races Run	1st	2nd	3rd	Unpl	Win £
On The Catwalk		2	6	3	1	1	1	14,837
Ink By Drum		4	3	1	1	0	1	2,243
Lute And Lyre		3	10	1	0	0	9	1,935

Favourites	2-6	33.3%	- 1.60	Total winning prize-money				£19,015

1991 Form	6-106	5.7%	- 16.00	1989 Form	5-112	4.5%	- 83.75
1990 Form	4-136	2.9%	-128.35	1988 Form	12-173	6.9%	- 89.25

PAT O'LEARY

	No. of Horses	Races Run	1st	2nd	3rd	Unpl	Per cent	£1 Level Stake
2-y-o	1	1	0	0	0	1	-	- 1.00
3-y-o	4	22	3	1	0	18	13.6	- 11.10
4-y-o+	1	3	0	1	1	1	-	- 3.00
Totals	6	26	3	2	1	20	11.5	- 15.10

Mar/Apr	May	Jun	Jul	Aug	Sep	Oct/Nov
1-9	0-4	1-4	1-2	0-1	0-2	0-4

Winning Jockeys	W-R	£1 Level Stake		W-R	£1 Level Stake
Mr S R Murphy	1-1	+ 0.90	M Fenton	1-4	0.00
P Carberry	1-2	+ 3.00			

Winning Courses					
Sligo	1-3	+ 1.00	The Curragh	1-9	- 4.00
Galway	1-3	- 1.10			

Winning Horses	Age	Races Run	1st	2nd	3rd	Unpl	Win £
Return Journey	3	7	2	0	0	5	4,660
Currency Basket	3	5	1	1	0	3	3,795

Favourites	1-2	50.0%	- 0.10	Total winning prize-money		£8,455

1991 Form	0-20			1989 Form	0-9		
1990 Form	0-18			1988 Form	1-17	5.9%	- 9.00

K F O'SULLIVAN

	No. of Horses	Races Run	1st	2nd	3rd	Unpl	Per cent	£1 Level Stake
2-y-o	2	7	0	0	1	6	-	- 7.00
3-y-o	3	24	2	1	4	17	8.3	- 13.67
4-y-o+	0	0	0	0	0	0	-	0.00
Totals	5	31	2	1	5	23	6.5	- 20.67

Mar/Apr	May	Jun	Jul	Aug	Sep	Oct/Nov
0-0	0-1	0-6	2-9	0-5	0-7	0-3

Winning Jockey	W-R	£1 Level Stake			W-R	£1 Level Stake
M Fenton	2-12	- 1.67				

Winning Courses						
Killarney	1-2	+ 2.33	Galway	1-5	+ 1.00

Winning Horse	Age	Races Run	1st	2nd	3rd	Unpl	Win £
Johnny Gringo	3	11	2	1	2	6	6,902

Favourites	1-1	100.0%	+ 3.33	Total winning prize-money	£6,902
1991 Form	0-8				

M A O'TOOLE

	No. of Horses	Races Run	1st	2nd	3rd	Unpl	Per cent	£1 Level Stake
2-y-o	2	5	0	0	0	5	-	- 5.00
3-y-o	8	54	3	2	5	44	5.6	- 43.35
4-y-o+	12	48	6	2	4	36	12.5	- 15.58
Totals	22	107	9	4	9	85	8.4	- 63.93

Mar/Apr	May	Jun	Jul	Aug	Sep	Oct/Nov
0-13	3-21	2-20	2-16	2-20	0-9	0-8

Winning Jockeys	W-R	£1 Level Stake		W-R	£1 Level Stake
M J Kinane	3-9	- 2.10	R Hughes	1-8	0.00
Mr D Marnane	2-5	- 0.83	J F Egan	1-17	- 10.50
C Asmussen	1-1	+ 12.00	M F Ryan	1-32	- 27.50

Winning Courses					
Laytown	2-6	+ 3.00	Down Royal	1-4	+ 0.50
Bellewstown	2-9	- 5.08	Limerick	1-6	- 4.10
Downpatrick	1-2	+ 6.00	The Curragh	1-17	- 4.00
Clonmel	1-2	+ 0.75			

Winning Horses	Age	Races Run	1st	2nd	3rd	Unpl	Win £
Outgoing	5	5	1	1	0	3	6,900
Enqelaab	4	8	2	0	1	5	5,180
Imprimatur	3	17	1	0	2	14	2,762
Head Of Chambers	4	3	1	1	1	0	2,417
Every One Knows	3	5	1	1	1	2	2,245
Buffet	3	5	1	1	1	2	2,072
Joker In The Pack	4	6	2	0	1	3	2,070

Favourites	5-12	41.7%	- 0.93	Total winning prize-money		£23,646
1991 Form	6-120	5.0%	- 82.50	1989 Form	19-151	12.6%	- 48.09
1990 Form	12-126	9.5%	- 18.75	1988 Form	8-144	5.6%	- 87.40

JOHN M OXX

	No. of Horses	Races Run	1st	2nd	3rd	Unpl	Per cent	£1 Level Stake
2-y-o	37	84	20	18	10	36	23.8	- 20.76
3-y-o	56	241	63	36	39	103	26.1	+ 6.26
4-y-o+	9	31	2	2	4	23	6.5	- 21.50
Totals	102	356	85	56	53	162	23.9	- 36.00

BY MONTH

2-y-o	W-R	Per cent	£1 Level Stake	3-y-o	W-R	Per cent	£1 Level Stake
Mar/Apr	0-1	-	- 1.00	Mar/Apr	7-28	25.0	+ 0.48
May	0-2	-	- 2.00	May	7-31	22.6	- 12.73
June	0-5	-	- 5.00	June	20-52	38.5	+ 35.51
July	1-4	25.0	- 2.60	July	10-37	27.0	- 14.00
August	4-12	33.3	+ 0.94	August	8-40	20.0	- 9.50
September	3-22	13.6	- 14.25	September	8-25	32.0	+ 23.75
Oct/Nov	12-38	31.6	+ 3.15	Oct/Nov	3-28	10.7	- 17.25

4-y-o+	W-R	Per cent	£1 Level Stake	Totals	W-R	Per cent	£1 Level Stake
Mar/Apr	0-5	-	- 5.00	Mar/Apr	7-34	20.6	- 5.52
May	1-5	20.0	+ 0.50	May	8-38	21.1	- 14.23
June	0-9	-	- 9.00	June	20-66	30.3	+ 21.51
July	1-6	16.7	- 2.00	July	12-47	25.5	- 18.60
August	0-2	-	- 2.00	August	12-54	22.2	- 10.56
September	0-2	-	- 2.00	September	11-49	22.4	+ 7.50
Oct/Nov	0-2	-	- 2.00	Oct/Nov	15-68	22.1	- 16.10

DISTANCE

2-y-o	W-R	Per cent	£1 Level Stake	3-y-o	W-R	Per cent	£1 Level Stake
5f-6f	10-42	23.8	- 6.24	5f-6f	19-78	24.4	- 5.06
7f-8f	7-37	18.9	- 19.00	7f-8f	15-64	23.4	+ 11.12
9f-13f	1-1	100.0	+ 4.00	9f-13f	19-64	29.7	- 8.30
14f+	2-4	50.0	+ 0.48	14f+	10-35	28.6	+ 8.50

4-y-o+	W-R	Per cent	£1 Level Stake	Totals	W-R	Per cent	£1 Level Stake
5f-6f	1-7	14.3	- 1.50	5f-6f	30-127	23.6	- 12.80
7f-8f	0-5	-	- 5.00	7f-8f	22-106	20.8	- 12.88
9f-13f	1-9	11.1	- 5.00	9f-13f	21-74	28.4	- 9.30
14f+	0-10	-	- 10.00	14f+	12-49	24.5	- 1.02

TYPE OF RACE

Non-Handicaps	W-R	Per cent	£1 Level Stake	Handicaps	W-R	Per cent	£1 Level Stake
2-y-o	20-82	24.4	- 18.76	2-y-o	0-2	-	- 2.00
3-y-o	47-173	27.2	+ 1.84	3-y-o	14-66	21.2	+ 2.85
4-y-o+	1-7	14.3	- 3.00	4-y-o+	0-20	-	- 20.00
Apprentice	1-1	100.0	+ 0.57	Apprentice	2-3	66.7	+ 4.50
Amat/Ladies	0-1	-	- 1.00	Amat/Ladies	0-1	-	- 1.00
Totals	69-264	26.1	- 20.35	Totals	16-92	17.4	- 15.65

FIRST TIME OUT

	W-R	Per cent	£1 Level Stake
2-y-o	9-37	24.3	- 3.45
3-y-o	13-56	23.2	+ 22.90
4-y-o+	0-9	-	- 9.00
Totals	22-102	21.6	+ 10.45

JOCKEYS RIDING

	W-R	Per cent	£1 Level Stake		W-R	Per cent	£1 Level Stake
J P Murtagh	35-122	28.7	- 3.33	M J Kinane	8-25	32.0	- 4.81
D G O'Shea	17-57	29.8	+ 37.92	W R Swinburn	1-3	33.3	+ 1.50
R Hughes	13-42	31.0	+ 4.60	S Cauthen	1-4	25.0	- 2.00
D Hogan	9-79	11.4	- 47.88	W J O'Connor	1-5	20.0	- 3.00

D Duggan	0-5	L Piggott	0-1	Pat Eddery	0-1
W J Supple	0-2	M Roberts	0-1	R M Burke	0-1
D O'Donoghue	0-1	Miss S Collen	0-1	S Craine	0-1
J McAuley	0-1	Mr A J Martin	0-1	T Jarnet	0-1
J Reid	0-1	P V Gilson	0-1		

COURSE RECORD

	Total W-R	Non-Handicaps 2-y-o	3-y-o+	Handicaps 2-y-o	3-y-o+	Per cent	£1 Level Stake
The Curragh	19-125	7-37	9-60	0-1	3-27	15.2	- 15.58
Leopardstown	17-75	4-12	8-35	0-0	5-28	22.7	- 5.93
Naas	7-26	1-3	4-13	0-1	2-9	26.9	- 4.38
Dundalk	6-10	1-2	5-8	0-0	0-0	60.0	+ 2.68
Fairyhouse	5-14	1-5	2-5	0-0	2-4	35.7	+ 3.17
Tipperary	5-16	1-4	4-9	0-0	0-3	31.3	- 0.15
Wexford	4-5	0-0	3-4	0-0	1-1	80.0	+ 8.92
Mallow	4-6	1-2	3-4	0-0	0-0	66.7	+ 1.53
Roscommon	4-9	1-1	2-5	0-0	1-3	44.4	+ 5.25
Tralee	3-8	1-1	2-5	0-0	0-2	37.5	- 0.31
Down Royal	2-3	0-0	2-3	0-0	0-0	66.7	+ 0.33
Listowel	2-6	1-3	0-2	0-0	1-1	33.3	+ 2.00

Gowran Park	2-20	1-9	1-8	0-0	0-3	10.0	- 16.47
Ballinrobe	1-1	0-0	1-1	0-0	0-0	100.0	+ 1.00
Bellewstown	1-3	0-0	0-2	0-0	1-1	33.3	+ 1.00
Navan	1-5	0-2	1-3	0-0	0-0	20.0	- 3.20
Clonmel	1-5	0-0	1-4	0-0	0-1	20.0	- 3.86
Galway	1-10	0-0	1-4	0-0	0-6	10.0	- 3.00

Limerick	0-3	Killarney	0-1	Tramore	0-1
Punchestown	0-3	Sligo	0-1		

WINNING HORSES

	Age	Races Run	1st	2nd	3rd	Unpl	Win £
Sinntara	3	6	4	0	1	1	26,977
Ebaziya	3	6	3	1	1	1	25,532
Foresee	2	2	2	0	0	0	17,825
Khizarabad	3	9	3	3	0	3	16,610
Sinissipi	2	3	2	1	0	0	14,145
Shakanda	3	8	3	1	1	3	13,455
Khanata	3	5	1	0	2	2	12,500
Tijara	3	8	2	2	2	2	12,330
West Chazy	3	8	3	0	1	4	12,077
Dabtiya	3	5	2	1	0	2	12,075
Chanzi	2	2	2	0	0	0	11,903
Equal Eloquence	3	6	2	1	0	3	11,385
Polar Wind	3	10	3	0	2	5	11,140
Kaskazi	3	6	2	0	0	4	9,315
Calounia	3	4	1	0	1	2	8,627
Poolesta	3	6	1	3	2	0	8,625
Garabagh	3	5	2	0	2	1	7,000
Darayna	3	6	2	1	1	2	6,904
Ladakiya	2	2	1	0	1	0	6,855
Mawara	3	5	2	0	1	2	6,385
Durshan	3	5	2	2	0	1	6,345
Khalidi	3	5	2	0	2	1	6,212
Hazaradjat	3	2	1	0	0	1	5,672
Mirana	3	6	1	2	3	0	5,520
Khoraz	2	4	1	1	1	1	5,520
Dawnsio	2	4	1	2	0	1	5,520
Massyar	2	3	1	0	0	2	5,520
Dark Reef	2	2	1	1	0	0	5,520
Idris	2	1	1	0	0	0	5,520
Nicea	2	1	1	0	0	0	5,520
Faraghan	3	7	2	1	1	3	5,350
Annonay	3	10	2	1	1	6	5,007
Mariyda	3	5	2	2	0	1	5,007
Ridiya	3	4	2	0	1	1	5,005
Khazari	4	6	1	0	2	3	4,142
Sumy	2	4	1	2	1	0	4,140
Kariniyd	2	1	1	0	0	0	4,140
Adira	3	5	1	0	1	3	3,797
Avenue Foch	3	3	1	0	1	1	3,452
Home Counties	3	4	1	1	0	2	3,452

Coopers Spot-On	4	5	1	0	0	4	3,452
Nadjati	3	3	1	0	1	1	3,450
Shawar	3	2	1	0	0	1	3,450
Oleari	3	2	1	0	0	1	3,450
Kadi	3	4	1	2	0	1	3,450
Kharandiz	3	2	1	0	0	1	3,450
Oiseau De Feu	2	2	1	1	0	0	3,450
Shaikala	2	2	1	0	0	1	3,450
Timourid	2	1	1	0	0	0	3,450
Shawiya	3	6	1	2	2	1	2,935
Seven Ages	3	4	1	1	0	2	2,762
Miami Sands	2	2	1	1	0	0	2,760
Tirizi	2	2	1	1	0	0	2,760
Tadila	3	5	1	1	1	2	2,245
Madiya	3	3	1	0	0	2	2,243
Badastan	3	2	1	0	0	1	2,243

WINNING OWNERS

	Races Won	Value £		Races Won	Value £
H H Aga Khan	52	244,741	Mrs J M Oxx	1	3,452
Sheikh Mohammed	20	95,216	M Fitzgibbon	1	3,452
Lady Clague	3	16,905	M E Parrish	1	3,450
Dundalk Racing Club	3	13,455	J F Maille	1	3,450
Malcolm Parrish	1	8,625	Dieter H Hofemeier	1	2,760
Peter Austin	1	5,520			

Favourites	53-102	52.0%	+ 24.79	Total winning prize-money		£401,026
Longest winning sequence			4	Average SP of winner		2.8/1
Longest losing sequence			15	Return on stakes invested		-10.1%
1991 Form	93-403	23.1%	+ 7.22	1989 Form	47-296	15.9%	- 81.25
1990 Form	65-376	17.3%	- 95.59	1988 Form	53-349	15.2%	- 63.98

F W PENNICOTT

	No. of Horses	Races Run	1st	2nd	3rd	Unpl	Per cent	£1 Level Stake
2-y-o	0	0	0	0	0	0	-	0.00
3-y-o	0	0	0	0	0	0	-	0.00
4-y-o+	1	7	1	1	0	5	14.3	+ 1.00
Totals	1	7	1	1	0	5	14.3	+ 1.00

Mar/Apr	May	Jun	Jul	Aug	Sep	Oct/Nov
1-3	0-0	0-0	0-3	0-0	0-0	0-1

Winning Jockey	W-R	£1 Level Stake	Winning Course	W-R	£1 Level Stake
D J O'Donohoe	1-6	+ 2.00	Leopardstown	1-3	+ 5.00

Winning Horse	Age	Races Run	1st	2nd	3rd	Unpl	Win £
Old Talka River	5	7	1	1	0	5	4,140

Favourites	0-0		Total winning prize-money		£4,140

1991 Form	0-22		1989 Form	1-13	7.7%	+ 4.00
1990 Form	0-22					

P PHELAN

	No. of Horses	Races Run	1st	2nd	3rd	Unpl	Per cent	£1 Level Stake
2-y-o	0	0	0	0	0	0	-	0.00
3-y-o	2	5	0	0	0	5	-	- 5.00
4-y-o+	3	7	1	0	0	6	14.3	+ 4.00
Totals	5	12	1	0	0	11	8.3	- 1.00

Mar/Apr	May	Jun	Jul	Aug	Sep	Oct/Nov
0-3	0-3	0-3	0-0	0-0	0-1	1-2

Winning Jockey	W-R	£1 Level Stake	Winning Course	W-R	£1 Level Stake
P Shanahan	1-5	+ 6.00	Naas	1-1	+ 10.00

Winning Horse	Age	Races Run	1st	2nd	3rd	Unpl	Win £
Raysulid	7	2	1	0	0	1	2,760

Favourites	0-1		Total winning prize-money		£2,760

1991 Form	0-16		1989 Form	1-9	11.1%	0.00
1990 Form	0-0					

K PRENDERGAST

	No. of Horses	Races Run	1st	2nd	3rd	Unpl	Per cent	£1 Level Stake
2-y-o	28	95	9	13	20	53	9.5	- 32.33
3-y-o	27	225	19	22	27	157	8.4	-132.52
4-y-o+	8	53	2	3	6	42	3.8	- 32.00
Totals	63	373	30	38	53	252	8.0	-196.85

BY MONTH

2-y-o	W-R	Per cent	£1 Level Stake	3-y-o	W-R	Per cent	£1 Level Stake
Mar/Apr	1-5	20.0	+ 2.00	Mar/Apr	1-22	4.5	- 17.50
May	1-6	16.7	- 1.50	May	2-32	6.3	- 20.17
June	0-11	-	- 11.00	June	7-41	17.1	- 14.45
July	1-10	10.0	- 8.33	July	0-34	-	- 34.00
August	2-17	11.8	- 5.50	August	6-37	16.2	- 15.40
September	3-14	21.4	+ 11.00	September	3-21	14.3	+ 7.00
Oct/Nov	1-32	3.1	- 19.00	Oct/Nov	0-38	-	- 38.00

4-y-o+	W-R	Per cent	£1 Level Stake	Totals	W-R	Per cent	£1 Level Stake
Mar/Apr	0-4	-	- 4.00	Mar/Apr	2-31	6.5	- 19.50
May	0-5	-	- 5.00	May	3-43	7.0	- 26.67
June	0-9	-	- 9.00	June	7-61	11.5	- 34.45
July	0-12	-	- 12.00	July	1-56	1.8	- 54.33
August	1-9	11.1	+ 1.00	August	9-63	14.3	- 19.90
September	0-5	-	- 5.00	September	6-40	15.0	+ 13.00
Oct/Nov	1-9	11.1	+ 2.00	Oct/Nov	2-79	2.5	- 55.00

DISTANCE

2-y-o	W-R	Per cent	£1 Level Stake	3-y-o	W-R	Per cent	£1 Level Stake
5f-6f	5-46	10.9	- 16.00	5f-6f	10-84	11.9	- 20.90
7f-8f	4-42	9.5	- 9.33	7f-8f	1-63	1.6	- 58.67
9f-13f	0-2	-	- 2.00	9f-13f	5-41	12.2	- 27.83
14f+	0-5	-	- 5.00	14f+	3-37	8.1	- 25.12

4-y-o+	W-R	Per cent	£1 Level Stake	Totals	W-R	Per cent	£1 Level Stake
5f-6f	1-11	9.1	- 1.00	5f-6f	16-141	11.3	- 37.90
7f-8f	0-19	-	- 19.00	7f-8f	5-124	4.0	- 87.00
9f-13f	0-9	-	- 9.00	9f-13f	5-52	9.6	- 38.83
14f+	1-14	7.1	- 3.00	14f+	4-56	7.1	- 33.12

TYPE OF RACE

Non-Handicaps	W-R	Per cent	£1 Level Stake	Handicaps	W-R	Per cent	£1 Level Stake
2-y-o	7-86	8.1	- 32.83	2-y-o	2-9	22.2	+ 0.50
3-y-o	10-124	8.1	- 85.52	3-y-o	9-88	10.2	- 34.00
4-y-o+	0-9	-	- 9.00	4-y-o+	2-40	5.0	- 19.00
Apprentice	0-2	-	- 2.00	Apprentice	0-13	-	- 13.00
Amat/Ladies	0-0	-	0.00	Amat/Ladies	0-2	-	- 2.00
Totals	17-221	7.7	-129.35	Totals	13-152	8.6	- 67.50

FIRST TIME OUT

	W-R	Per cent	£1 Level Stake
2-y-o	1-28	3.6	- 21.00
3-y-o	0-26	-	- 26.00
4-y-o+	0-7	-	- 7.00
Totals	1-61	1.6	- 54.00

JOCKEYS RIDING

	W-R	Per cent	£1 Level Stake		W-R	Per cent	£1 Level Stake
R Griffiths	22-224	9.8	- 98.93	D J Walsh	1-1	100.0	+ 10.00
B J Walsh	6-46	13.0	- 10.25	S Craine	1-8	12.5	- 3.67

R M Burke	0-53	A P Colgan	0-2	J F Egan	0-1
E A Leonard	0-9	Mr J R Banahan	0-2	M C G Laurence	0-1
J F Clarke	0-7	A J Reddington	0-1	M J Kinane	0-1
B P Harding	0-6	D Holland	0-1	P V Gilson	0-1
E M O'Riordan	0-3	J Cornally	0-1	A J Nolan	0-1
W J Supple	0-3	J D Eddery	0-1		

COURSE RECORD

	Total W-R	Non-Handicaps 2-y-o	Non-Handicaps 3-y-o+	Handicaps 2-y-o	Handicaps 3-y-o+	Per cent	£1 Level Stake
Leopardstown	8-67	1-14	3-25	0-0	4-28	11.9	- 12.09
The Curragh	7-101	2-27	1-31	1-3	3-40	6.9	- 53.50
Tipperary	5-23	2-7	1-10	0-0	2-6	21.7	+ 2.19
Roscommon	2-12	0-1	2-6	0-0	0-5	16.7	+ 1.33
Tramore	1-4	0-0	1-2	0-0	0-2	25.0	- 2.00
Wexford	1-4	0-0	1-4	0-0	0-0	25.0	- 2.83
Tralee	1-5	0-0	0-2	0-0	1-3	20.0	+ 1.50
Killarney	1-6	0-1	1-3	0-0	0-2	16.7	- 3.62
Bellewstown	1-6	1-2	0-2	0-0	0-2	16.7	- 4.33
Gowran Park	1-15	0-3	0-5	0-2	1-5	6.7	- 9.00
Fairyhouse	1-17	1-5	0-6	0-1	0-5	5.9	- 4.00
Galway	1-17	0-4	0-3	1-1	0-9	5.9	- 14.50

Naas	0-23	Ballinrobe	0-5	Listowel	0-2
Navan	0-20	Clonmel	0-4	Downpatrick	0-1
Dundalk	0-13	Laytown	0-4	Limerick	0-1
Down Royal	0-10	Punchestown	0-3		
Mallow	0-6	Sligo	0-3		

WINNING HORSES

	Age	Races Run	1st	2nd	3rd	Unpl	Win £
Bahi	3	12	3	3	4	2	17,599
Millie's Choice	3	15	4	4	2	5	13,802
Ebony And Ivory	3	15	3	5	1	6	11,732
Stripped Clean	3	14	2	2	1	9	8,629

Prendergast K

Boranwood	2	3	1	1	0	1	6,900
Earl Of Barking	2	5	2	0	3	0	6,730
Tony's Fen	3	14	2	2	5	5	6,385
Arlington Heights	3	11	2	0	1	8	5,695
Shahik	2	6	1	3	1	1	5,520
Sabaya	2	4	1	2	1	0	5,520
John Peel	2	5	1	1	1	2	4,140
Tony's Delight	4	11	1	2	2	6	4,140
Ukud	2	4	1	2	0	1	3,452
Fanny Blankers	2	8	1	1	1	5	3,452
Ibda	2	6	1	0	3	2	3,450
Thin Ice	4	9	1	0	2	6	3,207
Lakeshore	3	15	1	0	1	13	2,762
Desert Calm	3	6	1	2	0	3	2,760
Murahin	3	8	1	0	1	6	2,408

WINNING OWNERS

	Races Won	Value £		Races Won	Value £
Hamdan Al-Maktoum	8	37,949	Mrs Kevin Prendergast	2	6,902
Mrs C McNulty	5	18,119	Edward M Tynan	1	6,900
Colm McEvoy	4	13,802	G Berger	2	5,695
Michael W J Smurfit	3	11,732	Oliver Lehane	1	3,452
Mrs Chris Harrington	3	10,525	P Conlan	1	3,207

Favourites	11-33	33.3%	- 2.84	Total winning prize-money			£118,283
Longest winning sequence			2	Average SP of winner			4.9/1
Longest losing sequence			76	Return on stakes invested			-52.8%
1991 Form	36-467	7.7%	-214.25	1989 Form	52-435	12.0%	-169.60
1990 Form	59-533	11.1%	-159.45	1988 Form	61-453	13.5%	- 73.45

P PRENDERGAST

	No. of Horses	Races Run	1st	2nd	3rd	Unpl	Per cent	£1 Level Stake
2-y-o	5	17	5	3	0	9	29.4	+ 12.53
3-y-o	8	43	6	5	4	28	14.0	- 16.90
4-y-o+	4	22	0	0	1	21	-	- 22.00
Totals	17	82	11	8	5	58	13.4	- 26.37

BY MONTH

2-y-o	W-R	Per cent	£1 Level Stake	3-y-o	W-R	Per cent	£1 Level Stake
Mar/Apr	0-0	-	0.00	Mar/Apr	0-7	-	- 7.00
May	1-2	50.0	- 0.27	May	0-7	-	- 7.00
June	1-2	50.0	- 0.20	June	0-6	-	- 6.00
July	0-0	-	0.00	July	2-6	33.3	+ 3.50
August	0-2	-	- 2.00	August	2-8	25.0	- 1.40
September	1-6	16.7	+ 9.00	September	2-4	50.0	+ 6.00
Oct/Nov	2-5	40.0	+ 6.00	Oct/Nov	0-5	-	- 5.00

4-y-o+	W-R	Per cent	£1 Level Stake	Totals	W-R	Per cent	£1 Level Stake
Mar/Apr	0-6	-	- 6.00	Mar/Apr	0-13	-	- 13.00
May	0-1	-	- 1.00	May	1-10	10.0	- 8.27
June	0-1	-	- 1.00	June	1-9	11.1	- 7.20
July	0-1	-	- 1.00	July	2-7	28.6	+ 2.50
August	0-10	-	- 10.00	August	2-20	10.0	- 13.40
September	0-2	-	- 2.00	September	3-12	25.0	+ 13.00
Oct/Nov	0-1	-	- 1.00	Oct/Nov	2-11	18.2	0.00

DISTANCE

2-y-o	W-R	Per cent	£1 Level Stake	3-y-o	W-R	Per cent	£1 Level Stake
5f-6f	3-8	37.5	+ 4.80	5f-6f	3-20	15.0	- 4.50
7f-8f	2-9	22.2	+ 7.73	7f-8f	3-16	18.8	- 5.40
9f-13f	0-0	-	0.00	9f-13f	0-1	-	- 1.00
14f+	0-0	-	0.00	14f+	0-6	-	- 6.00

4-y-o+	W-R	Per cent	£1 Level Stake	Totals	W-R	Per cent	£1 Level Stake
5f-6f	0-7	-	- 7.00	5f-6f	6-35	17.1	- 6.70
7f-8f	0-7	-	- 7.00	7f-8f	5-32	15.6	- 4.67
9f-13f	0-6	-	- 6.00	9f-13f	0-7	-	- 7.00
14f+	0-2	-	- 2.00	14f+	0-8	-	- 8.00

TYPE OF RACE

Non-Handicaps	W-R	Per cent	£1 Level Stake	Handicaps	W-R	Per cent	£1 Level Stake
2-y-o	3-15	20.0	- 6.47	2-y-o	2-2	100.0	+ 19.00
3-y-o	4-27	14.8	- 11.40	3-y-o	2-12	16.7	- 1.50
4-y-o+	0-5	-	- 5.00	4-y-o+	0-15	-	- 15.00
Apprentice	0-2	-	- 2.00	Apprentice	0-3	-	- 3.00
Amat/Ladies	0-0	-	0.00	Amat/Ladies	0-1	-	- 1.00
Totals	7-49	14.3	- 24.87	Totals	4-33	12.1	- 1.50

FIRST TIME OUT

	W-R	Per cent	£1 Level Stake
2-y-o	0-5	-	- 5.00
3-y-o	0-8	-	- 8.00
4-y-o+	0-4	-	- 4.00
Totals	0-17	-	- 17.00

JOCKEYS RIDING

	W-R	Per cent	£1 Level Stake		W-R	Per cent	£1 Level Stake
J J Behan	3-13	23.1	+ 2.00	J D Eddery	1-1	100.0	+ 5.00
S Craine	2-6	33.3	- 0.40	M Fenton	1-7	14.3	- 1.00
R Hughes	2-17	11.8	- 13.47	K J Manning	1-10	10.0	+ 5.00
D G O'Shea	1-1	100.0	+ 3.50				

E A Leonard	0-4	R Griffiths	0-2	L Piggott	0-1
P Lowry	0-4	W R Swinburn	0-2	M Roberts	0-1
P Shanahan	0-3	D Hogan	0-1	Mr A J Martin	0-1
C F Swan	0-2	D Holland	0-1	Pat Eddery	0-1
C Roche	0-2	L P Aspell	0-1	Y Okabe	0-1

COURSE RECORD

	Total W-R	Non-Handicaps 2-y-o	Non-Handicaps 3-y-o+	Handicaps 2-y-o	Handicaps 3-y-o+	Per cent	£1 Level Stake
Fairyhouse	2-2	1-1	0-0	1-1	0-0	100.0	+ 14.73
Galway	2-2	1-1	1-1	0-0	0-0	100.0	+ 6.50
Down Royal	2-3	0-0	1-1	0-0	1-2	66.7	+ 9.00
Ballinrobe	1-3	0-1	1-1	0-0	0-1	33.3	+ 1.00
Tipperary	1-5	0-1	1-4	0-0	0-0	20.0	- 2.90
Leopardstown	1-6	0-1	0-1	0-0	1-4	16.7	- 1.50
Mallow	1-8	1-1	0-6	0-0	0-1	12.5	- 6.20
The Curragh	1-24	0-4	0-7	1-1	0-12	4.2	- 18.00

Tralee	0-6	Listowel	0-3	Gowran Park	0-1
Navan	0-5	Laytown	0-2	Naas	0-1
Sligo	0-4	Roscommon	0-2	Punchestown	0-1
Killarney	0-3	Downpatrick	0-1		

WINNING HORSES

	Age	Races Run	1st	2nd	3rd	Unpl	Win £
Forest Concert	3	9	2	2	2	3	6,557
Take No Chances	2	6	2	0	0	4	5,865
Soundproof	2	4	1	1	0	2	4,830
Dr Phillips	3	6	2	0	0	4	4,487
Great Diplomat	2	2	1	1	0	0	3,450
Little Munchkin	2	2	1	1	0	0	2,762
Lady President	3	9	1	3	1	4	2,760
Morning Wings	3	5	1	0	0	4	690

WINNING OWNERS

	Races Won	Value £		Races Won	Value £
Y Akazawa	4	14,147	Mrs Patrick Prendergast	2	3,452
Mrs Nerys Dutfield	2	5,865	High Seas Leisure Ltd	1	3,450
J D Clague	2	4,487			

Favourites	6-15	40.0%	+ 5.13	Total winning prize-money			£31,401
Longest winning sequence			2	Average SP of winner			4.1/1
Longest losing sequence			22	Return on stakes invested			-32.2%
1991 Form	5-69	7.2%	- 31.50	1989 Form	9-110	8.2%	- 50.50
1990 Form	7-69	10.1%	- 33.95	1988 Form	8-115	7.0%	- 71.50

M QUAID

	No. of Horses	Races Run	1st	2nd	3rd	Unpl	Per cent	£1 Level Stake
2-y-o	0	0	0	0	0	0	-	0.00
3-y-o	1	1	0	0	0	1	-	- 1.00
4-y-o+	1	5	1	1	0	3	20.0	+ 21.00
Totals	2	6	1	1	0	4	16.7	+ 20.00

Mar/Apr	May	Jun	Jul	Aug	Sep	Oct/Nov
0-0	0-0	0-0	0-0	1-3	0-1	0-2

Winning Jockey	W-R	£1 Level Stake	Winning Course	W-R	£1 Level Stake
P P Murphy	1-3	+ 23.00	The Curragh	1-2	+ 24.00

Winning Horse	Age	Races Run	1st	2nd	3rd	Unpl	Win £
Pharella	4	5	1	1	0	3	3,450

Favourites	0-0			Total winning prize-money		£3,450
1991 Form	0-15			1989 Form	0-6	
1990 Form	1-11	9.1%	- 2.00	1988 Form	2-25	8.0% - 3.50

J QUEALLY

	No. of Horses	Races Run	1st	2nd	3rd	Unpl	Per cent	£1 Level Stake
2-y-o	0	0	0	0	0	0	-	0.00
3-y-o	0	0	0	0	0	0	-	0.00
4-y-o+	2	4	1	1	0	2	25.0	+ 3.00
Totals	2	4	1	1	0	2	25.0	+ 3.00

Queally J

Mar/Apr	May	Jun	Jul	Aug	Sep	Oct/Nov
0-0	0-0	0-0	0-1	0-1	1-2	0-0

Winning Jockey	W-R	£1 Level Stake	Winning Course	W-R	£1 Level Stake
Mr J Queally	1-3	+ 4.00	Listowel	1-2	+ 5.00

Winning Horse	Age	Races Run	1st	2nd	3rd	Unpl	Win £
Cock Cockburn	6	3	1	1	0	1	6,900

Favourites	0-1		Total winning prize-money	£6,900

1991 Form	1-3	33.3%	- 0.75

W M ROPER

	No. of Horses	Races Run	1st	2nd	3rd	Unpl	Per cent	£1 Level Stake
2-y-o	0	0	0	0	0	0	-	0.00
3-y-o	6	29	1	0	2	26	3.4	- 24.00
4-y-o+	1	2	0	0	0	2	-	- 2.00
Totals	7	31	1	0	2	28	3.2	- 26.00

Mar/Apr	May	Jun	Jul	Aug	Sep	Oct/Nov
0-1	0-4	1-5	0-4	0-8	0-5	0-4

Winning Jockey	W-R	£1 Level Stake	Winning Course	W-R	£1 Level Stake
W J Supple	1-7	- 2.00	Ballinrobe	1-1	+ 4.00

Winning Horse	Age	Races Run	1st	2nd	3rd	Unpl	Win £
Philberg	3	5	1	0	0	4	2,245

Favourites	0-0		Total winning prize-money	£2,245

1991 Form	2-33	6.1%	- 11.00	1989 Form	1-20	5.0%	- 5.00
1990 Form	0-17			1988 Form	1-18	5.6%	- 10.00

COUNTESS SCHULENBURG

	No. of Horses	Races Run	1st	2nd	3rd	Unpl	Per cent	£1 Level Stake
2-y-o	0	0	0	0	0	0	-	0.00
3-y-o	1	3	1	0	0	2	33.3	+ 12.00
4-y-o+	2	4	0	0	1	3	-	- 4.00
Totals	3	7	1	0	1	5	14.3	+ 8.00

Mar/Apr	May	Jun	Jul	Aug	Sep	Oct/Nov
0-0	0-0	0-1	0-0	0-0	1-4	0-2

Winning Jockey	W-R	£1 Level Stake	Winning Course	W-R	£1 Level Stake
B P Gowran	1-6	+ 9.00	Listowel	1-1	+ 14.00

Winning Horse	Age	Races Run	1st	2nd	3rd	Unpl	Win £
El Louisa	3	3	1	0	0	2	4,140

Favourites	0-0		Total winning prize-money	£4,140
1991 Form	0-4			

T STACK

	No. of Horses	Races Run	1st	2nd	3rd	Unpl	Per cent	£1 Level Stake
2-y-o	17	58	3	5	10	40	5.2	- 37.70
3-y-o	17	85	12	9	8	56	14.1	- 17.00
4-y-o+	13	56	5	3	5	43	8.9	- 24.00
Totals	47	199	20	17	23	139	10.1	- 78.70

BY MONTH

2-y-o	W-R	Per cent	£1 Level Stake	3-y-o	W-R	Per cent	£1 Level Stake
Mar/Apr	0-3	-	- 3.00	Mar/Apr	1-21	4.8	- 13.00
May	0-4	-	- 4.00	May	5-16	31.3	- 1.25
June	1-6	16.7	- 4.20	June	3-24	12.5	+ 1.25
July	0-3	-	- 3.00	July	0-7	-	- 7.00
August	2-13	15.4	+ 5.50	August	0-6	-	- 6.00
September	0-17	-	- 17.00	September	2-8	25.0	+ 2.00
Oct/Nov	0-12	-	- 12.00	Oct/Nov	1-3	33.3	+ 7.00

4-y-o+	W-R	Per cent	£1 Level Stake	Totals	W-R	Per cent	£1 Level Stake
Mar/Apr	4-14	28.6	+ 9.00	Mar/Apr	5-38	13.2	- 7.00
May	1-12	8.3	- 3.00	May	6-32	18.8	- 8.25
June	0-7	-	- 7.00	June	4-37	10.8	- 9.95
July	0-10	-	- 10.00	July	0-20	-	- 20.00
August	0-6	-	- 6.00	August	2-25	8.0	- 6.50
September	0-5	-	- 5.00	September	2-30	6.7	- 20.00
Oct/Nov	0-2	-	- 2.00	Oct/Nov	1-17	5.9	- 7.00

DISTANCE

2-y-o	W-R	Per cent	£1 Level Stake	3-y-o	W-R	Per cent	£1 Level Stake
5f-6f	2-28	7.1	- 9.50	5f-6f	4-35	11.4	- 14.00
7f-8f	1-25	4.0	- 23.20	7f-8f	2-29	6.9	- 19.00
9f-13f	0-1	-	- 1.00	9f-13f	2-11	18.2	+ 8.75
14f+	0-4	-	- 4.00	14f+	4-10	40.0	+ 7.25

4-y-o+	W-R	Per cent	£1 Level Stake	Totals	W-R	Per cent	£1 Level Stake
5f-6f	1-17	5.9	- 10.00	5f-6f	7-80	8.8	- 33.50
7f-8f	1-12	8.3	- 3.00	7f-8f	4-66	6.1	- 45.20
9f-13f	2-19	10.5	- 5.50	9f-13f	4-31	12.9	+ 2.25
14f+	1-8	12.5	- 5.50	14f+	5-22	22.7	- 2.25

TYPE OF RACE

Non-Handicaps	W-R	Per cent	£1 Level Stake	Handicaps	W-R	Per cent	£1 Level Stake
2-y-o	2-50	4.0	- 33.20	2-y-o	1-8	12.5	- 4.50
3-y-o	9-58	15.5	- 14.00	3-y-o	3-24	12.5	0.00
4-y-o+	0-13	-	- 13.00	4-y-o+	3-35	8.6	- 12.50
Apprentice	0-1	-	- 1.00	Apprentice	1-6	16.7	- 3.50
Amat/Ladies	1-1	100.0	+ 6.00	Amat/Ladies	0-3	-	- 3.00
Totals	12-123	9.8	- 55.20	Totals	8-76	10.5	- 23.50

FIRST TIME OUT

	W-R	Per cent	£1 Level Stake
2-y-o	2-17	11.8	- 0.20
3-y-o	1-17	5.9	- 12.00
4-y-o+	3-13	23.1	+ 10.00
Totals	6-47	12.8	- 2.20

JOCKEYS RIDING

	W-R	Per cent	£1 Level Stake		W-R	Per cent	£1 Level Stake
S Craine	17-158	10.8	- 64.20	Mr K Whelan	1-4	25.0	+ 3.00
M Roberts	1-3	33.3	+ 14.00	J J Stack	1-15	6.7	- 12.50

D W O'Sullivan	0-8	D G O'Shea	0-1	M Fenton		0-1
R Hughes	0-3	E A Leonard	0-1	W J Smith		0-1
J G Power	0-2	M C G Laurence	0-1	W J Supple		0-1

COURSE RECORD

	Total W-R	Non-Handicaps 2-y-o	3-y-o+	Handicaps 2-y-o	3-y-o+	Per cent	£1 Level Stake
The Curragh	8-57	1-10	5-22	0-2	2-23	14.0	- 0.45
Tipperary	3-22	1-4	1-12	1-2	0-4	13.6	- 1.00
Leopardstown	3-30	0-8	0-8	0-0	3-14	10.0	- 7.50
Mallow	2-8	0-0	1-4	0-1	1-3	25.0	- 1.50
Navan	1-5	0-2	1-2	0-0	0-1	20.0	- 1.50
Killarney	1-5	0-0	1-2	0-0	0-3	20.0	- 1.75
Galway	1-7	0-1	1-2	0-0	0-4	14.3	- 2.00
Tralee	1-10	0-2	0-4	0-0	1-4	10.0	- 8.00

Naas	0-10	Gowran Park	0-4	Thurles	0-1
Listowel	0-9	Sligo	0-4	Tramore	0-1
Limerick	0-7	Dundalk	0-3	Wexford	0-1
Ballinrobe	0-6	Fairyhouse	0-2		
Roscommon	0-5	Punchestown	0-2		

WINNING HORSES

	Age	Races Run	1st	2nd	3rd	Unpl	Win £
Gentle Step	3	6	1	0	0	5	15,000
Firing Line	3	5	2	2	0	1	10,695
Dawn Bird	3	9	2	1	0	6	6,912
Suntan	3	10	2	1	3	4	6,902
Gaelic Myth	5	9	2	0	2	5	6,555
Purple Emperor	3	5	2	0	2	1	5,695
Glendower	3	7	2	3	0	2	5,522
El Zorro Dorado	2	2	1	0	1	0	5,520
Tartan Lady	2	2	1	0	0	1	3,452
Practitioner	5	5	1	0	0	4	3,105
Side Winger	4	6	1	0	0	5	3,105
Paint The Wind	2	8	1	1	4	2	2,762
Stylish Aristocrat	3	4	1	0	0	3	2,417
Moldavia	6	6	1	1	2	2	2,243

WINNING OWNERS

	Races Won	Value £		Races Won	Value £
R E Sangster	5	17,597	John Thompson	1	3,452
David F Jefferson	1	15,000	Glenn S Bromagen	1	3,105
T Corden	4	13,814	R D Hubbard	1	3,105
Mrs John Magnier	2	10,695	Mrs J Donnelly	1	2,762
Mrs T Stack	3	7,938	Prestonwood Farm Inc	1	2,417

Favourites	6-16	37.5%	+ 4.30	Total winning prize-money	£79,885

Longest winning sequence	1	Average SP of winner	5.0/1
Longest losing sequence	36	Return on stakes invested	-39.5%

1991 Form	49-263	18.6%	+ 22.70	1989 Form	23-167	13.8%	- 54.60
1990 Form	22-216	10.2%	- 101.10	1988 Form	12-98	12.2%	- 22.67

ADRIAN TAYLOR

	No. of Horses	Races Run	1st	2nd	3rd	Unpl	Per cent	£1 Level Stake
2-y-o	0	0	0	0	0	0	-	0.00
3-y-o	1	9	1	0	0	8	11.1	+ 6.00
4-y-o+	3	13	1	1	0	11	7.7	+ 8.00
Totals	4	22	2	1	0	19	9.1	+ 14.00

Mar/Apr	May	Jun	Jul	Aug	Sep	Oct/Nov
1-2	0-5	0-3	1-2	0-2	0-4	0-4

Winning Jockey	W-R	£1 Level Stake			W-R	£1 Level Stake
J J Behan	2-11	+ 25.00				

Winning Courses						
Galway	1-3	+ 18.00	The Curragh		1-11	+ 4.00

Winning Horses	Age	Races Run	1st	2nd	3rd	Unpl	Win £
Madam Picasso	3	9	1	0	0	8	4,140
Loving Memory	4	6	1	1	0	4	3,795

Favourites	0-0			Total winning prize-money		£7,935
1991 Form	1-22	4.5%	- 1.00	1989 Form	0-26	
1990 Form	1-28	3.6%	- 15.00			

WILBERT TOLERTON

	No. of Horses	Races Run	1st	2nd	3rd	Unpl	Per cent	£1 Level Stake
2-y-o	0	0	0	0	0	0	-	0.00
3-y-o	0	0	0	0	0	0	-	0.00
4-y-o+	5	13	1	2	1	9	7.7	+ 8.00
Totals	5	13	1	2	1	9	7.7	+ 8.00

Mar/Apr	May	Jun	Jul	Aug	Sep	Oct/Nov
0-0	0-0	1-1	0-4	0-4	0-1	0-3

Winning Jockey	W-R	£1 Level Stake	Winning Course	W-R	£1 Level Stake
W J Smith	1-7	+ 14.00	Sligo	1-1	+ 20.00

Winning Horse	Age	Races Run	1st	2nd	3rd	Unpl	Win £
Dustscreen	7	4	1	1	1	1	2,245

Favourites	0-0		Total winning prize-money			£2,245
1991 Form	0-2		1989 Form	1-10	10.0%	- 2.00
1990 Form	0-0		1988 Form	0-20		

F TOWEY

	No. of Horses	Races Run	1st	2nd	3rd	Unpl	Per cent	£1 Level Stake
2-y-o	0	0	0	0	0	0	-	0.00
3-y-o	0	0	0	0	0	0	-	0.00
4-y-o+	1	4	1	0	1	2	25.0	+ 7.00
Totals	1	4	1	0	1	2	25.0	+ 7.00

Mar/Apr	May	Jun	Jul	Aug	Sep	Oct/Nov
0-1	0-0	1-2	0-0	0-0	0-1	0-0

Winning Jockey	W-R	£1 Level Stake	Winning Course	W-R	£1 Level Stake
D G O'Shea	1-3	+ 8.00	The Curragh	1-1	+ 10.00

Winning Horse	Age	Races Run	1st	2nd	3rd	Unpl	Win £
Dashing Rose	4	4	1	0	1	2	4,155

Favourites	0-1	Total winning prize-money	£4,155
1991 Form	0-2		

JOHN J WALSH

	No. of Horses	Races Run	1st	2nd	3rd	Unpl	Per cent	£1 Level Stake
2-y-o	0	0	0	0	0	0	-	0.00
3-y-o	0	0	0	0	0	0	-	0.00
4-y-o+	1	10	1	0	1	8	10.0	- 1.00
Totals	1	10	1	0	1	8	10.0	- 1.00

Mar/Apr	May	Jun	Jul	Aug	Sep	Oct/Nov
0-2	0-2	0-1	0-1	0-2	1-1	0-1

Winning Jockey	W-R	£1 Level Stake	Winning Course	W-R	£1 Level Stake
M Fenton	1-2	+ 7.00	Sligo	1-2	+ 7.00

Winning Horse	Age	Races Run	1st	2nd	3rd	Unpl	Win £
Tajanama	4	10	1	0	1	8	2,243

Favourites	0-0	Total winning prize-money	£2,243

1991 Form	0-7	1989 Form	0-3
1990 Form	0-9	1988 Form	0-1

T M WALSH

	No. of Horses	Races Run	1st	2nd	3rd	Unpl	Per cent	£1 Level Stake
2-y-o	2	4	1	0	0	3	25.0	+ 7.00
3-y-o	5	29	1	5	2	21	3.4	- 26.00
4-y-o+	6	12	1	0	0	11	8.3	+ 3.00
Totals	13	45	3	5	2	35	6.7	- 16.00

Mar/Apr	May	Jun	Jul	Aug	Sep	Oct/Nov
1-10	0-3	0-2	0-5	1-7	1-8	0-10

Winning Jockeys	W-R	£1 Level Stake				W-R	£1 Level Stake
W J Supple	2-11	+ 15.00		R V Skelly		1-8	- 5.00

Winning Courses	W-R	£1 Level Stake				W-R	£1 Level Stake
The Curragh	2-20	- 2.00		Ballinrobe		1-5	+ 6.00

Winning Horses	Age	Races Run	1st	2nd	3rd	Unpl	Win £
Alligator Joe	4	4	1	0	0	3	6,900
Classical Affair	3	12	1	4	0	7	2,760
Down The Lane	2	2	1	0	0	1	2,760

Favourites	1-5	20.0%	- 2.00	Total winning prize-money	£12,420
1991 Form	1-26	3.8%	- 18.50		

D K WELD

	No. of Horses	Races Run	1st	2nd	3rd	Unpl	Per cent	£1 Level Stake
2-y-o	50	135	21	26	18	70	15.6	- 64.61
3-y-o	69	318	56	55	25	182	17.6	- 74.42
4-y-o+	35	144	29	14	15	86	20.1	- 41.60
Totals	154	597	106	95	58	338	17.8	-180.63

BY MONTH

2-y-o	W-R	Per cent	£1 Level Stake	3-y-o	W-R	Per cent	£1 Level Stake
Mar/Apr	0-7	-	- 7.00	Mar/Apr	4-53	7.5	- 34.85
May	1-12	8.3	- 10.50	May	15-46	32.6	+ 10.37
June	3-21	14.3	- 13.40	June	7-49	14.3	- 17.50
July	3-21	14.3	- 14.25	July	11-59	18.6	- 13.67
August	5-27	18.5	- 10.04	August	12-51	23.5	- 3.77
September	6-21	28.6	- 3.42	September	4-28	14.3	- 6.00
Oct/Nov	3-26	11.5	- 6.00	Oct/Nov	3-32	9.4	- 9.00

4-y-o+	W-R	Per cent	£1 Level Stake	Totals	W-R	Per cent	£1 Level Stake
Mar/Apr	0-13	-	- 13.00	Mar/Apr	4-73	5.5	- 54.85
May	7-22	31.8	+ 9.15	May	23-80	28.8	+ 9.02
June	6-25	24.0	- 0.60	June	16-95	16.8	- 31.50
July	8-23	34.8	- 0.20	July	22-103	21.4	- 28.12
August	5-23	21.7	- 7.08	August	22-101	21.8	- 20.89
September	2-21	9.5	- 16.12	September	12-70	17.1	- 25.54
Oct/Nov	1-17	5.9	- 13.75	Oct/Nov	7-75	9.3	- 28.75

DISTANCE

2-y-o	W-R	Per cent	£1 Level Stake	3-y-o	W-R	Per cent	£1 Level Stake
5f-6f	8-61	13.1	- 40.57	5f-6f	17-111	15.3	- 41.20
7f-8f	12-64	18.8	- 17.54	7f-8f	13-91	14.3	- 27.86
9f-13f	0-0	-	0.00	9f-13f	16-60	26.7	+ 4.06
14f+	1-10	10.0	- 6.50	14f+	10-56	17.9	- 9.42

4-y-o+	W-R	Per cent	£1 Level Stake	Totals	W-R	Per cent	£1 Level Stake
5f-6f	9-41	22.0	- 6.47	5f-6f	34-213	16.0	- 88.24
7f-8f	8-42	19.0	- 17.68	7f-8f	33-197	16.8	- 63.08
9f-13f	5-34	14.7	- 17.17	9f-13f	21-9⅂	22.3	- 13.11
14f+	7-27	25.9	- 0.28	14f+	18-93	19.4	- 16.20

TYPE OF RACE

Non-Handicaps	W-R	Per cent	£1 Level Stake	Handicaps	W-R	Per cent	£1 Level Stake
2-y-o	19-121	15.7	- 60.24	2-y-o	2-14	14.3	- 4.37
3-y-o	42-187	22.5	- 22.05	3-y-o	14-109	12.8	- 30.37
4-y-o+	13-44	29.5	- 5.15	4-y-o+	16-83	19.3	- 19.45
Apprentice	0-3	-	- 3.00	Apprentice	0-17	-	- 17.00
Amat/Ladies	0-14	-	- 14.00	Amat/Ladies	0-5	-	- 5.00
Totals	74-369	20.1	-104.44	Totals	32-228	14.0	- 76.19

FIRST TIME OUT

	W-R	Per cent	£1 Level Stake
2-y-o	6-50	12.0	- 23.92
3-y-o	10-68	14.7	- 12.68
4-y-o+	6-34	17.6	- 8.52
Totals	22-152	14.5	- 45.12

JOCKEYS RIDING

	W-R	Per cent	£1 Level Stake		W-R	Per cent	£1 Level Stake
M J Kinane	81-339	23.9	- 41.29	W J Smith	9-82	11.0	- 47.22
P Shanahan	14-115	12.2	- 44.22	D J O'Donohoe	2-8	25.0	+ 5.10

Mr J A Nash	0-10	A Slattery	0-1	Miss M Ashburner	0-1
W J Walsh	0-7	D G O'Shea	0-1	Miss M Olivefalk	0-1
P Lowry	0-6	D O'Callaghan	0-1	Mr D J Donegan	0-1
R Carroll	0-6	D O'Donoghue	0-1	Mr K M Hickey	0-1
Miss U Smyth	0-5	E A Malone	0-1	S Craine	0-1
B Coogan	0-4	M Roberts	0-1		
J J Byrne	0-3	Miss C Duffy	0-1		

COURSE RECORD

	Total W-R	Non-Handicaps 2-y-o	Non-Handicaps 3-y-o+	Handicaps 2-y-o	Handicaps 3-y-o+	Per cent	£1 Level Stake
Leopardstown	18-113	4-20	10-46	1-1	3-46	15.9	- 53.98
The Curragh	17-122	2-25	8-45	1-3	6-49	13.9	- 45.75
Tipperary	9-33	0-8	8-17	0-0	1-8	27.3	- 7.05
Galway	8-31	2-5	2-10	0-1	4-15	25.8	+ 3.13
Tralee	6-16	1-3	3-6	0-1	2-6	37.5	- 0.18
Gowran Park	6-26	2-5	3-10	0-3	1-8	23.1	- 7.05
Naas	6-51	1-12	1-21	0-2	4-16	11.8	- 21.85
Killarney	4-14	0-1	3-6	0-0	1-7	28.6	- 2.93
Limerick	4-16	2-2	1-8	0-1	1-5	25.0	- 4.67
Fairyhouse	4-25	0-5	2-9	0-1	2-10	16.0	- 1.50
Bellewstown	3-9	1-1	2-2	0-0	0-6	33.3	+ 4.50
Listowel	3-13	1-3	1-4	0-1	1-5	23.1	- 4.42
Mallow	3-16	0-5	3-10	0-0	0-1	18.8	+ 1.80
Dundalk	3-21	0-5	2-7	0-0	1-9	14.3	- 14.95
Clonmel	2-6	0-0	2-4	0-0	0-2	33.3	+ 10.00
Sligo	2-11	1-4	0-4	0-0	1-3	18.2	+ 1.00
Down Royal	2-12	0-4	2-7	0-0	0-1	16.7	- 8.23
Navan	2-18	2-4	0-9	0-0	0-5	11.1	- 2.00
Downpatrick	1-3	0-0	1-3	0-0	0-0	33.3	+ 1.00
Tramore	1-3	0-0	1-2	0-0	0-1	33.3	+ 3.00
Laytown	1-5	0-0	0-2	0-0	1-3	20.0	- 2.50
Roscommon	1-17	0-5	0-7	0-0	1-5	5.9	- 12.00

Ballinrobe	0-7	Wexford	0-3
Punchestown	0-4	Thurles	0-2

WINNING HORSES

	Age	Races Run	1st	2nd	3rd	Unpl	Win £
Market Booster	3	5	3	2	0	0	46,375
Asema	2	4	3	1	0	0	34,080
Brief Truce	3	4	2	1	1	0	31,625
Tropical	2	6	3	0	1	2	30,779
Pre-Eminent	5	8	3	0	0	5	28,547

Sleet Skier	5	7	3	2	1	1	23,809
Flowing	4	5	2	0	2	1	23,502
Misako-Togo	3	7	3	0	0	4	22,425
Cherry Grove Lad	4	5	3	0	0	2	20,355
Vintage Crop	5	4	2	0	1	1	15,910
Onesixnine	4	5	2	3	0	0	14,102
Ormsby	3	3	2	0	0	1	12,765
Be My Hostage	4	4	3	1	0	0	12,107
Private Guy	3	8	2	5	0	1	11,822
Judicial Field	3	7	2	3	1	1	11,507
Rami	5	3	1	0	1	1	11,500
Sharp Review	4	6	2	0	2	2	10,440
Viscardo	2	7	3	2	0	2	8,800
Committed Dancer	5	7	1	1	0	5	8,627
Seek The Faith	3	2	2	0	0	0	8,280
Milieu	7	3	1	0	1	1	7,682
Rare Chic	4	4	1	0	1	2	7,680
Lifewatch Vision	5	5	1	0	1	3	7,680
Garboni	3	9	3	3	1	2	7,248
Sparkness	3	6	2	2	0	2	7,245
Cliveden Gail	3	5	2	0	0	3	6,559
Arabic Treasure	2	6	1	1	1	3	5,522
Topographe	2	3	1	0	1	1	5,520
Viney	2	5	1	1	1	2	5,520
Unusual Heat	2	1	1	0	0	0	5,520
Just Society	3	4	2	0	0	2	5,177
Supportive	3	6	2	0	0	4	5,040
Mysuma	3	9	1	2	1	5	4,485
Looking Brill	3	4	1	1	1	1	4,142
In A Tiff	3	5	1	1	1	2	4,140
Trade Survivor	3	3	1	0	0	2	4,140
Evasive Tactic	2	3	1	0	1	1	4,140
Elegant Bloom	2	1	1	0	0	0	4,140
Clear Procedure	3	6	1	2	2	1	4,050
Open Market	3	5	1	2	0	2	3,797
Political Fact	3	1	1	0	0	0	3,795
Sylvia Fox	5	1	1	0	0	0	3,795
Royal Firm	3	2	1	0	1	0	3,654
Best Academy	3	4	1	0	0	3	3,452
Private Viewing	2	2	1	0	1	0	3,452
Beautiful France	3	1	1	0	0	0	3,452
Strategic Break	3	2	1	1	0	0	3,452
Jury Service	3	5	1	0	1	3	3,450
Saibot	3	5	1	2	0	2	3,450
Jalila	4	3	1	1	0	1	3,450
Best Swinger	3	4	1	1	0	2	3,450
Caslin's Grove	2	1	1	0	0	0	3,450
Atlantic Adios	2	1	1	0	0	0	3,450
Laatansa	2	3	1	0	0	2	3,280
Palace Charm	3	7	1	0	0	6	2,762
Puppet Theatre	3	4	1	0	1	2	2,762
Standing Cast	3	8	1	0	2	5	2,762
Damisters Pet	3	5	1	0	0	4	2,762
One For Twenty Six	2	11	1	5	2	3	2,760
Sir Slaves	2	3	1	0	0	2	2,760
Duharra	4	3	1	1	0	1	2,760

Weld D K

Azorica	3	5	1	0	0	4	2,245
Maxwelton Braes	3	5	1	1	0	3	2,245
Dark Chieftain	3	8	1	2	1	4	2,245
Cloncarrig	4	5	1	0	0	4	2,245
Desert Palace	3	5	1	0	1	3	2,245
Gaelic River	3	7	1	3	2	1	2,245
Persian Tactics	3	6	1	2	1	2	2,245
Miss Lenora	3	3	1	1	0	1	2,245
Steel Chimes	3	10	1	1	0	8	1,727
Markham Fair	3	5	1	0	0	4	828
Modjeska	3	3	1	0	0	2	828
Royal Birkdale	3	7	1	2	0	4	690

WINNING OWNERS

	Races Won	Value £		Races Won	Value £
Moyglare Stud Farms Ltd	21	143,309	Inte Thoroughbred Breeders Inc	2	6,559
Allen E Paulson	14	83,735	H N Khan	2	5,697
Michael W J Smurfit	10	61,194	Raymond J Rooney	1	5,522
The Sussex Stud Ltd	3	30,779	Mrs W Whitehead	2	5,040
Andrea Schiavi	6	25,662	Mrs David Nagle	1	4,485
A J O'Reilly	3	23,809	Ascagnano Ireland	2	4,140
P Monahan	4	23,805	Mrs C L Weld	1	3,795
Mrs J Maxwell Moran	2	23,502	Michael Fennessy	1	2,762
Hamdan Al-Maktoum	3	18,230	Ascagnano S P A	1	2,762
Y Akazawa	3	14,927	Mrs M Togher	1	2,760
Peter Wetzel	2	12,765	Sheikh Mohammed	1	2,245
T Lucas	3	12,107	Mrs J R Mullion	1	2,245
Mrs A J F O'Reilly	3	11,730	George M Steinbrenner III	1	2,245
Stablemate Racing Plc	2	11,507	Mrs M J Downey	1	2,245
Thomas T S Liang	2	9,174	Christopher McHale	1	2,245
M G Hynes	2	8,280	Sean O'Shea	1	1,727
Oliver Murphy	1	7,680	Mrs A W Stollery	1	828
Dr Anne J F Gillespie	1	7,680			

Favourites	55-141	39.0%	- 19.26	Total winning prize-money			£587,177
Longest winning sequence			3	Average SP of winner			2.9/1
Longest losing sequence			41	Return on stakes invested			-30.1%
1991 Form	120-645	18.6%	-119.34	1989 Form	104-511	20.4%	-130.30
1990 Form	82-559	14.7%	-266.83	1988 Form	103-555	18.6%	- 60.35

O WELDON

	No. of Horses	Races Run	1st	2nd	3rd	Unpl	Per cent	£1 Level Stake
2-y-o	3	6	0	0	0	6	-	- 6.00
3-y-o	4	18	0	1	0	17	-	- 18.00
4-y-o+	5	23	1	2	0	20	4.3	- 14.50
Totals	12	47	1	3	0	43	2.1	- 38.50

Mar/Apr	May	Jun	Jul	Aug	Sep	Oct/Nov
0-4	1-9	0-7	0-3	0-8	0-5	0-11

Winning Jockey	W-R	£1 Level Stake	Winning Course	W-R	£1 Level Stake
W J Smith	1-5	+ 3.50	Leopardstown	1-11	- 2.50

Winning Horse	Age	Races Run	1st	2nd	3rd	Unpl	Win £
Clandolly	4	6	1	1	0	4	3,107

Favourites	0-0		Total winning prize-money		£3,107

1991 Form	3-14	21.4%	+ 15.00	1989 Form	1-26	3.8%	- 17.00
1990 Form	0-20						

PATRICK WOODS

	No. of Horses	Races Run	1st	2nd	3rd	Unpl	Per cent	£1 Level Stake
2-y-o	2	6	0	0	1	5	-	- 6.00
3-y-o	2	13	0	0	0	13	-	- 13.00
4-y-o+	2	7	1	1	2	3	14.3	+ 44.00
Totals	6	26	1	1	3	21	3.8	+ 25.00

Mar/Apr	May	Jun	Jul	Aug	Sep	Oct/Nov
0-2	0-0	0-0	1-8	0-8	0-5	0-3

Winning Jockey	W-R	£1 Level Stake	Winning Course	W-R	£1 Level Stake
D G O'Shea	1-10	+ 41.00	Ballinrobe	1-4	+ 47.00

Winning Horse	Age	Races Run	1st	2nd	3rd	Unpl	Win £
Dunsford	6	5	1	1	1	2	2,762

Favourites	0-0		Total winning prize-money		£2,762

1991 Form	0-11		1989 Form	0-8
1990 Form	0-22		1988 Form	0-8

TRAINERS WITH NO WINNERS IN IRELAND 1992

	No. of Horses	Races Run	2nd	3rd	Unpl
P Aspell	1	10	4	0	6
J R Banahan	3	11	0	0	11
Thomas Bergin	5	15	2	0	13
F Berry	5	10	2	0	8
J A Berry	2	4	0	0	4
J Boyers	2	8	1	1	6
J Brassil	2	2	0	0	2
J Brennan	1	4	0	0	4
M Brew	2	5	0	0	5
P Burke	1	1	0	0	1
H Butler	1	1	0	0	1
T Carberry	1	12	1	3	8
P Carey	1	3	0	0	3
J A Carolan	1	1	0	0	1
P J Casserly	2	4	0	0	4
Noel T Chance	7	21	1	2	18
Luke Comer	4	18	0	0	18
J C Connor	1	2	0	0	2
M J Corbett	2	4	0	0	4
R J Cotter	1	2	0	0	2
M Cunningham	12	54	4	4	46
R F Dalton	5	23	0	0	23
J P Daly	2	10	0	0	10
P J Deegan	8	34	2	1	31
P Delaney	3	9	0	0	9
C P Donoghue	1	2	0	0	2
R Donoghue	3	9	0	0	9
F Doyle	1	1	0	0	1
Mrs P V Doyle	2	4	0	0	4
J Dreaper	1	1	0	0	1
T Duggan	2	3	0	0	3
M Dunne	1	2	0	0	2
H Eastwood	3	5	0	0	5
Francis Ennis	3	4	0	0	4
J J Enright	1	1	0	0	1
A D Evans	3	9	2	1	6
W Fennin	1	2	0	0	2
I Ferguson	3	3	0	0	3
Mrs E Finn	1	1	0	0	1
T M Finnegan	1	1	0	0	1
Mrs Ian Fox	4	22	4	1	17
Noel Furlong	7	9	0	0	9
Colm Gainey	1	3	0	0	3
P Griffin	1	6	1	0	5
W M Halley	1	1	0	0	1
W Harney	2	5	1	1	3
E P Harty	6	15	2	2	11
J L Hassett	1	7	0	1	6
Patrick J F Hassett	1	1	0	0	1
P Henley	2	7	0	2	5
W Hennessy	1	2	0	0	2
Martin Higgins	1	1	0	1	0
Peter Hill	7	22	0	1	21
G W Hillis	1	2	0	0	2

	No. of Horses	Races Run	2nd	3rd	Unpl
John Houghton	3	9	1	0	8
M Hourigan	4	10	1	0	9
R Jennings	1	1	0	0	1
P Keane	1	1	0	0	1
T Keaney	3	3	0	0	3
E J Kearns	4	12	3	0	9
Paul Kelly	3	10	2	4	4
J M Kennedy	1	2	0	0	2
David A Kiely	3	10	0	0	10
J E Kiely	1	6	0	0	6
P Kiely	1	1	0	0	1
C Kinane	2	7	0	0	7
T Kinane	3	7	0	0	7
Basil King	2	4	0	0	4
F J Lacy	3	11	0	0	11
P J Lally	3	16	0	0	16
J Lalor	1	8	1	0	7
B Lawlor	4	10	2	0	8
F Lennon	2	6	0	0	6
R Lister	6	22	0	0	22
P M Lynch	1	1	0	0	1
J Madden	1	1	0	0	1
Niall Madden	1	3	0	0	3
M V Manning	4	13	0	0	13
R Marrs	1	1	0	0	1
W J Martin	3	14	0	0	14
Peadar Matthews	6	21	0	1	20
A J Maxwell	14	58	2	4	52
D G McArdle	2	5	0	0	5
H McCaffrey	1	9	0	1	8
M McCausland	2	6	0	0	6
R J McCormick	2	10	1	0	9
Peter McCreery	7	16	0	1	15
L McHugh	1	2	1	0	1
Malachy McKenna	5	17	3	2	12
D A McMillan	6	21	0	3	18
A J McNamara	6	14	0	0	14
E McNamara	4	13	1	1	11
K McQuillan	1	5	0	0	5
P G Molony	1	7	0	0	7
P Mooney	4	9	0	0	9
Ms J Morgan	2	4	0	0	4
Thomas Morgan	3	10	0	0	10
Anthony Mullins	6	11	0	1	10
J G Murphy	3	6	0	0	6
M Murray	2	4	0	0	4
J F Myers	1	1	0	0	1
T B Naughton	1	4	0	0	4
P O'Brady	1	3	0	0	3
F M O'Brien	2	2	0	0	2
M J P O'Brien	7	16	1	4	11
V T O'Brien	1	1	0	0	1
G O'Callaghan	1	1	0	0	1
D O'Connell	2	5	0	0	5
E O'Connell	4	8	0	1	7
J A O'Connell	1	4	0	0	4

	No. of Horses	Races Run	2nd	3rd	Unpl
J J O'Connor	2	3	0	0	3
C G O'Donovan	1	2	0	0	2
G O'Hagen	2	2	0	0	2
J O'Haire	1	1	0	0	1
T O'Neill	1	3	0	0	3
E M O'Sullivan	1	6	0	0	6
F Oakes	6	19	1	2	16
A Persse	2	9	0	2	7
N Power	3	9	0	0	9
M Purcell	2	9	1	0	8
D J Reddan	3	3	0	0	3
A Redmond	13	52	5	3	44
T A Regan	5	13	0	1	12
L T Reilly	3	8	0	0	8
W Rock	1	1	0	0	1
Ms Rosemary Rooney	2	5	1	0	4
C C Ryan	2	8	0	0	8
J C Shearman	1	3	0	0	3
J Bryce Smith	1	2	0	0	2
F Sutherland	1	4	0	2	2
Capt D G Swan	9	22	0	3	19
S Treacy	1	6	0	0	6
T Walker	3	14	0	0	14
E Walsh	2	2	0	0	2
J Weld	2	5	0	0	5

J BERRY (England)

	No. of Horses	Races Run	1st	2nd	3rd	Unpl	Per cent	£1 Level Stake
2-y-o	1	2	1	0	0	1	50.0	- 0.47
3-y-o	0	0	0	0	0	0	-	0.00
4-y-o+	1	1	0	0	0	1	-	- 1.00
Totals	2	3	1	0	0	2	33.3	- 1.47

Mar/Apr	May	Jun	Jul	Aug	Sep	Oct/Nov
1-1	0-1	0-1	0-0	0-0	0-0	0-0

Winning Jockey	W-R	£1 Level Stake	Winning Course	W-R	£1 Level Stake
J Carroll	1-1	+ 0.53	Leopardstown	1-2	- 0.47

Winning Horse	Age	Races Run	1st	2nd	3rd	Unpl	Win £
Sober Lad	2	2	1	0	0	1	5,520

Favourites	1-1	100.0%	+ 0.53	Total winning prize-money		£5,520
1991 Form	0-7			1989 Form	0-2	
1990 Form	2-9	22.2%	+ 3.00	1988 Form	0-1	

C E BRITTAIN (England)

	No. of Horses	Races Run	1st	2nd	3rd	Unpl	Per cent	£1 Level Stake
2-y-o	3	3	2	0	0	1	66.7	+ 5.10
3-y-o	4	4	1	0	1	2	25.0	- 2.27
4-y-o+	2	2	1	0	0	1	50.0	+ 2.00
Totals	9	9	4	0	1	4	44.4	+ 4.83

Mar/Apr	May	Jun	Jul	Aug	Sep	Oct/Nov
0-0	0-0	1-3	1-2	0-0	2-4	0-0

Winning Jockeys	W-R	£1 Level Stake		W-R	£1 Level Stake
M Roberts	3-5	+ 7.10	G Duffield	1-1	+ 0.73

Winning Courses					
The Curragh	3-6	+ 1.83	Leopardstown	1-3	+ 3.00

Winning Horses	Age	Races Run	1st	2nd	3rd	Unpl	Win £
User Friendly	3	1	1	0	0	0	121,000
Mr Martini	2	1	1	0	0	0	98,000
Sayyedati	2	1	1	0	0	0	86,100
Sikeston	6	1	1	0	0	0	26,250

Favourites	2-2	100.0%	+ 1.83	Total winning prize-money		£331,350
1991 Form	0-1			1989 Form	0-0	
1990 Form	2-7	28.6%	+ 2.50	1988 Form	0-5	

N CALLAGHAN (England)

	No. of Horses	Races Run	1st	2nd	3rd	Unpl	Per cent	£1 Level Stake
2-y-o	0	0	0	0	0	0	-	0.00
3-y-o	1	1	1	0	0	0	100.0	+ 6.00
4-y-o+	0	0	0	0	0	0	-	0.00
Totals	1	1	1	0	0	0	100.0	+ 6.00

Mar/Apr	May	Jun	Jul	Aug	Sep	Oct/Nov
0-0	0-0	1-1	0-0	0-0	0-0	0-0

Winning Jockey	W-R	£1 Level Stake	Winning Course	W-R	£1 Level Stake
J Reid	1-1	+ 6.00	Leopardstown	1-1	+ 6.00

Winning Horse	Age	Races Run	1st	2nd	3rd	Unpl	Win £
Freddie Lloyd (USA)	3	1	1	0	0	0	14,625

Favourites	0-0		Total winning prize-money	£14,625

1991 Form	0-0	1989 Form	0-0
1990 Form	0-1	1988 Form	0-1

P CHAPPLE-HYAM (England)

	No. of Horses	Races Run	1st	2nd	3rd	Unpl	Per cent	£1 Level Stake
2-y-o	3	3	0	1	1	1	-	- 3.00
3-y-o	2	3	2	1	0	0	66.7	+ 3.23
4-y-o+	0	0	0	0	0	0	-	0.00
Totals	5	6	2	2	1	1	33.3	+ 0.23

Mar/Apr	May	Jun	Jul	Aug	Sep	Oct/Nov
0-0	1-1	0-1	0-0	0-1	1-2	0-1

Winning Jockeys	W-R	£1 Level Stake		W-R	£1 Level Stake
L Piggott	1-2	- 0.27	J Reid	1-3	+ 1.50

Winning Courses					
Leopardstown	1-2	+ 2.50	The Curragh	1-4	- 2.27

Winning Horses	Age	Races Run	1st	2nd	3rd	Unpl	Win £
Rodrigo De Triano	3	1	1	0	0	0	122,000
Dr Devious	3	2	1	1	0	0	86,300

Favourites	1-2	50.0%	- 0.27	Total winning prize-money	£208,300
1991 Form	0-1				

J L DUNLOP (England)

	No. of Horses	Races Run	1st	2nd	3rd	Unpl	Per cent	£1 Level Stake
2-y-o	0	0	0	0	0	0	-	0.00
3-y-o	1	1	1	0	0	0	100.0	+ 9.00
4-y-o+	1	1	0	0	0	1	-	- 1.00
Totals	2	2	1	0	0	1	50.0	+ 8.00

Mar/Apr	May	Jun	Jul	Aug	Sep	Oct/Nov
0-0	0-0	0-1	0-0	0-0	1-1	0-0

Winning Jockey	W-R	£1 Level Stake	Winning Course	W-R	£1 Level Stake
M Roberts	1-1	+ 9.00	The Curragh	1-2	+ 8.00

Winning Horse	Age	Races Run	1st	2nd	3rd	Unpl	Win £
Cloud Of Dust	3	1	1	0	0	0	14,375

Favourites	0-0			Total winning prize-money	£14,375

1991 Form	0-2			1989 Form	1-9	11.1%	- 4.00
1990 Form	2-8	25.0%	- 2.63	1988 Form	2-11	18.2%	- 3.67

J H M GOSDEN (England)

	No. of Horses	Races Run	1st	2nd	3rd	Unpl	Per cent	£1 Level Stake
2-y-o	0	0	0	0	0	0	-	0.00
3-y-o	1	1	0	0	0	1	-	- 1.00
4-y-o+	3	3	1	0	1	1	33.3	+ 0.75
Totals	4	4	1	0	1	2	25.0	- 0.25

Mar/Apr	May	Jun	Jul	Aug	Sep	Oct/Nov
0-1	0-1	0-1	0-0	0-0	1-1	0-0

Winning Jockey	W-R	£1 Level Stake	Winning Course	W-R	£1 Level Stake
S Cauthen	1-1	+ 2.75	The Curragh	1-4	- 0.25

Winning Horse	Age	Races Run	1st	2nd	3rd	Unpl	Win £
Mashaallah	4	1	1	0	0	0	84,600

Favourites	1-2	50.0%	+ 1.75	Total winning prize-money	£84,600

1991 Form	0-2		1989 Form	0-1
1990 Form	0-2			

R HANNON (England)

	No. of Horses	Races Run	1st	2nd	3rd	Unpl	Per cent	£1 Level Stake
2-y-o	2	2	1	0	0	1	50.0	+ 9.00
3-y-o	2	2	0	0	0	2	-	- 2.00
4-y-o+	0	0	0	0	0	0	-	0.00
Totals	4	4	1	0	0	3	25.0	+ 7.00

Mar/Apr	May	Jun	Jul	Aug	Sep	Oct/Nov
0-0	0-1	0-0	0-0	1-2	0-0	0-1

Winning Jockey	W-R	£1 Level Stake	Winning Course	W-R	£1 Level Stake
L Dettori	1-1	+ 10.00	Leopardstown	1-2	+ 9.00

Winning Horse	Age	Races Run	1st	2nd	3rd	Unpl	Win £
Pips Pride	2	1	1	0	0	0	87,250

Favourites	0-2	Total winning prize-money	£87,250

1991 Form	2-4	50.0%	+ 6.50	1989 Form	1-2	50.0%	+ 0.10
1990 Form	2-4	50.0%	+ 2.75	1988 Form	0-2		

W R HERN (England)

	No. of Horses	Races Run	1st	2nd	3rd	Unpl	Per cent	£1 Level Stake
2-y-o	0	0	0	0	0	0	-	0.00
3-y-o	0	0	0	0	0	0	-	0.00
4-y-o+	1	2	1	0	0	1	50.0	+ 0.50
Totals	1	2	1	0	0	1	50.0	+ 0.50

Mar/Apr	May	Jun	Jul	Aug	Sep	Oct/Nov
0-0	0-0	0-0	0-0	1-1	0-1	0-0

Winning Jockey	W-R	£1 Level Stake	Winning Course	W-R	£1 Level Stake
W Carson	1-2	+ 0.50	The Curragh	1-2	+ 0.50

Winning Horse	Age	Races Run	1st	2nd	3rd	Unpl	Win £
Jahafil	4	2	1	0	0	1	11,500

Favourites	1-1	100.0%	+ 1.50	Total winning prize-money	£11,500

1991 Form	0-1			1989 Form	0-0		
1990 Form	1-2	50.0%	+ 1.00	1988 Form	1-1	100.0%	+ 7.00

B W HILLS (England)

	No. of Horses	Races Run	1st	2nd	3rd	Unpl	Per cent	£1 Level Stake
2-y-o	1	1	0	0	0	1	-	- 1.00
3-y-o	1	1	0	1	0	0	-	- 1.00
4-y-o+	3	5	1	2	1	1	20.0	- 1.00
Totals	5	7	1	3	1	2	14.3	- 3.00

Mar/Apr	May	Jun	Jul	Aug	Sep	Oct/Nov
0-1	0-0	0-2	0-0	0-1	1-3	0-0

Winning Jockey	W-R	£1 Level Stake	Winning Course	W-R	£1 Level Stake
S Cauthen	1-1	+ 3.00	The Curragh	1-7	- 3.00

Winning Horse	Age	Races Run	1st	2nd	3rd	Unpl	Win £
Norwich	5	2	1	1	0	0	11,500

Favourites	0-1			Total winning prize-money		£11,500

1991 Form	1-8	12.5%	- 1.00	1989 Form	5-12	41.7%	+ 10.00
1990 Form	4-15	26.7%	- 0.87	1988 Form	2-11	18.2%	- 2.00

M R STOUTE (England)

	No. of Horses	Races Run	1st	2nd	3rd	Unpl	Per cent	£1 Level Stake
2-y-o	0	0	0	0	0	0	-	0.00
3-y-o	2	3	0	1	0	2	-	- 3.00
4-y-o+	2	2	1	0	0	1	50.0	+ 1.50
Totals	4	5	1	1	0	3	20.0	- 1.50

Mar/Apr	May	Jun	Jul	Aug	Sep	Oct/Nov
0-0	1-2	0-1	0-1	0-0	0-1	0-0

Winning Jockey	W-R	£1 Level Stake	Winning Course	W-R	£1 Level Stake
S Cauthen	1-1	+ 2.50	The Curragh	1-5	- 1.50

Winning Horse	Age	Races Run	1st	2nd	3rd	Unpl	Win £
Opera House	4	1	1	0	0	0	43,125

Favourites	0-0			Total winning prize-money		£43,125

1991 Form	0-4			1989 Form	1-7	14.3%	- 2.50
1990 Form	1-4	25.0%	- 1.75	1988 Form	2-7	28.6%	+ 5.50

G WRAGG (England)

	No. of Horses	Races Run	1st	2nd	3rd	Unpl	Per cent	£1 Level Stake
2-y-o	0	0	0	0	0	0	-	0.00
3-y-o	1	1	1	0	0	0	100.0	+ 0.80
4-y-o+	0	0	0	0	0	0	-	0.00
Totals	1	1	1	0	0	0	100.0	+ 0.80

Mar/Apr	May	Jun	Jul	Aug	Sep	Oct/Nov
0-0	1-1	0-0	0-0	0-0	0-0	0-0

	Winning Jockey	W-R	£1 Level Stake	Winning Course	W-R	£1 Level Stake
	W R Swinburn	1-1	+ 0.80	The Curragh	1-1	+ 0.80

Winning Horse	Age	Races Run	1st	2nd	3rd	Unpl	Win £
Marling	3	1	1	0	0	0	121,000

Favourites	1-1	100.0%	+ 0.80	Total winning prize-money	£121,000

1991 Form	0-1	1989 Form	0-1
1990 Form	0-2		

OVERSEAS TRAINERS WITH NO WINNERS IN IRELAND 1992

	No. of Horses	Races Run	2nd	3rd	Unpl
D W Arbuthnot (Eng)	1	1	0	0	1
R W Armstrong (Eng)	1	1	1	0	0
I A Balding (Eng)	2	2	1	0	1
M Bell (Eng)	4	4	1	0	3
H R A Cecil (Eng)	1	1	0	0	1
M R Channon (Eng)	1	1	0	0	1
P F I Cole (Eng)	7	7	4	1	2
L Cumani (Eng)	1	1	0	0	1
A Fabre (Fra)	1	1	0	0	1
J E Hammond (Fra)	1	1	0	0	1
B Hanbury (Eng)	1	1	0	0	1
G Harwood (Eng)	1	1	0	1	0
Lord Huntingdon (Eng)	1	1	0	1	0
M S Johnston (Eng)	5	5	2	1	2
Mrs G E Jones (Eng)	2	3	0	0	3
P Leach (Eng)	1	1	0	0	1
M McCormack (Eng)	1	1	0	0	1
B A McMahon (Eng)	1	1	0	0	1
M Moubarak (Eng)	1	1	0	0	1
Sir M Prescott (Eng)	1	1	0	1	0
A A Scott (Eng)	1	1	0	0	1
M H Tompkins (Eng)	1	1	0	0	1
P T Walwyn (Eng)	1	1	0	0	1
J W Watts (Eng)	2	2	0	0	2
M Zilber (Fra)	3	3	0	1	2

COURSE SECTION

(IRISH FLAT 1988-92)

BALLINROBE

Leading Trainers 1988-92

	Total W-R	Non-handicaps 2-y-o	3-y-o+	Handicaps 2-y-o	3-y-o+	Per cent	£1 Level Stake
D K Weld	9-38	1-10	4-14	0-0	4-14	23.7	- 9.05
J S Bolger	8-36	1-6	2-19	0-0	5-11	22.2	- 6.50
John M Oxx	5-7	0-1	4-5	0-0	1-1	71.4	+ 7.47
D Gillespie	5-17	0-2	2-8	0-0	3-7	29.4	+ 3.53
Augustine Leahy	3-8	0-1	2-3	0-0	1-4	37.5	+ 4.75
P O'Brady	2-4	0-0	0-0	0-0	2-4	50.0	+ 7.50
P Prendergast	2-6	1-2	1-3	0-0	0-1	33.3	+ 7.00
C Collins	2-11	0-2	1-3	0-0	1-6	18.2	- 5.13
D T Hughes	2-11	0-1	1-5	0-0	1-5	18.2	+ 2.33
Edward Lynam	2-17	0-2	1-5	0-0	1-10	11.8	- 9.67
K Prendergast	2-21	0-7	1-8	0-0	1-6	9.5	- 5.25
H De Bromhead	1-1	0-0	0-0	0-0	1-1	100.0	+ 12.00
W M Roper	1-1	0-0	0-0	0-0	1-1	100.0	+ 4.00
T G McCourt	1-1	0-0	0-0	0-0	1-1	100.0	+ 10.00
J Burns	1-3	0-0	0-1	0-0	1-2	33.3	+ 2.00
J L Hassett	1-3	0-1	1-2	0-0	0-0	33.3	+ 5.00
J G Coogan	1-3	1-2	0-0	0-0	0-1	33.3	+ 0.25
Patrick Woods	1-4	0-0	0-2	0-0	1-2	25.0	+ 47.00
Daniel J Murphy	1-4	0-1	0-1	0-0	1-2	25.0	+ 13.00
D Hanley	1-4	0-1	1-2	0-0	0-1	25.0	+ 6.00
J Bryce Smith	1-5	0-0	0-4	0-0	1-1	20.0	- 1.00
D J Reddan	1-5	0-0	1-2	0-0	0-3	20.0	+ 0.50

Leading Jockeys

	Total W-R	Per cent	£1 Level Stake	Best Trainer	W-R	Per cent	£1 Level Stake
M J Kinane	11-39	28.2	+ 0.83	D K Weld	7-30	23.3	- 8.05
W J Supple	8-28	28.6	+ 14.40	J S Bolger	4-13	30.8	+ 1.50
J P Murtagh	6-18	33.3	+ 10.47	John M Oxx	4-6	66.7	+ 6.47
C Roche	3-16	18.8	- 7.00	J S Bolger	3-15	20.0	- 6.00
P Shanahan	3-20	15.0	- 12.87	C Collins	2-7	28.6	- 1.12
N G McCullagh	3-20	15.0	- 7.50	Augustine Leahy	1-1	100.0	+ 2.50
K J Manning	3-21	14.3	0.00	D McDonogh	1-1	100.0	+ 5.00
J F Egan	3-26	11.5	- 14.25	P O'Brady	1-2	50.0	+ 5.00
R Hughes	3-29	10.3	- 11.67	D T Hughes	2-7	28.6	+ 6.33
A J Roche	2-5	40.0	+ 12.00	J Bryce Smith	1-1	100.0	+ 3.00
R Carroll	2-6	33.3	+ 1.00	D K Weld	1-1	100.0	+ 3.00
M Fenton	2-15	13.3	- 4.75	Augustine Leahy	1-2	50.0	+ 1.25

How the Favourites Fared

Non-handicaps	W-R	Per cent	£1 Level Stake	Handicaps	W-R	Per cent	£1 Level Stake
2-y-o	4-10	40.0	+ 2.00	2-y-o	0-0	-	0.00
3-y-o	1-2	50.0	+ 1.25	3-y-o	1-4	25.0	- 1.62
Weight-for-age	12-28	42.9	+ 7.16	All-aged	11-29	37.9	- 1.12
Totals	17-40	42.5	+ 10.41	Totals	12-33	36.4	- 2.74
All favs	29-73	39.7	+ 7.67				

BELLEWSTOWN

Leading Trainers 1988–92

	Total W-R	Non-handicaps 2-y-o	Non-handicaps 3-y-o+	Handicaps 2-y-o	Handicaps 3-y-o+	Per cent	£1 Level Stake
D K Weld	9-40	2-8	5-14	0-0	2-18	22.5	− 9.40
John M Oxx	4-13	0-0	3-9	0-0	1-4	30.8	+ 6.00
J S Bolger	4-23	1-5	2-7	0-0	1-11	17.4	− 9.00
M Kauntze	4-31	1-9	1-10	0-0	2-12	12.9	− 16.55
K Prendergast	4-36	2-9	1-10	0-0	1-17	11.1	− 21.33
M A O'Toole	3-23	1-6	2-8	0-0	0-9	13.0	− 13.08
E J O'Grady	2-5	1-1	0-2	0-0	1-2	40.0	+ 30.00
P Hughes	2-5	1-2	0-0	0-0	1-3	40.0	+ 18.00
T G Curtin	2-13	0-0	1-5	0-0	1-8	15.4	0.00
B V Kelly	2-14	0-3	0-3	0-0	2-8	14.3	+ 17.50
M J Grassick	2-18	0-2	1-11	0-0	1-5	11.1	− 8.00
M V O'Brien	1-2	0-0	1-2	0-0	0-0	50.0	− 0.20
P Prendergast	1-3	0-1	0-1	0-0	1-1	33.3	+ 0.50
J T Gorman	1-4	0-0	0-0	0-0	1-4	25.0	+ 5.00
Mrs P V Doyle	1-5	0-1	1-1	0-0	0-3	20.0	+ 16.00
C Kinane	1-5	0-0	0-1	0-0	1-4	20.0	− 2.00
J C Hayden	1-6	1-2	0-1	0-0	0-3	16.7	− 3.00
T Keaney	1-6	0-0	0-1	0-0	1-5	16.7	− 0.50
Daniel J Murphy	1-6	0-2	0-1	0-0	1-3	16.7	− 2.00
V Kennedy	1-7	0-0	1-2	0-0	0-5	14.3	+ 10.00
A Redmond	1-7	0-1	0-2	0-0	1-4	14.3	− 2.50
F Dunne	1-7	0-2	0-4	0-0	1-1	14.3	+ 4.00

Leading Jockeys

	Total W-R	Per cent	£1 Level Stake	Best Trainer	W-R	Per cent	£1 Level Stake
M J Kinane	14-48	29.2	+ 0.47	D K Weld	9-35	25.7	− 4.40
J P Murtagh	8-32	25.0	+ 27.50	John M Oxx	3-10	30.0	+ 5.00
P V Gilson	4-26	15.4	+ 22.80	Daniel J Murphy	1-1	100.0	+ 3.00
C Roche	3-28	10.7	− 19.68	J S Bolger	2-12	16.7	− 5.25
S Craine	3-36	8.3	− 13.50	P Hughes	1-1	100.0	+ 7.00
Mr A P O'Brien	2-3	66.7	+ 4.25	J S Bolger	2-3	66.7	+ 4.25
D V Smith	2-14	14.3	− 6.50	P Prendergast	1-1	100.0	+ 2.50
R Griffiths	2-14	14.3	− 8.83	K Prendergast	2-14	14.3	− 8.83
M Fenton	2-17	11.8	+ 9.50	Edward Lynam	1-3	33.3	+ 2.50
N G McCullagh	2-21	9.5	− 4.00	E J O'Grady	1-1	100.0	+ 8.00
R M Burke	2-21	9.5	− 5.00	F Dunne	1-1	100.0	+ 10.00
Mr R Neylon	1-1	100.0	+ 1.00	M J Grassick	1-1	100.0	+ 1.00

How the Favourites Fared

Non-handicaps	W-R	Per cent	£1 Level Stake	Handicaps	W-R	Per cent	£1 Level Stake
2-y-o	5-11	45.5	− 1.46	2-y-o	0-0	−	0.00
3-y-o	0-0	−	0.00	3-y-o	0-0	−	0.00
Weight-for-age	8-22	36.4	− 4.68	All-aged	12-24	50.0	+ 7.42
Totals	13-33	39.4	− 6.14	Totals	12-24	50.0	+ 7.42
All favs	25-57	43.9	+ 1.28				

CLONMEL

Leading Trainers 1988-92

	Total W-R	Non-handicaps 2-y-o	3-y-o+	Handicaps 2-y-o	3-y-o+	Per cent	£1 Level Stake
J S Bolger	7-34	0-0	4-21	0-0	3-13	20.6	- 5.60
J J McLoughlin	6-13	0-0	2-5	0-0	4-8	46.2	+ 24.58
D K Weld	5-16	0-0	4-11	0-0	1-5	31.3	+ 10.55
John M Oxx	5-17	0-0	5-14	0-0	0-3	29.4	- 6.56
P J Flynn	5-35	0-0	3-19	0-0	2-16	14.3	- 8.83
Capt D G Swan	4-11	0-0	1-8	0-0	3-3	36.4	+ 20.83
Noel Meade	3-14	0-0	3-12	0-0	0-2	21.4	+ 0.90
E J O'Grady	3-26	0-0	1-15	0-0	2-11	11.5	- 9.10
K Prendergast	3-26	0-0	2-15	0-0	1-11	11.5	- 10.10
V Kennedy	2-4	0-0	2-2	0-0	0-2	50.0	+ 15.00
Daniel J Murphy	2-8	0-0	1-5	0-0	1-3	25.0	- 0.25
C Collins	2-9	0-0	1-8	0-0	1-1	22.2	+ 9.00
Liam Browne	2-16	0-0	2-12	0-0	0-4	12.5	- 7.50
P Griffin	1-1	0-0	1-1	0-0	0-0	100.0	+ 3.00
P F O'Donnell	1-2	0-0	1-2	0-0	0-0	50.0	+ 4.00
David A Kiely	1-3	0-0	0-0	0-0	1-3	33.3	0.00
F Flood	1-3	0-0	1-3	0-0	0-0	33.3	- 0.50
T A Regan	1-4	0-0	0-2	0-0	1-2	25.0	- 1.75
J P Byrne	1-4	0-0	1-3	0-0	0-1	25.0	- 1.00
Mrs Crowley-O'Brien	1-4	0-0	1-3	0-0	0-1	25.0	- 1.75
P Prendergast	1-5	0-0	1-3	0-0	0-2	20.0	- 3.10
J P Kavanagh	1-5	0-0	1-3	0-0	0-2	20.0	- 2.50

Leading Jockeys

	Total W-R	Per cent	£1 Level Stake	Best Trainer	W-R	Per cent	£1 Level Stake
M J Kinane	7-21	33.3	+ 4.45	D K Weld	4-8	50.0	+ 10.55
C Roche	6-32	18.8	- 13.12	J S Bolger	3-16	18.8	- 5.60
J P Murtagh	5-25	20.0	- 13.81	John M Oxx	4-12	33.3	- 3.06
S Craine	5-28	17.9	- 5.43	Noel Meade	3-6	50.0	+ 8.90
T J O'Sullivan	3-16	18.8	+ 10.00	E J O'Grady	2-10	20.0	+ 5.00
E A Leonard	3-18	16.7	- 0.77	J J McLoughlin	2-4	50.0	+ 11.33
W J Supple	3-20	15.0	- 9.00	J S Bolger	3-7	42.9	+ 4.00
W J O'Connor	3-25	12.0	- 8.50	Liam Browne	1-1	100.0	+ 1.50
N G McCullagh	3-26	11.5	- 9.75	J J McLoughlin	3-6	50.0	+ 10.25
J F Egan	3-33	9.1	- 13.00	P J Flynn	3-17	17.6	+ 3.00
P V Gilson	2-18	11.1	- 6.50	V Kennedy	1-1	100.0	+ 7.00
P Shanahan	2-23	8.7	- 5.00	C Collins	2-6	33.3	+ 12.00

How the Favourites Fared

Non-handicaps	W-R	Per cent	£1 Level Stake	Handicaps	W-R	Per cent	£1 Level Stake
2-y-o	0-0	-	0.00	2-y-o	0-0	-	0.00
3-y-o	7-13	53.8	+ 3.84	3-y-o	2-4	50.0	- 0.10
Weight-for-age	19-30	63.3	+ 11.42	All-aged	7-20	35.0	- 2.68
Totals	26-43	60.5	+ 15.26	Totals	9-24	37.5	- 2.78
All favs	35-67	52.2	+ 12.48				

THE CURRAGH

Leading Trainers 1988-92

	Total W-R	Non-handicaps 2-y-o	3-y-o+	Handicaps 2-y-o	3-y-o+	Per cent	£1 Level Stake
J S Bolger	102-609	45-183	34-232	2-19	21-175	16.7	- 45.83
John M Oxx	74-494	20-142	30-221	2-5	22-126	15.0	- 47.42
M V O'Brien	63-205	27-82	34-109	0-0	2-14	30.7	+ 8.27
D K Weld	61-578	17-161	31-224	2-10	11-183	10.6	-278.21
K Prendergast	34-528	8-139	12-179	2-17	12-193	6.4	-292.38
C Collins	27-284	8-67	6-93	3-8	10-116	9.5	- 72.30
T Stack	24-225	6-59	12-97	1-7	5-62	10.7	- 46.37
M Kauntze	21-181	8-59	7-68	0-3	6-51	11.6	- 43.91
P J Flynn	10-101	1-13	4-29	0-3	5-56	9.9	- 7.50
P Prendergast	9-114	2-31	4-34	1-8	2-41	7.9	- 37.60
M J Grassick	9-125	3-30	1-51	1-6	4-38	7.2	- 61.00
P Mullins	7-97	0-13	6-33	0-5	1-46	7.2	- 39.25
M A O'Toole	7-131	1-33	1-40	0-4	5-54	5.3	- 66.50
F Dunne	6-67	0-9	2-22	0-1	4-35	9.0	+ 7.00
Liam Browne	6-194	4-66	1-73	0-11	1-44	3.1	-136.50
H R A Cecil (Eng)	5-13	1-1	4-12	0-0	0-0	38.5	- 3.55
P F I Cole (Eng)	5-15	0-2	5-12	0-0	0-1	33.3	+ 4.63
J L Dunlop (Eng)	5-19	1-5	4-14	0-0	0-0	26.3	+ 5.70
Noel Meade	5-152	0-34	4-46	1-6	0-66	3.3	-109.00
C E Brittain (Eng	4-14	1-4	3-10	0-0	0-0	28.6	- 2.17
B W Hills (Eng)	4-33	1-8	2-24	0-0	1-1	12.1	- 16.50
E P Harty	4-47	1-14	0-12	0-0	3-21	8.5	- 9.00

Leading Jockeys

	Total W-R	Per cent	£1 Level Stake	Best Trainer	W-R	Per cent	£1 Level Stake
C Roche	91-464	19.6	- 38.08	J S Bolger	78-332	23.5	+ 26.67
M J Kinane	66-507	13.0	-199.26	D K Weld	56-404	13.9	-149.70
J Reid	41-186	22.0	+ 9.57	M V O'Brien	27-83	32.5	- 3.76
P Shanahan	30-344	8.7	-140.80	C Collins	18-129	14.0	- 3.30
S Craine	27-389	6.9	-204.87	T Stack	21-180	11.7	- 46.37
L Piggott	26-90	28.9	+ 4.90	M V O'Brien	23-55	41.8	+ 15.17
J P Murtagh	25-252	9.9	- 67.83	John M Oxx	19-163	11.7	- 55.83
W J O'Connor	17-208	8.2	- 99.16	M Kauntze	12-87	13.8	- 21.16
R Hughes	17-245	6.9	-115.13	John M Oxx	6-22	27.3	+ 5.47
W J Supple	14-207	6.8	- 42.50	J S Bolger	6-90	6.7	- 35.50
P V Gilson	14-240	5.8	-127.75	C Collins	6-68	8.8	- 9.50
S Cauthen	12-42	28.6	+ 2.47	H R A Cecil (Eng)	3-8	37.5	- 3.53

How the Favourites Fared

Non-handicaps	W-R	Per cent	£1 Level Stake	Handicaps	W-R	Per cent	£1 Level Stake
2-y-o	71-177	40.1	- 28.73	2-y-o	8-17	47.1	+ 15.85
3-y-o	42-94	44.7	+ 0.39	3-y-o	5-17	29.4	+ 0.63
Weight-for-age	48-165	29.1	- 42.02	All-aged	38-143	26.6	+ 9.19
Totals	161-436	36.9	- 70.36	Totals	51-177	28.8	+ 25.67
All favs	212-613	34.6	- 44.69				

657

DOWN ROYAL

Leading Trainers 1988-92

	Total W-R	Non-handicaps 2-y-o	3-y-o+	Handicaps 2-y-o	3-y-o+	Per cent	£1 Level Stake
M Kauntze	13-47	5-15	4-20	0-0	4-12	27.7	+ 6.53
D K Weld	10-38	1-7	7-23	0-1	2-7	26.3	- 5.23
J S Bolger	9-29	1-9	6-16	1-1	1-3	31.0	+ 8.31
M J Grassick	6-26	1-4	3-13	0-0	2-9	23.1	- 2.50
J C Hayden	5-14	2-4	3-7	0-0	0-3	35.7	+ 13.80
John M Oxx	5-21	0-2	5-18	0-0	0-1	23.8	- 7.83
B V Kelly	5-33	2-11	2-11	0-0	1-11	15.2	- 13.50
Liam Browne	3-13	2-4	1-8	0-0	0-1	23.1	+ 3.35
C Collins	3-19	2-4	0-10	0-0	1-5	15.8	- 11.25
K Prendergast	3-37	1-9	1-20	0-0	1-8	8.1	- 27.58
P Prendergast	2-4	0-0	1-2	0-0	1-2	50.0	+ 8.00
J J McLoughlin	2-12	0-0	0-3	0-0	2-9	16.7	- 3.50
V Bowens	2-13	0-2	0-6	0-0	2-5	15.4	+ 2.25
F Dunne	2-13	0-2	1-7	0-0	1-4	15.4	- 4.75
Noel Meade	2-24	1-5	1-13	0-0	0-6	8.3	- 8.50
G T Hourigan	1-1	0-0	0-0	0-0	1-1	100.0	+ 14.00
J Burns	1-2	1-2	0-0	0-0	0-0	50.0	+ 4.50
T Stack	1-3	0-0	1-3	0-0	0-0	33.3	+ 2.00
L T Reilly	1-4	0-0	1-2	0-0	0-2	25.0	+ 5.00
N O'Callaghan	1-4	0-0	1-3	0-0	0-1	25.0	+ 9.00
Daniel J Murphy	1-5	1-2	0-0	0-1	0-2	20.0	- 0.50
M A O'Toole	1-7	0-0	0-3	0-1	1-3	14.3	- 2.50

Leading Jockeys

	Total W-R	Per cent	£1 Level Stake	Best Trainer	W-R	Per cent	£1 Level Stake
P Shanahan	11-41	26.8	- 1.02	M Kauntze	7-14	50.0	+ 11.09
P V Gilson	7-22	31.8	+ 0.25	C Collins	3-7	42.9	+ 0.75
C Roche	6-10	60.0	+ 15.53	J S Bolger	5-7	71.4	+ 15.03
J P Murtagh	5-18	27.8	- 0.17	John M Oxx	3-8	37.5	- 3.17
M J Kinane	5-19	26.3	+ 1.00	D K Weld	3-9	33.3	+ 1.50
M Fenton	4-16	25.0	+ 9.25	P Prendergast	1-1	100.0	+ 5.00
W J Supple	4-23	17.4	- 6.00	J S Bolger	3-12	25.0	+ 2.00
K J Manning	4-24	16.7	- 5.75	M J Grassick	3-8	37.5	+ 1.25
W J O'Connor	4-25	16.0	+ 13.44	M Kauntze	3-17	17.6	+ 0.44
N G McCullagh	3-14	21.4	- 5.20	M Kauntze	1-1	100.0	+ 3.00
D Duggan	3-27	11.1	- 7.50	Daniel J Murphy	1-1	100.0	+ 3.50
W Carson	2-2	100.0	+ 6.50	B V Kelly	2-2	100.0	+ 6.50

How the Favourites Fared

Non-handicaps	W-R	Per cent	£1 Level Stake	Handicaps	W-R	Per cent	£1 Level Stake
2-y-o	12-22	54.5	+ 4.04	2-y-o	1-1	100.0	+ 0.50
3-y-o	3-16	18.8	- 8.90	3-y-o	0-1	-	- 1.00
Weight-for-age	11-31	35.5	- 11.01	All-aged	13-26	50.0	+ 6.35
Totals	26-69	37.7	- 15.87	Totals	14-28	50.0	+ 5.85
All favs	40-97	41.2	- 10.02				

DOWNPATRICK

Leading Trainers 1988-92

	Total W-R	Non-handicaps 2-y-o	Non-handicaps 3-y-o+	Handicaps 2-y-o	Handicaps 3-y-o+	Per cent	£1 Level Stake
D K Weld	5-17	0-0	5-17	0-0	0-0	29.4	+ 9.75
Peter Casey	3-12	0-0	2-10	0-0	1-2	25.0	+ 6.50
K Prendergast	3-13	0-0	3-11	0-0	0-2	23.1	+ 2.50
J F C Maxwell	2-5	0-0	2-4	0-0	0-1	40.0	+ 5.00
M J Grassick	2-14	0-0	2-13	0-0	0-1	14.3	- 7.20
J F Bailey Jnr	1-1	0-0	1-1	0-0	0-0	100.0	+ 20.00
P Prendergast	1-2	0-0	1-2	0-0	0-0	50.0	+ 1.50
F Dunne	1-2	0-0	1-2	0-0	0-0	50.0	+ 1.50
T O'Neill	1-2	0-0	1-2	0-0	0-0	50.0	+ 11.00
J Burns	1-2	0-0	1-2	0-0	0-0	50.0	+ 13.00
P Hughes	1-2	0-0	1-2	0-0	0-0	50.0	- 0.33
F Flood	1-2	0-0	1-2	0-0	0-0	50.0	- 0.60
T Stack	1-2	0-0	1-1	0-0	0-1	50.0	0.00
Liam Browne	1-3	0-0	1-3	0-0	0-0	33.3	0.00
E P Harty	1-3	0-0	1-3	0-0	0-0	33.3	- 1.43
M A O'Toole	1-4	0-0	0-3	0-0	1-1	25.0	+ 4.00
J S Bolger	1-4	0-0	1-4	0-0	0-0	25.0	+ 3.50
Daniel J Murphy	1-4	0-0	1-3	0-0	0-1	25.0	+ 1.00
A Redmond	1-5	0-0	0-4	0-0	1-1	20.0	0.00
Noel Meade	1-6	0-0	1-5	0-0	0-1	16.7	- 2.50
V Bowens	1-7	0-0	0-6	0-0	1-1	14.3	- 2.00
M Cunningham	1-7	0-0	1-7	0-0	0-0	14.3	- 5.33

Leading Jockeys

	Total W-R	Per cent	£1 Level Stake		Best Trainer	W-R	Per cent	£1 Level Stake
S Craine	3-4	75.0	+ 3.07		E P Harty	1-1	100.0	+ 0.57
W J Smith	3-9	33.3	+ 8.00		J P Byrne	1-1	100.0	+ 6.00
D V Smith	3-15	20.0	+ 16.00		D K Weld	2-5	40.0	+ 11.00
C O'Dwyer	2-2	100.0	+ 2.40		F Flood	1-1	100.0	+ 0.40
J A Heffernan	2-5	40.0	+ 23.50		J F Bailey Jnr	1-1	100.0	+ 20.00
N Byrne	2-12	16.7	+ 6.00		M J Grassick	1-1	100.0	+ 4.00
E A Leonard	2-13	15.4	- 5.00		K Prendergast	1-1	100.0	+ 3.50
D Duggan	2-15	13.3	- 0.50		Peter Casey	1-4	25.0	- 0.50
F Berry	1-2	50.0	- 1.00		J F C Maxwell	1-1	100.0	+ 20.00
M Fenton	1-2	50.0	+ 5.00		Peter Casey	1-1	100.0	+ 6.00
R M Burke	1-4	25.0	- 0.50		F Dunne	1-1	100.0	+ 2.50
R V Skelly	1-4	25.0	+ 1.00		Daniel J Murphy	1-3	33.3	+ 2.00

How the Favourites Fared

Non-handicaps	W-R	Per cent	£1 Level Stake	Handicaps	W-R	Per cent	£1 Level Stake
2-y-o	0-0	-	0.00	2-y-o	0-0	-	0.00
3-y-o	2-7	28.6	- 3.18	3-y-o	0-0	-	0.00
Weight-for-age	8-25	32.0	- 6.96	All-aged	1-6	16.7	- 2.50
Totals	10-32	31.3	- 10.14	Totals	1-6	16.7	- 2.50
All favs	11-38	28.9	- 12.64				

DUNDALK

Leading Trainers 1988-92

	Total W-R	Non-handicaps 2-y-o	3-y-o+	Handicaps 2-y-o	3-y-o+	Per cent	£1 Level Stake
J S Bolger	21-82	8-29	7-31	1-1	5-21	25.6	- 11.37
John M Oxx	18-60	7-18	9-30	0-0	2-12	30.0	- 6.60
D K Weld	15-108	4-35	5-27	0-2	6-44	13.9	- 50.32
M Kauntze	10-61	2-17	5-19	0-0	3-25	16.4	+ 2.10
K Prendergast	8-81	2-17	1-24	0-1	5-39	9.9	- 36.23
F Dunne	7-33	0-7	4-13	0-0	3-13	21.2	+ 20.75
C Collins	7-43	1-14	4-16	0-0	2-13	16.3	- 3.25
M J Grassick	6-37	0-7	1-10	0-0	5-20	16.2	- 2.83
Liam Browne	4-28	3-16	1-9	0-0	0-3	14.3	- 14.88
J C Hayden	4-29	1-10	0-5	0-0	3-14	13.8	+ 2.25
Noel Meade	4-47	1-13	1-10	0-0	2-24	8.5	- 28.04
M V O'Brien	3-3	1-1	2-2	0-0	0-0	100.0	+ 2.90
Peter Casey	3-15	0-1	2-7	0-0	1-7	20.0	+ 39.50
V Kennedy	2-12	0-1	0-1	0-0	2-10	16.7	+ 3.00
D Gillespie	2-19	0-5	0-4	0-1	2-9	10.5	- 13.10
Edward Lynam	2-22	1-6	0-1	0-0	1-15	9.1	+ 1.00
Mrs Crowley-O'Brien	1-1	1-1	0-0	0-0	0-0	100.0	+ 1.75
A L T Moore	1-2	0-0	1-2	0-0	0-0	50.0	+ 7.00
L T Reilly	1-2	0-0	0-0	0-0	1-2	50.0	+ 13.00
J F C Maxwell	1-3	0-0	1-2	0-0	0-1	33.3	- 1.20
M J P O'Brien	1-5	1-2	0-1	0-0	0-2	20.0	+ 4.00
J C Harley	1-6	0-0	0-1	0-0	1-5	16.7	+ 2.00

Leading Jockeys

	Total W-R	Per cent	£1 Level Stake	Best Trainer	W-R	Per cent	£1 Level Stake
M J Kinane	19-90	21.1	- 12.60	D K Weld	13-70	18.6	- 16.35
C Roche	16-55	29.1	- 2.09	J S Bolger	15-42	35.7	+ 2.91
J P Murtagh	14-70	20.0	- 1.90	John M Oxx	11-25	44.0	+ 4.10
P Shanahan	12-68	17.6	+ 4.22	M Kauntze	5-16	31.3	+ 11.30
P V Gilson	7-45	15.6	- 4.85	M V O'Brien	3-3	100.0	+ 2.90
R Hughes	7-62	11.3	- 28.95	M J Grassick	4-10	40.0	+ 12.67
W J Supple	6-48	12.5	- 24.52	J S Bolger	4-17	23.5	- 3.27
J A Heffernan	4-14	28.6	+ 12.75	Mrs C-O'Brien	1-1	100.0	+ 1.75
D Hogan	4-22	18.2	+ 9.50	Edward Lynam	2-6	33.3	+ 17.00
K J Manning	4-48	8.3	- 23.00	J S Bolger	2-12	16.7	0.00
N G McCullagh	4-52	7.7	- 16.50	M J Grassick	2-4	50.0	+ 7.50
W J O'Connor	4-63	6.3	- 41.70	M Kauntze	2-27	7.4	- 16.70

How the Favourites Fared

Non-handicaps	W-R	Per cent	£1 Level Stake	Handicaps	W-R	Per cent	£1 Level Stake
2-y-o	18-37	48.6	+ 2.76	2-y-o	0-1	-	- 1.00
3-y-o	11-20	55.0	+ 4.34	3-y-o	3-7	42.9	+ 0.51
Weight-for-age	13-29	44.8	- 3.21	All-aged	14-47	29.8	- 9.80
Totals	42-86	48.8	+ 3.89	Totals	17-55	30.9	- 10.29
All favs	59-141	41.8	- 6.40				

FAIRYHOUSE

Leading Trainers 1988-92

	Total W-R	Non-handicaps 2-y-o	Non-handicaps 3-y-o+	Handicaps 2-y-o	Handicaps 3-y-o+	Per cent	£1 Level Stake
John M Oxx	15-53	5-19	6-19	0-0	4-15	28.3	- 1.83
D K Weld	12-92	3-29	7-39	0-1	2-23	13.0	- 38.52
J S Bolger	7-70	4-25	3-25	0-1	0-19	10.0	- 52.85
K Prendergast	5-56	1-18	3-25	0-1	1-12	8.9	- 22.00
T Stack	4-15	1-7	3-5	0-1	0-2	26.7	- 4.58
M Kauntze	4-42	1-13	3-16	0-0	0-13	9.5	- 28.75
D Hanley	3-7	3-3	0-3	0-0	0-1	42.9	+ 16.50
J C Hayden	3-12	2-5	0-2	0-1	1-4	25.0	+ 37.00
D Gillespie	3-13	0-6	1-4	0-0	2-3	23.1	+ 0.75
P Prendergast	2-6	1-4	0-0	1-1	0-1	33.3	+ 10.73
P J Flynn	2-8	1-1	0-2	0-1	1-4	25.0	+ 3.00
V Bowens	2-11	0-4	1-4	0-0	1-3	18.2	+ 3.00
J J McLoughlin	2-15	0-2	0-4	0-0	2-9	13.3	- 3.25
P Mullins	2-16	0-2	1-10	0-0	1-4	12.5	- 3.00
M Halford	2-17	0-4	1-9	0-0	1-4	11.8	+ 5.00
C Collins	2-28	0-10	1-12	0-0	1-6	7.1	- 13.00
Noel Meade	2-29	0-7	1-16	0-1	1-5	6.9	- 14.50
Liam Browne	2-33	0-14	2-15	0-0	0-4	6.1	- 11.00
B W Hills (Eng)	1-1	0-0	1-1	0-0	0-0	100.0	+ 6.00
E J Kearns	1-2	0-0	1-2	0-0	0-0	50.0	+ 32.00
Lord Huntingdon (Eng)	1-2	1-1	0-1	0-0	0-0	50.0	+ 7.00
Noel T Chance	1-3	0-2	0-0	0-0	1-1	33.3	+ 5.00

Leading Jockeys

	Total W-R	Per cent	£1 Level Stake	Best Trainer	W-R	Per cent	£1 Level Stake
M J Kinane	14-66	21.2	- 8.52	D K Weld	12-59	20.3	- 5.52
R Hughes	9-41	22.0	+ 6.73	D Hanley	3-4	75.0	+ 19.50
J P Murtagh	7-31	22.6	- 2.58	John M Oxx	6-15	40.0	+ 5.42
C Roche	7-53	13.2	- 27.45	J S Bolger	5-33	15.2	- 22.45
S Craine	5-55	9.1	- 39.83	T Stack	3-12	25.0	- 5.33
P V Gilson	4-45	8.9	- 8.00	C Collins	2-7	28.6	+ 8.00
D G O'Shea	3-18	16.7	- 3.25	John M Oxx	2-6	33.3	+ 5.50
N G McCullagh	3-27	11.1	- 4.25	J J McLoughlin	2-7	28.6	+ 4.75
Miss S Kauntze	2-3	66.7	+ 4.00	M Kauntze	2-3	66.7	+ 4.00
K J Manning	2-28	7.1	+ 8.00	P Prendergast	1-1	100.0	+ 14.00
W J O'Connor	2-48	4.2	- 35.75	Liam Browne	1-2	50.0	+ 9.00
P Shanahan	2-50	4.0	- 34.00	Liam Browne	1-5	20.0	+ 6.00

How the Favourites Fared

Non-handicaps	W-R	Per cent	£1 Level Stake	Handicaps	W-R	Per cent	£1 Level Stake
2-y-o	14-26	53.8	+ 3.14	2-y-o	0-1	-	- 1.00
3-y-o	7-12	58.3	+ 5.84	3-y-o	3-4	75.0	+ 6.75
Weight-for-age	8-26	30.8	- 8.57	All-aged	4-16	25.0	- 2.25
Totals	29-64	45.3	+ 0.41	Totals	7-21	33.3	+ 3.50
All favs	36-85	42.4	+ 3.91				

GALWAY

Leading Trainers 1988-92

	Total W-R	Non-handicaps 2-y-o	3-y-o+	Handicaps 2-y-o	3-y-o+	Per cent	£1 Level Stake
D K Weld	39-149	10-30	13-44	0-4	16-71	26.2	+ 0.48
J S Bolger	16-142	5-25	5-39	0-6	6-72	11.3	- 83.03
C Collins	12-76	2-12	4-25	1-2	5-37	15.8	- 7.13
P J Flynn	11-54	0-5	7-18	0-0	4-31	20.4	- 11.00
John M Oxx	10-53	2-6	5-23	0-0	3-24	18.9	+ 14.75
T Stack	9-35	1-5	5-13	1-1	2-16	25.7	+ 20.05
Noel Meade	6-83	1-18	1-15	0-3	4-47	7.2	- 59.17
M Kauntze	4-24	1-7	1-4	0-3	2-10	16.7	+ 12.50
P Prendergast	4-30	1-7	1-12	0-2	2-9	13.3	- 10.00
J J McLoughlin	4-39	0-1	1-6	1-2	2-30	10.3	0.00
K Prendergast	4-64	0-16	0-15	1-3	3-30	6.3	- 28.00
Augustine Leahy	3-25	0-7	1-6	0-1	2-11	12.0	- 5.50
M J Grassick	3-34	0-3	1-12	0-1	2-18	8.8	+ 5.00
P Mullins	3-37	1-4	0-9	0-1	2-23	8.1	+ 34.00
M Cunningham	3-38	0-5	0-8	0-0	3-25	7.9	- 7.00
E J O'Grady	2-29	0-5	0-14	0-0	2-10	6.9	- 17.50
A Redmond	2-38	1-11	0-6	0-3	1-18	5.3	- 14.50
M A O'Toole	2-39	0-2	1-9	1-3	0-25	5.1	- 27.00
J C Shearman	1-1	0-0	1-1	0-0	0-0	100.0	+ 1.25
J Nicholson	1-1	1-1	0-0	0-0	0-0	100.0	+ 3.00
M A McCullagh	1-2	0-0	0-1	0-0	1-1	50.0	+ 15.00
J E Kiely	1-2	0-0	0-0	0-0	1-2	50.0	+ 1.50

Leading Jockeys

	Total W-R	Per cent	£1 Level Stake	Best Trainer	W-R	Per cent	£1 Level Stake
M J Kinane	38-139	27.3	- 0.51	D K Weld	37-123	30.1	+ 10.49
P Shanahan	16-103	15.5	- 7.87	C Collins	12-51	23.5	+ 17.88
S Craine	15-121	12.4	- 49.12	T Stack	7-28	25.0	+ 11.05
C Roche	9-86	10.5	- 57.20	J S Bolger	8-57	14.0	- 38.70
J P Murtagh	7-58	12.1	+ 32.25	P J Flynn	2-3	66.7	+ 10.75
P V Gilson	6-62	9.7	+ 16.50	M J Grassick	1-2	50.0	+ 9.00
M Fenton	5-43	11.6	- 6.00	Augustine Leahy	2-11	18.2	+ 4.00
K J Manning	5-66	7.6	- 33.32	J S Bolger	3-28	10.7	- 20.32
N G McCullagh	5-76	6.6	- 12.00	M A McCullagh	1-1	100.0	+ 16.00
J F Egan	5-82	6.1	- 33.00	P J Flynn	3-22	13.6	- 9.00
R M Burke	4-48	8.3	- 16.00	K Prendergast	2-15	13.3	+ 5.50
R Hughes	4-79	5.1	- 49.50	John M Oxx	1-1	100.0	+ 6.00

How the Favourites Fared

Non-handicaps	W-R	Per cent	£1 Level Stake	Handicaps	W-R	Per cent	£1 Level Stake
2-y-o	15-29	51.7	- 0.27	2-y-o	2-5	40.0	+ 2.50
3-y-o	6-10	60.0	+ 6.62	3-y-o	5-8	62.5	+ 3.98
Weight-for-age	16-44	36.4	- 10.81	All-aged	19-75	25.3	- 12.04
Totals	37-83	44.6	- 4.46	Totals	26-88	29.5	- 5.56
All favs	63-171	36.8	- 10.02				

GOWRAN PARK

Leading Trainers 1988-92

	Total W-R	Non-handicaps 2-y-o	3-y-o+	Handicaps 2-y-o	3-y-o+	Per cent	£1 Level Stake
D K Weld	37-135	12-34	19-61	2-13	4-27	27.4	- 7.45
J S Bolger	27-136	10-36	9-53	3-11	5-36	19.9	- 3.62
John M Oxx	15-72	3-24	9-31	0-2	3-15	20.8	- 12.59
M Kauntze	8-53	5-17	1-14	2-7	0-15	15.1	- 15.45
K Prendergast	7-100	0-25	5-37	0-11	2-27	7.0	- 72.45
Noel Meade	5-53	1-14	2-18	1-8	1-13	9.4	- 27.52
J J McLoughlin	4-27	0-3	1-9	1-4	2-11	14.8	+ 5.75
F Dunne	4-38	0-8	3-17	0-4	1-9	10.5	+ 3.00
M A O'Toole	4-42	0-9	0-9	0-2	4-22	9.5	- 16.25
C Collins	4-46	1-13	3-20	0-5	0-8	8.7	- 23.00
M V O'Brien	3-12	1-4	1-7	0-0	1-1	25.0	- 4.53
M Halford	3-19	0-2	1-8	0-1	2-8	15.8	- 2.00
M Cunningham	3-19	0-1	2-9	0-1	1-8	15.8	+ 0.50
Liam Browne	3-36	2-11	1-13	0-6	0-6	8.3	- 26.52
P Mullins	3-43	0-7	1-19	1-4	1-13	7.0	- 31.75
W P Mullins	2-14	0-4	0-2	2-4	0-4	14.3	+ 3.00
D Gillespie	2-16	0-5	0-3	0-4	2-4	12.5	- 1.00
P J Flynn	2-47	1-14	0-18	0-4	1-11	4.3	- 33.50
David A Kiely	1-2	0-0	0-1	0-0	1-1	50.0	+ 19.00
B Lawlor	1-2	0-0	0-1	0-0	1-1	50.0	+ 7.00
Peter McCreery	1-5	0-1	1-3	0-0	0-1	20.0	+ 12.00
Noel T Chance	1-7	1-1	0-3	0-1	0-2	14.3	0.00

Leading Jockeys

	Total W-R	Per cent	£1 Level Stake	Best Trainer	W-R	Per cent	£1 Level Stake
M J Kinane	39-131	29.8	- 0.72	D K Weld	35-105	33.3	+ 12.05
C Roche	16-98	16.3	- 35.74	J S Bolger	13-66	19.7	- 22.74
J P Murtagh	9-71	12.7	- 37.64	John M Oxx	7-29	24.1	- 5.14
W J O'Connor	8-71	11.3	- 28.45	M Kauntze	7-27	25.9	+ 6.55
K J Manning	8-74	10.8	- 36.50	J S Bolger	6-22	27.3	+ 5.00
W J Supple	6-64	9.4	- 25.37	J S Bolger	5-25	20.0	+ 7.63
N G McCullagh	5-63	7.9	- 17.25	J J McLoughlin	3-11	27.3	+ 6.75
R Hughes	5-65	7.7	- 28.25	John M Oxx	1-1	100.0	+ 5.50
E A Leonard	4-41	9.8	- 17.50	K Prendergast	2-10	20.0	- 5.50
P V Gilson	4-73	5.5	- 52.18	M V O'Brien	1-5	20.0	- 3.43
P Shanahan	4-89	4.5	- 70.00	C Collins	3-32	9.4	- 20.00
S Craine	4-99	4.0	- 79.77	Noel Meade	2-24	8.3	- 14.27

How the Favourites Fared

Non-handicaps	W-R	Per cent	£1 Level Stake	Handicaps	W-R	Per cent	£1 Level Stake
2-y-o	20-40	50.0	+ 2.81	2-y-o	5-13	38.5	+ 4.25
3-y-o	11-27	40.7	+ 2.80	3-y-o	3-9	33.3	+ 0.40
Weight-for-age	16-35	45.7	- 2.53	All-aged	12-32	37.5	+ 3.55
Totals	47-102	46.1	+ 3.08	Totals	20-54	37.0	+ 8.20
All favs	67-156	42.9	+ 11.28				

KILLARNEY

Leading Trainers 1988-92

	Total W-R	Non-handicaps 2-y-o	3-y-o+	Handicaps 2-y-o	3-y-o+	Per cent	£1 Level Stake
J S Bolger	17-62	1-5	8-26	0-0	8-31	27.4	- 11.87
T Stack	12-36	3-5	6-16	0-0	3-15	33.3	+ 7.73
D K Weld	10-41	1-3	8-20	0-0	1-18	24.4	- 16.76
T G Curtin	6-29	0-0	1-11	0-0	5-18	20.7	+ 12.05
M V O'Brien	5-6	1-1	2-2	0-0	2-3	83.3	+ 4.25
P J Flynn	5-25	0-0	1-6	0-0	4-19	20.0	- 12.85
K Prendergast	3-18	0-1	3-12	0-0	0-5	16.7	- 7.13
R Lister	2-4	0-0	1-2	0-0	1-2	50.0	+ 15.00
Neil S McGrath	2-7	0-0	0-2	0-0	2-5	28.6	+ 1.50
M Kauntze	2-9	0-1	2-3	0-0	0-5	22.2	- 5.28
M J Grassick	2-12	0-0	2-9	0-0	0-3	16.7	+ 2.80
P Mullins	2-18	0-0	1-9	0-0	1-9	11.1	- 8.75
Liam Browne	2-19	0-3	2-10	0-0	0-6	10.5	- 11.75
J J McLoughlin	2-19	0-1	0-3	0-0	2-15	10.5	- 11.43
Noel T Chance	1-2	0-0	0-1	0-0	1-1	50.0	+ 3.50
M Quaid	1-2	0-0	0-0	0-0	1-2	50.0	+ 15.00
J E Kiely	1-2	0-0	0-0	0-0	1-2	50.0	+ 0.38
P F O'Donnell	1-2	0-0	0-0	0-0	1-2	50.0	+ 6.00
K F O'Sullivan	1-2	0-0	0-1	0-0	1-1	50.0	+ 2.33
H De Bromhead	1-3	0-0	0-0	0-0	1-3	33.3	+ 14.00
J C Harley	1-3	0-0	1-1	0-0	0-2	33.3	+ 12.00
W P Mullins	1-5	0-0	0-2	0-0	1-3	20.0	+ 8.00

Leading Jockeys

	Total W-R	Per cent	£1 Level Stake	Best Trainer	W-R	Per cent	£1 Level Stake
S Craine	17-66	25.8	+ 2.88	T Stack	11-34	32.4	+ 7.83
C Roche	15-59	25.4	- 15.06	J S Bolger	9-31	29.0	- 10.39
M J Kinane	11-47	23.4	- 19.38	D K Weld	9-28	32.1	- 5.26
J F Egan	6-32	18.8	+ 0.10	P J Flynn	2-10	20.0	- 4.65
P Shanahan	5-15	33.3	+ 6.37	Liam Browne	1-1	100.0	+ 4.00
K J Manning	4-24	16.7	- 5.00	J S Bolger	4-10	40.0	+ 9.00
Miss C Hutchinson	3-4	75.0	+ 4.90	J S Bolger	1-1	100.0	+ 0.40
L Piggott	3-5	60.0	+ 1.43	M V O'Brien	3-3	100.0	+ 3.43
J P Murtagh	3-25	12.0	- 9.00	R Lister	1-1	100.0	+ 7.00
W J O'Connor	3-28	10.7	- 2.78	H McMahon	1-1	100.0	+ 6.00
W J Supple	3-37	8.1	- 27.62	J S Bolger	1-9	11.1	- 4.00
D Duggan	2-8	25.0	+ 2.33	M Cunningham	1-1	100.0	+ 3.33

How the Favourites Fared

Non-handicaps	W-R	Per cent	£1 Level Stake	Handicaps	W-R	Per cent	£1 Level Stake
2-y-o	4-6	66.7	+ 1.33	2-y-o	0-0	-	0.00
3-y-o	12-16	75.0	+ 11.25	3-y-o	4-7	57.1	+ 0.62
Weight-for-age	16-29	55.2	+ 1.38	All-aged	16-42	38.1	- 4.05
Totals	32-51	62.7	+ 13.96	Totals	20-49	40.8	- 3.43
All favs	52-100	52.0	+ 10.53				

LAYTOWN

Leading Trainers 1988-92

	Total W-R	Non-handicaps 2-y-o	3-y-o+	Handicaps 2-y-o	3-y-o+	Per cent	£1 Level Stake
D K Weld	6-14	0-0	3-7	0-0	3-7	42.9	+ 12.75
M A O'Toole	5-24	0-0	1-9	0-0	4-15	20.8	- 8.02
P Martin	2-7	0-0	1-3	0-0	1-4	28.6	+ 14.50
K Prendergast	2-20	0-0	0-7	0-0	2-13	10.0	- 3.20
C Kinane	1-2	0-0	1-2	0-0	0-0	50.0	+ 3.50
B V Kelly	1-3	0-0	1-2	0-0	0-1	33.3	+ 1.33
Daniel J Murphy	1-4	0-0	1-1	0-0	0-3	25.0	- 2.43
P Prendergast	1-5	0-0	1-1	0-0	0-4	20.0	+ 1.00
R Donoghue	1-5	0-0	1-4	0-0	0-1	20.0	+ 2.00
D J Reddan	1-8	0-0	0-3	0-0	1-5	12.5	- 0.50
M Halford	1-9	0-0	0-5	0-0	1-4	11.1	+ 2.00
J T Gorman	1-9	0-0	1-6	0-0	0-3	11.1	- 1.00
Peter Casey	1-10	0-0	0-3	0-0	1-7	10.0	+ 3.00

Leading Jockeys

	Total W-R	Per cent	£1 Level Stake	Best Trainer	W-R	Per cent	£1 Level Stake
R Carroll	3-6	50.0	+ 9.25	D K Weld	3-5	60.0	+ 10.25
W J Smith	3-9	33.3	+ 9.50	D K Weld	2-4	50.0	+ 1.50
J F Egan	3-13	23.1	+ 2.00	M A O'Toole	2-6	33.3	+ 3.50
P V Gilson	2-10	20.0	+ 5.50	M Halford	1-2	50.0	+ 9.00
R M Burke	2-11	18.2	+ 21.00	P Martin	1-1	100.0	+ 16.00
S Craine	2-13	15.4	- 0.67	B V Kelly	1-1	100.0	+ 3.33
Miss C Hutchinson	1-1	100.0	+ 5.00	P Prendergast	1-1	100.0	+ 5.00
Mr D Marnane	1-1	100.0	+ 1.50	M A O'Toole	1-1	100.0	+ 1.50
D J Walsh	1-1	100.0	+ 0.80	K Prendergast	1-1	100.0	+ 0.80
Mr A J Martin	1-3	33.3	+ 4.00	R Donoghue	1-1	100.0	+ 6.00
B Bowens	1-3	33.3	+ 4.50	D J Reddan	1-1	100.0	+ 6.50
C Roche	1-4	25.0	- 1.75	M A O'Toole	1-4	25.0	- 1.75

How the Favourites Fared

Non-handicaps	W-R	Per cent	£1 Level Stake	Handicaps	W-R	Per cent	£1 Level Stake
2-y-o	0-0	-	0.00	2-y-o	0-0	-	0.00
3-y-o	0-0	-	0.00	3-y-o	0-0	-	0.00
Weight-for-age	4-12	33.3	- 1.68	All-aged	6-13	46.2	+ 1.28
Totals	4-12	33.3	- 1.68	Totals	6-13	46.2	+ 1.28
All favs	10-25	40.0	- 0.40				

LEOPARDSTOWN

Leading Trainers 1988-92

	Total W-R	Non-handicaps 2-y-o	3-y-o+	Handicaps 2-y-o	3-y-o+	Per cent	£1 Level Stake
D K Weld	85-454	17-101	52-188	2-8	14-157	18.7	- 126.81
J S Bolger	84-449	28-112	27-179	3-10	26-148	18.7	- 72.87
John M Oxx	51-310	11-68	26-142	1-3	13-97	16.5	- 66.38
K Prendergast	41-364	10-78	13-142	2-11	16-133	11.3	- 90.73
M V O'Brien	25-77	9-24	14-49	0-0	2-4	32.5	- 6.61
T Stack	16-130	3-34	7-54	0-3	6-39	12.3	- 25.25
C Collins	13-152	6-38	4-71	0-2	3-41	8.6	- 63.50
M A O'Toole	9-104	0-23	3-25	1-2	5-54	8.7	- 29.00
Noel Meade	8-131	1-21	3-45	0-5	4-60	6.1	- 69.47
Liam Browne	8-135	3-51	4-57	0-6	1-21	5.9	- 46.17
M Kauntze	8-168	1-38	5-68	0-6	2-56	4.8	- 119.00
J E Mulhern	6-67	0-7	1-21	0-1	5-38	9.0	- 14.50
P Mullins	5-59	0-7	4-19	0-3	1-30	8.5	- 24.38
J J McLoughlin	4-95	0-25	2-30	0-3	2-37	4.2	- 50.50
F Dunne	4-105	0-11	2-35	0-3	2-56	3.8	- 57.00
Daniel J Murphy	3-19	1-4	1-9	0-1	1-5	15.8	+ 13.00
R Lister	3-20	0-5	1-12	0-0	2-3	15.0	+ 11.00
W P Mullins	3-20	0-0	0-7	0-0	3-13	15.0	+ 2.00
P Prendergast	3-28	0-8	0-11	0-1	3-8	10.7	- 8.50
Neil S McGrath	3-28	1-13	0-7	0-0	2-8	10.7	+ 7.00
T G Curtin	3-39	0-4	2-11	0-0	1-24	7.7	+ 10.00
J M Canty	3-53	1-11	1-15	0-0	1-27	5.7	- 38.20

Leading Jockeys

	Total W-R	Per cent	£1 Level Stake	Best Trainer	W-R	Per cent	£1 Level Stake
M J Kinane	81-365	22.2	- 46.42	D K Weld	80-330	24.2	- 35.42
C Roche	72-340	21.2	- 37.58	J S Bolger	60-234	25.6	+ 20.82
S Craine	35-286	12.2	- 39.84	T Stack	15-110	13.6	- 10.75
J P Murtagh	32-202	15.8	- 15.03	John M Oxx	26-109	23.9	+ 24.97
P V Gilson	18-196	9.2	- 66.56	M V O'Brien	8-22	36.4	+ 1.19
P Shanahan	18-237	7.6	- 148.62	C Collins	8-80	10.0	- 35.50
R Hughes	14-133	10.5	- 30.60	M A O'Toole	4-11	36.4	+ 24.25
J Reid	13-89	14.6	- 27.15	M V O'Brien	7-23	30.4	- 4.65
R Griffiths	10-102	9.8	- 29.19	K Prendergast	10-94	10.6	- 21.19
W J Supple	9-128	7.0	- 67.25	J S Bolger	7-66	10.6	- 24.25
E A Leonard	8-95	8.4	+ 27.50	K Prendergast	3-24	12.5	- 7.00
W J O'Connor	8-198	4.0	- 115.75	M Kauntze	3-79	3.8	- 65.75

How the Favourites Fared

Non-handicaps	W-R	Per cent	£1 Level Stake	Handicaps	W-R	Per cent	£1 Level Stake
2-y-o	55-106	51.9	+ 13.14	2-y-o	5-12	41.7	+ 0.48
3-y-o	35-72	48.6	+ 2.44	3-y-o	3-10	30.0	- 1.50
Weight-for-age	59-129	45.7	+ 1.50	All-aged	28-130	21.5	- 26.58
Totals	149-307	48.5	+ 17.08	Totals	36-152	23.7	- 27.60
All favs	185-459	40.3	- 10.52				

LIMERICK

Leading Trainers 1988-92

	Total W-R	Non-handicaps 2-y-o	3-y-o+	Handicaps 2-y-o	3-y-o+	Per cent	£1 Level Stake
J S Bolger	12-41	4-7	4-22	0-0	4-12	29.3	+ 10.34
P J Flynn	8-36	0-4	2-13	0-1	6-18	22.2	+ 6.25
D K Weld	8-51	4-10	3-28	0-1	1-12	15.7	- 23.73
Liam Browne	5-20	1-5	4-12	0-0	0-3	25.0	- 4.88
Mrs Crowley-O'Brien	3-5	0-0	0-2	0-0	3-3	60.0	+ 14.00
J C Hayden	3-16	1-5	0-7	0-0	2-4	18.8	+ 7.00
Neil S McGrath	2-6	1-2	1-4	0-0	0-0	33.3	+ 24.00
M A O'Toole	2-12	0-1	2-7	0-0	0-4	16.7	- 8.10
J J McLoughlin	2-12	0-0	0-4	0-0	2-8	16.7	0.00
C Collins	2-19	0-2	1-11	0-0	1-6	10.5	- 4.00
K Prendergast	2-25	0-2	2-13	0-1	0-9	8.0	- 18.20
T Stack	2-25	0-8	1-10	0-1	1-6	8.0	- 19.25
E J O'Grady	2-27	0-1	1-17	1-1	0-8	7.4	- 17.75
D P Kelly	1-2	0-0	1-1	0-0	0-1	50.0	+ 15.00
M V O'Brien	1-4	0-0	1-3	0-0	0-1	25.0	- 1.00
M Kauntze	1-5	0-0	1-3	0-0	0-2	20.0	- 2.25
J T Gorman	1-5	0-1	1-1	0-0	0-3	20.0	+ 16.00
J Morrison	1-6	0-0	1-3	0-0	0-3	16.7	+ 3.00
H McMahon	1-7	0-4	1-2	0-0	0-1	14.3	- 2.50
Daniel J Murphy	1-8	0-1	1-4	0-0	0-3	12.5	- 2.00
D T Hughes	1-9	0-0	1-5	0-0	0-4	11.1	- 4.00
D Gillespie	1-10	0-3	0-3	0-1	1-3	10.0	- 7.90

Leading Jockeys

	Total W-R	Per cent	£1 Level Stake	Best Trainer	W-R	Per cent	£1 Level Stake
M J Kinane	10-43	23.3	- 12.03	D K Weld	8-32	25.0	- 4.73
C Roche	8-31	25.8	+ 8.29	J S Bolger	6-19	31.6	+ 8.54
J F Egan	4-26	15.4	- 6.75	P J Flynn	4-13	30.8	+ 6.25
S Craine	4-40	10.0	- 25.87	Liam Browne	2-5	40.0	+ 2.38
W J Supple	3-25	12.0	- 5.50	J S Bolger	2-8	25.0	+ 2.50
K J Manning	3-25	12.0	- 14.20	J S Bolger	2-3	66.7	+ 0.80
W J O'Connor	3-25	12.0	- 5.50	C Collins	1-1	100.0	+ 6.00
N G McCullagh	3-26	11.5	+ 1.00	Mrs C-O'Brien	1-1	100.0	+ 6.00
P V Gilson	3-30	10.0	- 17.50	Liam Browne	1-2	50.0	+ 0.50
Mr A P O'Brien	2-3	66.7	+ 6.50	J S Bolger	2-3	66.7	+ 6.50
E A Leonard	2-17	11.8	- 2.20	K Prendergast	1-1	100.0	+ 0.80
R M Burke	2-21	9.5	- 7.00	Mrs C-O'Brien	1-1	100.0	+ 8.00

How the Favourites Fared

Non-handicaps	W-R	Per cent	£1 Level Stake	Handicaps	W-R	Per cent	£1 Level Stake
2-y-o	8-14	57.1	+ 0.07	2-y-o	0-1	-	- 1.00
3-y-o	5-15	33.3	- 4.05	3-y-o	0-2	-	- 2.00
Weight-for-age	8-18	44.4	- 0.47	All-aged	5-24	20.8	- 11.15
Totals	21-47	44.7	- 4.45	Totals	5-27	18.5	- 14.15
All favs	26-74	35.1	- 18.60				

LISTOWEL

Leading Trainers 1988-92

	Total W-R	Non-handicaps 2-y-o	3-y-o+	Handicaps 2-y-o	3-y-o+	Per cent	£1 Level Stake
D K Weld	12-48	4-14	2-10	0-3	6-21	25.0	- 1.33
J S Bolger	8-53	5-12	2-21	0-4	1-16	15.1	- 23.03
John M Oxx	5-27	1-4	2-10	0-1	2-12	18.5	- 10.00
T Stack	4-32	1-9	2-13	0-1	1-9	12.5	- 17.70
K Prendergast	3-20	2-6	0-5	0-4	1-5	15.0	+ 2.00
M Kauntze	3-24	0-3	1-3	2-3	0-15	12.5	- 2.00
P Mullins	3-26	1-5	1-8	0-1	1-12	11.5	- 10.25
P J Flynn	3-40	1-11	0-12	0-0	2-17	7.5	- 12.50
M Halford	2-14	0-3	0-1	0-0	2-10	14.3	- 0.50
Countess Schulenburg	1-1	0-0	1-1	0-0	0-0	100.0	+ 14.00
Ms J Morgan	1-2	0-0	1-1	0-1	0-0	50.0	+ 7.00
M V O'Brien	1-2	0-0	1-2	0-0	0-0	50.0	- 0.20
M Purcell	1-2	0-0	1-1	0-0	0-1	50.0	+ 3.50
J Queally	1-2	0-0	1-2	0-0	0-0	50.0	+ 5.00
Noel T Chance	1-3	1-1	0-0	0-0	0-2	33.3	+ 10.00
David A Kiely	1-3	0-0	0-1	0-0	1-2	33.3	+ 6.00
H De Bromhead	1-4	0-2	0-0	0-0	1-2	25.0	+ 1.00
F Flood	1-4	0-1	0-2	0-0	1-1	25.0	+ 4.00
J M Canty	1-5	0-1	0-1	0-1	1-2	20.0	+ 16.00
J G Coogan	1-5	0-3	1-2	0-0	0-0	20.0	+ 16.00
Mrs Crowley-O'Brien	1-5	0-1	0-0	0-0	1-4	20.0	- 1.75
Neil S McGrath	1-6	0-1	1-1	0-2	0-2	16.7	+ 5.00

Leading Jockeys

	Total W-R	Per cent	£1 Level Stake	Best Trainer	W-R	Per cent	£1 Level Stake
M J Kinane	12-54	22.2	- 4.29	D K Weld	10-38	26.3	+ 3.33
C Roche	8-37	21.6	- 0.63	J S Bolger	6-22	27.3	- 2.13
S Craine	7-48	14.6	- 16.45	T Stack	3-24	12.5	- 14.20
R M Burke	5-32	15.6	- 1.25	M Halford	2-2	100.0	+ 11.50
N G McCullagh	4-43	9.3	+ 5.00	J M Canty	1-1	100.0	+ 20.00
J P Murtagh	3-33	9.1	- 24.00	John M Oxx	3-16	18.8	- 7.00
W J O'Connor	3-37	8.1	- 9.00	M Kauntze	2-14	14.3	+ 1.00
B Bowens	2-10	20.0	+ 8.00	J Morrison	1-3	33.3	+ 5.00
P V Gilson	2-23	8.7	- 14.20	M V O'Brien	1-1	100.0	+ 0.80
M Fenton	2-23	8.7	- 14.67	Liam Browne	1-2	50.0	+ 2.00
K J Manning	2-28	7.1	- 22.90	T F Lacy	1-1	100.0	+ 2.00
J F Egan	2-41	4.9	- 16.00	P J Flynn	2-22	9.1	+ 3.00

How the Favourites Fared

Non-handicaps	W-R	Per cent	£1 Level Stake	Handicaps	W-R	Per cent	£1 Level Stake
2-y-o	8-17	47.1	+ 1.00	2-y-o	1-5	20.0	- 1.50
3-y-o	0-6	-	- 6.00	3-y-o	0-0	-	0.00
Weight-for-age	7-16	43.8	- 0.34	All-aged	12-32	37.5	+ 9.16
Totals	15-39	38.5	- 5.34	Totals	13-37	35.1	+ 7.66
All favs	28-76	36.8	+ 2.32				

MALLOW

Leading Trainers 1988-92

	Total W-R	Non-handicaps 2-y-o	Non-handicaps 3-y-o+	Handicaps 2-y-o	Handicaps 3-y-o+	Per cent	£1 Level Stake
John M Oxx	13-37	3-9	7-20	0-0	3-8	35.1	- 7.31
J S Bolger	8-46	4-16	3-16	0-1	1-13	17.4	- 11.15
D K Weld	8-53	4-13	4-30	0-1	0-9	15.1	- 17.34
J J McLoughlin	6-17	0-1	1-7	0-1	5-8	35.3	+ 8.00
Liam Browne	5-23	2-5	2-10	0-0	1-8	21.7	+ 8.75
M J Grassick	4-31	0-5	4-18	0-0	0-8	12.9	- 17.08
T Stack	4-33	0-4	3-21	0-1	1-7	12.1	- 20.70
K Prendergast	4-35	2-7	0-17	0-0	2-11	11.4	- 12.00
T G Curtin	3-7	0-0	0-4	0-0	3-3	42.9	+ 20.00
D Gillespie	3-13	1-2	0-4	1-2	1-5	23.1	+ 4.10
E J O'Grady	3-33	0-5	2-16	1-1	0-11	9.1	- 21.60
P J Flynn	3-39	0-12	1-13	0-0	2-14	7.7	- 11.50
B V Kelly	2-5	0-0	2-4	0-1	0-0	40.0	+ 2.00
M V O'Brien	2-5	2-4	0-1	0-0	0-0	40.0	+ 6.38
Neil S McGrath	2-7	0-0	2-7	0-0	0-0	28.6	+ 5.00
Noel Meade	2-15	0-3	1-6	0-0	1-6	13.3	+ 12.00
C Collins	2-17	0-3	2-8	0-0	0-6	11.8	+ 2.50
J P Kavanagh	1-2	1-1	0-0	0-0	0-1	50.0	- 0.60
E O'Connell	1-5	0-0	0-1	0-0	1-4	20.0	- 2.00
J G Coogan	1-5	0-2	1-2	0-1	0-0	20.0	+ 2.00
M J Corbett	1-8	0-2	0-1	0-0	1-5	12.5	- 0.50
V Bowens	1-10	0-4	0-3	0-0	1-3	10.0	- 1.00

Leading Jockeys

	Total W-R	Per cent	£1 Level Stake	Best Trainer	W-R	Per cent	£1 Level Stake
C Roche	11-57	19.3	- 9.85	J S Bolger	7-31	22.6	+ 2.35
S Craine	10-61	16.4	- 23.95	T Stack	3-27	11.1	- 17.20
M J Kinane	9-46	19.6	+ 2.29	D K Weld	6-32	18.8	- 5.34
J P Murtagh	8-28	28.6	- 8.80	John M Oxx	8-15	53.3	+ 4.20
N G McCullagh	5-32	15.6	- 6.00	J J McLoughlin	2-6	33.3	0.00
P Shanahan	5-38	13.2	- 19.25	J S Bolger	1-1	100.0	+ 0.50
E A Leonard	4-25	16.0	- 6.00	J J McLoughlin	4-8	50.0	+ 11.00
J F Egan	4-30	13.3	+ 20.00	P J Flynn	2-19	10.5	+ 2.00
D V Smith	2-12	16.7	- 4.00	D K Weld	1-3	33.3	0.00
R M Burke	2-23	8.7	- 11.00	K Prendergast	2-12	16.7	0.00
R Hughes	2-36	5.6	- 32.47	John M Oxx	1-1	100.0	+ 0.73
P Carberry	1-2	50.0	+ 0.10	D Gillespie	1-1	100.0	+ 1.10

How the Favourites Fared

Non-handicaps	W-R	Per cent	£1 Level Stake	Handicaps	W-R	Per cent	£1 Level Stake
2-y-o	11-21	52.4	+ 0.29	2-y-o	1-2	50.0	+ 0.10
3-y-o	10-16	62.5	+ 7.02	3-y-o	2-6	33.3	- 0.45
Weight-for-age	9-24	37.5	- 5.64	All-aged	6-19	31.6	- 5.33
Totals	30-61	49.2	+ 1.67	Totals	9-27	33.3	- 5.68
All favs	39-88	44.3	- 4.01				

NAAS

Leading Trainers 1988-92

	Total W-R	Non-handicaps 2-y-o	3-y-o+	Handicaps 2-y-o	3-y-o+	Per cent	£1 Level Stake
D K Weld	31-170	8-46	13-68	1-8	9-48	18.2	- 41.41
J S Bolger	23-134	10-39	5-38	3-20	5-37	17.2	- 36.91
John M Oxx	20-98	4-24	8-37	0-4	8-33	20.4	- 11.68
K Prendergast	13-150	3-40	7-52	0-15	3-43	8.7	- 80.00
C Collins	10-82	6-27	1-29	0-5	3-21	12.2	- 43.33
M V O'Brien	6-15	1-4	3-8	1-2	1-1	40.0	+ 7.52
Liam Browne	6-54	4-22	2-15	0-3	0-14	11.1	- 6.25
J J McLoughlin	5-38	2-7	0-12	0-2	3-17	13.2	- 2.38
M Kauntze	5-51	1-15	2-15	1-5	1-16	9.8	- 20.00
Noel Meade	5-63	0-19	2-20	0-6	3-18	7.9	- 31.25
F Dunne	4-42	1-9	2-15	0-0	1-18	9.5	- 8.17
P J Flynn	3-19	0-2	0-3	0-0	3-14	15.8	+ 11.50
M J Grassick	3-32	1-5	1-15	0-4	1-8	9.4	- 12.50
M A O'Toole	3-44	2-13	1-14	0-4	0-13	6.8	- 32.40
J G Coogan	2-17	1-7	0-4	0-2	1-4	11.8	- 2.00
N O'Callaghan	2-17	1-7	1-2	0-0	0-8	11.8	- 5.00
E J O'Grady	2-36	0-10	1-14	1-2	0-10	5.6	- 14.00
T Stack	2-36	0-11	1-15	0-1	1-9	5.6	- 22.50
A Geraghty	1-2	0-1	1-1	0-0	0-0	50.0	+ 11.00
Oliver Finnegan	1-2	0-0	0-0	0-0	1-2	50.0	+ 9.00
F Flood	1-2	0-0	0-0	0-0	1-2	50.0	+ 5.00
C Kinane	1-2	0-0	1-2	0-0	0-0	50.0	+ 4.00

Leading Jockeys

	Total W-R	Per cent	£1 Level Stake	Best Trainer	W-R	Per cent	£1 Level Stake
M J Kinane	24-102	23.5	- 6.79	D K Weld	22-80	27.5	+ 1.71
C Roche	23-101	22.8	- 11.10	J S Bolger	20-57	35.1	+ 17.60
P Shanahan	15-102	14.7	- 21.83	C Collins	8-41	19.5	- 10.58
J P Murtagh	10-80	12.5	- 14.55	John M Oxx	9-44	20.5	+ 0.45
D G O'Shea	7-33	21.2	+ 0.37	John M Oxx	4-12	33.3	- 3.63
P V Gilson	7-90	7.8	- 44.81	M V O'Brien	4-10	40.0	+ 6.94
W J O'Connor	6-80	7.5	- 36.00	M Kauntze	3-26	11.5	- 8.50
R Hughes	6-85	7.1	- 38.50	Noel Meade	2-8	25.0	+ 4.00
J F Egan	5-69	7.2	- 22.00	P J Flynn	2-11	18.2	+ 15.00
N G McCullagh	5-75	6.7	- 29.37	J J McLoughlin	3-20	15.0	- 3.37
S Craine	5-114	4.4	- 80.75	N O'Callaghan	1-2	50.0	+ 4.00
E A Leonard	4-45	8.9	- 21.00	K Prendergast	3-14	21.4	+ 2.00

How the Favourites Fared

Non-handicaps	W-R	Per cent	£1 Level Stake	Handicaps	W-R	Per cent	£1 Level Stake
2-y-o	27-53	50.9	+ 14.77	2-y-o	3-12	25.0	+ 0.30
3-y-o	11-27	40.7	- 2.30	3-y-o	3-16	18.8	- 8.00
Weight-for-age	13-31	41.9	+ 1.76	All-aged	16-38	42.1	+ 18.74
Totals	51-111	45.9	+ 14.23	Totals	22-66	33.3	+ 11.04
All favs	73-177	41.2	+ 25.27				

NAVAN

Leading Trainers 1988-92

	Total W-R	Non-handicaps 2-y-o	Non-handicaps 3-y-o+	Handicaps 2-y-o	Handicaps 3-y-o+	Per cent	£1 Level Stake
J S Bolger	13-79	8-25	4-28	0-2	1-24	16.5	- 32.63
D K Weld	11-91	5-28	5-40	1-2	0-21	12.1	- 20.81
K Prendergast	11-99	6-30	3-32	0-2	2-35	11.1	- 42.00
M Kauntze	6-45	1-16	2-15	0-1	3-13	13.3	- 14.75
John M Oxx	6-50	2-19	4-21	0-1	0-9	12.0	- 30.98
C Collins	6-52	0-13	5-26	0-0	1-13	11.5	- 17.50
Noel Meade	5-63	2-20	1-18	0-0	2-25	7.9	- 27.00
Liam Browne	3-22	3-7	0-10	0-1	0-4	13.6	- 3.50
D T Hughes	3-22	1-7	0-6	0-0	2-9	13.6	+ 9.00
M J Grassick	3-42	0-11	1-17	0-0	2-14	7.1	- 12.50
M V O'Brien	2-7	2-6	0-1	0-0	0-0	28.6	- 1.13
V Kennedy	2-16	0-2	0-9	0-0	2-5	12.5	+ 9.00
T F Lacy	2-19	0-4	1-9	0-0	1-6	10.5	- 8.25
J J McLoughlin	2-22	0-2	0-10	0-0	2-10	9.1	- 10.50
E J O'Grady	2-27	1-8	1-13	0-0	0-6	7.4	- 14.00
M Halford	2-29	1-7	1-12	0-0	0-10	6.9	- 13.00
M A O'Toole	2-31	0-7	2-9	0-3	0-12	6.5	- 23.90
T Stack	2-32	0-7	2-18	0-0	0-7	6.3	- 24.00
Mrs Ian Fox	1-1	0-0	0-0	0-0	1-1	100.0	+ 14.00
C P Magnier	1-2	0-0	0-0	0-0	1-2	50.0	+ 7.00
J E Mulhern	1-4	0-1	1-2	0-0	0-1	25.0	+ 4.00
W P Mullins	1-5	0-1	0-1	0-0	1-3	20.0	+ 4.00

Leading Jockeys

	Total W-R	Per cent	£1 Level Stake	Best Trainer	W-R	Per cent	£1 Level Stake
C Roche	15-76	19.7	- 9.31	J S Bolger	12-43	27.9	- 5.64
M J Kinane	11-79	13.9	- 14.31	D K Weld	9-63	14.3	- 8.81
J P Murtagh	9-47	19.1	+ 11.23	John M Oxx	5-19	26.3	- 1.77
P Shanahan	9-80	11.3	- 19.00	C Collins	4-27	14.8	- 4.50
S Craine	6-83	7.2	- 50.00	Noel Meade	2-21	9.5	- 11.00
P V Gilson	5-65	7.7	- 38.62	M V O'Brien	1-1	100.0	+ 1.38
M Fenton	4-21	19.0	+ 14.00	Liam Browne	2-5	40.0	+ 7.00
W J O'Connor	4-56	7.1	- 36.75	M Kauntze	3-14	21.4	- 1.75
E A Leonard	3-42	7.1	- 13.00	P Henley	1-1	100.0	+ 14.00
P P Murphy	2-6	33.3	+ 14.00	D T Hughes	2-5	40.0	+ 15.00
R M Burke	2-33	6.1	- 8.00	J E Mulhern	1-2	50.0	+ 6.00
N G McCullagh	2-42	4.8	- 29.50	W P Mullins	1-1	100.0	+ 8.00

How the Favourites Fared

Non-handicaps	W-R	Per cent	£1 Level Stake	Handicaps	W-R	Per cent	£1 Level Stake
2-y-o	16-34	47.1	+ 2.51	2-y-o	1-2	50.0	+ 0.75
3-y-o	8-31	25.8	- 12.46	3-y-o	2-10	20.0	- 4.10
Weight-for-age	7-12	58.3	+ 5.88	All-aged	2-20	10.0	- 16.20
Totals	31-77	40.3	- 4.07	Totals	5-32	15.6	- 19.55
All favs	36-109	33.0	- 23.62				

PUNCHESTOWN

Leading Trainers 1988-92

	Total W-R	Non-handicaps 2-y-o	3-y-o+	Handicaps 2-y-o	3-y-o+	Per cent	£1 Level Stake
J S Bolger	5-12	2-3	0-5	0-0	3-4	41.7	+ 2.71
D K Weld	3-24	0-6	2-8	0-0	1-10	12.5	- 8.00
M Kauntze	2-11	1-4	0-2	0-0	1-5	18.2	+ 4.00
John M Oxx	2-17	2-9	0-3	0-0	0-5	11.8	- 7.50
Mrs Crowley-O'Brien	1-1	0-0	1-1	0-0	0-0	100.0	+ 2.00
J E Mulhern	1-2	0-0	1-2	0-0	0-0	50.0	+ 2.00
Peadar Matthews	1-5	0-1	0-1	0-0	1-3	20.0	+ 6.00
P Prendergast	1-5	1-3	0-0	0-0	0-2	20.0	+ 2.00
M Cunningham	1-5	0-1	1-2	0-0	0-2	20.0	+ 10.00
J P Kavanagh	1-5	0-2	0-1	0-0	1-2	20.0	+ 6.00
Anthony Mullins	1-5	0-1	0-0	0-0	1-4	20.0	+ 5.00
M A O'Toole	1-6	1-1	0-1	0-0	0-4	16.7	- 2.50
J C Hayden	1-9	1-4	0-1	0-0	0-4	11.1	+ 6.00
P Mullins	1-10	0-2	1-3	0-0	0-5	10.0	- 8.00
Noel Meade	1-11	1-2	0-3	0-0	0-6	9.1	- 7.50
M J Grassick	1-13	0-6	1-3	0-0	0-4	7.7	0.00
K Prendergast	1-20	0-6	0-4	0-0	1-10	5.0	- 13.50

Leading Jockeys

	Total W-R	Per cent	£1 Level Stake	Best Trainer	W-R	Per cent	£1 Level Stake
K J Manning	3-11	27.3	+ 23.00	J S Bolger	1-1	100.0	+ 5.00
C Roche	3-14	21.4	- 2.12	J S Bolger	2-6	33.3	- 1.12
J F Egan	2-12	16.7	+ 6.00	Mrs C-O'Brien	1-1	100.0	+ 2.00
W J O'Connor	2-12	16.7	+ 3.00	M Kauntze	2-8	25.0	+ 7.00
M J Kinane	2-17	11.8	- 3.00	D K Weld	2-15	13.3	- 1.00
A J Beale	1-1	100.0	+ 3.00	J E Mulhern	1-1	100.0	+ 3.00
C Everard	1-2	50.0	+ 0.50	J S Bolger	1-2	50.0	+ 0.50
J A Heffernan	1-6	16.7	+ 4.00	Anthony Mullins	1-1	100.0	+ 9.00
J P Murtagh	1-11	9.1	- 7.50	John M Oxx	1-4	25.0	- 0.50
W J Supple	1-12	8.3	- 10.67	J S Bolger	1-2	50.0	- 0.67
S Craine	1-13	7.7	- 9.50	Noel Meade	1-4	25.0	- 0.50
R Hughes	1-14	7.1	- 7.00				

How the Favourites Fared

Non-handicaps	W-R	Per cent	£1 Level Stake	Handicaps	W-R	Per cent	£1 Level Stake
2-y-o	5-9	55.6	+ 5.46	2-y-o	0-0	-	0.00
3-y-o	0-3	-	- 3.00	3-y-o	0-4	-	- 4.00
Weight-for-age	4-4	100.0	+ 6.40	All-aged	4-6	66.7	+ 10.25
Totals	9-16	56.3	+ 8.86	Totals	4-10	40.0	+ 6.25
All favs	13-26	50.0	+ 15.11				

ROSCOMMON

Leading Trainers 1988-92

	Total W-R	Non-handicaps 2-y-o	3-y-o+	Handicaps 2-y-o	3-y-o+	Per cent	£1 Level Stake
J S Bolger	17-71	9-22	3-32	0-0	5-17	23.9	- 2.33
K Prendergast	17-88	2-19	9-42	0-0	6-27	19.3	+ 34.08
John M Oxx	15-55	2-5	9-35	0-0	4-15	27.3	- 12.99
D K Weld	10-79	6-25	2-34	0-0	2-20	12.7	- 28.53
T Stack	7-28	1-6	5-16	0-0	1-6	25.0	+ 24.00
Noel Meade	5-37	3-11	1-13	0-0	1-13	13.5	- 9.20
M Kauntze	3-22	0-3	2-12	0-0	1-7	13.6	- 6.17
D Gillespie	3-22	0-4	1-7	0-0	2-11	13.6	- 6.00
J J McLoughlin	3-24	0-4	0-7	0-0	3-13	12.5	- 6.75
M J Grassick	3-33	0-5	3-16	0-0	0-12	9.1	- 13.00
V Kennedy	2-4	1-2	1-1	0-0	0-1	50.0	+ 11.63
T G Curtin	2-9	0-0	1-5	0-0	1-4	22.2	- 1.00
P Prendergast	2-11	0-4	2-5	0-0	0-2	18.2	- 5.60
M A O'Toole	2-18	0-5	0-2	0-0	2-11	11.1	+ 4.00
M Halford	2-25	0-5	2-12	0-0	0-8	8.0	- 10.25
C Collins	2-30	1-3	1-16	0-0	0-11	6.7	- 22.27
W P Browne	1-1	0-0	1-1	0-0	0-0	100.0	+ 0.50
R O'Donovan	1-2	0-0	1-2	0-0	0-0	50.0	+ 6.00
C P Donoghue	1-2	0-0	0-0	0-0	1-2	50.0	+ 3.00
T Kinane	1-4	0-0	1-4	0-0	0-0	25.0	- 1.50
T B Naughton	1-4	0-0	0-3	0-0	1-1	25.0	+ 7.00
M J P O'Brien	1-6	0-1	0-2	0-0	1-3	16.7	- 1.00

Leading Jockeys

	Total W-R	Per cent	£1 Level Stake	Best Trainer	W-R	Per cent	£1 Level Stake
C Roche	12-44	27.3	+ 10.26	J S Bolger	9-33	27.3	+ 3.26
S Craine	11-67	16.4	+ 0.80	Noel Meade	5-16	31.3	+ 11.80
M J Kinane	11-73	15.1	- 29.78	D K Weld	7-55	12.7	- 23.53
J P Murtagh	7-56	12.5	- 34.33	John M Oxx	6-22	27.3	- 4.66
R Griffiths	5-27	18.5	+ 20.33	K Prendergast	5-26	19.2	+ 21.33
W J Supple	5-33	15.2	- 7.00	J S Bolger	5-19	26.3	+ 7.00
N G McCullagh	4-43	9.3	- 20.75	J J McLoughlin	2-11	18.2	- 1.75
K J Manning	4-48	8.3	- 27.77	J S Bolger	1-4	25.0	- 2.27
P Shanahan	4-54	7.4	- 28.20	J S Bolger	1-1	100.0	+ 0.80
R Hughes	4-59	6.8	- 39.10	R O'Donovan	1-1	100.0	+ 7.00
R M Burke	3-28	10.7	- 5.00	K Prendergast	3-10	30.0	+ 13.00
P V Gilson	3-49	6.1	- 31.62	M Halford	2-14	14.3	+ 0.75

How the Favourites Fared

Non-handicaps	W-R	Per cent	£1 Level Stake	Handicaps	W-R	Per cent	£1 Level Stake
2-y-o	8-24	33.3	- 7.06	2-y-o	0-0	-	0.00
3-y-o	5-21	23.8	- 11.55	3-y-o	5-10	50.0	+ 5.08
Weight-for-age	12-28	42.9	- 0.18	All-aged	3-28	10.7	- 22.13
Totals	25-73	34.2	- 18.79	Totals	8-38	21.1	- 17.05
All favs	33-111	29.7	- 35.84				

SLIGO

Leading Trainers 1988-92

	Total W-R	Non-handicaps 2-y-o	Non-handicaps 3-y-o+	Handicaps 2-y-o	Handicaps 3-y-o+	Per cent	£1 Level Stake
D K Weld	10-54	5-11	2-25	0-0	3-18	18.5	- 13.32
Noel Meade	7-27	1-5	2-10	0-0	4-12	25.9	- 4.15
M J Grassick	7-40	0-4	4-24	0-0	3-12	17.5	+ 0.63
John M Oxx	5-18	0-3	4-13	0-0	1-2	27.8	+ 4.23
Edward Lynam	4-35	0-6	2-15	0-0	2-14	11.4	- 17.25
T G Curtin	3-5	1-1	2-2	0-0	0-2	60.0	+ 16.50
M Halford	3-10	1-1	1-5	0-0	1-4	30.0	+ 9.00
P J Flynn	3-14	0-1	1-2	0-0	2-11	21.4	- 2.88
K Prendergast	3-34	0-7	3-16	0-0	0-11	8.8	- 23.50
J S Bolger	3-37	0-10	2-15	0-0	1-12	8.1	- 10.00
J Burns	2-3	1-2	1-1	0-0	0-0	66.7	+ 11.00
Wilbert Tolerton	2-5	0-0	1-2	0-0	1-3	40.0	+ 24.00
Anthony Mullins	2-5	0-1	2-3	0-0	0-1	40.0	+ 1.25
O Weldon	2-5	0-0	0-2	0-0	2-3	40.0	+ 15.00
J C Hayden	2-9	1-3	1-4	0-0	0-2	22.2	+ 3.25
M McDonagh	2-10	0-0	0-5	0-0	2-5	20.0	- 0.50
C Collins	2-16	0-2	1-9	0-0	1-5	12.5	- 4.25
A Redmond	2-22	0-5	1-8	0-0	1-9	9.1	- 5.50
Liam Browne	2-27	2-9	0-13	0-0	0-5	7.4	- 18.60
John J Walsh	1-2	0-0	0-0	0-0	1-2	50.0	+ 7.00
C P Magnier	1-2	0-0	0-1	0-0	1-1	50.0	+ 3.00
Thomas Bergin	1-2	0-0	1-2	0-0	0-0	50.0	+ 7.00

Leading Jockeys

	Total W-R	Per cent	£1 Level Stake	Best Trainer	W-R	Per cent	£1 Level Stake
M J Kinane	10-33	30.3	+ 8.68	D K Weld	9-29	31.0	+ 9.18
P Shanahan	7-33	21.2	+ 1.75	J Burns	2-3	66.7	+ 11.00
R Hughes	7-37	18.9	- 2.40	Noel Meade	2-4	50.0	+ 1.60
S Craine	6-35	17.1	- 14.75	Anthony Mullins	2-3	66.7	+ 3.25
J P Murtagh	5-32	15.6	- 6.50	John M Oxx	4-9	44.4	+ 11.50
J F Egan	4-29	13.8	- 8.87	P J Flynn	2-8	25.0	+ 0.88
J A Heffernan	3-12	25.0	+ 18.00	O Weldon	2-2	100.0	+ 18.00
W J Supple	3-34	8.8	- 10.50	M Halford	1-2	50.0	+ 4.00
N G McCullagh	3-37	8.1	- 20.00	Noel Meade	1-1	100.0	+ 5.00
D G O'Shea	2-11	18.2	+ 2.50	M McDonagh	1-1	100.0	+ 4.50
M Fenton	2-13	15.4	0.00	John J Walsh	1-1	100.0	+ 8.00
W J Smith	2-18	11.1	+ 11.00	Wilbert Tolerton	2-4	50.0	+ 25.00

How the Favourites Fared

Non-handicaps	W-R	Per cent	£1 Level Stake	Handicaps	W-R	Per cent	£1 Level Stake
2-y-o	5-14	35.7	- 3.15	2-y-o	0-0	-	0.00
3-y-o	9-19	47.4	+ 4.84	3-y-o	0-1	-	- 1.00
Weight-for-age	9-22	40.9	+ 4.01	All-aged	10-31	32.3	- 5.49
Totals	23-55	41.8	+ 5.70	Totals	10-32	31.3	- 6.49
All favs	33-87	37.9	- 0.79				

THURLES

Leading Trainers 1988-92

	Total W-R	Non-handicaps 2-y-o	Non-handicaps 3-y-o+	Handicaps 2-y-o	Handicaps 3-y-o+	Per cent	£1 Level Stake
Noel Meade	3-6	0-0	3-5	0-0	0-1	50.0	+ 11.00
Edward Lynam	2-7	0-0	2-7	0-0	0-0	28.6	+ 15.00
D K Weld	2-13	0-0	2-11	0-0	0-2	15.4	+ 17.00
P J Flynn	2-14	0-0	2-11	0-0	0-3	14.3	- 10.55
J S Bolger	2-20	0-0	1-14	0-0	1-6	10.0	+ 10.00
T G Curtin	1-2	0-0	0-0	0-0	1-2	50.0	+ 3.00
Mrs Crowley-O'Brien	1-2	0-0	1-2	0-0	0-0	50.0	+ 1.50
F Flood	1-3	0-0	0-1	0-0	1-2	33.3	- 0.25
F J Lacy	1-3	0-0	0-0	0-0	1-3	33.3	+ 6.00
K Prendergast	1-4	0-0	1-4	0-0	0-0	25.0	- 0.25
B V Kelly	1-4	0-0	1-3	0-0	0-1	25.0	+ 1.00
R Lister	1-4	0-0	1-4	0-0	0-0	25.0	- 0.75
John M Oxx	1-5	0-0	1-5	0-0	0-0	20.0	0.00
T Stack	1-6	0-0	1-5	0-0	0-1	16.7	- 4.27
Capt D G Swan	1-9	0-0	0-6	0-0	1-3	11.1	- 6.00
Augustine Leahy	1-9	0-0	1-9	0-0	0-0	11.1	+ 4.00
E J O'Grady	1-10	0-0	1-6	0-0	0-4	10.0	- 7.75

Leading Jockeys

	Total W-R	Per cent	£1 Level Stake	Best Trainer	W-R	Per cent	£1 Level Stake
S Craine	5-15	33.3	+ 15.73	B V Kelly	1-1	100.0	+ 4.00
J P Murtagh	3-11	27.3	+ 8.25	F J Lacy	1-1	100.0	+ 8.00
M J Kinane	3-17	17.6	- 3.00	F Flood	1-1	100.0	+ 1.75
P Shanahan	2-9	22.2	+ 19.00	D K Weld	1-2	50.0	+ 19.00
C Roche	2-16	12.5	- 1.00	J S Bolger	1-9	11.1	0.00
A P McCoy	1-2	50.0	+ 19.00	J S Bolger	1-2	50.0	+ 19.00
M F Ryan	1-3	33.3	+ 2.00	Noel Meade	1-1	100.0	+ 4.00
J A Heffernan	1-3	33.3	+ 0.50	Mrs C-O'Brien	1-1	100.0	+ 2.50
M Duffy	1-4	25.0	- 2.27	P J Flynn	1-2	50.0	- 0.27
J F Egan	1-7	14.3	- 5.27	P J Flynn	1-4	25.0	- 2.27
D Duggan	1-7	14.3	- 3.00				
D V Smith	1-7	14.3	0.00	Edward Lynam	1-1	100.0	+ 6.00

How the Favourites Fared

Non-handicaps	W-R	Per cent	£1 Level Stake	Handicaps	W-R	Per cent	£1 Level Stake
2-y-o	0-0	-	0.00	2-y-o	0-0	-	0.00
3-y-o	3-10	30.0	- 3.02	3-y-o	0-0	-	0.00
Weight-for-age	3-10	30.0	- 3.29	All-aged	2-8	25.0	- 2.25
Totals	6-20	30.0	- 6.31	Totals	2-8	25.0	- 2.25
All favs	8-28	28.6	- 8.56				

TIPPERARY

Leading Trainers 1988-92

	Total W-R	Non-handicaps 2-y-o	3-y-o+	Handicaps 2-y-o	3-y-o+	Per cent	£1 Level Stake
J S Bolger	34-156	12-43	16-79	0-2	6-32	21.8	- 47.81
D K Weld	31-152	4-34	23-83	1-1	3-34	20.4	- 38.63
K Prendergast	16-92	6-27	4-43	0-0	6-22	17.4	- 14.98
John M Oxx	15-79	5-14	10-47	0-0	0-18	19.0	- 27.52
T Stack	15-87	4-19	9-51	1-3	1-14	17.2	- 4.94
M V O'Brien	9-26	2-3	7-22	0-0	0-1	34.6	- 3.82
Noel Meade	5-35	2-8	2-16	0-0	1-11	14.3	- 15.38
M J Grassick	4-30	2-5	2-22	0-0	0-3	13.3	- 3.60
Liam Browne	4-49	1-14	2-29	0-0	1-6	8.2	- 20.25
Augustine Leahy	4-49	1-13	1-21	0-0	2-15	8.2	- 21.25
P Mullins	4-54	1-17	2-22	0-0	1-15	7.4	- 24.75
J G Coogan	3-13	3-10	0-1	0-1	0-1	23.1	+ 3.50
B V Kelly	3-18	0-0	0-8	0-0	3-10	16.7	+ 12.00
D Gillespie	3-20	2-6	0-5	0-1	1-8	15.0	- 1.88
T F Lacy	3-27	0-8	1-13	0-0	2-6	11.1	- 10.50
C Collins	3-45	1-8	2-31	0-0	0-6	6.7	- 33.00
J Burns	2-8	1-6	1-2	0-0	0-0	25.0	+ 3.25
Daniel J Murphy	2-8	0-1	1-5	0-0	1-2	25.0	+ 12.00
M Kauntze	2-14	0-2	2-10	0-0	0-2	14.3	- 8.50
J J McLoughlin	2-36	0-9	0-11	0-0	2-16	5.6	- 16.00
B W Hills (Eng)	1-1	0-0	1-1	0-0	0-0	100.0	+ 2.50
J Queally	1-1	0-0	1-1	0-0	0-0	100.0	+ 1.25

Leading Jockeys

	Total W-R	Per cent	£1 Level Stake	Best Trainer	W-R	Per cent	£1 Level Stake
C Roche	29-117	24.8	- 20.60	J S Bolger	25-81	30.9	- 7.64
M J Kinane	27-131	20.6	- 24.47	D K Weld	26-106	24.5	- 2.22
S Craine	22-136	16.2	- 19.78	T Stack	14-68	20.6	+ 10.06
J P Murtagh	12-67	17.9	- 14.12	John M Oxx	8-29	27.6	- 4.12
P Shanahan	11-75	14.7	- 24.08	D K Weld	3-8	37.5	- 1.83
R Griffiths	8-29	27.6	+ 20.91	K Prendergast	8-27	29.6	+ 22.91
K J Manning	8-69	11.6	- 2.06	J S Bolger	4-22	18.2	- 5.56
P V Gilson	5-81	6.2	- 45.00	M V O'Brien	2-9	22.2	- 0.25
E A Leonard	4-48	8.3	- 11.90	K Prendergast	2-7	28.6	+ 2.10
W J Supple	4-56	7.1	- 29.40	D Hanley	1-1	100.0	+ 1.10
J F Egan	4-58	6.9	- 32.50	Peter McCreery	1-1	100.0	+ 8.00
N G McCullagh	4-67	6.0	- 37.25	P Mullins	2-13	15.4	+ 1.25

How the Favourites Fared

Non-handicaps	W-R	Per cent	£1 Level Stake	Handicaps	W-R	Per cent	£1 Level Stake
2-y-o	21-50	42.0	- 9.41	2-y-o	2-2	100.0	+ 1.85
3-y-o	15-36	41.7	- 0.96	3-y-o	2-6	33.3	- 1.00
Weight-for-age	37-66	56.1	+ 11.89	All-aged	9-39	23.1	- 17.22
Totals	73-152	48.0	+ 1.52	Totals	13-47	27.7	- 16.37
All favs	86-199	43.2	- 14.85				

TRALEE

Leading Trainers 1988-92

	Total W-R	Non-handicaps 2-y-o	3-y-o+	Handicaps 2-y-o	3-y-o+	Per cent	£1 Level Stake
D K Weld	26-88	4-16	11-29	1-4	10-39	29.5	+ 13.40
J S Bolger	16-94	11-22	2-35	0-3	3-34	17.0	- 39.54
John M Oxx	9-41	1-6	7-22	0-0	1-13	22.0	- 16.25
Liam Browne	8-45	4-19	4-16	0-2	0-8	17.8	- 3.60
C Collins	6-54	0-9	1-21	0-2	5-22	11.1	- 28.25
T G Curtin	5-37	0-0	1-10	0-0	4-27	13.5	+ 19.50
T Stack	5-45	2-9	2-19	0-2	1-15	11.1	- 26.33
P Prendergast	4-33	1-9	1-7	0-2	2-15	12.1	- 10.75
Augustine Leahy	4-38	0-10	0-8	0-2	4-18	10.5	- 18.50
M Kauntze	3-15	1-1	2-5	0-2	0-7	20.0	- 0.20
A Redmond	3-22	0-3	1-3	1-4	1-12	13.6	- 7.70
K Prendergast	3-26	0-2	0-8	1-2	2-14	11.5	+ 1.50
M McDonagh	2-8	0-1	0-0	0-0	2-7	25.0	+ 5.75
M A O'Toole	2-11	0-0	1-4	0-0	1-7	18.2	0.00
Edward Lynam	2-12	0-2	1-6	1-1	0-3	16.7	+ 20.00
J C Hayden	2-13	1-7	0-3	0-1	1-2	15.4	+ 4.50
P Mullins	2-13	0-1	2-5	0-1	0-6	15.4	- 5.00
M Halford	2-14	0-2	1-6	0-0	1-6	14.3	- 2.00
B V Kelly	2-15	0-2	1-5	0-2	1-6	13.3	- 6.50
D Gillespie	2-16	0-3	2-4	0-1	0-8	12.5	- 8.00
E J O'Grady	2-27	0-6	0-6	0-2	2-13	7.4	- 18.50
B Lawlor	1-1	0-0	1-1	0-0	0-0	100.0	+ 4.50

Leading Jockeys

	Total W-R	Per cent	£1 Level Stake	Best Trainer	W-R	Per cent	£1 Level Stake
M J Kinane	25-84	29.8	+ 21.62	D K Weld	20-66	30.3	+ 10.87
J P Murtagh	11-56	19.6	- 0.23	John M Oxx	4-14	28.6	- 6.48
C Roche	11-60	18.3	- 20.36	J S Bolger	8-37	21.6	- 14.36
S Craine	9-71	12.7	- 26.00	T Stack	3-28	10.7	- 13.75
K J Manning	7-44	15.9	- 10.34	T Stack	2-2	100.0	+ 2.43
P Shanahan	6-57	10.5	- 32.10	D K Weld	2-5	40.0	+ 2.40
W J Supple	6-65	9.2	- 40.05	J S Bolger	3-23	13.0	- 13.90
W J O'Connor	5-48	10.4	- 24.90	M Kauntze	2-9	22.2	+ 0.30
R M Burke	4-32	12.5	+ 14.00	P Hughes	1-1	100.0	+ 6.00
P V Gilson	4-36	11.1	- 15.00	C Collins	2-8	25.0	+ 1.50
W J Smith	3-16	18.8	+ 26.50	Edward Lynam	1-2	50.0	+ 19.00
M Fenton	3-43	7.0	- 30.15	Augustine Leahy	2-16	12.5	- 5.25

How the Favourites Fared

Non-handicaps	W-R	Per cent	£1 Level Stake	Handicaps	W-R	Per cent	£1 Level Stake
2-y-o	14-26	53.8	+ 0.14	2-y-o	0-5	-	- 5.00
3-y-o	4-10	40.0	- 1.15	3-y-o	0-1	-	- 1.00
Weight-for-age	19-37	51.4	+ 7.32	All-aged	20-58	34.5	- 6.10
Totals	37-73	50.7	+ 6.31	Totals	20-64	31.3	- 12.10
All favs	57-137	41.6	- 5.79				

TRAMORE

Leading Trainers 1988-92

	Total W-R	Non-handicaps 2-y-o	3-y-o+	Handicaps 2-y-o	3-y-o+	Per cent	£1 Level Stake
K Prendergast	8-33	0-0	5-17	0-0	3-16	24.2	- 1.75
P Mullins	6-23	0-0	4-12	0-0	2-11	26.1	+ 4.78
T Stack	4-8	0-0	3-5	0-0	1-3	50.0	+ 10.50
C Collins	4-12	0-0	3-10	0-0	1-2	33.3	- 0.88
W P Mullins	3-11	0-0	1-6	0-0	2-5	27.3	+ 4.00
M A McCullagh	2-3	0-0	0-1	0-0	2-2	66.7	+ 4.50
W P Browne	2-3	0-0	2-3	0-0	0-0	66.7	+ 6.67
John M Oxx	2-4	0-0	2-3	0-0	0-1	50.0	+ 0.30
Mrs Crowley-O'Brien	2-5	0-0	0-2	0-0	2-3	40.0	- 0.52
P Hughes	2-8	0-0	0-3	0-0	2-5	25.0	+ 15.00
M J Grassick	2-10	0-0	1-2	0-0	1-8	20.0	+ 3.50
Augustine Leahy	2-14	0-0	1-5	0-0	1-9	14.3	+ 7.00
A Redmond	2-18	0-0	0-9	0-0	2-9	11.1	- 7.00
D McDonogh	1-1	0-0	0-0	0-0	1-1	100.0	+ 10.00
A L T Moore	1-1	0-0	1-1	0-0	0-0	100.0	+ 1.25
R Donoghue	1-1	0-0	1-1	0-0	0-0	100.0	+ 3.50
D J McGrath	1-1	0-0	1-1	0-0	0-0	100.0	+ 1.00
J S Bolger	1-2	0-0	0-1	0-0	1-1	50.0	+ 0.10
F Dunne	1-2	0-0	0-1	0-0	1-1	50.0	+ 4.00
M Kauntze	1-2	0-0	1-2	0-0	0-0	50.0	+ 4.00
Mrs John Harrington	1-2	0-0	1-1	0-0	0-1	50.0	+ 7.00
Pat O'Leary	1-2	0-0	1-2	0-0	0-0	50.0	+ 6.00

Leading Jockeys

	Total W-R	Per cent	£1 Level Stake	Best Trainer	W-R	Per cent	£1 Level Stake
N G McCullagh	9-46	19.6	+ 1.92	P Mullins	2-6	33.3	+ 1.17
W J O'Connor	7-25	28.0	+ 9.50	C Collins	1-1	100.0	+ 3.00
R Hughes	6-29	20.7	+ 3.15	W P Browne	2-2	100.0	+ 7.67
J P Murtagh	5-35	14.3	- 4.70	John M Oxx	2-3	66.7	+ 1.30
S Craine	4-13	30.8	+ 5.75	T Stack	3-5	60.0	+ 10.25
P Shanahan	3-10	30.0	- 3.12	C Collins	2-5	40.0	- 0.50
D G O'Shea	3-10	30.0	+ 15.00	W P Mullins	1-1	100.0	+ 4.00
D V Smith	3-22	13.6	+ 20.10	E P Harty	1-1	100.0	+ 33.00
D Duggan	3-23	13.0	- 7.50	R Donoghue	1-1	100.0	+ 3.50
T J O'Sullivan	3-24	12.5	+ 1.50	Augustine Leahy	1-3	33.3	+ 3.00
E A Leonard	3-28	10.7	- 19.25	K Prendergast	3-11	27.3	- 2.25
R Griffiths	2-4	50.0	+ 1.00	K Prendergast	2-4	50.0	+ 1.00

How the Favourites Fared

Non-handicaps	W-R	Per cent	£1 Level Stake	Handicaps	W-R	Per cent	£1 Level Stake
2-y-o	0-0	-	0.00	2-y-o	0-0	-	0.00
3-y-o	2-7	28.6	- 2.00	3-y-o	2-2	100.0	+ 3.00
Weight-for-age	20-36	55.6	+ 7.88	All-aged	12-35	34.3	- 4.82
Totals	22-43	51.2	+ 5.88	Totals	14-37	37.8	- 1.82
All favs	36-80	45.0	+ 4.06				

WEXFORD

Leading Trainers 1988-92

	Total W-R	Non-handicaps 2-y-o	3-y-o+	Handicaps 2-y-o	3-y-o+	Per cent	£1 Level Stake
John M Oxx	13-28	0-0	11-23	0-0	2-5	46.4	+ 11.38
T G Curtin	5-11	0-0	3-4	0-0	2-7	45.5	+ 18.75
P Mullins	5-22	0-0	2-13	0-0	3-9	22.7	+ 6.08
P J Flynn	4-17	0-0	0-6	0-0	4-11	23.5	+ 10.03
K Prendergast	4-19	0-0	3-13	0-0	1-6	21.1	+ 1.67
M J Grassick	3-10	0-0	2-6	0-0	1-4	30.0	+ 4.00
J S Bolger	3-35	0-0	2-21	0-0	1-14	8.6	- 15.50
J J McLoughlin	2-8	0-0	0-4	0-0	2-4	25.0	+ 11.50
C Collins	2-10	0-0	2-6	0-0	0-4	20.0	+ 7.00
D K Weld	2-16	0-0	1-13	0-0	1-3	12.5	- 5.00
J C Shearman	1-1	0-0	1-1	0-0	0-0	100.0	+ 5.00
J E Kiely	1-2	0-0	0-0	0-0	1-2	50.0	+ 1.50
J Morrison	1-2	0-0	0-0	0-0	1-2	50.0	+ 7.00
Mrs Crowley-O'Brien	1-2	0-0	1-1	0-0	0-1	50.0	+ 5.00
F Flood	1-3	0-0	1-3	0-0	0-0	33.3	+ 2.50
H De Bromhead	1-4	0-0	1-4	0-0	0-0	25.0	- 2.00
W M Roper	1-4	0-0	0-2	0-0	1-2	25.0	+ 11.00
D T Hughes	1-6	0-0	1-3	0-0	0-3	16.7	- 1.50
J M Canty	1-6	0-0	1-1	0-0	0-5	16.7	- 4.56
Noel Meade	1-7	0-0	0-4	0-0	1-3	14.3	- 2.67
J C Hayden	1-7	0-0	1-3	0-0	0-4	14.3	+ 2.00
R Lister	1-7	0-0	1-3	0-0	0-4	14.3	0.00

Leading Jockeys

	Total W-R	Per cent	£1 Level Stake	Best Trainer	W-R	Per cent	£1 Level Stake
J P Murtagh	11-28	39.3	+ 9.63	John M Oxx	8-13	61.5	+ 6.13
C Roche	7-32	21.9	- 15.08	J S Bolger	2-19	10.5	- 14.50
M J Kinane	5-22	22.7	+ 1.25	T G Curtin	2-4	50.0	+ 7.00
S Craine	4-22	18.2	- 7.53	P Mullins	2-3	66.7	+ 8.50
J F Egan	4-24	16.7	+ 15.00	P J Flynn	2-10	20.0	+ 9.00
P V Gilson	3-20	15.0	+ 12.00	C Collins	2-6	33.3	+ 11.00
R Hughes	3-22	13.6	- 9.67	Noel Meade	1-2	50.0	+ 2.33
B P Harding	2-3	66.7	+ 5.50	F Flood	1-1	100.0	+ 4.50
D G O'Shea	2-7	28.6	+ 1.25	John M Oxx	2-2	100.0	+ 6.25
J R Barry	2-8	25.0	+ 5.33	P Mullins	2-6	33.3	+ 7.33
K J Manning	2-16	12.5	- 5.50	M J Grassick	2-2	100.0	+ 8.50
Mr J Queally	1-1	100.0	+ 1.00	H De Bromhead	1-1	100.0	+ 1.00

How the Favourites Fared

Non-handicaps	W-R	Per cent	£1 Level Stake	Handicaps	W-R	Per cent	£1 Level Stake
2-y-o	0-0	-	0.00	2-y-o	0-0	-	0.00
3-y-o	5-16	31.3	- 4.46	3-y-o	2-2	100.0	+ 2.25
Weight-for-age	12-23	52.2	- 0.13	All-aged	8-22	36.4	+ 1.86
Totals	17-39	43.6	- 4.59	Totals	10-24	41.7	+ 4.11
All favs	27-63	42.9	- 0.48				

TRAINERS' FAVOURITES AT THE CURRAGH 1988-92

	Total W-R	Non-handicaps 2-y-o	3-y-o+	Handicaps 2-y-o	3-y-o+	Per cent	£1 Level Stake
M V O'Brien	44-93	23-45	19-42	0-0	2-6	47.3	+ 12.71
J S Bolger	40-100	24-45	11-29	1-5	4-21	40.0	- 5.49
D K Weld	29-112	8-28	14-51	1-2	6-31	25.9	- 23.20
John M Oxx	27-85	8-22	7-30	2-2	10-31	31.8	+ 7.59
K Prendergast	12-31	1-7	4-10	2-4	5-10	38.7	+ 12.13
C Collins	7-19	1-2	2-5	1-1	3-11	36.8	+ 5.70
M Kauntze	4-14	1-2	3-9	0-1	0-2	28.6	- 6.66
T Stack	4-21	1-6	2-9	0-0	1-6	19.0	- 9.95
P J Flynn	3-4	0-0	0-0	0-0	3-4	75.0	+ 15.50
H R A Cecil (Eng)	3-8	0-0	3-8	0-0	0-0	37.5	- 4.30
P F I Cole (Eng)	3-8	0-1	3-7	0-0	0-0	37.5	- 0.37
J M Canty	2-2	0-0	0-0	0-0	2-2	100.0	+ 9.50
P T Walwyn (Eng)	2-2	0-0	2-2	0-0	0-0	100.0	+ 2.67
C E Brittain (Eng)	2-4	1-2	1-2	0-0	0-0	50.0	- 0.17
L Cumani (Eng)	2-4	0-0	2-4	0-0	0-0	50.0	+ 0.43
M J Grassick	2-7	1-3	1-1	0-1	0-2	28.6	- 1.50
P Prendergast	2-13	0-2	1-4	1-2	0-5	15.4	- 5.10
Capt D G Swan	1-1	0-0	1-1	0-0	0-0	100.0	+ 3.50
T G Curtin	1-1	0-0	1-1	0-0	0-0	100.0	+ 2.00
P J Deegan	1-1	0-0	0-0	0-0	1-1	100.0	+ 3.00
R Hannon (Eng)	1-1	0-0	1-1	0-0	0-0	100.0	+ 1.25
I A Balding (Eng)	1-1	1-1	0-0	0-0	0-0	100.0	+ 1.75
W R Hern (Eng)	1-1	0-0	1-1	0-0	0-0	100.0	+ 1.50
H T Jones (Eng)	1-1	0-0	1-1	0-0	0-0	100.0	+ 1.10

TRAINERS' FAVOURITES AT LEOPARDSTOWN 1988-92

	Total W-R	Non-handicaps 2-y-o	3-y-o+	Handicaps 2-y-o	3-y-o+	Per cent	£1 Level Stake
D K Weld	51-131	11-23	34-70	0-0	6-38	38.9	- 2.67
J S Bolger	40-92	16-35	14-30	3-5	7-22	43.5	+ 6.64
John M Oxx	25-62	8-15	12-26	0-0	5-21	40.3	+ 10.87
M V O'Brien	17-38	7-10	9-26	0-0	1-2	44.7	- 1.52
K Prendergast	12-30	3-4	5-10	1-2	3-14	40.0	+ 6.86
M Kauntze	4-15	1-4	2-6	0-0	1-5	26.7	- 1.75
P Mullins	3-7	0-0	3-4	0-0	0-3	42.9	+ 5.63
H R A Cecil (Eng)	2-2	0-0	2-2	0-0	0-0	100.0	+ 0.75
Lord Huntingdon	2-2	1-1	1-1	0-0	0-0	100.0	+ 1.80
Noel Meade	2-3	0-0	1-1	0-0	1-2	66.7	+ 2.03
B W Hills (Eng)	2-3	0-0	2-3	0-0	0-0	66.7	+ 3.25
M A O'Toole	2-7	0-1	1-3	1-1	0-2	28.6	- 1.50
C Collins	2-9	2-3	0-4	0-1	0-1	22.2	- 3.25
T Stack	2-9	0-0	1-4	0-2	1-3	22.2	+ 0.25
P Prendergast	1-1	0-0	0-0	0-0	1-1	100.0	+ 3.50
J C Hayden	1-1	1-1	0-0	0-0	0-0	100.0	+ 3.00
M J Grassick	1-1	1-1	0-0	0-0	0-0	100.0	+ 0.50
P F I Cole (Eng)	1-1	0-0	1-1	0-0	0-0	100.0	+ 3.00
J Berry (Eng)	1-1	1-1	0-0	0-0	0-0	100.0	+ 0.53
B V Kelly	1-2	0-0	1-1	0-0	0-1	50.0	+ 1.25
D T Hughes	1-2	0-0	0-0	0-0	1-2	50.0	+ 1.25
R Hannon (Eng)	1-2	1-2	0-0	0-0	0-0	50.0	+ 1.00
J E Hammond (Fra)	1-2	0-0	1-2	0-0	0-0	50.0	- 0.33
T F Lacy	1-3	0-0	0-0	0-0	1-3	33.3	+ 1.50

TOP PERCENTAGE COURSES FOR FAVOURITES 1988-92

	W-R	Per cent	£1 Level Stake		W-R	Per cent	£1 Level Stake
Clonmel	35-67	52.2	+ 12.48	Down Royal	40-97	41.2	- 10.02
Killarney	52-100	52.0	+ 10.53	Leopardstown	185-459	40.3	- 10.52
Punchestown	13-26	50.0	+ 15.11	Laytown	10-25	40.0	- 0.40
Tramore	36-80	45.0	+ 4.06	Ballinrobe	29-73	39.7	+ 7.67
Mallow	39-88	44.3	- 4.01	Sligo	33-87	37.9	- 0.79
Bellewstown	25-57	43.9	+ 1.28	Galway	63-171	36.8	- 10.02
Tipperary	86-199	43.2	- 14.85	Listowel	28-76	36.8	+ 2.32
Gowran	67-156	42.9	+ 11.28	Limerick	26-74	35.1	- 18.60
Wexford	27-63	42.9	- 0.48	The Curragh	212-613	34.6	- 44.69
Fairyhouse	36-85	42.4	+ 3.91	Navan	36-109	33.0	- 23.62
Dundalk	59-141	41.8	- 6.40	Roscommon	33-111	29.7	- 35.84
Tralee	57-137	41.6	- 5.79	Downpatrick	11-38	28.9	- 12.64
Naas	73-177	41.2	+ 25.27	Thurles	8-28	28.6	- 8.56

FAVOURITES' PERFORMANCE BY TYPE OF RACE 1988-92

Non-h'caps	W-R	Per cent	£1 Level Stake	Handicaps	W-R	Per cent	£1 Level Stake
2-y-o	374-816	45.8	- 11.61	2-y-o	33-86	38.4	+ 19.79
3-y-o	230-546	42.1	- 19.78	3-y-o	53-151	35.1	+ 0.80
Weight/age	437-1023	42.7	- 35.89	All-aged	307-1033	29.7	- 99.90
Totals	1041-2385	43.6	- 67.28	Totals	393-1270	30.9	- 79.31
All Favs	1434-3655	39.2	-146.59				

When there is more than one favourite in a race then the £1 stake has been equally divided on each one. Only one favourite is counted for each race.

IRISH TRAINER SUMMARIES

WINNING FLAT TRAINERS IN IRELAND 1992

	Total W-R	2-y-o	3-y-o	4-y-o+	Per cent	£1 Level Stake
J S Bolger	119-671	48-192	58-349	13-130	17.7	-160.84
D K Weld	106-597	21-135	56-318	29-144	17.8	-179.63
John M Oxx	85-356	20-84	63-241	2-31	23.9	- 36.00
K Prendergast	30-373	9-95	19-225	2-53	8.0	-196.85
P J Flynn	22-181	2-39	9-58	11-84	12.2	- 71.72
T Stack	20-199	3-58	12-85	5-56	10.i	- 78.70
M V O'Brien	19-53	6-17	13-36	0-0	35.8	+ 1.32
Noel Meade	18-170	4-43	4-51	10-76	10.6	- 61.54
M Kauntze	16-142	7-50	8-77	1-15	11.3	- 55.33
C Collins	16-167	6-40	8-89	2-38	9.6	- 78.45
J J McLoughlin	15-162	0-0	9-120	6-42	9.3	- 75.18
M J Grassick	14-134	2-37	12-76	0-21	10.4	- 31.20
D Gillespie	14-199	3-47	7-120	4-32	7.0	-129.50
P Prendergast	11-82	5-17	6-43	0-22	13.4	- 26.37
F Dunne	10-138	0-26	4-59	6-53	7.2	- 53.92
M A O'Toole	9-107	0-5	3-54	6-48	8.4	- 63.93
Augustine Leahy	8-91	1-29	6-49	1-13	8.8	- 44.67
Liam Browne	8-130	4-47	4-65	0-18	6.2	- 83.04
J Burns	7-56	3-33	2-10	2-13	12.5	- 4.25
Mrs Crowley-O'Brien	7-62	1-18	6-36	0-8	11.3	- 20.25
J G Coogan	7-75	5-46	1-14	1-15	9.3	- 41.50
V Bowens	7-85	0-21	4-26	3-38	8.2	- 16.75
W P Mullins	7-99	1-22	4-42	2-35	7.1	- 56.75
Daniel J Murphy	6-79	1-27	4-39	1-13	7.6	- 14.50
D Hanley	5-35	0-1	5-34	0-0	14.3	- 7.90
J C Hayden	5-45	1-18	4-25	0-2	11.1	- 15.75
T G Curtin	5-47	0-0	2-30	3-17	10.6	- 2.00
Edward Lynam	5-92	2-37	2-43	1-12	5.4	- 35.50
M Halford	5-103	1-18	1-50	3-35	4.9	- 79.17
E J O'Grady	5-108	3-20	1-83	1-5	4.6	- 86.10
C E Brittain (Eng)	4-9	2-3	1-4	1-2	44.4	+ 4.83
J E Mulhern	4-76	0-6	1-44	3-26	5.3	- 35.00
J C Harley	4-79	2-23	1-31	1-25	5.1	- 48.75
B V Kelly	4-98	1-28	2-20	1-50	4.1	- 73.67
M A McCullagh	3-11	0-0	3-11	0-0	27.3	+ 13.50
H De Bromhead	3-17	0-0	3-11	0-6	17.6	+ 14.00
W P Browne	3-18	0-5	0-0	3-13	16.7	- 6.00
P F O'Donnell	3-25	0-0	0-16	3-9	12.0	- 3.00
Pat O'Leary	3-26	0-1	3-22	0-3	11.5	- 15.10
D P Kelly	3-35	1-15	0-9	2-11	8.6	+ 10.00
D T Hughes	3-40	0-3	1-13	2-24	7.5	- 11.00
P Martin	3-45	0-0	1-21	2-24	6.7	- 12.50
T M Walsh	3-45	1-4	1-29	1-12	6.7	- 16.00
Neil S McGrath	3-51	1-16	2-34	0-1	5.9	- 14.00
P Mullins	3-56	1-22	2-20	0-14	5.4	+ 6.00
T F Lacy	3-87	0-19	1-41	2-27	3.4	- 75.25
P Chapple-Hyam (Eng)	2-6	0-3	2-3	0-0	33.3	+ 0.23
C P Magnier	2-17	0-0	2-15	0-2	11.8	- 3.00
J P Kavanagh	2-22	0-3	0-9	2-10	9.1	- 14.00
Adrian Taylor	2-22	0-0	1-9	1-13	9.1	+ 14.00
K F O'Sullivan	2-31	0-7	2-24	0-0	6.5	- 20.67
Arthur Bunyan	2-32	0-3	1-14	1-15	6.3	- 21.33
H McMahon	2-35	0-7	2-28	0-0	5.7	- 23.50
N Callaghan (Eng)	1-1	0-0	1-1	0-0	100.0	+ 6.00

	Total W–R	2-y-o	3-y-o	4-y-o+	Per cent	£1 Level Stake
G Wragg (Eng)	1–1	0–0	1–1	0–0	100.0	+ 0.80
J L Dunlop (Eng)	1–2	0–0	1–1	0–1	50.0	+ 8.00
W R Hern (Eng)	1–2	0–0	0–0	1–2	50.0	+ 0.50
J Berry (Eng)	1–3	1–2	0–0	0–1	33.3	− 1.47
R Hannon (Eng)	1–4	1–2	0–2	0–0	25.0	+ 7.00
J H M Gosden (Eng)	1–4	0–0	0–1	1–3	25.0	− 0.25
F Towey	1–4	0–0	0–0	1–4	25.0	+ 7.00
J Queally	1–4	0–0	0–0	1–4	25.0	+ 3.00
M McDonagh	1–5	0–2	0–0	1–3	20.0	+ 0.50
M R Stoute (Eng)	1–5	0–0	0–3	1–2	20.0	− 1.50
A Geraghty	1–6	0–0	1–3	0–3	16.7	+ 7.00
M Quaid	1–6	0–0	0–1	1–5	16.7	+ 20.00
J F C Maxwell	1–6	0–0	0–1	1–5	16.7	− 5.00
B W Hills (Eng)	1–7	0–1	0–1	1–5	14.3	− 3.00
R O'Donovan	1–7	0–0	1–7	0–0	14.3	+ 1.00
F W Pennicott	1–7	0–0	0–0	1–7	14.3	+ 1.00
Countess Schulenburg	1–7	0–0	1–3	0–4	14.3	+ 8.00
Robert Norris	1–7	0–1	1–6	0–0	14.3	+ 10.00
Mrs John Harrington	1–8	0–0	1–7	0–1	12.5	+ 1.00
J Nicholson	1–8	1–4	0–0	0–4	12.5	− 4.00
John J Walsh	1–10	0–0	0–0	1–10	10.0	− 1.00
J Morrison	1–11	0–1	0–5	1–5	9.1	− 2.00
D J McGrath	1–11	0–0	0–0	1–11	9.1	− 5.00
J P Byrne	1–12	0–5	1–3	0–4	8.3	+ 1.00
F Flood	1–12	0–7	0–0	1–5	8.3	− 5.00
P Phelan	1–12	0–0	0–5	1–7	8.3	− 1.00
E P Mitchell	1–12	0–0	0–6	1–6	8.3	+ 14.00
Wilbert Tolerton	1–13	0–0	0–0	1–13	7.7	+ 8.00
P Hughes	1–15	0–3	0–1	1–11	6.7	− 11.75
A L T Moore	1–18	0–0	0–4	1–14	5.6	− 9.00
C Cassidy	1–18	0–0	1–13	0–5	5.6	− 9.00
T G McCourt	1–19	0–0	1–12	0–7	5.3	− 8.00
J F Bailey Jnr	1–20	0–4	0–9	1–7	5.0	+ 1.00
G T Hourigan	1–21	0–8	1–11	0–2	4.8	− 6.00
Peter Casey	1–25	0–0	0–10	1–15	4.0	− 18.00
D McDonogh	1–26	0–0	0–10	1–16	3.8	− 20.50
Patrick Woods	1–26	0–6	0–13	1–7	3.8	+ 25.00
Oliver Finnegan	1–29	0–0	1–10	0–19	3.4	− 8.00
W M Roper	1–31	0–0	1–29	0–2	3.2	− 26.00
N O'Callaghan	1–31	0–12	1–13	0–6	3.2	− 18.00
G M Connolly	1–36	0–4	1–21	0–11	2.8	− 28.00
V Kennedy	1–37	0–0	0–21	1–16	2.7	− 28.00
O Weldon	1–47	0–6	0–18	1–23	2.1	− 38.50
J M Canty	1–58	0–18	0–20	1–20	1.7	− 56.56
J T Gorman	1–72	0–22	1–24	0–26	1.4	− 51.00

WINNING FLAT JOCKEYS IN IRELAND 1992

	1st	2nd	3rd	Unpl	Total Mts	Per cent	£1 Level Stake
M J Kinane	100	82	45	200	427	23.4	- 74.18
C Roche	93	74	57	162	386	24.1	- 29.90
J P Murtagh	50	33	33	112	228	21.9	+ 49.92
R Hughes	35	36	40	238	349	10.0	-170.16
D G O'Shea	32	18	20	187	257	12.5	- 30.03
S Craine	29	32	43	241	345	8.4	-200.75
P Shanahan	27	25	21	202	275	9.8	-134.80
P V Gilson	24	24	29	203	280	8.6	-144.69
R Griffiths	22	27	35	157	241	9.1	-115.93
W J O'Connor	21	19	30	188	258	8.1	-130.45
M Fenton	19	14	25	168	226	8.4	-113.59
K J Manning	19	30	21	170	240	7.9	-131.39
W J Supple	19	23	23	207	272	7.0	-114.75
J J Behan	16	18	5	124	163	9.8	- 15.64
W J Smith	16	16	13	137	182	8.8	- 58.05
N G McCullagh	14	22	29	214	279	5.0	-200.18
D Hogan	12	11	21	98	142	8.5	- 80.88
J A Heffernan	11	9	10	92	122	9.0	- 43.00
J F Egan	10	5	8	90	113	8.8	- 45.75
L Piggott	8	3	6	19	36	22.2	- 15.89
J R Barry	7	6	2	25	40	17.5	- 9.95
B J Walsh	7	8	13	44	72	9.7	- 31.25
P P Murphy	7	9	7	103	126	5.6	- 48.50
B Coogan	6	6	7	44	63	9.5	- 35.50
P Carberry	6	5	7	58	76	7.9	- 30.15
Joanna Morgan	6	5	2	98	111	5.4	- 54.50
D Marnane	5	0	1	6	12	41.7	+ 11.60
S R Murphy	5	2	3	4	14	35.7	+ 3.90
M Roberts	5	0	3	7	15	33.3	+ 24.10
R V Skelly	5	8	8	70	91	5.5	- 51.00
R M Burke	5	19	18	163	205	2.4	-165.17
S Cauthen	4	0	1	4	9	44.4	+ 4.25
J Reid	4	4	3	13	24	16.7	- 1.40
C Everard	4	8	6	54	72	5.6	- 44.25
B Bowens	4	2	4	69	79	5.1	- 30.00
J D Eddery	4	8	9	79	100	4.0	- 83.25
Miss C Hutchinson	3	0	0	5	8	37.5	+ 0.78
W R Swinburn	3	2	2	9	16	18.8	- 6.82
T P Treacy	3	3	2	27	35	8.6	- 13.00
D J O'Donohoe	3	4	2	42	51	5.9	- 29.90
D V Smith	3	1	2	79	85	3.5	- 46.00
Miss A Marshall	2	1	0	3	6	33.3	+ 11.00
K Whelan	2	0	0	4	6	33.3	+ 10.00
W Carson	2	1	1	3	7	28.6	- 2.00
T J Daly	2	2	3	14	21	9.5	- 1.00
N Byrne	2	4	6	81	93	2.2	- 81.00
G Starkey	1	0	0	0	1	100.0	+ 7.00
L Dettori	1	0	0	0	1	100.0	+ 10.00
J Carroll	1	0	0	0	1	100.0	+ 0.53
John O'Connor	1	0	0	0	1	100.0	+ 1.25
Miss J Lewis	1	0	0	0	1	100.0	+ 2.00
C Asmussen	1	0	0	1	2	50.0	+ 11.00
F Berry	1	1	0	0	2	50.0	- 1.00
D J Walsh	1	0	0	1	2	50.0	+ 9.00

	1st	2nd	3rd	Unpl	Total Mts	Per cent	£1 Level Stake
J Walsh	1	0	0	1	2	50.0	+ 5.00
John Tarrant	1	0	0	1	2	50.0	+ 7.00
G Duffield	1	0	0	2	3	33.3	− 1.27
J Queally	1	1	0	1	3	33.3	+ 4.00
D M McCullagh	1	0	0	3	4	25.0	− 1.50
D O'Donoghue	1	0	1	2	4	25.0	+ 7.00
W P Mullins	1	0	1	2	4	25.0	+ 7.00
E Norris	1	0	0	3	4	25.0	− 1.25
F J Flood	1	1	0	3	5	20.0	+ 2.00
Miss S Kauntze	1	2	0	2	5	20.0	0.00
J A Hayes	1	0	0	4	5	20.0	− 3.33
Miss A Gilsenan	1	0	1	3	5	20.0	+ 10.00
B P Gowran	1	0	1	4	6	16.7	+ 9.00
K D Maher	1	0	0	6	7	14.3	+ 10.00
A J Martin	1	0	1	5	7	14.3	+ 3.00
M Duffy	1	1	0	6	8	12.5	− 6.27
A J Roche	1	1	1	6	9	11.1	+ 6.00
P Fenton	1	4	2	3	10	10.0	− 4.50
B A Hunter	1	0	1	9	11	9.1	+ 1.00
T E Durcan	1	1	0	9	11	9.1	− 6.50
J J Mullins	1	0	0	15	16	6.3	− 13.37
A P McCoy	1	2	2	19	24	4.2	− 3.00
J J Stack	1	2	1	23	27	3.7	− 24.50
M C G Laurence	1	1	5	22	29	3.4	− 20.00
L O'Shea	1	5	2	26	34	2.9	− 21.00
D Duggan	1	2	3	29	35	2.9	− 30.50
M F Ryan	1	0	3	39	43	2.3	− 38.50
R Fitzpatrick	1	1	4	50	56	1.8	− 35.00
E A Leonard	1	4	4	87	96	1.0	− 70.00

LEADING TRAINERS' AND OWNERS' PRIZE MONEY 1992

	Races Won	Value £		Races Won	Value £
J S Bolger	119	973,704	Mrs V Kraft Payson	14	431,344
D K Weld	106	587,177	H H Aga Khan	52	244,741
John M Oxx	85	401,026	Sheikh Mohammed	28	168,306
C E Brittain (Eng)	4	331,350	Mrs M V O'Brien	8	143,512
M V O'Brien	19	228,294	Moyglare Stud Farms	21	143,309
P Chapple-Hyam (Eng)	2	208,300	R E Sangster	6	139,597
G Wragg (Eng)	1	121,000	E J Loder	1	121,000
K Prendergast	30	118,283	W J Gredley	1	121,000
P J Flynn	22	94,311	Michael W J Smurfit	18	99,847
C Collins	16	92,668	Circlechart Ltd	1	98,000
R Hannon (Eng)	1	87,250	D H W Dobson	17	93,493
J H M Gosden (Eng)	1	84,600	Maktoum Al Maktoum	15	92,171
T Stack	20	79,885	Mrs V S Grant	1	87,250
Noel Meade	18	68,320	Sidney H Craig	1	86,300
M Kauntze	16	59,836	Mohamed Obaida	1	86,100
J J McLoughlin	15	46,768	A J O'Reilly	14	85,452
M J Grassick	14	46,652	Sheikh Ahmed Al Maktoum	1	84,600
M R Stoute (Eng)	1	43,125	Allen E Paulson	14	83,735
D Gillespie	14	39,011	Hamdan Al Maktoum	12	67,679
J E Mulhern	4	34,660	John J McLoughlin	15	46,768

LEADING IRISH TRAINERS FIRST TIME OUT 1988-92

	Total W-R	2-y-o	3-y-o	4-y-o+	Per cent	£1 Level Stake
J S Bolger	117-616	59-238	32-239	26-139	19.0	-158.01
D K Weld	104-718	37-286	49-294	18-138	14.5	-282.18
John M Oxx	75-497	31-190	41-273	3-34	15.1	-131.34
M V O'Brien	61-202	29-93	29-98	3-11	30.2	- 10.89
T Stack	32-239	11-94	11-103	10-42	13.4	- 32.79
K Prendergast	25-370	10-160	11-165	4-45	6.8	-175.94
M Kauntze	21-198	14-89	5-87	2-22	10.6	- 76.65
C Collins	18-278	9-103	7-108	2-67	6.5	-123.08
Liam Browne	11-205	5-84	4-90	2-31	5.4	-146.50
P J Flynn	9-142	0-31	2-44	7-67	6.3	- 86.77
M J Grassick	8-178	3-49	5-79	0-50	4.5	-127.25
T G Curtin	7-68	1-3	3-24	3-41	10.3	- 15.00
F Flood	5-26	1-4	0-3	4-19	19.2	+ 13.25
Daniel J Murphy	5-72	2-29	2-26	1-17	6.9	- 23.00
F Dunne	5-80	1-22	1-37	3-21	6.3	- 19.00
B V Kelly	5-86	1-31	3-34	1-21	5.8	- 31.00
P Mullins	5-129	0-20	1-32	4-77	3.9	- 88.87
Noel Meade	5-218	1-73	3-83	1-62	2.3	-182.75

LEADING IRISH TRAINERS BY MONTH 1988-92

March/April

	Total W-R	2-y-o	3-y-o	4-y-o+	Per cent	£1 Level Stake
J S Bolger	69-276	16-30	36-174	17-72	25.0	+ 56.59
D K Weld	45-334	2-19	40-237	3-78	13.5	- 180.04
John M Oxx	23-165	0-1	21-143	2-21	13.9	- 51.29
K Prendergast	20-238	5-32	14-157	1-49	8.4	- 110.94
T Stack	18-125	0-3	9-83	9-39	14.4	- 9.29
M V O'Brien	17-44	0-0	16-40	1-4	38.6	+ 5.84
C Collins	12-182	3-22	7-116	2-44	6.6	- 79.00
M Kauntze	10-93	0-3	7-70	3-20	10.8	- 2.25
Noel Meade	10-160	1-17	9-104	0-39	6.3	- 102.00
M J Grassick	7-99	2-4	5-74	0-21	7.1	- 76.33
T F Lacy	6-90	1-18	3-40	2-32	6.7	- 56.65
E J O'Grady	6-101	0-2	6-69	0-30	5.9	- 86.35
Liam Browne	5-112	3-13	2-72	0-27	4.5	- 75.00

May

	Total W-R	2-y-o	3-y-o	4-y-o+	Per cent	£1 Level Stake
D K Weld	76-365	7-54	51-219	18-92	20.8	- 41.92
J S Bolger	55-338	15-69	21-157	19-112	16.3	- 98.19
John M Oxx	38-196	1-11	33-163	4-22	19.4	- 43.53
T Stack	21-146	3-15	11-95	7-36	14.4	- 38.17
M Kauntze	21-147	5-32	14-90	2-25	14.3	- 41.79
K Prendergast	21-269	6-50	11-176	4-43	7.8	- 152.17
C Collins	20-169	7-31	9-90	4-48	11.8	- 55.88
M V O'Brien	19-74	0-1	17-63	2-10	25.7	- 9.94
Liam Browne	15-120	2-17	10-76	3-27	12.5	- 54.00
J J McLoughlin	13-84	5-14	6-44	2-26	15.5	+ 19.08
M A O'Toole	12-96	0-18	6-48	6-30	12.5	+ 6.23
M J Grassick	11-93	0-6	7-62	4-25	11.8	- 22.20
P J Flynn	10-94	0-1	3-34	7-59	10.6	- 35.73
Noel Meade	10-137	2-23	5-74	3-40	7.3	- 68.62
T G Curtin	6-44	0-1	3-21	3-22	13.6	+ 12.00
F Dunne	6-71	0-3	2-46	4-22	8.5	- 12.50

June

	Total W-R	2-y-o	3-y-o	4-y-o+	Per cent	£1 Level Stake
D K Weld	64-366	13-80	37-196	14-90	17.5	- 136.27
J S Bolger	56-342	23-75	25-170	8-97	16.4	- 81.21
John M Oxx	51-238	2-23	46-186	3-29	21.4	- 19.05
K Prendergast	50-315	10-62	32-199	8-54	15.9	- 34.82
M V O'Brien	22-60	5-8	16-51	1-1	36.7	+ 6.97
C Collins	21-144	7-25	9-72	5-47	14.6	- 18.37
Noel Meade	19-142	1-26	11-75	7-41	13.4	- 22.50
T Stack	14-118	3-21	10-71	1-26	11.9	- 38.47
Liam Browne	14-145	7-41	7-85	0-19	9.7	- 51.79
J J McLoughlin	12-74	1-11	8-42	3-21	16.2	- 15.10
M J Grassick	10-95	0-9	8-54	2-32	10.5	- 43.57
M Kauntze	10-131	3-29	6-77	1-25	7.6	- 76.08
P Mullins	9-97	0-9	1-28	8-60	9.3	- 27.62
D Gillespie	7-52	0-10	4-32	3-10	13.5	- 13.10
Edward Lynam	7-59	1-9	4-39	2-11	11.9	- 4.50
P J Flynn	7-68	0-7	1-28	6-33	10.3	- 39.82
P Prendergast	6-39	2-10	1-20	3-9	15.4	+ 2.45
M Halford	6-64	1-7	2-33	3-24	9.4	- 16.00
E J O'Grady	6-86	1-16	1-44	4-26	7.0	- 46.50
T G Curtin	5-43	0-0	3-23	2-20	11.6	- 13.25
F Dunne	5-73	0-13	2-36	3-24	6.8	- 20.50

July

	Total W-R	2-y-o	3-y-o	4-y-o+	Per cent	£1 Level Stake
J S Bolger	105-451	31-111	42-210	32-130	23.3	- 13.77
D K Weld	95-454	25-118	43-228	27-108	20.9	- 90.94
John M Oxx	60-274	11-44	44-203	5-27	21.9	- 48.40
K Prendergast	37-360	8-95	22-204	7-61	10.3	- 141.60
C Collins	17-147	5-29	8-73	4-45	11.6	- 33.62
M Kauntze	17-150	7-45	7-80	3-25	11.3	- 75.53
T Stack	16-126	5-30	7-67	4-29	12.7	- 59.07
Noel Meade	16-150	6-29	6-71	4-50	10.7	- 81.10
M V O'Brien	14-50	4-9	10-36	0-5	28.0	- 19.92
M A O'Toole	13-109	2-19	6-63	5-27	11.9	- 30.83
M J Grassick	12-93	2-12	9-53	1-28	12.9	- 21.60
P Mullins	11-100	2-23	4-28	5-49	11.0	+ 12.90
Liam Browne	10-143	7-57	2-70	1-16	7.0	- 67.02
J J McLoughlin	9-114	1-26	8-55	0-33	7.9	- 29.00
T G Curtin	8-55	0-1	3-21	5-33	14.5	+ 2.05
P Prendergast	8-57	2-17	5-26	1-14	14.0	- 21.50
D Gillespie	8-61	1-15	7-33	0-13	13.1	- 22.37
P J Flynn	8-64	0-6	2-15	6-43	12.5	- 13.50
F Dunne	8-101	0-21	3-45	5-35	7.9	- 31.67
Augustine Leahy	6-76	0-16	3-38	3-22	7.9	- 47.50
M Cunningham	5-72	1-7	1-23	3-42	6.9	- 31.67

August

	Total W-R	2-y-o	3-y-o	4-y-o+	Per cent	£1 Level Stake
D K Weld	116-548	35-162	59-279	22-107	21.2	- 93.73
J S Bolger	81-495	50-170	22-215	9-110	16.4	-168.13
John M Oxx	64-297	13-80	49-197	2-20	21.5	- 34.06
K Prendergast	50-403	10-114	32-243	8-46	12.4	-117.35
C Collins	30-196	8-58	12-92	10-46	15.3	- 53.26
T Stack	27-172	10-63	11-84	6-25	15.7	+ 1.05
M V O'Brien	18-59	9-23	9-34	0-2	30.5	- 6.03
M Kauntze	18-148	6-48	10-78	2-22	12.2	- 44.67
M A O'Toole	16-134	3-38	9-72	4-24	11.9	- 27.52
T G Curtin	15-72	1-5	6-27	8-40	20.8	+ 70.00
P J Flynn	13-91	2-20	4-25	7-46	14.3	- 21.22
P Mullins	13-96	0-20	8-35	5-41	13.5	- 37.63
Noel Meade	13-149	4-43	7-77	2-29	8.7	- 86.01
J J McLoughlin	12-129	1-33	7-58	4-38	9.3	- 40.75
Liam Browne	12-157	7-82	4-61	1-14	7.6	- 92.87
J C Hayden	9-101	4-41	5-49	0-11	8.9	- 38.50
M J Grassick	9-102	1-20	5-50	3-32	8.8	- 37.00
P Prendergast	9-103	0-31	6-48	3-24	8.7	- 56.80
F Dunne	9-111	0-28	6-51	3-32	8.1	- 51.75
W P Mullins	8-40	0-6	3-7	5-27	20.0	+ 11.00
Augustine Leahy	7-75	0-20	6-31	1-24	9.3	- 30.00
A Redmond	7-97	2-29	3-32	2-36	7.2	- 42.50
B V Kelly	6-60	1-23	5-25	0-12	10.0	- 15.17
M Halford	6-75	0-9	2-36	4-30	8.0	- 42.17
E J O'Grady	6-108	2-24	2-75	2-9	5.6	- 76.00
E P Harty	5-41	1-15	4-18	0-8	12.2	+ 13.57
T F Lacy	5-62	0-17	0-19	5-26	8.1	- 24.50

September

	Total W-R	2-y-o	3-y-o	4-y-o+	Per cent	£1 Level Stake
D K Weld	66-394	33-154	25-167	8-73	16.8	- 92.32
John M Oxx	53-290	20-112	32-160	1-18	18.3	- 2.10
J S Bolger	43-327	21-130	13-143	9-54	13.1	-117.89
K Prendergast	31-276	10-99	17-141	4-36	11.2	- 71.61
M V O'Brien	22-84	11-51	10-31	1-2	26.2	- 14.09
M Kauntze	22-129	9-47	10-64	3-18	17.1	- 5.91
T Stack	20-147	9-66	10-65	1-16	13.6	- 53.15
C Collins	14-164	5-60	7-72	2-32	8.5	- 81.75
P J Flynn	12-130	1-30	5-51	6-49	9.2	- 61.27
M J Grassick	9-116	1-29	5-58	3-29	7.8	- 43.08
Liam Browne	8-113	5-64	3-41	0-8	7.1	- 24.62
F Dunne	6-45	0-7	3-22	3-16	13.3	+ 4.75
P Prendergast	6-57	1-23	4-24	1-10	10.5	- 21.20
Noel Meade	6-103	1-45	3-41	2-17	5.8	- 63.47
Capt D G Swan	5-36	0-4	0-7	5-25	13.9	- 0.87
D Gillespie	5-60	1-19	4-34	0-7	8.3	- 35.62
J C Hayden	5-64	1-23	4-37	0-4	7.8	- 16.75
E J O'Grady	5-89	1-31	2-49	2-9	5.6	- 59.60
J J McLoughlin	5-114	2-33	0-60	3-21	4.4	- 84.00

October/November

	Total W-R	2-y-o	3-y-o	4-y-o+	Per cent	£1 Level Stake
J S Bolger	64-413	35-196	24-163	5-54	15.5	-136.75
John M Oxx	54-320	33-174	21-134	0-12	16.9	- 71.17
D K Weld	53-406	27-186	13-146	13-74	13.1	-120.23
M V O'Brien	40-107	27-77	12-28	1-2	37.4	+ 46.62
K Prendergast	29-400	11-165	13-177	5-58	7.3	-185.11
P J Flynn	17-163	1-46	7-58	9-59	10.4	- 22.52
T Stack	10-109	3-60	7-37	0-12	9.2	- 37.27
M Kauntze	10-138	7-75	3-54	0-9	7.2	- 78.95
M J Grassick	9-146	3-56	4-57	2-33	6.2	- 78.25
C Collins	8-179	2-73	6-72	0-34	4.5	-114.50
Liam Browne	7-135	4-80	2-40	1-15	5.2	- 79.50
J C Hayden	6-92	5-58	1-33	0-1	6.5	- 27.00
Mrs Crowley-O'Brien	5-35	1-12	4-19	0-4	14.3	- 5.75
E J O'Grady	5-90	3-41	2-39	0-10	5.6	- 26.00
J J McLoughlin	5-93	1-32	3-44	1-17	5.4	- 52.87
Noel Meade	5-146	1-66	4-62	0-18	3.4	- 99.50

LEADING IRISH TRAINERS BY TYPE OF RACE 1988-92

2-y-o Non-Handicaps

	W-R	Per cent	£1 Level Stake		W-R	Per cent	£1 Level Stake
J S Bolger	177-693	25.5	- 142.98	D K Weld	132-711	18.6	-227.81
John M Oxx	77-427	18.0	- 106.64	M V O'Brien	55-167	32.9	- 9.94
K Prendergast	54-540	10.0	- 225.02	Liam Browne	34-317	10.7	-105.41
M Kauntze	32-247	13.0	- 116.48	C Collins	32-272	11.8	- 79.43
T Stack	29-234	12.4	- 62.26	Noel Meade	14-213	6.6	-141.95
J C Hayden	13-141	9.2	- 30.45	P Prendergast	10-116	8.6	- 68.72
J G Coogan	8-98	8.2	- 46.25	M J Grassick	8-121	6.6	- 79.85
J J McLoughlin	8-136	5.9	- 77.17	M A O'Toole	5-143	3.5	-123.90

3-y-o Non-Handicaps

	W-R	Per cent	£1 Level Stake		W-R	Per cent	£1 Level Stake
D K Weld	210-924	22.7	- 140.72	John M Oxx	171-788	21.7	- 94.60
J S Bolger	117-775	15.1	- 177.00	M V O'Brien	82-255	32.2	+ 0.94
K Prendergast	80-753	10.6	- 325.34	T Stack	49-339	14.5	- 96.86
C Collins	37-423	8.7	- 223.54	M Kauntze	32-272	11.8	-106.83
Noel Meade	27-244	11.1	- 94.79	Liam Browne	27-294	9.2	-135.14
M J Grassick	23-261	8.8	- 131.48	P Mullins	14-107	13.1	- 21.25
T G Curtin	13-87	14.9	- 1.00	M A O'Toole	12-142	8.5	- 76.42
F Dunne	12-144	8.3	- 52.00	P Prendergast	11-125	8.8	- 76.40
B V Kelly	9-107	8.4	- 56.92	E J O'Grady	9-205	4.4	-171.10
P J Flynn	8-111	7.2	- 50.40	Edward Lynam	8-165	4.8	-108.92
Daniel J Murphy	7-62	11.3	- 14.93	M Halford	7-144	4.9	- 88.25
D Hanley	6-29	20.7	+ 5.10	D Gillespie	6-91	6.6	- 69.85
Mrs C-O'Brien	5-24	20.8	+ 2.00	A Redmond	5-90	5.6	- 78.40
J J McLoughlin	5-123	4.1	- 90.25				

4-y-o+ Non-Handicaps

	W-R	Per cent	£1 Level Stake		W-R	Per cent	£1 Level Stake
D K Weld	42-189	22.2	- 22.77	J S Bolger	32-191	16.8	- 59.82
T Stack	12-71	16.9	- 11.65	P J Flynn	9-78	11.5	- 34.91
K Prendergast	8-69	11.6	- 31.50	M J Grassick	7-77	9.1	- 31.70
Augustine Leahy	6-42	14.3	+ 29.50	Noel Meade	5-63	7.9	- 36.97
P Mullins	5-70	7.1	- 28.48	W P Browne	4-13	30.8	+ 0.67
M V O'Brien	4-21	19.0	+ 8.17	M Kauntze	4-41	9.8	- 4.00
C Collins	4-42	9.5	- 22.87	John M Oxx	4-49	8.2	- 27.25
Liam Browne	4-62	6.5	- 36.25	F Flood	3-10	30.0	- 0.60
R Lister	3-13	23.1	+ 6.25	J M Canty	3-24	12.5	- 14.26
P Prendergast	3-27	11.1	- 16.10	T G Curtin	3-28	10.7	+ 8.00

Apprentice Non-Handicaps

	W-R	Per cent	£1 Level Stake		W-R	Per cent	£1 Level Stake
John M Oxx	4-9	44.4	+ 2.95	D K Weld	4-30	13.3	+ 2.00
K Prendergast	3-22	13.6	- 7.20	J C Hayden	2-5	40.0	+ 11.00
M Kauntze	2-7	28.6	- 3.33				

Amateur Non-Handicaps

	W-R	Per cent	£1 Level Stake		W-R	Per cent	£1 Level Stake
J S Bolger	12-76	15.8	- 34.20	D K Weld	8-53	15.1	- 23.92
P Mullins	7-48	14.6	- 11.87	M Kauntze	6-16	37.5	+ 14.75
M A O'Toole	5-18	27.8	- 1.83	P J Flynn	5-20	25.0	+ 4.75
F Dunne	5-23	21.7	+ 28.00	T Stack	5-25	20.0	- 2.60
C Collins	5-29	17.2	+ 4.23	K Prendergast	4-16	25.0	+ 0.05
John M Oxx	4-16	25.0	- 1.92				

2-y-o Handicaps

	W-R	Per cent	£1 Level Stake		W-R	Per cent	£1 Level Stake
J S Bolger	14-86	16.3	- 28.45	D K Weld	10-62	16.1	- 4.44
K Prendergast	6-75	8.0	- 37.27	C Collins	5-26	19.2	+ 2.48
M Kauntze	5-32	15.6	- 2.25	E J O'Grady	4-22	18.2	+ 19.00
T Stack	4-24	16.7	- 3.50	W P Mullins	3-12	25.0	+ 14.00
John M Oxx	3-18	16.7	- 3.00	J J McLoughlin	3-22	13.6	+ 3.00
M A O'Toole	3-23	13.0	- 10.75	A Redmond	3-25	12.0	- 3.00
P Mullins	2-20	10.0	- 8.50	B V Kelly	2-24	8.3	- 13.00
J C Hayden	2-27	7.4	- 10.00	P Prendergast	2-28	7.1	- 7.00
Noel Meade	2-36	5.6	- 25.50				

3-y-o Handicaps

	W-R	Per cent	£1 Level Stake		W-R	Per cent	£1 Level Stake
John M Oxx	63-350	18.0	- 6.52	J S Bolger	56-394	14.2	- 65.73
K Prendergast	53-466	11.4	- 49.27	D K Weld	51-448	11.4	-204.30
J J McLoughlin	26-203	12.8	- 23.93	C Collins	20-138	14.5	+ 11.00
M Kauntze	17-209	8.1	- 68.17	P J Flynn	16-105	15.2	+ 3.50
Noel Meade	16-230	7.0	- 107.32	M J Grassick	15-114	13.2	- 2.50
Augustine Leahy	12-76	15.8	- 10.92	D Gillespie	12-92	13.0	- 27.62
T Stack	12-131	9.2	- 54.50	M A O'Toole	10-127	7.9	- 48.00
B V Kelly	9-82	11.0	+ 8.00	M V O'Brien	8-28	28.6	- 0.72
E P Harty	6-44	13.6	+ 8.00	P Prendergast	6-78	7.7	- 41.50
M Halford	6-79	7.6	- 36.00	J C Hayden	6-112	5.4	- 62.25
E J O'Grady	6-161	3.7	- 107.75	V Bowens	4-36	11.1	- 7.00
T G Curtin	4-38	10.5	- 3.00	J T Gorman	4-50	8.0	- 5.00
Daniel J Murphy	4-64	6.3	- 18.00				

4-y-o+ Handicaps

	W-R	Per cent	£1 Level Stake		W-R	Per cent	£1 Level Stake
D K Weld	54-358	15.1	- 62.99	J S Bolger	53-340	15.6	- 26.89
K Prendergast	25-237	10.5	- 76.43	P J Flynn	24-186	12.9	- 41.00
C Collins	17-202	8.4	- 91.50	F Dunne	15-118	12.7	+ 25.33
T G Curtin	13-109	11.9	+ 10.80	M A O'Toole	13-111	11.7	+ 16.00
T F Lacy	11-97	11.3	- 36.00	P Mullins	11-143	7.7	- 78.75
T Stack	10-79	12.7	+ 8.00	John M Oxx	10-89	11.2	- 32.37
M Kauntze	10-97	10.3	- 23.87	W P Mullins	8-75	10.7	- 13.00
J J McLoughlin	8-119	6.7	- 42.50	Noel Meade	7-142	4.9	-101.54
P Hughes	6-40	15.0	+ 13.25	E J O'Grady	6-47	12.8	- 3.50
D T Hughes	6-67	9.0	- 27.75	M J Grassick	6-93	6.5	- 53.00
M Cunningham	6-128	4.7	- 85.67	P Prendergast	5-45	11.1	+ 9.00
L T Reilly	5-52	9.6	+ 14.00	V Kennedy	5-68	7.4	- 12.00
J M Canty	5-79	6.3	- 51.75	M Halford	5-100	5.0	- 55.00

Apprentice Handicaps

	W-R	Per cent	£1 Level Stake		W-R	Per cent	£1 Level Stake
John M Oxx	7-33	21.2	+ 0.75	J S Bolger	7-56	12.5	- 14.75
J J McLoughlin	5-31	16.1	+ 1.63	M J Grassick	5-40	12.5	+ 4.50
D Gillespie	4-19	21.1	+ 4.40	K Prendergast	4-76	5.3	- 56.42
Capt D G Swan	3-10	30.0	+ 13.25	T Stack	3-25	12.0	- 11.00
Noel Meade	3-30	10.0	- 6.25	D K Weld	3-85	3.5	- 68.50

Amateur Handicaps

	W-R	Per cent	£1 Level Stake		W-R	Per cent	£1 Level Stake
J S Bolger	5-20	25.0	+ 0.60	P J Flynn	3-14	21.4	- 3.00
W Fennin	2-3	66.7	+ 7.00	M A O'Toole	2-5	40.0	- 0.77
F Flood	2-5	40.0	+ 10.00	Noel Meade	2-6	33.3	+ 5.50
David A Kiely	2-7	28.6	+ 6.00	M Cunningham	2-9	22.2	+ 1.25
D Gillespie	2-9	22.2	+ 6.10				

LEADING IRISH TRAINERS' FAVOURITES 1988-1992

	W-R	Per cent	£1 Level Stake	% of Runners that Started Favourite	% of Winners that Started Favourite
D K Weld	275-758	36.3	- 76.85	26.4	53.4
J S Bolger	232-557	41.7	- 23.81	21.1	49.0
John M Oxx	190-437	43.5	+ 69.73	24.6	55.4
M V O'Brien	109-226	48.2	+ 24.83	47.3	71.7
K Prendergast	77-251	30.7	- 27.96	11.1	32.4
C Collins	44-117	37.6	+ 15.12	9.9	36.1
M Kauntze	42-113	37.2	- 7.51	12.1	38.9
T Stack	41-106	38.7	+ 5.80	11.2	32.5
P J Flynn	28-63	44.4	+ 26.19	9.6	39.4
Noel Meade	25-81	30.9	- 14.28	8.2	31.6
Liam Browne	21-66	31.8	- 11.76	7.1	29.6
M A O'Toole	20-56	35.7	- 4.25	8.6	37.0
P Mullins	17-47	36.2	+ 8.82	8.1	35.4
M J Grassick	17-51	33.3	- 5.53	6.9	25.4
D Gillespie	14-38	36.8	- 0.37	10.5	45.2
P Prendergast	14-46	30.4	- 4.57	10.3	35.0
J J McLoughlin	13-30	43.3	+ 8.20	4.4	22.4
A Redmond	9-31	29.0	- 4.52	6.3	42.9
T F Lacy	8-18	44.4	+ 10.35	4.4	47.1
E J O'Grady	8-30	26.7	- 9.95	4.7	25.0
Mrs Crowley-O'Brien	7-13	53.8	+ 5.23	11.0	46.7
Augustine Leahy	7-27	25.9	- 2.67	6.4	26.9
J C Hayden	6-14	42.9	+ 3.80	3.0	20.0
Edward Lynam	6-23	26.1	+ 1.25	4.6	28.6
T G Curtin	6-23	26.1	- 5.20	7.4	15.4
Capt D G Swan	5-16	31.3	+ 1.13	10.1	50.0
J M Canty	5-19	26.3	- 0.51	6.7	35.7
M Halford	5-20	25.0	+ 0.25	4.5	20.0
B V Kelly	5-23	21.7	- 7.25	5.6	18.5
F Dunne	4-15	26.7	- 2.00	2.9	10.5
J E Kiely	3-6	50.0	+ 1.28	14.0	75.0
Anthony Mullins	3-6	50.0	+ 2.75	4.1	60.0
F Flood	3-7	42.9	- 0.35	13.2	37.5
W P Browne	3-7	42.9	- 1.33	28.0	75.0
J G Coogan	3-8	37.5	+ 0.50	4.4	21.4
M Cunningham	3-10	30.0	- 2.83	2.3	17.6
E P Harty	3-12	25.0	- 3.93	5.8	25.0
D T Hughes	3-20	15.0	- 6.75	7.2	18.8
Lord Huntingdon (Eng)	2-2	100.0	+ 1.80	15.4	50.0
Oliver Finnegan	2-3	66.7	+ 5.50	2.5	50.0
D Hanley	2-3	66.7	+ 9.10	4.2	22.2
J P Kavanagh	2-4	50.0	- 0.10	2.6	33.3
M A McCullagh	2-4	50.0	+ 3.50	15.4	66.7
N O'Callaghan	2-4	50.0	+ 5.75	2.1	22.2
V Bowens	2-7	28.6	- 1.75	2.5	16.7
C Kinane	2-7	28.6	+ 2.00	15.9	40.0
P Hughes	2-8	25.0	- 3.08	6.8	22.2
V Kennedy	2-11	18.2	- 5.12	4.7	16.7
J E Mulhern	2-12	16.7	- 4.50	5.7	15.4
Daniel J Murphy	2-14	14.3	- 9.68	5.4	11.8

TRAINER TIPS FOR 1993

H R A Cecil	–	Runners at Catterick, Chepstow, Royal Ascot and Newbury
L M Cumani	–	Runners at Brighton
J H M Gosden	–	Runners at Doncaster, Haydock and York
B Hanbury	–	Runners at Hamilton with Bruce Raymond riding
G Harwood	–	Runners at Folkestone
B W Hills	–	Runners at Catterick and Chester
M H Tompkins	–	Runners at Edinburgh
Favourites	–	2-y-o non-handicap races at Goodwood, Newcastle and Pontefract

TRAINER INDEX

COURSE INDEX

NOTES

NOTES

NOTES

NOTES

NOTES

NOTES

NOTES

NOTES

NOTES

NOTES

NOTES

NOTES

NOTES

NOTES